Goldmine
45 RPM
PICTURE
SLEEVE
PRICE GUIDE

CHARLES SZABLA

Published by

krause
publications

700 E. State Street • Iola, WI 54990-0001
Telephone: 715/445-2214

Please call or write for our free catalog of music publications.
Our toll-free number to place an order or obtain a free catalog is 800-258-0929
or please use our regular business telephone 715-445-2214
for editorial comment and further information.

Library of Congress Catalog Number: 97-80621
ISBN: 0-87341-594-9
Printed in the United States of America

Design, layout, and cover concept by
Charles Szabla

Introduction

For those of us who collect picture sleeves, no introduction is necessary. For the people who are only briefly acquainted or unfamiliar with this area of collecting, this is for you.

I'm sure you recall going to the record store to buy the latest single by one of your favorite recording artists. It could have been the spring of 1957 and "Love Letters In The Sand" by Pat Boone was the tune you secretly loved to croon along to. Or perhaps it was September of 1965, the Beatles had released "Yesterday," and even though your folks thought it was a pretty song you still wanted to buy the 45. Or maybe it was 1979, new wave was ebbing onto your local airwaves, and the Police's "Can't Stand Losing You" was one of the tunes you wanted to play at your next party. All three of these songs were released on a 45 RPM (the little record with the big hole) and each one was issued with its own distinctive picture sleeve. The sleeve usually would have a picture of the artist and the title of the song. Often the b-side, or flip side, of the record was also listed on the sleeve.

After digging into your pockets for change, you paid for the record and rushed it home to your turntable. You gingerly slid the adapter onto the spindle, slapped the 45 on the record player and tossed the sleeve under the bed. Or, like me, maybe you saved that picture sleeve and took good care of it until one day, your mother decided to go on a cleaning binge and tossed that treasured item in the trash. Aaaarghhh!

Well, as it turns out, those 45 RPM picture sleeves are now often more valuable than the record they held. So you may want to check out your attic, a forgotten corner of the basement, or your mother's garage, to find those long-forgotten treasures. They may actually be worth some substantial moolah.

How To Use This Book

The Goldmine Price Guide to 45 RPM Picture Sleeves is arranged alphabetically by artist/group name. A letter by letter system is employed. All spaces and punctuation between words are ignored in this process. The individual sleeves for each artist are listed chronologically by date of release from earliest to latest. The a-side of the 45 is indicated in all caps. If the b-side is listed on the sleeve, it is shown after the a-side title with initial caps. There are some entries that have a slash following the a-side title which means the b-side is most likely listed on the sleeve but documentation is currently unavailable.

The focus of this first edition is 45 RPM major label U.S. releases. Independent issues are included if the individual or group was issued at some point in their career on a major label. A major label is a record company with the resources to produce, market, and distribute their product nationally and internationally.

A recurring problem in the identification of sleeves is imports being confused with U.S. releases. Beyond the obvious method of looking for identification of the country of origin in the text, another overlooked indicator is the manner in which the seams of the sleeve are sealed. In order to close up the sides of the sleeve tabs are folded in, the back is folded up, and then glued closed. Imports often fold up the back first then seal the tabs on the outside of the sleeve instead of hiding them inside. There is a small number of U.S. indies that employ the outside sealed tab method so examine carefully. Also look for unknown or unusual phrases, periods instead of dashes between numbers, or catalog numbers that do not match known U.S. titles.

This detail of identification is necessary to avoid "phantom" sleeves. There are a couple of examples noted in this book (specifically by Big Brother and the Holding Company) where an import was mistakenly identified as a U.S. release and offered for sale. Many people would see this sleeve listed and begin looking for another copy. Others would add it to their want lists and begin searching for their own copy. Thus is born a "phantom" sleeve.

For many years I had believed U.S. sleeves existed for "The Man With The Child In His Eyes" by Kate Bush and "Baby Jane" by Rod Stewart. After searching for many years I became convinced I was dealing with imports and an honest-to-goodness U.S. release did not exist. But on the other hand, if somebody would have told me a couple of years ago there was a U.S. sleeve for "Time" by David Bowie or "Time Has Come Today" by the Chambers Brothers, I would not have believed them. Even "All Tomorrow's Parties" by the Velvet Underground didn't turn up for sale until 1992.

Bootleg sleeves, items that are illegally created without the permission of the record label, publishing company, or recording artist are an issue to be aware of. Sometimes bootlegs are made by impassioned fans paying homage to their idols. The Left Banke's "Pedestal/ Myra" is an example that comes to mind. But usually it's a pathetic attempt to deceive consumers and hoodwink collectors. Elvis Presley, Beatles, and Rolling Stones fans report the highest incidence of bootleg releases. Valuable and highly desirable authentic sleeves such as "Can't Buy Me Love" by the Beatles and "The Last Time" by the Rolling Stones seem to be targets of this charade. Just be wary of a known valuable sleeve being offered in mint condition for an unusually low price. Chances are you're getting ripped off.

The cross referencing used in this book has been designed to help locate related artists, actors, or songs. When a group is referenced, an attempt has been made to list in parentheses the members that were involved. For instance, under Jefferson Airplane, a cross reference is made to SVT (Jack Casady). This means when the sleeves were released Casady was a member of Jefferson Airplane and was also a member of the group SVT that had sleeves too. Since this book deals specifically with picture sleeves, only artists that had sleeves are cross referenced.

Actors and actresses who did not release 45s with sleeves are given individual listings and referenced to the specific place to find the sleeve their image appears on. These are usually movie and television related. Many recording artists have done songs for or lent songs to motion picture soundtracks. These films are given individual listings with a reference to the specific artist and title.

Condition and Demand

This book lists two prices, one for VG (very good) and one for NM (near mint) condition. Near mint is fairly self-explanatory–almost perfect. The sleeve will be flat and unwrinkled, the colors will be rich and vibrant, and the edges and corners are not torn or folded.

Near mint is generally the highest grade you'll find a sleeve in. Mint condition is unusual to come across in its true form. That is to say, absolutely, without a doubt, pristine, perfect. If you do land a mint condition sleeve, expect to pay a 25% premium above the near mint price listed in this book.

Very good condition is a highly subjective grade. A VG sleeve will show some signs of wear and age such as slight color fading, bent corners, a wrinkled top edge, slight abrasions, printing misregistration, price stickers, or small amounts of writing. The degree to which a sleeve exhibits these flaws and the number of different types of damage will affect its value. More severe conditions such as large holes and rips, substantial writing (other than the artist's autograph), and missing pieces of the sleeve will degrade sleeves to VG- (very good minus), G+ (good plus), G (good), and P (poor). These grades are usually "filler" pieces that a collector will purchase only to fill a hole in the collection until a better grade can be found.

A popular grade in use is VG+ (very good plus). These sleeves are just shy of being graded as near mint but not flawed enough to warrant a very good grade. A VG+ would place a sleeve's value halfway between VG and NM.

The demand of collectors will also dictate the value of a picture sleeve. Simply because a sleeve is rare and hard to find does not necessarily translate into big bucks. A quick flip through this book will show a higher interest in Elvis Presley and the Beatles. Their sleeve output was relatively substantial. All but fifteen of Presley's singles on RCA were released with picture sleeves. Presley and the Beatles, along with the Rolling Stones, the Beach Boys, and Bob Dylan regularly fetch three to four figures for select sleeves.

Buying and Selling

The best place to purchase picture sleeves is either through music collecting magazines or at record shows. Magazines such as *Goldmine* and *Discoveries* offer items for sale at a set price (set sale) or by auction. Generally the more valuable and desirable sleeves will be offered through a mail auction process. You send the seller your bid and keep your fingers crossed. Record shows appear on a regular basis at hotels, convention centers, union halls, fairgrounds, and other public meeting places. A broad range of material is offered for sale at these shows: albums, 45s, CDs, magazines, posters, concert ephemera, and of course, picture sleeves. Dealers come from across the country in hopes of selling something to you. Other sources for picture sleeves are flea markets, garage sales, mail order record dealers, auction houses, second-hand shops, and used record stores.

The process of selling sleeves is somewhat more complex than buying them. You can establish your own mail order business if you have the time and patience. Of course, that involves purchasing, sorting, storing, grading, pricing, and listing the sleeves, typesetting and printing the catalog, compiling a mailing list, sending out the list, answering availability queries, processing, packing, and mailing orders—whew! That sounds like a full-time job to me. If you only have a handful of sleeves you're trying to unload, the easiest way is to take them to a record show. The dealers can often be pretty particular about what they will purchase. Since they have to make a profit at what they do, a dealer will not usually pay more than 50% of the list price. Remember, they make a buck by maximizing their profit–it's the American way! The best way to get the most cash for your sleeves is to run a classified or display ad in one of the previously mentioned record collector's magazines. This is a bit more involved but you will get top dollar for choice items.

My Story

My collection started out not so much out of a love for the hobby as a love for the music. After all, without the music there would be no need for picture sleeves. Originally I bought 45s with picture sleeves only if I liked the music. At the time my musical scope of interest was fairly narrow. As my collection slowly grew I expanded the boundaries of the types of music I purchased. Eventually my passion for sleeves encompassed every type of recorded material on a major label.

I had always felt there was a need for this type of book. The reference material on picture sleeves was scant and as a compulsive, anal-retentive collector I found this a frustrating situation. It wasn't until around 1994 that specific documentation on individual sleeves began showing up in print. This convinced me I wasn't the only person interested in collecting picture sleeves. It was like finding other life on another planet.

The ability to fulfill my dream of creating a comprehensive reference source for picture sleeves was realized when my wife Leslie went back to college for her bachelor's degree. It was necessary for us to purchase a computer for Leslie to do her schoolwork. The computer offered me the means to document my collection and start on my book.

I limited my research to U.S. major label releases. The daunting task of accumulating information on all independent labels was too mind-boggling. I decided to limit the listing of indies to artists that released on a major at some point during their career. For instance, the B-52's signed with Warner Brothers in 1979, but in 1978 they had released their first record on the independent Athens, Georgia label Boo-Fant. This would qualify the listing of this independent release for the book.

Attending local record shows was and still is an exciting experience for me. The morning of the show I find my pulse quickening and my breathing sharp, pretty odd huh? The immediate pleasure and thrill of finding a previously unknown sleeve is still a real kick. When I first started attending record shows I would always make a point of purchasing one expensive item. At the time, expensive to me meant at least $10 which is either an indication of how long ago this was or a statement of my financial status. The first expensive sleeve I bought was "Surfin' Safari" by the Beach Boys. It's still one of my favorite sleeves. I continue to attend local record shows and I always manage to find a cool sleeve I've never seen before.

Even though the era of picture sleeve production reached its peak almost ten years ago, the availability of quality items for sale is thriving in this field of collecting. Long Live The Picture Sleeve!

Credits

I would like to thank my wife Leslie for her unending support and constant words of encouragement. Her patience with my obsession made this process a manageable one. Thank you Leslie for going back to school and for asking "Are you working on that book tonight?" in the most innocent and innocuous manner possible. I'm glad to see that my daughter Jessica Mae is following in her mother's footsteps. She too exhibits a sensitivity and empathy I admire.

Thanks to Deborah Faupel for her enthusiastic support of the book. I'm fortunate that we saw eye-to-eye on the concept and she acted as a successful advocate for me at Krause. Don Gulbrandsen was quite encouraging to me while he shepherded my book through the production process.

A few more thanks go to Bob Fuller at Record Revolution on Coventry for letting me rummage through his 45s; too bad about that R.E.M. poster sleeve. I hope you find your Kinks "mirror label" record. An acknowledgment goes out to Ray Peters for allowing me to come out to his house and photograph a ton of sleeves. Plus he had a terrific selection at reasonable prices. My research was aided by the equally obsessive folks at Vinyl Vendors. Their huge catalogs have aided in my research. And a final tip of the hat to Heather Carpenter for her help in cross referencing many of the modern rock artists.

Glossary

Coated Paper Paper having a surface coating which produces a smooth finish

Duotone A two-color halftone reproduction from a one-color photograph.

Envelope Sleeve Has an additional flap on top that can be folded over, sealed, and shipped in the mail.

Extended Plays A record that contains more than three songs.

Folding Sleeve A single sheet of paper that is usually printed on one side only and folded in half. The edges of the sleeve are not sealed with tabs.

Halftone The reproduction of continuous-tone artwork, such as a photograph, which converts the image into dots of various sizes.

Half Sleeve The same outside dimensions of a picture sleeve but has a large hole die-cut in its center to expose the label on the 45.

Insert An additional printed piece that is included inside the picture sleeve to accompany the record.

Picture Sleeve A paper product, generally 7-1/4 inches square, designed to hold a 7 inch record. A design or representation made by various means (as a photograph, illustration, graphic, or text) is employed to identify the sleeve's contents.

Promotional An item that is distributed without charge to radio stations, music distributors, disc jockeys, etc. to help promote the artist.

Small-Hole Record Most 45s have a 1-1/2 inch hole but these records have a 1/4 inch hole identical to albums.

Split Single Two different artists share the same 45 with one artist on one side and the other artist on the other side of the record. The sleeve can use the same method of separate sides or feature both artists' names together.

Stock An item that is sold to the general public.

Uncoated Paper Paper with no surface coating which will have a non-glossy appearance

Correspondence

I'm not presumptious enough to assume I have catalogued every sleeve ever made. Your help in making additions and corrections to this book would be greatly appreciated. Please write to Charles Szabla, c/o Krause Publications, 700 East State Street, Iola, WI 54990-0001. Include your own address (snail mail and e-mail if you have one) in case I have any questions concerning your contributions. Thank you for buying this book.

A

AARON, HANK
(Baseball Player)
    See Bill Slayback (*Move Over Babe*), Richard "Popcorn" Wylie (*Move Over Babe*)

ABBA

TITLE	LABEL AND NUMBER	VG	NM	YR
WATERLOO	(Atlantic 3035)	3.75	15.00	74
(Promotional issue only)				
KNOWING ME, KNOWING YOU / Happy Hawaii	(Atlantic 3387)	1.00	4.00	76
MONEY, MONEY, MONEY / Crazy World	(Atlantic 3434)	1.25	5.00	76
TAKE A CHANCE ON ME / I'm A Marionette	(Atlantic 3457)	1.00	4.00	77
DOES YOUR MOTHER KNOW / Kisses Of Fire	(Atlantic 3574)	1.00	4.00	79
VOULEZ-VOUS / Angeleyes	(Atlantic 3609)	1.00	4.00	79
SUPER TROUPER / The Piper	(Atlantic 3806)	1.00	4.00	80
WHEN ALL IS SAID AND DONE / Should I Laugh Or Cry	(Atlantic 3889)	1.00	4.00	81
THE VISITORS / Head Over Heels	(Atlantic 4031)	1.00	4.00	81
ONE OF US / Should I Laugh Or Cry	(Atlantic 7-89881)	1.25	5.00	83

EXTENDED PLAYS

TITLE	LABEL AND NUMBER	VG	NM	YR
FERNANDO / WATERLOO	(Atlantic OP-7501)	1.25	5.00	78

(Promotional issue only titled *Profiles In Gold Album 1*, issued with a small-hole 33-1/3 RPM record. Sold only at Burger King for 59¢ with the purchase of a Coke. Also includes two songs each by Spinners, Firefall, and England Dan and John Ford Coley.)

Also see Agnetha Faltskog, Murray Head (Benny Andersson and Björn Ulvaeus), Elaine Paige (Benny Andersson and Björn Ulvaeus)

ABBOTT, GREGORY

TITLE	LABEL AND NUMBER	VG	NM	YR
SHAKE YOU DOWN / Wait Until Tomorrow	(Columbia 38-06191)	1.25	5.00	78
I GOT THE FEELIN' (IT'S OVER) / Rhyme And Reason	(Columbia 38-06632)	.75	3.00	87
I GOT THE FEELIN' (IT'S OVER)	(Columbia 38-06632)	1.00	4.00	87
(Promotional issue, *Demonstration–Not For Sale* printed on sleeve)				
I'LL PROVE IT TO YOU /	(Columbia 38-07774)	.75	3.00	88
LET ME BE YOUR HERO / She's An Entertainer	(Columbia 38-08027)	.75	3.00	88

ABC

TITLE	LABEL AND NUMBER	VG	NM	YR
THE LOOK OF LOVE (PART ONE) / Theme From Mantrap	(Mercury 76168)	1.00	4.00	82
POISON ARROW / Tears Are Not Enough	(Mercury 8810 340-7)	1.25	5.00	83
THAT WAS THEN BUT THIS IS NOW / Vertigo	(Mercury 888 661-1 M-1)	.75	3.00	83
BE NEAR ME / A To Z	(Mercury 888 626-7 M-1)	.75	3.00	85
HOW TO BE A MILLIONAIRE!	(Mercury 888 382-1)	.75	3.00	85
WHEN SMOKEY SINGS / Chicago (Part 1)	(Mercury 888 604-7)	.75	3.00	87
THE NIGHT YOU MURDERED LOVE / Minneapolis	(Mercury 888 783-7)	.75	3.00	87

ABDUL, PAULA

TITLE	LABEL AND NUMBER	VG	NM	YR
KNOCKED OUT / Opposites Attract	(Virgin 7-99329)	.75	3.00	88
(IT'S JUST) THE WAY THAT YOU LOVE ME / (It's Just) The Way That You Love Me (7" Dub)	(Virgin 7-99282)	.75	3.00	88
FOREVER YOUR GIRL / Next To You	(Virgin 7-99230)	.75	3.00	89
COLD HEARTED / One Or The Other	(Virgin 7-99196)	.75	3.00	89
OPPOSITES ATTRACT / One Or The Other	(Virgin 7-99158)	.75	3.00	89
(Back of sleeve credits a-side as *Duet with the Wild Pair, Rap by Derrick Delite from The Soul Purpose*)				
MY LOVE IS FOR REAL / Didn't I Say I Love You	(Virgin 38493 7)	.50	2.00	95

"ABOUT LAST NIGHT..."
(Motion Picture)
    See Sheena Easton (*So Far So Good*), John Waite (*If Anybody Had A Heart*)

MISS ABRAMS AND THE STRAWBERRY POINT FOURTH GRADE CLASS

ABRAMS, MISS, & THE STRAWBERRY POINT SCHOOL THIRD GRADE CLASS

TITLE	LABEL AND NUMBER	VG	NM	YR
MILL VALLEY	(Warner Bros./Reprise 0928)	1.25	5.00	70

ABRAMS, MISS, & THE STRAWBERRY POINT FOURTH GRADE CLASS

TITLE	LABEL AND NUMBER	VG	NM	YR
AMERICA (LET'S GET STARTED AGAIN)	(Warner Bros./Reprise 1322)	1.25	5.00	75
(Photography by Annie Leibovitz)				

A. B. SKHY

TITLE	LABEL AND NUMBER	VG	NM	YR
CAMEL BACK	(MGM K-14086)	2.00	8.00	69

ABSOLUTE BEGINNERS
(Motion Picture)
    See David Bowie (*Absolute Beginners*)

ABSTRAC'

TITLE	LABEL AND NUMBER	VG	NM	YR
RIGHT AND HYPE	(Reprise 22872)	.75	3.00	89

ACCEPT THIS FREE

ACADEMY OF ST. MARTIN'S IN THE FIELDS, THE

TITLE	LABEL AND NUMBER	VG	NM	YR
W.A. MOZART: SYMPHONY NO. 25 IN G MINOR, K. 183; 1ST MOVEMENT / W.A. Mozart: Concerto For Two Pianos, K. 365; 3rd movement	(Fantasy 956)	1.00	4.00	85

(Promotional issue only, *For Promotion Only Not For Sale* printed on sleeve, issued with a small-hole 33-1/3 RPM record. From the motion picture *Amadeus*, conducted by Neville Marriner.)

ACCEPT

TITLE	LABEL AND NUMBER	VG	NM	YR
MIDNIGHT MOVER / Screaming For A Love Bite	(Portrait PAE7 2049)	1.00	4.00	85

(Promotional issue only, *Not For Sale* printed on sleeve, issued with a small-hole 33-1/3 RPM record)

AC/DC

TITLE	LABEL AND NUMBER	VG	NM	YR
LET'S GET IT UP / Snowballed	(Atlantic 3894)	1.00	4.00	81
FOR THOSE ABOUT TO ROCK (WE SALUTE YOU) / T.N.T.	(Atlantic 4029)	1.00	4.00	82
GUNS FOR HIRE / Landslide	(Atlantic 7-89774)	1.00	4.00	83
FLICK OF THE SWITCH / Badlands	(Atlantic 7-89722)	1.00	4.00	83
JAILBREAK / Show Business	(Atlantic 7-89614)	1.00	4.00	84
DANGER / Back In Business	(Atlantic 7-89532)	1.00	4.00	85
WHO MADE WHO / Guns For Hire (Live Version)	(Atlantic 7-89425)	1.00	4.00	86
HEAT SEEKER / Go Zone	(Atlantic 7-89136)	1.00	4.00	88
THAT'S THE WAY I WANNA ROCK N ROLL / Kissin' Dynamite	(Atlantic 7-89098)	1.00	4.00	88

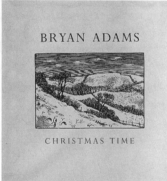

TITLE	LABEL AND NUMBER	VG	NM	YR

ACKLIN, BARBARA
JUST AIN'T NO LOVE/Please Sunrise Please .... (Brunswick 55388)   2.50   10.00   68

ACTION JACKSON
(Motion Picture)
 See Pointer Sisters (He Turned Me Out)

ACOUSTIC ALCHEMY
MR. CHOW/The Stone Circle .... (MCA 53166)   .75   3.00   87

ACUFF, ROY
 See Nitty Gritty Dirt Band (Honky Tonkin')

ADAM AND THE ANTS
STAND & DELIVER/Beat My Guest .... (Epic AE7-1236)   1.50   6.00   81
 (Promotional issue only, Demonstration–Not For Sale printed on sleeve)
 Also see Adam Ant, Bow Wow Wow (Matthew Ashman, Dave Barbarossa)

ADAMS, BRYAN
LET ME TAKE YOU DANCING .... (A&M 474)   3.75   15.00   79
STRAIGHT FROM THE HEART/One Good Reason .... (A&M 2536)   1.00   4.00   83
CUTS LIKE A KNIFE/Lonely Nights .... (A&M 2553)   1.00   4.00   83
THIS TIME/Fits Ya Good .... (A&M 2574)   1.00   4.00   83
RUN TO YOU/I'm Ready .... (A&M 2686)   .75   3.00   84
SOMEBODY/Long Gone .... (A&M 2701)   .75   3.00   84
HEAVEN/Heaven "Live" .... (A&M 2729)   .75   3.00   85
SUMMER OF '69/The Best Was Yet To Come .... (A&M 2739)   .75   3.00   85
ONE NIGHT LOVE AFFAIR/Lonely Nights .... (A&M 2770)   .75   3.00   85
IT'S ONLY LOVE/The Only One .... (A&M 2791)   .75   3.00   85
 (A-side shown as by Bryan Adams/Tina Turner, both pictured)
CHRISTMAS TIME/Reggae Christmas .... (A&M 8651)   1.00   4.00   85
 (First printing with "wrapping" art, issued with green vinyl)
CHRISTMAS TIME/Reggae Christmas .... (A&M 8651)   1.00   4.00   85
 (Second printing with landscape art, issued with green vinyl)
HEAT OF THE NIGHT/Another Day .... (A&M 2921)   .75   3.00   87
HEARTS ON FIRE/The Best Was Yet To Come .... (A&M 2948)   .75   3.00   87
VICTIM OF LOVE/Into The Fire .... (A&M 2964)   .75   3.00   87
THE ONLY THING THAT LOOKS GOOD ON ME IS YOU/Hey Elvis .... (A&M 31458-1578-7)   .50   2.00   96

ADAMS, EYDIE, AND BOB HOPE
CALL ME BWANA/The Flip Side .... (United Artists 603)   6.25   25.00   63

ADAMS, JOHNNY
 See Lou Reed (b-side of September Song)

ADAMS, OLETA
 See Tears For Fears (Woman In Chains)

ADCOCK, C.C.
CINDY LOU/Done Most Everything .... (Island 422-858 348-7)   .50   2.00   94

ADDAMS FAMILY, THE
(Television Series)
 Related see Ted Cassidy (The Lurch)

ADDERLY, CANNONBALL
TAURUS/Scorpio .... (Capitol 3406)   1.50   6.00   72

ADDRISI BROTHERS, THE
GHOST DANCER .... (Scotti Brothers 500)   1.00   4.00   79

ADRENALIN
ROAD OF THE GYPSY .... (MCA 52833)   .75   3.00   86
 (From the motion picture Iron Eagle)

ADRIAN AND THE SUNSETS
BREAKTHROUGH .... (Sunset 63-602)   25.00   100.00   63

ADVENTURES, THE
SEND MY HEART/Lost In Hollywood .... (Chrysalis VS4 42894)   .75   3.00   85
BROKEN LAND .... (Elektra 68414)   .75   3.00   88

AEROSMITH
SHEILA .... (Geffen 28814-7)   1.00   4.00   85
DUDE (LOOKS LIKE A LADY) .... (Geffen 28240-7)   1.00   4.00   87
ANGEL .... (Geffen 28249-7)   1.00   4.00   87
RAG DOLL .... (Geffen 27915-7)   .75   3.00   87
LOVE IN AN ELEVATOR .... (Geffen 22845-7)   .75   3.00   89
FALLING IN LOVE (IS HARD ON THE KNEES)/Fall Together .... (Columbia 38 78499)   .50   2.00   97
 (Issued with a small-hole 45 RPM record)
HOLE IN MY SOUL/Falling Off .... (Columbia 38 78569)   .50   2.00   97
 Also see Run-D.M.C. (Walk This Way)

AFGHAN WHIGS
I AM THE STICKS/White Trash Party .... (Sub Pop 32)   5.00   20.00   89
 (Issued with either white or lavender vinyl)
SISTER BROTHER/Hey Cuz .... (Sub Pop 84)   2.50   10.00   90
 (First 2000 issued with red vinyl)
CONJURE ME/My World Is Empty .... (Sub Pop 142)   2.50   10.00   92

AFRICAN BEAVERS
FIND MY BABY .... (RCA 47-8530)   2.50   10.00   65

AFTER 7
HEAT OF THE MOMENT/Heat Of The Moment (Instrumental) .... (Virgin 7-99204)   .75   3.00   89

AFTER THE FOX
(Motion Picture)
 See Peter Sellers (After The Fox)

AGAINST ALL ODDS
(Motion Picture)
    See Phil Collins *(Against All Odds)*, Peter Gabriel *(Walk Through The Fire)*

AGE OF CHANCE
KISS/Crash Conscious .... (Virgin 7-99472)   .75   3.00   87

A-HA
TAKE ON ME/Love Is Reason .... (Warner Bros. 29011-7)   2.00   8.00   85
    (Promotional issue only, 8-page book format with back pocket for record)
TAKE ON ME .... (Warner Bros. 29011-7)   1.00   4.00   85
THE SUN ALWAYS SHINES ON T.V. .... (Warner Bros. 28846-7)   .75   3.00   85
HUNTING HIGH AND LOW .... (Warner Bros. 28684-7)   .75   3.00   86
I'VE BEEN LOSING YOU .... (Warner Bros. 28594-7)   .75   3.00   86
CRY WOLF .... (Warner Bros. 28500-7)   .75   3.00   86
THE LIVING DAYLIGHTS .... (Warner Bros. 28305-7)   1.00   4.00   87
    (From the motion picture *The Living Daylights*)
STAY ON THESE ROADS .... (Warner Bros. 27886-7)   .75   3.00   88

AINLEY, CHARLIE
(YOU TELL ME) LIES/Walk A Mile .... (Nemperor ZS8-7517)   1.00   4.00   85
    (Promotional issue only, *Demonstration–Not For Sale* printed on sleeve)

AIRRACE
I DON'T CARE/Caught In The Fire .... (Atco 7-99702)   .75   3.00   84

AIR SUPPLY
THE ONE THAT YOU LOVE/I Want To Give It All .... (Arista 0604)   .75   3.00   81
EVEN THE NIGHTS ARE BETTER/One Step Closer .... (Arista 0692)   .75   3.00   82
MAKING LOVE OUT OF NOTHING AT ALL/Late Again (Recorded Live) .... (Arista 9056)   .75   3.00   83
JUST AS I AM/Crazy Love .... (Arista 9353)   .75   3.00   85
THE POWER OF LOVE/ .... (Arista 9391)   .75   3.00   85
LONELY IS THE NIGHT/ .... (Arista 9521)   .75   3.00   86

ALABAMA
WHY LADY WHY/I Wanna Come Over .... (RCA PB-12091)   1.00   4.00   80
FORTY HOUR WEEK (FOR A LIVIN') .... (RCA PB-14085)   .75   3.00   85
SHE AND I .... (RCA PB-14281)   .75   3.00   85
TAR TOP .... (RCA 5222-7-RAA)   1.50   6.00   88
    (Promotional issue only, folding sleeve)
PASS IT ON DOWN/The Borderline .... (RCA 2519-7-R)   .75   3.00   90
PASS IT ON .... (RCA 2519)   1.50   6.00   90
    (Promotional issue only, originally issued with Public Service Announcement script)
    Also see Lionel Richie *(Deep River Woman)*

ALAMO, THE
(Motion Picture)
    See the Brothers Four *(The Green Leaves Of Summer)*, Marty Robbins *(Ballad Of The Alamo)*

ALAN, BUDDY
WHEN I TURN TWENTY-ONE/ .... (Capitol 2305)   1.25   5.00   68
    Also see Buck Owens & Buddy Alan and the Buckaroos

ALARM, THE
THE STAND/Reason 41 .... (I.R.S. 9922)   2.00   8.00   83
SIXTY-EIGHT GUNS/Pavilion Steps .... (I.R.S. 9924)   1.50   6.00   84
THE DECEIVER/Second Generation .... (I.R.S. 9929)   1.50   6.00   84
STRENGTH/Majority .... (I.R.S. 52736)   1.00   4.00   85
SPIRIT OF '76/Reason 36 .... (I.R.S. 52792)   1.00   4.00   85
ABSOLUTE REALITY/Room At The Top .... (I.R.S. 52828)   1.00   4.00   87
RAIN IN THE SUMMERTIME/Rose Beyond The Wall .... (I.R.S. 53219)   1.00   4.00   87
PRESENCE OF LOVE/The Hurricane Sessions (My Land Your Land) .... (I.R.S. 53259)   1.00   4.00   88
SOLD ME DOWN THE RIVER/ .... (I.R.S. 73002)   1.25   5.00   89
    Also see Ferry Aid

ALBANO, CAPTAIN LOU
    See Junk Yard Dog *(Grab Them Cakes)*, the Wrestlers *(Land Of 1,000 Dances)*

ALBERT, EDDIE
(Singer/actor best known for his role of Oliver Douglas on the television series *Green Acres*)
LITTLE CHILD/Jenny Kissed Me .... (Kapp 134)   3.75   15.00   56
    (A-side shown as by Eddie Albert and Sondra Lee)

ALBRIGHT, GERALD
SO AMAZING/Just Between Us .... (Atlantic 7-89163)   .75   3.00   87
FEELING INSIDE .... (Atlantic 7-88989)   .75   3.00   88

ALCATRAZZ
ISLAND IN THE SUN/Hiroshima Mon Amour .... (Rocshire XR95047)   1.25   5.00   83
    Also see Yngwie J. Malmsteen's Rising Force *(Yngwie J. Malmsteen)*

ALDER, DEXTER, Pfc.
PAPER DOLL/Don't Blame Me .... (Columbia 4-43595)   3.00   12.00   66

ALDERMEN, THE
    See Cannibal and the Headhunters (shared a-side with *Land Of 1000 Dances*)

ALEPH
TOCCATA .... (Roulette 7089)   2.50   10.00   70

ALESSI
ALL FOR A REASON .... (A&M 2045)   1.00   4.00   78

ALEXANDER, WILLIE
BURNING CANDLES/In Your Car .... (Arf Arf 017)   .75   3.00   84
YOU GOT A HARD TIME COMING/Larry Bird .... (Stanton Park 011)   .75   3.00   88

TITLE	LABEL AND NUMBER	VG	NM	YR

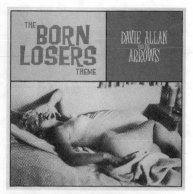

ALFIE
STAR/ .... (Motown 1777MF) | .75 | 3.00 | 85
STAR .... (Motown 1777MF) | 1.00 | 4.00 | 85
   (Promotional issue, *For Promotional Use Only Not For Sale* printed on sleeve)
JUST GETS BETTER WITH TIME/ .... (Motown 1827) | .75 | 3.00 | 85
JUST GETS BETTER WITH TIME .... (Motown 1827) | 1.00 | 4.00 | 85
   (Promotional issue, *For Promotional Use Only Not For Sale* printed on sleeve)

ALHONA, RICHIE
ONE DESIRE .... (Fantasy 553) | 3.75 | 15.00 |

ALI, MUHAMMAD
   See Cassius Clay, Michael Masser & Mandrill (*Ali Bombaye*)

ALISHA
INTO MY SECRET/Do You Dream About Me .... (RCA 5219-7-R) | .75 | 3.00 | 87

ALLAN, DAVIE, AND THE ARROWS
THE BORN LOSERS THEME/The Glory Stompers .... (Get Hip 209) | .50 | 2.00 | 97
   (Hard cover folding sleeve)

ALLEN, DEBORAH
BABY I LIED/Time Is Taking You Away From Me .... (RCA PB-13600) | 1.00 | 4.00 | 83
HEARTACHE AND A HALF .... (RCA PB-13921) | 1.00 | 4.00 | 84

ALLEN, DONNA
MAKE IT MY NIGHT/Red Hot .... (Atlantic 7-89152) | .75 | 3.00 | 87
   (B-side shown as by Debbie Gibson. From the motion picture *Fatal Beauty*, Whoopi Goldberg pictured.)
HEAVEN ON EARTH/ .... (Oceana/Atlantic 7-99265) | .75 | 3.00 | 88
CAN WE TALK/Come For Me .... (Oceana/Atlantic 7-99213) | .75 | 3.00 | 89

ALLEN, JIMMY
WHEN SANTA COMES OVER THE BROOKLYN BRIDGE/
   What Would You Like To Have For Christmas?(*Al-Brite 1300*) .... 12.50 | 50.00 | 59

ALLEN, LLOYD
I KEEP LOOKING AT YOU/ .... (Epic 34-04252) | .75 | 3.00 | 83
I KEEP LOOKING AT YOU .... (Epic 34-04252) | 1.00 | 4.00 | 83
   (Promotional issue, *Demonstration Only–Not For Sale* printed on sleeve)

ALLEN, REX, JR.
LAST OF THE SILVER SCREEN COWBOYS/Round Up Time .... (Warner Bros. 50035) | 1.50 | 6.00 | 82
   (Shown as by Rex Allen, Jr. With Guest Stars Roy Rogers & Rex Allen, Sr.)

ALLEN, REX, SR.
   See Rex Allen, Jr. (*Last Of The Silver Screen Cowboys*)

ALLEN, WOODY
EXCERPTS FROM A GREAT NEW COMEDY ALBUM .... (*Colpix* number unknown) | 7.50 | 30.00 | 64
   (Promotional issue only, specific excerpted titles unknown)
THE NIGHTCLUB YEARS 1964–1968 .... (*United Artists* number unknown) | 2.50 | 10.00 | 72
   (Promotional issue only, specific banded titles unknown)
   Also see Tom Jones (*What's New Pussycat?*)

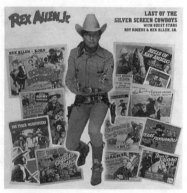

ALLISON, FRAN
AT THE FAIR .... (RCA WY 2004) | 6.25 | 25.00 | 52
   (Shown as by Kukla, Fran & Ollie. Fold-open sleeve with 12-page coloring book and detachable puppet
   pieces)
HAPPY MOTHER GOOSE .... (RCA WY-423) | 6.25 | 25.00 | 53
   (Shown as by Kukla, Fran & Ollie)
DRAGON RETREAT .... (RCA WY-425) | 6.25 | 25.00 | 53
   (Shown as by Kukla, Fran & Ollie)

ALLISON, KE!TH
SWEET LITTLE ROCK 'N ROLLER/The Girl Can't Help It .... (Warner Bros. 5681) | 6.25 | 25.00 | 65
LOOK AT ME/I Ain't Blaming You .... (Columbia 43619) | 6.25 | 25.00 | 66
FREEBORN MAN/Louise .... (Columbia 44028) | 6.25 | 25.00 | 67
   Also see Paul Revere and the Raiders

ALLISONS, THE
ARE YOU SURE?/There's One Thing More .... (London 45-1977) | 1.25 | 5.00 | 61

ALLMAN BROTHERS BAND, THE
STRAIGHT FROM THE HEART/Leavin' .... (Arista 0618) | 1.25 | 5.00 | 81
   Also see Hourglass

ALL MY CHILDREN
(Television Soap Opera)
   Related see the Soaps and Hearts Ensemble

ALL SPORTS BAND
YOUNG GIRL .... (Radio 4071) | 1.00 | 4.00 | 82

ALL THIS AND WORLD WAR II
(Motion Picture)
   See Richard Cocciante (*Michelle*)

ALMOND, MARC
TEARS RUN RINGS/Everything I Wanted Love To Be .... (Capitol B-44240) | .75 | 3.00 | 88
   Also see Soft Cell

ALOHA FROM HAWAII VIA SATELLITE
(Television Special)
   See Elvis Presley (*Steamroller Blues*)

ALPERT, HERB
THIS GUY'S IN LOVE WITH YOU/Quiet Tear .... (A&M 929) | 1.25 | 5.00 | 68
TO WAIT FOR LOVE/Bud .... (A&M 964) | 1.25 | 5.00 | 68

|---|---|---|---|---|

ROTATION	(A&M 2202)	1.00	4.00	79
STREET LIFE	(A&M 2221)	1.00	4.00	79
BEYOND	(A&M 2246)	1.00	4.00	80
MAGIC MAN/Fantasy Island	(A&M 2356)	1.00	4.00	81
ROUTE 101	(A&M 2422)	1.00	4.00	82
KEEP YOUR EYE ON ME	(A&M 2915)	.75	3.00	87
DIAMONDS	(A&M 2929)	.75	3.00	87

(Front of sleeve credits lead & background vocals by Janet Jackson & Lisa Keith)

| MAKING LOVE IN THE RAIN | (A&M 2949) | .75 | 3.00 | 87 |

(Front of sleeve credits lead & background vocals by Lisa Keith)
Also see Herb Alpert & the Tijuana Brass

ALPERT, HERB, & THE TIJUANA BRASS

| WHAT NOW MY LOVE/Spanish Flea | (A&M 792) | 1.50 | 6.00 | 66 |

(—B-side used as the theme for the television series *The Dating Game*)

THE WORK SONG/Plucky	(A&M 805)	1.25	5.00	66
FLAMINGO/So What's New?	(A&M 813)	1.25	5.00	66
MAME/Our Day Will Come	(A&M 823)	1.25	5.00	66
WADE IN THE WATER/Mexican Road Race	(A&M 840)	1.25	5.00	67
CASINO ROYALE/The Wall Street Rag	(A&M 850)	1.25	5.00	67

(A-side from the motion picture *Casino Royale*)

THE HAPPENING/Town Without Pity	(A&M 860)	1.25	5.00	67
A BANDA (AH BAHN–DA)/Miss Frenchy Brown	(A&M 870)	1.25	5.00	67
CARMEN/Love So Fine	(A&M 890)	1.25	5.00	68
CABARET/Slick	(A&M 925)	1.25	5.00	68
MY FAVORITE THINGS/The Christmas Song	(A&M 1001)	1.25	5.00	69
ZAZUEIRA/Treasure Of San Miguel	(A&M 1043)	1.25	5.00	69
WITHOUT HER/Sandbox	(A&M 1065)	1.25	5.00	69
JERUSALEM/Strike Up The Band	(A&M 1225)	1.25	5.00	70
SUMMERTIME/Hurt So Bad	(A&M 1261)	1.25	5.00	71
BULLISH	(A&M 2655)	.75	3.00	84

Also see Herb Alpert

ALPHAVILLE

BIG IN JAPAN/Seeds	(Atlantic 7-89665)	1.25	5.00	84
DANCE WITH ME/The Nelson High Rise Sector Two	(Atlantic 7-89415)	1.00	4.00	86
RED ROSE/Next Generation	(Atlantic 7-89292)	.75	3.00	86
FOREVER YOUNG/Lies	(Atlantic 7-89013)	.75	3.00	88

(*Forever Young* was previously released in 1985 with catalog number 89578, but without a picture sleeve)

ALTERED IMAGES

| DON'T TALK TO ME ABOUT LOVE/Last Goodbye | (Portrait 37-03841) | 1.25 | 5.00 | 83 |

ALVARADO, TRINI
(Actress)
See Marcy Levy and Robin Gibb (*Help Me!*)

AMADEUS
(Motion Picture)
See the Academy of St. Martin's in the Fields

AMBROSIA
See David Pack

AMERICA

I NEED YOU/Riverside	(Warner Bros. 7580)	1.25	5.00	74
LONELY PEOPLE/Mad Dog	(Warner Bros. 8048)	1.25	5.00	74
CALIFORNIA DREAMING	(American International 700-DJ)	1.25	5.00	78

(Promotional issue only, from the motion picture *California Dreaming*)

| RIGHT BEFORE YOUR EYES | (Capitol B-5177) | 1.00 | 4.00 | 82 |
| THE BORDER | (Capitol B-5236) | 1.00 | 4.00 | 84 |

AMERICAN ANTHEM
(Motion Picture)
See John Parr (*Don't Worry 'Bout Me*)

AMERICAN BREED, THE

| GREEN LIGHT/Don't It Make You Cry | (Acta 821) | 3.00 | 12.00 | 68 |

AMERICAN DREAM, THE

| I AIN'T SEARCHIN'/Good News | (Ampex 11001) | 2.00 | 8.00 | 70 |

AMERICAN GIGOLO
(Motion Picture)
See Blondie

AMERICAN GIRLS

| AMERICAN GIRL/Sharkskin Suit | (I.R.S. 52878) | 1.00 | 4.00 | 86 |

AMERICAN MUSIC CLUB

| GOODBYE TO LOVE | (A&M 31458 0706 7) | .50 | 2.00 | 94 |

(Side 1 of a 7-record box set titled *If I Were A Carpenter*. Each sleeve has a different face shot of Karen Carpenter on the front, Richard Carpenter on the back. No artist name or song titles indicated on sleeve. Complete set valued at $30.00 near mint.)

AMERICAN NOISE

| ANOTHER GIRL LIKE YOU/Statutory Sue | (Kriminal 45003) | 2.00 | 8.00 | 82 |

(Folding sleeve)

AMERICAN SPRING

| SHYIN' AWAY | (Columbia 4-45834) | 7.50 | 30.00 | 73 |

Also see the Honeys (Diane Rovell, Marilyn Rovell-Wilson), Rodney and the Brunettes (Diane Rovell, Marilyn Rovell-Wilson)

AMES, ED

| WHO WILL ANSWER/My Love Is Gone From Me | (RCA Victor 47-9400) | 2.00 | 8.00 | 67 |

Also see the Ames Brothers

TITLE	LABEL AND NUMBER	VG	NM	YR
AMES, NANCY				
FRIENDS AND LOVERS FOREVER	(RCA 47-8365)	1.00	4.00	64
AMES BROTHERS, THE				
CHINA DOLL / Christopher Sunday	(RCA Victor 47-7655)	3.00	12.00	60
LOVE IS AN OCEAN OF EMOTION / Love Me With All Your Heart	(Epic 9530)	2.00	8.00	62
Also see Ed Ames				
AMOS, TORI				
See Y Kant Tori Read				
ANA				
SHY BOYS	(Parc/CBS ZS4-07056)	.75	3.00	87
AN AMERICAN TAIL				
(Motion Picture)				
See Linda Ronstadt (*Somewhere Out There*), James Ingram (*Somewhere Out There*)				
ANDAL, LINDA				
SUMMER VALENTINE	(Columbia 4-43354)	2.00	8.00	66
ANDERSEN, BETH				
See Deborah Harry (b-side of *Rush Rush*)				
ANDERSON, BILL				
8 X 10 / One Mile Over–Two Miles Back	(Decca 31521)	2.00	8.00	63
PO' FOLKS CHRISTMAS / Christmas Time's A Comin'	(Decca 32417)	2.00	8.00	69
ANDERSON, CARL				
FRIENDS AND LOVERS	(Carrere 06122)	.75	3.00	86
(Shown as by Gloria Loring & Carl Anderson)				
ANDERSON, JON				
HOLD ON TO LOVE	(Columbia 38-07766)	1.00	4.00	88
Also see Anderson, Bruford, Wakeman, Howe, Yes				
ANDERSON, LAURIE				
O SUPERMAN / Walk The Dog	(Warner Bros. 49876)	5.00	20.00	81
(Hard cover with picture sleeve insert, issued with a small-hole 33-1/3 RPM record)				
ANDERSON, LYNN				
DING-A-LING THE CHRISTMAS BELL	(Columbia 4-45251)	1.50	6.00	70
(Promotional issue only)				
FRANK JONES INTERVIEW WITH LYNN ANDERSON	(Columbia AS7 1024)	1.25	5.00	70
(Promotional issue only envelope sleeve with 3" flap. Sleeve reads *...an Exclusive Interview with Lynn Anderson...including musical excerpts from "Rose Garden," "Snowbird," "No Love At All," "Honey Come Back," "You're My Man" and "For The Good Times."* Issued with a small-hole 33-1/3 RPM record.)				
FROSTY THE SNOWMAN / Don't Wish Me Merry Christmas	(Columbia AE7 1056)	1.25	5.00	72
(Promotional issue only)				
ANDERSON, BRUFORD, WAKEMAN, HOWE				
BROTHER OF MINE / Vultures	(Arista 9852)	1.00	4.00	89
Also see Jon Anderson, GTR (Steve Howe), Rick Wakeman, Yes				
ANDREWS, JULIE				
SUPER-CALI-FRAGIL-ISTIC-EXPI-ALI-DOCIOUS / A Spoonful Of Sugar	(Buena Vista F-434)	3.00	12.00	65
(A-side shown as by Julie Andrews, Dick Van Dyke, and the Pearlies. From the motion picture *Mary Poppins*.)				
THOROUGHLY MODERN MILLIE / Jimmy	(Decca 32102)	2.00	8.00	67
(From the Broadway musical *Thoroughly Modern Millie*)				
ANDREWS SISTERS				
BEI MIR BIST DU SCHÖN / In Apple Blossom Time	(Decca 1-705)	3.00	12.00	51
(Part of the Decca "Curtain Call" Series of reissues)				
ANELLO, ANN				
AMERICA	(Spi Discs 254-1)	.75	3.00	80s
(Hard cover)				
ANGEL, JIMMY				
TOUCH ME WITH MAGIC	(Mega 106)	1.25	5.00	73
ANGEL CITY				
NO SECRETS	(Epic 9-50927)	1.25	5.00	80
(Promotional issue only, *For Promotional Use Only* printed on sleeve)				
ANGELLE, LISA				
LOVE-IT'S THE PITS / Biloxi Blue	(EMI America B-8258)	.75	3.00	85
THE FIRST TIME I LOVED FOREVER	(Capitol B-44292)	1.00	4.00	89
(From the television series *Beauty And The Beast*. Lyrics credited to Melanie.)				
ANGEL				
See the Cherry People (Punky Meadows), Giuffria (Gregg Giuffra), House Of Lords (Gregg Giuffra)				
ANGEL LISTENER, THE				
PREVIEW HIGHLIGHTS	(Angel SPRO-9527)	.75	3.00	80
(Camelot Music and Angel Records promotional issue only, issued with a small-hole 33-1/3 RPM record. Sleeve advertises sale prices for six albums. Album covers pictured include those by pianist Leonard Pennario, violinist Itzhak Perlman, soprano Maria Callas, and conductor/pianist Andre Previn.)				
ANGELS, THE				
DREAM BOY / Jamaica Joe	(Smash 1915)	5.00	20.00	64
I ADORE HIM / Thank You And Goodnight	(Smash 1854)	6.25	25.00	63
THE BOY FROM 'CROSS TOWN / A World Without Love	(Smash 1931)	6.25	25.00	64
ANGIE				
PEPPERMINT LUMP	(Stiff/Epic 9-50793)	2.00	8.00	79
(Pete Townshend also pictured on sleeve)				
PEPPERMINT LUMP	(Stiff/Epic 9-50793)	1.50	6.00	79
(Promotional issue, *Demonstration–Not For Sale* printed on sleeve. Pete Townshend also pictured on sleeve)				

ANGRY SAMOANS
DOPE ON THE SCARECROW / Heroin .... (Bad Trip 019)   1.00   4.00   95
   (Parody of John Mellencamp's *Rain On The Scarecrow* with lyrics referring to the Grateful Dead's Jerry Garcia. Garcia pictured on sleeve. Reportedly only 900 copies were made.)

ANIMAL HOUSE
(Motion Picture)
   See Stephen Bishop

ANIMALS
THE HOUSE OF THE RISING SUN / Talkin' 'Bout You .... (MGM K-13264)   5.00   20.00   64
I'M CRYING / Take It Easy .... (MGM K-13274)   7.50   30.00   64
   (First printing with b-side incorrectly shown without the word *Baby*)
I'M CRYING / Take It Easy Baby .... (MGM K-13274)   5.00   20.00   64
   (Second printing with correct title)
BOOM BOOM / Blue Feeling .... (MGM K-13298)   5.00   20.00   65
BRING IT ON HOME TO ME / For Miss Caulker .... (MGM K-13339)   3.75   15.00   65
SAN FRANCISCAN NIGHTS .... (MGM K-13769)   3.00   12.00   67
   (Shown as by Eric Burdon and the Animals)
MONTEREY .... (MGM K-13868)   3.00   12.00   67
   (Shown as by Eric Burdon and the Animals)
   Also see Eric Burdon, Alan Price

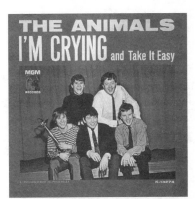

ANIMOTION
OBSESSION / Turn Around .... (Mercury 880 266-7)   1.00   4.00   85
LET HIM GO / Holding You .... (Mercury 880 737-7 M-1)   .75   3.00   85
I ENGINEER / The Essence .... (Casablanca 884 433-7)   .75   3.00   86
I WANT YOU / Staring Down The Demons .... (Casablanca 884 729-7)   .75   3.00   86
STRANGE BEHAVIOR / One Step Ahead .... (Casablanca 884 916-7)   .75   3.00   86
ROOM TO MOVE / Send It Over .... (Polydor 871 418-7)   .75   3.00   88
   (From the motion picture *My Stepmother Is An Alien*)
CALLING IT LOVE / The Way Into Your Heart .... (Polydor 889 054-7)   .75   3.00   89
   Also see Device (Paul Engemann), Giorgio Moroder (*Reach Out*)

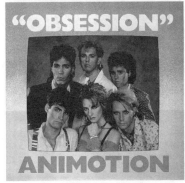

ANKA, PAUL
JUST YOUNG / So It's Goodbye .... (ABC-Paramount 9956)   12.50   50.00   58
(YOU CAN) SHARE YOUR LOVE / I Talk To You (On The Telephone) ... (ABC-Paramount PRO-104)   12.50   50.00   58
   (Fan club issue only)
I MISS YOU / Late Last Night .... (ABC-Paramount 10011)   6.25   25.00   59
PUT YOUR HEAD ON MY SHOULDER / Don't Ever Leave Me .... (ABC-Paramount 10040)   6.25   25.00   59
IT'S TIME TO CRY / Something Has Changed Me .... (ABC-Paramount 10064)   6.25   25.00   60
PUPPY LOVE / Adam And Eve .... (ABC-Paramount 10082)   6.25   25.00   60
MY HOME TOWN / Something Happened .... (ABC-Paramount 10106)   3.75   15.00   60
HELLO YOUNG LOVERS / I Love You In The Same Old Way .... (ABC-Paramount 10132)   3.75   15.00   60
SUMMER'S GONE / I'd Have To Share .... (ABC-Paramount 10147)   3.75   15.00   60
THE STORY OF MY LOVE / Don't Say You're Sorry .... (ABC-Paramount 10168)   3.75   15.00   60
IT'S CHRISTMAS EVERYWHERE / Rudolph The Red-Nosed Reindeer .... (ABC-Paramount 10169)   5.00   20.00   60
TONIGHT–MY LOVE–TONIGHT / I'm Just A Fool Anyway .... (ABC-Paramount 10194)   3.75   15.00   61
DANCE ON, LITTLE GIRL / I Talk To You .... (ABC-Paramount 10220)   3.75   15.00   61
KISSIN' ON THE PHONE / Cinderella .... (ABC-Paramount 10239)   3.75   15.00   61
LOVE ME WARM AND TENDER / I'd Like To Know .... (RCA Victor 47-7977)   3.00   12.00   62
A STEEL GUITAR AND A GLASS OF WINE / I Never Knew Your Name .... (RCA Victor 47-8030)   3.00   12.00   62
EVERY NIGHT / There You Go .... (RCA Victor 47-8068)   3.00   12.00   62
ESO BESO / Give Me Back My Heart .... (RCA Victor 47-8097)   3.00   12.00   62
LOVE (MAKES THE WORLD GO ROUND) / Crying In The Wind .... (RCA Victor 47-8115)   3.00   12.00   62
REMEMBER DIANA / At Night .... (RCA Victor 47-8170)   3.00   12.00   63
HELLO, JIM / You've Got The Nerve To Call This Love .... (RCA Victor 47-8195)   3.00   12.00   63
HURRY UP AND TELL ME / Wondrous Are The Ways Of Love .... (RCA Victor 47-8237)   3.00   12.00   63
DID YOU HAVE A HAPPY BIRTHDAY? / For No Good Reason At All .... (RCA Victor 47-8272)   3.00   12.00   63
FROM ROCKING HORSE TO ROCKING CHAIR / Cheer Up .... (RCA Victor 47-8311)   2.50   10.00   64
MY BABY'S COMING HOME / No, No .... (RCA Victor 47-8349)   2.50   10.00   64
IT'S EASY TO SAY / In My Imagination .... (RCA Victor 47-8396)   2.50   10.00   64
CINDY GO HOME / Ogni Volta .... (RCA Victor 47-8441)   2.50   10.00   65
THE LONELIEST BOY IN THE WORLD / Dream Me Happy .... (RCA Victor 47-8595)   2.50   10.00   65
AS IF THERE WERE NO TOMORROW / Every Day A Heart Is Broken .... (RCA Victor 47-8662)   2.50   10.00   65
I DON'T LIKE TO SLEEP ALONE .... (United Artists XW615-X)   1.00   4.00   75
TIMES OF YOUR LIFE / Water Runs Deep .... (United Artists UAST 16430/15288)   1.00   4.00   75
BROUGHT UP IN NEW YORK (BROUGHT DOWN IN L.A.) / Love Me Lady .... (RCA PB-11351)   .75   3.00   78
BROUGHT UP IN NEW YORK (BROUGHT DOWN IN L.A.) .... (RCA JH-11351)   1.25   5.00   78
   (Promotional issue, *Promotion Copy Not For Sale* printed front and back)
HOLD ME 'TIL THE MORNIN' COMES / This Is The First Time .... (Columbia 38-03897)   .75   3.00   83
YOU ARE MY DESTINY / Let The Bells Keep Ringing .... (Eric 199)   .75   3.00   84
DIANA / Don't Gamble With Love .... (Eric 200)   .75   3.00   84
NO WAY OUT .... (Columbia 38-07358)   .75   3.00   87
   (Shown as by Julia Migenes and Paul Anka. From the motion picture *No Way Out*, Kevin Costner pictured.)
   Also see Annette (*Talk To Me, Baby*)

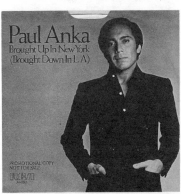

ANNETTE
(Annette Funicello)
HOW WILL I KNOW MY LOVE / Annette .... (Disneyland LG 758)   10.00   40.00   57
   (B-side shown as by Jimmie Dodd)
HOW WILL I KNOW MY LOVE? / Don't Jump To Conclusions .... (Disneyland F-102)   7.50   30.00   58
MEETIN' AT THE MALT SHOP .... (Disneyland F-105)   12.50   50.00   58
LONELY GUITAR / Wild Willie .... (Buena Vista F-339)   7.50   30.00   59
FIRST NAME INITIAL / My Heart Became Of Age .... (Buena Vista F-349)   7.50   30.00   59
O DIO MIO / It Took Dreams .... (Buena Vista F-354)   10.00   40.00   60
TRAIN OF LOVE / Tell Me Who's The Girl .... (Buena Vista F-359)   10.00   40.00   60
PINEAPPLE PRINCESS / Luau Cha Cha Cha .... (Buena Vista F-362)   6.25   25.00   60
TALK TO ME, BABY / I Love You, Baby .... (Buena Vista F-369)   6.25   25.00   60
   (Sleeve pictures Annette with Paul Anka)
DREAM BOY / Please, Please Signore .... (Buena Vista F-374)   6.25   25.00   61
INDIAN GIVER / Mama, Mama Rosa .... (Buena Vista F-375)   7.50   30.00   61

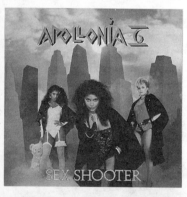

TITLE	LABEL AND NUMBER	VG	NM	YR
HAWAIIAN LOVE TALK/Blue Muu Muu	(Buena Vista F-384)	15.00	60.00	61
DREAMIN' ABOUT YOU/Strummin' Song	(Buena Vista F-388)	7.50	30.00	61
THE PARENT TRAP/Let's Get Together	(Buena Vista F-802)	10.00	40.00	61
(Shown as by Annette and Tommy Sands. From the motion picture *The Parent Trap*.)				
THAT CRAZY PLACE FROM OUTER SPACE/Seven Moons	(Buena Vista F-392)	6.25	25.00	62
THE TRUTH ABOUT YOUTH/I Can't Do The Swim	(Buena Vista F-394)	7.50	30.00	62
MISTER PIANO MAN/He's My Ideal	(Buena Vista F-405)	6.25	25.00	62
BELLA BELLA FLORENCE/Canzone D'Amore	(Buena Vista F-407)	18.75	75.00	62
(From the television special *Escapade In Florence*. Shown as by Annette and Gianni Marzocchi, both pictured on front; Annette and Tommy Kirk pictured on back.)				
TEENAGE WEDDING/Walking And Talking	(Buena Vista F-414)	50.00	200.00	63
PROMISE ME ANYTHING/Treat Him Nicely	(Buena Vista F-427)	15.00	60.00	63
MERLIN JONES/The Scrambled Egghead	(Buena Vista F-431)	10.00	40.00	63
(Sleeve pictures Annette with Tommy Kirk)				
CUSTOM CITY/Rebel Rider	(Buena Vista F-432)	12.50	50.00	63
MUSCLE BEACH PARTY/I Dream About Frankie	(Buena Vista F-433)	6.25	25.00	64
(From the motion picture *Muscle Beach Party*)				
BIKINI BEACH PARTY/The Clyde	(Buena Vista F-436)	7.50	30.00	64
SOMETHING BORROWED, SOMETHING BLUE/How Will I Know My Love?	(Buena Vista F-438)	12.50	50.00	64
THE MONKEY'S UNCLE	(Buena Vista F-440)	6.25	25.00	65
(From the motion picture *The Monkey's Uncle*)				
TOGETHER WE CAN MAKE A MERRY CHRISTMAS	(Pacific Star 569)	1.25	5.00	81
(Shown as by Frankie Avalon & Annette Funicello.)				
THE PROMISED LAND/In Between And Out Of Love	(Starview 3001)	3.75	15.00	83
(Picture sleeve mailing envelope)				

ANNIE
(Broadway Musical)
See Aileen Quinn and the Orphans (*Tomorrow*)

ANNIE AND THE ORPHANS

TITLE	LABEL AND NUMBER	VG	NM	YR
MY GIRL'S BEEN BITTEN BY THE BEATLE BUG/ A Place Called Happiness	(Capitol 5144)	5.00	20.00	64

ANN-MARGRET

TITLE	LABEL AND NUMBER	VG	NM	YR
I JUST DON'T UNDERSTAND/I Don't Hurt Anymore	(RCA Victor 47-7894)	3.75	15.00	61
IT DO ME SO GOOD/Gimme Love	(RCA Victor 47-7952)	3.75	15.00	61
WHAT AM I SUPPOSED TO DO/Let's Stop Kidding Each Other	(RCA Victor 47-7986)	5.00	20.00	62
JIM DANDY/I Was Only Kidding	(RCA Victor 47-8061)	5.00	20.00	62
NO MORE/So Did I	(RCA Victor 47-8130)	6.25	25.00	62
BYE BYE BIRDIE/Take All The Kisses	(RCA Victor 47-8168)	6.25	25.00	63
Also see Wayne Newton (*Stagecoach To Cheyenne*).				

ANOTHER WORLD
(Television Soap Opera)
Related see the Soaps and Hearts Ensemble

ANT, ADAM

TITLE	LABEL AND NUMBER	VG	NM	YR
PUSS 'N BOOTS/Kiss The Drummer	(Epic 34-04461)	.75	3.00	83
STRIP/Yours, Yours, Yours	(Epic 34-04337)	.75	3.00	84
STRIP	(Epic 34-04337)	1.00	4.00	84
(Promotional issue, *Demonstration–Not For Sale* printed on sleeve)				
VIVE LE ROCK/Greta X	(Epic 34-05574)	.75	3.00	85
VIVE LE ROCK	(Epic 34-05574)	1.25	5.00	85
(Promotional issue, *Demonstration–Not For Sale* printed on sleeve) Also see Adam and the Ants				

ANTHONY AND THE CAMP

TITLE	LABEL AND NUMBER	VG	NM	YR
WHAT I LIKE	(Warner Bros. 7-28730)	.75	3.00	88
HOW MANY LOVERS	(Warner Bros. 7-28613)	.75	3.00	88
SUSPENSE	(Warner Bros. 7-28144)	.75	3.00	88

ANTON, SUSAN

TITLE	LABEL AND NUMBER	VG	NM	YR
LISTEN TO MY SMILE	(Columbia 3-10740)	3.75	15.00	78
(Promotional issue only, *Demonstration Not For Sale* printed on sleeve)				

APARTMENT, THE
(Motion Picture)
See Ferrante And Teicher (*The Theme From The Apartment*), Jack Lemmon (*The Theme From The Apartment*)

APHRODITE'S CHILD
See Demis Roussos, Vangelis

APOLLONIA 6

TITLE	LABEL AND NUMBER	VG	NM	YR
SEX SHOOTER/In A Spanish Villa	(Warner Bros. 29182-7)	.75	3.00	84
BLUE LIMOUSINE/Some Kind Of Lover	(Warner Bros. 29092-7)	.75	3.00	84
Also see Prince (*Take Me With U*), Vanity 6 (Brenda Bennett, Susan Moonsie)				

APPARITIONS, THE

TITLE	LABEL AND NUMBER	VG	NM	YR
SHE'S SO SATISFYIN'/Midnight Hour	(Caped Crusader 71)	2.50	10.00	66

APPLE RECORDS

TITLE	LABEL AND NUMBER	VG	NM	YR
GENERIC APPLE RECORDS HALF SLEEVE	(Apple no #)	.50	2.00	68
(Issued with any 45 on Apple from 1968-1974, no song titles listed)				

APRIL WINE

TITLE	LABEL AND NUMBER	VG	NM	YR
SAY HELLO/Before The Dawn	(Capitol 4802)	1.00	4.00	81
JUST BETWEEN YOU AND ME	(Capitol 4975)	1.50	6.00	81
(Poster sleeve)				
JUST BETWEEN YOU AND ME	(Capitol 4975)	1.00	4.00	81
SIGN OF THE GYPSY QUEEN	(Capitol 5001)	1.00	4.00	81
TELL ME WHY	(Capitol 5168)	.75	3.00	82
ENOUGH IS ENOUGH	(Capitol B-5133)	.75	3.00	82
THIS COULD BE THE RIGHT ONE	(Capitol B-5319)	.75	3.00	84

TITLE	LABEL AND NUMBER	VG	NM	YR

ROCK MYSELF TO SLEEP .... (Capitol B-5506) .75 3.00 85
(From the motion picture *Fright Night*)

APSARAS
APSARAS/Children Of The Sunshine .... (CBS MAE7-2021) 1.00 4.00 85
(Promotional issue only)

ARBOGAST & ROSS
CHAOS .... (Liberty 55197) 6.25 25.00 59

ARCADIA

ELECTION DAY/She's Moody and Grey, She's Mean and She's Restless .... (Capitol B-5501) 1.50 6.00 85
(Grace Jones provides narration on the 45 but she is not credited on the sleeve)
GOODBYE IS FOREVER .... (Capitol B-5542) 1.50 6.00 86
THE FLAME .... (Capitol B-5570) 1.50 6.00 86
SAY THE WORD/Say The Word (Instrumental) .... (Atlantic 7-89370) 2.50 10.00 86
(From the motion picture *Playing For Keeps*)
Also see Duran Duran, Roger Taylor

ARCHANGEL, NATHALIE
I CAN'T REACH YOU .... (Columbia 38-07397) .75 3.00 87

ARCHIES, THE

BANG-SHANG-A-LANG/Truck Driver .... (Calendar 63-1006) 3.75 15.00 68
FEELIN' SO GOOD/Love Light .... (Calendar 63-1007) 3.75 15.00 68
A SUMMER PRAYER FOR PEACE/Maybe I'm Wrong .... (Kirshner 5014) 3.75 15.00 68
Also see the Cuff Links (Ron Dante), the Detergents (Ron Dante), Ron Dante

ARKADE
MORNING OF OUR LIVES .... (ABC/Dunhill 4268) 1.25 5.00 71

ARM, MARK
MASTERS OF WAR/My Life With Rickets .... (Sub Pop 87) 1.25 5.00 90
(Titled on front *The Freewheelin'*, issued with either black, purple, or green vinyl)
Also see Mudhoney

ARMATRADING, JOAN

DROP THE PILOT/Business Is Business .... (A&M 2538) 1.25 5.00 83
TEMPTATION/Talking To The Wall .... (A&M 2712) 1.00 4.00 85
KIND WORDS (AND A REAL GOOD HEART)/Figure Of Speech .... (A&M 2837) 1.00 4.00 86
EXTENDED PLAYS
ME MYSELF I/TALL IN THE SADDLE/SHOW SOME EMOTION/
Love And Affection/Rosie/Back To The Night/People .... (A&M 2391) 2.00 8.00 81
(Promotional issue only titled *Free Joan Armatrading*, issued with a small-hole 33-1/3 RPM record)

ARMSTRONG, LOUIS
FIVE PENNIES SAINTS .... (Dot 15941) 2.50 10.00 59
(Shown as by Danny Kaye and Louis Armstrong, from the motion picture *The Five Pennies*)
THE BEAT GENERATION/Some Day You'll Be Sorry .... (MGM K12809) 2.50 10.00 59
(Shown as by Louis Armstrong and His All-Stars. From the motion picture *The Beat Generation*. Mamie Van Doren, Steve Cochran, and Armstrong individually pictured.)
HELLO, DOLLY! .... (Kapp 573) 2.50 10.00 64
(From the Broadway musicals *Hello, Dolly!* and *Bye Bye Birdie*)
I STILL GET JEALOUS/Someday .... (Kapp 597) 2.50 10.00 64
SO LONG DEARIE .... (Mercury 72338) 2.50 10.00 64
FAITH .... (Mercury 72371) 2.50 10.00 64
(From the Broadway Musical *I Had A Ball*)
TEN FEET OFF THE GROUND/'Bout Time .... (Buena Vista 465) 2.00 8.00 68
(Shown as by Louis Armstrong and His Orchestra. From the motion picture *The One And Only, Genuine, Original Family Band*.)
THE NIGHT BEFORE CHRISTMAS/
When The Saints Go Marching In .... (Continental 1001) 1.50 6.00 71
WHAT A WONDERFUL WORLD .... (A&M 3010) .75 3.00 88
(From the motion picture *Good Morning, Vietnam*. Robin Williams pictured front and back.)
Also see Red Nichols (*Selmer Sampler*)

ARMSTRONG, VANESSA BELL
YOU BRING OUT THE BEST IN ME/Always .... (Jive/RCA 1051-7-J) .75 3.00 87

ARNAZ, DESI, JR.
(Son of Lucille Ball and Desi Arnaz)
See Dino, Desi & Billy

ARNOLD, EDDY
LITTLE MISS SUNBEAM/ .... (RCA Victor 47-7040) 2.50 10.00 58
DOES HE MEAN THAT MUCH TO YOU?/Tender Touch .... (RCA Victor 47-8102) 2.00 8.00 62
NO MORE/ .... (RCA Victor 47-8130) 2.00 8.00 63
YESTERDAY'S MEMORIES/Lonely Balladeer .... (RCA Victor 47-8160) 2.00 8.00 63
JUST A RIBBON/A Million Years Or So .... (RCA Victor 47-8207) 1.50 6.00 63
HE'S MY MAN/ .... (RCA Victor 47-8446) 1.50 6.00 64
MAKE THE WORLD GO AWAY/The Easy Way .... (RCA Victor 47-8679) 1.50 6.00 65
I WANT TO GO WITH YOU/You'd Better Stop Tellin' Lies (About Me) .... (RCA Victor 47-8749) 1.50 6.00 66
THE LAST WORD IN LONESOME IS ME/Mary Claire Melvina Rebecca Jane (RCA Victor 47-8818) 1.50 6.00 66
TIP OF MY FINGERS/Long, Long Friendship .... (RCA Victor 47-8869) 1.50 6.00 66
SOMEBODY LIKE ME/Taking Chances .... (RCA Victor 47-8965) 1.50 6.00 66
Also see Chet Atkins (*Chet's Tune*), Elvis Presley (*Old Shep EP*)

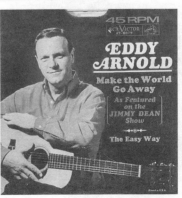

AROUND THE WORLD IN 80 DAYS
(Motion Picture)
See Mantovani (*Around The World*)

ARROWS, THE
See Davie Allan and the Arrows

ART BEARS
RATS & MONKEYS/Collapse .... (Ralph 7904) .50 2.00 96
Also see Fred Frith

TITLE	LABEL AND NUMBER	VG	NM	YR

ART COLLECTION
I GO TO SCHOOL / Morning .... (Sundazed 119) | .50 | 2.00 | 96
(Issued with yellow vinyl)

ARTHUR
(Motion Picture)
See Christopher Cross

ARTISTS UNITED AGAINST APARTHEID
SUN CITY / Not So Far Away .... (Manhattan B50017) | 1.00 | 4.00 | 85

Also see Afrika Bambaataa, Stiv Bators, Pat Benatar, Jackson Browne, Clarence Clemons, Jimmy Cliff, George Clinton, Peter Gabriel, Bob Geldof, Daryl Hall, Herbie Hancock, Little Steven, Bonnie Raitt, Lou Reed, Run-DMC, Bruce Springsteen, Ringo Starr, Pete Townshend, and Peter Wolf

ART OF NOISE
CLOSE (TO THE EDIT) / do DONNA do .... (Chrysalis 7-99754)	1.00	4.00	84
LEGS / Hoops And Mallets .... (Chrysalis VS4 42932)	1.00	4.00	85
PETER GUNN / Something Always Happens .... (Chrysalis VS4 42986)	1.00	4.00	86

(A-side shown as by the Art Of Noise Featuring Duane Eddy, Eddy pictured)

| PARANOIMIA / Why Me? .... (Chrysalis VS4 43002) | 1.00 | 4.00 | 86 |

(A-side shown as by the Art Of Noise With Max Headroom 7)

| LEGACY / Opus III .... (Chrysalis VS4 43055) | 1.00 | 4.00 | 86 |
| DRAGNET / Acton Art .... (Chrysalis VS4 43134) | 1.00 | 4.00 | 87 |

(From the motion picture *Dragnet*. Dan Aykroyd and Tom Hanks pictured on front.)

| KISS / E.F.L. .... (Chrysalis 871 038-7) | 1.00 | 4.00 | 88 |

(Hard cover, a-side shown as by the Art Of Noise Featuring Tom Jones)

ASHFORD, MATTHEW
(Actor)
See the Soaps and Hearts Ensemble

ASHFORD & SIMPSON
LOVE DON'T MAKE IT RIGHT / Finally Got To Me .... (Warner Bros. 49269)	1.00	4.00	80
STREET CORNER .... (Capitol B-5109)	.75	3.00	82
HIGH-RISE .... (Capitol B-5250)	.75	3.00	83
IT'S MUCH DEEPER .... (Capitol B-5284)	.75	3.00	83
I'M NOT THAT TOUGH .... (Capitol B-5310)	.75	3.00	84
SOLID .... (Capitol B-5397)	.75	3.00	84
OUTTA THE WORLD .... (Capitol B-5435)	.75	3.00	84
BABIES .... (Capitol B-5468)	.75	3.00	84
COUNT YOUR BLESSINGS / Side Effect .... (Capitol B-5598)	.75	3.00	84
WHAT BECOMES OF LOVE .... (Capitol B-5637)	.75	3.00	86
I'LL BE THERE FOR YOU .... (Capitol B-44326)	.75	3.00	86

Also see Maria Vidal (b-side of *Body Rock*)

ASHMAN, CHARLES
AN AMERICAN'S ANSWER (TO GORDON SINCLAIR) /
The Middle Class Is In The Middle Now .... (Dot 17507) | 1.25 | 5.00 | 74

ASIA
HEAT OF THE MOMENT / Ride Easy .... (Geffen 50040)	1.00	4.00	82
ONLY TIME WILL TELL / Time Again .... (Geffen 29970-7)	1.00	4.00	82
SOLE SURVIVOR / Here Comes The Feeling .... (Geffen 29871-7)	1.00	4.00	82
DON'T CRY / Daylight .... (Geffen 29571-7)	1.00	4.00	83
THE SMILE HAS LEFT YOUR EYES / Lying To Yourself ...... (Geffen 29475-7)	1.00	4.00	83
GO .... (Geffen 28872-7)	1.00	4.00	85

Also see Emerson, Lake & Palmer (Carl Palmer)

ASLEEP AT THE WHEEL
LOUISIANA .... (Capitol PRO-8868) | 2.00 | 8.00 | 78
(Promotional issue only)

ASSOCIATION, THE
PANDORA'S GOLDEN HEEBIE JEEBIES / Standing Still .... (Valiant 755) | 2.50 | 10.00 | 66

AS THE WORLD TURNS
(Television Soap Opera)
Related see the Soaps and Hearts Ensemble

ASTRONAUTS, THE
HOT-DOGGIN' / Every One But Me .... (RCA Victor 47-8224) | 10.00 | 40.00 | 63

ASTLEY, JON
JANE'S GETTING SERIOUS / The Animal .... (Atlantic 7-89258)	1.00	4.00	87
BEEN THERE, DONE THAT / Welcome To The Circus ...... (Atlantic 7-88965)	.75	3.00	88
PUT THIS LOVE TO THE TEST / Been There, Done That ...... (Atlantic 7-89027)	.75	3.00	88

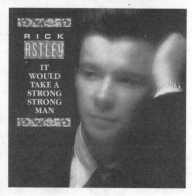

ASTLEY, RICK
NEVER GONNA GIVE YOU UP (Vocal) / Never Gonna Give You Up (Instrumental) ..... (RCA 5347)	.75	3.00	87
TOGETHER FOREVER / I'll Never Set You Free .... (RCA 83197-R)	.75	3.00	88
IT WOULD TAKE A STRONG MAN / You Move Me .... (RCA 8663-7)	.75	3.00	88
SHE WANTS TO DANCE WITH ME / She Wants To Dance With Me (Instrumental) (RCA 8838-7)	.75	3.00	88
GIVING UP ON LOVE / I'll Be Time .... (RCA 8872-7-R)	.75	3.00	89
AIN'T TOO PROUD TO BEG / I Don't Want To Be Your Lover .... (RCA 9030-7-R)	.75	3.00	89

Also see Ferry Aid

ASWAD
DON'T TURN AROUND / Woman .... (Mango/Island MS123) | .75 | 3.00 | 88
(The a-side is the original version of the song later recorded by Ace Of Base)
BEAUTY'S ONLY SKIN DEEP / Smokey Blues .... (Mango/Island MS125) | .75 | 3.00 | 89

ATHENS, GA—INSIDE/OUT
(Motion Picture)
See the Squalls (*Na, Na, Na, Na*)

ATKINS, CHET
THE SLOP/Hot Mocking Bird .... (RCA Victor 47-7847)   2.00   8.00   61
CHET'S TUNE/Country Gentleman .... (RCA Victor 47-9229)   1.50   6.00   67
   (A-side shown as By Some Of Chet's Friends, tribute song by various artists, Atkins pictured. The artists
   credited on the sleeve are Jerry Reed, Floyd Cramer, Eddy Arnold, Dottie West, Archie Campbell, Bobby Bare,
   Norma Jean, George Hamilton IV, Skeeter Davis, Jimmy Dean, Hank Locklin, Jim Ed Brown, Hank Snow,
   John D. Loudermilk, Connie Smith, Homer & Jethro, Waylon Jennings, Willie Nelson, Porter Wagoner, and
   Don Bowman. B-side shown as by Chet Atkins.)
SAILS/My Song .... (Columbia CS7 2712)   1.25   5.00   87
   (Promotional issue only issued with small-hole 33-1/3 RPM record)
   Also see the Country Hams

ATKINS, CHRISTOPHER
(Juvenile Actor)
HOW CAN I LIVE WITHOUT HER .... (Polydor 2210)   .75   3.00   82
   (From the motion picture *The Pirate Movie*)

ATLANTICS, THE
See Cannibal and the Headhunters (b-side of *Land Of 1000 Dances*)

ATLANTIC STARR
TOUCH A FOUR LEAF CLOVER .... (A&M 2580)   .75   3.00   83
FREAK A RISTIC/Island Dream .... (A&M 2718)   .75   3.00   85
IF YOUR HEART ISN'T IN IT/One Love .... (A&M 2822)   .75   3.00   85
ALWAYS .... (Warner Bros. 28455-7)   .75   3.00   87
ONE LOVER AT A TIME .... (Warner Bros. 28327-7)   .75   3.00   87
ALL IN THE NAME OF LOVE .... (Warner Bros. 28215-7)   .75   3.00   87
MY FIRST LOVE .... (Warner Bros. 27525-7)   .75   3.00   89

AUBREY TWINS
POOR BOY .... (Epic 5-10135)   2.50   10.00   66

AUGER, BRIAN
See Julie Driscoll and Brian Auger

AUSTIN, GENE
TOO LATE .... (RCA 47-6880)   2.50   10.00   57
   (From the television special *The Gene Austin Story*)

AUTOGRAPH
TURN UP THE RADIO .... (RCA PB-13953)   .75   3.00   84
   (First printing states on back *Special extended mix not available on the album*)
TURN UP THE RADIO .... (RCA PB-13953)   .75   3.00   84
   (Second printing states on back *Special extended mix*)
SEND HER TO ME/All I'm Gonna Take .... (RCA PB-14055)   .75   3.00   85

AUTRY, GENE
FROSTY THE SNOWMAN/When Santa Claus Gets Your Letter ...... (Columbia MJV 4-75)   2.50   10.00   51
   (Shown as by Gene Autry and The Cass County Boys. Half sleeve, children's series)
PETER COTTONTAIL/Funny Little Bunny .... (Columbia 68)   2.50   10.00   53
   (Children's series)
THE STORY OF LITTLE CHAMP .... (Columbia 104)   2.50   10.00   53
   (Children's series, two-record set)
THE THREE LITTLE DWARFS .... (Columbia 121)   2.50   10.00   53
   (Children's series)
MERRY TEXAS CHRISTMAS, YOU ALL .... (Columbia 150)   3.00   12.00   53
   (Half sleeve)
SANTA'S COMIN' IN A WHIRLYBIRD .... (Republic 2002)   2.50   10.00   59
RUDOLPH THE RED-NOSED REINDEER/Up On The Housetop .... (Mistletoe 801)   1.50   6.00   67
   (The 45 issued with this sleeve was on the Trip label with the same catalog number. Both Trip and Mistletoe
   were products of Springboard International Records.)
RUDOLPH THE RED-NOSED REINDEER .... (Columbia 33165)   3.00   12.00   69
   (Promotional issue only for Hall of Fame series)

AVALON, FRANKIE
SHY GUY/Too Young To Love .... (Chancellor C-1)   10.00   40.00   58
   (Promotional issue only sponsored by Acnecare products)
GINGER BREAD/Blue Betty .... (Chancellor 1021)   7.50   30.00   58
I'LL WAIT FOR YOU/What Little Girl .... (Chancellor 1026)   7.50   30.00   59
VENUS/I'm Broke .... (Chancellor 1031)   7.50   30.00   59
A BOY WITHOUT A GIRL/Bobby Sox To Stockings .... (Chancellor 1036)   6.25   25.00   59
JUST ASK YOUR HEART/Two Fools .... (Chancellor 1040)   5.00   20.00   60
WHY/Swingin On A Rainbow .... (Chancellor 1045)   6.25   25.00   60
DON'T THROW AWAY ALL THOSE TEARDROPS/Talk, Talk, Talk ...... (Chancellor 1048)   5.00   20.00   60
WHERE ARE YOU/Tuxedo Junction .... (Chancellor 1052)   5.00   20.00   60
TOGETHERNESS/Don't Let Love Pass Me By .... (Chancellor 1056)   5.00   20.00   60
A PERFECT LOVE/The Puppet Song .... (Chancellor 1065)   5.00   20.00   60
ALL OF EVERYTHING/Call Me Anytime .... (Chancellor 1071)   5.00   20.00   61
VOYAGE TO THE BOTTOM OF THE SEA/Summer Of '61 ..... (Chancellor 1081)   5.00   20.00   61
   (From the motion picture *Voyage to the Bottom of the Sea*)
TRUE, TRUE LOVE/Married .... (Chancellor 1087)   5.00   20.00   61
SLEEPING BEAUTY/The Lonely Bit .... (Chancellor 1095)   5.00   20.00   61
AFTER YOU'VE GONE/If You Don't Think I'm Leaving .... (Chancellor 1101)   5.00   20.00   61
YOU ARE MINE/Ponchinella .... (Chancellor 1107)   3.75   15.00   62
A MIRACLE/Don't Let Me Stand In Your Way .... (Chancellor 1115)   3.75   15.00   62
WELCOME HOME/Dance To The Bossa Nova .... (Chancellor 1125)   3.75   15.00   63
MY LOVE IS HERE TO STAY/
   New Fangled Jingle Jangle Swimming Suit From Paris .... (United Artists 748)   3.75   15.00   64
VENUS/Venus (Disco Version) .... (De-Lite 1578)   2.00   8.00   76
BEAUTY SCHOOL DROPOUT/Midnight Lady .... (De-Lite 907)   2.00   8.00   78
TOGETHER WE CAN MAKE A MERRY CHRISTMAS .... (Pacific Star 569)   2.00   8.00   81
   (Shown as by Frankie Avalon & Annette Funicello)
   Also see Annette (*Talk To Me, Baby*)

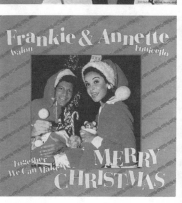

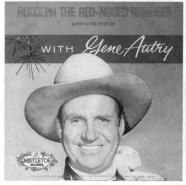

AVEDON, RICHARD
(Fashion Photographer)
   See the Wild Ones (*Come On Back*)

TITLE	LABEL AND NUMBER	VG	NM	YR

AVONS, THE
PUSH A LITTLE HARDER/Oh, Gee Baby .... (Groove 58-0022) — 5.00 — 20.00 — 63

AXTON, HOYT
SAN FERNANDO/Ten Thousand Sunsets .... (Colgems 66-1005) — 1.50 — 6.00 — 67

AYERS, ROY
2000 BLACK/The Way Of The World .... (Polydor 14294) — 1.25 — 5.00 — 75

AYKROYD, DAN
(Comic Actor)
CITY OF CRIME .... (MCA 53086) — .75 — 3.00 — 87
    (Shown as by Dan Aykroyd & Tom Hanks. From the motion picture *Dragnet*, both pictured.)
    Also see the Art Of Noise *(Dragnet)*, the Blues Brothers, Paul McCartney *(Spies Like Us)*, U.S.A. For Africa, Voices Of America

AZNAVOUR, CHARLES
(Actor)
YOU'VE LET YOURSELF GO/You've Got To Learn .... (Mercury 72031) — 5.00 — 20.00 — 62
    (Possibly a promotional issue only, brief biography on back)

AZTEC CAMERA
ALL I NEED IS EVERYTHING/Jump .... (Sire 29153-7) — 1.00 — 4.00 — 84
DEEP AND WIDE AND TALL/Bad Education .... (Sire 28155-7) — 1.00 — 4.00 — 87
SOMEWHERE IN MY HEART/
    Everybody Is A Number One (Boston '86 Version) .... (Sire 27819-7) — .75 — 3.00 — 88
    Also see the Smiths (Craig Gannon)

AZTECS, THE
THE AZTEC ROCK/Dreamy .... (Sultan 2) — 12.50 — 50.00 — 59

AZTEC TWO-STEP
EXTENDED PLAYS
MEET AZTEC TWO-STEP .... (RCA JF-10381) — 1.00 — 4.00 — 75
    (Promotional issue only, *For DJs Only* printed on sleeve, issued with a small-hole 33-1/3 RPM record)
ONE THING I FORGOT TO TELL YOU .... (RCA JF-11225) — 1.25 — 5.00 — 78
    (Promotional issue only titled *The Music's On Us*, issued with a small-hole 33-1/3 RPM record. Also includes
    one song each by Bill Quateman, Scorpions, and Fandango.)

B

BABES IN TOYLAND
DUST CAKE BOY/Spit To See The Shine .... (Treehouse 017) — 6.25 — 25.00 — 89
HOUSE/Arriba .... (Sub Pop 66) — 2.50 — 10.00 — 90
    (Limited to 3500 copies with 2000 on gold vinyl and 1500 on black)
CALLING OCCUPANTS OF INTERPLANETARY CRAFT .... (A&M 31458 0714 7) — .50 — 2.00 — 94
    (Side 10 of a 7-record box set titled *If I Were A Carpenter*. Each sleeve has a different face shot of Karen
    Carpenter on the front, Richard Carpenter on the back. No artist name or song titles indicated on sleeve.
    Complete set valued at $30.00 near mint.)

BABIES, THE
YOU MAKE ME FEEL LIKE SOMEONE/The Hands Of Fate .... (Dunhill 4085) — 5.00 — 20.00 — 67

BABINEAU, MARKO
    See Tesla

BABY BUGS, THE
BINGO .... (Vee-Jay 594) — 12.50 — 50.00 — 64
    (Promotional issue only, *Promotion Copy* printed on sleeve)

BABYS, THE
BACK ON MY FEET AGAIN/Turn Around In Tokyo .... (Chrysalis 2398) — 1.00 — 4.00 — 79
    Also see Journey (Jonathan Cain), John Waite

BACHARACH, BURT
ALL KINDS OF PEOPLE/She's Gone Away .... (A&M 1241) — 1.25 — 5.00 — 71
ONE LESS BELL TO ANSWER/Freefall .... (A&M 1290) — 1.25 — 5.00 — 71
    Also see Carole Bayer Sager *(Stronger Than Before)*, Dionne Warwick *(That's What Friends Are For)*

BACHELOR PARTY
(Motion Picture)
    See Fleshtones *(American Beat '84)*

BACHELORS, THE
I BELIEVE .... (London 45-9672) — 2.50 — 10.00 — 64
I WOULDN'T TRADE YOU FOR THE WORLD .... (London 45-9693) — 2.50 — 10.00 — 64
CHAPEL IN THE MOONLIGHT .... (London 45-9793) — 2.50 — 10.00 — 65

BACHMAN-TURNER OVERDRIVE
DOWN TO THE LINE/She's A Devil .... (Mercury 73724) — 1.50 — 6.00 — 75
    Also see the Guess Who (Randy Bachman), Union (Randy Bachman)

BACKBEAT BAND, THE
MONEY/Dizzy Miss Lizzy .... (Dry Hump 010) — 1.25 — 5.00 — 94
    (Originally issued with an insert advertising other Dry Hump releases)
    Also see Ciccone Youth (Thurston Moore), Hindu Love Gods (Mike Mills), Nirvana (Dave Grohl), R.E.M. (Mike Mills), Thurston Moore,
    Sonic Youth (Thurston Moore)

BACK STREET CRAWLER
EXTENDED PLAYS
HOO DOO WOMEN/ALL THE GIRLS ARE CRAZY/
    Survivor/The Band Plays On .... (Atco E.P. PR-247) — 1.50 — 6.00 — 75
    (Promotional issue only, *For Promotion Use Only* printed on sleeve. Issued with a small-hole 33-1/3 RPM
    record.)
STONE COLD SOBER .... (CBS AE7-1128 AE7-1129) — 2.00 — 8.00 — 77
    (Shown as by Crawler. Promotional issue only titled *Music For Every Ear*, double single release issued with two
    small-hole 33-1/3 RPM records. Also includes one song each by Joan Baez, Cheap Trick, Burton Cummings,
    Ram Jam, and Dennis Wilson.)
    Also see Free (Paul Kossoff)

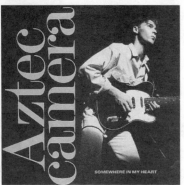

BACK PORCH MAJORITY, THE

SMASH FLOPS .... (Epic 5-9769) — 2.00 — 8.00 — 64

GENERIC BACK PORCH MAJORITY SLEEVE .... (Epic no #) — 1.25 — 5.00 — 60s

   (Used for a variety of singles, no song titles listed)

   Also see the New Christy Minstrels (Randy Sparks), Randy Sparks

BACK TO SCHOOL

(Motion Picture)

   See Jude Cole (Back To School)

BACK TO THE BEACH

(Motion Picture)

   See Dick Dale (Pipeline), Pee-Wee Herman (Surfin' Bird), Stevie Ray Vaughan (Pipeline)

BACK TO THE FUTURE

(Motion Picture)

   See Huey Lewis and the News (The Power Of Love), Marty McFly and the Starlighters (Johnny B. Goode)

BACK TO THE FUTURE PART III

(Motion Picture)

   See ZZ Top (Doubleback)

BACON, KEVIN

(Actor)

   See Roger Daltrey (Quicksilver Lightning), Ray Parker, Jr. (One Sunny Day/Dueling Bikes From Quicksilver), Dave Wakeling (She's Having A Baby)

BAD BRAINS

PAY TO CUM/Stay Close To Me .... (Bad Brains 001) — 2.50 — 10.00 — 80

   (Originally issued with a lyric insert)

PAY TO CUM/At The Movies .... (Caroline 1460) — 1.00 — 4.00 — 90

   (Issued with small-hole, yellow vinyl)

GOD OF LOVE/Longtime .... (Maverick 1001) — 1.50 — 6.00 — 94

   (Promotional issue only, individually numbered, issued with small-hole 45 RPM red vinyl)

BAD COMPANY

ROCK 'N' ROLL FANTASY/Crazy Circles .... (Swan Song 70119) — 1.25 — 5.00 — 79

   (Hard cover)

GONE GONE GONE/Take The Time .... (Swan Song 71000) — 1.25 — 5.00 — 79

   (Hard cover)

ELECTRICLAND/Untie The Knot .... (Swan Song 7-99966) — 1.00 — 4.00 — 82

THIS LOVE/Tell It Like It Is .... (Atlantic 7-89355) — .75 — 3.00 — 86

NO SMOKE WITHOUT A FIRE/Love Attack .... (Atlantic 89035-7) — .75 — 3.00 — 88

SHAKE IT UP/Dangerous Age .... (Atlantic 7-88939) — .75 — 3.00 — 88

   Also see the Firm (Paul Rodgers), Foreigner (Mick Jones), Free (Paul Rodgers), Mott The Hoople (Mick Ralphs), Paul Rodgers, Willie and the Poor Boys (Paul Rodgers)

BAD MANNERS

WHAT THE PAPERS SAY .... (Portrait 37-05725) — 1.00 — 4.00 — 85

WHAT THE PAPERS SAY .... (Portrait 37-05725) — 1.25 — 5.00 — 85

   (Promotional issue, Demonstration–Not For Sale printed on sleeve)

BADFINGER

BABY BLUE .... (Apple 1844) — 3.00 — 12.00 — 72

BADLANDS

DREAMS IN THE DARK/Hard Driver .... (Atlantic 7-88888) — .75 — 3.00 — 89

BADOWSKI, HENRY

MY FACE/Making Love With My Wife .... (I.R.S. 9013) — 1.25 — 5.00 — 85

BAD RELIGION

ATOMIC GARDEN .... (Sympathy For The Record Industry 158) — 1.00 — 4.00 — 91

AMERICAN JESUS .... (Sympathy For The Record Industry 232) — .75 — 3.00 — 92

STRANGER THAN FICTION .... (Sympathy For The Record Industry 326) — .75 — 3.00 — 94

PUNK SONG/The Universal Cynic/The Dodo .... (Unplayable 87079) — .75 — 3.00 — 96

   (Issued with small-hole, gray marbled vinyl)

   Also see Daredevils (Brett Gurewitz)

BAEZ, JOAN

THERE BUT FOR FORTUNE .... (Vanguard 35031) — 6.25 — 25.00 — 65

PACK UP YOUR SORROWS .... (Vanguard 35040) — 5.00 — 20.00 — 66

THE LITTLE DRUMMER BOY .... (Vanguard 35046) — 5.00 — 20.00 — 66

BE NOT TOO HARD .... (Vanguard 35055) — 5.00 — 20.00 — 66

MARIA DOLORES/Plane Wreck At Los Gatos (Deportee) ...... (Vanguard SPV-6) — 2.50 — 10.00 — 70

   (Black background extends to all four sides on the front. Included with the album Blessed Are, issued with a small-hole 33-1/3 RPM record.)

MARIA DOLORES/Plane Wreck At Los Gatos (Deportee) ...... (Vanguard SPV-6) — 2.50 — 10.00 — 70

   (1/8" white border on front. Included with the album Blessed Are, issued with a small-hole 33-1/3 RPM record.)

THE BALLAD OF SACCO AND VANZETTI/Here's To You ...... (RCA Victor 74-0568) — 2.00 — 8.00 — 71

   (From the motion picture Sacco & Vanzetti)

SONG OF BANGLADESH/Prison Trilogy (Billy Rose) .... (A&M 1334) — 1.50 — 6.00 — 72

IN THE QUIET MORNING (FOR JANIS JOPLIN)/To Bobby ...... (A&M 1362) — 1.50 — 6.00 — 72

EXTENDED PLAYS

TIME RAG .... (CBS AE7-1128 AE7-1129) — 2.00 — 8.00 — 77

   (Promotional issue only titled Music For Every Ear, double single release issued with two small-hole 33-1/3 RPM records. Also includes one song each by Cheap Trick, Crawler, Burton Cummings, Ram Jam, and Dennis Wilson.)

BAILEY, MILDRED

ROCKIN' CHAIR/Georgia On My Mind .... (Decca 1-725) — 3.00 — 12.00 — 53

   (Decca "Curtain Call" series of reissues)

BAILEY, PHILIP

I KNOW/The Good Guy's Supposed To Get The Girls ...... (Columbia 38-03968) — .75 — 3.00 — 83

EASY LOVER .... (Columbia 38-04679) — .75 — 3.00 — 84

   (Credited front and back as Duet With Phil Collins, only Bailey pictured)

TITLE	LABEL AND NUMBER	VG	NM	YR

EASY LOVER .... (Columbia 38-04679) | 1.00 | 4.00 | 83

(Promotional issue, *Demonstration–Not For Sale* printed on sleeve. Credited front and back as *Duet With Phil Collins*, only Bailey pictured.)

WALKING ON THE CHINESE WALL / Children Of The Ghetto .... (Columbia 38-04826) | .75 | 3.00 | 85
WALKING ON THE CHINESE WALL .... (Columbia 38-04826) | 1.00 | 4.00 | 85

(Promotional issue, *Demonstration–Not For Sale* printed on sleeve)

STATE OF THE HEART / .... (Columbia 38-05861) | .75 | 3.00 | 86
STATE OF THE HEART .... (Columbia 38-05861) | 1.00 | 4.00 | 86

(Promotional issue only, *Demonstration Only Not For Sale* printed on back)
Also see Earth Wind & Fire

BAILEY, RAZZY
I KEEP COMING BACK / True Life Country Music .... (RCA PB-12120) | .75 | 3.00 | 80

BAIO, SCOTT
(Juvenile Actor)
WHAT WAS IN THAT KISS / Looking For The Right Girl .... (RCA PB-13256) | 1.50 | 6.00 | 82
WANTED FOR LOVE / Woman I Love Only You .... (RCA PB-13356) | 1.50 | 6.00 | 82

BAJA MARIMBA BAND, THE
SPANISH MOSS .... (A&M 833) | 1.25 | 5.00 | 67
ALONG COMES MARY / The Wall Street Rag .... (A&M 862) | 1.25 | 5.00 | 67
YES SIR, THAT'S MY BABY / Brasilia .... (A&M 937) | 1.25 | 5.00 | 68

BAKER, ANITA
AIN'T NO NEED TO WORRY .... (Qwest 29274-7) | .75 | 3.00 | 85

(Shown as by the Winans and Anita Baker)

CAUGHT UP IN THE RAPTURE / Mystery .... (Elektra 7-69511) | .75 | 3.00 | 86
SAME OLE LOVE (365 DAYS A YEAR) /
  Same Ole Love (365 Days A Year) (Live Version) .... (Elektra 7-69484) | .75 | 3.00 | 87
NO ONE IN THE WORLD / Watch Your Step .... (Elektra 7-69456) | .75 | 3.00 | 86
GIVING YOU THE BEST THAT I GOT / Good Enough .... (Elektra 7-69371) | .75 | 3.00 | 88
JUST BECAUSE / Good Enough .... (Elektra 7-69327) | .75 | 3.00 | 89
LEAD ME INTO LOVE / Good Enough .... (Elektra 7-69299) | .75 | 3.00 | 89

BAKER, CARROLL
(Actress)
See Bobby Vinton *(Theme From Harlow)*

BAKER, GEORGE, SELECTION
DEAR ANN .... (Colossus 117) | 2.00 | 8.00 | 70

BAKER, PENNY, AND THE PILLOWS
BRING BACK THE BEATLES / Gonna Win Him .... (Witch 123) | 5.00 | 20.00 | 64

BAKER, SCOTT THOMPSON
(Actor)
See the Soaps and Hearts Ensemble

BAKKER, TAMMY FAYE
(Co-founder of the P.T.L. Club, a television talk-show, with her ex-husband and former televangelist Jim Bakker. Jim Bakker resigned his ministry in 1987 and was tried and convicted of fraud and conspiracy in 1989.)
IF IT HAD NOT BEEN / Gone .... (PTL R45-1821) | 3.00 | 12.00 | 80

(Tammy and Jim Bakker pictured on back)

THE BALLAD OF JIM AND TAMMY / Farewell, We Love You .... (Sutra 165) | 2.50 | 10.00 | 87

BALAAM & THE ANGEL
I LOVE THE THINGS YOU DO TO ME / Warm Again .... (Virgin 7-99340) | .75 | 3.00 | 88

BALDRY, LONG JOHN
MOTHER AIN'T DEAD / You Can't Judge A Book By Its Cover .... (Warner Bros. 7617) | 1.25 | 5.00 | 72
YOU'VE LOST THAT LOVING FEELING / Baldry's Out .... (EMI America 8018) | .75 | 3.00 | 79

(Shown as by Long John Baldry & Kathi McDonald)

BALIN, MARTY
HEARTS / Freeway .... (EMI America 8084) | 1.00 | 4.00 | 81
WHAT LOVE IS / Will You Forever .... (EMI America B-8153) | 1.25 | 5.00 | 83
DO IT FOR LOVE / Heart Of Stone .... (EMI America B-8160) | .75 | 3.00 | 83

Also see Jefferson Airplane, Jefferson Starship

BALLARD, FLORENCE
LOVE AIN'T LOVE / Forever Faithful .... (ABC 11114) | 7.50 | 30.00 | 68

Also see the Supremes

BALLARD, HANK, & THE MIDNIGHTERS
THE CONTINENTAL WALK / What Is This I See? .... (King 5491) | 10.00 | 40.00 | 61

BALLARD, RUSS
VOICES / Living Without You .... (EMI America B-8204) | .75 | 3.00 | 83
THE FIRE STILL BURNS / Hold On .... (EMI America B-8275) | .75 | 3.00 | 85

BALTIMORA
TARZAN BOY / Tarzan Boy (Dub Version) .... (Manhattan B 50018) | 1.25 | 5.00 | 85

BAMBAATAA, AFRIKA, AND FAMILY
RECKLESS / Mind Body And Soul .... (Capitol/EMI B-44163) | .75 | 3.00 | 88

(A-side featuring UB40)
Also see Artists United Against Apartheid

BANANARAMA
SHY BOY (DON'T IT MAKE YOU FEEL GOOD) /
  Give Us Back Our Cheap Fares .... (London 810 112-7) | 1.00 | 4.00 | 83
NA NA HEY HEY KISS HIM GOODBYE / Tell Tale Signs .... (London 810 117-7) | 1.00 | 4.00 | 83
ROBERT DE NIRO'S WAITING . . . / Push! .... (London 820 033-7) | 1.00 | 4.00 | 84
THE WILD LIFE / The State I'm In .... (London 886 019-7) | 1.00 | 4.00 | 84

(A-side from the motion picture *The Wild Life*)

TITLE	LABEL AND NUMBER	VG	NM	YR
VENUS/White Train	(London 886 056-7)	1.00	4.00	86
MORE THAN PHYSICAL/Scarlett	(London 886 080-7)	.75	3.00	86
A TRICK OF THE NIGHT/Cut Above The Rest	(London 886 119-7)	.75	3.00	86
I HEARD A RUMOUR/Clean Cut Boy (Party Size)	(London 886 165-7)	.75	3.00	87

(A-side from the motion picture *Disorderlies*)

I CAN'T HELP IT/Mr. Sleaze	(London 886 212-7)	.75	3.00	87
LOVE IN THE FIRST DEGREE/Ecstasy	(London 886 255-7)	.75	3.00	87
LOVE, TRUTH & HONESTY/Strike It Rich	(London 886 362-7)	.75	3.00	88
NATHAN JONES/Once In A Lifetime	(London 886 400-7)	.75	3.00	88
HELP!/Help	(London 886 492-7)	.75	3.00	89

(Shown as by Bananarama and Lananeeneenoonoo, all six women pictured. Record credits only Bananarama.)
Also see Band Aid, Ferry Aid

BANANA SPLITS, THE

THE TRA LA LA SONG/Toy Piano Melody	(Decca 32429)	6.25	25.00	68
LONG LIVE LOVE/Pretty Painted Carousel	(Decca 32536)	6.25	25.00	69

BAND, THE

RAG MAMA RAG/The Unfaithful Servant	(Capitol 2705)	2.00	8.00	70

Also see Robbie Robertson

BAND AID

DO THEY KNOW IT'S CHRISTMAS?/Feed The World	(Columbia 38-04749)	1.00	4.00	84
DO THEY KNOW IT'S CHRISTMAS?	(Columbia 38-04749)	1.50	6.00	84

(Promotional issue, *Demonstration–Not For Sale* printed on sleeve)
Also see Bananarama, Phil Collins, Culture Club, Duran Duran, Heaven 17, Paul McCartney, Spandau Ballet, Sting, Style Council, Ultravox, U2, Wham, Paul Young (Bob Geldof, Kool and the Gang, Jody Watley, and Paul Weller participated but were not credited on sleeve)

BAND WITHOUT A NAME, THE

TURN ON YOUR LOVELIGHT/A Perfect Girl	(Tower 246)	7.50	30.00	66

BANDY, MOE & JOE

THE BOY'S NIGHT OUT/	(Columbia 38-04601)	.75	3.00	84
THE BOY'S NIGHT OUT	(Columbia 38-04601)	1.00	4.00	84

(Promotional issue, *Demonstration–Not For Sale* printed on sleeve)

BANG-BANG

THIS IS LOVE	(Epic 34-04712)	.75	3.00	84
THIS IS LOVE	(Epic 34-04712)	1.00	4.00	84

(Promotional issue, *Demonstration–Not For Sale* printed on sleeve)

BANGLES

GETTING OUT OF HAND/Call On Me	(Downkiddie 001)	12.50	50.00	81

(Shown as by the Bangs. First printing features a Christmas message.)

GETTING OUT OF HAND/Call On Me	(Downkiddie 001)	10.00	40.00	81

(Shown as by the Bangs. Second printing deletes Christmas message.)

GETTING OUT OF HAND/Call On Me	(Downkiddie 001)	7.50	30.00	81

(Back of sleeve indicates Downkiddie address in Los Angeles, California)

GETTING OUT OF HAND/Call On Me	(Downkiddie 001)	6.25	25.00	81

(Back of sleeve indicates Downkiddie address in Torrance, California)

HERO TAKES A FALL/Where Were You When I Needed You	(Columbia 38-04479)	2.00	8.00	84

(First stock printing)

HERO TAKES A FALL	(Columbia 38-04770)	1.50	6.00	84

(Second stock printing, no b-side listed)

HERO TAKES A FALL	(Columbia 38-04479)	2.50	10.00	84

(Promotional issue, *Demonstration Only–Not For Sale* printed on sleeve)

MANIC MONDAY	(Columbia 38-05757)	1.00	4.00	85
MANIC MONDAY	(Columbia 38-05757)	1.50	6.00	85

(Promotional issue, *Demonstration Only/Not For Sale* printed on sleeve)

IF SHE KNEW WHAT SHE WANTS	(Columbia 38-05886)	1.00	4.00	86
IF SHE KNEW WHAT SHE WANTS	(Columbia 38-05886)	1.50	6.00	86

(Promotional issue, *Demonstration Only–Not For Sale* printed on sleeve)

WALKING DOWN YOUR STREET/Let It Go	(Columbia 38-06674)	1.00	4.00	87
HAZY SHADE OF WINTER	(Def Jam/Columbia 38-07630)	1.00	4.00	87

(From the motion picture *Less Than Zero*)

IN YOUR ROOM	(Columbia 38-08090)	1.00	4.00	88

Also see the Hoodoo Gurus (*Good Times*)

BANG ORCHESTRA!

SAMPLE THAT! (SHORT)	(Geffen 28621-7)	.75	3.00	86

BANGS, THE

GETTING OUT OF HAND/Call On Me	(Downkiddie 001)	12.50	50.00	81

(First printing features a Christmas message)

GETTING OUT OF HAND/Call On Me	(Downkiddie 001)	10.00	40.00	81

(Second printing deletes Christmas message)
Also see the Bangles

BANNED, THE

IT COULDN'T HAPPEN HERE	(Fontana 1616)	5.00	20.00	68

BANTAMS, THE

FOLLOW ME/Meet Me Tonight, Little Girl	(Warner Bros. 5695)	3.75	15.00	66

BARBER'S, CHRIS, JAZZ BAND

PETITE FLEUR/Wild Cat Blues	(Laurie 3022)	2.00	8.00	59

BARBUSTERS, THE

See Joan Jett and the Blackhearts

BARDENS, PETE

IN DREAMS	(Capitol B-44080)	.75	3.00	87
GOLD	(Capitol B-44192)	.75	3.00	88

Also see Them

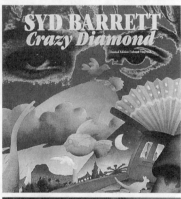

TITLE	LABEL AND NUMBER	VG	NM	YR

BARDEUX
MAGIC CARPET RIDE / When We Kiss .... (Enigma/Synthicide B-75016) .75 | 3.00 | 87
 (Hard cover)

BARDOT, BRIGITTE
(Actress)
SIDONIE .... (MGM K13099) | 7.50 | 30.00 | 61

BARDS, THE
THE OWL AND THE PUSSYCAT .... (Capitol 2148) | 6.25 | 25.00 | 68

BARE, BOBBY
I DON'T BELIEVE I'LL FALL IN LOVE TODAY / To Whom It May Concern ... (RCA Victor 47-8083) | 2.50 | 10.00 | 62
I'D FIGHT THE WORLD / Dear Waste Basket .... (RCA Victor 47-8146) | 2.50 | 10.00 | 63
DETROIT CITY / Heart Of Ice .... (RCA Victor 47-8183) | 2.50 | 10.00 | 63
NEW CUT ROAD .... (CBS AE7 1429) | 1.00 | 4.00 | 82
 (Promotional issue only titled *Kickin Rock & Roll*, co-sponsored by Busch Beer and WBCN 104 FM and
 included in *The Phoenix* magazine. Also includes songs by George Jones, Merle Haggard, Larry Gatlin and the
 Gatlin Brothers Band, the Burrito Brothers, and Ricky Skaggs.)
 Also see Chet Atkins (*Chet's Tune*)

BARNABY BYE
EXTENDED PLAYS
SHE'S LEAVING HOME .... (Atlantic PR 195) | 1.25 | 5.00 | 73
 (Promotional issue only titled *Something For Nothing*. Also includes one song each, the titles are not listed on
 sleeve, by Daryl Hall & John Oates, John Prine, and Delbert & Glen.)

BARNES, BILL
SLOOP JOHN B .... (Columbia 4-43491) | 2.00 | 8.00 | 66

BARNES, JIMMY
I'D DIE TO BE WITH YOU TONIGHT / Piece Of My Heart .... (Geffen 28693-7) | .75 | 3.00 | 86
GOOD TIMES / Laying Down The Law .... (Atlantic 7-89237) | .75 | 3.00 | 86
 (Shown as by INXS and Jimmy Barnes. From the motion picture *The Lost Boys*)
TOO MUCH AIN'T ENOUGH LOVE / .... (Geffen 27920-7) | .75 | 3.00 | 88

BARNES, KATHY
SLEEPING WITH A MEMORY .... (Republic 223) | 1.50 | 6.00 | 76

BARNES & BARNES
A DAY IN THE LIFE OF GREEN ACRES .... (Asinine no #) | 3.75 | 15.00 | 79
 (Parody of the Beatles *A Day In The Life* with lyrics from the television series Green Acres)

BARNETT, BOBBY
MOANIN' THE BLUES .... (Sims 198) | 3.00 | 12.00 | 63

BARNUM, H.B.
IT HURTS TOO MUCH TO CRY / Lonely Hearts .... (RCA Victor 47-8112) | 20.00 | 80.00 | 62

BARR, JULIA
(Actress)
 See the Soaps and Hearts Ensemble

BARRACUDA
THE DANCE OF ST. FRANCIS / Lady Fingers .... (RCA Victor 47-9660) | 5.00 | 20.00 | 68

BARRETT, SYD
TERRAPIN / OCTOPUS /
Baby Lemonade / Effervescing Elephant .... (Capitol NR 7243 8 58186 7) | 1.00 | 4.00 | 93
 (Issued with pink vinyl and titled *Crazy Diamond*)
 Also see Pink Floyd

BARRIS, CHUCK
(Television producer and host of the game show *The Gong Show*. Barris also wrote the Freddy Cannon hit *Palisades Park*.)
THEME THEME FROM GENE GENE / Lovee's Come Back .... (Gong Show 100) | 2.50 | 10.00 | 78

BARRON KNIGHTS
YOU'RE ALL I NEED / Nothin' Doin' .... (Mercury 73302) | 1.50 | 6.00 | 72

BARRY, JOE
TEARDROPS IN MY HEART / For You, Sunshine .... (Smash 1710) | 15.00 | 60.00 | 61

BARRY, JOHN
JAMES BOND THEME / March Of The Mandarins .... (United Artists 581) | 2.50 | 10.00 | 63

BARRY, LEN
JUST THE TWO OF US / Diggin' Life .... (Buddah 284) | 1.25 | 5.00 | 72
 Also see the Dovells

BARTON, BOB
AIN'T I'M A MESS .... (EEM 1651) | 7.50 | 30.00 | 58

BARTON, DIANE
(Actress)
 See the Soaps and Hearts Ensemble

BARTON, EILEEN
 See the Triplets (*Loyalty*)

BARTON, LOU ANN
TEAR ME APART / Quittin' Time .... (Spindletop 7-107) | 1.00 | 4.00 | 86

BARYSHNIKOV, MIKHAIL
(Ballet Dancer)
 See Lou Reed (*My Love Is Chemical*), Lionel Richie (*Say You, Say Me*)

BASIL, TONI
MICKEY / Thief On The Loose .... (Chrysalis 2638) | 1.25 | 5.00 | 82
SHOPPIN' FROM A TO Z / Time After Time .... (Chrysalis VS4 03537) | .75 | 3.00 | 83
OVER MY HEAD / Best Performance .... (Chrysalis VS4 42753) | .75 | 3.00 | 83

BASINGER, KIM
(Actress)
See Gary Morris and Jennifer Warnes (*Simply Meant To Be*), Alan Silvestri (*No Mercy Main Title*), Billy Vera & the Beaters (*Let You Get Away*)

BASKERVILLE HOUNDS, THE
CHRISTMAS IS HERE/Make Me Your Man .... (Tema 131)	7.50	30.00	66

BASSEY, SHIRLEY
NEVER NEVER NEVER .... (United Artists XW211)	1.25	5.00	73

BATMAN
(Comic Book)
See Dan and Dale (*Batman Theme*)

BATMAN
(Motion Picture)
See Danny Elfman (*The Batman Theme*), Prince (*The Arms Of Orion, Partman, Scandalous*)

BATMAN
(Television Series)
See Frank Gorshin (*The Riddler*), Neal Hefti (*Batman Theme*)

BATORS, STIV
IT'S COLD OUTSIDE/The Last Year .... (Bomp 124)	1.50	6.00	79

(Issued with small-hole 45 RPM record)
NOT THAT WAY ANYMORE/Circumstantial Evidence .... (Bomp 128)	2.00	8.00	79

Also see Artists United Against Apartheid, the Dead Boys, the Lords of the New Church

BAUHAUS
ZIGGY STARDUST/Lagartija-Nick/Third Uncle .... (A&M 2524)	6.25	25.00	83

Also see Love And Rockets (Daniel Ash, David J, Kevin Haskins), Peter Murphy

BAXTER, ANNE
(Actress)
See Brook Benton (*Walk On The Wild Side*)

BAXTER, LES
THEME FROM THE MANCHURIAN CANDIDATE .... (Reprise 20120)	15.00	60.00	62

(From the motion picture *The Manchurian Candidate*, Frank Sinatra credited on sleeve.)

BAY CITY ROLLERS, THE
GIVE A LITTLE LOVE .... (Arista 0149)	1.50	6.00	75
SATURDAY NIGHT .... (Arista 0149)	1.50	6.00	75

(Two records were released with the same catalog number; the promotional issue of *Give A Little Love* and the stock issue of *Saturday Night* on Arista 0149. Identical sleeves, that did not show song titles, were used for both.)
MONEY HONEY .... (Arista 170)	1.50	6.00	76
DEDICATION/Rock N' Roller .... (Arista 0239)	1.50	6.00	77
WHERE WILL I BE NOW .... (Arista 0363)	1.50	6.00	78

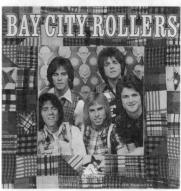

BEACH BOYS, THE
SURFIN' SAFARI/409 .... (Capitol 4777)	15.00	60.00	62
TEN LITTLE INDIANS/County Fair .... (Capitol 4880)	50.00	200.00	62
SPIRIT OF AMERICA .... (Capitol no #)	150.00	600.00	63

(Promotional issue only, sleeve reads *I Was There KFWB Day! Wallich's Music City South Bay Store Opening Nov. 16, 1963.*)
A SURPRISE GIFT FROM THE BEATLES, THE BEACH BOYS & THE KINGSTON TRIO .... (Capitol/Evatone 8464)	500.00	2000.00	64

(6" x 9" mailer issued with a 5" flexidisc)
FUN, FUN, FUN/Why Do Fools Fall In Love .... (Capitol 5118)	6.25	25.00	64
DON'T WORRY BABY/I Get Around .... (Capitol 5174)	6.25	25.00	64
WHEN I GROW UP (TO BE A MAN)/She Knows Me Too Well .... (Capitol 5245)	6.25	25.00	64

(Blue border)
WHEN I GROW UP (TO BE A MAN)/She Knows Me Too Well .... (Capitol 5245)	7.50	30.00	64

(Green border)

DANCE, DANCE, DANCE/The Warmth Of The Sun .... (Capitol 5306)	10.00	40.00	64
DO YOU WANNA DANCE?/Please Let Me Wonder .... (Capitol 5372)	6.25	25.00	65
HELP ME, RHONDA/Kiss Me, Baby .... (Capitol 5395)	6.25	25.00	65
CALIFORNIA GIRLS/Let Him Run Wild .... (Capitol 5464)	6.25	25.00	65
THE LITTLE GIRL I ONCE KNEW/No Other (Like My Baby) .... (Capitol 5540)	6.25	25.00	65
BARBARA ANN/Girl Don't Tell Me .... (Capitol 5561)	30.00	120.00	65

(Glossy coated paper)
BARBARA ANN/Girl Don't Tell Me .... (Capitol 5561)	37.50	150.00	65

(Non-glossy uncoated paper)

SLOOP JOHN B/You're So Good To Me .... (Capitol 5602)	5.00	20.00	66
GOOD VIBRATIONS .... (Capitol 5676)	6.25	25.00	66
HEROES AND VILLAINS .... (Capitol 5826)	125.00	500.00	67

(Originally planned for U.S. release, but after the decision to issue it as Brother Records debut 45, this sleeve was used for foreign distribution of the Capitol pressing)
HEROES AND VILLAINS/You're Welcome .... (Brother 1001)	12.50	50.00	67

(Different design from the Capitol version)
DARLIN'/Here Today .... (Capitol 2068)	5.00	20.00	67
GETCHA BACK/Male Ego .... (CBS ZS4-04913)	1.00	4.00	85
GETCHA BACK .... (CBS ZS4-04913)	2.00	8.00	85

(Promotional issue, *Demonstration Only–Not For Sale* printed on sleeve)
IT'S GETTIN' LATE/It's OK .... (CBS ZS4-05433)	1.00	4.00	85
IT'S GETTIN' LATE .... (CBS ZS4-05433)	2.00	8.00	85

(Promotional issue, *Demonstration Only–Not For Sale* printed on sleeve)
SHE BELIEVES IN LOVE AGAIN .... (CBS ZS4-05624)	1.00	4.00	85
SHE BELIEVES IN LOVE AGAIN .... (CBS ZS4-05624)	2.00	8.00	85

(Promotional issue, *Demonstration Only–Not For Sale* printed on sleeve)
ROCK 'N' ROLL TO THE RESCUE .... (Capitol B-5595)	1.00	4.00	86
HAPPY ENDINGS/California Girls .... (Critique 7-99392)	1.00	4.00	87

(A-side shown as by the Beach Boys & Little Richard)

TITLE	LABEL AND NUMBER	VG	NM	YR
I JUST WASN'T MADE FOR THESE TIMES (STEREO MIX)/WOULDN'T IT BE NICE (VOCALS ONLY)/Here Today (Stereo Backing Track) (Folding hard cover)	(Sub Pop 363)	.75	3.00	96

EXTENDED PLAYS

| WENDY/DON'T BACK DOWN/Little Honda/Hushabye (Titled 4–By The Beach Boys, issued with a small-hole 33-1/3 RPM record) | (Capitol R-5267) | 12.50 | 50.00 | 64 |
| MOUNT VERNON AND FAIRWAY (A FAIRY TALE) | (Warner Bros. MS 2118) | 2.50 | 10.00 | 73 |

("Magic Transistor Radio" artwork, no specific identification on sleeve other than the catalog number and Warner Bros. copyright date. 6-track EP included with the album Holland, issued with a small-hole 33-1/3 RPM record.)

Also see the Everly Brothers (Don't Worry Baby), Fat Boys (Wipeout), Julio Iglesias (The Air That I Breathe), Bruce Johnston, the Legendary Masked Surfers, Mike & Dean (Mike Love), the Rip Chords (Bruce Johnston), Brian Wilson

BEACHES
(Motion Picture)

See Bette Midler (Under The Boardwalk, Wind Beneath My Wings)

BEACH NUTS, THE
| SURF BEAT '65/The Last Ride | (Coronado 131) | 18.75 | 75.00 | 63 |

BEAGLES, THE
| DEEP IN THE HEART OF TEXAS/Let's All Sing Like The Birdies Sing | (Era 3132) | 6.25 | 25.00 | 64 |

BEARS, THE
| TRUST/Save Me (Illustration by Mort Drucker) | (I.R.S. 53197) | .75 | 3.00 | 85 |

BEASLEY, WALTER
| ON THE EDGE/Where | (Polydor 887 413-7) | .75 | 3.00 | 87 |

BEASTIE BOYS
SHE'S ON IT/Slow And Low	(Def Jam 38 05683)	1.00	4.00	85
SHE'S ON IT (Promotional issue, Demonstration–Not For Sale printed on sleeve)	(Def Jam 38 05683)	1.50	6.00	85
NO SLEEP TILL BROOKLYN/She's Crafty	(Def Jam 38 06675)	1.00	4.00	87

Also see Mike Watt (Mike D on E-Ticket Ride)

BEAT, THE
EXTENDED PLAYS
| DON'T WAIT UP FOR ME | (Columbia AE7-1187) | 1.00 | 4.00 | 79 |

(Promotional issue only titled The Now Wave Sampler, issued with small-hole 33-1/3 RPM record. Also includes one song each by Hounds, Jules and the Polar Bears, and the Sinceros.)

Also see the Nerves (Paul Collins), MnMs (Paul Collins)

BEAT FARMERS
| BIGGER STONES/California Kid | (Rhino 021) | 1.00 | 4.00 | 85 |

BEAT GENERATION, THE
(Motion Picture)

See Louis Armstrong (The Beat Generation)

BEAT HAPPENING
EXTENDED PLAYS
| NOT A CARE IN THE WORLD | (Sub Pop 171) | 2.50 | 10.00 | 92 |

(Limited edition of 3,000 copies issued with green vinyl and insert. Promotional item given away to Sassy magazine readers on request. Also includes one song each by Velocity Girl, Codeine, and Sebadoh.)

BEATLES, THE
MY BONNIE/The Saints (When The Saints Go Marching In) (Shown as by the Beatles with Tony Sheridan)	(MGM 13213)	25.00	100.00	64
WHY/Cry For A Shadow (Shown as by the Beatles with Tony Sheridan)	(MGM 13227)	50.00	200.00	64
PLEASE, PLEASE ME/From Me To You	(Vee-Jay 581)	75.00	300.00	64
PLEASE, PLEASE ME/From Me To You (Promotional issue which reads The Record That Started Beatlemania! across the top. The Beatles not pictured.)	(Vee-Jay 581)	500.00	2000.00	64
DO YOU WANT TO KNOW A SECRET/Thank You Girl	(Vee-Jay 587)	25.00	100.00	64
SHE LOVES YOU	(Swan 4152)	25.00	100.00	64
LOVE ME DO/P.S. I Love You	(Tollie 9008)	20.00	80.00	64
AIN'T SHE SWEET	(Atco 6308)	125.00	500.00	64
THE BEATLES ARRIVE IN AMERICA	(Foto-Fi number unknown)	125.00	500.00	64

(Promotional issue only, sleeve reads The Beatles arrive in America! Have fun running the film with this specially scored recording. Title on the record is Stand Up And Holler. The film was footage of the Beatles departing their plane in New York.)

I WANT TO HOLD YOUR HAND/I Saw Her Standing There (Paul shown with cigarette and George's head is within border)	(Capitol 5112)	15.00	60.00	64
I WANT TO HOLD YOUR HAND/I Saw Her Standing There (Paul shown with cigarette and George's head is cropped on top)	(Capitol 5112)	15.00	60.00	64
I WANT TO HOLD YOUR HAND/I Saw Her Standing There	(Capitol 5112)	375.00	1500.00	64

(Promotional issue only "WMCA Good Guys Sleeve." Front is identical to commercial release, back of sleeve pictures six WMCA disc jockeys. Released with standard stock single.)

CAN'T BUY ME LOVE/You Can't Do That (A-side from the motion picture A Hard Day's Night)	(Capitol 5150)	150.00	600.00	64
A SURPRISE GIFT FROM THE BEATLES, THE BEACH BOYS & THE KINGSTON TRIO (6" x 9" mailer issued with a 5" flexidisc)	(Capitol/Evatone 8464)	500.00	2000.00	64
MUSIC CITY KFWBEATLES/You Can't Do That	(Capitol RB 2637/38)	1000.00	4000.00	64

(Promotional issue only mailer which reads The Beatles Talk And Sing! Wallichs Music City KFWB/98. Souvenir Record. A Limited Pressing Celebrating The Opening Of Wallichs Music City, Topanga Plaza, Canoga Park.)

A HARD DAY'S NIGHT/I Should Have Known Better (Straight cut top of sleeve, from the motion picture A Hard Day's Night)	(Capitol 5222)	12.50	50.00	64
A HARD DAY'S NIGHT/I Should Have Known Better (Tab cut at top of sleeve, from the motion picture A Hard Day's Night)	(Capitol 5222)	10.00	40.00	64
I'LL CRY INSTEAD/I'm Happy Just To Dance With You (Straight cut top of sleeve, from the motion picture A Hard Day's Night)	(Capitol 5234)	20.00	80.00	64
I'LL CRY INSTEAD/I'm Happy Just To Dance With You (Tab cut at top of sleeve, from the motion picture A Hard Day's Night)	(Capitol 5234)	15.00	60.00	64

TITLE	LABEL AND NUMBER	VG	NM	YR
AND I LOVE HER / If I Fell .... (Straight cut top of sleeve, from the motion picture *A Hard Day's Night*)	(Capitol 5235)	20.00	80.00	64
AND I LOVE HER / If I Fell .... (Tab cut at top of sleeve, from the motion picture *A Hard Day's Night*)	(Capitol 5235)	15.00	60.00	64
MATCHBOX / Slow Down .... (Straight cut top of sleeve)	(Capitol 5255)	20.00	80.00	64
MATCHBOX / Slow Down .... (Tab cut at top of sleeve)	(Capitol 5255)	15.00	60.00	64
I FEEL FINE / She's A Woman .... (Straight cut top of sleeve)	(Capitol 5327)	10.00	40.00	64
I FEEL FINE / She's A Woman .... (Tab cut at top of sleeve)	(Capitol 5327)	7.50	30.00	64
EIGHT DAYS A WEEK / I Don't Want To Spoil The Party .... (Straight cut top of sleeve)	(Capitol 5371)	7.50	30.00	65
EIGHT DAYS A WEEK / I Don't Want To Spoil The Party .... (Tab cut at top of sleeve)	(Capitol 5371)	5.00	20.00	65
TICKET TO RIDE / Yes It Is .... (Straight cut top of sleeve, a-side from the motion picture *Help!*)	(Capitol 5407)	25.00	100.00	65
TICKET TO RIDE / Yes It Is .... (Tab cut at top of sleeve, a-side from the motion picture *Help!*)	(Capitol 5407)	20.00	80.00	65
HELP! / I'm Down .... (Straight cut top of sleeve, a-side from the motion picture *Help!*)	(Capitol 5476)	10.00	40.00	65
HELP! / I'm Down .... (Tab cut at top of sleeve, a-side from the motion picture *Help!*)	(Capitol 5476)	7.50	30.00	65
YESTERDAY / Act Naturally .... (Straight cut top of sleeve)	(Capitol 5498)	10.00	40.00	65
YESTERDAY / Act Naturally .... (Tab cut at top of sleeve)	(Capitol 5498)	7.50	30.00	65
WE CAN WORK IT OUT / Day Tripper .... (Straight cut top of sleeve)	(Capitol 5555)	10.00	40.00	65
WE CAN WORK IT OUT / Day Tripper .... (Tab cut at top of sleeve)	(Capitol 5555)	7.50	30.00	65
AS IT HAPPENED .... (Shown as by The Beatles & Murray the 'K')	(No label or # indicated)	10.00	40.00	65
NOWHERE MAN / What Goes On .... (Straight cut top of sleeve)	(Capitol 5587)	7.50	30.00	66
NOWHERE MAN / What Goes On .... (Tab cut at top of sleeve)	(Capitol 5587)	5.00	20.00	66
PAPERBACK WRITER / Rain .... (Straight cut top of sleeve)	(Capitol 5651)	12.50	50.00	66
PAPERBACK WRITER / Rain .... (Tab cut at top of sleeve)	(Capitol 5651)	10.00	40.00	66
YELLOW SUBMARINE / Eleanor Rigby .... (Straight cut top of sleeve, a-side from the motion picture *Yellow Submarine*)	(Capitol 5715)	15.00	60.00	66
YELLOW SUBMARINE / Eleanor Rigby .... (Tab cut at top of sleeve, a-side from the motion picture *Yellow Submarine*)	(Capitol 5715)	10.00	40.00	66
PENNY LANE / Strawberry Fields Forever .... (Straight cut top of sleeve, from the motion picture *Magical Mystery Tour*)	(Capitol 5810)	20.00	80.00	67
PENNY LANE / Strawberry Fields Forever .... (Tab cut at top of sleeve, from the motion picture *Magical Mystery Tour*)	(Capitol 5810)	15.00	60.00	67
ALL YOU NEED IS LOVE / Baby, You're A Rich Man .... (Straight cut top of sleeve, from the motion picture *Magical Mystery Tour*)	(Capitol 5964)	7.50	30.00	67
ALL YOU NEED IS LOVE / Baby, You're A Rich Man .... (Tab cut at top of sleeve, from the motion picture *Magical Mystery Tour*)	(Capitol 5964)	5.00	20.00	67
HELLO GOODBYE / I Am The Walrus .... (Straight cut top of sleeve, from the motion picture *Magical Mystery Tour*)	(Capitol 2056)	7.50	30.00	67
HELLO GOODBYE / I Am The Walrus .... (Tab cut at top of sleeve, from the motion picture *Magical Mystery Tour*)	(Capitol 2056)	5.00	20.00	67
LADY MADONNA / The Inner Light .... (Straight cut top of sleeve. Originally issued with a glossy, coated insert for a poster offer from the Official Beatles Fan Club. This insert is valued at $20 in near mint condition.)	(Capitol 2138)	20.00	80.00	68
THE BALLAD OF JOHN AND YOKO / Old Brown Shoe	(Apple 2531)	10.00	40.00	69
LET IT BE / You Know My Name (Look Up My Number) .... (Straight cut top of sleeve, a-side from the motion picture *Let It Be*)	(Apple 2764)	10.00	40.00	70
LET IT BE / You Know My Name (Look Up My Number) .... (Straight cut top of sleeve, a-side from the motion picture *Let It Be*)	(Apple 2764)	7.50	30.00	70
THE LONG AND WINDING ROAD / For You Blue .... (From the motion picture *Let It Be*)	(Apple 8232)	10.00	40.00	70
GOT TO GET YOU INTO MY LIFE	(Capitol 4274)	1.50	6.00	76
OB-LA-DI, OB-LA-DA / Julia .... (Each sleeve individually numbered, those under #1000 are in greater demand have a higher value)	(Capitol 4347)	1.50	6.00	76
GIRL / You're Going To Lose That Girl .... (The stock record for this sleeve was never pressed but many sleeves found their way onto the market. The single exists only as a promo and is valued at $200 near mint.)	(Capitol 4506)	2.50	10.00	77
SGT. PEPPER'S LONELY HEARTS CLUB BAND / WITH A LITTLE HELP FROM MY FRIENDS / A Day In The Life	(Capitol 4612)	1.50	6.00	78
THE BEATLES' MOVIE MEDLEY / I'm Happy Just To Dance With You	(Capitol B-5107)	1.25	5.00	82
THE BEATLES' MOVIE MEDLEY / Fab Four On Film	(Capitol B-5107)	5.00	20.00	82
LOVE ME DO	(Capitol B-5189)	1.00	4.00	82
I WANT TO HOLD YOUR HAND / I Saw Her Standing There .... (Paul shown without cigarette, dated 1984 in lower left corner of one side, and *I Want To Hold Your Hand* is listed as a-side on both sides)	(Capitol 5112)	1.00	4.00	84
LEAVE MY KITTEN ALONE / Ob La Di Ob La Da (Alternate Version) .... (Unreleased sleeve, no record exists)	(Capitol B-5439)	50.00	200.00	85
HELP! OPEN END INTERVIEW	(Cicadelic/BIOdisc 002)	1.25	5.00	90
LOVE ME DO / P.S. I Love You	(Capitol 7PRO-79551/2)	6.25	25.00	92
I WANT TO HOLD YOUR HAND / I Saw Her Standing There .... (Identical to original 1964 release except REG. U.S. PAT. OFF. type in Capitol logo has periods. Issued in a plastic sleeve with a *30th Anniversary* sticker.)	(Capitol 5112)	1.25	5.00	94
FREE AS A BIRD / Christmas Time (Is Here Again) .... (Issued with small-hole 45 RPM record)	(Apple NR 7243 8 58497 7 0)	.75	3.00	95

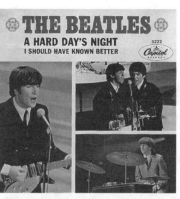

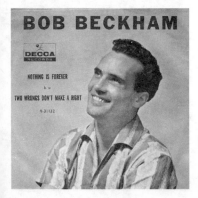

TITLE	LABEL AND NUMBER	VG	NM	YR
REAL LOVE/Baby's In Black	(Apple NR 7243 8 58544 7 7)	.75	3.00	96
(Issued with small-hole 45 RPM record)				
EXTENDED PLAYS				
MISERY/TASTE OF HONEY/Ask Me Why/Anna	(Vee-Jay 1-903)	15.00	60.00	64
(Cardboard sleeve titled *Souvenir of Their Visit to America*)				
MISERY/TASTE OF HONEY/Ask Me Why/Anna	(Vee-Jay 1-903)	2000.00	8000.00	64
(Promotional issue only, sleeve reads *Ask Me Why/The Beatles*)				
OPEN-END INTERVIEW WITH THE BEATLES/I WANT TO HOLD YOUR HAND/				
This Boy/It Won't Be Long	(Capitol PRO 2548/49)	375.00	1500.00	64
(Promotional issue only commonly referred to as *Open-End Interview With The Beatles*)				
OPEN-END INTERVIEW WITH THE BEATLES/ROLL OVER BEETHOVEN/				
Please Mr. Postman/Thank You Girl	(Capitol PRO 2548/49)	250.00	1000.00	64
(Promotional issue only commonly referred to as *The Beatles Second Open-End Interview*)				
HONEY DON'T/I'M A LOSER/Mr. Moonlight/Everybody's Trying To Be My Baby	(Capitol R-5365)	50.00	200.00	65
(Cardboard sleeve titled *4 By 4 The Beatles*)				
ROLL OVER BEETHOVEN/THIS BOY/All My Loving/Please, Mr. Postman	(Capitol EAP 1-2121)	75.00	300.00	64
(Cardboard sleeve titled *Four By The Beatles*)				
BABY IT'S YOU/I'LL FOLLOW THE SUN/Devil In Her Heart/Boys ..	(Apple NR 7243 8 58348 1 3)	.75	3.00	95
CHRISTMAS SLEEVES				
WE WISH YOU A MERRY CHRISTMAS AND A HAPPY NEW YEAR	(Vee-Jay no #)	15.00	60.00	64
(Half sleeve issued with various Vee Jay and Tollie singles during the holiday season)				
THE BEATLES THIRD CHRISTMAS RECORD	(Lyntone 948)	25.00	100.00	65
(Distributed to the Official Beatles Fan Club members)				
THE BEATLES 1968 CHRISTMAS RECORD	(Lyntone 948 H-2041)	20.00	80.00	68
(Distributed to the Official Beatles Fan Club members. The front is the same artwork used on the 1967 Christmas message mailer which was designed by John Lennon and Ringo Starr. The back features art by John Lennon's 5 year old son, Julian.)				
HAPPY CHRISTMAS 1969	(Lyntone 948 H-2565)	15.00	60.00	69
(Distributed to the Official Beatles Fan Club members. Sleeve design by Richard Starkey, a.k.a. Ringo Starr, and his son Zak.)				
Also see Pete Best, George Harrison, Billy J. Kramer *(From A Window)*, John Lennon, George Martin and His Orchestra, Paul McCartney, Ringo Starr, the Traveling Wilburys (George Harrison)				

BEATLES COSTELLO, THE

EXTENDED PLAYS				
WASHING THE DEFECTIVES/SOLDIER OF LOVE/				
I Feel Fine/Theme From A Summer Place/Out Of Limits	(Pious 310)	1.25	5.00	78
Also see the Paley Brothers				

BEAT RODEO

WHAT'S THE MATTER/Mimi	(Coyote 005)	1.50	6.00	83
EVERYTHING I'M NOT/It Could Happen Here	(I.R.S. 52918)	.75	3.00	86

BEAT STREET

(Motion Picture)
See Jenny Burton *(Strangers In A Strange World)*, Patrick Jude *(Strangers In A Strange World)*, Grandmaster Melle Mel & the Furious Five *(Beat Street Breakdown)*, Juicy *(Beat Street Strut)*

BEAU BRUMMELS, THE

LAUGH LAUGH/Just A Little	(Rhino 4506)	1.00	4.00	84

BEAUTY AND THE BEAST

(Television Series)
See Lisa Angelle

BEAUVOIR, JEAN

FEEL THE HEAT/Standing In The Line Of Fire	(Columbia 38-05904)	.75	3.00	86
FEEL THE HEAT	(Columbia 38-05904)	1.00	4.00	86
(Promotional issue, *Demonstration–Not For Sale* printed on sleeve)				
MISSING THE YOUNG DAYS/Crazy	(Columbia 38-06288)	.75	3.00	86
MISSING THE YOUNG DAYS	(Columbia 38-06288)	1.00	4.00	86
(Promotional issue, *Demonstration–Not For Sale* printed on sleeve)				
JIMMY/Dangerously	(Columbia 38-07741)	.75	3.00	88
Also see Little Steven				

BECAUSE THEY'RE YOUNG

(Motion Picture)
See Duane Eddy *(Shazam!, Because They're Young)*, Bobby Rydell *(Swingin' School)*

BECK

STEVE THREW UP/Mutherfucker	(Bongload 11)	1.50	6.00	94
IT'S ALL IN YOUR MIND/	(K Records # unknown)	1.00	4.00	94

BECK, JEFF

PEOPLE GET READY/Back On The Street	(Epic 34-05416)	1.00	4.00	85
(Shown as by Jeff Beck and Rod Stewart)				
PEOPLE GET READY	(Epic 34-05416)	1.50	6.00	85
(Promotional issue, *Demonstration–Not For Sale* printed on sleeve. Shown as by Jeff Beck and Rod Stewart.)				
EXTENDED PLAYS				
GOT THE FEELING	(Columbia AS 53)	1.50	6.00	71
(Part of a series of promotional issues titled *Playback* issued with a small-hole 33-1/3 RPM record. Price includes generic *Playback* sleeve with folding insert. Also includes one song each by Lesley Duncan, Firesign Theatre, Grootna, the Mahavishnu Orchestra With John McLaughlin, and Mylon.)				
Also see Donovan, the Honeydrippers, the Yardbirds				

BECKHAM, BOB

JUST AS MUCH AS EVER	(Decca 9-30861)	2.50	10.00	59
CRAZY ARMS	(Decca 9-31029)	2.50	10.00	60
NOTHING IS FOREVER/Two Wrongs Don't Make A Right	(Decca 9-31132)	2.50	10.00	60

BEDLAM FOUR, THE

NO ONE LEFT TO LOVE/Psychedelic Mantra	(Caped Crusader 73)	1.25	5.00	91
(Originally issued with insert)				

BEE, MOLLY

KEEP IT A SECRET	(MGM K-13356)	2.50	10.00	65

BEE GEES, THE
MARLEY PURT DRIVE/Sound Of Love .... (Atco EP 4535)   3.75   15.00   69
   (Promotional issue only)
THE WOMAN IN YOU/Stayin' Alive .... (RSO 813 173-7)   1.25   5.00   83
   (From the motion picture *Staying Alive*)
SOMEONE BELONGING TO SOMEONE .... (RSO 815 235-7)   1.25   5.00   83
   (From the motion picture *Staying Alive*)
YOU WIN AGAIN .... (Warner Bros. 28351-7)   1.00   4.00   87
E•S•P/Overnight .... (Warner Bros. 28139-7)   1.00   4.00   87
ONE/Wing And A Prayer .... (Warner Bros. 22899-7)   1.00   4.00   89
EXTENDED PLAYS
(OUR LOVE) DON'T THROW IT ALL AWAY/IF I CAN'T HAVE YOU/
Rest Your Love On Me/Wind Of Change .... (RSO EP 200)   2.00   8.00   79
   (Promotional issue only, *Not For Sale–For Promotional Use Only* printed on sleeve. Issued with a small-hole
   33-1/3 RPM record.)
   Also see the Bunburys, Barry Gibb, Robin Gibb

BEETLEJUICE
(Motion Picture)
   See Harry Belafonte (*Day-O*)

BEHOLD A PALE HORSE
(Motion Picture)
   See Maurice Jarre (*Theme From Behold A Pale Horse*)

BELAFONTE, HARRY
TROUBLES/Hello Everybody .... (RCA Victor 47-6249)   3.00   12.00   55
THE BLUES IS MAN–PARTS 1 & 2 .... (RCA Victor 47-6458)   3.00   12.00   56
JAMAICA FAREWELL/Once Was .... (RCA Victor 47-6663)   2.50   10.00   56
MARY'S BOY CHILD/Venezuela .... (RCA Victor 47-6735)   2.50   10.00   56
BANANA BOAT (DAY-O)/Star-O .... (RCA Victor 47-6771)   2.50   10.00   56
JOHN HENRY/Tol' My Captain .... (RCA Victor 47-6780)   2.50   10.00   56
MO MARY/Lord Randall .... (RCA Victor 47-6781)   2.50   10.00   56
MAN PIABA/The Fox .... (RCA Victor 47-6782)   2.50   10.00   56
MAN SMART/Chimney Smoke .... (RCA Victor 47-6783)   2.50   10.00   56
UNCHAINED MELODY/A-Roving .... (RCA Victor 47-6784)   2.50   10.00   56
IN THAT GREAT GETTIN' UP MORNIN'/Jump Down, Spin Around .... (RCA Victor 47-6785)   2.50   10.00   56
WILL HIS LOVE BE LIKE HIS RUM/Dolly Dawn .... (RCA Victor 47-6786)   2.50   10.00   56
HOSANNA/I Do Adore Her .... (RCA Victor 47-6787)   2.50   10.00   56
COME BACK LIZA/Brown Skin Girl .... (RCA Victor 47-6788)   2.50   10.00   56
WATER BOY/Noah .... (RCA Victor 47-6789)   2.50   10.00   56
DANNY BOY/Take My Mother Home .... (RCA Victor 47-6790)   2.50   10.00   56
SUZANNE/Matilda, Matilda! .... (RCA Victor 447-0320)   2.50   10.00   57
SHENANDOAH/Scarlet Ribbons .... (RCA Victor 447-0321)   2.50   10.00   57
HOLD 'EM JOE/I'm Just A Country Boy .... (RCA Victor 447-0322)   2.50   10.00   57
MAMA LOOK AT BUBU/Don't Ever Look At Me .... (RCA Victor 47-6830)   2.50   10.00   57
MARY MARY/ .... (RCA Victor 47-7425)   2.50   10.00   58
FIFTEEN/Round The Bay Of Mexico .... (RCA Victor 47-7550)   2.50   10.00   59
STRANGE SONG/ .... (RCA Victor 47-9263)   2.50   10.00   67
DAY-O .... (Geffen 7-27859)   .75   3.00   88
   (From the motion picture *Beetlejuice*)
   Also see U.S.A. For Africa, Voices Of America

BELEW, ADRIAN
OH DADDY/Peaceable Kingdom .... (Atlantic 7-88904)   .75   3.00   89

BEL GEDDES, BARBARA
(Actress)
   See Floyd Cramer (*Theme From Dallas*)

BELL, CHRIS
I AM THE COSMOS/You And Your Sister .... (Car 6)   7.50   30.00   78

BELL, MAGGIE
HOLD ME/Spring Greens .... (Swan Song 72006)   .75   3.00   81
   (Shown as by B.A. Robertson & Maggie Bell)
PUT ANGELS AROUND YOU/Here, There And Everywhere .... (Swan Song 7-99907)   .75   3.00   83
   (Shown as by Maggie Bell & Bobby Whitlock, both pictured on back)

BELL, RANDY
DON'T DO ME/Someone's Fantasy .... (Epic 34-04497)   .75   3.00   84
DON'T DO ME .... (Epic 34-04497)   1.00   4.00   84
   (Promotional issue, *Demonstration Only–Not For Sale* printed on sleeve)

BELLE, REGINA
SO MANY TEARS/Gotta Give It Up .... (Columbia 38-07388)   .75   3.00   87
   Also see Peabo Bryson (*Without You*)

BELLE STARS, THE
SIGN OF THE TIMES/Madness .... (Warner Bros. 29672-7)   .75   3.00   82

BELL HEIRS, THE
CALIFORNIA SUN/Shaking It Down .... (Visa 501)   .75   3.00   78

BELLS ARE RINGING
(Motion Picture)
   See Maurice Chevalier (*Just In Time*), Dean Martin (*I Met A Girl*)

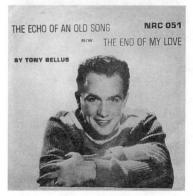

BELLUS, TONY
HEY LITTLE DARLIN'/Only Your Heart .... (NRC 035)   12.50   50.00   59
THE ECHO OF AN OLD SONG/The End Of My Love .... (NRC 051)   10.00   40.00   60

BELUSHI, JOHN
   See Stephen Bishop (*Animal House*), the Blues Brothers

TITLE	LABEL AND NUMBER	VG	NM	YR

BENATAR, PAT

HEARTBREAKER/My Clone Sleeps Alone .... (Chrysalis 2395)	1.50	6.00	80
WE LIVE FOR LOVE/So Sincere .... (Chrysalis 2419)	1.25	5.00	80
HIT ME WITH YOUR BEST SHOT/Prisoner Of Love .... (Chrysalis 2464)	1.00	4.00	80
TREAT ME RIGHT/Never Wanna Leave You .... (Chrysalis 2487)	1.00	4.00	81
FIRE AND ICE/Hard To Believe .... (Chrysalis 2529)	1.00	4.00	81
PROMISES IN THE DARK/Evil Genius .... (Chrysalis 2555)	1.00	4.00	81
SHADOWS OF THE NIGHT/The Victim .... (Chrysalis 2647)	1.00	4.00	82
LOOKING FOR A STRANGER/I'll Do It .... (Chrysalis VS4 42688)	1.00	4.00	83
LITTLE TOO LATE/Fight It Out .... (Chrysalis VS4 03536)	1.00	4.00	83
LOVE IS A BATTLEFIELD/Hell Is For Children (Live Version) .... (Chrysalis VS4-42732)	1.00	4.00	85
WE BELONG/Suburban King .... (Chrysalis VS4-42826)	.75	3.00	84
WE BELONG .... (Chrysalis VS4-42826)	2.00	8.00	84
(Promotional issue gatefold with insert)			
SEX AS A WEAPON/Red Vision .... (Chrysalis VS4 42927)	.75	3.00	85
OOH OOH SONG/La Cancion Ooh Ooh .... (Chrysalis VS4-42843)	.75	3.00	84
INVINCIBLE/Invincible (Instrumental) .... (Chrysalis VS4 42877)	.75	3.00	85
(From the motion picture The Legend Of Billie Jean)			
ALL FIRED UP/Cool Zero .... (Chrysalis VS4 43268)	.75	3.00	88
LET'S STAY TOGETHER/Wide Awake In Dreamland .... (Chrysalis VS4 43314)	.75	3.00	88
Also see Artists United Against Apartheid			

BEN CASEY
(Television Series)
    See Valjean (Theme From Ben Casey)
    Related see Vincent Edwards

BENNETT, LINDA

IF YOU LET ME MAKE LOVE TO YOU .... (Command 4134)	2.50	10.00	69

BENNETT, ROBERT RUSSELL

BENEATH THE SOUTHERN CROSS (NO OTHER LOVE)/			
Guadalcanal March .... (RCA Victor 61-8507)	2.00	8.00	54
(Hard cover, from the television special Victory At Sea composed by Richard Rodgers)			

BENNETT, TONY

STRANGER IN PARADISE/Why Does It Have To Be Me .... (Columbia 4-40121)	3.00	12.00	53
FIREFLY/The Night That Heaven Fell .... (Columbia 4-41237)	2.50	10.00	58
FOLLOW ME/Ramona .... (Columbia 4-41874)	2.50	10.00	60
(A-side from the Broadway musical Camelot)			
I LEFT MY HEART IN SAN FRANCISCO/Once Upon A Time .... (Columbia 4-42332)	2.50	10.00	62
THEME FROM OSCAR/Baby Dream Your Dream .... (Columbia 4-43508)	2.00	8.00	66
(A-side from the motion picture Oscar)			
MY FAVORITE THINGS/I Love The Winter Weather .... (Columbia # unknown)	2.00	8.00	70
(Promotional issue only, theme song for 1970 Christmas Seal campaign. No catalog number indicated on sleeve.)			
ALL THAT LOVE WENT TO WASTE/Some Of These Days .... (Brut 813)	1.50	6.00	73
THERE'S ALWAYS TOMORROW/I Wish I Were In Love Again .... (Improv TB713)	1.50	6.00	76
(Hard cover, theme song for the United Way of America)			
WHITE CHRISTMAS/All Of My Life .... (Columbia 38-07658)	1.00	4.00	87
(The painting pictured on the front is by Bennett)			

BENNY & THE BEDBUGS

THE BEATLE BEAT/Roll Over Beethoven .... (DCP 1008)	6.25	25.00	64

BENSON, GEORGE

THE GREATEST LOVE OF ALL .... (Arista 0251)	1.25	5.00	77
(From the motion picture The Greatest)			
ON BROADWAY .... (Warner Bros. 8542)	1.00	4.00	78
LOVE BALLAD/You're Never Too Far From Me .... (Warner Bros. 8759)	.75	3.00	79
GIVE ME THE NIGHT .... (Warner Bros. 49505)	.75	3.00	81
TURN YOUR LOVE AROUND/Nature Boy .... (Warner Bros. 49846)	.75	3.00	81
NEVER GIVE UP ON A GOOD THING/Livin' Inside Your Love .... (Warner Bros. 50005)	.75	3.00	81
INSIDE LOVE (SO PERSONAL)/In Search Of A Dream .... (Warner Bros. 29649-7)	.75	3.00	83
20/20 .... (Warner Bros. 29120-7)	.75	3.00	84
KISSES IN THE MOONLIGHT .... (Warner Bros. 28640-7)	.75	3.00	86
DREAMIN' .... (Warner Bros. 28244-7)	.75	3.00	86
(Shown as by George Benson & Earl Klugh)			
SINCE YOU'RE GONE/Love Theme From Romeo & Juliet .... (Warner Bros. 27975-7)	.75	3.00	87
(Shown as by George Benson & Earl Klugh)			
LET'S DO IT AGAIN .... (Warner Bros. 27780-7)	.75	3.00	87
TWICE THE LOVE .... (Warner Bros. 27658-7)	.75	3.00	88

BENSON, ROBBIE
(Actor)
    See Bobbie Gentry (Ode To Billy Joe)

BENTON, BARBI

WELCOME STRANGER/That Country Boy Of Mine .... (Playboy 6008)	1.25	5.00	74
NOW I LAY ME DOWN TO SLEEP WITH YOU/If You Can't Do It, That's All Right (Playboy 6018)	1.25	5.00	74
ROLL YOU LIKE A WHEEL/Let's Sing A Song Together .... (Playboy 6045)	1.25	5.00	75
(Shown as by Mickey Gilley and Barbi Benton)			
STAYING POWER .... (Playboy 6078)	1.25	5.00	76

BENTON, BROOK

THE TIES THAT BIND/Hither And Thither And Yon .... (Mercury 71566)	3.75	15.00	60
A ROCKIN' GOOD WAY .... (Mercury 71629)	3.75	15.00	60
(Shown as by Brook Benton and Dinah Washington)			
THE SAME ONE/Kiddio .... (Mercury 71652)	3.75	15.00	60
FOOLS RUSH IN/Someday You'll Want Me To Want You .... (Mercury 71722)	3.75	15.00	60
THINK TWICE/For My Baby .... (Mercury 71774)	3.75	15.00	60
THE BOLL WEEVIL SONG/Your Eyes .... (Mercury 71820)	3.75	15.00	61
FRANKIE AND JOHNNY/It's Just A House Without You .... (Mercury 71859)	3.75	15.00	61

REVENGE/Really Really .... (Mercury 71903)	3.75	15.00	61
SHADRACK/The Lost Penny .... (Mercury 71912)	3.75	15.00	62
WALK ON THE WILD SIDE/Somewhere In The Used To Be .... (Mercury 71925)	3.75	15.00	62

(From the motion picture *Walk On The Wild Side*, Lawrence Harvey, Capucine, Jane Fonda, Anne Baxter, and Barbara Stanwyck pictured)

HIT RECORD/Thanks To The Fool .... (Mercury 71962)	3.75	15.00	62

(There are two versions of this sleeve, their differences are currently unknown)

LIE TO ME/With The Touch Of Your Hand .... (Mercury 72024)	3.75	15.00	62
HOTEL HAPPINESS/Still Waters Run Deep .... (Mercury 72055)	3.75	15.00	62
I GOT WHAT I WANTED/Dearer Than Life .... (Mercury 72099)	3.75	15.00	63
MY TRUE CONFESSION/Tender Years .... (Mercury 72135)	3.75	15.00	63
TWO TICKETS TO PARADISE/Don't Hate Me .... (Mercury 72177)	3.75	15.00	63

(There are two versions of this sleeve, their differences are currently unknown)

YOU'RE ALL I WANT FOR CHRISTMAS/This Time Of The Year .... (Mercury 72214)	3.75	15.00	63
GOING GOING GONE/After Midnight .... (Mercury 72230)	3.75	15.00	64
TOO LATE TO TURN BACK NOW/Another Cup Of Coffee .... (Mercury 72266)	3.75	15.00	64
A HOUSE IS NOT A HOME/Come On Back .... (Mercury 72303)	3.75	15.00	64

(From the motion picture *A House Is Not A Home*)

LUMBERJACK/Don't Do What I Did (Do What I Say) .... (Mercury 72333)	3.75	15.00	64
DO IT RIGHT/Please, Please Make It Easy .... (Mercury 72365)	3.75	15.00	64
MOTHER NATURE, FATHER TIME/You're Mine .... (RCA Victor 47-8693)	3.00	12.00	65

EXTENDED PLAYS

IF YOU'VE GOT THE TIME .... (Miller Beer 621)	3.75	15.00	66

(Promotional issue only radio spots for Miller Beer; three by the Troggs, two by Brook Benton, and one by Johnny Mack)

BERGMAN, PETER
(Actor)
   See the Soaps and Hearts Ensemble

BERLIN

A MATTER OF TIME/Overload .... (Zone-H 001)	3.00	12.00	80
A MATTER OF TIME/French Reggae .... (I.R.S./Zone-H 9015)	2.50	10.00	80

(Issued with small-hole 45 RPM record)

THE METRO/Tell Me Why .... (M.O.A. F-4)	3.00	12.00	81
SEX (I'M A...)/Tell Me Why .... (Geffen 29747-7)	1.50	6.00	83
THE METRO/World Of Smiles .... (Geffen 29638-7)	1.00	4.00	83
MASQUERADE/Live Sex .... (Geffen 29504-7)	1.00	4.00	83
NO MORE WORDS/Rumor Of Love .... (Geffen 29360-7)	1.00	4.00	84
NOW IT'S MY TURN/Lost In The Crowd .... (Geffen 29283-7)	1.00	4.00	84
LIKE FLAMES/Hideaway .... (Geffen 28563-7)	.75	3.00	86
YOU DON'T KNOW .... (Geffen 28486-7)	.75	3.00	86
TAKE MY BREATH AWAY .... (Columbia 38-05903)	.75	3.00	86

(From the motion picture *Top Gun*)

TAKE MY BREATH AWAY .... (Columbia 38-05903)	1.00	4.00	86

(Promotional issue, *Demonstration Only–Not For Sale* printed on sleeve. From the motion picture *Top Gun*.)

BERNIE, BEN

AU REVOIR–PLEASANT DREAMS/It's A Lonesome Old Town .... (Decca 1-713)	3.00	12.00	53

(Decca "Curtain Call" series of reissues)

BERRY, CHUCK

NO PARTICULAR PLACE TO GO/You Two .... (Chess 1898)	6.25	25.00	64
YOU NEVER CAN TELL/Brenda Lee .... (Chess 1906)	6.25	25.00	64
LITTLE MARIE/Go, Bobby Soxer .... (Chess 1912)	6.25	25.00	64
PROMISED LAND/Things I Used To Do .... (Chess 1916)	6.25	25.00	64
IT WASN'T ME/Welcome Back Pretty Baby .... (Chess 1943)	6.25	25.00	64
IT'S TOO DARK IN THERE/Good Lookin' Woman .... (Mercury 72963)	5.00	20.00	69

BERRY, JAN

THE UNIVERSAL COWARD/I Can't Wait To Love You .... (Liberty 55845)	37.50	150.00	65

   Also see Jan & Dean, the Legendary Masked Surfers

BERTRAND, PLASTIC

CA PLANE POUR MOI/Pogo Pogo .... (Sire 1020)	2.00	8.00	78

BERWICK, BRAD

I'M BETTER THAN THE BEATLES/Walkin' Down Easy Street .... (Clinton 1012)	6.25	25.00	64

BEST, PETE
Best was an early member of the Beatles from 1960-1962. He was replaced by Ringo Starr before the group released any songs in America.

BOYS/Kansas City .... (Cameo 391)	12.50	50.00	66

BEST LITTLE WHOREHOUSE IN TEXAS, THE
(Motion Picture)
   See Dolly Parton (*I Will Always Love You*)

BEST OF EVERYTHING, THE
(Motion Picture)
   See Johnny Mathis (*The Best Of Everything*)

BETTIE SERVEERT

FOR ALL WE KNOW .... (A&M 31458 0710 7)	.50	2.00	94

(Side 5 of a 7-record box set titled *If I Were A Carpenter*. Each sleeve has a different face shot of Karen Carpenter on the front, Richard Carpenter on the back. No artist name or song titles indicated on sleeve. Complete set valued at $30.00 near mint.)

SOMETHING SO WILD/What Friends? .... (Matador OLE 150)	1.25	5.00	95

BEVAN, ALEX, & THE BUZZARD BAND

THE BUZZARD SONG/Ho For The Weekend .... (Buzzard 101)	1.50	6.00	78

(Cleveland area release commemorating radio station WMMS 101 FM's tenth anniversary)

BEVERLY, FRANKIE
   See Maze Featuring Frankie Beverly

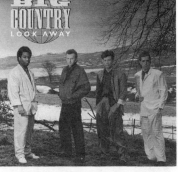

BEVERLY HILLBILLIES, THE
(Television Series)
> See Flatt & Scruggs (*Pearl Pearl Pearl*)
> Related see Buddy Ebsen, Irene Ryan

BEVERLY HILLS COP
(Motion Picture)
> See Danny Elfman (*Gratitude*), Harold Faltermeyer (*Axel F Theme*), Glenn Frey (*The Heat Is On*), Patti LaBelle
> (*New Attitude, Stir It Up*)

BEVERLY HILLS COP II
(Motion Picture)
> See the Jets (*Cross My Broken Heart*), George Michael (*I Want Your Sex*), Pointer Sisters (*Be There*), Bob Seger (*Shakedown*), Charlie Sexton (*In Deep*)

B-52'S

Title	Label and Number	VG	NM	YR
ROCK LOBSTER/52 Girls	(Boo-Fant DB-52)	6.25	25.00	78
(Black and white photo on front)				
ROCK LOBSTER/52 Girls	(Boo-Fant DB-52)	6.25	25.00	78
(Green and white photo on front)				
ROCK LOBSTER/6060-842	(Warner Bros. 49173)	2.00	8.00	79
PLANET CLAIRE/There's A Moon In The Sky (Called The Moon)	(Warner Bros. 49212)	2.00	8.00	79
PRIVATE IDAHO/Party Out Of Bounds (Instrumental Version)	(Warner Bros. 49537)	2.00	8.00	80
DEEP SLEEP/Nip It In The Bud	(Warner Bros. 50064)	1.25	5.00	82
LEGAL TENDER	(Warner Bros. 29579-7)	1.25	5.00	83
SONG FOR A FUTURE GENERATION/Trism	(Warner Bros. 29561-7)	1.25	5.00	83
SUMMER OF LOVE	(Warner Bros. 28561-7)	1.25	5.00	86
LOVE SHACK/Channel Z	(Reprise 22817-7)	1.00	4.00	89

BIAFRA, JELLO

Title	Label and Number	VG	NM	YR
DIE FOR OIL SUCKER/Pledge Of Allegiance	(Alternative Tentacles 146 VIRUS 90/90C)	1.00	4.00	91
(Poster sleeve issued with a small-hole 45 RPM record)				
WILL THE FETUS BE ABORTED?/The Lost World	(Alternative Tentacles VIRUS 136)	1.00	4.00	93
(Shown as by Jello Biafra and Mojo Nixon, 6-page folding sleeve)				
Also see Dead Kennedys				

BIG AUDIO DYNAMITE

Title	Label and Number	VG	NM	YR
MEDICINE SHOW/This Is Big Audio Dynamite	(Columbia 38-05841)	1.00	4.00	86
MEDICINE SHOW	(Columbia 38-05841)	1.25	5.00	86
(Promotional issue, *Demonstration–Not For Sale* printed on sleeve)				
E=MC²/A Party	(Columbia 38-06053)	1.00	4.00	86
E=MC²	(Columbia 38-06053)	1.25	5.00	86
(Promotional issue, *Demonstration–Not For Sale* printed on sleeve)				
C'MON EVERY BEATBOX/Badrock City	(Columbia 38-06364)	1.00	4.00	86
JUST PLAY MUSIC!/Much Worse	(Columbia 38-07955)	1.00	4.00	88
OTHER 99/What Happened To Eddie?	(Columbia 38-08094)	1.00	4.00	88
Also see the Clash (Mick Jones)				

BIG BAM BOO

Title	Label and Number	VG	NM	YR
SHOOTING FROM MY HEART	(Uni 50019)	.75	3.00	89

BIG BROTHER AND THE HOLDING COMPANY

Title	Label and Number	VG	NM	YR
PIECE OF MY HEART/Turtle Blues	(Columbia 44626)	—	—	68
(A "phantom" sleeve that some have heard of but none have seen and probably does not exist. It is most likely that an import was mistakenly identified as a U.S. printing.)				

BIG COUNTRY

Title	Label and Number	VG	NM	YR
IN A BIG COUNTRY/All Of Us	(Mercury 814 467-7)	1.25	5.00	83
FIELDS OF FIRE	(Mercury 811 450-7)	1.50	6.00	83
(Poster sleeve)				
WONDERLAND/Lost Patrol	(Mercury 818 834-7)	1.00	4.00	84
WHERE THE ROSE IS SOWN/Prairie Rose	(Mercury 880 412-7)	1.00	4.00	84
LOOK AWAY/Restless Natives	(Mercury 884 645-7)	.75	3.00	86
KING OF EMOTION/The Travellers	(Reprise 27737-7)	.75	3.00	88

BIG DISH, THE

Title	Label and Number	VG	NM	YR
SLIDE/Reverend Killer	(Virgin 28474-7)	.75	3.00	86

BIG F, THE

Title	Label and Number	VG	NM	YR
PATIENCE PEREGRINE/Three Headed Boris	(Chrsalis 04534)	1.00	4.00	93
(Promotional issue only issued with yellow vinyl)				

BIG PIG

Title	Label and Number	VG	NM	YR
HUNGRY TOWN/Charlie	(A&M 1216)	.75	3.00	88
BREAKAWAY	(A&M 3014)	.75	3.00	88

BIG SANDY WITH LOS STRAIGHTJACKETS

Title	Label and Number	VG	NM	YR
LA PLAGA/¡Qué Mala!	(Spinout 45-015)	.50	2.00	96
Also see Los Straightjackets				

BIG STAR
> See Chris Bell

"BIG SURPRISE" TRIO

Title	Label and Number	VG	NM	YR
ME AND MY SHADOW/Five-Foot-Two, Eyes Of Blue	(RCA Victor 47-6449)	3.75	15.00	56
(Sleeve reads *The George Wright $100,000 Prize Winner of NBC-TV's "The Big Surprise"*)				

BIG TOWN, THE
(Motion Picture)
> See Bobby Darin (*Beyond The Sea*), Little Willie John (*Fever*)

BIG TROUBLE

Title	Label and Number	VG	NM	YR
CRAZY WORLD	(Epic 34-07432)	.75	3.00	87
WHEN THE LOVE IS GOOD	(Epic 34-07677)	.75	3.00	87

BIKEL, THEODORE

Title	Label and Number	VG	NM	YR
IF I WERE A RICH MAN/Sunrise, Sunset	(Elektra 45632)	2.50	10.00	79

BIKINI KILL
Members of the group were involved in the formation of the feminist movement *Riot Grrrl* (also spelled *Riot Girl*)
NEW RADIO/REBEL GIRL/Demirap .... (*Kill Rock Stars 212*)   1.00   4.00   93
    (Joan Jett credited with 2nd guitar, vocals and production. Folding sleeve with lyric insert, bumper sticker,
    and small-hole 45 RPM record.)
I LIKE FUCKING/I Hate Danger .... (*Kill Rock Stars 253*)   .75   3.00   95
    (Folding sleeve with small-hole 45 RPM record)

BILLY & LISA
SHOULD'VE KNOWN BETTER .... (*MCA 53309*)   .75   3.00   88

BILLY & THE BEATERS
See Billy Vera and the Beaters

BILLY SATELLITE
SATISFY ME .... (*Capitol B-5356*)   .75   3.00   84
I WANNA GO BACK .... (*Capitol B-5409*)   .75   3.00   84

BINGENHEIMER, RODNEY
See Rodney and the Brunettes

BINGHAM, MARK
See Lou Reed (b-side of *September Song*)

BINGO LONG TRAVELING ALL-STARS & MOTOR KINGS, THE
(Motion Picture)
See Thelma Houston (*The Bingo Long Song*)

BIRCH, MO
See UB40 (*Sing Our Own Song*)

BISHOP, STEPHEN
ANIMAL HOUSE/Dream Girl .... (*MCA AB-12435*)   2.50   10.00   78
    (From the motion picture *Animal House,* John Belushi and Bishop pictured)

BIZARROS, THE
EXTENDED PLAYS
LADY DOBONETTE/I BIZARRO/Without Reason/Nova .... (*Gorilla NR-7639*)   3.00   12.00   76
LADY DOBONETTE/I BIZARRO/Without Reason/Nova .... (*Clone 000*)   2.00   8.00   76

BIZ MARKIE
JUST A FRIEND .... (*Cold Chillin' 22784*)   .75   3.00   89

BLACK, CILLA
LOVE'S JUST A BROKEN HEART/Yesterday .... (*Capitol 5595*)   6.25   25.00   66

BLACK, JAY
WHAT WILL MARY SAY?/Return To Me .... (*United Artists 50116*)   5.00   20.00   67
    Also see Jay & the Americans

BLACK, JIMMY CARL
JIMMY CARL BLACK RAPS ABOUT GERONIMO BLACK .... (*MCA 1914*)   2.50   10.00   71
    (Promotional issue only issued with small-hole 33-1/3 RPM record)

BLACK, TERRY
EVERYONE CAN TELL/Say It Again .... (*Tollie 9041*)   5.00   20.00   65

BLACK'S, BILL, COMBO
(Bill Black played bass for Elvis Presley)
JOSEPHINE/Dry Bones .... (*Hi 45-2022*)   2.00   8.00   60
DON'T BE CRUEL/Rollin' .... (*Hi 45-2026*)   2.00   8.00   60
BLUE TANGO/Willie .... (*Hi 45-2027*)   2.00   8.00   60
YOGI/Ole Buttermilk Sky .... (*Hi 45-2036*)   2.00   8.00   61
    (The b-side peaked at #25 while the a-side didn't chart in Billboard's Top 100)
TWISTIN' WHITE SILVER SANDS/My Babe .... (*Hi 45-2052*)   2.00   8.00   62

BLACK BRITAIN
FUNKY NASSAU .... (*Virgin 7-99462*)   .75   3.00   87

BLACK CROWES, THE
REMEDY .... (*Def American 5474*)   1.50   6.00   92
    (Promotional issue only, *Promotion Copy Not For Sale* printed on back)

BLACK FLAG
NERVOUS BREAKDOWN/Fix Me/I've Had It/Wasted .... (*SST 001*)   2.50   10.00   78
    (First printing, black and white version)
NERVOUS BREAKDOWN/Fix Me/I've Had It/Wasted .... (*SST 001*)   1.25   5.00   78
    (Second printing, red version)
NERVOUS BREAKDOWN/Fix Me/I've Had It/Wasted .... (*SST 001*)   .75   3.00   78
    (Third printing, blue version with bar code on back)
SIX PACK/I've Heard It All Before/American Waste .... (*SST 005*)   1.00   4.00   81
TV PARTY/I've Got Run/My Rules .... (*SST 012*)   1.00   4.00   81
    (Black and white version)
TV PARTY .... (*SST 95006*)   3.75   15.00   81
    (Color sleeve, promotional issue giveaway)
LOUIE LOUIE/Damaged 1 .... (*SST 175*)   1.00   4.00   81
LOUIE LOUIE/Damaged 1 .... (*Posh Boy 13*)   2.50   10.00   81
TV PARTY/I've Got Run/My Rules .... (*SST 012*)   1.00   4.00   85
    (Color version)
    Also see the Rollins Band (Henry Rollins)

BLACK FLAMES, THE
ARE YOU MY WOMAN?/Bring The Noise .... (*Def Jam/Columbia 38-07651*)   .75   3.00   87
    (B-side shown as by Public Enemy. From the motion picture *Less Than Zero.*)

BLACKFOOT
TEENAGE IDOL/Run For Cover .... (*Atco 7-99851*)   1.00   4.00   83
MORNING DEW/Livin' In The City .... (*Atco 7-99690*)   1.00   4.00   84

TITLE	LABEL AND NUMBER	VG	NM	YR

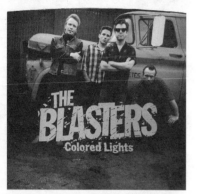

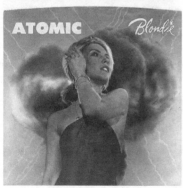

BLACKFOOT, J. D.
EPITAPH FOR A HEAD .... (Philips 40625) — 6.25 — 25.00 — 69

BLACK N BLUE
SWING TIME/Rockin' On Heaven's Door .... (Geffen 2358) — 1.25 — 5.00 — 85
    (Promotional issue only)

BLACKWELLS, THE
HONEY, HONEY/Always It's You .... (Jamie 1150) — 6.25 — 25.00 — 60

BLADES, RUBÉN
TÚ CARIÑO/CARMEN'S THEME/
    Tú Cariño/Carmen's Theme (English Version) .... (Atlantic 7-89658) — .75 — 3.00 — 84

BLAKE, BETTY ANN
THE LADY SINGS THE BLUES/Jersey Boy .... (Golden Crest 115) — 2.50 — 10.00 — 50s

BLAKE, NORMAN
    See Nitty Gritty Dirt Band (Honky Tonkin')

BLAKE, ROBERT
(Actor)
    See James William Guercio (Tell Me)

BLANCMANGE
LIVING ON THE CEILING/Running Thin .... (Island 7-99929) — 1.50 — 6.00 — 82

BLANDA, GEORGE
(Football quarterback and kicker active for 26 years from 1949-1975)
IT'S NEVER TOO LATE/This Old House .... (Daybreak 1002) — 2.00 — 8.00 — 71

BLASTERS, THE
I'M SHAKIN'/No Other Girl .... (Slash 110) — 1.50 — 6.00 — 81
SO LONG BABY GOODBYE/Border Radio .... (Slash/Warner Bros. 29975-7) — 1.25 — 5.00 — 81
BAREFOOT ROCK/Bus Station .... (Slash/Warner Bros. 29678-7) — 1.00 — 4.00 — 85
COLORED LIGHTS/Help You Dream .... (Slash/Warner Bros. 29055-7) — 1.00 — 4.00 — 85
    Also see Dan Hartman (b-side of I Can Dream About You)

BLAZING SADDLES
(Motion Picture)
    See Frankie Laine (Blazing Saddles)

BLESS THE BEASTS AND CHILDREN
(Motion Picture)
    See Carpenters (b-side of Superstar)

BLEYER, ARCHIE
MUSTAFA .... (Cadence 1383) — 2.50 — 10.00 — 61
    Also see Arthur Godfrey ('Twas The Night Before Christmas)

BLIND DATE
(Motion Picture)
    See Billy Vera & The Beaters (Let You Get Away), Gary Morris and Jennifer Warnes (Simply Meant To Be)

BLIND MELON
TONES OF HOME .... (Capitol 7PRO-79448) — 1.25 — 5.00 — 92
    (Promotional issue only)

BLINKER THE STAR
BLUISH BOY/Transona 5 .... (A&M PRO 00306) — .75 — 3.00 — 96
    (Promotional issue only with separate front and back sheets, not a true picture sleeve)

BLOCH, RAY, & ORCHESTRA
FROM HERE TO ETERNITY .... (Coral 9-1327) — 125.00 — 500.00 — 53
    (From the motion picture From Here To Eternity, Frank Sinatra, Burt Lancaster, Montgomery Clift, Donna Reed, and Deborah Kerr pictured.)

BLOND
DEEP INSIDE MY HEART/I Will Bring You Flowers In The Morning .... (Fontana 1673) — 2.50 — 10.00 — 68

BLOND, JEFFREY
MY SKIES WERE BLACK .... (Decca 32479) — 2.50 — 10.00 — 68

BLONDIE
HANGING ON THE TELEPHONE/Fade Away And Radiate .... (Chrysalis 2271) — 1.50 — 6.00 — 78
HEART OF GLASS/11:59 .... (Chrysalis 2295) — 1.25 — 5.00 — 79
THE HARDEST PART/Sound-A-Sleep .... (Chrysalis 2408) — 1.00 — 4.00 — 79
ATOMIC/Die Young Stay Pretty .... (Chrysalis 2410) — 1.25 — 5.00 — 80
CALL ME/Call Me (Instrumental) .... (Chrysalis 2414) — .75 — 3.00 — 80
    (B-side shown as by Giorgio Moroder. From the motion picture American Gigolo, Debbie Harry pictured.)
CALL ME/Call Me (Instrumental) .... (Chrysalis 2414) — .75 — 3.00 — 80
    (B-side shown as by Giorgio Moroder. From the motion picture American Gigolo, Richard Gere pictured.)
THE TIDE IS HIGH/Suzy And Jeffrey .... (Chrysalis 2465) — .75 — 3.00 — 80
RAPTURE/Walk Like Me .... (Chrysalis 2485) — .75 — 3.00 — 81
ISLAND OF LOST SOULS/Dragonfly .... (Chrysalis 2603) — .75 — 3.00 — 82
    Also see Debbie Harry, Rodney and the Brunettes. Gary Valentine left Blondie in 1977 and was replaced by Frank Infante.

BLOODROCK
HELP IS ON THE WAY/Bloodrock Interview .... (Capitol PRO-6579) — 3.75 — 15.00 — 72
    (Promotional issue only. B-side shown as by Sol Smaizys/Dennis Gray WXFM–Chicago. Back of sleeve reads "On the flip-side of this disc, Bloodrock discusses their transition from music about death to music about life.")

BLOODSTONE
GIVE ME YOUR HEART .... (London 1062) — 1.50 — 6.00 — 75

BLOOD, SWEAT & TEARS
GO DOWN GAMBLIN'/Valentine's Day .... (Columbia 4-45427) — 1.50 — 6.00 — 71
SO LONG DIXIE/Alone .... (Columbia 4-45661) — 1.50 — 6.00 — 72

TITLE	LABEL AND NUMBER	VG	NM	YR

EXTENDED PLAYS

SMILING PHASES .... (Columbia Special Products CSS 1491) — 1.50 — 6.00 — 70
(Promotional issue only titled *The Great American Sound*, issued with a small-hole 33-1/3 RPM record and a 6" x 6" insert for a mail-order Hershey Poster Offer. Also includes one song each by Chicago, Aretha Franklin, and Santana.)
Also see the Blues Project (Steve Katz)

BLOSSOMS, THE
THINGS ARE CHANGING .... (E.E.O.C. no #) — 50.00 — 200.00 — 65
(Promotional issue sponsored by the Equal Employment Opportunities Commission. Similar releases by Jay & the Americans and the Supremes.)

BLOW MONKEYS, THE
DIGGING YOUR SCENE / Digging Your Scene (U.K. Mix) .... (RCA PB-14325) — 1.00 — 4.00 — 86
WICKED WAYS / Walking The Blue Beat .... (RCA PB-14423) — .75 — 3.00 — 86
IT DOESN'T HAVE TO BE THIS WAY / Ask For More .... (RCA 5138-7-R) — .75 — 3.00 — 87

BLU, PEGGI
TENDER MOMENTS .... (Capitol B-5676) — .75 — 3.00 — 88

BLUE BELLES, THE
I SOLD MY HEART TO THE JUNKMAN .... (Peak 7042) — 12.50 — 50.00 — 62
(Credited to the Blue Belles but actually recorded by the Starlets. The existence of this sleeve has been questioned.)
YOU'LL NEVER WALK ALONE .... (Parkway 896) — 10.00 — 40.00 — 64
(Shown as by Patti LaBelle and Her Blue Bells)
Also see Nona Hendryx, Patti LaBelle, the Supremes (Cindy Birdsong)

BLUE CHEER
SUMMERTIME BLUES .... (Philips 40516) — 5.00 — 20.00 — 68
FEATHERS FROM YOUR TREE .... (Philips 40561) — 6.25 — 25.00 — 68

BLUE CITY
(Motion Picture)
See Pops and 'Timer (*Tell Me Something Slick*)

BLUE COMETS, THE
BLUE EYES .... (Epic 5-10066) — 2.00 — 8.00 — 66

BLUE HAWAII
(Motion Picture)
See Elvis Presley (*Can't Help Falling In Love*)

BLUE IGUANA, THE
(Motion Picture)
See James Brown (*Sex Machine*)

BLUE MERCEDES
I WANT TO BE YOUR PROPERTY .... (MCA 53262) — .75 — 3.00 — 87

BLUE MINK
MELTING POT .... (Philips 40658) — 2.00 — 8.00 — 70
Also see Roger Cook, David & Jonathan

BLUENOTES, THE
I'M GONNA FIND OUT / Forever On My Mind .... (Brooke 116) — 6.25 — 25.00 — 60

BLUE OYSTER CULT
CITIES ON FLAME WITH ROCK AND ROLL / Before The Kiss, A Redcap .... (Columbia 4-45598) — 3.75 — 15.00 — 72
HOT RAILS TO HELL / 7 Screaming Diz-Busters .... (Columbia 4-45879) — 2.50 — 10.00 — 73
GODZILLA LIVE / Godzilla (Studio Version) .... (Columbia AE 71156) — 6.25 — 25.00 — 78
(Promotional issue only, *Special pressing for radio. Demonstration–not for sale* printed on front of sleeve)
BURNIN' FOR YOU / Vengeance (The Pact) .... (Columbia 18-02415) — 1.00 — 4.00 — 81
SHOOTING SHARK / Dragon Lady .... (Columbia 38 04298) — 1.00 — 4.00 — 83
SHOOTING SHARK .... (Columbia 38 04298) — 1.50 — 6.00 — 83
(Promotional issue, *Demonstration–Not For Sale* printed on sleeve)
Also see Hear 'N Aid

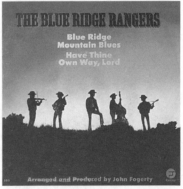

BLUE RIDGE RANGERS, THE
BLUE RIDGE MOUNTAIN BLUES / Have Thine Own Way, Lord .... (Fantasy 683) — 5.00 — 20.00 — 72
Also see Creedence Clearwater Revival (John Fogerty), John Fogerty

BLUE RODEO
TRY / Piranha Pool .... (Atlantic 7-89119) — .75 — 3.00 — 87

BLUES, ELWOOD, REVUE FEATURING WILSON PICKETT
LAND OF A THOUSAND DANCES (PART 1) /
Land Of A Thousand Dances (Part 2) .... (Atlantic 7-89062) — 1.00 — 4.00 — 88
(From the motion picture *The Great Outdoors*, Dan Aykroyd, a.k.a. Elwood Blues, and John Candy pictured)
Also see Dan Aykroyd, Blues Brothers, Elwood Blues Revue, Paul McCartney (*Spies Like Us*), U.S.A. For Africa (Dan Aykroyd)

BLUES BROTHERS
(Dan Aykroyd a.k.a. Elwood Blues and John Belushi a.k.a. Jake Blues)
SOUL MAN / Excusez Moi Mon Cherie .... (Atlantic 3545) — 1.00 — 4.00 — 78
GIMME SOME LOVIN' / She Caught The Katy .... (Atlantic 3666) — 1.00 — 4.00 — 80
(Stock sleeve used for both promotional blue vinyl and stock black vinyl. From the motion picture *The Blues Brothers*.)
Also see Dan Aykroyd, Stephen Bishop (*Animal House*), Elwood Blues Revue, Paul McCartney (*Spies Like Us*), U.S.A. For Africa (Dan Aykroyd)

BLUES IMAGE
CLEAN LOVE / Pay My Dues / Parchman Farm .... (Atco 33-317) — 1.25 — 5.00 — 70
(Promotional issue only issued with small-hole 33-1/3 RPM record)

BLUES MAGOOS, THE
PIPE DREAM / There's A Chance We Can Make It .... (Mercury 72660) — 3.75 — 15.00 — 67
ONE BY ONE .... (Mercury 72692) — 3.75 — 15.00 — 67

BLUES PROJECT, THE
WHERE'S THERE'S SMOKE THERE'S FIRE! / Louisiana .... (Verve/Folkways KF-5019) — 5.00 — 20.00 — 67
Also see Blood, Sweat and Tears (Steve Katz), Al Kooper, Tommy Flanders

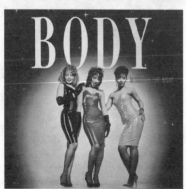

TITLE	LABEL AND NUMBER	VG	NM	YR
BLUE SWEDE				
SILLY MILLY/Lonely Sunday Afternoon	(EMI 3893)	1.00	4.00	73
NEVER MY LOVE/Pinewood Rally	(EMI 3938)	1.00	4.00	73
BLUE THINGS, THE				
LA DO DA DA/I Must Be Doing Something Wrong	(RCA Victor 47-8692)	5.00	20.00	66
BLUE VELVET				
(Motion Picture)				
See Bobby Vinton *(Blue Velvet)*				
BLUE YONDER				
WINDSONG/Only For A Moment	(Atlantic 7-89307)	.75	3.00	87
BLUE ZONE U.K.				
JACKIE/Chance It	(Arista 9725)	.75	3.00	88
(Issued with stock black and promotional blue vinyl)				
Also see Coldcut (Lisa Stansfield), Lisa Stansfield				
BLYTHE, ARTHUR				
ILLUSIONS/Miss Nancy	(Columbia AE7 1227)	1.00	4.00	81
(Promotional issue only, *Demonstration–Not For Sale* printed on back)				
BOB & KIT				
AUTUMN TOO LONG	(HBR 475)	2.50	10.00	67
BODEANS				
ONLY LOVE/Stella	(Reprise/Slash 281792-7)	1.00	4.00	87
DREAMS/Ooh	(Reprise/Slash 28102-7)	1.00	4.00	87
BODINE				
KEEP LOOKIN' THROUGH MY WINDOW/Easy To See	(MGM K14088)	2.50	10.00	69
BODY				
MIDDLE OF THE NIGHT	(MCA 53111)	.75	3.00	87
POSSESSION	(MCA 53265)	.75	3.00	88
BODY ROCK				
(Motion Picture)				
See Dwight Twilley *(Why You Wanna Break My Heart)*, Maria Vidal *(Body Rock)*				
BOFILL, ANGELA				
I JUST WANNA STOP	(Capitol B-44169)	.75	3.00	88
BOLD AND THE BEAUTIFUL, THE				
(Television Soap Opera)				
Related see the Soaps and Hearts Ensemble				
BOLGER, RAY				
(Actor, famous for playing the Scarecrow in the motion picture *The Wizard Of Oz*)				
ONCE IN LOVE WITH AMY/Make A Miracle	(Decca 9-40065)	10.00	40.00	52
BOLT, BENT				
THE MECHANICAL MAN	(MGM K 13635)	2.50	10.00	67
BOLTON, MICHAEL				
(SITTIN' ON) THE DOCK OF THE BAY/Call My Name	(Columbia 38-07680)	.75	3.00	88
(SITTIN' ON) THE DOCK OF THE BAY	(Columbia 38-07680)	1.25	5.00	88
(Promotional issue with a quote from Otis Redding's widow on the back)				
WAIT ON LOVE/	(Columbia 38-07794)	.75	3.00	88
BOMB THE BASS				
BEAT DIS/Dub Dis	(4th & Broadway 7462)	.75	3.00	88
BONADUCE, DANNY				
DREAMLAND	(Lion 145)	3.75	15.00	72
Also see the Partridge Family				
BONDS, GARY U.S.				
QUARTER TO THREE/Time Ole Story	(Legrand 1008)	5.00	20.00	61
(Shown as by U. S. Bonds)				
SCHOOL IS OUT/One Million Tears	(Legrand 1009)	5.00	20.00	61
THIS LITTLE GIRL/Way Back When	(EMI America 8079)	.75	3.00	82
OUT OF WORK/Bring Her Back	(EMI America B-8117)	.75	3.00	82
STANDING IN THE LINE OF FIRE	(Phoenix 0071)	1.25	5.00	84
(Shown as by Gary U.S. Bonds and the American Men)				
SUMMERTIME FUN	(Phoenix 008)	2.50	10.00	84
(Infamous nude female sleeve does not credit Bonds)				
BONE SYMPHONY				
IT'S A JUNGLE OUT THERE	(Capitol B-5260)	.75	3.00	83
BONEY M				
MARY'S BOY CHILD/OH MY LORD/Dancing In The Streets	(Sire 1036)	1.00	4.00	79
BONGOS, THE				
TELEPHOTO LENS/Glow In The Dark	(Fetish 003)	1.25	5.00	80
BON JOVI				
RUNAWAY/Love Lies	(Mercury 818 309-7)	1.50	6.00	84
SHE DON'T KNOW ME/Burning For Love	(Mercury 818 958-7)	1.50	6.00	84
ONLY LONELY/Always Run To You	(Mercury 880 736-7)	1.00	4.00	85
YOU GIVE LOVE A BAD NAME/Raise Your Hands	(Mercury 884 953-7)	.75	3.00	86
LIVIN' ON A PRAYER/Wild In The Streets	(Mercury 888 184-7)	.75	3.00	86
WANTED DEAD OR ALIVE/I'd Die For You	(Mercury 888 467-7)	.75	3.00	87
BAD MEDICINE/99 In The Shade	(Mercury 870 657-7)	.75	3.00	88
BORN TO BE MY BABY/Love For Sale	(Mercury 872 156-7)	.75	3.00	88
I'LL BE THERE FOR YOU/Homebound Train	(Mercury 872 564-7)	.75	3.00	89

TITLE	LABEL AND NUMBER	VG	NM	YR
LAY YOUR HANDS ON ME/Runaway (Live)	(Mercury 874 452-7)	.75	3.00	89
LIVING IN SIN/Love Is War	(Mercury 876 070-7)	.75	3.00	89

BONNAVILLS, THE

HIGH NOON STOMP/Dirty Herb	(Question Mark 101)	15.00	60.00	62

BONNER, GARY

THE HEART OF JULIET JONES/Me About You	(Columbia 4-44306)	5.00	20.00	67

BONNIE AND CLYDE

(Motion Picture)
    See Flatt & Scruggs (*Foggy Mountain Breakdown, Theme From Bonnie & Clyde*)

BONOFF, KARLA

KARLA BONOFF
SOMEBODY'S EYES

PERSONALLY/Dream	(Columbia 18-02805)	.75	3.00	82
PERSONALLY	(Columbia 18-02805)	1.00	4.00	82
(Promotional issue, *Demonstration–Not For Sale* printed on sleeve)				
SOMEBODY'S EYES	(Columbia 38-04472)	.75	3.00	84
(From the motion picture *Footloose*)				
SOMEBODY'S EYES	(Columbia 38-04472)	1.00	4.00	84
(Promotional issue, *Demonstration Only–Not For Sale* printed on sleeve)				

BOOKER T. & MG'S

TIME IS TIGHT	(Stax 0028)	5.00	20.00	69
(Promotional issue only, catalog number not listed on sleeve)				
Also see Booker T. & Priscilla				

BOOKER T. & PRISCILLA

SHE/The Wedding Song	(A&M 1298)	.75	3.00	87
Also see Booker T. & MG's				

BOOK OF LOVE

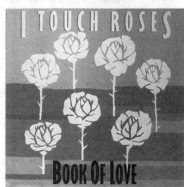

I TOUCH ROSES
BOOK OF LOVE

I TOUCH ROSES	(Sire 28428-7)	.75	3.00	86
PRETTY BOYS AND PRETTY GIRLS/Tubular Bells	(Sire 28858-7)	.75	3.00	88

BOOMERANG

WHEN THE PHONE STOPS RINGING/Money, Men And Makeup	(Atlantic 7-89393)	.75	3.00	86
THESE BOOTS ARE MADE FOR WALKIN'/ Guess You Know I'll Always Be Around	(Atlantic 7-89330)	.75	3.00	86

BOONE, DEBBY

(Daughter of Pat Boone)

Debby Boone / Baby, I'm Yours

CALIFORNIA/Hey Everybody	(Warner Bros./Curb 8511)	1.00	4.00	78
BABY I'M YOURS/God Knows	(Warner Bros./Curb 8554)	1.25	5.00	78
WHEN YOU'RE LOVED	(Warner Bros./Curb 8633)	1.00	4.00	78

BOONE, PAT

BERNADINE/Love Letters In The Sand	(Dot 15570)	5.00	20.00	57
(Red background, from the motion picture *Bernadine* starring Boone. The b-side charted higher than the a-side, it hit #1.)				
BERNADINE/Love Letters In The Sand	(Dot 15570)	3.75	15.00	57
(Orange background, from the motion picture *Bernadine* starring Boone. The b-side charted higher than the a-side, it hit #1.)				
SUGAR MOON/Cherie, I Love You	(Dot 15750)	3.75	15.00	58
I'LL REMEMBER TONIGHT/The Mardi Gras March	(Dot 15840)	3.75	15.00	58
(From the motion picture *Mardi Gras* starring Boone)				
TWIXT TWELVE AND TWENTY/Roll, Boll Weevil	(Dot 15955)	3.75	15.00	59
FOOLS HALL OF FAME/Brightest Wishing Star	(Dot 15982)	3.75	15.00	59
(WELCOME) NEW LOVERS/Words	(Dot 16048)	3.00	12.00	60
SPRING RAIN/Walking The Floor Over You	(Dot 16073)	3.00	12.00	60

BOO RADLEYS, THE

AT THE SOUND OF SPEED/Let Me Be Your Faith	(Spin Art 17)	1.25	5.00	92
(Issued with red splatter vinyl)				

BOOTSY'S RUBBER BAND

BOOTSY'S RUBBER BAND
HOLLYWOOD SQUARES

HOLLYWOOD SQUARES	(Warner Bros. 8575)	1.50	6.00	78
Also see Bootsy Collins, Parliament (Bootsy Collins)				

BOSÈ

LAY DOWN ON ME/Seems Like It's Midnight Forever	(Atlantic 7-89090)	.75	3.00	88

BOSTON

AMANDA	(MCA 52756)	.75	3.00	86
WE'RE READY	(MCA 52985)	.75	3.00	86
CAN'TCHA SAY (YOU BELIEVE IN ME)	(MCA 53029)	.75	3.00	87
HOLLYANN	(MCA 53114)	.75	3.00	87

BOSTON POPS ORCHESTRA CONDUCTED BY ARTHUR FIEDLER

I WANT TO HOLD YOUR HAND	(RCA Victor 47- 8378)	3.75	15.00	64

BOSWELL, CONNEE

MARTHA (AH SO PURE)/Stormy Weather	(Decca 1-722)	3.00	12.00	53
(Decca "Curtain Call" series of reissues)				

BOTKIN, PERRY, JR.

CAN'TCHA SAY
(YOU BELIEVE IN ME)
BOSTON

NADIA'S THEME (THE YOUNG AND THE RESTLESS)	(A&M 1856)	.75	3.00	76
(Blue background, shown as by Barry DeVorzon and Perry Botkin, Jr.)				
NADIA'S THEME (THE YOUNG AND THE RESTLESS)	(A&M 1856)	.75	3.00	76
(Green background, shown as by Barry DeVorzon and Perry Botkin, Jr.)				
NADIA'S THEME (THE YOUNG AND THE RESTLESS)	(A&M 1856)	.75	3.00	76
(Black background, shown as performed by Perry Botkin, Jr., written and produced by Barry DeVorzon and Perry Botkin, Jr.)				

BO-WEEVELS, THE

THE BEETLES WILL GETCHA	(United States 1934)	2.50	10.00	64

BOWEN, JIMMY

TEENAGE DREAM WORLD/It's Against The Law	(Capehart 5005)	10.00	40.00	62

TITLE	LABEL AND NUMBER	VG	NM	YR

BOWIE, DAVID

TITLE	LABEL AND NUMBER	VG	NM	YR
STARMAN/Suffragette City	(RCA 74-0719)	7.50	30.00	72
SPACE ODDITY/The Man Who Sold The World	(RCA 74-0876)	3.75	15.00	73
TIME/The Prettiest Star	(RCA APB0-0001)	150.00	600.00	73
ASHES TO ASHES/It's No Game	(RCA PB-12078)	1.50	6.00	80
ASHES TO ASHES (Edited Version)	(RCA JH-12078)	3.75	15.00	80
(Promotional issue, *Not For Sale–Promotional Use Only* printed on sleeve)				
FASHION/Scream Like A Baby	(RCA PB-12134)	1.50	6.00	80
UNDER PRESSURE/Soul Brother	(Elektra 47235)	1.25	5.00	81
(A-side shown as by Queen & David Bowie)				
CAT PEOPLE (PUTTING OUT FIRE)	(Backstreet 1767)	1.50	6.00	82
(From the motion picture *Cat People*)				
CAT PEOPLE (PUTTING OUT FIRE)	(Backstreet 52024)	1.00	4.00	82
(From the motion picture *Cat People*)				
PEACE ON EARTH/LITTLE DRUMMER BOY	(RCA PH-13400)	2.00	8.00	83
(Shown as by David Bowie and Bing Crosby)				
WHITE LIGHT/WHITE HEAT	(RCA PB-13660)	1.25	5.00	83
(From the motion picture Ziggy Stardust/The Motion Picture)				
WHITE LIGHT/WHITE HEAT	(RCA JK-13660)	2.00	8.00	83
(Promotional issue, *Not For Sale* printed on sleeve. From the motion picture *Ziggy Stardust/The Motion Picture*)				
LET'S DANCE/Cat People (Putting Out Fire)	(EMI America B-8158)	1.00	4.00	83
CHINA GIRL/Shake It	(EMI America B-8165)	1.00	4.00	83
MODERN LOVE/Modern Love (Live Version)	(EMI America B-8177)	1.00	4.00	83
WITHOUT YOU/Criminal World	(EMI America B-8190)	1.00	4.00	84
1984/TVC 15	(RCA PB-13769)	1.00	4.00	84
BLUE JEAN/Dancing With The Big Boys	(EMI America B-8231)	.75	3.00	84
(Originally issued with blue vinyl)				
TONIGHT/Tumble And Twirl	(EMI America B-8246)	1.50	6.00	84
(Poster sleeve)				
THIS IS NOT AMERICA/This Is Not America (Instrumental)	(EMI America B-8251)	1.00	4.00	85
(Shown as by David Bowie/Pat Metheny Group. From the motion picture *The Falcon And The Snowman* by Pat Metheny Group. Round sticker applied to sleeve credits film's director and stars.)				
LOVING THE ALIEN/Don't Look Down	(EMI America BG-8271)	1.50	6.00	85
(Hard cover, double pocket folder)				
DANCING IN THE STREET	(EMI America B-8288)	.75	3.00	85
(Shown as by David Bowie and Mick Jagger)				
ABSOLUTE BEGINNERS/Absolute Beginners (dub mix)	(EMI America B8308)	1.00	4.00	86
(From the motion picture *Absolute Beginners* starring Bowie)				
UNDERGROUND/Underground (Instrumental)	(EMI America B-8323)	1.00	4.00	86
(From the motion picture *Labyrinth* starring Bowie)				
DAY-IN DAY-OUT/Julie	(EMI America B-8380)	.75	3.00	87
TIME WILL CRAWL/Girls	(EMI America B-43020)	2.50	10.00	87
NEVER LET ME DOWN/'87 And Cry	(EMI America B43031)	.75	3.00	87
EXTENDED PLAYS				
SPACE ODDITY/MOONAGE DAYDREAM/Life On Mars/It Ain't Easy	(RCA EP-45-103)	6.25	25.00	72
(Promotional issue only sent to fan club members, *For Promotional Use Only* printed on sleeve)				
Also see Robin Clark (*Too Many Fish In The Sea*)				

BOWIE, JIM

TITLE	LABEL AND NUMBER	VG	NM	YR
THE PRAIRIE CHIEFS/Old Chisholm Trail	(RCA Victor Bluebird WBY-73)	2.00	8.00	57

BOWMAN, DON

See Chet Atkins (*Chet's Tune*)

BOWN, ANDY

TITLE	LABEL AND NUMBER	VG	NM	YR
OPEN YOUR EYES/Oh James	(Mercury 73282)	1.00	4.00	73

BOW WOW WOW

TITLE	LABEL AND NUMBER	VG	NM	YR
CHIHUAHUA/Golly! Golly! Go Buddy!	(RCA PB-12338)	1.00	4.00	81
ORANG-OUTANG/Mickey, Put It Down	(RCA PB-13060)	.75	3.00	82
I WANT CANDY/Elimination Dancing	(RCA PB-13204)	.75	3.00	82
BABY, OH NO/Cowboy	(RCA PB-13291)	.75	3.00	82
Also see Adam and the Ants (Matthew Ashman, Dave Barbarossa)				

BOXCAR WILLIE

TITLE	LABEL AND NUMBER	VG	NM	YR
TRIBUTE TO JIMMIE RODGERS/'T' For Texas	(Main Street no #)	2.00	8.00	83

BOXER

TITLE	LABEL AND NUMBER	VG	NM	YR
ALL THE TIME IN THE WORLD/Save Me	(Virgin ZS8 9506)	1.25	5.00	75
(Promotional issue only, *Demonstration–Not For Sale* printed on sleeve)				

BOYCE, TOMMY, & BOBBY HART

TITLE	LABEL AND NUMBER	VG	NM	YR
OUT AND ABOUT/My Little Chickadee	(A&M 858)	3.00	12.00	67
SOMETIMES SHE'S A LITTLE GIRL/Love Every Day	(A&M 874)	3.00	12.00	67
I'M GONNA BLOW YOU A KISS IN THE WIND/Smilin'	(Aquarian 380)	2.00	8.00	68
I WONDER WHAT SHE'S DOING TONIGHT?/The Ambushers	(A&M 893)	3.00	12.00	67
GOODBYE BABY (I DON'T WANT TO SEE YOU CRY)/ Where Angels Go (Trouble Follows)	(A&M 919)	3.00	12.00	68
ALICE LONG (YOU'RE STILL MY FAVORITE GIRLFRIEND)/P. O. Box 9847	(A&M 948)	3.00	12.00	68
WE'RE ALL GOING TO THE SAME PLACE/6 + 6	(A&M 993)	3.00	12.00	68
L.U.V. (LET US VOTE)/I Wanna Be Free	(A&M 1031)	3.00	12.00	69
Also see Bobby Hart				

BOYD, JIMMY

TITLE	LABEL AND NUMBER	VG	NM	YR
I SAW MOMMY KISSING SANTA CLAUS	(Columbia 152)	5.00	20.00	52
(Half sleeve)				
I SAW MOMMY DO THE MAMBO	(Columbia J4-225)	3.75	15.00	54

BOYD, WILLIAM

(Actor who played the role of western hero Hopalong Cassidy)

TITLE	LABEL AND NUMBER	VG	NM	YR
HOPALONG CASSIDY AND THE STORY OF TOPPER	(Capitol 3110)	2.50	10.00	55

BOYFRIENDS

TITLE	LABEL AND NUMBER	VG	NM	YR
I DON'T WANT NOBODY (I WANT YOU)/You're The One	(Bomp 117)	.75	3.00	78

BOY GEORGE
EVERYTHING I OWN / Use Me .... (Virgin 7-99445)   .75   3.00   87
YOU FOUND ANOTHER GUY / I Go Where I Go .... (Virgin 7-99200)   .75   3.00   89
    Also see Culture Club, Ferry Aid

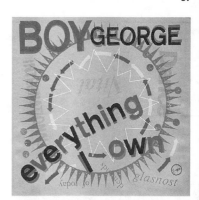

BOY IN THE PLASTIC BUBBLE, THE
(Motion Picture)
    See John Travolta (Razzamatazz)

BOYLE, PETER
(Actor)
    See Buster Poindexter (Hit The Road Jack)

BOY MEETS GIRL
OH GIRL / Kissing, Falling, Flying .... (A&M 2713)   ..75   3.00   85
THE TOUCH / Pieces .... (A&M 2741)   .75   3.00   85
WAITING FOR A STAR TO FALL / No Apologies .... (RCA 8691-7-R)   .75   3.00   88
BRING DOWN THE MOON / Restless Dreamer .... (RCA 8807-7-R)   .75   3.00   88

BOYS, THE
SPLENDOR IN THE GRASS .... (Kama Sutra 203)   1.25   5.00

BOYS, THE
DIAL MY HEART .... (Motown 53301)   .75   3.00   88
A LITTLE ROMANCE .... (Motown 1965)   .75   3.00   89

BOYS BAND, THE
PLEASE DON'T STOP ME BABY (I'M ON FIRE) / We're Lovers .... (Elektra 47406)   .75   3.00   85

BOYS BRIGADE
MELODY .... (Capitol B-5311)   .75   3.00   84

BOYS CLUB
I REMEMBER HOLDING YOU .... (MCA 53430)   .75   3.00   88
THE LONELIEST HEART .... (MCA 53507)   .75   3.00   89
    Also see the Jets (Eugene Wolfgramm a.k.a. Gene Hunt)

BOYS DON'T CRY
CITIES ON FIRE / Lipstick .... (Profile 5114)   .75   3.00   86
WHO THE AM DAM DO YOU THINK I AM? / The Cure .... (Atlantic 7-89196)   .75   3.00   87
WE GOT THE MAGIC / Love Talk .... (Atlantic 7-89085)   .75   3.00   87

BOYS' NIGHT OUT, THE
(Motion Picture)
    See Patti Page (The Boys' Night Out)

BOYZZ, THE
WAKE IT UP, SHAKE IT UP / Hoochie Cootchie .... (Epic-Cleveland International 8-50610)   1.00   4.00   78

BOZUM, ALEX
SO MUCH FOR LOVE .... (Warner Bros. 27680-7)   .75   3.00   88

BOZZIO, DALE
SIMON SIMON .... (Paisley Park 7-28142)   .75   3.00   88
RIOT IN ENGLISH .... (Paisley Park 7-27731)   .75   3.00   88
    Also see Missing Persons

BOZZIO, TERRY
    See Missing Persons, Andy Taylor (Take It Easy)

BRADSHAW, TERRY
(Quarterback for the Pittsburgh Steelers and television football commentator)
UNTIL YOU .... (Benson R2001)   2.50   10.00   80

BRADY BUNCH, THE
(Television Series)
    Related see the Brady Bunch, Annie Davis, Chris Knight, Mike Lookinland

BRADY BUNCH, THE
FROSTY THE SNOWMAN / Silver Bells .... (Paramount 0062)   5.00   20.00   71
ZUCKERMAN'S FAMOUS PIG / Charlotte's Web .... (Paramount 0205)   3.75   15.00   73
    Also see Chris Knight, Mike Lookinland

BRAINS, THE
MONEY CHANGES EVERYTHING / Quick With Your Lip .... (Gray Matter 1-A)   3.75   15.00   79
    (Band members pictured individually on back)
MONEY CHANGES EVERYTHING / Quick With Your Lip .... (Gray Matter 1-A)   3.00   12.00   79
    (Group photo on back)

BRANDO, MARLON
(Actor)
    See Ferrante and Teicher (Love Theme From One Eyed Jacks)

BRANDON, JOHNNY
SANTA CLAUS, JR. / Theme From Santa Claus, Jr. .... (Laurie 3042)   6.25   25.00   59

BRANIGAN, BILLY
MAYBE TONIGHT / Written In Stone .... (Polydor 885 276-7)   .75   3.00   86

BRANIGAN, LAURA
SOLITAIRE / I'm Not The Only One .... (Atlantic 7-89868)   .75   3.00   83
HOW AM I SUPPOSED TO LIVE WITHOUT YOU / Mama .... (Atlantic 7-89805)   .75   3.00   83
SELF CONTROL / Silent Partners .... (Atlantic 7-89676)   .75   3.00   84
THE LUCKY ONE / .... (Atlantic 7-89636)   .75   3.00   84
TI AMO / .... (Atlantic 7-89608)   .75   3.00   84
SPANISH EDDIE / Tenderness .... (Atlantic 7-89531)   .75   3.00   85
HOLD ME / Tenderness .... (Atlantic 7-89496)   .75   3.00   85
I FOUND SOMEONE / .... (Atlantic 7-89451)   .75   3.00   86

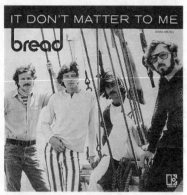

TITLE	LABEL AND NUMBER	VG	NM	YR
SHATTERED GLASS/Statue In The Rain	(Atlantic 7-89245)	.75	3.00	87
POWER OF LOVE/Spirit Of Love	(Atlantic 7-89191)	.75	3.00	87
CRY WOLF/Whatever I Do	(Atlantic 7-89121)	.75	3.00	87
COME INTO MY LIFE/Believe In Me	(Atco 7-99280)	.75	3.00	88

(A-side shown as by Laura Branigan and Joe Esposito, both pictured. From the motion picture *Coming To America*.)

BRASS CONSTRUCTION
WALKIN' THE LINE	(Capitol B-5219)	.75	3.00	83

BRASS RING
LOVE IN THE OPEN AIR	(Dunhill 4090)	6.25	25.00	67

(Credited on sleeve as *Paul McCartney's First Non Beatles Song*)

BRAUN, BOB
TILL DEATH DO US PART/So It Goes	(Decca 31355)	2.50	10.00	62

BREAD
IT DON'T MATTER TO ME	(Elektra 45701)	1.50	6.00	70
IF/Take Comfort	(Elektra 45720)	1.50	6.00	71

Also see Duane Eddy (keyboard player Larry Knechtel was a member of Eddy's band, the Rebels)

BREAKFAST CLUB
RIGHT ON TRACK	(MCA 52954)	.75	3.00	87
KISS AND TELL	(MCA 53128)	.75	3.00	87
EXPRESSWAY TO YOUR HEART	(MCA 53273)	.75	3.00	88
DRIVE MY CAR	(MCA 53348)	.75	3.00	88

(From the motion picture *License To Drive*, Corey Haim and Corey Feldman pictured)

BREAKFAST CLUB, THE
(Motion Picture)
See Simple Minds (*Don't You Forget About Me*), Wang Chung (*Fire In The Twilight*)

BREATHE
HANDS TO HEAVEN/Life And Times	(A&M 2991)	.75	3.00	87
HOW CAN I FALL/Monday Morning Blues	(A&M 1224)	.75	3.00	87
DON'T TELL ME LIES/Liberties Of Love	(A&M 1267)	.75	3.00	87

BREATHLESS
(Motion Picture)
See X (*Breathless*)

BREEDERS, THE
HEAD TO TOE/SHOCKER IN GLOOMTOWN/Freed Pig	(Elektra 7-64533)	.75	3.00	94

(Hard cover issued with small-hole 45 RPM lime green vinyl)

BREEN, BOBBY
WAIT/If The Night Could Tell You	(Chic 1003)	5.00	20.00	56
HERE COMES THAT HEARTACHE/You're Just Like You	(Motown 1059)	3.00	12.00	64

BREMERS, BEVERLY
WE'RE FREE/Colors Of Love	(Scepter 12348)	1.50	6.00	72
I JUST NEED SOME MUSIC/Let It Play On	(Brut 45-513)	1.50	6.00	73

BRENNAN, WALTER
DUTCHMAN'S GOLD/Back To The Farm	(Dot 16066)	3.75	15.00	60

(Shown as by Walter Brennan with Billy Vaughn and His Orchestra)

SPACE MICE/The Thievin' Stranger	(Dot 16136)	3.75	15.00	60
HOUDINI/The Old Kelly Place	(Liberty 55477)	3.00	12.00	62
WHITE CHRISTMAS/Henry Had A Merry Christmas	(Liberty 55518)	3.00	12.00	62

BRENT, FRANKIE, REVUE, FEATURING LITTLE LINDA LOU
RIP IT UP/Summertime	(Epic 5-9712)	2.50	10.00	64

BREWER, SPENCER
EXTENDED PLAYS
THE LAST SNOW LEOPARD	(Narada S33-17254)	1.00	4.00	86

(Promotional issue only titled *Narada Sampler–Excellence In New Acoustic Music*, issued with a small-hole 33-1/3 RPM record. Also includes one song each by Tingstad–Rumbel, Randy Mead, William Ellwood, Michael Jones, Matthew Montfort, David Lanz, and Gabriel Lee.)

BREWER, TERESA
I LOVE MICKEY/Keep Your Cotton Pickin' Paddies Offa My Heart	(Coral 9-61700)	6.25	25.00	56

(Shown as by Teresa Brewer With Mickey Mantle)

LOST/	(Coral 9-61944)	2.50	10.00	58
PEACE OF MIND/	(Coral 9-62167)	2.50	10.00	60
ANYMORE/That Piano Man	(Coral 9-62219)	2.50	10.00	60
SOME SONGS/A Natural Feelin' For You	(Signature 101)	1.00	4.00	80
COME FOLLOW THE BAND/The Colors Of My Life	(Project 3 100)	1.00	4.00	81

BREWER & SHIPLEY
YANKEE LADY	(Kama Sutra 547)	1.25	5.00	72

BRICKELL, EDIE, AND NEW BOHEMIANS
WHAT I AM/I Do	(Geffen 27696-7)	1.00	4.00	88
LOVE LIKE WE DO/Plain Jane	(Geffen 22937-7)	.75	3.00	89
CIRCLE/Now	(Geffen 27580-7)	.75	3.00	89

BRICKLIN
EVEN WHEN YOU'RE DONE WITH ME/How Come I?	(A&M 2852)	.75	3.00	86

BRIDGES, JEFF
(Actor)
See Phil Collins (*Against All Odds*)

BRIGGS, BRIAN
NERVOUS BREAKDOWN/Lifer	(Bearsville 49167)	1.25	5.00	79

BRIGHT LIGHTS, BIG CITY
(Motion Picture)
    See Donald Fagen (*Century's End*), Bryan Ferry (*Kiss And Tell*)

BRIGHTMAN, SARAH
PIE JESU / Recordare .... (EMI Angel B-5467)   .75   3.00   85
    (A-side shown as by Sarah Brightman and Paul Miles-Kingston, both pictured on back. From Andrew Lloyd
    Webber's *Requiem*.)
ALL I ASK OF YOU / The Phantom Of The Opera–Overture (Act II) .... (Polydor 885 336-7)   1.00   4.00   86
    (Shown as by Cliff Richard and Sarah Brightman, both pictured on front. B-side by The Royal Philharmonic
    Orchestra. From the musical *The Phantom Of The Opera*.)

BRILEY, MARTIN
I DON'T FEEL BETTER / Medley: A Little Knowledge Is A Dangerous Thing /
    The Man I Feel / I Don't Feel Better / Fear Of The Unknown .... (Mercury 76137)   .75   3.00   81
ONE NIGHT WITH A STRANGER / Put Your Hands On The Screen .... (Mercury 814 182-7)   .75   3.00   83
DANGEROUS MOMENTS .... (Mercury 880 245-7)   .75   3.00   84

BRILL, MARTY & LARRY FOSTER
THE MAN FROM T.A.N.T.E. / Dr. Nu? / Goldflaker .... (Colpix 790)   2.50   10.00   65

BRILLIANT
IT'S A MAN'S MAN'S MAN'S WORLD / Crash The Car .... (Atlantic 7-89315)   .75   3.00   86

BRITNY FOX
SAVE THE WEAK .... (Columbia 38-68561)   .75   3.00   88

BROKEN ARROW
(Television Series)
    See the Prairie Chiefs (*Broken Arrow*)

BRONCO BILLY
(Motion Picture)
    See Penny DeHaven (*Bayou Lullaby*), Clint Eastwood (*Bar Room Buddies*), Merle Haggard (*Bar Room Buddies*), Ronnie Milsap (*Cowboys And
    Clowns*)

BRONNER BROTHERS
I'M NOT THAT BAD A MAN TO LOVE .... (*Neighbor* number unknown)   .75   3.00   84

BRONSKI BEAT
SMALLTOWN BOY / Memories .... (MCA 52494)   .75   3.00   84
WHY? / Cadillac Car .... (MCA 52565)   .75   3.00   84
HIT THAT PERFECT BEAT .... (MCA 52750)   .75   3.00   85
C'MON C'MON / Something Special .... (MCA 52831)   .75   3.00   86
    Also see the Communards (Jimmy Sommerville)

BROOKINS, ROBERT
WHERE IS THE LOVE .... (MCA 53283)   .75   3.00   88
    (Shown as by Stephanie Mills and Robert Brookins)

BROOKS, DONNIE
DOLL HOUSE / Round Robin .... (Era 3028)   5.00   20.00   60
MEMPHIS / That's Why .... (Era 3042)   5.00   20.00   61
ALL I CAN GIVE / Wishbone .... (Era 3049)   5.00   20.00   61

BROOKS, MEL
HIGH ANXIETY / Springtime For Hitler .... (Asylum 45458)   2.00   8.00   78
    (From the motion picture *High Anxiety*)
    Also see Frankie Laine (*Blazing Saddles*), Lionel Newman (*The Silent Movie March*)

BROOKS, RANDY
(Actor)
    See the Soaps and Hearts Ensemble

BROS
WHEN WILL I BE FAMOUS? / Love To Hate You .... (Epic 34-07905)   .75   3.00   88
I OWE YOU NOTHING / Shocked .... (Epic 34-08006)   .75   3.00   88

BROTHER BEYOND
HE AIN'T NO COMPETITION .... (Capitol P-B-44340)   .75   3.00   88

BROTHERHOOD
JUMP OUT THE WINDOW / Box Guitar .... (RCA Victor 47-9621)   3.75   15.00   68
    Also see Paul Revere & the Raiders

BROTHERHOOD, THE
(Motion Picture)
    See Lyn Roman (*The Taste Of Love*)

BROTHERS FOUR, THE
GREENFIELDS .... (Columbia 4-41571)   2.50   10.00   60
MY TANI / Ellie Lou .... (Columbia 4-41692)   2.50   10.00   60
THE GREEN LEAVES OF SUMMER / Beautiful Brown Eyes .... (Columbia 4-41808)   2.50   10.00   60
    (From the motion picture *The Alamo*)
FROGG / Sweet Rosyanne .... (Columbia 4-41958)   2.50   10.00   61
MY WOMAN LEFT ME / Nobody Knows .... (Columbia 4-42142)   2.50   10.00   61
BLUE WATER LINE / Summer Days Alone .... (Columbia 4-42256)   2.50   10.00   61
THEME FROM LAFAYETTE / .... (Columbia 4-42391)   2.50   10.00   62
THIS TRAIN / .... (Columbia 4-42450)   2.50   10.00   62
FIVE WEEKS IN A BALLOON / .... (Columbia 4-42507)   2.50   10.00   62
25 MINUTES TO GO / The Tavern Song .... (Columbia 4-42586)   2.50   10.00   62
55 DAYS AT PEKING / .... (Columbia 4-42787)   2.50   10.00   63

BROTHERS JOHNSON, THE
I'LL BE GOOD TO YOU / The Devil .... (A&M 1806)   1.25   5.00   76
GET THE FUNK OUT MA FACE / Tomorrow .... (A&M 1851)   1.25   5.00   76
STRAWBERRY LETTER #23 / Dancin' And Prancin' .... (A&M 1949)   1.25   5.00   76
RUNNIN' FOR YOUR LOVIN' / Q .... (A&M 1982)   1.25   5.00   77
    Also see Quincy Jones (*Is It Love That We're Missin'*)

TITLE	LABEL AND NUMBER	VG	NM	YR

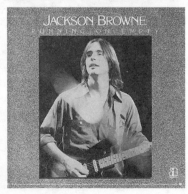

BROWN, BOBBY

GIRLFRIEND	(MCA 52866)	.75	3.00	86
GIRL NEXT DOOR	(MCA 53022)	.75	3.00	87
SEVENTEEN	(MCA 53135)	.75	3.00	87
DON'T BE CRUEL	(MCA 53327)	.75	3.00	88
MY PREROGATIVE	(MCA 53383)	.75	3.00	88
RONI	(MCA 53463)	.75	3.00	88
EVERY LITTLE STEP	(MCA 53618)	.75	3.00	89

Also see New Edition

BROWN, CLARENCE 'GATEMOUTH'

See Professor Longhair (Mardi Gras In New Orleans)

BROWN, JAMES

OH BABY DON'T YOU WEEP	(King 5842)	3.75	15.00	64
CALDONIA/Evil	(Smash 1898)	5.00	20.00	64
THE THINGS THAT I USED TO DO/Out Of The Blue	(Smash 1908)	5.00	20.00	64
OUT OF SIGHT/Maybe The Last Time	(Smash 1919)	5.00	20.00	64
HEY AMERICA	(King 6339)	3.75	15.00	70
SANTA CLAUS IS DEFINITELY HERE TO STAY	(King 6340)	3.75	15.00	70
KING HEROIN	(Polydor 14116)	2.00	8.00	72
THE PAYBACK	(Polydor 14223)	2.00	8.00	74
BRING IT ON!	(Churchill/Augusta 94023)	1.25	5.00	83
LIVING IN AMERICA	(Scotti Bros. ZS4-05682)	.75	3.00	85
LIVING IN AMERICA	(Scotti Bros. ZS4-05682)	1.00	4.00	85
(Promotional issue, Demonstration Only–Not For Sale printed on sleeve)				
GRAVITY/Gravity (Dub Mix)	(Scotti Bros. ZS4-06275)	.75	3.00	86
GRAVITY	(Scotti Bros. ZS4-06275)	1.00	4.00	86
(Promotional issue, Demonstration Only–Not For Sale printed on sleeve)				
HOW DO YOU STOP	(Scotti Bros. ZS4-06568)	.75	3.00	86
HOW DO YOU STOP	(Scotti Bros. ZS4-06568)	1.00	4.00	86
(Promotional issue, Demonstration Only–Not For Sale printed on sleeve)				
I'M REAL/Tribute	(Scotti Bros. ZS4-07783)	.75	3.00	88
(Sleeve credits music and background vocals by Full Force)				
(GET UP I FEEL LIKE BEING LIKE A) SEX MACHINE	(Polydor 887-500-7)	.75	3.00	88
(From the motion picture The Blue Iguana)				

Also see Martha and the Vandellas (b-side of Nowhere To Run)

BROWN, JIM ED

See Chet Atkins (Chet's Tune)

BROWN, JOCELYN

EGO MANIAC	(Warner Bros. 28698-7)	.75	3.00	87

BROWN, JOYCE

WORKING GIRL	(Mega 14)	1.50	6.00	71

BROWN, JULIE

I LIKE 'EM BIG AND STUPID/Homecoming Queen	(Bulletz 767-7)	2.00	8.00	83
TRAPPED IN THE BODY OF A WHITE GIRL	(Sire 28251-7)	1.25	5.00	87
GIRL FIGHT TONIGHT!	(Sire 27983-7)	1.25	5.00	88

BROWN, KAY

See the Triplets (Loyalty)

BROWN, LES, AND HIS ORCHESTRA

See Bing Crosby (A Time To Be Jolly)

BROWN, MAXINE

ASK ME/Yesterday's Kisses	(Wand 135)	5.00	20.00	63
ALL IN MY MIND/Funny	(Wham 7036)	5.00	20.00	

BROWN, O'CHI

TWO HEARTS BEATING AS ONE/Another Broken Heart	(Mercury 888 300-7)	.75	3.00	86

BROWN, PETER

THEY ONLY COME OUT AT NIGHT	(Columbia 38-04381)	1.00	4.00	83
(Promotional issue only, Demonstration–Not For Sale printed on sleeve)				

BROWN, SAM

STOP	(A&M 1234)	.75	3.00	89

BROWN, T. GRAHAM

SHE COULDN'T LOVE ME ANYMORE	(Capitol B-44061)	.75	3.00	87

BROWNE, JACKSON

STAY/Rosie	(Asylum 45485)	1.00	4.00	77
YOU LOVE THE THUNDER/The Road	(Asylum 45543)	1.50	6.00	77
RUNNING ON EMPTY/Nothing But Time	(Asylum 45460)	2.00	8.00	78
BOULEVARD/Call It A Loan	(Asylum 47003)	1.25	5.00	80
SOMEBODY'S BABY/The Crow On The Cradle	(Asylum 7-69982)	1.00	4.00	82
(From the motion picture Fast Times At Ridgemont High)				
LAWYERS IN LOVE/Say It Isn't True	(Asylum 7-69791)	1.00	4.00	83
TENDER IS THE NIGHT/On The Day	(Asylum 7-69791)	1.00	4.00	83
FOR A ROCKER/Downtown	(Asylum 7-69764)	.75	3.00	84
FOR AMERICA/Till I Go Down	(Asylum 7-69566)	.75	3.00	86
IN THE SHAPE OF A HEART/Voice Of America	(Asylum 7-69543)	.75	3.00	86
Also Artists United Against Apartheid, Clarence Clemons (You're A Friend Of Mine)				

BROWNE, SEVERIN

LOVE SONG	(Motown 1303)	2.00	8.00	74

BROWNS, FEATURING JIM EDWARD BROWN, THE

THE OLD LAMPLIGHTER/Teen-Ex	(RCA Victor 47-7700)	2.00	8.00	60
MARGO/Lonely Little Robin	(RCA Victor 47-7755)	2.00	8.00	60
WHIFFENPOOF SONG/Brighten The Corner Where You Are	(RCA Victor 47-7780)	2.00	8.00	60

BRUBECK, DAVE, QUARTET, THE

		VG	NM	YR
UNSQUARE DANCE/It's A Raggy Waltz	(Columbia 4-42228)	2.50	10.00	61
COUNTDOWN/	(Columbia 4-42404)	2.50	10.00	62
BOSSA NOVA U.S.A./Camptown Races	(Columbia 4-42675)	2.50	10.00	63
SUMMER SONG/Three To Get Ready	(Columbia 4-42804)	2.50	10.00	63

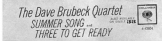

BRUCE, LENNY
EXTENDED PLAYS

		VG	NM	YR
THE LAW, LANGUAGE AND LENNY BRUCE	(Warner/Spector PRO 598)	5.00	20.00	74

(Promotional issue only, *Promotion Not For Sale* printed on sleeve. Originally included a letter from Phil Spector on Warner/Spector color letterhead briefly detailing the recording's background. Issued with a 13-track, small-hole 33-1/3 RPM record, titles listed on back.)

BRYAN, WES

		VG	NM	YR
LONESOME LOVE/Tiny Spaceman	(United Artists 102X)	6.25	25.00	58

BRYANT, ANITA

		VG	NM	YR
THE WEDDING (LA NOVIA)/Seven Kinds Of Lonesome	(Columbia 4-42148)	2.00	8.00	61
COLD COLD WINTER/Step By Step, Little By Little	(Columbia 4-42257)	2.00	8.00	61
ONE MORE TIME WITH BILLY/	(Columbia 4-42438)	2.00	8.00	62
MOONLIGHT MELODY/	(Columbia 4-42515)	2.00	8.00	62
A-SLEEPIN' AT THE FOOT OF MY BED/	(Columbia 4-42629)	2.00	8.00	63
HEY GOOD LOOKIN'/	(Columbia 4-42847)	2.00	8.00	63
MAN IN THE RAINCOAT/	(Columbia 4-44193)	2.00	8.00	67
DO YOU HEAR WHAT I HEAR/	(Columbia 4-44341)	2.00	8.00	67
THE ORANGE BIRD SONG/Orange Tree	(Disneyland 560)	1.50	6.00	71

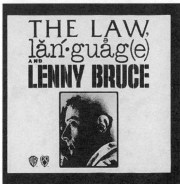

BRYANT, RAY

		VG	NM	YR
MADISON TIME	(Columbia 4-41628)	2.00	8.00	60

(Originally issued with a four-page insert illustrating the "Madison" dance steps)

		VG	NM	YR
MADISON TIME	(MCA 53322)	.75	3.00	88

(From the motion picture *Hairspray*)

BRYANT, SHARON

		VG	NM	YR
LET GO	(Wing 871 722-7)	.75	3.00	89

BRYSON, PEABO

		VG	NM	YR
TURN THE HANDS OF TIME	(Capitol 4989)	.75	3.00	81
TONIGHT, I CELEBRATE MY LOVE	(Capitol B-5242)	.75	3.00	83

(Shown as by Peabo Bryson and Roberta Flack)

		VG	NM	YR
MAYBE	(Capitol B-5283)	.75	3.00	83

(Shown as by Peabo Bryson and Roberta Flack. From the motion picture *Romantic Comedy*.)

		VG	NM	YR
YOU'RE LOOKIN' LIKE LOVE TO ME	(Capitol B-5307)	.75	3.00	83

(Shown as by Peabo Bryson and Roberta Flack)

		VG	NM	YR
TAKE NO PRISONERS (IN THE GAME OF LOVE)/Love Means Forever	(Elektra 7-69632)	.75	3.00	85
WITHOUT YOU/The Higher You Climb	(Elektra 7-69426)	.75	3.00	87

(A-side shown as by Peabo Bryson & Regina Belle. From the motion picture *Leonard Part 6*, Bill Cosby pictured.)

		VG	NM	YR
SHOW AND TELL	(Capitol P-B-44347)	.75	3.00	89

Also see Peabo Bryson and Roberta Flack

BUCKAROOS, THE

		VG	NM	YR
CHICKEN PICKIN'	(Capitol 2010)	2.00	8.00	67

Also see Buck Owens

BUCKINGHAM, LINDSEY

		VG	NM	YR
TROUBLE/Mary Lee Jones	(Asylum 47223)	1.00	4.00	81
GO INSANE/Play In The Rain	(Elektra 7-69714)	1.00	4.00	84

Also see Buckingham Nicks, Fleetwood Mac, U.S.A. For Africa, Voices Of America

BUCKINGHAM NICKS

		VG	NM	YR
CRYING IN THE NIGHT/Stephanie	(Polydor 14428)	7.50	30.00	73

Also see Lindsey Buckingham, Fleetwood Mac, Stevie Nicks, U.S.A. For Africa (Lindsey Buckingham), Voices Of America (Lindsey Buckingham)

BUCKINGHAMS, THE

		VG	NM	YR
DON'T YOU CARE/Why Don't You Love Me	(Columbia 4-44053)	2.50	10.00	67
MERCY, MERCY, MERCY/You Are Gone	(Columbia 4-44182)	2.50	10.00	67
HEY BABY (THEY'RE PLAYING OUR SONG)/And Our Love	(Columbia 4-44254)	2.50	10.00	67
SUSAN/Foreign Policy	(Columbia 4-44378)	2.50	10.00	67
BACK IN LOVE AGAIN/You Misunderstand Me	(Columbia 4-44533)	2.50	10.00	68
WHERE DID YOU COME FROM?/Song Of The Breeze	(Columbia 4-44672)	3.00	12.00	68
THIS IS HOW MUCH I LOVE YOU/Can't Find The Words	(Columbia 4-44790)	3.00	12.00	68
VERONICA	(Red Label B-71001)	1.00	4.00	85

Also see the Fabulous Rhinestones (Marty Grebb)

BUCKNER AND GARCIA

		VG	NM	YR
DO THE DONKEY KONG/Do The Donkey Kong (Instrumental)	(Columbia 18-02867)	.75	3.00	82

BUCK PETS, THE

		VG	NM	YR
PEARLS/Hey Sunshine	(Island 422-878 346-7)	2.50	10.00	90

(Individually numbered, promotional issue only. Hard cover edition of 4000 produced by Independent Project Press, issued with small-hole 45 RPM record.)

		VG	NM	YR
CAR CHASE/Shave/Bargain	(Sing Fat 04)	1.00	4.00	93

BUCKWHEAT ZYDECO

		VG	NM	YR
MY GIRL LIL/On A Night Like This	(Island 7-99396)	1.00	4.00	87

BUDD, JULIE

		VG	NM	YR
ALL'S QUIET ON WEST 23RD	(MGM K-13925)	1.50	6.00	68

BUELL, BEBE

		VG	NM	YR
GARGOYLE/Bored Baby	(Ultra Under 001)	.75	3.00	92

(Folding hard cover)

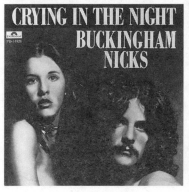

BUFFALO, GRANT LEE
WE'VE ONLY JUST BEGUN .... (A&M 31458 0718 7)   .50   2.00   94
(Side 14 of a 7-record box set titled *If I Were A Carpenter*. Each sleeve has a different face shot of Karen Carpenter on the front, Richard Carpenter on the back. No artist name or song titles indicated on sleeve. Complete set valued at $30.00 near mint.)

BUFFALO SPRINGFIELD
See Richie Furay, Jim Messina, Stephen Stills, Neil Young

BUFFALO TOM
SODAJERK/Witches .... (Beggars Banquet 7-98366)   1.50   6.00   93
(Individually numbered, hard cover edition produced by Independent Project Press. Issued with a small-hole 45 RPM record.)

BUFFETT, JIMMY
CHANGES IN LATITUDES, CHANGES IN ATTITUDES .... (ABC 12305)   1.50   6.00   77
HELLO TEXAS/Lyin' Eyes .... (Full Moon/Asylum 47073)   1.00   4.00   80
(B-side shown as by Eagles. From the motion picture *Urban Cowboy*, John Travolta pictured.)
WHEN THE WILD LIFE BETRAYS ME/Ragtop Day .... (MCA 52438)   1.00   4.00   84
GYPSIES IN THE PALACE/Jolly Mon Sing .... (MCA 52607)   1.00   4.00   85
IF THE PHONE DOESN'T RING, IT'S ME .... (MCA 52664)   1.00   4.00   85
CREOLA .... (MCA 52932)   1.00   4.00   86
BRING BACK THE MAGIC .... (MCA 53396)   .75   3.00   88

BUHL, DAVEY
A DEDICATION .... (Mega 5)   1.50   6.00   70

BULL DURHAM
(Motion Picture)
See Joe Cocker

BULLET BOYS
FOR THE LOVE OF MONEY .... (Warner Bros. 27554-7)   .75   3.00   89

BUNBURYS, THE
FIGHT (NO MATTER HOW LONG)/Fight (No Matter How Long) .... (Arista 9760)   .75   3.00   88
Also see the Bee Gees, Eric Clapton

BUOYS, THE
TIMOTHY .... (Scepter 12275)   2.00   8.00   71

BURDON, ERIC
SPILL THE WINE/Magic Mountain .... (MGM 70L 1277)   2.50   10.00   70
(Shown as by Eric Burdon & War)
THE REAL ME/Ring Of Fire .... (Capitol 4007)   3.00   12.00   74
(Shown as by the Eric Burdon Band)
Also see the Animals

BURGLAR
(Motion Picture)
See Jacksons (*Time Out For The Burglar*)

BURKE, SOLOMON
See the Soul Clan

BURKE, SONNY, AND HIS ORCHESTRA
HENNESSEY/Martha .... (Decca 9-31069)   2.50   10.00   60
(From the television series *Hennessey*, Jackie Cooper and Abby Dalton pictured)

BURNETTE, DORSEY
THE RIVER AND THE MOUNTAIN/This Hotel .... (Era 3033)   10.00   40.00   60
FOUR FOR TEXAS/Foolish Pride .... (Reprise 0246)   7.50   30.00   63
BE A NAVY MAN .... (U.S. Navy no #)   6.25   25.00   60s
(Promotional issue only for U.S. Navy recruitment)

BURNETTE, JOHNNY
YOU'RE SIXTEEN/I Beg Your Pardon .... (Liberty 55285)   6.25   25.00   60
LITTLE BOY SAD/(I Go) Down To The River .... (Liberty 55298)   6.25   25.00   61
BIG BIG WORLD/Ballad Of The One Eyed Jacks .... (Liberty 55285)   6.25   25.00   61
BIGGER MAN/Less Than A Heart Beat .... (Magic Lamp 515)   25.00   100.00   64

BURNETTE, SMILEY
(Character actor, Gene Autrey's sidekick)
BLUE BOTTLE FLY/Smart Alec Crow .... (Capitol F 30129)   7.50   30.00   48
GRANDADDY FROG/Courtin' Cricket .... (Capitol F 30130)   7.50   30.00   48

BURNING SLICKS, THE
MIDNIGHT DRAG/Hard Drivin' Man .... (Battle 45926)   10.00   40.00   63

BURNS, GEORGE
I WISH I WAS EIGHTEEN AGAIN/One Of The Mysteries Of Life ... (Mercury 57011)   1.25   5.00   79

BURRITO BROTHERS, THE
EXTENDED PLAYS
CLOSER TO YOU .... (CBS AE7 1429)   1.00   4.00   82
(Promotional issue only titled *Kickin Rock & Roll*, co-sponsored by Busch Beer and WBCN 104 FM and included in *The Phoenix* magazine. Also includes songs by George Jones, Merle Haggard, Larry Gatlin and the Gatlin Brothers Band, Bobby Bare, and Ricky Skaggs.)
Also see the Flying Burrito Brothers

BURTNICK, GLEN
FOLLOW YOU .... (A&M 2968)   .75   3.00   87

BURTON, JENNY
STRANGERS IN A STRANGE WORLD .... (Atlantic 7-89660)   .75   3.00   84
(Shown as by Jenny Burton and Patrick Jude. From the motion picture *Beat Street*.)
DON'T YOU WANT IT BAD ENUFF .... (Atlantic 7-89343)   .75   3.00   86
Also see Lou Reed (b-side of *My Love Is Chemical*)

BUS BOYS, THE
CLEANIN' UP THE TOWN .... (Arista 9229)   1.00   4.00   84
(From the motion picture *Ghostbusters*)

BUSH, KATE
WUTHERING HEIGHTS/Kite ....(EMI America 8003)   10.00   40.00   78
THE MAN WITH THE CHILD IN HIS EYES/Moving ....(EMI America 8006)   —   —   78
(Another "phantom" sleeve that some have heard of but none have seen and probably does not exist. It is most likely that an import was mistakenly identified as a U.S. printing.)
RUNNING UP THAT HILL/Under The Ivy .... (EMI America B-8285)   2.50   10.00   85
(Artist name and song titles in light gold metallic ink. The type is slightly thicker than the dark gold version and the smaller type on back appears fuzzy. This may have been issued with promotional copies and after seeing the results was subsequently corrected for the stock printing.)
RUNNING UP THAT HILL/Under The Ivy .... (EMI America B-8285)   1.50   6.00   85
(Artist name and song titles in dark gold metallic ink. Smaller gold type on back is clear and sharp.)
HOUNDS OF LOVE/Burning Bridge .... (EMI America B-8302)   1.50   6.00   85
THE BIG SKY/Not This Time .... (EMI America B-8327)   1.50   6.00   85
EXPERIMENT IV/Wuthering Heights (New Vocal) .... (EMI America B8363)   1.25   5.00   86
CLOUDBUSTING/The Man With The Child In His Eyes .... (EMI America B-8386)   1.25   5.00   86
Also see Ferry Aid, Peter Gabriel (*Don't Give Up*)

BUSH TETRAS
PAGE 18/Find A Lie .... (Tim Kerr 644 830 139-7)   .75   3.00   96
(Hard cover with small-hole 45 RPM record)

BUSSE, HENRY
HOT LIPS/When Day Is Done .... (Decca 1-720)   3.00   12.00   53
(Decca "Curtain Call" series of reissues)

BUSTER
SUNDAY/Salt Lake City-Silver Gun .... (RCA JH 10726)   1.50   6.00   76
(Promotional issue only, *For DJ's Only–Not For Sale* printed on sleeve)

BUSTER
(Motion Picture)
See Phil Collins (*Two Hearts*)

BUTCHER, JON
SOUNDS OF YOUR VOICE .... (Capitol B-5534)   1.00   4.00   85
(Shown as by the Jon Butcher Axis)
GOODBYE SAVING GRACE .... (Capitol B-5693)   1.00   4.00   87
HOLY WAR .... (Capitol B-44006)   1.00   4.00   87
WISHES .... (Capitol B-44046)   1.00   4.00   87
SEND ME SOMEBODY .... (Capitol B-44334)   .75   3.00   89

BUTLER, BILL
PRELUDE IN BLUE .... (Epic 5-9493)   2.50   10.00   61
(From the motion picture *Les Liaisons Dangereuses*)

BUTLER, CHRIS
A HOLE IN THE SKY/Davey's Sister's Home From College .... (Future Fossil DIG1-FF)   .75   3.00   95
(Folding sleeve titled *The Wilderness Years Volume 1*, issued with small-hole 45 RPM record)
THE MAN IN THE RAZOR SUIT/The Bottom Of A Workingman's Beer .... (Future Fossil DIG3-FF)   .75   3.00   95
(Folding sleeve titled *The Wilderness Years Volume 3*, issued with small-hole 45 RPM record. In the tradition of the Traveling Wilburys, there is no Volume 2.)
Also see Tin Huey, the Waitresses

BUTLER, DAWS
(Provided the voices for many Hanna-Barbera cartoon characters including Beany of *Beany and Cecil*, Elroy of *The Jetsons*, Huckleberry Hound, Quickdraw McGraw, and Yogi Bear)
BINGO, RINGO/Clementine .... (Merri 6011)   7.50   30.00   64

BUTLER, JERRY
THEME FROM TARAS BULBA (WISHING STAR)/You Go Right Through Me .... (Vee-Jay 475)   5.00   20.00   62
I STAND ACCUSED/I Don't Want To Hear Anymore .... (Vee-Jay 598)   5.00   20.00   64
OPEN END INTERVIEW .... (Mercury DJ 132)   2.50   10.00   60s
(Promotional issue only)
SPICE OF LIFE EXCERPTS .... (Mercury SRM2 7502)   1.25   5.00   72
(Promotional issue only)
THE DEVIL IN MRS. JONES .... (Motown 1403F)   1.00   4.00   76

BUTLER, JOE
REVELATION, REVOLUTION '69 .... (Kama Sutra 264)   2.00   8.00   69

BUTLER, JONATHAN
LIES/Haunted By Your Love .... (Jive/RCA 1038-7-J)   .75   3.00   87
HOLDING ON/7th Avenue South .... (Jive/RCA 1063-7-J)   .75   3.00   87
TAKE GOOD CARE OF ME/Barenese .... (Jive/RCA 1083-7-J)   .75   3.00   87
Also see Ruby Turner (*If You're Ready*)

BUTTERFIELD, PAUL, BLUES BAND, THE
RUN OUT OF TIME/One More Heartache .... (Elektra 45620)   5.00   20.00   67

BUTTHOLE SURFERS, THE
HURDY GURDY MAN/Barking Dogs .... (Rough Trade RUS 97-3)   1.50   6.00   90
(Issued with gold vinyl)

BUTTONS, RED
(Comic Actor)
See Wayne Newton (*Stagecoach To Cheyenne*)

BUTT TRUMPET
PRIMITIVE ENEMA/Yesterday II, The Sequel .... (EMI/Chrysalis PB-19925)   .75   3.00   84
(Issued with a small-hole 45 RPM record)

BUZZCOCKS
EVERYBODY'S HAPPY NOWADAYS/Why Can't I Touch It? .... (I.R.S. 9001)   2.00   8.00   79
I BELIEVE/Something's Gone Wrong Again .... (I.R.S. 9010)   2.00   8.00   80

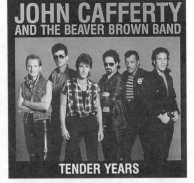

TITLE	LABEL AND NUMBER	VG	NM	YR
ARE EVERYTHING/Why She's A Girl From The Chainstore	(I.R.S. 9017)	1.50	6.00	80
(Issued with small-hole 45 RPM record)				
STRANGE THING/Airwaves Dream	(I.R.S. 9019)	1.50	6.00	80
(Issued with small-hole 45 RPM record)				
RUNNING FREE/What Do You Know?	(I.R.S. 9020)	1.50	6.00	80
Also see Pete Shelley				

BYE BYE BIRDIE
(Broadway Musical)
    See Louis Armstrong (*Hello, Dolly!*)

BYRDS, THE

TITLE	LABEL AND NUMBER	VG	NM	YR
MR. TAMBOURINE MAN	(Columbia 4-43271)	50.00	200.00	65
(Promotional issue only issued with red vinyl)				
EIGHT MILES HIGH/Why?	(Columbia 4-43578)	6.25	25.00	66
5D/The 5D Open-End Interview	(Columbia ZLP-116003-4)	75.00	300.00	66
(Promotional issue only)				
HAVE YOU SEEN HER FACE/Don't Make Waves	(Columbia 4-44157)	10.00	40.00	67

EXTENDED PLAYS

TITLE	LABEL AND NUMBER	VG	NM	YR
LOVER OF THE BAYOU/SO YOU WANT TO BE A ROCK AND ROLL STAR/ Goin' Back/Chimes Of Freedom	(Scholastic 1602)	3.75	15.00	70

Also see Gene Clark, Crosby, Stills & Nash (David Crosby), Crosby, Stills, Nash & Young (David Crosby), Firefall (Michael Clarke), the New Christy Minstrels (Gene Clark), the Textones (Gene Clark). Gram Parsons and Kevin Kelley, of the International Submarine Band, were with the group for two albums in 1968.

BYRNE, MARTHA
(Actress)
    See the Soaps and Hearts Ensemble

BYRNES, EDWARD

TITLE	LABEL AND NUMBER	VG	NM	YR
KOOKIE, KOOKIE (LEND ME YOUR COMB)/You're The Top	(Warner Bros. 5047)	5.00	20.00	59
(A-side shown as by Edward Byrnes With Connie Stevens)				
LIKE I LOVE YOU/Kookie's Mad Pad	(Warner Bros. 5087)	3.75	15.00	59
KOOKIE'S LOVE SONG	(Warner Bros. 5114)	3.75	15.00	59
(Shown as by Edd "Kookie" Byrnes and the Mary Kaye Trio. Front of sleeve reads *"Kookie's Love Song"* [*While Dancing*] *with Joanie Sommers*.)				
YULESVILLE/Lonely Christmas	(Warner Bros. 5121)	3.75	15.00	59

BYRON, D.L.

TITLE	LABEL AND NUMBER	VG	NM	YR
DOWN IN THE BOONDOCKS/21st Century Man	(Arista 0524)	1.00	4.00	80

C

CADDILL, SHIRLEY

TITLE	LABEL AND NUMBER	VG	NM	YR
PART TIME GAL	(Columbia 4-40939)	2.50	10.00	57

CADDY SHACK II
(Motion Picture)
    See Lisa Lisa and Cult Jam (*Go For Yours*), Kenny Loggins (*Nobody's Fool*)

CAESAR, VIC

TITLE	LABEL AND NUMBER	VG	NM	YR
NIXON'S THE ONE	(Caesar Productions 37)	1.25	5.00	
(Richard Nixon pictured)				

CAESAR & CLEO
    See Sonny and Cher

CAFFERTY, JOHN, AND THE BEAVER BROWN BAND

TITLE	LABEL AND NUMBER	VG	NM	YR
WILD SUMMER NIGHTS/Tender Years	(Coastline 01)	3.75	15.00	80
TENDER YEARS	(Scotti Brothers ZS4-04682)	.75	3.00	84
(From the motion picture *Eddie And The Cruisers*)				
TENDER YEARS	(Scotti Brothers ZS4-04682)	1.00	4.00	84
(Promotional issue, *Demonstration Only/Not For Sale* printed on sleeve. From the motion picture *Eddie And The Cruisers*.)				
TOUGH ALL OVER/Strangers In Paradise	(Scotti Brothers ZS4-04891)	.75	3.00	85
TOUGH ALL OVER	(Scotti Brothers ZS4-04891)	1.00	4.00	85
(Promotional issue, *Demonstration Only–Not For Sale* printed on sleeve)				
CITY	(Scotti Brothers ZS4-05452)	.75	3.00	85
CITY	(Scotti Brothers ZS4-05452)	1.00	4.00	85
(Promotional issue, *Demonstration Only–Not For Sale* printed on sleeve)				
SMALL TOWN GIRL/More Than Just One Of The Boys	(Scotti Brothers ZS4-05668)	.75	3.00	85
SMALL TOWN GIRL	(Scotti Brothers ZS4-05668)	1.00	4.00	85
(Promotional issue, *Demonstration Only–Not For Sale* printed on sleeve)				
HEART'S ON FIRE	(Scotti Brothers ZS4-05774)	.75	3.00	86
(Shown as by John Cafferty. From the motion picture *Rocky IV*.)				
HEART'S ON FIRE	(Scotti Brothers ZS4-05774)	1.00	4.00	86
(Promotional issue, *Demonstration Only–Not For Sale* printed on sleeve. Shown as by John Cafferty. From the motion picture *Rocky IV*.)				
VOICE OF AMERICA'S SONS	(Scotti Brothers ZS4-060484)	.75	3.00	86
(From the motion picture *Cobra*, Sylvester Stallone pictured)				
VOICE OF AMERICA'S SONS	(Scotti Brothers ZS4-060484)	1.00	4.00	86
(Promotional issue, *Demonstration Only–Not For Sale* printed on sleeve. From the motion picture *Cobra*, Sylvester Stallone pictured.)				
SONG & DANCE	(Atlantic 4031)	.75	3.00	88

CAIN, TANÉ

TITLE	LABEL AND NUMBER	VG	NM	YR
MY TIME TO FLY/Suspicious Eyes	(RCA PB-13392)	1.25	5.00	82

CAKE

TITLE	LABEL AND NUMBER	VG	NM	YR
I KNOW/You Can Have Him	(Decca 32212)	3.00	12.00	67

CALDWELL, BOBBY
    See Gloria Loring (*One Love, One Heart*)

CALE, JOHN
MERCENARIES (READY FOR WAR)/Rosegarden Funeral Of Sores .... (SPY/I.R.S. 9008)   1.50   6.00   80
    Also see the Velvet Underground

CALIFORNIA DREAMING
(Motion Picture)
    See America (California Dreaming)

CALIFORNIA RAISINS, THE
I HEARD IT THROUGH THE GRAPEVINE .... (Priority 9719)   1.00   4.00   87
SIGNED, SEALED, DELIVERED I'M YOURS/Green Onions .... (Atlantic 7-89009)   1.00   4.00   88
RUDOLPH THE RED NOSED REINDEER/Hark! .... (Atlantic 7-89008)   1.00   4.00   88
    (From the television special Claymation Christmas Celebration)

CALIGULA
(Motion Picture)
    See Lydia (We Are One)

CALL, THE
THE WALLS CAME DOWN/Upperbirth .... (Mercury 811 487-7)   1.50   6.00   83
EVERYWHERE I GO/Tore The Old Place Down .... (Elektra 7-69546)   1.00   4.00   86
I DON'T WANNA/Day Or Night .... (Elektra 7-69461)   1.00   4.00   87

CALLAHAN, MIKE
I CAN'T HELP IT .... (Protone 204)   6.25   25.00   58

CALLAS, MARIA
    See the Angel Listener (Preview Highlights)

CAMELOT
(Broadway Musical)
    See Tony Bennett (Follow Me), Johnny Mathis (How To Handle A Woman)

CAMEO
WORD UP!/Urban Warrior .... (Atlanta Artists 884 933-7)   .75   3.00   86
CANDY/She's Strange .... (Atlanta Artists 888 193-7)   .75   3.00   86
SHE'S MINE .... (Atlanta Artists 888 876-7)   .75   3.00   86
BACK AND FORTH/You Can Have The World .... (Atlanta Artists 888 385-7)   .75   3.00   87
SKIN I'M IN/Honey .... (Atlanta Artists 872 314-7)   .75   3.00   88
YOU MAKE ME WORK/DKWIG .... (Atlanta Artists 870 587-7)   .75   3.00   88
PRETTY GIRLS/Pretty Girls (Dub) .... (Atlanta Artists 874 050-7)   .75   3.00   89

CAMEOS, THE
BEST OF THE CAN CAN .... (Cameo 176)   2.50   10.00   59

CAMERON, JOHNNY
FANTASTIC .... (20th Century 179)   2.00   8.00   62

CAMERON, KIRK
    See Steve Dorff and Friends (Theme From Growing Pains)

CAMERON, ROBERT
NO SUCH THING AS LOVE .... (Epic 5-10071)   2.00   8.00   66

CAMOUFLAGE
THE GREAT COMMANDMENT/Pompeji .... (Atlantic 7-89031)   .75   3.00   88
THAT SMILING FACE/Every Now And Then .... (Atlantic 7-88920)   .75   3.00   88

CAMPBELL, ARCHIE
    See Chet Atkins (Chet's Tune)

CAMPBELL, DICK
THE PEOPLE PLANNERS .... (Mercury 72511)   2.50   10.00   66

CAMPBELL, GLEN
LONG BLACK LIMOUSINE/Here I Am .... (Capitol 4856)   5.00   20.00   62
SUMMER, WINTER, SPRING AND FALL/Heartaches Can Be Fun .... (Capitol 4856)   3.75   15.00   64
HEY LITTLE ONE/My Baby's Gone .... (Capitol 4856)   2.50   10.00   68
IT'S JUST A MATTER OF TIME/Gene Autry, My Hero .... (Atlantic America 7-99600)   .75   3.00   85
    Also see the Legendary Masked Surfers

CAMPBELL, STAN
DON'T LET ME BE MISUNDERSTOOD/'Til We Meet Again .... (Elektra 7-69442)   .75   3.00   87
YEARS GO BY/ .... (Elektra 7-69473)   .75   3.00   87

CAMPERS, THE
(Also recorded as the Camps)
THE BALLAD OF BATMAN/Batmobile .... (Parkway 974)   10.00   40.00   65
    Also see the Crickets

CAMPI, RAY
WITH YOU/My Screamin' Screamin' Mimi .... (Domino 700)   18.75   75.00   58
    (Single sheet insert, not a true picture sleeve)

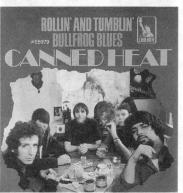

CAN
MOONSHAKE/Future Days .... (United Artists XW446-W)   1.50   6.00   74

CANDI
DANCING UNDER A LATIN MOON/Luna Latina Tu Y Yo .... (I.R.S. 53436)   .75   3.00   88

CANDY
WHATEVER HAPPENED TO FUN.../Kids In The City .... (Mercury 880 919-7)   .75   3.00   85

CANNED HEAT
ROLLIN' AND TUMBLIN'/Bullfrog Blues .... (Liberty 55979)   2.50   10.00   67
GOING UP THE COUNTRY/One Kind Favor .... (Liberty 56077)   2.00   8.00   68
WHISKEY AND WIMMEN/Let's Make It .... (United Artists 50779)   1.50   6.00   71
    (Shown as by Canned Heat and John Lee Hooker. Promotional issue only issued with blue jean patch.)

TITLE	LABEL AND NUMBER	VG	NM	YR

CANNIBAL AND THE HEADHUNTERS
LAND OF 1000 DANCES (NON EDITED VERSION /
    HOUSE OF WAX/Fine, Fine, Fine/Beaver Shot .... (Rampart 45.BA05) | .50 | 2.00 | 95
    (Only *Land Of 1000 Dances* is by Cannibal and the Headhunters. *House Of Wax* shown as by the Aldermen and
    both b-side tracks by The Atlantics.)

CANNON, ACE
COTTONFIELDS/Mildew .... (Hi 2065) | 2.50 | 10.00 | 63
SWANEE RIVER/Moanin' The Blues .... (Hi 2070) | 2.00 | 8.00 | 63

CANNON, FREDDY
WAY DOWN YONDER IN NEW ORLEANS/Fractured .... (Swan 4043) | 5.00 | 20.00 | 59
CHATTANOOGA SHOE SHINE BOY/Boston .... (Swan 4050) | 5.00 | 20.00 | 60
JUMP OVER/The Urge .... (Swan 4053) | 5.00 | 20.00 | 60
HAPPY SHADES OF BLUE/Cuernavaca Choo Choo .... (Swan 4057) | 5.00 | 20.00 | 60
HUMDINGER/My Blue Heaven .... (Swan 4061) | 5.00 | 20.00 | 60
MUSKRAT RAMBLE/Two Thousand 88s .... (Swan 4066) | 5.00 | 20.00 | 60
TRANSISTOR SISTER/Walk To The Moon .... (Swan 4078) | 5.00 | 20.00 | 61
PALISADES PARK/June, July And August .... (Swan 4106) | 5.00 | 20.00 | 62
LITTLE MISS A-GO-GO/In The Night .... (Warner Bros. 5615) | 10.00 | 40.00 | 64
KENNYWOOD PARK .... (HQ no #) | 5.00 | 20.00 | 87
    (Promotional issue in conjunction with radio station KDKA, Pittsburgh, Pennsylvania)

CANOVA, DIANE
(Actress)
WHO YOU FOOLIN' .... (20th Century-Fox 2486) | 1.50 | 6.00 | 81

CANTOR, EDDIE
NOW'S THE TIME TO FALL IN LOVE/Makin' Whoopee .... (Decca 1-701) | 3.00 | 12.00 | 51
    (Decca "Curtain Call" series of reissues)

CAN'T STOP THE MUSIC
(Motion Picture)
    See Village People (*Can't Stop The Music*)

CAPALDI, JIM
THAT'S LOVE/Runaway .... (Atlantic 7-89849) | 1.00 | 4.00 | 83
    Also see Traffic

CAPELLI, RACHELE
I'M SORRY .... (Atlantic 7-89011) | .75 | 3.00 | 88

CAPTAIN AND TENNILLE, THE
LOVE WILL KEEP US TOGETHER/Gentle Stranger .... (A&M 1672) | 1.25 | 5.00 | 75
THE WAY I WANT TO TOUCH YOU/Broddy Bounce .... (A&M 1725) | 1.25 | 5.00 | 75
LONELY NIGHT (ANGEL FACE)/Smile For Me One More Time .... (A&M 1782) | 1.25 | 5.00 | 76
SHOP AROUND/Butterscotch Castle .... (A&M 1817) | 1.25 | 5.00 | 76
MUSKRAT LOVE/Honey Come Love Me .... (A&M 1870) | 1.25 | 5.00 | 76
CAN'T STOP DANCIN'/Mis Canciones .... (A&M 1912) | 1.25 | 5.00 | 77
COME IN FROM THE RAIN/We Never Really Say Goodbye .... (A&M 1944) | 1.25 | 5.00 | 77
I'M ON MY WAY/We Never Really Say Goodbye .... (A&M 2027) | 1.25 | 5.00 | 77
SONG OF JOY/Wedding Song .... (A&M 8601) | 1.25 | 5.00 | 77
YOU NEVER DONE IT LIKE THAT/"D" Keyboard Blues .... (A&M 2063) | 1.25 | 5.00 | 78
YOU NEED A WOMAN TONIGHT/Love Me Like A Baby .... (A&M 2106) | 1.25 | 5.00 | 78

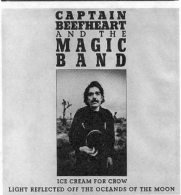

CAPTAIN BEEFHEART AND THE MAGIC BAND
CLICK CLACK/Glider .... (Reprise PRO 514) | 6.25 | 25.00 | 71
    (Promotional issue only, issued with a small-hole 33-1/3 RPM record)
TOO MUCH TIME/Lo Yo-Yo Stuff .... (Reprise PRO 547) | 6.25 | 25.00 | 72
    (Promotional issue only, issued with a small-hole 33-1/3 RPM record)
ICE CREAM FOR CROW/Light Reflected Off The Oceands Of The Moon .... (Virgin/Epic 14-03190) | 3.00 | 12.00 | 82

CAPTAIN Q. B. & THE BIG BOYS
SAN DIEGO SUPER CHARGERS .... (Air Records no #) | 1.25 | 5.00 | 79
    (Official theme song for the San Diego Chargers football team)

CAPUCINE
(Actor)
    See Brook Benton (*Walk On The Wild Side*)

CARA, IRENE
WHY ME? .... (Geffen 29464-7) | .75 | 3.00 | 83

CARDENAS, LUIS
RUNAWAY/Still Waiting .... (Capitol B-72500) | 1.00 | 4.00 | 86
HUNGRY FOR YOUR LOVE/Blasting Off .... (Capitol B 72502) | .75 | 3.00 | 86

CAREFREES, THE
WE LOVE YOU BEATLES .... (London International 10614) | 7.50 | 30.00 | 64

CAREY, MARIAH
ALWAYS BE MY BABY/Long Ago .... (Columbia 38 78276) | .50 | 2.00 | 96
HONEY (LP VERSION)/Honey (Bad Boy Remix Featuring Mase & The Lox) .. (Columbia 38 78648) | .50 | 2.00 | 97

CAREY, TONY
WEST COAST SUMMER NIGHTS/Sing Along .... (Rocshire XR95037) | 1.25 | 5.00 | 82
    (Hard cover)
A FINE, FINE DAY .... (MCA 52343) | 1.00 | 4.00 | 84
    Also see Planet P

CARILLO
I WANNA LIVE AGAIN/Let's Get It Up .... (Atlantic 3492) | .75 | 3.00 | 78

CARL, MAX
THE CIRCLE/Tell Me Where Your Sister's Hiding .... (MCA 52568) | .75 | 3.00 | 85

CARLIN, GEORGE
11 O'CLOCK NEWS/The Hair Piece/Divorce Game Werds .... (Atlantic/Little David 77214) | 1.50 | 6.00 | 72
    (Promotional issue only)

TITLE	LABEL AND NUMBER	VG	NM	YR

NEW NEWS (PART ONE)/New News (Part Two) .... (Little David 731)   2.00   8.00   75
(Promotional issue only titled *New News Is Good News*. Originally came with a 3" x 6" ticket.)

EXTENDED PLAYS

GOOFY SH*T/TOLEDO WINDOW BOX/NURSERY RHYMES/
Some Werds .... (Little David PRO 594)   1.50   6.00   74
(Promotional issue only, issued with a small-hole 33-1/3 RPM record.)

HEADLINES/SUICIDE & REINCARNATION/
Kids Are Too Small/Laugh, I Thought I'd Die .... (Little David PR 279)   1.50   6.00   77
(Promotional issue only titled *The George Carlin E.P.*)

HAVE A NICE DAY–RICE KRISPIES/SECOND ANNOUNCEMENTS, THIRD
ANNOUNCEMENTS, FIFTH ANNOUNCEMENTS, SIXTH ANNOUNCEMENTS/
JOIN THE BOOK CLUB/Ice Box Man .... (Atlantic EP-PR-409)   1.50   6.00   81
(Promotional issue only titled *A Place For My Stuff*. *Promotion Copy Not For Sale* printed on sleeve.)

CARLISLE, BELINDA
MAD ABOUT YOU/I Never Wanted A Rich Man .... (I.R.S. 52815)   1.00   4.00   86
I FEEL THE MAGIC/From The Heart .... (I.R.S. 52889)   1.25   5.00   86
HEAVEN IS A PLACE ON EARTH .... (MCA 53181)   .75   3.00   87
I GET WEAK .... (MCA 53242)   .75   3.00   88
CIRCLE IN THE SAND .... (MCA 53308)   .75   3.00   88
I FEEL FREE .... (MCA 53377)   1.00   4.00   88
Also see the Go-Go's

CARLOS, WALTER
(Changed his name to Wendy Carlos after a sex change)
SWITCHED ON BACH (BRANDENBURG CONCERTO NO. 3–
FINAL MOVEMENT) .... (Columbia 8-3322)   1.00   4.00   68
(Promotional issue only titled *A Second Chance For Bach!*)

CARLTON, LARRY
SMILES AND SMILES TO GO/Carrying You .... (MCA 52844)   .75   3.00   86
Also see Mike Post (*The Theme From Hill Street Blues*)

CARMAN, PAULI
IN THE HEAT OF THE NIGHT/ .... (Columbia 38-07290)   .75   3.00   87
IN THE HEAT OF THE NIGHT .... (Columbia 38-07290)   .75   3.00   87
(Promotional issue only, *Demonstration Only Not For Sale* printed on back)

CARMEN, ERIC
SHE DID IT .... (Arista 266)   1.25   5.00   77
BOATS AGAINST THE CURRENT .... (Arista 295)   2.00   8.00   77
(Promotional issue only)
I WANNA HEAR IT FROM YOUR LIPS .... (Geffen 29118-7)   1.00   4.00   84
I'M THROUGH WITH LOVE .... (Geffen 29032-7)   1.00   4.00   85
THE ROCK STOPS HERE .... (Cool 101)   1.00   4.00   86
(Benefit for the Greater Cleveland Growth Association Rock and Roll Hall of Fame Foundation)
MAKE ME LOSE CONTROL/That's Rock And Roll .... (Arista 9686)   .75   3.00   88
REASON TO CRY/Sunrise .... (Arista 9746)   .75   3.00   88
Also see Raspberries

CARNES, KIM
MORE LOVE/Changin' .... (EMI America 8045)   1.00   4.00   80
BETTE DAVIS EYES/Miss You Tonight .... (EMI America 8077)   1.00   4.00   81
DRAW OF THE CARDS/Break The Rules Tonight (Out Of School) .... (EMI America A8087)   .75   3.00   81
MISTAKEN IDENTITY/Jamaica Sunday Morning .... (EMI America A-8098)   .75   3.00   81
VOYEUR/Thrill Of The Grill .... (EMI America B-8127)   .75   3.00   82
DOES IT MAKE YOU REMEMBER/Take It On The Chin .... (EMI America B-8147)   .75   3.00   82
INVISIBLE HANDS/I'll Be Here Where The Heart Is .... (EMI America B-8181)   .75   3.00   83
YOU MAKE MY HEART BEAT FASTER (AND THAT'S ALL THAT MATTERS)/
Hangin' On By A Thread (A Sad Affair Of The Heart) .... (EMI America B-8191)   .75   3.00   83
I PRETEND/Hurricane .... (EMI America B-8202)   .75   3.00   84
INVITATION TO DANCE/Breakthrough .... (EMI America B-8250)   .75   3.00   85
CRAZY IN THE NIGHT (BARKING AT AIRPLANES)/
Oliver (Voice On The Radio) .... (EMI America B-8267)   .75   3.00   85
ABADABADANGO .... (EMI America B-8281)   .75   3.00   85
DIVIDED HEARTS .... (EMI America B-8322)   .75   3.00   86
Also see Kenny Rogers (*Don't Fall In Love With A Dreamer, What About Me?*), Barbra Streisand (*Make No Mistake, He's Mine*), U.S.A. For Africa,
Voices Of America

CARNEY, ART
(Comic actor, played Ed Norton in *The Honeymooners* sketches from the television series *The Jackie Gleason Show*)
THEM/The Dodo Bird .... (Columbia J4-204)   6.25   25.00   59
(Half sleeve)
THE SONG OF THE BASSOON/Where Did The Chickie Lay The Eggie? .... (Columbia J4-228)   6.25   25.00   59

CARO, NYDIA
ASK WHAT I WANT FOR CHRISTMAS .... (Roulette 4588)   1.50   6.00   64

CARPENTERS
WE'VE ONLY JUST BEGUN/All Of My Life .... (A&M 1217)   1.50   6.00   70
MERRY CHRISTMAS, DARLING/Mr. Guder .... (A&M 1236)   1.50   6.00   70
FOR ALL WE KNOW/Don't Be Afraid .... (A&M 1243)   1.50   6.00   71
(Red and black duotone, red dominant, with textured cloth background)
FOR ALL WE KNOW/Don't Be Afraid .... (A&M 1243)   1.50   6.00   71
(Red and black duotone, black dominant, with flat background)
RAINY DAYS AND MONDAYS/Saturday .... (A&M 1260)   1.25   5.00   71
SUPERSTAR/Bless The Beasts And Children .... (A&M 1289)   1.25   5.00   71
(Medium blue background with Carpenters portrait graphic in black. B-side from the motion picture *Bless The Beasts And Children*)
SUPERSTAR/Bless The Beasts And Children .... (A&M 1289)   1.25   5.00   71
(Royal blue background with Carpenters portrait graphic in white. B-side from the motion picture *Bless The Beasts And Children*)
HURTING EACH OTHER/Maybe It's You .... (A&M 1322)   1.25   5.00   72
(Glossy coated paper)
HURTING EACH OTHER/Maybe It's You .... (A&M 1322)   1.25   5.00   72
(Non-glossy uncoated paper)

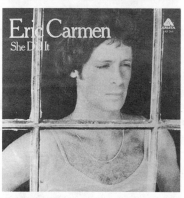

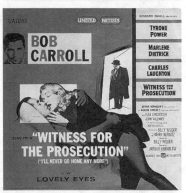

TITLE	LABEL AND NUMBER	VG	NM	YR
IT'S GOING TO TAKE SOME TIME/Flat Baroque	(A&M 1351)	1.25	5.00	72
GOODBYE TO LOVE/Crystal Lullaby	(A&M 1367)	1.50	6.00	72
SING/Druscilla Penny	(A&M 1413)	1.25	5.00	73
YESTERDAY ONCE MORE/Road Ode	(A&M 1446)	1.25	5.00	73
TOP OF THE WORLD/Heather	(A&M 1468)	1.25	5.00	73
I WON'T LAST A DAY WITHOUT YOU/One Love	(A&M 1521)	1.50	6.00	74
PLEASE MR. POSTMAN/The Masquerade	(A&M 1646)	1.25	5.00	74
SANTA CLAUS IS COMING TO TOWN/Merry Christmas, Darling	(A&M 1648)	2.00	8.00	74
ONLY YESTERDAY/Happy	(A&M 1677)	1.00	4.00	75
SOLITAIRE/Love Me For What I Am	(A&M 1721)	1.00	4.00	75
THERE'S A KIND OF HUSH/Goodbye And I Love You	(A&M 1800)	1.00	4.00	76
ALL YOU GET FROM LOVE IS A LOVE SONG/I Have You	(A&M 1940)	1.00	4.00	77
CALLING OCCUPANTS OF INTERPLANETARY CRAFT/Can't Smile Without You	(A&M 1978)	1.00	4.00	77
THE CHRISTMAS SONG/Merry Christmas Darling	(A&M 1991)	1.00	4.00	77
SWEET, SWEET, SMILE/I Have You	(A&M 2008)	1.00	4.00	78
TOUCH ME WHEN WE'RE DANCING/Because We Are In Love	(A&M 2344)	1.00	4.00	81
MAKE BELIEVE IT'S YOUR FIRST TIME/Look To Your Dreams	(A&M 2585)	1.00	4.00	83
YESTERDAY ONCE MORE	(A&M 2735)	3.75	15.00	84
(Promotional issue only)				
THE CHRISTMAS SONG/Merry Christmas Darling	(A&M 8620)	1.00	4.00	87
HONOLULU CITY LIGHTS/I Just Fall In Love Again	(A&M 88667)	1.00	4.00	88

Also see American Music Club (Goodbye To Love), Babes In Toyland (Calling Occupants Of Interplanetary Craft), Bettie Serveert (For All We Know), Grant Lee Buffalo (We've Only Just Begun), Cracker (Rainy Days And Mondays), the Cranberries (Close To You), Sheryl Crow (Solitaire), Dishwalla (It's Going To Take Some Time), 4 Non Blondes (Bless The Beasts And Children), Johnette Napolitano (Hurting Each Other), Redd Kross (Yesterday Once More), Shonen Knife (Top Of The World), Sonic Youth (Superstar), Matthew Sweet (Let Me Be The One)

CARR, VIKKI
THE SILENCERS/Santiago	(Liberty 55857)	1.50	6.00	67
THE LESSON/One More Mountain	(Liberty 56012)	1.50	6.00	67
DON'T BREAK MY PRETTY BALLOON/Nothing To Lose	(Liberty 56039)	1.50	6.00	68
ETERNITY	(Liberty 56132)	1.50	6.00	69
IT HAPPENED ON A MIDNIGHT CLEAR	(Columbia AS585)	1.25	5.00	74

CARRACK, PAUL
DON'T SHED A TEAR/Merilee	(Chrysalis VS4 43164)	.75	3.00	87
ONE GOOD REASON/All Your Love Is In Vain	(Chrysalis VS4 43204)	.75	3.00	88
WHEN YOU WALK IN THE ROOM/	(Chrysalis VS4 43252)	.75	3.00	88

Also see Mike and the Mechanics, Squeeze, Roger Waters (Sunset Strip)

CARRADINE, ROBERT
(Actor)

See Mike + the Mechanics (Revolution)

CARRASCO, JOE "KING"
PARTY WEEKEND/Houston El Mover	(Gee Bee 101)	1.00	4.00	80
(Record shown as by Joe "King" Carrasco and the Crowns)				

CARROLL, ANDREA
GEE DAD/The Charm On My Arm	(Epic 5-9471)	10.00	40.00	61
SALLY FOOL	(RCA Victor 47-8618)	3.75	15.00	65
THE WORLD ISN'T BIG ENOUGH	(United Artists 982)	5.00	20.00	66
HEY BEACH BOY	(United Artists 50039)	5.00	20.00	66

CARROLL, BOB
SONG FROM WITNESS FOR THE PROSECUTION (I'LL NEVER GO HOME ANY MORE)/ Lovely Eyes	(United Artists 106X)	5.00	20.00	58
(From the motion picture Witness For The Prosecution, Tyrone Power, Marlene Dietrich, Charles Laughton, and Carroll pictured)				
HI HO SILVER/Tonto The Brave	(United Artists 129X)	5.00	20.00	59
(From the motion picture The Lone Ranger And The Lost City Of Gold)				

CARROLL, CORKY
SKATEBOARD BILL/Pocket Rocket	(Jet 1001)	1.25	5.00	77
(Shown as by Corky Carroll and the Corkettes. Issued with either stock black or promotional blue vinyl.)				
TAN PUNKS ON BOARDS/From Pizza Towers To Defeat	(Pacific Arts 45-103)	1.25	5.00	78
(Shown as by Corky Carroll and the Cool Water Casuals)				

CARROLL, JIM
SAVE ME/I Got Plenty	(A&M 1360)	1.50	6.00	72

CARROLL, JIMMY
RUMBLE/Big Man	(Bell 84)	10.00	40.00	58

CARS, THE
JUST WHAT I NEEDED/I'm In Touch With Your World	(Elektra 45491)	1.25	5.00	78
(Originally issued with red vinyl)				
IT'S ALL I CAN DO/Got A Lot On My Head	(Elektra 46546)	1.25	5.00	79
(Illustration by Alberto Vargas)				
SHAKE IT UP/Cruiser	(Elektra 47250)	1.00	4.00	81
SINCE YOU'RE GONE/Think It Over	(Elektra 47433)	1.00	4.00	81
YOU MIGHT THINK/Heartbeat City	(Elektra 7-69744)	.75	3.00	84
YOU ARE THE GIRL/Ta Ta Wayo Wayo	(Elektra 7-69446)	.75	3.00	87
COMING UP YOU/Double Trouble	(Elektra 7-69432)	.75	3.00	87

Also see Ric Ocasek, Benjamin Orr, Jonathan Richman and the Modern Lovers (David Robinson)

CARSON, SAL
See Vicky Spinosa

CARTER, CARLENE
NEVER TOGETHER BUT CLOSE SOMETIMES	(Warner Bros. 8576)	1.25	5.00	78

CARTER, MOTHER MAYBELLE
See Nitty Gritty Dirt Band (Honky Tonkin')

CARTER, VALERIE
See Tom Snow (Hurry Boy), Jack Wagner (Love Can Take Us All The Way)

CARTER FAMILY, THE
See Johnny Cash (Busted)

CASABLANCA
(Motion Picture)
See Dooley Wilson (As Time Goes By)

CASADY, JACK
See Hot Tuna, Jefferson Airplane, SVT

CASCADES, THE

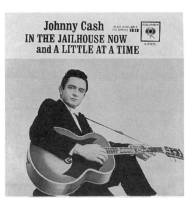

A LITTLE LIKE LOVIN'/Cinderella .... (RCA Victor 47-8206)	5.00	20.00	63
EVERYONE IS BLOSSOMING/Two Sided Man .... (Probe 543)	3.75	15.00	68

CASH, JOHNNY

GUESS THINGS HAPPEN THAT WAY/Come In, Stranger .... (Sun 295)	6.25	25.00	58
ALL OVER AGAIN/What Do I Care .... (Columbia 4-41251)	5.00	20.00	58
DON'T TAKE YOUR GUNS TO TOWN/I Still Miss Someone .... (Columbia 4-41313)	5.00	20.00	59
THE LITTLE DRUMMER BOY/I'll Remember You .... (Columbia 4-41481)	5.00	20.00	59
THE REBEL–JOHNNY YUMA/Forty Shades Of Green .... (Columbia 4-41995)	5.00	20.00	61
TENNESSEE FLAT-TOP BOX/Tall Men .... (Columbia 4-42147)	3.00	12.00	61
THE BIG BATTLE/When I've Learned .... (Columbia 4-42301)	3.00	12.00	60
IN THE JAILHOUSE NOW/A Little At A Time .... (Columbia 4-42425)	3.00	12.00	62
BONANZA!/Pick A Gale O' Cotton .... (Columbia 4-42512)	3.00	12.00	62
PEACE IN THE VALLEY/Were You There .... (Columbia 4-42615)	3.00	12.00	63
BUSTED/Send A Picture Of Mother .... (Columbia 4-42665)	3.00	12.00	63

(Shown as by Johnny Cash With The Carter Family)

RING OF FIRE/I'd Still Be There .... (Columbia 4-42788)	3.75	15.00	63
THE MATADOR/Still In Town .... (Columbia 4-42880)	3.00	12.00	63
IT AIN'T ME BABE/Time And Time Again .... (Columbia 4-43145)	5.00	20.00	64

(Promotional issue only issued with red vinyl)

ROSANNA'S GOING WILD/Roll Call .... (Columbia 4-44373)	2.50	10.00	67
FOLSOM PRISON BLUES/The Folk Singer .... (Columbia 4-44513)	3.00	12.00	68
(GHOST) RIDERS IN THE SKY .... (Columbia 3-10961)	1.25	5.00	79
WINGS IN THE MORNING/What On Earth .... (Cachet CS4-4506)	1.50	6.00	79
HIGHWAYMAN .... (Columbia 38-04881)	1.00	4.00	85

(Shown as by Willie Nelson, Kris Kristofferson, Johnny Cash, and Waylon Jennings)

CASH, ROSEANNE

SEVEN YEAR ACHE .... (Columbia 3-11426)	1.25	5.00	81
I DON'T KNOW WHY YOU DON'T WANT ME/ What You Gonna Do About It .... (Columbia 38-04809)	.75	3.00	85
I DON'T KNOW WHY YOU DON'T WANT ME/ Pink Bedroom/Never Gonna Hurt .... (Columbia CS7 2139)	1.25	5.00	85

(Promotional issue only titled *Limited Edition Sampler Record*, titles listed on back. *Not For Sale Promotional Only* printed on sleeve, issued with a small-hole 33-1/3 RPM record.)

RUNAWAY TRAIN/Seven Year Ache (Live) .... (Columbia 38-07988)	.75	3.00	88
I DON'T WANT TO SPOIL THE PARTY/Look What Our Love Is Coming To .. (Columbia 38-68599)	.75	3.00	89

CASHMAN, TERRY

TALKIN' BASEBALL .... (Lifesong 45096)	1.25	5.00	76
TALKIN' BASEBALL .... (Lifesong 45097)	1.25	5.00	76
TALKIN' BASEBALL .... (Lifesong 45098)	1.25	5.00	76
TALKIN' BASEBALL .... (Lifesong 45099)	1.25	5.00	76
TALKIN' BASEBALL .... (Lifesong 45100)	1.25	5.00	76
TALKIN' BASEBALL .... (Lifesong 45101)	1.25	5.00	76
TALKIN' BASEBALL .... (Lifesong 45102)	1.25	5.00	76
TALKIN' BASEBALL .... (Lifesong 45103)	1.25	5.00	76
TALKIN' BASEBALL .... (Lifesong 45104)	1.25	5.00	76
TALKIN' BASEBALL .... (Lifesong 45105)	1.25	5.00	76
TALKIN' BASEBALL .... (Lifesong 45106)	1.25	5.00	76
TALKIN' BASEBALL .... (Lifesong 45107)	1.25	5.00	76
TALKIN' BASEBALL .... (Lifesong 45108)	1.25	5.00	76
TALKIN' BASEBALL .... (Lifesong 45109)	1.25	5.00	76
TALKIN' BASEBALL .... (Lifesong 45110)	1.25	5.00	76
TALKIN' BASEBALL .... (Lifesong 45111)	1.25	5.00	76
TALKIN' BASEBALL .... (Lifesong 45112)	1.25	5.00	76
TALKIN' BASEBALL .... (Lifesong 45113)	1.25	5.00	76
TALKIN' BASEBALL .... (Lifesong 45114)	1.25	5.00	76
TALKIN' BASEBALL .... (Lifesong 45115)	1.25	5.00	76

(20 different variations; each for a specific major league baseball team. Individual sleeves would command a higher price in their hometowns.)

WILLIE, MICKEY & "THE DUKE" (TALKIN' BASEBALL) .... (Lifesong 45086)	2.50	10.00	82

Also see Cashman & West

CASHMAN & WEST

THE AMERICAN CITY SUITE .... (ABC/Dunhill 4324)	1.25	5.00	72

(Promotional issue only)
Also see Terry Cashman

CASINO ROYALE
(Motion Picture)
See Herb Alpert and the Tijuana Brass (*Casino Royale*), Sergio Mendes and Brasil '66 (*The Look Of Love*)

CASS, MAMA
See Mama Cass Elliot, the Mamas and the Papas

CASSIDY, DAVID
(Son of actor Jack Cassidy and stepson of Shirley Jones)

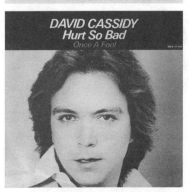

CHERISH/All I Wanna Do Is Touch You .... (Bell 45-150)	1.50	6.00	71
COULD IT BE FOREVER/Blind Hope .... (Bell 45-187)	1.50	6.00	71
HURT SO BAD/Once A Fool .... (MCA 41101)	2.00	8.00	79

Also see the Partridge Family

TITLE	LABEL AND NUMBER	VG	NM	YR

CASSIDY, SHAUN
(Brother of David Cassidy)
DA DOO RON RON	(Warner Bros./Curb 8365)	1.00	4.00	77
THAT'S ROCK 'N' ROLL	(Warner Bros./Curb 8423)	1.00	4.00	77
HEY DEANIE	(Warner Bros./Curb 8488)	1.00	4.00	77
DO YOU BELIEVE IN MAGIC	(Warner Bros./Curb 8533)	1.00	4.00	77
OUR NIGHT	(Warner Bros./Curb 8634)	1.00	4.00	78
MIDNIGHT SUN	(Warner Bros./Curb 8698)	1.00	4.00	78
YOU'RE USIN' ME	(Warner Bros./Curb 8859)	1.00	4.00	79

CASSIDY, TED
(Actor popularly known for playing Lurch in the television series *The Addams Family*)
| THE LURCH/Wesley | (Capitol 5503) | 12.50 | 50.00 | 65 |

CASTLE SISTERS, THE
| GOODBYE DAD/Wishing Star | (Terrace 7506) | 5.00 | 20.00 | 62 |

CASUAL GODS
    See Jerry Harrison

CASWELL, ELAINE
    See Joe Jackson (*Happy Ending*)

CAT BALLOU
(Motion Picture)
    See Nat King Cole

CATCHERS
| SHIFTING/Beauty No. 3 | (Discovery 74505-7) | .75 | 3.00 | 95 |
    (Promotional issue only with gold stamped promo disclaimer on front)

CATES, THE
| MAKE LOVE TO ME | (Ovation 1126) | 1.00 | 4.00 | 79 |

CATES, PHOEBE
(Actress)
| THEME FROM PARADISE/Paradise Part 2 | (Columbia 38-05603) | 1.25 | 5.00 | 82 |
| THEME FROM PARADISE | (Columbia 38-05603) | 1.50 | 6.00 | 82 |
    (Promotional issue, *Demonstration–Not For Sale* printed on sleeve)

CATHOLIC GIRLS, THE
| PRIVATE SCHOOL/Where Did I Go Wrong | (Cinema 008037) | 2.50 | 10.00 | 80 |
    (Shown as by the Double Cross School Girls. The group name was later blackened out on some sleeves and a sticker added stating: Debut single by Catholic Girls [limited edition])
| BOYS CAN CRY | (MCA 52135) | 1.25 | 5.00 | 82 |
| PRIVATE SCHOOL/God Made You For Me | (MCA 52212) | 1.00 | 4.00 | 83 |

CATHY JEAN & THE ROOMMATES
| MAKE ME SMILE AGAIN | (Valmor 016) | 5.00 | 20.00 | 61 |
    Also see the Roommates

CAT PEOPLE
(Motion Picture)
    See David Bowie (*Cat People*)

CAUDELL, LANE
| HANGING ON A STAR | (MCA 40901) | .75 | 3.00 | 78 |

CAVE, NICK
| WHAT A WONDERFUL WORLD/Rainy Night In Soho/Lucy | (Sub Pop 194) | 1.25 | 5.00 | 92 |
    (A-side shown as by Nick Cave and Shane MacGowan. *Rainy Night In Soho* shown as by Nick Cave, *Lucy* shown as by Shane MacGowan.)

CELENTANO, ADRIANO
| SABATO TRISTE | (Reprise 0266) | 1.50 | 6.00 | 64 |

CELL
| WILD/Auf Wiedersehen | (DGC 19143) | 1.00 | 4.00 | 92 |
    (Promotional issue only issued with yellow vinyl)

CELLARFUL OF NOISE
| I'D WALK THE LINE/Something Goin' On With Us | (CBS Associated ZS4-05432) | .75 | 3.00 | 85 |
| I'D WALK THE LINE | (CBS Associated ZS4-05432) | 1.00 | 4.00 | 85 |
    (Promotional issue, *Demonstration–Not For Sale* printed on sleeve)
    Also see the Innocent (Kevin Valentine)

CERTAIN SMILE, A
(Motion Picture)
    See Johnny Mathis (*A Certain Smile*)

CERVENKA, EXENE
| TOMBS/Woman Of The Year/Rage | (Kill Rock Stars 107) | .75 | 3.00 | 94 |
    (Folding sleeve titled *Wordcore Volume 7*. Issued with small-hole 45 RPM white vinyl.)
    Also see X

CETERA, PETER
| GLORY OF LOVE | (Warner Bros. 28662-7) | .75 | 3.00 | 86 |
    (First printing with a blue and black duotone of Cetera and artist name in green. From the motion picture *The Karate Kid Part II*.)
| GLORY OF LOVE | (Warner Bros. 28662-7) | .75 | 3.00 | 86 |
    (Second printing with a color photo of Cetera and artist name in red. From the motion picture *The Karate Kid Part II*.)
| THE NEXT TIME I FALL | (Warner Bros. 28597-7) | .75 | 3.00 | 86 |
    (Shown as by Peter Cetera w/ Amy Grant)
BIG MISTAKE	(Warner Bros. 28507-7)	.75	3.00	86
ONLY LOVE KNOWS WHY	(Warner Bros. 27383-7)	.75	3.00	87
ONE GOOD WOMAN	(Warner Bros. 27824-7)	.75	3.00	88
BEST OF TIMES	(Warner Bros. 27712-7)	.75	3.00	88

HOLDING OUT .... (Warner Bros. 27563-7) .75 3.00 89
    Also see Cher (After All), Chicago, Agnetha Fältskog (I Wasn't The One)

CHAD AND JEREMY
WILLOW WEEP FOR ME/If She Were Mine .... (World Artists 1034) 3.75 15.00 64
IF I LOVED YOU/Donna, Donna .... (World Artists 1041) 3.75 15.00 65
BEFORE AND AFTER/Fare Thee Well .... (Columbia 4-43277) 3.00 12.00 65
I DON'T WANNA LOSE YOU BABY/Pennies .... (Columbia 4-43339) 3.00 12.00 65
I HAVE DREAMED/Should I? .... (Columbia 4-43414) 3.00 12.00 65
TEENAGE FAILURE/Early Morning Rain .... (Columbia 4-43490) 3.00 12.00 66
DISTANT SHORES/Last Night .... (Columbia 4-436827) 3.00 12.00 66
YOU ARE SHE/I Won't Cry .... (Columbia 4-43807) 3.00 12.00 66
PAXTON QUIGLEY'S HAD THE COURSE .... (Columbia 4-44660) 3.00 12.00 67
    (Promotional issue only)
    Also see Chad & Jill Stuart

CHAINSAW KITTENS
MOTHER (OF THE ANCIENT BIRTH)/Death Sex Rattletrap .... (Mammoth # unknown) 1.00 4.00 90

CHAIRMEN OF THE BOARD
PAY TO THE PIPER/Bless You .... (Invictus 9081) 1.25 5.00 70

CHAKIRIS, GEORGE
(Actor)
MARIA/Once Upon A Time .... (Capitol 4844) 2.50 10.00 62

CHAMBERLAIN, RICHARD
(Played the title role in the television series Dr. Kildare and appeared in a number of television mini-series)
THEME FROM DR. KILDARE/A Kiss To Build A Dream On .... (MGM K13075) 2.50 10.00 62
LOVE ME TENDER/All I Do Is Dream Of You .... (MGM K13097) 2.50 10.00 62
ALL I HAVE TO DO IS DREAM/Hi-Lili, Hi-Lo .... (MGM K13121) 2.50 10.00 63
I WILL LOVE YOU/True Love .... (MGM K13148) 2.50 10.00 63
THEY LONG TO BE CLOSE TO YOU/Blue Guitar .... (MGM K13170) 2.50 10.00 63
GEORGIA ON MY MIND/Stella By Starlight .... (MGM K13205) 2.50 10.00 64
ROME WILL NEVER LEAVE YOU/You Always Hurt The One You Love .... (MGM K-13285) 2.50 10.00 64
    (A-side from the three-part television movie Rome Will Never Leave You)
APRIL LOVE/Joy In The Morning .... (MGM K13340) 2.50 10.00 65
    Also see Henry Mancini (The Thorn Birds Theme)

CHAMBERS BROTHERS, THE
TIME HAS COME TODAY .... (Columbia 4-43816) 20.00 80.00 66
    (Possibly a promotional issue only)
I CAN'T TURN YOU LOOSE/Do Your Thing .... (Columbia 4-44679) 2.50 10.00 68

CHAMPAGNE
ROCK AND ROLL STAR .... (Ariola America 7658) 1.25 5.00 77

CHAMPLIN, BILL
    See Patti LaBelle (The Last Unbroken Heart)

CHAMPS, THE
I'VE JUST SEEN HER/What A Country .... (Challenge 9143) 7.50 30.00 62
TEQUILA '76 .... (Republic 246) 1.50 6.00 76
    Also see Seals and Crofts. Glen Campbell was with the group for a short time in 1960.

CHANCELLORS, THE
LITTLE LATIN LUPE LU/Yo Yo .... (Soma 1421) 3.75 15.00 64

CHANCES ARE
(Motion Picture)
    See Cher (After All)

CHANGE OF HABIT
(Motion Picture)
    See Elvis Presley (Don't Cry Daddy)

CHANNEL, BRUCE
SOMEWHERE IN THIS TOWN/Stand Tough .... (Smash 1780) 3.75 15.00 62
NIGHT PEOPLE/No Other Baby .... (Smash 1826) 3.75 15.00 63
SEND HER HOME/Dipsy Doodle .... (Smash 1838) 3.75 15.00 63

CHANTS, THE
CLOSE FRIENDS/Lost And Found .... (Capitol 3949) 5.00 20.00 58

CHAPIN, HARRY
    See the Chapins

CHAPINS, THE
OLD TIME MOVIES .... (Rock-Land 664) 5.00 20.00 66
    (Shown as by The Chapins With Will Jordan And Friends)

CHAPMAN, TRACY
TALKIN' BOUT A REVOLUTION/Behind The Wall .... (Elektra 7-69383) 1.00 4.00 88
BABY CAN I HOLD YOU/If Not Now... .... (Elektra 7-69356) 1.00 4.00 88
CROSSROADS/Born To Fight .... (Elektra 7-69273) .75 3.00 89

CHAPTER 8
GIVE A CHANCE .... (Capitol P-B-44170) .75 3.00 88

CHARADE
(Motion Picture)
    See Henry Mancini (Charade)

CHARIOTS OF FIRE
(Motion Picture)
    See Vangelis

TITLE	LABEL AND NUMBER	VG	NM	YR

CHARLATANS, THE
THE SHADOW KNOWS / 32-20 .... (Kapp 779) — 12.50 — 50.00 — 66
HIGH COIN / When We Go Sailin' By .... (Philips 40610) — 12.50 — 50.00 — 69
    (Promotional issue only)

CHARLENE
FREDDIE .... (Prodigal/Motown 0633F) — 1.00 — 4.00 — 77
USED TO BE / I Want To Come Back As A Song .... (Motown 1650MF) — .75 — 3.00 — 82
    (A-side shown as by Charlene & Stevie Wonder, b-side shown as by Charlene)

CHARLES, JIMMY
THE AGE FOR LOVE .... (Promo 1003) — 6.25 — 25.00 — 61
I SAW MOMMY (MY BABY) KISSING SANTA CLAUS .... (Promo 1004) — 5.00 — 20.00 — 61
CHRISTMASVILLE U.S.A. .... (Promo 1005) — 5.00 — 20.00 — 61

CHARLES, RAY
I USED TO BE SO HAPPY / See See Rider .... (Baronet 7111) — 6.25 — 25.00 — 62
WALKIN' AND TALKIN' / I Can't Stop Loving You .... (Bonus 7019) — 5.00 — 20.00 — 60s
THAT'S A LIE / Go On Home .... (ABC/TRC 11045) — 2.50 — 10.00 — 68
    Also see Billy Joel (Baby Grand), Quincy Jones (I'll Be Good To You), U.S.A. For Africa, Voices Of America

CHARLIE
JOHNNY HOLD BACK .... (Janus 272) — 1.25 — 5.00 — 77
    (Promotional issue only)
KILLER CUT .... (Arista 0449) — 1.50 — 6.00 — 79
IT'S INEVITABLE / Can't Wait 'Til Tomorrow .... (Mirage 7-99862) — 1.00 — 4.00 — 83

CHARLOTTE'S WEB
(Motion Picture)
    See Debbie Reynolds (Mother Earth And Father Time)

CHARMAINES
CHRISTMAS IS FOR KIDS .... (Allied Artists PB-72501) — .75 — 3.00 — 86

CHARM FARM
SICK / Dear Laura Jones .... (PRA 2011-7) — .75 — 3.00 — 96
    (Folding sleeve)

CHARO
OLÉ, OLÉ .... (Salsoul 2075) — 2.00 — 8.00 — 78

CHASE, CHEVY
(Comic Actor)
    See Harold Faltermeyer (Fletch Theme), Paul McCartney (Spies Like Us)

CHEAP TRICK
I WANT YOU TO WANT ME / Clock Strikes Ten .... (Epic 8-50680) — 1.25 — 5.00 — 79
I WANT YOU TO WANT ME / I Want You To Want Me (Mono) ..... (Epic 8-50680) — 2.00 — 8.00 — 79
    (Promotional issue, Demonstration/Not For Sale printed on sleeve)
DREAM POLICE .... (Epic 9-50774) — 1.25 — 5.00 — 79
VOICES .... (Epic 9-50814) — 1.50 — 6.00 — 79
    (Promotional issue only, Demonstration–Not For Sale printed on sleeve only)
REACH OUT / I Must Be Dreamin' .... (Full Moon/Asylum 47187) — 1.25 — 5.00 — 81
    (From the motion picture Heavy Metal)
SHE'S TIGHT / All I Really Want To Do .... (Epic 34-03233) — .75 — 3.00 — 82
SHE'S TIGHT .... (Epic 34-03233) — 1.25 — 5.00 — 82
    (Promotional issue, Demonstration–Not For Sale printed on sleeve)
DANCING THE NIGHT AWAY / Don't Make Our Love A Crime ... (Epic 34-04078) — .75 — 3.00 — 83
DANCING THE NIGHT AWAY .... (Epic 34-04078) — 1.25 — 5.00 — 83
    (Promotional issue, Demonstration–Not For Sale printed on sleeve)
TONIGHT IT'S YOU / Wild Wild Women .... (Epic 34-05431) — .75 — 3.00 — 85
TONIGHT IT'S YOU .... (Epic 34-05431) — 1.25 — 5.00 — 85
    (Promotional issue, Demonstration–Not For Sale printed on sleeve)
MIGHTY WINGS .... (Columbia 38-06137) — .75 — 3.00 — 86
    (From the motion picture Top Gun)
MIGHTY WINGS .... (Columbia 38-06137) — 1.00 — 4.00 — 86
    (Promotional issue, Demonstration Only/Not For Sale printed on sleeve. From the motion picture Top Gun)
THE FLAME / Through The Night .... (Epic 34-07745) — .75 — 3.00 — 88
DON'T BE CRUEL / I Know What I Want (Live) .... (Epic 34 07965) — .75 — 3.00 — 88
GHOST TOWN / Wrong Side Of Love .... (Epic 34-08097) — .75 — 3.00 — 88
BABY TALK / Brontosaurus .... (Sub Pop 393) — .50 — 2.00 — 97
    (Hard cover)

EXTENDED PLAYS
I WANT YOU TO WANT ME .... (CBS AE7-1128 AE7-1129) — 2.00 — 8.00 — 77
    (Promotional issue only titled Music For Every Ear, double single release issued with two small-hole 33-1/3
    RPM records. Also includes one song each by Joan Baez, Crawler, Burton Cummings, Ram Jam, and Dennis
    Wilson.)
I KNOW WHAT I WANT .... (Epic AE71185) — 2.50 — 10.00 — 79
    (Promotional issue only released in conjunction with Washington DC radio station DC 101 to benefit the
    Special Olympics. Includes one song by David Werner and Molly Hatchett. Issued with a small-hole
    33-1/3 RPM yellow vinyl record.)
I WANT YOU TO WANT ME .... (Columbia Special Products PV 16174) — 1.25 — 5.00 — 81
    (Promotional issue only used as an advertising tool for Nestle's $100,000 candy bar, issued with a small-hole
    33-1/3 RPM record. Also includes one song each by Journey, Molly Hatchet, and REO Speedwagon.)
    Also see Robin Zander

CHECKER, CHUBBY
THE TWIST / Twistin' U.S.A. .... (Parkway 811) — 3.75 — 15.00 — 61
LET'S TWIST AGAIN / Everything's Gonna Be Alright .... (Parkway 824) — 3.00 — 12.00 — 61
JINGLE BELL ROCK / Jingle Bell Imitations .... (Cameo 205) — 3.75 — 15.00 — 61
    (Shown as by Bobby Rydell and Chubby Checker)
SWINGIN' TOGETHER / Teach Me To Twist .... (Cameo 214) — 3.75 — 15.00 — 62
    (Shown as by Bobby Rydell and Chubby Checker)
THE FLY / That's The Way It Goes .... (Parkway 830) — 3.00 — 12.00 — 62
THAT'S THE WAY IT GOES / Spencer & Tracy .... (Parkway 830) — 3.00 — 12.00 — 62

		VG	NM	YR
SLOW TWISTIN'/La Paloma Twist .... (Parkway 835)		3.00	12.00	62
(A-side shown as by Chubby Checker With Dee Dee Sharp)				
DANCIN' PARTY/Gotta Get Myself Together .... (Parkway 842)		3.00	12.00	62
LIMBO ROCK/Popeye (The Hitch-Hiker) .... (Parkway 849)		3.00	12.00	62
TWENTY MILES/Let's Limbo Some More .... (Parkway 862)		3.00	12.00	63
BIRDLAND/Black Cloud .... (Parkway 873)		3.00	12.00	63
TWIST IT UP/Surf Party .... (Parkway 879)		3.00	12.00	63
LODDY LO/Everything's Gonna Be Alright .... (Parkway 890)		3.00	12.00	63
LODDY LO/Hooka Tooka .... (Parkway 890)		3.00	12.00	63
HEY BOBBA NEEDLE/Spread Joy .... (Parkway 907)		3.00	12.00	64
LAZY ELSIE MOLLY/Rosie .... (Parkway 920)		3.00	12.00	64
SHE WANTS T' SWIM/You Better Believe It, Baby .... (Parkway 922)		3.00	12.00	64
LOVELY LOVELY/The Weekend's Here .... (Parkway 936)		3.00	12.00	65

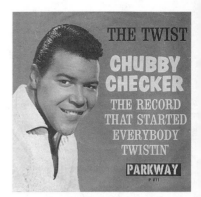

EXTENDED PLAYS

		VG	NM	YR
THE RAY CHARLES-TON/THE MESS AROUND/ The Jet/The Continental Walk .... (Parkway PC 5001)		2.00	8.00	61
(Half sleeve for Compact 33 Double)				
Also see Fat Boys (The Twist)				

CHEECH & CHONG

		VG	NM	YR
SANTA CLAUS AND HIS OLD LADY .... (Ode 66021)		2.00	8.00	73
BASKETBALL JONES .... (Ode 66038)		2.00	8.00	73
SISTER MARY ELEPHANT .... (Ode 66041)		2.00	8.00	73
EARACHE MY EYE .... (Ode 66102)		2.00	8.00	74
BLACK LASSIE .... (Ode 66104)		2.00	8.00	74
BLOAT ON/Just Say Right On (The Bloaters Creed) .... (Ode 8-50471)		1.50	6.00	77
UP IN SMOKE/Rock Fight .... (Warner Bros. 8666)		1.50	6.00	78
BORN IN EAST L.A. .... (MCA 52655)		1.00	4.00	85
I'M NOT HOME RIGHT NOW! .... (MCA 52732)		1.00	4.00	85
Also see Mike + the Mechanics (Revolution)				

CHEEK

EXTENDED PLAYS

		VG	NM	YR
DO YOU HAVE A SOUL/TAKE ME FOR WHAT I'M WORTH/ So Much In Love/Still In Love .... (Voxx vep-3302)		1.25	5.00	
(Back of sleeve pictures band with producers Vanda & Young in the studio. Issued with a small-hole 33-1/3 RPM record.)				

CHEERS

(Television Series)

See Gary Portnoy (Theme From Cheers)

CHELSEA

		VG	NM	YR
DECIDE/I'm On Fire .... (I.R.S. 9004)		1.50	6.00	79

CHER

		VG	NM	YR
DREAM BABY .... (Imperial 66223)		6.25	25.00	66
(The existence of this sleeve is in question)				
RUDY .... (Columbia 18-02850)		1.50	6.00	82
(Promotional issue only, Demonstration–Not For Sale printed on sleeve)				
I FOUND SOMEONE .... (Geffen 28191-7)		.75	3.00	87
WE ALL SLEEP ALONE .... (Geffen 27986-7)		.75	3.00	88
SKIN DEEP .... (Geffen 27894-7)		.75	3.00	88
MAIN MAN .... (Geffen 27742-7)		.75	3.00	88
AFTER ALL .... (Geffen 27529-7)		.75	3.00	89
(Shown as by Cher & Peter Cetera. From the motion picture Chances Are.)				
IF I COULD TURN BACK TIME/Some Guys .... (Geffen 22886-7)		.75	3.00	89
Also see Sonny and Cher				

CHEROKEES, THE

		VG	NM	YR
CHEROKEE/Harlem Nocturne .... (Guyden 2044)		5.00	20.00	60

CHERRELLE

		VG	NM	YR
SATURDAY LOVE .... (Tabu ZS4-05767)		.75	3.00	86
(Shown as by Cherrelle with Alexander O'Neal)				
EVERYTHING I MISS AT HOME .... (Tabu ZS4-08052)		.75	3.00	88
Also see Alexander O'Neal (Never Knew Love Like This)				

CHERRY, AVA

		VG	NM	YR
GOOD INTENTIONS .... (Capitol 7PRO 79093)		.75	3.00	87
(Promotional issue only)				

CHERRY, NENEH

		VG	NM	YR
BUFFALO STANCE/Buffalo Stance (Electro Ski Mix) .... (Virgin 7-99231)		.75	3.00	89
KISSES ON THE WIND/Buffalo Blues .... (Virgin 7-99183)		.75	3.00	89
MANCHILD/Phoney Ladies .... (Virgin 7-99154)		.75	3.00	89

CHERRY BOMB

See Dolby's Cube Featuring Cherry Bomb

CHERRY PEOPLE, THE

		VG	NM	YR
AND SUDDENLY .... (Heritage 801)		2.50	10.00	68
GOTTA GET BACK TO THE GOOD LIFE .... (Heritage 807)		2.50	10.00	68
FEELINGS .... (Heritage 810)		2.50	10.00	68

CHESS

(Stage Musical)

See Murray Head (One Night In Bangkok), Elaine Paige (Heaven Help My Heart)

CHESSMAN SQUARE

		VG	NM	YR
CIRCLES/Try .... (Lion 1002)		30.00	120.00	60s

CHEVALIER, MAURICE

		VG	NM	YR
JUST IN TIME/If You Knew Suzie .... (MGM K-12920)		5.00	20.00	60
(From the motion picture Bells Are Ringing)				

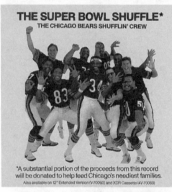

TITLE	LABEL AND NUMBER	VG	NM	YR
ENJOY IT/Let's Climb	(Buena Vista 409)	5.00	20.00	62

(Shown as by Hayley Mills and Maurice Chevalier)

CHEVELLE FIVE, THE

DANGLING LITTLE FRIENDS/Stone And Steel Man	(Titan 1737)	10.00	40.00	67

CHEVELLES, THE

BLUE CHEVELLE/Mala Boo	(Bangar 603)	20.00	80.00	63

CHIC

LE FREAK/Savoir Faire	(Atlantic 3519)	1.25	5.00	78
I WANT YOUR LOVE/(Funny) Bone	(Atlantic 3557)	1.25	5.00	78
GOOD TIMES/A Warm Summer Night	(Atlantic 3584)	1.00	4.00	79

EXTENDED PLAYS

DANCE, DANCE, DANCE (YOWSAH, YOWSAH, YOWSAH)/ EVERYBODY DANCE	(Atlantic OP-7502)	1.25	5.00	78

(Promotional issue only titled *Profiles In Gold Album 2*, issued with a small-hole 33-1/3 RPM record. Sold only at Burger King for 59¢ with the purchase of a Coke. Also includes two songs each by Roberta Flack, Genesis, and Leif Garrett.)

Also see Chic, the Honeydrippers (Nile Rodgers), Power Station (Tony Thompson), Nile Rodgers, Carly Simon (b-side of *Why*)

CHICAGO

QUESTIONS 67 AND 68/Listen	(Columbia 4-44909)	2.00	8.00	69
MAKE ME SMILE/Colour My World	(Columbia 4S-45127)	1.25	5.00	70
DOES ANYBODY REALLY KNOW WHAT TIME IT IS/Listen	(Columbia 4-45264)	1.25	5.00	70
FREE/Free Country	(Columbia 4-45331)	2.00	8.00	71
LOWDOWN/Loneliness Is Just A Word	(Columbia 4-45370)	1.25	5.00	71
BEGINNINGS/Colour My World	(Columbia 4-45417)	1.25	5.00	71
DIALOGUE/Now That You're Gone	(Columbia 4-45683)	1.50	6.00	72
HARRY TRUMAN/Til We Meet Again	(Columbia 3-10092)	1.25	5.00	75
BABY WHAT A BIG SURPRISE/Takin' It On Uptown	(Columbia 3-10620)	1.00	4.00	77
BABY WHAT A BIG SURPRISE/Takin' It On Uptown	(Columbia 3-10620)	2.00	8.00	77

(Promotional issue, sleeve lists b-side although the 45 has *Baby What A Big Surprise* on both sides)

STAY THE NIGHT/Only You	(Warner Bros. 29306-7)	.75	3.00	84
HARD HABIT TO BREAK	(Warner Bros. 29214-7)	.75	3.00	84
25 OR 6 TO 4	(Warner Bros. 28628-7)	.75	3.00	86
IF SHE WOULD HAVE BEEN FAITHFUL...	(Warner Bros. 28424-7)	.75	3.00	87
NIAGARA FALLS	(Warner Bros. 28283-7)	.75	3.00	87
I DON'T WANNA LIVE WITHOUT YOUR LOVE	(Reprise 27855-7)	.75	3.00	88
LOOK AWAY	(Reprise 27766-7)	.75	3.00	88
YOU'RE NOT ALONE	(Reprise 27757-7)	.75	3.00	88
WHAT KIND OF MAN WOULD I BE?/25 Or 6 To 4	(Reprise 22741-7)	.75	3.00	89

EXTENDED PLAYS

DOES ANYBODY REALLY KNOW WHAT TIME IT IS?	(Columbia Special Products CSS 1491)	1.50	6.00	70

(Promotional issue only titled *The Great American Sound*, issued with a small-hole 33-1/3 RPM record and a 6" x 6" insert for a mail-order Hershey Poster Offer. Also includes one song each by Blood Sweat and Tears, Aretha Franklin, and Santana.)

Also see Peter Cetera, James William Guercio, the Sons of Champlin (Bill Champlin)

CHICAGO BEARS SHUFFLIN' CREW, THE

(Members of the Chicago Bears football team)

THE SUPER BOWL SHUFFLE	(Red Label B71012)	1.50	6.00	85

CHICAGO WHITE SOX

(Baseball Team)

See Steam (*Na Na Hey Hey Kiss Him Goodbye*)

CHILDE, HAROLD

BRINK OF DEATH	(Limelight 3084)	3.75	15.00	60s

CHILDS, TONI

DON'T WALK AWAY	(A&M 1237)	.75	3.00	88
WALK AND TALK LIKE ANGELS/Tin Drum	(A&M 1253)	.75	3.00	88

CHILL FACTOR

CONVERSATION	(Warner Bros. 28364-7)	.75	3.00	87
NEVER MY LOVE	(Warner Bros. 28159-7)	.75	3.00	87

CHINA CRISIS

ARIZONA SKY/Trading In Gold	(A&M 2902)	.75	3.00	86

CHINNOCK, BILLY

SOMEWHERE IN THE NIGHT/	(CBS Associated ZS4-06330)	.75	3.00	86
SOMEWHERE IN THE NIGHT	(CBS Associated ZS4-06330)	1.00	4.00	86

(Promotional issue, *Demonstration–Not For Sale* printed on sleeve)

CHIPMUNKS, THE

RAGTIME COWBOY JOE/Flip Side	(Liberty 55200)	3.00	12.00	59

(Shown as by David Seville and the Chipmunks)

ALVIN'S ORCHESTRA	(Liberty 55233)	3.00	12.00	60

(Shown as by David Seville and the Chipmunks)

COMIN' 'ROUND THE MOUNTAIN/Sing A Goofy Song	(Liberty 55246)	3.75	15.00	60
THE CHIPMUNK SONG (CHRISTMAS DON'T BE LATE!)/Alvin's Harmonica	(Liberty 55250)	3.00	12.00	59

(This was the first year this popular reissue was released. The record has a green label, all other reissues are on a multi-colored label.)

ALVIN FOR PRESIDENT/Sack Time	(Liberty 55277)	3.75	15.00	60

(Shown as by David Seville and the Chipmunks)

RUDOLPH THE RED-NOSED REINDEER/Spain	(Liberty 55289)	3.00	12.00	60

(Shown as by Alvin, Simon & Theodore With David Seville)

ALVIN'S ALL-STAR CHIPMUNK BAND/Old MacDonald Cha Cha	(Liberty 55544)	3.75	15.00	63
THE NIGHT BEFORE CHRISTMAS/Wonderful Day	(Liberty 55635)	3.00	12.00	63
TALK TO THE ANIMALS/My Friend The Doctor	(Sunset 61002)	2.50	10.00	68
CHITTY CHITTY BANG BANG/Hushabye Mountain	(Sunset 61003)	2.50	10.00	68
CALL ME/Refugee	(Excelsior SIS-1003)	1.25	5.00	80

(Hard cover)

ON THE ROAD AGAIN	(RCA JH-12247)	1.00	4.00	81
SLEIGH RIDE / The Chipmunk Song	(RCA 12354)	1.00	4.00	81
BETTE DAVIS EYES	(RCA 13098)	1.00	4.00	82

Also see David Seville

CHiPs
(Television Series)

See Corniche *(Theme From CHiPs)*

CHIPS, THE
(More than one group recorded under this name)

| MIXED UP SHOOK UP GIRL / Break It Gently | (Philips 40520) | 2.50 | 10.00 | 68 |

CHOCOLATE WATCHBAND
EXTENDED PLAYS

| SITTING THERE STANDING / TILL THE END OF THE DAY / Sweet Young Thing / Are You Gonna Be There (At The Love-In) | (Sundazed 109) | .50 | 2.00 | 95 |

(Hard cover issued with pink vinyl)

CHORDETTES, THE

| ZORRO | (Cadence 1349) | 5.00 | 20.00 | 58 |
| NO WHEELS | (Cadence 1366) | 6.25 | 25.00 | 59 |

(Promotional issue, shown as by the Chordettes with Jeff Kron and Jackie Ertel)

| NO WHEELS / A Girl's Work Is Never Done | (Cadence 1366) | 3.75 | 15.00 | 59 |

(Shown as by the Chordettes with Jeff Kron and Jackie Ertel)

| LOLLIPOP / Never On Sunday | (Atlantic 7-89310) | .75 | 3.00 | 86 |

Also see Arthur Godfrey *('Twas The Night Before Christmas)*

CHRIS & KATHY
(Chris Montez and Kathy Young)

| SHOOT THAT CURL / It Takes Two | (Monogram 520) | 20.00 | 80.00 | 63 |

CHRISTEN, NADIA

| TAKE IT EASY / Take Me Back | (Liberty 56058) | 2.00 | 8.00 | 68 |

CHRISTIAN, CHRIS

| I WANT YOU, I NEED YOU | (Boardwalk 126) | 1.00 | 4.00 | 81 |

CHRISTIE, LOU

BIG TIME / Cryin' On My Knees	(Colpix 799)	5.00	20.00	66
RHAPSODY IN THE RAIN / Trapeze	(MGM K-13473)	3.75	15.00	66
PAINTER / Du Ronda	(MGM K-13533)	3.75	15.00	66
IF MY CAR COULD ONLY TALK / Song Of Lita	(MGM K-13576)	7.50	30.00	66
SING ME, SING ME / The Paper Song	(Buddah 285)	2.50	10.00	72

(Promotional issue only)

CHRISTIE, SUSAN
(Sister of Lou Christie)

| I LOVE ONIONS | (Columbia 4-43595) | 5.00 | 20.00 | 66 |

CHRISTOPHER, GAVIN

| ONE STEP CLOSER TO YOU | (Manhattan 50028) | .75 | 3.00 | 86 |
| YOU ARE WHO YOU LOVE (SHORT VERSION) / You Are Who You Love (Lovers Version 1) | (EMI Manhattan B-50108) | .75 | 3.00 | 88 |

CHRISTOPHER, JORDAN

| GOODBYE MY LOVE | (Jubilee 5440) | 2.00 | 8.00 | 63 |

CHRISTOPHER, LYN

| I DON'T WANT TO HEAR IT ANYMORE / She Used To Wanna Be A Ballerina | (Paramount 0221) | 1.50 | 6.00 | 73 |

CHRISTY, CHARLES

| YOUNG AND BEAUTIFUL / In The Arms Of A Girl | (HBR 473) | 6.25 | 25.00 | 66 |

CHUNKY A
(Arsenio Hall)

| OWWWW! / Owwww (Plumpapella) | (MCA 53736) | .75 | 3.00 | 89 |

CHURCH, THE

COLUMBUS / As You Will	(Arista 28700-7)	1.00	4.00	86
REPTILE / Under The Milky Way, Tantalized	(Arista 9733)	.75	3.00	88
UNDER THE MILKY WAY / Musk	(Arista 9673)	.75	3.00	88

(Issued with small-hole 45 RPM record)

CHURCHILL, WINSTON
(British statesman and author)

| MEMOIRES AND SPEECHES EXCERPTS | (London PE 1) | 2.00 | 8.00 | |

(Promotional issue only issued with one-sided, small-hole 33-1/3 RPM record)

CICCONE YOUTH

| BURNIN' UP / Tuff Titty Rap / Into The Groovey | (New Alliance 030) | 2.50 | 10.00 | 86 |

Also see the Backbeat Band (Thurston Moore), Thurston Moore, Sonic Youth

CINDERELLA

NOBODY'S FOOL / Push Push	(Mercury 884 851-7)	.75	3.00	86
SOMEBODY SAVE ME / Hell On Wheels	(Mercury 888 483-7)	.75	3.00	87
DON'T KNOW WHAT YOU GOT (TILL IT'S GONE) / Fire And Ice	(Mercury 870 644-7)	.75	3.00	88
THE LAST MILE / Long Cold Winter	(Mercury 872 148-7)	.75	3.00	88
COMING HOME / Take Me Back	(Mercury 872 982-7)	.75	3.00	89

CIRCLE JERKS

| JERKS ON 45 | (Avenue PR 7103) | 2.00 | 8.00 | 94 |

(Promotional issue only)

| TEENAGE ELECTRIC / Fable | (Mercury 1182) | 1.50 | 6.00 | 95 |

(Promotional issue only)

TITLE	LABEL AND NUMBER	VG	NM	YR

CIRCUS OF HORRORS
(Motion Picture)
    See Gary Miles (*Look For A Star*)

CIRCUS OF POWER

HEAVEN & HELL/Evil Woman .... (Columbia CS7-4873)		1.00	4.00	92
(Promotional issue only)				

CITIZENS BAND

DAILY NEWS .... (Claridge 407)		.75	3.00	75

CITY, THE

WALKAWAY/Fatal Attraction .... (Chrysalis VS4 43064)		.75	3.00	86
PLANETS IN MOTION/ .... (Chrysalis VS4 43098)		.75	3.00	87

CITY BOY

5.7.0.5./Bad For Business .... (Mercury 73999)		1.50	6.00	78

CLAMBAKE
(Motion Picture)
    See Elvis Presley (*Big Boss Man, Guitar Man*)

CLANTON, JIMMY

MY OWN TRUE LOVE/Little Boy In Love .... (Ace 567)		3.75	15.00	59
GO, JIMMY, GO/I Trusted You .... (Ace 575)		3.75	15.00	59
ANOTHER SLEEPLESS NIGHT/I'm Gonna Try .... (Ace 585)		3.75	15.00	60
THE SLAVE .... (Ace 51860)		7.50	30.00	60
(Promotional issue only included with the album *Jimmy's Happy–Jimmy's Blue*)				
COME BACK/Wait .... (Ace 600)		5.00	20.00	60
WHAT AM I GONNA DO?/If I .... (Ace 607)		5.00	20.00	61
DOWN THE AISLE/No Longer Blue .... (Ace 616)		5.00	20.00	61
(Shown as by Jimmy Clanton & Mary Ann Mobley; both pictured. Purchaser had the option to mail their sleeve to Ace Records in Jackson, Mississippi to have it autographed by the artists. It is unknown if these autographs are authentic or the work of office staffers.)				
I JUST WANNA MAKE LOVE/Don't Look At Me .... (Ace 622)		5.00	20.00	61
LUCKY IN LOVE WITH YOU/Not Like A Brother .... (Ace 634)		5.00	20.00	61
TWIST ON, LITTLE GIRL/Wayward Love .... (Ace 641)		5.00	20.00	62
BECAUSE I DO/Just A Moment .... (Ace 655)		5.00	20.00	62
ENDLESS NIGHT/Another Day, Another Heartache .... (Ace 8006)		3.75	15.00	63
I'LL STEP ASIDE/I Won't Cry Anymore .... (Philips 40181)		3.00	12.00	64

CLAPTON, ERIC

ANOTHER TICKET/Rita Mae .... (RSO 1064)		1.25	5.00	81
FOREVER MAN .... (Warner Bros./Duck 29081-7)		1.00	4.00	85
IT'S IN THE WAY THAT YOU USE IT .... (Warner Bros./Duck 28514-7)		.75	3.00	86
(From the motion picture *The Color Of Money*)				
TEARING US APART/Hold On .... (Warner Bros./Duck 28279-7)		.75	3.00	87
(Shown as by Eric Clapton with Tina Turner)				
AFTER MIDNIGHT/I Can't Stand It .... (Polydor 887 403-7)		.75	3.00	88
PRETENDING/Before You Accuse Me .... (Reprise/Duck 22732-7)		.75	3.00	89
Also see the Bunburys, Randy Crawford, the Yardbirds				

CLARK, DAVE, FIVE, THE

I KNEW IT ALL THE TIME/That's What I Said .... (Congress 212)		7.50	30.00	64
GLAD ALL OVER .... (Epic 5-9656)		3.75	15.00	64
CAN'T YOU SEE THAT SHE'S MINE? .... (Epic 5-9692)		3.75	15.00	64
BECAUSE (Epic 5-9704)		3.75	15.00	64
EVERYBODY KNOWS (I STILL LOVE YOU) .... (Epic 5-9722)		3.75	15.00	64
COME HOME/Your Turn To Cry .... (Epic 5-9763)		3.75	15.00	65
I LIKE IT LIKE THAT/Hurtin' Inside .... (Epic 5-9811)		3.75	15.00	65
CATCH US IF YOU CAN .... (Epic 5-9833)		3.75	15.00	65
(From the motion picture *Having A Wild Weekend*)				
OVER AND OVER .... (Epic 5-9863)		3.75	15.00	65
AT THE SCENE .... (Epic 5-9882)		3.00	12.00	66
TRY TOO HARD .... (Epic 5-10004)		3.75	15.00	66
PLEASE TELL ME WHY/Look Before You Leap .... (Epic 5-10031)		3.00	12.00	66
SATISFIED WITH YOU .... (Epic 5-10053)		3.75	15.00	66
NINETEEN DAYS .... (Epic 5-10076)		3.75	15.00	66
I'VE GOT TO HAVE A REASON .... (Epic 5-10114)		3.75	15.00	67
YOU GOT WHAT IT TAKES .... (Epic 5-10144)		3.75	15.00	67
YOU MUST HAVE BEEN A BEAUTIFUL BABY .... (Epic 5-10179)		5.00	20.00	67
A LITTLE BIT NOW .... (Epic 5-10209)		3.00	12.00	67
RED AND BLUE .... (Epic 5-10244)		5.00	20.00	67
EVERYBODY KNOWS .... (Epic 5-10265)		6.25	25.00	67
THE RED BALLOON .... (Epic 5-10375)		5.00	20.00	68
PARADISE .... (Epic 5-10474)		6.25	25.00	69
BRING IT ON HOME TO ME .... (Epic 5-10547)		3.75	15.00	70
GOOD OLD ROCK & ROLL .... (Epic 5-10684)		6.25	25.00	70
OVER AND OVER/You Got What It Takes .... (Hollywood 65909-7)		1.25	5.00	93
I LIKE IT LIKE THAT/Reelin' And Rockin' .... (Hollywood 65910-7)		1.25	5.00	93
GLAD ALL OVER/Bits And Pieces .... (Hollywood 65911-7)		1.25	5.00	93
DO YOU LOVE ME/Can't You See That She's Mine .... (Hollywood 65912-7)		1.25	5.00	93
CATCH US IF YOU CAN/Try Too Hard .... (Hollywood 65913-7)		1.25	5.00	93
BECAUSE/Everybody Knows (I Still Love You) .... (Hollywood 65914-7)		1.25	5.00	93
ANY WAY YOU WANT IT/Come Home .... (Hollywood 65915-7)		1.25	5.00	93

CLARK, DEE

HEY, LITTLE GIRL/If It Wasn't For Love .... (Abner 1029)		7.50	30.00	59

CLARK, GENE

ECHOES/I Found You .... (Columbia 4-43903)		50.00	200.00	66
Also see the Byrds, the New Christy Minstrels, the Textones				

CLARK, ROBIN
TOO MANY FISH IN THE SEA .... (HME WS4-04705) | 1.00 | 4.00 | 84
   (Features a quote from David Bowie touting Clark's talent)
   Also see Simple Minds (*All The Things She Said*)

CLARK, ROY
TOBACCO ROAD/Black Sapphire .... (Silver Dollar 70001) | 1.00 | 4.00 | 86

CLARKE, GARY
THEME FROM THE VIRGINIAN (LONESOME TREE)/One Summer In A Million .... (Decca 31511) | 5.00 | 20.00 | 63

CLARKE, STANLEY
WHAT IF I SHOULD FALL IN LOVE/Stereotypica .... (Epic 34-05584) | .75 | 3.00 | 85

CLASH, THE
SHOULD I STAY OR SHOULD I GO?/First Night Back In London .... (Epic 14-03061) | 3.00 | 12.00 | 82
   ("Special Limited Edition" first version picturing Ronald Reagan)
SHOULD I STAY OR SHOULD I GO?/Cool Confusion .... (Epic 34-03547) | 1.25 | 5.00 | 83
   (Second version picturing group members)
SHOULD I STAY OR SHOULD I GO? .... (Epic 34-03547) | 2.00 | 8.00 | 83
   (Promotional issue, *Demonstration–Not For Sale* printed on sleeve, group pictured)
   Also see Big Audio Dynamite (Mick Jones), Dave Wakeling (Topper Headon on b-side of *She's Having A Baby*)

CLASSMATES, THE
SOME OF THESE DAYS .... (Radar 3962) | 7.50 | 30.00 | 62

CLAUDINE
(Motion Picture)
   See Gladys Knight & the Pips (*On And On*)

CLAY, CASSIUS
(Muhammad Ali)
I AM THE GREATEST/Stand By Me .... (Columbia 4-43007) | 10.00 | 40.00 | 64
   (Sleeve shown as by the given name of former World Heavyweight Champion boxer Muhammad Ali)
I AM THE GREATEST .... (Columbia JZSP 75716) | 12.50 | 50.00 | 64
   (Promotional issue)

CLAYBURGH, JILL
(Actress)
   See Diana Ross (*It's My Turn*)

CLAYDERMAN, RICHARD
THE WAY I LOVED YOU .... (Columbia 38-04631) | .75 | 3.00 | 84
THE WAY I LOVED YOU .... (Columbia 38-04631) | 1.00 | 4.00 | 84
   (Promotional issue, *Demonstration–Not For Sale* printed on sleeve)

CLAYMATION CHRISTMAS CELEBRATION
(Television Special)
   See the California Raisins

CLEGG, JOHNNY, & SAVUKA
SCATTERLINGS OF AFRICA .... (Capitol P-B-44324) | .75 | 3.00 | 89

CLEMENTINO, CLAIRETTE
SEE ME/Everywhere .... (Capitol 5003) | 2.50 | 10.00 | 63

CLEMENTS, VASSAR
   See Nitty Gritty Dirt Band (*Honky Tonkin'*)

CLEMONS, CLARENCE
YOU'RE A FRIEND OF MINE/Let The Music Say It .... (Columbia 38-05660) | .75 | 3.00 | 85
   (A-side shown as by Clarence Clemons and Jackson Browne)
YOU'RE A FRIEND OF MINE .... (Columbia 38-05660) | 1.00 | 4.00 | 85
   (Promotional issue, *Demonstration–Not For Sale* printed on sleeve. Shown as by Clarence Clemons and Jackson Browne.)
   Also see Jersey Artists For Mankind, Ronnie Spector (*Say Goodbye To Hollywood*), Bruce Springsteen (Clemons was a member of the E Street Band)

CLEOPATRA JONES
(Motion Picture)
   See Joe Simon (*Theme From Cleopatra Jones*)

CLEVELAND BROWNS
(Football Team)
   See the Michael Stanley Band (*Hard Die The Heroes*)

CLEVELAND INDIANS
(Baseball Team)
INDIAN FEVER .... (Cleveland Indians 004010X) | 2.50 | 10.00 | 80
   (Folding sleeve titled *Catch Indian Fever*. Advertising jingle used for commercials and televised baseball games, no players pictured on sleeve or featured on recording.)

CLIFF, JIMMY
WONDERFUL WORLD, BEAUTIFUL PEOPLE/Waterfall .... (A&M 1146) | 2.00 | 8.00 | 69
SEVEN-DAY WEEKEND .... (Columbia 38-06135) | 1.00 | 4.00 | 86
   (Shown as by Jimmy Cliff & Elvis Costello and the Attractions. From the motion picture *Club Paradise*)
   Also see Artists United Against Apartheid

CLIFFORD, BUZZ
HELLO, MR. MOONLIGHT/Blue Lagoon .... (Columbia 4-41774) | 7.50 | 30.00 | 60
BABY SITTIN' BOOGIE/Driftwood .... (Columbia 4-41876) | 7.50 | 30.00 | 60
SIMPLY BECAUSE/Three Little Fishes .... (Columbia 4-41979) | 7.50 | 30.00 | 61
I'LL NEVER FORGET/The Awakening .... (Columbia 4-42019) | 12.50 | 50.00 | 61
MOVING DAY/Loneliness .... (Columbia 4-42177) | 7.50 | 30.00 | 61
FOREVER/Magic Circle .... (Columbia 4-42290) | 7.50 | 30.00 | 62

CLIFFORD, DOUG
LATIN MUSIC/Take A Train .... (Fantasy 686) | 2.00 | 8.00 | 73
   Also see Creedence Clearwater Revival

TITLE	LABEL AND NUMBER	VG	NM	YR

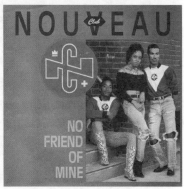

CLIFFORD, MIKE

POOR LITTLE SINGER/Stranger	(Columbia 4-41862)	3.75	15.00	61
BOMBAY/When We Marry	(Columbia 4-42226)	3.75	15.00	61

CLIFT, MONTGOMERY
(Actor)
See Joni James (Never Till Now), Ray Bloch & Orchestra (From Here To Eternity)

CLIMIE FISHER

LOVE CHANGES (EVERYTHING)	(Capitol B-44137)	.75	3.00	88
RISE TO THE OCCASION	(Capitol B-44197)	.75	3.00	88

CLINE, PATSY

GENERIC PATSY CLINE SLEEVE	(Everest no #)	1.50	6.00	56

(Half sleeve used for miscellaneous Patsy Cline singles on Everest from 1956-1958. No titles listed, sleeve reads Patsy Cline's On Everest.)

WALKIN' AFTER MIDNIGHT/A Poor Man's Roses (Or A Rich Man's Gold)	(Decca 30221)	6.25	25.00	57
WHEN I GET THROUGH WITH YOU/Imagine That	(Decca 31377)	5.00	20.00	62
LEAVIN' ON YOUR MIND/Tra Le La Le La Triangle	(Decca 31455)	5.00	20.00	63

CLINTON, GEORGE

ATOMIC DOG	(Capitol B-5201)	1.25	5.00	82
GET DRESSED	(Capitol B-5222)	1.25	5.00	82
NUBIAN NUT	(Capitol B-5296)	1.25	5.00	83
QUICKIE	(Capitol B-5324)	1.50	6.00	84
DOUBLE OH-OH	(Capitol B-5473)	1.25	5.00	85
R&B SKELETONS IN THE CLOSET	(Capitol B-5642)	1.25	5.00	86

Also see Artists United Against Apartheid, Funkadelic, Mudhoney (b-side of Pump It Up), Parliament, Well Red (Get Lucky)

CLOONEY, ROSEMARY

MANY A WONDERFUL MOMENT	(RCA Victor 47-7754)	2.00	8.00	60

Also see Jose Ferrer (Woman)

CLOSE ENCOUNTERS OF THE THIRD KIND
(Motion Picture)
See John Williams (Theme From Close Encounters Of The Third Kind)

CLOUSEAU, INSPECTOR
See Inspector Clouseau

CLUB NOUVEAU

IT'S A COLD COLD WORLD	(Warner Bros. 28101-7)	.75	3.00	88
NO FRIEND OF MINE	(Warner Bros. 22769-7)	.75	3.00	89

CLUB PARADISE
(Motion Picture)
See Jimmy Cliff (Seven-Day Weekend), Elvis Costello (Seven-Day Weekend)

COAL MINER'S DAUGHTER
(Motion Picture)
See Sissy Spacek (Coal Miner's Daughter)

COASTERS, THE
See Ben E. King (b-side of Stand By Me)

COBHAM, BILLY

STRATUS (PART 1)	(Atlantic 2998)	1.50	600	76

COBRA
(Motion Picture)
See John Cafferty and the Beaver Brown Band (Voice Of America's Sons)

COCCIANTE, RICHARD

MICHELLE/Lucia	(RCA PB-10867)	1.00	4.00	76

(Shown as by Richard Cocciante with the London Symphony Orchestra. From the motion picture All This And World War II)

COCHRAN, EDDIE

MEAN WHEN I'M MAD/One Kiss	(Liberty F-55070)	250.00	1000.00	57
ROUGH STUFF/Our Love	(Capehart 5003)	37.50	150.00	60

COCHRAN, STEVE
(Actor)
See Louis Armstrong (The Beat Generation)

COCHRAN, WAYNE

HARLEM SHUFFLE/Somebody Please	(Mercury 72507)	5.00	20.00	65
WHEN MY BABY CRIES/Some A Your Sweet Lovin'	(Chess 2020)	3.75	15.00	67

COCHRANE, TOM

BOY INSIDE THE MAN/Lasting Song	(Capitol B-5591)	.75	3.00	86

(Shown as by Tom Cochrane and Red Rider)

BIG LEAGUE/Vacation (In My Mind)	(RCA 8750-7-R)	.75	3.00	88

(Shown as by Tom Cochrane and Red Rider)
Also see Red Rider

COCKER, JOE

SHE CAME IN THROUGH THE BATHROOM WINDOW/Change In Louise	(A&M 1147)	1.50	6.00	69
THE LETTER/Space Captain	(A&M 1174)	1.50	6.00	70
CRY ME A RIVER/Give Peace A Chance	(A&M 1200)	1.50	6.00	70
BLACK EYED BLUES/High Time We Went	(A&M 1258)	2.00	8.00	71
MIDNIGHT RIDER/Woman To Woman	(A&M 1370)	1.50	6.00	72
PARDON ME SIR/St. James Infirmary Blues	(A&M 1407)	1.50	6.00	72
PUT OUT THE LIGHT/If I Love You	(A&M 1539)	1.25	5.00	74
FUN TIME/Watching The River Flow	(Asylum 45540)	1.25	5.00	78
UP WHERE WE BELONG	(Island 7-99996)	1.00	4.00	82

(Shown as by Joe Cocker and Jennifer Warnes. From the motion picture An Officer and a Gentleman, Richard Gere and Debra Winger pictured front and back.)

		VG	NM	YR
CIVILIZED MAN	(Capitol B-5338)	.75	3.00	84
EDGE OF A DREAM	(Capitol B-5412)	.75	3.00	84
(From the motion picture *Teachers*)				
YOU CAN LEAVE YOUR HAT ON	(Capitol B-5589)	.75	3.00	86
UNCHAIN MY HEART	(Capitol B-44072)	.75	3.00	87
LOVE LIVES ON	(MCA 53077)	.75	3.00	87
(From the motion picture *Harry And The Hendersons*)				
A MAN LOVES A WOMAN	(Capitol B-44182)	1.00	4.00	86
(From the motion picture *Bull Durham*, Kevin Costner and Susan Sarandon pictured)				

COCK ROBIN

		VG	NM	YR
WHEN YOUR HEART IS WEAK/Because It Keeps On Working	(Columbia 38-04875)	.75	3.00	85
WHEN YOUR HEART IS WEAK	(Columbia 38-04875)	1.00	4.00	85
(Promotional issue, *Demonstration Only–Not For Sale* printed on sleeve)				
THOUGHT YOU WERE ON MY SIDE/Little Innocence	(Columbia 38-05635)	.75	3.00	85
THOUGHT YOU WERE ON MY SIDE	(Columbia 38-05635)	1.00	4.00	85
(Promotional issue, *Demonstration Only–Not For Sale* printed on sleeve)				
THE PROMISE YOU MADE/Have You Any Sympathy?	(Columbia 38-05720)	.75	3.00	86
THE PROMISE YOU MADE	(Columbia 38-05720)	1.00	4.00	86
(Promotional issue, *Demonstration Only/Not For Sale* printed on sleeve)				
THE PROMISE YOU MADE	(Columbia 38-05720)	1.50	6.00	86
(Promotional issue only, *Demonstration Only–Not For Sale* printed on sleeve. Completely different design from previous two versions.)				
JUST AROUND THE CORNER/Open Book	(Columbia 38-07123)	.75	3.00	87
THE BIGGEST FOOL OF ALL	(Columbia 38-07639)	.75	3.00	87

COCKTAIL
(Motion Picture)
See the Georgia Satellites (*Sheila*), John Cougar Mellencamp (*Rave On*), Starship (*Wild Again*)

COCONUTS, THE

		VG	NM	YR
IF I ONLY HAD A BRAIN/Indiscreet	(EMI America B-8173)	.75	3.00	83
Also see Kid Creole and the Coconuts				

COCOON
(Motion Picture)
See Michael Sembello (*Gravity*)

CODEINE

		VG	NM	YR
REALIZE/Broken-Hearted Wine	(Sub Pop 155)	1.25	5.00	92
(Issued with either clear or white vinyl)				
TOM/Something New	(Sub Pop 242)	1.25	5.00	93

EXTENDED PLAYS

		VG	NM	YR
HARD TO FIND	(Sub Pop 171)	2.50	10.00	92
(Limited edition of 3,000 copies issued with green vinyl and insert. Promotional item given away to *Sassy* magazine readers on request. Also includes one song each by Velocity Girl, Beat Happening, and Sebadoh.)				

COE, DAVID ALLAN

		VG	NM	YR
CHEAP THRILLS/You Never Even Called Me By My Name	(Columbia 38-03997)	.75	3.00	83
CHEAP THRILLS	(Columbia 38-03997)	1.00	4.00	83
(Promotional issue, *Demonstration–Not For Sale* printed on sleeve.)				

COFIELD, PETER

		VG	NM	YR
ASK ME IN THE MORNING	(Coral 762563)	1.50	6.00	68

COHN, MARC

		VG	NM	YR
THE HEART OF THE CITY	(Morning 86-1067)	1.00	4.00	86
(Cohn's name not credited on sleeve. Benefit for the Rock & Roll Hall of Fame.)				

COLBERT, CLAUDETTE
(Actress)
See George Greeley (*Allison's Theme From "Parrish"*)

COLDCUT

		VG	NM	YR
DOCTORIN' THE HOUSE/	(Columbia 38-07935)	.75	3.00	88
PEOPLE HOLD ON/People Hold On (a capella)	(Tommy Boy/Reprise 22848-7)	.75	3.00	89
(Shown as by Coldcut Featuring Lisa Stansfield)				

COLE, COZY

		VG	NM	YR
ALA TOPSY	(Random 602)	2.50	10.00	60

COLE, GARDNER

		VG	NM	YR
LIVE IT UP/Got Me Curious	(Warner Bros. 27793-7)	.75	3.00	88

COLE, JUDE

		VG	NM	YR
BACK TO SCHOOL	(MCA 52886)	.75	3.00	86
(From the motion picture *Back To School*)				
LIKE LOVERS DO	(Warner Bros. 28358-7)	.75	3.00	87
YOU WERE IN MY HEART	(Warner Bros. 28202-7)	.75	3.00	87
Also see the Records				

COLE, LLOYD, AND THE COMMOTIONS

		VG	NM	YR
MY BAG	(Capitol B-44253)	1.00	4.00	87

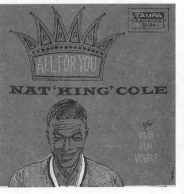

COLE, NAT KING

		VG	NM	YR
ALL FOR YOU/Vom-Vim-Veedle	(Tampa 134)	5.00	20.00	57
SWEET BIRD OF YOUTH/Midnight Flyer	(Capitol F4248)	3.00	12.00	59
THE HAPPIEST CHRISTMAS TREE/Buon Natale	(Capitol 4301)	3.00	12.00	59
GOODNIGHT LITTLE LEAGUER/The First Baseball Game	(Capitol 4555)	3.00	12.00	61
RAMBLIN' ROSE/The Good Times	(Capitol 4804)	3.00	12.00	62
DEAR LONELY HEARTS/Who's Next In Line?	(Capitol 48704)	3.00	12.00	62
THOSE LAZY–HAZY–CRAZY DAYS OF SUMMER/In The Cool Of The Day	(Capitol 4965)	3.00	12.00	63
(B-side from the motion picture *In The Cool Of The Day*)				
THE BALLAD OF CAT BALLOU/They Can't Make Her Cry	(Capitol 54124)	2.50	10.00	65
(A-side shown as by Nat King Cole and Stubby Kaye, both pictured. From the motion picture *Cat Ballou*)				
FRANK AND SARAH AND NAT AND VIC SALUTE HAROLD ADAMSON	(Harold Adamson Music Co. 100)	2.50	10.00	73
(Shown as by Frank Sinatra, Sarah Vaughan, Nat King Cole, and Vic Damone)				

TITLE	LABEL AND NUMBER	VG	NM	YR

COLE, NATALIE
(Daughter of Nat King Cole)
DANGEROUS/Love Is On The Way .... (Modern 99648) | .75 | 3.00 | 85
JUMP START/More Than The Stars .... (Manhattan B 50073) | .75 | 3.00 | 87
I LIVE FOR YOUR LOVE/More Than The Stars .... (Manhattan B 50094) | .75 | 3.00 | 87
WHEN I FALL IN LOVE/Pink Cadillac .... (EMI-Manhattan B 50138) | .75 | 3.00 | 88
MISS YOU LIKE CRAZY/Good To Be Back .... (EMI-Manhattan B 50185) | .75 | 3.00 | 89
    Also see Ray Parker Jr. (Over You)

COLEMAN, CARLTON "KING"
THE BOO BOO SONG .... (King 6365) | 2.00 | 8.00 | 71

COLLINS, AL "JAZZBO"
LITTLE RED RIDING HOOD/Three Little Pigs .... (Brunswick 86001) | 7.50 | 30.00 | 53

COLLINS, BOOTSY
HOLLYWOOD SQUARES .... (Warner Bros. 8575) | 1.50 | 6.00 | 78
    (Shown as by Bootsy's Rubber Band)
MUG PUSH .... (Warner Bros. 49599) | 1.50 | 6.00 | 80
    (Shown as by Bootsy)
PARTY ON PLASTIC/ .... (Columbia 38-07991) | .75 | 3.00 | 88
    Also see Parliament, Mudhoney (Pump It Up)

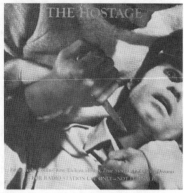

COLLINS, JUDY
CHELSEA MORNING/Pretty Polly .... (Elektra 45657) | 3.00 | 12.00 | 69
THE HOSTAGE/Che .... (Elektra PR-JC-3) | 2.00 | 8.00 | 73
    (Promotional issue only, For Radio Station Use Only–Not For Sale printed on sleeve. Issued with a small-hole
    33-1/3 RPM record. Cuban revolutionary Ernesto "Che" Guevara pictured on back.)
BREAD & ROSES .... (Elektra 45355) | 1.25 | 5.00 | 76
HARD TIMES FOR LOVERS/Happy End .... (Elektra 46020) | 1.00 | 4.00 | 79

COLLINS, PHIL
I MISSED AGAIN/I'm Not Moving .... (Atlantic 3790) | 1.00 | 4.00 | 81
IN THE AIR TONIGHT/The Roof Is Leaking .... (Atlantic 3824) | 1.00 | 4.00 | 81
YOU CAN'T HURRY LOVE/Do You Know, Do You Care? .... (Atlantic 7-89933) | .75 | 3.00 | 82
I DON'T CARE ANYMORE/The West Side .... (Atlantic 7-89877) | .75 | 3.00 | 83
AGAINST ALL ODDS (TAKE A LOOK AT ME NOW) .... (Atlantic 7-89700) | .75 | 3.00 | 84
    (From the motion picture Against All Odds, Rachel Ward and Jeff Bridges pictured)
ONE MORE NIGHT/The Man With The Horn .... (Atlantic 7-89588) | .75 | 3.00 | 85
SUSSUDIO/I Like The Way .... (Atlantic 7-89560) | .75 | 3.00 | 85
DON'T LOSE MY NUMBER/We Said Hello Goodbye .... (Atlantic 7-89536) | .75 | 3.00 | 85
SEPARATE LIVES (LOVE THEME FROM WHITE NIGHTS)/
    I Don't Wanna Know .... (Atlantic 7-89498) | 1.00 | 4.00 | 85
    (Shown as by Phil Collins and Marilyn Martin, b-side shown as by Phil Collins. Collins and Martin pictured
    on the front, Mikhail Baryshnikov and Gregory Hines pictured on the back. From the motion picture White
    Nights.)
SEPARATE LIVES (LOVE THEME FROM WHITE NIGHTS)/
    I Don't Wanna Know .... (Atlantic 7-89498) | 1.00 | 4.00 | 85
    (Shown as by Phil Collins and Marilyn Martin, b-side shown as by Phil Collins. Movie art pictured on the
    front, Mikhail Baryshnikov and Gregory Hines pictured on the back. From the motion picture White Nights.)
TAKE ME HOME/Only You Know And I Know .... (Atlantic 7-89472) | .75 | 3.00 | 85
GROOVY KIND OF LOVE/Big Noise .... (Atlantic 7-89017) | .75 | 3.00 | 88
    (From the motion picture Buster)
TWO HEARTS/The Robbery .... (Atlantic 7-88980) | .75 | 3.00 | 88
    (From the motion picture Buster)
ANOTHER DAY IN PARADISE/Heat On The Street .... (Atlantic 7/88774) | .75 | 3.00 | 89
I WISH IT WOULD RAIN DOWN/
    You've Been In Love (That Little Bit Too Long) .... (Atlantic 7-88738) | .75 | 3.00 | 90
    Also see Band Aid, Philip Bailey (Easy Lover), Genesis, Tears For Fears (Woman In Chains)

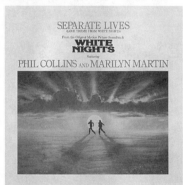

COLLINS, TYLER
WHATCHA GONNA DO?/Give And Take .... (RCA 9094-7-R) | .75 | 3.00 | 89

COLONEL ABRAMS
HOW SOON WE FORGET .... (MCA 53121) | .75 | 3.00 | 87
SOON YOU'LL BE GONE .... (MCA 53282) | .75 | 3.00 | 87

COLOR OF MONEY, THE
(Motion Picture)
    See Eric Clapton (It's In The Way That You Use It)

COLOR PURPLE, THE
(Motion Picture)
    See Tata Vega (Miss Celie's Blues)

COLORS
(Motion Picture)
    See Ice-T (Colors)

COLOURFIELD, THE
RUNNING AWAY/Digging It Deep .... (Chrysalis VS4 43092) | .75 | 3.00 | 88

COMBONATION
GIRLS LIKE YOU .... (Warner Bros. 29240-7) | .75 | 3.00 | 88

COME BLOW YOUR HORN
(Motion Picture)
    See Nelson Riddle (Come Blow Your Horn)

COME SEPTEMBER
(Motion Picture)
    See Bobby Darin (Theme From "Come September", Irresistible You)

COMING TO AMERICA
(Motion Picture)
    See the Cover Girls (Better Late Than Never), the System (Coming To America), Laura Branigan and Joe Esposito (Come Into My Life)

COMMANDER CODY AND HIS LOST PLANET AIRMEN

LOST IN THE OZONE / Midnight Shift .... (Paramount 0130)	1.25	5.00	72
BEAT ME DADDY, EIGHT TO THE BAR .... (Paramount 0169)	1.00	4.00	72
MAMA HATED DIESELS / Truck Stop Rock .... (Paramount 0178)	1.00	4.00	73
SMOKE SMOKE SMOKE .... (Paramount 0216)	1.00	4.00	73
TWO TRIPLE CHEESE / Roll The Dice .... (Peter Pan 109)	1.50	6.00	81

(Shown as by Commander Cody Band. Issued with yellow vinyl.)

COMMODORES

NIGHTSHIFT .... (Motown 1773MF)	.75	3.00	84
GOIN' TO THE BANK / Serious Love .... (Polydor 885 358-7)	.75	3.00	86
TAKE IT FROM ME / I Wanna Rock You .... (Polydor 885 538-7)	.75	3.00	87
SOLITAIRE / Stretchhh .... (Polydor 887 939-7)	.75	3.00	88

Lionel Richie left the group in 1982, two years before the first sleeve was released

COMMUNARDS, THE

DON'T LEAVE ME THIS WAY / Sanctified .... (MCA 52928)	.75	3.00	86
NEVER CAN SAY GOODBYE .... (MCA 53224)	.75	3.00	88

Also see Bronski Beat (Jimmy Sommerville)

COMO, PERRY

NO OTHER LOVE / Keep It Gay .... (RCA Victor 47-5317)	3.75	15.00	53
SOMEBODY UP THERE LIKES ME / On My Way To A Star ... (RCA Victor 47-6590)	2.50	10.00	56
(From the motion picture *Somebody Up There Likes Me*)			
JINGLE BELLS / Santa Claus Is Coming To Town ..... (RCA Victor Bluebird WBY-57)	2.50	10.00	56
(Children's series)			
ROUND AND ROUND / Mi Casa, Su Casa .... (RCA Victor 47-6815)	2.50	10.00	57
I KNOW / You Are In Love .... (RCA Victor 47-7541)	2.50	10.00	59
CATCH A FALLING STAR / Chin-Cher-In-Chee .... (RCA Victor Bluebird WBY-90)	2.50	10.00	60s
(Children's series)			
CATERINA / The Island Of Forgotten Lovers .... (RCA Victor 47-8004)	2.50	10.00	62
ONE MORE MOUNTAIN / (I Love You) Don't You Forget It ... (RCA Victor 47-8186)	2.50	10.00	63
DREAM ON LITTLE DREAMER / My Own Peculiar Way ..... (RCA Victor 47-8533)	2.50	10.00	65
CHRISTMAS BELLS / .... (RCA Victor 47-9637)	2.50	10.00	69
THE BEST OF TIMES / Song On The Sand .... (RCA JB-13690)	1.00	4.00	83

COMPANY B

FULL CIRCLE .... (Atlantic 7-89218)	.75	3.00	87

COMPTON BROTHERS

PINE GROVE .... (Dot 17378)	1.50	6.00	71

CONCRETE BLONDE

STILL IN HOLLYWOOD / Cold Part Of Town .... (IRS 52982)	1.25	5.00	86
(Issued with small-hole 45 RPM record)			
TRUE / True II .... (IRS 53053)	1.00	4.00	86
DANCE ALONG THE EDGE / (You're The Only One) Can Make Me Cry ... (IRS 53113)	.75	3.00	87

Also see Johnette Napolitano

CONIGLIARO, TONY

(Baseball player for the Boston Red Sox)

I CAN'T GET OVER YOU / Little Red Scooter .... (RCA Victor 47-8577)	5.00	20.00	65

CONLEY, ARTHUR

See the Soul Clan

CONLEY, EARL THOMAS

HOLDING HER AND LOVING YOU .... (RCA PB-13596)	.75	3.00	83
ANGEL IN DISGUISE .... (RCA PB-13758)	.75	3.00	84
HONOR BOUND .... (RCA PB-13960)	.75	3.00	84

CONLEY, MICHAEL

TELL ME PRETTY BABY .... (Elvis Classic 5478)	2.50	10.00	78

(This release was masquerading as a 1954 recording by Elvis Presley. Pictures an artist's sketch of Presley.)

CONNELLY, CHRIS

(Actor)

THEME FROM PEYTON PLACE / Young Love .... (Philips 40274)	2.00	8.00	65

(From the television series *Peyton Place*)

CONNIFF, RAY

CHRISTMAS BRIDE .... (Columbia 4-41484)	2.00	8.00	60

Also see Johnny Mathis (b-side of *Wild Is The Wind*), Guy Mitchell (*Knee Deep In The Blues*)

CONNORS, CAROL

(a.k.a. Annette Bard and a.k.a. Annette Kleinbard as a member of the Teddy Bears)

YUM YUM YAMAHA .... (N.T.C. 3131)	25.00	100.00	64
(Issued with one-sided single)			
LONELY LITTLE BEACH GIRL / My Baby Looks, But He Don't Touch ... (Mira 219)	12.50	50.00	66

CONNORS, MICHAEL

(Actor)

See Wayne Newton (*Stagecoach To Cheyenne*)

CONRAD, BOB

(Actor)

BALLIN' THE JACK / I Want You (Pretty Baby) ...... (Warner Bros. 5211)	5.00	20.00	61
BYE BYE BABY / Love You .... (Warner Bros. 5242)	5.00	20.00	61

CONSIDINE, TIM

(Juvenile actor, appeared on *The Mickey Mouse Club* and played the eldest brother, Mike, on the television series *My Three Sons*)

THE TRIPLE R SONG .... (Disneyland F-58)	6.25	25.00	58

CONTINENTAL MINIATURES

STAY AWHILE / Glad All Over .... (London 266)	1.25	5.00	78

62

TITLE	LABEL AND NUMBER	VG	NM	YR

CONTOURS, THE
DO YOU LOVE ME?/Shake, Shake, Sherrie .... (Motown Y448F) .75 3.00 88
  (A-side from the motion picture *Dirty Dancing*, Patrick Swayze and Jennifer Grey pictured)

CONTROLLERS
PLAY TIME .... (MCA 53214) .75 3.00 88

CONWAY, TIM
(Comic actor)
  See Marvin Hamlisch (*Love Theme*)

CONWELL, TOMMY, AND THE YOUNG RUMBLERS
I'M NOT YOUR MAN/Workout (Part 2) .... (Columbia 38-07980) .75 3.00 88
I'M NOT YOUR MAN .... (Columbia 38-07980) 1.00 4.00 88
  (Promotional issue, *Demonstration–Not For Sale* printed on sleeve)
  Also see the Hooters (Rob Miller)

COODER, RY
MONEY HONEY/Billy The Kid .... (Reprise PRO-514) 3.75 15.00 72
  (Promotional issue only)
  Also see John Cougar Mellencamp (*Lonely Ol' Night*)

COOK, ROGER
SWEET AMERICA .... (Kama Sutra 554) 1.00 4.00 72
  Also see Blue Mink, David & Jonathan

COOKE, SAM
YOU UNDERSTAND ME/I Belong To Your Heart .... (RCA Victor 47-7730) 6.25 25.00 60
CHAIN GANG/I Fall In Love Every Day .... (RCA Victor 47-7783) 5.00 20.00 60
CUPID/Farewell My Darling .... (RCA Victor 47-7883) 5.00 20.00 61
FEEL IT/It's All Right .... (RCA Victor 47-7927) 5.00 20.00 61
NOTHING CAN CHANGE THIS LOVE/Somebody Have Mercy .... (RCA Victor 47-8088) 5.00 20.00 62
SEND ME SOME LOVIN'/Baby, Baby, Baby .... (RCA Victor 47-8129) 5.00 20.00 63
ANOTHER SATURDAY NIGHT/Love Will Find A Way .... (RCA Victor 47-8164) 5.00 20.00 63
FRANKIE AND JOHNNY/Cool Train .... (RCA Victor 47-8215) 5.00 20.00 63
LITTLE RED ROOSTER/You Gotta Move .... (RCA Victor 47-8247) 5.00 20.00 63
SUGAR DUMPLING/Bridge Of Tears .... (RCA Victor 47-8631) 5.00 20.00 65

COOLIDGE, RITA
FEVER/My Crew .... (A&M 1398) 1.50 6.00 72
A SONG I'D LIKE TO SING/From The Bottle To The Bottom .... (A&M 1475) 1.25 5.00 73
  (Shown as by Kris Kristofferson & Rita Coolidge, both pictured)
(YOUR LOVE HAS LIFTED ME) HIGHER AND HIGHER/
  Who's To Bless And Who's To Blame .... (A&M 1922) 1.00 4.00 77
WE'RE ALL ALONE/Southern Lady .... (A&M 1965) 1.00 4.00 77
THE WAY YOU DO THE THINGS YOU DO/
  I Feel The Burden (Being Lifted Off My Shoulders) .... (A&M 2004) 1.00 4.00 77
YOU/Only You Know And I Know .... (A&M 2058) 1.00 4.00 78
ALL TIME HIGH/All Time High .... (A&M 2551) 1.00 4.00 83
  (From the motion picture *Octopussy*)

COOPER, ALICE
SCHOOL'S OUT/Gutter Cat .... (Warner Bros. 7596) 2.50 10.00 72
ELECTED/Luney Tune .... (Warner Bros. 7631) 2.50 10.00 72
YOU AND ME/It's Hot Tonight .... (Warner Bros. 8349) 1.50 6.00 77
CLONES (WE'RE ALL)/Model Citizen .... (Warner Bros. 49204) 1.25 5.00 80
HE'S BACK (THE MAN IN THE MASK)/Billion Dollar .... (MCA 52904) 1.00 4.00 86
  (From the motion picture *Friday The 13th, Part IV: Jason Lives*)
FREEDOM/Time To Kill .... (MCA 53212) 1.00 4.00 87

COOPER, GARY
(Actor)
  See Jane Morgan (*Fascination*)

COOPER, MICHAEL
DINNER FOR TWO .... (Warner Bros. 27934-7) .75 3.00 87

COPE, JULIAN
WORLD SHUT YOUR MOUTH/Umpteenth Unnatural Blues .... (Island 7-99479) 1.00 4.00 86
5 O'CLOCK WORLD/S. P. Q. R. .... (Island 7-99241) .75 3.00 88

COPELAND, STEWART
DON'T BOX ME IN/Drama At Home .... (A&M 2604) 1.00 4.00 83
  (A-side shown as by Stewart Copeland and Stanard Ridgway, both pictured. From the motion picture *Rumble Fish*)
  Also see Klark Kent, the Police

COPLAND, AARON
COPLAND REHEARSES APPALACHIAN SPRING .... (Columbia BTS 34) 2.00 8.00 74
  (Promotional issue only with 2-1/4" envelope flap. Issued with 33-1/3 small-hole record.)

COQUETTES, THE
THE SIAMESE CAT SONG .... (RCA Victor Bluebird WBY-26) 3.75 15.00
  (Children's series)

CORBETTA, JERRY
I GOT A SONG .... (Brut 815) 1.50 6.00 73
  (Shown as by Sugarloaf/Jerry Corbetta)
  Also see Sugarloaf

CORD, ALEX
(Actor)
  See Wayne Newton (*Stagecoach To Cheyenne*)

CORDS
AMERICAN WOMAN/Storm .... (Fuel 3612-0) .75 3.00 94
  (Issued with small-hole 45 RPM yellow vinyl)

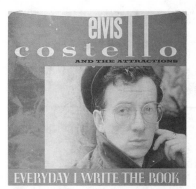

CORLEY, AL
SQUARE ROOMS/Don't Play With Me .... (Mercury 822 241-7) | .75 | 3.00 | 84

CORNICHE
THEME FROM CHiPs .... (Windsong 11552) | 1.50 | 6.00 | 79
(From the television series CHiPs)

COSBY, BILL
EXTENDED PLAYS
STREET FOOTBALL/SHOP/The Playground/The Water Bottle .... (Warner Bros. 274) | 2.50 | 10.00 | 68
(Promotional issue only titled *A Taste Of Cosby*, no titles listed on sleeve. Released to commemorate "The Bill Cosby Special". Issued with large-hole 45 RPM record.)
Also see Peabo Bryson *(Without You)*

COSTA, DON, ORCHESTRA
NEVER ON SUNDAY/Sound Of Love .... (United Artists 234) | 2.50 | 10.00 | 60

COSTELLO, ELVIS, AND THE ATTRACTIONS
WATCH YOUR STEP/Luxembourg .... (Columbia 11-60519) | 1.25 | 5.00 | 81
EVERYDAY I WRITE THE BOOK/Heathen Town .... (Columbia 38 04045) | 1.25 | 5.00 | 83
EVERYDAY I WRITE THE BOOK .... (Columbia 38 04045) | 2.00 | 8.00 | 83
(Promotional issue, *Demonstration–Not For Sale* printed on sleeve)
THE ONLY FLAME IN TOWN/Turning The Town Red .... (Columbia 38-04502) | 1.25 | 5.00 | 84
THE ONLY FLAME IN TOWN .... (Columbia 38-04502) | 2.00 | 8.00 | 84
(Promotional issue, *Demonstration Not For Sale* printed on sleeve)
SEVEN-DAY WEEKEND .... (Columbia 38-06135) | 1.00 | 4.00 | 86
(Shown as by Jimmy Cliff & Elvis Costello and the Attractions. From the motion picture *Club Paradise*)
SEVEN-DAY WEEKEND .... (Columbia 38-06135) | 1.00 | 4.00 | 86
(Promotional issue, *Demonstration Not For Sale* printed on sleeve. Shown as by Jimmy Cliff & Elvis Costello and the Attractions. From the motion picture *Club Paradise*.)
VERONICA/You're No Good .... (Warner Bros. 22981-7) | 1.00 | 4.00 | 89
(Shown as by Elvis Costello)
EXTENDED PLAYS
ADCIENTS WILL HAPPEN/ALISON/Watching The Detectives .... (Columbia AE7 1171) | 2.00 | 8.00 | 78
(Promotional issue only titled *Live At Hollywood High*, included with the album *Armed Forces*, *Not For Sale* printed on sleeve. Issued with a small-hole 33-1/3 RPM. Note intentional misspelling of *Accidents Will Happen* on sleeve only.)
I CAN'T STAND UP FOR FALLING DOWN/GIRLS TALK/
Secondary Modern/King Horse .... (Columbia 1-11251) | 1.50 | 6.00 | 80
(Sleeve does not credit the Attractions but the record does)
I CAN'T STAND UP FOR FALLING DOWN/GIRLS TALK/
Secondary Modern/King Horse .... (Columbia 1-11251) | 2.00 | 8.00 | 80
(Promotional issue, *Demonstration–Not For Sale* printed on back of sleeve. Sleeve does not credit the Attractions but the record does.)
Also see the Special AKA *(Free Nelson Mandela)*

COSTNER, KEVIN
(Actor)
See Julia Migenes and Paul Anka *(No Way Out)*

COTTON, JOSIE
JOHNNY ARE YOU QUEER?/(Let's Do) The Blackout .... (Elektra 47255) | 1.25 | 5.00 | 82
HE COULD BE THE ONE/Systematic Way .... (Elektra 47481) | 1.00 | 4.00 | 82
(Originally issued with pink vinyl)
JIMMY LOVES MARYANN/No Pictures Of Dad .... (Elektra 7-69748) | .75 | 3.00 | 84

COUNTERFEIT TRAITOR, THE
(Motion Picture)
See Johnny Mathis *(Marianna)*

COUNTRY COALITION
KEEPIN' FREE .... (ABC 11286) | 1.25 | 5.00 | 70

COUNTRY HAMS, THE
(Paul and Linda McCartney, Chet Atkins, and Floyd Cramer)
WALKING IN THE PARK WITH ELOISE/Bridge On The River Suite .... (EMI 3977) | 18.75 | 75.00 | 74
Also see Band Aid (Paul McCartney), the Beatles (Paul McCartney), Brass Ring (Paul McCartney on *Love In The Open Air*), Ferry Aid (Paul McCartney), Billy J. Kramer (Paul McCartney on *From A Window*), Paul McCartney, Chet Atkins, Floyd Cramer

COUNTRY JOE & THE FISH
WHO AM I? .... (Vanguard 35061) | 5.00 | 20.00 | 68

COURY, AL
See Tesla

COVEN
WICKED WOMAN/White Witch Of Rosehall .... (Mercury 72973) | 6.25 | 25.00 | 69
Also see Ozzy Osbourne

COVER GIRLS, THE
BECAUSE OF YOU/ .... (Fever 1914) | .75 | 3.00 | 87
INSIDE OUTSIDE/Inside Outside (Instrumental) .... (Fever 1916) | .75 | 3.00 | 88
PROMISE ME!/One Night Affair .... (Fever 1917) | .75 | 3.00 | 88
BETTER LATE THAN NEVER/Better Late Than Never .... (Fever 1918) | .75 | 3.00 | 88
(From the motion picture *Coming To America*)

COWBOY CHURCH SUNDAY SCHOOL, THE
OPEN UP YOUR HEART (AND LET THE SUNSHINE IN)/
The Lord Is Counting On You .... (Decca 1-299) | 3.75 | 15.00 | 55

COWBOY JUNKIES
SWEET JANE/200 More Miles .... (RCA 8879-7-R) | 1.00 | 4.00 | 89
MISGUIDED ANGEL/Postcard Blues .... (RCA 8977-7-R) | 1.00 | 4.00 | 89

COWSILLS, THE
MOST OF ALL/Siamese Cat .... (Philips 40382) | 3.00 | 12.00 | 66
THE RAIN, THE PARK & OTHER THINGS/River Blue .... (MGM K-13810) | 2.50 | 10.00 | 67
WE CAN FLY .... (MGM K-13886) | 2.50 | 10.00 | 68

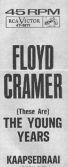

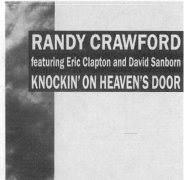

TITLE	LABEL AND NUMBER	VG	NM	YR
IN NEED OF A FRIEND/Mister Flynn	(MGM K-13909)	2.50	10.00	68
INDIAN LAKE/Newspaper Blanket	(MGM K-13944)	2.50	10.00	68
SILVER THREADS AND GOLDEN NEEDLES/Love American Style	(MGM K-14084)	3.00	12.00	69
CHRISTMASTIME (SONG FOR MARISSA)/Some Good Years	(Rockville 6139-7)	1.25	5.00	93

(Issued with either black or green vinyl)

COX, WALLY

(Comic actor who starred in the television series *Mr. Peepers,* was a regular on *Hollywood Squares,* and provided the voice for the cartoon character Underdog)

TITLE	LABEL AND NUMBER	VG	NM	YR
WHAT A CRAZY GUY/There's A Tavern In The Town	(RCA Victor 47-5278)	10.00	40.00	53

COYOTE SISTERS, THE

STRAIGHT FROM THE HEART	(Morocco 1742)	1.00	4.00	84

CRACKER

RAINY DAYS AND MONDAYS	(A&M 31458 0716 7)	.50	2.00	94

(Side 11 of a 7-record box set titled *If I Were A Carpenter.* Each sleeve has a different face shot of Karen Carpenter on the front, Richard Carpenter on the back. No artist name or song titles indicated on sleeve. Complete set valued at $30.00 near mint.)

CRACKERJACK SOCIETY

WALK IN THE SKY/Listen To This Side	(Columbia 4-44434)	2.50	10.00	67

CRACK THE SKY

MR. DJ/Needles & Pins	(Criminal 1712)	1.25	5.00	83

Also see B. E. Taylor Group

CRADDOCK, CRASH

DON'T DESTROY ME/Boom Boom Baby	(Columbia 4-41470)	7.50	30.00	59
ALL I WANT IS YOU/Letter Of Love	(Columbia 4-41619)	7.50	30.00	60
JUST ANOTHER MISERABLE DAY (HERE IN PARADISE)/Softly Diana	(Atlantic 7-88851)	.75	3.00	89

(Shown as by Billy "Crash" Craddock)

CRAMER, FLOYD

ON THE REBOUND/Mood Indigo	(RCA Victor 47-7840)	2.50	10.00	61
YOUR LAST GOODBYE/Hang On	(RCA Victor 47-7907)	2.50	10.00	61
SWING LOW/Losers Weepers	(RCA Victor 47-8084)	2.50	10.00	62
(THESE ARE) THE YOUNG YEARS/ Kaapsedraai ("cop-se-dry") (The South African Cape Reel)	(RCA Victor 47-8171)	2.50	10.00	63
HOW HIGH THE MOON/	(RCA Victor 47-8217)	2.50	10.00	63
THEME FROM DALLAS	(RCA Victor PB-11916)	1.25	5.00	79

(From the television series *Dallas,* Jim Davis, Barbara Bel Geddes, Larry Hagman, Linda Gray, Patrick Duffy, Victoria Prinipal, and Ken Kercheval pictured)

Also see Chet Atkins (*Chet's Tune*), the Country Hams

CRAMPS, THE

SURFIN' BIRD/The Way I Walk	(Vengeance 666)	10.00	40.00	78
DOMINO/Human Fly	(Vengeance 668)	10.00	40.00	78
GARBAGEMAN/Drug Train	(IRS 9014)	5.00	20.00	80

(Issued with small-hole 45 RPM record)

GOOGOO MUCK/She Said	(I.R.S. 9021)	3.00	12.00	81

CRANBERRIES, THE

(THEY LONG TO BE) CLOSE TO YOU	(A&M 31458 0708 7)	.50	2.00	94

(Side 4 of a 7-record box set titled *If I Were A Carpenter.* Each sleeve has a different face shot of Karen Carpenter on the front, Richard Carpenter on the back. No artist name or song titles indicated on sleeve. Complete set valued at $30.00 near mint.)

CRANE, BOB

(Comic actor, starred in the television series *Hogan's Heroes* from 1965-1971)

HAPPY FEET/Theme from Get Smart	(Epic 5-10038)	3.75	15.00	66

CRANE, JIMMY

SHIG-A-SHAG	(Spangle 1422)	12.50	50.00	58

CRANE, LES

DESIDERATA	(Warner Bros. 7520)	1.50	6.00	71

CRAWFORD, JOHNNY

(Juvenile actor, played Chuck Connor's son in the television series *The Rifleman* from 1958-1963)

DAYDREAMS/So Goes The Story	(Del-Fi 4162)	3.75	15.00	61
YOUR LOVE IS GROWING COLD/The Treasure	(Del-Fi 4165)	3.75	15.00	61
CINDY'S BIRTHDAY/Something Special	(Del-Fi 4178)	3.75	15.00	62
YOUR NOSE IS GONNA GROW/Mr. Blue	(Del-Fi 4181)	3.75	15.00	62
RUMORS/No One Really Loves A Clown	(Del-Fi 4188)	3.75	15.00	62
GOOD BUDDIES/You Gotta Wear Shoes	(Del-Fi 4191)	3.75	15.00	62

(Shown as by the Crawford Brothers)

ANGELICA/Everybody Has Their Day	(Sidewalk 941)	2.50	10.00	68
EVERYONE SHOULD OWN A DREAM (LOVE SONG FROM THE SAVAGE SEVEN)/ Good Guys Finish Last	(Sidewalk 941)	2.50	10.00	68

(A-side from the motion picture *The Savage Seven*)

Also see the Crawford Brothers

CRAWFORD, RANDY

KNOCK ON WOOD/	(Columbia 4-45693)	2.50	10.00	72
KNOCKIN' ON HEAVEN'S DOOR/ Medley: The Shipyard/Knockin'On Heaven's Door	(Warner Bros. 22865-7)	.75	3.00	89

(Shown as by Randy Crawford Featuring Eric Clapton and David Sanborn)

Also see Rick Springfield (*Bop 'Til You Drop*)

CRAWFORD BROTHERS, THE

(Johnny and Bobby Crawford)

GOOD BUDDIES/You Gotta Wear Shoes	(Del-Fi 4191)	3.75	15.00	62

CRAWLER

EXTENDED PLAYS

HOO DOO WOMEN/ALL THE GIRLS ARE CRAZY/ Survivor/The Band Plays On	(Atco E.P. PR-247)	2.00	8.00	75

(Shown as by Back Street Crawler. Promotional issue only, *For Promotion Use Only* printed on sleeve. Issued with small-hole 33-1/3 RPM record.)

STONE COLD SOBER .... (CBS AE7-1128 AE7-1129)   2.00   8.00   77
    (Promotional issue only titled *Music For Every Ear*, double single release issued with two small-hole
    33-1/3 RPM records. Also includes one song each by Joan Baez, Cheap Trick, Burton Cummings, Ram Jam,
    and Dennis Wilson.)
    Also see Free (Paul Kossoff)

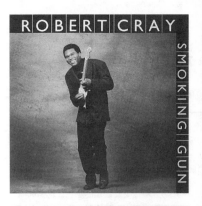

CRAY, ROBERT
SMOKING GUN/Fantasized .... (Mercury 888 343-7)   .75   3.00   87
RIGHT NEXT DOOR (BECAUSE OF ME)/New Blood .... (Mercury 888 327-7)   .75   3.00   87
ACTING THIS WAY/Laugh Out Loud .... (Mercury 872 208-7)   .75   3.00   88
    (Shown as by the Robert Cray Band)
DON'T BE AFRAID OF THE DARK/ .... (Mercury 870 569-7)   .75   3.00   88
    (Shown as by the Robert Cray Band)

CRAZY HORSE
See Neil Young (*Rust Never Sleeps*)

CREAM
CROSSROADS/As You Said/Those Were The Days .... (Atco EP 4525)   12.50   50.00   68
    (Promotional issue only)

CREATIONS, THE
(A number of different groups recorded under this name)
CRASH/Chickie Darlin .... (Top Hat 1003)   20.00   80.00   64
DON'T BE MEAN .... (Top Hat 1004)   25.00   100.00   65

CREATIVE SOURCE
YOU CAN'T HIDE LOVE/Lovesville .... (Sussex 501)   1.50   6.00   76

CREATURES, THE
TURN OUT THE LIGHT/It Must Be Love .... (Columbia 4-43480)   3.00   12.00   66

CREDIBILITY GAP, THE
SOMETHING FOR MARY (SHORT BITS) .... (Warner Bros. 517)   1.50   6.00   73
    (Promotional issue only)
    Also see Spinal Tap (Michael McKean a.k.a. David St. Hubbins, Harry Shearer a.k.a. Derek Smalls)

CREEDENCE CLEARWATER REVIVAL
45 REVOLUTIONS PER MINUTE .... (Fantasy 2838)   7.50   30.00   69
    (Promotional issue only)
FORTUNATE SON/Down On The Corner .... (Fantasy 634)   2.00   8.00   69
TRAVELIN' BAND/Who'll Stop The Rain .... (Fantasy 637)   2.00   8.00   70
RUN THROUGH THE JUNGLE/Up Around The Bend .... (Fantasy 641)   2.00   8.00   70
LOOKIN' OUT MY BACK DOOR/Long As I Can See The Light .... (Fantasy 645)   2.00   8.00   70
SWEET HITCH-HIKER/Door To Door .... (Fantasy 565)   2.00   8.00   71
I HEARD IT THROUGH THE GRAPEVINE/Good Golly Miss Molly .... (Fantasy 759)   1.50   6.00   75
    Also see Blue Ridge Mountain Rangers, Doug Clifford, John Fogerty, Tom Fogerty

CRENSHAW, MARSHALL
WHENEVER YOU'RE ON MY MIND/Jungle Rock .... (Warner Bros. 29630-7)   1.00   4.00   83
LITTLE WILD ONE (NO. 5)/Like A Vague Memory .... (Warner Bros. 28865-7)   .75   3.00   85
SOME HEARTS .... (Warner Bros. 22878-7)   .75   3.00   89

CRESCENDOS, THE
GENERIC CRESCENDOS SLEEVE .... (Nasco no #)   10.00   40.00   57
    (Half sleeve picturing the group, possibly issued only with the single *Oh Julie* on Nasco)
SCHOOL GIRL/Crazy Hop .... (Nasco 6009)   10.00   40.00   57
YOUNG AND IN LOVE/Rainy Sunday .... (Nasco 6021)   10.00   40.00   58
OH! JULIE/Angel Face .... (Tap 7027)   6.25   25.00   62
    Also see Dale Ward

CRETONES, THE
REAL LOVE/Ways Of The Heart .... (Planet 45911)   1.00   4.00   80

CREW CUTS, THE
SH-BOOM/I Spoke Too Soon .... (Mercury 70404)   25.00   100.00   54
    (Issued with 7-inch 78 RPM record)

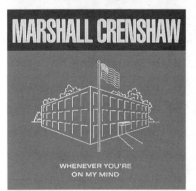

CREWE, BOB, GENERATION
MINI SKIRTS IN MOSCOW, OR.../Theme For A Lazy Girl .... (DynoVoice 233)   1.50   6.00   67

CRIB AND BEN
EMILY .... (Decca 32453)   1.25   5.00   69

CRICKETS, THE
T-SHIRT .... (Epic 08028)   1.50   6.00   88
    (Promotional issue only)
    Also see the Campers, Bobby Vee (b-side of *Punish Her*)

CRISTINA
THINGS FALL APART/What's A Girl To Do .... (Island 7-99946)   .75   3.00   82

CRITTERS, THE
MR. DIEINGLY SAD/It Just Won't Be That Way .... (Kapp 769)   3.75   15.00   66
GOOD MORNING SUNSHINE/A Moment Of Being With You .... (Project 3 1326)   2.00   8.00   67

CROCE, JIM
IT DOESN'T HAVE TO BE THAT WAY/Roller Derby Queen .... (ABC 11413)   1.50   6.00   73

CROCKETT, DAVY
(Five episodes, based on the American folk hero, that appeared from 1954-1955 on the television series *Disneyland*)
See Fess Parker (*Ballad Of Davy Crockett* and *Old Betsy*), the Sandpipers (*The Ballad Of Davy Crockett*)

CROSBY, BING
A CROSBY CHRISTMAS .... (Decca 1-134)   10.00   40.00   50
    (Shown as by Gary, Phillip, Dennis, Lindsay & Bing Crosby)
I SURRENDER DEAR/When The Blue Of The Night Meets The Gold Of The Day ..... (Decca 1-704)   3.75   15.00   51
    (Decca "Curtain Call" series of reissues)

TITLE	LABEL AND NUMBER	VG	NM	YR

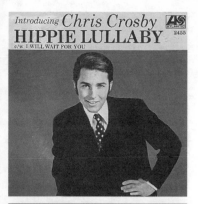

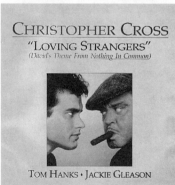

TITLE	LABEL AND NUMBER	VG	NM	YR
WHITE CHRISTMAS/God Rest Ye Merry Gentlemen	(Decca 9-23778)	2.50	10.00	55

(This was the first year this sleeve was used and would appear through at least 1962. *White Christmas* was originally released in 1942 and was featured in the 1954 motion picture *White Christmas*.)

TITLE	LABEL AND NUMBER	VG	NM	YR
SILENT NIGHT/Adestes Fideles	(Decca 9-23777)	2.50	10.00	57
MISSISSIPPI MUD/Around The World	(Decca 9-30262)	3.00	12.00	57
HOW LOVELY IS CHRISTMAS	(Kapp 196X)	3.00	12.00	57
HOW LOVELY IS CHRISTMAS/Boy At A Window	(Golden EP407)	3.00	12.00	57

(8" tall hard cover, Golden 3-on-1 series)

TITLE	LABEL AND NUMBER	VG	NM	YR
THE OLDEST ESTABLISHED (PERMANENT FLOATING CRAP GAME IN NEW YORK)/ Fugue For Tinhorns	(Reprise 20,217)	15.00	60.00	63

(Shown as by Frank Sinatra, Bing Crosby, and Dean Martin)

TITLE	LABEL AND NUMBER	VG	NM	YR
WE WISH YOU THE MERRIEST/Go Tell It On The Mountain	(RCA Victor 0317)	7.50	30.00	64

(Shown as by Frank Sinatra, Bing Crosby, and Fred Waring)

TITLE	LABEL AND NUMBER	VG	NM	YR
A TIME TO BE JOLLY/And The Bells Rang	(Daybreak 1001)	1.50	6.00	71

(Also credited on sleeve are Jack Halloran and the Voices of Christmas with Orchestra conducted by Les Brown)

TITLE	LABEL AND NUMBER	VG	NM	YR
WHITE CHRISTMAS/Where The Blue Of The Night Meets The Gold Of The Day	(MCA 40830)	1.00	4.00	77

Also see Wayne Newton (*Stagecoach To Cheyenne*)

CROSBY, CHRIS
(Son of Bob Crosby, Bing's brother)

TITLE	LABEL AND NUMBER	VG	NM	YR
ALL I HAVE TO DO IS DREAM	(MGM K13234)	2.50	10.00	64
HIPPIE LULLABY/I Will Wait For You	(Atlantic 2455)	3.75	15.00	67

CROSBY, STILLS & NASH

TITLE	LABEL AND NUMBER	VG	NM	YR
JUST A SONG BEFORE I GO/Dark Star	(Atlantic 3401)	1.00	4.00	79
WASTED ON THE WAY/Delta	(Atlantic 4058)	1.00	4.00	82
SOUTHERN CROSS/Into The Darkness	(Atlantic 7-89969)	1.00	4.00	82
WAR GAMES/Shadow Captain	(Atlantic 7-89812)	1.00	4.00	83

Also see the Byrds (David Crosby), Crosby, Stills, Nash & Young, the Hollies (Graham Nash), Graham Nash, Stephen Stills

CROSBY, STILLS, NASH & YOUNG

TITLE	LABEL AND NUMBER	VG	NM	YR
OHIO/Find The Cost Of Freedom	(Atlantic 2740)	2.00	8.00	70
AMERICAN DREAM/Compass	(Atlantic 7-89003)	1.00	4.00	88
GOT IT MADE/This Old House	(Atlantic 7-88966)	1.00	4.00	89

Also see the Byrds (David Crosby), Crosby, Stills & Nash, the Hollies (Graham Nash), Graham Nash, Stephen Stills, Neil Young

CROSS, THE

TITLE	LABEL AND NUMBER	VG	NM	YR
SHOVE IT/Feel The Force	(Virgin 7-99327)	.75	3.00	88

Also see Queen (Roger Taylor), Roger Taylor

CROSS, CHRISTOPHER

TITLE	LABEL AND NUMBER	VG	NM	YR
ARTHUR'S THEME (BEST THAT YOU CAN DO)/Minstrel Gigolo	(Warner Bros. 49787)	.75	3.00	81

(From the motion picture *Arthur*)

TITLE	LABEL AND NUMBER	VG	NM	YR
ALL RIGHT	(Warner Bros. 29843-7)	.75	3.00	83
A CHANCE FOR HEAVEN	(Columbia 38-04492)	.75	3.00	84

(Swimming theme from the official music of the XXIIIrd Olympiad Los Angeles 1984)

TITLE	LABEL AND NUMBER	VG	NM	YR
A CHANCE FOR HEAVEN	(Columbia 38-04492)	1.00	4.00	84

(Promotional issue, *Demonstration–Not For Sale* printed on sleeve. Swimming theme from the official music of the XXIIIrd Olympiad Los Angeles 1984)

TITLE	LABEL AND NUMBER	VG	NM	YR
CHARM THE SNAKE	(Warner Bros. 28864-7)	.75	3.00	85
LOVING STRANGERS/Seven Summers	(Arista 9530)	.75	3.00	86

(B-side shown as by Cruzados. From the motion picture *Nothing In Common*, Tom Hanks and Jackie Gleason pictured.)

TITLE	LABEL AND NUMBER	VG	NM	YR
I WILL (TAKE YOU FOREVER)	(Reprise 27795-7)	.75	3.00	88
SWEPT AWAY	(Reprise 27673-7)	.75	3.00	88

(The "Aloha Show Theme" from the television series *Growing Pains*)

CROW, SHERYL

TITLE	LABEL AND NUMBER	VG	NM	YR
SOLITAIRE	(A&M 31458 0712 7)	.50	2.00	94

(Side 7 of a 7 record box set titled *If I Were A Carpenter*. Each sleeve has a different face shot of Karen Carpenter on the front, Richard Carpenter on the back. No artist name or song titles indicated on sleeve. Complete set valued at $30.00 near mint.)

TITLE	LABEL AND NUMBER	VG	NM	YR
CAN'T CRY ANYMORE/We Do What We Can	(A&M 31458 0638 7)	.75	3.00	95

CROWDED HOUSE

TITLE	LABEL AND NUMBER	VG	NM	YR
DON'T DREAM IT'S OVER	(Capitol B-5614)	.75	3.00	86
SOMETHING SO STRONG	(Capitol B-5695)	.75	3.00	87
WORLD WHERE YOU LIVE	(Capitol B-44033)	.75	3.00	87
NOW WE'RE GETTING SOMEWHERE	(Capitol B-44083)	.75	3.00	87
BETTER BE HOME SOON	(Capitol B-44164)	.75	3.00	88
INTO TEMPTATION	(Capitol B-44226)	.75	3.00	88

Also see Tim Finn, Split Enz (Tim Finn)

CROWN HEIGHTS AFFAIR

TITLE	LABEL AND NUMBER	VG	NM	YR
(DO IT) THE FRENCH WAY	(De-Lite 1592)	1.25	5.00	77

CRUISE, TOM
(Actor)

See John Cougar Mellencamp (*Rave On*), Bob Seger (*Old Time Rock & Roll*)

CRUMB, ROBERT
(Artist)

See Larry Groce (*Turn On Your TV*)

CRUSADERS

TITLE	LABEL AND NUMBER	VG	NM	YR
THIS WORLD'S TOO FUNKY FOR ME	(MCA 51222)	1.00	4.00	81

(Promotional issue only)

CRUZADOS

TITLE	LABEL AND NUMBER	VG	NM	YR
MOTORCYCLE GIRL/1,000 Miles	(Arista 9436)	.75	3.00	85
BED OF LIES/Chains Of Freedom	(Arista 9610)	.75	3.00	87
SMALL TOWN LOVE/Blue Sofa (Still A Fool)	(Arista 9634)	.75	3.00	87
TIME FOR WAITING/Young And On Fire	(Arista 9654)	.75	3.00	87

(Back of sleeve credits background vocals to E.G. Daily)

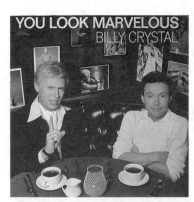

YOU LOOK MARVELOUS
BILLY CRYSTAL

EXTENDED PLAYS
MOTORCYCLE GIRL/HANGING OUT IN CALIFORNIA/
Crying Eyes/Just Like Roses .... (Arista 9433)   1.00   4.00   85
(Promotional issue only)
Also see Christopher Cross (Loving Strangers)

CRYAN' SHAMES, THE
IT COULD BE WE'RE IN LOVE/I Was Lonely When .... (Columbia 4-44191)   3.00   12.00   67

CRYER, JON
(Actor)
See Orchestral Manœuvres In The Dark (If You Leave)

CRYSTAL, BILLY
(Comedian/Actor)
YOU LOOK MARVELOUS/You Look Marvelous (Dub Version) .... (A&M 2764)   .75   3.00   85
I HATE WHEN THAT HAPPENS/I Hate When That Happens (Dub Version) .... (A&M 2774)   .75   3.00   85
(Billy Crystal and Christopher Guest pictured)
THE CHRISTMAS SONG .... (A&M 2795)   .75   3.00   85
Also see Michael McDonald (Sweet Freedom), New Edition (Once In A Lifetime Groove)

CUFF LINKS, THE
TRACY .... (Decca 32533)   2.50   10.00   69
(Promotional issue only, gatefold sleeve)
Also see the Archies (Ron Dante), the Detergents (Ron Dante), Ron Dante

CULT, THE
LI'L DEVIL/Memphis Hip Shake .... (Sire 28290-7)   1.00   4.00   87
WILD FLOWER/Love Trooper .... (Sire 28213-7)   1.50   6.00   87
(Poster sleeve)
FIRE WOMAN/Automatic Blues .... (Sire 27543-7)   1.00   4.00   89

CULTURE CLUB
TIME (CLOCK OF THE HEART)/Romance Beyond The Alphabet .... (Epic/Virgin 34-03796)   1.00   4.00   82
I'LL TUMBLE 4 YA!/Mystery Boy .... (Epic/Virgin 34-03912)   .75   3.00   83
I'LL TUMBLE 4 YA! .... (Epic/Virgin 34-03912)   1.00   4.00   83
(Promotional issue, Demonstration–Not For Sale printed on sleeve)
CHURCH OF THE POISON MIND/Mystery Boy .... (Epic/Virgin 34-04144)   .75   3.00   83
CHURCH OF THE POISON MIND .... (Epic/Virgin 34-04144)   1.00   4.00   83
(Promotional issue, Demonstration–Not For Sale printed on sleeve)
KARMA CHAMELEON/That's The Way .... (Epic/Virgin 34-04221)   .75   3.00   83
KARMA CHAMELEON .... (Epic/Virgin 34-04221)   1.00   4.00   83
(Promotional issue, Demonstration–Not For Sale printed on sleeve)
IT'S A MIRACLE/Love Twist .... (Epic/Virgin 34-04457)   .75   3.00   84
IT'S A MIRACLE .... (Epic/Virgin 34-04457)   1.00   4.00   84
(Promotional issue, Demonstration–Not For Sale printed on sleeve)
MISS ME BLIND/Colour By Numbers .... (Epic/Virgin 34-04388)   .75   3.00   84
MISS ME BLIND .... (Epic/Virgin 34-04388)   1.00   4.00   84
(Promotional issue, Demonstration–Not For Sale printed on sleeve)
THE WAR SONG/La Cancion De Guerra .... (Epic/Virgin 34-04638)   .75   3.00   84
THE WAR SONG .... (Epic/Virgin 34-04638)   1.00   4.00   84
(Promotional issue, Demonstration–Not For Sale printed on sleeve)
MOVE AWAY/Sexuality .... (Epic/Virgin 34-05847)   .75   3.00   86
MOVE AWAY .... (Epic/Virgin 34-05847)   1.00   4.00   86
(Promotional issue, Demonstration–Not For Sale printed on sleeve)
GUSTO BLUSTO/From Luxury To Heartache .... (Epic/Virgin 34-06133)   .75   3.00   86
GUSTO BLUSTO .... (Epic/Virgin 34-06133)   1.00   4.00   86
(Promotional issue, Demonstration–Not For Sale printed on sleeve)
Also see Band Aid, Boy George

CULTURE CLUB
Karma Chameleon

CUMMINGS, BOB
(Actor)
See Wayne Newton (Stagecoach To Cheyenne)

CUMMINGS, BURTON
BREAK IT TO THEM GENTLY/Roll With The Punches .... (Portrait 6-70016)   1.25   5.00   78
YOU SAVED MY SOUL .... (Alfa 7008)   1.00   4.00   81
EXTENDED PLAYS
MY OWN WAY TO ROCK .... (CBS AE7-1128 AE7-1129)   2.00   8.00   77
(Promotional issue only titled Music For Every Ear, double single release issued with two small-hole
33-1/3 RPM records. Also includes one song each by Joan Baez, Cheap Trick, Crawler, Ram Jam, and Dennis
Wilson.)
MY OWN WAY TO ROCK/COME ON BY/
Charlemagne/Gotta Find Another Way .... (Portrait AE 7 1125)   2.00   8.00   77
(Promotional issue only)
Also see the Guess Who

BURTON CUMMINGS
MY OWN WAY TO ROCK

CUNNINGHAM
NORMA JEAN WANTS TO BE A MOVIE STAR/Cross My Mind .... (Capitol 7005)   1.00   4.00   74

CURBSTONES, THE
SCRUMPDILLYISHUS LAND .... (MGM Special Products PK-1010)   1.50   6.00   73
(This appears to be a promotional tie-in with Dairy Queen)

PK-1010   THE CURBSTONES
Scrumpdillyishus Land

CURE, THE
IN BETWEEN DAYS/Stop Dead .... (Elektra 7-69604)   2.00   8.00   85
CLOSE TO ME/Sinking .... (Elektra 7-69551)   2.00   8.00   86
LET'S GO TO BED/Boys Don't Cry .... (Elektra 7-69537)   2.00   8.00   86
JUST LIKE HEAVEN/Breathe .... (Elektra 7-66793)   1.50   6.00   87
WHY CAN'T I BE YOU?/A Japanese Dream .... (Elektra 7-69474)   1.50   6.00   87
JUST LIKE HEAVEN/Breathe .... (Elektra 7-69443)   1.25   5.00   87
HOT HOT HOT!!!/Hey You!!! (Remix) .... (Elektra 7-69424)   1.25   5.00   87
FASCINATION STREET/Babble .... (Elektra 7-69300)   1.25   5.00   89

THE CURE · LET'S GO TO BED

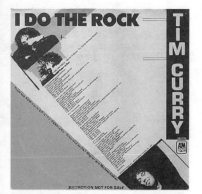

CURIOSITY KILLED THE CAT
DOWN TO EARTH/Down To Earth (Instrumental)	(Mercury 888-167-7)	.75	3.00	86
MISFIT/Man	(Mercury 888 674-7)	.75	3.00	87
ORDINARY DAY/Bullet	(Mercury 870 101-7)	.75	3.00	87

CURLESS, DICK
THE BARON/Good Job	(Tower 255)	2.00	8.00	66

CURRIE, CHERIE & MARIE
SINCE YOU'VE BEEN GONE/Longer Than Forever	(Capitol 4754)	2.00	8.00	79

CURRY, TIM
SWEET TRANSVESTITE/I'm Going Home	(Ode 66103)	2.50	10.00	74

(Shown as by Tim Curry and the Original Roxy Cast. From the stage musical *The Rocky Horror Show*.)

I DO THE ROCK	(A&M 2166)	3.75	15.00	79

(Promotional issue only, *Promotion Not For Sale* printed on sleeve)

WORKING ON MY TAN/On A Roll	(A&M 2353)	1.50	6.00	81

CURTOLA, BOBBY
I CRY AND CRY/Big Time Spender	(Del-Fi 4182)	5.00	20.00	62
ALADDIN/I Don't Want To Go On Without You	(Del-Fi 4185)	5.00	20.00	62

CUTTING CREW
(I JUST) DIED IN YOUR ARMS/For The Longest Time	(Virgin 7-99481)	.75	3.00	87
ONE FOR THE MOCKINGBIRD/Mirror And A Blade (Live)	(Virgin 99464-7)	.75	3.00	87
I'VE BEEN IN LOVE BEFORE/Life In A Dangerous Time	(Virgin 7-99425)	.75	3.00	87
(BETWEEN A) ROCK AND A HARD PLACE/Card House	(Virgin 7-99215)	.75	3.00	87

CYMBAL, JOHNNY
GO VW, GO/Sorrow and Pain	(DCP 1135)	7.50	30.00	65

CYMONE, ANDRE
THE DANCE ELECTRIC/	(Columbia 38-05435)	.75	3.00	85
THE DANCE ELECTRIC	(Columbia 38-05435)	1.00	4.00	85

(Promotional issue, *Demonstration–Not For Sale* printed on sleeve)

CYRKLE, THE
RED RUBBER BALL/How Can I Leave Her	(Columbia 4-43589)	6.25	25.00	66
TURN-DOWN DAY/Big, Little Woman	(Columbia 4-43729)	2.50	10.00	66
CAMARO/SS 396	(Columbia CSM-466)	7.50	30.00	67

(Promotional issue for Chevrolet. Flip side shown as by Paul Revere and the Raiders.)

I WISH YOU COULD BE HERE	(Columbia 4-43965)	2.50	10.00	67

D

D'ABO, MARYAM
(Actress)

See the Pretenders (*If There Was A Man*)

D.A.D
SLEEPING MY DAY AWAY	(Warner Bros. 22775-7)	.75	3.00	89

DADDY BOB
WELCOME HOME ELVIS/Poppa's Gone	(Bertram-International 1835)	2.50	10.00	77

(Originally issued with insert picturing Elvis Presley)

DAHL, STEVE, & TEENAGE RADIATION
DO YOU THINK I'M DISCO/Coho Lip Blues	(Ovation 1132)	1.25	5.00	79

DAILY, E.G.
LOVE IN THE SHADOWS/Little Toy	(A&M 2862)	.75	3.00	85
SAY IT, SAY IT/Don't Let Them Take The Child Away	(A&M 2825)	.75	3.00	86
MIND OVER MATTER/Mind Over Matter (Instrumental)	(Chrysalis VS4-43152)	.75	3.00	87

Also see Cruzados (*Time For Waiting*)

DAKIS, SOPHIE SARA
OLDER WOMAN/Dear Johnny	(CBS ZS4-04525)	.75	3.00	84

DAL BELLO, LISA
PRETTY GIRLS	(Talisman US-1)	1.50	6.00	78

(Promotional issue only, fold-out hard cover)

SHE WANTS TO KNOW	(Capitol 5006)	1.00	4.00	81

DALE, CYNTHIA
(Actress)

See Cheryl Lynn (*At Last You're Mine*), Bonnie Pointer (*The Beast In Me*)

DALE, DICK, AND THE DEL-TONES
ENLISTMENT TWIST	(Overland 1301/2)	7.50	30.00	62

(Promotional issue only for the United States Army. Shown as by Dick Dale [and His Del-Tones] & Francine York [Honorary Army Recruiter])

PEPPERMINT MAN/Open End Interview/Misirlou	(Capitol PRO-2320)	25.00	50.00	63

(Promotional issue only for Compact 33 Single)

KING OF THE SURF GUITARS/Hava Nagila	(Capitol 4963)	7.50	30.00	63
WE'LL NEVER HEAR THE END OF IT/The Fairest Of Them All	(Yes 7014)	5.00	20.00	63
PIPELINE	(Columbia 38-07340)	1.25	5.00	87

(Shown as by Stevie Ray Vaughan & Dick Dale, both pictured. From the motion picture *Back To The Beach*.)

DALLAS
(Television Series)

See Floyd Cramer (*Theme From Dallas*), Crystal Gayle (*Makin' Up For Lost Time*), Gary Morris (*Makin' Up For Lost Time*)

DALTON, BOB
MAMA CALL ME HOME	(Mega 3)	2.00	8.00	70

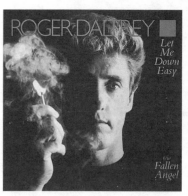

DALTON, TIMOTHY
(Actor)
    See the Pretenders (If There Was A Man)

DALTREY, ROGER
FREE ME/McVicar	(Polydor 2105)	1.25	5.00	80
WALKING IN MY SLEEP/Somebody Told Me	(Atlantic 7-89704)	1.00	4.00	84
AFTER THE FIRE/It Don't Satisfy Me	(Atlantic 7-89491)	1.00	4.00	85
LET ME DOWN EASY/Fallen Angel	(Atlantic 7-89471)	1.00	4.00	85
QUICKSILVER LIGHTNING/Love Me Like You Do	(Atlantic 7-89457)	1.00	4.00	86

    (From the motion picture Quicksilver, Daltrey pictured on front and Kevin Bacon on back)
    Also see the Who

DAMIAN, MICHAEL
SHE DID IT	(Legrand 007)	1.00	4.00	81
COVER OF LOVE/Cover Of Love (Instrumental)	(A&M/Cypress YY-1430)	.75	3.00	89

DAMITA JO
I'LL BE THERE/Love Laid Its Hands On Me	(Mercury 71840)	2.50	10.00	61
DANCE WITH DOLLY/	(Mercury 71871)	2.00	8.00	61
I BUILT MY WORLD AROUND A DREAM/	(Mercury 71929)	2.00	8.00	62
YOU'RE NOBODY TILL SOMEBODY LOVES YOU/	(Mercury 71944)	2.00	8.00	62
TENNESSEE WALTZ/	(Mercury 72019)	2.00	8.00	62
DANCE HIM BY ME/	(Mercury 72056)	2.00	8.00	62
LITTLE THINGS/	(Mercury 72086)	2.00	8.00	62
MELANCHOLY BABY/	(Mercury 72162)	2.00	8.00	63
TOMORROW NIGHT/Silver Dollar	(Epic 5-9766)	1.50	6.00	65
IF YOU GO AWAY/	(Epic 5-10061)	1.50	6.00	66

DAMNED, THE
ALONE AGAIN OR	(MCA 53051)	1.00	4.00	87

DAMONE, VIC
FRANK AND SARAH AND NAT AND VIC SALUTE HAROLD ADAMSON	(Harold Adamson Music Co. 100)	2.50	10.00	73

    (Shown as by Frank Sinatra, Sarah Vaughan, Nat King Cole, and Vic Damone)

DANA, BILL
(Comic Actor and Writer)
THE ASTRONAUT	(Kapp 409)	2.50	10.00	61

    (Shown as by Jose Jimenez)
SHINE ON HARVEST MOON/Jingle Bells	(Kapp 434)	5.00	20.00	61

DANA, VIC
I WILL/Proud	(Dolton 51)	2.00	8.00	62
DANGER/Heart, Hand & Teardrop	(Dolton 73)	2.00	8.00	63
LOVE IS ALL WE NEED/I Need You Now	(Dolton 95)	2.00	8.00	64
GARDEN IN THE RAIN/Stairway To The Stars	(Dolton 99)	2.00	8.00	64
BRING A LITTLE SUNSHINE (TO MY HEART)/That's All	(Dolton 305)	2.00	8.00	66

DAN AND DALE
BATMAN THEME	(Tifton 45-125)	7.50	30.00	66

    (Comic book illustrations of Batman and Robin pictured)

DANCER, PRANCER & NERVOUS
THE HAPPY REINDEER/Dancer's Waltz	(Capitol 4300)	2.50	10.00	59

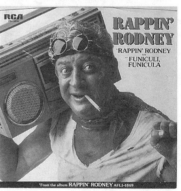

DANGERFIELD, RODNEY
RAPPIN' RODNEY/Funiculi, Funicula	(RCA PB-13656)	1.00	4.00	83

    (Shown as by Rappin' Rodney)

DANIELS, CHARLIE, BAND, THE
RIDING WITH JESSE JAMES	(A&M 2290)	1.00	4.00	80

    (Generic half sleeve for the album The Legend Of Jessse James. No artist or song title on sleeve.)
CAROLINA (I REMEMBER YOU)–LONG VERSION/ Carolina (I Remember You)–Short Version	(Epic 19-50955)	1.25	5.00	80

    (Promotional issue only, Demonstration: Not For Sale printed on sleeve)
AMERICAN FARMER/Runnin' With That Crowd	(Epic 34-05638)	.75	3.00	85
AMERICAN FARMER	(Epic 34-05638)	1.00	4.00	85

    (Promotional issue, Demonstration Only–Not For Sale printed on sleeve)
STILL HURTIN' ME	(Epic 34-05699)	.75	3.00	85
STILL HURTIN' ME	(Epic 34-05699)	1.00	4.00	85

    (Promotional issue, Demonstration Only–Not For Sale printed on sleeve)

EXTENDED PLAYS
VOLUNTEER JAM PART (1)/ Volunteer Jam contd. Part (2)/ Volunteer Jam contd. Part (3)	(Kama Sutra EP-10)	1.50	6.00	74

    (Included with the album Fire On The Mountain, issued with small-hole 45 RPM record)

DANNY & THE JUNIORS
CANDY CANE, SUGARY PLUM	(Swan 4064)	37.50	150.00	60
BACK AT THE HOP	(Swan 4082)	20.00	80.00	61

DANNY WILSON
MARY'S PRAYER/Monkey's Shiny Day	(Virgin 99465-7)	.75	3.00	87
A GIRL I USED TO KNOW/I Won't Forget	(Virgin 7-99399)	.75	3.00	87
IF EVERTHING YOU SAID WAS TRUE/I'll Be Waiting	(Virgin 7-99195)	.75	3.00	89

DANTE, RON
LET ME BRING YOU UP/How Do You Know?	(Kirshner 1010)	2.50	10.00	70

    Also see the Archies, the Cuff Links, the Detergents

DANTE, STEVEN
    See Jellybean (The Real Thing)

D'ARBY, TERENCE TRENT
IF YOU LET ME STAY/Loving You Is Another Word For Lonely	(Columbia 38-07398)	.75	3.00	87
WISHING WELL/Elevators And Hearts	(Columbia 38-07675)	.75	3.00	87

TITLE	LABEL AND NUMBER	VG	NM	YR
SIGN YOUR NAME/Greasy Chicken	(Columbia 38-07911)	.75	3.00	87
DANCE LITTLE SISTER/Dance Little Sister (Part Two)	(Columbia 38-08023)	.75	3.00	87

DARE
ABANDON/The Last Time	(A&M 1251)	.75	3.00	88

DAREDEVILS
HATE YOU/Rules, Hearts	(Sympathy For The Record Industry 436)	.75	3.00	96

(Hard cover folding sleeve issued with small hole 45 RPM record)
Also see Bad Religion (Brett Gurewitz)

DARIN, BOBBY
PLAIN JANE/While I'm Gone	(Atco 6133)	5.00	20.00	59
DREAM LOVER/Bullmoose	(Atco 6140)	5.00	20.00	59
MACK THE KNIFE/Was There A Call For Me	(Atco 6147)	5.00	20.00	59
BEYOND THE SEA/That's The Way Love Is	(Atco 6158)	5.00	20.00	60
CLEMENTINE/Tall Story	(Atco 6161)	5.00	20.00	60
WON'T YOU COME HOME, BILL BAILEY/I'll Be There	(Atco 6167)	3.75	15.00	60
BEACHCOMBER/Autumn Blues	(Atco 6173)	3.75	15.00	60
ARTIFICIAL FLOWERS/Somebody To Love	(Atco 6179)	3.75	15.00	60
CHRISTMAS AULD LANG SYNE/Child Of God	(Atco 6183)	3.75	15.00	60
LAZY RIVER/Oo-Ee Train	(Atco 6188)	3.75	15.00	61
NATURE BOY/Look For My True Love	(Atco 6196)	3.75	15.00	61
THEME FROM "COME SEPTEMBER"/Walk Bach To Me	(Atco 6200)	5.00	20.00	61

(Note the misspelling in the b-side title which should read *Walk Back To Me*. From the motion picture *Come September* starring Darin and Sandra Dee)

YOU MUST HAVE BEEN A BEAUTIFUL BABY/Sorrow Tomorrow	(Atco 6206)	3.75	15.00	61
AVE MARIA/O Come All Ye Faithful	(Atco 6211)	30.00	120.00	61
IRRESISTIBLE YOU/Multiplication	(Atco 6214)	3.75	15.00	61

(From the motion picture *Come September* starring Darin and Sandra Dee)

WHAT'D I SAY (PARTS 1 & 2)	(Atco 6221)	3.75	15.00	62
IF A MAN ANSWERS/A True, True Love	(Capitol 4837)	3.00	12.00	62

(From the motion picture *If A Man Answers* starring Darin and Sandra Dee)

YOU'RE THE REASON I'M LIVING/Now You're Gone	(Capitol 4897)	3.00	12.00	63
18 YELLOW ROSES/Not For Me	(Capitol 4970)	3.00	12.00	63
SALLY WAS A GOOD OLD GIRL/Who Can I Count On?	(Capitol PRO-2354)	5.00	20.00	63
WHEN I GET HOME/Lonely Road	(Capitol 5443)	3.00	12.00	65
LONG LINE RIDER/Change	(Direction 350)	3.00	12.00	69
BEYOND THE SEA/Mack The Knife	(Atlantic 89166)	.75	3.00	87

(From the motion picture *The Big Town*)

DARK HORSE RECORDS
GENERIC DARK HORSE RECORDS HALF SLEEVE	(Dark Horse no #)	.50	2.00	76

(Issued with any 45 on Dark Horse from 1976-1987, no song titles listed)

DARK SHADOWS
(Television Series)
See the First Theremin Era

DARLING LILI
(Motion Picture)
See Henry Mancini (*Whistling Away The Dark*)

DARRELL, JOHNNY
SON OF HICKORY HOLLER'S TRAMP	(United Artists 50235)	1.50	6.00	67

DARREN, JIMMY
(Actor)
THERE'S NO SUCH THING	(Colpix 102)	5.00	20.00	58

(From the motion picture *Gidget* starring Darren and Sandra Dee)

ANGEL FACE	(Colpix 119)	5.00	20.00	58
BECAUSE THEY'RE YOUNG	(Colpix 142)	5.00	20.00	60
GOODBYE CRUEL WORLD	(Colpix 609)	3.75	15.00	61

(Shown as by James Darren)

DAS DAMEN
SAD MILE/Making Time	(Sub Pop 39)	3.00	12.00	89
NOON DAYLIGHT/Damen Dance	(Twin Tone 89139)	2.00	8.00	89

DATING GAME, THE
(Television Series)
See Herb Alpert and the Tijuana Brass (*Spanish Flea*; b-side for *What Now My Love*)

DAVID & DAVID
WELCOME TO THE BOOMTOWN/A Rock For The Forgotten	(A&M 2857)	.75	3.00	86
AIN'T SO EASY/Swimming In The Ocean	(A&M 2905)	.75	3.00	86

DAVID & JONATHAN
MICHELLE/How Bitter The Taste Of Love	(Capitol 5563)	3.00	12.00	66
SPEAK HER NAME/I Know	(Capitol 5625)	2.00	8.00	66

Also see Blue Mink (Roger Cook), Roger Cook

DAVIDSON, JOHN
I CAN'T HELP THIS FEELING I FEEL/I Still Send Her Flowers	(Columbia 4-43531)	2.00	8.00	65
I'LL ALWAYS REMEMBER/Daydream	(Columbia 4-44005)	2.00	8.00	66

DAVIDSON, MICHAEL
TURN IT UP	(Sire 28219-7)	.75	3.00	87

(From the motion picture *Who's That Girl*)

DAVIES, DAVE
IMAGINATIONS REAL/Wild Man	(RCA PB-12089)	5.00	20.00	80

Also see the Kinks

DAVIES, GAIL
JAGGED EDGE OF A BROKEN HEART	(RCA JK-13912)	1.00	4.00	84

(Poster sleeve)

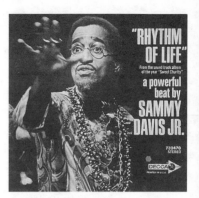

DAVINCI, PAUL
EVERY SINGLE WORD (LULLABY FOR GROWN-UPS)/Take Me Now .... (Epic 8-50336)   1.00   4.00   77
    (1/2" die-cut hole in center of sleeve instead of the standard 3-1/4" hole for half sleeves)

DAVIS, ANNIE
(Actress Ann B. Davis, played the maid Alice on the television series The Brady Bunch)
ANNIE OAKLEY .... (RCA Victor Bluebird WBY-88)   6.25   25.00   60s

DAVIS, BETTE
WHATEVER HAPPENED TO BABY JANE/I've Written A Letter To Daddy .... (MGM K13107)   3.75   15.00   62

DAVIS, JIM
(Actor)
    See Floyd Cramer (Theme From Dallas)

DAVIS, JIMMY, & JUNCTION
KICK THE WALL/Over The Top .... (MCA/QMI 53107)   .75   3.00   87
JUST A LITTLE BIT/ .... (MCA/QMI 53240)   .75   3.00   87

DAVIS, MAC
WHOEVER FINDS THIS, I LOVE YOU .... (Columbia 4-45117)   1.50   6.00   70

DAVIS, MARTHA
DON'T TELL ME THE TIME .... (Capitol B-44057)   .75   3.00   87
TELL IT TO THE MOON .... (Capitol B-44114)   .75   3.00   87
    Also see the Motels

DAVIS, MARY
STEPPIN' OUT/I'm Gonna Love You Better .... (Tabu ZS4-07612)   .75   3.00   87

DAVIS, PAUL
    See Marie Osmond (You're Still New To Me)

DAVIS, SAMMY, JR.
ME & MY SHADOW/Sam's Song .... (Reprise 20,128)   6.25   25.00   62
    (A-side shown as by Frank Sinatra and Sammy Davis, Jr., b-side by Dean Martin and Sammy Davis, Jr., all
    three pictured)
RHYTHM OF LIFE .... (Decca 732470)   2.50   10.00   69
    (From the motion picture Sweet Charity)
YOU RASCAL YOU .... (MGM PK-1013)   2.50   10.00
    (Promotional issue only issued with one-sided record)
THE HOUSE I LIVE IN .... (A.L.B.B. 38032)   2.50   10.00
    Also see Lena Horne (I Wish I'd Met You)

DAVIS, SKEETER
I CAN'T STAY MAD AT YOU/It Was Only A Heart .... (RCA Victor 47-8219)   2.00   8.00   63
    Also see Chet Atkins (Chet's Tune)

DAVIS, SPENCER, GROUP, THE
TIME SELLER .... (United Artists 50202)   3.00   12.00   67
    Also see Traffic (Steve Winwood), Steve Winwood

DAVY D.
FEEL FOR YOU .... (Def Jam 38-07420)   .75   3.00   87
OHHH GIRL .... (Def Jam 38-07712)   .75   3.00   87

DAY, DENNIS
THE WIND IN THE WILLOWS/Let There Be Peace .... (Daydream 100)   1.25   5.00
MY IRISH ROSE/WHEN IRISH EYES ARE SMILING/
    Clancy Lowered The Boom .... (Glendale 45-102)   1.25   5.00

DAY, DORIS
EVERBODY LOVES A LOVER/Instant Love .... (Columbia 4-41195)   3.75   15.00   58
TUNNEL OF LOVE/Runaway, Skidaddle, Skidoo .... (Columbia 4-41252)   3.75   15.00   58
PILLOW TALK/Inspiration .... (Columbia 4-41463)   3.75   15.00   59
    (From the motion picture Pillow Talk, Doris Day, Rock Hudson, Tony Randall, and Thelma Ritter pictured on
    back)
PLEASE DON'T EAT THE DAISIES/ .... (Columbia 4-41630)   3.75   15.00   61
    (From the motion picture Please Don't Eat The Daisies)

DAY, MORRIS
THE OAK TREE .... (Warner Bros. 28899-7)   .75   3.00   85
COLOR OF SUCCESS .... (Warner Bros. 28809-7)   .75   3.00   85
LOVE ADDICTION .... (Warner Bros. 28734-7)   .75   3.00   85
THE CHARACTER .... (Warner Bros. 28729-7)   .75   3.00   86
FISHNET/Maybe .... (Warner Bros. 28201-7)   .75   3.00   87
DAYDREAMING .... (Warner Bros. 27917-7)   .75   3.00   88
LOVE IS A GAME .... (Warner Bros. 27831-7)   .75   3.00   88
ARE YOU READY .... (Warner Bros. 27642-7)   .75   3.00   88
    Also see Vanity (Mechanical Emotion)

DAY, TERRY
(a.k.a. Terry Melcher, son of Doris Day)
I WAITED TOO LONG/That's All I Want .... (Columbia 4-42427)   10.00   40.00   63
BE A SOLDIER/I Love You, Betty .... (Columbia 4-42678)   10.00   40.00   63

DAYLIGHTERS, THE
SOMETHING IS WRONG/I'll Never Let You Go .... (Domino 904)   12.50   50.00   59
    (Single sheet insert, not a true picture sleeve)

DAYNE, TAYLOR
TELL IT TO MY HEART/Tell It To My Heart .... (Arista 9612)   .75   3.00   87
PROVE YOUR LOVE/Upon The Journey's End .... (Arista 9676)   .75   3.00   88
I'LL ALWAYS LOVE YOU/Where Does That Boy Hang Out .... (Arista 9700)   .75   3.00   88
DON'T RUSH ME/In The Darkness .... (Arista 9722)   .75   3.00   88
WITH EVERY BEAT OF MY HEART/All I Ever Wanted .... (Arista 9895)   .75   3.00   89
LOVE WILL LEAD YOU BACK/You Meant The World To Me .... (Arista 9938)   .75   3.00   90

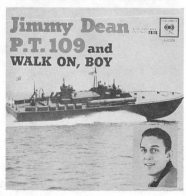

DAY OF THE DEAD
(Motion Picture)
> See Sputzy Sparacino and Delilah (*The World Inside Your Eyes*)

DAYS OF OUR LIVES
(Television Soap Opera)
> Related see Gloria Loring, the Soaps and Hearts Ensemble

DAYS OF WINE AND ROSES
(Motion Picture)
> See Four Saints (*Days Of Wine And Roses*), Henry Mancini (*Days Of Wine And Roses*)

dB'S, THE

Title	Label and Number	VG	NM	YR
IF AND WHEN/(I Thought) You Wanted To Know	(Car 7)	3.75	15.00	78
(Individually numbered, shown as by Chris Stamey and the dB's)				
BLACK AND WHITE/Soul Kiss	(Shake 100)	1.50	6.00	80
I LIE/Sharon	(I.R.S. 53198)	1.00	4.00	87

Also see Peter Holsapple, Holly Robinson (b-side of *21 Jump Street*), Chris Stamey

DEAD BOYS, THE

Title	Label and Number	VG	NM	YR
SONIC REDUCER/Down In Flames	(Sire 1004)	3.00	12.00	77
TELL ME/Not Anymore/Ain't Nothin' To Do	(Sire 6038)	3.00	12.00	78

Also see Stiv Bators, the Lords of the New Church

DEAD KENNEDYS

Title	Label and Number	VG	NM	YR
CALIFORNIA ÜBER ALLES/The Man With The Dogs	(Alternative Tentacles 95-41)	3.75	15.00	79
(Originally issued with lyric insert)				
CALIFORNIA ÜBER ALLES/The Man With The Dogs	(Optional Music 2)	3.75	15.00	79
HOLIDAY IN CAMBODIA/Policetruck	(I.R.S./Faulty 9016)	2.50	10.00	80
HOLIDAY IN CAMBODIA/Policetruck	(Optional Music 4)	2.50	10.00	80
(Originally issued with lyric insert)				
NAZI PUNKS FUCK OFF/ Moral Majority	(Alternative Tentacles/Subterranean SUB 24/VIRUS 6)	1.50	6.00	81
(Screenprinted on two separate sheets of clear plastic with armband, packaged in a clear plastic sleeve, not a true picture sleeve. Issued with small hole 45 RPM record.)				
TOO DRUNK TO FUCK/The Prey	(I.R.S./Faulty VIRUS 2)	2.00	8.00	81
(Issued with lyric insert and small hole 45 RPM record)				
BLEED FOR ME/Life Sentence	(Alternative Tentacles VIRUS 23)	2.00	8.00	82
HALLOWEEN/Saturday Night Holocaust	(Alternative Tentacles VIRUS 28)	2.00	8.00	82

Also see Jello Biafra

DEAD OR ALIVE

Title	Label and Number	VG	NM	YR
LOVER COME BACK TO ME/Far Too Hard	(Epic 34-05607)	.75	3.00	85
LOVER COME BACK TO ME	(Epic 34-05607)	1.00	4.00	85
(Promotional issue, *Demonstration–Not For Sale* printed on sleeve)				
BRAND NEW LOVER/In Too Deep (Live)	(Epic 34-06374)	.75	3.00	86
BRAND NEW LOVER	(Epic 34-06374)	1.00	4.00	86
(Promotional issue, *Demonstration–Not For Sale* printed on sleeve)				
SOMETHING IN MY HOUSE/D.J. Hit That Button	(Epic 34-07022)	.75	3.00	86
SOMETHING IN MY HOUSE	(Epic 34-07022)	1.00	4.00	86
(Promotional issue, *Demonstration–Not For Sale* printed on sleeve)				

DEAF SCHOOL

Title	Label and Number	VG	NM	YR
WHAT A WAY TO END IT ALL/Hi Jo Hi (Record 1), CAPALDI'S CAFE/Taxi (Record 2)	(Warner Bros. PRO 675)	1.00	4.00	85
(Promotional issue only, hard cover gatefold double-pocket, double single release. Issued with two small hole 33-1/3 RPM records.)				

DEAL, BILL, & THE RONDELLS

Title	Label and Number	VG	NM	YR
I'VE BEEN HURT	(Heritage 812)	3.00	12.00	69
SWINGIN' TIGHT	(Heritage 818)	3.00	12.00	69

DEAN, DEBBIE

Title	Label and Number	VG	NM	YR
EVERYBODY'S TALKING ABOUT MY BABY/I Cried All Night	(Motown 1025)	20.00	80.00	62

DEAN, JAMES

Title	Label and Number	VG	NM	YR
JUNGLE RHYTHM/Dean's Lament	(Romeo 100)	20.00	80.00	55
(Shown as by James Dean on Conga Drums and Bob Romeo on Flute in an Ad-Lib Jam Session)				

Also see Ray Heindorf (*Tribute To James Dean*), Mantovani (*Let Me Be Loved*), Art Mooney (*Rebel Without A Cause*)

DEAN, JIMMY

Title	Label and Number	VG	NM	YR
FALSE PRIDE/	(Mercury 70691)	3.00	12.00	56
LITTLE SANDY SLEIGHFOOT/When They Ring The Golden Bells	(Columbia 4-41025)	5.00	20.00	57
SING ALONG/	(Columbia 4-41391)	2.00	8.00	59
BIG BAD JOHN/ I Won't Go Huntin' With You Jake (But I'll Go Chasin' Wimmin)	(Columbia 4-42175)	2.00	8.00	61
DEAR IVAN/Smoke, Smoke, Smoke That Cigarette	(Columbia 4-42259)	2.00	8.00	62
TO A SLEEPING BEAUTY/The Cajun Queen	(Columbia 4-42282)	2.00	8.00	62
P.T. 109/Walk On, Boy	(Columbia 4-42338)	2.00	8.00	62
STEEL MEN/Litty Bitty Big John	(Columbia 4-42483)	2.00	8.00	62
PLEASE PASS THE BISCUITS/Little Black Book	(Columbia 4-42529)	2.00	8.00	62
A DAY THAT CHANGED THE WORLD/Gonna Raise A Ruckus Tonight	(Columbia 4-42600)	2.00	8.00	62
(*A Day That Changed The World* is listed first as the a-side on the sleeve but it was *Gonna Raise A Ruckus Tonight* that made it to #73 in Billboard's Top 100)				
MILE LONG TRAIN/This Ole House	(Columbia 4-42738)	2.00	8.00	63
THE FUNNIEST THING I EVER HEARD/	(Columbia 4-42861)	2.00	8.00	63
I REALLY DON'T WANT TO KNOW/	(Columbia 4-42934)	2.00	8.00	63
YES PATRICIA THERE IS A SANTA CLAUS/	(Columbia 4-43457)	2.00	8.00	66

Also see Chet Atkins (*Chet's Tune*)

DEAR HEART
(Motion Picture)
> See Jack Jones (*Dear Heart*), Henry Mancini (*Dear Heart*)

DEAUVILLE, RONNIE

Title	Label and Number	VG	NM	YR
LAURA/It Wasn't Much Of A Town	(Era 1056)	7.50	30.00	58

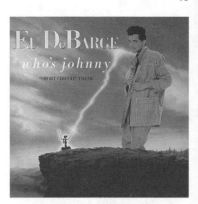

DeBARGE

RHYTHM OF THE NIGHT .... (Gordy 1770GF) .75 3.00 86
(From the motion picture *The Last Dragon*)
WHO'S HOLDING DONNA NOW/Be My Lady .... (Gordy 1793GF) .75 3.00 85
    Also see Chico DeBarge, El DeBarge

DeBARGE, CHICO

TALK TO ME .... (Gordy 1858GF) .75 3.00 86
THE GIRL NEXT DOOR/You're Much Too Fast .... (Motown 1875MF) .75 3.00 87
THE GIRL NEXT DOOR .... (Motown 1875MF) 1.00 4.00 87
    (Promotional issue, *For Promotional Use Only Not For Sale* printed on sleeve)
KISS SERIOUS/Shame Shame .... (Motown 1935MF) .75 3.00 87

DeBARGE, EL

YOU WEAR IT WELL/Baby Won't Cha Come Quick .... (Gordy 1804GF) .75 3.00 85
    (Shown as by El DeBarge with DeBarge)
THE HEART IS NOT SO SMART .... (Gordy 1822GF) .75 3.00 85
    (Shown as by El DeBarge with DeBarge)
WHO'S JOHNNY .... (Gordy 1842GF) .75 3.00 86
    (From the motion picture *Short Circuit*)
LOVE ALWAYS .... (Gordy 1857GF) .75 3.00 86
LOVE ALWAYS .... (Gordy 1857GF) 1.00 4.00 86
    (Promotional issue, *For Promotional Use Only Not For Sale* printed on sleeve)
SOMEONE .... (Gordy 1867GF) .75 3.00 86
SOMEONE .... (Gordy 1867GF) 1.00 4.00 86
    (Promotional issue, *For Promotional Use Only Not For Sale* printed on sleeve)
THE SECRET GARDEN .... (Qwest 19992) .75 3.00 90
    (Shown as by Quincy Jones, Al B. Sure, James Ingram, El DeBarge, and Barry White)
    Also see DeBarge

DE BURGH, CHRIS

I LOVE THE NIGHT (THE ECSTASY OF FLIGHT)/Moonlight And Vodka .... (A&M 2674) 1.00 4.00 84
THE LADY IN RED/The Vision .... (A&M 2848) 1.00 4.00 86
THE SPIRIT OF MAN/The Vision .... (A&M 2848) 1.00 4.00 86
    (This sleeve shares the same catalog number and b-side as *The Lady In Red*. The existence of a 45 with these
    titles and catalog number is unknown.)

DEDICATIONS, THE

WHY DON'T YOU WRITE ME?/Boppin' Around .... (Card 335/6) 12.50 50.00 61

DEE, JOEY, AND THE STARLITERS

HEY, LET'S TWIST/Roly Poly .... (Roulette 4408) 5.00 20.00 62
SHOUT PART 1 & 2 .... (Roulette 4416) 5.00 20.00 62
WHAT KIND OF LOVE IS THIS?/Wing Ding .... (Roulette 4438) 5.00 20.00 62
I LOST MY BABY/Keep Your Mind On What You're Doin' ..... (Roulette 4456) 5.00 20.00 62
PEPPERMINT TWIST .... (Vaseline Hair Tonic R-12) 5.00 20.00 62
    (Sleeve states *Joey Dee Teaches You How To Dance The Authentic Peppermint Twist*. Add $5 if insert is included.)
LORRAINE/The Girl I Walk To School .... (Bonus 7009) 15.00 60.00 63

DEE, JOHNNY

SITTIN' IN THE BALCONY .... (Colonial 430) 10.00 40.00 57
    Also see John D. Loudermilk

DEE, KIKI

THE DAY WILL COME BETWEEN SUNDAY & MONDAY .... (Tamla 54193) 2.00 8.00 70
DON'T GO BREAKING MY HEART/Snow Queen .... (Rocket/MCA PIG-40585) 1.00 4.00 76
    (Shown as by Elton John and Kiki Dee)

DEE, SANDRA

(Actress)
WHEN I FALL IN LOVE/Dear Johnny .... (Decca 9-31042) 5.00 20.00 60
DO IT WHILE YOU'RE YOUNG/Questions .... (Decca 9-31063) 5.00 20.00 60

DEE, TOMMY, WITH CAROL KAY AND THE TEEN-AIRES

    See Waylon Jennings

DEE JAY AND THE RUNAWAYS

LOVE TENDER LOVE/While You Were Sleeping .... (Dee Jay 101) 1.25 5.00 82
    (Issued with an insert which adds $3 to the value)

DEEP FOREST

SWEET LULLABY/Forest Hymn .... (Sony 36 77371) .50 2.00 94

DEEP PURPLE

HUSH/One More Rainy Day .... (Tetragrammaton 1503) 7.50 30.00 68
KENTUCKY WOMAN/Hard Road .... (Tetragrammaton 1508) 3.75 15.00 68
KNOCKIN' AT YOUR BACK DOOR/Wasted Sunsets .... (Mercury 880 477-7) 1.00 4.00 84
CALL OF THE WILD/Dead Or Alive .... (Mercury 885 617-7) .75 3.00 87
    Also see Rainbow (Ritchie Blackmore), Whitesnake (Jon Lord, Ian Paice). Roger Glover (of Rainbow) was with Deep Purple from 1969-73 and
    David Coverdale (of Whitesnake) was a member from 1973-1976.

DEEP RIVER BOYS

I DON'T KNOW WHY .... (Gallant 2001) 6.25 25.00 59

DEES, RICK

MR. BIGFOOT .... (Stax 3207) 1.25 5.00 78
    (Record shows title as *Bigfoot*)
GET NEKKED/Eat My Shorts .... (Atlantic 89601) 1.25 5.00 84

DEF LEPPARD

PHOTOGRAPH/Action! Not Words .... (Mercury 811 215-7) 1.50 6.00 83
BRINGIN' ON THE HEARTBREAK/Me & My Wine .... (Mercury 818 779-7) 1.25 5.00 84
WOMEN/Tear It Down .... (Mercury 888 757-7) 1.00 4.00 87
ANIMAL/I Wanna Be Your Hero .... (Mercury 888 832-7) 1.00 4.00 87
HYSTERIA/Ride Into The Sun .... (Mercury 870-004-7) 1.00 4.00 87
POUR SOME SUGAR ON ME/Ring Of Fire .... (Mercury 870 298-7) 1.00 4.00 88

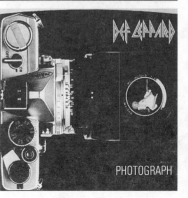

PHOTOGRAPH

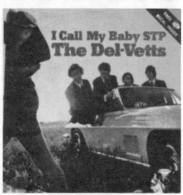

TITLE	LABEL AND NUMBER	VG	NM	YR
LOVE BITES / Billy's Got A Gun (Live)	(Mercury 870 402-7)	1.00	4.00	88
ARMAGEDDON IT / Release Me	(Mercury 870 692-7)	1.00	4.00	88
(B-side shown as by Stumpus Maximus and the Good Ol' Boys. Stumpus pictured on the back.)				
ROCKET / Women (Live)	(Mercury 872-614-7)	1.00	4.00	89
(Reportedly, Mercury planned to release 9 different picture sleeves that when put together, as a puzzle, would recreate the cover of the album *Hysteria*. Only the last 7 sleeves listed here were produced.)				

DeFRANCO FAMILY, FEATURING TONY DeFRANCO, THE

HEARTBEAT, IT'S A LOVEBEAT	(20th Century 2030)	1.25	5.00	73
ABRA-CA-DABRA	(20th Century 2070)	1.25	5.00	73
SAVE THE LAST DANCE FOR ME	(20th Century 2088)	1.25	5.00	74
WRITE ME A LETTER	(20th Century 2128)	1.25	5.00	74

DeHAVEN, PENNY

BAYOU LULLABY	(Elektra 46645)	.75	3.00	80
(From the motion picture *Bronco Billy*, illustration featuring Clint Eastwood pictured on back)				

DÉJÀ

YOU AND ME TONIGHT /	(Virgin 7-99422)	.75	3.00	87
THAT'S WHERE YOU'LL FIND ME /	(Virgin 7-99375)	.75	3.00	87
MADE TO BE TOGETHER / Sexy Dancer	(Virgin 7-99226)	.75	3.00	89

DELBERT & GLEN
EXTENDED PLAYS

LUCKY BOY (YOUR RAMBLIN' DAYS ARE THROUGH)	(Atlantic PR 195)	1.25	5.00	73
(Promotional issue only titled *Something For Nothing*. Also includes one song each, the titles are not listed on sleeve, by Daryl Hall & John Oates, John Prine, and Barnaby Bye.)				

DEL CADES, THE

WORLD'S FAIR U.S.A. / (It Takes) Two To Fall In Love	(United Sound 175)	10.00	40.00	64

DEL FUEGOS, THE

I CAN'T SLEEP / I Always Call Her Back	(Czech 71)	2.00	8.00	83
I STILL WANT YOU	(Warner Bros./Slash 28822-7)	.75	3.00	85
I'LL SLEEP WITH YOU (CHA CHA D'AMOUR)	(Warner Bros./Slash 28262-7)	.75	3.00	87

DELILAH & SPUTZY
See Sputzy Sparacino and Delilah

DELITE, DERRICK
See Paula Abdul (*Opposites Attract*)

DEL-LORDS, THE

SOLDIER'S HOME / No Waitress No More	(EMI America B-8314)	.75	3.00	86

DELLS, THE

SHY GIRL / What Do We Prove?	(Vee-Jay 595)	5.00	20.00	64

DEL SATINS, THE

FEELIN' NO PAIN / Who Cares?	(Columbia 4-42802)	10.00	40.00	63

DeLUISE, DOM
(Comic Actor)
See Lionel Newman (*The Silent Movie March*)

DEL-VETTS, THE

I CALL MY BABY STP	(Dunwich 142)	6.25	25.00	66
(Originally issued with an STP decal)				

DEL-VIKINGS

THE SUN	(Alpine 66)	18.75	75.00	60

DeMARCO, RALPH

OLD SHEP / More Than Riches	(Guaranteed 202)	5.00	20.00	59

DEMENSIONS, THE

MY FOOLISH HEART	(Coral 62344)	7.50	30.00	63

DeMORNAY, REBECCA
(Actress)

OH JIMMY / Little Red Corvette	(MCA 52534)	1.00	4.00	85

DENIMS, THE

SALTY DOG / Salty Dog Man	(Cavort 122333)	3.00	12.00	63

DE NIRO, ROBERT
(Actor)
See Ennio Morricone (*Theme From The Mission*)

DENNY, MARTIN

A TASTE OF HONEY / The Brighter Side	(Liberty 55470)	1.50	6.00	62

DENTISTS, THE
BOXED SET

GAS / TREMENDOUS MANY / This Is Not My Flag / Faces On Stone	(EastWest 7-98362-A)	.50	2.00	93
(Part of a 3 record boxed set. This sleeve titled *Big Bang*, no individual song titles on sleeve. Complete set, including cardboard folder, valued at $10.)				
SPACE MAN / SORRY IS NOT ENOUGH / Apple Beast / Water For A Man On Fire	(EastWest 7-98362-B)	.50	2.00	93
(Part of a 3 record boxed set. This sleeve titled *Red Shift*, no individual song titles on sleeve. Complete set, including cardboard folder, valued at $10 near mint.)				
YOUR KIND OF DAY / THE QUALITY OF MERCY / Ace Of Spades / Eyes	(EastWest 7-98362-C)	.50	2.00	93
(Part of a 3 record boxed set. This sleeve titled *Black Holes*, no individual song titles on sleeve. Complete set, including cardboard folder, valued at $10 near mint.)				

DENVER, JOHN

ROCKY MOUNTAIN HIGH	(RCA 2008)	3.75	15.00	72
(Promotional issue only)				

		VG	NM	YR
HAVE YOURSELF A MERRY LITTLE CHRISTMAS/WE WISH YOU A MERRY CHRISTMAS/				
Baby Just Like You .... (RCA PB-11767)		1.25	5.00	79
(Shown as by John Denver & the Muppets)				
AUTOGRAPH/The Mountain Song .... (RCA PB 11915)		1.25	5.00	80
DREAMLAND EXPRESS .... (RCA PB-14227)		1.00	4.00	85
FLYING OR ME .... (Cherry Mountain 02)		1.25	5.00	86
COUNTRY GIRL IN PARIS/Bread And Roses .... (Allegiance B-75720)		1.00	4.00	88
FOR YOU/Rocky Mountain High .... (Legacy 33 77993)		.75	3.00	95
Also see the New Christy Minstrels				

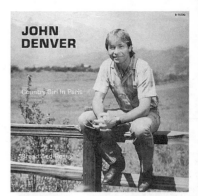

JOHN DENVER
Country Girl In Paris
Bread And Roses

DEODATO

		VG	NM	YR
RHAPSODY IN BLUE/Super Strut .... (CTI OJ 16)		1.00	4.00	86

DEPECHE MODE

		VG	NM	YR
EVERYTHING COUNTS/Work Hard .... (Sire 29482-7)		2.00	8.00	83
PEOPLE ARE PEOPLE/In Your Memory .... (Sire 29221-7)		1.50	6.00	84
MASTER AND SERVANT .... (Sire 28918-7)		1.50	6.00	84
(Hard cover)				
SHAKE THE DISEASE/Flexible .... (Sire 28835-7)		1.25	5.00	85
A QUESTION OF LUST/Christmas Island .... (Sire 28697-7)		1.00	4.00	86
BUT NOT TONIGHT .... (Sire 28564-7)		1.00	4.00	86
STRANGELOVE/FPMIP .... (Sire 28366-7)		1.00	4.00	87
NEVER LET ME DOWN AGAIN/Pleasure, Little Treasure .... (Sire 28189-7)		1.00	4.00	87
ROUTE 66/BEHIND THE WHEEL/Behind The Wheel .... (Sire 27991-7)		1.00	4.00	88
STRANGELOVE/Nothing .... (Sire 27777-7)		1.00	4.00	88
Vince Clarke left the group in 1981 and later formed Yazoo and Erasure				

DEPECHE MODE
A QUESTION OF LUST

DEREK & CYNDI

		VG	NM	YR
YOU BRING OUT THE BEST IN ME .... (Thunder ZS8 5251)		1.50	6.00	74

DEREK, BO

(Actress)

See Henry Mancini (Ravel's Bolero)

DERN, BRUCE

(Actor)

		VG	NM	YR
MIDDLE AGE CRAZY .... (Backstage 144)		1.50	6.00	80
(Promotional issue only)				

DERRINGER, RICK

See Barbra Streisand (Left In The Dark), "Weird Al" Yankovic (Ricky)

DES BARRES, MICHAEL

		VG	NM	YR
MONEY DON'T COME EASY .... (Sire 29221-7)		.75	3.00	86
TOO GOOD TO BE BAD/Is There Someone Else? .... (MCA 52938)		.75	3.00	86

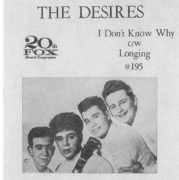

THE DESIRES
I Don't Know Why
c/w
Longing
#195
20th FOX Record Corporation

DESERTERS

		VG	NM	YR
ALIEN/Innervisions .... (Capitol 72856)		.75	3.00	81

DeSHANNON, JACKIE

		VG	NM	YR
FADED LOVE/Dancing Silhouettes .... (Liberty 55526)		12.50	50.00	63

DESIRES, THE

		VG	NM	YR
I DON'T KNOW WHY/Longing .... (20th Fox 195)		10.00	40.00	60

DESMOND, JOHNNY

		VG	NM	YR
TOGETHERNESS .... (Coral 61410)		2.50	10.00	55

DETERGENTS, THE

		VG	NM	YR
LEADER OF THE LAUNDROMAT/Ulcers .... (Roulette 4590)		7.50	30.00	64
Also see the Archies (Ron Dante), the Cuff Links (Ron Dante), Ron Dante				

DEVICE

		VG	NM	YR
HANGING ON A HEART ATTACK/				
Hanging On A Heart Attack (extended version) .... (Chrysalis VS4-42996)		.75	3.00	86
Also see Animotion (Paul Engemann), Holly Knight, Giorgio Moroder (Paul Engemann on Reach Out), Spider (Holly Knight)				

MARK KNOPFLER • WILLY DEVILLE
THEME FROM THE PRINCESS BRIDE
STORYBOOK LOVE

DEVILLE, WILLY

		VG	NM	YR
STORYBOOK LOVE/The Friends' Song .... (Warner Bros. 28242-7)		1.00	4.00	87
(Shown as by Mark Knopfler and Willy DeVille. From the motion picture The Princess Bride, Cary Elwes and Robin Wright pictured.)				

DEVILS ANVIL

		VG	NM	YR
KARKADON/Hala Laya .... (Columbia # unknown)		5.00	20.00	66

DEVO

		VG	NM	YR
MONGOLOID/Jocko Homo .... (Booji Boy 7033-14)		1.50	6.00	77
(Hard cover gatefold)				
(I CAN'T GET ME NO) SATISFACTION/				
Sloppy (I Saw My Baby Getting) .... (Bomp/Booji Boy 72843-1)		1.50	6.00	77
FREEDOM OF CHOICE/Snowball .... (Warner Bros. 49621)		.75	3.00	80
BEAUTIFUL WORLD/Enough Said .... (Warner Bros. 49834)		.75	3.00	81
WORKING IN THE COAL MINE/Planet Earth .... (Full Moon/Asylum 47204)		.75	3.00	81
(From the motion picture Heavy Metal)				
PEEK-A-BOO/Find Out .... (Warner Bros. 29931-7)		.75	3.00	82
ARE U X-PERIENCED?/Growing Pains .... (Warner Bros. 29133-7)		.75	3.00	84
DISCO DANCER (7-Inch Version)/Disco Dancer (Karaoke Version) .... (Enigma B-75023)		1.00	4.00	88
(Printed in Canada for U.S. distribution)				
BABY DOLL/Baby Doll (Devo Mix) .... (Enigma 7 75029-7)		1.00	4.00	88
(Printed in Canada for U.S. distribution)				

(I can't get me no) SATISFACTION
SLOPPY (I saw my baby getting)
DEVO
another fine product of THE DE-EVOLUTION BAND

DEVOL, FRANK, ORCHESTRA

		VG	NM	YR
GUESS WHO'S COMING TO DINNER .... (Colgems 1615)		1.25	5.00	68
(From the motion picture Guess Who's Coming To Dinner)				

DEVON SQUARE

		VG	NM	YR
WALKING ON ICE/The Sandman .... (Atlantic 7-89100)		.75	3.00	87

TITLE	LABEL AND NUMBER	VG	NM	YR

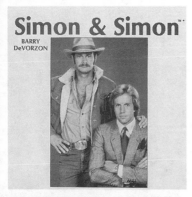

DeVORZON, BARRY
THEME FROM SIMON & SIMON .... (Earthtone 7005) | 1.50 | 6.00 | 84
  (From the television series *Simon & Simon*. Gerald McRaney and Jameson Parker pictured.)
NADIA'S THEME (THE YOUNG AND THE RESTLESS) .... (A&M 1856) | .75 | 3.00 | 76
  (Blue background, shown as by Barry DeVorzon and Perry Botkin, Jr.)
NADIA'S THEME (THE YOUNG AND THE RESTLESS) .... (A&M 1856) | .75 | 3.00 | 76
  (Green background, shown as by Barry DeVorzon and Perry Botkin, Jr.)
NADIA'S THEME (THE YOUNG AND THE RESTLESS) .... (A&M 1856) | .75 | 3.00 | 76
  (Black background, shown as performed by Perry Botkin, Jr., written and produced by Barry DeVorzon and Perry Botkin, Jr.)

DEXYS MIDNIGHT RUNNERS
COME ON EILEEN/Let's Make This Precious .... (Mercury 76189) | 1.00 | 4.00 | 82
  (Shown as by Dexys Midnight Runners & the Emerald Express)
THE CELTIC SOUL BROTHERS (MORE, PLEASE, THANK YOU)/
Reminisce Part One .... (Mercury 811 142-7) | .75 | 3.00 | 83
  (Shown as by Kevin Rowland and Dexys Midnight Runners)
THE CELTIC SOUL BROTHERS (MORE, PLEASE, THANK YOU)/
Reminisce Part One .... (Mercury DEXYP 12/811 142-7) | 1.25 | 5.00 | 83
  (Poster sleeve, shown as by Kevin Rowland and Dexys Midnight Runners)

DEY, SUSAN
(Actress)
  See the Partridge Family

DE YOUNG, CLIFF
MY SWEET LADY/Sunshine .... (MCA 40156) | 1.00 | 4.00 | 73
  (De Young not credited on sleeve. From the television movie *Sunshine*.)

DE YOUNG, DENNIS
DESERT MOON/Gravity .... (A&M 2666) | 1.00 | 4.00 | 84
CALL ME/Please .... (A&M 2816) | 1.00 | 4.00 | 86
BOOMCHILD .... (MCA 53376) | 1.00 | 4.00 | 88
  Also see Styx

DHARMA BUMS
GIVIN IN/Shake Some Action .... (Frontier/BMG 34676) | 1.00 | 4.00 | 91
  (Issued with red vinyl)

DIABLOS
VILLAGE OF LOVE .... (Fortune 563) | 6.25 | 25.00 | 64

DIAMOND, NEIL
TWO-BIT MANCHILD .... (Uni 55075) | 3.75 | 15.00 | 68
SOOLAIMÓN/And The Green Grass Won't Pay No Mind .... (Uni 55224) | 3.00 | 12.00 | 70
BE/Flight Of The Gull .... (Columbia 4-45942) | 1.50 | 6.00 | 73
  (From the motion picture *Jonathan Livingston Seagull*)
LOVE ON THE ROCKS .... (Capitol 4939) | 1.00 | 4.00 | 80
  (From the motion picture *The Jazz Singer* starring Diamond)
HELLO AGAIN (LOVE THEME FROM "THE JAZZ SINGER") .... (Capitol 4960) | 1.00 | 4.00 | 81
  (From the motion picture *The Jazz Singer* starring Diamond)
AMERICA .... (Capitol 4994) | 1.00 | 4.00 | 81
  (From the motion picture *The Jazz Singer* starring Diamond)
YESTERDAY'S SONGS/Guitar Heaven .... (Columbia 38-02604) | 1.00 | 4.00 | 81
YESTERDAY'S SONGS .... (Columbia 38-02604) | 1.25 | 5.00 | 81
  (Promotional issue, *Demonstration/Not For Sale* printed on sleeve)
ON THE WAY TO THE SKY/Save Me .... (Columbia 38-02712) | 1.00 | 4.00 | 81
HEARTLIGHT/You Don't Know Me .... (Columbia 38-03219) | 1.00 | 4.00 | 82
FRONT PAGE STORY .... (Columbia 38-03801) | 1.00 | 4.00 | 83
FRONT PAGE STORY .... (Columbia 38-03801) | 1.25 | 5.00 | 83
  (Promotional issue, *Demonstration Only–Not For Sale* printed on sleeve)
TURN AROUND/Brooklyn On A Saturday Night .... (Columbia 38-04541) | .75 | 3.00 | 84
TURN AROUND .... (Columbia 38-04541) | 1.25 | 5.00 | 84
  (Promotional issue, *Demonstration–Not For Sale* printed on sleeve)
YOU MAKE IT FEEL LIKE CHRISTMAS/Crazy .... (Columbia 38-04719) | 1.50 | 6.00 | 86
HEADED FOR THE FUTURE .... (Columbia 38-05889) | .75 | 3.00 | 86
HEADED FOR THE FUTURE .... (Columbia 38-05889) | .1.00 | 4.00 | 86
  (Promotional issue, *Demonstration–Not For Sale* printed on sleeve)
THE STORY OF MY LIFE .... (Columbia 38-06136) | .75 | 3.00 | 86
THE STORY OF MY LIFE .... (Columbia 38-06136) | 1.00 | 4.00 | 86
  (Promotional issue, *Demonstration–Not For Sale* printed on sleeve)
I DREAMED A DREAM .... (Columbia 38-07614) | .75 | 3.00 | 87

DIAMOND REO
BOYS WILL BE BOYS/Lover Boy .... (Buddah 559) | 1.00 | 4.00 | 77
  Also see the Silencers (Frank Czuri)

DIAMONDS, THE
HIGH SIGN/Don't Let Me Down .... (Mercury 71291) | 12.50 | 50.00 | 58

DICK & DEE DEE
THE RIVER TOOK MY BABY/My Lonely Self .... (Warner Bros. 5320) | 6.25 | 25.00 | 63
THOU SHALT NOT STEAL/River 'Round The Bend .... (Warner Bros. 5482) | 6.25 | 25.00 | 64
  (The sleeve's major emphasis is promoting Triumph motorcycles)

DICKIES, THE
SILENT NIGHT/Sounds Of Silence .... (A&M 2092) | 2.50 | 10.00 | 78
  (Issued with white vinyl)
NIGHTS IN WHITE SATIN/Manny, Moe And Jack .... (A&M 2225) | 2.50 | 10.00 | 80
BANANA SPLITS (THE TRA LA LA SONG)/Sounds Of Silence .... (A&M 2241) | 2.50 | 10.00 | 80

DICKINSON, ANGIE
(Actress)
  See Melba Moore (*My Sensitive, Passionate Man*)

DIETRICH, MARLENE
(Actress)
THE BOYS IN THE BACKROOM / Falling In Love Again .... (Decca 1-714)   3.75   15.00   53
    (Decca "Curtain Call" series of reissues)
OPEN-END INTERVIEW / Makin' Whoopee! .... (Columbia ZSP 49718)   3.75   15.00   60
    (Promotional issue only titled *An Interview With Marlene Dietrich*)

DIFFORD & TILBROOK
    See Ferry Aid, Squeeze

DIGITAL AIR
DIG DUG .... (Atlantic 7-89716)   .75   3.00   84

DILCHER, CHERYL
LOVIN' WOMAN / Follow The Love .... (Butterfly CM1202)   .75   3.00   77
    (Issued with either stock black or promotional white vinyl)

DILLON, DEAN
BROTHERLY LOVE(RCA 13049)   1.25   5.00   82
    (Shown as by Gary Stewart and Dean Dillon)

DILLON, MATT
(Actor)
    See Little Willie John (*Fever*)

DINNER, MICHAEL
THE PROMISED LAND .... (Fantasy 750)   1.00   4.00   75
    (Back of sleeve credits Joe Walsh, Glenn Frey, and Tim Schmit)
SILVER BULLETS .... (Fantasy 781)   1.00   4.00   76

DINNING, MARK
A STAR IS BORN (A LOVE HAS DIED) / You Win Again .... (MGM K12888)   5.00   20.00   60
THE LOVIN' TOUCH / Come Back To Me (My Love) .... (MGM K12929)   5.00   20.00   60

DINO
24/7 / Nighttime Lovekind (Edit) .... (4th & B'Way 7471)   .75   3.00   89
SUNSHINE / Sunshine (Instrumental) .... (4th & B'Way 7489)   .75   3.00   89

DINO, DESI & BILLY
(Dino Martin, Jr., Desi Arnaz, Jr., and Billy Hinsche)
I'M A FOOL / So Many Ways .... (Reprise 0367)   3.00   12.00   65
NOT THE LOVIN' KIND / Chimes Of Freedom .... (Reprise 0401)   3.00   12.00   65
PLEASE DON'T FIGHT IT / The Rebel Kind .... (Reprise 0426)   3.00   12.00   65
MY, WHAT A SHAME / The Inside Outside Caspar Milquetoast Eskimo Flash .... (Reprise 0653)   3.00   12.00   68

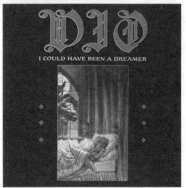

DINOSAUR JR
REPULSION / Bulbs Of Passion .... (Homestead 032)   2.50   10.00   85
    (Shown as by Dinosaur)
FREAK SCENE / Keep The Glove .... (SST 220)   1.25   5.00   88
    (Issued with either large-hole clear vinyl or small-hole black vinyl)
JUST LIKE HEAVEN / Throw Down-Chunks .... (SST 224)   3.00   12.00   90
THE WAGON / Better Than Gone .... (Sub Pop 68)   1.25   5.00   88
    (Limited edition of 10,000 copies with 9,800 on white and 200 on purple vinyl)
    Also see Mike Watt (J Mascis on *Big Train* and *E-Ticket Ride* b-side), Sebadoh (Lou Barlow)

DIO
I COULD HAVE BEEN A DREAMER .... (Warner Bros. 28255-7)   .75   3.00   87
    Also see Hear 'N Aid

DION
LONELY TEENAGER / Little Miss Blue .... (Laurie 3070)   7.50   30.00   60
HAVIN' FUN / Northeast End Of The Corner .... (Laurie 3081)   7.50   30.00   61
KISSIN' GAME / Heaven Help Me .... (Laurie 3090)   7.50   30.00   61
RUNAROUND SUE / Runaround Girl .... (Laurie 3110)   5.00   20.00   61
THE WANDERER / The Majestic .... (Laurie 3115)   5.00   20.00   61
LOVERS WHO WANDER / (I Was) Born To Cry .... (Laurie 3123)   5.00   20.00   62
LITTLE DIANE / Lost For Sure .... (Laurie 3134)   5.00   20.00   62
RUBY BABY / He'll Only Hurt You .... (Columbia 4-42662)   3.75   15.00   62
RUBY BABY .... (Columbia 4-42662)   10.00   40.00   62
    (Promotional issue only, neither song title nor catalog number listed. Sleeve states *Dion Is Now On Columbia Records*.)
I'M YOUR HOOTCHY KOOTCHY MAN / The Road I'm On .... (Columbia 4-42977)   3.75   15.00   64
TOMORROW WON'T BRING THE RAIN / You Move Me Babe .... (Columbia 4-43423)   5.00   20.00   66
SANCTUARY .... (Warner Bros. 7537)   2.50   10.00   71
AND THE NIGHT STOOD STILL / Tower Of Love .... (Arista 9797)   .75   3.00   89
    Also see Dion and the Belmonts

DION AND THE BELMONTS
EVERY LITTLE THING I DO / A Lover's Prayer .... (Laurie 3035)   7.50   30.00   59
WHERE OR WHEN / That's My Desire .... (Laurie 3044)   7.50   30.00   59
WHEN YOU WISH UPON A STAR / Wonderful Girl .... (Laurie 3052)   7.50   30.00   60
IN THE STILL OF THE NIGHT / A Funny Feeling .... (Laurie 3059)   7.50   30.00   60
    Also see Dion

DIRE STRAITS
LADY WRITER .... (Warner Bros. 49006)   1.00   4.00   79
SKATEAWAY / Solid Rock .... (Warner Bros. 49632)   1.00   4.00   80
MONEY FOR NOTHING .... (Warner Bros. 28950-7)   .75   3.00   85
WALK OF LIFE .... (Warner Bros. 28878-7)   .75   3.00   85
SO FAR AWAY .... (Warner Bros. 28789-7)   .75   3.00   85
    Also see Ferry Aid, Mark Knopfler / Willy DeVille

DIRKSEN, SENATOR EVERETT McKINLEY
GALLANT MEN / New Colossus .... (Capitol F5805)   2.00   8.00   66

TITLE	LABEL AND NUMBER	VG	NM	YR

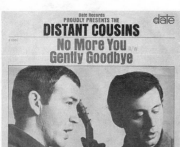

DIRTY DANCING
(Motion Picture)
    See the Contours (*Do You Love Me?*), Bill Medley and Jennifer Warnes (*The Time Of My Life*), Patrick Swayze (*She's Like The Wind*)

DIRTY FILTHY MUD
THE FOREST OF BLACK/Morning Sunflower .... (Worex 2340) | | 6.25 | 25.00 | 69

DISHWALLA
IT'S GOING TO TAKE SOME TIME .... (A&M 31458 0710 7) | | .50 | 2.00 | 94
    (Side 6 of a 7-record box set titled *If I Were A Carpenter*. Each sleeve has a different face shot of Karen Carpenter on the front, Richard Carpenter on the back. No artist name or song titles indicated on sleeve. Complete set valued at $30.00 near mint.)

DISORDERLIES
(Motion Picture)
    See Bananarama (*I Heard A Rumour*)

DISTANT COUSINS
NO MORE YOU/Gently Goodbye .... (Date 2-1501) | | 2.00 | 8.00 | 66

DIVINYLS
PLEASURE & PAIN/Heart Telegraph .... (Chrysalis VS4 42916) | | 1.00 | 4.00 | 85
HEY LITTLE BOY/Fighting .... (Chrysalis VS4 43241) | | .75 | 3.00 | 88

DIXON, JEANNE
(Astrologer)
A GIFT OF PROPHECY .... (Bell 657) | | 2.00 | 8.00 |

D.J. JAZZY JEFF & THE FRESH PRINCE
PARENTS JUST DON'T UNDERSTAND/
    Parents Just Don't Understand (Instrumental) .... (Jive 1099-7) | | .75 | 3.00 | 88
A NIGHTMARE ON MY STREET/A Nightmare On My Street (Instrumental) .... (Jive 1124-7) | | .75 | 3.00 | 88
GIRLS AIN'T NOTHING BUT TROUBLE/Brand New Funk .... (Jive 1147-7) | | .75 | 3.00 | 88
I THINK I CAN BEAT MIKE TYSON/I Think I Can Beat Mike Tyson (Instrumental) ... (Jive 1282-7) | | .75 | 3.00 | 89

DOBKINS, CARL, JR.
LUCKY DEVIL/(There's A Little Song A-Singing) In My Heart .... (Decca9- 31020) | | 6.25 | 25.00 | 59
EXCLUSIVELY YOURS/One Little Girl .... (Decca 9-31088) | | 5.00 | 20.00 | 60

DOBSON, TAMARA
(Actress)
    See Joe Simon (*Theme From Cleopatra Jones*)

DOCTOR & THE MEDICS
SPIRIT IN THE SKY/Laughing At The Pieces .... (I.R.S. 52880) | | .75 | 3.00 | 86
BURN/Barbara Can't Dance .... (I.R.S. 52970) | | .75 | 3.00 | 86
    Also see Scarlett and Black (*Sue West*)

DR. HOOK
CARRY ME CARRIE/True Love .... (Columbia 4-45667) | | 1.50 | 6.00 | 72
A FREE STIMU FROM DR. HOOK .... (Capitol SPRO-8220/8221) | | 2.00 | 8.00 | 75
    (Promotional issue only, *Not For Sale* printed on sleeve)
YEARS FROM NOW .... (Capitol 4885) | | 1.00 | 4.00 | 80
BABY MAKES HER BLUE JEANS TALK/The Turn On .... (Casablanca 2347) | | .75 | 3.00 | 82

DR. KILDARE
(Television Series)
    See Valjean (*Theme From Dr. Kildare*)
    Related see Richard Chamberlain

DR. WEST'S MEDICINE SHOW
GONDOLIERS, SHAKESPEARES, OVERSEERS, PLAYBOYS AND BUMS/
    Daddy, I Know .... (Go Go 102) | | 5.00 | 20.00 | 67
    Also see Norman Greenbaum

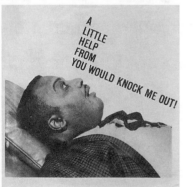

DODD, DICK
LITTLE SISTER/Lonely Weekends .... (Tower 447) | | 5.00 | 20.00 | 68

DODD, JIMMIE
(Adult mouseketeer on the television series *The Mickey Mouse Club*)
MOUSEKEDANCES/Mickey Mouse Mambo .... (Disneyland F-754) | | 3.00 | 12.00 | 57
PUSSY CAT POLKA/Mousekedance .... (Disneyland LG-754) | | 3.00 | 12.00 | 57
    (Shown as by Jimmie Dodd and the Mouseketeers)
    Also see Annette (b-side of *How Will I Know My Love*)

DOGGETT, BILL
CHOO CHOO/Oops .... (Columbia 4-42531) | | 3.75 | 15.00 | 62
A LITTLE HELP FROM YOU WOULD KNOCK ME OUT .... (Columbia no #) | | 3.75 | 15.00 | 62
    (Generic promotional issue only which was probably used for any Doggett promo)

DOHERTY, DENNY
INDIAN GIRL .... (Columbia 4-45779) | | 1.50 | 6.00 | 73
    Also see the Mamas and the Papas

DOKKEN
DREAM WARRIORS/Back For The Attack .... (Elektra 7-69483) | | .75 | 3.00 | 87
    (A-side from the motion picture *A Nightmare On Elm Street 3*)
BURNING LIKE A FLAME/Lost Behind The Wall .... (Elektra 7-69435) | | .75 | 3.00 | 87
HEAVEN SENT/Mr. Scary .... (Elektra 7-69405) | | .75 | 3.00 | 88
ALONE AGAIN (LIVE)/It's Not Love (Live) .... (Elektra 7-69353) | | .75 | 3.00 | 88
    Also see Hear 'N Aid

DOLBY, THOMAS
EUROPA AND THE PIRATE TWINS .... (Capitol B-5238) | | 1.00 | 4.00 | 81
HYPER-ACTIVE! .... (Capitol B-5321) | | .75 | 3.00 | 83
I SCARE MYSELF/Dissidents .... (Capitol B-5355) | | .75 | 3.00 | 84
DISSIDENTS: THE SEARCH FOR TRUTH .... (Capitol B-5374) | | .75 | 3.00 | 84

		VG	NM	YR
AIRHEAD/Budapest By Blimp	(EMI-Manhattan B-50125)	.75	3.00	88
HOT SAUCE/Salsa Picante	(EMI-Manhattan B-50148)	.75	3.00	88

Also see Bruce Wooley & The Camera Club

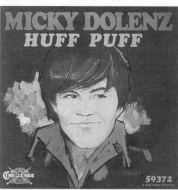

DOLBY'S CUBE FEATURING CHERRY BOMB
HOWARD THE DUCK	(MCA 52868)	1.00	4.00	86

(From the motion picture *Howard The Duck*)

DOLDINGER, KLAUS
THE TITLE MELODY FROM DAS BOOT (THE BOAT)/ The Return Home Of The U 96	(Atlantic 4045)	.75	3.00	82

DOLENZ, MICKEY
DON'T DO IT	(Challenge 59353)	6.25	25.00	67
HUFF PUFF	(Challenge 59372)	10.00	40.00	67

Also see Dolenz, Jones & Tork, the Monkees

DOLENZ, JONES & TORK
CHRISTMAS IS MY TIME OF YEAR/White Christmas	(Fan Club/CDS 700)	6.25	25.00	76

Also see Mickey Dolenz, David Jones, the Monkees

DOLPHIN DOLLS, THE
WE LOVE YOU DOLPHINS/Go-Go-Go, Dolphins	(Scarpa 621)	1.00	4.00	

DOMINATION
YOU HAVEN'T HEARD NOTHING/I Need A Rolex	(Warner Bros. 27542-7)	.75	3.00	89

("Double Artist Single", flip side shown as by Toddy Tee)

DOMINGO, PLACIDO
A LOVE UNTIL THE END OF TIME/Save Your Nights For Me	(CBS 38-05425)	1.00	4.00	85

(A-side shown as by Placido Domingo With Maureen McGovern)

DOMINIQUE
CHANGES OF HEART/The Way That Love Goes	(Atlantic 7-89690)	.75	3.00	84

DOMINO, FATS
I'M WALKIN'/I'm In The Mood For Love	(Imperial 5428)	7.50	30.00	57
THE BIG BEAT/I Want You To Know	(Imperial 5477)	12.50	50.00	57
I WANT TO WALK YOU HOME/I'm Gonna Be A Wheel Some Day	(Imperial 5606)	7.50	30.00	59
BE MY GUEST/I've Been Around	(Imperial 5629)	7.50	30.00	59
WHAT'S THAT YOU GOT?/It's Never Too Late	(Mercury 72485)	5.00	20.00	65

DOMINO RECORDS
Based in Austin, Texas, this independent label released 16 singles. Their repertoire of artists include Ray Campi, the Daylighters, Joyce Harris, Rod McCullough, the Slades, Barney Tall, Dub Walker, and Joyce Webb. The 45s were issued with a single sheet insert which served as Domino's version of a picture sleeve. The inserts are included in this book to distinguish them from true picture sleeves.

DONAHUE, TROY
(Actor)
SOMEBODY LOVES ME/Like Young	(Warner Bros. 5394)	6.25	25.00	62

Also see George Greeley (*Allison's Theme From "Parrish"*)

DONALD DUCK
See Willio & Phillio (*Goin' Quackers*)

DONALDSON, BO, AND THE HEYWOODS
DEEPER AND DEEPER	(ABC 11402)	2.00	8.00	73
THE HEARTBREAK KID	(ABC 12039)	1.25	5.00	74

DON AND THE GALAXIES
SUNDOWN/Avalanche	(Fox-Fidel 3)	10.00	40.00	62

DON AND THE GOODTIMES
I COULD BE SO GOOD TO YOU	(Epic 5-10145)	3.75	15.00	67
HAPPY AND ME	(Epic 5-10199)	5.00	20.00	67

Also see the Kingsmen (Don Gallucci)

DONNA MARIE
THE PENTHOUSE/Pretty Thing	(Columbia 4-44402)	3.75	15.00	68

DONNER, RAL
I GOT BURNED/A Tear In My Eye	(Reprise 20141)	37.50	150.00	63
(ALL OF A SUDDEN) MY HEART SINGS/Lovin' Place	(MJ 222)	2.50	10.00	70

(Sleeve reads*Whatever Happened To Ral Donner...*, no titles listed)
CHRISTMAS DAY/Second Miracle (Of Christmas)	(Starfire 103)	2.50	10.00	78

(Issued with green vinyl)
RIP IT UP/Don't Leave Me Now	(Starfire 114)	2.50	10.00	79

DONOVAN
SUNSHINE SUPERMAN	(Epic 5-10045)	2.50	10.00	66
MELLOW YELLOW	(Epic 5-10098)	2.50	10.00	66
EPISTLE TO DIPPY	(Epic 5-10127)	2.50	10.00	67
WEAR YOUR LOVE LIKE HEAVEN/Oh Gosh	(Epic 5-10253)	2.50	10.00	67
JENNIFER JUNIPER/Poor Cow	(Epic 5-10300)	2.50	10.00	68

(B-side from the motion picture *Poor Cow*)
THE HURDY GURDY MAN/Teen Angel	(Epic 5-10345)	2.50	10.00	68
LALÉNA	(Epic 5-10393)	2.50	10.00	68
ATLANTIS/To Susan On The West Coast Waiting	(Epic 5-10434)	2.50	10.00	69
BARABAJAGAL (LOVE IS HOT)	(Epic 5-10510)	2.50	10.00	69

(Shown as by Donovan With The Jeff Beck Group)
RIKI TIKI TAVI/Roots Of Oak	(Epic 5-10649)	2.50	10.00	70
CELIA OF THE SEALS/Song Of The Wandering Aengus	(Epic 5-10694)	2.50	10.00	71

(Shown as by Donovan with Danny Thomson, concert bass fiddle)

DONOVAN, JASON
(Son of Donovan)
TOO MANY BROKEN HEARTS/Wrap My Arms Around You	(Atlantic 7-88855)	.75	3.00	89

80

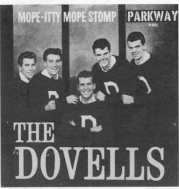

TITLE	LABEL AND NUMBER	VG	NM	YR
DOOBIE BROTHERS, THE				
WHAT A FOOL BELIEVES/Don't Stop To Watch The Wheels	(Warner Bros. 8725)	1.00	4.00	78
REAL LOVE/Thank You Love	(Warner Bros. 49503)	1.00	4.00	80
WYNKEN, BLYNKEN AND NOD/In Harmony	(Warner Bros./Sesame Street 49642)	1.00	4.00	80
(B-side shown as by Kate Taylor and the Simon-Taylor Family)				
YOU BELONG TO ME/South City Midnight Lady	(Warner Bros. 29552-7)	.75	3.00	83
THE DOCTOR	(Capitol B-44376)	.75	3.00	89
Also see Michael McDonald				
DOORS, THE				
BREAK ON THROUGH/End Of The Night	(Elektra 45611)	15.00	60.00	67
PEOPLE ARE STRANGE/Unhappy Girl	(Elektra 45621)	6.25	25.00	67
THE UNKNOWN SOLDIER/We Could Be So Good Together	(Elektra 45628)	5.00	20.00	68
TELL ALL THE PEOPLE	(Elektra 45663)	5.00	20.00	69
PEOPLE ARE STRANGE/Not To Touch The Earth	(Elektra 47097)	1.25	5.00	80
(Originally issued with an insert advertising the Doors albums)				
DORFF, STEVE, & FRIENDS				
THEME FROM GROWING PAINS–AS LONG AS WE GOT EACH OTHER	(Reprise 27878-7)	1.00	4.00	88
(Back of sleeve states Performed by B.J. Thomas and Dusty Springfield. From the television series Growing Pains, cast from the series pictured; Alan Thicke, Joanna Kerns, Kirk Cameron, Tracey Gold, and Jeremy Miller. Photography by Annie Leibovitz.)				
DORSEY, JIMMY				
CONTRASTS/Green Eyes	(Decca 1-711)	3.00	12.00	52
(Decca "Curtain Call" series of reissues)				
DOUBLE				
THE CAPTAIN OF HER HEART/Your Prayer Takes Me Off Part II (Dub)	(A&M 2838)	.75	3.00	86
WOMAN OF THE WORLD/Woman Of The World (Instrumental)	(A&M 2869)	.75	3.00	86
DOUBLE TROUBLE				
(Motion Picture)				
See Elvis Presley (Long Legged Girl)				
DOUGLAS, CAROL				
WE DID IT	(Midland International 10979)	1.25	5.00	77
DOUGLAS, KIRK				
(Actor)				
See Kenny Rogers (They Don't Make Them Like They Used To)				
DOUGLAS, MICHAEL				
(Actor, son of Kirk Douglas)				
See Diana Ross (It's My Turn)				
DOUGLAS, MIKE				
PASS ME BY/Ev'ryone Here Loves Kelly	(Epic 5-9760)	2.00	8.00	65
(A-side from the motion picture Father Goose)				
THE MEN IN MY LITTLE GIRL'S LIFE/Stranger On The Shore	(Epic 5-9876)	2.00	8.00	65
HERE'S TO MY JENNY/While We're Young	(Epic 5-10002)	2.00	8.00	66
THE PARENTS OF THE KIDS IN LOVE/Real Love	(Epic 5-10041)	2.00	8.00	66
WHAT IS A SQUARE/That's How Love Goes	(Epic 5-10126)	2.00	8.00	67
DOVE, RONNIE				
HAPPY SUMMER DAYS/Long After	(Diamond 205)	2.00	8.00	66
DOVELLS, THE				
DO THE NEW CONTINENTAL/Mope-Itty Mope Stomp	(Parkway 833)	3.00	12.00	62
BRISTOL TWISTIN' ANNIE/The Actor	(Parkway 838)	3.00	12.00	62
HULLY GULLY BABY/Your Last Chance	(Parkway 845)	3.00	12.00	62
THE JITTERBUG/Kissin' In The Kitchen	(Parkway 855)	3.00	12.00	62
SAVE ME BABY/You Can't Run Away From Yourself	(Parkway 861)	3.75	15.00	63
YOU CAN'T SIT DOWN/Wildwood Days	(Parkway 867)	3.00	12.00	63
YOU CAN'T SIT DOWN/Stompin' Everywhere	(Parkway 867)	3.00	12.00	63
BETTY IN BERMUDAS/Dance The Froog	(Parkway 882)	3.00	12.00	63
STOP MONKEYIN' AROUN'/No, No, No	(Parkway 889)	3.75	15.00	63
WATUSI WITH LUCY/What In The World's Come Over You	(Parkway 925)	3.75	15.00	62
Also see Len Barry				
DOWELL, JOE				
WOODEN HEART/Little Bo Peep	(Smash 1708)	3.75	15.00	61
THE BRIDGE OF LOVE/Just Love Me	(Smash 1717)	2.50	10.00	61
(I WONDER) WHO'S SPENDING CHRISTMAS WITH YOU/A Kiss For Christmas	(Smash 1728)	2.50	10.00	61
THE SOUND OF SADNESS/Thorn On The Rose	(Smash 1730)	2.50	10.00	62
LITTLE RED RENTED ROWBOAT/One I Left For You	(Smash 1759)	2.50	10.00	62
POOR LITTLE CUPID/No Secrets	(Smash 1786)	2.50	10.00	62
OUR SCHOOL DAYS/Bringa-Branga-Brought	(Smash 1799)	2.50	10.00	63
THOSE DARNED INFLATION BLUES	(Journey 413)	1.50	6.00	73
DOWN AND OUT IN BEVERLY HILLS				
(Motion Picture)				
See Little Richard (Great Gosh A'mighty)				
DOWNEY, ROBERT, JR.				
(Actor)				
See the Judas Priest (Johnny B. Goode), Pretenders (Windows Of The World)				
DOWNS, HUGH				
(Television announcer from The Today Show, Over Easy, and 20/20)				
FIRST MAN ON THE MOON	(MGM PX-101)	2.00	8.00	69
DOZY, BEAKY, MICK & TICH				
TONIGHT TODAY/Bad News	(Cotillion 44061)	2.50	10.00	70

DRAGNET
(Motion Picture)
See the Art Of Noise *(Dragnet)*, Dan Aykroyd *(City Of Crime)*, Tom Hanks *(City Of Crime)*

DRAMA
PARALYZE/Let It Breathe .... (RCA PB-14114)   .75   3.00   85
    Also see Susanne Jerome Taylor

DREAD ZEPPELIN
WHOLE LOTTA LOVE/Tour-Telvis: A Bad Trip .... (Birdcage 45-2690)   1.50   6.00   89
    (Issued with pink vinyl)
IMMIGRANT SONG/Hey, Hey, What Can I Do .... (Birdcage 45-2777)   1.50   6.00   89
    (Issued with yellow vinyl)

DREAM ACADEMY, THE
LIFE IN A NORTHERN TOWN/Test Tape No. 3 .... (Reprise 28841-7)   1.00   4.00   85
THE LOVE PARADE/Girl In A Million .... (Reprise 28750-7)   .75   3.00   86
INDIAN SUMMER .... (Reprise 28199-7)   .75   3.00   87
THE LESSON OF LOVE .... (Reprise 28118-7)   .75   3.00   88

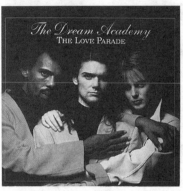

DREAMS SO REAL
EVERYWHERE GIRL/Whirl .... (Coyote # unknown)   1.25   5.00   86
RED LIGHTS (MERRY CHRISTMAS)/Bearing Witness .... (Arista 9784)   .75   3.00   88
    (Issued with green vinyl)
BEARING WITNESS/Cinnamon Girl .... (Arista 9794)   .75   3.00   88

DREAM SYNDICATE, THE
BALLAD OF DWIGHT FRYE/Low Rider .... (Forced Exposure 004)   3.75   15.00   86

DREAM TEAM, THE
(Motion Picture)
    See Buster Poindexter *(Hit The Road Jack)*

DREW, DAVID
GREEN-EYED LADY .... (MCA 53384)   .75   3.00   88
    (Issued with green vinyl)

DRIFTERS, THE
SATURDAY NIGHT AT THE MOVIES/Spanish Lace .... (Atlantic 2260)   5.00   20.00   64
THE CHRISTMAS SONG/I Remember Christmas .... (Atlantic 2261)   6.25   25.00   64
    (Both sleeves feature the same picture of the group)
EXTENDED PLAYS
SWINGERS FOR COKE .... (Coca-Cola no #)   12.50   50.00   66
    (Promotional issue only with one "Coke" song each by the Drifters, Lesley Gore, Los Bravos, and Roy Orbison)
    Also see Ferry Aid, Little Willie John *(Fever).* Clyde McPhatter was lead vocalist from 1953-54. Ben E. King was a member of the revamped Drifters from 1958-60. The vocal line-up for these sleeves was Johnny Moore, Gene Pearson, Johnny Terry, and Charles Thomas with Billy Davis on guitar.)

DRISCOLL, JULIE, AND BRIAN AUGER
THIS WHEEL'S ON FIRE/A Kind Of Love In .... (Atco 6593)   2.50   10.00   67

DRUCKER, MORT
(Artist best known for his work in *Mad* magazine)
    See the Bears *(Trust)*

DRUIDS, THE
IT'S A DAY/A Man Should Never Cry .... (Columbia 4-43450)   2.50   10.00   65

DRUSKY, ROY
PEEL ME A NANNER/The Room Across The Hall .... (Mercury 72204)   1.50   6.00   63

DRYSDALE, DON
(Baseball pitcher for the Los Angeles Dodgers)
GIVE HER LOVE/One Love .... (Reprise 20,162)   5.00   20.00   63

DUDLEY, DAVE
YOUR ONLY ONE/Maybe I Do .... (Curio 7029)   2.00   8.00   60s

DUFFY, PATRICK
(Actor)
    See Floyd Cramer *(Theme From Dallas)*

DUKE, GEORGE
LOVE BALLAD .... (Elektra 7-69296)   .75   3.00   89

DUKE, PATTY
DON'T JUST STAND THERE/Everything But Love .... (United Artists 875)   3.75   15.00   65
FUNNY LITTLE BUTTERFLIES .... (United Artists 915)   3.75   15.00   65
THE WORLD IS WATCHING US/Little Things Mean A Lot .... (United Artists 50034)   3.75   15.00   66

DUKES OF HAZZARD, THE
(Television Series)
    See Waylon Jennings *(Theme From The Dukes Of Hazzard)*
    Related see John Schneider

DUNCAN, JOHNNY
LOOKING FOR SOMEONE LONELY .... (Columbia 4-43988)   2.00   8.00   66
I'M THE ONE .... (Columbia 4-44484)   2.00   8.00   68

DUNCAN, LESLEY
EXTENDED PLAYS
HELP ME JESUS/SING CHILD SING .... (Columbia AS 53)   1.50   6.00   71
    (Part of a series of promotional issues titled *Playback* issued with a small hole 33-1/3 RPM record. Price includes generic *Playback* sleeve with folding insert. Also includes one song each by Jeff Beck, Firesign Theatre, Grootna, the Mahavishnu Orchestra With John McLaughlin, and Mylon.)

DUPREE, ROBBIE
BROOKLYN GIRLS/Lonely Runner .... (Elektra 47145)   1.00   4.00   81

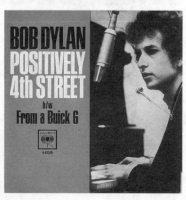

DUPREES, THE

GOODNIGHT MY LOVE	(Heritage 805)	3.00	12.00	68
MY LOVE, MY LOVE	(Heritage 808)	3.00	12.00	69
TWO DIFFERENT WORLDS	(Heritage 811)	3.00	12.00	69

Also see the Italian Asphalt & Pavement Company (I.A.P. Co.)

DURAN DURAN

HUNGRY LIKE THE WOLF (Long and Short Version)	(Harvest 5195)	1.25	5.00	82
RIO	(Capitol B-5215)	1.25	5.00	82
IS THERE SOMETHING I SHOULD KNOW?	(Capitol B-5233)	1.00	4.00	83
UNION OF THE SNAKE/Secret Oktober	(Capitol B-5290)	1.00	4.00	83
NEW MOON ON MONDAY	(Capitol B-5309)	1.00	4.00	84
THE REFLEX	(Capitol B-5345)	1.00	4.00	84
THE REFLEX	(Capitol B-5345)	1.50	6.00	84
(Poster sleeve)				
THE WILD BOYS/(I'm Looking For) Cracks In The Pavement (1984)	(Capitol B-5417)	1.00	4.00	84
SAVE A PRAYER/Save A Prayer (From The Arena)	(Capitol B-5438)	1.00	4.00	84
A VIEW TO A KILL/A View To A Kill (That Fatal Kiss)	(Capitol B-5475)	1.00	4.00	85
(From the motion picture A View To A Kill)				
NOTORIOUS	(Capitol B-5648)	1.00	4.00	86
SKIN TRADE/We Need You	(Capitol B-5670)	1.00	4.00	87
MEET EL PRESIDENTE/Vertigo (Do The Demolition)	(Capitol B-44001)	1.50	6.00	87
(Poster sleeve)				
I DON'T WANT YOUR LOVE	(Capitol B-44237)	.75	3.00	88
ALL SHE WANTS IS	(Capitol B-44287)	.75	3.00	88
DO YOU BELIEVE IN SHAME?	(Capitol B-44337)	.75	3.00	89

Also see Arcadia (Simon LeBon, Nick Rhodes, Roger Taylor), Band Aid, Power Station (Andy Taylor, John Taylor), Andy Taylor, John Taylor. Wayne Cuccurullo, formerly of Missing Persons, joined the group in 1990.

DURANT, DON
(Actor)

JOHNNY RINGO/The Whistlin' Wind	(RCA Victor 47-7760)	3.75	15.00	60

DURANTE, JIMMY

START OFF EACH DAY WITH A SONG/Inka Dinka Doo	(Decca 1-702)	3.00	12.00	51
(Decca "Curtain Call" series of reissues)				

DUROCS

IT HURTS TO BE IN LOVE/No Fool No Fun	(Capitol 4756)	1.00	4.00	79

DURY, IAN, AND THE BLOCKHEADS

REASONS TO BE CHEERFUL (PART THREE)	(Stiff-Epic 9-50800)	1.50	6.00	79
HIT ME WITH YOUR RHYTHM STICK/ There Ain't Half Been Some Clever Bastards	(CBS/Stiff-Epic AE7-1179)	1.50	6.00	79
(Promotional issue only included with the album Do It Yourself)				

DUST

LOVE ME HARD	(Kama Sutra 541)	1.50	6.00	71

Also see the Ramones (Marc Bell a.k.a. Marky Ramone), Stories

DUSTIN, ALTA

ONE MAN WOMAN (LUONGO MIX)/One Man Woman (Edit)	(Atlantic 7-88930)	.75	3.00	89

DUVALL, SHELLEY
(Actress)

See Robin Williams (I Yam What I Yam)

DWEEZIL

See Dweezil Zappa

DYER, ADA

I DON'T FEEL LIKE CRYING	(Motown 1943)	.75	3.00	88

DYLAN, BOB

BLOWIN' IN THE WIND/Don't Think Twice	(Columbia 4-42856)	250.00	1000.00	63
(Promotional issue only which features the headline Rebel With A Cause. Not a true picture sleeve, but a single sheet insert printed on one side with three paragraphs promoting Dylan's release.)				
SUBTERRANEAN HOMESICK BLUES	(Columbia 4-43242)	375.00	1500.00	65
(Promotional issue only issued with black vinyl, Dylan pictured. The red vinyl 45 was not issued with this picture sleeve.)				
SUBTERRANEAN HOMESICK BLUES	(Columbia 4-43242)	15.00	60.00	65
(Columbia Hit Pack Series issued with red vinyl)				
POSITIVELY 4TH STREET/From A Buick 6	(Columbia 4-43389)	10.00	40.00	66
I WANT YOU	(Columbia 4-43683)	10.00	40.00	66
HURRICANE	(Columbia 3-10245)	2.50	10.00	79
(Sleeve does not credit artist or title on sleeve. Boxer Rubin "Hurricane" Carter pictured. This sleeve was used for both the 45 RPM and 33-1/3 RPM versions of the record.)				
HURRICANE	(Columbia 3-10245)	5.00	20.00	79
(Promotional issue, Demonstration–Not For Sale printed on sleeve. Sleeve does not credit artist or title on sleeve. Boxer Rubin "Hurricane" Carter pictured. Some promos have Demonstration Not For Sale rubber stamped on the sleeve and should be valued the same as the commercial version.)				
SLOW TRAIN/Do Right To Me Baby (Do Unto Others)	(Columbia 1-11235)	2.50	10.00	79
SLOW TRAIN/Do Right To Me Baby (Do Unto Others)	(Columbia 1-11235)	3.75	15.00	79
(Promotional issue, Demonstration–Not For Sale printed on sleeve)				
HEART OF MINE/The Groom's Still Waiting At The Altar	(Columbia 18 02510)	1.50	6.00	81
HEART OF MINE	(Columbia 18 02510)	3.00	12.00	81
(Promotional issue, Demonstration–Not For Sale printed on sleeve)				
SWEETHEART LIKE YOU/Union Sundown	(Columbia 38-04301)	1.25	5.00	83
SWEETHEART LIKE YOU	(Columbia 38-04301)	2.50	10.00	83
(Promotional issue, Demonstration–Not For Sale printed on sleeve)				
TIGHT CONNECTION TO MY HEART (HAS ANYBODY SEEN MY LOVE)/ We Better Talk This Over	(Columbia 38-04933)	1.00	4.00	85
TIGHT CONNECTION TO MY HEART (HAS ANYBODY SEEN MY LOVE)	(Columbia 38-04933)	2.00	8.00	85
(Promotional issue, Demonstration–Not For Sale printed on sleeve)				
BAND OF THE HAND	(MCA 52811)	1.00	4.00	86
(Shown as by Bob Dylan With the Heartbreakers)				

Also see U.S.A. For Africa, Voices Of America

DYNATONES, THE

LOVE CITY / Twine Time (Solid Smoke 45-711)	1.00	4.00	82
(Folding sleeve)			
ITALIAN SHOES (Warner Bros. 27865-7)	.75	3.00	88

DYSON, RONNIE

ONE MAN BAND (PLAYS ALL ALONE) / I Think I'll Tell Her (Columbia 4-45776)	1.50	6.00	73

E

EAGLES

PLEASE COME HOME FOR CHRISTMAS / Funky New Year (Asylum 45555)	1.00	4.00	78
(Coated paper)			
PLEASE COME HOME FOR CHRISTMAS / Funky New Year (Asylum 45555)	1.00	4.00	78

(Uncoated paper, possibly used for promotional copies of the record)

Also see Jimmy Buffett (b-side of *Hello Texas*), Don Felder, Glenn Frey, Don Henley, Johnny Lee (b-side of *Lookin' For Love*), Poco (Timothy B. Schmit), Timothy B. Schmit, Joe Walsh. Randy Meisner left the group in 1977 and was replaced by Schmit.

EARLE, STEVE

A LITTLE BIT IN LOVE / (Epic 04784)	1.00	4.00	85
A LITTLE BIT IN LOVE (Epic 04784)	1.25	5.00	85
(Promotional issue, *Demonstration–Not For Sale* printed on back of sleeve)			

EXTENDED PLAYS

NOTHIN' BUT YOU / CONTINENTAL TRAILWAYS BLUES / Squeeze Me In / My Baby Worships Me (LSI 8209)	2.50	10.00	82
(Titled on front *Pink And Black*)			

EARONS, THE

LAND OF HUNGER / Working Hard (Island 7-99776)	.75	3.00	84

EARTH GIRLS ARE EASY

(Motion Picture)
See Daryl Hall & John Oates

EARTH QUAKE

I GET THE SWEETEST FEELING / Live And Let Live (A&M 1338)	1.50	6.00	72
FRIDAY ON MY MIND / Road Runner (Beserkley 5701)	2.50	10.00	74
(B-side by Jonathan Richman)			

EXTENDED PLAYS

LOVIN' CUP (Beserkley AE7-1120)	1.25	5.00	77

(Promotional issue only titled *Great Ideas From Beserkley*, issued with a small-hole 33-1/3 RPM record. Also includes one song each, the titles are not listed on sleeve, by the Rubinoos, Greg Kihn, and Jonathan Richman & the Modern Lovers.)

EARTH WIND & FIRE

MIGHTY MIGHTY / Drum Song (Columbia 4-46007)	1.25	5.00	74
SHINING STAR / Yearnin' Learnin' (Columbia 3-10090)	1.25	5.00	75
GETAWAY / Getaway (Instrumental) (Columbia 1-10373)	1.00	4.00	76
LET ME TALK / Let Me Talk (Instrumental) (Columbia 1-11366)	.75	3.00	80
LET ME TALK (Columbia 1-11366)	1.00	4.00	80
(Promotional issue, *Demonstration Only Not For Sale* printed on sleeve)			
FALL IN LOVE WITH ME / Lady Sun (Columbia 38-03375)	.75	3.00	83
FALL IN LOVE WITH ME (Columbia 38-03375)	1.00	4.00	83
(Promotional issue, *Demonstration Only Not For Sale* printed on sleeve)			
MAGNETIC (Columbia 38-04210)	.75	3.00	83
MAGNETIC (Columbia 38-04210)	1.00	4.00	83
(Promotional issue, *Demonstration Only Not For Sale* printed on sleeve)			
TOUCH (Columbia 38-04329)	.75	3.00	83
TOUCH (Columbia 38-04329)	1.00	4.00	83
(Promotional issue, *Demonstration Only Not For Sale* printed on sleeve)			
STAND BY ME / Can't Stop Love (Columbia 38-05571)	.75	3.00	87
SYSTEM OF SURVIVAL (Columbia 38-07608)	.75	3.00	87
EVIL ROY (Columbia 38-07687)	.75	3.00	87
THINKING OF YOU (Columbia 38-07695)	.75	3.00	88

Also see Philip Bailey, Maurice White

EASTON, SHEENA

MORNING TRAIN (NINE TO FIVE) / Calm Before The Storm (EMI America 8071)	1.25	5.00	81
MODERN GIRL / Summer's Over (EMI America 8080)	1.00	4.00	81
YOU COULD HAVE BEEN WITH ME / Savoir Faire (EMI America A-8101)	1.00	4.00	81
MACHINERY / So We Say Goodbye (EMI America B-8131)	1.00	4.00	82
TELEFONE (LONG DISTANCE LOVE AFFAIR) / Wish You Were Here Tonight (EMI America B-8172)	1.00	4.00	83
DEVIL IN A FAST CAR / Sweet Talk (EMI America B-8201)	1.00	4.00	84
STRUT / Letters From The Road (EMI America B-8227)	1.00	4.00	84
SUGAR WALLS / Straight Talking (EMI America B-8259)	1.00	4.00	85
SWEAR / Fallen Angels (EMI America B-8263)	.75	3.00	85
DO IT FOR LOVE / Can't Wait Till Tomorrow (EMI America B-8295)	.75	3.00	85
JIMMY MACK (EMI America B-8309)	.75	3.00	86
MAGIC OF LOVE (EMI America B8305)	.75	3.00	86
SO FAR SO GOOD / Magic Of Love (EMI America B-8332)	.75	3.00	86
(From the motion picture "*About Last Night...*")			
ETERNITY / Shockwave (EMI America B-43011)	1.25	5.00	87
(Poster sleeve)			
THE LOVER IN ME (MCA 53416)	.75	3.00	88
DAYS LIKE THIS (MCA 53499)	.75	3.00	89

Also see Prince (*The Arms Of Orion, U Got The Look*), Kenny Rogers (*We've Got Tonight*)

EASTWOOD, CLINT

(Actor/Director)

ROWDY / Cowboy Wedding Song (Cameo 240)	12.50	50.00	63
GET YOURSELF ANOTHER FOOL! / For You, For Me, Forevermore (GNP Crescendo 177)	18.75	75.00	63

TITLE	LABEL AND NUMBER	VG	NM	YR
UNKNOWN GIRL/For All We Know	(Gothic 005)	20.00	40.00	63
BURNING BRIDGES/When I Loved Her	(Certron 10010)	3.75	15.00	70
BAR ROOM BUDDIES	(Elektra 46634)	1.00	4.00	80

(Shown as by Merle Haggard and Clint Eastwood, both pictured. From the motion picture *Bronco Billy*.)
Also see Penny DeHaven (*Bayou Lullaby*), Ronnie Milsap (*Cowboys And Clowns*)

EASYBEATS, THE

IN MY BOOK/Make You Feel Alright (Women)	(Ascot 2214)	7.50	30.00	66

Also see Cheek

EASY RIDER
(Motion Picture)
See Steppenwolf (*Born To Be Wild*)

EBSEN, BUDDY

MAIL ORDER BRIDE/Ballad Of Jed Clampett	(MGM K 13210)	2.00	8.00	63

(A-side from the motion picture *Mail Order Bride*, Ebsen and Keir Dullea pictured. B-side from the television series *The Beverly Hillbillies*.)

ECHO & THE BUNNYMEN

BRING ON THE DANCING HORSES	(Sire 28791-7)	1.00	4.00	85
LIPS LIKE SUGAR/Rollercoaster	(Sire 28260-7)	1.00	4.00	87
BEDBUGS AND BALLYHOO/Run, Run, Run	(Sire 28113-7)	1.00	4.00	88

ECKSTINE, BILLY

THE BEST THING/Faraway Forever (Love Theme From 'The Getaway')	(A&M 1858)	1.00	4.00	76

EDDIE, JOHN

JUNGLE BOY/Mary's Ghost	(Columbia 38-05858)	.75	3.00	86
JUNGLE BOY	(Columbia 38-05858)	1.00	4.00	86

(Promotional issue, *Demonstration–Not For Sale* printed on sleeve)

STRANDED/Living Doll	(Columbia 38-06277)	.75	3.00	86
STRANDED	(Columbia 38-06277)	1.00	4.00	86

(Promotional issue, *Demonstration–Not For Sale* printed on sleeve)

EDDIE AND THE CRUISERS
(Motion Picture)
See John Cafferty and the Beaver Brown Band

EDDIE AND THE TIDE

WAITING FOR THE ONE/This Life Is Ours	(Atco 7-99447)	.75	3.00	87

Also see Lou Gramm (b-side of *Lost In The Shadows*)

EDDY, DUANE

YEP!/Three-30-Blues	(Jamie 1122)	6.25	25.00	59

(Shown as by Duane Eddy and The Rebels)

FORTY MILES OF BAD ROAD/The Quiet Three	(Jamie 1126)	5.00	20.00	59

(Shown as by Duane Eddy and The Rebels)

SOME KIND-A EARTHQUAKE/First Love, First Tears	(Jamie 1130)	5.00	20.00	59

(Shown as by Duane Eddy and The Rebels)

BONNIE CAME BACK/Lost Island	(Jamie 1144)	3.75	15.00	59

(Shown as by Duane Eddy and The Rebels)

SHAZAM!/The Secret Seven	(Jamie 1151)	3.75	15.00	60

(Shown as by Duane Eddy and The Rebels. From the motion picture *Because They're Young*)

BECAUSE THEY'RE YOUNG/Rebel Walk	(Jamie 1156)	5.00	20.00	60

(Shown as by Duane Eddy and The Rebels. From the motion picture *Because They're Young*)

KOMMOTION/Theme For Moon Children	(Jamie 1163)	3.75	15.00	60
PETER GUNN/Along The Navajo Trail	(Jamie 1168)	3.75	15.00	60
PEPE/Lost Friend	(Jamie 1175)	5.00	20.00	60

(Red background, a-side from the motion picture *Pepe*)

PEPE/Lost Friend	(Jamie 1175)	3.75	15.00	60

(Yellow background, a-side from the motion picture *Pepe*)

THEME FROM DIXIE/Gidget Goes Hawaiian	(Jamie 1183)	3.75	15.00	61
RING OF FIRE/Bobbie	(Jamie 1187)	3.75	15.00	61
DRIVIN' HOME/Tammy	(Jamie 1195)	3.75	15.00	61
MY BLUE HEAVEN/Along Came Linda	(Jamie 1200)	3.75	15.00	61
DEEP IN THE HEART OF TEXAS/Saints And Sinners	(RCA Victor 47-7999)	3.00	12.00	62
THE BALLAD OF PALADIN/The Wild Westerners	(RCA Victor 47-8047)	3.75	15.00	62

(From the television series *Have Gun Will Travel*)

(DANCE WITH THE) GUITER MAN/Stretchin' Out	(RCA Victor 47-8087)	3.75	15.00	63
BOSS GUITAR/The Desert Rat	(RCA Victor 47-8131)	3.00	12.00	63
LONELY BOY, LONELY GUITAR/Joshin'	(RCA Victor 47-8180)	3.00	12.00	63
YOUR BABY'S GONE SURFIN'/Shuckin'	(RCA Victor 47-8214)	3.75	15.00	63
THE SON OF REBEL ROUSER/The Story Of Three Loves	(RCA Victor 47-8276)	3.00	12.00	64
GUITAR CHILD/Jerky Jalopy	(RCA Victor 47-8335)	3.00	12.00	64
WATER SKIING/(Theme From) A Summer Place	(RCA Victor 47-8376)	3.00	12.00	64
GUITAR STAR/The Iguana	(RCA Victor 47-8442)	3.00	12.00	64
MOONSHOT/Roughneck	(RCA Victor 47-8507)	3.00	12.00	65
DON'T THINK TWICE, IT'S ALRIGHT/House Of The Rising Sun	(Colpix 788)	5.00	20.00	66
SPIES	(Capitol B-44018)	1.25	5.00	87

Also see the Art Of Noise (*Peter Gunn*). The Rebels pianist, Larry Knechtel, was a member of Bread.

EDELWEISS

BRING ME EDELWEISS! (SINGLE VERSION)/ Bring Me Edelweiss! (Yodel Version)	(Atlantic 7-88911)	.75	3.00	88

EDEN, BARBARA
(Actress best known for her role as Jeannie in the television series *I Dream Of Jeannie*)
See Jeannie C. Riley (*Harper Valley P.T.A.*)

EDEN, CHANCE

YOU'D BETTER GO	(Roulette 4592)	2.50	10.00	64

EDMUNDS, DAVE

ALMOST SATURDAY NIGHT/You'll Never Get Me Up (In One Of Those)	(Swan Song 72000)	1.25	5.00	81

RUN RUDOLPH RUN / Deep In The Heart Of Texas .... *(Columbia 38-03428)*   1.00   4.00   82
: (Shown as by Dave Edmunds Band. From the motion picture *Party Party*)

RUN RUDOLPH RUN / Deep In The Heart Of Texas .... *(Columbia 38-03428)*   1.50   6.00   82
: (Promotional issue, *Demonstration Not For Sale* printed on sleeve. Shown as by Dave Edmunds Band. From the motion picture *Party Party*)

HIGH SCHOOL NIGHTS / Porky's Revenge! .... *(Columbia 38-04762)*   .75   3.00   85
: (B-side title in green on front and shown on back as by Dave Edmunds with Chuck Leavell, Michael Shrieve & Kenny Aaronson. From the motion picture *Porky's Revenge!*)

HIGH SCHOOL NIGHTS / Porky's Revenge! .... *(Columbia 38-04762)*   1.00   4.00   85
: (B-side title in red on front. Promotional issue, *Demonstration Only–Not For Sale* printed on sleeve. From the motion picture *Porky's Revenge!*)

GONNA MOVE / Red River Rock .... *(MCA 53256)*   .75   3.00   88
: (B-side shown as by Silicone Teens. From the motion picture *Planes, Trains, And Automobiles.*)
: Also see Rockpile

EDWARD BEAR
LAST SONG .... *(Capitol 3452)*   1.25   5.00   72
CLOSE YOUR EYES .... *(Capitol 3581)*   1.25   5.00   73
WALKING ON BACK .... *(Capitol 3683)*   1.25   5.00   73

EDWARDS, TOMMY
I REALLY DON'T WANT TO KNOW / Unloved .... *(MGM K12890)*   3.75   15.00   60

EDWARDS, VINCENT
(Actor who played the title role in the television series *Ben Casey*)
I GOT IT BAD (AND THAT AIN'T GOOD) / Say It Isn't So .... *(Decca 31426)*   2.50   10.00   62
SEE THAT GIRL / No Not Much .... *(Colpix 771)*   2.50   10.00   65
TO BE WITH YOU / Nylon Stockings .... *(Kama Sutra 221)*   2.50   10.00   66

EGAN, WALTER
FULL MOON FIRE / Tammy Ann .... *(Backstreet 52200)*   .75   3.00   83

EIGHTH DAY, THE
HEY BOY! / A Million Lights .... *(Kapp 826)*   2.00   8.00   67

EIGHTH WONDER
CROSS MY HEART .... *(CBS/WTG 31-08036)*   .75   3.00   88

EIGHT SECONDS
KISS YOU (WHEN IT'S DANGEROUS) / Land Of The Monster .... *(Polydor 885 352-7)*   .75   3.00   86
SINCERE (I SHALL RETURN) / Commissioner St. .... *(Polydor 885 769-7)*   .75   3.00   87

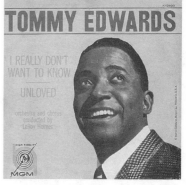

EKBERG, ANITA
(Actress)
: See Ray Ellis (*La Dolce Vita*)

ELASTICA
STUTTER / Pussycat .... *(Sub Pop 275)*   1.25   5.00   95
: (Originally issued as part of a 4-record set titled *Helter Shelter*, which also included singles by S*M*A*S*H, Supergrass, and Gene. Envelope sleeve issued with colored vinyl.)

ELASTIC OZ BAND, THE
GOD SAVE US / Do The Oz .... *(Apple 1835)*   2.50   10.00   71

ELECTRAS, THE
SOUL SEARCHIN' / Action Woman .... *(Get Hip 5067)*   .75   3.00   93

ELECTRIC FLAG, THE
GROOVIN' IS EASY / Over-Lovin' You .... *(Columbia 4-44307)*   3.00   12.00   67
: Also see the Goldberg-Miller Blues Band (Barry Goldberg), Nick Gravenites, the Textones (Barry Goldberg)

ELECTRIC LIGHT ORCHESTRA
CAN'T GET IT OUT OF MY HEAD / Illusion In G Major .... *(United Artists XW573-X)*   1.50   6.00   74
STRANGE MAGIC / New World Rising .... *(United Artists/Jet XW770-Y)*   1.00   4.00   76
: (Shown as by ELO)
TELEPHONE LINE / Poorboy (The Greenwood) .... *(United Artists/Jet XW1000)*   1.00   4.00   77
: (Originally issued with green vinyl)
SWEET TALKIN' WOMAN / Fire On High .... *(United Artists/Jet XW 1145)*   1.00   4.00   77
: (Originally issued with purple vinyl)
TURN TO STONE / Mister Kingdom .... *(United Artists/Jet XW1099)*   1.00   4.00   77
SHINE A LITTLE LOVE .... *(CBS/Jet ZS8-5057)*   1.00   4.00   79
DON'T BRING ME DOWN / Dreaming Of 4000 .... *(CBS/Jet ZS8-5060)*   12.50   50.00   79
I'M ALIVE .... *(MCA 41246)*   .75   3.00   80
: (From the motion picture *Xanadu*)
XANADU .... *(MCA 41285)*   1.00   4.00   80
: (Shown as by Olivia Newton-John / Electric Light Orchestra. From the motion picture *Xanadu*)
ALL OVER THE WORLD .... *(MCA 41289)*   .75   3.00   80
: (From the motion picture *Xanadu*)
CALLING AMERICA / Caught In A Trap .... *(CBS Associated ZS4-05766)*   .75   3.00   86
CALLING AMERICA .... *(CBS Associated ZS4-05766)*   1.25   5.00   86
: (Promotional issue, *Demonstration Only/Not For Sale* printed on sleeve)
SO SERIOUS .... *(CBS Associated ZS4-05892)*   .75   3.00   86
: Also see the Traveling Wilburys (Jeff Lynne)

ELEGANTS, THE
A DREAM CAN COME TRUE / Dressin' Up .... *(Photo 2662)*   15.00   60.00   63
: (Add $10-20 if original single sheet insert is included)

ELEKTRICS
SOME LOVIN' TONIGHT .... *(Capitol P-4905)*   .75   3.00   80

ELEPHANT'S MEMORY
MONGOOSE .... *(Metromedia 182)*   2.00   8.00   70
LIBERATION SPECIAL .... *(Apple 1854)*   3.00   12.00   72
: Also see John Lennon (*Woman Is The Nigger Of The World*)

ELEVATOR DROPS, THE
LENNON'S DEAD / Strange .... *(Time Bomb 7501)*   .50   2.00   95
: (Sleeve pictures a profile head shot of John Lennon, issued with small-hole 45 RPM)

TITLE	LABEL AND NUMBER	VG	NM	YR

ELFMAN, DANNY
GRATITUDE/Tough As Nails .... (MCA 52560) — .75 — 3.00 — 85
    (From the motion picture *Beverly Hills Cop*, Eddie Murphy pictured)
THE BATMAN THEME (EDIT)/The Batman Theme (Action Mix) .... (Warner Bros. 22756-7) — .75 — 3.00 — 89
    (From the motion picture *Batman*)
    Also see Oingo Boingo

ELIAS, JONATHAN
    See Mike + the Mechanics *(Revolution)*

ELLEDGE, JIMMY
A GOLDEN TEAR/I'll Get By .... (RCA Victor 47-8081) — 2.50 — 10.00 — 62
    (This release is mentioned in the promotional insert for Elvis Presley's *King Of The Whole Wide World*)
PLEASE LOVE ME FOREVER/ .... (RCA Victor 47-8191) — 2.50 — 10.00 — 63

ELLIMAN, YVONNE
MOMENT BY MOMENT/Sailing Ships .... (RSO 915) — 1.25 — 5.00 — 78
    (From the motion picture *Moment by Moment*, John Travolta and Lily Tomlin pictured)

ELLINGTON, DUKE
HOOKED ON ELLINGTON .... (RCA 13023) — 1.00 — 4.00 — 81
    (Promotional issue only, gatefold sleeve)

ELLIOT, MAMA CASS
THE GOOD TIMES ARE COMING/Welcome To The World .... (Dunhill 4253) — 5.00 — 20.00 — 70
SOMETHING TO MAKE YOU HAPPY .... (ABC/Dunhill & Blue Thumb D-4266) — 1.25 — 5.00 — 71
    (Shown as by Dave Mason & Mama Cass)
    Also see the Mamas and the Papas

ELLIS, CINDY
DO YOU THINK OF ME .... (Laurie 3045) — 2.00 — 8.00 — 60

ELLIS, DON
EXTENDED PLAYS
ELI'S COMIN (Excerpt) .... (Columbia AS 1) — 1.25 — 5.00 — 70
    (Promotional issue only titled *Dig This*, issued with a small-hole 33-1/3 RPM record. Also includes excerpts
    by Pacific Gas and Electric, Moondog, Nick Gravenites, Pete Seeger, Santana, Raven, Firesign Theatre, and
    Tony Kosinec.)

ELLIS, JIMMY
I'M NOT TRYING TO BE LIKE ELVIS/The Games You've Been Playing .... (Boblo 536) — 1.25 — 5.00 — 78

ELLIS, RAY, AND HIS ORCHESTRA
LA DOLCE VITA/Parlami Di Me (Speak To Me) .... (RCA Victor 47-7888) — 1.50 — 6.00 — 61
    (From the motion picture *La Dolce Vita*, Anita Ekberg pictured)
    Also see Johnny Mathis *(Wild Is The Wind)*

ELLIS, SHIRLEY
THE NAME GAME .... (Congress 230) — 3.00 — 12.00 — 64
THE CLAPPING SONG (CLAP-PAT-CLAP-SLAP) .... (Congress 234) — 3.00 — 12.00 — 64

ELLWOOD, WILLIAM
EXTENDED PLAYS
ETERNAL HOLLY .... (Narada S33-17254) — 1.00 — 4.00 — 86
    (Promotional issue only titled *Narada Sampler–Excellence In New Acoustic Music*, issued with a small-hole
    33-1/3 RPM record. Also includes one song each by Tingstad–Rumbel, Randy Mead, Michael Jones, Matthew
    Montfort, Spencer Brewer, David Lanz, and Gabriel Lee.)

ELMO & PATSY
DEAD SKUNK IN THE MIDDLE OF THE ROAD/I'd Walk With You .... (Oink 8381) — 2.00 — 8.00 — 83
GRANDMA GOT RUN OVER BY A REINDEER/Percy, The Puny Poinsettia .... (Epic 15-5479) — 1.00 — 4.00 — 84

ELM STREET GROUP, THE
IN THE MIDNIGHT HOUR/Do The Freddy .... (RIC 4500) — 1.00 — 4.00 — 84
    (Sleeve pictures Robert Englund as Freddy Krueger from the *Nightmare on Elm Street* motion picture series)

ELVIS
(Television Special)
    See Elvis Presley *(Memories)*

ELVIS BROTHERS, THE
HIDDEN IN A HEARTBEAT/Full Speed Straight Ahead .... (Portrait 37-04106) — .75 — 3.00 — 83
HIDDEN IN A HEARTBEAT .... (Portrait 37-04106) — 1.00 — 4.00 — 83
    (Promotional issue, *Demonstration–Not For Sale* printed on back of sleeve)
MOTORMOUTH/Rock For It .... (Recession 88144) — .75 — 3.00 — 93
    (Issued with small-hole, green vinyl)

ELVIS ON TOUR
(Motion Picture)
    See Elvis Presley *(Separate Ways)*

ELWES, CARY
(Actor)
    See Willy DeVille *(Storybook Love)*, Mark Knopfler *(Storybook Love)*

ELY, JOE, BAND, THE
EXTENDED PLAYS
CRAZY LEMON/NOT FADE AWAY/
    Treat Me Like A Saturday Night/Wishin' For You .... (SouthCoast EPS 33-1736) — 1.25 — 5.00 — 81
    (Included with the album *Texas Special*, issued with a small-hole 33-1/3 RPM record)

ELY, RICK
(Television actor who appeared in only one series, *The Young Rebels*)
CIRCLE GAME .... (RCA Victor 74-0389) — 1.25 — 5.00 — 70

EMERSON, LAKE & PALMER
BRAIN SALAD SURGERY .... (Manticore 2003) — 2.00 — 8.00 — 74
    (Possibly a promotional issue only)

EXTENDED PLAYS

TAKE A PEBBLE/LUCKY MAN/Lookin' For A Love/Sometime In The Morning ...... (Atco PR176) — 3.00 — 12.00 — 72
(Promotional issue only from the live Puerto Rico Pop Festival album *Mar-Y-Sol*. Song one on the b-side shown as by J. Geils Band, song two on the b-side by Jonathan Edwards.)
Also see Asia (Carl Palmer), Greg Lake, Emerson, Lake & Powell

EMERSON, LAKE & POWELL
TOUCH AND GO/Learning To Fly .... (Polydor 885 101-7) — .75 — 3.00 — 86
Also see Asia, Greg Lake, Emerson, Lake & Palmer

ENCHANTED ISLAND
(Motion Picture)
See the Four Lads (*Enchanted Island*)

ENCHANTMENT
SUNSHINE .... (United Artists XW991) — 1.50 — 6.00 — 76
SUNSHINE .... (Roadshow 991) — 1.00 — 4.00 — 77

ENGEL, SCOTT
THE LIVIN' END/Good For Nothin' .... (Orbit 506) — 10.00 — 40.00 — 58
CHARLEY BOP/All I Do Is Dream .... (Orbit 511) — 12.50 — 50.00 — 58
PAPER DOLL/Bluebell .... (Orbit 512) — 10.00 — 40.00 — 58
GOLDEN RULE OF LOVE/Sunday .... (Orbit 537) — 10.00 — 40.00 — 58
Also see the Walker Brothers

ENGLAND DAN AND JOHN FORD COLEY
EXTENDED PLAYS
GONE TOO FAR/WE'LL NEVER HAVE TO SAY GOODBYE AGAIN .... (Atlantic OP-7501) — 1.25 — 5.00 — 78
(Promotional issue only titled *Profiles In Gold Album 1*, issued with a small-hole 33-1/3 RPM record. Sold only at Burger King for 59¢ with the purchase of a Coke. Also includes two songs each by Abba, Spinners, and Firefall.)
Also see Dan Seals (Dan Seals' brother is Jimmy Seals, of Seals & Crofts)

ENGLUND, ROBERT
(Portrayed horror film character Freddy Krueger in the *Nightmare On Elm Street* series)
See the Elm Street Group

ENGLISH BEAT, THE
SAVE IT FOR LATER/Jeanette .... (I.R.S. 9909) — 1.00 — 4.00 — 82
GENERIC ENGLISH BEAT SLEEVE .... (I.R.S. no #) — 1.00 — 4.00 — 82
(Generic half sleeve used for any English Beat single)
Also see Fine Young Cannibals (David Steele), General Public (Ranking Roger, Dave Wakeling), the Special AKA (Rankin Roger, Dave Wakeling), Dave Wakeling

ENO, BRIAN
WIMOWEH (LION SLEEPS TONITE)/Deadly 7 Finns .... (Was Trash 101) — 12.50 — 50.00 — 79
(Promotional issue only, folding sleeve with no song titles or label identification on sleeve)
BABY'S ON FIRE/Fever .... (unknown) — 12.50 — 50.00
(Folding sleeve with no label identification on sleeve)

ENUFF Z'NUFF
NEW THING/Kiss The Clown .... (Atco 7-99207) — .75 — 3.00 — 87

ENVY
I BELIEVE IN YOU/Hurt Me .... (Atco 7-99443) — .75 — 3.00 — 87

ENYA
ORINOCO FLOW (SAIL AWAY)/Out Of The Blue .... (Geffen 27633-7) — 1.50 — 6.00 — 88

EPIC SPLENDOR
IT COULD BE WONDERFUL/She's High On Life .... (Hot Biscuit 1452) — 3.00 — 12.00 — 68

ERASURE
WHO NEEDS LOVE LIKE THAT/Push Me Shove Me .... (Sire 28728-7) — 1.50 — 6.00 — 87
SOMETIMES/It Doesn't Have To Be .... (Sire 28362-7) — 1.25 — 5.00 — 87
VICTIM OF LOVE/Soldier's Return .... (Sire 28238-7) — 1.25 — 5.00 — 87
CHAINS OF LOVE/Don't Suppose .... (Sire 27844-7) — 1.00 — 4.00 — 88
A LITTLE RESPECT/Like Zsa Zsa Gabor .... (Sire 27738-7) — 1.00 — 4.00 — 88
Also see Yazoo (Vince Clarke). Clarke was also a founding member of Depeche Mode but left after their first album in 1981.

ERIC B. & RAKIM
Microphone Fiend .... (Uni 50005) — .75 — 3.00 — 88

ERICKSON, ROKY
BERMUDA/The Interpreter .... (Rhino 003) — 1.25 — 5.00 — 77

ERIK
LOOK WHERE I AM (WELL, IT'S RIGHT OVER HERE) .... (Vanguard 35056) — 1.50 — 6.00 — 68

ESCAPADE IN FLORENCE
(Television Special)
See Annette (*Bella Bella Florence*)

ESCAPE CLUB, THE
WILD, WILD WEST/We Can Run .... (Atlantic 7-89048) — .75 — 3.00 — 88
SHAKE FOR THE SHEIK/Working For The Fatman .... (Atlantic 7-88983) — .75 — 3.00 — 88
WALKING THROUGH WALLS/Standing On A Bridge .... (Atlantic 7-88951) — .75 — 3.00 — 89

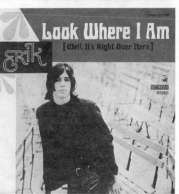

ESPOSITO, JOE
COME INTO MY LIFE/ .... (Atco 7-99280) — .75 — 3.00 — 88
(A-side shown as by Laura Branigan and Joe Esposito, both pictured, b-side by Laura Branigan. From the motion picture *Coming To America*.)
Also see Brenda Russell (*Piano In The Dark*)

ESQUERITA
HEY MISS LUCY .... (Capitol 1075) — 750.00 — 3000.00 — 59
(Promotional issue only, sleeve reads *Presenting The Rocking Vocals And Rolling Piano Of Esquerita*. Reportedly four copies are known to exist, the near mint price is speculation.)

TITLE	LABEL AND NUMBER	VG	NM	YR

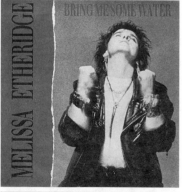

ESSEX, DAVID

TITLE	LABEL AND NUMBER	VG	NM	YR
ROCK ON/On And On	(Columbia 4-45940)	1.50	6.00	73
LAMPLIGHT/We All Insane	(Columbia 4-46041)	1.25	5.00	74
AMERICA	(Columbia 3-10005)	1.25	5.00	74
GONNA MAKE YOU A STAR/Window	(Columbia 3-10039)	1.25	5.00	74
ROLLING STONE/Coconut Ice	(Columbia 3-10183)	1.25	5.00	75

ESTEFAN, GLORIA, AND MIAMI SOUND MACHINE

TITLE	LABEL AND NUMBER	VG	NM	YR
CONGA/Mucho Money	(Epic 34-05457)	.75	3.00	85
(Shown as by Miami Sound Machine)				
CONGA	(Epic 34-05457)	1.00	4.00	85
(Promotional issue, *Demonstration Only–Not For Sale* printed on sleeve. Shown as by Miami Sound Machine)				
BAD BOY/Surrender Paradise	(Epic 34-05805)	.75	3.00	85
(Shown as by Miami Sound Machine)				
BAD BOY	(Epic 34-05805)	1.00	4.00	85
(Promotional issue, *Demonstration Only–Not For Sale* printed on sleeve. Shown as by Miami Sound Machine)				
FALLING IN LOVE (UH-OH)/Primitive Love	(Epic 34-06352)	.75	3.00	86
(Shown as by Miami Sound Machine)				
FALLING IN LOVE (UH-OH)	(Epic 34-06352)	1.00	4.00	86
(Promotional issue, *Demonstration Only–Not For Sale* printed on sleeve. Shown as by Miami Sound Machine)				
RHYTHM IS GONNA GET YOU	(Epic 34-07059)	.75	3.00	87
RHYTHM IS GONNA GET YOU	(Epic 34-07059)	1.00	4.00	87
(Promotional issue, *Demonstration Only–Not For Sale* printed on sleeve)				
BETCHA SAY THAT	(Epic 34-07371)	.75	3.00	87
CAN'T STAY AWAY FROM YOU	(Epic 34-07641)	.75	3.00	87
ANYTHING FOR YOU	(Epic 34-07759)	.75	3.00	88
1 2 3	(Epic 34-07921)	.75	3.00	88

ESTEVEZ, EMILIO
(Actor, son of Martin Sheen and brother of Charlie Sheen)
See John Parr (*St. Elmo's Fire*), Wang Chung (*Fire In The Twilight*)

E STREET BAND, THE
See Clarence Clemons, Little Steven, Ronnie Spector (*Say Goodbye To Hollywood*), Bruce Springsteen, Jim Steinman (*The Storm*), Barbra Streisand (*Left In The Dark*), Warren Zevon (*Reconsider Me*)

ESTUS, DEON

TITLE	LABEL AND NUMBER	VG	NM	YR
HEAVEN HELP ME/It's A Party	(Polydor 871 538-7)	.75	3.00	89
(Shown as by Deon Estus with additional vocals by George Michael)				

ETERNITY'S CHILDREN

TITLE	LABEL AND NUMBER	VG	NM	YR
MRS. BLUEBIRD/Little Boy	(Tower 416)	3.75	15.00	68
SUNSHINE AMONG US/Rupert White	(Tower 416)	3.75	15.00	68

ETHERIDGE, MELISSA

TITLE	LABEL AND NUMBER	VG	NM	YR
BRING ME SOME WATER/Occasionally	(Island 7-99287)	1.00	4.00	88
SIMILAR FEATURES/Bring Me Some Water (Live)	(Island 7-99251)	1.00	4.00	88
NO SOUVENIRS/No Souvenirs (Live)	(Island 7-99176)	1.00	4.00	89

E.T. THE EXTRA TERRESTRIAL
(Motion Picture)
See John Williams (*Theme From E.T.*)

E-TYPES, THE

TITLE	LABEL AND NUMBER	VG	NM	YR
I CAN'T DO IT/Long Before	(Link 1)	5.00	20.00	66

E.U.

TITLE	LABEL AND NUMBER	VG	NM	YR
DA BUTT	(EMI Manhattan 50115)	.75	3.00	88
(Featured in the motion picture *School Daze*, film's director Spike Lee pictured)				
BUCK WILD/Express	(Virgin 7-99232)	.75	3.00	89
Also see Salt-N-Pepa (*Spinderella's Not A Fella*)				

EUCLID BEACH BAND

TITLE	LABEL AND NUMBER	VG	NM	YR
THERE'S NO SURF IN CLEVELAND/Laugh In The Dark	(Scene 45001)	1.50	6.00	78

EUPHORIA

TITLE	LABEL AND NUMBER	VG	NM	YR
YOU MUST FORGET	(Heritage 831)	2.50	10.00	69

EUROGLIDERS

TITLE	LABEL AND NUMBER	VG	NM	YR
CAN'T WAIT TO SEE YOU/I Like To Hear It	(Columbia 38-05797)	.75	3.00	86
CAN'T WAIT TO SEE YOU	(Columbia 38-05797)	1.00	4.00	86
(Promotional issue, *Demonstration–Not For Sale* printed on sleeve)				

EUROPE

TITLE	LABEL AND NUMBER	VG	NM	YR
CARRIE/Love Chaser	(Epic 34-07282)	.75	3.00	86
ROCK THE NIGHT/Seven Doors Hotel	(Epic 34-07091)	.75	3.00	87
CHEROKEE/Heart Of Stone	(Epic 34-07638)	.75	3.00	87
SUPERSTITIOUS/Light & Shadows	(Epic 34-07979)	.75	3.00	88
OPEN YOUR HEART/Tower's Callin'	(Epic 34-08102)	.75	3.00	88
LET THE GOOD TIMES ROCK/Never Say Die	(Epic 34-68547)	.75	3.00	89

EURYTHMICS

TITLE	LABEL AND NUMBER	VG	NM	YR
SWEET DREAMS (ARE MADE OF THIS)/I Could Give You (A Mirror)	(RCA PB-13533)	1.00	4.00	83
LOVE IS A STRANGER/I've Got An Angel	(RCA PB-13618)	1.00	4.00	83
HERE COMES THE RAIN AGAIN (LONG VERSION)/Paint A Rumour	(RCA PB-13725)	.75	3.00	83
WHO'S THAT GIRL?/Aqua	(RCA PB-13800)	.75	3.00	83
RIGHT BY YOUR SIDE/Right By Your Side (Party-Mix)	(RCA PB-13695)	.75	3.00	83
SEXCRIME (NINETEEN EIGHTY-FOUR)/I Did It Just The Same	(RCA PB-13956)	.75	3.00	84
(From the motion picture *1984*)				
JULIA/Theme From "1984" (Sexcrime)	(RCA PB-14015)	.75	3.00	85
(From the motion picture *1984*, Suzanna Hamilton pictured)				
WOULD I LIE TO YOU?/Here Comes That Sinking Feeling	(RCA PB-14078)	.75	3.00	85
THERE MUST BE AN ANGEL (PLAYING WITH MY HEART)/Grown Up Girls	(RCA PB-14160)	.75	3.00	85
SISTERS ARE DOIN' IT FOR THEMSELVES/I Love You Like A Ball And Chain	(RCA PB-14214)	.75	3.00	85
(Shown as by Eurythmics and Aretha Franklin)				

Title	Label and Number	VG	NM	YR
IT'S ALRIGHT–(BABY'S COMING BACK)/Conditioned Soul	(RCA PB-14284)	.75	3.00	85
MISSIONARY MAN (EDITED VERSION)/Take Your Pain Away	(RCA PB-14414)	.75	3.00	86
THORN IN MY SIDE/In This Town	(RCA 5058-7-R)	.75	3.00	86
I NEED A MAN/Heaven	(RCA 5361-7-R)	1.00	4.00	87
YOU HAVE PLACED A CHILL IN MY HEART (CHILL MIX)/ You Have Placed A Chill In My Heart	(RCA 7615-7-RX)	5.00	20.00	88
DON'T ASK ME WHY/Rich Girl	(Arista 9880)	.75	3.00	89
ANGEL/Precious	(Arista 9917)	1.50	6.00	89
(MY MY) BABY'S GONNA CRY/(My My) Baby's Gonna Cry (Acoustic Version)	(Arista 9939)	1.50	6.00	90

Also see Annie Lennox and Al Green, Etta James (Dave A. Stewart)

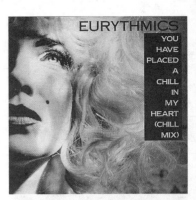

EVENTUALS, THE
CHARLIE CHAN	(Okeh 7142)	3.75	15.00	62

EVERCLEAR
NERVOUS & WEIRD/Electra Made Me Blind	(Tim Kerr 937055)	1.00	4.00	93

(Hard cover with lyric insert, issued with half red/half clear vinyl)

EXTENDED PLAYS
LIVE ON THE RADIO	(Capitol/Tim Kerr 7PRO-79594)	1.00	4.00	95

(Issued with red vinyl, included with the album *Sparkle And Fade*)

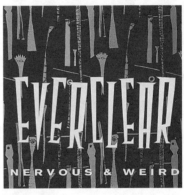

EVERGREEN BLUES, THE
MIDNIGHT CONFESSIONS/That's My Baby (Yes)	(Mercury 72756)	2.00	8.00	68
LAURA/Yesterday's Coming	(Mercury 72780)	2.00	8.00	68

EVERLY BROTHERS, THE
WAKE UP, LITTLE SUSIE/Maybe Tomorrow	(Cadence 1337)	37.50	150.00	57
PROBLEMS/Love Of My Life	(Cadence 1355)	10.00	40.00	58
('TIL) I KISSED YOU/Oh, What A Feeling	(Cadence 1369)	10.00	40.00	59
LET IT BE ME/Since You Broke My Heart	(Cadence 1376)	10.00	40.00	59
CATHY'S CLOWN/Always It's You	(Warner Bros. 5151)	6.25	25.00	60
SO SAD/Lucille	(Warner Bros. 5163)	5.00	20.00	60
EBONY EYES/Walk Right Back	(Warner Bros. 5199)	5.00	20.00	61
TEMPTATION/Stick With Me Baby	(Warner Bros. 5220)	5.00	20.00	61
DON'T BLAME ME/WALK RIGHT BACK/Muskrat/Lucille	(Warner Bros. 5501)	6.25	25.00	61

(*Plus 2 Oldies* series which offered "4 Songs For The Price Of 2")

CRYING IN THE RAIN/I'm Not Angry	(Warner Bros. 5250)	5.00	20.00	61
THAT'S OLD FASHIONED/How Can I Meet Her	(Warner Bros. 5273)	5.00	20.00	62
I'M HERE TO GET MY BABY OUT OF JAIL/Lightning Express	(Cadence 1429)	6.25	25.00	62
DON'T ASK ME TO BE FRIENDS/No One Can Make My Sunshine Smile	(Warner Bros. 5297)	5.00	20.00	62
LOVE IS STRANGE/Man With Money	(Warner Bros. 5649)	5.00	20.00	65
ON THE WINGS OF A NIGHTINGALE/Asleep	(Mercury 880 213-7)	1.25	5.00	83
I KNOW LOVE/These Shoes	(Mercury 884 694-7)	1.00	4.00	86
DON'T WORRY BABY	(Capitol B-44297)	1.00	4.00	88

(Shown as by the Everly Brothers With the Beach Boys. From the motion picture *Tequila Sunrise*, Mel Gibson, Michelle Pfeiffer, and Kurt Russell pictured on back.)

EVERY MOTHER'S SON
PUT YOUR MIND AT EASE	(MGM K-13788)	2.00	8.00	67

EVERYTHING BUT THE GIRL
I ALWAYS WAS YOUR GIRL	(Sire 7-27892)	.75	3.00	88

EXCITERS, THE
I WANT YOU TO BE MY BOY/Tonight, Tonight	(Roulette 4591)	7.50	30.00	64

EXILE
GIVE ME ONE MORE CHANCE/Ain't That A Pity	(Epic 34-04567)	.75	3.00	84

EXPERIMENT IN TERROR
(Motion Picture)

See Henry Mancini (*Experiment In Terror*)

EXPOSÉ
COME GO WITH ME/December	(Arista 9555)	.75	3.00	87
POINT OF NO RETURN/Extra Extra	(Arista 9579)	.75	3.00	87
LET ME BE THE ONE/Love Is Our Destiny	(Arista 9617)	.75	3.00	87
SEASONS CHANGE/December	(Arista 9640)	.75	3.00	87
WHAT YOU DON'T KNOW/Walk Along With Me	(Arista 9836)	.75	3.00	89
WHEN I LOOKED AT HIM/When I Looked At Him "Suave Mix" (Acoustic Version)	(Arista 9868)	.75	3.00	89
TELL ME WHY/Let Me Down Easy	(Arista 9916)	.75	3.00	89

F

FABARES, SHELLEY
JOHNNY ANGEL/Where's It Gonna Get Me?	(Colpix 621)	37.50	150.00	62

(The cast of the Donna Reed Show is pictured which includes Fabares.)

WHAT DID THEY DO BEFORE ROCK AND ROLL?/Very Unlikely	(Colpix 631)	15.00	60.00	62

(Shown as by Shelley Fabares With Paul Petersen)

JOHNNY LOVES ME/I'm Growing Up	(Colpix 636)	25.00	100.00	62

Also see Paul Petersen (B-side of *She Can't Find Her Keys*)

FABIAN
I AM A MAN	(Chancellor 1029)	6.25	25.00	59

(Record shows a-side title correctly as *I'm A Man*)

TURN ME LOOSE/Stop, Thief!	(Chancellor 1033)	6.25	25.00	59
TIGER/Mighty Cold (To A Warm, Warm Heart)	(Chancellor 1037)	6.25	25.00	59
COME ON AND GET ME/Got The Feeling	(Chancellor 1041)	6.25	25.00	59
HOUND DOG MAN/This Friendly World	(Chancellor 1044)	6.25	25.00	59

(There are reported to be 2 variations)

ABOUT THIS THING CALLED LOVE/String Along	(Chancellor 1047)	6.25	25.00	60
STROLLIN' IN THE SPRINGTIME/ I'm Gonna Sit Right Down And Write Myself A Letter	(Chancellor 1051)	6.25	25.00	60

TITLE	LABEL AND NUMBER	VG	NM	YR

KING OF LOVE/Tomorrow .... (Chancellor 1055) 6.25 25.00 60
KISSIN' AND TWISTIN'/Long Before .... (Chancellor 1061) 6.25 25.00 60
YOU KNOW YOU BELONG TO SOMEONE ELSE/Hold On .... (Chancellor 1067) 6.25 25.00 61
THE LOVE THAT I'M GIVING TO YOU/You're Only Young Once .... (Chancellor 1079) 6.25 25.00 61
A GIRL LIKE YOU/Dream Factory .... (Chancellor 1084) 7.50 30.00 61
WILD PARTY/Made You .... (Chancellor 1092) 7.50 30.00 61
THE AMERICAN EAST/Ease On Into My Life .... (Cream 7717) 1.25 5.00 77

FABRIC, BENT
ALLEY CAT .... (Atco 6226) 3.75 15.00 62

FABULOUS PACK, THE
WIDETRACKIN' .... (Lucky Eleven 007) 3.75 15.00 65
    Also see Mark Farner and Don Brewer, Grand Funk

FABULOUS RHINESTONES, THE
WHAT A WONDERFUL THING WE HAVE .... (Just Sunshine 500) 1.50 6.00 72
    Also see the Buckinghams (Marty Grebb)

FABULOUS THUNDERBIRDS, THE
TUFF ENUFF/Look At That, Look At That .... (CBS Associated ZS4-05838) .75 3.00 86
TUFF ENUFF .... (CBS Associated ZS4-05838) 1.00 4.00 86
    (Promotional issue, *Demonstration–Not For Sale* printed on sleeve)
WRAP IT UP/True Love .... (CBS Associated ZS4-06270) .75 3.00 86
WRAP IT UP .... (CBS Associated ZS4-06270) 1.00 4.00 86
    (Promotional issue, *Demonstration–Not For Sale* printed on sleeve)
WHY GET UP/I Don't Care .... (CBS Associated ZS4 06396) .75 3.00 86
WHY GET UP .... (CBS Associated ZS4 06396) 1.00 4.00 86
    (Promotional issue, *Demonstration–Not For Sale* printed on sleeve)
STAND BACK/It Takes A Big Man To Cry .... (CBS Associated ZS4-07230) .75 3.00 87

FACES
REAL GOOD TIME .... (Warner Bros. 7442) 5.00 20.00 70
    (Promotional issue only. Sleeve shows group name as Small Faces but record credits Faces.)
CINDY, INCIDENTALLY .... (Warner Bros. 7681) 3.00 12.00 73
    (Possibly a promotional issue only)
    Also see Ronnie Lane, the Rolling Stones (Ron Wood), the Small Faces (Kenney Jones, Ronnie Lane), Rod Stewart, the Who (Kenney Jones)

FACE TO FACE
10-9-8/Heaven On Earth .... (Epic 34-04430) .75 3.00 84
10-9-8 .... (Epic 34-04430) 1.00 4.00 84
    (Promotional issue, *Demonstration–Not For Sale* printed on sleeve)
UNDER THE GUN/Over The Edge .... (Epic 34-04582) .75 3.00 84
UNDER THE GUN .... (Epic 34-04582) 1.00 4.00 84
    (Promotional issue, *Demonstration Not For Sale* printed on sleeve)

FACHIN, ERIA
SAVIN' MYSELF .... (Critique 99356) .75 3.00 88

FAGEN, DONALD
I.G.Y./Walk Between Raindrops .... (Warner Bros. 29900-7) 1.00 4.00 82
CENTURY'S END/Shanghai Confidential .... (Warner Bros. 27972-7) .75 3.00 88
    (From the motion picture *Bright Lights, Big City*)

FAIRGROUND ATTRACTION
PERFECT/Mythology .... (RCA 8789-7-R) .75 3.00 88

FAITH, PERCY, AND HIS ORCHESTRA
THEME FROM "A SUMMER PLACE" .... (Columbia 4-41490) 2.00 8.00 60
    (From the motion picture *A Summer Place*)
THEME FOR YOUNG LOVERS/Dimini Goombay .... (Columbia 4-41655) 2.00 8.00 60

FAITH, RUSSELL
THEME FROM JACQUELINE .... (Chancellor 1076) 1.50 6.00 61

FAITHFULL, MARIANNE
GO AWAY FROM MY WORLD .... (London 45-9802) 5.00 20.00 65
COUNTING .... (London 45-20012) 5.00 20.00 66

FAITH NO MORE
QUIET IN HEAVEN/Song Of Liberty .... (Ministry Of Propaganda FNM1) 5.00 20.00 83
    (Shown as by Faith No Man)
EASY/Slide (Live) .... (Soil X Samples 5847) 2.50 10.00 92
    (Split single, flip side shown as by L7)

FALCO
VIENNA CALLING/Tango In The Night .... (A&M 2832) .75 3.00 85
JEANNY/Manner Des Westens-Any Kind Of Land .... (A&M 2851) .75 3.00 85
EMOTIONAL .... (Sire 28375-7) .75 3.00 86
THE SOUND OF MUSIK .... (Sire 28590-7) .75 3.00 86

FALCON AND THE SNOWMAN, THE
(Motion Picture)
    See David Bowie (*This Is Not America*)

FALCONER, RODERICK
PLAY IT AGAIN/New Nation .... (United Artists 900) 1.25 5.00 76

FALTERMEYER, HAROLD
AXEL F THEME .... (MCA 52536) .75 3.00 85
    (From the motion picture *Beverly Hills Cop*)
FLETCH THEME .... (MCA 52641) .75 3.00 85
    (From the motion picture *Fletch*, Chevy Chase pictured)
TOP GUN ANTHEM .... (Columbia 38-06282) .75 3.00 86
    (Shown as by Harold Faltermeyer and Steve Stevens. From the motion picture *Top Gun*.)
TOP GUN ANTHEM .... (Columbia 38-06282) 1.00 4.00 86
    (Shown as by Harold Faltermeyer and Steve Stevens. Promotional issue, *Demonstration Only–Not For Sale* printed on sleeve. From the motion picture *Top Gun*.)

FÄLTSKOG, AGNETHA
CAN'T SHAKE LOOSE/Man .... (Polydor 815 230-7)	1.50	6.00	83
I WASN'T THE ONE/Maybe It Was Magic .... (Atlantic 7-89145)	1.00	4.00	88

(A-side shown as by Agnetha Fältskog and Peter Cetera)

LET IT SHINE/Maybe It Was Magic .... (Atlantic 7-89055)   1.00   4.00   88

Also see Abba

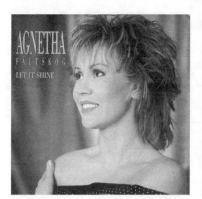

FAME
(Television Series)

See the Kids From Fame (Be Your Own Hero)

FAMILY
IN MY OWN TIME/Seasons .... (United Artists 50832)   3.00   12.00   71

FAMILY, THE
THE SCREAMS OF PASSION .... (Paisley Park 28953-7)   .75   3.00   85

FAMILY AFFAIR
(Television Series)

Related see Johnny Whitaker

FAMILY ALBUM, THE
WALK ALONG BESIDE ME/Candy .... (Columbia 4-44570)   3.00   12.00   68

FANDANGO
LAST KISS .... (RCA JH-11357)   1.25   5.00   78

(Promotional issue only, For D.J.'s Only Not For Sale printed on front)

EXTENDED PLAYS

HEADLINER .... (RCA JF-11225)   1.25   5.00   78

(Promotional issue only titled The Music's On Us, issued with a small-hole 33-1/3 RPM record. Also includes one song each by Bill Quateman, Aztec Two-Step, and Scorpions.)

FAR CORPORATION
STAIRWAY TO HEAVEN/Financial Controller .... (Atco 7-99509)   .75   3.00   86

Also see Toto (Bobby Kimball, Steve Lukather, Dave Paich)

FARGO, DONNA
THE HAPPIEST GIRL IN THE WHOLE U.S.A. .... (Dot 17409)	1.50	6.00	71
LITTLE GIRL GONE .... (Dot 17476)	1.50	6.00	72
U. S. OF A. .... (ABC/Dot 17523)	1.50	6.00	74
LONESTAR COWBOY/The Utah Song .... (Warner Bros. 49757)	1.25	5.00	81

FARNER, MARK, AND DON BREWER
WE GOTTA HAVE LOVE/Harlem Shuffle .... (Lucky Eleven 74011)   3.75   15.00   68

Also see the Fabulous Pack, Grand Funk

FARRENHEIT
FOOL IN LOVE .... (Warner Bros. 28427-7)   .75   3.00   87

FARROW, CEE
SHOULD I LOVE YOU .... (Rocshire 95032)   .75   3.00   83

FASHION
THE INNOCENT .... (I.R.S. 9502)   1.00   4.00   79

FASTBACKS, THE
IT'S YOUR BIRTHDAY/You Can't Be Happy .... (No Threes 005)   6.25   25.00   81

Also see Guns N' Roses (Duff McKagan), Silly Killers (Duff McKagan)

FASTER PUSSYCAT
BABYLON/Smash Alley .... (Elektra 7-69413)   .75   3.00   87

FAST TIMES AT RIDGEMONT HIGH
(Motion Picture)

See Jackson Browne (Somebody's Baby), Ravyns (Raised On The Radio), Joe Walsh (Waffle Stomp)

FATAL BEAUTY
(Motion Picture)

See Donna Allen (Make It My Night), Shannon (Criminal)

FAT BOYS
FALLING LOVE/Protect Yourself/My Nuts .... (Tin Pan Apple/Polydor 885 766-7)	.75	3.00	87
WIPEOUT/Crushin' .... (Tin Pan Apple/Polydor 885 960-7)	.75	3.00	88

(Shown as by Fat Boys and the Beach Boys, sleeve pictures both groups)

THE TWIST (YO TWIST)/The Twist (Buffapella) .... (Tin Pan Apple/Polydor 887 571-7)   .75   3.00   88

(Shown as by Fat Boys With Stupid Def Vocals By Chubby Checker)

ARE YOU READY FOR FREDDY/Back And Forth .... (Tin Pan Apple/Polydor 887 894-7)   .75   3.00   88

LOUIE LOUIE/All Day Lover (7" Version) .... (Tin Pan Apple/Mercury 871 010-7)   .75   3.00   88

FATHER GOOSE
(Motion Picture)

See Mike Douglas (Pass Me By)

FAWCETT MAJORS, FARRAH
YOU (TOÍ) (SI)/Let Me Get To Know You .... (Nelson Barry/TK 7900)   1.50   6.00   77

(Farrah Fawcett Majors pictured on the front and Jean-Paul Vignon on the back, titles not listed on sleeve. Record shows a-side by Farrah Fawcett and Jean-Paul Vignon, b-side by Jean-Paul Vignon.)

Also see Jean-Paul Vignon

FEAR
I LOVE LIVIN' IN THE CITY/Now You're Dead .... (Criminal no #)	25.00	100.00	78
FUCK CHRISTMAS/*uck Christmas .... (Slash 900)	2.50	10.00	79

(Plain white sleeve stamped with a Christmas tree graphic)

FEARON, PHIL
AIN'T NOTHING BUT A HOUSE PARTY .... (Chrysalis VS4-43073)   .75   3.00   86

TITLE	LABEL AND NUMBER	VG	NM	YR

FELDER, DON
HEAVY METAL (TAKIN' A RIDE)/All Of You .... (Full Moon/Asylum 47175) | 1.00 | 4.00 | 81
(From the motion picture *Heavy Metal*)
Also see the Eagles, Ravyns (*Raised On The Radio*)

FELDER, WILTON
I'LL STILL BE LOOKING UP TO YOU .... (MCA 52467) | .75 | 3.00 | 85
(Shown as by Bobby Womack and Wilton Felder)
SECRETS .... (MCA 52599) | .75 | 3.00 | 85
(Shown as by Bobby Womack and Wilton Felder)

FELDMAN, COREY
(Juvenile Actor)
See Breakfast Club (*Drive My Car*)

FELDMAN, MARTY
(Comic Actor)
See Lionel Newman (*The Silent Movie March*)

FELDON, BARBARA
(Actress/entertainer best known for her role as Agent 99 in the telvision series *Get Smart*)
MAX/99 .... (RCA Victor 47-8954) | 5.00 | 20.00 | 65

FELONY
THE FANATIC/Positively Negative .... (CBX DR-1004) | 2.00 | 8.00 | 82

FEMALE BODY INSPECTORS
THE GIRL PULLED A DOG .... (Warner Bros. 28637-7) | .75 | 3.00 | 86

FEMME FATALE
FALLING IN & OUT OF LOVE .... (MCA 53445) | .75 | 3.00 | 88

FENHOLT, JEFF
SIMPLE MAN/Billy Is Dead .... (Columbia 4-45604) | 1.25 | 5.00 | 72

FERRANTE AND TEICHER
THE THEME FROM THE APARTMENT .... (United Artists 231) | 2.00 | 8.00 | 60
(From the motion picture *The Apartment*, Jack Lemmon, Shirley MacLaine, and Fred MacMurray pictured)
THE THEME FROM EXODUS .... (United Artists 274) | 2.00 | 8.00 | 60
LOVE THEME FROM ONE EYED JACKS/
Tara's Theme From Gone With The Wind .... (United Artists 300) | 2.00 | 8.00 | 61
(From the motion picture *One Eyed Jacks*, illustration of Marlon Brando pictured)
THE WISHING STAR .... (United Artists 537) | 2.00 | 8.00 | 63
THE 7TH DAWN/You're Too Much .... (United Artists 735) | 2.00 | 8.00 | 64
GREATEST STORY EVER TOLD .... (United Artists 816) | 2.00 | 8.00 | 65
KHARTOUM (MAIN THEME)/Firebird .... (United Artists 50038) | 1.50 | 6.00 | 67

FERRER, JOSE
WOMAN (UH-HUH)/Man .... (Columbia 4-40144) | 2.00 | 8.00 | 53
(B-side shown as by Rosemary Clooney)
YES VIRGINIA THERE IS A SANTA CLAUS/Santa's Marching Song .... (RCA Victor 47-7823) | 2.00 | 8.00 | 61
(Shown as by Jose Ferrer With The Little Ferrers)

FERRIS BUELLER'S DAY OFF
(Motion Picture)
See General Public (b-side of *Too Much Or Nothing*), Yello (*Oh Yeah*)

FERRY, BRYAN
SLAVE TO LOVE/Valentine .... (Warner Bros. 289902-7) | 1.00 | 4.00 | 85
DON'T STOP THE DANCE/Nocturne .... (Warner Bros. 28887-7) | 1.00 | 4.00 | 85
IS YOUR LOVE STRONG ENOUGH/Windswept (Instrumental) .... (MCA 52788) | 1.00 | 4.00 | 86
(From the motion picture *Legend*)
HELP ME/Broken Wings .... (Warner Bros. 28582-7) | 1.00 | 4.00 | 86
(From the motion picture *The Fly*)
KISS AND TELL/Zamba .... (Reprise 28117-7) | 1.00 | 4.00 | 87
(A-side featured in the motion picture *Bright Lights, Big City*)
LIMBO (Latin Version)/Limbo (Brooklyn Version) .... (Reprise 28116-7) | 1.00 | 4.00 | 88
Also see Roxy Music

FERRY AID
LET IT BE .... (Profile 5147) | 1.00 | 4.00 | 87
Also see the Alarm, Rick Astley, Bananarama, Boy George, Kate Bush, Difford & Tilbrook, the Drifters, Frankie Goes To Hollywood, Go West, Nick Kamen, Nik Kershaw, Paul King, Mark Knopfler, Annabel Lamb, Paul McCartney, the New Seekers, Hazel O'Connor, Pepsi & Shirlie, Maxi Priest, Suzi Quatro, Bonnie Tyler, Kim Wilde

FIALKA, KAREL
HEY MATTHEW/The Things I Saw .... (I.R.S. 53427) | .75 | 3.00 | 88

FIDDLER ON THE ROOF
(Broadway Musical)
See Zero Mostel (*If I Were A Rich Man*)

FIEDLER, ARTHUR
See the Boston Pops Orchestra Conducted By Arthur Fiedler

FIELD, SALLY
(Actress who was starring in the television series *The Flying Nun* at the time of this release)
FELICIDAD/Find Yourself A Rainbow .... (Colgems 66-1008) | 2.00 | 8.00 | 67

FIELDS, KIM
(Juvenile actress who played Tootie in the television series *The Facts Of Life* from 1979-1988)
DEAR MICHAEL/Dear Michael (Instrumental) .... (Critique 705) | 2.50 | 10.00 | 84

FIENSTEIN, DIANNE
(Mayor of San Francisco, California)
See Vicky Spinosa

FIENSTEIN, MICHAEL
WHAT CHANCE HAVE I WITH YOU .... (Elektra 7-69460) | 1.00 | 4.00 | 87

5TH DIMENSION, THE
		VG	NM	YR
GO WHERE YOU WANNA GO	(Soul City 753)	3.75	15.00	69
ANOTHER DAY, ANOTHER HEARTACHE/Rosecrans Blvd.	(Soul City 755)	2.50	10.00	67
STONED SOUL PICNIC/The Sailboat Song	(Soul City 766)	2.50	10.00	68
SWEET BLINDNESS	(Soul City 768)	2.50	10.00	68
AQUARIUS/LET THE SUNSHINE IN	(Soul City 772)	2.50	10.00	69
PUPPET MAN/A Love Like Ours	(Bell 880)	3.00	12.00	70

52ND STREET
		VG	NM	YR
TELL ME (HOW IT FEELS)/Tell Me (How It Feels) (Dub)	(MCA 52805)	.75	3.00	85
YOU'RE MY LAST CHANCE	(MCA 52887)	.75	3.00	86

FIGGS, THE
GIRL, KILL YOUR BOYFRIEND/What Became Of It .... (Capitol 11250) | 1.25 | 5.00 | 96
(5" promotional issue only)

FIGURES ON A BEACH
YOU AIN'T SEEN NOTHING YET .... (Sire 27628-7) | .75 | 3.00 | 89

FINE MESS, A
(Motion Picture)
See Mary Jane Girls (Walk Like A Man), The Temptations (A Fine Mess)

FINESSE AND SYNQUIS
BASS GAME/He Cuts So Fresh .... (MCA 53043) | .75 | 3.00 | 87
(Double artist single, flip side shown as by Marley Marl Featuring M.C. Shan)

FINE YOUNG CANNIBALS
		VG	NM	YR
JOHNNY COME HOME/Love For Sale	(I.R.S. 52760)	.75	3.00	85
SUSPICIOUS MINDS/Prick Up Your Ears	(I.R.S. 52836)	.75	3.00	86
EVER FALLEN IN LOVE	(I.R.S./MCA 52981)	1.00	4.00	86
(From the motion picture Something Wild)				
SHE DRIVES ME CRAZY	(I.R.S./MCA 53483)	.75	3.00	88

Also see the English Beat

FINN, TIM
HOW'M I GONNA SLEEP .... (Capitol B-44339) | .75 | 3.00 | 89
Also see Crowded House, Split Enz

FINN AND THE SHARKS
WHEELS START TURNING .... (HME WS4-04827) | .75 | 3.00 | 85

FIONA
		VG	NM	YR
LOVE MAKES YOU BLIND/	(Atlantic 7-89610)	.75	3.00	85
(From the motion picture No Small Affair)				
LOVE MAKES YOU BLIND/Over Now	(Atlantic 7-89543)	.75	3.00	85
LIVING IN A BOY'S WORLD/Keeper Of The Flame	(Atlantic 7-89432)	.75	3.00	86
HOPELESSLY LOVE YOU/Keeper Of The Flame	(Atlantic 7-89408)	.75	3.00	86
EVERYTHING YOU DO (YOU'RE SEXING ME)/Calling On You	(Atlantic 7-88823)	.75	3.00	89

(A-side credited as a Duet With Kip Winger)

FIORENTINO, LINDA
(Actress)
See John Waite (Change)

FIORILLO, ELISA
		VG	NM	YR
WHO FOUND WHO/The Real Thing (Part 2 Instrumental)	(Chrysalis VS4 43120)	.75	3.00	87
(Shown as by Jellybean Featuring Elisa Fiorillo)				
HOW CAN I FORGET YOU/More Than Love	(Chrysalis VS4 43189)	.75	3.00	87
FORGIVE ME FOR DREAMING/	(Chrysalis VS4 43237)	.75	3.00	88

FIRE AND RAIN
ALRIGHT TONIGHT/Home To You .... (Mercury 73358) | 2.50 | 10.00 | 73

FIREBALLS, THE
CALLIN' THE SHERIFF/Don't Stop .... (Seven Arts 714) | 12.50 | 50.00 | 61

FIREFALL
		VG	NM	YR
STRANGE WAY/Anymore	(Atlantic 3518)	1.25	5.00	78
GOODBYE, I LOVE YOU/Baby	(Atlantic 3544)	1.25	5.00	78
BODY AND SOUL/It's Not Too Late	(Atlantic 7-89963)	1.00	4.00	82

EXTENDED PLAYS
YOU ARE THE WOMAN/JUST REMEMBER I LOVE YOU .... (Atlantic OP-7501) | 1.25 | 5.00 | 78
(Promotional issue only titled Profiles In Gold Album 1, issued with a small-hole 33-1/3 RPM record. Sold only at Burger King for 59¢ with the purchase of a Coke. Also includes two songs each by Abba, Spinners, and England Dan and John Ford Coley.)
Also see the Byrds (Michael Clarke), the Flying Burrito Brothers (Rick Roberts), Heart (Mark Andes), Spirit (Mark Andes)

FIRE INC.
TONIGHT IS WHAT IT MEANS TO BE YOUNG .... (MCA 52377) | .75 | 3.00 | 84
(From the motion picture Streets of Fire)

FIRESIGN THEATRE, THE
		VG	NM	YR
STATION BREAK/Forward, Into The Past	(Columbia 4-45052)	5.00	20.00	69
THIS SIDE/The Other Side	(Columbia AE 30)	2.50	10.00	70
(Promotional issue only)				

EXTENDED PLAYS
YANKEE DOODLE CAME TO TERMS (Excerpt) .... (Columbia AS 1) | 1.25 | 5.00 | 70
(Promotional issue only titled Dig This, issued with a small-hole 33-1/3 RPM record. Also includes excerpts by Pacific Gas and Electric, Moondog, Nick Gravenites, Pete Seeger, Santana, Don Ellis, Raven, and Tony Kosinec.)
THE HOLYGRAM'S SONG .... (Columbia AS 53) | 1.50 | 6.00 | 71
(Part of a series of promotional issues titled Playback issued with a small-hole 33-1/3 RPM record. Price includes generic Playback sleeve with folding insert. Also includes one song each by Jeff Beck, Lesley Duncan, Grootna, the Mahavishnu Orchestra With John McLaughlin, and Mylon.)
Also see Proctor & Bergman (Phil Proctor, Peter Bergman)

TITLE	LABEL AND NUMBER	VG	NM	YR

FIRE TOWN
CARRY THE TORCH/The Mystery Field .... (Atlantic 7-89242) .75 3.00 87

FIRE WITH FIRE
(Motion Picture)
See Wild Blue (Fire With Fire)

FIRM, THE
RADIOACTIVE/Together .... (Atlantic 7-89586) 1.00 4.00 85
SATISFACTION GUARANTEED/Closer .... (Atlantic 7-89561) 1.00 4.00 85
ALL THE KINGS HORSES/Fortune Hunter .... (Atlantic 7-88823) 1.00 4.00 86
    Also see Bad Company (Paul Rodgers), Free (Paul Rodgers), Led Zeppelin (Jimmy Page), Jimmy Page, Paul Rodgers, Chris Slade (Manfred Mann's Earth Band, joined AC/DC in 1990), the Yardbirds (Jimmy Page)

FIRST THEREMIN ERA, THE
THE BARNABAS THEME FROM "DARK SHADOWS"/Sunset In Siberia .... (Epic 5-10440) 3.75 15.00 69
    (Jonathan Frid, in character as the vampire Barnabas Collins, pictured)

FISHBONE
HE'S A FLYGUY/He's A Flyguy (Instrumental) .... (Arista 9806) .75 3.00 89
    (Shown as by Curtis Mayfield and Fishbone. From the motion picture I'm Gonna Git You Sucka.)

FISHER, EDDIE
EVEN NOW/ .... (RCA Victor 47-5106) 6.25 25.00 53
WITH THESE HANDS/When I Was Young .... (RCA Victor 47-5365) 2.50 10.00 53
OH MY PAPA/Until You Said Goodbye .... (RCA Victor 47-5552) 2.50 10.00 53
EDDIE FISHER SINGS .... (RCA Victor no #) 2.50 10.00 53
    (Generic half sleeve used for a variety of 45s. Sleeve also promotes Fisher's TV and radio series Coke Time which aired from 1953-57.)
WEDDING BELLS/A Man Chases A Girl .... (RCA Victor 47-6015) 2.50 10.00 55
    ("This Is His Life" cartoon strip style sleeve)
WITHOUT YOU/ .... (RCA Victor 47-6470) 2.50 10.00 56
SCENT OF MYSTERY/The Chase .... (Ramrod no #) 2.50 10.00 60
    (From the motion picture Scent Of Mystery)

FITZGERALD, ELLA
A–TISKET A–TASKET/Undecided .... (Decca 1-724) 3.00 12.00 53
    (Decca "Curtain Call" series of reissues. Shown as by Ella Fitzgerald and Chick Webb and His Orchestra)
BEALE STREET BLUES/ .... (Verve 10128) 5.00 20.00 59
MR. PAGANINI/You're Driving Me Crazy .... (Verve 10237) 3.00 12.00 60
    (Sleeve issued with either stock black or promotional yellow vinyl)
CLAP HANDS (HERE COMES CHARLIE!)/Cry Me A River .... (Verve 10241) 3.75 15.00 60

FIVE AMERICANS, THE
EVOL–NOT LOVE/Don't Blame Me .... (HBR 468) 5.00 20.00 66
STOP LIGHT/Tell Ann I Love Her .... (Abnak 125) 3.75 15.00 67
7:30 GUIDED TOUR/See-Saw Man .... (Abnak 126) 3.75 15.00 68
RAIN MAKER/No Communication .... (Abnak 128) 3.75 15.00 68

FIVE PENNIES, THE
(Motion Picture)
    See Louis Armstrong (The Five Pennies Saints), Danny Kaye (The Five Pennies Saints), Red Nichols (Selmer Sampler)

FIVE SATINS
WHEN THE SWALLOWS COME BACK TO CAPISTRANO/Dance Girl Dance .... (X-Bat 1000) .75 3.00 95
    (B-side shown as by Gerry Granahan with the Five Satins, Granahan pictured. Issued with red vinyl.)

FIVE STAIRSTEPS, THE, & CUBIE
SOMETHING'S MISSING/Tell Me Who .... (Buddah 20) 2.50 10.00 67
A MILLION TO ONE/You Make Me So Mad .... (Buddah 26) 2.50 10.00 68

FIVE STAR
LET ME BE THE ONE .... (RCA PB-14229) .75 3.00 86
CAN'T WAIT ANOTHER MINUTE .... (RCA PB-14421) .75 3.00 86
IF I SAY YES .... (RCA 5083-7-R) .75 3.00 86
WHENEVER YOU'RE READY .... (RCA 5292-7-R) .75 3.00 87

FIVE STRANGERS, THE
MOCKING BIRD HILL/Fare Thee Well .... (MGM K-13239) .75 3.00 64

FIXX, THE
SAVED BY ZERO/Going Overboard .... (MCA 52213) 1.00 4.00 83
ONE THING LEADS TO ANOTHER/Opinions .... (MCA 52264) 1.00 4.00 83
THE SIGN OF FIRE .... (MCA 52316) 1.00 4.00 83
ARE WE OURSELVES?/Deeper And Deeper .... (MCA 52444) .75 3.00 84
SUNSHINE IN THE SHADE/Question .... (MCA 52498) .75 3.00 84
LESS CITIES, MORE MOVING PEOPLE/Woman On A Train .... (MCA 52529) .75 3.00 84
BUILT FOR THE FUTURE .... (MCA 52902) .75 3.00 86
RED SKIES .... (MCA 53066) .75 3.00 87
DRIVEN OUT/Shred Of Evidence .... (RCA 8837-7-R) .75 3.00 88

FIZZY QUICK
HANGIN' OUT .... (Motown 1838) .75 3.00 86
HANGIN' OUT .... (Motown 1838) 1.00 4.00 86
    (Promotional issue, For Promotional Use Only Not For Sale printed on sleeve)

FLACK, ROBERTA
MAKING LOVE/Jesse .... (Atlantic 4005) 1.00 4.00 82
    (From the motion picture Making Love, Michael Ontkean, Kate Jackson, and Harry Hamlin pictured)
TONIGHT, I CELEBRATE MY LOVE .... (Capitol B-5242) .75 3.00 83
    (Shown as by Peabo Bryson and Roberta Flack)
MAYBE .... (Capitol B-5283) .75 3.00 83
    (Shown as by Peabo Bryson and Roberta Flack. From the motion picture Romantic Comedy.)
YOU'RE LOOKIN' LIKE LOVE TO ME .... (Capitol B-5307) .75 3.00 83
    (Shown as by Peabo Bryson and Roberta Flack)

OASIS/ You Know What It's Like .... (Atlantic 7-88996) .75 3.00 88
UH-UH OOH-OOH LOOK OUT (HERE IT COMES)/ You Know What It's Like .. (Atlantic 7-88941) .75 3.00 89
EXTENDED PLAYS
THE FIRST TIME EVER I SAW YOUR FACE/ KILLING ME SOFTLY WITH HIS
SONG .... (Atlantic OP-7502) 1.25 5.00 78
(Promotional issue only titled *Profiles In Gold Album 2*, issued with a small-hole 33-1/3 RPM record. Sold only
at Burger King for 59¢ with the purchase of a Coke. Also includes two songs each by Genesis, Chic, and Leif
Garrett.)
Also see Peabo Bryson and Roberta Flack

FLAMING LIPS, THE
STRYCHNINE/
Drug Machine/ What's So Funny 'Bout Peace Love And Understanding .... (Sub Pop 28) 3.75 15.00 89

FLAMIN' GROOVIES, THE
YOU TORE ME DOWN/ Him Or Me .... (Bomp 101) 2.50 10.00 75

FLANDERS, TOMMY
THE MOONSTONE/ Between Purple And Blue .... (Verve 3075) 2.50 10.00 69
Also see the Blues Project

FLARES, THE
JUMP AND BUMP .... (Felsted 8607) 7.50 30.00 60

FLASH GORDON
(Motion Picture)
See Queen (*Flash's Theme*)

FLAT DUO JETS
I'LL HAVE A MERRY CHRISTMAS WITHOUT YOU/ Caravan .... (Norton 45-031) .50 2.00 94
Also see the Squalls (b-side of *Na, Na, Na, Na*)

FLATT & SCRUGGS
THE BALLAD OF JED CLAMPETT .... (Columbia 4-42606) 2.50 10.00 63
(From the television series *Beverly Hillbillies*)
PEARL PEARL PEARL/ Hard Travelin' .... (Columbia 4-42755) 2.50 10.00 63
(Shown as by Lester Flatt and Earl Scruggs and The Foggy Mountain Boys. A-side featured on the television
series *Beverly Hillbillies*. Flatt and Scruggs pictured with Bea Benaderet who played Pearl on the show.)
CALIFORNIA UP TIGHT BAND/ Last Train To Clarksville .... (Columbia 4-44194) 2.00 8.00 67
(Shown as by Lester Flatt and Earl Scruggs)
FOGGY MOUNTAIN BREAKDOWN .... (Columbia 4-44380) 1.50 6.00 68
(From the motion picture *Bonnie & Clyde*. This version was recorded in 1968.)
THEME FROM BONNIE & CLYDE .... (Mercury 72739) 1.50 6.00 68
(From the motion picture *Bonnie & Clyde*. Sleeve pictures a man and woman impersonating the film's stars.
The song is the original 1949 recording.)

FLAVOR
SALLY HAD A PARTY/ Shop Around .... (Columbia 4-44521) 2.00 8.00 68
HEART TEASER .... (Columbia 4-44673) 2.00 8.00 68

FLEETWOOD MAC
ALBATROSS .... (Epic JZSP 139609) 5.00 20.00 68
(Promotional issue only)
DON'T STOP/ Never Going Back Again .... (Warner Bros. 8413) 1.25 5.00 77
TUSK/ Never Make Me Cry .... (Warner Bros. 49077) 1.00 4.00 79
(Color sleeve with 2" x 3" photo of dog)
TUSK/ Never Make Me Cry .... (Warner Bros. 49077) 1.50 6.00 79
(Black and white sleeve with 3.5" x 5" photo of dog)
SARA/ That's Enough For Me .... (Warner Bros. 49150) 1.00 4.00 79
THINK ABOUT ME/ Save Me A Place .... (Warner Bros. 49196) 1.00 4.00 79
THE FARMER'S DAUGHTER/ Monday Morning .... (Warner Bros. 49700) 1.00 4.00 80
FIREFLIES/ Over My Head .... (Warner Bros. 49660) 1.00 4.00 81
HOLD ME/ Eyes Of The World .... (Warner Bros. 29966-7) 1.00 4.00 82
GYPSY/ Cool Water .... (Warner Bros. 29918-7) 1.00 4.00 82
BIG LOVE/ You And I, Part I .... (Warner Bros. 28398-7) .75 3.00 87
SEVEN WONDERS/ Book Of Miracles .... (Warner Bros. 28317-7) .75 3.00 87
LITTLE LIES/ Ricky .... (Warner Bros. 28291-7) .75 3.00 87
EVERYWHERE/ When I See You Again .... (Warner Bros. 28143-7) .75 3.00 87
FAMILY MAN/ Down Endless Street .... (Warner Bros. 28114-7) .75 3.00 87
AS LONG AS YOU FOLLOW/ Oh Well (Live) .... (Warner Bros. 27644-7) .75 3.00 88
SILVER SPRINGS/ Go Your Own Way .... (Reprise 17300-7-7) .50 2.00 97
Also see Lindsey Buckingham, Buckingham Nicks, Mick Fleetwood's Zoo, Christine McVie, Stevie Nicks, U.S.A. For Africa (Lindsey
Buckingham), Voices Of America (Lindsey Buckingham)

Fleetwood Mac
SILVER SPRINGS

FLEETWOODS, THE
RUNAROUND/ Truly Do .... (Dolton 22) 3.75 15.00 60

FLEETWOOD'S ZOO, MICK
I WANT YOU BACK/ Put Me Right .... (RCA PB-13621) 1.00 4.00 83
Also see Fleetwood Mac

FLEMING, SHERWOOD
PEACE, LOVE AND UNDERSTANDING .... (Kent 4528) 1.25 5.00 70

FLESH FOR LULU
I GO CRAZY .... (MCA 53036) 1.00 4.00 87
(From the motion picture *Some Kind Of Wonderful*, Eric Stoltz, Mary Stuart Masterson, and Lea Thompson
pictured)
POSTCARDS FROM PARADISE .... (Capitol B-44074) .75 3.00 87

FLESHTONES
THE WORLD HAS CHANGED!/ All Around The World .... (I.R.S. 9024) 1.00 4.00 81
RIDE YOUR PONY/ Roman Gods .... (I.R.S. 9905) 1.00 4.00 82
AMERICAN BEAT '84/ Hall Of Fame .... (I.R.S. 9930) .75 3.00 84
(From the motion picture *Bachelor Party*)

TITLE	LABEL AND NUMBER	VG	NM	YR

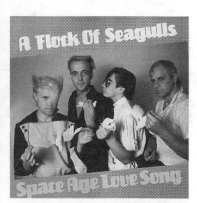

FLETCH
(Motion Picture)
    See Harold Faltermeyer (*Fletch Theme*), Stephanie Mills (*Bit By Bit*)

FLETCHER, SAM
    See Elvis Presley (*Me And The One That I Love/The Answer To Everything* is mentioned in the promotional insert for Elvis' *King Of The Whole Wide World*)

FLINTSTONES, THE
(Animated Television Series)
    Related see Pebbles and Bamm Bamm, Bruce Springstone (parody)

FLIP

THAT'S WHAT THEY SAY ABOUT LOVE/	(CBS/Private I ZS4-05775)	.75	3.00	86
THAT'S WHAT THEY SAY ABOUT LOVE	(CBS/Private I ZS4-05775)	1.00	4.00	86

    (Promotional issue, *Demonstration Only–Not For Sale* printed on sleeve)

FLO & EDDIE
(Phlorescent Leech & Eddie a.k.a. Mark Volman and Howard Kaylan)

FLO & EDDIE MEET THE WOLFMAN	(Reprise PRO 564)	1.50	6.00	75

    (Promotional issue only, hard cover. Issued with a 33-1/3 record, no individual song titles listed)
    Also see Andy Taylor (*Take It Easy*), the Turtles

FLOATERS, THE

FLOAT ON	(ABC 12284)	1.00	4.00	77

FLOCK OF SEAGULLS, A

SPACE AGE LOVE SONG/Windows	(Arista/Jive 2003)	1.00	4.00	82
WISHING (IF I HAD A PHOTOGRAPH OF YOU)/Committed	(Arista/Jive 2006)	1.00	4.00	83
WISHING (IF I HAD A PHOTOGRAPH OF YOU)/Committed	(Arista/Jive 9018)	1.00	4.00	83

    (A small sticker with the number JS1-9018 placed over the original VS 2006 catalog number. This appears to be an interim version until the revised 9018 number sleeves could be printed.)

WISHING (IF I HAD A PHOTOGRAPH OF YOU)/Committed	(Arista/Jive 9018)	.75	3.00	83

    (It is assumed that this sleeve, with revised catalog number, was printed)

(IT'S NOT ME) TALKING/I Ran (live)	(Arista/Jive 9069)	.75	3.00	83
THE MORE YOU LIVE THE MORE YOU LOVE/Lost Control	(Arista/Jive JS1 9220)	.75	3.00	84

FLOWER

RUN TO ME	(United Artists XW 1092)	1.00	4.00	77

FLOWERS, PHIL
    See Bill Haley (B-side of *The A.B.C. Boogie*)

CURTIS, KING
    See King Curtis

FLOYD, KING
    See King Floyd

FLUBBER
(Motion Picture)
    See Fred MacMurray (*The Flubber Song*)

FLUID
    See Nirvana (b-side of *Molly's Lips*)

FLY, THE
(Motion Picture)
    See Bryan Ferry (*Help Me*)

FLYING BURRITO BROS, THE

WHITE LINE FEVER/Colorado	(A&M 1277)	3.00	12.00	72

    Also see the Burrito Brothers, the Byrds (Chris Hillman, Michael Clarke), Firefall (Rick Roberts). Gram Parsons left the group for a solo career in 1970; Bernie Leadon left in 1971 to join the Eagles; ex-Canned Heat bassist Joel Scott Hill joined the re-formed group in 1975.

FLYING LIZARDS, THE

MONEY/Money B	(Virgin 67003)	1.00	4.00	79
MONEY/Money B	(Virgin 67003)	1.25	5.00	79

    (Hard cover)

TV/Tube	(Virgin 67006)	1.00	4.00	79

FOGELBERG, DAN

NETHERLANDS	(Full Moon/Epic 8-50462)	1.25	5.00	77
SAME OLD LANG SYNE/Hearts And Crafts	(Full Moon/Epic 19-50961)	1.00	4.00	80
THE LANGUAGE OF LOVE/Windows And Walls	(Full Moon/Epic 34-04314)	.75	3.00	84
THE LANGUAGE OF LOVE/Windows And Walls	(Full Moon/Epic 34-04314)	1.00	4.00	84

    (Promotional issue, *Demonstration Only/Not For Sale* printed on sleeve)

SHE DON'T LOOK BACK	(Full Moon/Epic 34-07044)	.75	3.00	87
SHE DON'T LOOK BACK	(Full Moon/Epic 34-07044)	1.00	4.00	87

    (Promotional issue, *Demonstration Only/Not For Sale* printed on sleeve)

LONELY IN LOVE	(Full Moon/Epic 34-07275)	.75	3.00	87
LONELY IN LOVE	(Full Moon/Epic 34-07275)	1.00	4.00	87

    (Promotional issue, *Demonstration Only/Not For Sale* printed on sleeve)

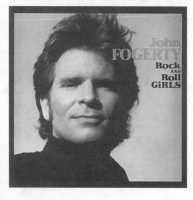

FOGERTY, JOHN

THE OLD MAN DOWN THE ROAD	(Warner Bros. 291005-7)	.75	3.00	84

    (First printing, blue and black ink)

THE OLD MAN DOWN THE ROAD	(Warner Bros. 291005-7)	.75	3.00	84

    (Second printing, blue ink only; the images, especially the one of Fogerty on the back, appear cleaner and less muddy)

ROCK AND ROLL GIRLS	(Warner Bros. 29053-7)	.75	3.00	85
EYE OF THE ZOMBIE/I Confess	(Warner Bros. 28657-7)	.75	3.00	86
CHANGE IN THE WEATHER/My Toot Toot	(Warner Bros. 28535-7)	.75	3.00	86

    Also see Blue Ridge Rangers, Creedence Clearwater Revival

FOGERTY, TOM
GOODBYE MEDIA MAN (PARTS I AND II) .... (Fantasy 661) — 2.00 — 8.00 — 71
    Also see Creedence Clearwater Revival

FOGGY MOUNTAIN BOYS, THE
    See Flatt & Scruggs *(Pearl Pearl Pearl)*

FOGHAT
THIRD TIME LUCKY (FIRST TIME I WAS A FOOL) .... (Bearsville 49125) — 1.00 — 4.00 — 79
WIDE BOY/Love Zone .... (Bearsville 49779) — 1.00 — 4.00 — 81
GOIN' HOME FOR CHRISTMAS/
    Santa Claus Is Back In Town .... (Mark-O-Hildenen Productions no #) — 1.50 — 6.00 — 86

FOLEY, BRIAN
LOVE ME, PLEASE LOVE ME .... (Kapp 861) — 1.50 — 6.00 — 67

FOLEY, ELLEN
SAD SONG .... (Epic/Cleveland International 9-50839) — 1.25 — 5.00 — 80
    (Promotional issue only, *Demonstration–Not For Sale* printed on sleeve)

FOLLOW THE BOYS
(Motion Picture)
    See Connie Francis *(Follow The Boys)*

FONDA, HENRY
(Actor)
THE CHEYENNE SOCIAL CLUB/Lonely Rolling Stone .... (National General 007) — 3.75 — 15.00 — 70
    (Shown as by James Stewart and Henry Fonda)

FONDA, JANE
(Actress, daughter of Henry Fonda)
    See Brook Benton *(Walk On The Wild Side)*

FONTAINE, FRANK
(Played the character Crazy Guggenheim on the *Jackie Gleason Show*)
WHEN YOUR HAIR HAS TURNED TO SILVER/Heart Of My Heart .... (ABC Paramount 45-10384) — 2.50 — 10.00 — 62
THE SWEEPSTAKES WINNER .... (Capitol F-4929) — 2.50 — 10.00 — 63

FONTANE SISTERS, THE
KISSING BRIDGE .... (RCA Victor 47-5524) — 3.75 — 15.00 — 54

FOOLS, THE
I WON'T GROW UP/Easy For You .... (EMI America 8046) — 1.25 — 5.00 — 80

FOOTLOOSE
(Motion Picture)
    See Karla Bonoff *(Somebody's Eyes)*, Kenny Loggins *(I'm Free, Footloose)*, Mike Reno and Ann Wilson *(Almost Paradise)*, Bonnie Tyler *(Holding Out For A Hero)*, Deniece Williams *(Let's Hear It For The Boy)*

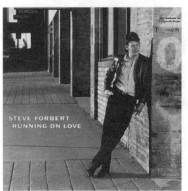

FORBERT, STEVE
RUNNING ON LOVE/I Blinked Once .... (Geffen 27846-7) — .75 — 3.00 — 88
EXTENDED PLAYS
YOU CANNOT WIN IF YOU DO NOT PLAY/Steve Forbert's Midsummer Night's Toast/
    Steve Forbert's Moon River .... (Nemperor/CBS AE7-1174) — 1.50 — 6.00 — 79
    (Promotional issue only titled *"Arriving Live" Live FM Special. Demonstration/Not For Sale* printed on sleeve, issued with a small-hole 33-1/3 RPM record.)

FORBIDDEN PLANET
(Motion Picture)
    See David Rose and His Orchestra

FORCE M.D.'S
TENDER LOVE/Tender Love (Instrumental) .... (Warner Bros. 28818-7) — .75 — 3.00 — 85
    (From the motion picture *Krush Groove*)
HERE I GO AGAIN .... (Tommy Boy 28742-7) — .75 — 3.00 — 85
ONE PLUS ONE .... (Tommy Boy 28619-7) — .75 — 3.00 — 86
LOVE IS A HOUSE .... (Tommy Boy 28300-7) — .75 — 3.00 — 87
COULDN'T CARE LESS .... (Tommy Boy 27978-7) — .75 — 3.00 — 87

FORD, FRANKIE
CHINATOWN/What's Going On .... (Ace 592) — 6.25 — 25.00 — 60

FORD, HARRISON
(Actor)
    See Carly Simon *(Let The River Run)*

FORD, LITA
KISS ME DEADLY/Broken Dreams .... (Dreamland/RCA 6866-7-R) — 1.00 — 4.00 — 88
BACK TO THE CAVE/Under The Gun .... (Dreamland/RCA 8640-7-R) — 1.00 — 4.00 — 88
CLOSE MY EYES FOREVER (Remix)/Under The Gun .... (Dreamland/RCA 8899-7-R) — 1.00 — 4.00 — 89
    (A-side shown as Duet With Ozzy Osbourne)
FALLING IN AND OUT OF LOVE (Remix)/Fatal Passion .... (Dreamland/RCA 9008-7-R) — 1.00 — 4.00 — 89

FORD, PETER
(Son of actor Glenn Ford)
DON'T KEEP IT TO YOURSELF .... (Philips 40336) — 5.00 — 20.00 — 65

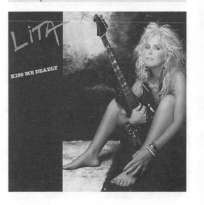

FORD, ROBBEA
TALK TO YOUR DAUGHTER .... (Warner Bros. 27744-7) — .75 — 3.00 — 88

FORD, TENNESSEE ERNIE
LITTLE KLINKER .... (Capitol 4446) — 2.00 — 8.00 — 60
EXTENDED PLAYS
NATIONAL WILDLIFE FEDERATION ANNOUNCEMENTS .... (ADS Audio 1964) — 2.50 — 10.00 — 64
    (Promotional issue only featuring spots by Ford, Lorne Greene, and Andy Griffith; all three individually pictured)

TITLE	LABEL AND NUMBER	VG	NM	YR
FORD FAIRLANE				
(Motion Picture)				
See Billy Idol				
FORDHAM, JULIA				
HAPPY EVER AFTER/Behind Closed Doors	(Virgin 7-99294)	.75	3.00	88
(Top of sleeve die cut on a curve causing title to be removed)				
HAPPY EVER AFTER/Behind Closed Doors	(Virgin 7-99294)	1.00	4.00	88
(Top of sleeve straight cut)				
COMFORT OF STRANGERS/I Wish	(Virgin 7-99224)	1.00	4.00	89
FOREIGNER				
DOUBLE VISION/Lonely Children	(Atlantic 3514)	1.00	4.00	78
DIRTY WHITE BOY/Rev On The Red Line	(Atlantic 3618)	1.00	4.00	79
HEAD GAMES/Do What You Like	(Atlantic 3633)	1.00	4.00	79
URGENT/Girl On The Moon	(Atlantic 3831)	.75	3.00	81
WAITING FOR A GIRL LIKE YOU/I'm Gonna Win	(Atlantic 3868)	.75	3.00	81
JUKE BOX HERO/Night Life	(Atlantic 4017)	.75	3.00	82
BREAK IT UP/Head Games (Live)	(Atlantic 4044)	.75	3.00	82
I WANT TO KNOW WHAT LOVE IS/Street Thunder (Instrumental)	(Atlantic 7-89596)	.75	3.00	84
THAT WAS YESTERDAY/Two Different Worlds	(Atlantic 7-89571)	.75	3.00	84
REACTION TO ACTION/She's Too Tough	(Atlantic 7-89542)	.75	3.00	84
SAY YOU WILL/A Night To Remember	(Atlantic 7-89169)	.75	3.00	87
I DON'T WANT TO LIVE WITHOUT YOU/Face To Face	(Atlantic 7-89101)	.75	3.00	88
HEART TURNS TO STONE/Counting Every Minute	(Atlantic 7-89046)	.75	3.00	88
Also see Lou Gramm, Mick Jones, Roxy Music (Rick Wills)				
FORESTER SISTERS, THE				
DON'T YOU/All I Need	(Warner Bros. 22943-7)	.75	3.00	89
Also see Crystal Gayle (b-side of *Makin' Up For Lost Time*)				
FORM, THE				
HAPPENS THAT WAY/All The Young Dudes	(Twin Tone 8552)	1.00	4.00	85
FOR REAL				
LIKE I DO (Main Mix)/Like I Do (Instrumental)	(Rowdy 75444-35079-7)	.50	2.00	96
FORREST, JACKIE				
BREAKIN' YOUR HEART FOR FUN/				
Mama Don't Sit Up & Wait For Me	(Hitsville number unknown)	3.00	12.00	50s
(Promotional issue only)				
FORSEY, KEITH				
See Wang Chung (*Fire In The Twilight*)				
FORTUNE				
STACY	(MCA/Camel 52727)	.75	3.00	85
FOSTER, BRUCE				
PLATINUM HEROES	(Millennium/Casablanca 602)	1.50	6.00	77
(Promotional issue only, *Promotion Copy Not For Sale* printed on sleeve)				
FOSTER, DAVID				
LOVE THEME FROM ST. ELMO'S FIRE (INSTRUMENTAL)/Georgetown	(Atlantic 7-89528)	.75	3.00	85
(From the motion picture *St. Elmo's Fire*. Rob Lowe, Demi Moore, Emilio Estevez, Ally Sheedy, Judd Nelson, Mare Winningham, and Andrew McCarthy pictured on front, Foster on back.)				
THE BEST OF ME/Sajé	(Atlantic 7-89420)	1.00	4.00	86
(A-side shown as by David Foster & Olivia Newton-John, both pictured on front. B-side by David Foster.)				
RENDEZ-VOUS (LOVE LIGHTS THE WORLD)/Flight Of The Snowbirds	(Atlantic 7-89323)	.75	3.00	87
(On back the a-side credits and pictures David Foster with the Red Army Chorus)				
WINTER GAMES/Piano Concerto In G	(Atlantic 7-89140)	.75	3.00	88
Also see John Parr (b-side of *St. Elmo's Fire*)				
FOSTER, IAN				
OUT FOR THE COUNT	(MCA 53059)	.75	3.00	87
FOSTER & LLOYD				
(Radney Foster and Bill Lloyd)				
CRAZY OVER YOU	(RCA 5210-7-RAA)	1.00	4.00	87
(Promotional issue only, *Promotional Use Only–Not For Sale* printed on back)				
FOTO-FI FOUR, THE				
STAND UP AND HOLLAR	(Foto-Fi 107)	10.00	40.00	64
(Promotional issue only cardboard sleeve that reads *The Beatles Arrive In America! Have Fun Running The Film With This Specially Scored Recording*. Issued with a film of the Beatles departing a plane, etc.)				
FOUL PLAY				
(Motion Picture)				
See Barry Manilow (*Ready To Take A Chance Again*)				
FOUR ACES				
SEARCHING	(ABC/Paramount 10166)	2.50	10.00	60
4 BY FOUR				
WANT YOU FOR MY GIRLFRIEND	(Capitol B-5690)	.75	3.00	87
FOUR COINS, THE				
MY LOVE LOVES ME/New World	(Epic 5-9258)	2.50	10.00	57
FOUR FRESHMEN, THE				
SUMMERTIME	(Capitol 5007)	2.00	8.00	63
DEMO RECORD COMMERCIAL	(Charles H. Stern Co. TB 256)	2.50	10.00	60s
EXTENDED PLAYS				
IT'S A BLUE WORLD/POINCIANA/You're So Far Above Me/Brazil Me	(Capitol PRO 863)	3.75	15.00	59
(Promotional issue only)				
EV'RY TIME WE SAY GOODBYE/CIRCUS/				
Whistle Me Some Blues/It Never Occured To Me	(Capitol PRO 864)	3.75	15.00	59
(Promotional issue only)				

FOUR-IN-LEGION

		VG	NM	YR
PARTY IN MY PANTS .... (CBS Associated ZS4-04678)		.75	3.00	84
PARTY IN MY PANTS .... (CBS Associated ZS4-04678)		1.00	4.00	84
(Promotional issue, *Demonstration Only–Not For Sale* printed on sleeve)				

FOUR LADS, THE

		VG	NM	YR
WHO NEEDS YOU / It's So Easy To Forget .... (Columbia 4-40811)		2.50	10.00	57
THE EYES OF GOD / .... (Columbia 4-40974)		2.50	10.00	57
ENCHANTED ISLAND / Guess What The Neighbors'll Say .... (Columbia 4-41194)		2.50	10.00	58
(A-side from the motion picture *Enchanted Island*)				
HAPPY ANNIVERSARY / .... (Columbia 4-41497)		2.50	10.00	59
JUST YOUNG .... (Kapp 359)		2.50	10.00	61

FOUR LEAVES

		VG	NM	YR
SEASON OF THE SUN / Chotto Matte Kudasai .... (MGM K-14326)		1.50	6.00	70

4 NON BLONDES

		VG	NM	YR
BLESS THE BEASTS AND CHILDREN .... (A&M 31458 0718 7)		.50	2.00	94
(Side 13 of a 7-record box set titled *If I Were A Carpenter*. Each sleeve has a different face shot of Karen Carpenter on the front, Richard Carpenter on the back. No artist name or song titles indicated on sleeve. Complete set valued at $30.00 near mint.)				

FOUR PREPS, THE

		VG	NM	YR
MORE MONEY FOR YOU AND ME / Swing Down, Chariot .... (Capitol 4599)		3.00	12.00	61
THE BIG DRAFT / Suzy Cockroach .... (Capitol 4599)		3.00	12.00	62

FOUR SAINTS, THE

		VG	NM	YR
DAYS OF WINE AND ROSES / Wendy .... (Warner Bros. 5335)		3.75	15.00	63
(From the motion picture *Days Of Wine And Roses*, Jack Lemmon and Lee Remick pictured front and back)				

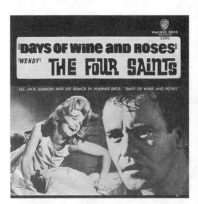

FOUR SEASONS, THE

		VG	NM	YR
CANDY GIRL / Marlena .... (Vee-Jay 539)		12.50	50.00	63
LONG LONELY NIGHTS / Alone .... (Vee-Jay 597)		10.00	40.00	64
(*Long Lonely Nights* is listed as the a-side and charted at #102 while the b-side made it to #28)				
I SAW MOMMY KISSING SANTA CLAUS / Christmas Tears .... (Vee-Jay 626)		10.00	40.00	64
RONNIE / Born To Wander .... (Philips 40185)		5.00	20.00	64
RAG DOLL / Silence Is Golden .... (Philips 40211)		5.00	20.00	64
(Green version)				
RAG DOLL / Silence Is Golden .... (Philips 40211)		5.00	20.00	64
(Yellow version)				
BIG MAN IN TOWN / Little Angel .... (Philips 40238)		5.00	20.00	64
BYE BYE BABY (BABY, GOODBYE) .... (Philips 40260)		5.00	20.00	65
TOY SOLDIER .... (Philips 40278)		5.00	20.00	65
GIRL COME RUNNING .... (Philips 40305)		5.00	20.00	65
OPUS 17 (DON'T YOU WORRY 'BOUT ME) .... (Philips 40370)		5.00	20.00	66
I'VE GOT YOU UNDER MY SKIN .... (Philips 40393)		5.00	20.00	66
TELL IT TO THE RAIN .... (Philips 40412)		5.00	20.00	66
BEGGIN' .... (Philips 40433)		5.00	20.00	67
C'MON MARIANNE .... (Philips 40460)		5.00	20.00	67
WATCH THE FLOWERS GROW .... (Philips 40490)		5.00	20.00	67
SATURDAY'S FATHER .... (Philips 40542)		2.50	10.00	68
SATURDAY'S FATHER .... (Philips 40542)		3.75	15.00	68
(Poster sleeve)				
IDAHO .... (Philips 40597)		2.00	8.00	69
AND THAT REMINDS ME / The Singles Game .... (Crewe 333)		2.50	10.00	69
A PATCH OF BLUE .... (Philips 40662)		2.00	8.00	70
Also see Frankie Valli, the Wonder Who?				

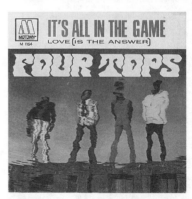

FOUR STARS, THE

		VG	NM	YR
BLUE DAWN / The Frog .... (Era 3021)		5.00	20.00	60
(Issued with blue vinyl)				

4-3-1

		VG	NM	YR
ANIMAL .... (Recovery 3001)		1.00	4.00	84
(Promotional issue only)				

FOUR TOPS, THE

		VG	NM	YR
ASK THE LONELY / Where Did You Go .... (Motown 1073)		12.50	50.00	65
REACH OUT I'LL BE THERE / Until You Love Someone .... (Motown 1098)		7.50	30.00	66
IT'S ALL IN THE GAME / Love (Is The Answer) .... (Motown 1164)		3.75	15.00	70
JUST SEVEN NUMBERS (CAN STRAIGHTEN OUT MY LIFE) .... (Motown 1175)		3.75	15.00	71
BACK TO SCHOOL AGAIN .... (RSO 1069)		1.00	4.00	82
(From the motion picture *Grease 2*)				
INDESTRUCTIBLE / Are You With Me .... (Arista 9706)		.75	3.00	88
IF EVER A LOVE THERE WAS / Indestructible .... (Arista 9766)		.75	3.00	88
(A-side shown as a Duet with Aretha Franklin and sax solo by Kenny G)				
Also see Aretha Franklin (*It Isn't, It Wasn't, It Ain't Never Gonna Be*)				

FOWLER, RED

		VG	NM	YR
TIMES ARE CHANGIN' .... (Chrysalios VS4 43261)		.75	3.00	88

FOX, CHARLIE

		VG	NM	YR
ALL .... (Ambassador 219)		2.00	8.00	66

FOX, MICHAEL J.
(Actor)

See Joan Jett and the Blackhearts (*Light Of Day*), Marty McFly and the Starlighters (*Johnny B. Goode*)

FOX, SAMANTHA

		VG	NM	YR
TOUCH ME (I WANT YOUR BODY) / Drop Me A Line .... (Jive/RCA 1006-7-J RE)		1.00	4.00	86
TOUCH ME (I WANT YOUR BODY) / Drop Me A Line .... (Jive/RCA 1006-7-J)		1.50	6.00	86
(Poster sleeve)				
DO YA DO YA (WANNA PLEASE ME) / Want You To Want Me .... (Jive/RCA 1012-1-J)		.75	3.00	87
NOTHING'S GONNA STOP ME NOW / Dream City .... (Jive/RCA 1072-7-J)		.75	3.00	87

TITLE	LABEL AND NUMBER	VG	NM	YR
NAUGHTY GIRLS (NEED LOVE TOO)(FULL FORCE MIX)/				
Naughty Girls (Need Love Too)(U.K. Mix)	(Jive/RCA 1089-7-J)	.75	3.00	87
(Full Force credited with writing, producing, and remixing)				
I WANNA HAVE SOME FUN/Don't Cheat On Me	(Jive/RCA 1150-1-J)	.75	3.00	88
I ONLY WANNA BE WITH YOU/Confession	(Jive/RCA 1192-7-J)	.75	3.00	89
LOVE HOUSE/Don't Cheat On Me	(Jive/RCA 1233-7-J)	.75	3.00	89

FOXX, RED
(Comedian and comic actor)

TITLE	LABEL AND NUMBER	VG	NM	YR
"YOU GOTTA WASH YOUR ASS" PROGRAMMING TEASERS	(Atlantic EP PR 250)	1.25	5.00	75
(Promotional issue only, Promotion Not For Sale printed on back)				

FRAMPTON, PETER

TITLE	LABEL AND NUMBER	VG	NM	YR
SHOW ME THE WAY/The Crying Clown	(A&M 1693)	1.25	5.00	75
SHOW ME THE WAY/Shine On	(A&M 1795)	1.00	4.00	76
BABY, I LOVE YOUR WAY/It's A Plain Shame	(A&M 1832)	1.00	4.00	76
I'M IN YOU/St. Thomas (Know How I Feel)	(A&M 1941)	1.00	4.00	77
SIGNED, SEALED, DELIVERED (I'M YOURS)/Rocky's Hot Club	(A&M 1972)	1.00	4.00	77
TRIED TO LOVE/You Don't Have To Worry	(A&M 1988)	1.00	4.00	77
I CAN'T STAND IT NO MORE/May I Baby	(A&M 2148)	1.00	4.00	79
BREAKING ALL THE RULES/Night Town	(A&M 2350)	1.00	4.00	81
LYING/Into View	(Atlantic 7-89463)	.75	3.00	86
ALL EYES ON YOU/So Far Away	(Atlantic 7-89426)	.75	3.00	86
Also see Humble Pie				

FRANCIS, CONNIE

TITLE	LABEL AND NUMBER	VG	NM	YR
MY HAPPINESS/Never Before	(MGM K12738)	6.25	25.00	58
(White sleeve)				
MY HAPPINESS/Never Before	(MGM K12738)	5.00	20.00	58
(Pink sleeve)				
IF I DIDN'T CARE/Toward The End Of The Day	(MGM K12769)	5.00	20.00	59
EVERYBODY'S SOMEBODY'S FOOL/Jealous Of You	(MGM K12899)	3.75	15.00	60
MY HEART HAS A MIND OF ITS OWN/Malaguena	(MGM K12923)	3.75	15.00	60
MANY TEARS AGO/Senza Mama (With No One)	(MGM K12964)	3.75	15.00	60
WHERE THE BOYS ARE	(MGM K12971)	3.75	15.00	61
(From the motion picture Where The Boys Are, Francis, Dolores Hart, Yvette Mimieux, Barbara Nichols, and Paula Prentiss pictured)				
BREAKIN' IN A BRAND NEW HEART/Someone Else's Boy	(MGM K12995)	3.75	15.00	61
TOGETHER/Too Many Rules	(MGM K13019)	3.00	12.00	61
HOLLYWOOD/(He's My) Dreamboat	(MGM K13039)	3.00	12.00	61
(Hollywood listed as the a-side although the b-side charted higher on the Billboard charts at #14 versus #42)				
WHEN THE BOY IN YOUR ARMS (IS THE BOY IN YOUR HEART)/				
Baby's First Christmas	(MGM K13051)	3.00	12.00	61
DON'T BREAK THE HEART/Drop It, Joe	(MGM K13059)	3.00	12.00	62
(A-side title shown on 45 as Don't Break The Heart That Loves You)				
SECOND HAND LOVE/Gonna Git That Man	(MGM K 13074)	3.00	12.00	62
VACATION/The Biggest Sin Of All	(MGM K 13087)	3.00	12.00	62
I WAS SUCH A FOOL (TO FALL IN LOVE WITH YOU)/He Thinks I Still Care	(MGM K13096)	2.50	10.00	62
I'M GONNA BE WARM THIS WINTER/Al Di La	(MGM K-13116)	2.50	10.00	62
FOLLOW THE BOYS/Waiting For Billy	(MGM K-13127)	2.50	10.00	62
(From the motion picture Follow The Boys starring Francis)				
IF MY PILLOW COULD TALK/You're The Only One Who Can Hurt Me	(MGM K-13143)	2.50	10.00	63
DROWNIN' MY SORROWS/Mala Femmena (Evil Woman)	(MGM K 13160)	2.50	10.00	63
YOUR OTHER LOVE/Whatever Happened To Rosemarie	(MGM K-13176)	2.50	10.00	63
IN THE SUMMER OF HIS YEARS/My Buddy	(MGM K-13203)	2.50	10.00	63
BLUE WINTER/You Know You Don't Want Me	(MGM K-13214)	2.50	10.00	64
BE ANYTHING (BUT BE MINE)/Tommy	(MGM K13237)	2.50	10.00	64
LOOKING FOR LOVE/This Is My Happiest Moment	(MGM K-13256)	2.50	10.00	64
(From the motion picture Looking For Love starring Francis)				
DON'T EVER LEAVE ME/We Have Something More	(MGM K-13287)	2.50	10.00	64
WHOSE HEART ARE YOU BREAKING TONIGHT/C'mon Jerry	(MGM K-13303)	3.00	12.00	65
WISHING IT WAS YOU/You're Mine	(MGM K-13331)	3.00	12.00	65
LOVE IS ME, LOVE IS YOU/I'd Let You Break My Heart All Over Again	(MGM K-13470)	3.00	12.00	66
IT'S A DIFFERENT WORLD/Empty Chapel	(MGM K-13505)	3.75	15.00	66
SPANISH NIGHTS AND YOU/Games That Lovers Play	(MGM K-13610)	3.75	15.00	66
MY HEART CRIES FOR YOU/Someone Took The Sweetness Out Of Sweetheart	(MGM K-13773)	3.75	15.00	67
GONE LIKE THE WIND/Am I Blue?	(MGM K14058)	5.00	20.00	69
MR. LOVE/Zingara	(MGM K14091)	5.00	20.00	69

FRANCISCUS, JAMES

TITLE	LABEL AND NUMBER	VG	NM	YR
DROPPITY DROP OUTS/Oh Friday Day	(MGM K13319)	6.25	25.00	65

FRANKE & THE KNOCKOUTS

TITLE	LABEL AND NUMBER	VG	NM	YR
SWEETHEART	(Millennium JH-11801)	1.25	5.00	81
(Promotional issue only, Not For Sale For Promotional Use Only printed on sleeve. No song title listed, sleeve states "For Your Sweetheart–Love, Franke & the Knockouts". Issued with red vinyl.)				

FRANKIE GOES TO HOLLYWOOD

TITLE	LABEL AND NUMBER	VG	NM	YR
RELAX	(Island 7-99805)	1.00	4.00	83
(First printing with an illustration of a man and woman)				
RELAX	(Island 7-99805)	.75	3.00	83
(Second printing with graphics)				
TWO TRIBES	(Island 7-99695)	.75	3.00	84
WELCOME TO THE PLEASURE DOME/Relax International (Live)	(Island 7-99653)	.75	3.00	85
RAGE HARD/(Don't Lose What's Left) Of Your Little Mind	(Island 7-99502)	.75	3.00	86
WARRIOR (OF THE WASTELAND)	(Island 7-99486)	.75	3.00	86
Also see Ferry Aid				

FRANKLIN, ARETHA

TITLE	LABEL AND NUMBER	VG	NM	YR
ROUGH LOVER/I Surrender, Dear	(Columbia 4-42266)	6.25	25.00	62
DON'T CRY BABY/Without The One You Love	(Columbia 4-42546)	6.25	25.00	62
HERE'S WHERE I CAME IN/Say It Isn't So	(Columbia 4-42796)	6.25	25.00	63
FREEWAY OF LOVE/Until You Say You Love Me	(Arista 9354)	1.00	4.00	85
(Stock 45 is black vinyl, promo is pink and both used the same sleeve)				

TITLE	LABEL AND NUMBER	VG	NM	YR
WHO'S ZOOMIN' WHO/Sweet Bitter Love	(Arista 9410)	1.00	4.00	85
JUMPIN' JACK FLASH/Integrity	(Arista AS1-9528)	1.00	4.00	86

(A-side from the motion picture *Jumpin' Jack Flash*, Aretha and Keith Richards pictured. Issued with black vinyl)

TITLE	LABEL AND NUMBER	VG	NM	YR
JUMPIN' JACK FLASH/Integrity	(Arista ASC-9528)	1.00	4.00	86

(A-side from the motion picture *Jumpin' Jack Flash*, Aretha and Keith Richards pictured. Issued with clear vinyl, note the catalog number variation.)

TITLE	LABEL AND NUMBER	VG	NM	YR
JIMMY LEE/If You Need My Love Tonight	(Arista 9546)	.75	3.00	86

(B-side shown as a Duet with Larry Graham)

TITLE	LABEL AND NUMBER	VG	NM	YR
I KNEW YOU WERE WAITING (FOR ME)/ I Knew You Were Waiting (For Me) (Instrumental)	(Arista 9559)	.75	3.00	87

(A-side shown as by Aretha Franklin & George Michael)

TITLE	LABEL AND NUMBER	VG	NM	YR
ROCK-A-LOTT/Look To The Rainbow	(Arista 9574)	.75	3.00	87
OH HAPPY DAY/The Lord's Prayer	(Arista 9672)	.75	3.00	87
THROUGH THE STORM/Come To Me	(Arista 9809)	.75	3.00	89

(A-side shown as by Aretha & Elton. Artwork by Peter Max.)

TITLE	LABEL AND NUMBER	VG	NM	YR
IT ISN'T, IT WASN'T, IT AIN'T NEVER GONNA BE/If Ever A Love There Was	(Arista 9850)	.75	3.00	89

(A-side shown as by Aretha & Whitney, both pictured, b-side shown as by Aretha Featuring the Four Tops and Kenny G.)

EXTENDED PLAYS

TITLE	LABEL AND NUMBER	VG	NM	YR
CRY LIKE A BABY	(Columbia Special Products CSS 1491)	1.50	6.00	70

(Promotional issue only titled *The Great American Sound*, issued with a small-hole 33-1/3 RPM record and a 6" x 6" insert for a mail-order Hershey Poster Offer. Also includes one song each by Blood Sweat and Tears, Chicago, and Santana.)
Also see Eurythmics (*Sisters Are Doin' It For Themselves*), the Four Tops (*If Ever A Love There Was*)

FRANKLIN, ERMA
(Sister of Aretha Franklin)

TITLE	LABEL AND NUMBER	VG	NM	YR
EACH NIGHT I CRY/Time After Time	(Epic 9559)	6.25	25.00	62

FRANKS, MICHAEL

TITLE	LABEL AND NUMBER	VG	NM	YR
WHEN I GIVE MY LOVE TO YOU	(Warner Bros. 28819-7)	.75	3.00	85

(Shown as by Michael Franks Featuring Brenda Russell)

TITLE	LABEL AND NUMBER	VG	NM	YR
THE CAMERA NEVER LIES	(Warner Bros. 27997-7)	.75	3.00	87

FRASER, ANDY

TITLE	LABEL AND NUMBER	VG	NM	YR
DO YOU LOVE ME	(Island 7-99784)	1.25	5.00	84

(Promotional issue only, *Licensed For Promotion Only–Sale Is Prohibited* printed on sleeve)
Also see Free

FREBERG, STAN

TITLE	LABEL AND NUMBER	VG	NM	YR
WUN'ERFUL WUN'ERFUL!	(Capitol 3815)	7.50	30.00	57

(Promotional issue only with one-sided record which bears the catalog number PRO 415)

TITLE	LABEL AND NUMBER	VG	NM	YR
GREEN CHRITMA/The Meaning Of Christmas	(Capitol F4097)	3.75	15.00	58
THE OLD PAYOLA ROLL BLUES	(Capitol 4329)	6.25	25.00	60
THE FLACKMAN AND REAGAN	(Capitol 5726)	5.00	20.00	66

EXTENDED PLAYS

TITLE	LABEL AND NUMBER	VG	NM	YR
SELECTIONS FROM THE UNITED STATES OF AMERICA	(Capitol PRO 564)	5.00	20.00	61

(Promotional issue only)

TITLE	LABEL AND NUMBER	VG	NM	YR
SWIMSUITSMANSHIP	(Capitol 2080)	15.00	60.00	64

(Promotional issue only, sleeve reads *Fit Facts And Figures, You And Rose Marie Reid*)

TITLE	LABEL AND NUMBER	VG	NM	YR
MUSIC TO BUBBLE UP BY	(Coca Cola 2227)	12.50	50.00	65

(Promotional issue only for radio spots, gatefold sleeve)

TITLE	LABEL AND NUMBER	VG	NM	YR
COKE	(Coca Cola 2227)	12.50	50.00	67

(Same EP and sleeve as previous listing)

TITLE	LABEL AND NUMBER	VG	NM	YR
A COLORFUL COLLECTION OF RADIO COMMERCIALS FROM PITTSBURGH PAINTS	(Freberg Ltd. no #)	10.00	40.00	67

(Issued with seven track EP which includes the cut *Painting On Radio*)

FREDDIE AND THE DREAMERS

TITLE	LABEL AND NUMBER	VG	NM	YR
I LOVE YOU BABY/Don't Make Me Cry	(Mercury 72285)	3.00	12.00	65
I DON'T KNOW/Windmill In Old Amsterdam	(Mercury 72487)	3.00	12.00	65

FREE

TITLE	LABEL AND NUMBER	VG	NM	YR
STEALER/Broad Daylight	(A&M 1230)	1.50	6.00	86

Also see Back Street Crawler (Paul Kossoff), Bad Company (Simon Kirke, Paul Rodgers), Andy Fraser, Paul Rodgers, Willie and the Poor Boys (Paul Rodgers)

FREE BEER

TITLE	LABEL AND NUMBER	VG	NM	YR
QUEEN OF THE PURPLE SAGE/California	(RCA PB-10881)	.75	3.00	77

FREEBIE AND THE BEAN
(Motion Picture)
   See Bobby Hart (*Hard Core Man*)

FREE SPIRITS, THE

TITLE	LABEL AND NUMBER	VG	NM	YR
GIRL OF THE MOUNTAIN/Tattoo Man	(ABC 10872)	3.00	12.00	66

FREHLEY, ACE

TITLE	LABEL AND NUMBER	VG	NM	YR
INTO THE NIGHT/Fractured Too	(Atlantic/Megaforce 7-89255)	1.25	5.00	87

   Also see Kiss

FREUR

TITLE	LABEL AND NUMBER	VG	NM	YR
DOOT DOOT/Hold Me Mother	(Epic 34-03909)	2.00	8.00	83

FREY, GLENN

TITLE	LABEL AND NUMBER	VG	NM	YR
I FOUND SOMEBODY/She Can't Let Go	(Asylum 47466)	1.00	4.00	82
SEXY GIRL	(MCA 52413)	1.00	4.00	84
THE ALLNIGHTER	(MCA 52461)	.75	3.00	84
THE HEAT IS ON	(MCA 52512)	.75	3.00	84

(From the motion picture *Beverly Hills Cop*, Eddie Murphy pictured)

TITLE	LABEL AND NUMBER	VG	NM	YR
SMUGGLER'S BLUES/New Love	(MCA 52546)	.75	3.00	85
YOU BELONG TO THE CITY/Smugglers Blues	(MCA 52651)	.75	3.00	85

(From the television series *Miami Vice*)

TITLE	LABEL AND NUMBER	VG	NM	YR
TRUE LOVE	(MCA 53363)	.75	3.00	88
SOUL SEARCHIN'	(MCA 53452)	.75	3.00	88

   Also see the Eagles, Michael Dinner (*The Promised Land*)

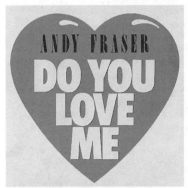

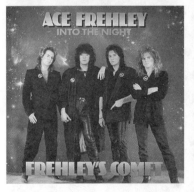
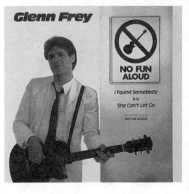

TITLE	LABEL AND NUMBER	VG	NM	YR

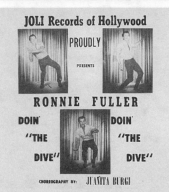

FRICKIE, JANIE
ALWAYS HAVE ALWAYS WILL .... (Columbia 38-06144) .75 3.00 86

FRIDAY THE 13TH, PART IV: JASON LIVES
(Motion Picture)
   See Alice Cooper (*He's Back*)

FRIEND AND LOVER
HARD LOVIN'/Colorado Exile .... (Cadet Concept 7019) 2.50 10.00 68

FRIGHT NIGHT
(Motion Picture)
   See April Wine, the J. Geils Band

FRITH, FRED
DANCING IN THE STREET/What A Dilemma .... (Ralph 8056) 1.00 4.00 80
   Also see Art Bears, Golden Palaminos

FROGS, THE
HERE COMES SANTA'S PUSSY/Have A Merry X-Mas/Snow Kisses .... (Matador ELO 069-7) .75 3.00 95
   (Issued with small-hole, green vinyl)
   Also see Pearl Jam (b-side of *Immortality*, but not credited on sleeve)

FROST
ROCK AND ROLL MUSIC/Donny's Blues .... (Vanguard 35111) 2.00 8.00 69

FROST, MAX, AND THE TROOPERS
52% .... (Tower 452) 7.50 30.00 68
PAXTON QUIGLEY'S HAD THE COURSE/Sittin' In Circles .... (Tower 478) 5.00 20.00 68

FROSTED
BED/Call Me Crazy .... (Sugar Fix 003) 2.00 8.00 95
   (Promotional issue only issued with blue vinyl)
   Also see the Go-Go's (Jane Wiedlin), Jane Wiedlin

FROZEN GHOST
PAUPER IN PARADISE/Suspended Humanation .... (Atlantic 7-88986) .75 3.00 88
   Also see Sheriff

FULLER, RANDY
IT'S LOVE, COME WHAT MAY/Revelation .... (Show Town 466) 5.00 20.00 67

FULLER, RONNIE
DOIN' "THE DIVE" .... (Joli 074) 5.00 20.00 65

FULLER BROTHERS, THE
WHY DO FOOLS FALL IN LOVE/Judge Me With Your Heart .... (Monument 45-925) 2.50 10.00 66

FULL FORCE
OLD FLAMES NEVER DIE/Body Heavenly .... (Columbia 38-06600) .75 3.00 87
ALL IN MY MIND/ .... (Columbia 38-07705) .75 3.00 87
YOUR LOVE IS SO DEF/ .... (Columbia 38-07920) .75 3.00 87
   Also see Samantha Fox (*Naughty Girls*), Lisa Lisa and Cult Jam (*Go For Yours, Can You Feel The Beat, Someone To Love Me For Me*), James Brown (*I'm Real*)

FULL METAL JACKET
(Motion Picture)
   See Abigail Mead (*Full Metal Jacket*)

FULSON, LOWELL
MAKE A LITTLE LOVE/I'm Sinkin' .... (Kent 463) 2.00 8.00 67
   (Sleeve mistakenly shows his last name as Fulsom)

FULTON, RICHARD
POOR LITTLE PAPER BOY .... (RCA Victor 47-9412) 2.00 8.00 67

FUNICELLO, ANNETTE
   See Annette

FUN IN ACAPULCO
(Motion Picture)
   See Elvis Presley (*Bossa Nova Baby*)

FUNKADELIC
ONE NATION UNDER A GROOVE, PART I/
   One Nation Under A Groove, Part II .... (Warner Bros. 8618) 2.50 10.00 78
UNCLE JAM, PART I/Uncle Jam, Part II .... (Warner Bros. 49667) 3.75 15.00 81
THE ELECTRIC SPANKING OF WAR BABIES .... (Warner Bros. 49667) 2.50 10.00 81
   Also see George Clinton, Mudhoney (b-side of *Pump It Up*)

FUNKY WORM, THE
HUSTLE! (TO THE MUSIC...) RADIO I/Hustle! (To The Music...) Radio II .... (Atlantic 7-88995) .75 3.00 88

FUN WITH ANIMALS
THE TEST OF LOVE AND SEX/A.D. 3623 .... (A&M 2223) 1.00 4.00 80

FUN WITH DICK AND JANE
(Motion Picture)
   See the Movies (*Ahead Of The Game*)

FURAY, RICHIE
   See Poco

FURST, CHRISTOPHER
(Actor)
   See Buster Poindexter (*Hit The Road Jack*)

FURTER, FRANK, AND HIS HOT DOGS
THE GREEN WEENIE .... (Uptown 738) 2.50 10.00 60

FUZZBOX
LOVE IS THE SLUG .... (Geffen 28416-7) .75 3.00 86

FUZZY BUNNIES, THE
MAKE US ONE/Strength To Carry On .... (Decca 32420) 3.00 12.00 69

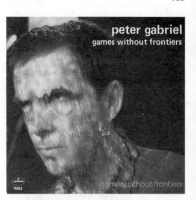

peter gabriel
games without frontiers

G

GABRIEL, PETER
GAMES WITHOUT FRONTIERS/Lead A Normal Life .... (Mercury 76063) 1.25 5.00 80
WALK THROUGH THE FIRE/Making A Big Mistake .... (Atlantic 7-89668) .1.00 4.00 84
    (From the motion picture *Against All Odds*. B-side shown as by Mike Rutherford.)
SLEDGEHAMMER/Don't Break This Rhythm .... (Geffen 28247-7) .75 3.00 86
IN YOUR EYES/In Your Eyes (Special Mix) .... (Geffen 28622-7) .75 3.00 86
BIG TIME/We Do What We're Told (milgram's 37) .... (Geffen 28503-7) .75 3.00 86
DON'T GIVE UP/Curtains .... (Geffen 28463-7) .75 3.00 87
    (A-side shown as by Peter Gabriel and Kate Bush)
RED RAIN/Ga-Ga (I Go Swimming Instrumental) .... (Geffen 28247-7) .75 3.00 87
    Also see Artists United Against Apartheid

GAINES, STEVE
IT'S ALRIGHT .... (MCA 53324) .75 3.00 88
    Gaines was a member of Lynyrd Skynyrd when he was killed in a plane crash in 1977 with his sister Cassie and Ronnie Van Zant also of
    Lynyrd Skynyrd

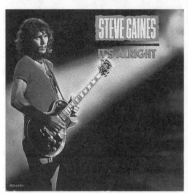

STEVE GAINES
IT'S ALRIGHT

GALLERY
I BELIEVE IN MUSIC .... (Sussex 239) 1.50 6.00 72

GALLOP, FRANK
THE SON OF IRVING/The One Love I'll Never Forget .... (Musicor 1191) 2.00 8.00 66

GAP BAND, THE
EARLY IN THE MORNING .... (Total Experience 8201) 1.25 5.00 82
BEEP A FREAK .... (Total Experience 2405) 1.00 4.00 84
DESIRE .... (Total Experience 2427) 1.00 4.00 85
I'M GONNA GIT YOU SUCKA/Clean Up Your Act .... (Arista 9788) .75 3.00 88
    (From the motion picture *I'm Gonna Git You Sucka*. B-side shown as by Jermaine Jackson.)

Early in the Morning

GARBAGE
See Spooner (Doug "Duke" Erikson, Butch Vig)

GARCIA, JERRY
DEAL/The Wheel .... (Warner Bros. PRO-514) 6.25 25.00 72
    (Promotional issue only)
    Also see the Grateful Dead, Angry Samoans (parody)

GARFUNKEL, ART
ALL I KNOW/Mary Was An Only Child .... (Columbia 4-45926) 2.00 8.00 73
    (Shown as by Garfunkel)
A HEART IN NEW YORK/Is This Love .... (Columbia 18-02307) 1.00 4.00 81
CAROL OF THE BIRDS/The Decree .... (Columbia 38-06590) 1.00 4.00 86
    (Shown as by Art Garfunkel With Amy Grant)
    Also see Simon & Garfunkel

GARFUNKEL · ALL I KNOW

GARI, FRANK
LULLABYE OF LOVE/Tonight Is Our Last Night .... (Crusade 1021) 5.00 20.00 61
PRINCESS/The Last Bus Left At Midnight .... (Crusade 1022) 5.00 20.00 61
YOU BETTER KEEP RUNNIN'/There's Lots More Where This Came From ...... (Crusade 1024) 5.00 20.00 62

GARLAND, JUDY
AFTER YOU'VE GONE/When You're Smiling .... (Capitol no #) 7.50 30.00 59
    (Sleeve reads *Two Of The Top Tunes From "Garland At The Grove"*)

GARNER, ERROLL
MORE/It Ain't Necessarily So .... (MGM K-13677) 5.00 20.00 66

GARNETT, GALE
LOVIN' PLACE/I Used To Live Here .... (RCA Victor 47-8472) 2.50 10.00 64

GARRETT, HOLLY
IT'S THE RIDER .... (Mega 4) 1.50 6.00 70

GARRETT, LEIF
SURFIN' USA/Special Kind Of Girl .... (Atlantic 3423) 1.00 4.00 77
RUNAROUND SUE/I Wanna Share A Dream With You .... (Atlantic 3440) 1.00 4.00 77
THE WANDERER/Love On The Run .... (Atlantic 3476) 1.00 4.00 78
I WAS MADE FOR DANCIN'/Living Without Your Love .... (Scotti Brothers 403) 1.00 4.00 78
FEEL THE NEED/New York City Lights .... (Scotti Brothers 407) 1.00 4.00 79
RUNAWAY RITA/Just Like A Brother .... (Scotti Brothers ZS5-02579) 1.00 4.00 81
EXTENDED PLAYS
RUNAROUND SUE/SURFIN' USA .... (Atlantic OP-7502) 1.25 5.00 78
    (Promotional issue only titled *Profiles In Gold Album 2*, issued with a small-hole 33-1/3 RPM record. Sold only
    at Burger King for 59¢ with the purchase of a Coke. Also includes two songs each by Roberta Flack, Genesis,
    and Chic.)

GARRETT, SIEDAH
CURVES .... (Qwest 7-28975) .75 3.00 85
K.I.S.S.I.N.G. .... (Qwest 7-27928) .75 3.00 88
REFUSE TO BE LOOSE .... (Qwest 7-27829) .75 3.00 88
    Also see Michael Jackson (*I Just Can't Stop Loving You*)

ERROLL GARNER
More
b/w It Ain't Necessarily So

GARVER, KATHY
(Played Cissy on the television series Family Affair from 1966-1971)
LEN THE ORPHAN REINDEER/Opus .... (Aquarian 381) 3.75 15.00

TITLE	LABEL AND NUMBER	VG	NM	YR

GARY & THE HORNETS
HI HI HAZEL/Patti Girl .... (Smash 2061) — 2.50 — 10.00 — 66
KIND OF HUSH/That's All For Now Sugar Baby .... (Smash 2078) — 2.50 — 10.00 — 67

GASKIN, BARBARA
IT'S MY PARTY ....:........ (Platinum 4) — 1.50 — 6.00 — 81
 (Shown as by Dave Stewart and Barbara Gaskin)

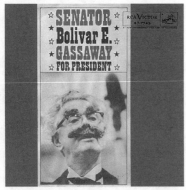

GASSAWAY, SENATOR BOLIVAR E.
SENATOR BOLIVAR E. GASSAWAY FOR PRESIDENT .... (RCA Victor 47-7743) — 2.00 — 8.00 — 60

GATES, DAVID
CLOUDS/I Use The Soap .... (Elektra 45857) — 1.50 — 6.00 — 73
GOODBYE GIRL/Sunday Rider .... (Elektra 45450) — 1.00 — 4.00 — 77
 (Sleeve pictures David Gates on front, titles on back. From the motion picture *The Goodbye Girl*)
GOODBYE GIRL/Sunday Rider .... (Elektra 45450) — 1.00 — 4.00 — 77
 (Titles printed on front and back, no picture of Gates. From the motion picture *The Goodbye Girl*)
 Also see Bread

GATEWAY TRIO, THE
OPEN END INTERVIEW/Foolish Questions .... (Capitol PRO 2340) — 2.50 — 10.00 — 64
 (Promotional issue only)

GATLIN, LARRY, AND THE GATLIN BROTHERS
I JUST WISH YOU WERE SOMEONE I LOVE .... (Monument 45-234) — 1.25 — 5.00 — 77
 (Shown as by Larry Gatlin)
EXTENDED PLAYS
ALL THE GOLD IN CALIFORNIA/IN LIKE WITH EACH OTHER .... (CBS AE7 1429) — 1.00 — 4.00 — 82
 (Promotional issue only titled *Kickin Rock & Roll*, co-sponsored by Busch Beer and WBCN 104 FM and included in *The Phoenix* magazine. Also includes songs by George Jones, Merle Haggard, the Burrito Brothers, Bobby Bare, and Ricky Skaggs.)

GAUTIER, DICK
(Comic television actor known for his role as the robot Hymie from the series *Get Smart*)
HONESTLY SINCERE .... (Columbia 50662) — 2.50 — 10.00
 (Promotional issue only)

GAYE, MARVIN
WHAT'S THE MATTER WITH YOU BABY/Once Upon A Time .... (Motown 1057) — 10.00 — 40.00 — 64
 (Shown as by Marvin Gaye and Mary Wells)
TRY IT BABY/If My Heart Could Sing .... (Tamla 54095) — 10.00 — 40.00 — 64
BABY DON'T YOU DO IT/Walk On The Wild Side .... (Tamla 54101) — 10.00 — 40.00 — 64
LITTLE DARLIN' I NEED YOU/Hey Diddle Diddle .... (Tamla 54138) — 12.50 — 50.00 — 66
GOT TO GIVE IT UP .... (Tamla 54280) — 1.25 — 5.00 — 77
THE WORLD IS RATED X .... (Tamla 1836) — 1.50 — 6.00 — 86
 (Promotional issue only)
THIS LOVE STARVED HEART OF MINE (IT'S KILLING ME)/
 It's A Desperate Situation .... (Tamla 42286-0288) — 1.00 — 4.00 — 95

GAYLE, CRYSTAL
DON'T IT MAKE MY BROWN EYES BLUE .... (United Artists 1016) — 2.00 — 8.00 — 77
MAKIN' UP FOR LOST TIME (THE DALLAS LOVERS' SONG)/
 A Few Good Men (Pam And Jenna's Song For Bobby) .... (Warner Bros. 28856-7) — 1.00 — 4.00 — 85
 (A-side shown as by Crystal Gayle and Gary Morris, b-side by The Forester Sisters. From the television series *Dallas*.)

GAYLORD, MITCH
(Olympic Athlete)
 See John Parr (*Don't Worry 'Bout Me*)

GAYNOR, MITZI
HAPPY ANNIVERSARY .... (Laurie 3050) — 2.00 — 8.00 — 60

GEFFRIES, EVON, AND THE STAND
STAND AND DELIVER .... (Atlantic 7-89018) — .75 — 3.00 — 88

GEILS, J., BAND, THE
MAKE UP YOUR MIND/Southside Shuffle .... (Atlantic 2974) — 2.00 — 8.00 — 73
I DO/Trying To Live My Life Without You .... (Atlantic 3454) — 1.50 — 6.00 — 77
 (Shown as by Geils)
ONE LAST KISS .... (EMI America 8007) — 1.25 — 5.00 — 78
WILDMAN/Jus' Can't Stop Me .... (EMI America 8016) — 1.25 — 5.00 — 79
LOVE STINKS/Till The Walls Come Tumblin' Down .... (EMI America 8039) — 1.00 — 4.00 — 80
CENTERFOLD/Rage In The Cage .... (EMI America A-8102) — 2.50 — 10.00 — 81
 (Unusually hard to find considering the availablity of their other sleeves)
FREEZE-FRAME/Flamethrower .... (EMI America B-8108) — 1.00 — 4.00 — 81
ANGEL IN BLUE/River Blindness .... (EMI America B-8100) — 1.00 — 4.00 — 82
I DO (LIVE VERSION)/Sanctuary (Live Version) .... (EMI America B-8148) — 1.00 — 4.00 — 82
CONCEALED WEAPONS/Tell 'Em Jonesy .... (EMI America B-8242) — 1.00 — 4.00 — 84
FRIGHT NIGHT .... (Private I ZS4-05462) — 1.00 — 4.00 — 85
 (From the motion picture *Fright Night*)
 Also see Artists United Against Apartheid (Peter Wolf), Peter Wolf

GELDOF, BOB
THIS IS THE WORLD CALLING/Talk Me Up .... (Atlantic 7-89341) — .75 — 3.00 — 86
HEARTLESS HEART/Pulled Apart By Horses .... (Atlantic 7-89261) — .75 — 3.00 — 86
 Also see Artists United Against Apartheid, Band Aid, U.S.A. For Africa, Voices Of America

GENE
I CAN'T HELP MYSELF/Be My Light, Be My Guide .... (Sub Pop 294) — 1.00 — 4.00 — 95
 (Originally issued as part of a 4-record set titled *Helter Shelter*, which also included singles by Elastica, S*M*A*S*H, and Supergrass. Envelope sleeve issued with blue vinyl.)

GENE LOVES JEZEBEL
THE MOTION OF LOVE/Bugg's Bruises .... (Geffen 28183-7) — .75 — 3.00 — 87
SUSPICION/ .... (Geffen 28104-7) — .75 — 3.00 — 87

GENERAL HOSPITAL
(Television Soap Opera)
Related see Shaun Cassidy, Tuesday Knight, Nia Peeples, the Soaps and Hearts Ensemble, Rick Springfield, Jack Wagner

GENERAL KANE

		VG	NM	YR
CRACK KILLED APPLEJACK	(Gordy 1865GF)	.75	3.00	86
HAIRDOOZ	(Gordy 1872GF)	.75	3.00	86
HAIRDOOZ	(Gordy 1872GF)	1.00	4.00	86

(Promotional issue, *For Promotional Use Only Not For Sale* printed on sleeve)

GENERAL PUBLIC

		VG	NM	YR
TENDERNESS/Limited Balance	(I.R.S. 9934)	.75	3.00	84
NEVER YOU DONE THAT/All The Rage	(I.R.S. 9935)	.75	3.00	85
TOO MUCH OR NOTHING/Taking The Day Off	(I.R.S. 52941)	.75	3.00	86

(B-side from the motion picture *Ferris Bueller's Day Off*)

		VG	NM	YR
COME AGAIN/Cheque In The Post	(I.R.S. 53016)	.75	3.00	86

Also see the English Beat (Dave Wakeling), the Special AKA (Rankin Roger, Dave Wakeling), the Specials

GENESIS

		VG	NM	YR
MISUNDERSTANDING/Behind The Lines	(Atlantic 3662)	1.25	5.00	80
ABACAB/Who Dunnit?	(Atlantic 3891)	.75	3.00	81
MAN ON THE CORNER/Submarine	(Atlantic 4025)	.75	3.00	82
PAPERLATE/You Might Recall	(Atlantic 4053)	.75	3.00	82
MAMA/It's Gonna Get Better	(Atlantic 7-89770)	.75	3.00	83
THAT'S ALL/Second Home By The Sea	(Atlantic 7-89724)	1.00	4.00	83
THAT'S ALL/Second Home By The Sea	(Atlantic 7-89724)	.75	3.00	83

(Half sleeve)

		VG	NM	YR
ILLEGAL ALIEN/Turn It On Again (Live Version)	(Atlantic 7-89698)	.75	3.00	84
TAKING IT ALL TOO HARD/Silver Rainbow	(Atlantic 7-89656)	.75	3.00	84
INVISIBLE TOUCH/The Last Domino	(Atlantic 7-89407)	.75	3.00	86
THROWING IT ALL AWAY/Do The Neurotic	(Atlantic 7-89372)	.75	3.00	86
LAND OF CONFUSION/Feeding The Fire	(Atlantic 7-89336)	.75	3.00	86
IN TOO DEEP/I'd Rather Be With You	(Atlantic 7-89316)	.75	3.00	87
TONIGHT, TONIGHT, TONIGHT/In The Glow Of The Night	(Atlantic 7-89290)	.75	3.00	87

(Color version)

		VG	NM	YR
TONIGHT, TONIGHT, TONIGHT/In The Glow Of The Night	(Atlantic 7-89290)	1.00	4.00	87

(Black and white version)

EXTENDED PLAYS

		VG	NM	YR
FOLLOW YOU, FOLLOW ME/YOUR OWN SPECIAL WAY	(Atlantic OP-7502)	1.25	5.00	78

(Promotional issue only titled *Profiles In Gold Album 2*, issued with a small-hole 33-1/3 RPM record. Sold only at Burger King for 59¢ with the purchase of a Coke. Also includes two songs each by Roberta Flack, Chic, and Leif Garrett.)
Also see Phil Collins, Mike + the Mechanics (Mike Rutherford), Mike Rutherford. Peter Gabriel left Genesis in 1975, before any U.S. picture sleeves were issued.

GENTILI, PHIL

		VG	NM	YR
MAMA LIED/It's Your Love I Need	(Portrait 24-02400)	.75	3.00	81
MAMA LIED/It's Your Love I Need	(Portrait 24-02400)	1.00	4.00	81

(Promotional issue, *Demonstration–Not For Sale* printed on front)

GENTLE SOUL

		VG	NM	YR
TELL ME LOVE/You Move Me	(Columbia # unknown)	6.25	25.00	67

(Promotional issue only)

GENTRY, BOBBIE

		VG	NM	YR
PAPPA WONCHA LET ME GO TO TOWN WITH YOU/I Saw An Angel Die	(Capitol 5992)	2.00	8.00	67
OKOLONA RIVER BOTTOM BAND/Penduli Pendulum	(Capitol 2044)	2.00	8.00	67
THE GIRL FROM CINCINNATI/You And Me Together	(Capitol 3413)	1.50	6.00	72
ODE TO BILLY JOE	(Warner Bros. 8210)	1.25	5.00	76

(From the motion picture *Ode To Billy Joe*. Robbie Benson and Glynnis O'Connor pictured)

GENTRYS, THE

		VG	NM	YR
SPREAD IT ON THICK/Brown Paper Sack	(MGM 13432)	3.00	12.00	65

GEORGE, ROBIN

		VG	NM	YR
HEARTLINE/The Dangerous Music Story-An Audiobiography	(Bronze/Island 7-99658)	.75	3.00	85

GEORGE, TEDDY, AND THE CONDORS

		VG	NM	YR
SO I CRY	(Philips 40364)	2.50	10.00	66

GEORGIA SATELLITES, THE

		VG	NM	YR
KEEP YOUR HANDS TO YOURSELF/Can't Stand The Pain	(Elektra 7-69502)	.75	3.00	86
BATTLESHIP CHAINS/Golden Light	(Elektra 7-69497)	.75	3.00	86
OPEN ALL NIGHT/Dunk 'N' Dine	(Elektra 7-69393)	.75	3.00	88
SHEILA/Hippy Hippy Shake	(Elektra 7-69328)	.75	3.00	88

(B-side from the motion picture *Cocktail*)

GEORGIO

		VG	NM	YR
SEXAPPEAL	(Motown 1882MF)	.75	3.00	87
TINA CHERRY	(Motown 1892MF)	.75	3.00	87
LOVER'S LANE	(Motown 1906MF)	.75	3.00	87

GERE, RICHARD
(Actor)
See Blondie (*Call Me*), Joe Cocker (*Up Where We Belong*), Alan Silvestri (*No Mercy Main Title*), X (*Breathless*)

GERMS, THE

		VG	NM	YR
FORMING/Sex Boy	(What? 01)	5.00	20.00	77

(Originally included a lyric insert. Sleeve states *This Record Causes Ear Cancer*. First pressing records have a label on one side only; second pressings have labels on both sides. It is unknown if the second pressings have a different sleeve. If they exist, they would be valued at 50% less.)

		VG	NM	YR
LEXICON DEVIL/Circle One/No God	(Slash 101)	5.00	20.00	78
FORMING/Sexboy	(Iloki ILSO 101)	2.00	8.00	90

(Limited edition of 1000, issued with clear vinyl)

GERONIMO BLACK
See Jimmy Carl Black

TITLE	LABEL AND NUMBER	VG	NM	YR

GETAWAY, THE
(Motion Picture)
    See Quincy Jones (*The Love Theme*)

GET WET
JUST SO LONELY .... (Boardwalk NB7-02-018) .75 3.00 87

GHOSTBUSTERS
(Motion Picture)
    See the Bus Boys (*Cleanin' Up The Town*)

GHOULIES II
(Motion Picture)
    See W.A.S.P. (*Scream Until You Like It*)

GIBB, ANDY
(Brother of Barry, Robin, and Maurice Gibb but not a member of the Bee Gees)
I JUST WANT TO BE YOUR EVERYTHING/In The End .... (RSO 872) 1.25 5.00 77
(OUR LOVE) DON'T THROW IT ALL AWAY/One More Look At The Night .... (RSO 911) 1.00 4.00 78
ALL I HAVE TO DO IS DREAM/Good Feeling .... (RSO 1065) 1.25 5.00 78
    (Shown as by Andy Gibb and Victoria Principal, both pictured)

GIBB, BARRY
SHINE SHINE .... (MCA 52443) 1.00 4.00 84
FINE LINE/Stay Alone .... (MCA 52501) 1.50 6.00 84
    Also see the Bee Gees, the Bunburys

GIBB, CYNTHIA
(Actress, no relation to the Gibb brothers Andy, Barry, Robin, and Maurice)
    See Mickey Thomas (*Stand In The Fire*)

GIBB, ROBIN
HELP ME! .... (RSO 1047) 1.50 6.00 80
    (Shown as by Marcy Levy and Robin Gibb. From the motion picture *Times Square*, Robin Johnson and Trini
    Alvarado pictured)
JULIET/Hearts On Fire .... (Polydor 810 895-7) 1.25 5.00 83
BOYS DO FALL IN LOVE/Diamonds .... (Mirage/Atco 7-99743) 1.25 5.00 84
LIKE A FOOL/Possession .... (EMI America B8291) 1.25 5.00 85
TOYS .... (EMI America B-8304) 1.25 5.00 86
    Also see the Bee Gees, the Bunburys

GIBBONS, STEVE, BAND
NO SPITTING ON THE BUS .... (Polydor 14501) 1.50 6.00 86
    (Promotional issue only)

GIBBS, TERRI
I'M A LADY .... (MCA S-33-1754) 1.00 4.00 81
    (Promotional issue only titled *McDonald's Menu Music Chant*, issued with a small-hole 33-1/3 RPM record. Also
    includes one song each, the titles are not listed on sleeve, by Donnie Iris, One Way, and Rufus.)

GIBSON, DEBBIE
ONLY IN MY DREAMS/Only In My Dreams (Dub) .... (Atlantic 7-89322) 1.00 4.00 86
SHAKE YOUR LOVE/Shake Your Love (Bad Dubb Version) .... (Atlantic 7-89187) .75 3.00 87
OUT OF THE BLUE/Out Of The Blue (Dub Edit) .... (Atlantic 7-89129) .75 3.00 87
FOOLISH BEAT/Foolish Beat (Instrumental) .... (Atlantic 7-89109) .75 3.00 88
STAYING TOGETHER/Staying Together (Dub) .... (Atlantic 7-89034) .75 3.00 88
LOST IN YOUR EYES/Silence Speaks (A Thousand Words) .... (Atlantic 7-88970) .75 3.00 89
ELECTRIC YOUTH/We Could Be Together .... (Atlantic 7-88919) .75 3.00 89
NO MORE RHYME/Over The Wall .... (Atlantic 7-88885) .75 3.00 89
WE COULD BE TOGETHER/No More Rhyme .... (Atlantic 7-88896) .75 3.00 89
    Also see Donna Allen (b-side of *Make It My Night*)

GIBSON, DON
SO HOW COME/Baby We're Really In Love .... (RCA Victor 47-8085) 2.00 8.00 62
HEAD OVER HEELS IN LOVE WITH YOU/It Was Worth It All .... (RCA Victor 47-8144) 2.00 8.00 63
AFTER THE HEARTACHE/ .... (RCA Victor 47-8192) 2.00 8.00 63

GIBSON, MEL
(Actor)
    See the Everly Brothers With the Beach Boys (*Don't Worry Baby*), Tina Turner (*We Don't Need Another Hero*), Ann Wilson and Robin Zander
    (*Surrender To Me*)

GIDGET
(Motion Picture)
    See James Darren (*There's No Such Thing*)

GILDER, NICK
HERE COMES THE NIGHT/Rockaway .... (Chrysalis 2264) 1.25 5.00 78
LET ME IN/Don't Forget .... (RCA PB-14177) 1.00 4.00 85

GILKYSON, TERRY, AND THE EASY RIDERS
MARIANNE/Goodbye Chiquita .... (Columbia 4-40817) 3.75 15.00 57

GILL, JOHNNY
HALF CRAZY/Chemistry .... (Cotillion 7-99671) .75 3.00 84
    Also see New Edition

GILLES, GENEVIEVE
(Actress)
HELLO–GOODBYE .... (20th Century-Fox 6717) 1.50 6.00 70
    (Promotional issue only from the motion picture *Hello–Goodbye*. Issued with a 5" x 7" glossy photo of Gilles.)

GILLESPIE, DANA
    See Mick Ronson

GILLEY, MICKEY
ROLL YOU LIKE A WHEEL / Let's Sing A Song Together .... (Playboy 6045)   1.25   5.00   75
    (Shown as by Mickey Gilley and Barbi Benton)

GILLEY'S "URBAN COWBOY" BAND
    See Bonnie Raitt (Don't It Make Ya Wanna Dance)

GILMOUR, DAVID
BLUE LIGHT / Cruise .... (Columbia 38-04378)   1.25   5.00   84
BLUE LIGHT .... (Columbia 38-04378)   2.00   8.00   84
    (Promotional issue, *Demonstration–Not For Sale* printed on sleeve)
    Also see Pink Floyd, Pete Townshend (Give Blood)

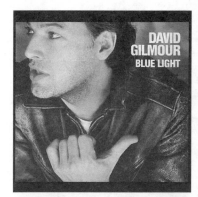

GIN BLOSSOMS
    See the Psalms (Doug Hopkins, Bill Lean)

GIRL NAMED TOMIKO, A
(Motion Picture)
    See Jackie Wilson (A Girl Named Tomiko)

GIRLS! GIRLS! GIRLS!
(Motion Picture)
    See Elvis Presley (Return To Sender)

GIUFFRIA
CALL TO THE HEART / Out Of The Blue .... (Camel/MCA 52497)   .75   3.00   84
LONELY IN LOVE / Do Me Right .... (Camel/MCA 52558)   .75   3.00   85
LOVE YOU FOREVER .... (Camel/MCA 52882)   .75   3.00   86
    Also see Hear 'N Aid, House Of Lords (Lanny Cordola, Gregg Giuffria, Chuck Wright)

GIVE MY REGARDS TO BROAD STREET
(Motion Picture)
    See Paul McCartney (No More Lonely Nights)

GLASS TIGER
DON'T FORGET ME (WHEN I'M GONE) / Ancient Evenings .... (Manhattan B 50037)   .75   3.00   86
SOMEDAY / Vanishing Tribe .... (Manhattan B 50048)   .75   3.00   86
I WILL BE THERE / Do You Wanna Dance With Me .... (Manhattan B 50066)   .75   3.00   87
FAR AWAY FROM HERE / This Island Earth .... (EMI-Manhattan B-50144)   .75   3.00   88
I'M STILL SEARCHING / Suffer In Silence .... (EMI-Manhattan B-50116)   .75   3.00   88

GLAZER, TOM
ON TOP OF SPAGHETTI / Battle Hymn Of The Children .... (Kapp 526)   2.50   10.00   63
    (Shown as by Tom Glazer and the Do-Re-Mi Children's Chorus)
CHISHOLM TRAIL .... (Young People's Records 45x 409)   1.50   6.00
    (Artist's name not credited on sleeve)

GLEASON, JACKIE
(Actor/Comedian/Conductor, played Ralph Kramden in *The Honeymooners* sketches from the television series *The Jackie Gleason Show*)
SEASON'S GREETINGS FROM BULOVA .... (Bulova/Capitol no #)   10.00   40.00   55
    (Promotional issue only, hard cover)
    Also see Christopher Cross (Loving Strangers)

GLEASON, JACKIE, SHOW
(Television Series)
    Related see Frank Fontaine, Jackie Gleason

GLENN, DARRELL
THE WAYS OF THE WORLD .... (Longhorn 546)   3.75   15.00   60s

GLOBETROTTERS, THE
GRAVY / Cheer Me Up .... (Kirshner 63-5006)   3.00   12.00   70
    Also see Meadowlark Lemon

GLOVER, ROGER
    See Rainbow (was also with Deep Purple from 1969-73)

GOANNA
SOLID ROCK / Four Weeks Gone .... (Atco 7-99895)   1.00   4.00   82

GO-BETWEENS, THE
STREETS OF YOUR TOWN .... (Capitol/Beggars Banquet B-44262)   1.00   4.00   88

GODFREY, ARTHUR
'TWAS THE NIGHT BEFORE CHRISTMAS / Jingle Bells .... (Columbia 4-90092)   2.50   10.00   51
    (Half sleeve. A-side credit reads *Music composed and conducted by Archie Bleyer.* B-side credit reads *With the Mariners and the Chordettes.*)

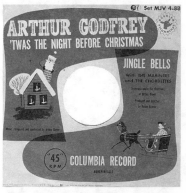

GODFREY, RAY
KEEP YOUR CHIN UP SOLDIER .... (Columbia 4-43618)   1.50   6.00   68

GODLEY & CREME
CRY (REMIX VERSION) / Love Bombs .... (Polydor 881 786-7)   1.00   4.00   85
A LITTLE PIECE OF HEAVEN / Bits Of Blue Sky .... (Polydor 887 301-7)   1.00   4.00   88
    Also see 10cc

GOFFIN, LOUISE
(Daughter of Carole King and Gerry Goffin)
BRIDGE OF SIGHS .... (Warner Bros. 27949-7)   1.00   4.00   88
SURRENDER .... (Sire 22821-7)   1.00   4.00   89
    (From the motion picture *Shag, The Movie*)

GO-GO'S, THE
OUR LIPS ARE SEALED / Surfing And Spying .... (I.R.S. 9901)   1.25   5.00   81
WE GOT THE BEAT / Can't Stop The World .... (I.R.S. 9903)   1.25   5.00   81
VACATION / Beatnik Beach .... (I.R.S. 9907)   1.00   4.00   82

TITLE	LABEL AND NUMBER	VG	NM	YR

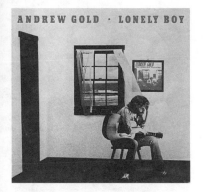

| GET UP AND GO/Speeding | (I.R.S. 9910) | 1.00 | 4.00 | 82 |
| GENERIC GO-GO'S SLEEVE | (I.R.S. no #) | 1.00 | 4.00 | 82 |

(Generic yellow Go-Go's half sleeve used for singles released between 1982-1984. No song titles or catalog number indicated.)

| HEAD OVER HEELS/Good For Gone | (I.R.S. 9926) | 1.00 | 4.00 | 84 |
| TURN TO YOU/I'm With You | (I.R.S. 9928) | 1.00 | 4.00 | 84 |

Also see Belinda Carlisle, Frosted (Jane Wiedlin), House Of Schock (Gina Schock), Sparks (Jane Wiedlin), the Textones (Kathy Valentine), the Ventures (*Surfin' and Spyin'*), Jane Wiedlin

GOLD, ANDREW

| LONELY BOY/Must Be Crazy | (Elektra/Asylum 45384) | 1.25 | 5.00 | 76 |
| NEVER LET HER SLIP AWAY/Genevieve | (Elektra/Asylum 45489) | 1.25 | 5.00 | 78 |

GOLD, TRACEY
(Juvenile Actress)
See Steve Dorff and Friends (*Theme From Growing Pains*)

GOLDBERG, WHOOPI
(Actress/Comedian)
See Donna Allen (*Make It My Night*), Shannon (*Criminal*)

GOLDBERG-MILLER BLUES BAND, THE

| THE MOTHER SONG | (Epic 5-9865) | 10.00 | 40.00 | 65 |

(Possibly a promotional release only. Issued with 2-page press release and blue vinyl.)
Also see the Electric Flag (Barry Goldberg), Steve Miller, the Textones (Barry Goldberg)

GOLDEN, ANNIE
See Darlene Love (*River Deep, Mountain High*), the Shirts

GOLDEN CHILD, THE
(Motion Picture)
See Ann Wilson (*The Best Man In The World*)

GOLDEN EARRING

BACK HOME/As Long As The Wind Blows	(Dwarf 2000)	2.50	20.00	69
WHEN THE LADY SMILES/Orwell's Year	(21 Records 7-99533)	1.00	4.00	84
QUIET EYES/Love In Motion	(21 Records 7-99533)	1.00	4.00	86

GOLDEN PALAMINOS

| OMAHA/I.D. (Like A Version) | (Celluloid 56) | 1.25 | 5.00 | 85 |

(Sleeve printed in Canada for distribution in the U.S.)

| KIND OF TRUE/Brides Of Jesus | (Celluloid 59) | 1.25 | 5.00 | 86 |

Also see Fred Frith, R.E.M. (Michael Stipe), Chris Stamey

GOLDSBORO, BOBBY

WHENEVER HE HOLDS YOU/If She Was Mine	(United Artists 710)	3.00	12.00	64
I KNOW YOU BETTER THAN THAT/When Your Love Has Gone	(United Artists 50,018)	2.00	8.00	67
AUTUMN OF MY LIFE	(United Artists 50318)	2.00	8.00	68
SUMMER (THE FIRST TIME)/Childhood–1949	(United Artists XW251-W)	1.25	5.00	73

GOLDSMITH, JERRY
See Michael Sembello (b-side of *Gremlins...Mega Madness*)

GOLDTONES, THE

| STRIKE/Gutterball | (A&R 714) | 7.50 | 30.00 | 63 |

GOODBYE GIRL, THE
(Motion Picture)
See David Gates

GOODMAN, DICKIE

| WHITE HOUSE HAPPENING/President Johnson | (Davy Jones 663) | 7.50 | 30.00 | 66 |

GOODMAN, JOHN
(Comic Actor)
See Talking Heads (*Wild Wild Life*)

GOODMAN, STEVE

| THE DUTCHMAN/Spinning Ball | (Buddah 348) | 2.00 | 8.00 | 73 |

GOOD MORNING, VIETNAM
(Motion Picture)
See Louis Armstrong (*What A Wonderful World*)

GOOD QUESTION

| GOT A NEW LOVE | (Paisley Park 27861-7) | .75 | 3.00 | 85 |

GOODWYN, MILES

| CAVIAR | (Atlantic 7-89110) | .75 | 3.00 | 88 |

GOO GOO DOLLS

| ONLY ONE/Slave Girl/Disconnected | (Warner Bros. PRO-S-7440) | 1.25 | 5.00 | 95 |

(Promotional issue only issued with pink vinyl)

GOONIES, THE
(Motion Picture)
See the Goon Squad (*8 Arms To Hold You*), Cyndi Lauper (*The Goonies 'R' Good Enough*), Teena Marie (*14K*)

GOON SQUAD

| 8 ARMS TO HOLD YOU | (Epic 34-05449) | .75 | 3.00 | 85 |

(From the motion picture *The Goonies*)

| 8 ARMS TO HOLD YOU | (Epic 34-05449) | 1.00 | 4.00 | 85 |

(Promotional issue, *Demonstration–Not For Sale* printed on sleeve. From the motion picture *The Goonies*)

GORDON, BARRY

| NUTTIN' FOR CHRISTMAS/Santa Claus Looks Just Like Daddy | (MGM K-12092) | 5.00 | 20.00 | 55 |

(Shown as by Art Mooney and His Orchestra With Barry Gordon)

| I CAN'T WHISTLE/The Milkman's Polka | (MGM K-12222) | 5.00 | 20.00 | 56 |
| I LIKE CHRISTMAS/ | (MGM K-12243) | 5.00 | 20.00 | 56 |

GORDON, KELLY
I CAN'T FACE THE DAY .... (Mercury 72081) — 2.00 — 8.00 — 62

GORDON, ROBERT
FIRE .... (Private Stock 45203) — 2.00 — 8.00 — 78
   (Shown as by Robert Gordon and Link Wray)
IT'S ONLY MAKE BELIEVE/Rock Billy Boogie .... (RCA PB-11471) — 1.50 — 6.00 — 79
IT'S ONLY MAKE BELIEVE .... (RCA JH-11471) — 2.50 — 10.00 — 79
   (Promotional issue, *Promotion Copy Not For Sale* printed on sleeve. Issued with white vinyl)
   Also see Tuff Darts

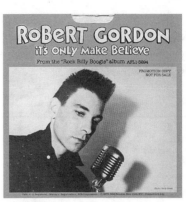

GORE, LESLEY
IT'S MY PARTY .... (Mercury 72119) — 3.75 — 15.00 — 63
JUDY'S TURN TO CRY/Just Let Me Cry .... (Mercury 72143) — 3.75 — 15.00 — 63
SHE'S A FOOL/The Old Crowd .... (Mercury 72180) — 3.75 — 15.00 — 63
YOU DON'T OWN ME/Run Bobby Run .... (Mercury 72206) — 3.75 — 15.00 — 63
THAT'S THE WAY BOYS ARE/That's The Way The Ball Bounces .... (Mercury 72259) — 3.75 — 15.00 — 64
IT'S GOTTA BE YOU/I Don't Wanna Be A Loser .... (Mercury 72270) — 3.75 — 15.00 — 64
MAYBE I KNOW/Wonder Boy .... (Mercury 72309) — 3.75 — 15.00 — 64
SOMETIMES I WISH I WERE A BOY/Hey Now .... (Mercury 72352) — 3.75 — 15.00 — 64
THE LOOK OF LOVE/Little Girl Go Home .... (Mercury 72372) — 3.75 — 15.00 — 64
ALL OF MY LIFE/I Cannot Hope For Anyone .... (Mercury 72412) — 3.75 — 15.00 — 65
SUNSHINE, LOLLIPOPS AND RAINBOWS/You've Come Back .... (Mercury 72433) — 3.75 — 15.00 — 65
MY TOWN, MY GUY AND ME/A Girl In Love .... (Mercury 72475) — 3.75 — 15.00 — 65
I WON'T LOVE YOU ANYMORE (SORRY)/No Matter What You Did .... (Mercury 72513) — 3.75 — 15.00 — 65
CALIFORNIA NIGHTS/I'm Going Out .... (Mercury 72649) — 5.00 — 20.00 — 67
SUMMER AND SANDY/I'm Fallin' Down .... (Mercury 72683) — 3.75 — 15.00 — 67
GIVE IT TO ME SWEET THING/Immortality .... (A&M 1710) — 3.00 — 12.00 — 75

EXTENDED PLAYS
SWINGERS FOR COKE .... (Coca-Cola no #) — 12.50 — 50.00 — 66
   (Promotional issue only with one "Coke" song each by the Drifters, Lesley Gore, Los Bravos, and Roy Orbison)

GORMAN, MRS. DOROTHY
HAPPY BIRTHDAY SON .... (Tower 391) — 2.00 — 8.00 — 67

GORME, EYDIE
YES MY DARLING DAUGHTER/ .... (Columbia 4-42424) — 2.00 — 8.00 — 62
BLAME IT ON THE BOSSA NOVA/Guess I Should Have Loved Him More ...... (Columbia 4-42661) — 2.00 — 8.00 — 63

GORSHIN, FRANK
THE RIDDLER/Never Let Her Go .... (A&M 804) — 5.00 — 20.00 — 66

GORTNER, MARJOE
(Actor and former child evangelist)
LO AND BEHOLD! .... (Chelsea 78-0107) — 1.50 — 6.00 — 72
   (Shown as by Marjoe)

GOULET, MICHELLE
I'M IN LOVE/Slow Down .... (Island 7-99508) — .75 — 3.00 — 86

GOULET, ROBERT
TOO SOON/Two Different Worlds .... (Columbia 4-42369) — 1.50 — 6.00 — 62
WHAT KIND OF FOOL AM I/Where Do I Go From Here .... (Columbia 4-42519) — 1.50 — 6.00 — 62
WHAT KIND OF FOOL AM I/Where Do I Go From Here .... (Columbia JZSP 58203) — 2.00 — 8.00 — 62
   (Promotional issue with yellow vinyl)
YOUNG AT LOVE/ .... (Columbia 4-42612) — 1.50 — 6.00 — 63
THESE ARE THE CLOSING CREDITS/ .... (Columbia 4-42740) — 1.50 — 6.00 — 63
THE MOON WAS YELLOW .... (Columbia 59227) — 2.50 — 10.00 — 63
   (Promotional issue only)
THIS CHRISTMAS I SPEND WITH YOU .... (Columbia JZSP 111805) — 2.50 — 10.00 — 65
   (Promotional issue only, theme song for the 1965 Christmas Seal campaign. No catalog number indicated on sleeve.)
HURRY HOME FOR CHRISTMAS/A Wonderful World Of Christmas ...... (Columbia 4-44710) — 1.50 — 6.00 — 68

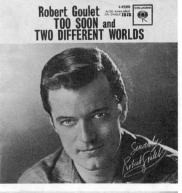

GO WEST
WE CLOSE OUR EYES/Missing Persons .... (Chrysalis VS4 42850) — .75 — 3.00 — 85
CALL ME/Haunted .... (Chrysalis VS4 42865) — .75 — 3.00 — 85
EYE TO EYE/Man In My Mirror .... (Chrysalis VS4 42903) — .75 — 3.00 — 85
DON'T LOOK DOWN (THE SEQUEL)/Let's Build A Boat .... (Chrysalis VS4 43141) — .75 — 3.00 — 87
FROM BALTIMORE TO PARIS/ .... (Chrysalis VS4 43191) — .75 — 3.00 — 87
   Also see Ferry Aid

GRACE POOL
AWAKE WITH THE RAIN .... (Reprise 27761-7) — .75 — 3.00 — 88

GRADY, DON
(Actor who played Robbie on the television series *My Three Sons*)
THE CHILDREN OF ST. MONICA .... (Canterbury 501) — 3.75 — 15.00 — 66

GRAHAM, LARRY
ONE IN A MILLION YOU/The Entertainer .... (Warner Bros. 49221) — 1.00 — 4.00 — 80
SOONER OR LATER/I Feel Good .... (Warner Bros. 29956-7) — 1.00 — 4.00 — 82
   Also see Aretha Franklin (*Jimmy Lee*), Sly and the Family Stone

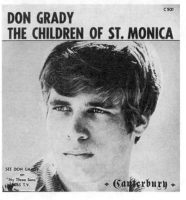

GRAMM, LOU
MIDNIGHT BLUE/Chain Of Love .... (Atlantic 7-89304) — .75 — 3.00 — 87
READY OR NOT/Lover Come Back .... (Atlantic 7-89269) — .75 — 3.00 — 87
LOST IN THE SHADOWS (THE LOST BOYS)/Power Play .... (Atlantic 7-89236) — .75 — 3.00 — 87
   (B-side shown as by Eddie and the Tide. From the motion picture *The Lost Boys*.)
   Also see Foreigner

GRAMMER, BILLY
WABASH CANNONBALL .... (Tap 7031) — 2.50 — 10.00

GRANAHAN, GERRY
LOOK FOR ME/It Hurts .... (Gone 5081) — 7.50 — 30.00 — 60
   Also see Five Satins

TITLE	LABEL AND NUMBER	VG	NM	YR

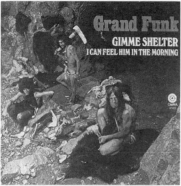

GRANATA, ROCCO, AND THE INTERNATIONAL QUINTET
MARINA .... (Laurie 3041) | 2.00 | 8.00 | 59

GRAND FENWICK PHIL
MOUSE ON THE MOON / Care For Me .... (United Artists 610) | 1.25 | 5.00 | 63

GRAND FUNK
GIMME SHELTER / I Can Feel Him In The Morning .... (Capitol 3160) | 2.00 | 8.00 | 71
FOOTSTOMPIN' MUSIC .... (Capitol 3255) | 1.50 | 6.00 | 72
   (Shown as by Grand Funk Railroad. Song title not listed on silver sleeve)
WE'RE AN AMERICAN BAND .... (Capitol 3660) | 1.25 | 5.00 | 73
   (Originally issued with yellow vinyl)
WALK LIKE A MAN .... (Capitol 3760) | 1.25 | 5.00 | 73
THE LOCO-MOTION .... (Capitol 3840) | 1.25 | 5.00 | 74
SHININ' ON .... (Capitol 3917) | 1.25 | 5.00 | 74
SOME KIND OF WONDERFUL .... (Capitol 4002) | 1.25 | 5.00 | 74
TAKE ME .... (Capitol 4199) | 1.25 | 5.00 | 75
SALLY .... (Capitol 4235) | 1.25 | 5.00 | 76
CAN YOU DO IT .... (MCA 40590) | 1.00 | 4.00 | 76
Y.O.U. / Testify .... (Full Moon / Warner Bros. 49823) | 1.00 | 4.00 | 81
   Also see the Fabulous Pack (Mark Farner, Don Brewer), Mark Farner and Don Brewer

GRANDMASTER MELLE MEL & THE FURIOUS FIVE
BEAT STREET BREAKDOWN .... (Atlantic 7-89659) | .75 | 3.00 | 84
   (From the motion picture Beat Street)
VICE .... (MCA 52740) | .75 | 3.00 | 85
   (Shown as by Grandmaster Melle Mel. From the television series Miami Vice.)

GRAND PRIX
(Motion Picture)
   See Maurice Jarre (Theme From Grand Prix)

GRANT, AMY
TENNESSEE CHRISTMAS / Little Town .... (A&M 2777) | 1.50 | 6.00 | 83
FIND A WAY / Angels .... (A&M 2734) | 1.00 | 4.00 | 85
WISE UP / Straight Ahead .... (A&M 2762) | 1.00 | 4.00 | 85
LEAD ME ON / .... (A&M 1218) | 1.00 | 4.00 | 88
   Also see Peter Cetera (The Next Time I Fall), Art Garfunkel (Carol Of The Birds)

GRANT, EDDY
ROMANCING THE STONE / My Turn To Love You .... (Portrait 37-04433) | .75 | 3.00 | 84
ROMANCING THE STONE .... (Portrait 37-04433)) | 1.00 | 4.00 | 84
   (Promotional issue, Demonstration–Not For Sale printed on sleeve)
BOYS IN THE STREET / Time To Let Go .... (Portrait 37-04620) | .75 | 3.00 | 84
BOYS IN THE STREET .... (Portrait 37-04620) | 1.00 | 4.00 | 84
   (Promotional issue, Demonstration–Not For Sale printed on sleeve)

GRASS ROOTS, THE
THINGS I SHOULD HAVE SAID .... (Dunhill 4094) | 3.00 | 12.00 | 67
BABY, HOLD ON .... (Dunhill 4237) | 2.00 | 8.00 | 70
COME ON SAY IT .... (Dunhill 4249) | 2.00 | 8.00 | 70
   P. F. Sloan and Steve Barri recorded the band's first 4 singles in 1966. After that time, a Los Angeles bar band, the Thirteenth Floor, was recruited to play as the Grass Roots. This group consisted of Rob Grill, Creed Braton, Warren Entner, and Ricky Coonce, later replaced by Dennis Provisor in 1969.

GRATEFUL DEAD
DARK STAR / Born Crosseyed .... (Warner Bros. 7186) | 75.00 | 300.00 | 68
U.S. BLUES .... (Grateful Dead 45-03) | 5.00 | 20.00 | 74
ALABAMA GETAWAY / Far From Me .... (Arista 0519) | 1.50 | 6.00 | 80
TOUCH OF GREY / My Brother Esau .... (Arista 9606) | 1.25 | 5.00 | 87
   (Poster sleeve originally issued with grey vinyl. A 50% premium would be added if the sleeve were still shrink-wrapped with sticker intact.)
THROWING STONES (ASHES ASHES) / When Push Comes To Shove .... (Arista 9643) | 1.00 | 4.00 | 87
FOOLISH HEART / We Can Run .... (Arista 9899) | 1.00 | 4.00 | 89
   Also see Angry Samoans (Dope On The Scarecrow), Jerry Garcia

GRAVENITES, NICK
EXTENDED PLAYS
KILLING MY LOVE (Excerpt) .... (Columbia AS 1) | 1.25 | 5.00 | 70
   (Promotional issue only titled Dig This, issued with a small-hole 33-1/3 RPM record. Also includes excerpts by Pacific Gas and Electric, Moondog, Pete Seeger, Santana, Don Ellis, Raven, Firesign Theatre, and Tony Kosinec.)
   Also see the Electric Flag

GRAVES, TERESA
(Star of television series Get Christie Love and a regular on Rowan & Martin's Laugh-In from 1969-1970)
A TIME FOR US (LOVE THEME FROM ROMEO AND JULIET) /
We're On Our Way .... (Calendar 63-5001) | 1.50 | 6.00 | 69

GRAY, JENNIFER
(Actress)
   See Bill Medley (The Time Of My Life)

GRAY, LINDA
(Actress)
   See Floyd Cramer (Theme From Dallas)

GREASE
(Motion Picture)
   See John Travolta (Greased Lightnin', You're The One That I Want), Olivia Newton-John (You're The One That I Want)

GREASE 2
(Motion Picture)
   See the Four Tops (Back To School Again)

GREAT BALLS OF FIRE
(Motion Picture)
   See Jerry Lee Lewis (Great Balls Of Fire)

GREAT BUILDINGS
HOLD ON TO SOMETHING / Combat Zone .... (Columbia 11-02008)   1.00   4.00   81
   (Promotional issue only, *Demonstration–Not For Sale* printed on sleeve)
   Also see Danny Wilde

GREAT CARUSO, THE
(Motion Picture)
   See Mario Lanza (*Generic Mario Lanza Sleeve*)

GREATEST, THE
(Motion Picture)
   See George Benson (*The Greatest Love Of All*), Michael Masser and Mandrill (*Ali Bombaye*)

GREATEST AMERICAN HERO, THE
(Television Series)
   See Joey Scarbury (*Theme From The Greatest American Hero*)

GREAT IMPOSTOR, THE
(Motion Picture)
   See Henry Mancini (*The Great Impostor*)

GREAT OUTDOORS, THE
(Motion Picture)
   See the Elwood Blues Revue Featuring Wilson Pickett (*Land Of A Thousand Dances*)

GREAT RACE, THE
(Motion Picture)
   See Henry Mancini (*The Sweetheart Tree*)

GREAT WHITE
ROCK ME .... (Capitol B-44042)   .75   3.00   87
   (Back of sleeve shows title as *Rock Me [The Short Of It]*)
SAVE YOUR LOVE .... (Capitol B-44104)   .75   3.00   88
ONCE BITTEN TWICE SHY .... (Capitol B-44366)   .75   3.00   89

GRECO, BUDDY
THE LADY IS A TRAMP / Like Young .... (Epic 5-9387)   2.00   8.00   61
OOOH LOOK-A-THERE, AIN'T SHE PRETTY /
   This Could Be The Start Of Something .... (Epic 5-9404)   2.00   8.00   61
MORE .... (Epic 5-9666)   1.50   6.00   64
THAT DARN CAT .... (Epic 5-9864)   1.50   6.00   65

GREELEY, GEORGE
ALLISON'S THEME FROM "PARRISH" / Lucy's Theme From "Parrish" .... (Warner Bros. 5218)   2.00   8.00   62
   (From the motion picture *Parrish*, Troy Donahue and Claudette Colbert pictured)

GREEN, AL
BELLE .... (Hi 77505)   1.25   5.00   78
TO SIR WITH LOVE .... (Hi 78522)   1.25   5.00   78
EVERYTHING'S GONNA BE ALRIGHT / So Real To Me .... (A&M 2919)   .75   3.00   87
   Also see Scrooged

GREENBAUM, NORMAN
I. J. FOXX .... (Reprise 0956)   2.50   10.00   70
   (Promotional issue only)
   Also see Dr. West's Medicine Show

GREEN DAY
EXTENDED PLAYS
1,000 HOURS / DRY ICE / Only Of You / The One I Want .... (Lookout 17)   .75   3.00   89
   (Hard cover titled *1,000 Hours*, issued with small-hole 45 RPM record)
PAPER LANTERNS / WHY DO YOU WANT HIM? /
   409 In Your Coffeemaker / Knowledge .... (Lookout 35)   .75   3.00   90
   (Hard cover titled *Slappy E.P.*, issued with small-hole 45 RPM record)

GREENE, LORNE
(Played the role of Ben Cartwright in the television series *Bonanza* from 1959-1971)
LOVE FINDS A WAY / I'm The Same Old Me .... (RCA Victor 47-8229)   2.50   10.00   63
AN OL' TIN CUP / Sand .... (RCA Victor 47-8554)   2.50   10.00   65
EXTENDED PLAYS
NATIONAL WILDLIFE FEDERATION ANNOUNCEMENTS .... (ADS Audio 1964)   2.50   10.00   64
   (Promotional issue only featuring spots by Greene, Ernie Ford, and Andy Griffith; all three individually
   pictured)

GREEN RIVER
TOGETHER WE'LL NEVER / Ain't Nothing To Do .... (Tasque Force ICP 01)   —   —   84
   (This sleeve has turned up for auction but it's authenticity is highly questionable. Verification is needed before
   any value can be assigned.)
   Also see Mudhoney (Mark Arm, Steve Turner), Pearl Jam (Jeff Ament, Stone Gossard)

GREENWOOD, LEE
I.O.U. .... (MCA 52199)   .75   3.00   83
TO ME .... (MCA 52415)   .75   3.00   84
   (Shown as by Barbara Mandrell / Lee Greenwood, both pictured)
DIXIE ROAD .... (MCA 52564)   .75   3.00   85
DON'T UNDERESTIMATE MY LOVE FOR YOU /
   Leave My Heart The Way You Found It .... (MCA 52741)   .75   3.00   85

GREENWOOD COUNTY SINGERS, THE
FRANKIE AND JOHNNY .... (Kapp 591)   1.50   6.00   64

GREGORY, DICK
EXTENDED PLAYS
CAUGHT IN THE ACT .... (United Artists 94)   1.50   6.00   73
   (Promotional issue only)

GREMLINS
(Motion Picture)
   See Michael Sembello (*Gremlins...Mega Madness*)

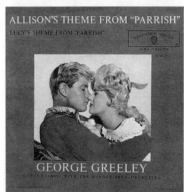

TITLE	LABEL AND NUMBER	VG	NM	YR

GREN
SHE SHINES / Pop Songs .... (I.R.S. 10520) 1.50 6.00 95
   (Promotional issue only issued with gold vinyl)
POP SONGS / Ayayo / Kiss Ass .... (I.R.S. 10742) 1.50 6.00 95
   (Promotional issue only issued with orange vinyl)

GRETA
ROCKING CHAIR / Insomnia .... (Stardog 1032) 1.25 5.00 93
   (Promotional issue only)

GREY, JENNIFER
(Actress)
   See the Contours (Do You Love Me?)

GRIFFIN, PAUL
YOU ARE THE RAIN .... (Golden Crest 511) 1.50 6.00

GRIFFIN, PORTIA
   See Jeffrey Osborne (You Should Be Mine)

GRIFFITH, ANDY
ROMEO & JULIET PARTS 1 & 2 .... (Capitol 2571) 5.00 20.00 70
EXTENDED PLAYS
NATIONAL WILDLIFE FEDERATION ANNOUNCEMENTS .... (ADS Audio 1964) 2.50 10.00 64
   (Promotional issue only featuring spots by Griffith, Ernie Ford, and Lorne Greene; all three individually
   pictured)

GRIFFITH, BOBBY
THE SOUND OF PEACE .... (Ranwood 933) 1.25 5.00

GRIFFITH, JOE
CRAZY SACK .... (Reelfoot 1250) 7.50 30.00 60s

GRIFFITH, MELANIE
(Actress)
   See Carly Simon (Let The River Run)

GRIFFITH, RONI
MONDO MAN .... (Vanguard 35218) .75 3.00 80

GRIGGS, ROBYN
(Actress)
   See the Soaps and Hearts Ensemble

GRIMES, TAMMY
I'M JUST WILD ABOUT YOU HARRY / You Came A Long Way From St Louis ..... (Columbia 57151) 2.00 8.00
   (Promotional issue only)

GRIM REAPER
THE SHOW MUST GO ON / Dead On Arrival .... (RCA/Ebony PB-13932) 1.00 4.00 84
   (Issued with small-hole 45 RPM record)

GROCE, LARRY
JUNKFOOD JUNKIE / The Little Old Lady In Cowboy Boots .... (Peaceable 45003) 1.50 6.00 75
TURN ON YOUR TV / The Hog And Dog Faction .... (Warner Bros. PRO 687) 1.50 6.00 77
   (Promotional issue only, illustration by Robert Crumb)

GROOTNA
EXTENDED PLAYS
FULL TIME WOMAN .... (Columbia AS 53) 1.50 6.00 71
   (Part of a series of promotional issues titled Playback issued with a small-hole 33-1/3 RPM record. Price
   includes generic Playback sleeve with folding insert. Also includes 1 song each by Jeff Beck, Lesley Duncan,
   Firesign Theatre, the Mahavishnu Orchestra With John McLaughlin, and Mylon.)

GROWING PAINS
(Television Series)
   See Christopher Cross (Swept Away), Steve Dorff and Friends (Theme From Growing Pains)

GRUPPO SPORTIVO
EXTENDED PLAYS
BERNADETTE / DISCO REALLY MADE IT / ARE YOU READY? /
   Girls Never Know / Tokyo / Rubber Gun .... (Sire EP 6066) 1.00 4.00 79
   (Issued with a small-hole 33-1/3 RPM record)

GTR
WHEN THE HEART RULES THE MIND / Reach Out (Never Say No) .... (Arista 9470) .75 3.00 86
THE HUNTER / Sketches In The Sun .... (Arista 9512) .75 3.00 86
   Also see Anderson, Bruford, Wakeman, Howe (Steve Howe), Yes (Steve Howe)

GUADALCANAL DIARY
ALWAYS SATURDAY / Kiss Of Fire .... (Elektra 7-69316) .75 3.00 89

GUERCIO, JAMES WILLIAM
TELL ME .... (Columbia 4-45886) 2.00 8.00 73
   (From the motion picture Electra Glide In Blue, Robert Blake pictured)
   Also see Chicago

GUESS WHO, THE
SHARE THE LAND / Bus Rider .... (RCA 74-0388) 1.50 6.00 70
HANG ON TO YOUR LIFE / Do You Miss Me Darlin' .... (RCA 74-0414) 12.50 50.00 71
   Also see Bachman-Turner Overdrive (Randy Bachman), Burton Cummings, Union (Randy Bachman)

GUESS WHO'S COMING TO DINNER
(Motion Picture)
   See Frank Devol Orchestra (Guess Who's Coming To Dinner)

GUEST, CHRISTOPHER
(Actor)
   See Billy Crystal (I Hate When That Happens), Spinal Tap (a.k.a. Nigel Tufnel)

GUIDING LIGHT
(Television Soap Opera)
    Related see the Soaps and Hearts Ensemble

GUILLOTEENS, THE
FOR MY OWN / Don't Let The Rain Get You Down .... (HBR 451) — 3.75 — 15.00 — 65

GUITARS INC., THE
    See Efrem Zimbalist, Jr.

GULAGER, CLU
(Actor)
BILLY THE KID .... (Deville 116) — 7.50 — 30.00 — 60

GUMBALL
UNDER MY WHEELS .... (Sub Pop 121) — 2.50 — 10.00 — 91
    (Alice Cooper Tribute double single release limited to 5,500 copies with an unknown number on blue-gray vinyl. Also includes one song each by Sonic Youth, These Immortal Souls, and Laughing Hyenas.)
WHATCHA GONNA DO / Read The News .... (Dry Hump 013) — .75 — 3.00 — 94
    (Issued with a small-hole 45 RPM)
    Also see Velvet Monkeys (Don Fleming, Jay Spiegel)

GUNS N' ROSES
WELCOME TO THE JUNGLE .... (Geffen PRO-S-3094) — 2.50 — 10.00 — 87
    (Promotional issue which requests radio stations *Don't Report This Record*. Completely different sleeve from the 1988 stock copy.)
SWEET CHILD O' MINE .... (Geffen 27963-7) — 1.25 — 5.00 — 88
WELCOME TO THE JUNGLE .... (Geffen 27759-7) — 1.25 — 5.00 — 88
PARADISE CITY .... (Geffen 27570-7) — 1.25 — 5.00 — 89
PATIENCE / Rocket Queen .... (Geffen 22996-7) — 1.00 — 4.00 — 89
    Also see the Fastbacks (Duff McKagan), Silly Killers (Duff McKagan), Y Kant Tori Read (Matt Sorum)

GURUS, THE
COME GIRL / Blue Snow Night .... (United Artists 50089) — 5.00 — 20.00 — 66

GUTHRIE, ARLO
(Son of folk legend Woody Guthrie)
VALLEY TO PRAY / Gabriel's Mother's Highway Ballad #16 Blues .... (Reprise 0951) — 2.50 — 10.00 — 70
ARLO GUTHRIE ON GUTHRIE THOMAS .... (Capitol SPRO 8216/8217) — 1.50 — 6.00 — 75
    (Promotional issue only, *Promotion Copy–Not For Sale* printed on sleeve. Guthrie Thomas pictured.)

GUTHRIE, GWEN
AIN'T NOTHIN' GOIN' ON BUT THE RENT / Passion Eyes .... (Polydor 885 106-7) — .75 — 3.00 — 86
OUTSIDE IN THE RAIN / Save Your Love For Me .... (Polydor 885 362-7) — .75 — 3.00 — 86

GUTTENBERG, STEVE
(Actor)
    See Village People (*Can't Stop The Music*)

GUY
GROOVE ME .... (MCA 53300) — .75 — 3.00 — 88

GUZMAN, ENRIQUE
I'M NOT THE MARRYING KIND .... (Columbia 4-43652) — 2.00 — 8.00 — 66

H

HAGAR, SAMMY
(SITTIN' ON) THE DOCK OF THE BAY / I've Done Everything For You .... (Capitol 4699) — 1.25 — 5.00 — 79
PIECE OF MY HEART / Sweet Hitchhiker .... (Geffen 50059) — 1.00 — 4.00 — 81
NEVER GIVE UP / Fast Times At Ridgemont High .... (Geffen 29718-7) — 1.00 — 4.00 — 82
TWO SIDES OF LOVE / Burnin' Down The City .... (Geffen 29246-7) — 1.00 — 4.00 — 84
    (Originally issued with red vinyl)
I CAN'T DRIVE 55 .... (Geffen 29173-7) — 1.00 — 4.00 — 84
WINNER TAKES IT ALL .... (Columbia 38-06647) — .75 — 3.00 — 87
    (From the motion picture *Over The Top*)
WINNER TAKES IT ALL .... (Columbia 38-06647) — 1.00 — 4.00 — 87
    (Promotional issue, *Demonstration–Not For Sale* printed on sleeve. From the motion picture *Over The Top*)
GIVE TO LIVE .... (Geffen 28314-7) — .75 — 3.00 — 87
EAGLES FLY .... (Geffen 28185-7) — .75 — 3.00 — 87
    Also see Hagar-Schon-Aaronson-Shrieve, Van Halen

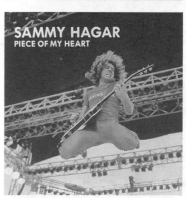

HAGAR-SCHON-AARONSON-SHRIEVE
WHITER SHADE OF PALE / Hot And Dirty .... (Geffen 29280-7) — 1.00 — 4.00 — 84
    Also see Dave Edmunds (Kenny Aaronson and Michael Schrieve on b-side of *High School Nights*), Sammy Hagar, Hear 'N Aid (Neal Schon), Journey (Neal Schon), Santana (Neal Schon, Michael Shrieve)

HAGERTY, JULIE
(Actress)
    See Mike + the Mechanics (*Revolution*)

HAGGARD, MERLE
I THREW AWAY THE ROSE .... (Capitol 5844) — 2.00 — 8.00 — 67
BRANDED MAN / You Don't Have Very Far To Go .... (Capitol 5931) — 2.00 — 8.00 — 67
SING ME BACK HOME .... (Capitol 2017) — 2.00 — 8.00 — 67
MAMA TRIED / You'll Never Love Me Now .... (Capitol 2219) — 2.00 — 8.00 — 68
I TAKE A LOT OF PRIDE IN WHAT I AM / Keep Me From Cryin' Today .... (Capitol 2289) — 2.00 — 8.00 — 68
HUNGRY EYES .... (Capitol 2383) — 2.00 — 8.00 — 68
WORKING MAN BLUES .... (Capitol 2503) — 2.00 — 8.00 — 69
OKIE FROM MUSKOGEE .... (Capitol 2626) — 2.00 — 8.00 — 69
THE FIGHTIN' SIDE OF ME .... (Capitol 2719) — 2.00 — 8.00 — 70
SIDEWALKS OF CHICAGO / I Can't Be Myself .... (Capitol 2891) — 2.00 — 8.00 — 70
SOLDIER'S LAST LETTER .... (Capitol 3024) — 2.00 — 8.00 — 70
DADDY FRANK (THE GUITAR MAN) / My Heart Would Know .... (Capitol 3198) — 2.00 — 8.00 — 71

TITLE	LABEL AND NUMBER	VG	NM	YR

MISERY & GIN .... (MCA 41255)		1.00	4.00	80
BAR ROOM BUDDIES .... (Elektra 46634)		1.00	4.00	80
(Shown as by Merle Haggard and Clint Eastwood, both pictured. From the motion picture *Bronco Billy*.)				

EXTENDED PLAYS

BIG CITY / MY FAVORITE MEMORY .... (CBS AE7 1429)		1.00	4.00	82

(Promotional issue only titled *Kickin Rock & Roll*, co-sponsored by Busch Beer and WBCN 104 FM and included in *The Phoenix* magazine. Also includes songs by George Jones, Larry Gatlin and the Gatlin Brothers Band, the Burrito Brothers, Bobby Bare, and Ricky Skaggs.)

HAGMAN, LARRY
(Actor)

BALLAD OF THE GOOD LUCK CHARM / My Favorite Sins .... (Portrait 12-70044)		1.50	6.00	80

Also see Floyd Cramer (*Theme From Dallas*)

HAIM, COREY
(Actor)

See Breakfast Club (*Drive My Car*)

HAIR
(Broadway Musical)

HAIR MEDLEY / Aquarius .... (RCA SP-45-184)		2.50	10.00	68

(Promotional issue only, *For Disk Jockeys Only Not For Sale* printed on back of sleeve)

HAIRCUT ONE HUNDRED
See Nick Heyward

HAIRCUTS, THE

SHE LOVES YOU .... (Parkway 899)		7.50	30.00	64

HAIRSPRAY
(Motion Picture)

See Ray Bryant (*Madison Time*), Rachel Sweet (*Hairspray*)

HALEY, BILL, AND THE COMETS

(YOU HIT THE WRONG NOTE) BILLY GOAT / Rockin' Rollin' Rover .... (Decca 30314)		18.75	75.00	57
IT'S A SIN / Mary, Mary Lou .... (Decca 30530)		10.00	40.00	57
THE A.B.C. BOOGIE / Rock Around The Clock .... (Kasey 7006)		10.00	40.00	61
(B-side shown as by Phil Flowers)				
YODEL YOUR BLUES AWAY / With This Broken Heart Of Mine .... (Arzee 4677)		5.00	20.00	78

HALIFAX THREE, THE

THE MAN WHO WOULDN'T SING ALONG WITH MITCH .... (Epic 5-9572)		2.50	10.00	62

HALL, ANTHONY MICHAEL
(Actor)

See Judas Priest (*Johnny B. Goode*), Wang Chung (*Fire In The Twilight*)

HALL, ARSENIO
See Chunky A

HALL, DARYL

SOMETHING IN 4/4 TIME / Sacred Songs .... (RCA PB-12001)		1.00	4.00	80
DREAMTIME / Let It Out .... (RCA PB-14387)		.75	3.00	86
FOOLISH PRIDE / What's Gonna Happen To Us .... (RCA 5038-7-R)		.75	3.00	86
SOMEONE LIKE YOU (WITH GUITAR SOLO) / Someone Like You (With Sax Solo) (RCA 5105-7-R)		.75	3.00	87

Also see Artists United Against Apartheid, Daryl Hall & John Oates, U.S.A. For Africa, Voices Of America

HALL, DARYL, & JOHN OATES

RICH GIRL / London Luck, & Love .... (RCA PB-10860)		1.25	5.00	77
MANEATER / Delayed Reaction .... (RCA PB-13354)		1.00	4.00	82
ONE ON ONE / Art Of Heartbreak .... (RCA PB-13421)		1.00	4.00	83
SAY IT ISN'T SO / Kiss On My List .... (RCA PB-13654)		1.00	4.00	83
SAY IT ISN'T SO .... (RCA JK-13654)		1.50	6.00	83
(Promotional issue, *Not For Sale* printed on sleeve)				
ADULT EDUCATION / Maneater .... (RCA PB-13714)		1.00	4.00	84
OUT OF TOUCH / Cold, Dark And Yesterday .... (RCA PB-13916)		.75	3.00	84
METHOD OF MODERN LOVE / Bank On Your Love .... (RCA PB-13970)		.75	3.00	84
SOME THINGS ARE BETTER LEFT UNSAID / All American Girl .... (RCA PB-14035)		.75	3.00	85
POSSESSION OBSESSION / Dance On Your Knees .... (RCA PB-14098)		.75	3.00	85
THE WAY YOU DO THE THINGS YOU DO / My Girl .... (RCA PB-14178)		.75	3.00	85
(Shown as by Hall & Oates with David Ruffin & Eddie Kendrick. Note misspelling of Kendricks last name.)				
JINGLE BELL ROCK / Jingle Bell Rock .... (RCA JB-14259)		1.25	5.00	85
(A-side by Daryl Hall and b-side by John Oates, originally issued with red vinyl)				
JINGLE BELL ROCK / Jingle Bell Rock .... (RCA JB-14259)		2.50	10.00	85
(Promotional issue, a-side by Daryl Hall and b-side by John Oates, issued with either red or green vinyl)				
EVERYTHING YOUR HEART DESIRES / .... (Arista 9684)		.75	3.00	88
MISSED OPPORTUNITY / .... (Arista 9727)		.75	3.00	88
DOWNTOWN LIFE (ALBUM VERSION) / Downtown Life (Urban Mix) ..... (Arista 9753)		.75	3.00	88
LOVE TRAIN / Earth Girls Are Easy .... (Sire/Reprise 22967-7)		1.00	4.00	89
(B-side shown as by the N. From the motion picture *Earth Girls Are Easy*.)				

EXTENDED PLAYS

LADY RAIN .... (Atlantic PR 195)		1.25	5.00	73

(Promotional issue only titled *Something For Nothing*. Also includes one song each, the titles are not listed on sleeve, by John Prine, Barnaby Bye, and Delbert & Glen.)
Also see Daryl Hall, U.S.A. For Africa, Voices Of America

HALL, JENNIFER

ICE CREAM DAYS .... (Warner Bros. 27965-7)		.75	3.00	86

HALL, LANI

LOVE SONG / How Can I Tell You .... (A&M 1385)		1.25	5.00	72
BANQUET / .... (A&M 1433)		1.25	5.00	73
I DON'T WANT YOU TO GO / Only You .... (A&M 2232)		1.00	4.00	80
(Sleeve pictures Hall with her husband Herb Alpert)				
NEVER SAY NEVER AGAIN .... (A&M 2596)		1.00	4.00	83

(From the motion picture *Never Say Never Again*)
Also Sergio Mendes (Hall was a member of Brasil '66)

HALL, RANDY
I'VE BEEN WATCHING YOU (JAMIE'S GIRL) .... (MCA 52405) | .75 | 3.00 | 84

HALLORAN, JACK, AND THE VOICES OF CHRISTMAS
See Bing Crosby (*A Time To Be Jolly*)

HALLYDAY, DAVID
(Son of Johnny Hallyday)
HE'S MY GIRL .... (Scotti Brothers ZS4-07777) | .75 | 3.00 | 88
   (From the motion picture *He's My Girl* starring Hallyday)
MOVE .... (Scotti Brothers ZS4-07777) | .75 | 3.00 | 88

HALLYDAY, JOHNNY
BE BOP A LULA/I Got A Woman .... (Philips 40024) | 6.25 | 25.00 | 62

HAMILTON, GEORGE
(Actor)
LITTLE BITTY FALLING STAR/Don't Envy Me .... (MGM K13178) | 2.50 | 10.00 | 63
LONELINESS/So Small .... (ABC 10734) | 2.50 | 10.00 | 65

HAMILTON, GEORGE, IV
See Chet Atkins (*Chet's Tune*)

HAMILTON, ROY
A GREAT ROMANCE/On My Way Back Home .... (Epic 5-9342) | 3.75 | 15.00 | 59
YOU CAN HAVE HER/Abide With Me .... (Epic 5-9434) | 2.50 | 10.00 | 61
YOU'RE GONNA NEED MAGIC/To The One I Love .... (Epic 5-9443) | 2.50 | 10.00 | 61
NO SUBSTITUTE FOR LOVE/Please Louise .... (Epic 5-9449) | 2.50 | 10.00 | 61
IF ONLY I HAD KNOWN/Don't Come Cryin' To Me .... (Epic 5-9492) | 2.50 | 10.00 | 62
CLIMB EV'RY MOUNTAIN/I'll Come Running Back To You .... (Epic 5-9520) | 2.50 | 10.00 | 62
I AM/Earthquake .... (Epic 9538) | 2.50 | 10.00 | 62

HAMILTON, SUZANNA
(Actress)
See Eurythmics (*Julia*)

HAMILTON, JOE FRANK & DENNISON
LIGHT UP THE WORLD WITH SUNSHINE .... (Playboy 6077) | 1.00 | 4.00 | 76
DON'T FIGHT THE HANDS .... (Playboy 6088) | 1.00 | 4.00 | 76

HAMLIN, HARRY
(Actor)
See Roberta Flack (*Making Love*)

HAMLISCH, MARVIN
LOVE THEME/Teeny Tim's Theme .... (Buena Vista F-491) | 3.00 | 12.00 | 73
   (Hard cover, from the motion picture *The World's Greatest Athlete*, Jan-Michael Vincent pictured on front and Vincent, Tim Conway, and female co-star on back. Sleeve included a 6-3/4" x 6-3/4" color "photograph" of Jan-Michael Vincent.)

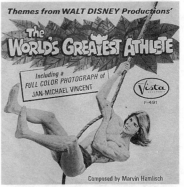

HAMMER, JAN
MIAMI VICE THEME .... (MCA 52666) | 1.25 | 5.00 | 85
   (First printing without *The Original Version As Heard On Miami Vice* text, but the phrase was printed on a sticker that was placed on front of some sleeves. The top of the sleeve is straight cut.)
MIAMI VICE THEME .... (MCA 52666) | 1.00 | 4.00 | 85
   (Second printing with *The Original Version As Heard On Miami Vice* printed at the top. The top of the sleeve is curved.)
CROCKETT'S THEME .... (MCA 53239) | .75 | 3.00 | 88
   (From the television series *Miami Vice*)
   Also see the Mahavishnu Orchestra, Van Stephenson (b-side of *No Secrets*)

HAMMOND, ALBERT
See Bruce Springsteen (*The Circus Song*). Hammond was a member of the Magic Lanterns in 1971.

HAMPTON, PAUL
I'M IN LOVE WITH A BUNNY .... (Battle 45919) | 2.50 | 10.00 | 63
THE LONG DRIVE HOME/Somebody– Someone– Something .... (ABC/Dunhill 4167) | 1.50 | 6.00 | 68
   (Promotional issue only)

HANCOCK, HERBIE
OSTINATO .... (Warner Bros. 457) | 2.00 | 8.00 | 70s
   (Promotional issue only)
HARDROCK .... (Columbia 38-04565) | .75 | 3.00 | 84
VIBE ALIVE .... (Columbia 38-07718) | .75 | 3.00 | 88
   Also see Artists United Against Apartheid

HANGING TREE, THE
(Motion Picture)
See Marty Robbins (*The Hanging Tree*)

HANKS, TOM
(Comic Actor)
CITY OF CRIME .... (MCA 53086) | .75 | 3.00 | 87
   (Shown as by Dan Aykroyd & Tom Hanks. From the motion picture *Dragnet*, both pictured.)
   Also see the Art Of Noise (*Dragnet*), Christopher Cross (*Loving Strangers*)

HANSON
I WILL COME TO YOU/With You In Your Dreams .... (Mercury 314 568 066-7) | .50 | 2.00 | 97

HAPPENINGS, THE
MY MAMMY/I Believe In Nothing .... (B.T. Puppy 45-530) | 3.00 | 12.00 | 67
WHY DO FOOLS FALL IN LOVE/When The Summer Is Through .... (B.T. Puppy 45-532) | 3.00 | 12.00 | 67
MUSIC MUSIC MUSIC/When I Lock My Door .... (B.T. Puppy 45-538) | 3.00 | 12.00 | 68
RANDY/The Love Song Of Mommy And Dad .... (B.T. Puppy 45-540) | 3.00 | 12.00 | 68

HAPPY ANNIVERSARY
(Motion Picture)
See Jane Morgan (*Happy Anniversary*)

TITLE	LABEL AND NUMBER	VG	NM	YR

HAPPY DAYS
(Television Series)
Related see Scott Baio (Chachi), Donnie Most (Ralph Malph), the Heyettes (Fonzie For President), Suzi Quatro (Leather Tuscadero), Anson Williams (Potsie)

HAPPY LOUIE
FOREVER AND EVER '66/Apples, Peaches, Pumpkin Pie .... (MGM K-13620) 1.50 6.00 66

HARBRINGERS, THE
DOWN AROUND THE RIVER/Come Into My World .... (Columbia 4-44290) 2.50 10.00 67
(Promotional issue only)

HARDCASTLE, PAUL
19/Fly By Night .... (Chrysalis VS4-42860) .75 3.00 85
JUST FOR MONEY/Back In Time .... (Chrysalis VS4 42922) .75 3.00 85

HARD DAY'S NIGHT, A
(Motion Picture)
See the Beatles (Can't Buy Me Love, A Hard Day's Night, I'll Cry Instead, And I Love Her)

HARDEN, ARLENE
CRYING/It's Over .... (Columbia 4-45203) 1.50 6.00 70
(Back of sleeve has a statement about Harden by Roy Orbison)

HARDEN, BOBBY
TULSA .... (Mega 6) 1.50 6.00 70

HARDEN TRIO, THE
See Arlene Harden, Bobby Harden

HARDIN, TIM
DON'T MAKE PROMISES/Lady Came From Baltimore .... (Verve 3078) 2.00 8.00 68

HARD TO HOLD
(Motion Picture)
See Rick Springfield (Bop 'Til You Drop, Don't Walk, Love Somebody)

HARLEM CHILDREN'S CHORUS, THE
BLACK CHRISTMAS/Do You Hear What I Hear .... (Cur 3003) 1.25 5.00

HARLEM COMMUNITY CHOIR, THE
See John Lennon (Happy Xmas)

HARLEM GLOBETROTTERS, THE
See the Globetrotters, Meadowlark Lemon

HARLOW
(Motion Picture)
See Bobby Vinton (Theme From "Harlow")

HARMONICATS
See Jerry Murad's Harmonicats

HARPER VALLEY P.T.A.
(Motion Picture)
See Jeannie C. Riley (Harper Valley P.T.A.)

HARRIS, EMMYLOU
LIGHT OF THE STABLE .... (Reprise 1341) 1.50 6.00 75
(Back of sleeve credits Harris, Dolly Parton, Linda Ronstadt, and Neil Young as "The Singers")
WAYFARING STRANGER/Green Pastures .... (Warner Bros. 49239) 1.25 5.00 80
WISH WE WERE BACK IN MISSOURI .... (A&M 2290) 1.00 4.00 80
(Generic half sleeve for the album The Legend Of Jessse James. No artist or song title on sleeve.)
TO KNOW HIM IS TO LOVE HIM .... (Warner Bros. 28492-7) 1.00 4.00 87
(Shown as by Dolly Parton, Linda Ronstadt, Emmylou Harris)
THOSE MEMORIES OF YOU .... (Warner Bros. 28248-7) 1.00 4.00 87
(Shown as by Dolly Parton, Linda Ronstadt, Emmylou Harris)
Also see Gram Parsons and the Fallen Angels

HARRIS, JOYCE
DO YOU KNOW WHAT IT'S LIKE TO BE LONESOME/I Cheated .... (Domino 903) 12.50 50.00 60
(Single sheet insert, not a true picture sleeve)
NO WAY OUT/Dreamer .... (Domino 905) 12.50 50.00 61
(Single sheet insert, not a true picture sleeve)

HARRIS, PHIL
THE THING/The Mountaineer And The Jabberwock .... (RCA Victor WBY-87) 3.00 12.00 50

HARRIS, RICHARD
MACARTHUR PARK .... (ABC/Dunhill 4134) 1.50 6.00 68
MACARTHUR PARK .... (ABC/Dunhill 4134) 3.00 12.00 68
(Promotional issue)
FILL THE WORLD WITH LOVE .... (ABC/Dunhill 4218) 1.50 6.00 69
THERE ARE TOO MANY SAVIORS ON MY CROSS .... (ABC/Dunhill 4322) 1.50 6.00 72
ON CRIME AND PUNISHMENT/Trilogy From The Prophet .... (Atlantic 3128) 1.25 5.00 74

HARRIS, ROLF
TIE ME KANGAROO DOWN, SPORT/The Big Black Hat .... (Epic 5-9596) 3.00 12.00 63
NICK TEEN AND AL K. HALL/I Know A Man .... (Epic 5-9615) 3.00 12.00 63
LOST LITTLE BOY/Six White Boomers .... (Epic 5-9641) 3.00 12.00 63

HARRIS, SAM
SUGAR DON'T BITE/You Keep Me Hangin' On .... (Motown 1743) .75 3.00 84
SUGAR DON'T BITE/You Keep Me Hangin' On .... (Motown 1743) 1.00 4.00 84
(Promotional issue, For Promotional Use Only/Not For Sale printed on sleeve)
OVER THE RAINBOW/I've Heard It All Before .... (Motown 1780) .75 3.00 84
OVER THE RAINBOW/I've Heard It All Before .... (Motown 1780) 1.00 4.00 84
(Promotional issue, For Promotional Use Only/Not For Sale printed on sleeve)

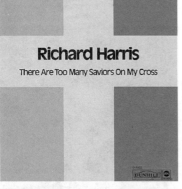

TITLE	LABEL AND NUMBER	VG	NM	YR
I'D DO IT ALL AGAIN .... (Motown 1829)		.75	3.00	85
(Back of sleeve credits, among others, Lauren Wood on keyboards)				
I'D DO IT ALL AGAIN .... (Motown 1829)		1.00	4.00	85
(Promotional issue, *For Promotional Use Only/Not For Sale* printed on sleeve. Back of sleeve credits, among others, Lauren Wood on keyboards.)				
FOREVER FOR YOU .... (Motown 1840)		.75	3.00	86
FOREVER FOR YOU .... (Motown 1840)		1.00	4.00	86
(Promotional issue, *For Promotional Use Only/Not For Sale* printed on sleeve)				

The Story Behind "This Song"

HARRISON, GEORGE

TITLE	LABEL AND NUMBER	VG	NM	YR
MY SWEET LORD/Isn't It A Pity .... (Apple 2995)		6.25	25.00	70
WHAT IS LIFE/Apple Scruffs .... (Apple 1828)		7.50	30.00	71
(WE'VE GOT TO RELIEVE) BANGLA DESH .... (Apple 1836)		5.00	20.00	71
DARK HORSE .... (Apple 1877)		25.00	100.00	74
DING DONG; DING DONG/Hari's On Tour (Express) .... (Apple 1879)		3.75	15.00	74
YOU .... (Apple 1884)		3.00	12.00	75
THIS SONG .... (Dark Horse 8294)		5.00	20.00	76
THIS SONG .... (Dark Horse 8294)		12.50	50.00	76
(Promotional issue titled *The Story Behind "This Song"*)				
BLOW AWAY/Soft-Hearted Hana .... (Dark Horse 8763)		1.50	6.00	79
LOVE COMES TO EVERYONE/Soft Touch .... (Dark Horse 8844)		150.00	600.00	79
ALL THOSE YEARS AGO/Writing's On The Wall .... (Dark Horse 49725)		1.25	5.00	81
GOT MY MIND SET ON YOU/Lay His Head .... (Dark Horse 28178-7)		1.00	4.00	87
WHEN WE WAS FAB/Zig Zag .... (Dark Horse 28131-7)		1.00	4.00	88
THIS IS LOVE/Breath Away From Heaven .... (Dark Horse 27913-7)		1.00	4.00	88
CHEER DOWN .... (Warner Bros. 22807-7)		1.25	5.00	89
(From the motion picture *Lethal Weapon 2*)				
Also see the Beatles, the Traveling Wilburys				

HARRISON, JERRY

TITLE	LABEL AND NUMBER	VG	NM	YR
REV IT UP/Bobby .... (Sire 27977-7)		.75	3.00	88
(Shown as by Jerry Harrison: Casual Gods)				
Also see Jonathan Richman and the Modern Lovers, Talking Heads				

HARRISON, NOEL

TITLE	LABEL AND NUMBER	VG	NM	YR
CHERYL'S GOING HOME/In A Dusty Old Room .... (London 20017)		2.00	8.00	66

HARRISON, WES

TITLE	LABEL AND NUMBER	VG	NM	YR
FUN WITH SOUND .... (IRC 6930)		1.25	5.00	

HARRY, DEBBIE

TITLE	LABEL AND NUMBER	VG	NM	YR
BACKFIRED/Military Rap .... (Chrysalis 2526)		1.00	4.00	81
RUSH RUSH/Dance, Dance, Dance .... (Chrysalis VS4 42745)		1.00	4.00	83
(From the motion picture *Scarface*. B-side shown as by Beth Andersen.)				
FRENCH KISSIN .... (Geffen 28546-7)		1.00	4.00	86
IN LOVE WITH LOVE .... (Geffen 28476-7)		1.00	4.00	87
LIAR, LIAR/Queen Of VouDou .... (Reprise 27792-7)		1.00	4.00	88
(From the motion picture *Married To The Mob*. B-side shown as by the Voodooist Corporation.)				
DENIS '88 (THE DANCIN' DANNY D REMIX)/ Rapture (The Teddy Riley Remix) .... (Chrysalis VS4 43328)		1.00	4.00	88
I WANT THAT MAN/Bike Boy .... (Sire/Reprise 22816-7)		1.00	4.00	89
(Shown as by Deborah Harry)				
Also see Blondie, Rodney and the Brunettes				

HARRY AND THE HENDERSONS

(Motion Picture)
See Joe Cocker (*Love Lives On*)

HART, BOBBY

TITLE	LABEL AND NUMBER	VG	NM	YR
HARD CORE MAN/To Keep From Crying .... (Warner Bros. 8058)		1.50	6.00	74
(From the motion picture *Freebie And The Bean*)				
Also see Tommy Boyce & Bobby Hart				

HART, COREY

TITLE	LABEL AND NUMBER	VG	NM	YR
SUNGLASSES AT NIGHT/At The Dance .... (EMI America B-8203)		1.00	4.00	84
IT AIN'T ENOUGH/Araby (She's Just A Girl) .... (EMI America B-8236)		.75	3.00	84
NEVER SURRENDER/Water From The Moon .... (EMI America B-8268)		1.00	4.00	85
(Poster sleeve)				
BOY IN THE BOX .... (EMI America B-8287)		.75	3.00	85
EVERYTHING IN MY HEART .... (EMI America B8300)		.75	3.00	85
I AM BY YOUR SIDE/Political Cry .... (EMI America B-8348)		.75	3.00	86
CAN'T HELP FALLING IN LOVE/Broken Arrow .... (EMI America B8368)		1.00	4.00	86
(Poster sleeve printed on white paper)				
CAN'T HELP FALLING IN LOVE/Broken Arrow .... (EMI America B8368)		1.00	4.00	86
(Poster sleeve printed on tan paper)				
IN YOUR SOUL/Chippin' Away .... (EMI-Manhattan B50134)		.75	3.00	88

HART, DOLORES

(Actress)
See Connie Francis (*Where The Boys Are*)

HART, FREDDIE

TITLE	LABEL AND NUMBER	VG	NM	YR
TOGETHERNESS .... (Kapp 879)		1.50	6.00	68
SURE THING .... (Sunbird 7550)		1.25	5.00	80

HART, ROBERT

TITLE	LABEL AND NUMBER	VG	NM	YR
WHITE LIES AND PROMISES/She's On The List .... (Atlantic 7-88867)		.75	3.00	89

HARTMAN, DAN

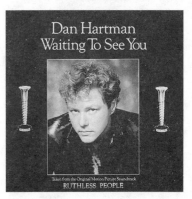

TITLE	LABEL AND NUMBER	VG	NM	YR
I CAN DREAM ABOUT YOU .... (MCA 52378)		1.00	4.00	84
(From the motion picture *Streets Of Fire*. The Blasters' *Blue Shadows* appears on the b-side of the 45 but is not credited on the sleeve.)				
WE ARE THE YOUNG/I'm Not A Rolling Stone .... (MCA 52471)		.75	3.00	84
SECOND NATURE/I Can't Get Enough .... (MCA 52519)		.75	3.00	85
WAITING TO SEE YOU .... (Epic 34-06130)		.75	3.00	86
(From the motion picture *Ruthless People*)				

TITLE	LABEL AND NUMBER	VG	NM	YR

WAITING TO SEE YOU .... (Epic 34-06130) | 1.00 | 4.00 | 86
(Promotional issue, *Demonstration Only–Not For Sale* printed on sleeve. From the motion picture *Ruthless People*)
Also see the Legends, the Edgar Winter Group

HARTMAN, LISA
(Actress)

TEMPT ME (IF YOU WANT TO)/How Many Rivers .... (Atlantic 7-89179)	1.00	4.00	87
I DON'T NEED LOVE/Tender Kiss .... (Atlantic 7-89139)	1.00	4.00	87
THE DRESS/Tender Kiss .... (Atlantic 7-89070)	1.00	4.00	88

HARVEY, ALEX
EXTENDED PLAYS
ALEX HARVEY TALKS ABOUT EVERYTHING .... (Vertigo VEPL-2) | 6.25 | 25.00 | 74
(Promotional issue only with script included)

HARVEY, LAWRENCE
(Actor)
See Brook Benton (*Walk On The Wild Side*)

HASH
I FORGOT MY BLANKET/I Am The Walrus .... (Elektra 64625) | .75 | 3.00 | 93

HASKELL, JACK
(Television Announcer)
See Jack Paar (*I-M-4-U*)

HASKELL, JIMMIE
BYE BYE BIRDIE/The James Bond Theme .... (Capitol 4954) | 1.50 | 6.00 | 63

HASSELHOFF, DAVID
(Actor best known from the television series *Knight Rider* and *Baywatch*)

DO YOU LOVE ME .... (Silver Blue ZS4-04699)	1.00	4.00	84
DO YOU LOVE ME .... (Silver Blue ZS4-04699)	1.25	5.00	84

(Promotional issue, *Demonstration Only/Not For Sale* printed on sleeve)

HASSLES, THE
YOU'VE GOT ME HUMMIN' .... (United Artists 50215) | 3.75 | 15.00 | 67
Also see Billy Joel

HATARI!
(Motion Picture)
See Henry Mancini (*Theme From Hatari!*)

HATFIELD, JULIANA, THREE, THE
MY SISTER/A Dame With A Rod/Put It Away .... (Atlantic/Mammoth 0053-7) | 1.00 | 4.00 | 93
(Hard cover, hand numbered edition of 1,500 issued with grey vinyl)

HAVE GUN WILL TRAVEL
(Television Series)
See Duane Eddy (*The Ballad Of Paladin*)

HAVENS, RICHIE

FREEDOM/Handsome Johnny .... (Stormy Forest 666)	2.00	8.00	71
EYESIGHT TO THE BLIND/Underture .... (Ode 66032)	2.00	8.00	72

(B-side shown as by London Symphony Orchestra and English Chamber Choir)

HAVING A WILD WEEKEND
(Motion Picture)
See the Dave Clark Five (*Catch Us If You Can*)

HAWKINS, DALE

POOR LITTLE RHODE ISLAND/Every Little Girl .... (Checker 944)	25.00	100.00	60
NUMBER NINE TRAIN/On Account Of You .... (Norton 45-055)	.50	2.00	97

(Hard cover)

HAWN, GOLDIE
(Actress who originally gained fame as the scatter-brained blonde on the television series *Rowan & Martin's Laugh-In*)
PITTA PATTA .... (Reprise 1126) | 3.00 | 12.00 | 72

HAY, COLIN JAMES

HOLD ME/Home Sweet Home .... (Columbia 38-06580)	.75	3.00	87
HOLD ME .... (Columbia 38-06580)	1.00	4.00	87

(Promotional issue, *Demonstration–Not For Sale* printed on sleeve)

CAN I HOLD YOU?/Nature Of The Beast .... (Columbia 38-07042)	.75	3.00	87
CAN I HOLD YOU? .... (Columbia 38-07042)	1.00	4.00	87

(Promotional issue, *Demonstration–Not For Sale* printed on sleeve)

LOOKING FOR JACK/ .... (Columbia 38-07265)	.75	3.00	87
LOOKING FOR JACK .... (Columbia 38-07265)	1.00	4.00	87

(Promotional issue, *Demonstration–Not For Sale* printed on sleeve)
Also see Men At Work

HAYES, BILL
WRINGLE WRANGLE .... (ABC Paramount 9785) | 3.00 | 12.00 | 57
(From the motion picture *Westward Ho The Wagons*)

HAYES, BONNIE, WITH THE WILD COMBO
SHELLY'S BOYFRIEND/Coverage .... (Slash 113) | 1.50 | 6.00 | 82
Also see the Punts

HAYES, ISAAC

IKE'S RAP/Hey Girl .... (Columbia 38-06363)	.75	3.00	86
IKE'S RAP .... (Columbia 38-06363)	1.00	4.00	86

(Promotional issue, *Demonstration–Not For Sale* printed on sleeve)

HAYSI FANTAYZEE
SHINY SHINY/Shiny Shiny Bon Temps .... (RCA PB-13534) | 1.00 | 4.00 | 83

HAYWARD, JUSTIN
BLUE GUITAR .... (Threshold 67021) | 3.75 | 15.00 | 75

(Shown as by Justin Hayward and John Lodge)
Also see the Moody Blues

HEAD, MURRAY
SUPERSTAR .... (Decca 732603) | 1.50 | 6.00 | 69

("Jesus" graphics on front, text on back. Shown as by Murray Head with the Trinidad Singers. Identifies song as "from the Rock Opera *Jesus Christ* now in preparation.")

SUPERSTAR .... (Decca 732603) | 1.50 | 6.00 | 69

("Angel" graphics on front, text and album cover on back. Shown as by Murray Head with the Trinidad Singers. From the Rock Opera *Jesus Christ/Superstar.*)

SUPERSTAR .... (Decca 732603) | 1.50 | 6.00 | 69

(Text and album cover from the back of the "angel" version used as the front of this sleeve, back is unprinted. Shown as by Murray Head with the Trinidad Singers. From the Rock Opera *Jesus Christ/Superstar.*)

(TOO MUCH) HEAVEN ON THEIR MINDS .... (Decca 32709) | 1.50 | 6.00 | 69

(Head credited as performing the role of Judas in the Rock Opera *Jesus Christ/Superstar*)

ONE NIGHT IN BANGKOK/Merano .... (RCA PB-13988) | .75 | 3.00 | 84

(From the stage musical *Chess*. B-side shown as by London Symphony Orchestra and the Ambrosian Singers. Benny Andersson, Tim Rice, and Björn Ulvaeus credited on front.)
Also see the Smiths (*Stop Me If You Think You've Heard This One Before*)

HEAD EAST
SINCE YOU'VE BEEN GONE/Pictures .... (A&M 2026) | 2.00 | 8.00 | 78

HEADPINS
JUST ONE MORE TIME .... (SGR 90001) | .75 | 3.00 | 83

HEADROOM, MAX
(Computer manipulated image of actor Matt Frewer)

MERRY CHRISTMAS SANTA CLAUS (YOU'RE A LOVELY GUY)/
Gimme Shades .... (Chrysalis VS4 44000) | 1.00 | 4.00 | 86

Also see the Art Of Noise (*Paranoimia*)

HEALEY, JEFF BAND, THE
CONFIDENCE MAN/That's What They Say .... (Arista 9790) | .75 | 3.00 | 88
ANGEL EYES/Don't Let Your Chance Go By .... (Arista 9808) | .75 | 3.00 | 89

HEAR 'N AID
STARS/The 4-1/2 Minute News .... (Mercury 884 004-7) | 1.00 | 4.00 | 86

Also see Blue Oyster Cult, Dio, Dokken, Giuffria, Iron Maiden, Judas Priest, King Kobra, Mötley Crüe, Night Ranger, Ted Nugent, Quiet Riot, Neal Schon, Spinal Tap, Twisted Sister, Y & T

HEART
THIS MAN IS MINE/America .... (Epic 14-02925) | 1.00 | 4.00 | 83
THIS MAN IS MINE/America .... (Epic 14-02925) | 1.50 | 6.00 | 83

(Promotional issue, *Demonstration Only–Not For Sale* printed on sleeve)

HOW CAN I REFUSE .... (Epic 34-04047) | 1.00 | 4.00 | 83
HOW CAN I REFUSE .... (Epic 34-04047) | 1.50 | 6.00 | 83

(Promotional issue, *Demonstration Only–Not For Sale* printed on sleeve)

ALLIES/Together Now .... (Epic 34-04184) | 1.00 | 4.00 | 83
WHAT ABOUT LOVE .... (Capitol B-5481) | .75 | 3.00 | 85
NEVER .... (Capitol B-5512) | .75 | 3.00 | 85
THESE DREAMS .... (Capitol B-5541) | .75 | 3.00 | 86
NOTHIN' AT ALL .... (Capitol B-5572) | .75 | 3.00 | 86
IF LOOKS COULD KILL/What He Don't Know .... (Capitol B-5605) | .75 | 3.00 | 86
ALONE .... (Capitol B-44002) | .75 | 3.00 | 87
WHO WILL YOU RUN TO/Magic Man (Live) .... (Capitol B-44040) | .75 | 3.00 | 87
THERE'S THE GIRL .... (Capitol B-44089) | .75 | 3.00 | 87
ALL I WANNA DO IS MAKE LOVE TO YOU .... (Capitol B-44507) | .75 | 3.00 | 90

Also see Spirit (Mark Andes), Firefall (Mark Andes), Ann Wilson

HEARTBREAK HOTEL
(Motion Picture)
See Elvis Presley (*Heartbreak Hotel*)

HEARTBURN
(Motion Picture)
See Carly Simon (*Coming Around Again*)

HEATHERTON, JOEY
THAT'S HOW IT GOES/I'll Be Seeing You .... (Coral 62422) | 6.25 | 25.00 | 64
GONE/The Road I Took To You .... (MGM K14387) | 2.50 | 10.00 | 72

HEAVENLY BODIES
(Motion Picture)
See Cheryl Lynn (*At Last You're Mine*), Bonnie Pointer (*The Beast In Me*)

HEAVEN ON EARTH
ON AN ANGEL'S WINGS .... (Atlantic 7-89007) | .75 | 3.00 | 88

HEAVEN 17
WE LIVE SO FAST/The Best Kept Secret .... (Arista 9027) | 1.25 | 5.00 | 83
CONTENDERS/Diary Of A Contender .... (Virgin 7-99468) | 1.00 | 4.00 | 87

Also see Band Aid, the Human League (Martyn Ware)

HEAVY D. AND THE BOYZ
THE OVERWEIGHT LOVERS .... (MCA 53195) | .75 | 3.00 | 87

HEAVY METAL
(Motion Picture)
See Cheap Trick (*Reach Out*), Devo (*Working In The Coal Mine*), Don Felder (*Heavy Metal*)

HEBB, BOBBY
A SATISFIED MIND/Love, Love, Love .... (Philips 40400) | 2.00 | 8.00 | 66

TITLE	LABEL AND NUMBER	VG	NM	YR

HEFLIN, VAN
(Actor)
   See Wayne Newton (*Stagecoach To Cheyenne*)

HEFTI, NEAL
THE YEAR OF THE DUCK .... (*United Artists 972*)   1.50   6.00   66
   (From the motion picture *Lord Love A Duck*. Shown as by Neal Hefti And His Orchestra.)
BATMAN THEME .... (*RCA Victor 47-8755*)   2.50   10.00   66
   (From the television series *Batman*)

HEINDORF, RAY
TRIBUTE TO JAMES DEAN .... (*Columbia 4-40754*)   3.75   15.00   56

HELIX
HEAVY METAL LOVE .... (*Capitol B-5294*)   .75   3.00   83
ROCK YOU .... (*Capitol B-5391*)   .75   3.00   84

HELL, RICHARD, & THE VOIDOIDS
BLANK GENERATION/Love Comes In Spurts .... (*Sire 1003*)   3.75   15.00   77
ANOTHER WORLD/Blank Generation/You Gotta Lose .... (*Ork 81976*)   6.25   25.00   77
   Also see Neon Boys (Richard Hell)

HELMS, BOBBY
FRAULEIN .... (*Decca 30194*)   5.00   20.00   57
JINGLE BELL ROCK/Captain Santa Claus (And His Reindeer Space Patrol) .... (*Decca 9-30513*)   3.75   15.00   57
NEW SINGING SENSATION .... (*Decca no #*)   5.00   20.00   57
   (Generic half sleeve pictures Helms, no song titles or number indicated.)
JINGLE BELL ROCK/Jingle Bells .... (*Mistletoe 802*)   2.00   8.00   74

HELLO, DOLLY!
(Broadway Musical)
   See Louis Armstrong

HELLO–GOODBYE
(Motion Picture)
   See Genevieve Gilles

HELLO PEOPLE, THE
PAISLEY TEDDY BEAR/Stranger At Her Door .... (*Philips 40522*)   2.00   8.00   68

HELP!
(Motion Picture)
   See the Beatles (*Ticket To Ride, Help!*)

HENDRIX, JIMI
HEY JOE/51st Anniversary .... (*Reprise 0572*)   125.00   500.00   67
NO SUCH ANIMAL .... (*Audio Fidelity 167*)   6.25   25.00   70
LITTLE DRUMMER BOY/SILENT NIGHT/Auld Lang Syne .... (*Reprise PRO-595*)   37.50   150.00   74
   (Promotional issue only titled *...And A Happy New Year*)
GLORIA .... (*Reprise HS 2293*)   2.00   8.00   79
   (Included with the album *The Essential Jimi Hendrix Volume Two*, issued with a small-hole 33-1/3 RPM record.
   Two variations exist of this record, one has the same song on both sides and the other is a one-sided disc. Both
   can be found with this sleeve.)

HENDRYX, NONA
I SWEAT .... (*Arista 9370*)   1.00   4.00   84
IF LOOKS COULD KILL .... (*RCA PB-14168*)   1.00   4.00   85
WHY SHOULD I CRY?/Funkyland .... (*EMI America B-8382*)   .75   3.00   87
BABY GO-GO/Drive Me Wild .... (*EMI America B-43028*)   .75   3.00   87
   Also see the Blue Belles

HENLEY, DON
JOHNNY CAN'T READ/Long Way Home .... (*Asylum 7-69971*)   1.00   4.00   82
DIRTY LAUNDRY/Lilah .... (*Asylum 7-69894*)   1.00   4.00   82
THE BOYS OF SUMMER/A Month Of Sundays .... (*Geffen 29141-7*)   .75   3.00   84
ALL SHE WANTS TO DO IS DANCE .... (*Geffen 29065-7*)   .75   3.00   85
NOT ENOUGH LOVE IN THE WORLD/Man With A Mission .... (*Geffen 29012-7*)   .75   3.00   85
THE END OF THE INNOCENCE .... (*Geffen 22925-7*)   .75   3.00   89
THE LAST WORTHLESS EVENING .... (*Geffen 22771-7*)   .75   3.00   89
   Also see the Eagles, Stevie Nicks (*Leather And Lace*), the Textones (*Midnight Mission*), Warren Zevon (*Reconsider Me*)

HENNESSEY
(Television Series)
   See Sonny Burke and His Orchestra (*Hennessey*)

HENRY COW
   See Art Bears (Fred Frith, Chris Cutler, Dagmar Krause), Fred Frith

HEPBURN, AUDREY
   See Henry Mancini (*Moon River*), Jane Morgan (*Fascination*)

HERMAN, BONNIE
STAY WITH ME .... (*Columbia 4-43672*)   2.00   8.00   66

HERMAN, PEE-WEE
(Comic actor Paul Reubens)
SURFIN' BIRD .... (*Columbia 38-07301*)   1.50   6.00   87
   (From the motion picture *Back To The Beach*)

HERMAN, WOODY
WOODCHOPPER'S BALL/ .... (*Decca 1-727*)   2.50   10.00   53
   (Decca "Curtain Call" series of reissues)

HERMAN'S HERMITS
CAN'T YOU HEAR MY HEART BEAT/I Know Why .... (*MGM K-13310*)   3.75   15.00   65
MRS. BROWN YOU'VE GOT A LOVELY DAUGHTER/I Gotta Dream On .... (*MGM K-13341*)   3.00   12.00   65
WONDERFUL WORLD/Traveling Light .... (*MGM K-13354*)   3.00   12.00   65

TITLE	LABEL AND NUMBER	VG	NM	YR
I'M HENRY VIII I AM/The End Of The World	(MGM K-13367)	3.00	12.00	65
JUST A LITTLE BIT BETTER/Sea Cruise	(MGM K-13398)	3.00	12.00	65
DANDY/My Reservations Been Confirmed	(MGM K-13603)	3.00	12.00	66
THERE'S A KIND OF HUSH/No Milk Today	(MGM K-13681)	3.00	12.00	67
DON'T GO OUT INTO THE RAIN (YOU'RE GOING TO MELT)/Moonshine Man	(MGM K-13761)	3.75	15.00	67
MUSEUM/The Last Bus Home	(MGM K-13787)	3.75	15.00	67

HE'S MY GIRL
(Motion Picture)
    See David Hallyday *(He's My Girl)*

HESS, BERNIE

THE BALLAD OF JIMMIE RODGERS	(Showland 241973)	10.00	40.00	61

    (Shown as by Bernie Hess and Tom Swatzell)

HEWETT, HOWARD

STAY/Eye On You	(Elektra 69499)	.75	3.00	86
I'M FOR REAL/Eye On You	(Elektra 69527)	.75	3.00	86
ANOTHER CHANCE TO LOVE/Cry On Me	(Arista 9656)	.75	3.00	87

    (A-side shown as by Dionne Warwick and Howard Hewett, b-side by Warwick)
    Also see Shalamar

HEYETTES, THE

FONZIE FOR PRESIDENT	(London 237)	2.00	8.00	76

HEYWARD, NICK

YOU'RE MY WORLD	(Reprise27835-7)	1.00	4.00	88

HIATT, JOHN

SNAKE CHARMER/This Is Your Day	(Atlantic 7-89461)	1.00	4.00	85

    (From the motion picture *White Nights*. B-side shown as by Sandy Stewart and Nile Rodgers.)

THANK YOU GIRL/Lipstick Sunset	(A&M 2950)	.75	3.00	87

HICKMAN, DWAYNE
(Actor who played the role of Dobie Gillis in the television series *The Many Loves Of Dobie Gillis*)

SCHOOL DANCE/Pretty Baby-O	(ABC-Paramount 9908)	6.25	25.00	58

HICKS, DAN, AND HIS HOT LICKS
    See the Charlatans, David LaFlamme

HIDING OUT
(Motion Picture)
    See Roy Orbison *(Crying)*, Pretty Poison *(Catch Me I'm Falling)*

HIGH ANXIETY
(Motion Picture)
    See Mel Brooks

HIGHLANDER
(Motion Picture)
    See Queen *(Princes Of The Universe)*

HIGH NUMBERS, THE
    See the Who

HIGH SCHOOL CONFIDENTIAL
(Motion Picture)
    See Jerry Lee Lewis *(High School Confidential)*

HIGHWAY 101

SOMEWHERE TONIGHT	(Warner Bros. 28223-7)	.75	3.00	87
CRY, CRY, CRY	(Warner Bros. 28105-7)	.75	3.00	88
(DO YOU LOVE ME) JUST SAY YES/I'll Be Missing You	(Warner Bros. 27867-7)	.75	3.00	88

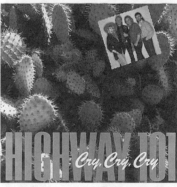

HILL, BUNKER
    See Link Wray *(Friday Night Dance Party)*

HILL, DAN

LET THE SONG LAST FOREVER	(20th Century 2392)	1.25	5.00	78

HILL STREET BLUES
(Television Series)
    See Mike Post *(The Theme From Hill Street Blues)*

HI-LOS

LIFE IS JUST A BOWL OF CHERRIES	(Columbia 4-40840)	2.00	8.00	57

HINDSIGHT

SMALL CHANGE/	(Virgin 7-99316)	.75	3.00	86
STAND UP/Stand Up (Work It Down Groove Dub)	(Virgin 7-99391)	.75	3.00	87

HINDU LOVE GODS

GONNA HAVE A GOOD TIME TONIGHT/Narrator	(I.R.S. 52867)	1.00	4.00	86

    (Issued with small-hole 45 RPM record)
    Also see the Backbeat Band (Mike Mills), R.E.M., Warren Zevon

HINES, GREGORY
THERE'S NOTHING BETTER THAN LOVE/

There's Nothing Better Than Love (Instrumental)	(Epic 34-06978)	.75	3.00	87

    (Shown as by Luther Vandross and Gregory Hines)

THERE'S NOTHING BETTER THAN LOVE	(Epic 34-06978)	1.00	4.00	86

    (Promotional issue, *Demonstration Not For Sale* printed on sleeve. Shown as by Luther Vandross and Gregory Hines.)

THAT GIRL WANTS TO DANCE WITH ME/	(Epic 34-07793)	.75	3.00	88

    Also see Michael McDonald *(Sweet Freedom)*, New Edition *(Once In A Lifetime Groove)*, Lou Reed *(My Love Is Chemical)*, Lionel Richie *(Say You, Say Me)*

HINES, HINES AND DAD

WHY MUST I FEEL THIS WAY	(Columbia 4-44052)	2.00	8.00	67

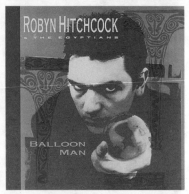

HINSCHE, BILLY
See Dino, Desi & Billy

HINTON, JOE
PRETTY LITTLE MAMA .... (Backbeat 526) | 2.00 | 8.00 | 63

HIPSWAY
THE HONEYTHIEF .... (Columbia 38-06579) | .75 | 3.00 | 86
THE HONEYTHIEF .... (Columbia 38-06579) | 1.00 | 4.00 | 86
  (Promotional issue, *Demonstration Only–Not For Sale* printed on sleeve)
ASK THE LORD .... (Columbia 38-07118) | .75 | 3.00 | 87
LONG WHITE CAR .... (Columbia 38-07330) | .75 | 3.00 | 87

HIROSHIMA
ONE WISH .... (Epic 34-05875) | .75 | 3.00 | 86
ONE WISH (SPECIAL MIX) .... (Epic 34-05875) | 1.00 | 4.00 | 86
  (Promotional issue, *Demonstration Only–Not For Sale* printed on sleeve)
GO .... (Epic 34-07428) | .75 | 3.00 | 87
HAWAIIAN ELECTRIC .... (Epic 34-07604) | .75 | 3.00 | 87

HIRT, AL
ELGIE .... (RCA Victor 47-7854) | 2.00 | 8.00 | 61
PICKIN' COTTON .... (RCA Victor 47-8128) | 2.00 | 8.00 | 63
WHITE CHRISTMAS .... (RCA Victor 47-8478) | 2.00 | 8.00 | 65
SANTA CLAUS IS COMING TO TOWN .... (RCA Victor 47-8706) | 2.00 | 8.00 | 65
MAME/Seven Days To Tahiti .... (RCA Victor 47-8774) | 2.00 | 8.00 | 66

HITCHCOCK, ROBYN
BALLOON MAN/A Globe Of Frogs (Electric) .... (A&M 3023) | 1.00 | 4.00 | 88
  (Shown as by Robyn Hitchcock & the Egyptians. B-side credit states *Featuring Peter Buck on 12 string guitar*.)
I SOMETHING YOU/ZIPPER IN MY SPINE/
Man With A Womans Shadow .... (International Pop Underground 55) | 1.00 | 4.00 | 94
  Also see Squeeze (Andy Metcalfe of the Egyptians was a member of Squeeze from 1985-90)

HODGE, CATFISH
BOOGIE MAN GONNA GET YA .... (Eastbound 607) | 1.00 | 4.00 |

HODGE, CHRIS
WE'RE ON OUR WAY .... (Apple 1850) | 2.00 | 8.00 | 72

HODGES, EDDIE
I'M GONNA KNOCK ON YOUR DOOR/Ain't Gonna Wash For A Week .... (Cadence 1397) | 5.00 | 20.00 | 61
SEEIN' IS BELIEVIN'/Secret .... (Columbia 4-42649) | 3.00 | 12.00 | 62
FLITTERIN'/Beautiful Beulah .... (Buena Vista 420) | 5.00 | 20.00 | 62
  (Shown as by Hayley Mills & Eddie Hodges, both pictured. From the motion picture *Summer Magic*.)
JUST A KID IN LOVE/Avalanche .... (MGM K-13219) | 3.00 | 12.00 | 64
EXTENDED PLAYS
SUMMER MAGIC/FLITTERIN'/BEAUTIFUL BEULAH/UGLY BUG BALL/
On The Front Porch/Pink Of Perfection/Femininity .... (Buena Vista 4023) | 3.75 | 15.00 | 63
  (Promotional issue sponsored by Alcoa Wrap. Shown as by Burl Ives, Hayley Mills, Eddie Hodges, and Deborah Walley. From the motion picture *Summer Magic*, Burl Ives and Hayley Mills pictured on front.)

HOEHN, TOMMY
BLOW YOURSELF UP/Love You (All Day Long) .... (Power Play 1954) | 1.50 | 6.00 | 77

HOENIG, MICHAEL
EXTENDED PLAYS
DEPARTURE FROM THE NORTHERN WASTELAND: EXCERPT 1/EXCERPT II/Excerpt from:
Hanging Garden Transfer/Excerpt from: Sun And Moon .... (Warner Bros. PRO-E-712) | 1.00 | 4.00 | 78
  (Promotional issue only)

HOLE
RETARD GIRL/Phonebillsong/Johnnie's In The Bathroom .. (Sympathy For The Record Industry 53) | 2.00 | 8.00 | 90
  (Originally issued with pink vinyl)
DICKNAIL/Burn Black .... (Sub Pop 93) | 2.00 | 8.00 | 91
  (Limited edition of 5,000 copies with 3,500 on grey marbled vinyl and 1,500 on black)
MISS WORLD/Over The Edge .... (Tim Kerr 947081) | 1.00 | 4.00 | 96
  (Issued with pink vinyl)
  Also see Courtney Love

HOLE IN THE HEAD, A
(Motion Picture)
  See Frank Sinatra (*High Hopes*)

HOLIDAY, BILLIE
DON'T WORRY 'BOUT ME/Just One More Chance .... (MGM K-12813) | 3.75 | 15.00 | 59
MY MAN/Them There Eyes .... (United Artists 50999) | 2.00 | 8.00 | 72
  Also see U2 (*Angel Of Harlem*)

HOLLAND, AMY
HOW DO I SURVIVE .... (Capitol 4884) | .75 | 3.00 | 80

HOLLAND, EDDIE
IF CLEOPATRA TOOK A CHANCE/What About Me .... (Motown 1030) | 12.50 | 50.00 | 62

HOLLAND, JOOLS, AND HIS MILLIONAIRES
BUMBLE BOOGIE/Like I Do To You .... (I.R.S. 9906) | 1.00 | 4.00 | 82
  Also see Squeeze

HOLLAWAY, BRENDA
WHEN I'M GONE/I've Been Good To You .... (Tamla 54111) | 2.50 | 10.00 | 64

HOLLIDAY, JENNIFER
HARD TIMES FOR LOVERS .... (Geffen 28958-7) | .75 | 3.00 | 85
NO FRILLS LOVE .... (Geffen 28845-7) | .75 | 3.00 | 86
I LOVE YOU SO MUCH JESUS/Too Close To Heaven .... (JPL 7880) | 1.25 | 5.00 |

HOLLIER, JILL
MANY TEARS AGO .... (Warner Bros. 27585-7)   .75   3.00   89

HOLLIES, THE
ON A CAROUSEL / All The World Is Love .... (Imperial 66231)   5.00   20.00   67
CARRIE ANNE .... (Epic 5-10180)   5.00   12.00   67
CARRIE ANNE / Silence Is Golden .... (Epic 5-10180/84)   12.50   50.00   67
     (Promotional issue only issued with red vinyl. Flip side shown as by the Tremeloes.)
KING MIDAS IN REVERSE .... (Epic 5-10234)   3.00   12.00   67
DEAR ELOISE .... (Epic 5-10251)   3.00   12.00   67
THE BABY / Oh Granny .... (Epic 5-10842)   7.50   30.00   72
STOP IN THE NAME OF LOVE / Musical Pictures .... (Atlantic 7-89819)   1.00   4.00   83
     Also see Crosby/Stills/Nash, Crosby/Stills/Nash/Young, Graham Nash, the Alan Parsons Project (Allan Clarke), Bruce Springsteen (*Rosalita*), Terry Sylvester

HOLLOWAY, BRENDA
WHEN I'M GONE / I've Been Good To You .... (Tamla 54111)   10.00   40.00   65

HOLLY, BUDDY
LOVE IS STRANGE / You're The One .... (Coral 62558)   7.50   30.00   69
IT DOESN'T MATTER ANYMORE .... (MCA 40905)   1.25   5.00   78
     (Shown as by Buddy Holly/The Crickets)

HOLLY, PETE, & THE LOOKS
BABY, PLEASE BELIEVE ME / What Did I Say, Look Out Below .... (Bomp 130)   1.25   5.00   81

HOLLYWOOD STARS, THE
ALL THE KIDS ON THE STREET / Sleepwalker .... (Arista SP-5)   3.75   15.00   77
     (Promotional issue only, flip side shown as by the Kinks which accounts for its value. Issued with yellow vinyl.)

HOLMAN, LIBBY
LOVE FOR SALE / Moanin' Low .... (Decca 1-715)   3.00   12.00   53
     (Decca "Curtain Call" series of reissues)

HOLMES, JAKE
YOU CAN'T GET LOVE .... (Tower 313)   1.50   6.00   67

HOLMES, RUPERT
I DON'T WANT TO HOLD YOUR HAND / Man Behind The Woman .... (Epic 8-50096)   1.25   5.00   75
TERMINAL .... (Epic 8-50161)   1.50   6.00   75
     (Promotional issue only)

HOLMES, SCOTT
(Actor)
     See the Soaps and Hearts Ensemble

HOLSAPPLE, PETER
BIG BLACK TRUCK / Death Garage / 96 Second Blowout .... (Car 5)   3.75   15.00   78
     Also see the dB's

HOMEMADE THEATRE
SANTA JAWS / Santa Jaws (Part 2) .... (A&M 407)   1.25   5.00   76

HOMER & JETHRO
(ALL I WANT FOR CHRISTMAS IS) MY UPPER PLATE /
   I Saw Mommy Smoochin' Santy Claus .... (RCA Victor 47-5456)   3.00   12.00   53
I WANT TO HOLD YOUR HAND / .... (RCA Victor 47-8345)   1.50   6.00   64
     Also see Chet Atkins (*Chet's Tune*)

HONDELLS, THE
MY BUDDY SEAT / You're Gonna Ride With Me .... (Mercury 72366)   5.00   20.00   64
SEA CRUISE / You Meet The Nicest People On A Honda .... (Mercury 72479)   5.00   20.00   65

HONEYCOMBS, THE
I CAN'T STOP / I'll Cry Tomorrow .... (Interphon 7713)   5.00   20.00   64
COLOR SLIDE / That's The Way .... (Interphon 7716)   5.00   20.00   64

HONEYDRIPPERS, THE
SEA OF LOVE / Rockin' At Midnight .... (Es Paranza 7-99701)   1.00   4.00   84
     (First printing)
SEA OF LOVE / I Get A Thrill .... (Es Paranza 7-99701)   .75   3.00   84
     (Second printing, identical art as the first printing on the front but with a different b-side listed on the back)
ROCKIN' AT MIDNIGHT / Young Boy Blues .... (Es Paranza 7-99686)   .75   3.00   84
     Also see Jeff Beck, Chic (Nile Rodgers), Led Zeppelin (Jimmy Page, Robert Plant), Jimmy Page, Robert Plant, Nile Rodgers, the Yardbirds (Jimmy Page)

HONEYMOON SUITE
NEW GIRL NOW / It's Your Heart .... (Warner Bros. 29208-7)   1.00   4.00   84
FEEL IT AGAIN / Wounded .... (Warner Bros. 28779-7)   .75   3.00   85
WHAT DOES IT TAKE .... (Warner Bros. 28670-7)   .75   3.00   85
     (From the motion picture *One Crazy Summer*)
LETHAL WEAPON .... (Warner Bros. 28379-7)   .75   3.00   87
LOVE CHANGES EVERYTHING .... (Warner Bros. 27935-7)   .75   3.00   88
COLD LOOK .... (Warner Bros. 27791-7)   .75   3.00   88

HONEYS, THE
SURFIN' DOWN THE SWANEE RIVER / Shoot The Curl .... (Capitol 4952)   250.00   1000.00   63
     Also see American Spring (Diane Rovell, Marilyn Rovell-Wilson), Rodney and the Brunettes (Diane Rovell, Marilyn Rovell-Wilson)

HOODOO GURUS, THE
LIKE WOW—WIPEOUT / Bring The Hoodoo Down .... (Big Time 1503)   1.25   5.00   85
BITTERSWEET / Bring The Hoodoo Down .... (Elektra 7-69544)   1.00   4.00   86
GOOD TIMES / Heart Of Darkness .... (Elektra 7-69481)   .75   3.00   87
     (A-side credits the Bangles' Susanna Hoffs, Debbie Peterson, Vicki Peterson, Michael Steele)
WHAT'S MY SCENE / Heart Of Darkness .... (Elektra 7-69440)   .75   3.00   87
     Rick Grossman, of the Divinyls, did not join the group until 1988

TITLE	LABEL AND NUMBER	VG	NM	YR
HOOKER, EARL				
BOOGIE DON'T BLOT	(Blue Thumb 103)	1.50	6.00	70
HOOKER, JOHN LEE				
WHISKEY AND WIMMEN / Let's Make It	(United Artists 50779)	1.50	6.00	71
(Shown as by Canned Heat and John Lee Hooker. Promotional issue only issued with blue jean patch.)				
HOOTERS				
FIGHTIN' ON THE SAME SIDE / Wireless.....................	(Eighty Percent HOO 80)	2.50	10.00	81
ALL YOU ZOMBIES (Live) / Rescue Me	(Eighty Percent HOO 82)	2.50	10.00	82
HANGING ON A HEARTBEAT / Concubine	(Antenna HOO84)	1.50	6.00	84
AND WE DANCED / Blood From A Stone	(Columbia 38-05568)	.75	3.00	85
AND WE DANCED	(Columbia 38-05568)	1.00	4.00	85
(Promotional issue, *Demonstration–Not For Sale* printed on sleeve)				
DAY BY DAY / South Ferry Road	(Columbia 38-05730)	.75	3.00	85
DAY BY DAY	(Columbia 38-05730)	1.00	4.00	85
(Promotional issue, *Demonstration–Not For Sale* printed on sleeve)				
WHERE DO THE CHILDREN GO / Nervous Night	(Columbia 38-05854)	.75	3.00	86
WHERE DO THE CHILDREN GO (SHORT VERSION)/ Where Do The Children Go (Long Version)	(Columbia 38-05854)	1.00	4.00	86
(Promotional issue, *Demonstration Not For Sale* printed on sleeve)				
JOHNNY B / Lucy In The Sky With Diamonds	(Columbia 38-07241)	.75	3.00	87
SATELLITE / One Way Home	(Columbia 38-07607)	.75	3.00	87
Also see Tommy Conwell and the Young Rumblers (Rob Miller)				
HOOTIE & THE BLOWFISH				
OLD MAN & ME (WHEN I GET TO HEAVEN) / Before The Heartache Rolls In ..	(Atlantic 7-87074)	.75	3.00	96
(Hard cover issued with a small-hole 45 RPM record)				
HOPE, BOB, AND EYDIE ADAMS				
CALL ME BWANA / The Flip Side	(United Artists 603)	6.25	25.00	63
HOPKIN, MARY				
GOODBYE / Sparrow	(Apple 1806)	2.50	10.00	69
TEMMA HARBOUR / Lont Ano Dagli Ochli	(Apple 1816)	2.50	10.00	70
THINK ABOUT YOUR CHILDREN / Heritage	(Apple 1825)	2.50	10.00	70
HOPKINS, NICKY				
Session keyboardist who recorded with the Kinks, the Rolling Stones, the Beatles, the Who, the Small Faces, the Jeff Beck Group, Quicksilver Messenger Service, Steve Miller, the Jefferson Airplane, Graham Parker, the Jerry Garcia Band, and others.				
See Night				
HORNE, LENA				
WHERE IS LOVE / Come On Strong	(RCA Victor 47-8092)	2.00	8.00	62
I WISH I'D MET YOU / When I Fall In Love	(Three Cherries 7301)	1.00	4.00	88
(A-side featuring Sammy Davis Jr., both pictured on back)				
HORNER, JAMES, & GROUP 87				
THE SEARCH FOR SPOCK (THEME FROM STAR TREK III)	(Capitol B-5365)	1.25	5.00	84
(From the motion picture *Star Trek III–The Search For Spock,* stylized Spock artwork on sleeve)				
HORNSBY, BRUCE, & THE RANGE				
MANDOLIN RAIN / The Red Plains (Live)	(RCA 5087-7-R)	.75	3.00	86
THE VALLEY ROAD / The Long Race	(RCA 7645-7-R)	.75	3.00	88
LOOK OUT ANY WINDOW / The Way It Is................	(RCA 8678-7-R)	.75	3.00	88
Also see Stevie Nicks (*Two Kinds Of Love*)				
HORTON, JOHNNY				
PLAID AND CALICO / Shadows On The Old Bayou	(Dot 15966)	3.00	12.00	59
WHEN IT'S SPRINGTIME IN ALASKA	(Columbia 4-41308)	5.00	20.00	59
(Black and white promotional issue only)				
THE BATTLE OF NEW ORLEANS	(Columbia 4-41339)	3.75	15.00	59
SINK THE BISMARK / The Same Old Tale The Crow Told Me	(Columbia 4-41568)	3.75	15.00	60
JOHNNY FREEDOM / Comanche	(Columbia 4-41685)	3.75	15.00	60
NORTH TO ALASKA / The Mansion You Stole	(Columbia 4-41782)	3.75	15.00	60
(A-side from the motion picture *North To Alaska*)				
SLEEPY-EYED JOHN / They'll Never Take Her Love From Me	(Columbia 4-41963)	3.00	12.00	61
OLE SLEWFOOT / Miss Marcy	(Columbia 4-42063)	3.00	12.00	61
HONKY TONK MAN / Words	(Columbia 4-42302)	3.00	12.00	62
ALL GROWN UP / I'm A One-Woman Man	(Columbia 4-42653)	3.00	12.00	62
WHEN IT'S SPRINGTIME IN ALASKA / Sugar Coated Baby	(Columbia 4-42774)	3.00	12.00	63
HOORAY FOR THAT LITTLE DIFFERENCE / Tell My Baby I Love Her	(Columbia 4-42993)	3.00	12.00	64
HOTHOUSE FLOWERS				
DON'T GO / Saved	(London 886 279-7)	.75	3.00	88
I'M SORRY / Mountains	(London 886 317-7)	.75	3.00	88
HOT TUNA				
BEEN SO LONG / Candy Man	(RCA 74-0528)	2.00	8.00	71
KEEP ON TRUCKIN' / Water Song	(Grunt 65-0502)	2.00	8.00	72
Also see Jefferson Airplane, KBC Band (Jack Casady), SVT (Jack Casady)				
HOUNDS				
EXTENDED PLAYS				
DOO WAH DIDDY DIDDY	(Columbia AE7-1187)	1.00	4.00	79
(Promotional issue only titled *The Now Wave Sampler,* issued with small-hole 33-1/3 RPM record. Also includes one song each by the Beat, Jules and the Polar Bears, and the Sinceros.)				
HOURGLASS				
NOTHING BUT TEARS / Heartbeat	(Liberty 56002)	10.00	40.00	68
Also see the Allman Brothers Band				
HOUSE IS NOT A HOME, A				
(Motion Picture)				
See Brook Benton (*A House Is Not A Home*)				

HOUSEMARTINS, THE
HAPPY HOUR/The Mighty Ship .... (Elektra/Go! Discs 7-69515) .75 3.00 86
FLAG DAY/The Mighty Ship .... (Elektra/Go! Discs 7-69491) .75 3.00 86
CARAVAN OF LOVE/When I First Met Jesus .... (Elektra/Go! Discs 7-69436) .75 3.00 87

HOUSE OF FREAKS
BOTTOM OF THE OCEAN/I'll Treat You Right .... (Rhino 74409) .75 3.00 87

HOUSE OF LARGE SIZES
NORTH CEDAR/The Blow-Bye .... (Columbia CS7-77255) .75 3.00 93

HOUSE OF LORDS
I WANNA BE LOVED/Call My Name .... (RCA/Simmons 8805-7-R) .75 3.00 88
   Also see Giuffria (Lanny Cordola, Gregg Giuffria, Chuck Wright)

HOUSE OF PAIN
SHAMROCKS AND SHENANIGANS (IN THE DIRT MIX)/
  Shamrocks And Shenanigans (Buds & Brew Mix) .... (Sub Pop 188) 1.25 5.00 92
  (Issued with green vinyl)

HOUSE OF SCHOCK
MIDDLE OF NOWHERE .... (Capitol B-44135) .75 3.00 88
   Also see the Go-Go's (Gina Schock)

HOUSTON, DAVID
SAMMY .... (Epic 5-9884) 2.00 8.00 66
WHERE COULD I GO BUT TO HER .... (Epic 5-10102) 2.00 8.00 67
WITH ONE EXCEPTION .... (Epic 5-10154) 2.00 8.00 67
YOU MEAN THE WORLD TO ME .... (Epic 5-10224) 2.00 8.00 67
HAVE A LITTLE FAITH .... (Epic 5-10291) 2.00 8.00 68
ALREADY IT'S HEAVEN .... (Epic 5-10338) 2.00 8.00 68
MY WOMAN'S GOOD TO ME/Come On Home And Sing The Blues To Daddy (Epic JZSP 138795) 2.50 10.00 69
  (Promotional issue only programming re-service single. Flip side shown as by Bob Luman with a different
  catalog number on the record.)

HOUSTON, PENELOPE
GLAD I'M A GIRL/Sweetheart .... (Iloki 104) .75 3.00 92

HOUSTON, THELMA
EVERYBODY GETS TO GO TO THE MOON .... (ABC/Dunhill SPD-11) 3.75 15.00 69
  (Apollo 11 promotional issue)
THE BINGO LONG SONG .... (Motown 1385F) 1.25 5.00 76
  (From the motion picture The Bingo Long Traveling All-Stars & Motor Kings, caricatures of the cast pictured)
LEAN ON ME .... (Warner Bros. 27533-7) .75 3.00 89
  (Shown as by Thelma Houston and the Winans)

HOUSTON, WHITNEY
YOU GIVE GOOD LOVE/Greatest Love Of All .... (Arista 9274) .75 3.00 85
SAVING ALL MY LOVE FOR YOU/All At Once .... (Arista 9381) .75 3.00 86
THINKING ABOUT YOU/Someone For Me .... (Arista 9412) .75 3.00 85
HOW WILL I KNOW/Someone For Me .... (Arista 9434) .75 3.00 85
GREATEST LOVE OF ALL/Thinking About You .... (Arista 9466) .75 3.00 86
I WANNA DANCE WITH SOMEBODY/Moment Of Truth .... (Arista 9598) .75 3.00 87
DIDN'T WE ALMOST HAVE IT ALL/Shock Me .... (Arista 9616) .75 3.00 87
  (B-side shown as by Whitney Houston & Jermaine Jackson)
SO EMOTIONAL/For The Love Of You .... (Arista 9642) .75 3.00 87
WHERE DO BROKEN HEARTS GO/Where You Are .... (Arista 9674) .75 3.00 88
LOVE WILL SAVE THE DAY/How Will I Know (Edited Remix) .... (Arista 9720) .75 3.00 88
ONE MOMENT IN TIME/Love Is A Contact Sport .... (Arista 9743) .75 3.00 88
   Also see Aretha Franklin (It Isn't, It Wasn't, It Ain't Never Gonna Be), Teddy Pendergrass (Hold Me)

HOWARD, DANNY
TWO LONELY WEEKS/Dating An Angel .... (Birthstone 1035) 2.00 8.00 60s

HOWARD, GEORGE
LOVE WILL CONQUER ALL .... (MCA 53280) .75 3.00 88
   Also see Patti LaBelle (Kiss Away The Pain)

HOWARD, MIKI
COME SHARE MY LOVE/I Surrender .... (Atlantic 7-89351) .75 3.00 86
CRAZY/In Too Deep .... (Atlantic 7-89068) .75 3.00 87

HOWARD, RANDY
ALL AMERICAN REDNECK .... (Viva 7-29781) 1.00 4.00 83

HOWARD THE DUCK
(Motion Picture)
   See Dolby's Cube Featuring Cherry Bomb

HOWELL, C. THOMAS
(Actor)
   See Van Stephenson (No Secrets)

HOWELL, REUBEN
WHEN YOU TAKE ANOTHER CHANCE ON LOVE/
  You Can't Stop A Man In Love .... (Motown 1274) 1.25 5.00 73

HOW THE WEST WAS WON
(Motion Picture)
   See Debbie Reynolds (Home In The Meadow)

H. P. LOVECRAFT
WAYFARING STRANGER/The Time Machine .... (Philips 40491) 3.75 15.00 67

HUB KAPP AND THE WHEELS
LET'S REALLY HEAR IT/Work, Work .... (Take Five 631) 5.00 20.00 63
SIGH, CRY, ALMOST DIE/Bony Marony .... (Capitol 5215) 5.00 20.00 64

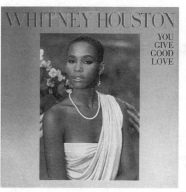

TITLE	LABEL AND NUMBER	VG	NM	YR

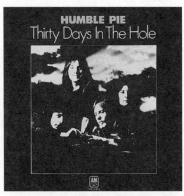

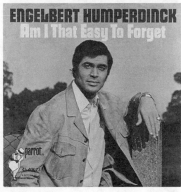

HUDSON, LAVINE
INTERVENTION/It's Me .... (Virgin 7-99318) .75 3.00 88

HUDSON, ROCK
(Actor)
PILLOW TALK .... (Decca 9-30966) 2.50 10.00 59
    (From the motion picture *Pillow Talk*. Originally issued with a 4" x 5" black and white photograph of Hudson.)
    Also see Doris Day (*Pillow Talk*)

HUDSON BROTHERS, THE
LONELY SCHOOL YEAR .... (MCA/Rocket 40464) 1.25 5.00 75

HUE AND CRY
LABOUR OF LOVE .... (Virgin 7-99311) .75 3.00 88

HUGH, GRAYSON
TALK IT OVER/Empty As The Wind .... (RCA 8802-7-R) .75 3.00 88
BRING IT ALL BACK/Who Are You And How Are You? (Live) .... (RCA 9093-7-R) .75 3.00 89

HUGO & LUIGI
CHA HUA HUA .... (Roulette 4074) 2.00 8.00 58
THEME FROM THE RULING CLASS .... (Avco 4605) 1.50 6.00 72
    (From the motion picture *Ruling Class*)

HULL, GENE
PICO PEAK A BOO (PART 1)/Pico Peak A Boo (Part 2) .... (Columbia 4-44132) 1.50 6.00 67
    (Promotional issue only)

HULLABALOOS, THE
I'M GONNA LOVE YOU TOO/Party Doll .... (Roulette 4587) 5.00 20.00 64
DID YOU EVER/Beware .... (Roulette 4593) 5.00 20.00 65
LEARNING THE GAME/Don't Stop .... (Roulette 4612) 5.00 20.00 65
I WON'T TURN AWAY NOW/My Heart Keeps Telling Me .... (Roulette 4662) 5.00 20.00 65

HUMAN BEINZ, THE
TURN ON YOUR LOVE LIGHT/It's Fun To Be Clean .... (Capitol 2119) 5.00 20.00 68

HUMAN LEAGUE, THE
DON'T YOU WANT ME/Seconds .... (A&M/Virgin 2397) 1.00 4.00 82
LOVE ACTION (I BELIEVE IN LOVE)/Hard Times .... (A&M/Virgin 2425) .75 3.00 82
(KEEP FEELING) FASCINATION/Total Panic .... (A&M/Virgin 2547) .75 3.00 83
MIRROR MAN/Non-Stop .... (A&M/Virgin 2587) .75 3.00 83
THE LEBANON/Thirteen .... (A&M/Virgin 2641) .75 3.00 84
HUMAN/Human (Instrumental) .... (A&M/Virgin 2861) .75 3.00 86
I NEED YOUR LOVING/Are You Ever Coming Back? .... (A&M/Virgin 2893) .75 3.00 86
    Also see Heaven 17 (Martyn Ware), Philip Oakey

HUMANS, THE
I LIVE IN THE CITY/EARTHLING/Electric Bodies/Play .... (Beat HIT 1234) 1.50 6.00 79
I LIVE IN THE CITY/PLAY/Tracy Pipeline .... (I.R.S. 7700) 1.50 6.00 80
    (Gatefold sleeve with 12-page booklet)
I LIVE IN THE CITY/Wild Thing .... (I.R.S. 9009) 1.25 5.00 80

HUMBLE PIE
I DON'T NEED NO DOCTOR/A Song For Jenny .... (A&M 1282) 1.50 6.00 71
HOT 'N' NASTY/You're So Good For Me .... (A&M 1349) 2.00 8.00 72
THIRTY DAYS IN THE HOLE/Sweet Peace And Time .... (A&M 1366) 2.00 8.00 72
BLACK COFFEE/Say No More .... (A&M 1406) 2.00 8.00 73
    Also see Peter Frampton, the Small Faces (Steve Marriott)

HUMPERDINCK, ENGELBERT
THE LAST WALTZ .... (Parrot 45-40019) 1.50 6.00 67
AM I THAT EASY TO FORGET .... (Parrot 45-40023) 1.50 6.00 67
LES BICYCLETTES DE BELSIZE .... (Parrot 45-40032) 1.25 5.00 68
THE WAY IT USED TO BE .... (Parrot 45-40036) 1.25 5.00 69
WINTER WORLD OF LOVE .... (Parrot 45-40044) 1.25 5.00 69
MY MARIE .... (Parrot 45-40049) 1.25 5.00 70
SWEETHEART .... (Parrot 45-40054) 1.25 5.00 70
WHEN THERE'S NO YOU .... (Parrot 45-40059) 1.25 5.00 71
CHRISTMAS SONG/Silent Night .... (Epic AE7-1170) 1.25 5.00 78
    (Promotional issue only)

HUNTER, JOHN
VALENTINE/Take Your Chances .... (Private I ZS4-04878) .75 3.00 84
VALENTINE .... (Private I ZS4-04878) 1.00 4.00 84
    (Promotional issue, *Demonstration Only–Not For Sale* printed on sleeve)

HUNTER, TAB
JEALOUS HEART/Lonesome Road .... (Warner Bros. 5008) 5.00 20.00 58
I'LL BE WITH YOU IN APPLE BLOSSOM TIME/My Only Love .... (Warner Bros. 5032) 5.00 20.00 59
THERE'S NO FOOL LIKE A YOUNG FOOL/I'll Never Smile Again ..... (Warner Bros. 5051) 5.00 20.00 59
WAITIN' FOR FALL/Our Love .... (Warner Bros. 5093) 5.00 20.00 60
AGAIN/Love Is Just Around The Corner .... (Warner Bros. 5160) 5.00 20.00 61

HUNTSBERRY, HOWARD
LONELY TEARDROPS .... (Slash 28166-7) .75 3.00 87
    (From the motion picture *La Bamba*)
SLEEPLESS WEEKEND .... (MCA 53305) .75 3.00 88

HÜSKER DÜ
STATUES/Amusement .... (Reflex 38285) 5.00 20.00 80
IN A FREE LAND/What Do I Want/M.I.C. .... (New Alliance 010) 3.75 15.00 82
EIGHT MILES HIGH/Masochism World .... (SST 025) 1.00 4.00 84
CELEBRATED SUMMER/New Day Rising .... (SST 031) 2.00 8.00 84
    (Rubber stamped sleeve with sticker and press release insert)
MAKES NO SENSE AT ALL/Love Is All Around ..... (SST 051) 1.00 4.00 85

HUSKEY, JUNIOR
See Nitty Gritty Dirt Band (Honky Tonkin')

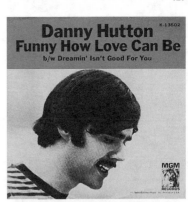

HUSKY, FERLIN
THE WALTZ YOU SAVED FOR ME/Out Of A Clear Blue Sky .... (Capitol 4650)	2.00	8.00	62
DON'T HURT ME ANYMORE/Just For You .... (Capitol 2048)	2.00	8.00	68
YOU SHOULD LIVE MY LIFE/I Promised You The World .... (Capitol 2154)	2.00	8.00	68

HUSSEY, OLIVIA
(Actress)
See Nino Rota (What Is Youth)

HUTCH, WILLIE
SLICK .... (Motown 1252)   1.50   6.00   73
(From the motion picture The Mack)

HUTTON, DANNY
ROSES & RAINBOWS/Monster Shindig .... (HBR 447)   5.00   20.00   65
FUNNY HOW LOVE CAN BE/Dreamin' Isn't Good For You .... (MGM K-13502)   3.75   15.00   66
     Also see Three Dog Night

HYDE, PAUL, AND THE PAYOLAS
CHINA BOYS/TNT/Rose/Juke Box .... (I.R.S. 7701)   1.00   4.00   80
     (Hard cover gatefold titled Introducing Payolas, issued with a small-hole 33-1/3 RPM record. Shown as by Payolas.)
YOU'RE THE ONLY LOVE/Eyes Of A Stranger .... (A&M 2733)   .75   3.00   85
IT MUST BE LOVE/Little Boys .... (A&M 2761)   .75   3.00   85
     Also see Rock and Hyde (Bob Rock, Paul Hyde)

HYLAND, BRIAN
ITSY BITSY TEENIE WEENIE YELLOW POLKADOT BIKINI .... (Kapp 342-x)	5.00	20.00	60
FOUR LITTLE HEELS/That's How Much .... (Kapp 352)	5.00	20.00	60
(Color version)			
FOUR LITTLE HEELS/That's How Much .... (Kapp 352)	7.50	30.00	60
(Black and white promotional issue)			
I GOTTA GO/Lop-Sided Over-Loaded .... (Kapp 363)	6.25	25.00	60
I'LL NEVER STOP WANTING YOU/The Night I Cried .... (ABC-Paramount 10262)	3.75	15.00	61
GINNY COME LATELY/I Should Be Getting Better .... (ABC-Paramount 10294)	3.75	15.00	62
SEALED WITH A KISS/Summer Job .... (ABC-Paramount 10336)	3.75	15.00	62
WARMED OVER KISSES (LEFT OVER LOVE)/Walk A Lonely Mile .... (ABC-Paramount 10359)	3.75	15.00	62
I MAY NOT LIVE TO SEE TOMORROW/It Ain't That Way .... (ABC-Paramount 10374)	3.75	15.00	62
IF MARY'S THERE/Remember Me .... (ABC-Paramount 10400)	3.75	15.00	63
HERE'S TO OUR LOVE/Two Kinds Of Girls .... (Philips 40179)	2.50	10.00	63
DEVOTED TO YOU/Pledging My Love .... (Philips 40203)	2.50	10.00	63
HE DON'T UNDERSTAND YOU/Love Will Find A Way .... (Philips 40203)	2.50	10.00	64
HUNG UP IN YOUR EYES/Why Mine? .... (Philips 40424)	2.50	10.00	66

HYMAN, DICK
MORITAT (A THEME FROM "THE THREE PENNY OPERA") .... (MGM 12149)   3.75   15.00   56
     (Song title popularly known as Mack The Knife)

HYMAN, PHYLLIS
LIVING ALL ALONE/What You Won't Do For Love .... (Philadelphia International B 50059)   .75   3.00   86

I

IAM SIAM
TALK TO ME (I CAN HEAR YOU NOW) .... (Columbia 38-04580)	.75	3.00	84
TALK TO ME (I CAN HEAR YOU NOW) .... (Columbia 38-04580)	1.00	4.00	84
(Promotional issue, Demonstration–Not For Sale printed on sleeve)			
SHE WENT POP .... (Columbia 38-04763)	.75	3.00	85
SHE WENT POP .... (Columbia 38-04763)	1.00	4.00	85
(Promotional issue, Demonstration Not For Sale printed on sleeve)			

IAN, JANIS
AT SEVENTEEN/Stars .... (Columbia 3-10154)   2.00   8.00   75

IAN & THE ZODIACS
SO MUCH IN LOVE WITH YOU/This Empty Place .... (Philips 40291)   5.00   20.00   65

ICEHOUSE
WE CAN GET TOGETHER/Not My Kind .... (Chrysalis 2530)	1.00	4.00	81
NO PROMISES/Into The Wild .... (Chrysalis VS4-42978)	.75	3.00	86
CRAZY/No Promises (Live) .... (Chrysalis VS4 43156)	.75	3.00	87
ELECTRIC BLUE/Over My Head .... (Chrysalis VS4 43201)	.75	3.00	87
MY OBSESSION/Your Confession .... (Chrysalis VS4 43240)	.75	3.00	87

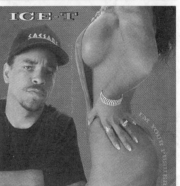

ICE-T
COLORS .... (Warner Bros./Sire 27902-7)   1.00   4.00   88
     (From the motion picture Colors)
I'M YOUR PUSHER .... (Sire 27768-7)   1.00   4.00   88

IDOL, BILLY
HOT IN THE CITY/Hole In The Wall .... (Chrysalis 2605)	1.00	4.00	82
DANCING WITH MYSELF/Love Calling (Rub A Dub Dub Mix) .... (Chrysalis VS4 42723)	1.00	4.00	83
REBEL YELL/Crank Call .... (Chrysalis VS4-42762)	1.00	4.00	83
EYES WITHOUT A FACE/Blue Highway .... (Chrysalis VS4-42786)	.75	3.00	84
FLESH FOR FANTASY/The Dead Next Door .... (Chrysalis VS4-42809)	.75	3.00	84
TO BE A LOVER/All Summer Single .... (Chrysalis VS4 43024)	.75	3.00	86
DON'T NEED A GUN/Fatal Charm .... (Chrysalis VS4 43087)	.75	3.00	86
SWEET SIXTEEN/Beyond Belief .... (Chrysalis VS4 43114)	.75	3.00	86
MONY MONY (LIVE)/Shakin' All Over (Live) .... (Chrysalis VS4 43161)	.75	3.00	87

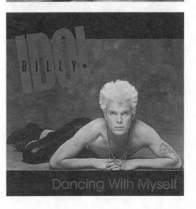

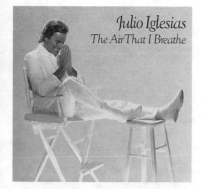

Julio Iglesias
The Air That I Breathe

The Illinois Speed Press

i love you

she's the one/i.n.s.e.t.   hang straight up

India
DANCING ON THE F R E

INDUSTRY
WHAT HAVE I GOT TO LOSE
STATE OF THE NATION

TITLE	LABEL AND NUMBER	VG	NM	YR
HOT IN THE CITY / Catch My Fall	(Chrysalis VS4 43203)	.75	3.00	87
CRADLE OF LOVE / 311 Man	(Chrysalis B-23509)	.75	3.00	90
(From the motion picture *Ford Fairlane*)				

IF A MAN ANSWERS
(Motion Picture)
See Bobby Darin (*If A Man Answers*)

IGGY AND THE STOOGES

I'M SICK OF YOU / Tight Pants / Scene Of The Crime	(Bomp 113)	2.00	8.00	77
JESUS LOVES THE STOOGES / Consolation Prizes / Johanna	(Bomp 114)	2.00	8.00	77
I GOT A RIGHT / Gimme Some Skin	(Siamese 001)	1.50	6.00	77
I GOT A RIGHT / Gimme Some Skin	(Bomp 139)	.75	3.00	91
Also see Iggy Pop				

IGLESIAS, JULIO

AMOR / Nostalgie (Nostalgia) (French)	(Columbia 38 03805)	1.25	5.00	84
THE AIR THAT I BREATHE	(Columbia 38-04726)	1.00	4.00	84
(Vocals credited to the Beach Boys and Julio Iglesias)				
THE AIR THAT I BREATHE	(Columbia 38-04726)	1.25	5.00	84
(Promotional issue, *Demonstration Only–Not For Sale* printed on sleeve. Vocals credited to the Beach Boys and Julio Iglesias.)				
AS TIME GOES BY	(Columbia 38-04495)	3.75	15.00	84
(Shown as by Julio Iglesias & Willie Nelson)				
TO ALL THE GIRLS I'VE LOVED BEFORE	(Columbia 38-04217)	1.00	4.00	84
(Shown as by Julio Iglesias & Willie Nelson in upper and lower case letters, both pictured)				
TO ALL THE GIRLS I'VE LOVED BEFORE	(Columbia 38-04217)	.75	3.00	84
(Shown as by Julio Iglesias & Willie Nelson in all upper case letters, both pictured)				
TO ALL THE GIRLS I'VE LOVED BEFORE	(Columbia 38-04217)	1.00	4.00	84
(Promotional issue, *Demonstration Only–Not For Sale* printed on sleeve. Shown as by Julio Iglesias & Willie Nelson.)				
ALL OF YOU / The Last Time	(Columbia 38-04507)	.75	3.00	84
(A-side shown as by Julio Iglesias and Diana Ross)				
ALL OF YOU / The Last Time	(Columbia 38-04507)	1.00	4.00	84
(Promotional issue, *Demonstration Only–Not For Sale* printed on sleeve. A-side shown as by Julio Iglesias and Diana Ross.)				
MOONLIGHT LADY / If (E Poi)	(Columbia 38-04645)	.75	3.00	84
MOONLIGHT LADY / If (E Poi)	(Columbia 38-04645)	1.00	4.00	84
(Promotional issue, *Demonstration Only–Not For Sale* printed on sleeve)				
NI TE TENGO, NI TE OLVIDO / Todo Y Nada	(Columbia 38-05671)	.75	3.00	85
NI TE TENGO, NI TE OLVIDO	(Columbia 38-05671)	1.00	4.00	85
(Promotional issue, *Demonstration Only–Not For Sale* printed on sleeve)				
AMERICA / Too Many Women	(Columbia 38-06173)	.75	3.00	86
AMERICA	(Columbia 38-06173)	1.00	4.00	86
(Promotional issue, *Demonstration Only–Not For Sale* printed on sleeve)				
MY LOVE / Words And Music	(Columbia 38-07781)	.75	3.00	88
(A-side shown as by Julio Iglesias Featuring Stevie Wonder. Record shows b-side title as *My Love* by Julio Iglesias.)				
AE AO	(Columbia 38-08011)	.75	3.00	88

I HAD A BALL
(Broadway Musical)
See Louis Armstrong (*Faith*)

ILLINOIS SPEED PRESS, THE

GET IN THE WIND	(Columbia 4-44564)	3.00	12.00	68
Also see Poco (Paul Cotton)				

I LOVE YOU

SHE'S THE ONE / I.N.S.E.T. / Hang Straight Up	(Geffen PRO-S-4221)	1.00	4.00	91
(Promotional issue only issued with small-hole 33-1/3 RPM purple vinyl. Sleeves are autographed by various combinations of band members.)				

IMAGINE: JOHN LENNON
(Motion Picture)
See John Lennon (*Jealous Guy*)

I'M GONNA GIT YOU SUCKA
(Motion Picture)
See the Gap Band (*I'm Gonna Git You Sucka*)

IMPALAS, THE

MY HERO	(U.G.H.A. 17)	1.25	5.00	82

IMPRESSIONS, THE

FOOL FOR YOU	(Curtom 1932)	3.00	12.00	68
Also see Curtis Mayfield. Jerry Butler left the group for solo career in 1958.				

INDEPENDENT PROJECT PRESS
A printing company that has specialized in limited edition letterpress picture sleeves.
See the Buck Pets, Buffalo Tom, Scritti Politti

INDIA

DANCING ON THE FIRE / Bailando En El Fuego (Spanish Mix)	(Warner Bros. 27925-7)	.75	3.00	88

INDIANA JONES AND THE LAST CRUSADE
(Motion Picture)
See John Williams (*Raiders March*)

INDUSTRY

WHAT HAVE I GOT TO LOSE / State Of The Nation	(Capitol B-5341)	.75	3.00	84

INFORMATION SOCIETY

WHAT'S ON YOUR MIND (CLUB RADIO EDIT) / What's On Your Mind (Pure Energy Edit)	(Tommy Boy/Reprise 27826-7)	.75	300	88
WALKING AWAY / Make It Funkier	(Tommy Boy/Reprise 27736-7)	.75	300	88

INGRAM, JAMES

THERE'S NO EASY WAY / Come A Da Machine (To Take My Place) .... (Qwest 29316-7)	.75	3.00	83
ALWAYS .... (Qwest 28669-7)	.75	3.00	86
SOMEWHERE OUT THERE .... (MCA 52973A)	1.00	4.00	86

(Shown as by Linda Ronstadt and James Ingram. From the motion picture *An American Tail*.)

BETTER WAY .... (MCA 53125)	.75	3.00	87
IT'S REAL / Aren't You Tired .... (Warner Bros. 22975-7)	.75	3.00	89
THE SECRET GARDEN .... (Qwest 19992)	.75	3.00	90

(Shown as by Quincy Jones, Al B. Sure, James Ingram, El DeBarge, and Barry White)
Also see Kenny Rogers (*What About Me?*), Boz Scaggs (*Heart Of Mine*), U.S.A. For Africa, Voices Of America

INK SPOTS

IF I DIDN'T CARE / Do I Worry? .... (Decca 1-706)	2.50	10.00	51

(Decca "Curtain Call" series of reissues)

INNER CITY

GOOD LIFE (RADIO MIX) / Good Life (Magic Juan 7") .... (Virgin 99236-7)	.75	300	89

INNERSPACE

(Motion Picture)
See Rod Stewart (*Twistin' The Night Away*)

INNOCENT, THE

LIVIN' IN THE STREET .... (Red Label B-71002)	1.25	5.00	85

Also see Cellarful Of Noise (Kevin Valentine), Nine Inch Nails (Trent Reznor)

INN OF THE SIXTH HAPPINESS

(Motion Picture)
See Mitch Miller (*The Children's Marching Song*)

IN SEARCH OF THE CASTAWAYS

(Motion Picture)
See Hayley Mills (*Castaway*)

INSIDERS, THE

GHOST ON THE BEACH .... (Epic 34-07352)	.75	3.00	87

INSPECTOR CLOUSEAU

THANK HEAVEN FOR LITTLE GIRLS / Singin' In The Rain .... (United Artists X1221-Y)	1.50	6.00	78

(A-side from the motion picture *Revenge Of The Pink Panther*. Peter Sellers pictured in character as Inspector Clouseau spoofing the artist Henri de Toulouse-Lautrec. B-side shown as by Inspector Clouseau With The Sureté Brass Band.)

INSPIRATIONS, THE

THE GENIE / The Feeling Of Her Kiss .... (Sultan 1)	12.50	50.00	59

INTERNATIONAL SUBMARINE BAND, THE

THE RUSSIANS ARE COMING / Truck Driving Man .... (Ascot 2218)	10.00	40.00	66

Also see Gram Parsons and the Fallen Angels (Gram Parsons)

IN THE COOL OF THE DAY

(Motion Picture)
See Nat King Cole (*Those Lazy–Hazy–Crazy Days Of Summer*)

INTIMATE STRANGERS

LET GO / My Brilliant Career (Instrumental Mix) .... (I.R.S. 52921)	.75	3.00	86

(From the motion picture *My Demon Lover*, Scott Valentine and Michelle Little pictured)

INTRUDERS, THE

DEVIL WITH AN ANGEL'S SMILE / A Book For The Broken Hearted .... (Gamble 203)	2.50	10.00	67

IN TUA NUA

ALL I WANTED / Meeting Of The Waters .... (Virgin 7-99278)	.75	3.00	88

IN VITRO

I CHOOSE YOU / Lightning In The Dark .... (EMI Manhattan B 50100)	.75	3.00	87

INXS

THE ONE THING / Phantim Of The Opera .... (Atco 7-99905)	1.00	4.00	82

(Spelling is correct as shown for b-side)

TO LOOK AT YOU / The Sax Thing (Instrumental) .... (Atco 7-99833)	2.50	10.00	82

(It has been reported that this is an unusually rare sleeve for INXS. Prices have ranged from $4 to $30 accompanied by the 45, so the actual rarity is yet to be determined. This price averages these sales.)

ORIGINAL SIN (DREAM ON) / Stay Young .... (Atco 7-99766)	1.00	4.00	84
I SEND A MESSAGE / Mechanical .... (Atco 7-99731)	1.00	4.00	84
BURN FOR YOU (REMIXED VERSION) / Johnson's Aeroplane .... (Atco 7-99703)	1.00	4.00	84
DON'T CHANGE / Long In Tooth .... (Atco 7-99874)	1.00	4.00	83
THIS TIME / I'm Over You .... (Atlantic 7-89497)	1.00	4.00	85
WHAT YOU NEED / Sweet As Sin .... (Atlantic 7-89460)	1.00	4.00	85
LISTEN LIKE THIEVES / Begotten .... (Atlantic 7-89429)	.75	3.00	86
KISS THE DIRT (FALLING DOWN THE MOUNTAIN) / Six Knots / The One Thing .... (Atlantic 7-89418)	.75	3.00	86
GOOD TIMES / Laying Down The Law .... (Atlantic 7-89237)	.75	3.00	86

(Shown as by INXS and Jimmy Barnes. From the motion picture *The Lost Boys*.)

NEED YOU TONIGHT / I'm Coming Home (Live) .... (Atlantic 7-89188)	.75	3.00	87
DEVIL INSIDE / On The Rocks .... (Atlantic 7-89144)	.75	3.00	87
NEW SENSATION / Guns In The Sky (Kookaburra Mix) .... (Atlantic 7-89080)	.75	3.00	88
NEVER TEAR US APART / Different World (7" Mix) .... (Atlantic 7-89038)	.75	3.00	88
DISAPPEAR / Middle Beast .... (Atlantic 7-87784)	.75	3.00	90

IRIS, DONNIE

TOUGH WORLD .... (MCA 52127)	.75	3.00	82
DO YOU COMPUTE? .... (MCA 52230)	.75	3.00	83
INJURED IN THE GAME OF LOVE .... (HME WS4-04734)	.75	3.00	85

EXTENDED PLAYS

THE LAST TO KNOW .... (MCA S-33-1754)	1.00	4.00	81

(Promotional issue only titled *McDonald's Menu Music Chant*, issued with a small-hole 33-1/3 RPM record. Also includes one song each, the titles are not listed on sleeve, by Terri Gibbs, One Way, and Rufus.)

TITLE	LABEL AND NUMBER	VG	NM	YR

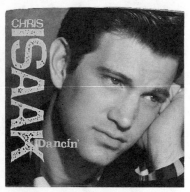

IRISH ROVERS, THE
RHYMES AND REASONS .... (Decca 732616) | | 2.00 | 8.00 | 70

IRON EAGLE
(Motion Picture)
    See Adrenalin *(Road Of The Gypsy)*, Queen *(One Vision)*

IRON MAIDEN
FLIGHT OF ICARUS/I've Got The Fire .... (Capitol B-5248) | | 1.50 | 6.00 | 83
CAN I PLAY WITH MADNESS/Black Bart Blues .... (Capitol B-44154) | | 1.00 | 4.00 | 88
    Also see Hear 'N Aid

IRONS, JEREMY
(Actor)
    See Ennio Morricone *(Theme From The Mission)*

ISAAK, CHRIS
DANCIN'/Unhappiness .... (Warner Bros. 29073-7) | | 1.50 | 6.00 | 85
GONE RIDIN' .... (Warner Bros. 28907-7) | | 1.50 | 6.00 | 85
LIVIN' FOR YOUR LOVER/Talk To Me .... (Warner Bros. 28971-7) | | 1.50 | 6.00 | 85
BLUE HOTEL .... (Warner Bros. 28374-7) | | 1.25 | 5.00 | 87

ISH
FASTER THAN A SPEEDING BULLET/Don't Stop .... (Clouds 13) | | 1.00 | 4.00 | 79
YOU'RE MY ONLY LOVER/It Ain't Necessarily So .... (Geffen 28760-7) | | .75 | 3.00 | 86

ISLE OF MAN
AM I FORGIVEN/Afraid Of Heights .... (Pasha ZS4-05900) | | .75 | 3.00 | 86
DESPERATE SURRENDER (AMOR MORIENDO)/Only The Brave ..... (Pasha ZS4-06323) | | .75 | 3.00 | 86

ISLEY BROTHERS, THE
SMOOTH SAILIN' TONIGHT .... (Warner Bros. 28385-7) | | .75 | 3.00 | 87
I WISH .... (Warner Bros. 28129-7) | | .75 | 3.00 | 88
IT TAKES A GOOD WOMAN .... (Warner Bros. 27954-7) | | .75 | 3.00 | 88
SPEND THE NIGHT .... (Warner Bros. 22900-7) | | .75 | 3.00 | 89

ITALIAN ASPHALT & PAVEMENT COMPANY, THE (I.A.P. CO.)
THE SKY'S THE LIMIT/Check Yourself .... (Colossus 110) | | 1.50 | 6.00 | 70
    Also see the Duprees

IT BITES
WHOLE NEW WORLD .... (Geffen/Virgin 28618-7) | | .75 | 3.00 | 86

IT HAPPENED AT THE WORLD'S FAIR
(Motion Picture)
    See Elvis Presley *(One Broken Heart For Sale,* b-side of *If Every Day Was Like Christmas)*

IVES, BURL
ON THE FRONT PORCH/Ugly Bug Ball .... (Buena Vista 419) | | 2.50 | 10.00 | 63
EXTENDED PLAYS
SUMMER MAGIC/FLITTERIN'/BEAUTIFUL BEULAH/UGLY BUG BALL/
  On The Front Porch/Pink Of Perfection/Femininity .... (Buena Vista 4023) | | 3.75 | 15.00 | 63
    (Promotional issue sponsored by Alcoa Wrap. Shown as by Burl Ives, Hayley Mills, Eddie Hodges, and
    Deborah Walley. From the motion picture *Summer Magic,* Burl Ives and Hayley Mills pictured on front.)

IVY LEAGUE, THE
TOSSIN' & TURNIN'/Graduation Day .... (Cameo 377) | | 3.75 | 15.00 | 65
I COULD MAKE YOU FALL IN LOVE/Our Love Is Slipping Away .... (Cameo 388) | | 3.75 | 15.00 | 66
GENERIC IVY LEAGUE SLEEVE .... (Cameo no #) | | 3.75 | 15.00 | 66
    (No song titles or catalog number indicated, band pictured)

J

JABARA, PAUL
TRAPPED IN A STAIRWAY .... (Casablanca NB 930) | | 1.25 | 5.00 | 78
    (From the motion picture *Thank God It's Friday)*

JACKSON, CHUCK
TELL HIM I'M NOT HOME/Lonely Am I .... (Wand 132) | | 3.75 | 15.00 | 63

JACKSON, FREDDIE
ROCK ME TONIGHT (FOR OLD TIMES SAKE) .... (Capitol B-5459) | | .75 | 3.00 | 85
YOU ARE MY LADY .... (Capitol B-5495) | | .75 | 3.00 | 85
HE'LL NEVER LOVE YOU (LIKE I DO) .... (Capitol B-5535) | | .75 | 3.00 | 85
TASTY LOVE .... (Capitol B-5616) | | .75 | 3.00 | 86
HAVE YOU EVER LOVED SOMEBODY .... (Capitol B-5661) | | .75 | 3.00 | 86
NICE 'N' SLOW .... (Capitol B-44171) | | .75 | 3.00 | 88

JACKSON, JANET
YOUNG LOVE/The Magic Is Working .... (A&M 2440) | | 1.50 | 6.00 | 82
COME GIVE YOUR LOVE TO ME/Forever Yours .... (A&M 2522) | | 1.25 | 5.00 | 83
DON'T STAND ANOTHER CHANCE/Rock N Roll .... (A&M 2660) | | 1.25 | 5.00 | 84
WHAT HAVE YOU DONE FOR ME LATELY/He Doesn't Know I'm Alive .... (A&M 2812) | | .75 | 3.00 | 86
NASTY/You'll Never Find (A Love Like Mine) .... (A&M 2830) | | .75 | 3.00 | 86
WHEN I THINK OF YOU/Pretty Boy .... (A&M 2855) | | .75 | 3.00 | 86
CONTROL/Fast Girls .... (A&M 2877) | | .75 | 3.00 | 86
LET'S WAIT AWHILE/Pretty Boy .... (A&M 2906) | | .75 | 3.00 | 86
THE PLEASURE PRINCIPLE/Fast Girls .... (A&M 2927) | | .75 | 3.00 | 86
RUNAWAY/When I Think Of You (Morales House Mix '95) .... (A&M 31458 1194 7) | | .50 | 2.00 | 95
    Also see Herb Alpert *(Diamonds)*

JACKSON, JERMAINE
DYNAMITE/Tell Me I'm Not Dreamin' (Too Good To Be True) .... (Arista 9190) | | .75 | 3.00 | 84
    (Issued with either stock black or promotional red vinyl)

WHEN THE RAIN BEGINS TO FALL/Substitute .... (MCA/Curb 52521) | .75 | 3.00 | 84

(A-side shown as by Jermaine Jackson and Pia Zadora, both pictured. B-side shown as by Pia Zadora. A-side from the motion picture *Voyage Of The Rock Aliens* starring Zadora.)

(CLOSEST THING TO) PERFECT/(Closest Thing To) Perfect (Instrumental Version) . (Arista 9356) | .75 | 3.00 | 85

(From the motion picture *Perfect*, John Travolta and Jamie Lee Curtis pictured)

I THINK IT'S LOVE/Voices In The Dark .... (Arista 9444) | .75 | 3.00 | 86
DO YOU REMEMBER ME?/Whatcha Doin' .... (Arista 9502) | .75 | 3.00 | 86
DON'T TAKE IT PERSONAL/Clean Up Your Act .... (Arista 9875) | .75 | 3.00 | 89
TWO SHIPS/Next To You .... (Arista 9933) | .75 | 3.00 | 89

Also see the Gap Band (*I'm Gonna Git You Sucka*), Whitney Houston (*Didn't We Almost Have It All*), Jackson Five, Jacksons

JACKSON, JOE
IS SHE REALLY GOING OUT WITH HIM?/(Do The) Instant Mash .... (A&M 2132) | 1.25 | 5.00 | 79
IT'S DIFFERENT FOR GIRLS/Come On .... (A&M 2186) | 1.25 | 5.00 | 79
ON YOUR RADIO/The Band Wore Blue Shirts .... (A&M SP-18000-A/B) | .50 | 2.00 | 79

(Originally included in the boxed set *I'm The Man*. No song titles on sleeve but can be identified by the number 1 on the back. Issued with small-hole 45 RPM record.)

GERALDINE AND JOHN/Don't Wanna Be Like That .... (A&M SP-18000-C/D) | .50 | 2.00 | 79

(Originally included in the boxed set *I'm The Man*. No song titles on sleeve but can be identified by the number 2 on the back. Issued with small-hole 45 RPM.)

KINDA KUTE/Amateur Hour .... (A&M SP-18000-E/F) | .50 | 2.00 | 79

(Originally included in the boxed set *I'm The Man*. No song titles on sleeve but can be identified by the number 3 on the back. Issued with small-hole 45 RPM.)

IT'S DIFFERENT FOR GIRLS/Get That Girl .... (A&M SP-18000-G/H) | .50 | 2.00 | 79

(Originally included in the boxed set *I'm The Man*. No song titles on sleeve but can be identified by the number 4 on the back. Issued with small-hole 45 RPM record.)

I'M THE MAN/Friday .... (A&M SP-18000-I/J) | .50 | 2.00 | 79

(Originally included in the boxed set *I'm The Man*. No song titles on sleeve but can be identified by the number 5 on the back. Issued with small-hole 45 RPM record.)

STEPPIN' OUT/Chinatown .... (A&M 2428) | 1.00 | 4.00 | 82
BREAKING US IN TWO/Target .... (A&M 2510) | 1.00 | 4.00 | 82
MEMPHIS/Breakdown .... (A&M 2601) | 1.00 | 4.00 | 83

(From the motion picture *Mike's Murder*)

YOU CAN'T GET WHAT YOU WANT (TILL YOU KNOW WHAT YOU WANT) .... (A&M 2628) | .75 | 3.00 | 84
HAPPY ENDING/Loisaida .... (A&M BR-2635) | .75 | 3.00 | 84

(Back of sleeve credits and pictures Elaine Caswell)

RIGHT AND WRONG/Breaking Us In Two (Live Version) .... (A&M 2829) | .75 | 3.00 | 86
HOME TOWN/I'm The Man (Live) .... (A&M 2847) | .75 | 3.00 | 86

BOXED SET
I'M THE MAN .... (A&M SP-18000) | 5.00 | 20.00 | 79

(Complete set including five records in picture sleeves, hinged cardboard box, and poster. See individual descriptions above.)

JACKSON, KATE
(Actress)

See Roberta Flack (*Making Love*)

JACKSON, LA TOYA
HEART DON'T LIE/Without You .... (Private I ZS4-04439) | .75 | 3.00 | 84

Also see U.S.A. For Africa, Voices Of America

JACKSON, MAHALIA
SILENT NIGHT, HOLY NIGHT .... (Apollo 750) | 2.50 | 10.00 | 62

JACKSON, MICHAEL
I WANNA BE WHERE YOU ARE/We've Got A Good Thing Going .... (Motown 1202F) | 2.50 | 10.00 | 72
EASE ON DOWN THE ROAD .... (MCA 40947) | 1.25 | 5.00 | 78

(Shown as by Diana Ross and Michael Jackson. From the motion picture *The Wiz*.)

SOMEONE IN THE DARK .... (MCA S45-1786) | 12.50 | 50.00 | 82

(Promotional issue only)

THE GIRL IS MINE .... (Epic 34-03288) | 1.00 | 4.00 | 82

(Shown as by Michael Jackson/Paul McCartney)

THE GIRL IS MINE .... (Epic 34-03288) | 2.00 | 8.00 | 82

(Promotional issue, *Demonstration–Not For Sale* printed on sleeve. Shown as by Michael Jackson/Paul McCartney.)

WANNA BE STARTIN' SOMETHIN' .... (Epic 34-03914) | 1.00 | 4.00 | 83
WANNA BE STARTIN' SOMETHIN' .... (Epic 34-03914) | 1.25 | 5.00 | 83

(Promotional issue, *Demonstration Only–Not For Sale* printed on sleeve)

HUMAN NATURE .... (Epic 34-04026) | 1.00 | 4.00 | 83
HUMAN NATURE .... (Epic 34-04026) | 1.25 | 5.00 | 83

(Promotional issue, *Demonstration Only–Not For Sale* printed on sleeve)

P.Y.T. (PRETTY YOUNG THING) .... (Epic 34-04165) | 1.00 | 4.00 | 83
P.Y.T. (PRETTY YOUNG THING) .... (Epic 34-04165) | 1.25 | 5.00 | 83

(Promotional issue, *Demonstration Only–Not For Sale* printed on sleeve)

SAY SAY SAY/Ode To A Koala Bear .... (Columbia 38-04168) | 1.00 | 4.00 | 83

(Shown as by Paul McCartney and Michael Jackson. B-side by Paul McCartney.)

SAY SAY SAY .... (Columbia 38-04168) | 2.00 | 8.00 | 83

(Promotional issue, *Demonstration–Not For Sale* printed on sleeve. Shown as by Paul McCartney and Michael Jackson.)

FAREWELL MY SUMMER LOVE .... (Motown 1739MF) | 1.25 | 5.00 | 84
TWENTY FIVE MILES .... (Motown 1914MF) | 2.00 | 8.00 | 84
TWENTY FIVE MILES .... (Motown 1914MF) | 2.00 | 8.00 | 84

(Promotional issue, *Demonstration–Not For Sale* printed on sleeve)

I JUST CAN'T STOP LOVING YOU .... (Epic 34-07253) | .75 | 3.00 | 87

(Back of sleeve credits and pictures Siedah Garrett with Jackson)

BAD .... (Epic 34-07418) | .75 | 3.00 | 87
THE WAY YOU MAKE ME FEEL .... (Epic 34-07645) | .75 | 3.00 | 87
MAN IN THE MIRROR/Man In The Mirror (Instrumental) .... (Epic 34-07668) | .75 | 3.00 | 87
DIRTY DIANA .... (Epic 34-07739) | .75 | 3.00 | 88

(Back of sleeve credits and pictures Steve Stevens)

GET IT .... (Motown 1930MF) | .75 | 3.00 | 88

(Shown as by Stevie Wonder and Michael Jackson)

ANOTHER PART OF ME/(Instrumental) .... (Epic 34-07962) | .75 | 3.00 | 88
SMOOTH CRIMINAL/Smooth Criminal (Instrumental) .... (Epic 34-08044) | .75 | 3.00 | 88

Also see Jackson Five, Jacksons, U.S.A. For Africa, Voices Of America, Stevie Wonder (*Get It*)

TITLE	LABEL AND NUMBER	VG	NM	YR

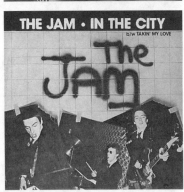

JACKSON, MILLIE

ACT OF WAR (PART 1)/Act Of War (Part 2) .... (Geffen 28958-7)		.75	3.00	85
(Shown as by Elton John and Millie Jackson)				
HOT! WILD! UNRESTRICTED! CRAZY LOVE/				
Hot! Wild! Unrestricted! Crazy Love (Short Instrumental Version) .... (Jive 1007-7-J)		.75	3.00	86
LOVE IS A DANGEROUS GAME/				
Love Is A Dangerous Game (Instrumental Version) .... (Jive 1009-7-J)		.75	3.00	86
THE TIDE IS TURNING/ .... (Jive 1108-7-J)		.75	3.00	88

JACKSON, REBBIE

CENTIPEDE/Centipede (Instrumental) .... (Columbia 38-04547)		1.00	4.00	84
R U TUFF ENUFF/ .... (Columbia 38-07799)		.75	3.00	88
PLAYTHING/Distant Conversation .... (Columbia 38-07685)		.75	3.00	88

JACKSON, SAMMY

LIVE FAST/Are You My Baby .... (Orbit 536)		6.25	25.00	59
TEEN AGE MISS/Single And Searchin' .... (Orbit 583)		6.25	25.00	60

JACKSON, STONEWALL

WATERLOO .... (Columbia 4-41393)		2.50	10.00	59
THE MINUTE MAN .... (Columbia 4-43552)		2.00	8.00	66
I BELIEVE IN LOVE/Drinking And Driving .... (Columbia 4-44501)		2.00	8.00	68

JACKSON, WALTER

IT'S AN UPHILL CLIMB TO THE BOTTOM .... (Okeh 7247)		3.75	15.00	66
SPEAK HER NAME .... (Okeh 7272)		3.75	15.00	67

JACKSON, WANDA

IF I CRIED EVERYTIME YOU HURT ME/Let My Love Walk In .... (Capitol 4723)		3.00	12.00	62

JACKSON FIVE

MAMA'S PEARL .... (Motown 1177)		2.50	10.00	71
Also see Jermaine Jackson, Michael Jackson, Jacksons, U.S.A. For Africa, Voices Of America				

JACKSONS

STATE OF SHOCK .... (Epic 34-04503)		1.00	4.00	84
(Sleeve credits lead vocals by Michael Jackson and Mick Jagger)				
STATE OF SHOCK .... (Epic 34-04503)		1.25	5.00	84
(Promotional issue, Demonstration Only–Not For Sale printed on sleeve. Sleeve credits lead vocals by Michael Jackson and Mick Jagger)				
TORTURE .... (Epic 34-04575)		.75	3.00	84
TORTURE .... (Epic 34-04575)		1.00	4.00	84
(Promotional issue, Demonstration Only–Not For Sale printed on sleeve)				
BODY .... (Epic 34-04673)		.75	3.00	84
BODY .... (Epic 34-04673)		1.00	4.00	84
(Promotional issue, Demonstration Only–Not For Sale printed on sleeve)				
TIME OUT FOR THE BURGLAR .... (MCA 6201)		.75	3.00	87
(From the motion picture Burglar, Whoopi Goldberg pictured)				
Also see Jermaine Jackson, Michael Jackson, Jackson Five, U.S.A. For Africa, Voices Of America				

JAGGER, MICK

JUST ANOTHER NIGHT/Turn The Girl Loose .... (Columbia 38-04743)		1.00	4.00	85
JUST ANOTHER NIGHT (ALBUM VERSION)/				
Just Another Night (Edited Version) .... (Columbia 38-04743)		1.50	6.00	85
(Promotional issue, Demonstration–Not For Sale printed on sleeve)				
LUCKY IN LOVE/Running Out Of Luck .... (Columbia 38-04893)		1.00	4.00	85
LUCKY IN LOVE (3:57)/Lucky In Love (4:45) .... (Columbia 38-04893)		1.50	6.00	85
(Promotional issue, Demonstration–Not For Sale printed on sleeve)				
DANCING IN THE STREET .... (EMI America B-8288)		.75	3.00	85
(Shown as by David Bowie and Mick Jagger)				
RUTHLESS PEOPLE .... (Epic 34-06211)		1.00	4.00	86
(From the motion picture Ruthless People)				
RUTHLESS PEOPLE .... (Epic 34-06211)		1.25	5.00	86
(Promotional issue, Demonstration Only–Not For Sale printed on sleeve. From the motion picture Ruthless People.)				
LET'S WORK/Catch As Catch Can .... (Columbia 38-07306)		1.00	4.00	87
THROWAWAY/Peace For The Wicked .... (Columbia 38-07653)		1.00	4.00	87
SAY YOU WILL/Shoot Of Your Mouth .... (Columbia 38-07703)		1.00	4.00	88
Also see Jacksons (State Of Shock), the Rolling Stones, Peter Tosh (Don't Look Back)				

JAILHOUSE ROCK

(Motion Picture)
See Elvis Presley (Jailhouse Rock, Jailhouse Rock Media Preview)

JAK

I GO WILD/I Go Wild (Instrumental) .... (Epic 34-04751)		.75	3.00	85
I GO WILD .... (Epic 34-04751)		1.00	4.00	85
(Promotional issue, Demonstration Only–Not For Sale printed on sleeve)				

JAKATA

HELL IS ON THE RUN .... (Morocco 1750CF)		1.00	4.00	84
(Promotional issue only)				

J.A.M.

See Jersey Artists For Mankind

JAM, THE

IN THE CITY/Takin' My Love .... (Polydor 14442)		5.00	20.00	77
START!/When You're Young .... (Polydor 2155)		2.00	8.00	81
Also see the Style Council (Paul Weller)				

JAMES, BRIAN

AIN'T THAT A SHAME/Living In Sin/I Can Make You Cry .... (I.R.S. 9501)		1.25	5.00	79

JAMES, BOB

MAIN THEME FROM STAR TREK–THE MOTION PICTURE/				
I Want To Thank You (Very Much) .... (Columbia/Tappan Zee 1-11171)		1.25	5.00	79

Title	Label and Number	VG	NM	YR
MAIN THEME FROM STAR TREK–THE MOTION PICTURE/				
I Want To Thank You (Very Much) .... (Columbia/Tappan Zee 1-11171)		1.50	6.00	79
(Promotional issue, *Demonstration–Not For Sale* printed on sleeve)				

JAMES, COLIN

FIVE LONG YEARS/Three Sheets To The Wind .... (Virgin 7-99262)		.75	3.00	88

JAMES, ETTA

AVENUE D .... (Capitol B-44333)		.75	3.00	89
(Shown as by Etta James Featuring Dave A. Stewart, both pictured on back. From the motion picture *Rooftops*.)				

JAMES, HARRY

BALLAD FOR BEATNICKS/The Blues About Manhattan .... (MGM K12798)		2.00	8.00	59

JAMES, JONI

NEVER TILL NOW .... (MGM K12565)		6.25	25.00	57
(From the motion picture *Raintree County*, pictured, in addition to James, are Montgomery Clift, Elizabeth Taylor, and Eva Marie Saint)				
THERE GOES MY HEART/Funny .... (MGM K12706)		12.50	50.00	58
I STILL GET A THRILL (THINKING OF YOU)/Perhaps .... (MGM K12779)		5.00	20.00	59
WE KNOW/They Really Don't Know You .... (MGM K12895)		5.00	20.00	60
MY LAST DATE (WITH YOU)/I Can't Give You Anything But Love ...... (MGM K12933)		5.00	20.00	60
BE MY LOVE/Tall As A Tree .... (MGM K12948)		5.00	20.00	61
YOU WERE WRONG/Somebody Else Is Taking My Place .... (MGM K13037)		5.00	20.00	62

JAMES, MELVIN

LOVING YOU IS STRANGE .... (MCA 53217)		.75	3.00	87

JAMES, RICK

HIGH ON YOUR LOVE SUITE/Stone City Band, Hi! .... (Gordy 7164F)		1.50	6.00	79
DANCE WIT ME .... (Gordy 1619GF)		1.00	4.00	82
CAN'T STOP/Oh What A Night (4 Luv) .... (Gordy 1776GF)		.75	3.00	85
CAN'T STOP .... (Gordy 1776GF)		1.00	4.00	85
(Promotional issue, *Not For Sale/For Promotional Use Only* printed on sleeve)				
FOREVER AND A DAY .... (Gordy 1776GF)		.75	3.00	86
FOREVER AND A DAY .... (Gordy 1776GF)		1.00	4.00	86
(Promotional issue, *Not For Sale/For Promotional Use Only* printed on sleeve)				
LOOSEY'S RAP .... (Reprise 27885-7)		.75	3.00	88

JAMES, RONNIE

I MUST HAVE DONE IT RIGHT .... (Philadelphia International ZS8-3662)		1.00	4.00	78
(Promotional issue only, *Demonstration–Not For Sale* printed on sleeve)				

JAMES, SONNY

WHO'S NEXT IN LINE .... (Capitol 4268)		2.50	10.00	59
JENNY LOU/Passin' Through .... (NRC 050)		3.75	15.00	60
IT'S JUST A MATTER OF TIME/This World Of Ours .... (Capitol PRO-4906)		2.50	10.00	63
(Promotional issue only)				
THE MINUTE YOU'RE GONE/Gold And Silver .... (Capitol 4969)		2.00	8.00	63
YOU'RE THE ONLY WORLD I KNOW/Tying The Pieces Together ... (Capitol 5280)		2.00	8.00	64
I'LL KEEP HOLDING ON .... (Capitol 5375)		2.00	8.00	65
BEHIND THE TEAR .... (Capitol 5454)		2.00	8.00	65
TRUE LOVE'S A BLESSING .... (Capitol 5536)		2.00	8.00	65
TAKE GOOD CARE OF HER/On The Finger Of One Hand .... (Capitol 5612)		2.00	8.00	66
ROOM IN YOUR HEART .... (Capitol 5690)		2.00	8.00	66
BAREFOOT SANTA CLAUS/My Christmas Dream .... (Capitol 5733)		2.00	8.00	66
(Shown as by Sonny James The Southern Gentleman...With A Bunch Of Kids)				
NEED YOU/On And On .... (Capitol 5833)		2.00	8.00	67
I'LL NEVER FIND ANOTHER YOU/Goodbye, Maggie, Goodbye ... (Capitol 5914)		1.50	6.00	67
IT'S THE LITTLE THINGS/Don't Cut Timber On A Rainy Day ... (Capitol 5987)		1.50	6.00	67
ENDLESSLY/Happy Memories .... (Capitol PRO-6029)		2.00	8.00	67
(Promotional issue only)				
EMPTY ARMS/Everything Begins And Ends With You .... (Capitol 6148)		1.50	6.00	67
A WORLD OF OUR OWN/An Old Sweetheart Of Mine .... (Capitol 2067)		1.50	6.00	67
HEAVEN SAYS HELLO/Fairy Tales .... (Capitol 2155)		1.50	6.00	68
BORN TO BE WITH YOU .... (Capitol 2271)		1.50	6.00	68
ONLY THE LONELY .... (Capitol 2370)		1.50	6.00	68
RUNNING BEAR .... (Capitol 2486)		1.50	6.00	69
SINCE I MET YOU BABY .... (Capitol 2595)		1.50	6.00	69
IT'S JUST A MATTER OF TIME .... (Capitol 2700)		1.25	5.00	70
MY LOVE .... (Capitol 2782)		1.25	5.00	70
DON'T KEEP ME HANGIN' ON/Woodbine Valley .... (Capitol 2834)		1.25	5.00	70
ENDLESSLY .... (Capitol 2914)		1.25	5.00	70
EMPTY ARMS .... (Capitol 3015)		1.25	5.00	71
BRIGHT LIGHTS, BIG CITY .... (Capitol 3114)		1.25	5.00	71
HERE COMES HONEY AGAIN .... (Capitol 3174)		1.25	5.00	71
ONLY LOVE CAN BREAK A HEART/He Has Walked This Way Before ... (Capitol 3232)		1.25	5.00	72
WHEN THE SNOW IS ON THE ROSES .... (Columbia 4-45644)		1.25	5.00	72
I LOVE YOU MORE AND MORE EVERYDAY .... (Columbia 4-45770)		1.25	5.00	72
A MI ESPOSA CON AMOR (TO MY WIFE WITH LOVE) .... (Columbia 3-10001)		1.25	5.00	74
A LITTLE BIT SOUTH OF SASKATOON .... (Columbia 3-10072)		1.25	5.00	75
A LITTLE BAND OF GOLD .... (Columbia 3-10121)		1.25	5.00	75
THE PRISONER'S SONG/Back In The Saddle Again .... (Columbia 3-10276)		1.25	5.00	76
A PLACE IN THE SUN .... (Dimension 1033)		1.25	5.00	76
I'M LOOKING OVER A RAINBOW .... (Dimension 1036)		1.25	5.00	76
THIS IS THE LOVE .... (Columbia 3-10703)		1.25	5.00	78
Most sleeves are shown as by Sonny James The Southern Gentleman				

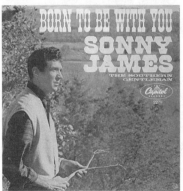

JAMES, TOMMY

I LOVE YOU LOVE ME LOVE/Devil Gate Drive .... (Fantasy 761)		3.75	15.00	76
NO HAY DOS SIN TRES/I Just Wanna Play The Music .... (Millenium 11787)		2.00	8.00	77
SAY PLEASE/Two Time Lover .... (21 Records 105)		1.00	4.00	83
Also see Tommy James and the Shondells				

TITLE	LABEL AND NUMBER	VG	NM	YR

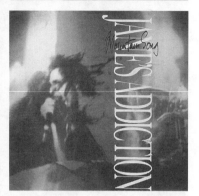

JAMES, TOMMY, AND THE SHONDELLS
SAY I AM/Lots Of Pretty Girls	(Roulette 4695)	3.00	12.00	66
I THINK WE'RE ALONE NOW/Gone, Gone, Gone	(Roulette 4720)	3.00	12.00	67
MIRAGE/Run Run Run	(Roulette 4736)	3.00	12.00	67
GETTIN' TOGETHER/Real Girl	(Roulette 4762)	3.00	12.00	67

Also see Tommy James

JAMES BOYS, THE
BAD REPUTATION/Sometimes You Walk In The Sunshine	(Columbia 4-43488)	1.50	6.00	65
OVER AND OVER/Same Old Way	(Bell/Penny Farthing 55,022)	1.25	5.00	73

JAMES DEAN STORY, THE
(Motion Picture)

See Mantovani (*Let Me Be Loved*)

JAMIES, THE
SUMMERTIME, SUMMERTIME/Searching For You	(Epic 9281)	5.00	20.00	58

(Song was re-released in 1962 with the same sleeve)

JAN & DEAN
(Jan Berry and Dean Torrence)
WE GO TOGETHER	(Dore 555)	15.00	60.00	60
GEE/Such A Good Night For Dreaming	(Dore 576)	37.50	150.00	60
SURF CITY/She's My Summer Girl	(Liberty 55580)	6.25	25.00	63
HONOLULU LULU/Someday (You'll Go Walking By)	(Liberty 55613)	6.25	25.00	63
DRAG CITY/Schlock Rock	(Liberty 55724)	6.25	25.00	64
DEAD MAN'S CURVE/The New Girl In School	(Liberty 55672)	6.25	25.00	64
THE LITTLE OLD LADY FROM PASADENA	(Liberty 55704)	5.00	20.00	64
RIDE THE WILD SURF	(Liberty 55724)	6.25	25.00	64

(A-side from the motion picture *Ride The Wild Surf*)
SIDEWALK SURFIN'/When It's Over	(Liberty 55727)	7.50	30.00	64
FROM ALL OVER THE WORLD/Freeway Flyer	(Liberty 55766)	37.50	150.00	65

(From the concert motion picture *The T.A.M.I. Show*)
YOU REALLY KNOW HOW TO HURT A GUY	(Liberty 55792)	5.00	20.00	65
A BEGINNING FROM AN END/Folk City	(Liberty 55849)	10.00	40.00	65
JENNY LEE/Vegetables	(United Artists 50859)	6.25	25.00	71

EXTENDED PLAYS
YELLOW BALLOON/RAINDROPS/California Lullaby/Here Comes The Rain	(Sundazed 125)	.50	2.00	96

(Hard cover issued with light pastel green vinyl, titled on front *Sounds For A Rainy Day*)

Also see Jan Berry, the Legendary Masked Surfers, Mike & Dean (Dean Torrence)

JAN & KJELD
PENNY MELODY/Ting-A-Ling (My Banjo Sings)	(Jaro International 77032)	2.50	10.00	60
BANJO BOY/Don't Raise A Storm (Mach Doch Nicht So Viel Wind)	(Kapp 335)	2.50	10.00	60

JANE'S ADDICTION
MOUNTAIN SONG	(Warner Bros. 27520-7)	1.00	4.00	89

Also see Mike Watt (Perry Ferrell on *Big Train* b-side, Stephen Perkins on *E-Ticket Ride* and *Big Train* b-side)

JANET & JAY
PRETEND A WEDDING	(Leader 810)	2.00	8.00	

JANKOWSKI, HORST, AND HIS ORCHESTRA AND CHORUS
SIMPEL GIMPEL	(Mercury 72465)	1.50	6.00	65

JANSSEN, DAVID
(Actor)

See Melba Moore (*My Sensitive, Passionate Man*)

JARRE, JEAN-MICHEL
FOURTH RENDEZ-VOUS/First Rendez-vous	(Polydor/Dreyfus 883 892-7)	.75	3.00	86

JARRE, MAURICE
THEME FROM BEHOLD A PALE HORSE PART 1–PART 2	(Colpix 746)	2.00	8.00	64

(From the motion picture *Behold A Pale Horse*, Gregory Peck, Anthony Quinn, and Omar Sharif pictured on front, Jarre on back)
THEME FROM GRAND PRIX	(MGM K13669)	2.00	8.00	66

(From the motion picture *Grand Prix*)

JARREAU, AL
THE CHRISTMAS SONG	(Warner Bros. 29446-7)	1.00	4.00	82

(Song title is not listed on sleeve, instead, sleeve reads "*And God bless us all...Jarreau.*" Possibly a promotional issue only.)
MORNIN'/Not Like This	(Warner Bros. 29720-7)	.75	3.00	83

(Shown as by Jarreau)
TROUBLE IN PARADISE/Step By Step	(Warner Bros. 29501-7)	.75	3.00	83

(Shown as by Jarreau)
AFTER ALL/I Keep Callin'	(Warner Bros. 29262-7)	.75	3.00	84
L IS FOR LOVER	(Warner Bros. 28686-7)	.75	3.00	86
THE MUSIC OF GOODBYE (LOVE THEME FROM OUT OF AFRICA)	(MCA 52784)	1.00	4.00	86

(Shown as by Melissa Manchester and Al Jarreau. From the motion picture *Out Of Africa*, Robert Redford and Meryl Streep pictured.)
MOONLIGHTING THEME	(MCA 53124)	1.25	5.00	87

(From the television series *Moonlighting*)
SINCE I FELL FOR YOU	(MCA 53187)	1.25	5.00	87

(From the television series *Moonlighting*, Bruce Willis and Cybill Shepherd pictured on front, Jarreau on back.)
SO GOOD	(Reprise 27664-7)	.75	3.00	88

Also see U.S.A. For Africa, Voices Of America

JARVIS, JOHN
WIDE OPEN SPACES	(MCA 53188)	.75	3.00	87

JASON & THE SCORCHERS
SHOP IT AROUND	(EMI America B-8269)	.75	3.00	85
GOLDEN BALL AND CHAIN	(EMI America B-8369)	.75	3.00	86

JASPER, CHRIS

SUPERBAD .... (CBS Associated ZS4-07657)	.75	3.00	87
SUPERBAD .... (CBS Associated ZS4-07657)	1.00	4.00	87

(Promotional issue, *Demonstration–Not For Sale* printed on sleeve)
Jasper was a member of the Isley Brothers from 1969-1984

JAY, MORTY, AND THE SURFERIN' CATS

SALTWATER TAFFY / What Is Surfin' All About .... (Legend 124)	5.00	20.00	63

JAY & THE AMERICANS

THINGS ARE CHANGING .... (E.E.O.C. no #)	50.00	200.00	65

(Promotional issue sponsored by the Equal Employment Opportunities Commission. Similar releases by the Blossoms and the Supremes.)

SOME ENCHANTED EVENING / Girl .... (United Artists 919)	3.00	12.00	65
CRYING / I Don't Need A Friend .... (United Artists 50 016)	2.50	10.00	66
LIVIN' ABOVE YOUR HEAD / Look At Me–What Do You See .... (United Artists 50 046)	2.50	10.00	66

Also see Jay Black

JAY & THE TECHNIQUES

KEEP THE BALL ROLLIN' .... (Smash 2124)	2.00	8.00	67
STRAWBERRY SHORTCAKE .... (Smash 2142)	2.00	8.00	68
BABY MAKE YOUR OWN SWEET MUSIC .... (Smash 2154)	2.00	8.00	68
SINGLES GAME .... (Smash 2171)	2.00	8.00	68

JAYE, ICEY

ICEY (SHE'S BAD) .... (Arista 9878)	.75	3.00	89

JAYE, MILES

I'VE BEEN A FOOL FOR YOU .... (Island 7-99379)	.75	3.00	87

JAZZ SINGER, THE

(Motion Picture)

See Neil Diamond (*Love On The Rocks, Hello Again, America*)

JAZZY JEFF & THE FRESH PRINCE

See D.J. Jazzy Jeff & The Fresh Prince

JEFFERSON AIRPLANE

CROWN OF CREATION / Lather .... (RCA Victor 47-9644)	5.00	20.00	68
PLASTIC FANTASTIC LOVER / Other Side Of This Life .... (RCA Victor 74-0150)	5.00	20.00	69
VOLUNTEERS / We Can Be Together .... (RCA Victor 74-0245)	3.75	15.00	70
HAVE YOU SEEN THE SAUCERS / Mexico .... (RCA Victor 74-0343)	3.75	15.00	70
PRETTY AS YOU FEEL / Wild Turkey .... (Grunt 65-0500)	2.50	10.00	71
LONG JOHN SILVER / Milk Train .... (Grunt 65-0506)	3.75	15.00	72
WHITE RABBIT / Plastic Fantastic Lover .... (RCA 5156-7-R)	1.25	5.00	87

(Issued with white vinyl)

Also see Marty Balin, Hot Tuna (Jack Casady, Jorma Kaukonen), Jefferson Starship, Paul Kantner, KBC Band (Marty Balin, Jack Casady, Paul Kantner), Grace Slick, Starship, SVT (Jack Casady). Skip Spence left the group after their first album was released in 1966 to join Moby Grape.

JEFFERSON STARSHIP

COUNT ON ME / Show Yourself .... (Grunt FB-11196)	1.00	4.00	78
RUNAWAY / Hot Water .... (Grunt FB-11274)	1.00	4.00	78
RUNAWAY .... (Grunt JB-11274)	1.50	6.00	78

(Promotional issue, *For DJ's Only Not For Sale* printed on sleeve)

CRAZY FEELIN' / Love Too Good .... (Grunt FB-11374)	1.00	4.00	78
LIGHT THE SKY ON FIRE .... (Grunt FB-11426-2)	1.00	4.00	78

(Gold half sleeve included with the album *Gold*. No identification other than the catalog number in the lower right corner.)

LIGHT THE SKY ON FIRE .... (Grunt JB-11426)	1.50	6.00	78

(Promotional issue only, *Promo Record...Not For Sale* printed on sleeve. Copy promotes album *Gold* and *Star Wars* Holiday Special Friday, November 17th.)

JANE / Freedom At Point Zero .... (Grunt FB-11750)	1.00	4.00	79
GIRL WITH THE HUNGRY EYES / Just The Same .... (Grunt FB-11921)	1.00	4.00	80
LAYIN' IT ON THE LINE / Showdown .... (Grunt FB-13872)	1.00	4.00	84

AS STARSHIP (AFTER PAUL KANTNER LEFT THE GROUP)

WE BUILT THIS CITY / Private Room (Instrumental) .... (Grunt FB-14170)	1.00	4.00	85
SARA / Hearts Of The World (Will Understand) .... (Grunt FB-14253)	1.00	4.00	86

(Issued with either blue or black vinyl.)

TOMORROW DOESN'T MATTER TONIGHT / Love Rusts .... (Grunt FB-14332)	7.50	30.00	86
BEFORE I GO / Cut You Down To Size .... (Grunt FB-14393)	1.00	4.00	86
NOTHING'S GONNA STOP US NOW / Layin' It On The Line (Live) ...... (Grunt 5109-7-G)	.75	3.00	87

(From the motion picture *Mannequin*, Andrew McCarthy pictured on front.)

NOTHING'S GONNA STOP US NOW / Layin' It On The Line (Live) ...... (Grunt 5109-7-G-1)	1.50	6.00	87

(Promotional issue only, *Special Holiday Re-Service* printed on sleeve, band pictured on front.)

IT'S NOT OVER ('TIL IT'S OVER) / Babylon .... (RCA/Grunt 5225-7-G)	.75	3.00	87
BEAT PATROL / Girls Like You .... (Grunt 5308-7-G)	.75	3.00	87
WILD AGAIN / Layin' It On The Line .... (Elektra 7-69349)	.75	3.00	88

(From the motion picture *Cocktail*)

IT'S NOT ENOUGH / Love Among The Cannibals .... (RCA 9032-7-R)	.75	3.00	89

Also see Marty Balin, Jefferson Airplane, Paul Kantner, KBC Band (Marty Balin, Paul Kantner), Grace Slick, Mickey Thomas

JEFFREYS, GARLAND

REELIN' / One-Eyed Jack .... (A&M 2030)	1.00	4.00	78

(A-side shown as by Garland Jeffreys and Phoebe Snow)

EXTENDED PLAYS

LOVER'S WALK / CHRISTINE / Miami Beach / We The People .... (Epic AE7-1223)	1.50	6.00	81

(Promotional issue only titled *Escapades* included with the album *Escape Artist*, issued with a small-hole 33-1/3 RPM record)

INTERVIEW / Interview (continued) / 96 Tears .... (Epic AE7 1225)	1.50	6.00	81

(Promotional issue only titled *Ways Of Escape*. *Demonstration–Not For Sale* printed on sleeve, issued with a small-hole 33-1/3 RPM record.)

JELLYBEAN

THE MEXICAN / .... (EMI PB-8240)	1.00	4.00	84
WHO FOUND WHO / The Real Thing (Part 2 Instrumental) .... (Chrysalis VS4 43120)	.75	3.00	87

(Shown as by Jellybean Featuring Elisa Fiorillo)

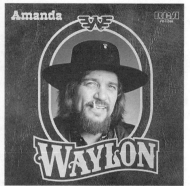

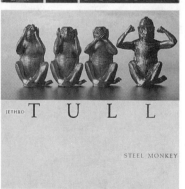

TITLE	LABEL AND NUMBER	VG	NM	YR
THE REAL THING/Am I Dreaming (Instrumental)	(Chrysalis VS4 43167)	.75	3.00	87
(Shown as by Jellybean Featuring Steven Dante)				

JENKINS, TOMMY
TELLING YOU HOW IT IS	(Elektra 69301-7)	.75	3.00	89

JENNER, BRUCE
(Olympic Athlete)
See Village People (Can't Stop The Music)

JENNIFER
DO IT FOR ME	(Motown 1417)	1.25	5.00	76

JENNINGS, WAYLON
AMANDA/Lonesome, On'ry And Mean	(RCA PB-11596)	1.00	4.00	79
THEME FROM THE DUKES OF HAZZARD	(RCA PB-12067)	1.00	4.00	80
HIGHWAYMAN	(Columbia 38-04881)	.75	3.00	85
(Shown as by Willie Nelson, Kris Kristofferson, Johnny Cash, and Waylon Jennings)				
THREE STARS	(Crest 1057)	1.50	6.00	80s
(Title sleeve released with a Waylon Jennings interview dubbed into the 1959 hit song by Tommy Dee with Carol Kay and the Teen-Aires)				
Also see Chet Atkins (Chet's Tune), Willie Nelson (Take It To The Limit), U.S.A. For Africa, Voices Of America				

JENSEN, KRIS
POOR UNLUCKY ME/	(Hickory 1203)	3.75	15.00	64
BIG AS I CAN DREAM/Donna Donna	(Hickory 1224)	3.75	15.00	64

JERSEY ARTISTS FOR MANKIND (J.A.M.)
WE'VE GOT THE LOVE/Save Love, Save Life	(Arista 9498)	1.00	4.00	86
Also see Clarence Clemons, Nils Lofgren, Carolyn Mas, Bruce Springsteen, Southside Johnny				

JESSEL, GEORGE
HELLO MOMMA PARTS 1 AND 2	(Decca 1-717)	2.50	10.00	53
(Decca "Curtain Call" series of reissues)				

JESSE'S GANG
NOIZ WITHOUT WORDS	(Geffen 28557-7)	.75	3.00	86
BACK-UP	(Geffen 28449-7)	.75	3.00	87
I'M BACK AGAIN	(Geffen 28149-7)	.75	3.00	87

JESUS AND MARY CHAIN, THE
UPSIDE DOWN/Vegetable Man	(Rough Trade 006)	2.00	8.00	84
SURFIN' USA/Kill Surf City	(Warner Bros. 27754-7)	1.00	4.00	88

JESUS CHRIST SUPERSTAR
(Rock Opera)
See Murray Head (Heaven On Their Minds, Superstar), Frank Pourcel (I Only Want To Say)

JETHRO TULL
BUNGLE IN THE JUNGLE	(Chrysalis 2101)	2.00	8.00	74
STEEL MONKEY/Steel Monkey	(Chrysalis VS4 43172)	1.25	5.00	87
(Sleeve shows same song on both sides although the 45 has Down At The End Of Your Road as the b-side)				
Also see London Symphony Orchestra (Bourree)				

JETS, THE
CURIOSITY	(MCA 52682)	.75	3.00	85
CRUSH ON YOU/Right Before My Eyes	(MCA 52774)	.75	3.00	86
PRIVATE NUMBER	(MCA 52846)	.75	3.00	86
CROSS MY BROKEN HEART	(MCA 53123)	.75	3.00	87
(From the motion picture Beverly Hills Cop II, Eddie Murphy pictured on front, the Jets on back)				
I DO YOU	(MCA 53193)	.75	3.00	87
ROCKET 2 U	(MCA 53254)	.75	3.00	88
MAKE IT REAL	(MCA 53311)	.75	3.00	88
SENDIN' ALL MY LOVE	(MCA 53380)	.75	3.00	89
Also see Boys Club (Eugene Wolfgramm a.k.a. Gene Hunt)				

JETT, JOAN, AND THE BLACKHEARTS
I LOVE ROCK 'N ROLL/You Don't Know What You've Got	(Boardwalk NB7-11-135)	1.50	6.00	82
CRIMSON AND CLOVER/Oh Woe Is Me	(Boardwalk NB7-11-144)	1.00	4.00	82
DO YOU WANNA TOUCH ME (OH YEAH)/Victim Of Circumstance	(Boardwalk NB-11-150-7)	1.00	4.00	82
FAKE FRIENDS/Nitetime	(MCA/Blackheart 52240)	1.00	4.00	83
EVERYDAY PEOPLE/Why Can't We Be Happy	(MCA/Blackheart 52272)	1.00	4.00	83
I LOVE YOU LOVE/Talkin Bout My Baby (Live)	(MCA/Blackheart 52472)	1.00	4.00	84
GOOD MUSIC/Fantasy	(CBS Associated/Blackheart ZS4-06336)	.75	3.00	86
GOOD MUSIC	(CBS Associated/Blackheart ZS4-06336)	1.25	5.00	86
(Promotional issue, Demonstration–Not For Sale printed on sleeve)				
LIGHT OF DAY/Roadrunner (Radio On)	(CBS Associated/Blackheart ZS4-08095)	.75	3.00	87
(Shown as by the Barbusters, a.k.a. Joan Jett and the Blackhearts. From the motion picture Light Of Day, Joan Jett and Michael J. Fox pictured.)				
I HATE MYSELF FOR LOVING YOU/Love Is Pain	(CBS Associated/Blackheart ZS4-07919)	.75	3.00	88
LITTLE LIAR/What Can I Do For You	(CBS Associated/Blackheart ZS4-08095)	.75	3.00	88
SPINSTER/Go Home/Hostility	(Blackheart 15)	.50	2.00	94
(Hard cover issued with blue vinyl)				
Also see Bikini Kill (New Radio)				

JEWEL OF THE NILE, THE
(Motion Picture)
See Billy Ocean (When The Going Gets Tough, The Tough Get Going)

JIMENEZ, JOSE
(Character created and played by Bill Dana)
THE ASTRONAUT	(Kapp 409)	2.00	8.00	61
SING ALONG WITH JOSE	(Kapp 434)	2.00	8.00	62
Also see Bill Dana				

JIVE BUNNY AND THE MASTERMIXERS
SWING THE MOOD	(Music Factory 99140)	.75	3.00	89

J.J. FAD
SUPERSONIC .... (Ruthless 99328-7) .75 3.00 88
WAY OUT .... (Ruthless 99285-7) .75 3.00 88
IS IT LOVE .... (Ruthless 99257-7) .75 3.00 88

JOEL, BILLY

YOU MAY BE RIGHT/Close To The Borderline .... (Columbia 1-11231) 1.00 4.00 80
IT'S STILL ROCK AND ROLL TO ME/Through The Long Night .... (Columbia 1-11276) 1.00 4.00 80
DON'T ASK ME WHY/C'Etait Toi (You Were The One) .... (Columbia 1-11331) 1.00 4.00 80
SOMETIMES A FANTASY/All For Leyna .... (Columbia 1-11379) 1.00 4.00 80
SAY GOODBYE TO HOLLYWOOD/Summer, Highland Falls .... (Columbia 18-02518) 1.00 4.00 81
SHE'S GOT A WAY/The Ballad Of Billy The Kid .... (Columbia 18-02628) 1.00 4.00 81
PRESSURE/Laura .... (Columbia 38-03244) .75 3.00 82
ALLENTOWN/Elvis Presley Blvd. .... (Columbia 38-03413) .75 3.00 82
GOODNIGHT SAIGON/A Room Of Our Own .... (Columbia 38-03780) .75 3.00 83
GOODNIGHT SAIGON .... (Columbia 38-03780) 1.00 4.00 83
    (Promotional issue, *Demonstration–Not For Sale* printed on sleeve)

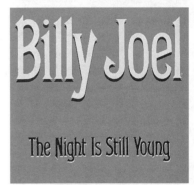

TELL HER ABOUT IT/Easy Money .... (Columbia 38-04149) .75 3.00 83
TELL HER ABOUT IT .... (Columbia 38-04149) 1.00 4.00 83
    (Promotional issue, *Demonstration–Not For Sale* printed on sleeve)
UPTOWN GIRL/Careless Talk .... (Columbia 38-04149) .75 3.00 83
UPTOWN GIRL .... (Columbia 38-04149) 1.00 4.00 83
    (Promotional issue, *Demonstration–Not For Sale* printed on sleeve)
AN INNOCENT MAN/I'll Cry Instead (Live) .... (Columbia 38-04259) .75 3.00 83
AN INNOCENT MAN .... (Columbia 38-04259) 1.00 4.00 83
    (Promotional issue, *Demonstration–Not For Sale* printed on sleeve)
THE LONGEST TIME/Christie Lee .... (Columbia 38-04400) .75 3.00 84
THE LONGEST TIME .... (Columbia 38-04400) 1.00 4.00 84
    (Promotional issue, *Demonstration–Not For Sale* printed on sleeve)
LEAVE A TENDER MOMENT ALONE/This Night .... (Columbia 38-04514) .75 3.00 84
    (Back of sleeve credits a-side harmonica solo to "Toots" Thielemans)
LEAVE A TENDER MOMENT ALONE .... (Columbia 38-04514) 1.00 4.00 84
    (Promotional issue, *Demonstration–Not For Sale* printed on sleeve. Back of sleeve credits a-side harmonica solo to "Toots" Thielemans.)
KEEPING THE FAITH/She's Right On Time .... (Columbia 38-04681) .75 3.00 84
KEEPING THE FAITH .... (Columbia 38-04681) 1.00 4.00 84
    (Promotional issue, *Demonstration–Not For Sale* printed on sleeve)
YOU'RE ONLY HUMAN (SECOND WIND)/Surprises .... (Columbia 38-05417) .75 3.00 85
YOU'RE ONLY HUMAN (SECOND WIND) .... (Columbia 38-05417) 1.00 4.00 85
    (Promotional issue, *Demonstration–Not For Sale* printed on sleeve)
THE NIGHT IS STILL YOUNG/Summer, Highland Falls .... (Columbia 38-05657) .75 3.00 85
THE NIGHT IS STILL YOUNG .... (Columbia 38-05657) 1.50 6.00 85
    (Promotional issue only, *Demonstration–Not For Sale* printed on sleeve. Completely different design from the stock issue.)
MODERN WOMAN/Sleeping With The Television On .... (Epic 34-06118) .75 3.00 86
    (From the motion picture *Ruthless People*)
MODERN WOMAN .... (Epic 34-06118) 1.00 4.00 86
    (Promotional issue, *Demonstration Only–Not For Sale* printed on sleeve. From the motion picture *Ruthless People*)
THIS IS THE TIME/Code Of Silence .... (Columbia 38-06526) .75 3.00 86
    (Back of sleeve credits Cyndi Lauper as guest vocalist on b-side)
THIS IS THE TIME .... (Columbia 38-06526) 1.00 4.00 86
    (Promotional issue, *Demonstration–Not For Sale* printed on sleeve)
BABY GRAND/Big Man On Mulberry Street .... (Columbia 38-06994) .75 3.00 87
    (Shown as by Billy Joel Featuring Ray Charles, both pictured on back)
BACK IN THE U.S.S.R./Big Shot .... (Columbia 38-07626) .75 3.00 87
    Also see U.S.A. For Africa, Voices Of America

JOHANNA
OUT OF SPACE AND TIME/Johnny Kissed A Girl .... (Kapp 319X) 2.50 10.00 60

JOHANSEN, DAVID
FUNKY BUT CHIC/The Rope (The Let Go Song) .... (Blue Sky ZS8-2771) 1.50 6.00 78
    Also see the New York Dolls, Buster Poindexter

JOHN, ELTON

LUCY IN THE SKY WITH DIAMONDS/One Day At A Time .... (MCA 40344) 1.25 5.00 74
    (Back of sleeve credits the reggae guitars of Doctor Winston O'Boogie a.k.a. John Lennon)
PHILADELPHIA FREEDOM/I Saw Her Standing There .... (MCA 40364) 1.25 5.00 75
    (Back of sleeve credits John Lennon With The Muscle Shoals Horns on b-side)
PHILADELPHIA FREEDOM .... (MCA 40364) 7.50 30.00 75
    (Souvenir issue for Philadelphia radio station WFIL 56)
DON'T GO BREAKING MY HEART/Snow Queen .... (Rocket/MCA PIG-40585) 1.00 4.00 76
    (Shown as by Elton John and Kiki Dee, both pictured)
EGO/Flintstone Boy .... (MCA 40892) 1.25 5.00 78
PART-TIME LOVE/I Cry At Night .... (MCA 40973) 1.00 4.00 78
SONG FOR GUY .... (MCA 40993) 1.00 4.00 79
MAMA CAN'T BUY YOU LOVE/Three Way Love Affair .... (MCA 41042) 1.00 4.00 79
LITTLE JEANNIE/Conquer The Sun .... (MCA 41236) 1.00 4.00 80
NOBODY WINS .... (Geffen 49722) 1.00 4.00 81
EMPTY GARDEN (HEY HEY JOHNNY)/Take Me Down To The Ocean ... (Geffen 50049) 1.00 4.00 82
BLUE EYES/Hey Papa Legba .... (Geffen 29954-7) .75 3.00 82
I'M STILL STANDING/Love So Cold .... (Geffen 29639-7) .75 3.00 83
KISS THE BRIDE/Choc Ice Goes Mental .... (Geffen 29568-7) .75 3.00 83
I GUESS THAT'S WHY THEY CALL IT THE BLUES/The Retreat .... (Geffen 29460-7) .75 3.00 83
COLD AS CHRISTMAS .... (Geffen # unknown) 75.00 300.00 83
    (Reportedly this was supposed to be the fourth single from the album *Too Low For Zero* but was withdrawn. Only six copies are known to exist. An image of an iceberg is pictured.)
WHO WEARS THESE SHOES? .... (Geffen 29189-7) .75 3.00 84
ACT OF WAR (PART 1)/Act Of War (Part 2) .... (Geffen 28958-7) .75 3.00 85
    (Shown as by Elton John and Millie Jackson)
WRAP HER UP/The Man Who Never Died .... (Geffen 28873-7) .75 3.00 85

EGO

TITLE	LABEL AND NUMBER	VG	NM	YR
THAT'S WHAT FRIENDS ARE FOR/Two Ships Passing In The Night	(Arista 9422)	.75	3.00	85
(Shown as by Dionne & Friends Featuring Elton John, Gladys Knight and Stevie Wonder. Warwick, John, Knight, and Wonder pictured on front. Warwick, John, Knight, Wonder, and the song's authors, Burt Bacharach and Carole Bayer Sager, pictured on back.)				
NIKITA/Restless	(Geffen 28800-7)	.75	3.00	85
HEARTACHE ALL OVER THE WORLD/Highlander	(Geffen 28578-7)	.75	3.00	86
CANDLE IN THE WIND	(MCA 53196)	.75	3.00	87
(Yellow background on front and "Available on these two albums" promo on back)				
CANDLE IN THE WIND	(MCA 53196)	.75	3.00	87
(Ivory background on front and red background on back)				
TAKE ME TO THE PILOT/Tonight	(MCA 53260)	.75	3.00	88
I DON'T WANNA GO ON WITH YOU LIKE THAT/Rope Around A Fool	(MCA 53345)	.75	3.00	88
A WORD IN SPANISH	(MCA 53408)	.75	3.00	88
BELIEVE/The One (Live)	(Rocket/Island 422-856 014-7)	.50	2.00	95
Also see Aretha Franklin (Through The Storm), Jennifer Rush (Flames Of Paradise)				

JOHN, LITTLE WILLIE
TITLE	LABEL AND NUMBER	VG	NM	YR
FEVER/Ruby Baby	(Atlantic 7-89189)	.75	3.00	87
(B-side shown as by the Drifters. From the motion picture The Big Town, Matt Dillon and Diane Lane pictured.)				

JOHNNY AND HIS LEISURE SUITS
TITLE	LABEL AND NUMBER	VG	NM	YR
THE SNOWBIRD SONG	(Loon 002)	1.50	6.00	81

JOHNNY & THE DWELLERS
TITLE	LABEL AND NUMBER	VG	NM	YR
DEPRESSION/Rudolf The Red Nosed Reindeer	(EMI 19949)	1.50	6.00	94
(Promotional issue only)				

JOHNNY & THE HURRICANES
TITLE	LABEL AND NUMBER	VG	NM	YR
BEATNIK FLY/Sand Storm	(Warwick 520)	7.50	30.00	60
DOWN YONDER/Sheba	(Big Top 45-3036)	5.00	20.00	60
ROCKING GOOSE/Revival	(Big Top 45-3051)	5.00	20.00	60
(Uses the same color image of the band as the previous sleeve Down Yonder)				
YOU ARE MY SUNSHINE/Molly-O	(Big Top 45-3056)	5.00	20.00	60
JA-DA/Mr. Lonely	(Big Top 45-3063)	5.00	20.00	61
OLD SMOKIE/High Voltage	(Big Top 45-3076)	5.00	20.00	61

JOHNNY BE GOOD
(Motion Picture)
   See Judas Priest (Johnny B. Goode)

JOHNNY DANGEROUSLY
(Motion Picture)
   See "Weird Al" Yankovic (This Is The Life)

JOHNNY HATES JAZZ
TITLE	LABEL AND NUMBER	VG	NM	YR
SHATTERED DREAMS/My Secret Garden	(Virgin 7-99383)	.75	3.00	88
TURN BACK THE CLOCK/Cracking Up	(Virgin 7-99308)	.75	3.00	88
I DON'T WANT TO BE A HERO/The Cage	(Virgin 7-99304)	.75	3.00	88

JOHNS, SARAH
TITLE	LABEL AND NUMBER	VG	NM	YR
GLORY, TENNESSEE/I'm Making Love To A Memory	(RCA PB-10203)	1.00	4.00	75

JOHNSON, DON
TITLE	LABEL AND NUMBER	VG	NM	YR
HEARTBEAT/Can't Take Your Memory	(Epic 34-06285)	.75	3.00	86
(First printing with Johnson against a black background)				
HEARTBEAT	(Epic 34-06285)	1.00	4.00	86
(Promotional issue, Demonstration Not For Sale printed on sleeve. First printing with Johnson against a black background.)				
HEARTBEAT/Can't Take Your Memory	(Epic 34-06285)	.75	3.00	86
(Second printing with Johnson against a yellow background)				
HEARTBEAT	(Epic 34-06285)	1.00	4.00	86
(Promotional issue, Demonstration Not For Sale printed on sleeve. Second printing with Johnson against a yellow background.)				
HEARTACHE AWAY/Love Roulette	(Epic 34-06426)	.75	3.00	86
HEARTACHE AWAY	(Epic 34-06426)	1.00	4.00	86
(Promotional issue, Demonstration Not For Sale printed on sleeve)				
TILL I LOVED YOU	(Columbia 38-08062)	1.00	4.00	88
(Shown as by Barbra Streisand and Don Johnson, both pictured)				
Also see Chaka Khan (Own The Night) , Patti LaBelle (The Last Unbroken Heart)				

JOHNSON, JANICE MARIE
TITLE	LABEL AND NUMBER	VG	NM	YR
LOVE ME TONITE/Catch 22	(Capitol B-5359)	1.25	5.00	84
Also see A Taste Of Honey				

JOHNSON, JEANIE
TITLE	LABEL AND NUMBER	VG	NM	YR
WISHING WELL	(RCA Victor 47-7782)	2.00	8.00	61

JOHNSON, JESSE
TITLE	LABEL AND NUMBER	VG	NM	YR
BE YOUR MAN	(A&M 2702)	.75	3.00	85
(Shown as by Jesse Johnson's Revue)				
I WANT MY GIRL	(A&M 2749)	.75	3.00	85
(Shown as by Jesse Johnson's Revue)				
CRAZAY	(A&M 2878)	1.00	4.00	86
(Shown as by Jesse Johnson Featuring Sly Stone)				
BABY LET'S KISS	(A&M 2912)	.75	3.00	86
LOVE STRUCK	(A&M 3020)	.75	3.00	88

JOHNSON, MICHAEL
TITLE	LABEL AND NUMBER	VG	NM	YR
ALMOST LIKE BEING IN LOVE/Ridin' In The Sky	(EMI America 8004)	.75	3.00	78

JOHNSON, ROY LEE
TITLE	LABEL AND NUMBER	VG	NM	YR
BLACK PEPPER WILL MAKE YOU SNEEZE	(Okeh 7160)	2.50	10.00	63

JOHNSON & MIRIAM
TITLE	LABEL AND NUMBER	VG	NM	YR
YOUNG AND INNOCENT	(Jamie 1181)	2.00	8.00	61

JOHNSON, ROBIN
(Actress)
    See Marcy Levy and Robin Gibb (Help Me!)

JOHNSTON, BRUCE

DO THE SURFER STOMP	(Donna 1354)	10.00	40.00	62

    Also see the Beach Boys, the Rip Chords

JOLI, FRANCE

DOES HE DANCE	(Epic 34-04863)	.75	3.00	85
DOES HE DANCE	(Epic 34-04863)	1.00	4.00	85

    (Promotional issue, *Demonstration–Not For Sale* printed on sleeve)

JOLSON, AL

SONNY BOY/My Mammy	(Decca 1-716)	2.50	10.00	52

    (Decca "Curtain Call" series of reissues)

JONATHAN LIVINGSTON SEAGULL
(Motion Picture)
    See Neil Diamond (Be)

JONES, DAVID

DREAM GIRL/Take Me To Paradise	(Colpix 764)	6.25	25.00	65
WHAT ARE WE GOING TO DO?/This Bouquet	(Colpix 784)	6.25	25.00	65
THEME FOR A NEW LOVE/Girl From Chelsea	(Colpix 789)	7.50	30.00	65
GENERIC DAVY JONES SLEEVE	(Davy Jones no #)	3.75	15.00	60s

    (Generic half sleeve featuring an illustration of Jones. No titles listed. Used for any release on Jones' self-named record label.)
    Also see Dolenz, Jones & Tork, the Monkees

JONES, DAVID LYNN

BONNIE JEAN (LITTLE SISTER)/Valley Of A Thousand Years	(Mercury 888 733-7)	.75	3.00	87

JONES, DOROTHY

IT'S UNBEARABLE/Takin' That Long Walk Home	(Columbia 4-42062)	2.50	10.00	61

JONES, GEORGE

SHE THINKS I STILL CARE/Sometimes You Just Can't Win ...	(United Artists 424)	3.00	12.00	62
TENDER YEARS/Battle Of Love	(Mercury 71804)	2.50	10.00	62
ACHING BREAKING HEART/	(Mercury 71910)	2.50	10.00	62
WHEN MY HEART HURTS NO MORE/	(Mercury 71960)	2.50	10.00	62
I LOVE YOU BECAUSE/	(Mercury 72087)	2.50	10.00	62
COLD COLD HEART/You're Still On My Mind	(Mercury 72010)	2.50	10.00	63

    (Uses the same front and back as *Tender Years* but with different titles and catalog number which are letterpressed, as opposed to offset printed, onto sleeve; a slight recess can be felt on the letter edges.)

YOU COMB HER HAIR	(United Artists 538)	2.50	10.00	63
AIN'T IT FUNNY WHAT A FOOL WILL DO	(United Artists 578)	2.50	10.00	63
TARNISHED ANGEL/	(Mercury 72233)	2.50	10.00	64
OH LONESOME ME/Life To Go	(Mercury 72293)	2.00	8.00	64

    (Uses the same front and back as *Tender Years* but with different titles and catalog number)

THINGS HAVE GONE TO PIECES/Wearing My Heart Away	(Musicor 1067)	2.00	8.00	65
I'M A FOOL TO CARE/Louisiana Man	(Musicor 1097)	2.00	8.00	65

    (Shown as by George Jones and Gene Pitney)

YOUR OLD STANDBY/Big Job	(Musicor 1115)	2.00	8.00	65

    (Shown as by George Jones and Gene Pitney)

YOU'RE IN MY HEART	(Curio 7020)	2.50	10.00	60s

    (Shown as by George Jones and Melba Montgomery)

YA BA DA BA DO (SO ARE YOU)	(Epic 34-68743)	.75	3.00	88

EXTENDED PLAYS

INTERVIEW AND EXCERPTS	(Epic AS 44)	1.50	6.00	73

    (Promotional issue only, shown as by George Jones and Tammy Wynette)

HE STOPPED LOVING HER TODAY/STILL DOIN' TIME	(CBS AE7 1429)	1.00	4.00	82

    (Promotional issue only titled *Kickin Rock & Roll*, co-sponsored by Busch Beer and WBCN 104 FM and included in *The Phoenix* magazine. Also includes songs by Merle Haggard, Larry Gatlin and the Gatlin Brothers Band, the Burrito Brothers, Bobby Bare, and Ricky Skaggs.)

JONES, GLENN

OH GIRL/Love Me Through The Night	(Jive/RCA 5364-7-J)	.75	3.00	87
WE'VE ONLY JUST BEGUN (THE ROMANCE IS NOT OVER)/ We've Only Just Begun (The Romance Is Not Over) (Instrumental Version)	(Jive/RCA 1049-7-J)	.75	3.00	87

JONES, GRACE

SLAVE TO THE RHYTHM	(Manhattan/Island B-50020)	.75	3.00	85
I'M NOT PERFECT (BUT I'M PERFECT FOR YOU)/Scary But Fun	(Manhattan B-50052)	.75	3.00	86
CRUSH/White Collar Crime	(Manhattan B-50064)	.75	3.00	87
PARTY GIRL/Party Girl (Dub Version)	(Manhattan B-50072)	.75	3.00	87

    Also see Arcadia (Election Day)

JONES, HOWARD

NEW SONG/Conditioning	(Elektra 7-69766)	.75	3.00	83
WHAT IS LOVE?/It Just Doesn't Matter	(Elektra 7-69737)	.75	3.00	83
THINGS CAN ONLY GET BETTER/Why Look For The Key	(Elektra 7-69651)	.75	3.00	85
LIFE IN ONE DAY/Learning How To Love	(Elektra 7-69631)	.75	3.00	85
NO ONE IS TO BLAME/The Chase	(Elektra 7-69549)	.75	3.00	86
YOU KNOW I LOVE YOU...DON'T YOU?/Roll Right Up	(Elektra 7-69512)	.75	3.00	86
ALL I WANT/Dig This Well Deep	(Elektra 7-69494)	.75	3.00	86
WILL YOU STILL BE THERE/Will You Still Be There (Acoustic)	(Elektra 7-69479)	.75	3.00	87
EVERLASTING LOVE/The Brutality Of Fact	(Elektra 7-69308)	.75	3.00	89

JONES, JACK

MAKE ROOM FOR JOY	(Capitol 4161)	2.00	8.00	60
WIVES AND LOVERS/Toys In The Attic	(Kapp 551)	1.50	6.00	63

    (B-side from the motion picture *Toys In The Attic*)

LOVE WITH THE PROPER STRANGER/The Mood I'm In	(Kapp 571)	1.50	6.00	63

    (A-side from the motion picture *Love With The Proper Stranger*)

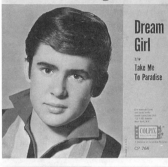

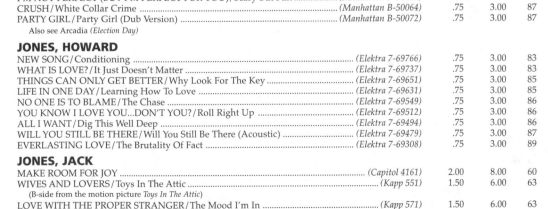

TITLE	LABEL AND NUMBER	VG	NM	YR

THE FIRST NIGHT OF THE FULL MOON .... (Kapp 589) | 1.50 | 6.00 | 64
WHERE LOVE HAS GONE .... (Kapp 608) | 1.50 | 6.00 | 64
   (From the motion picture *Where Love Has Gone*)
LULLABY FOR CHRISTMAS EVE .... (Kapp 629) | 1.50 | 6.00 | 64
DEAR HEART .... (Kapp 635) | 1.50 | 6.00 | 64
   (From the motion picture *Dear Heart*)
THE RACE IS ON .... (Kapp 651) | 1.50 | 6.00 | 65
LOVE BUG .... (Kapp 722) | 1.50 | 6.00 | 66
A DAY IN THE LIFE OF A FOOL .... (Kapp 781) | 1.50 | 6.00 | 66

JONES, JILL
MIA BOCCA .... (Paisley Park 7-28438) | .75 | 3.00 | 87
G-SPOT .... (Paisley Park 7-28280) | .75 | 3.00 | 87

JONES, JIMMY
THAT'S WHEN I CRIED / I Just Go For You .... (Cub 9072) | 7.50 | 30.00 | 60

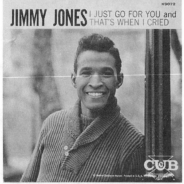

JONES, KEN
THEME FROM ROOM 43 .... (Warner Bros. 5078) | 2.50 | 10.00 | 60
   (From the motion picture *The Room*)

JONES, MICHAEL
EXTENDED PLAYS
MEXICAN MEMORIES .... (Narada S33-17254) | 1.00 | 4.00 | 86
   (Promotional issue only titled *Narada Sampler–Excellence In New Acoustic Music*, issued with a small-hole
   33-1/3 RPM record. Also includes one song each by Tingstad–Rumbel, Randy Mead, William Ellwood,
   Matthew Montfort, Spencer Brewer, David Lanz, and Gabriel Lee.)

JONES, MICK
JUST WANNA HOLD / You Are My Friend .... (Atlantic 7-88954) | .75 | 3.00 | 89
   Also see Foreigner

JONES, QUINCY
LONELY BOTTLES .... (Colgems 1016) | 2.00 | 8.00 | 68
THE LOVE THEME (FARAWAY FOREVER)(INSTRUMENTAL)/
  The Love Theme (Faraway Forever)(Vocal) .... (A&M 1404) | 1.25 | 5.00 | 73
   (From the motion picture *The Getaway*, Steve McQueen and Ali MacGraw pictured)
IS IT LOVE THAT WE'RE MISSIN' .... (A&M 1743) | 1.00 | 4.00 | 75
   (Shown as by Quincy Jones Featuring the Brothers Johnson)
"ROOTS" MEDLEY / Many Rains Ago (Oluwa) .... (A&M 1909) | 1.00 | 4.00 | 77
   (B-side featuring Letta Mbulu)
STUFF LIKE THAT .... (A&M 2043) | .75 | 3.00 | 78
I'LL BE GOOD TO YOU .... (Qwest 22697) | .75 | 3.00 | 89
   (Shown as by Quincy Jones Featuring Ray Charles and Chaka Khan)
THE SECRET GARDEN .... (Qwest 19992) | .75 | 3.00 | 90
   (Shown as by Quincy Jones, Al B. Sure, James Ingram, El DeBarge, and Barry White)
   Also see Frank Sinatra (*L.A. Is My Lady*), U.S.A. For Africa, Voices Of America

JONES, RICKIE LEE
THE REAL END .... (Warner Bros. 29191-7) | .75 | 3.00 | 84

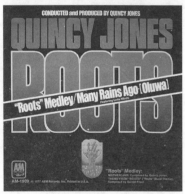

JONES, SAM
(Actor)
   See Queen (*Flash's Theme*)

JONES, SAMANTHA
I WOKE UP CRYING .... (United Artists 909) | 2.00 | 8.00 | 66

JONES, SHIRLEY
   See the Partridge Family

JONES, SPIKE, AND HIS CITY SLICKERS
I SAW MOMMY KISSING SANTA CLAUS! / Winter .... (RCA Victor 47-5067) | 7.50 | 30.00 | 53
I'M IN THE MOOD FOR LOVE / Secret Love .... (RCA Victor 47-5742) | 7.50 | 30.00 | 54

JONES, STEVE
   See Andy Taylor (*Take It Easy*)

JONES, TOM
LITTLE LONELY ONE / That's What We'll All Do .... (Tower 126) | 5.00 | 20.00 | 65
I WAS A FOOL / Lonely Joe .... (Tower 176) | 5.00 | 20.00 | 65
WHAT'S NEW PUSSYCAT? .... (Parrot 9765) | 2.00 | 8.00 | 65
   (From the motion picture *What's New Pussycat?* Front pictures caricatures of the film's cast including Peter
   Sellers, Peter O'Toole, and Woody Allen.)
WITH THESE HANDS .... (Parrot 9787) | 2.00 | 8.00 | 65
THUNDERBALL .... (Parrot 9801) | 3.75 | 15.00 | 65
   (First printing picturing a woman and a spear gun. From the motion picture *Thunderball*.)
THUNDERBALL .... (Parrot 9801) | 2.00 | 8.00 | 65
   (Second printing picturing Jones. From the motion picture *Thunderball*.)
LOVE ME TONIGHT .... (Parrot 45-40038) | 1.50 | 6.00 | 69
WITHOUT LOVE (THERE IS NOTHING) .... (Parrot/London 45-40045) | 1.50 | 6.00 | 69
DAUGHTER OF DARKNESS .... (Parrot/London 45-40048) | 1.50 | 6.00 | 70
I WHO HAVE NOTHING .... (Parrot/London 45-40051) | 1.50 | 6.00 | 70
CAN'T STOP LOVING YOU .... (Parrot/London 45-40038) | 1.50 | 6.00 | 70
SHE'S A LADY .... (Parrot/London 45-40058) | 1.50 | 6.00 | 71
PUPPET MAN .... (Parrot/London 45-40062) | 1.50 | 6.00 | 71
HIT MEDLEY / Rock And Roll Medley .... (Parrot/London DPAS 49/50) | 3.75 | 15.00 | 71
   (Promotional issue only)
   Also see the Art Of Noise (*Kiss*)

JONESES, THE
LOVE INFLATION .... (Mercury 73689) | 1.50 | 6.00 | 75

JOSEPH, IRVING
MARCH OF THE HORSE SOLDIERS .... (United Artists 178) | 1.50 | 6.00 |

JOSEPH CONSORTIUM, THE
JACOB & SONS / Any Dream Will Do .... (Scepter 12308) | 1.50 | 6.00 | 69

JOSIE, L.T.
DONNA'S GONE / I Gotta Know .... (Tower 343) | 2.00 | 8.00 | 67

JOSIE AND THE PUSSYCATS
LETTER TO MAMA / Inside, Outside, Upside Down .... (Capitol CP 58-1) | 6.25 | 25.00 | 70
WITH EVERY BEAT OF MY HEART / Josie .... (Capitol CP 59-2) | 6.25 | 25.00 | 70
VOODOO / If That Isn't Love .... (Capitol CP 60-3) | 6.25 | 25.00 | 70
I WANNA MAKE YOU HAPPY / It's Gotta Be Him .... (Capitol CP 61-4) | 6.25 | 25.00 | 72
    Also see Cheryl Ladd

JOURNEY
WHO'S CRYING NOW / Mother, Father .... (Columbia 18-02241) | .75 | 3.00 | 81
WHO'S CRYING NOW (LONG VERSION)/
   Who's Crying Now (Short Version) .... (Columbia 18-02241) | 1.00 | 4.00 | 81
   (Promotional issue, *Demonstration/Not For Sale* printed on sleeve)
DON'T STOP BELIEVIN' / Natural Thing .... (Columbia 18-02567) | .75 | 3.00 | 81
DON'T STOP BELIEVIN' .... (Columbia 18-02567) | 1.00 | 4.00 | 81
   (Promotional issue, *Demonstration–Not For Sale* printed on sleeve)
OPEN ARMS / Little Girl .... (Columbia 18-02687) | .75 | 3.00 | 81
OPEN ARMS / Little Girl .... (Columbia 18-02687) | 1.00 | 4.00 | 81
   (Promotional issue, *Demonstration Not For Sale* printed on sleeve. Sleeve lists b-side although the 45 has *Open Arms* on both sides.)

STILL THEY RIDE / La Raza Del Sol .... (Columbia 18-02883) | .75 | 3.00 | 82
STILL THEY RIDE .... (Columbia 18-02883) | 1.00 | 4.00 | 82
   (Promotional issue, *Demonstration Not For Sale* printed on sleeve)
SEPARATE WAYS (WORLDS APART) / Frontiers .... (Columbia 38-03513) | .75 | 3.00 | 83
SEPARATE WAYS (WORLDS APART) .... (Columbia 38-03513) | 1.00 | 4.00 | 83
   (Promotional issue, *Demonstration–Not For Sale* printed on sleeve)
ONLY THE YOUNG .... (Geffen 29090-7) | .75 | 3.00 | 85
   (From the motion picture *Vision Quest*)
BE GOOD TO YOURSELF .... (Columbia 38-05869) | .75 | 3.00 | 86
BE GOOD TO YOURSELF .... (Columbia 38-05869) | 1.00 | 4.00 | 86
   (Promotional issue, *Demonstration Only–Not For Sale* printed on sleeve)
SUZANNE .... (Columbia 38-06134) | .75 | 3.00 | 86
SUZANNE .... (Columbia 38-06134) | 1.00 | 4.00 | 86
   (Promotional issue, *Demonstration Only–Not For Sale* printed on sleeve)
GIRL CAN'T HELP IT .... (Columbia 38-06302) | .75 | 3.00 | 86
GIRL CAN'T HELP IT .... (Columbia 38-06302) | 1.00 | 4.00 | 86
   (Promotional issue, *Demonstration Only–Not For Sale* printed on sleeve)
I'LL BE ALRIGHT WITHOUT YOU (Hot Mix) .... (Columbia 38-06301) | .75 | 3.00 | 86
I'LL BE ALRIGHT WITHOUT YOU (Hot Mix) .... (Columbia 38-06301) | 1.00 | 4.00 | 86
   (Promotional issue, *Demonstration Only–Not For Sale* printed on sleeve)
WHY CAN'T THIS NIGHT GO ON FOREVER .... (Columbia 38-07043) | .75 | 3.00 | 87
WHY CAN'T THIS NIGHT GO ON FOREVER .... (Columbia 38-07043) | 1.00 | 4.00 | 87
   (Promotional issue, *Demonstration Only–Not For Sale* printed on sleeve)
EXTENDED PLAYS
ANY WAY YOU WANT IT .... (Columbia Special Products PV 16174) | 1.25 | 5.00 | 81
   (Promotional issue only used as an advertising tool for Nestle's $100,000 candy bar, issued with a small-hole
33-1/3 RPM record. Also includes one song each by Cheap Trick, Molly Hatchet, and REO Speedwagon.)
   Also see the Babys (Jonathan Cain), Hagar-Schon-Aaronson-Shrieve, Hear 'N Aid, Steve Perry, Gregg Rolie, Santana (Gregg Rolie, Neal Schon),
U.S.A. For Africa (Steve Perry), Voices Of America (Steve Perry)

JOURNEYMEN, THE
HERE'S RAG MAMA / I Never Will Marry .... (Capitol 4943) | 7.50 | 30.00 | 63
   Also see the Mamas and the Papas (John Philips)

JOY DIVISION
LOVE WILL TEAR US APART / These Days .... (Factory 23) | 3.00 | 12.00 | 80
KOMAKINO / Incubation .... (Factory 28) | 6.25 | 25.00 | 80
   (Numbered sleeve for flexi-disc included with the magazine *The Other Sound*)
   Also see New Order (Bernard Sumner, Peter Hook, Stephen Morris)

J'S WITH JAMIE
FOR THE LAST TIME .... (Columbia 4-42855) | 2.00 | 8.00 | 63

JUDAS PRIEST
HEADING OUT TO THE HIGHWAY /
   Rock Forever (Live) / Hell Bent For Leather (Live) .... (Columbia 11-02083) | 1.50 | 6.00 | 81
HEADING OUT TO THE HIGHWAY /
   Rock Forever (Live) / Hell Bent For Leather (Live) .... (Columbia 11-02083) | 2.00 | 8.00 | 81
   (Promotional issue, *Demonstration Not For Sale* printed on sleeve. Sleeve lists b-sides although the 45 has
Heading Out To The Highway on both sides)
SOME HEADS ARE GONNA ROLL / Breaking The Law (Live) .... (Columbia 38-04371) | 1.25 | 5.00 | 84
SOME HEADS ARE GONNA ROLL .... (Columbia 38-04371) | 1.50 | 6.00 | 84
   (Promotional issue, *Demonstration–Not For Sale* printed on sleeve)
LOCKED IN / Hot For Love .... (Columbia 38-05856) | 1.00 | 4.00 | 86
LOCKED IN .... (Columbia 38-05856) | 1.25 | 5.00 | 86
   (Promotional issue, *Demonstration–Not For Sale* printed on sleeve)
TURBO LOVER / Reckless .... (Columbia 38-06142) | 1.00 | 4.00 | 86
TURBO LOVER .... (Columbia 38-06142) | 1.25 | 5.00 | 86
   (Promotional issue only, *Demonstration–Not For Sale* printed on sleeve. Completely different design from the
stock sleeve.)
JOHNNY B. GOODE / Rock You All Around The World .... (Atlantic 7-89114) | .75 | 3.00 | 88
   (From the motion picture *Johnny Be Good*, Uma Thurman, Anthony Michael Hall, and Robert Downey, Jr.
pictured)
   Also see Hear 'N Aid

JUDE, PATRICK
STRANGERS IN A STRANGE WORLD .... (Atlantic 7-89660) | .75 | 3.00 | 84
   (Shown as by Jenny Burton and Patrick Jude. From the motion picture *Beat Street*.)

JUDGE DREAD
BIG SIX / One Armed Bandit .... (20th Century 2014) | 2.00 | 8.00 | 72

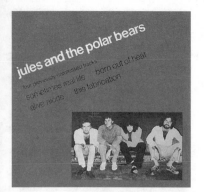

TITLE	LABEL AND NUMBER	VG	NM	YR

JUICY
BEAT STREET STRUT/Beat Street Strut (Instrumental) .... (Atlantic 7-89655) .75 3.00 84
    (From the motion picture *Beat Street*)

JULES AND THE POLAR BEARS
EXTENDED PLAYS
GOOD REASON ....(Columbia AE7-1187) 1.00 4.00 79
    (Promotional issue only titled *The Now Wave Sampler*, issued with small-hole 33-1/3 RPM record. Also includes
    one song each by the Beat, Hounds, and the Sinceros.)
SOMETIMES REAL LIFE/BORN OUT OF HEAT/
    Alive Alone/This Fabrication .... (Columbia 1-11204) 1.00 4.00 80
    (Issued with a small-hole 33-1/3 RPM record)
    Also see Reckless Sleepers, Jules Shear

JUMPING JACKS
YOU'LL WONDER WHERE THE YELLOW WENT/A Frantic Antic .... (Decca 29973) 2.50 10.00 56

JUMPIN' JACK FLASH
(Motion Picture)
    See Aretha Franklin (*Jumpin' Jack Flash*)

JUMP 'N THE SADDLE BAND
THE CURLY SHUFFLE/Jump For Joy .... (Acme 416) 1.50 6.00 83
    (The Three Stooges' Curly Howard pictured on the front)
THE CURLY SHUFFLE/Jump For Joy .... (Atlantic 7-89718) 1.00 4.00 83
    (Dance steps art on the front)

JUNGKLAS, ROB
MAKE IT MEAN SOMETHING/Memphis Thing .... (Manhattan B50054) .75 3.00 86

JUNIOR
    See Kim Wilde (*Another Step*)

JUNIOR
SAY THAT YOU CARE .... (London 886 331-7) .75 3.00 88

JUNKYARD DOG WITH VICKIE SUE ROBINSON
GRAB THEM CAKES/Captain Lou's History Of Music .... (Epic 34-05688) .75 3.00 85
    (B-side shown as by Captain Lou Albano)
GRAB THEM CAKES .... (Epic 34-05688) 1.00 4.00 85
    (Promotional issue, *Demonstration–Not For Sale* printed on back)

JUSTICE
(Television Series)
    See Gisele MacKenzie (*Hard To Get*)

JUSTIS, BILL
I'M GONNA LEARN TO DANCE/Tamoure .... (Smash 1812) 2.50 10.00 63

JUST US
WHAT ARE WE GONNA DO .... (Kapp 853) 2.50 10.00 67

K

KAEMPFERT, BERT
BYE BYE BLUES .... (Decca 31882) 2.00 8.00 66

KAHN, MADELINE
(Comic Actress)
    See Frankie Laine (*Blazing Saddles*)

KAJAGOOGOO
TOO SHY/Take Another View .... (EMI America B-8161) 1.00 4.00 82
HANG ON NOW/Kajagoogoo (Instrumental) .... (EMI America B-8171) .75 3.00 83
TURN YOUR BACK ON ME/The Pump Rooms Of Bath .... (EMI America B-8262) .75 3.00 84
    (Shown as by Kaja)
    Also see Limahl

KALIN TWINS, THE
WHY DON'T YOU BELIEVE/The Meaning Of The Blues .... (Decca 30997) 3.75 15.00 59

KALLEN, KITTY
IT'S NOT THE WHISTLE .... (Decca 290) 3.75 15.00 55

KAMEN, NICK
EACH TIME YOU BREAK MY HEART .... (Sire 28435-7) 1.00 4.00 86
    (Madonna and Kamen pictured on back)
NOBODY ELSE .... (Sire 28295-7) .75 3.00 87
    Also see Ferry Aid

KAMON, KAREN
LOVERBOY/You Can Do Better Than That .... (Columbia 38-04474) .75 3.00 84
LOVERBOY .... (Columbia 38-04474) 1.00 4.00 84
    (Promotional issue, *Demonstration–Not For Sale* printed on sleeve)
DA DOO RON RON/When You Got A Woman .... (Columbia 38-04597) .75 3.00 84
DA DOO RON RON .... (Columbia 38-04597) 1.00 4.00 84
    (Promotional issue, *Demonstration–Not For Sale* printed on sleeve)

KANE, BIG DADDY
I'LL TAKE YOU THERE .... (Cold Chillin' 7-27708) .75 3.00 88

KANE, MADLEEN
ROUGH DIAMOND .... (Warner Bros. 8573) 1.25 5.00 78

KANE GANG, THE
MOTORTOWN .... (Capitol 44062) .75 3.00 87

TITLE	LABEL AND NUMBER	VG	NM	YR

143

KANSAS
RIGHT AWAY / Windows	(Kirshner ZS5-03084)	1.25	5.00	82
FIGHT FIRE WITH FIRE / Incident On A Bridge	(CBS Associated ZS4-04057)	1.00	4.00	83
FIGHT FIRE WITH FIRE / Incident On A Bridge	(CBS Associated ZS4-04057)	1.25	5.00	83

(Promotional issue, *Demonstration Only–Not For Sale* printed on sleeve. Sleeve lists b-side although the 45 has *Fight Fire With Fire* on both sides)

| EVERYBODY'S MY FRIEND / End Of The Age | (CBS Associated ZS4-04213) | 1.00 | 4.00 | 83 |
| EVERYBODY'S MY FRIEND | (CBS Associated ZS4-04213) | 1.25 | 5.00 | 83 |

(Promotional issue, *Demonstration Only–Not For Sale* printed on sleeve)

ALL I WANTED	(MCA 52958)	.75	3.00	86
CAN'T CRY ANYMORE	(MCA 53070)	.75	3.00	87
POWER	(MCA 53027)	.75	3.00	87
STAND BESIDE ME	(MCA 53425)	.75	3.00	88

KANYE, MORY
| YE KE YE KE | (Polydor 887 048-7) | .75 | 3.00 | 87 |

KANTNER, PAUL
| SUNFIGHTER / China | (Grunt 65-0503) | 1.50 | 6.00 | 72 |

(Shown as by Paul Kantner & Grace Slick)

| A CHILD IS COMING / Lets Go Together | (RCA 74-0426) | 1.00 | 4.00 | 83 |

Also see Jefferson Airplane, Jefferson Starship, KBC Band

KAPLAN, GABRIEL
(Comedian who starred in the television series *Welcome Back Kotter* from 1975-1978)
| UP YOUR NOSE / Bye Centennial Minutes | (Elektra 45369) | 1.25 | 5.00 | 77 |

KAPRISKY, VALERIE
(Actress)
See X (*Breathless*)

KARATE KID PART II
(Motion Picture)
See Peter Cetera (*Glory Of Love*)

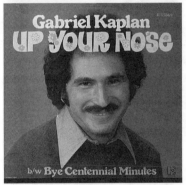

KAREN, KENNY
| OH SUSIE, FORGIVE ME | (Columbia 4-42264) | 3.75 | 15.00 | 62 |
| TO SANDY, WITH LOVE | (Columbia 4-43452) | 3.75 | 15.00 | 62 |

KAREN AND CUBBY
(Mouseketeers from the television series *The Mickey Mouse Club*)
| BIDIN' MY TIME / What The Well Dressed Hobo Will Wear | (Mickey Mouse Club DBR-75) | 2.50 | 10.00 | 62 |

KASHIF
| LOVE ON THE RISE / Virgin Island | (Arista 9336) | 1.00 | 4.00 | 85 |

(Shown as by Kenny G & Kashif)

| CONDITION OF THE HEART / Help Yourself To My Love (Live Version) | (Arista 9415) | .75 | 3.00 | 85 |
| LOVE CHANGES / Midnight Mood | (Arista 9626) | .75 | 3.00 | 87 |

(A-side shown as by Kashif + Meli'sa Morgan, both pictured)

| RESERVATIONS FOR TWO / For Everything You Are | (Arista 9638) | .75 | 3.00 | 87 |

(A-side shown as by Dionne Warwick and Kashif, b-side by Warwick. Warwick pictured on front and Kashif on back.)

| I'M IN LOVE | (Capitol B-44195) | .75 | 3.00 | 88 |

(Shown as by Melba Moore and Kashif)

| AIN'T NO WOMAN (LIKE THE ONE I GOT) / My Door | (Arista 9926) | .75 | 3.00 | 90 |

KATRINA & THE WAVES
WALKING ON SUNSHINE / Going Down To Liverpool	(Capitol B-5466)	.75	3.00	85
DO YOU WANT CRYING	(Capitol B-5450)	.75	3.00	85
QUE TE QUIERO (KAY-TEH-KEY-AIRO)	(Capitol B-5528)	.75	3.00	85
IS THAT IT?	(Capitol B-5566)	.75	3.00	86
SUN STREET	(Capitol B-5593)	.75	3.00	86
THAT'S THE WAY / Love Calculator	(SBK B-07303)	.75	3.00	89
ROCK N' ROLL GIRL / Rene (Live Version)	(SBK B-07310)	.75	3.00	89

KAYAK
| KEEP THE CHANGE | (Janus 278) | 1.00 | 4.00 | 79 |

KAYE, DANNY
| THE LITTLE WHITE DUCK / The Thing | (Decca 9-27350) | 3.75 | 15.00 | 51 |
| THE FIVE PENNIES SAINTS / Just The Blues | (Dot 45-15941) | 3.75 | 15.00 | 59 |

(Shown as by Danny Kaye and Louis Armstrong, from the motion picture *The Five Pennies*)

| D-O-D-G-E-R-S SONG (OH, REALLY? NO, O'MALLEY) / Myti Kaysi At The Bat | (Reprise 20,105) | 3.75 | 15.00 | 62 |
| THE PRINCESS AND THE PEA / The Tinderbox | (Wonderland WDP2014) | 2.00 | 8.00 | 66 |

(Hard cover, children's series)
Also see Red Nichols (*Selmer Sampler*)

KAYE, DEBBIE
| SOLDIER BOY | (Columbia 4-43454) | 2.50 | 10.00 | 66 |

KAYE, LENNY
| CHILD BRIDE / Tracks Of My Tears (Live) | (Mer 604) | 3.00 | 12.00 | 80 |

Also see Patti Smith (Kaye was a member of the Patti Smith Group)

KAYE, MARY, TRIO
See Edward Byrnes (*Kookie's Love Song*)

KAYE, SAMMIE
| I'M A BRASS BAND | (Decca 32442) | 2.00 | 8.00 | 68 |

KAYE, STUBBY
See Nat King Cole

KBC BAND
| IT'S NOT YOU, IT'S NOT ME / Dream Motorcycle | (Arista 9526) | .75 | 3.00 | 86 |
| AMERICA / Wrecking Crew | (Arista 9572) | .75 | 3.00 | 87 |

Also see Marty Balin, Jefferson Airplane, Jefferson Starship, Paul Kantner, Paul Kantner, SVT (Jack Casady)

TITLE	LABEL AND NUMBER	VG	NM	YR

KC AND THE SUNSHINE BAND
KEEP IT COMIN' LOVE/Baby I Love You ...... (TK 1023)		1.25	5.00	77
BOOGIE SHOES/I Get Lifted ...... (TK 1025)		1.25	5.00	78
(A-side featured in the motion picture *Saturday Night Fever*)				
IT'S THE SAME OLD SONG/ ...... (TK 1028)		1.25	5.00	78
DO YOU FEEL ALL RIGHT/I Will Love You Tomorrow ...... (TK 1030)		1.25	5.00	78
WHO DO YA LOVE/Sho-Nuff ...... (TK 1031)		1.25	5.00	78

KEATON, MICHAEL
(Actor)
    See Buster Poindexter (*Hit The Road Jack*)

KEEL
BECAUSE THE NIGHT ...... (MCA/Gold Mountain 52783)		.75	3.00	86
TEARS OF FIRE ...... (MCA/Gold Mountain 52861)		.75	3.00	86

KEENE, TOMMY
LISTEN TO ME/Faith In Love ...... (Geffen 28678-7)		.75	3.00	86
Also see Bruce Springstone				

KEITH
98.6 ...... (Mercury 72639)		2.00	8.00	66
TELL ME TO MY FACE ...... (Mercury 72652)		2.00	8.00	67
DAYLIGHT SAVIN' TIME ...... (Mercury 72695)		1.50	6.00	67
SUGAR MAN ...... (Mercury 72715)		1.50	6.00	67
CANDY CANDY/I'm So Proud ...... (Mercury 72746)		1.50	6.00	67
THE PLEASURE OF YOUR COMPANY ...... (Mercury 72794)		1.50	6.00	68

KEITH, DAVID
    See Elvis Presley (b-side of *Heartbreak Hotel*)

KEITH, LISA
    See Herb Alpert (*Diamonds, Making Love In The Rain*)

KELLER, JERRY
HERE COMES SUMMER/Time Has A Way ...... (Kapp 277)		5.00	20.00	59
IF I HAD A GIRL/Lovable ...... (Kapp 295)		5.00	20.00	59

KELLY, PAUL
I NEED YOUR LOVE SO BAD/Nine Out Of Ten Times ...... (Philips 40409)		3.75	15.00	66

KENDRICKS, EDDIE
    See Daryl Hall & John Oates (*The Way You Do The Things You Do*), the Temptations

KENNEDY, JOHN FITZGERALD, PRESIDENT
VOICE OF THE PRESIDENT/Inaugural Address, January 20, 1961 ...... (Golden 766)		2.50	10.00	60s
(A-side is Kennedy's acceptance speech from July 15, 1960 and oath of office from January 20, 1961)				
Also see the Sickniks				

KENNEDY, JOYCE
STRONGER THAN BEFORE/Chain Reaction ...... (A&M 2685)		.75	3.00	84

KENNEDY, RAY
JUST FOR THE MOMENT/Isn't It Time? ...... (ARC/Columbia 1-11242)		1.00	4.00	80
(Promotional issue only, *Demonstration–Not For Sale* printed on sleeve)				

KENNEDY, ROBERT F.
    See Andy Williams (*Battle Hymn Of The Republic*)

KENNY & CORKY
NUTTIN' FOR CHRISTMAS/Suzy Snowflake ...... (Big Top 3031)		1.25	5.00	78

KENNY G
LOVE ON THE RISE/Virgin Island ...... (Arista 9336)		1.00	4.00	85
(Shown as by Kenny G & Kashif)				
DON'T MAKE ME WAIT FOR LOVE/Esther ...... (Arista 9544)		1.00	4.00	86
SONGBIRD ...... (Arista 9573)		1.25	5.00	87
(Promotional issue, black and gray artwork on front with a white border)				
SONGBIRD/Midnight Motion ...... (Arista 9588)		.75	3.00	87
(Black and gold artwork bleeds all 4 sides on front. Note the different catalog numbers.)				
DON'T MAKE ME WAIT FOR LOVE/Midnight Motion ...... (Arista 9625)		.75	3.00	87
(A-side vocal by Lenny Williams, credited on front)				
DON'T MAKE ME WAIT FOR LOVE/Midnight Motion ...... (Arista 9625)		.75	3.00	87
AGAINST DOCTOR'S ORDERS ...... (Arista 9630)		.75	3.00	88
SILHOUETTE/Home ...... (Arista 9751)		.75	3.00	88
WE'VE SAVED THE BEST FOR LAST/Silhouette ...... (Arista 9785)		.75	3.00	88
(A-side credits *Vocal By Smokey Robinson*, both pictured on front)				
Also see the Four Tops (*If Ever A Love There Was*), Aretha Franklin (*It Isn't, It Wasn't, It Ain't Never Gonna Be*), Smokey Robinson (*One Heartbeat*)				

KENT, KLARK
(Stewart Copeland)
DON'T CARE/Thrills/Office Girls ...... (Kryptone 1)		1.50	6.00	80
(Hard cover issued with small-hole, green vinyl)				
AWAY FROM HOME/Office Talk ...... (I.R.S./Kryptone 9012)		1.25	5.00	80
(Issued with small-hole, green vinyl)				
Also see Stewart Copeland, the Police				

KENTON, STAN
STAN KENTON PROLOGUE: THIS IS AN ORCHESTRA ...... (Capitol # unknown)		5.00	20.00	50s
MAMA SANG A SONG ...... (Creative World ST 45-1075)		1.25	5.00	70s

KERCHEVAL, KEN
(Actor)
    See Floyd Cramer (*Theme From Dallas*)

KERNS, JOANNA
(Actress)
    See Steve Dorff and Friends (*Theme From Growing Pains*)

KERR, DEBORAH
(Actress)
    See Ray Bloch & Orchestra *(From Here To Eternity)*

KERSEY, PAUL
(Actor)
    See the Soaps and Hearts Ensemble

KERSHAW, NIK

WOULDN'T IT BE GOOD	(MCA 52371)	1.00	4.00	84
THE RIDDLE/Progress	(MCA 52544)	.75	3.00	84
WIDE BOY/So Quiet	(MCA 52601)	.75	3.00	85

    Also see Ferry Aid

KESSLER, KEITH

DON'T CROWD ME/Sunshine Morning	(M.T.W. 102)	3.00	12.00	60s

KEY WITNESS
(Motion Picture)
    See Tobin Matthews *(Ruby Duby Du)*

KHAN, CHAKA

I'M EVERY WOMAN/A Woman In A Man's World	(Warner Bros. 8683)	1.25	5.00	78
(Shown as by Chaka)				
CLOUDS	(Warner Bros. 49216)	1.50	6.00	80
I FEEL FOR YOU/Chinatown	(Warner Bros. 29195-7)	1.00	4.00	84
THIS IS MY NIGHT	(Warner Bros. 29097-7)	1.00	4.00	84
THE OTHER SIDE OF THE WORLD/ The Other Side Of The World (Instrumental)	(Atlantic 89449-7)	1.00	4.00	85
OWN THE NIGHT	(MCA 52730)	1.00	4.00	85
(From the television series *Miami Vice*, Don Johnson and Philip Michael-Thomas pictured on back)				
(KRUSH GROOVE) CAN'T STOP THE STREET	(Warner Bros. 28923-7)	1.00	4.00	85
(From the motion picture *Krush Groove*)				
LOVE OF A LIFETIME	(Warner Bros. 28671-7)	.75	3.00	86
TIGHT FIT	(Warner Bros. 28576-7)	.75	3.00	86
IT'S MY PARTY	(Warner Bros. 27678-7)	.75	3.00	88

    Also see Quincy Jones *(I'll Be Good To You)*, Rufus

KHAN, SAJID
(Juvenile Actor)

SOMEDAY/Dream	(Colgems 1034)	2.50	10.00	68

KIARA

THIS TIME/Wait So Long	(Arista 9772)	.75	3.00	89
(Shown as by Kiara & Shanice Wilson)				
EVERY LITTLE TIME/	(Arista 9800)	.75	3.00	89

KID BROTHER

TELL ME ANOTHER ONE	(MCA 41111)	1.00	4.00	79

KID CREOLE AND THE COCONUTS

THERE BUT FOR THE GRACE OF GOD GO I/He's Not Such A Bad Guy (After All)	(Antilles 103)	1.25	5.00	80
(Issued with small-hole 45 RPM record)				
ANNIE, I'M NOT YOUR DADDY/Imitation	(Sire/Ze 29738-7)	.75	3.00	83
HEY MAMBO/When October Goes	(Arista 9666)	.75	3.00	88
(A-side shown as by Barry Manilow with Kid Creole and the Coconuts, b-side by Barry Manilow. Manilow and Kid Creole pictured.)				
PEOPLE WILL TALK/Another Tribe	(Elektra Musician 7-69306)	.75	3.00	89
(A-side from the motion picture *New York Stories*)				

    Also see the Coconuts

KIDS FROM FAME, THE

BE YOUR OWN HERO	(RCA 13372)	1.25	5.00	82
(From the television series *Fame*, entire cast pictured)				

KIDS IN THE KITCHEN

CURRENT STAND	(Sire 28726-7)	.75	3.00	86

KIDS NEXT DOOR, THE

INKY DINKY SPIDER	(4 Corners of the World 129)	2.50	10.00	65

KIHN, GREG

LOVE'S MADE A FOOL OF YOU/Sorry	(Beserkley B-5744)	1.25	5.00	76
THE BREAKUP SONG (THEY DON'T WRITE 'EM)/When The Music Starts	(Beserkley B-47149)	1.00	4.00	81
(Shown as by Greg Kihn Band)				
HAPPY MAN/Trouble In Paradise	(Beserkley B-47463)	1.00	4.00	82
(Shown as by Greg Kihn Band)				
LUCKY/Sad Situation	(EMI America B-8255)	.75	3.00	85
BOYS WON'T (LEAVE THE GIRLS ALONE)	(EMI America B-8272)	.75	3.00	85

EXTENDED PLAYS

MADISON AVENUE	(Beserkley AE7-1120)	1.25	5.00	77
(Promotional issue only titled *Great Ideas From Beserkley*, issued with a small-hole 33-1/3 RPM record. Also includes 1 song each, the titles are not listed on sleeve, by the Rubinoos, Earthquake, and Jonathan Richman & the Modern Lovers.)				

KILZER, JOHN

MEMORY IN THE MAKING/Maria	(Geffen 27775-7)	.75	3.00	88

KIM, ANDY

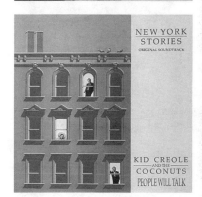

SO GOOD TOGETHER/I Got To Know	(Steed 720)	1.50	6.00	69
A FRIEND IN THE CITY	(Steed 723)	1.50	6.00	70
I BEEN MOVED	(Steed 734)	1.50	6.00	71
FIRE, BABY I'M ON FIRE/Here Comes The Mornin'	(Capitol 3962)	1.25	5.00	74

KIMMEL, TOM

THAT'S FREEDOM/No Tech	(Mercury 888 571-7)	.75	3.00	87
TRYIN' TO DANCE/On The Defensive	(Mercury 888-803-7)	.75	3.00	87

TITLE	LABEL AND NUMBER	VG	NM	YR

KING
LOVE & PRIDE / Don't Stop .... (Epic 34-04917) | .75 | 3.00 | 84
LOVE & PRIDE .... (Epic 34-04917) | 1.00 | 4.00 | 84
   (Promotional issue, *Demonstration Only–Not For Sale* printed on sleeve)
ALONE WITHOUT YOU / Crazy Party .... (Epic 34-05843) | .75 | 3.00 | 86
ALONE WITHOUT YOU .... (Epic 34-05843) | 1.00 | 4.00 | 86
   (Promotional issue, *Demonstration Only–Not For Sale* printed on sleeve)
   Also see Ferry Aid, Paul King

KING, B. B.
THE THRILL IS GONE / You're Mean .... (ABC BluesWay 61032) | 3.00 | 12.00 | 69
INTO THE NIGHT .... (MCA 52530) | 1.00 | 4.00 | 85
MY LUCILLE .... (MCA 52574) | 1.00 | 4.00 | 85
HABIT TO ME .... (MCA 53269) | 1.00 | 4.00 | 88
WHEN LOVE COMES TO TOWN / Dancing Barefoot .... (Island 7-99225) | 1.00 | 4.00 | 89
   (Shown as by U2 With BB King, hard cover)

KING, BEN E.
STAND BY ME / Yakety Yak .... (Atlantic 7-89361) | .75 | 3.00 | 86
   (B-side shown as by the Coasters. From the motion picture *Stand By Me*.)
STAND BY ME .... (Atlantic 7-89361) | 1.50 | 6.00 | 86
   (Promotional issue with the same artwork on the front but different graphics on the back. From the motion
   picture *Stand By Me*.)
SAVE THE LAST DANCE FOR ME .... (Manhattan PB-50078) | .75 | 3.00 | 87
   Also see the Soul Clan

KING, CAROLE
IT'S TOO LATE / I Feel The Earth Move .... (Ode 66015) | 1.25 | 5.00 | 71
SO FAR AWAY / Smackwater Jack .... (Ode 66019) | 1.25 | 5.00 | 71
SWEET SEASONS / Pocket Money .... (Ode 66022) | 1.25 | 5.00 | 72
BEEN TO CANAAN / Bitter With The Sweet .... (Ode 66031) | 1.25 | 5.00 | 72
YOU LIGHT UP MY LIFE / Believe In Humanity .... (Ode 66035) | 1.25 | 5.00 | 73
JAZZMAN / You Go Your Way, I'll Go Mine .... (Ode 66101) | 1.25 | 5.00 | 74
PIERRE / Chicken Soup With Rice .... (Ode 66112SP) | 1.50 | 6.00 | 75
   (Issued with a small-hole 33-1/3 RPM record)
HARD ROCK CAFE .... (Capitol 4455) | 1.25 | 5.00 | 77
MOVE LIGHTLY / Whiskey .... (Capitol 4718) | 1.25 | 5.00 | 79
ONE FINE DAY / Recipients Of History .... (Capitol 4864) | 2.00 | 8.00 | 80
   (Sleeve was printed with the wrong b-side title. The record shows b-side title as *Rulers Of This World*)
ONE FINE DAY .... (Capitol 4864) | 1.00 | 4.00 | 80
   (Second printing eliminating b-side from sleeve)
ONE TO ONE / Goat Annie .... (Atlantic 4026) | 1.00 | 4.00 | 82
CITY STREETS / Time Heals All Wounds .... (Capitol B-44336) | 1.00 | 4.00 | 89
CITY STREETS .... (Capitol 7PRO-79520) | 1.50 | 6.00 | 89
   (Promotional issue, *Promotional Use Only Not For Sale* printed on sleeve)

KING, CLAUDE
THE COMANCHEROS / .... (Columbia 4-42196) | 2.00 | 8.00 | 61
WOLVERTON MOUNTAIN / Little Bitty Heart .... (Columbia 4-42352) | 2.00 | 8.00 | 62
THE BURNING OF ATLANTA / .... (Columbia 4-42581) | 2.00 | 8.00 | 62
I'VE GOT THE WORLD BY THE TAIL / .... (Columbia 4-42630) | 2.00 | 8.00 | 63
SHEEPSKIN VALLEY / I Backed Out .... (Columbia 4-42688) | 2.00 | 8.00 | 63
BUILDING A BRIDGE / .... (Columbia 4-42782) | 2.00 | 8.00 | 63
HEY LUCILLE / Scarlet O'Hara .... (Columbia 4-42833) | 2.00 | 8.00 | 63
ALL FOR THE LOVE OF A GIRL / .... (Columbia 4-44833) | 2.00 | 8.00 | 69

KING, EVELYN "CHAMPAGNE"
I DON'T KNOW IF IT'S RIGHT .... (RCA PB-11386) | 1.25 | 5.00 | 77
I'M IN LOVE .... (RCA PB-12243) | 1.00 | 4.00 | 81
JUST FOR THE NIGHT / So In Love .... (RCA PB-13914) | 1.00 | 4.00 | 84
YOUR PERSONAL TOUCH / Talking In My Sleep .... (RCA PB-14201) | 1.00 | 4.00 | 85
FLIRT .... (Manhattan 50101) | .75 | 3.00 | 88

KING, JEAN
WATERMELON MAN / The In Crowd .... (Hanna Barbera 463) | 2.00 | 8.00 | 66

KING, MARTIN LUTHER, JR., REV.
I'VE BEEN TO THE MOUNTAIN TOP / EULOGY / I Have A Dream .... (Mercury 72814) | 6.25 | 25.00 | 65
   Also see U2 (*Pride*)

KING, MORGANA
YOU ARE THE SUNSHINE OF MY LIFE .... (Paramount 245) | 1.25 | 5.00 | 73

KING, PAUL
I KNOW / .... (Epic 34-07138) | .75 | 3.00 | 87
I KNOW .... (Epic 34-07138) | 1.00 | 4.00 | 87
   (Promotional issue, *Demonstration–Not For Sale* printed on sleeve)
   Also see Ferry Aid, King

KING, PERRY
BON VOYAGE .... (Buena Vista 397) | 2.50 | 10.00 | 62

KINGBEES
WHAT SHE DOES TO ME / That Ain't Love .... (RCA Victor 47-8688) | 10.00 | 40.00 | 65

KINGBEES, THE
SHE CAN'T 'MAKE-UP' HER MIND / Stick It Out! .... (RSO 1062) | 1.00 | 4.00 | 81

KING CURTIS
YOUR CHEATIN' HEART / Beautiful Brown Eyes .... (Capitol 4841) | 5.00 | 20.00 | 62
BILL BAILEY / Soul Twine .... (Capitol 5377) | 3.00 | 12.00 | 65

KINGDOM COME
GET IT ON / 17 .... (Polydor 887 436-7) | .75 | 3.00 | 88
WHAT LOVE CAN BE / The Shuffle .... (Polydor 887 570-7) | .75 | 3.00 | 88
   Also see Stone Fury (Lenny Wolf)

KING FLASH
ZOMBIE JAMBOREE .... (Columbia 4-40866)	2.50	10.00	58

KING FLOYD
BABY LET ME KISS YOU .... (Chimneyville 437)	1.50	6.00	71

KING GUIM
MONTE CARLO .... (Canadian American 170)	2.00	8.00	63

KING KOBRA
HUNGER .... (Capitol B-5449)	.75	3.00	85

Also see Hear 'N Aid, Vanilla Fudge (Carmen Appice)

KINGSMEN, THE
THE KRUNCH/The Climb .... (Wand 1118)	6.25	25.00	66

Also see Don and the Goodtimes (Don Gallucci)

KINGS OF THE SUN
BLACK LEATHER/Bad Love .... (RCA 8646-7-R)	.75	3.00	88

KINGSTON TRIO, THE
MOLLY DEE/Haul Away .... (Capitol Special Products 2782/3)	6.25	25.00	59

(Promotional issue only for the New March Of Dimes)

FAREWELL ADELITA/Corey, Corey .... (Capitol Special Products 2006/7)	6.25	25.00	60

(Promotional issue only. Sleeve reads *A Collector's Record Made Expressly For Lion Of Troy Shirt Customers By The Kingston Trio.*)

EL MATADOR/Home From The Hill .... (Capitol 4338)	5.00	20.00	60
SOMERSET GLOUCESTERSHIRE WASSAIL/Goodnight My Baby .... (Capitol 4475)	5.00	20.00	60
SCOTCH AND SODA/Jane, Jane, Jane .... (Capitol 4740)	3.75	15.00	62
ONE MORE TOWN/She Was Good To Me .... (Capitol 4842)	3.75	15.00	62
GREENBACK DOLLAR/The New Frontier .... (Capitol 4898)	3.75	15.00	63
A SURPRISE GIFT FROM THE BEATLES, THE BEACH BOYS & THE KINGSTON TRIO .... (Capitol/Evatone 8464)	500.00	2000.00	64

(6" x 9" mailer issued with a 5" flexidisc)

MY RAMBLIN' BOY/Hope You Understand .... (Decca 31702)	5.00	20.00	64
STAY AWHILE/Yes, I Can Feel It .... (Decca 31790)	5.00	20.00	65
RUNAWAY SONG/Parchment Farm (Blues) .... (Decca 31860)	5.00	20.00	65
LOOKING FOR THE SUNSHINE/Reverend Mr. Black .... (Xeres 10004)	1.00	4.00	82

Also see John Stewart

KING SWAMP
IS THIS LOVE?/Glow .... (Virgin 7-99212)	.75	3.00	89

KINKS, THE
SLEEPWALKER/All The Kids On The Street .... (Arista SP-5)	3.75	15.00	77

(Promotional issue only, flip side shown as by the Hollywood Stars. Issued with yellow vinyl.)

FATHER CHRISTMAS .... (Arista 0296)	1.25	5.00	77
FATHER CHRISTMAS/(Wish I Could Fly Like) Superman .... (Arista Flashback 106)	2.00	8.00	80

(Promotional issue given away at their 1980 New Year's Eve performance at the Palladium)

CELLULOID HEROES/Lola .... (Arista 0541)	1.25	5.00	80

(*Celluloid Heroes* listed as the a-side and failed to make the Billboard Top 100 but *Lola* managed to chart at #81)

COME DANCING/Noise .... (Arista 1054)	1.00	4.00	83
COME DANCING/Noise .... (Arista 9016)	1.00	4.00	83

(Identical to previous sleeve with the exception of the catalog number)

DO IT AGAIN/Guilty .... (Arista 9309)	1.00	4.00	84
ROCK 'N' ROLL CITIES .... (MCA 52960)	.75	3.00	86
LOST AND FOUND .... (MCA 53015)	.75	3.00	87

Also see Dave Davies

KIRBY, PETE OSWALD
See Nitty Gritty Dirt Band (*Honky Tonkin'*)

KIRK, JIM, AND THE TM SINGERS
VOICE OF FREEDOM/Star Spangled Banner .... (Capitol 4834)	1.00	4.00	80

KIRK, TOMMY
See Annette (*Bella Bella Florence, Merlin Jones*)

KISS
FLAMING YOUTH .... (Casablanca NB 858)	7.50	30.00	75
I LOVE IT LOUD .... (Casablanca NB2365)	3.00	12.00	82
TEARS ARE FALLING/Anyway You Slice It .... (Mercury 884 141-7 M-1)	1.25	5.00	85
CRAZY CRAZY NIGHTS/No, No, No .... (Mercury 888-796-7)	1.25	5.00	87
TURN ON THE NIGHT/Hell Or High Water .... (Mercury 870 215-7)	1.25	5.00	87
REASON TO LIVE/Thief In The Night .... (Mercury 870 022-7)	1.25	5.00	87
LET'S PUT THE X IN SEX/Calling Dr. Love .... (Mercury 872 246-7)	1.25	5.00	88

Also see Ace Frehley, the Mighty Mighty Bosstones (*Detroit Rock City*), Vinnie Vincent Invasion (Vinnie Vincent). Eric Singer, formerly of Badlands, joined Kiss in 1991.

KISSIN' COUSINS
(Motion Picture)
See Elvis Presley (*Kissin' Cousins*)

KISSING THE PINK
See KTP

KITT, EARTHA
SANTA BABY/Under The Bridges Of Paris .... (RCA Victor 47-5502)	5.00	20.00	54
(THIS YEAR'S) SANTA BABY .... (RCA Victor 47-5914)	5.00	20.00	55

KIX
GET IT WHILE IT'S HOT/Don't Close Your Eyes .... (Atlantic 7-88902)	.75	3.00	89

KLAATU
MADMAN/Around The Universe In Eighty Days .... (Capitol SPRO 8697)	2.50	10.00	77

(Promotional issue only, no group name or song titles listed. *Dear Programmer: Capitol Records is now readying...* statement on front, issued with a small-hole 33-1/3 RPM record.)

WE'RE OFF YOU KNOW/Around The Universe In Eighty Days .... (Capitol 4516)	1.50	6.00	77

TITLE	LABEL AND NUMBER	VG	NM	YR

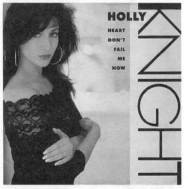

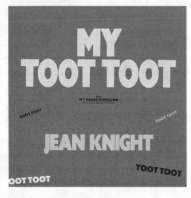

KLEMMER, JOHN
See Dan Siegel (b-side of *Friday*)

KLF, THE
See the Timelords

KLOVER
COMMON FACTOR/Nothing .... (Mercury PRO 1189-7) — 1.25 — 5.00 — 95
(Promotional issue only with small-hole, red vinyl)

KLOWNS, THE
LADY LOVE .... (RCA 74-0393) — 1.50 — 6.00 — 70

KLUGH, EARL
DREAMIN' .... (Warner Bros. 28244-7) — .50 — 2.00 — 86
(Shown as by George Benson & Earl Klugh)

KLYMAXX
MEETING IN THE LADIES ROOM/Ask Me No Questions .... (MCA/Constellation 52545) — .75 — 3.00 — 85
THE MEN ALL PAUSE .... (MCA/Constellation 52486) — .75 — 3.00 — 85
MAN SIZE LOVE .... (MCA 52841) — .75 — 3.00 — 85
(From the motion picture *Running Scared*)
I'D STILL SAY YES .... (MCA/Constellation 53028) — .75 — 3.00 — 87
DIVAS NEED LOVE TOO .... (MCA/Constellation 53117) — .75 — 3.00 — 87

KNACK, THE
TIME WAITS FOR NO ONE/I'm Aware .... (Capitol 5774) — 3.75 — 15.00 — 67

KNACK, THE
MY SHARONA/Let Me Out .... (Capitol 4731) — 2.00 — 8.00 — 79
GOOD GIRLS DON'T/Frustrated .... (Capitol 4771) — 1.50 — 6.00 — 79
BABY TALKS DIRTY/End Of The Game .... (Capitol 4822) — 2.50 — 10.00 — 80
PAY THE DEVIL (OOO BABY OOO) .... (Capitol A-5054) — 1.25 — 5.00 — 81
MY SHARONA/Tempted .... (A&M/RCA/Capitol 62800-7) — 1.00 — 4.00 — 94
(Both songs listed as the a-side, *Tempted* shown as by Squeeze. From the motion picture *Reality Bites*.)
MY SHARONA/Tempted .... (A&M/RCA/Capitol 62800-7) — 2.00 — 8.00 — 94
(Promotional issue with either brown or black vinyl. Both songs listed as the a-side, *Tempted* shown as by Squeeze. From the motion picture *Reality Bites*.)
Also see the Sunset Bombers (Doug Feiger)

KNIEVEL, EVEL
See John Culliton Mahoney (*The Ballad Of Evel Knievel*)

KNIGHT, CHRIS
(Juvenile actor who played Peter Brady in the television series *The Brady Bunch*)
OVER AND OVER/Good For Each Other .... (Paramount 0177) — 3.00 — 12.00 — 72
Also see the Brady Bunch

KNIGHT, GLADYS, AND THE PIPS
WHERE PEACEFUL WATERS FLOW/Perfect Love .... (Buddah 363) — 1.50 — 6.00 — 73
ON AND ON/The Makings Of You .... (Buddah 423) — 1.50 — 6.00 — 74
(From the motion picture *Claudine*)
SILENT NIGHT/Do You Hear What I Hear .... (Buddah 1974) — 1.50 — 6.00 — 74
FOREVER YESTERDAY (FOR THE CHILDREN) .... (Columbia 11-02113) — 1.00 — 4.00 — 81
THAT'S WHAT FRIENDS ARE FOR/Two Ships Passing In The Night .... (Arista 9422) — .75 — 3.00 — 85
(Shown as by Dionne & Friends Featuring Elton John, Gladys Knight and Stevie Wonder. Warwick, John, Knight, and Wonder pictured on front. Warwick, John, Knight, Wonder, and the song's authors, Burt Bacharach and Carole Bayer Sager, pictured on back.)
MY TIME/My Time (Instrumental) .... (Columbia 38-04761) — .75 — 3.00 — 85
MY TIME/My Time (Instrumental) .... (Columbia 38-04761) — 1.00 — 4.00 — 85
(Promotional issue, *Demonstration Only–Not For Sale* printed on sleeve)
LOVE OVERBOARD .... (MCA 53210) — .75 — 3.00 — 87
LOVIN' ON NEXT TO NOTHIN' .... (MCA 53211) — .75 — 3.00 — 88

KNIGHT, HOLLY
HEART DON'T FAIL ME NOW/Howling At The Moon .... (Columbia 38-07932) — .75 — 3.00 — 88
Also see Device, Spider

KNIGHT, JEAN
MY TOOT TOOT/My Heart Is Willing (And My Body Is Too) .... (Mirage/Atco 7-99643) — 1.00 — 4.00 — 85

KNIGHT, MARIE
COME TOMORROW .... (Okeh 7141) — 2.50 — 10.00 — 61

KNIGHT, SONNY
LOVE ME (AS THOUGH THERE WERE NO TOMORROW)/A Fool Like Me .... (Aura X4505) — 5.00 — 20.00 — 64

KNIGHT, TED
(Actor best known for the role of Ted Baxter on the television series *The Mary Tyler Moore Show*)
THE MAN WHO USED TO BE/May The Bird Of Paradise Fly Up Your Nose .... (Ranwood 1045) — 2.00 — 8.00 — 76

KNIGHT, TERRY, AND THE PACK
See the Fabulous Pack

KNIGHT, TUESDAY
(Actress/Singer)
OUT OF CONTROL .... (Parc ZS4-07625) — .75 — 3.00 — 87

KNOPFLER, MARK
STORYBOOK LOVE/The Friends' Song .... (Warner Bros. 28242-7) — 1.00 — 4.00 — 87
(Shown as by Mark Knopfler and Willy DeVille. From the motion picture *The Princess Bride*, Cary Elwes and Robin Wright pictured.)
Also see Dire Straits, Ferry Aid, Randy Newman (*It's Money That Matters*)

K-9 POSSE
AIN'T NOTHIN' TO IT .... (Arista 9765) — .75 — 3.00 — 88

KNOX, BUDDY
LING-TING-TONG/The Kisses (They're All Mine) .... (Liberty 55305)   6.25   25.00   61

KOKOMO
ASIA MINOR .... (Felsted 45-8612)   2.00   8.00   61
THEME FROM A SILENT MOVIE/Humorous .... (Felsted 45-8622)   2.00   8.00   61

KONGOS, JOHN
HE'S GONNA STEP ON YOU AGAIN .... (Elektra 45729)   1.25   5.00   71

KON KAN
HARRY HOUDINI .... (Atlantic 7-88900)   .75   3.00   89

KOOL AND THE GANG
COUNTRY JUNKY .... (De-Lite 555)   1.00   4.00   72
FRESH/In The Heart .... (De-Lite 880 623-7)   .75   3.00   84
CHERISH/Cherish (Instrumental) .... (De-Lite 880 869-7)   .75   3.00   85
VICTORY/Bad Woman .... (Mercury 888 074-7)   .75   3.00   86
STONE LOVE/Dance Champion .... (Mercury 888 292-7)   .75   3.00   86
HOLIDAY/Holiday (Jam Mix) .... (Mercury 888 712-7)   .75   3.00   87
SPECIAL WAY/God's Country .... (Mercury 888 867-7)   .75   3.00   87
STRONG/Funky Stuff .... (Mercury 872 038-7)   .75   3.00   88
RAGS TO RICHES/ .... (Mercury 870 621-7)   .75   3.00   88
     Also see Band Aid

KOOL G RAP & DJ POLO
ROAD TO THE RICHES .... (Warner Bros. 27559-7)   .75   3.00   89

KOOL MOE DEE
NO RESPECT .... (Jive 1116)   .75   3.00   87
THEY WANT MONEY .... (Jive 1217)   .75   3.00   89

KOOPER, AL
YOU NEVER KNOW WHO YOUR FRIENDS ARE/Soft Landing On The Moon (Columbia 4-44748)   1.50   6.00   69
     Also see the Blues Project

KÖRBERG, TOMMY
     See Elaine Paige (Heaven Help My Heart)

KOSINEC, TONY
EXTENDED PLAYS
FEATHER OF A BOY (Excerpt) .... (Columbia AS 1)   1.25   5.00   70
     (Promotional issue only titled Dig This, issued with a small-hole 33-1/3 RPM record. Also includes excerpts
     by Pacific Gas and Electric, Moondog, Nick Gravenites, Pete Seeger, Santana, Don Ellis, Raven, and Firesign
     Theatre.)

KRAFTWERK
RADIOACTIVITY/Antenna .... (Capitol 4211)   2.00   8.00   75
POCKET CALCULATOR/Dentaku .... (Warner Bros. 49723)   1.00   4.00   81
     (Clear plastic sleeve with black printing. Issued with both lime green and black vinyl)
MUSIQUE NON STOP .... (Warner Bros. 28532-7)   .75   3.00   86
THE TELEPHONE CALL/Der Telefon Anruf German Version .... (Warner Bros. 28441-7)   .75   3.00   87

KRAMER, BILLY J.
FROM A WINDOW/I'll Be On My Way .... (Imperial 66051)   5.00   20.00   65
     (Sleeve states on front Both Songs Written By John Lennon and Paul McCartney)

KRAMER, WAYNE
NEGATIVE GIRLS/Street Warfare .... (Pure And Easy 017)   1.25   5.00   83
     (Hard cover folding sleeve)
EXTENDED PLAYS
NEW YORK CITY/I'D MUCH RATHER BE WITH THE BOYS/
     Endless Party/Just Because I'm White .... (Zodiac 800)   1.50   6.00   87
     (Shown as by Wayne Kramer's "Gang War" Featuring Johnny Thunders. Issued with red vinyl, small-hole
     33-1/3 RPM record.)
     Also see MC5

KREVISS
     See Mecca Normal (b-side of You Heard It All)

KRISTOFFERSON, KRIS
A SONG I'D LIKE TO SING/From The Bottle To The Bottom .... (A&M 1475)   1.25   5.00   73
     (Shown as by Kris Kristofferson & Rita Coolidge, both pictured)
WATCH CLOSELY NOW .... (Columbia 3-10525)   1.00   4.00   77
     (From the motion picture A Star Is Born co-starring Kristofferson)
HIGHWAYMAN .... (Columbia 38-04881)   .75   3.00   85
     (Shown as by Willie Nelson, Kris Kristofferson, Johnny Cash, and Waylon Jennings)
     Also see Barbra Streisand (Love Theme From A Star Is Born)

KROKUS
MIDNITE MANIAC/Ready To Rock .... (Arista 9248)   .75   3.00   84
SCHOOL'S OUT/Screaming In The Night .... (Arista 9468)   .75   3.00   86

KRUSH GROOVE
(Motion Picture)
     See Force M.D.'s (Tender Love), Chaka Khan (Can't Stop The Street), Sheila E (Holly Rock)

KTP
ONE STEP/Footsteps .... (Mercury 884 990-7)   .75   3.00   85
CERTAIN THINGS ARE LIKELY (GARAGE MIX)/Certain Things Are Likely . (Mercury 885 727-7)   .75   3.00   86
     The same group also recorded as Kissing The Pink but released no U.S. sleeves under that name

KUKLA, FRAN & OLLIE
AT THE FAIR .... (RCA WY 2004)   6.25   25.00   52
     (Fold-open sleeve with 12-page coloring book and detachable puppet pieces)
HAPPY MOTHER GOOSE .... (RCA WY 423)   6.25   25.00   53
DRAGON RETREAT .... (RCA WY 425)   6.25   25.00   53

TITLE	LABEL AND NUMBER	VG	NM	YR

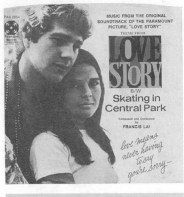

L

LA BAMBA
(Motion Picture)
See Howard Huntsberry (*Lonely Teardrops*), Los Lobos (*La Bamba*)

LABAN
LOVE IN SIBERIA .... (Mega 2143) | .75 | 3.00 | 86
(Sleeve printed for multi-country release, the record is on the U.S. Critique label)

LaBELLE, PATTI
YOU'LL NEVER WALK ALONE .... (Parkway 896) | 10.00 | 40.00 | 64
(Shown as by Patti LaBelle and Her Blue Bells)
NEW ATTITUDE .... (MCA 52517) | .75 | 3.00 | 85
(From the motion picture *Beverly Hills Cop*, LaBelle pictured on front, Eddie Murphy on back.)
STIR IT UP .... (MCA 52610) | .75 | 3.00 | 85
(From the motion picture *Beverly Hills Cop*, LaBelle pictured on front, Eddie Murphy on back.)
ON MY OWN .... (MCA 52770) | .75 | 3.00 | 86
(Shown as by Patti LaBelle and Michael McDonald)
OH, PEOPLE .... (MCA 52877) | .75 | 3.00 | 86
KISS AWAY THE PAIN .... (MCA 52945) | .75 | 3.00 | 86
(Front of sleeve credits George Howard on saxophone)
THE LAST UNBROKEN HEART .... (MCA 53064) | .75 | 3.00 | 87
(Shown as by Patti LaBelle and Bill Champlin. From the television series *Miami Vice*, Don Johnson and Philip-Michael Thomas pictured on back.)
JUST THE FACTS .... (MCA 53100) | .75 | 3.00 | 87
Also see the Blue Belles

LABYRINTH
(Motion Picture)
See David Bowie (*Underground*)

LADD, CHERYL
(Actress)
MAMA DON'T BE BLUE/The Family .... (Warner Bros. 7821) | 2.00 | 8.00 | 74
THINK IT OVER/Here Is A Song .... (Capitol 4599) | 1.25 | 5.00 | 78
CAN'T SAY NO TO YOU .... (Capitol B-5115) | 1.25 | 5.00 | 82
(Shown as by Frankie Valli and Cheryl Ladd)
Also see Josie and the Pussycats

LA DOLCE VITA
(Motion Picture)
See Ray Ellis and His Orchestra (*La Dolce Vita*)

LA DREAM TEAM
RUDY AND SNAKE .... (MCA 53176) | .75 | 3.00 | 87

LADY SINGS THE BLUES
(Motion Picture)
See Diana Ross (*Good Morning Heartache*)

LAFLAMME, DAVID
WHITE BIRD .... (Amherst 717) | 1.00 | 4.00 | 76

LAI, FRANCES
A MAN AND A WOMAN ("UN HOMME ET UNE FEMME") .... (United Artists 50052) | 1.25 | 5.00 | 66
(From the motion picture *A Man and a Woman*)
THEME FROM LOVE STORY/Skating In Central Park .... (Paramount 0064) | 1.00 | 4.00 | 70
(Top of sleeve straight cut. From the motion picture *Love Story*, Ryan O'Neal and Ali MacGraw pictured.)
THEME FROM LOVE STORY/Skating In Central Park .... (Paramount 0064) | 1.00 | 4.00 | 70
(Top of sleeve curved. From the motion picture *Love Story*, Ryan O'Neal and Ali MacGraw pictured.)

LAING, SHONA
SOVIET SNOW/Drive Baby Drive .... (MCA 2475) | .75 | 3.00 | 87

LAINE, FRANKIE
MOONLIGHT GAMBLER/Lotus Land .... (Columbia 4-40780) | 3.75 | 15.00 | 56
BLAZING SADDLES/I'm Tired .... (Warner Bros. 7774) | 1.50 | 6.00 | 74
(B-side shown as by Madeline Kahn. From the motion picture *Blazing Saddles*.)

LAKE, GREG
I BELIEVE IN FATHER CHRISTMAS .... (Atlantic 3305) | 1.25 | 5.00 | 75

LAKESIDE
I WANT TO HOLD YOUR HAND/Magic Moments .... (Solar 48001) | 1.25 | 5.00 | 81

LA LA
MY LOVE IS ON THE MONEY/So Into Love .... (Arista 9620) | .75 | 3.00 | 87

L.A. LAW
(Television Series)
See Mike Post (*Theme From L.A. Law*)

LAMAS, LORENZO
(Actor)
FOOLS LIKE ME/Smooth Talker .... (Scotti Brothers ZS4 04686) | 1.25 | 5.00 | 84

LAMB, ANNABEL
INSIDE OF MY HEAD/Sisters Of Mercy .... (A&M 2663) | .75 | 3.00 | 84
Also see Ferry Aid

LAMBERT, CHRISTOPHER
(Actor)
See Queen (*Princes Of The Universe*)

LAMP OF CHILDHOOD, THE
FIRST TIME LAST TIME .... (Dunhill 4063) | 2.50 | 10.00 | 67

LANANEENEENOONOO
HELP!/Help .... (London 886 492-7)   .75   3.00   89
    (Shown as by Bananarama and Lananeeneenoonoo, all six women pictured. Record credits only Bananarama)

LANCASTER, BURT
(Actor)
    See Ray Bloch & Orchestra (*From Here To Eternity*), Kenny Rogers (*They Don't Make Them Like They Used To*)

LAND BEFORE TIME, THE
(Motion Picture)
    See Diana Ross (*If We Hold On Together*)

LANCELOT LINK, SECRET CHIMP
(Television Series)
    See Lancelot Link and the Evolution Revolution

LANCE, MAJOR
UM, UM, UM, UM, UM, UM .... (Okeh 4-7187)   3.75   15.00   64
RHYTHM .... (Okeh 4-7203)   3.00   12.00   64
COME SEE .... (Okeh 4-7216)   3.00   12.00   65
INVESTIGATE .... (Okeh 4-7250)   3.00   12.00   66
AIN'T NO SOUL (IN THESE SHOES) .... (Okeh 4-7266)   3.00   12.00   66

LANDERS, AUDREY
(Actress)
MANUEL GOODBYE .... (MCA/Curb 52339)   1.50   6.00   84

LANDON, MICHAEL
(Actor who began his television career as Little Joe Cartwright in the series *Bonanza* from 1959-1973)
GIMME A LITTLE KISS (WILL "YA" HUH)/Be Patient With Me .... (Fono Graf 1240)   10.00   40.00   60
LINDA IS LONESOME/Without You .... (RCA 47-8330)   10.00   40.00   64

LANE, CHRISTY
I HAVE A DREAM .... (Liberty 1396)   1.25   5.00   80

LANE, DIANE
(Actress)
    See Little Willie John (*Fever*)

LANE, ROBIN, & THE CHARTBUSTERS
WHEN THINGS GO WRONG/Why Did You Tell Lies/The Letter .... (Deli Platters RLC 1)   2.50   10.00   79
WHEN THINGS GO WRONG/Many Years Ago .... (Warner Bros. 49246)   1.00   4.00   80

LANE, RONNIE
HOW COME?/Tell Everyone/Done This One Before .... (A&M 1524)   1.50   6.00   73
    Also see Faces, the Small Faces

LANG, K.D., AND THE RECLINES
TURN ME AROUND/Diet Of Strange Places .... (Sire 28338-7)   .75   3.00   87
I'M DOWN TO MY LAST CIGARETTE/Western Stars .... (Sire 27919-7)   .75   3.00   88
LOCK, STOCK AND TEARDROPS .... (Sire 27813-7)   .75   3.00   88
    (Shown as by k.d. lang)
FULL MOON FULL OF LOVE .... (Sire 22932-7)   .75   3.00   89
    Also see Roy Orbison (*Crying*)

LANGFORD, FRANCES
THEN YOU'VE NEVER BEEN BLUE/Baltimore Oriole .... (Decca 1-723)   3.00   12.00   53
    (Decca "Curtain Call" series of reissues)

LANIN, LESTER, AND HIS ORCHESTRA
BLUE TANGO ROCK .... (Epic 5-9426)   2.00   8.00   61

LANZ, DAVID
EXTENDED PLAYS
LEAVES ON THE SEINE .... (Narada S33-17254)   1.00   4.00   86
    (Promotional issue only titled *Narada Sampler–Excellence In New Acoustic Music*, issued with a small-hole
    33-1/3 RPM record. Also includes one song each by Tingstad–Rumbel, Randy Mead, William Ellwood,
    Michael Jones, Matthew Montfort, Spencer Brewer, and Gabriel Lee.)

LANZA, MARIO
THE LOVELIEST NIGHT OF THE YEAR .... (RCA Victor 3300)   6.25   25.00   51
SONG OF INDIA .... (RCA Victor 4209)   6.25   25.00   51
GENERIC MARIO LANZA SLEEVE .... (RCA Victor Red Seal)   2.00   8.00   50s
    (Half sleeve promoting the motion picture *The Great Caruso*. Lanza head shot and Enrico Caruso in costume
    pictured. Eight titles by Caruso and four by Lanza listed on back as *Music Made Famous By "The Great Caruso"*.)

LARGE, BILLY
THE GOODIE WAGON .... (Columbia 4-43741)   2.00   8.00   66

LARSON, JACK
(Actor who played Jimmy Olsen in the television series *The Adventures Of Superman* from 1951-1957)
BACK TO SCHOOL BLUES/Lonely Part Of Town .... (Fraternity 844)   2.00   8.00   61

LARSON, NICOLETTE
LET ME GO, LOVE .... (Warner Bros. 49130)   1.00   4.00   79

LA RUE, EVA
(Actress)
    See the Soaps and Hearts Ensemble

LAST, THE
SHE DON'T KNOW WHY I'M HERE/Bombing Of London .... (Backlash 001)   7.50   30.00   78
    (Handmade sleeve art, not printed)
EVERY SUMMER DAY/Slave Driver .... (Backlash 002)   3.75   15.00   78
SHE DON'T KNOW WHY I'M HERE/Bombing Of London .... (Bomp 119)   1.50   6.00   78
EVERY SUMMER'S DAY/Slave Driver .... (Bomp 126)   1.50   6.00   79
L.A. EXPLOSION/Hitler's Brother .... (Backlash 003)   2.50   10.00   79

TITLE	LABEL AND NUMBER	VG	NM	YR

EXTENDED PLAYS

UP IN THE AIR/Wrong Turn/Leper Colony .... (Warfrat 1082) | | 1.25 | 5.00 | 82
   (Black and yellow sleeve issued with red label record)

UP IN THE AIR/Wrong Turn/Leper Colony .... (Warfrat 1082) | | 1.00 | 4.00 | 82
   (Black and orange sleeve issued with yellow label record)

LAST DRAGON, THE
(Motion Picture)
   See DeBarge (Rhythm Of The Night)

LATIN POETS, THE
VIVA LA MUSICA .... (Warner Bros. 27943-7) | | .75 | 3.00 | 88

LATIN RASCALS
DON'T LET ME BE MISUNDERSTOOD (LP EDIT)/
   Don't Let Me Be Misunderstood (12" Remix Edit) .... (Tin Pan Apple/Mercury 887 893-7) | | .75 | 3.00 | 88
   Also see Warren Zevon (Leave My Monkey Alone)

LATTISAW, STACY
WHEN YOU'RE YOUNG AND IN LOVE/Three Wishes .... (Cotillion 44250) | | 1.25 | 5.00 | 79
NAIL IT TO THE WALL .... (Motown 1859) | | .75 | 3.00 | 86
CALL ME .... (Motown 1945) | | .75 | 3.00 | 88

LAUGHING HYENAS
PUBLIC ANIMAL #9 .... (Sub Pop 121) | | 2.50 | 10.00 | 91
   (Alice Cooper Tribute double single release limited to 5,500 copies with an unknown number on blue-gray vinyl. Also includes one song each by Sonic Youth, These Immortal Souls, and Gumball.)

LAUGHNER, PETER
CINDERELLA BACKSTREET/White Light White Heat .... (Forced Exposure 018) | | 2.50 | 10.00 | 87
   Also see Pere Ubu

LAUPER, CYNDI
GIRLS JUST WANT TO HAVE FUN/Right Track Wrong Train .... (Portrait 37-04120) | | 1.00 | 4.00 | 84
GIRLS JUST WANT TO HAVE FUN .... (Portrait 37-04120) | | 1.25 | 5.00 | 84
   (Promotional issue, Demonstration–Not For Sale printed on sleeve)
SHE BOP .... (Portrait 37-04516) | | .75 | 3.00 | 84
SHE BOP .... (Portrait 37-04516) | | 1.00 | 4.00 | 84
   (Promotional issue, Demonstration–Not For Sale printed on sleeve)
ALL THROUGH THE NIGHT/Witness .... (Portrait 37-04639) | | .75 | 3.00 | 84
ALL THROUGH THE NIGHT .... (Portrait 37-04639) | | 1.00 | 4.00 | 84
   (Promotional issue, Demonstration–Not For Sale printed on sleeve)
MONEY CHANGES EVERYTHING .... (Portrait 37-04737) | | .75 | 3.00 | 84
MONEY CHANGES EVERYTHING .... (Portrait 37-04737) | | 1.00 | 4.00 | 84
   (Promotional issue, Demonstration–Not For Sale printed on sleeve)
THE GOONIES 'R' GOOD ENOUGH/What A Thrill .... (Portrait 34-04918) | | .75 | 3.00 | 85
   (From the motion picture The Goonies)
THE GOONIES 'R' GOOD ENOUGH/What A Thrill .... (Portrait 34-04918) | | 1.00 | 4.00 | 85
   (Promotional issue, Demonstration Only–Not For Sale printed on sleeve. Sleeve lists b-side although the 45 has The Goonies 'R' Good Enough on both sides. From the motion picture The Goonies.)
TRUE COLORS/Heading For The Moon .... (Portrait 37-06242) | | .75 | 3.00 | 86
TRUE COLORS .... (Portrait 37-06242) | | 1.00 | 4.00 | 86
   (Promotional issue, Demonstration–Not For Sale printed on sleeve)
CHANGE OF HEART/Witness .... (Portrait 37-06431) | | .75 | 3.00 | 86
CHANGE OF HEART .... (Portrait 37-06431) | | 1.00 | 4.00 | 86
   (Promotional issue, Demonstration Not For Sale printed on sleeve)
WHAT'S GOING ON/One Track Mind .... (Portrait 37-06970) | | .75 | 3.00 | 87
WHAT'S GOING ON .... (Portrait 37-06970) | | 1.00 | 4.00 | 87
   (Promotional issue, Demonstration–Not For Sale printed on sleeve)
BOY BLUE/The Faraway Nearby .... (Epic 34 07181) | | 1.25 | 5.00 | 88
HOLE IN MY HEART/Boy Blue (Recorded Live at Le Zenith) .... (Epic 34 07940) | | .75 | 3.00 | 88
   (A-side from the motion picture Vibes co-starring Lauper)
   Also see Billy Joel (This Is The Time), U.S.A. For Africa, Voices Of America

LAURA
WILD & FREE/Take Me Inside Your Heart .... (Ovation 14/1018) | | 1.50 | 6.00 | 71

LAUREN, ROD
IF I HAD A GIRL/No Wonder .... (RCA Victor 47-7645) | | 2.50 | 10.00 | 59
LISTEN MY LOVE/This I Know .... (RCA Victor 47-7720) | | 2.50 | 10.00 | 60

LAVERNE & SHIRLEY
(Penny Marshall and Cindy Williams)
CHAPEL OF LOVE/Sixteen Reasons .... (Atlantic 3367) | | 1.50 | 6.00 | 76

LAVERNE & SHIRLEY
(Television Series)
   Related see the Credibility Gap (Michael McKean who played Lenny and David L. Lander who played Squiggy), Laverne & Shirley (Penny Marshall and Cindy Williams), Spinal Tap (Michael McKean a.k.a. David St. Hubbins)

LaVOIE, DANIEL
NEVER BEEN TO NEW YORK .... (Capitol PB-44051) | | .75 | 3.00 | 86

LAWRENCE, EDDIE
ABNER THE BASEBALL .... (Coral 61821) | | 2.50 | 10.00 | 56
WORLD'S FAIR PHILOSOPHER .... (Epic 5-9804) | | 2.00 | 8.00 | 65

LAWRENCE, STEVE
I NEED/Tango Of The Roses .... (Big 7001) | | 3.75 | 15.00 |
TEARS FROM HEAVEN/Hansel & Gretel .... (United Artists 240) | | 2.50 | 10.00 | 60
MY CLAIRE DE LUNE/In Time .... (United Artists 335) | | 2.50 | 10.00 | 60
THE LADY WANTS TO TWIST/ .... (Columbia 4-42396) | | 2.00 | 8.00 | 62
HOUSE WITHOUT WINDOWS/The Endless Night (Greensleeves) .... (Columbia 4-42455) | | 2.00 | 8.00 | 62
GO AWAY LITTLE GIRL/If You Love Her Tell Her So .... (Columbia 4-42601) | | 2.00 | 8.00 | 62
DON'T BE AFRAID LITTLE DARLIN'/Don't Come Running .... (Columbia 4-42699) | | 2.00 | 8.00 | 63
WALKING PROUD/All The Way Home .... (Columbia 4-42865) | | 2.00 | 8.00 | 63

LEADER OF THE PACK
(Broadway Musical)
   See Darlene Love *(River Deep, Mountain High)*

LEAPY LEE
EVERY ROAD LEADS BACK TO YOU / Little Arrows .... (MCA 40470)   1.25   5.00   75

LEATHER BOY, THE
I'M A LEATHER BOY / Shadows .... (MGM 13724)   10.00   40.00   67

LE BLANC, SONNY
TERRORISTS .... (CBT 7205)   .75   3.00   85

LE CLERC, JEAN
(Actress)
   See the Soaps and Hearts Ensemble

LED ZEPPELIN
DAZED AND CONFUSED / Babe I'm Gonna Leave You .... (Atlantic 1019)   75.00   300.00   69
   (Promotional issue only released with 33-1/3 RPM record)
STAIRWAY TO HEAVEN .... (Atlantic PR-175)   25.00   100.00   73
   (Promotional issue only)
   Also see the Honeydrippers, Jimmy Page, Robert Plant, Willie and the Poor Boys (Jimmy Page)

LEE, ALBERT
HAVE YOU HEARD THE NEWS .... (A&M 2306)   1.00   4.00   80
   (Generic half sleeve for the album *The Legend Of Jessse James.* No artist or song title on sleeve.)

LEE, ALVIN
DETROIT DIESEL / Let's Go .... (21 Records 7-99526)   1.25   5.00   86

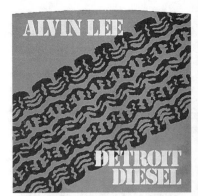

LEE, BILLY, & THE RIVIERAS
YOU KNOW / Won't You Dance With Me? .... (Sundazed 117)   .50   2.00   96
   (Issued with dark red vinyl)
   Also see Mitch Ryder and the Detroit Wheels, the Rockets (James McCarty, Johnny Badenjek)

LEE, BRENDA
I'M GONNA LASSO SANTA CLAUS / Christy Christmas .... (Decca 30107)   10.00   40.00   56
   (Shown as by Little Brenda Lee, 9 Years Old. Issued in Decca's Children Series.)
I'M GONNA LASSO SANTA CLAUS / Christy Christmas .... (Decca 88215)   18.75   75.00   56
   (Shown as by Little Brenda Lee, 9 Years Old. Issued in Decca's Children Series. This sleeve is for the 78 rpm.)
ROCKIN' AROUND THE CHRISTMAS TREE / Papa Noël .... (Decca 30776)   6.25   25.00   58
SWEET NOTHIN'S / Weep No More My Baby .... (Decca 30967)   12.50   50.00   59
I'M SORRY / That's All You Gotta Do .... (Decca 31093)   5.00   20.00   60
I WANT TO BE WANTED / Just A Little .... (Decca 31149)   5.00   20.00   60
EMOTIONS / I'm Learning About Love .... (Decca 31195)   3.75   15.00   61
YOU CAN DEPEND ON ME / It's Never Too Late .... (Decca 31231)   3.75   15.00   61
DUM DUM / Eventually .... (Decca 31272)   3.75   15.00   61
FOOL #1 / Anybody But Me .... (Decca 31309)   3.75   15.00   61
BREAK IT TO ME GENTLY / So Deep .... (Decca 31348)   3.75   15.00   62
ALL ALONE AM I / Save All Your Lovin' For Me .... (Decca 31424)   3.75   15.00   62
YOUR USED TO BE / She'll Never Know .... (Decca 31454)   3.00   12.00   63
LOSING YOU / He's So Heavenly .... (Decca 31478)   3.00   12.00   63
MY WHOLE WORLD IS FALLING DOWN / I Wonder .... (Decca 31510)   3.00   12.00   63
THE GRASS IS GREENER / Sweet Impossible You .... (Decca 31539)   3.00   12.00   63
THINK / The Waiting Game .... (Decca 31599)   3.00   12.00   64
ALONE WITH YOU / My Dreams .... (Decca 31628)   2.50   10.00   64
WHEN YOU LOVED ME / He's Sure To Remember Me .... (Decca 31654)   2.50   10.00   64
JINGLE BELL ROCK / Winter Wonderland .... (Decca 31687)   3.75   15.00   64
CHRISTMAS WILL BE JUST ANOTHER DAY / This Time Of The Year .... (Decca 31688)   3.00   12.00   64
IS IT TRUE / Just Behind The Rainbow .... (Decca 31690)   2.50   10.00   64
TRULY, TRULY, TRUE / I Still Miss Someone .... (Decca 31762)   2.50   10.00   65
JOHNNY ONE TIME / I Must Have Been Out Of My Mind .... (Decca 32428)   2.50   10.00   69
WHY YOU BEEN GONE SO LONG / He Can't Make Your Kind Of Love ..... (MCA 52720)   .75   3.00   85

LEE, CURTIS
PLEDGE OF LOVE / Then I'll Know .... (Dunes 45-2003)   7.50   30.00   61

LEE, DICK
I NEVER KNEW .... (Felsted 8603)   3.00   12.00   61

LEE, DONNA
GOOD TIMES ARE GONE .... (Columbia 4-43878)   2.00   8.00   68

LEE, GABRIEL
EXTENDED PLAYS
RUNNING DANCES .... (Narada S33-17254)   1.00   4.00   86
   (Promotional issue only titled *Narada Sampler–Excellence In New Acoustic Music,* issued with a small-hole
   33-1/3 RPM record. Also includes one song each by Tingstad–Rumbel, Randy Mead, William Ellwood,
   Michael Jones, Matthew Montfort, Spencer Brewer, and David Lanz.)

LEE, HAROLD
THE TWO SIDES OF ME .... (Columbia 4-44458)   1.50   6.00   67

LEE, JOHNNY
LOOKIN' FOR LOVE / Lyin' Eyes .... (Full Moon/Asylum 47004)   1.00   4.00   80
   (B-side shown as by the Eagles. From the motion picture *Urban Cowboy.*)

LEE, MAGGIE
RUNAROUND .... (Columbia 38-04397)   .75   3.00   84
RUNAROUND .... (Columbia 38-04397)   1.00   4.00   84
   (Promotional issue, *Demonstration Only–Not For Sale* printed on sleeve)

LEE, PEGGY
THE TREE / The Christmas List .... (Capitol 4311)   2.00   8.00   60

TITLE	LABEL AND NUMBER	VG	NM	YR
LEE, ROBIN				
BEFORE YOU CHEAT ON ME ONCE	(Atlantic America 7-99264)	.75	3.00	88
SHINE A LIGHT ON A LIE	(Atlantic America 7-99307)	.75	3.00	88
THIS OLD FLAME	(Atlantic America 7-99353)	.75	3.00	88
LEE, SONDRA				
See Eddie Albert				
LEE, SPIKE				
(Director / Writer / Actor)				
See E.U. (Da Butt)				
LEEK, ANDY				
HOLDIN' ON TO YOU /	(Atlantic 7-88997)	.75	3.00	88
PLEASE PLEASE / Entangled Hearts	(Atlantic 7-89054)	.75	3.00	89
LEFT BANKE, THE				
DESIRÉE	(Smash 2119)	5.00	20.00	67
PEDESTAL / Myra	(Smash 2243)	—	—	69
(Bootleg sleeve often mistaken for a legitimate release)				
Also see Stories (Michael Brown)				
LEGAL EAGLES				
(Motion Picture)				
See Rod Stewart (Love Touch)				
LEGEND				
(Motion Picture)				
See Bryan Ferry (Is Your Love Strong Enough)				
LEGENDARY MASKED SURFERS, THE				
SUMMER MEANS FUN / Gonna Hustle You	(United Artists XW270)	7.50	30.00	73
(Originally issued with an explanatory note insert from member Dean Torrance. Add $5 if included.)				
Also see the Beach Boys (Bruce Johnston, Brian Wilson), Jan Berry, Glen Campbell, Jan & Dean, Leon Russell, Brian Wilson				
LEGENDARY STARDUST COWBOY, THE				
I HATE CD'S / Linda	(Norton 012)	.50	2.00	92
LEGEND OF BILLIE JEAN, THE				
(Motion Picture)				
See Pat Benatar (Invincible)				
LEGENDS, THE				
HIGH TOWERS / Fever Games	(Railroad House 12003)	5.00	20.00	69
Also see Dan Hartman, the Edgar Winter Group (Dan Hartman)				
LEGENDS, THE				
LARIAT / Late Train	(Key 1002)	7.50	30.00	61
LARIAT / Gail	(Key 1002)	10.00	40.00	61
BOP-A-LENA / I Wish I Knew	(Ermine 43)	12.50	50.00	62
LEGENDS, THE				
SURF'S UP / Dance With The Drummer Man	(Doc Holliday 107)	12.50	50.00	63
LEGRAND, MICHEL, AND ORCHESTRA				
LARA'S THEME	(MGM K13816)	3.75	15.00	67
LEIBOVITZ, ANNIE				
(Photographer)				
See Miss Abrams & the Strawberry Point Fourth Grade Class (America), Steve Dorff and Friends (Theme From Growing Pains), Bruce Springsteen (One Step Up, Tunnel Of Love, Fire, My Hometown, I'm On Fire, Born In The U.S.A.)				
LEIGHTON, BERNIE				
THE WAR LOVER	(Colpix 658)	2.50	10.00	62
(From the motion picture War Lover)				
LEMMON, JACK				
(Actor)				
THE THEME FROM THE APARTMENT	(Epic 5-9399)	2.00	8.00	60
(From the motion picture The Apartment)				
Also see Ferrante And Teicher (The Theme From The Apartment)				
LEMON, MEADOWLARK				
PERSONALITY / Shoot-A-Basket	(RSVP 1125)	3.00	12.00	62
Also see the Globetrotters				
LEMONHEADS, THE				
LUKA / Strange / Mad	(Taang! 31)	1.25	5.00	89
(Issued with either, red, white, blue, black, or blue / yellow vinyl)				
STYLE / Acoustic Rick James Style	(Atlantic PR 5336)	1.50	6.00	89
(Promotional issue only with small-hole 45 RPM record)				
LEMON PIPERS, THE				
RICE IS NICE / Blueberry Blue	(Buddah 31)	3.00	12.00	68
LEN & GLEN				
A CARD FOR MY BABY	(Columbia 4-43350)	2.50	10.00	65
LENNEAR, CLAUDIA				
See Leon Russell (The Ballad Of Mad Dogs & Englishmen)				
LENNON, JOHN				
GIVE PEACE A CHANCE / Remember Love	(Apple 1809)	3.00	12.00	69
(Shown as by Plastic Ono Band)				
COLD TURKEY / Don't Worry Kyoko (Mummy's Only Looking For A Hand In The Snow)	(Apple 1813)	12.50	50.00	69
(Shown as by Plastic Ono Band)				
INSTANT KARMA! (WE ALL SHINE ON) / Who Has Seen The Wind?	(Apple 1818)	3.00	12.00	70
(A-side shown as by John Ono Lennon, b-side shown as by Yoko Ono Lennon. Yoko pictured on back.)				

MOTHER / Why .... (Apple 1827)   25.00   100.00   70
  (A-side shown as by John Lennon/Plastic Ono Band, b-side shown as by Yoko Ono/Plastic Ono Band.)
POWER TO THE PEOPLE / Touch Me .... (Apple 1830)   6.25   25.00   71
  (A-side shown as by John Lennon/Plastic Ono Band, b-side shown as by Yoko Ono/Plastic Ono Band. Yoko pictured on back.)
HAPPY XMAS (WAR IS OVER) / Listen, The Snow Is Falling .... (Apple 1842)   3.75   15.00   71
  (A-side shown as by John & Yoko, the Plastic Ono Band with the Harlem Community Choir. B-side shown as by Yoko Ono, the Plastic Ono Band. Issued with green vinyl.)
WOMAN IS THE NIGGER OF THE WORLD / Sisters O Sisters .... (Apple 1848)   2.50   20.00   72
  (A-side shown as by John Lennon/Plastic Ono Band with Elephant's Memory and Invisible Strings. B-side shown as by Yoko Ono/Plastic Ono Band with Elephant's Memory and Invisible Strings. Front pictures John and Yoko, back pictures John, Yoko, and Elephant's Memory.)
MIND GAMES .... (Apple 1868)   2.00   10.00   73
(JUST LIKE) STARTING OVER / Kiss Kiss Kiss .... (Geffen 49604)   1.00   4.00   81
  (B-side shown as by Yoko Ono, John and Yoko pictured)
WOMAN / Beautiful Boys .... (Geffen 49644)   1.00   4.00   81
  (B-side shown as by Yoko Ono, John and Yoko pictured)
WATCHING THE WHEELS / Yes, I'm Your Angel .... (Geffen 49695)   1.00   4.00   81
  (B-side shown as by Yoko Ono, John and Yoko pictured)
HAPPY XMAS (WAR IS OVER) / Beautiful Boy (Darling Boy) .... (Geffen 29855-7)   1.00   4.00   82
NOBODY TOLD ME / O' Sanity .... (Polydor 817 254-7)   1.00   4.00   83
  (B-side shown as by Yoko Ono, John and Yoko pictured on both sides)
I'M STEPPING OUT / Sleepless Night .... (Polydor 821 107-7)   1.00   4.00   84
  (B-side shown as by Yoko Ono)
BORROWED TIME / Your Hands .... (Polydor 821 204-7)   1.00   4.00   84
  (B-side shown as by Yoko Ono, Yoko pictured on back)
EVERY MAN HAS A WOMAN WHO LOVES HIM / It's Alright .... (Polydor 881 378-7)   1.00   4.00   84
  (B-side shown as by Sean Ono Lennon, John's son)
JEALOUS GUY .... (Capitol B-44230)   1.00   4.00   88
  (From the motion picture *Imagine: John Lennon*)
  Also see the Beatles, Elevator Drops (*Lennon's Dead*), Elton John (*Lucy In The Sky With Diamonds*, b-side of *Philadelphia Freedom*), Billy J. Kramer (*From A Window*)

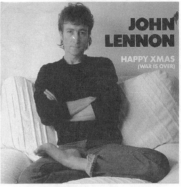

LENNON, JULIAN
(John Lennon's son with his first wife Cynthia Twist)
VALOTTE / Well I Don't Know .... (Atlantic 7-89609)   1.00   4.00   84
TOO LATE FOR GOODBYES / Let Me Be .... (Atlantic 7-89589)   1.00   4.00   84
SAY YOU'RE WRONG / Big Mama .... (Atlantic 7-89567)   1.00   4.00   85
JESSE / Bebop .... (Atlantic 7-89529)   1.00   4.00   84
STICK AROUND / Always Think Twice .... (Atlantic 7-89437)   .75   3.00   86
THIS IS MY DAY / Everyday .... (Atlantic 7-89385)   .75   3.00   86
WANT YOUR BODY / Everyday .... (Atlantic 7-89405)   .75   3.00   86
TIME WILL TEACH US ALL /
  Time Will Teach Us All (Special Instrumental Version) .... (Capitol B-5618)   1.50   6.00   86
  (Sleeve credits backing vocals by Stevie Wonder. From the musical *Time*.)
NOW YOU'RE IN HEAVEN / Second Time .... (Atlantic 7-88925)   .75   3.00   89
YOU'RE THE ONE / Sunday Morning .... (Atlantic 7-88890)   .75   3.00   89

LENNON, SEAN ONO
(John Lennon's son with his second wife Yoko Ono)
  See John Lennon (*Every Man Has A Woman Who Loves Him*)

LENNOX, ANNIE
  See Eurythmics, Scrooged

LEO AND LOREE
(Motion Picture)
  See Donny Most (*I Only Want What's Mine*)

LEONARD PART 6
(Motion Picture)
  See Peabo Bryson (*Without You*)

LEONETTI, TOMMY
LET'S TAKE A WALK .... (Columbia 4-44568)   2.00   8.00   68

LE ROUX
EXTENDED PLAYS
SEASONS GREETINGS / YOU KNOW HOW THOSE BOYS ARE /
  Addicted / The Last Safe Place On Earth .... (RCA JF-13012)   1.50   6.00   82
  (Promotional issue only issued with green vinyl)

LES LIAISONS DANGEREUSES
(Motion Picture)
  See Bill Butler (*Prelude In Blue*)

LESS THAN ZERO
(Motion Picture)
  See Bangles (*Hazy Shade Of Winter*) , L.L. Cool J. (*Going Back To Cali*), the Black Flames (*Are You My Woman?*)

LETHAL WEAPON 2
(Motion Picture)
  See George Harrison (*Cheer Down*)

LET IT BE
(Motion Picture)
  See the Beatles (*Let It Be, The Long And Winding Road*)

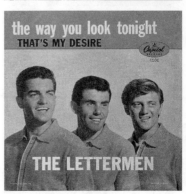

LETTA AND THE SAFARIS
WALKIN' AROUND .... (Columbia 4-43675)   3.75   15.00   66

LETTERMEN, THE
THE WAY YOU LOOK TONIGHT / That's My Desire .... (Capitol 4586)   2.00   8.00   61
WHEN I FALL IN LOVE / Smile .... (Capitol 4658)   2.00   8.00   61
COME BACK SILLY GIRL / A Song For Young Love .... (Capitol 4699)   2.00   8.00   62
HOW IS JULIE? / Turn Around, Look At Me .... (Capitol 4746)   2.00   8.00   62
SILLY BOY (SHE DOESN'T LOVE YOU) / I Told The Stars .... (Capitol 4810)   2.00   8.00   62
AGAIN / A Tree In The Meadow .... (Capitol 4851)   2.00   8.00   63

TITLE	LABEL AND NUMBER	VG	NM	YR
IT'S OVER/	(Capitol 5370)	2.00	8.00	65
SECRETLY/The Things We Did Last Summer	(Capitol 5499)	2.00	8.00	65
RUN TO MY LOVIN' ARMS/	(Capitol 5583)	2.00	8.00	66
I ONLY HAVE EYES FOR YOU/Love Letters	(Capitol 5649)	2.00	8.00	66
LOVE	(Capitol 3192)	1.50	6.00	71
ONE MORE SUMMER NIGHT/Theme From A Summer Place	(Alpha Omega 078701)	1.00	4.00	87

LEVEL 42

LEAVING ME NOW/I Sleep On My Heart	(Polydor 885 284-7)	.75	3.00	85
HOT WATER/Dream Crazy	(Polydor 885 155-7)	.75	3.00	86
LESSONS IN LOVE/Hot Water (Live)	(Polydor 883 956-7)	.75	3.00	87
RUNNING IN THE FAMILY/Fashion Fever	(Polydor 885 957-7)	.75	3.00	87
IT'S OVER/MICR Kid	(Polydor 887 227-7)	.75	3.00	88
HEAVEN IN MY HANDS/Gresham Blues	(Polydor 887 777-7)	.75	3.00	88
TRACIE/Man	(Polydor 871 438-7)	1.25	5.00	88

LEVERT

LET'S GO OUT TONIGHT/Grip	(Atlantic 7-89350)	.75	3.00	86
CASANOVA/Throwdown	(Atlantic 7-89217)	.75	3.00	87
SWEET SENSATION/	(Atlantic 7-89124)	.75	3.00	87
PULL OVER/Pull Over (Instrumental)	(Atlantic 7-88987)	.75	3.00	88
JUST COOLIN'/Just Coolin' (Hip Hop Version)	(Atlantic 7-88959)	.75	3.00	89
ADDICTED TO YOU/	(Atlantic 7-99292)	.75	3.00	89

LEVY, MARCY
(a.k.a. Marcella Detroit)

HELP ME!	(RSO 1047)	1.00	4.00	80

(Shown as by Marcy Levy and Robin Gibb. From the motion picture *Times Square*, Robin Johnson and Trini Alvarado pictured)
Also see Shakespear's Sister

LEWIS, BOBBY

AN ORDINARY MIRACLE	(United Artists 50263)	2.00	8.00	68

LEWIS, GARY, & THE PLAYBOYS

DOIN' THE FLAKE/This Diamond Ring/Little Miss Go-Go	(Liberty 65-227-1/2)	7.50	30.00	65

(Promotional issue only available by mail order for 35¢ and a Kellog's Corn Flakes box top)

EVERYBODY LOVES A CLOWN/Time Stands Still	(Liberty 55818)	2.50	10.00	65
SHE'S JUST MY STYLE	(Liberty 55846)	2.50	10.00	66
SURE GONNA MISS HER/I Don't Wanna Say Goodnight	(Liberty 55865)	2.50	10.00	66
GREEN GRASS/I Can Read Between The Lines	(Liberty 55880)	2.50	10.00	66
MY HEART'S SYMPHONY	(Liberty 55898)	2.00	8.00	66
(YOU DON'T HAVE TO) PAINT ME A PICTURE/Looking For The Stars	(Liberty 55914)	2.00	8.00	66
THE LOSER (WITH A BROKEN HEART)/Ice Melts In The Sun	(Liberty 55949)	2.00	8.00	67

LEWIS, HUEY, AND THE NEWS

SOME OF MY LIES ARE TRUE (SOONER OR LATER)	(Chrysalis 21-PDJ)	2.50	10.00	80

(Poster sleeve designed in a "Special Edition"newspaper format)

DO YOU BELIEVE IN LOVE/Is It Me	(Chrysalis 2589)	1.50	6.00	82

(Promotional issue only, hard cover, issued with red vinyl. No song titles or label number on sleeve. A heart-shaped graphic created with the group's name is on the front.)

HOPE YOU LOVE ME LIKE YOU SAY YOU DO/ Whatever Happened To True Love	(Chrysalis 2604)	1.00	4.00	82
HEART AND SOUL/You Crack Me Up	(Chrysalis VS4 42726)	.75	3.00	83
I WANT A NEW DRUG/Finally Found A Home	(Chrysalis VS4-42766)	.75	3.00	83
THE HEART OF ROCK & ROLL/Workin' For A Livin' (Live)	(Chrysalis VS4 42782)	.75	3.00	84
IF THIS IS IT/Change Of Heart	(Chrysalis VS4 42803)	.75	3.00	84
WALKING ON A THIN LINE/The Only One	(Chrysalis VS4-42825)	.75	3.00	84
THE POWER OF LOVE/Bad Is Bad	(Chrysalis VS4-42876)	.75	3.00	85

(A-side from the motion picture *Back To The Future*)

STUCK WITH YOU/Don't Ever Tell Me That You Love Me	(Chrysalis VS4 43019)	.75	3.00	86
HIP TO BE SQUARE/Some Of My Lies Are True	(Chrysalis VS4 43065)	.75	3.00	86
JACOB'S LADDER/Heart Of Rock & Roll (Live)	(Chrysalis VS4 43097)	.75	3.00	86
I KNOW WHAT I LIKE/Forest For The Trees	(Chrysalis VS4 43108)	.75	3.00	87
DOING IT ALL FOR MY BABY/	(Chrysalis VS4 43143)	.75	3.00	87
PERFECT WORLD/Slammin'	(Chrysalis VS4 43265)	.75	3.00	88
SMALL WORLD/Small World (Part One & Two)	(Chrysalis VS4 43306)	.75	3.00	88
GIVE ME THE KEYS (AND I'LL DRIVE YOU CRAZY)/It's All Right (Live)	(Chrysalis VS4 43335)	.75	3.00	88

Also see U.S.A. For Africa, Voices Of America

LEWIS, JERRY LEE

GREAT BALLS OF FIRE/You Win Again	(Sun 281)	12.50	50.00	57

(Lewis and "Florida starlet" Jeane Solomon pictured)

HIGH SCHOOL CONFIDENTIAL/Fools Like Me	(Sun 296)	12.50	50.00	58

(From the motion picture *High School Confidential*. Lewis, Russ Tamblyn, Jan Sterling, Mamie Van Doren and an unidentified couple pictured.)

GREAT BALLS OF FIRE/Breathless	(Polydor 889 312-7)	.75	3.00	89

(From the motion picture *Great Balls Of Fire*, Dennis Quaid pictured on the front, Quaid and Lewis pictured on the back)
Also see Carl Perkins (*Birth Of Rock And Roll*)

LEWIS, JUNIOR

WHERE THE WORLD BEGINS	(Columbia 4-42129)	2.00	8.00	61
TOO BAD	(Columbia 4-42236)	2.00	8.00	62
THE ONLY GIRL	(Columbia 4-42361)	2.00	8.00	62

LEWIS, SHARI
(Ventriloquist best known for her character Lamb Chop)

"SOME THINGS FOR XMAS" A SNAKE, SOME MICE, SOME GLUE AND A HOLE TOO	(Musicor 1140)	3.75	15.00	65
GOTTA HAVE RAIN/Piccolo Pete	(RCA Victor Bluebird WBY-96)	1.50	6.00	60s

(Children's series)

EXTENDED PLAYS

THE LOVE BUG/LET'S SING OUR FAVORITE SONG/ Get On Board Little Children/What Do You Do?	(Kimberly 45FC)	2.50	10.00	64

(Promotional release for Infanta sweaters)

LEWIS, TED
WHEN MY BABY SMILES AT ME / Wear A Hat With A Silver Lining .... (Decca 1-700) — 2.50 — 10.00 — 51
(Decca "Curtain Call" series of reissues)

LEWIS & CLARKE EXPEDITION, THE
(Michael Murphy and Boomer Castleman)
BLUE REVELATIONS / I Feel Good (I Feel Bad) .... (Colgems 66-1006) — 2.50 — 10.00 — 67
DESTINATION UNKNOWN / Freedom Bird .... (Colgems 66-1011) — 2.50 — 10.00 — 68
   Also see Michael Martin Murphey

LIBERACE
I LOVE YOU TRULY / Oh Promise Me .... (Columbia 4-48008) — 3.75 — 15.00 — 54

LICENSE TO DRIVE
(Motion Picture)
   See Breakfast Club (Drive My Car)

LIFE BY NIGHT
PHONE TO PHONE / Life By Night .... (Manhattan 50007) — .75 — 3.00 — 85

LIGHTFOOT, GORDON
THE WAY I FEEL / Peaceful Waters .... (United Artists 50152) — 5.00 — 20.00 — 67
ANYTHING FOR LOVE / Let It Ride .... (Warner Bros. 28655-7) — 1.00 — 4.00 — 86

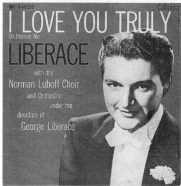

LIGHT OF DAY
(Motion Picture)
   See Joan Jett and the Blackhearts (Light Of Day)

LI'L WALLY
YOU WALTZ .... (Jay Jay 171) — 5.00 — 20.00 — 59
KISSED AGAIN WALTZ .... (Jay Jay 172) — 5.00 — 20.00 — 60
JULIDA .... (Jay Jay 173) — 3.75 — 15.00 — 60
LIVE IT UP .... (Jay Jay 177) — 3.75 — 15.00 — 60
YOU ARE MY SWEETHEART NOW POLKA .... (Jay Jay 211) — 3.75 — 15.00 — 63
CLAPPIN' POLKA .... (Jay Jay 217) — 3.75 — 15.00 — 63
   (Shown as by Lee Morgan)
THANKS FOR A WONDERFUL EVENING POLKA .... (Jay Jay 218) — 3.75 — 15.00 — 64

LIMAHL
THE NEVER ENDING STORY / Ivory Tower .... (EMI America B-8230) — .75 — 3.00 — 84
   (From the motion picture The Never Ending Story)
ONLY FOR LOVE / The Waiting Game .... (EMI America B-8277) — .75 — 3.00 — 84
LOVE IN YOUR EYES / Love Will Tear The Soul .... (EMI America B-8318) — .75 — 3.00 — 86
   Also see Kajagoogoo

LIMELITERS, THE
A DOLLAR DOWN / When Twice The Moon Has Come And Gone .... (RCA Victor 47-7859) — 2.00 — 8.00 — 61
WHO WILL BUY / .... (RCA Victor 47-8094) — 2.00 — 8.00 — 63
   Also see Glenn Yarbrough

LIME SPIDERS
EXTENDED PLAYS
SPACE CADET / JUST ONE SOLUTION / Action Woman / Stone Free .... (Virgin 7-99393) — 2.00 — 8.00 — 87
   (Promotional issue only issued with green vinyl)

LIMITED WARRANTY
VICTORY LINE / Yesterday's News .... (Atco 7-99541) — .75 — 3.00 — 86

LINDE, DENNIS
UNDER THE EYE .... (Monument 246) — 1.50 — 6.00 — 76

LINDEN, KATHY
ALLENTOWN JAIL .... (Monument 420) — 2.00 — 8.00 — 60

LINHART, BUZZY
YOU GOT WHAT IT TAKES .... (Kama Sutra 548) — 1.50 — 6.00 — 72
   (Promotional issue only)

LINK, LANCELOT, AND THE EVOLUTION REVOLUTION
SHA-LA LOVE YOU .... (ABC 11278) — 2.50 — 10.00 — 71
   (From the Saturday morning television series Lancelot Link, Secret Chimp. This group was literally a bunch of monkeys; the actual artists who dubbed the voices for the chimpanzees is unknown.)

LINKLETTER, ART & DIANE
WE LOVE YOU, CALL COLLECT .... (Word 1101) — 3.75 — 15.00 — 69
   (Cardboard sleeve)

LINN COUNTY
LET THE MUSIC BEGIN .... (Philips 40644) — 1.50 — 6.00 — 70

LINTON, SHERWIN
I'M NOT AMONG THE LOVING .... (Black Gold 6913) — 2.50 — 10.00 — 68

LINX
YOU'RE LYING .... (Chrysalis 2461) — 1.00 — 4.00 — 81

LIPTON, CELIA
CHILD / Puppet On A String .... (IRC 2359) — .75 — 3.00 — 87

LIPTON, PEGGY
(Actress who appeared in the television series The Mod Squad and Twin Peaks)
STONEY END / San Francisco Glide .... (Ode ZS7-114) — 2.00 — 8.00 — 69
LU / Let Me Pass By .... (Ode ZS7124) — 2.50 — 10.00 — 70
WEAR YOUR LOVE LIKE HEAVEN .... (Ode 66001) — 2.50 — 10.00 — 71
   (Back of sleeve reads On Mod Squad She's Julie Barnes On Ode '70 She's Peggy Lipton)

TITLE	LABEL AND NUMBER	VG	NM	YR

LISA LISA AND CULT JAM

CAN YOU FEEL THE BEAT/Beat The Feel You Can (Slick Mix) .... (Columbia 38-05669) — .75 — 3.00 — 85
   (Shown as by Lisa Lisa & Cult Jam With Full Force)
CAN YOU FEEL THE BEAT .... (Columbia 38-05669) — 1.00 — 4.00 — 85
   (Promotional issue, *Demonstration–Not For Sale* printed on sleeve. Shown as by Lisa Lisa & Cult Jam With Full Force)
HEAD TO TOE/You'll Never Change .... (Columbia 38-07008) — .75 — 3.00 — 87
LOST IN EMOTION/Motion Is Lost .... (Columbia 38 07267) — .75 — 3.00 — 87
SOMEONE TO LOVE ME FOR ME/Spanish Fly (The Full Force Groove) .... (Columbia 38-07619) — .75 — 3.00 — 87
   (Shown as by Lisa Lisa & Cult Jam Featuring Full Force, Full Force pictured on back)
EVERYTHING WILL B-FINE/Everything's Instrumental .... (Columbia 38-07737) — .75 — 3.00 — 88
GO FOR YOURS .... (Columbia 38-07982) — .75 — 3.00 — 88
   (Shown as by Lisa Lisa & Cult Jam With Full Force. From the motion picture *Caddyshack II.*)
LITTLE JACKIE WANTS TO BE A STAR/Star (The Jackie Mix) .... (Columbia 38-68674) — .75 — 3.00 — 89

LITTLE, CINDY

HAPPY BIRTHDAY JESUS .... (Columbia 4-41320) — 2.00 — 8.00 — 59
IT MUST HAVE BEEN THE EASTER BUNNY .... (Columbia 4-41346) — 2.00 — 8.00 — 59

LITTLE, MICHELLE

(Actress)
   See Intimate Strangers (*Let Go*)

LITTLE AMERICA

WALK ON FIRE .... (Geffen 28363-7) — .75 — 3.00 — 87

LITTLE ANTHONY AND THE IMPERIALS

HURT SO BAD/Reputation .... (DCP 1128) — 3.00 — 12.00 — 65
BETTER USE YOUR HEAD/The Wonder Of It All .... (Veep 1228) — 3.00 — 12.00 — 66

LITTLE EVA

MAKIN' WITH THE MAGILLA/Run To Her .... (Dimension 1035) — 7.50 — 30.00 — 64

LITTLE FEAT

HATE TO LOSE YOUR LOVIN' .... (Warner Bros. 27728-7) — 1.00 — 4.00 — 88
ONE CLEAR MOMENT .... (Warner Bros. 27684-7) — 1.00 — 4.00 — 88
   Also see Pure Prairie League (Craig Fuller)

LITTLE LINDA LOU

   See Frankie Brent Revue Featuring Little Linda Lou

LITTLE RICHARD

JENNY, JENNY/Miss Ann .... (Specialty 606) — 10.00 — 40.00 — 57
KEEP A KNOCKIN'/Can't Believe You Wanna Leave .... (Specialty 611) — 10.00 — 40.00 — 57
GOOD GOLLY, MISS MOLLY/Hey, Hey, Hey .... (Specialty 624) — 7.50 — 30.00 — 58
OOH! MY SOUL/True, Fine Mama .... (Specialty 633) — 7.50 — 30.00 — 58
HOLY MACKERAL/Baby, Don't You Want A Man Like Me .... (Modern 1018) — 7.50 — 30.00 — 58
POOR DOG (WHO CAN'T WAG HIS OWN TAIL)/Well .... (Okeh 4-7251) — 5.00 — 20.00 — 67
GREAT GOSH A'MIGHTY (IT'S A MATTER OF TIME) .... (MCA 52780) — .75 — 3.00 — 86
   (From the motion picture *Down And Out In Beverly Hills*)
   Also see the Beach Boys (*Happy Endings*), John Cougar Mellencamp (*Rave On*)

LITTLE RIVER BAND

LADY .... (Harvest 4667) — 1.25 — 5.00 — 79
TAKE IT EASY ON ME .... (Capitol B-5057) — 1.00 — 4.00 — 81
MAN ON YOUR MIND .... (Capitol B-5061) — 1.00 — 4.00 — 81
THE OTHER GUY .... (Capitol B-5185) — 1.00 — 4.00 — 82
YOU'RE DRIVING ME OUT OF MY MIND .... (Capitol B-5256) — 1.00 — 4.00 — 83
PLAYING TO WIN .... (Capitol B-5411) — 1.00 — 4.00 — 84
   (Shown as by LRB)
LOVE IS A BRIDGE .... (MCA 42193) — .75 — 3.00 — 88
IT'S COLD OUT TONIGHT .... (MCA 53424) — .75 — 3.00 — 88
   Also see Glenn Shorrock

LITTLE STEVEN

(Miami Steve Van Zandt)
FOREVER/Caravan .... (EMI America B-8144) — 1.00 — 4.00 — 82
   (Shown as by Little Steven and the Disciples of Soul. B-side from the motion picture *Men Without Women.*)
OUT OF THE DARKNESS/Fear .... (EMI America B-8207) — .75 — 3.00 — 84
NO MORE PARTY'S/Vote! .... (Manhattan B-50087) — .75 — 3.00 — 87
   Also see Artists United Against Apartheid, the Rascals (Dino Danelli was a member of the Disciples Of Soul), Ronnie Spector (*Say Goodbye To Hollywood*), Bruce Springsteen (Van Zandt was a member of the E Street Band)

LIVE A LITTLE, LOVE A LITTLE

(Motion Picture)
   See Elvis Presley (*A Little Less Conversation*)

LIVING DAYLIGHTS, THE

(Motion Picture)
   See A-Ha (*The Living Daylights*), the Pretenders (*If There Was A Man*)

LIVING IN A BOX

LIVING IN A BOX (SINGLE VERSION)/Living In A Box (Edited Dance Mix) (Chrysalis VS4 43104) — .75 — 3.00 — 87
SO THE STORY GOES/The Liam McCoy .... (Chrysalis VS4 43162) — .75 — 3.00 — 87
BLOW THE HOUSE DOWN/ .... (Chrysalis VS4 43364) — .75 — 3.00 — 89

L.L. COOL J.

GO CUT CREATOR GO/Kanday .... (Def Jam/Columbia 38-07620) — 1.00 — 4.00 — 87
GOING BACK TO CALI .... (Def Jam/Columbia 38-07679) — 1.00 — 4.00 — 87
   (From the motion picture *Less Than Zero*)

LLOYD, CHARLES

(Recorded and toured with the Beach Boys in the 70s)
MOON MAN/I Don't Care What You Tell Me .... (Kapp 2118) — 1.25 — 5.00 — 70

LLOYD, CHRISTOPHER
(Actor)
   See Buster Poindexter (*Hit The Road Jack*)

LLOYD, RICHARD
GET OFF OF MY CLOUD/Connection .... (Ice Water 27-001)   1.25   5.00   81
   (Hard cover issued with a small hole 45 RPM record)

LOCAL H
CYNIC/Talking Smack .... (Island 162-535 200-7)   .75   3.00   95
   (Issued with small-hole 45 RPM record)

LOCKLIN, HANK
   See Chet Atkins (*Chet's Tune*)

LODGE, JOHN
BLUE GUITAR .... (Threshold 67021)   3.75   15.00   75
   (Shown as by Justin Hayward and John Lodge)
   Also see the Moody Blues

LOFGREN, NILS
CRY TOUGH/Share A Little .... (A&M 1812)   1.25   5.00   76
   Also see Jersey Artists For Mankind, Bruce Springsteen (Lofgren was a member of the E Street Band)

LOGGINS, DAVE
   See Anne Murray (*Nobody Loves Me Like You Do*)

LOGGINS, KENNY
DON'T FIGHT IT/The More We Try .... (Columbia 18-03192)   1.00   4.00   82
   (A-side shown as by Kenny Loggins With Steve Perry)
DON'T FIGHT IT .... (Columbia 18-03192)   1.25   5.00   82
   (Shown as by Kenny Loggins With Steve Perry. Promotional issue, *Demonstration Only Not For Sale* printed on sleeve.)
WELCOME TO HEARTLIGHT/Only A Miracle .... (Columbia 38-03555)   1.00   4.00   82
WELCOME TO HEARTLIGHT .... (Columbia 38-03555)   1.25   5.00   82
   (Promotional issue, *Demonstration Only Not For Sale* printed on sleeve)
FOOTLOOSE .... (Columbia 38-04310)   .75   3.00   84
   (From the motion picture *Footloose*)
FOOTLOOSE .... (Columbia 38-04310)   1.00   4.00   84
   (Promotional issue, *Demonstration Only/Not For Sale* printed on sleeve. From the motion picture *Footloose*.)
I'M FREE (HEAVEN HELPS THE MAN) .... (Columbia 38-04452)   .75   3.00   84
   (From the motion picture *Footloose*)
I'M FREE (HEAVEN HELPS THE MAN) .... (Columbia 38-04452)   1.00   4.00   84
   (Promotional issue, *Demonstration Only–Not For Sale* printed on sleeve. From the motion picture *Footloose*.)
VOX HUMANA .... (Columbia 38-04849)   .75   3.00   85
VOX HUMANA .... (Columbia 38-04849)   1.00   4.00   85
   (Promotional issue, *Demonstration Only–Not For Sale* printed on sleeve)
FOREVER .... (Columbia 38-04931)   .75   3.00   85
FOREVER .... (Columbia 38-04931)   1.00   4.00   85
   (Promotional issue, *Demonstration Only–Not For Sale* printed on sleeve)
DANGER ZONE .... (Columbia 38-05893)   .75   3.00   86
(From the motion picture *Top Gun*)
DANGER ZONE .... (Columbia 38-05893)   1.00   4.00   86
   (Promotional issue, *Demonstration Only–Not For Sale* printed on sleeve. From the motion picture *Top Gun*.)
PLAYING WITH THE BOYS .... (Columbia 38-05902)   .75   3.00   86
(From the motion picture *Top Gun*)
PLAYING WITH THE BOYS .... (Columbia 38-05902)   1.00   4.00   86
   (Promotional issue, *Demonstration Only–Not For Sale* printed on sleeve. From the motion picture *Top Gun*.)
MEET ME HALFWAY .... (Columbia 38-06690)   .75   3.00   87
   (From the motion picture *Over The Top*)
MEET ME HALFWAY .... (Columbia 38-06690)   1.00   4.00   87
   (Promotional issue, *Demonstration Only Not For Sale* printed on sleeve. From the motion picture *Over The Top*.)
NOBODY'S FOOL .... (Columbia 38-07971)   .75   3.00   88
   (From the motion picture *Caddyshack II*)
I'M GONNA MISS YOU .... (Columbia 38-08091)   .75   3.00   88
   Also see Loggins and Messina, U.S.A. For Africa, Voices Of America

LOGGINS AND MESSINA
JUST BEFORE THE NEWS .... (Columbia AE 7-1060)   2.00   8.00   72
   (Promotional issue only)
ANGRY EYES .... (Columbia 3-10444)   1.25   5.00   76
   (Promotional issue only, half sleeve)
   Also see Kenny Loggins, Poco (Jim Messina), U.S.A. For Africa (Kenny Loggins), Voices Of America (Kenny Loggins)

LOLITA
COWBOY JIMMY JOE .... (Kapp 370)   3.75   15.00   61

LOLLIPOP SHOPPE, THE
YOU MUST BE A WITCH/Don't Close The Door .... (Uni 55050)   3.75   15.00   68

LOMAX, JACKIE
HOW THE WEB WAS WOVEN/(I) Fall Inside Your Eyes .... (Apple 1819)   2.50   10.00   70
LET THE PLAY BEGIN/Lavender Dream .... (Warner Bros. PRO-514)   1.50   6.00   72
   (Promotional issue only issued with a small-hole 33-1/3 RPM record)

LOMBARDO, GUY
AULD LANG SYNE/Humoresque .... (Decca 1-708)   2.50   10.00   52
   (Decca "Curtain Call" series of reissues)

LONDON, JULIE
TIME FOR LOVERS/In The Wee Small Hours Of The Morning .... (Liberty 55269)   3.75   15.00   61
MOTHERLESS CHILD .... (Yes 7002)   3.00   12.00

TITLE	LABEL AND NUMBER	VG	NM	YR

LONDON, LAURIE
I GOTTA ROBE/Joshua .... (Capitol 3973) | 3.75 | 15.00 | 58
(Promotional issue only with a 2" envelope flap)

LONDON PHILHARMONIC ORCHESTRA, THE
See Pia Zadora (I Am What I Am)

LONDON SYMPHONY ORCHESTRA
BOURREE/Elegy .... (RCA PB-14262) | 1.00 | 4.00 | 85
(Sleeve reads The London Symphony Orchestra plays the music of Jethro Yull featuring Ian Anderson)
Also see Richard Cocciante (Michelle), Richie Havens (Eyesight To The Blind), Murray Head (One Night In Bangkok)

LONE JUSTICE
WAYS TO BE WICKED .... (Geffen 29023-7) | .75 | 3.00 | 85
SWEET, SWEET BABY (I'M FALLING) (REMIX)/Don't Toss Us Away .... (Geffen 28965-7) | .75 | 3.00 | 85
SHELTER .... (Geffen 28520-7) | .75 | 3.00 | 86

LONE RANGER, THE
HE BECOMES THE LONE RANGER .... (Decca K-29) | 3.75 | 15.00 | 51
(Number one of a four-record 45 RPM set titled The Adventures Of The Lone Ranger. There also exists a similar set of sleeves produced for the 78 RPM series.)
HE FINDS SILVER .... (Decca K-30) | 3.75 | 15.00 | 51
(Number two of a four-record 45 RPM set titled The Adventures Of The Lone Ranger. There also exists a similar set of sleeves produced for the 78 RPM series.)
HE FINDS DAN REID .... (Decca K-31) | 3.75 | 15.00 | 51
(Number three of a four-record 45 RPM set titled The Adventures Of The Lone Ranger. There also exists a similar set of sleeves produced for the 78 RPM series.)
HE HELPS THE COLONEL'S SON .... (Decca K-32) | 3.75 | 15.00 | 51
(Number four of a four-record 45 RPM set titled The Adventures Of The Lone Ranger. There also exists a similar set of sleeves produced for the 78 RPM series.)

LONE RANGER AND THE LOST CITY OF GOLD, THE
(Motion Picture)
See Bob Carroll (Hi Ho Silver)

LONG, JOHNNY
IN A SHANTY IN OLD SHANTY TOWN/The White Star Of Sigma Nu .... (Decca 1-719) | 3.00 | 12.00 | 53
(Decca "Curtain Call" series of reissues)

LONG, SHORTY
THE LEGEND OF WYATT EARP/Jesse James .... (RCA Victor Bluebird WBY-59) | 2.50 | 10.00 | 50s
(Children's series)

LONGEST DAY, THE
(Motion Picture)
See Mitch Miller (The Longest Day)

LOOKING FOR LOVE
(Motion Picture)
See Connie Francis (Looking For Love)

LOOKING GLASS
GOLDEN RAINBOW/Jenny Lynne .... (Epic 10900) | 1.25 | 5.00 | 72
EXTENDED PLAYS
JIMMY LOVES MARY-ANNE .... (Columbia AS 53) | 1.50 | 6.00 | 73
(Promotional issue only titled New Comers As Featured In New Ingenue In August, issued with a small-hole 33-1/3 RPM record. Also includes one song each by Johnny Nash, Andy Pratt, and Jimmie Spheeris.)

LOOKINLAND, MIKE
(Juvenile Actor)
LOVE DOESN'T CARE WHO'S IN IT/Gum Drop .... (Capitol 3914) | 3.00 | 12.00 | 74
Also see the Brady Bunch

LOOSE ENDS
HANGIN' ON A STRING (CONTEMPLATING) .... (MCA 52570) | .75 | 3.00 | *85
STAY A LITTLE WHILE, CHILD .... (MCA 52820) | .75 | 3.00 | 86

LOOSE GRAVEL
FRISCO BAND/Waiting In Line .... (Kelly 26945) | 2.00 | 8.00 | 75

LOPEZ, DENISE
SAYING SORRY (DOESN'T MAKE IT RIGHT) .... (Vendetta 7200) | .75 | 3.00 | 88

LOPEZ, TRINI
SAD TOMORROWS/I've Lost My Love For You .... (Reprise 0328) | 2.50 | 10.00 | 65
LEMON TREE/Pretty Eyes .... (Reprise 0336) | 2.50 | 10.00 | 65
SINNER MAN/Double Trouble .... (Reprise 0405) | 2.50 | 10.00 | 65
(From the motion picture Marriage On The Rocks)
MADE IN PARIS/Pretty Little Girl .... (Reprise 0435) | 2.50 | 10.00 | 66
EXTENDED PLAYS
IF I HAD A HAMMER/A-ME-RI-CA/
Kansas City/The Blizzard Song .... (Columbia/Warner Bros. 124178) | 2.50 | 10.00 | 67
(Promotional issue given away free with each carton of the soft drink Fresca. Titled on front Trini Lopez Sings His Greatest Hits. Sleeve has a flap with a small die-cut hole to hang off of a bottle.)

LORAIN, A'ME
WHOLE WIDE WORLD/Stop Twistin' My Arm .... (RCA 9098-7-RE) | .75 | 3.00 | 90
(B-side shown as by Barrence Whitfield and the Savages. From the motion picture True Love.)

LORBER, JEFF
FACTS OF LOVE .... (Warner Bros. 28588-7) | .75 | 3.00 | 86
(Shown as by Jeff Lorber Featuring Karyn White)

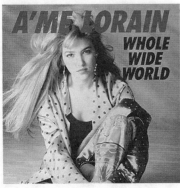

LORD, C. M.
YOUR LOVE IS LIKE THE MORNING SUN/Rushin' To Meet You .... (London 45-205) | 1.50 | 6.00 | 74

LORD DENT & THE INVADERS
WOLF CALL/The Greaser .... (Shelley 1001) | 6.25 | 25.00 | 60s

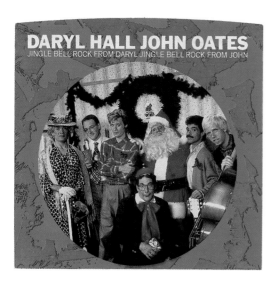

Bruce Springsteen *Santa Claus Is Comin' To Town* $20. Issued as a promotional item only.

The Brady Bunch *Frosty The Snowman* $20. Not a song I listen to but still a cool sleeve.

Daryl Hall & John Oates *Jingle Bell Rock* $5. This is the stock copy, the promotional issue sells for $10.

John Denver & The Muppets *Have Yourself A Merry Little Christmas/We Wish You A Merry Christmas* $5

Nat King Cole *The Happiest Christmas Tree* $12

Cheech & Chong *Santa Claus And His Old Lady* $8. A holiday favorite on my stereo each year.

Psychedelic Shack

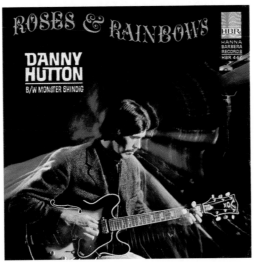

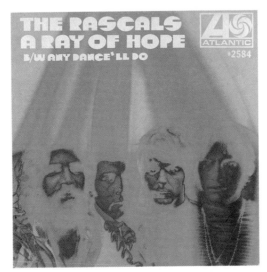

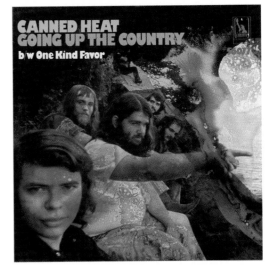

Hourglass *Nothing But Tears* $40. This group, with Duane and Greg Allman, was an early incarnation of the Allman Brothers Band.

Danny Hutton *Roses And Rainbows* $20. His first picture sleeve from 1965 before becoming one of Three Dog Night's lead vocalists.

The Rascals *A Ray Of Hope* $8. Groovy.

Keith *Tell Me To My Face* $8. Most sleeves from this time on Mercury were black and white. This sleeve is a colorful exception.

Jefferson Airplane *Crown of Creation* $20. A real beauty from 1968 with artwork characteristic of the times.

Canned Heat *Going Up The Country* $8. Fried effect for electric boogie.

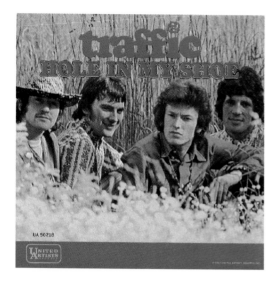

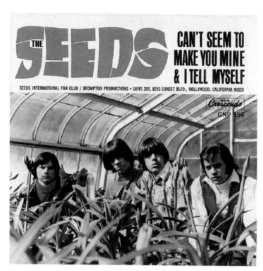

Trafffic *Hole In My Shoe* $20. Steve Winwood would release 12 sleeves as a solo artist but only one with Traffic.

Tommy James and the Shondells *Real Girl* $12

Livingston Taylor *Loving Arms* $3. The vocal similarities between Livingston, his older brother James, and James' and Carly Simon's son is remarkable.

Carly Simon *Why* $8. This is her hardest to find.

The Seeds *Can't Seem To Make You Mine* $20. Seeds...greenhouse...plants, yeah we get it.

Simon and Garfunkel *The Dangling Conversation* $20. Their first picture sleeve.

Paint Me A Picture

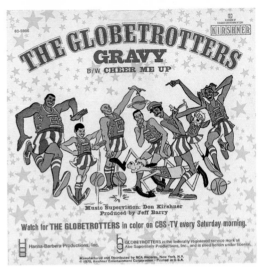

Andy Griffith *Romeo & Juliet (Parts 1 & 2)* $20

Cat Stevens *Oh Very Young* $5. Stevens' illustration style featured on this sleeve was employed in a children's book he wrote and illustrated for Scholastic Book Services in 1972 titled *Teaser and the Firecat*.

Tom Jones *What's New Pussycat?* $8. Wacky.

The Globetrotters *Gravy* $12. The clown princes of the basketball court had their own animated cartoon series on CBS from 1970–1972.

Faster Pussycat *Babylon* $3

The Rolling Stones *Harlem Shuffle* $3. Both the stock and promotional version ($6) are identical on the front and differ only slightly on the back.

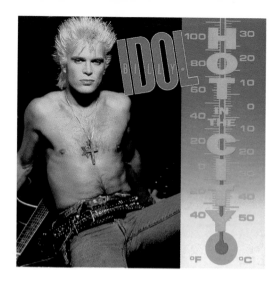

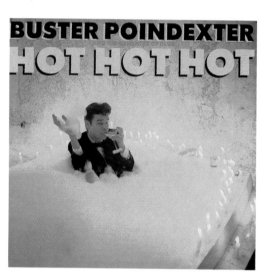

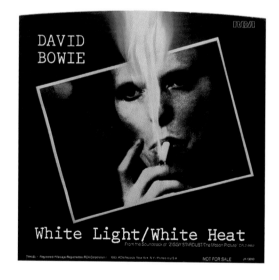

Billy Idol *Hot In The City* $3. This was the second release for Idol's popular tune, this one being a live version.

Blue Oyster Cult *Hot Rails To Hell* $10. A quote on the back from *Rolling Stone* states *... a brilliant exposition of what the Stones would be playing today if they hadn't turned into such bourgeois hedonist auteurs.*

Eno *Baby's On Fire* $50

Stevie Nicks *Rooms On Fire* $4. This was her last sleeve as a solo artist.

Buster Poindexter *Hot Hot Hot* $3. The lounge lizard image is a far cry from David Johansen's glitter-era days with the New York Dolls.

David Bowie *White Light/White Heat* $8. This live performance was from Bowie's last show with the Spiders From Mars.

Face The Face

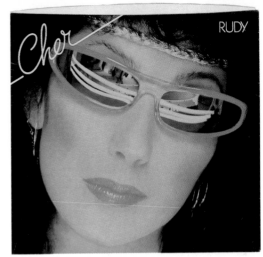

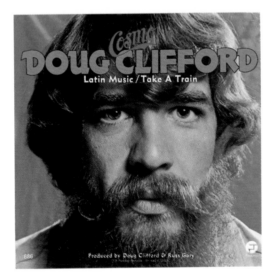

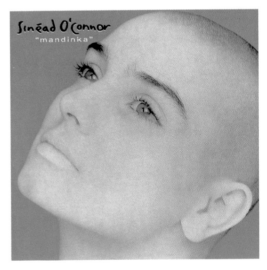

Sam Phillips *I Don't Know How To Say Goodbye To You* $4

Ellen Foley *Sad Song* $5. She was the heavy-breathing, commitment-seeking vocalist featured on Meatloaf's *Paradise By The Dashboard Light*.

Doug Clifford *Latin Music* $8. Drummer for Creedence Clearwater Revival.

Cher *Rudy* $6

Peggy Lipton *Wear Your Love Like Heaven* $10. Better known for fighting crime with the Mod Squad and waiting tables in Twin Peaks than for her recording career.

Sinéad O'Connor *Mandinka* $5. Her shaven pate was symbolic of O'Connor's disowning of the stereotypical female rock star image.

Kate Bush *Wuthering Heights* $40. Singer, songwriter, pianist, producer, director, and one day older than me.

Madonna *Keep It Together* $20. This was Madonna's last U.S. sleeve and, unlike most of her earlier releases, is hard to find.

Aretha Franklin *Rough Lover* $25. One of the most influential artists in the history of popular music.

The Pretenders *Hymn To Her* $3. Chrissie Hynde's self-assertive attitude has inspired many female rockers.

Joni Mitchell *Good Friends* $3. The artwork was created by Mitchell.

Joan Jett and the Blackhearts *I Love Rock 'N Roll* $6. A breakthrough #1 single for Jett who started her career with the all-female rock group The Runaways.

Saturday Night At The Movies

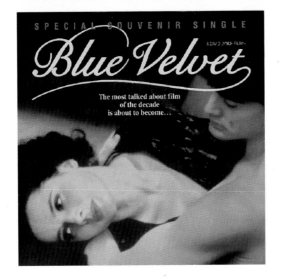

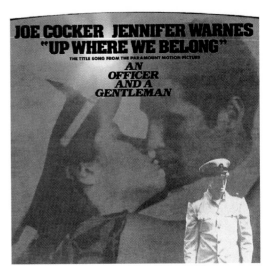

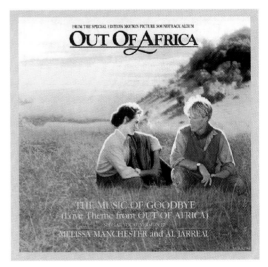

Bobby Vinton *Blue Velvet* $10. A strange yet effective pairing of Vinton's act of crooning and director David Lynch's vision of sadism.

John Travolta and Olivia Newton-John *You're The One That I Want* $5

Billy Vera and the Beaters *Let You Get Away* $4. This was printed on the standard sleeve text weight and also a heavier cover stock.

Henry Mancini *Moon River* $10. Audrey Hepburn as the wonderfully flighty Holly Golightly.

Joe Cocker and Jennifer Warnes *Up Where We Belong* $4. The song that brought Cocker back into the spotlight after a 7-year absence from the Top 40.

Melissa Manchester and Al Jarreau *The Music Of Goodbye* $4

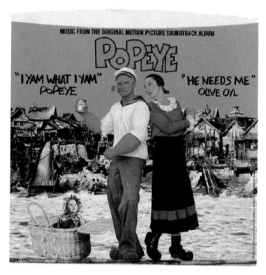

Ramones *Pet Sematary* $6

Lionel Newman *The Silent Movie March* $6. In typical Mel Brooks fashion, the only word spoken in the film is by mime Marcel Marceau.

Dick Van Dyke *Chim Chim Cheree* $12. I've always wondered how convincing is his cockney accent to a Brit?

John Williams *Star Wars Main Title* $6

Robin Williams *I Yam What I Yam* $6. Williams and Shelley Duvall sing tunes penned by Harry Nilsson.

Inspector Clouseau *Thank Heaven For Little Girls* $6. Peter Sellers' appearance in the fifth sequel as the bumbling detective features this vocal version of the song popularized by Maurice Chevalier.

U Got The Look

Julie London *Time For Lovers* $15. London recorded in the 50s and 60s, appeared in over a dozen films, and had a role in the television series *Emergency!* in the 70s.

Brenda Lee *Truly, Truly, True* $10. Singing professionally since she was 6, Lee's career spans five decades.

Olivia Newton-John *Can't We Talk It Over In Bed* $3

Marianne Faithfull *Go Away From My World* $20. She may have been better known in 1965 as Mick Jagger's girlfriend but that changed in 1978 with her landmark album *Broken English*.

Barbi Benton *Welcome Stranger* $5. A former Playboy playmate and a regular on *Hee Haw* from 1971-76.

The McGuire Sisters *Livin' Dangerously* $10

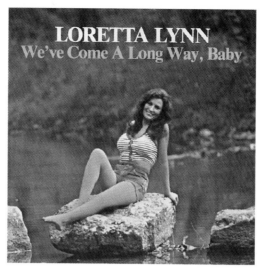

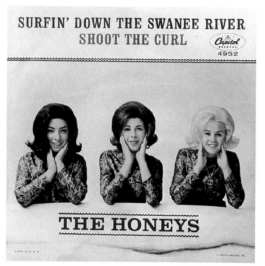

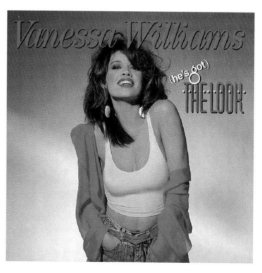

Ann-Margret *Jim Dandy* $20

The Honeys *Surfin' Down The Swanee River* $1000. One of the most valuable sleeves listed in this book. Group member Marilyn Rovell would later marry the Beach Boys' Brian Wilson.

Annette *First Name Initial* $30. Annette Funicello's sleeves are still popular, sentimental favorites of collectors.

Loretta Lynn *We've Come A Long Way Baby* $5. She had placed a string of singles in the country chart's Top Ten from 1962 through 1982.

Connie Francis *Follow The Boys* $10

Vanessa Williams *(He's Got) The Look* $3. Williams became the first black Miss America and followed that achievement with a successful recording career.

My Favorite Things

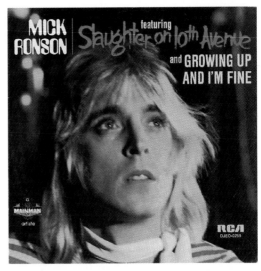

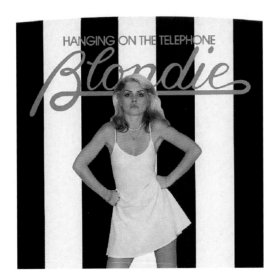

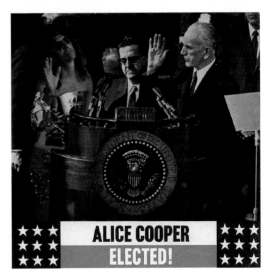

David Bowie *Time* $600. Reproduced for the first time, this elusive sleeve was relatively unknown for 20 years.

Steve Miller *Sitting In Circles* $25. Released in 1967, Capitol Records would not print another Miller sleeve until 14 years later.

Blondie *Hanging On The Telephone* $6. This song from 1978 was a cover version of the Nerves' 1976 power pop gem.

The Ren and Stimpy Show *Dog Pound Hop/ Happy, Happy, Joy, Joy* $10. Series creator John Kricfalusi originally provided the voice for the irascible chihuahua Ren and Billy West as the half-wit feline Stimpy.

Mick Ronson *Slaughter On 10th Avenue/ Growing Up And I'm Fine* $25

Alice Cooper *Elected* $10. Would you vote for this man?

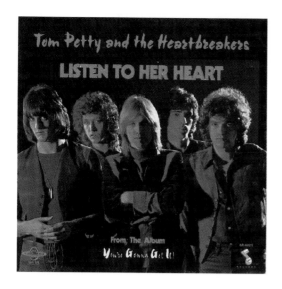

Tom Petty and the Heartbreakers *Listen To Her Heart* $6. From their second album.

Gordon Lightfoot *The Way I Feel* $20. One of Canada's most successful singer/ songwriters.

John Cougar *I Need A Lover That Won't Drive Me Crazy* $8. The Cougar moniker was eventually replaced with his given name of Mellencamp.

Pee-wee Herman *Surfin' Bird* $6. Paul Reuben's Saturday morning kids' show *Pee-wee's Playhouse* ran from 1986–1991.

Carole King *Sweet Seasons* $5. One of my early purchases before I considered myself a "collector".

The Beach Boys *Surfin' Safari* $60. A quintessential image of the group. Catch a wave dude!

Bits And Pieces

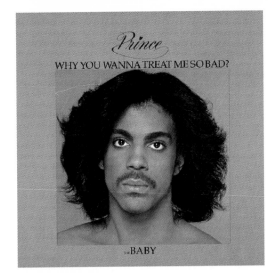

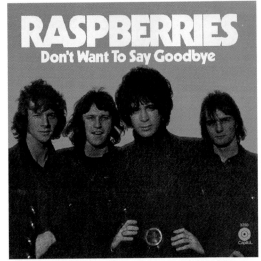

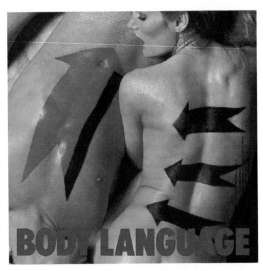

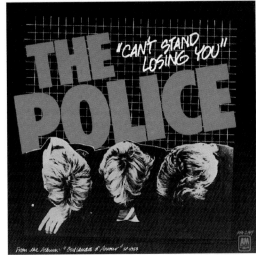

Prince *Why You Wanna Treat Me So Bad?* $50. This was Prince's third single to hit the R&B charts and his first commercial sleeve.

The Knack *My Sharona* $8. Gee I wonder who the target market was for this one?

Kiss *Flaming Youth* $30. Featuring the original line-up of Paul Stanley, Peter Criss, Ace Frehley, and Gene Simmons.

The Raspberries *Don't Want To Say Goodbye* $20. They released two sleeves, this one being the only one in color.

Queen *Body Language* $10. This is the first version before conservative minds issued a second variation with no flesh.

The Police *Can't Stand Losing You* $10. Sting once stated *"Three blond-hairs, the macho name...it's product."*

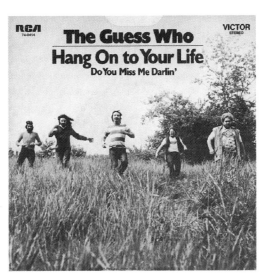

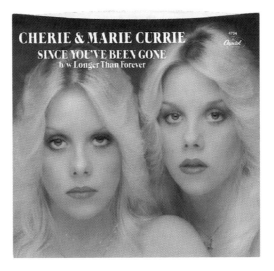

Tracey Ullman *They Don't Know* $4. In 1988 she landed the first Emmy for the Fox network with *The Tracey Ullman Show*.

Linda Ronstadt & the Stone Poneys *Up To My Neck In High Muddy Water* $30

Paul Kantner & Grace Slick *Sunfighter* $6. A commemoration in image and song of their baby daughter, China, born in 1971.

10cc *Art For Art's Sake* $8. A hit in the U.K. (#5), but the song made no headway in the states.

The Guess Who *Hang On To Your Life* $50. My favorite group.

Cherie & Marie Currie *Since You've Been Gone* $8. Cherie's post-Runaways career included an album with her sister and the 1980 film *Foxes*.

Takin' It To The Streets

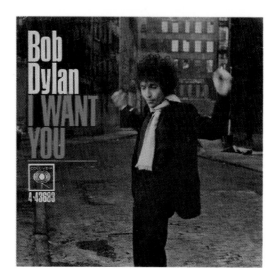

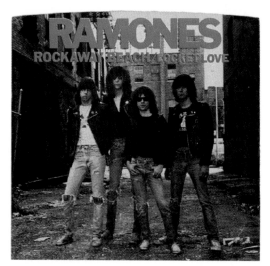

Crowded House *Something So Strong* $3

The Smashing Pumpkins *1979* $3. One of the few sleeves released in 1995 and a gem to boot.

Bob Dylan *I Want You* $40. The streets of New York appeared to be a favorite photo location judging by this sleeve and the album cover for *The Freewheelin'*.

Carole King *City Streets* $6. This is the promotional issue from her 1989 album of the same name.

Run DMC *Walk This Way* $4. These hardcore hip-hop artists teamed with Steve Tyler and Joe Perry on this record which helped revive Aerosmith's career.

Ramones *Rockaway Beach* $10. A no frills sleeve for a no frills band.

LORD LOVE A DUCK
(Motion Picture)
   See Neal Hefti (*The Year Of The Duck*)

LORDS, TRACI
   See Ronnie Mack (*I Love Traci Lords*)

LORDS OF THE NEW CHURCH, THE

OPEN YOUR EYES/Question Of Temperature .... (I.R.S. 9908)	1.25	5.00	82
LIVE FOR TODAY/Girls Girls Girls .... (I.R.S. 9921)	1.00	4.00	83

   Also see Stiv Bators, the Dead Boys (Stiv Bators)

LOREN, DONNA
BLOWING OUT THE CANDLES/Just A Little Girl .... (Capitol 5250)   3.00   12.00   64

LOREN, SOPHIA
(Actress)
LOVE SONG FROM HOUSEBOAT/Bing! Bang! Bong! .... (Columbia 4-41200)   6.25   25.00   58

LORING, GLORIA
(Actress)

FRIENDS AND LOVERS .... (Carrere 06122)   .75   3.00   86
   (Shown as by Gloria Loring & Carl Anderson)
ONE LOVE, ONE HEART (ONE HAND IN MINE)/New Moon Over Babylon ... (Atlantic 7-89079)   .75   3.00   88
   (A-side shown as by Gloria Loring Featuring Bobby Caldwell)

LOS ANGELES RAMS
(Football Team)
LET'S RAM IT .... (Red Entertainment 980-001)   1.00   4.00   86

LOS BRAVOS
EXTENDED PLAYS
SWINGERS FOR COKE .... (Coca-Cola no #)   12.50   50.00   66
   (Promotional issue only with one "Coke" song each by the Drifters, Lesley Gore, Los Bravos, and Roy Orbison)

LOS LOBOS

WILL THE WOLF SURVIVE? .... (Warner Bros./Slash 29093-7)	.75	3.00	84
LA BAMBA .... (Warner Bros./Slash 28336-7)	.75	3.00	87
   (From the motion picture *La Bamba*. Lou Diamond Phillips pictured on front, Los Lobos on back.)
| SET ME FREE ROSA LEE .... (Warner Bros./Slash 28390-7) | .75 | 3.00 | 87 |
| ONE TIME ONE NIGHT .... (Warner Bros./Slash 28464-7) | .75 | 3.00 | 87 |

LOS STRAIGHTJACKETS
PACIFICA/Kawanga .... (Spinout 45-012)   .75   3.00   95
LA PLAGA/¡Qué Mala! .... (Spinout 45-015)   .50   2.00   96
   (Shown as by Big Sandy With Los Straightjackets)

LOST BOYS, THE
(Motion Picture)
   See Lou Gramm (*Lost In The Shadows*), INXS and Jimmy Barnes (*Good Times*)

LOUDERMILK, JOHN D.
YEARBOOK/Susie's House .... (Columbia 4-41165)   7.50   30.00   58
ROAD HOG/Angela Jones .... (RCA 47-8101)   5.00   20.00   62
   Also see Chet Atkins (*Chet's Tune*), Johnny Dee

LOVE, COURTNEY
HIGHLIGHTS/Shaniko/Disappearing Lessons .... (IPU 22)   1.25   5.00   91
   Also see Hole

LOVE, DARLENE
(Darlene Love was a member of the sixties girl-groups, the Crystals, Bob B. Soxx and the Blue Jeans, and the Blossoms)
RIVER DEEP, MOUNTAIN HIGH/Leader Of The Pack .... (Elektra 7-69647)   1.25   5.00   85
   (B-side shown as by Annie Golden. From the Broadway Musical *Leader Of The Pack*.)

LOVE, MIKE
   See the Beach Boys, Mike & Dean

LOVE AFFAIR

ONE ROAD/Let Me Know .... (Date 2-1646)   3.00   12.00   69

LOVE AND MONEY
CANDYBAR EXPRESS/Love & Money (Dub) .... (Mercury 884 524-7)   .75   3.00   86
HALLELUIAH MAN/Love Is A Million Miles Away .... (Mercury 870 596-7)   .75   3.00   88
STRANGE KIND OF LOVE/Set The Night On Fire .... (Mercury 874 198-7)   .75   3.00   88

LOVE AND ROCKETS

SO ALIVE/Dreamtime .... (RCA/Beggars Banquet 8956-7-R)   .75   3.00   89
   Also see Bauhaus

LOVE BATTERY
FOOT/Mr. Soul .... (Sub Pop 135)   1.25   5.00   91
   Also see The Presidents Of The United States Of America (Jason Finn)

LOVE IN THE AFTERNOON
(Motion Picture)
   See Jane Morgan (*Fascination*)

LOVELESS, PATTY
LONELY DAYS LONELY NIGHTS .... (MCA 52694)   1.25   5.00   85

LOVENCRAFT, H.P.
WAYFARING STRANGER .... (Philips 40491)   2.00   8.00   68

LOVER SPEAKS, THE
EVERY LOVER'S SIGN (REMIX)/Every Lover's Sign (Remix) .... (A&M 2884)   .75   3.00   86

TITLE	LABEL AND NUMBER	VG	NM	YR

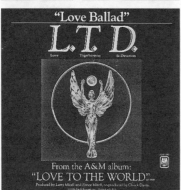

LOVERBOY
THE KID IS HOT TONITE/Teenage Overdose .... (Columbia 11-02068)		1.00	4.00	81
THE KID IS HOT TONITE/Teenage Overdose .... (Columbia 11-02068)		1.25	5.00	81

(Promotional issue, *Demonstration–Not For Sale* printed on sleeve. Sleeve lists b-side although the 45 has *The Kid Is Hot Tonite* on both sides.)

WORKING FOR THE WEEKEND/Emotional .... (Columbia 18-02589)		.75	3.00	81
WORKING FOR THE WEEKEND .... (Columbia 18-02589)		1.00	4.00	81

(Promotional issue, *Demonstration–Not For Sale* printed on sleeve)

WHEN IT'S OVER/It's Your Life .... (Columbia 18-02814)		.75	3.00	82

(Backing vocals credited on front to Nancy Nash)

WHEN IT'S OVER (LONG VERSION)/When It's Over (Short Version) .... (Columbia 18-02814)		1.00	4.00	82

(Promotional issue, *Demonstration: Not For Sale* printed on sleeve. Front of sleeve credits backing vocals to Nancy Nash.)

JUMP/Take Me To The Top .... (Columbia 38-03346)		.75	3.00	82
JUMP/Take Me To The Top .... (Columbia 38-03346)		1.00	4.00	82

(Promotional issue, *Demonstration–Not For Sale* printed on sleeve. Sleeve lists b-side although the 45 has *Jump* on both sides.)

HOT GIRLS IN LOVE/Meltdown .... (Columbia 38-03941)		.75	3.00	83
HOT GIRLS IN LOVE .... (Columbia 38-03941)		1.00	4.00	83

(Promotional issue, *Demonstration–Not For Sale* printed on sleeve)

QUEEN OF THE BROKEN HEARTS/Chance Of A Lifetime .... (Columbia 38 04096)		.75	3.00	83
QUEEN OF THE BROKEN HEARTS .... (Columbia 38 04096)		1.00	4.00	83

(Promotional issue, *Demonstration–Not For Sale* printed on sleeve)

LOVIN' EVERY MINUTE OF IT/Bullet In The Chamber .... (Columbia 38-05569)		.75	3.00	85
LOVIN' EVERY MINUTE OF IT .... (Columbia 38-05569)		1.00	4.00	85

(Promotional issue, *Demonstration–Not For Sale* printed on sleeve)

DANGEROUS/Too Much Too Soon .... (Columbia 38-05711)		.75	3.00	85
DANGEROUS .... (Columbia 38-05711)		1.00	4.00	85

(Promotional issue, *Demonstration–Not For Sale* printed on sleeve)

THIS COULD BE THE NIGHT/It's Your Life .... (Columbia 38-05765)		.75	3.00	85
THIS COULD BE THE NIGHT .... (Columbia 38-05765)		1.00	4.00	85

(Promotional issue, *Demonstration Not For Sale* printed on sleeve)

LEAD A DOUBLE LIFE/Steal The Thunder .... (Columbia 38-05867)		.75	3.00	86
LEAD A DOUBLE LIFE .... (Columbia 38-05867)		1.00	4.00	86

(Promotional issue, *Demonstration–Not For Sale* printed on sleeve)

HEAVEN IN YOUR EYES .... (Columbia 38-06178)		.75	3.00	86

(From the motion picture *Top Gun*)

HEAVEN IN YOUR EYES .... (Columbia 38-06178)		1.00	4.00	86

(Promotional issue, *Demonstration Only/Not For Sale* printed on sleeve. From the motion picture *Top Gun*.)

NOTORIOUS/Wildside .... (Columbia 38-07324)		.75	3.00	87
LOVE WILL RISE AGAIN/ .... (Columbia 38-07652)		.75	3.00	87

Also see Mike Reno *(Almost Paradise)*

LOVE STORY
(Motion Picture)

See Frances Lai *(Theme From Love Story)*

LOVE WITH THE PROPER STRANGER
(Motion Picture)

See Jack Jones *(Love With The Proper Stranger)*

LOVING
(Television Soap Opera)

Related see the Soaps and Hearts Ensemble

LOVIN' SPOONFUL, THE
YOU DIDN'T HAVE TO BE SO NICE/My Gal .... (Kama Sutra 205)		2.50	10.00	66
DAYDREAM .... (Kama Sutra 208)		3.00	12.00	66
DID YOU EVER HAVE TO MAKE UP YOUR MIND?/ Didn't Want To Have To Do It .... (Kama Sutra 209)		3.00	12.00	66
SUMMER IN THE CITY/Butchie's Tune .... (Kama Sutra 211)		3.00	12.00	66
RAIN ON THE ROOF/POW (Theme from "What's Up, Tiger Lily?") .... (Kama Sutra 216)		3.00	12.00	66
NASHVILLE CATS/Full Measure .... (Kama Sutra 219)		3.00	12.00	66
DARLING BE HOME SOON/Darlin' Companion .... (Kama Sutra 220)		3.00	12.00	67

(From the motion picture *You're A Big Boy Now*)

SIX O'CLOCK .... (Kama Sutra 225)		3.00	12.00	67
SHE IS STILL A MYSTERY/Only Pretty, What A Pity .... (Kama Sutra 239)		3.00	12.00	67

Also see John Sebastian, Zalman Yanovsky, Jerry Yester (Yester replaced Yanovsky in 1967 and was with the group on *She Is Still A Mystery*)

LOWE, ROB
(Actor)

See Mickey Thomas *(Stand In The Fire)*, John Parr *(St. Elmo's Fire)*

LRB
See Little River Band

L7
SHOVE/Packin' A Rod .... (Sub Pop 58)		2.50	10.00	90

(Limited edition of 3,000 with 1,200 on green vinyl and 1,800 on black)

SLIDE (LIVE)/Easy .... (Soil X Samples 5847)		2.50	10.00	92

(Split single, flip side shown as by Faith No More)

L.T.D.
LOVE BALLAD/Let The Music Keep Playing .... (A&M 1847)		1.25	5.00	76
(EVERY TIME I TURN AROUND) BACK IN LOVE AGAIN/Material Things .... (A&M 1974)		1.25	5.00	77
NEVER GET ENOUGH OF YOUR LOVE/Make Someone Smile, Today! .... (A&M 2005)		1.25	5.00	77
DANCE N SING N/Give It All .... (A&M 2142)		1.25	5.00	79

Also see Jeffrey Osborne

L'TRIMM
CUTTIE PIE .... (Atlantic 7-88973)		.75	3.00	88
CARS WITH THE BOOM .... (Atlantic 7-89005)		.75	3.00	88

LUBA
EVERYTIME I SEE YOUR PICTURE .... (Capitol B-5378)		.75	3.00	84

LUBOFF, NORMAN, CHOIR
WATER .... (Columbia 4-40886)		2.00	8.00	57
CONSIDER YOURSELF .... (RCA Victor 47-8095)		2.00	8.00	63

LUCAS, CARRIE
SUMMER IN THE STREET / Horsin' Around .... (MCA/Constellation 52449)		.75	3.00	84
CHARLIE .... (MCA/Constellation 52524)		.75	3.00	85

LUCKY CHARMS, THE
WHO DO YOU LOVE / Potential So And So .... (Starfire 111)		1.25	5.00	80
(Issued with red vinyl)				
YOU'RE THE GIRL FOR ME / Born To Be Lonely .... (Starfire 107)		1.25	5.00	80

LUFT, LORNA
(Actress/Entertainer, daughter of Judy Garland)
OUR DAY WILL COME / Is It Really Love At All .... (Epic 5-10993)		2.50	10.00	73

LUKE, ROBIN
SUSIE DARLIN' / Living's Loving You .... (Bertram International 206)		20.00	80.00	57
EVERLOVIN' / Well Oh, Well Oh .... (Dot 16096)		7.50	30.00	60

LULU
BEST OF BOTH WORLDS / Love Loves To Love Love .... (Epic 5-10260)		3.00	12.00	67
ME, THE PEACEFUL HEART .... (Epic 5-10302)		3.00	12.00	68
I COULD NEVER MISS YOU (MORE THAN I DO) .... (Alfa 7006)		1.50	6.00	81
(First printing picturing Lulu without headband)				
I COULD NEVER MISS YOU (MORE THAN I DO) .... (Alfa 7006)		1.25	5.00	81
(Second printing picturing Lulu with headband)				
IF I WERE YOU .... (Alfa 7011)		1.00	4.00	81

LUMAN, BOB
LET'S THINK ABOUT LIVING / You've Got Everything .... (Warner Bros. 5172)		7.50	30.00	60
BOSTON ROCKER / OLD FRIENDS / Bad Bad Day / Let's Think About Living .. (Warner Bros. 5506)		18.75	75.00	60
(Plus 2 Oldies series which offered "4 Songs For The Price Of 2.")				
OH, LONESOME ME / Why, Why, Bye, Bye .... (Warner Bros. 5184)		7.50	30.00	61
THE GREAT SNOWMAN / The Pig Latin Song .... (Warner Bros. 5204)		7.50	30.00	61
YOU'VE TURNED DOWN THE LIGHTS / Private Eye .... (Warner Bros. 5233)		7.50	30.00	61
COME ON HOME AND SING THE BLUES TO DADDY /				
My Woman's Good To Me .... (Epic JZSP 138804)		2.50	10.00	69
(Promotional issue only programming re-service single. Flip side shown as by David Houston with a different catalog number on the record.)				

LUSHUS DAIM & THE PRETTY VAIN
THE ONE YOU LOVE .... (Motown/Conceited 1826MF)		.75	3.00	85
THE ONE YOU LOVE .... (Motown/Conceited 1826MF)		1.00	4.00	85
(Promotional issue, For Promotional Use Only/Not For Sale printed front and back)				

LYDIA
WE ARE ONE .... (Penthouse 101)		1.50	6.00	80
(From the motion picture Caligula)				

LYMON, FRANKIE
I WANT YOU TO BE MY GIRL / Portable On My Shoulder .... (Big Kat 7008)		3.00	12.00	68

LYNDELL, LIZ
WE'VE BEEN STRONG LONG ENOUGH .... (Koala 321)		1.25	5.00	80
(Shown as by Del Reeves and Liz Lyndell, both pictured. Some promotional copies include a "Happy Birthday Grand Ole Opry" insert given away at the "Koala Records" Suite at Opryland Hotel during a trade convention.)				
I NEVER ONCE STOPPED LOVING YOU .... (Koala 335)		1.00	4.00	82

LYNN, CHERYL
AT LAST YOU'RE MINE / Look What You've Done To Me .... (Private I ZS4-04736)		.75	3.00	84
(B-side shown as by Marc Tanner. From the motion picture Heavenly Bodies, Cynthia Dale pictured.)				
AT LAST YOU'RE MINE .... (Private I ZS4-04736)		1.00	4.00	84
(Promotional issue, Demonstration–Not For Sale printed on sleeve. From the motion picture Heavenly Bodies, Cynthia Dale pictured.)				

LYNN, GERI
MY LIPS WILL NEVER TELL .... (Columbia 4-43574)		2.00	8.00	66

LYNN, JUDY
MAY I DRIVE YOU HOME .... (Columbia 4-44489)		2.00	8.00	68

LYNN, LORETTA
IT WON'T SEEM LIKE CHRISTMAS / .... (Decca 32043)		2.00	8.00	66
COAL MINER'S DAUGHTER / The Man Of The House .... (Decca 32749)		1.50	6.00	70
WE'VE COME A LONG WAY, BABY .... (MCA 40954)		1.25	5.00	78
HEART DON'T DO THIS TO ME / Adam's Rib .... (MCA 52621)		.75	3.00	85

LYNNE, GLORIA
BE ANYTHING (BUT BE MINE) / Soul Serenade .... (Fontana S-1890)		2.50	10.00	64

LYNYRD SKYNYRD
See Steve Gaines

LYONS, RUTH
EVERYWHERE THE BELLS ARE RINGING .... (Columbia 4-41810)		2.00	8.00	61

M

M
POP MUZIK / M Factor .... (Sire 49033)		1.25	5.00	79

MAC BAND
ROSES ARE RED .... (MCA 53177)		.75	3.00	88

TITLE	LABEL AND NUMBER	VG	NM	YR
MacGOWAN, SHANE				
WHAT A WONDERFUL WORLD/Rainy Night In Soho/Lucy	(Sub Pop 194)	1.25	5.00	92
(A-side shown as by Nick Cave and Shane MacGowan. *Rainy Night In Soho* shown as by Nick Cave, *Lucy* shown as by Shane MacGowan.)				
MacGRAW, ALI				
(Actress)				
See Quincy Jones (*The Love Theme*), Frances Lai (*Theme From Love Story*)				
MACHINATIONS				
NO SAY IN IT/5 Minutes Black	(Epic 34-05887)	.75	3.00	86
NO SAY IN IT	(Epic 34-05887)	1.00	4.00	86
(Promotional issue, *Demonstration–Not For Sale* printed on sleeve)				
MACK, THE				
(Motion Picture)				
See Willie Hutch (*Slick*)				
MACK, JOHNNY				
EXTENDED PLAYS				
IF YOU'VE GOT THE TIME	(Miller Beer 621)	3.75	15.00	66
(Promotional issue only radio spots for Miller Beer; three by the Troggs, two by Brook Benton, and one by Johnny Mack)				
MACK, RONNIE				
I LOVE TRACI LORDS/It Won't Take Much	(Lonesome Town 111)	1.50	6.00	86
(Porn star Traci Lords pictured)				
MACK, WARNER				
ROC-A-CHICKA/Since I Lost You	(Decca 30471)	5.00	20.00	64
THE EXCITING WARNER MACK	(Decca no #)	2.50	10.00	60s
(Generic half sleeve used for a number of different singles issued on Decca. No specific titles listed on sleeve.)				
(LET'S PUT AN OLE) BRUSH ARBOR IN THE WHITE HOUSE/She's A Sweet Talkin' Woman	(Pageboy 30)	1.50	6.00	77
MacKENZIE, GISELE				
HARD TO GET/Boston Fancy	(X Records 4X-0137)	2.50	10.00	55
(From the television series *Justice*)				
TOO FAT FOR THE CHIMNEY	(Vik 0300)	2.50	10.00	56
MACKEY, LINDA				
GOTTA FIND MY MAN/Yours For The Asking	(VJ International 721)	1.25	5.00	70s
(Sleeve reads *The Soul Sting Captured On VJ International*, no artist or titles credited. Black woman with machine gun, possibly Mackey, pictured.)				
MacLACHLAN, KYLE				
(Actor)				
See Bobby Vinton (*Blue Velvet*)				
MacLAINE, SHIRLEY				
(Actress/Entertainer)				
MY PERSONAL PROPERTY/Where Am I Going	(Decca 9-32446)	2.50	10.00	69
Also see Ferrante And Teicher (*The Theme From The Apartment*)				
MacMURRAY, FRED				
(Actor)				
THE FLUBBER SONG/Serendipity	(Buena Vista 381)	5.00	20.00	62
(From the motion picture *Flubber*)				
Also see Ferrante And Teicher (*The Theme From The Apartment*)				
MADAME X				
JUST THAT TYPE OF GIRL/Flirt	(Atlantic 7-89216)	.75	3.00	87
Also see Shannon (b-side of *Criminal*)				
MADHOUSE				
6/Six and 1/2	(Paisley Park 28485-7)	.75	3.00	86
(THE PERFECT) 10/Ten and 1/2	(Paisley Park 28182-7)	.75	3.00	87
MAD MAX–BEYOND THUNDERDOME				
(Motion Picture)				
See Tina Turner (*One Of The Living, We Don't Need Another Hero*)				
MADNESS				
OUR HOUSE/Cardiac Arrest	(Geffen 29668-7)	1.00	4.00	83
IT MUST BE LOVE/Calling Cards	(Geffen 29562-7)	.75	3.00	83
THE SUN AND THE RAIN/Time For Tea	(Geffen 29350-7)	.75	3.00	84
MADONNA				
BORDERLINE/Think Of Me	(Sire 29354-7)	7.50	30.00	84
(Poster sleeve)				
LIKE A VIRGIN	(Sire 29210-7)	1.00	4.00	84
MATERIAL GIRL	(Sire 29083-7)	1.00	4.00	85
CRAZY FOR YOU	(Geffen 29051-7)	.75	3.00	85
(From the motion picture *Vision Quest*)				
ANGEL	(Sire 29008-7)	.75	3.00	85
DRESS YOU UP	(Sire 28919-7)	7.50	30.00	85
(Reported to have a small distribution. It would not be unusual to see prices vary between $10 and $50.)				
LIVE TO TELL	(Sire 28717-7)	.75	3.00	86
PAPA DON'T PREACH	(Sire 28660-7)	.75	3.00	86
TRUE BLUE	(Sire 28591-7)	.75	3.00	86
(Issued with black vinyl)				
TRUE BLUE	(Sire 28591-7)	1.25	5.00	86
(Front of sleeve states *Limited Edition Blue Vinyl Pressing*)				
OPEN YOUR HEART	(Sire 28508-7)	.75	3.00	86
LA ISLA BONITA	(Sire 28425-7)	.75	3.00	87
WHO'S THAT GIRL	(Sire 28341-7)	.75	3.00	87
(From the motion picture *Who's That Girl*)				

		VG	NM	YR
CAUSING A COMMOTION	(Sire 28224-7)	.75	3.00	87

(From the motion picture *Who's That Girl*)

LIKE A PRAYER	(Sire 27539-7)	.75	3.00	89
EXPRESS YOURSELF	(Sire 22948-7)	.75	3.00	89
CHERISH/Supernatural	(Sire/Warner Bros. 22883-7)	.75	3.00	89
KEEP IT TOGETHER	(Sire 19986-7)	5.00	20.00	90

     Also see Nick Kamen *(Each Time You Break My Heart)*

MADSEN, VIRGINIA
(Actress)
     See Wild Blue *(Fire With Fire)*

MAGICAL MYSTERY TOUR
(Motion Picture)
     See the Beatles *(Penny Lane, All You Need Is Love, Hello Goodbye)*

MAGIC LANTERNS, THE
EXCUSE ME BABY/Greedy Girl	(Epic 10062)	3.75	15.00	66

MAGICIANS, THE
AN INVITATION TO CRY/Rain Don't Fall On Me No More	(Columbia 4-43435)	7.50	30.00	65

MAGNUM P.I.
(Television Series)
     See Mike Post *(Theme From Magnum P.I.)*

MAGNUSON, ANN
(Actress)
     See the Turtles *(Happy Together)*

MAHAL, TAJ
I WISH I COULD SHIMMY LIKE MY SISTER KATE	(Columbia 4-44051)	2.00	8.00	67

     Also see Bruce Springsteen *(The Circus Song)*

MAHARIS, GEORGE
(Actor)
TEACH ME TONIGHT/After The Lights Go Down Low	(Epic 5-9504)	1.50	6.00	62
LOVE ME AS I LOVE YOU/They Knew About You	(Epic 5-9522)	1.50	6.00	62
BABY HAS GONE BYE BYE/After One Kiss	(Epic 5-9555)	1.50	6.00	62
DON'T FENCE ME IN/Alright, Okay, You Win	(Epic 5-9569)	1.50	6.00	63
WHERE CAN YOU GO/Kiss Me	(Epic 5-9600)	1.50	6.00	63
THAT'S HOW IT GOES/It Isn't There	(Epic 5-9613)	1.50	6.00	63
TONIGHT YOU BELONG TO ME/The Object Of My Affection	(Epic 5-9696)	1.50	6.00	64

MAHAVISHNU ORCHESTRA, THE, WITH JOHN McLAUGHLIN
EXTENDED PLAYS
MEETINGS OF THE SPIRIT	(Columbia AS 53)	1.50	6.00	71

     (Part of a series of promotional issues titled *Playback* issued with a small-hole 33-1/3 RPM record. Price includes generic *Playback* sleeve with folding insert. Also includes one song each by Jeff Beck, Lesley Duncan, Firesign Theatre, Grootna, and Mylon.)
     Also see Jan Hammer

MAHOGANY
(Motion Picture)
     See Diana Ross *(Theme From Mahogany)*

MAHONEY, JOHN CULLITON
THE BALLAD OF EVEL KNIEVEL/Why	(Amherst 701)	2.00	8.00	74

     (Evel Knievel pictured, b-side is a narrative poem recited by Knievel.)

MAIL ORDER BRIDE
(Motion Picture)
     See Buddy Ebsen *(Mail Order Bride)*

MAIN INGREDIENT, THE
BLACK SEEDS KEEP ON GROWING/Baby Change Your Mind	(RCA 74-0517)	1.50	6.00	71
I ONLY HAVE EYES FOR YOU/Only	(RCA 12340)	2.00	8.00	81

     (Promotional issue only gatefold folder sleeve.)

MAINSTREETERS, THE
     See Joe Simon *(Theme From Cleopatra Jones)*

MAI TAI
FEMALE INTUITION	(Critique 722)	.75	3.00	86

MAITLAND, DEXTER
TAKE TEN TERRIFIC GIRLS	(United Artists 50484)	2.00	8.00	68

MAJORETTES, THE
WHITE LEVI'S	(Troy 1000)	3.00	12.00	62

MAKING LOVE
(Motion Picture)
     See Roberta Flack *(Making Love)*

MAKING MR. RIGHT
(Motion Picture)
     See the Turtles *(Happy Together)*

MALKOVICH, JOHN
(Actor)
     See the Turtles *(Happy Together)*

MALMSTEEN'S, YNGWIE J., RISING FORCE
HEAVEN TONIGHT/Riot In The Dungeons	(Polydor 887 518-7)	1.00	4.00	88

     Also see Alcatrazz *(Yngwie J. Malmsteen)*

TITLE	LABEL AND NUMBER	VG	NM	YR

MALTBY, RICHARD, AND ORCHESTRA
MAN WITH THE GOLDEN ARM .... (Vik 0196) | 3.75 | 15.00 | 56
(From the motion picture *Man With The Golden Arm*)

MALVIN, ARTIE
GARDEN OF EDEN/I Walk The Line .... (Bell 17) | 1.25 | 5.00 |
(Flip-side by Michael Stewart, neither performer credited on sleeve)

MAMAS AND THE PAPAS, THE
CALIFORNIA DREAMIN' .... (Dunhill 4020) | 18.75 | 75.00 | 66
(Promotional issue only)
CREEQUE ALLEY .... (Dunhill 4083) | 7.50 | 30.00 | 67
(Promotional issue only)
DANCING BEAR .... (Dunhill 4113) | 1.50 | 6.00 | 67
Also see Denny Doherty, Mama Cass Elliot, the Journeymen (John Philips), Michelle Phillips

MAN
SISTER SALVATION/ .... (Columbia 4-44806) | 2.00 | 8.00 | 69

MAN AND A WOMAN, A
(Motion Picture)
See Francis Lai (*A Man and a Woman*)

MAN AND HIS MUSIC, A
(Television Special)
See Frank Sinatra (*That's Life*)

MANCHESTER, MELISSA
MATHEMATICS/So Full Of Yourself .... (MCA 52575) | .75 | 3.00 | 85
ENERGY .... (MCA 52616) | .75 | 3.00 | 85
THE MUSIC OF GOODBYE (LOVE THEME FROM OUT OF AFRICA) .... (MCA 52784) | 1.00 | 4.00 | 86
(Shown as by Melissa Manchester and Al Jarreau. From the motion picture *Out Of Africa*, Robert Redford and Meryl Streep pictured.)
WALK ON BY/To Make You Smile Again .... (Mika/Polydor 873 012-7) | .75 | 3.00 | 89

MANCHURIAN CANDIDATE, THE
(Motion Picture)
See Les Baxter (*Theme From The Manchurian Candidate*)

MANCINI, HENRY
THEME FROM PETER GUNN/The Brothers Go To Mother's .... (RCA Victor 47-7460) | 2.50 | 10.00 | 59
SPOOK/ .... (RCA Victor 47-7512) | 2.50 | 10.00 | 59
THE BLUES/Big Noise From Winnetka .... (RCA Victor 47-7785) | 2.50 | 10.00 | 60
THE GREAT IMPOSTOR/Love Music .... (RCA Victor 47-7830) | 2.50 | 10.00 | 61
(From the motion picture *The Great Impostor*)
MOON RIVER/Breakfast At Tiffany's .... (RCA Victor 47-7916) | 2.50 | 10.00 | 61
(From the motion picture *Breakfast At Tiffany's*, Audrey Hepburn pictured)
EXPERIMENT IN TERROR/Tooty Twist .... (RCA Victor 47-8008) | 2.50 | 10.00 | 61
(A-side from the motion picture *Experiment In Terror*)
THEME FROM "HATARI!"/ .... (RCA Victor 47-8037) | 2.50 | 10.00 | 62
(From the motion picture *Hatari!*)
LOVE THEME FROM PHAEDRA/Dreamsville .... (RCA Victor 47-8099) | 2.00 | 8.00 | 63
DAYS OF WINE AND ROSES/Seventy Six Trombones .... (RCA Victor 47-8120) | 2.00 | 8.00 | 63
(From the motion picture *Days Of Wine And Roses*)
BANZAI PIPELINE/Rhapsody In Blue .... (RCA Victor 47-8184) | 2.50 | 10.00 | 63
CHARADE/Orange Tamoure .... (RCA Victor 47-8256) | 2.50 | 10.00 | 63
(From the motion picture *Charade*)
THE PINK PANTHER THEME/It Had Better Be Tonight (Meglio Stasera) ..... (RCA Victor 47-8286) | 2.50 | 10.00 | 64
(From the motion picture *The Pink Panther*)
A SHOT IN THE DARK/The Shadows Of Paris .... (RCA Victor 47-8381) | 2.50 | 10.00 | 64
DEAR HEART/How Soon .... (RCA Victor 47-8458) | 2.50 | 10.00 | 64
(From the motion picture *Dear Heart*)
THE SWEETHEART TREE/Pie In The Face Polka .... (RCA Victor 47-8624) | 2.50 | 10.00 | 65
(From the motion picture *The Great Race*)
MOMENT TO MOMENT/Soldier In The Rain .... (RCA Victor 47-8718) | 2.50 | 10.00 | 66
ARABESQUE/ .... (RCA Victor 47-8856) | 2.50 | 10.00 | 66
IN THE ARMS OF LOVE/The Swing March .... (RCA Victor 47-8857) | 2.50 | 10.00 | 66
TWO FOR THE ROAD/ .... (RCA Victor 47-9200) | 2.50 | 10.00 | 67
WAIT UNTIL DARK/Theme For Three .... (RCA Victor 47-9340) | 2.50 | 10.00 | 67
WHISTLING AWAY THE DARK .... (RCA Victor SPS-45-252) | 2.50 | 10.00 | 71
(Promotional issue only announcing Oscar Nomination for Best Song. From the motion picture *Darling Lili*.)
THEME FROM THE MANCINI GENERATION/Bluish Bag .... (RCA Victor 74-0756) | 2.00 | 8.00 | 72
(A-side from the television series *The Mancini Generation*)
THEME FROM THE THIEF WHO CAME TO DINNER .... (RCA Victor 45-430) | 2.00 | 8.00 | 73
(From the motion picture *The Thief Who Came To Dinner*)
THE TRAIL OF THE PINK PANTHER/The Inspector Clouseau Theme .... (Liberty B-1489) | 1.25 | 5.00 | 76
RAVEL'S BOLERO/It's Easy To Say .... (Warner Bros. 49139) | 1.50 | 6.00 | 79
(Poster sleeve, from the motion picture *10*. Bo Derek pictured.)
THE THORN BIRDS THEME/Luke And Meggie .... (Warner Bros. 29697-7) | 1.00 | 4.00 | 83
(From the television mini-series *The Thorn Birds*, Richard Chamberlain and Rachel Ward pictured)

MANCINI GENERATION, THE
(Television Series)
See Henry Mancini (*Theme From The Mancini Generation*)

MANDELL, HOWIE
(Comedian)
See Mary Jane Girls (*Walk Like A Man*)

MANDRELL, BARBARA
YEARS/Darlin' .... (MCA 41162) | 1.00 | 4.00 | 79
TO ME .... (MCA 52415) | .75 | 3.00 | 84
(Shown as by Barbara Mandrell/Lee Greenwood, both pictured)
THERE'S NO LOVE IN TENNESSEE/Sincerely I'm Yours .... (MCA 52537) | .75 | 3.00 | 85
FAST LANES AND COUNTRY ROADS/You Only You .... (MCA 52737) | .75 | 3.00 | 85

MANDRELL, LOUISE
(YOU SURE KNOW YOUR WAY) AROUND MY HEART .... (RCA PB-13039)   1.00   4.00   82

MANDRILL
     See Michael Masser & Mandrill

MANFRED MANN
SHA LA LA / John Hardy .... (Ascot 2165)   5.00   20.00   64
COME TOMORROW / What Did I Do Wrong .... (Ascot 2170)   5.00   20.00   65
JUST LIKE A WOMAN .... (Mercury 72607)   3.75   15.00   67
MY NAME IS JACK .... (Mercury 72822)   2.50   10.00   68
     Also see Manfred Mann's Earth Band

MANFRED MANN'S EARTH BAND
BLINDED BY THE LIGHT .... (Warner Bros. 8252)   1.25   5.00   76
     Also see Manfred Mann, Night (Chris Thompson), the Firm (Chris Slade), Chris Thompson

MANGIONE, CHUCK
MAIN SQUEEZE / Come Take A Ride With Me .... (A&M 1886)   1.50   6.00   75
FEELS SO GOOD / Maui-Waui .... (A&M 2001)   1.25   5.00   78
CHILDREN OF SANCHEZ / Doin' Everything With You .... (A&M 2088)   1.25   5.00   78
GIVE IT ALL YOU GOT / B'Bye .... (A&M 2211)   1.00   4.00   79
FUN AND GAMES / Children Of Sanchez Finale .... (A&M 2236)   1.00   4.00   79

MANHATTANS, THE
YOU SEND ME / You're Gonna Love Being Loved By Me .... (Columbia 38-04754)   .75   3.00   85

MANHATTAN TRANSFER, THE
AMERICAN POP / Why Not! .... (Atlantic 7-89720)   1.00   4.00   83
SPICE OF LIFE / .... (Atlantic 7-89786)   1.00   4.00   83
RAY'S ROCKHOUSE / .... (Atlantic 7-89533)   1.00   4.00   85
SOUL FOOD TO GO / Hear The Voices .... (Atlantic 7-89156)   .75   3.00   87
SO YOU SAY / Notes From The Underground .... (Atlantic 7-89094)   .75   3.00   88

MANILOW, BARRY
IT'S JUST ANOTHER NEW YEAR'S EVE .... (Arista SP-11)   2.50   10.00   77
     (Promotional issue only)
READY TO TAKE A CHANCE AGAIN .... (Arista SP-25)   2.00   8.00   78
     (Promotional issue only, from the motion picture *Foul Play*. Goldie Hawn and Chevy Chase pictured on the
     front, Manilow on the back.)
EVEN NOW .... (Arista 0330)   1.50   6.00   78
PARADISE CAFE .... (Arista 9318)   1.25   5.00   84
IN SEARCH OF LOVE / At The Dance .... (RCA PB-14223)   1.00   4.00   85
I'M YOUR MAN .... (RCA PB-14397)   1.00   4.00   86
HEY MAMBO / When October Goes .... (Arista 9666)   .75   3.00   88
     (A-side shown as by Barry Manilow With Kid Creole and the Coconuts)
KEEP EACH OTHER WARM / A Little Travelling Music, Please .... (Arista 9838)   .75   3.00   89

MANN, BARRY
ALMOST GONE / For No Reason At All .... (Warner Bros. 8752)   1.25   5.00   79

MANN, HERBIE
SUPERMAN .... (Atlantic 3547)   1.25   5.00   79

MANN, MANFRED
     See Manfred Mann, Manfred Mann'a Earth Band

MANNA, CHARLIE
THE ASTRONAUT .... (Decca 38238)   2.00   8.00   61

MANNEQUIN
(Motion Picture)
     See Starship (*Nothing's Gonna Stop Us Now*)

MANNHEIM STEAMROLLER
DECK THE HALLS / Silent Night .... (American Gramaphone 1984)   1.00   4.00   84

MAN OR ASTRO-MAN?
INTERPLANET JANE .... (Atlantic PR 6632-7)   1.00   4.00   95
     (Promotional issue only issued with orange vinyl)
EXTENDED PLAYS
ERIC ESTROTICA / LANDLOCKED / Adios Johnny Bravo / Joker's Wild .... (Homo Habilis no #)   1.50   6.00   92
     (Issued with blue vinyl)

MANRING, MICHAEL
WELCOMING .... (Windham Hill 0020)   .75   3.00   86

MANSFIELD, JAYNE
LITTLE THINGS MEAN A LOT / That Makes It .... (Original Sound 51)   10.00   40.00   64

MANTLE, MICKEY
(Baseball Player)
     See Teresa Brewer (*I Love Mickey*)

MANTOVANI
AROUND THE WORLD / The Road To Ballingarry .... (London 45-1746)   2.00   8.00   57
     (From the motion picture *Around The World In 80 Days*. Credit on front reads *Trumpet Solo Featuring Stan
     Newsome.*)
LET ME BE LOVED / Call Of The West .... (London 45-1761)   12.50   50.00   57
     (From the motion picture *The James Dean Story*. Two different illustrations of James Dean pictured, one on
     front and one on back. Credit on front reads *Trumpet Solo By Stan Newsome.*)
MAIN THEME FROM EXODUS .... (London 45-1953)   2.00   8.00   60
THE VALIANT YEARS .... (London 45-1983)   2.00   8.00   61
THEME FROM ROCCO AND HIS BROTHERS .... (London 45-2000)   2.00   8.00   62

MANTRONIX
SIMPLE SIMON (YOU GOTTA REGARD) .... (Capitol B-44120)   .75   3.00   88

TITLE	LABEL AND NUMBER	VG	NM	YR
MAN WITH THE GOLDEN ARM				
(Motion Picture)				
See Richard Maltby and Orchestra *(Man With The Golden Arm)*				
MAPPLETHORPE, ROBERT				
(Photographer)				
See Patti Smith *(People Have The Power)*				
MARAUDERS, THE				
SINCE I MET YOU/I Don't Know How	(Skyview 001)	5.00	20.00	66
MARC, BROWN				
See Prince *(Anotherloverholenyohead)*				
MARCELS, THE				
BLUE MOON	(Colpix 186)	12.50	50.00	61
HEARTACHES	(Colpix 612)	18.75	75.00	61
MERRY TWISTMAS/Don't Cry For Me This Christmas	(Colpix 624)	15.00	60.00	61
MARCH, LITTLE PEGGY				
I WISH I WERE A PRINCESS/My Teenage Castle (Is Tumblin' Down)	(RCA Victor 47-8189)	5.00	20.00	63
HELLO HEARTACHE, GOODBYE LOVE/Boy Crazy	(RCA Victor 47-8221)	5.00	20.00	63
MARC V.				
LET THEM STARE/Let Them Stare (Instrumental)	(Elektra 7-69318)	.75	3.00	89
MARCY BROS., THE				
THE THINGS I DIDN'T SAY	(Warner Bros. 27938-7)	.75	3.00	88
MARDI GRAS				
(Motion Picture)				
See Pat Boone *(I'll Remember Tonight)*, the Triplets *(Loyalty)*				
MARESCA, ERNIE				
DOWN ON THE BEACH	(Seville 45-119)	6.25	25.00	62
MARIE, DONNA				
THE PENTHOUSE	(Columbia 4-44402)	2.00	8.00	68
MARILLION				
KAYLEIGH	(Capitol B-5493)	.75	3.00	85
LADY NINA/Heart Of Lothian	(Capitol B-5561)	.75	3.00	86
SUGAR MICE	(Capitol B-44060)	.75	3.00	87
MARIN, CHEECH				
See Cheech & Chong, Mike + the Mechanics *(Revolution)*				
MARINERS, THE				
See Arthur Godfrey *('Twas The Night Before Christmas)*				
MARJOE				
See Marjoe Gortner				
MARKLEYS, THE				
See Irene Ryan *(Granny's Mini-Skirt)*				
MARK III, THE				
VALERIE/The Man	(BRB 100)	5.00	20.00	61
MARL, MARLEY				
DROPPIN' SCIENCE	(Cold Chillin' 27782-7)	.75	3.00	88
MARLEY, BOB, & THE WAILERS				
MIX UP, MIX UP/Trench Town	(Island/Tuff Gong 7-99837)	1.50	6.00	83
BUFFALO SOLDIER	(Island/Tuff Gong 7-99882)	1.25	5.00	83
MARLEY, ZIGGY, AND THE MELODY MAKERS				
(Ziggy is Bob Marley's son)				
TOMORROW PEOPLE/We A Guh Some Weh	(Virgin 7-99347)	.75	3.00	88
TUMBLIN' DOWN/Have You Ever Been To Hell	(Virgin 7-99299)	.75	3.00	88
LOOK WHO'S DANCING/	(Virgin 7-99182)	.75	3.00	89
MARLEY MARL FEATURING M.C. SHAN				
BASS GAME/He Cuts So Fresh	(MCA 53043)	.75	3.00	87
(Double artist single, flip side shown as by Finesse And Synquis)				
MARRIAGE ON THE ROCKS				
(Motion Picture)				
See Trini Lopez *(Sinner Man)*				
MARRIED TO THE MOB				
(Motion Picture)				
See Debbie Harry *(Liar, Liar)*				
M/A/R/R/S				
PUMP UP THE VOLUME/Anitina (Radio Edit)	(4th & Broadway 7452 C)	.75	3.00	87
MARSHALL, AMELIA				
(Actress)				
See the Soaps and Hearts Ensemble				
MARSHALL, MERI D.				
MY OBSESSION/Tears	(Atlantic 7-89503)	.75	3.00	85
MARSHALL, PENNY				
(Comic actress and director)				
See Laverne & Shirley				
MARSHALL TUCKER BAND				
LAST OF THE SINGING COWBOYS	(Warner Bros. 8841)	1.25	5.00	79

MARSHMELLOWS, THE
KNOT TIER/Just Like You And I .... (Columbia 4-44159) | 2.50 | 10.00 | 67

MARTHA AND THE MUFFINS
ECHO BEACH/1–4–6 .... (Virgin/Dindisc 68000) | 1.25 | 5.00 | 80

MARTHA AND THE VANDELLAS
DANCING IN THE STREET/There He Is (At My Door) .... (Gordy 7033) | 10.00 | 40.00 | 64
NOWHERE TO RUN/I Got You (I Feel Good) .... (A&M 3022) | .75 | 3.00 | 88
   (B-side shown as by James Brown)

MARTIKA
MORE THAN YOU KNOW .... (Columbia 38-08103) | .75 | 3.00 | 88

MARTIN, BOBBI
WHEN WILL THE TORCH GO OUT/I Love You So .... (Coral 62452) | 2.00 | 8.00 | 65

MARTIN, DEAN
VOLARE/Outa My Mind .... (Capitol F4028) | 6.25 | 25.00 | 58
SLEEP WARM .... (Capitol 987) | 50.00 | 200.00 | 59
   (Promotional issue only)
ON AN EVENING IN ROMA/You Can't Love 'Em All .... (Capitol F4222) | 6.25 | 25.00 | 59
I MET A GIRL .... (Capitol 1609) | 25.00 | 100.00 | 60
   (Promotional issue only, from the motion picture Bells Are Ringing)
FROM THE BOTTOM OF MY HEART (DAMMI, DAMMI, DAMMI)/
   Who's Got The Action .... (Reprise 20,116) | 5.00 | 20.00 | 62
ME & MY SHADOW/Sam's Song .... (Reprise 20,128) | 6.25 | 25.00 | 62
   (A-side shown as by Frank Sinatra and Sammy Davis, Jr., b-side by Dean Martin and Sammy
   Davis, Jr., all three pictured)
THE OLDEST ESTABLISHED (PERMANENT FLOATING CRAP GAME
   IN NEW YORK)/Fugue For Tinhorns .... (Reprise 20,217) | 15.00 | 60.00 | 63
   (Shown as by Frank Sinatra, Bing Crosby, and Dean Martin)
THAT'S AMORE .... (Capitol B-44153) | 1.00 | 4.00 | 88
   (From the motion picture Moonstruck)

MARTIN, ERIC
INFORMATION .... (Capitol B-5502) | .75 | 3.00 | 85
EVERYTIME I THINK OF YOU .... (Capitol B-5679) | .75 | 3.00 | 87
CONFESS .... (Capitol B-44016) | .75 | 3.00 | 87
   Also see Mr. Big

MARTIN, DINO, JR.
(Son of Dean Martin)
   See Dino, Desi & Billy

MARTIN, GEORGE, AND HIS ORCHESTRA
(The Beatles' producer from 1962-70)
AND I LOVE HER/Ringo's Theme (This Boy) .... (United Artists 745) | 37.50 | 150.00 | 64
   (Red sleeve that pictures the Beatles)
A HARD DAY'S NIGHT/I Should Have Known Better .... (United Artists 750) | 250.00 | 1000.00 | 64
   (Blue sleeve that pictures the Beatles)

MARTIN, JIMMY
   See Nitty Gritty Dirt Band (Honky Tonkin')

MARTIN, MARILYN
SEPARATE LIVES (LOVE THEME FROM WHITE NIGHTS)/
   I Don't Wanna Know .... (Atlantic 7-89498) | 1.00 | 4.00 | 85
   (Shown as by Phil Collins and Marilyn Martin, b-side shown as by Phil Collins. Collins and Martin pictured
   on the front, Mikhail Baryshnikov and Gregory Hines pictured on the back. From the motion picture White
   Nights.)
SEPARATE LIVES (LOVE THEME FROM WHITE NIGHTS)/
   I Don't Wanna Know .... (Atlantic 7-89498) | 1.00 | 4.00 | 85
   (Shown as by Phil Collins and Marilyn Martin, b-side shown as by Phil Collins. Movie art pictured on the
   front, Mikhail Baryshnikov and Gregory Hines pictured on the back. From the motion picture White Nights.)
NIGHT MOVES/Wildest Dreams .... (Atlantic 7-89465) | .75 | 3.00 | 85
MOVE CLOSER/The Dream Is Always The Same .... (Atlantic 7-89424) | .75 | 3.00 | 86
BODY AND THE BEAT (REMIX VERSION)/
   The Dream Is Always The Same .... (Atlantic 7-89386) | .75 | 3.00 | 86
POSSESSIVE LOVE/Homeless .... (Atlantic 7-89128) | .75 | 3.00 | 88
LOVE TAKES NO PRISONERS/Quiet Desperation .... (Atlantic 7-89075) | .75 | 3.00 | 88

MARTIN, RAY, ORCHESTRA
SONG FROM QUIET AMERICAN .... (United Artists 103) | 2.50 | 10.00 | 58
BOULEVARD OF BROKEN DREAMS/The Mime's Theme .... (RCA Victor 47-7920) | 2.00 | 8.00 | 61

MARTIN, STEVE
(Comedian/Actor)
GRANDMOTHER'S SONG/Let's Get Small .... (Warner Bros. 8503) | 1.25 | 5.00 | 77
KING TUT .... (Warner Bros. 8577) | 1.00 | 4.00 | 78
   (Shown as by Steve Martin and the Toot Uncommons)
WHAT I BELIEVE (A PATRIOTIC STATEMENT)/
   Freddie's Lilt Parts I & II .... (Warner Bros. 49845) | 1.00 | 4.00 | 81
   (Shown as by the Steve Martin Brothers)
   Also see John Stewart (Survivors)

MARTINDALE, WINK
(Television Game Show Host)
DECK OF CARDS/Now You Know How It Feels .... (Dot 15968) | 2.50 | 10.00 | 59
STEAL AWAY/Blue Bobby Sox .... (Dot 16051) | 2.50 | 10.00 | 60
THE GETTYSBURG ADDRESS .... (Dot 16083) | 2.50 | 10.00 | 60

MARTINEZ, NANCY
MOVE OUT/Without Love .... (Atlantic 7-89300) | .75 | 3.00 | 87

MARTINI RANCH
REACH .... (Sire 27985-7) | .75 | 3.00 | 88

TITLE	LABEL AND NUMBER	VG	NM	YR

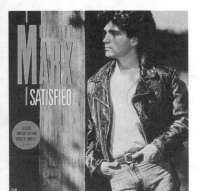

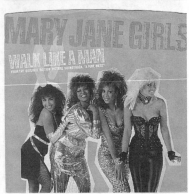

MARTINO, AL
DEAREST/Hello My Love .... (20th Fox 184) | 2.50 | 10.00 | 60
THERE'S NO TOMORROW .... (Maze 7025) | 3.00 | 12.00 | 62
MY HEART WOULD KNOW .... (Capitol 5341) | 2.50 | 10.00 | 65
WIEDERSEH'N/The Minute You're Gone .... (Capitol 5652) | 2.50 | 10.00 | 66

MARVELETTES
PLEASE MR. POSTMAN/So Long Baby .... (Tamla 54046) | 15.00 | 60.00 | 61
TWISTIN' POSTMAN/I Want A Guy .... (Tamla 54054) | 15.00 | 60.00 | 62
YOU'RE MY REMEDY/A Little Bit Of Sympathy, A Little Bit Of Love .... (Tamla 54097) | 10.00 | 40.00 | 64
    Also see Them (Baby Please Don't Go)

MARX, RICHARD
DON'T MEAN NOTHING/The Flame Of Love .... (Manhattan B 50079) | .75 | 3.00 | 87
SHOULD'VE KNOWN BETTER/Rhythm Of Life .... (Manhattan B-50083) | .75 | 3.00 | 87
ENDLESS SUMMER NIGHTS/Have Mercy (Live) .... (EMI Manhattan B-50113) | .75 | 3.00 | 87
HOLD ON TO THE NIGHTS/Lonely Heart .... (EMI Manhattan B50106) | .75 | 3.00 | 88
SATISFIED/Should've Known Better (Live Version) .... (EMI Manhattan B-50189) | 1.25 | 5.00 | 89
    (Poster sleeve)

MARY JANE GIRLS
IN MY HOUSE .... (Gordy 1741GF) | .75 | 3.00 | 85
WILD AND CRAZY LOVE .... (Gordy 1798GF) | .75 | 3.00 | 85
WALK LIKE A MAN .... (Motown 1851MF) | .75 | 3.00 | 86
    (From the motion picture A Fine Mess, Mary Jane Girls with Howie Mandell in drag pictured on back)
WALK LIKE A MAN .... (Motown 1851MF RE1) | 1.00 | 4.00 | 86
    (Promotional issue, For Promotional Use Only Not For Sale printed on sleeve. From the motion picture A Fine Mess, Mary Jane Girls with Howie Mandell in drag pictured on back.)

MARY POPPINS
(Motion Picture)
    See Julie Andrews (Super-Cali-Fragil-Istic-Expi-Ali-Docious), Dick Van Dyke (Super-Cali-Fragil-Istic-Expi-Ali-Docious, Chim Chim Cheree)

MARZOCCHI, GIANNI
    See Annette (Bella Bella Florence)

MAS, CAROLYN
SNOW .... (Mercury 76039) | 1.25 | 5.00 | 79
    Also see Jersey Artists For Mankind

MASEKELA, HUGH
U,-DWI (SMALL POX)/Emavungwani (Green Home) ..... (Mercury 72853) | 2.00 | 8.00 | 68

MASON, BARBARA, & THE FUTURES
WE GOT EACH OTHER .... (Buddah 481) | 1.50 | 6.00 | 75

MASON, DAVE
SOMETHING TO MAKE YOU HAPPY .... (ABC/Dunhill 4266) | 1.25 | 5.00 | 71
    (Shown as by Dave Mason & Mama Cass)
BRING IT ON HOME TO ME .... (Columbia 3-10074) | 1.50 | 6.00 | 74
    (Sleeve states As seen on Midnight Special, Friday, Feb. 7, 1975)
DREAMS I DREAM .... (MCA 53205) | .75 | 3.00 | 87
    (Credit on front reads Duet Vocal Performance by Phoebe Snow)
    Also see Traffic

MASON, JACKIE
EXTENDED PLAYS
SHRINK/IKNOW WHO I AM/SEX AND SOUP/REAGAN RAP/HOOKERS/
JEWISH PRESIDENT/Corporations/Trucking Business/Around The House/
Boats/Food And Drink/Portions .... (Warner Bros. PRO-S-2980) | 1.25 | 5.00 | 87
    (Promotional issue only titled King Of Deli Rap. For Promotional Use Only Not For Sale printed on back, issued with a small-hole 33-1/3 RPM record.)

MASON & DIXON
WORLD, I'M A MAN/Say You'd Like To .... (Tower 462) | 1.25 | 5.00 | 69

MASSER, MICHAEL, AND MANDRILL
ALI BOMBAYE .... (Arista 250) | 3.75 | 15.00 | 77
    (From the motion picture The Greatest, Muhammed Ali pictured. Record shows title as Ali Bom-Ba-Ye I.)

MASSEY, WAYNE
EASIN' ON BACK .... (MCA 52019) | .75 | 3.00 | 82
    Also see Charly McClain (With Just One Look In Your Eyes)

MASTERSON, MARY STUART
(Actress)
    See Flesh For Lulu (I Go Crazy)

MATERIAL ISSUE
KIM THE WAITRESS .... (Mercury 1095) | 1.25 | 5.00 | 94
    (Promotional issue only issued with clear vinyl)

MATHERS, JERRY
(Child actor who played the Beaver on the television series Leave It To Beaver)
DON'T CHA CRY/Wind Up Toy .... (Atlantic 2156) | 7.50 | 30.00 | 62

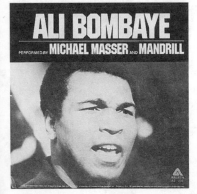

MATHIS, JOHNNY
CHANCES ARE/The Twelfth Of Never .... (Columbia 4-40993) | 5.00 | 20.00 | 57
WILD IS THE WIND/No Love .... (Columbia 4-41060) | 2.50 | 10.00 | 57
    (A-side shown as by Johnny Mathis with Ray Ellis and His Orchestra, b-side shown as by Johnny Mathis with Ray Conniff and His Orchestra)
A CERTAIN SMILE/Let It Rain .... (Columbia 4-41193) | 2.50 | 10.00 | 58
    (From the motion picture A Certain Smile)
CALL ME (SCALINATELLA)/Stairway To The Sea .... (Columbia 4-41253) | 2.50 | 10.00 | 58
MISTY .... (Columbia 4-41483) | 2.50 | 10.00 | 59

THE BEST OF EVERYTHING/Cherie	(Columbia 4-41491)	2.50	10.00	59
(From the motion picture *The Best Of Everything*)				
STARBRIGHT/	(Columbia 4-41583)	2.50	10.00	60
HOW TO HANDLE A WOMAN/While You're Young	(Columbia 4-41866)	2.50	10.00	60
YOU SET MY HEART TO MUSIC/Jenny	(Columbia 4-41980)	2.00	8.00	61
LAURIE, MY LOVE/Should I Wait	(Columbia 4-42048)	2.00	8.00	61
WASN'T THE SUMMER SHORT?/There You Are	(Columbia 4-42156)	2.00	8.00	61
CHRISTMAS EVE/	(Columbia 4-42238)	2.00	8.00	62
SWEET THURSDAY/One Look	(Columbia 4-42261)	2.00	8.00	62
MARIANNA/Unaccustomed As I Am	(Columbia 4-42420)	2.00	8.00	62
(A-side from the motion picture *The Counterfeit Traitor*)				
THAT'S THE WAY IT IS/	(Columbia 4-42509)	2.00	8.00	62
GINA/I Love Her That's Why	(Columbia 4-42582)	2.00	8.00	62
WHAT WILL MARY SAY/Quiet Girl	(Columbia 4-42666)	2.00	8.00	63
(Record shows a-side title as *What Will My Mary Say*)				
EVERY STEP OF THE WAY/No Man Can Stand Alone	(Columbia 4-42799)	2.00	8.00	63
TWO TICKETS AND A CANDY HEART/	(Mercury 72065)	2.00	8.00	63
YOUR TEENAGE DREAMS/Come Back	(Mercury 72184)	2.00	8.00	63
THE LITTLE DRUMMER BOY/	(Mercury 72217)	2.00	8.00	63
BYE BYE BARBARA/Great Night For Crying	(Mercury 72229)	2.00	8.00	64
LISTEN LONELY GIRL/	(Mercury 72339)	2.00	8.00	64
TAKE THE TIME/Dianacita	(Mercury 72432)	2.00	8.00	65
MIRAGE/	(Mercury 72464)	2.00	8.00	65
THE IMPOSSIBLE DREAM/So Nice	(Mercury 72610)	2.00	8.00	66
SATURDAY SUNSHINE/Two Tickets And A Candy Heart	(Mercury 72653)	2.00	8.00	66
GIVE ME YOUR LOVE FOR CHRISTMAS/Calypso Noel	(Columbia 4-45035)	2.00	8.00	69

MATT BIANCO

WHOSE SIDE ARE YOU ON?/Matt's Mood II	(Atlantic 7-89516)	.75	3.00	85
MORE THAN I CAN BEAR (REMIX)/Big Rosie (Remix)	(Atlantic 7-89483)	.75	3.00	85
(Artwork pictures a dancing couple)				
MORE THAN I CAN BEAR (RE-RECORDED VERSION)/ Summer Song	(Atlantic 7-89359)	.75	3.00	86
(Band member Mark Reilly pictured. Basia's vocals and Danny White's keyboards were removed from the mix after their departure from the band.)				
DON'T BLAME IT ON THAT GIRL/	(Atlantic 7-89040)	.75	3.00	88

MATTEA, KATHY

| GOIN' GONE/Every Love | (Mercury 888 874-7) | .75 | 3.00 | 87 |
| EIGHTEEN WHEELS AND A DOZEN ROSES/Like A Hurricane | (Mercury 870 148-7) | .75 | 3.00 | 88 |

MATTHAU, WALTER
(Actor)

| LOVE'S THE ONLY GAME IN TOWN/Theme From Pete 'N Tillie | (Decca 33050) | 2.00 | 8.00 | 72 |

MATTHEWS, IAN

| FOLLOWING EVERY FINGER/Smell Of Home | (Windham Hill 0027) | .75 | 3.00 | 88 |

MATTHEWS, TOBIN

| RUBY DUBY DU | (Chief 7022) | 5.00 | 20.00 | 60 |
| (From the motion picture *Key Witness*) | | | | |

MAULE, BRAD
(Actor)
See the Soaps and Hearts Ensemble

MAURIAT, PAUL, AND HIS ORCHESTRA

| LOVE IN EVERY ROOM (MÊME SI TU REVENAIS) | (Philips 40530) | 1.25 | 5.00 | 68 |

MAX, PETER
(Artist)
See Aretha Franklin *(Through The Storm)*

MAX DEMIAN BAND, THE

| PARADISE/Still Hosed | (RCA PB-11525) | 1.25 | 5.00 | 79 |

MAXIMUS, STUMPUS
See Def Leppard *(Armageddon It)*

MAY, BILLY

| OPEN END INTERVIEW/OPEN END INTERVIEW | (Capitol 2370) | 2.50 | 10.00 | 60s |
| (Promotional issue only, flip side is Jody Miller. Originally issued with a cue sheet.) | | | | |

MAY, BRIAN, & FRIENDS

| STAR FLEET/Son Of Star Fleet | (Capitol B-5278) | 1.00 | 4.00 | 83 |
| Also see Queen (Brian May), REO Speedwagon (Alan Gratzer), Van Halen (Edward Van Halen) | | | | |

MAYFIELD, CURTIS

SUPERFLY/Underground	(Curtom 1978)	1.50	6.00	72
(From the motion picture *Superfly*)				
KUNG FU/Right On For The Darkness	(Curtom 1999)	1.50	6.00	74
YOU ARE, YOU ARE/Get A Litle Bit	(Curtom 0135)	1.25	5.00	78
HE'S A FLYGUY/He's A Flyguy (Instrumental)	(Arista 9806)	.75	3.00	89
(Shown as by Curtis Mayfield and Fishbone. From the motion picture *I'm Gonna Git You Sucka*.)				
Also see the Impressions				

MAZARATI

100 MPH/Don't Leave Me Baby	(Paisley Park 28705-7)	1.00	4.00	86
PLAYER'S BALL/I Guess It's All Over	(Paisley Park 28759-7)	1.00	4.00	86
Also see Prince (Brown Marc)				

MAZE FEATURING FRANKIE BEVERLY

RUNNING AWAY	(Capitol B-5000)	1.00	4.00	80
BEFORE I LET GO	(Capitol A-5031)	1.00	4.00	81
LOVE IS THE KEY	(Capitol B-5221)	1.00	4.00	83
I WANNA THANK YOU	(Capitol B-5312)	1.00	4.00	83

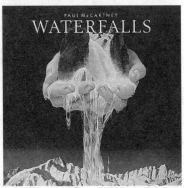

TITLE	LABEL AND NUMBER	VG	NM	YR
BACK IN STRIDE	(Capitol B-5431)	1.00	4.00	85
TOO MANY GAMES	(Capitol PB-5474)	1.00	4.00	85
I WANNA BE WITH YOU	(Capitol PB-5599)	1.00	4.00	86

MBULU, LETTA
See Quincy Jones ("Roots" Medley)

McCALLUM, DAVID
(Co-starred on the television series *The Man From U.N.C.L.E.* which aired from 1964-1968)

COMMUNICATION / My Carousel	(Capitol F5571)	3.00	12.00	66
THE HOUSE ON BRECKENRIDGE LANE / Three Bites Of The Apple	(Capitol F5721)	3.00	12.00	66

    (*Three Bites Of The Apple* is the only song McCallum has a vocal; he was conductor/composer for the other instrumentals)

McCANN, LES
ALL	(Limelight 3077)	1.50	6.00	65

McCARTERS, THE
THE GIFT	(Warner Bros. 27868-7)	.75	3.00	88

McCARTHY, ANDREW
(Actor)

    See Orchestral Manœuvres In The Dark (*If You Leave*), John Parr (*St. Elmo's Fire*), Starship (*Nothing's Gonna Stop Us Now*)

McCARTNEY, PAUL

GIVE IRELAND BACK TO THE IRISH	(Apple 1847)	5.00	20.00	72
(Shown as by Wings)				
MARY HAD A LITTLE LAMB / Little Woman Love	(Apple 1851)	7.50	30.00	72
(A-side listed on front, b-side listed on back. No artist name credited.)				
MARY HAD A LITTLE LAMB	(Apple 1851)	3.75	15.00	72
(Only a-side listed on front. No artist name credited.)				
LISTEN TO WHAT THE MAN SAID	(Capitol 4091)	1.50	6.00	75
(Shown as by Wings)				
GIRLS SCHOOL / Mull Of Kintyre	(Capitol 4504)	3.00	12.00	77
(Shown as by Wings)				
GETTING CLOSER / Spin It On	(Columbia 3-11020)	10.00	40.00	79
(Half sleeve, shown as by Wings)				
WONDERFUL CHRISTMASTIME /				
Rudolph The Red-Nosed Reggae	(Columbia 1-11162)	1.50	6.00	79
COMING UP / Coming Up (Live Version) / Lunch Box / Odd Sox	(Columbia 1-11263)	1.25	5.00	80
WATERFALLS / Check My Machine	(Columbia 1-11335)	5.00	20.00	80
EBONY AND IVORY / Rainclouds	(Columbia 18-02860)	1.00	4.00	82
(Shown as by Paul McCartney Additional Vocals By Stevie Wonder)				
EBONY AND IVORY	(Columbia 18-02860)	2.00	8.00	82
(Promotional issue, *Demonstration–Not For Sale* printed on sleeve. Shown as by Paul McCartney Additional Vocals By Stevie Wonder.)				
TAKE IT AWAY / I'll Give You A Ring	(Columbia 18-03018)	1.00	4.00	82
TAKE IT AWAY	(Columbia 18-03018)	2.00	8.00	82
(Promotional issue, *Demonstration–Not For Sale* printed on sleeve)				
THE GIRL IS MINE	(Epic 34-03288)	1.00	4.00	82
(Shown as by Michael Jackson / Paul McCartney)				
THE GIRL IS MINE	(Epic 34-03288)	2.00	8.00	82
(Promotional issue, *Demonstration–Not For Sale* printed on sleeve. Shown as by Michael Jackson / Paul McCartney.)				
SAY SAY SAY / Ode To A Koala Bear	(Columbia 38-04168)	1.00	4.00	83
(Shown as by Paul McCartney and Michael Jackson)				
SAY SAY SAY	(Columbia 38-04168)	2.00	8.00	83
(Promotional issue, *Demonstration–Not For Sale* printed on sleeve. Shown as by Paul McCartney and Michael Jackson.)				
SO BAD / Pipes Of Peace	(Columbia 38-04296)	1.00	4.00	83
SO BAD	(Columbia 38-04296)	2.00	8.00	83
(Promotional issue, *Demonstration–Not For Sale* printed on sleeve)				
NO MORE LONELY NIGHTS (BALLAD) /				
No More Lonely Nights (Playout Version)	(Columbia 38-04581)	1.00	4.00	84
(From the motion picture *Give My Regards To Broad Street* starring McCartney)				
NO MORE LONELY NIGHTS	(Columbia 38-04581)	2.00	8.00	84
(Promotional issue, *Demonstration–Not For Sale* printed on sleeve. From the motion picture *Give My Regards To Broad Street* starring McCartney.)				
SPIES LIKE US / My Carnival	(Capitol B-5537)	.75	3.00	85
(A-side from the motion picture *Spies Like Us*, McCartney, Chevy Chase, and Dan Aykroyd pictured)				
PRESS	(Capitol B-5597)	.75	3.00	86
STRANGLEHOLD / Angry	(Capitol B-5636)	.75	3.00	86
ONLY LOVE REMAINS / Tough On A Tightrope	(Capitol B-5672)	.75	3.00	86
MY BRAVE FACE	(Capitol B-44367)	.75	3.00	89

    Also see Band Aid, the Beatles, Brass Ring (*Love In The Open Air*), the Country Hams, Ferry Aid, Billy J. Kramer (*From A Window*)

McCLAIN, CHARLY

WITH JUST ONE LOOK IN YOUR EYES / Tangled In A Tightrope	(Epic 34-05398)	.75	3.00	85
(A-side shown as by Charly McClain With Wayne Massey)				
WITH JUST ONE LOOK IN YOUR EYES	(Epic 34-05398)	1.00	4.00	85
(Promotional issue, *Demonstration Only–Not For Sale* printed on sleeve. Shown as by Charly McClain With Wayne Massey.)				

McCLOUD, COYOTE, FEATURING CLARA PELLER
(Peller had a recurring role in television commercials for the fast-food restaurant Wendy's)

WHERE'S THE BEEF?	(Awesome 105 A)	1.25	5.00	84

McCOY, CHARLIE
SAMPLER AND INTERVIEW	(Columbia AE7-00001)	1.25	5.00	73

    (Promotional issue only)

McCOY, CLYDE
SUGAR BLUES / Tear It Down	(Decca 1-721)	3.00	12.00	53

    (Decca "Curtain Call" series of reissues)

McCOY, VAN
BUTTERFLY / Keep Loving Me .... (Columbia 4-43415) | 3.75 | 15.00 | 65

McCRANEY, GERALD
(Actor)
See Barry DeVorzon (*Theme From Simon & Simon*)

McCRORY, SUSAN
ROVIN' GAL .... (Arrow 1005) | 5.00 | 20.00 | 57

McCULLOUGH, ROD
MY LONELY NIGHT / Sweet Moments With You .... (Domino 902) | 12.50 | 50.00 | 59
(Single sheet insert, not a true picture sleeve)

McDANIEL, MEL
STAND ON IT .... (Capitol B-5620) | .75 | 3.00 | 86

McDONALD, KATHI
See Long John Baldry (*You've Lost That Loving Feeling*)

McDONALD, MICHAEL
I KEEP FORGETTIN' / Losin' End .... (Warner Bros. 29933-7) | .75 | 3.00 | 82
I GOTTA TRY / Believe In It .... (Warner Bros. 29862-7) | .75 | 3.00 | 82
NO LOOKIN' BACK .... (Warner Bros. 28960-7) | .75 | 3.00 | 85
LOST IN THE PARADE .... (Warner Bros. 28847-7) | .75 | 3.00 | 85
OUR LOVE .... (Warner Bros. 28596-7) | .75 | 3.00 | 85
ON MY OWN .... (MCA 52770) | .75 | 3.00 | 86
(Shown as by Patti LaBelle and Michael McDonald)
SWEET FREEDOM .... (MCA 52857) | .75 | 3.00 | 86
(From the motion picture *Running Scared*, McDonald, Billy Crystal, and Gregory Hines pictured)
Also see the Doobie Brothers, the Winans (*Love Has No Color*)

McDONALD, RONALD, & FRIENDS
(Ronald McDonald is the official "spokesclown" for the fast-food restaurant *McDonald's*)
SHARE A SONG FROM YOUR HEART / F-R-I-E-N-D-S .... (Casablanca KidWorks 5101) | 1.25 | 5.00 | 80

McDONOUGH, MEGAN
IF I COULD ONLY REACH YOU / (I'm Ready For) The Real Thing .... (Silver Star no#) | 1.00 | 4.00
(Hard cover, from the motion picture *You Never Gave Me Roses*)

McDOWELL, CARRIE
UH UH, NO NO CASUAL SEX .... (Motown 1903) | .75 | 3.00 | 87

McENTIRE, PAKE
BAD LOVE .... (RCA 5004-7-RAA) | 1.25 | 5.00 | 86
(Promotional issue poster sleeve)

McENTIRE, REBA
ONLY YOU (AND YOU ALONE) / Love By Love .... (Mercury 57062) | 1.50 | 6.00 | 81
JUST A LITTLE LOVE / If Your Heart's Not In It .... (MCA 52349) | 1.25 | 5.00 | 84
SOMEBODY SHOULD LEAVE / Don't You Believe Him .... (MCA 52527) | 1.25 | 5.00 | 85

McFADDEN, BOB, AND DOR
THE MUMMY / The Beat Generation .... (Brunswick 55140) | 7.50 | 30.00 | 59
Also see Rod McKuen (a.k.a..Dor)

McFERRIN, BOBBY
DON'T WORRY, BE HAPPY / Simple Pleasures .... (EMI Manhattan B-50146) | .75 | 3.00 | 88
GOOD LOVIN' / Don't Worry, Be Happy .... (EMI Manhattan B-50163) | .75 | 3.00 | 88

MC5
(Motor City Five)
LOOKING AT YOU / Borderline .... (A-Squared 333) | 50.00 | 200.00 | 67
(Hard cover)
Also see Wayne Kramer, the Secrets (Dennis Thompson), Patti Smith (Fred "Sonic" Smith was a member of MC5 and the Patti Smith Group. He was also Patti Smith's husband.)

McFLY, MARTY, AND THE STARLIGHTERS
(Michael J. Fox played the role of Marty McFly in the *Back To The Future* motion picture series)
JOHNNY B. GOODE .... (MCA 52650) | 1.00 | 4.00 | 85
(From the motion picture *Back To The Future*)

McGHEE, BROWNIE
BLUE BOYS HOLLER / Blues Last Walk .... (Brut 804) | 1.50 | 6.00 | 73
(Shown as by Sonny Terry and Brownie McGhee)

McGOVERN, ELIZABETH
(Actress)
See Dave Wakeling (*She's Having A Baby*)

McGOVERN, MAUREEN
LOVE SONGS ARE GETTING HARDER TO SING .... (20th Century 2234) | 1.50 | 6.00 | 75
(Promotional issue only, song title not credited on sleeve. Front of sleeve reads *The New Maureen McGovern...In More Ways Than One!*)
I COULD HAVE BEEN A SAILOR .... (CBS 39-06565) | 1.00 | 4.00 | 87
(Promotional issue only)
THE SAME MOON .... (CBS 39-07689) | .75 | 3.00 | 88
Also see Placido Domingo (*A Love Until The End Of Time*)

McGUFFEY LANE
MAKING A LIVING'S BEEN KILLING ME .... (Atlantic 7-99959) | 1.00 | 4.00 | 82

McGUIRE, BARRY
CHILD OF OUR TIMES / Upon A Painted Ocean .... (Dunhill 4014) | 2.50 | 10.00 | 65
TOP OF THE HILL .... (Dunhill 4124) | 3.00 | 12.00 | 68
Also see the New Christy Minstrels

TITLE	LABEL AND NUMBER	VG	NM	YR

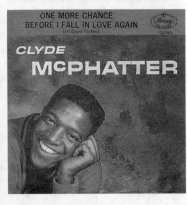

McGUIRE, NOVA
FEELIN' A SONG .... (ARC 402) 1.00 4.00 77

McGUIRE SISTERS, THE
WEARY BLUES/In The Alps .... (Coral 61670) 3.75 15.00 56
    (Shown as by the McGuire Sisters and Lawrence Welk, all four pictured)
LIVIN' DANGEROUSLY/Lovers Lullaby .... (Coral 9-62162) 2.50 10.00 60
JUST FOR OLD TIME'S SAKE .... (Coral 62249) 2.50 10.00 61
TEARS ON MY PILLOW/Will There Be Space In A Spaceship .... (Coral 62276) 2.50 10.00 61

McKENDREE, FRAN
LIKE I'VE NEVER BEEN GONE .... (Arista 281) 1.25 5.00 77

McKENDREE SPRING
GOD BLESS THE CONSPIRACY/Flying Dutchman .... (Decca 33000) 1.50 6.00 72

McKENZIE, BOB & DOUG
(Actor/Comedians Rick Moranis and Dave Thomas)
TAKE OFF .... (Mercury 76134) 1.00 4.00 81
    (Back of sleeve states *Featuring Geddy Lee*)

McKUEN, ROD
SCANDALOUS .... (Buena Vista 482) 1.50 6.00 69
THE CAROLS OF CHRISTMAS .... (Warner Bros. 7542) 1.50 6.00 71
    Also see Bob McFadden and Dor

McLACHLAN, SARAH
VOX/Touch .... (Arista 9804) 2.50 10.00 89

McLAREN, MALCOM
BUFFALO GALS .... (Island 7-99941) .75 3.00 82
    (Shown as by Malcom McLaren and the World's Famous Supreme Team)
DOUBLE DUTCH/Radio Show (D'Ya Like Scratchin'?) .... (Island 7-99864) .75 3.00 83
    (Originally issued with an American Double Dutch League Order Form insert)

McLAUGHLIN, JOHN
    See the Mahavishnu Orchestra With John McLaughlin

McLAUGHLIN, PAT
WRONG NUMBER .... (Capitol B-44138) .75 3.00 88

McLEAN, DON
AMERICAN PIE .... (United Artists 50856) 1.25 5.00 71
VINCENT/Castles In The Air .... (United Artists 50887) 1.25 5.00 72
SUPERMAN'S GHOST/To Have And To Hold .... (EMI B-43025) 1.50 6.00 87
    (Gatefold sleeve)

McNALLY, LARRY JOHN
MY OBSESSION (REMIX)/Long Drag Off A Cigarette .... (Atco 7-99493) .75 3.00 86

McNEELY, BIG JAY
ROCKIN' THE REEDS/California .... (Big J 105) 1.50 6.00 85

McNICHOL, KRISTY & JIMMY
(Actress/Actor, brother and sister)
HE'S SO FINE/He's A Dancer .... (RCA PB-11271) 1.50 6.00 78

McPHATTER, CLYDE
ONE RIGHT AFTER ANOTHER/This Is Not Goodbye .... (MGM 12949) 6.25 25.00 60
I JUST WANT TO LOVE YOU/You're For Me .... (Mercury 71692) 5.00 20.00 60
ONE MORE CHANCE/Before I Fall In Love Again (I'll Count To Ten) .... (Mercury 71740) 5.00 20.00 60
TOMORROW IS A-COMIN'/I'll Love You Till The Cows Come Home .... (Mercury 71783) 5.00 20.00 61
A WHOLE HEAP OF LOVE/You're Movin' Me .... (Mercury 71809) 5.00 20.00 61
I NEVER KNEW/Happiness .... (Mercury 71841) 5.00 20.00 61
SAME TIME, SAME PLACE/Your Second Choice .... (Mercury 71868) 5.00 20.00 61
LOVER PLEASE/Let's Forget About The Past .... (Mercury 71941) 5.00 20.00 61
LITTLE BITTY PRETTY ONE/Next To Me .... (Mercury 71987) 5.00 20.00 61
MAYBE/I Do Believe .... (Mercury 72025) 5.00 20.00 62
THE BEST MAN CRIED/Stop .... (Mercury 72051) 5.00 20.00 62
SO CLOSE TO BEING IN LOVE/Love One To One .... (Mercury 72166) 5.00 20.00 63
DEEP IN THE HEART OF HARLEM/Happy Good Times .... (Mercury 72220) 5.00 20.00 64
I FOUND MY LOVE/Crying Won't Help You Now .... (Mercury 72407) 5.00 20.00 65

McQUEEN, STEVE
(Actor)
    See Quincy Jones (*The Love Theme*)

McRAE, CARMEN
TAKE FIVE .... (Columbia 4-42292) 2.00 8.00 62

McVIE, CHRISTINE
GOT A HOLD ON ME/Who's Dreaming This Dream .... (Warner Bros. 29372-7) .75 3.00 84
LOVE WILL SHOW US HOW .... (Warner Bros. 29313-7) .75 3.00 84
    Also see Fleetwood Mac

McWILLIAMS, DAVID
DAYS OF PEARLY SPENCER/There's No Lock Upon My Door .... (Kapp 896) 1.50 6.00 69

MEAD, ABIGAIL
FULL METAL JACKET .... (Warner Bros. 28204-7) .75 3.00 87
    (From the motion picture *Full Metal Jacket*)

MEAD, RANDY
EXTENDED PLAYS
HILLSIDE VIEW .... (Narada S33-17254) 1.00 4.00 86
    (Promotional issue only titled *Narada Sampler–Excellence In New Acoustic Music*, issued with a small-hole
    33-1/3 RPM record. Also includes one song each by Tingstad–Rumbel, William Ellwood, Michael Jones,
    Matthew Montfort, Spencer Brewer, David Lanz, and Gabriel Lee.)

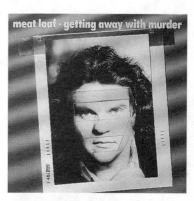

MEADOWS, AUDREY AND JANE
(Audrey played the character Alice Kramden in *The Honeymooners* sketches from the television series *The Jackie Gleason Show*. Jane, who is Audrey's sister, appeared as a panelist on the television series *I've Got A Secret* from 1952-1959, and is married to Steve Allen.)
HOT POTATO/Japanese Rhumba .... (RCA Victor 47-6132)   10.00   40.00   55

MEATBALLS
(Motion Picture)
     See David Naughton (*Makin' It*)

MEAT LOAF
(GIVE ME THE FUTURE WITH A) MODERN GIRL (SINGLE VERSION)/
     Sailor To A Siren .... (RCA PB-14101)   1.00   4.00   84
GETTING AWAY WITH MURDER/Rock 'N' Roll Hero .... (Atlantic 7-89340)   1.00   4.00   86
ROCK 'N' ROLL MERCENARIES/Execution Day .... (Atlantic 7-89303)   1.00   4.00   87
     (Shown as by Meat Loaf With John Parr, both pictured)

MEAT PUPPETS
SWIMMING GROUND/Up On The Sun .... (SST E39)   1.50   6.00   87
SAM/Bali Ha'i .... (London PRO 943-7)   1.25   5.00   91
     (Promotional issue only, *For Promotional Use Only–Not For Sale* printed on back)
     Also see Mike Watt (Cris and Curt Kirkwood on *Big Train*)

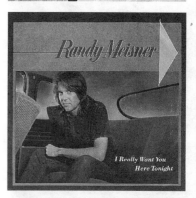

MECCA NORMAL
HOW MANY NOW/Horse Heaven Hills .... (Harriet 010)   1.50   6.00   91
YOU HEARD IT ALL/BROKEN FLOWERS/Going To Hell .... (Sub Pop 149)   1.25   5.00   92
     (B-side shown as by Kreviss. Limited to 3,200 copies on marbled forest green vinyl.)
FROM THE SURFACE/Upside Down Flame .... (Dionysus ID074539)   1.00   4.00   92
     (Folding sleeve with small-hole 45 RPM record)
     Also see Jean Smith

MECO
     See the Star Wars Intergalactic Droid Choir & Chorale

MEDEIROS, GLENN
NOTHING'S GONNA CHANGE MY LOVE FOR YOU/
     Nothing's Gonna Change My Love For You (Instrumental Version) .... (Amherst 311)   .75   3.00   87
WATCHING OVER YOU/You Left The Loneliest Heart .... (Amherst 314)   .75   3.00   87
LONELY WON'T LEAVE ME ALONE/ .... (Amherst 317)   .75   3.00   87
LONG AND LASTING LOVE (ONCE IN A LIFETIME)/
     You're My Woman, You're My Lady .... (Amherst 324)   .75   3.00   88
NEVER GET ENOUGH OF YOU/Pieces Of My Dreams .... (Amherst 326)   .75   3.00   88

MEDLEY, BILL
(I'VE HAD) THE TIME OF MY LIFE/Love Is Strange .... (RCA 5224-7-R)   1.00   4.00   87
     (A-side shown as by Bill Medley and Jennifer Warnes, b-side by Mickey and Sylvia. From the motion picture
     Dirty Dancing, Patrick Swayze and Jennifer Gray pictured.)
HE AIN'T HEAVY, HE'S MY BROTHER/The Bridge .... (Scotti Brothers ZS4 07938)   .75   3.00   88
     (B-side shown as by Giorgio Moroder. From the motion picture *Rambo III*.)
     Also see the Righteous Brothers

MEHTA, ZUBIN
     See Isaac Stern (*Happy Birthday, Isaac Stern*)

MEISNER, RANDY
I REALLY WANT YOU HERE TONIGHT/Heartsong .... (Asylum 45502)   1.00   4.00   78
     Also see Poco (Meisner was a member of the Eagles until 1977)

MEL & KIM
SHOWING OUT/ .... (Atlantic 7-89329)   .75   3.00   87
RESPECTABLE/Respectable (Instrumental) .... (Atlantic 7-89256)   .75   3.00   87

MELANIE
MY BEAUTIFUL PEOPLE .... (Columbia 4-44349)   6.25   25.00   68
WHY DIDN'T MY MOTHER TELL ME/Garden In The City .... (Columbia 4-44524)   6.25   25.00   68
LAY DOWN (CANDLES IN THE RAIN) .... (Buddah 167)   1.25   5.00   70
PEACE WILL COME (ACCORDING TO PLAN) .... (Buddah 186)   1.25   5.00   70
THE NICKEL SONG .... (Buddah 268)   1.25   5.00   72
I'M BACK IN TOWN .... (Buddah 304)   1.25   5.00   72
     (Generic "Melanie" sleeve with her name on the front and back. No song title or label number indicated.)
RING THE LIVING BELL/Railroad .... (Neighborhood 4202)   1.00   4.00   72
SOME DAY I'LL BE A FARMER/Steppin' .... (Neighborhood 4204)   1.00   4.00   72
TOGETHER ALONE/Center Of The Circle .... (Neighborhood 4207)   1.00   4.00   72
TOGETHER ALONE .... (Neighborhood 4207)   1.25   5.00   72
     (Promotional issue only. Completely different design from stock issue. Sleeve reads *URGENT September 14,*
     1972. This is a NEW PRESSING of MELANIE'S "Together Alone". Please destroy all previous copies of this record you
     have. We've found some records of the first shipment technically defective.)
BITTER BAD .... (Neighborhood 4210)   1.25   5.00   73
SEEDS/Some Say (I Got Devil) .... (Neighborhood 4212)   1.00   4.00   73
WILL YOU LOVE ME TOMORROW?/Here I Am .... (Neighborhood 4213)   1.00   4.00   73
LOVE TO LOSE AGAIN .... (Neighborhood 4214)   1.00   4.00   74
     Also see Lisa Angelle (*The First Time I Loved Forever*)

MELCHER, TERRY
     See Terry Day

MELLENCAMP, JOHN COUGAR
I NEED A LOVER THAT WON'T DRIVE ME CRAZY .... (Riva 202)   2.00   8.00   79
     (Shown as by John Cougar)
HURTS SO GOOD/Close Enough .... (Riva 209)   1.25   5.00   82
     (Shown as by John Cougar)
CRUMBLIN' DOWN/Golden Gates .... (Riva 214)   1.00   4.00   83
PINK HOUSES/Serious Business .... (Riva 215)   1.00   4.00   83
AUTHORITY SONG/Pink Houses (Acoustic Version) .... (Riva 216)   1.00   4.00   84
LONELY OL' NIGHT/The Kind Of Fella I Am .... (Riva 884 984-7 M-1)   .75   3.00   85
     (Back of sleeve credits Ry Cooder on slide guitar)

TITLE	LABEL AND NUMBER	VG	NM	YR

SMALL TOWN/Small Town (Acoustic Version)	(Riva 884 202-7)	.75	3.00	85
R.O.C.K. IN THE U.S.A./Under The Boardwalk	(Riva 884 455-7 M-1)	.75	3.00	86
RAIN ON THE SCARECROW/Pretty Ballerina	(Riva 884 635-7)	.75	3.00	86
RUMBLESEAT/Cold Sweat	(Riva 884 856-7)	.75	3.00	86
PAPER IN FIRE/Never Too Old	(Mercury 888-763-7)	.75	3.00	87
CHERRY BOMB/Shama Lama Ding Dong	(Mercury 888-934-7)	.75	3.00	87
CHECK IT OUT/We Are The People	(Mercury 870-126-7)	.75	3.00	88
ROOTY TOOT TOOT/Check It Out (Live)	(Mercury 870 327-7)	.75	3.00	88
RAVE ON/Tutti Frutti	(Elektra 7-69370)	.75	3.00	88

(B-side shown as by Little Richard. From the motion picture *Cocktail*, Tom Cruise pictured.)

POP SINGER/J.M.'s Question	(Mercury 874 012-7)	.75	3.00	89
JACKIE BROWN/Jackie Brown (Acoustic Version)	(Mercury 874 644-7)	.75	3.00	89
LET IT ALL HANG OUT/Country Gentleman	(Mercury 874 932-7)	.75	3.00	89

EXTENDED PLAYS

| KICKS/2000 A.D./Lou-ser/Hot Man | (Gulcher 005) | 2.50 | 10.00 | 78 |

(Single sheet insert titled *U.S. Male*, not a true picture sleeve. Song order on record is 2000 A.D./LOU-SER/Hot Man/Kicks.)

MELLON, LE GRAND
| MOVE IT ON OVER | (Columbia 4-43848) | 1.50 | 6.00 | 66 |

MELODEERS, THE

| RUDOLPH THE RED NOSED REINDEER/Wishing Is For Fools | (Studio 9908) | 7.50 | 30.00 | 60 |
| HAPPY TEENAGE TIMES/Goo Goo | (Studio 9909) | 5.00 | 20.00 | 60 |

MELVIN, HAROLD, AND THE BLUENOTES
| YESTERDAY I HAD THE BLUES | (Philadelphia International 3525) | 1.25 | 5.00 | 73 |
| BE FOR REAL/Ebony Woman/Let It Be You | (Philadelphia International ZS7-31648) | 1.50 | 6.00 | 75 |

MELVINS, THE
See Nirvana (b-side of *Here She Comes Now*)

MEN AT WORK
| OVERKILL/Til The Money Runs Out | (Columbia 38 03795) | .75 | 3.00 | 83 |
| OVERKILL | (Columbia AE7 1633) | 2.00 | 8.00 | 83 |

(Promotional issue only, *Demonstration–Not For Sale* printed on sleeve. Completely different design with a color photo of the band.)

| IT'S A MISTAKE/Shintaro | (Columbia 38 03959) | .75 | 3.00 | 83 |
| IT'S A MISTAKE | (Columbia 38 03959) | 1.00 | 4.00 | 83 |

(Promotional issue, *Demonstration–Not For Sale* printed on sleeve)

| DR. HECKYLL & MR. JIVE/I Like To (Live) | (Columbia 38-04111) | .75 | 3.00 | 83 |
| DR. HECKYLL & MR. JIVE | (Columbia 38-04111) | 1.00 | 4.00 | 83 |

(Promotional issue, *Demonstration–Not For Sale* printed on sleeve)

| EVERYTHING I NEED/Sail To You | (Columbia 38-04929) | .75 | 3.00 | 85 |
| EVERYTHING I NEED | (Columbia 38-04929) | 1.00 | 4.00 | 85 |

(Promotional issue, *Demonstration–Not For Sale* printed on sleeve)

| MARIA/Snakes And Ladders (Instrumental) | (Columbia 38-05454) | .75 | 3.00 | 85 |
| MARIA | (Columbia 38-05454) | 1.00 | 4.00 | 85 |

(Promotional issue, *Demonstration–Not For Sale* printed on sleeve)

MENDES, SERGIO, AND BRASIL '66
| THE FROG/Watch What Happens | (A&M 872) | 1.25 | 5.00 | 67 |
| THE LOOK OF LOVE/Like A Lover | (A&M 924) | 1.25 | 5.00 | 68 |

(From the motion picture *Casino Royale*)

THE FOOL ON THE HILL/So Many Stars	(A&M 961)	1.25	5.00	68
SCARBOROUGH FAIR/Canto Triste	(A&M 986)	1.25	5.00	68
PRETTY WORLD/Festa	(A&M 1049)	1.25	5.00	69
SITTIN' ON THE DOCK OF THE BAY/Song Of No Regrets	(A&M 1073)	1.25	5.00	69
MASQUERADE	(A&M 1164)	1.25	5.00	70
SO MANY PEOPLE	(A&M 1279)	1.25	5.00	71
THE CRAB	(A&M 1346)	1.25	5.00	72

(Shown as by Sergio Mendes and Brasil '72)

| OLYMPIA | (A&M 2623) | .75 | 3.00 | 84 |

(Shown as by Sergio Mendes)
Also see Lani Hall

MENTAL AS ANYTHING
| LIVE IT UP/Good Friday | (Columbia 38-05798) | .75 | 3.00 | 86 |
| LIVE IT UP | (Columbia 38-05798) | .75 | 3.00 | 86 |

(Promotional issue, *Demonstration: Not For Sale* printed on sleeve)

MENTHOL

| USA CAPABLE/Crystal Keg People | (Capitol CDP 7742 9 29308 2 D) | .75 | 3.00 | 95 |

(Hard cover with small-hole 45 RPM record)

MENUDO

IF YOU'RE NOT HERE (BY MY SIDE)/That's What You Do	(RCA PB-13771)	.75	3.00	84
MOTORCYCLE DREAMER/Gotta Get On Movin'	(RCA PB-13757)	.75	3.00	84
LIKE A CANNONBALL (ENGLISH)/Like A Cannonball (Spanish)	(RCA PB-13836)	.75	3.00	84
HOLD ME/	(RCA PB-14087)	.75	3.00	85

MEN WITHOUT HATS
THE SAFETY DANCE/Living In China	(Backstreet 52232)	1.00	4.00	84
I LIKE	(MCA 52293)	.75	3.00	83
WHERE DO THE BOYS GO?/Unsatisfaction	(MCA 52460)	.75	3.00	84
POP GOES THE WORLD/The End Of The World	(Mercury 888 859-7)	.75	3.00	88
MOONBEAM/Jenny Wore Black	(Mercury 870 153-7)	.75	3.00	88

MEN WITHOUT WOMEN
(Motion Picture)
See Little Steven (*Forever*)

MERCER, JOHNNY
See Ella Mae Morse (b-side of *Cow Cow Boogie*)

MERCURY, FREDDIE
LOVE KILLS .... (Columbia 38-04606) 1.00 4.00 84
  (From the motion picture *Metropolis*)
LOVE KILLS .... (Columbia 38-04606) 1.50 6.00 84
  (Promotional issue, *Demonstration Only Not For Sale* printed on sleeve. From the motion picture *Metropolis*.)
I WAS BORN TO LOVE YOU/Stop All The Fighting .... (Columbia 38-04869) 1.00 4.00 85
I WAS BORN TO LOVE YOU .... (Columbia 38-04869) 1.50 6.00 85
  (Promotional issue, *Demonstration–Not For Sale* printed on sleeve)
THE GREAT PRETENDER .... (Capitol B-5696) 1.00 4.00 87
  Also see Queen

MERRIL, LEE
BALLAD OF THE GREEN HORNET .... (Boom 60013) 2.50 10.00 60s

MESSINA, JIM
  See Loggins and Messina, Poco

METAL CHURCH
  See Sir Mix-A-Lot (*Iron Man*)

METALLICA
EYE OF THE BEHOLDER/Breadfan .... (Elektra 7-69357) 1.50 6.00 88
ONE/The Prince .... (Elektra 7-69329) 1.50 6.00 88

METHENY, PAT, GROUP
ARE YOU GOING WITH ME?/Au Lait .... (ECM/Warner Bros. 29999-7) 1.00 4.00 82
  Also see David Bowie (*This Is Not America*)

METROPOLIS
(Motion Picture)
  See Bonnie Tyler (*Here She Comes*)

MEYERS, AUGIE
  See Doug Sahm (*I'm Not A Fool Anymore*)

MIAMI DOLPHINS
(Football Team)
  See the Dolphin Dolls (*We Love You Dolphins*)

MIAMI SOUND MACHINE
  See Gloria Estefan and Miami Sound Machine

MIAMI VICE
(Television Series)
  See Glenn Frey (*You Belong To The City*), Grandmaster Melle Mel (*Vice*), Jan Hammer (*Miami Vice Theme, Crockett's Theme*), Chaka Khan (*Own The Night*), Patti LaBelle (*The Last Unbroken Heart*), Andy Taylor (*When The Rain Comes Down*)
  Related see Don Johnson, Philip Michael-Thomas

MICHAEL, GEORGE
A DIFFERENT CORNER/A Different Corner (Instrumental) .... (Columbia 38-05888) .75 3.00 86
A DIFFERENT CORNER .... (Columbia 38-05888) 1.00 4.00 86
  (Promotional issue, *Demonstration–Not For Sale* printed on sleeve)
I WANT YOUR SEX (RHYTHM 1 LUST)/
  I Want Your Sex (Rhythm 2 Brass In Love) .... (Columbia 38-07164) .75 3.00 87
  (From the motion picture *Beverly Hills Cop II*)
FAITH/Hand To Mouth .... (Columbia 38-07623) .75 3.00 87
FATHER FIGURE/Father Figure (Instrumental) .... (Columbia 38-07682) .75 3.00 87
ONE MORE TRY .... (Columbia 38-07773) .75 3.00 88
MONKEY .... (Columbia 38-07941) .75 3.00 88
KISSING A FOOL .... (Columbia 38-08050) .75 3.00 88
  Also see Deon Estus (*Heaven Help Me*), Aretha Franklin (*I Knew You Were Waiting*), Wham

MICHAELANGELO
300 WATT MUSIC BOX/Half A Tap .... (Columbia 4-45328) 1.25 5.00 71

MICHAELS, LEE
DO YOU KNOW WHAT I MEAN/Keep The Circle Turning .... (A&M 1262) 1.50 6.00 71
CAN I GET A WITNESS/You Are What You Do .... (A&M 1303) 1.25 5.00 71

MICHAELS, MARILYN
LUM MIR FRAYLICH ZEIN/Love Is Better Than Ever .... (Legend 123) 2.00 8.00
JOHNNY ONE NOTE/Heart Of Paris/Something I Dreamed Last Night .... (Warner Bros. 201) 2.00 8.00
  (Promotional issue only)

MICHAELS, TOMMY
(Actor)
  See the Soaps and Hearts Ensemble

MICKEY AND SYLVIA
  See Bill Medley (b-side of *The Time Of My Life*)

MICKEY MOUSE CLUB, THE
(Television Series)
  Related see Annette, Tim Considine, Johny Crawford, Jimmy Dodd, Shelly Fabares, Don Grady, Karen and Cubby, Paul Petersen, Roberta Shore, Lisa Whelchel

MIDAS TOUCH, THE
SWEET CAROLINE/Jean .... (Decca 732557) 1.50 6.00 69

MIDLER, BETTE
THE ROSE/Stay With Me .... (Atlantic 7-88976) 1.00 4.00 79
  (From the motion picture *The Rose* starring Midler)
ALL I NEED TO KNOW/My Eye On You .... (Atlantic 7-88789) 1.00 4.00 83
WIND BENEATH MY WINGS/Oh Industry .... (Atlantic 7-88972) 1.00 4.00 88
  (From the motion picture *Beaches* starring Midler)
UNDER THE BOARDWALK/The Friendship Theme .... (Atlantic 7-88976) 1.00 4.00 88
  (From the motion picture *Beaches* starring Midler)
  Also see U.S.A. For Africa, Voices Of America

TITLE	LABEL AND NUMBER	VG	NM	YR

MIDNIGHT ANGELS, THE
I'M SUFFERIN'/In The Moonlight .... (Apex 77073) | 7.50 | 30.00 | 67

MIDNIGHT OIL
POWER AND THE PASSION/Tin Legs And Tin Mines .... (Columbia 38-04349) | .75 | 3.00 | 83
POWER AND THE PASSION .... (Columbia 38-04349) | 1.00 | 4.00 | 83
    (Promotional issue, *Demonstration–Not For Sale* printed on sleeve)
THE DEAD HEART/Kosciusko .... (Columbia 38-07964) | .75 | 3.00 | 86
DREAMWORLD/Progress .... (Columbia 38-08093) | .75 | 3.00 | 88

MIDNIGHT STAR
HEADLINES .... (Solar 69547) | .75 | 3.00 | 86

MIGENES, JULIA, AND PAUL ANKA
NO WAY OUT .... (Columbia 38-07358) | .75 | 3.00 | 87
    (From the motion picture *No Way Out,* Kevin Costner pictured)

MIGHTY LEMON DROPS, THE
INSIDE OUT .... (Sire/Reprise 27906-7) | 1.00 | 4.00 | 88

MIGHTY MIGHTY BOSSTONES, THE
DETROIT ROCK CITY/Detroit Rock City .... (Mercury 858 894-7) | .75 | 3.00 | 94
    (Hard cover issued with small-hole, green vinyl. B-side shown as by Kiss, Paul Stanley and Gene Simmons pictured on back.)

MIKE & DEAN
(Mike Love and Dean Torrence)
JINGLE BELLS/Jingle Bells .... (Hitbound 102) | 3.75 | 15.00 | 82
    (Flip side shown as by Paul Revere and the Raiders)
DA DOO RON RON/Baby Talk .... (Premore 23/24) | 7.50 | 30.00 | 83
    Also see the Beach Boys (Mike Love), Jan & Dean (Dean Torrence)

MIKE + THE MECHANICS
SILENT RUNNING (ON DANGEROUS GROUND)/Par Avion .... (Atlantic 7-89488) | .75 | 3.00 | 85
ALL I NEED IS A MIRACLE/You Are The One .... (Atlantic 7-89450) | .75 | 3.00 | 85
TAKEN IN/A Call To Arms .... (Atlantic 7-89404) | .75 | 3.00 | 86
NOBODY'S PERFECT/Nobody Knows .... (Atlantic 7-88990) | .75 | 3.00 | 88
NOBODY'S PERFECT/Nobody Knows .... (Atlantic 7-88990) | .75 | 3.00 | 88
    (A sticker stating *Contains The Hit Nobody Knows* is placed over the *Nobody's Perfect* title on the front)
THE LIVING YEARS/Too Many Friends .... (Atlantic 7-88964) | .75 | 3.00 | 88
REVOLUTION/Leave Love Behind .... (Atlantic 7-69283) | .75 | 3.00 | 89
    (B-side shown as by Jonathan Elias. From the motion picture *Rude Awakening,* Cheech Marin, Eric Roberts, Julie Hagerty, and Robert Carradine pictured. Sticker reading "Mike + the Mechanics, Revolution, 7-69283 is pasted over the song title "Revolution" printed on sleeve)
SEEING IS BELIEVING/Don't .... (Atlantic 7-88921) | .75 | 3.00 | 89
    Also see Paul Carrack, Genesis (Mike Rutherford), Mike Rutherford, Sad Café (Paul Young), Squeeze (Paul Carrack), Paul Young

MIKE'S MURDER
(Motion Picture)
    See Joe Jackson *(Memphis)*

MILES, BUDDY
    See the California Raisins (vocalist for the Claymation characters)

MILES, GARRY
LOOK FOR A STAR .... (Liberty F-55261) | 5.00 | 20.00 | 60
    (From the motion picture *Circus Of Horrors*)

MILES, JOHN, BAND
BLINDED/Good So Bad .... (Valentino/Atco 7-99575) | .75 | 3.00 | 85

MILLENNIUM
IT'S YOU/I Just Want To Be Your Friend .... (Columbia 4-44546) | 3.00 | 12.00 | 68

MILLER, ANN
(Actress/Entertainer)
JIMMY McHUGH MELODY/Don't Blame Me .... (BER 842) | 1.50 | 6.00 |
    (Shown as by Mickey Rooney and Ann Miller)

MILLER, FRANKIE
TO DREAM THE DREAM .... (Capitol B-5131) | .75 | 3.00 | 82

MILLER, GLENN
GENERIC GLENN MILLER SLEEVE .... (RCA Victor) | 2.50 | 10.00 | 50s
    (Generic half sleeve titled *Glenn Miller Plays His Favorite Recordings.* Used for singles RCA Victor 447-0031 through 447-0047 which are individually listed on back.)

MILLER, JEREMY
(Child Actor)
    See Steve Dorff and Friends *(Theme From Growing Pains)*

MILLER, JODY
SILVER THREADS AND GOLDEN NEEDLES .... (Capitol 5429) | 2.50 | 10.00 | 65
HOME OF THE BRAVE .... (Capitol 5483) | 2.50 | 10.00 | 65
OPEN END INTERVIEW/OPEN END INTERVIEW .... (Capitol 2370) | 2.50 | 10.00 | 60s
    (Promotional issue only, flip side is Billy May. Originally issued with a cue sheet.)

MILLER, MARCUS
LOVIN' YOU .... (Warner Bros. 7-29768) | .75 | 3.00 | 83

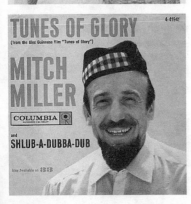

MILLER, MITCH
THE CHILDREN'S MARCHING SONG/Carolina In The Morning .... (Columbia 4-41317) | 2.50 | 10.00 | 59
    (From the motion picture *Inn Of The Sixth Happiness*)
DO-RE-MI .... (Columbia 4-41499) | 2.00 | 8.00 | 59
TUNES OF GLORY/Shlub-A-Dubba-Dub .... (Columbia 4-41941) | 2.00 | 8.00 | 61
    (A-side from the motion picture *Tunes Of Glory*)

TITLE	LABEL AND NUMBER	VG	NM	YR
TITLE THE TUNE CONTEST	(Columbia D-14)	2.20	10.00	61

(Promotional issue for members of the Columbia Record Club. Issued with a small-hole 33-1/3 RPM one-sided record titled *Theme For A Title*.)

BE A SANTA/Must Be Santa	(Columbia 4-42240)	2.00	8.00	62

(Shown as by Mitch Miller and the Gang)

THE LONGEST DAY	(Columbia 4-42585)	2.00	8.00	62

(From the motion picture *The Longest Day*)

THE GREAT ESCAPE MARCH	(Columbia 4-42813)	2.00	8.00	63

Also see the Sandpipers and Mitchell Miller and Orchestra

MILLER, MRS.
I SAID NO/The Weekend Of A Private Secretary

MILLER, ROGER
DANG ME/Got 2 Again	(Smash 1881)	2.50	10.00	64
DO-WACKA-DO/Love Is Not For Me	(Smash 1947)	2.00	8.00	64
ONE DYIN' AND A BURYIN'/It Happened Just That Way	(Smash 1994)	2.00	8.00	65
BALLAD OF WATERHOLE #3/Rainbow Valley	(Smash 2121)	1.50	6.00	67
OLD TOY TRAINS/Silent Night	(Smash 2130)	1.50	6.00	67
LITTLE GREEN APPLES/Our Little Love	(Smash 2148)	1.50	6.00	68
WHISTLE STOP/Not In Nottingham	(Buena Vista 493)	1.50	6.00	70

MILLER, STEVE

SITTING IN CIRCLES	(Capitol 2156)	6.25	25.00	67

(Song title not listed on sleeve)

HEART LIKE A WHEEL	(Capitol A-5068)	1.00	4.00	81
ABRACADABRA	(Capitol B-5126)	1.00	4.00	82
COOL MAGIC	(Capitol B-5162)	1.00	4.00	82
GIVE IT UP	(Capitol B-5194)	1.00	4.00	82
LIVING IN THE U.S.A.	(Capitol B-5223)	.75	3.00	83
SHANGRI-LA	(Capitol B-5407)	.75	3.00	84
BONGO BONGO	(Capitol B-5442)	.75	3.00	85
ITALIAN X RAYS	(Capitol B-5476)	1.25	5.00	85
I WANT TO MAKE THE WORLD TURN AROUND	(Capitol B-5646)	.75	3.00	86
NOBODY BUT YOU BABY	(Capitol B-5671)	.75	3.00	86
I WANNA BE LOVED	(Capitol B-5704)	.75	3.00	86
YA YA	(Capitol B-44222)	.75	3.00	88

Also see the Goldberg-Miller Blues Band, Boz Scaggs (Scaggs was a member of Miller's band from 1967-1968)

MILLER, TERRY

TEEN AGE LINGO JIVE/Too Lonesome To Cry	(Cavalier 877X45)	7.50	30.00	60s

MILLER, WARREN
EVERYONE'S GOT A BABY BUT ME	(United Artists 104)	2.00	8.00	61

MILLIONS, THE
SOMETIMES (RADIO EDIT)/Sometimes (LP Version)	(Smash PRO 963-7)	1.00	4.00	91

(Promotional issue only with small-hole 45 RPM record)

MILLIONS LIKE US
GUARANTEED FOR LIFE/Heaven Help The Child	(Virgin 7-99412)	.75	3.00	87
IN LOVE WITH YOURSELF/Heartbroken Man	(Virgin 7-99365)	.75	3.00	88

MILLI VANILLI
GIRL YOU KNOW IT'S TRUE/Magic Touch	(Arista 9781)	.75	3.00	88
BABY DON'T FORGET MY NUMBER/Too Much Monkey Business	(Arista 9832)	.75	3.00	89
GIRL I'M GONNA MISS YOU/All Or Nothing	(Arista 9870)	.75	3.00	89
BLAME IT ON THE RAIN/Dance With A Devil	(Arista 9904)	.75	3.00	89

MILLS, HAYLEY

LET'S GET TOGETHER/Cobbler, Cobbler	(Buena Vista F-385)	5.00	20.00	61

(A-side from the motion picture *The Parent Trap*)

JEEPERS CREEPERS/Johnny Jingo	(Buena Vista F-395)	5.00	20.00	62
SIDE BY SIDE/Ding Dong Ding	(Buena Vista F-401)	5.00	20.00	62
CASTAWAY/Sweet River	(Buena Vista F-408)	5.00	20.00	62

(From the motion picture *In Search Of The Castaways*)

ENJOY IT/Let's Climb	(Buena Vista F-409)	5.00	20.00	62

(Shown as by Hayley Mills and Maurice Chevalier)

FLITTERIN'/Beautiful Beulah	(Buena Vista F-420)	5.00	20.00	63

(Shown as by Hayley Mills & Eddie Hodges, both pictured. From the motion picture *Summer Magic*.)

EXTENDED PLAYS
SUMMER MAGIC/FLITTERIN'/BEAUTIFUL BEULAH/UGLY BUG BALL/ On The Front Porch/Pink Of Perfection/Femininity	(Buena Vista 4023)	3.75	15.00	63

(Promotional issue sponsored by Alcoa Wrap. Shown as by Burl Ives, Hayley Mills, Eddie Hodges, and Deborah Walley. From the motion picture *Summer Magic*, Burl Ives and Hayley Mills pictured on front.)

MILLS, STEPHANIE

SWEET SENSATION	(20th Century-Fox 2449)	1.00	4.00	80
BIT BY BIT	(MCA 52617)	.75	3.00	85

(From the motion picture *Fletch*)

STAND BACK	(MCA 52731)	.75	3.00	85
RISING DESIRE	(MCA 52843)	.75	3.00	86
I FELL GOOD ALL OVER	(MCA 53056)	.75	3.00	87
YOU'RE PUTTIN' A RUSH ON ME	(MCA 53151)	.75	3.00	87
SECRET LADY	(MCA 53209)	.75	3.00	87
IF I WERE YOUR WOMAN	(MCA 53275)	.75	3.00	88
WHERE IS THE LOVE	(MCA 53283)	.75	3.00	88

(Shown as by Stephanie Mills and Robert Brookins)

MILLS BROTHERS
TIGER RAG/Paper Doll	(Decca 1-707)	2.50	10.00	51

(Decca "Curtain Call" series of reissues)

TITLE	LABEL AND NUMBER	VG	NM	YR

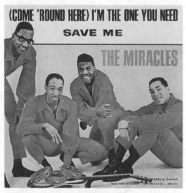

MILSAP, RONNIE
(I'D BE) A LEGEND IN MY TIME .... (RCA PB-10112)	1.25	5.00	74
COWBOYS AND CLOWNS/Misery Loves Company .... (RCA PB-12006)	1.00	4.00	80

(A-side from the motion picture *Bronco Billy,* illustration featuring Clint Eastwood pictured on front, Milsap pictured on back)

LOST IN THE FIFTIES TONIGHT (IN THE STILL OF THE NIGHT) .... (RCA PB-14135)	.75	3.00	85
OLD FOLKS/Earthquake .... (RCA 6896)	.75	3.00	88

(Shown as by Ronnie Milsap and Mike Reid)

MIMIEUX, YVETTE
(Actress)

See Connie Francis (*Where The Boys Are*)

MIMMS, GARNET, & THE ENCHANTERS
FOR YOUR PRECIOUS LOVE/Baby Don't You Weep .... (United Artists 658)	3.75	15.00	63

MINEO, SAL
(Actor)

START MOVIN'/Love Affair .... (Epic 5-9216)	7.50	30.00	57
LASTING LOVE/You Shouldn't Do That .... (Epic 5-9227)	5.00	20.00	57
PARTY TIME/The Words That I Whisper .... (Epic 5-9246)	5.00	20.00	57
LITTLE PIGEON/Cuttin' In .... (Epic 5-9260)	5.00	20.00	58
MAKE BELIEVE BABY/Young As We Are .... (Epic 5-9327)	5.00	20.00	58

MINER, RACHEL
(Actress)

See the Soaps and Hearts Ensemble

MINOGUE, KYLIE
I SHOULD BE SO LUCKY/I Should Be So Lucky (Instrumental) .. (Geffen/PWL/Mushroom 27922-7)	.75	3.00	87
THE LOCO-MOTION/I'll Still Be Loving You .... (Geffen/PWL/Mushroom 27752-7)	.75	3.00	88
IT'S NO SECRET/Made In Heaven .... (Geffen/PWL/Mushroom 27651-7)	.75	3.00	88
I STILL LOVE YOU/ .... (Geffen/PWL/Mushroom 27536-7)	.75	3.00	88

MINOR DETAIL
CANVAS OF LIFE/I'll Always Love You .... (Polydor 815 329-7)	.75	3.00	83
TAKE IT AGAIN/20th Century .... (Polydor 817 749-7)	.75	3.00	84

MINUTEMEN
JOY/BLACK SHEEP/More Joy .... (New Alliance 004)	1.50	6.00	81
COURAGE/WHAT IS IT/Stories .... (SST E58)	3.00	12.00	85
JOY/BLACK SHEEP/More Joy .... (SST 214)	1.50	6.00	89

Also see Mike Watt

MIRACLES, THE
MIGHTY GOOD LOVIN'/Broken Hearted .... (Tamla 54044)	25.00	100.00	61
EVERYBODY'S GOTTA PAY SOME DUES/I Can't Believe .... (Tamla 54048)	12.50	50.00	61
WHAT'S SO GOOD ABOUT GOOD-BY/I've Been Good To You .... (Tamla 54053)	12.50	50.00	61
I'LL TRY SOMETHING NEW/You Never Miss A Good Thing .... (Tamla 54059)	12.50	50.00	62
I LIKE IT LIKE THAT/You're So Fine And Sweet .... (Tamla 54098)	6.25	25.00	64
GOING TO A GO-GO/Choosey Beggar .... (Tamla 54127)	5.00	20.00	65
(COME 'ROUND HERE) I'M THE ONE YOU NEED/Save Me .... (Tamla 54140)	5.00	20.00	66
THE TRACKS OF MY TEARS/Ooo Baby Baby .... (Motown Yesteryear Y411F)	1.00	4.00	87

(Shown as by Smokey Robinson & the Miracles. From the motion picture *Platoon*.)

MI-SEX
CASTAWAY/ .... (Epic 34-04419)	.75	3.00	84
CASTAWAY .... (Epic 34-04419)	1.00	4.00	84

(Promotional issue, *Demonstration Only/Not For Sale* printed on sleeve)

MISFITS, THE
COUGH COOL/She .... (Blank A 101)	37.50	150.00	77

(Limited edition of 500)

BULLET/WE ARE 138/Attitude/Hollywood Babylon .... (Plan 9 1001)	18.75	75.00	78

(First printing of 2000 gatefold sleeves issued with red vinyl and lyric sheet)

BULLET/WE ARE 138/Attitude/Hollywood Babylon .... (Plan 9 1001)	18.75	75.00	78

(Second printing with *Better Dead In Red* on back)

HORROR BUSINESS/Teenagers From Mars/Children In Heat .... (Plan 9 1009)	18.75	75.00	79

(Limited edition of 5000 originally issued with insert and yellow vinyl. There are reportedly 25 copies pressed on black vinyl.)

NIGHT OF THE LIVING DEAD/Where Eagles Dare/Rat Fink .... (Plan 9 1010)	12.50	50.00	79
LONDON DUNGEON/Horror Hotel/Ghouls Night Out .... (Plan 9 1013)	12.50	50.00	81

(Titled *3 Hits From Hell*)

HALLOWEEN I/Halloween II .... (Plan 9 1017)	10.00	40.00	81

(Originally issued with lyric sheet)

EXTENDED PLAYS

EVILIVE .... (Plan 9 1019)	18.75	75.00	82

(Numbered edition of 800)

EVILIVE .... (Plan 9 1019)	10.00	40.00	82

(Unnumbered edition of 1400)

EVILIVE .... (Plan 9 1019)	25.00	100.00	82

(Total edition of 99 sleeves; 33 each of 3 different sleeves. Each pictures an individual band member, originally available through the fan club.)

MISS ALANS, THE
EXTENDED PLAYS

THE SAD LAST DAYS OF ELVIS ARON PRESLEY/ANATOMY/ Kangaroo/The Sad Last Days Of Elvis Aron Presley (Live) .... (Zoo/BMG 72445-14174-7)	1.00	4.00	94

(Hard cover, issued with red vinyl)

MISSING PERSONS
WORDS .... (Capitol B-5127)	1.25	5.00	82
DESTINATION UNKNOWN .... (Capitol B-5161)	1.25	5.00	82
WINDOWS .... (Capitol B-5200)	1.25	5.00	83
GIVE/Clandestine People .... (Capitol B-5326)	1.25	5.00	84

(Photography by Helmut Newton)

RIGHT NOW .... (Capitol B-5358) 1.50 6.00 84
    (Photography by Helmut Newton)
SURRENDER YOUR HEART .... (Capitol B-5381) 1.50 6.00 84
    (Photography by Helmut Newton)
I CAN'T THINK ABOUT DANCIN' .... (Capitol B-5569) 1.00 4.00 86
    Also see Dale Bozzio, Duran Duran (Warren Cuccurullo), Andy Taylor (Terry Bozzio)

MISSION, THE
SERPENTS KISS/Wake .... (Scatterbrainchild no #) 3.75 15.00 87

MISSION, THE
(Motion Picture)
    See Ennio Morricone (Theme From The Mission)

MR. BIG
ADDICTED TO THAT RUSH/Blame It On My Youth .... (Atlantic 7-88860) .75 3.00 89
    Also see Eric Martin

MR. MISTER
KYRIE .... (RCA PB-14258) .75 3.00 85
    (Originally issued with purple vinyl)
IS IT LOVE/32 .... (RCA PB-14313) .75 3.00 85
SOMETHING REAL (INSIDE ME/INSIDE YOU)/Bare My Soul .... (RCA 5273-7-R) .75 3.00 87
STAND AND DELIVER/Power Over Me .... (RCA 6991-7-R) .75 3.00 88
    (A-side from the motion picture Stand and Deliver, Edward James Olmos and Lou Diamond Phillips pictured
    on back)

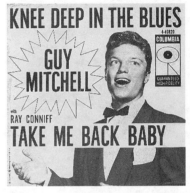

MR. T
(Actor and former bodyguard who appeared in the television series The A-Team and the motion picture Rocky III)
MR. T'S COMMANDMENT .... (Columbia 38-04589) 1.00 4.00 84
MR. T'S COMMANDMENT .... (Columbia 38-04589) 1.25 5.00 84
    (Promotional issue, Demonstration Only–Not For Sale printed on sleeve)

MITCHELL, CHAD, TRIO, THE
LIZZIE BORDEN/Super Skier .... (Kapp 439) 3.75 15.00 62
THE MARVELOUS TOY/Bonny Streets Of Fyve-10 .... (Mercury 72197) 3.00 12.00 63
TELL OLD BILL/ .... (Mercury 72234) 3.00 12.00 64
I CAN'T HELP BUT WONDER/Stewball And Griselda .... (Mercury 72340) 3.00 12.00 64
    (Shown as by the Mitchell Trio)
    Although John Denver was a member, he did not join the group until 1965. Roger McGuinn, later of the Byrds, was a session musician with the
    group and not an official member of the original trio.

MITCHELL, GUY
SINGING THE BLUES/Crazy With Love .... (Columbia 4-40769) 5.00 20.00 56
KNEE DEEP IN THE BLUES/Take Me Back Baby .... (Columbia 4-40820) 5.00 20.00 57
    (Shown as by Guy Mitchell With Ray Conniff)
ROCK-A-BILLY/Hoot Owl .... (Columbia 4-40877) 5.00 20.00 57
HEARTACHES BY THE NUMBER/Two .... (Columbia 4-41476) 3.75 15.00 60
SUNSHINE GUITAR/ .... (Columbia 4-41853) 3.75 15.00 60
SOFT RAIN/Big Big Change .... (Columbia 4-42231) 3.75 15.00 61

MITCHELL, JONI
(YOU'RE SO SQUARE) BABY, I DON'T CARE/Love .... (Geffen 29849-7) .75 3.00 82
GOOD FRIENDS/Smokin, (Empty, Try Another) .... (Geffen 28840-7) .75 3.00 85
    (Painting by Joni Mitchell)
SHINY TOYS .... (Geffen 28675-7) 1.00 4.00 86
    (Painting by Joni Mitchell)
MY SECRET PLACE .... (Geffen 27887-7) .75 3.00 88

MITCHELL, RUBIN
MY LIZA JANE/Spanish Eyes .... (Capitol PRO 4275) 2.50 10.00 59
    (Red and black promotional issue only titled Capitol Records Takes Pride In Presenting Rubin Mitchell. For
    Broadcast Use Only–Not For Sale printed on sleeve. Issued with a small-hole 33-1/3 RPM record.)
MY LIZA JANE/Spanish Eyes .... (Capitol SPRO 4276) 2.50 10.00 59
    (Blue and black promotional issue only titled Presenting Rubin Mitchell...The Most Sensational Pianist In A
    Decade. For Promotional Use Only–Not For Sale printed on sleeve. Issued with a small-hole 33-1/3 RPM record.)

MITCHELL, WILLIE
UP HARD .... (Hi/London 45-2151) 2.00 8.00 68

MITCHELL TRIO, THE
    See the Chad Mitchell Trio

MITCHUM, JIM
LONELY BIRTHDAY .... (20th Century 277) 1.50 6.00 61

MITCHUM, ROBERT
(Actor)
BALLAD OF THUNDER ROAD/My Honey's Lovin' Arms .... (Capitol F3986) 5.00 20.00 58

MIXMASTERS
DON'T CHA WANNA BE LOVED .... (MCA 53328) .75 3.00 88
TONY G.'S SO GOOD .... (MCA 53455) .75 3.00 88

MnMs
I'M TIRED/Knock Knock Knock .... (Quark/Bomp VOID 1) .75 3.00 79
    (A-side co-written with Paul Collins, a member of the Nerves and the Beat, and b-side written by Paul Collins.
    Neither credit is mentioned on sleeve. Issued with small-hole 45 RPM record.)

MOB, THE
GIVE IT TO ME .... (Colossus 134) 1.25 5.00 71

MOBLEY, MARY ANN
(Miss America 1959 and television actress)
DOWN THE AISLE .... (Ace 616) 5.00 20.00 61
    (Shown as by Jimmy Clanton & Mary Ann Mobley; both pictured. Purchaser had the option to mail their
    sleeve to Ace Records in Jackson, Mississippi to have it autographed by the artists. It is unknown if these
    autographs are authentic or the work of office staffers.)

182

TITLE	LABEL AND NUMBER	VG	NM	YR

MOBY GRAPE
FALL ON YOU/Changes ...... (Columbia 4-44170) — 6.25 — 25.00 — 67
SITTING BY THE WINDOW/Indifference ...... (Columbia 4-44171) — 6.25 — 25.00 — 67
8:05/Mister Blues ...... (Columbia 4-44172) — 6.25 — 25.00 — 67
OMAHA/Someday ...... (Columbia 4-44173) — 6.25 — 25.00 — 67
HEY GRANDMA/Come In The Morning ...... (Columbia 4-44174) — 6.25 — 25.00 — 67
(All five sleeves were released simultaneously and feature the same photo of the band. *Omaha* was the only record to make it to the Billboard Top 100; it peaked at #88.)

MODELS
OUT OF MIND OUT OF SIGHT/Down In The Garden ...... (Geffen/Mushroom 287624-7) — .75 — 3.00 — 85
COLD FEVER/Preacher From The Black Lagoon/
Out Of Mind Out Of Sight (Live) ...... (Geffen/Mushroom 28644-7) — .75 — 3.00 — 86

MODERN MAN
See Sputzy Sparacino and Delilah (b-side of *The World Inside Your Eyes*)

MODINE, MATTHEW
(Actor)
See John Waite (*Change*)

MOD SQUAD
(Television Series)
Related see Peggy Lipton

MOE, ADRIAN, AND THE SCULPTORS
SHOTGUN/Love Train ...... (Columbia 4-43445) — 3.75 — 15.00 — 65

MOLLY HATCHET
DREAMS I'LL NEVER SEE ...... (Epic 8-50669) — 1.25 — 5.00 — 78
DREAMS I'LL NEVER SEE ...... (Epic 8-50669) — 1.50 — 6.00 — 78
(Promotional issue, *Demonstration/Not For Sale* printed on sleeve)
STONE IN YOUR HEART ...... (Epic 34-04714) — .75 — 3.00 — 84
STONE IN YOUR HEART ...... (Epic 34-04714) — 1.00 — 4.00 — 84
(Promotional issue, *Demonstration Only–Not For Sale* printed on sleeve)
EXTENDED PLAYS
GATOR COUNTRY (Live) ...... (Epic AE71185) — 2.50 — 10.00 — 79
(Promotional issue only released in conjunction with Washington DC radio station DC 101 to benefit the Special Olympics. Includes one song each by Cheap Trick and David Werner. Issued with a yellow vinyl, small-hole 33-1/3 RPM record.)
FLIRTIN' WITH DISASTER ...... (Columbia Special Products PV 16174) — 1.25 — 5.00 — 81
(Promotional issue only used as an advertising tool for Nestle's $100,000 candy bar, issued with a small-hole 33-1/3 RPM record. Also includes one song each by Cheap Trick, Journey, and REO Speedwagon.)

MOMENT BY MOMENT
(Motion Picture)
See Yvonne Elliman (*Moment by Moment*)

MONAHAN, STEPHEN
CITY OF WINDOWS ...... (Kapp 835) — 1.25 — 5.00 — 67
PLAY WHILE SHE DANCES/The Iron Horse ...... (Kapp 857) — 1.25 — 5.00 — 69

MONDA, DICK
RIVER'S END ...... (Verve 5077) — 2.00 — 8.00 — 60s

MONDO CANE NO. 2
(Motion Picture)
See Kai Winding (*Mondo Cane No. 2*)

MONDO ROCK
COME SAID THE BOY ...... (Columbia 38-05458) — .75 — 3.00 — 85
COME SAID THE BOY ...... (Columbia 38-05458) — 1.00 — 4.00 — 85
(Promotional issue, *Demonstration–Not For Sale* printed on sleeve)

MONEY, EDDIE
THINK I'M IN LOVE/Drivin' Me Crazy ...... (Columbia/Wolfgang 18-02964) — .75 — 3.00 — 82
THINK I'M IN LOVE/Drivin' Me Crazy ...... (Columbia/Wolfgang 18-02964) — 1.00 — 4.00 — 82
(Promotional issue, *Demonstration Not For Sale* printed on sleeve)
THE BIG CRASH/Backtrack ...... (Columbia/Wolfgang 38-04199) — .75 — 3.00 — 83
THE BIG CRASH ...... (Columbia/Wolfgang 38-04199) — 1.00 — 4.00 — 83
(Promotional issue, *Demonstration Only–Not For Sale* printed on sleeve)
CLUB MICHELLE/Back On The Road ...... (Columbia/Wolfgang 38-04376) — .75 — 3.00 — 84
CLUB MICHELLE ...... (Columbia/Wolfgang 38-06569) — 1.00 — 4.00 — 84
(Promotional issue, *Demonstration Only–Not For Sale* printed on sleeve)
I WANNA GO BACK ...... (Columbia 38-06569) — .75 — 3.00 — 86
I WANNA GO BACK ...... (Columbia 38-06569) — 1.00 — 4.00 — 86
(Promotional issue, *Demonstration Only–Not For Sale* printed on sleeve)
ENDLESS NIGHTS ...... (Columbia 38-07035) — .75 — 3.00 — 87
ENDLESS NIGHTS ...... (Columbia 38-07035) — 1.00 — 4.00 — 87
(Promotional issue, *Demonstration Only–Not For Sale* printed on sleeve)
WE SHOULD BE SLEEPING ...... (Columbia 38-07359) — .75 — 3.00 — 87
WE SHOULD BE SLEEPING ...... (Columbia 38-07359) — 1.00 — 4.00 — 87
(Promotional issue, *Demonstration Only–Not For Sale* printed on sleeve)
WALK ON WATER ...... (Columbia 38-08060) — .75 — 3.00 — 88

MONKEES, THE
LAST TRAIN TO CLARKSVILLE/Take A Giant Step ...... (Colgems 66-1001) — 5.00 — 20.00 — 66
(Brown and black duotone photo of band with no text at bottom)
LAST TRAIN TO CLARKSVILLE/Take A Giant Step ...... (Colgems 66-1001) — 3.75 — 15.00 — 66
(Color photo of band with *Write To Monkees...Watch Them On NBC-TV* on the bottom front and *Ask For "The Monkees" LP Album* on the bottom back)
I'M A BELIEVER/(I'm Not Your) Steppin' Stone ...... (Colgems 66-1002) — 3.75 — 15.00 — 66
PLEASANT VALLEY SUNDAY/Words ...... (Colgems 66-1007) — 3.75 — 15.00 — 67
DAYDREAM BELIEVER/Goin' Down ...... (Colgems 66-1012) — 3.75 — 15.00 — 67
D.W. WASHBURN/It's Nice To Be With You ...... (Colgems 66-1031) — 3.75 — 15.00 — 68
PORPOISE SONG/As We Go Along ...... (Colgems 66-1031) — 3.75 — 15.00 — 68
(From the motion picture *Head*)

TITLE	LABEL AND NUMBER	VG	NM	YR

TEAR DROP CITY / A Man Without A Dream .... (Colgems 66-5000) | 6.25 | 25.00 | 69
SOMEDAY MAN / Listen To The Band .... (Colgems 66-5004) | 5.00 | 20.00 | 69
LISTEN TO THE BAND / Someday Man .... (Colgems 66-5004) | 6.25 | 25.00 | 69
   (Note the a-side versus b-side variations for the above two sleeves, both have identical images)
GOOD CLEAN FUN / Mommy And Daddy .... (Colgems 66-5005) | 6.25 | 25.00 | 69
OH MY MY / I Love You Better .... (Colgems 66-5011) | 7.50 | 30.00 | 70
   (Only Mickey Dolenz and Davey Jones pictured)
THAT WAS THEN, THIS IS NOW / (Theme From) The Monkees .... (Arista 9505) | 1.50 | 6.00 | 86
   (First printing shown as by the Monkees)
THAT WAS THEN, THIS IS NOW / (Theme From) The Monkees .... (Arista 9505) | .75 | 3.00 | 86
   (Second printing which shows the a-side as by Micky Dolenz and Peter Tork)
DAYDREAM BELIEVER / Randy Scouse Git .... (Arista 9532) | .75 | 3.00 | 86
   (Front of sleeve is a reproduction of the 1967 Colgems release but only the a-side is listed on the front, the back is completely different)
HEART AND SOUL / MGBGT (Live) .... (Rhino 74408) | .75 | 3.00 | 87
HEART AND SOUL / MGBGT (Live) .... (Rhino 74408) | 1.00 | 4.00 | 87
   (Hard cover originally issued with pink vinyl)
EVERY STEP OF THE WAY / (I'll) Love You Forever (Live) .... (Rhino 74410) | 1.25 | 5.00 | 87
   Also see Mickey Dolenz, Dolenz, Jones & Tork, David Jones, Michael Nesmith

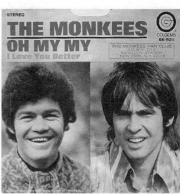

MONKEYS UNCLE, THE
(Motion Picture)
   See Annette (The Monkeys Uncle)

MONOCHROME SET
HE'S FRANK / Alphaville .... (I.R.S. 9002) | 2.50 | 10.00 | 79

MONROE, MARILYN
RIVER OF NO RETURN / I'm Gonna File My Claim .... (RCA Victor 47-5745) | 20.00 | 80.00 | 54
HEAT WAVE / After You Get What You Want .... (RCA Victor 47-6033) | 20.00 | 80.00 | 55
RIVER OF NO RETURN / One Silver Dollar .... (20th Fox 311) | 15.00 | 60.00 | 62

MONROE, VAUGHN
WRINGLE WRANGLE .... (RCA Victor Bluebird WBY-56) | 3.75 | 15.00 | 56
   (Children's series, from the motion picture Westward Ho The Wagons)
THE RIDE BACK .... (RCA Victor 47-6895) | 3.75 | 15.00 | 57

MONSTER MAGNET
LIZARD JOHNNY / Freak Shop USA .... (Circuit 7001) | 3.75 | 15.00 | 89
MURDER / Tractor .... (Primo Scree 2) | 2.50 | 10.00 | 90
CAGE AROUND THE SUN / Superjudge .... (A&M MM 1) | 1.25 | 5.00 | 93
   (Issued with blue vinyl)

MONTE, LOU
PEPINO THE ITALIAN MOUSE /
   What Did Washington Say (When He Crossed The Delaware) .... (Reprise 20,106) | 2.00 | 8.00 | 62
PEPINO'S FRIEND PASQUAL / I Like You, You Like Me, Eh Paisan .... (Reprise 20, 146) | 2.00 | 8.00 | 63
   (Sleeve credit reads Pepino and Pasqual Sing Along With Lou Monte)

MONTEZ, CHRIS
   See Chris & Kathy

MONTFORT, MATTHEW
EXTENDED PLAYS
MOUNTAIN SONG .... (Narada S33-17254) | 1.00 | 4.00 | 86
   (Promotional issue only titled Narada Sampler–Excellence In New Acoustic Music, issued with a small-hole 33-1/3 RPM record. Also includes one song each by Tingstad–Rumbel, Randy Mead, William Ellwood, Michael Jones, Spencer Brewer, David Lanz, and Gabriel Lee.)

MONTGOMERY, GENE
A PICTURE OF YOU .... (Columbia 4-42510) | 2.00 | 8.00 | 62

MONTGOMERY, MELBA
WON'T TAKE LONG .... (Musicor 1209) | 2.00 | 8.00 | 66

MONTY PYTHON
EXTENDED PLAYS
SPAM / ROYAL FESTIVAL HALL CONCERT / STAKE YOUR CLAIM /
   World Forum / Death Of Mary Queen Of Scots / Penguin On The T.V. .... (Charisma CMP-EP) | 2.50 | 10.00 | 72
   (Promotional issue only titled The Least Bizarre Of Monty Python's Comedy Album, issued with a small-hole 33-1/3 RPM record)

MOODY BLUES, THE
THE STORY IN YOUR EYES / Melancholy Man .... (Threshold 67006) | 2.00 | 8.00 | 83
THE VOICE .... (Threshold 602) | 1.00 | 4.00 | 81
SITTING AT THE WHEEL / Going Nowhere .... (Threshold 604) | 1.00 | 4.00 | 83
YOUR WILDEST DREAMS / Talkin' Talkin' .... (Polydor/Threshold 883 906-7) | .75 | 3.00 | 86
THE OTHER SIDE OF LIFE / The Spirit .... (Polydor/Threshold 885 201-7) | .75 | 3.00 | 86
   (Issued with blue vinyl. Sleeve reads Limited Edition Special Blue Vinyl Commemorating The Moody Blues 1986 U.S. Tour.)
THE OTHER SIDE OF LIFE / The Spirit .... (Polydor/Threshold 885 212-7) | .75 | 3.00 | 86
   (Issued with black vinyl)
I KNOW YOU'RE OUT THERE SOMEWHERE / Miracle .... (Polydor/Threshold 887 600-7) | .75 | 3.00 | 88
NO MORE LIES / River Of Endless Love .... (Polydor/Threshold 870 990-7) | .75 | 3.00 | 88
   Also see Justin Hayward, John Lodge

MOONDOG
EXTENDED PLAYS
SYMPHONIQUE #6 (Excerpt) .... (Columbia AS 1) | 1.25 | 5.00 | 70
   (Promotional issue only titled Dig This, issued with a small-hole 33-1/3 RPM record. Also includes excerpts by Pacific Gas and Electric, Nick Gravenites, Pete Seeger, Santana, Don Ellis, Raven, Firesign Theatre, and Tony Kosinec.)

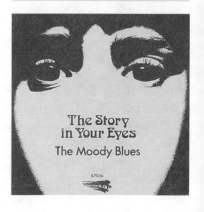

MOONEY, ART, AND HIS ORCHESTRA
NUTTIN' FOR CHRISTMAS .... (MGM 12092) | 5.00 | 20.00 | 55
   (Shown as by Art Mooney And His Orchestra With Barry Gordon)
REBEL WITHOUT A CAUSE / East Of Eden .... (MGM 12312) | 7.50 | 30.00 | 56
   (Sleeve states Tribute To James Dean)

MOONLIGHTING
(Television Series)
    See Al Jarreau (*Since I Fell For You, Moonlighting Theme*)

MOONSTRUCK
(Motion Picture)
    See Dean Martin (*That's Amore*)

MOORE, BOB
AUF WEIDERSEHN MARLENE .... (Monument 457)   2.00   8.00   62

MOORE, CLAYTON
    See the Lone Ranger

MOORE, DEMI
(Actress)
    See John Parr (*St. Elmo's Fire*)

MOORE, DONNY LEE
I'M BUGGIN' OUT, LITTLE BABY / Empty Arms, Empty Heart .... (Shelley 1000)   5.00   20.00   59
    (Promotional issue only)

MOORE, MELBA
THIS IS IT .... (Buddah 519)   1.25   5.00   76
MY SENSITIVE, PASSIONATE MAN .... (Buddah 572)   1.25   5.00   77
    (From the television movie *A Sensitive, Passionate Man*. Angie Dickinson and David Janssen pictured.)
KEEPIN' MY LOVER SATISFIED .... (Capitol B-5288)   .75   3.00   83
READ MY LIPS .... (Capitol B-5437)   .75   3.00   85
LOVE THE ONE I'M WITH .... (Capitol B-5577)   .75   3.00   86
FALLING .... (Capitol B-5651)   .75   3.00   86
I'M IN LOVE .... (Capitol B-44195)   .75   3.00   88
    (Shown as by Melba Moore and Kashif)

MOORE, THURSTON
CINDY (ROTTEN TANX) / Teenage Buddhist Daydream .... (Geffen DGCS7-19387)   1.00   4.00   95
    (Promotional issue only, hard cover)
    Also see Ciccone Youth, the Backbeat Band, Sonic Youth

MOORE, TIM
CHARMER / I'll Be Your Time .... (Asylum 45214)   1.25   5.00   75

MORALES, MICHAEL
WHO DO YOU GIVE YOUR LOVE TO? / Won't You Come Home .... (Wing 887 743-7)   .75   3.00   89

MORELAND, MARC
    See Johnette Napolitano

MORGAN, JANE
FASCINATION .... (Kapp 191-X)   3.00   12.00   57
    (Shown as by Jane Morgan and the Troubadors. From the motion picture *Love In The Afternoon*, Gary Cooper
    and Audrey Hepburn pictured.)
WITH OPEN ARMS / I Can't Begin To Tell You .... (Kapp 284)   2.50   10.00   59
HAPPY ANNIVERSARY .... (Kapp 305)   2.50   10.00   59
    (From the motion picture *Happy Anniversary*)
BLESS 'EM ALL .... (Colpix 713)   2.50   10.00   63
MAYBE .... (Epic 5-9819)   2.00   8.00   65
KISS AWAY .... (Epic # unknown)   2.00   8.00   65

MORGAN, LEE
    See Li'l Wally

MORGAN, MELI'SA
DO ME BABY .... (Capitol B-5523)   .75   3.00   85
LOVE CHANGES / Midnight Mood .... (Arista 9626)   .75   3.00   87
    (A-side shown as by Kashif + Meli'sa Morgan, b-side by Kashif)

MORGAN, RUSS
DOES YOUR HEART BEAT FOR ME? / Wabash Blues .... (Decca 1-709)   2.50   10.00   52
    (Decca "Curtain Call" series of reissues)

MORMON TABERNACLE CHOIR, THE
BATTLE HYMN OF THE REPUBLIC .... (Columbia 4-41459)   2.00   8.00   59

MORNING GLORY
NEED SOMEONE .... (Fontana 1613)   2.00   8.00   67

MORNING STARR
VIRGIN LOVER / If I Didn't Want To See You Anymore .... (Lion 45-1003)   1.25   5.00   70s

MORODER, GIORGIO
REACH OUT / .... (Columbia 38-04511)   .75   3.00   84
    (Shown as by Giorgio Moroder Featuring Paul Engemann)
GOODBYE BAD TIMES / Goodbye Bad Times (Instrumental) .... (A&M 2755)   .75   3.00   85
    (Shown as by Philip Oakey and Giorgio Moroder)
    Also see Blondie (b-side of *Call Me*), Bill Medley (b-side of *He Ain't Heavy, He's My Brother*)

MORPHINE
THURSDAY / Mary Won't You Call My Name? .... (Rykodisc RA7 1036)   .75   3.00   93
    (Folding sleeve issued with a small-hole 45 RPM record)

MORRICONE, ENNIO
THEME FROM THE MISSION / The Falls (Extended Remix) .... (Virgin 7-99484)   .75   3.00   86
    (From the motion picture *The Mission*, Jeremy Irons and Robert De Niro pictured on back)

MORRIS, GARY
MAKIN' UP FOR LOST TIME (THE DALLAS LOVERS' SONG) /
    A Few Good Men (Pam And Jenna's Song For Bobby) .... (Warner Bros. 28856-7)   1.00   4.00   85
    (A-side shown as by Crystal Gayle and Gary Morris, b-side by The Forester Sisters. From the television series
    Dallas.)

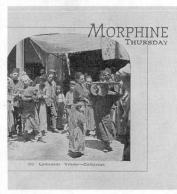

		VG	NM	YR
SIMPLY MEANT TO BE	(Warner Bros. 28388-7)	.75	3.00	87

(Shown as by Gary Morris and Jennifer Warnes. From the motion picture *Blind Date*. Kim Basinger and Bruce Willis pictured.)

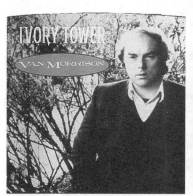

MORRIS, JENNY
BODY & SOUL / Animal Magnetism	(Atlantic 7-89115)	.75	3.00	87
YOU'RE GONNA GET HURT / Pass It Over	(Atlantic 7-89065)	.75	3.00	88

MORRISON, BOB
SANTA MOUSE / It Is Christmas	(Columbia 4-43786)	2.50	10.00	66

MORRISON, DOROTHY
ALL GOD'S CHILDREN GOT SOUL	(Elektra 45671)	2.00	8.00	69

MORRISON, JUNIE
STICK IT IN	(Island 7-99663)	.75	3.00	84

MORRISON, VAN
IVORY TOWER / New Kind Of Man	(Mercury 884 841-7)	1.00	4.00	86

Also see Them

MORRISSEY
SUEDEHEAD / I Know Very Well How I Got My Name	(Sire/Reprise 27907-7)	1.25	5.00	88
EVERYDAY IS LIKE SUNDAY / Disappointed	(Sire/Reprise 27837-7)	1.25	5.00	88

Also see the Smiths

MORSE, ELLA MAE
COW COW BOOGIE / Strip Polka	(Capitol 103)	3.00	12.00	

(B-side shown as by Johnny Mercer, 30th anniversary gatefold sleeve)

MORTIMER
DEDICATED MUSIC MAN	(Phillips 40254)	1.50	6.00	68

MOSBY, JOHNNY & JONIE
MY HAPPINESS	(Capitol 2865)	1.25	5.00	70

MOSS, GENE
I WANT TO BITE YOUR HAND / Ghoul Days	(RCA Victor 47-8438)	5.00	20.00	64

MOST, DONNY
(Actor best known as Ralph Malph on the television series *Happy Days*)
ALL ROADS LEAD BACK TO YOU / Better To Forget Him	(United Artists 871)	2.00	8.00	77
I ONLY WANT WHAT'S MINE	(Casablanca NB 2248)	2.00	8.00	80

(From the motion picture *Leo And Loree*)

MOSTEL, ZERO
(Actor / Entertainer)
IF I WERE A RICH MAN / Sunrise, Sunset	(RCA 447-0789)	2.00	8.00	71

(From the Broadway musical *Fiddler On The Roof*)

MOTELLO, ELTON
POP ART / 20th Century Fox	(Passport 7920)	1.00	4.00	80

MOTELS, THE
ONLY THE LONELY	(Capitol B-5114)	1.00	4.00	82
TAKE THE L	(Capitol B-5149)	.75	3.00	82
FOREVER MINE / So L.A.	(Capitol B-5182)	.75	3.00	82
SUDDENLY LAST SUMMER / Some Things Never Change	(Capitol B-5271)	.75	3.00	83
REMEMBER THE NIGHTS	(Capitol B-5246)	.75	3.00	83
SHAME	(Capitol B-5497)	.75	3.00	85
SHOCK	(Capitol B-5529)	.75	3.00	85

Also see Martha Davis

MOTHERS OF INVENTION
See Jimmy Carl Black, Captain Beefheart and the Magic Band (Captain Beefheart, Roy Estrada a.k.a. Orejon), George Duke, Flo & Eddie (Howard Kaylan and Mark Volman), Geronimo Black (Jimmy Carl Black, Bunk Gardner), Journey (Aynsley Dunbar), Turtles (Howard Kaylan and Mark Volman), Frank Zappa.

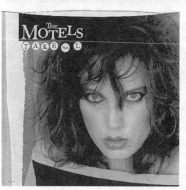

MOTHER TRUCKER
TONIGHT	(Paramount 0287)	1.00	4.00	74

MÖTLEY CRÜE
STICK TO YOUR GUNS / Toast Of The Town	(Leathür MC-001)	12.50	50.00	81
(Promotional issue given away at concerts)
LOOKS THAT KILL / Piece Of Your Action	(Elektra 7-69756)	1.00	4.00	83
TOO YOUNG TO FALL IN LOVE (REMIX) /				
Take Me To The Top (LP Version)	(Elektra 7-69732)	1.00	4.00	84
SMOKIN' IN THE BOYS ROOM / Use It Or Lose It	(Elektra 7-69625)	1.00	4.00	85
GIRLS GIRLS GIRLS / Sumthin' For Nuthin'	(Elektra 7-69465)	.75	3.00	87
WILD SIDE / Five Years Dead	(Elektra 7-69449)	.75	3.00	87
DR. FEELGOOD / Sticky Sweet	(Elektra 7-69271)	.75	3.00	89

Also see Hear 'N Aid

MOTOR BAND, THE
See Ray Parker, Jr. (*One Sunny Day/Dueling Bikes From Quicksilver*)

MOTORS, THE
LOVE AND LONELINESS / Time For Makeup	(Virgin 67007)	1.00	4.00	80
(Hard cover)

MOTT THE HOOPLE
ALL THE YOUNG DUDES / One Of The Boys	(Columbia 4-45673)	3.00	12.00	72
Also see Bad Company (Mick Ralphs)

MOURNING REIGN
SATISFACTION GUARANTEED / Our Fate	(Link 1)	125.00	500.00	66

MOUSE AND THE TRAPS
MAID OF SUGAR–MAID OF SPICE / I Am The One	(Fraternity 966)	25.00	100.00	66
SOMETIMES YOU JUST CAN'T WIN / Cryin' Inside	(Fraternity 1005)	15.00	60.00	68

TITLE	LABEL AND NUMBER	VG	NM	YR

MOUSKOURI, NANA
SCARBOROUGH FAIR CANTICLE .... (Fontana 1641) — 2.00 — 8.00 — 69
NICKELS AND DIMES/Roses Love Sunshine .... (Cachet 4-4500) — 1.25 — 5.00 — 79

MOUTH & MacNEAL
HELLO–A/Sing Along .... (Philips 40721) — 1.25 — 5.00 — 72

MOVIES, THE
AHEAD OF THE GAME/Satellite Touchdown .... (Arista 0235) — 1.25 — 5.00 — 77
(A-side from the motion picture *Fun With Dick And Jane*. George Segal and Jane Fonda pictured on front, the group, the Movies, pictured on back.)

MOVING PICTURES
WHAT ABOUT ME/Joni And The Romeo .... (Network 7-69952) — 1.00 — 4.00 — 82
Also see 1927 (Garry Frost)

MOYET, ALISON
INVISIBLE/Hitch Hike .... (Columbia 38-04781) — .75 — 3.00 — 85
INVISIBLE .... (Columbia 38-04781) — 1.00 — 4.00 — 85
(Promotional issue, *Demonstration–Not For Sale* printed on sleeve)
LOVE RESURRECTION/Baby I Do .... (Columbia 38-05411) — .75 — 3.00 — 85
LOVE RESURRECTION .... (Columbia 38-05411) — 1.00 — 4.00 — 85
(Promotional issue, *Demonstration: Not For Sale* printed on sleeve)
FOR YOU ONLY/Money Mile .... (Columbia 38-05614) — .75 — 3.00 — 85
FOR YOU ONLY .... (Columbia 38-05614) — 1.00 — 4.00 — 85
(Promotional issue, *Demonstration–Not For Sale* printed on sleeve)
IS THIS LOVE?/Blow Wind Blow .... (Columbia 38 07019) — .75 — 3.00 — 87
Also see Yazoo

MUDHONEY
HATE THE POLICE/Symptom Of The Universe .... (*Make 'Em Bleed And Suffer* no #) — 6.25 — 25.00 — 88
TOUCH ME I'M SICK/Sweet Young Thing Ain't Sweet No More .... (Sub Pop 18) — 2.00 — 8.00 — 88
(The first 800 issued with brown vinyl, the remainder on black. In error some 45s were pressed on red, yellow, blue, and purple vinyl. These 4 colors are rare and have reported values of $200 near mint.)
TOUCH ME I'M SICK/Sweet Young Thing Ain't Sweet No More .... (Sub Pop 18) — 1.00 — 4.00 — 88
(Second printing issued with green vinyl)
HALLOWEEN/Touch Me I'm Sick .... (Sub Pop 26) — 3.75 — 15.00 — 88
(Split single, *Touch Me I'm Sick* shown as by Sonic Youth. Limited to 3,000 copies with 500 on clear vinyl and 2,500 on black.)
YOU GOT IT (KEEP IT OUTTA MY FACE)/Burn Clean .... (Sub Pop 33) — 2.00 — 8.00 — 89
YOU GOT IT (KEEP IT OUTTA MY FACE)/Burn Clean .... (Sub Pop 33) — 3.75 — 15.00 — 89
(Limited edition of 3,000 poster sleeves)
THIS GIFT/Baby Help Me Forget .... (Sub Pop 44a) — 2.50 — 10.00 — 89
YOU'RE GONE/Thorn/You Make Me Die .... (Sub Pop 63) — 2.00 — 8.00 — 90
(The first 3,000 copies issued with pink vinyl)
LET IT SLIDE/Ounce Of Deception/Checkout Time .... (Sub Pop 95) — 1.50 — 6.00 — 91
(Issued with either yellow-green or black vinyl)
SHE'S JUST FIFTEEN/Jagged Time Lapse .... (Amphetamine Reptile SCALE 36) — 1.50 — 6.00 — 91
YOU STUPID ASSHOLE/Knife Manual .... (Empty # unknown) — 1.25 — 5.00
(Split single, *Knife Manual* shown as by Gas Huffer)
TONIGHT I'M GONNA GO DOWNTOWN/Blinding Sun .... (Sub Pop 248) — 1.25 — 5.00 — 94
(Split single, *Blinding Sun* shown as by Jimmie Dale Gilmore)
PUMP IT UP/Stomp .... (Fox 07822-10012-7) — .75 — 3.00 — 94
(B-side shown as by George Clinton/Parliament Funkadelic. Issued with red vinyl. From the motion picture *PCU*.)
Also see Mark Arm, Green River (Mark Arm, Steve Turner)

MUFFS, THE
NEW LOVE/I Don't Like You/You Lied To Me .... (Sympathy For The Record Industry 121) — 2.00 — 8.00 — 91
(Folding hard cover issued with small-hole 45 RPM record)
I NEED YOU/Beat Your Heart Out .... (Sub Pop 157) — 2.00 — 8.00 — 92
(Issued with pink vinyl)

MULL, MARTIN
(Comic Actor)
IN THE EYES OF MY DOG–HUMAN VERSION/
In The Eyes Of My Dog–Dog Version .... (Capricorn 0024) — 1.50 — 6.00 — 73

MUMPS
CROCODILE TEARS/I Like To Be Clean .... (Bomp BEJ-1) — 2.00 — 8.00 — 77

MUMY, BILLY
(Actor who appeared as Will Robinson in the television series *Lost In Space* from 1965-1966 and more recently in the series *Babylon 5*. Half of comedy duo Barnes & Barnes.)
See Barnes & Barnes

MUNDY, NICK
TRADE HIM IN .... (Warner Bros. 27933-7) — .75 — 3.00 — 87

MUPPET BABIES, THE
AMADOGUS .... (Columbia 38-07404) — .75 — 3.00 — 87

MUPPETS, THE
See John Denver (*Have Yourself A Merry Little Christmas*)

MURAD'S, JERRY, HARMONICATS
CHERRY PINK AND APPLE BLOSSOM WHITE/Lonely Love .... (Columbia 4-41816) — 2.50 — 10.00 — 60
THEME FROM HIPPIDROME/ .... (Columbia 4-41967) — 2.50 — 10.00 — 60

MURPHEY, MICHAEL MARTIN
GERONIMO'S CADILLAC/Boy From The Country .... (A&M 1368) — 1.50 — 6.00 — 72
(Shown as by Michael Murphey)
HOLY ROLLER/Rye By-The-Sea .... (Epic 5-11130) — 1.25 — 5.00 — 74
(Shown as by Michael Murphey)
DON'T COUNT THE RAINY DAYS/The Heart Never Lies .... (Liberty B-1505) — 1.00 — 4.00 — 83
WILL IT BE LOVE BY MORNING/Goodbye Money Mountain .... (Liberty B-1514) — 1.00 — 4.00 — 84

TITLE	LABEL AND NUMBER	VG	NM	YR
DISENCHANTED/Sacred Heart	(Liberty B-1517)	1.00	4.00	84
WHAT SHE WANTS/Still Taking Chances	(EMI America B-8243)	1.00	4.00	84
TALKIN' TO THE WRONG MAN/What Am I Doin' Hangin' 'Round?	(Warner Bros. 27947-7)	.75	3.00	88

(A-side shown as a Duet With Ryan Murphey)

NEVER GIVIN' UP ON LOVE	(Warner Bros. 22970-7)	.75	3.00	89

(From the motion picture *Pink Cadillac*)
Also see the Lewis & Clarke Expedition

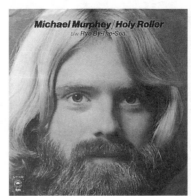

MURPHEY, RYAN
See Michael Martin Murphey (*Talkin' To The Wrong Man*)

MURPHY, EDDIE
(Comedian/Actor)

ENOUGH IS ENOUGH/"Buckwheat"/Talking Cars	(Columbia 38-05609)	1.00	4.00	82
ENOUGH IS ENOUGH/"Buckwheat"/Talking Cars	(Columbia 38-05609)	1.25	5.00	82

(Promotional issue, *Demonstration–Not For Sale* printed on sleeve)

PARTY ALL THE TIME/Party All The Time (Instrumental)	(Columbia 38-05609)	.75	3.00	85
PARTY ALL THE TIME/Party All The Time (Instrumental)	(Columbia 38-05609)	1.00	4.00	85

(Promotional issue, *Demonstration–Not For Sale* printed on sleeve)

HOW COULD IT BE/C-O-N Confused	(Columbia 38-05772)	.75	3.00	86
HOW COULD IT BE	(Columbia 38-05772)	1.00	4.00	86

(Promotional issue, *Demonstration–Not For Sale* printed on sleeve)
Also see Danny Elfman (*Gratitude*), Glenn Frey (*The Heat Is On*), the Jets (*Cross My Broken Heart*), Patti LaBelle (*New Attitude, Stir It Up*), Pointer Sisters (*Be There*), Bob Seger (*Shakedown*) , Charlie Sexton (*In Deep*)

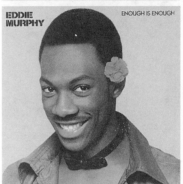

MURPHY, PETER

INDIGO EYES	(Beggars Banquet 8707-7)	1.25	5.00	88

(Promotional issue only)
Also see Bauhaus

MURPHY, WALTER

THEMES FROM E.T.	(MCA 52099)	1.00	4.00	82

MURRAY, ANNE

I JUST FALL IN LOVE AGAIN	(Capitol 4675)	1.00	4.00	79
COULD I HAVE THIS DANCE	(Capitol 4920)	1.00	4.00	80
BLESSED ARE THE BELIEVERS	(Capitol B-4987)	1.00	4.00	81
WE DON'T HAVE TO HOLD OUT	(Capitol B-5013)	1.00	4.00	81
HEY! BABY!	(Capitol B-5145)	1.00	4.00	82
SOMEBODY'S ALWAYS SAYING GOODBYE	(Capitol B-5183)	1.00	4.00	82
A LITTLE GOOD NEWS	(Capitol B-5264)	1.00	4.00	83
JUST ANOTHER WOMAN IN LOVE	(Capitol B-5344)	1.00	4.00	84
NOBODY LOVES ME LIKE YOU DO	(Capitol B-5401)	1.00	4.00	84

(Shown as by Anne Murray with Dave Loggins)

TIME DON'T RUN OUT ON ME	(Capitol B-5436)	1.00	4.00	84
I DON'T THINK I'M READY FOR YOU	(Capitol B-5472)	1.00	4.00	84

(From the motion picture *Stick*)

GO TELL IT ON THE MOUNTAIN/O Holy Night	(Capitol B-5536)	1.00	4.00	85
NOW AND FOREVER (YOU AND ME)	(Capitol B-5547)	.75	3.00	86
WHO'S LEAVING WHO	(Capitol B-5576)	.75	3.00	86
MY LIFE'S A DANCE	(Capitol B-5610)	.75	3.00	86
ARE YOU STILL IN LOVE WITH ME	(Capitol B-44005)	.75	3.00	87

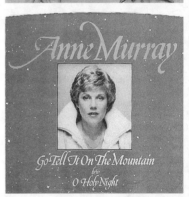

MURRAY, BILL
(Comedic Actor)
See Scrooged

MURRAY THE 'K'
(Disc Jockey)

AS IT HAPPENED	(No label or # indicated)	25.00	100.00	65

(Shown as by The Beatles & Murray the 'K'. Issued with 33-1/3 rpm record.)

AS IT HAPPENED	(IBC F4KM-0082/3)	2.50	10.00	76

(Shown as by The Beatles & Murray the 'K')

MUSCLE BEACH PARTY
(Motion Picture)
See Annette (*Muscle Beach Party*)

MUSICAL YOUTH

PASS THE DUTCHIE/Give Love A Chance	(MCA 52149)	.75	3.00	82
NEVER GONNA GIVE YOU UP/Jim'll Fix It	(MCA 52203)	.75	3.00	83
HEARTBREAKER/Rockers	(MCA 52216)	.75	3.00	83
SHE'S TROUBLE/Yard Style	(MCA 52312)	.75	3.00	84

MUSIC MACHINE, THE

HEY JOE/Wrong	(Original Sound 82)	6.25	25.00	67

(Half sleeve)

GENERIC MUSIC MACHINE SLEEVE	(Original Sound no #)	2.00	8.00	67

(Used for miscellaneous Music Machine singles, no titles listed.)

BOTTOM OF THE SOUL/Astrologically Incompatible	(Warner Bros. 7093)	3.75	15.00	68

MX-80 SOUND

SOMEDAY YOU'LL BE KING/White Night	(Ralph MX-8001)	1.25	5.00	80
O TYPE	(Ralph MX-8055)	1.25	5.00	80

MY DEMON LOVER
(Motion Picture)
See Intimate Strangers (*Let Go*)

MYLEKA

CONFESS	(MCA 53357)	.75	3.00	88

MY LIFE WITH THE THRILL KILL KULT

FINAL BLINDNESS	(Interscope/Atlantic 7-98391)	1.00	4.00	93

(Issued with a small-hole 45 RPM record)

TITLE	LABEL AND NUMBER	VG	NM	YR

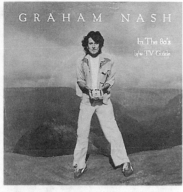

MYLON
extended plays
HOLY SMOKE DOO DAH BAND .... (Columbia AS 53) — 1.50 — 6.00 — 71
(Part of a series of promotional issues titled *Playback* issued with a small-hole 33-1/3 RPM record. Price includes generic *Playback* sleeve with folding insert. Also includes one song each by Jeff Beck, Lesley Duncan, Firesign Theatre, Grootna, the Mahavishnu Orchestra With John McLaughlin.)

MYRA BRECKINRIDGE
(Motion Picture)
See Mae West (*Hard To Handle*)

MYRICK, GARY, AND THE FIGURES
LIVING IN A MOVIE/My Girl (It's Simple) .... (Epic AE7 1303) — 1.25 — 5.00 — 81
(Promotional issue only with biographical insert)

MY STEPMOTHER IS AN ALIEN
(Motion Picture)
See Animotion (*Room To Move*)

N

N, THE
See Daryl Hall and John Oates (b-side of *Love Train*)

NAKED EYES
PROMISES, PROMISES/A Very Hard Act To Follow .... (EMI America B-8170) — .75 — 3.00 — 83
(WHAT) IN THE NAME OF LOVE/Two Heads Together .... (EMI America B-8219) — .75 — 3.00 — 84

NAPOLITANO, JOHNETTE, WITH MARC MORELAND
HURTING EACH OTHER .... (A&M 31458 0712 7) — .50 — 2.00 — 94
(Side 8 of a 7 record box set titled *If I Were A Carpenter*. Each sleeve has a different face shot of Karen Carpenter on the front, Richard Carpenter on the back. No artist name or song titles indicated on sleeve. Complete set valued at $30.00 near mint.)
Also see Concrete Blonde (Johnette Napolitano)

NARADA
(Narada Michael Walden)
DIVINE EMOTIONS .... (Reprise 27967-7) — .75 — 3.00 — 88

NARADA SAMPLER
EXCELLENCE IN NEW ACOUSTIC MUSIC .... (Narada S33-17254) — 1.00 — 4.00 — 86
(Promotional issue only with a small-hole 33-1/3 RPM record. Includes 1 song each by Eric Tingstad/Nancy Rumbel, Randy Mead, William Ellwood, Michael Jones, Matthew Montfort, Spencer Brewer, David Lanz, and Gabriel Lee)

NARDINI, NORM, & THE TIGERS
BURN'IN UP/Ready Freddy/Physco .... (Transport 9001) — 1.25 — 5.00 — 79
(Paper sleeve issued with a small-hole 33-1/3 RPM record. Note misplacement of apostrophe in a-side title.)
BURNIN' UP/Ready Freddy .... (Transport 7002) — 1.00 — 4.00 — 80
(Hard cover folding sleeve)
IF YOU DON'T WANT ME/Reptile Rock .... (CBS Associated ZS4-04780) — .75 — 3.00 — 85
IF YOU DON'T WANT ME .... (CBS Associated ZS4-04780) — 1.00 — 4.00 — 85
(Promotional issue, *Demonstration Only–Not For Sale* printed on sleeve)

NASH, GRAHAM
IN THE 80'S/TV Guide .... (Capitol 4812) — 1.00 — 4.00 — 79
INNOCENT EYES/I Got A Rock .... (Atlantic 7-89434) — .75 — 3.00 — 86

NASH, JOHNNY
AS TIME GOES BY/The Voice Of Love .... (ABC-Paramount 9996) — 5.00 — 20.00 — 59
I'VE GOT A LOT TO OFFER, DARLING/Helpless .... (Groove 0018) — 3.75 — 15.00 — 63
EXTENDED PLAYS
MY MERRY-GO-ROUND .... (Columbia AS 53) — 1.50 — 6.00 — 73
(Promotional issue only titled *New Comers As Featured In New Ingenue In August*, issued with a small-hole 33-1/3 RPM record. Also includes one song each by Looking Glass, Andy Pratt, and Jimmie Spheeris.)

NASH, NANCY
See Loverboy (*When It's Over*)

NATIONAL LAMPOON
HAVE A KUNG FU CHRISTMAS! .... (Epic AS 193) — 2.00 — 8.00 — 75
(Promotional issue only)
MR. ROBERTS .... (Label 21 201) — 2.50 — 10.00 — 77
WHAT WERE YOU EXPECTING–ROCK 'N' ROLL?/Perrier Junkie ...... (Label 21 202) — 1.50 — 6.00 — 80
(A-side shown as by Michael Simmons, b-side shown as by Alice Playten)

NATURALS, THE
MARTY .... (MGM K11970) — 2.50 — 10.00 — 55

NAUGHTON, DAVID
(Actor)
MAKIN' IT .... (RSO 916) — 1.00 — 4.00 — 79
(From the motion picture *Meatballs*)

NAUGHTY SWEETIES, THE
ALICE/A Fool For The City .... (Elektra/Dauntless 46554) — 1.25 — 5.00 — 79

NAZARETH
LOVE HURTS/Hair Of The Dog .... (A&M 1671) — 1.25 — 5.00 — 75

NAZZ
OPEN MY EYES/Hello It's Me .... (SGC 001) — 5.00 — 20.00 — 68
NOT WRONG LONG/Under The Ice .... (SGC 006) — 5.00 — 20.00 — 69
Also see Todd Rundgren, Utopia (Todd Rundgren)

NECESSARIES, THE
YOU CAN BORROW MY CAR/Runaway Child .... (I.R.S. 9003) — 1.00 — 4.00 — 79

NEELEY, TED

YOU PUT SOMETHING BETTER INSIDE OF ME/Rainbow .... (RCA APBO-0103)	1.50	6.00	73

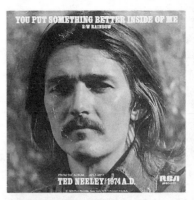

NELSON, JUDD

(Actor)

   See John Parr *(St. Elmo's Fire)*, Pops and 'Timer *(Tell Me Something Slick)*, Wang Chung *(Fire In The Twilight)*

NELSON, PHYLLIS

MOVE CLOSER/ .... (Carrere/CBS ZS4 05393)	.75	3.00	84
MOVE CLOSER .... (Carrere/CBS ZS4 05393)	1.00	4.00	84
(Promotional issue, *Demonstration–Not For Sale* printed on sleeve)			
I LIKE YOU/ .... (Carrere/CBS ZS4 05583)	.75	3.00	85
I LIKE YOU .... (Carrere/CBS ZS4 05583)	1.00	4.00	85
(Promotional issue, *Demonstration–Not For Sale* printed on sleeve)			

NELSON, RICK

BE-BOP BABY/Have I Told You Lately That I Love You .... (Imperial 5463)	10.00	40.00	57
STOOD UP/Waitin' In School .... (Imperial 5483)	7.50	30.00	57
BELIEVE WHAT YOU SAY/My Bucket's Got A Hole In It .... (Imperial 5503)	7.50	30.00	58
LONESOME TOWN/I Got A Feeling .... (Imperial 5545)	6.25	25.00	58
NEVER BE ANYONE ELSE BUT YOU/It's Late .... (Imperial 5565)	6.25	25.00	59
JUST A LITTLE TOO MUCH/Sweeter Than You .... (Imperial 5595)	6.25	25.00	59
I WANNA BE LOVED/Mighty Good .... (Imperial 5614)	6.25	25.00	59
YOUNG EMOTIONS/Right By My Side .... (Imperial 5663)	5.00	20.00	60
YES SIR, THAT'S MY BABY/I'm Not Afraid .... (Imperial 5685)	5.00	20.00	60
YOU ARE THE ONLY ONE/Milk Cow Blues .... (Imperial 5707)	5.00	20.00	60
TRAVELIN' MAN/Hello Mary Lou .... (Imperial 5741)	5.00	20.00	61
A WONDER LIKE YOU/Everlovin' .... (Imperial 5770)	5.00	20.00	61
YOUNG WORLD/Summertime .... (Imperial 5805)	5.00	20.00	62
TEEN AGE IDOL/I've Got My Eyes On You .... (Imperial 5864)	5.00	20.00	62
IT'S UP TO YOU/I Need You .... (Imperial 5901)	5.00	20.00	62
OLD ENOUGH TO LOVE/If You Can't Rock Me .... (Imperial 5935)	5.00	20.00	63
YOU DON'T LOVE ME ANYMORE/I Got A Woman .... (Decca 31475)	3.75	15.00	63
STRING ALONG/Gypsy Woman .... (Decca 31495)	3.75	15.00	63
FOOLS RUSH IN/Down Home .... (Decca 31533)	3.75	15.00	63
TODAY'S TEARDROPS/Thank You Darling .... (Imperial 66004)	5.00	20.00	63
FOR YOU/That's All She Wrote .... (Decca 31574)	3.75	15.00	63
THE VERY THOUGHT OF YOU/I Wonder .... (Decca 31612)	3.75	15.00	64
THERE'S NOTHING I CAN SAY/Lonely Corner .... (Decca 31656)	3.75	15.00	64
A HAPPY GUY/Don't Breathe A Word .... (Decca 31703)	3.75	15.00	64
MEAN OLD WORLD/When The Chips Are Down .... (Decca 31756)	3.75	15.00	65
YESTERDAY'S LOVE/Come Out Dancin' .... (Decca 31800)	3.75	15.00	65
LOVE AND KISSES/Say You Love Me .... (Decca 31845)	3.75	15.00	65
LOUISIANA MAN/You Just Can't Quit .... (Decca 31956)	3.75	15.00	66
THINGS YOU GAVE ME/Alone .... (Decca 32026)	3.75	15.00	66
I'M CALLED LONELY/Take A City Bride .... (Decca 32120)	3.75	15.00	67
EASY TO BE FREE/Come On In .... (Decca 32635)	2.50	10.00	70
YOU KNOW WHAT I MEAN/Don't Leave Me This Way .... (MCA/Silver Eagle 52781)	1.25	5.00	86
DREAM LOVER/Rave On .... (Epic 34-06066)	1.25	5.00	86
DREAM LOVER .... (Epic 34-06066)	1.50	6.00	86
(Promotional issue, *Demonstration Only–Not For Sale* printed on sleeve)			
Be-Bop Baby through *Travelin' Man* and *You Know What I Mean* shown as by Ricky Nelson			

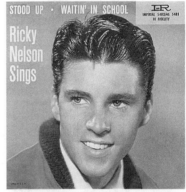

NELSON, TYKA

MARK ANTHONY'S TUNE .... (Chrysalis VS4-43238)	.75	3.00	88

NELSON, WILLIE

GOOD TIMES .... (RCA PB-12254)	1.00	4.00	81
TAKE IT TO THE LIMIT .... (Columbia 38-04131)	.75	3.00	83
(Shown as by Willie Nelson With Waylon Jennings)			
TAKE IT TO THE LIMIT .... (Columbia 38-04131)	1.00	4.00	83
(Promotional issue, *Demonstration Only–Not For Sale* printed on sleeve. Shown as by Willie Nelson With Waylon Jennings.)			
TO ALL THE GIRLS I'VE LOVED BEFORE .... (Columbia 38-04217)	1.00	4.00	84
(Shown as by Julio Iglesias & Willie Nelson in upper and lower case letters, both pictured)			
TO ALL THE GIRLS I'VE LOVED BEFORE .... (Columbia 38-04217)	.75	3.00	84
(Shown as by Julio Iglesias & Willie Nelson in all upper case letters, both pictured)			
TO ALL THE GIRLS I'VE LOVED BEFORE .... (Columbia 38-04217)	1.00	4.00	84
(Promotional issue, *Demonstration Only–Not For Sale* printed on sleeve. Shown as by Julio Iglesias & Willie Nelson.)			
AS TIME GOES BY .... (Columbia 38-04495)	3.75	15.00	84
(Shown as by Willie Nelson & Julio Iglesias. This single was reportedly withdrawn soon after its release.)			
CITY OF NEW ORLEANS .... (Columbia 38-04568)	1.00	4.00	84
CITY OF NEW ORLEANS .... (Columbia 38-04568)	1.25	5.00	84
(Promotional issue, *Demonstration–Not For Sale* printed on sleeve)			
HIGHWAYMAN .... (Columbia 38-04881)	.75	3.00	85
(Shown as by Willie Nelson, Kris Kristofferson, Johnny Cash, and Waylon Jennings)			
Also see Chet Atkins *(Chet's Tune)*, U.S.A. For Africa, Voices Of America			

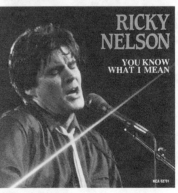

NEON BOYS

EXTENDED PLAYS

THAT'S ALL I KNOW (RIGHT NOW)/LOVE COMES IN SPURTS/Don't Die/Time ..... (Shake 101)	3.00	12.00	80
Also see Richard Hell & The Voidoids (Richard Hell)			

NERO, PETER

THEME FROM SUMMER AND SMOKE .... (RCA Victor 74-7956)	1.25	5.00	62
(From the motion picture *Summer And Smoke*)			
SPACE FLIGHT .... (RCA Victor 74-8161)	1.25	5.00	63
LADY SINGS THE BLUES .... (Columbia 4-45756)	1.25	5.00	73

NERVES, THE

HANGING ON THE TELEPHONE .... (Nerves 4501)	5.00	20.00	76
Also see the Beat (Paul Collins), MnMs (Paul Collins), the Plimsouls (Peter Case)			

TITLE	LABEL AND NUMBER	VG	NM	YR

NERVOUS EATERS
LORETTA/Rock With Me .... (Rat 5282)		2.50	10.00	79
LORETTA/Rock With Me .... (Rat 5282)		7.50	30.00	79
(Cardboard sleeve)				

NESMITH, MICHAEL
NEVADA FIGHTER .... (RCA Victor 74-0453)		5.00	20.00	71
(Shown as by Michael Nesmith & The First National Band)				
RIO/Casablanca Moonlight .... (Pacific Arts 104)		3.00	12.00	78
Also see the Monkees				

NETTO, LOZ
FADE AWAY/Show Me .... (21 Records 104)		.75	3.00	83
WE TOUCH/Do What You Want .... (Atlantic 7-89399)		.75	3.00	86

NEVER ENDING STORY, THE
(Motion Picture)
See Limahl (*The Never Ending Story*)

NEVER SAY NEVER AGAIN
(Motion Picture)
See Lani Hall (*Never Say Never Again*)

NEVIL, ROBBIE
C'EST LA VIE/Time Waits For No One .... (Manhattan B 50047)		.75	3.00	86
DOMINOES/Neighbor's .... (Manhattan B 50053)		.75	3.00	86
WOT'S IT TO YA/Wot's It To Ya (To Ya Remix) .... (Manhattan B-50075)		.75	3.00	87
BACK ON HOLIDAY/Too Soon .... (EMI Manhattan B-50152)		.75	3.00	88

NEVILLE, AARON
See Bonnie Raitt (*Baby Mine*), Lou Reed (b-side of *September Song*)

NEVILLE, IVAN
NOT JUST ANOTHER GIRL/Up To You .... (Polydor 887 814-7)		.75	3.00	88
FALLING OUT OF LOVE/Sun .... (Polydor 871 484-7)		.75	3.00	89

NEWBURY, MICKEY
ARE MY THOUGHTS WITH YOU/Weeping Annaleah .... (RCA Victor 74-9570)		2.00	8.00	68

NEW CHRISTY MINSTRELS, THE
THIS LAND IS YOUR LAND/Don't Cry Suzanne .... (Columbia 4-42592)		2.50	10.00	62
Also see the Back Porch Majority (Randy Sparks), the Byrds (Gene Clark), Gene Clark, Barry McGuire, Randy Sparks. Other members after 1962 included Kenny Rogers and the First Edition, John Denver, some members of the Association, Kim Carnes, and actress Karen Black.				

NEWCITY ROCKERS
REV IT UP/Break A Heart .... (Critique/Atco 7-99437)		.75	3.00	87

NEW COLONY SIX, THE
LOVE YOU SO MUCH/Let Me Love You .... (Sentar 1205)		12.50	50.00	66
TREAT HER GROOVY/Rap-A-Tap .... (Mercury 72737)		3.75	15.00	67
(Back of sleeve is unprinted)				
TREAT HER GROOVY/Rap-A-Tap .... (Mercury 72737)		2.00	8.00	67
(Fan club coupon on back)				
CAN'T YOU SEE ME CRY/Summertime's Another Name For Love .... (Mercury 72817)		2.00	8.00	68
EXTENDED PLAYS				
LAST NITE/ACCEPT MY RING/Cadillac/Rap-A-Tap .... (Sundazed 107)		.50	2.00	93
(Hard cover titled *Four By Six*, issued with a small-hole 45 RPM red vinyl record)				

NEW EDITION
COOL IT NOW/Cool It Now (Sing Along Version) .... (MCA 52455)		.75	3.00	84
MR. TELEPHONE MAN/Mr. Telephone Man (Instrumental) .... (MCA 52484)		.75	3.00	84
LOST IN LOVE/Gold Mine .... (MCA 52553)		.75	3.00	85
COUNT ME OUT .... (MCA 52703)		.75	3.00	85
IT'S CHRISTMAS (ALL OVER THE WORLD) .... (MCA 52745)		1.00	4.00	85
(Issued with red vinyl)				
A LITTLE BIT OF LOVE (IS ALL IT TAKES) .... (MCA 52768)		.75	3.00	86
WITH YOU ALL THE WAY .... (MCA 52829)		.75	3.00	86
ONCE IN A LIFETIME GROOVE .... (MCA 52959)		.75	3.00	86
(From the motion picture *Running Scared*, New Edition, Billy Crystal, and Gregory Hines pictured)				
TEARS ON MY PILLOW .... (MCA 53019)		.75	3.00	87
DUKE OF EARL .... (MCA 53079)		.75	3.00	87
IF IT ISN'T LOVE .... (MCA 53264)		.75	3.00	88
YOU'RE NOT MY KIND OF GIRL .... (MCA 53405)		.75	3.00	88
CAN YOU STAND THE RAIN .... (MCA 53464)		.75	3.00	88
CRUCIAL .... (MCA 53500)		.75	3.00	88
Also see Bobby Brown, Johnny Gill				

NEW ENGLAND
DDT/Elevator .... (Elektra 47155)		1.00	4.00	81

NEW KIDS ON THE BLOCK
PLEASE DON'T GO GIRL/Whatcha Gonna Do About It .... (Columbia 38-07700)		.75	3.00	88
YOU GOT IT (THE RIGHT STUFF)/You Got It (The Right Stuff) (Remix) .... (Columbia 38-08092)		.75	3.00	88
YOU GOT IT (REMIX) .... (Columbia CS7 01335)		1.25	5.00	88
(Promotional issue, *Demonstration Only–Not For Sale* printed on sleeve)				

NEWMAN, LIONEL
THE SILENT MOVIE MARCH/The Wrong Dog Rag .... (United Artists XW881-Y)		1.50	6.00	76
(From the motion picture *Silent Movie*, Mel Brooks, Marty Feldman, and Dom DeLuise pictured)				

NEWMAN, RANDY
THE BLUES/Same Girl .... (Warner Bros. 29803-7)		1.00	4.00	83
(Shown as by Randy Newman and Paul Simon, only Newman pictured)				
IT'S MONEY THAT MATTERS .... (Reprise 27709-7)		.75	3.00	88
(Back of sleeve states *Featuring Mark Knopfler*)				

NEW MONKEES
(Completely different group from the Monkees)

WHAT I WANT/Corner Of My Eye .... (Warner Bros. 28188-7)	.75	3.00	87

NEW ORDER

THE PERFECT KISS .... (Qwest 28968-7)	1.00	4.00	85
TRUE FAITH (THE MORNING SUN)/1963 .... (Qwest 28271-7)	.75	3.00	87
BLUE MONDAY 1988/Touched By The Hand Of God (Single Version) .... (Qwest 27979-7)	.75	3.00	88
ROUND & ROUND .... (Qwest 27524-7)	.75	3.00	89

Also see Joy Division (Bernard Sumner, Peter Hook, Stephen Morris)

NEW SEEKERS, THE

COME SOFTLY TO ME .... (MGM/Verve 10698)	1.25	5.00	73

Also see Ferry Aid, the Seekers

NEWSOME, STAN
See Mantovani (Around The World, Let Me Be Loved)

NEWTON, HELMUT
(Photographer)

See Missing Persons (Surrender Your Heart, Right Now, Give), Sade (Is It A Crime?)

NEWTON, JUICE

ANGEL OF THE MORNING .... (Capitol 4976)	1.00	4.00	81
QUEEN OF HEARTS .... (Capitol 4997)	.75	3.00	81
THE SWEETEST THING (I'VE EVER KNOWN) .... (Capitol A-5046)	.75	3.00	81
LOVE'S BEEN A LITTLE BIT HARD ON ME .... (Capitol B-5120)	.75	3.00	82
BREAK IT TO ME GENTLY .... (Capitol B-5148)	.75	3.00	82
HEART OF THE NIGHT .... (Capitol B-5192)	.75	3.00	82
TELL HER NO/Stranger At My Door .... (Capitol B-5265)	.75	3.00	83
DIRTY LOOKS .... (Capitol B-5289)	.75	3.00	83
A LITTLE LOVE/Waiting For The Sun .... (RCA PB-13823)	.75	3.00	84
CAN'T WAIT ALL NIGHT/Restless Heart .... (RCA PB 13863)	.75	3.00	84
YOU MAKE ME WANT TO MAKE YOU MINE .... (RCA PB-14139)	.75	3.00	85
HURT .... (RCA PB-14199)	.75	3.00	85
BOTH TO EACH OTHER (FRIENDS AND LOVERS) .... (RCA PB-14377)	.75	3.00	86

(Shown as by Eddie Rabbitt With Juice Newton)

NEWTON, WAYNE

AFTER THE LAUGHTER .... (Capitol 5518)	2.00	8.00	65
STAGECOACH TO CHEYENNE/Somebody To Love .... (Capitol 5643)	2.00	8.00	66

(A-side from the motion picture Stagecoach. Back of sleeve features Norman Rockwell drawings of the film's stars: Ann-Margret, Red Buttons, Michael Connors, Alex Cord, Bing Crosby, Bob Cummings, Van Heflin, Slim Pickens, Stefanie Powers, and Kennan Wynn.)

EXCUSE ME BABY/How Loud A Sound .... (Capitol 5692)	2.00	8.00	66

NEWTON-JOHN, OLIVIA

PLEASE MR. PLEASE .... (MCA 40418)	1.50	6.00	75
SOMETHING BETTER TO DO .... (MCA 40459)	1.25	5.00	75
DON'T STOP BELIEVIN' .... (MCA 40600)	1.25	5.00	76
I HONESTLY LOVE YOU/Don't Cry For Me Argentina .... (MCA 40811)	1.25	5.00	77
YOU'RE THE ONE THAT I WANT/Alone At A Drive-In Movie (Instrumental) .... (RSO 891)	1.25	5.00	78

(Shown as by John Travolta and Olivia Newton-John, both pictured. From the motion picture Grease.)

A LITTLE MORE LOVE/Borrowed Time .... (MCA 40975)	1.00	4.00	78
TOTALLY HOT/Dancin' 'Round And 'Round .... (MCA 41074)	1.00	4.00	79
MAGIC .... (MCA 41247)	1.00	4.00	80

(From the motion picture Xanadu)

XANADU .... (MCA 41285)	1.00	4.00	80

(Shown as by Olivia Newton-John/Electric Light Orchestra. From the motion picture Xanadu.)

SUDDENLY .... (MCA 51007)	1.00	4.00	80

(Shown as by Olivia Newton-John and Cliff Richard. From the motion picture Xanadu.)

LANDSLIDE .... (MCA 51155)	1.00	4.00	81
PHYSICAL .... (MCA 51182)	1.00	4.00	81
MAKE A MOVE ON ME .... (MCA 52000)	1.00	4.00	81
HEART ATTACK .... (MCA 52100)	1.00	4.00	82
TIED-UP .... (MCA 52155)	1.00	4.00	82
TWIST OF FATE .... (MCA 52284)	1.00	4.00	83

(From the motion picture Two Of A Kind)

LIVIN' IN DESPERATE TIMES .... (MCA 52341)	.75	3.00	84

(From the motion picture Two Of A Kind. Small inset photo on back picturing John Travolta and Newton-John.)

SOUL KISS/Electric .... (MCA 52686)	.75	3.00	85
THE BEST OF ME/Sajé .... (Atlantic 7-89420)	1.00	4.00	86

(A-side shown as by David Foster & Olivia Newton-John, both pictured on front. B-side by David Foster.)

TOUGHEN UP/Driving Music .... (MCA 52757)	.75	3.00	86
THE RUMOUR .... (MCA 53294)	.75	3.00	88
CAN'T WE TALK IT OVER IN BED .... (MCA 53438)	.75	3.00	88

NEW VOICES OF FREEDOM
See Scrooged

NEW WORLD SYMPHONY

WONDER WOMAN .... (Shady Brook 45-033)	2.00	8.00	77

(From the television series Wonder Woman)

NEW YORK DOLLS, THE

TRASH .... (Mercury 73414)	7.50	30.00	73
TRASH .... (Mercury DJ-378)	12.50	50.00	73

(Numbered promotional issue, it is unknown if the artwork is different from the stock issue)

Also see David Johansen, Wayne Kramer (Johnny Thunders), Buster Poindexter (a.k.a. David Johansen), Sylvain Sylvain

NEW YORK PHILHARMONIC ORCHESTRA
See Jim Steinman (The Storm)

NEW YORK STORIES
(Motion Picture)
See Kid Creole and the Coconuts (People Will Talk)

NICHOLS, BARBARA
(Actress)
See Connie Francis (Where The Boys Are)

NICHOLS, NICHELLE
(Actress best known for her role as Lieutenant Uhura in the television and motion picture series Star Trek)
I KNOW WHAT I MEAN/Why Don't You Do Right .... (Epic 5-10131)   5.00   20.00   68
BEYOND ANTARES/Uhura's Theme .... (R-Way 1001)   3.75   15.00   79
EXTENDED PLAYS
DARK SIDE OF THE MOON/IT'S BEEN ON MY MIND/Starry Eyed/Let's Trip (Americana EP 1)   5.00   20.00   74
   (Hard cover gatefold)

NICHOLS, RED
EXTENDED PLAYS
DANNY KAYE AND RED NICHOLS ANNOUNCEMENTS/BACK HOME AGAIN
   IN INDIANA/Wall Of The Winds (excerpt)/The Five Pennies Saints (excerpt)/
   Battle Hymn Of The Republic (excerpt) .... (Dot DEPR 102)   1.50   6.00   59
   (Promotional issue for Selmer horns titled Selmer Sampler, titles not listed on sleeve. From the motion picture
   The Five Pennies. Nichols pictured on the front, Louis Armstrong and Danny Kaye, who plays Nichols in the
   film, are pictured on the back.)

NICHOLSON, JACK
(Actor)
See Jack Nitzsche (One Flew Over The Cuckoo's Nest), Carly Simon (Coming Around Again)

NICKS, STEVIE
STOP DRAGGIN' MY HEART AROUND/Kind Of Woman .... (Modern/Atco 7336)   1.00   4.00   81
   (A-side shown as by Stevie Nicks With Tom Petty and the Heartbreakers)
LEATHER AND LACE/Bella Donna .... (Modern/Atco MR 7341)   1.00   4.00   81
   (A-side shown as by Stevie Nicks With Don Henley)
EDGE OF SEVENTEEN (JUST LIKE THE WHITE WINGED DOVE)/
   Edge Of Seventeen (Previously Unreleased Live Version) .... (Modern/Atco 7401)   1.00   4.00   82
AFTER THE GLITTER FADES/Think About It .... (Modern/Atco 7405)   1.00   4.00   82
STAND BACK/Garbo .... (Modern/Atco 7-99863)   .75   3.00   83
IF ANYONE FALLS/Wild Heart .... (Modern/Atco 7-99832)   .75   3.00   83
NIGHTBIRD/Gate And Garden .... (Modern/Atco 7-99179)   .75   3.00   83
   (A-side shown as by Stevie Nicks With Sandy Stewart)
TALK TO ME/One More Big Time Rock And Roll Star .... (Modern/Atco 7-99582)   .75   3.00   85
I CAN'T WAIT/The Nightmare .... (Modern/Atco 7-99565)   .75   3.00   86
I CAN'T WAIT(EDIT OF LP VERSION ROCK INTRO)/
   I Can't Wait (Soft Intro) .... (Modern/Atco 7-99565)   2.00   8.00   86
   (Promotional issue only with completely different design from stock copy)
HAS ANYONE EVER WRITTEN ANYTHING FOR YOU/Imperial Hotel ..... (Modern/Atco 7-99532)   .75   3.00   85
TWO KINDS OF LOVE/Real Tears .... (Modern/Atlantic 7-99179)   .75   3.00   89
   (A-side credited as a Duet With Bruce Hornsby)
ROOMS ON FIRE/Alice .... (Modern/Atlantic 7-99216)   1.00   4.00   89
   Also see Buckingham Nicks, Fleetwood Mac, Tom Petty and the Heartbreakers (Needles And Pins), the Rotters (a Stevie Nicks "tribute"),
   Tom Snow (Hurry Boy)

NICO
See the Velvet Underground (All Tomorrow's Parties)

NIGHT
HOT SUMMER NIGHTS/Party Shuffle .... (Planet 45903)   .75   3.00   79
LOVE ON THE AIRWAVES/Day After Day .... (Planet 47921)   .75   3.00   80
   Also see Manfred Mann's Earth Band (Chris Thompson), Chris Thompson, Toto (Steve Porcaro)

NIGHTCAPS, THE
NO PARKING .... (Vandan 3387)   7.50   30.00   60s

NIGHTINGALE, MAXINE
(BRINGING OUT) THE GIRL IN ME/Hideaway .... (Windsong 11729)   1.00   4.00   79

NIGHTMARE ON ELM STREET 3, A
(Motion Picture)
See Dokken (Dream Warriors)

NIGHT PEOPLE, THE
ISTANBUL/Zazerac .... (Seafair 103)   5.00   20.00   60

NIGHT RANGER
(YOU CAN STILL) ROCK IN AMERICA .... (MCA/Camel 52305)   1.25   5.00   84
   (Promotional issue only)
WHEN YOU CLOSE YOUR EYES .... (MCA/Camel 52420)   .75   3.00   84
SENTIMENTAL STREET/Night Machine .... (MCA/Camel 52591)   .75   3.00   85
FOUR IN THE MORNING (I CAN'T TAKE ANY MORE) .... (MCA/Camel 52661)   .75   3.00   85
GOODBYE .... (MCA/Camel 52729)   .75   3.00   85
THE SECRET OF MY SUCCESS .... (MCA/Camel 53013)   .75   3.00   87
   (From the motion picture The Secret Of My Success)
I DID IT FOR LOVE .... (MCA/Camel 53364)   .75   3.00   88
   Also see Hear 'N Aid

NIGHTROCKERS, THE
JUNCTION 1/Run Mary Run .... (Stereophonic Corporation 105)   2.50   10.00

NIKKI AND THE CORVETTES
HONEY BOP!/Shake It Up .... (Bomp 125)   1.00   4.00   79
   (Hard cover issued with small-hole 45 RPM red vinyl record)

NILSSON
(Harry Nilsson)
WITHOUT YOU/Gotta Get Up .... (RCA 74-0604)   2.00   8.00   71

DAYBREAK .... (RCA APBO-0246)   1.50   6.00   74
(From the motion picture *Son of Dracula,* first printing. Sleeve pictures Nilsson and Ringo Starr. The photo used is slightly different from the second printing and can be identified by Nilsson's fully illuminated face.)

DAYBREAK .... (RCA APBO-0246 re)   1.50   6.00   74
(From the motion picture *Son of Dracula.* Sleeve pictures Nilsson and Ringo Starr. Second printing identified by the "re" suffix on the catalog number. The photo used is slightly different from the first printing and can be identified by the deeper shadows in Nilsson's face.)

KOJAK COLUMBO / Turn Out The Light .... (RCA PB-10183)   1.25   5.00   75
WHO DONE IT? / Perfect Day .... (RCA PB-11059)   1.25   5.00   77

NIMOY, LEONARD
(Actor / Director who played the role of Mr. Spock in the television and motion picture series *Star Trek*)
A VISIT TO A SAD PLANET / Theme From "Star Trek" .... (Dot 17038)   12.50   50.00   68

NINE INCH NAILS
CRACK / Communique .... (Nothing 5948)   2.00   8.00   94
(Promotional issue only split single, *Communique* shown as by Prick)
Also see the Innocent (Trent Reznor)

9 1/2 WEEKS
(Motion Picture)
See the John Taylor (*I Do What I Do...*)

9.9
ALL OF ME FOR ALL OF YOU .... (RCA PB-14082)   .75   3.00   85
I LIKE THE WAY YOU DANCE .... (RCA PB-14203)   .75   3.00   85

1984
(Motion Picture)
See Eurythmics (*Julia, Sexcrime*)

1969
(Motion Picture)
See the Pretenders (*Windows Of The World*)

1927
THAT'S WHEN I THINK OF YOU / Alright .... (Atlantic 7-88878)   .75   3.00   89
Also see Moving Pictures (Garry Frost)

9 TO 5
(Motion Picture)
See Dolly Parton (*9 To 5*)

NIRVANA
LOVE BUZZ / Big Cheese .... (Sub Pop 23)   18.75   75.00   88
(Hand-numbered edition of 1000)
SLIVER / Dive .... (Sub Pop 73)   2.50   10.00   90
(First printing was a folding sleeve. The first 3,000 issued with blue vinyl.)
SLIVER / Dive .... (Sub Pop 73)   1.00   4.00   90
(Second printing was a standard, side-glued sleeve)
MOLLY'S LIPS / Candy .... (Sub Pop 97)   2.50   10.00   91
(Limited edition of 3,500. B-side shown as by Fluid.)
HERE SHE COMES NOW / Venus In Furs .... (Communion 23)   3.00   12.00   91
(B-side shown as by the Melvins, issued with both blue and green vinyl)
Also see the Backbeat Band (Dave Grohl), the Fastbacks (Duff McKagan), Silly Killers (Duff McKagan), Mike Watt (Dave Grohl on *Big Train*)

NITTY GRITTY DIRT BAND
THE TEDDY BEAR'S PICNIC / Truly Right .... (Liberty 55982)   5.00   20.00   67
HOUSE AT POOH CORNER / Travelin' Mood .... (United Artists 50769)   1.50   6.00   71
JAMBALAYA (ON THE BAYOU) .... (United Artists 50890)   1.50   6.00   71
HONKY TONKIN' / Will The Circle Be Unbroken .... (United Artists XW 177-W)   1.00   4.00   73
(Sleeve credits Mother Maybelle Carter, Earl Scruggs, Doc Watson, Roy Acuff, Merle Travis, Jimmy Martin, Vassar Clements, Junior Huskey, Norman Blake, and Pete Oswald Kirby)
BATTLE OF NEW ORLEANS / Mountain Whippoorwill .... (United Artists XW 544-X)   1.00   4.00   74
OH WHAT A LOVE / America, My Sweetheart .... (Warner Bros. 28173-7)   .75   3.00   87
EXTENDED PLAYS
AN INTERVIEW WITH THE NGDB .... (Liberty/United Artists 37)   2.00   8.00   70
(Promotional issue only issued with a small-hole 33-1/3 RPM record)

NITZSCHE, JACK
THE LONELY SURFER / Song For A Summer Night .... (Reprise 20,202)   12.50   50.00   63
ONE FLEW OVER THE CUCKOO'S NEST / The Last Dance .... (Fantasy 760)   3.00   12.00   76
(From the motion picture *One Flew Over The Cuckoo's Nest,* Jack Nicholson pictured)

NIXON, MOJO
WILL THE FETUS BE ABORTED? / The Lost World .... (Alternative Tentacles VIRUS 136)   1.00   4.00   93
(Shown as by Jello Biafra and Mojo Nixon, 6-page folding sleeve)

NIXON, RICHARD, PRESIDENT
See Vic Caesar (*Nixon's The One*)

NOBODYS, THE
NO GUARANTEES .... (Capitol B-5385)   .75   3.00   84

NOEL
(Female singer)
DANCING IS DANGEROUS / The Night They Invented Love .... (Virgin 67001)   1.00   4.00   79
(Hard cover)

NOEL
(Male singer Noel Pagan)
SILENT MORNING / Silent Morning (Instrumental) .... (4th & B'Way 7439)   .75   3.00   87
LIKE A CHILD (7" RADIO EDIT) / Like A Child (Heartthrob Dub) .... (4th & B'Way 7458)   .75   3.00   88

NOGUEZ, JACKY, AND HIS ORCHESTRA
AMAPOLA / Mahzel .... (Jamie 1148)   2.50   10.00   60

NO MERCY
(Motion Picture)
See Alan Silvestri (*No Mercy Main Title*)

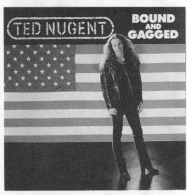

TITLE	LABEL AND NUMBER	VG	NM	YR

NOMO
RED LIPSTICK/Wailing Wall .... (Atco 7-99659) | .75 | 3.00 | 85

NORMA JEAN
See Chet Atkins (*Chet's Tune*)

NORMAL, THE
T.V.O.D./Warm Leatherette .... (Sire 1044) | 1.00 | 4.00 | 78

NORRIS, BOBBY
QUIET ROOM .... (Columbia 4-43498) | 2.00 | 8.00 | 66

NORTH, ALEX
CAESAR AND CLEOPATRA LOVE THEME .... (20th Century 408) | 2.00 | 8.00 | 60s

NORTH TO ALASKA
(Motion Picture)
See Johnny Horton (*North To Alaska*)

NO SMALL AFFAIR
(Motion Picture)
See Fiona (*Love Makes You Blind*)

NOTHING IN COMMON
(Motion Picture)
See Christopher Cross (*Loving Strangers*), Thompson Twins (*Nothing In Common*)

NOVA, ALDO
FANTASY/Under The Gun .... (Portrait 24-02799) | .75 | 3.00 | 82
ALWAYS BE MINE/Race Cars/Armageddon .... (Portrait 37-04207) | .75 | 3.00 | 83
RUMOURS OF YOU/Lay Your Love On Me .... (Portrait 37 05762) | .75 | 3.00 | 85
RUMOURS OF YOU .... (Portrait 37 05762) | 1.00 | 4.00 | 85
   (Promotional issue, *Demonstration–Not For Sale* printed on sleeve)

NO WAY OUT
(Motion Picture)
See Julia Migenes and Paul Anka (*No Way Out*)

NRBQ
(New Rhythm & Blues Quartet)
I GOT A ROCKET IN MY POCKET/Tapdancin' Bats .... (Red Rooster 1002) | 2.00 | 8.00 | 77
PEOPLE/ .... (Red Rooster 1005) | 2.00 | 8.00 | 77
CHRISTMAS WISH/Jolly Old St. Nicholas .... (Rounder 4525) | 1.50 | 6.00 | 79
ME AND THE BOYS/People .... (Rounder 4531) | 2.00 | 8.00 | 80
CAPTAIN LOU!/Boardin' House Pie .... (Rounder 1010) | 1.00 | 4.00 | 82

NUGENT, TED
BOUND AND GAGGED/Habitual Offender .... (Atlantic 7-89998) | 1.00 | 4.00 | 82
TIED UP IN LOVE/Lean Mean R & R Machine .... (Atlantic 7-89705) | 1.00 | 4.00 | 84
HIGH HEELS IN MOTION/Angry Young Man .... (Atlantic 7-89442) | 1.00 | 4.00 | 86
LITTLE MISS DANGEROUS/ Angry Young Man .... (Atlantic 7-89436) | 1.00 | 4.00 | 86
   Also see Hear 'N Aid

NU GIRLS
CAN WE TALK ABOUT IT?/Can We Talk About It? (Instrumental) .... (Atlantic 7-88968) | .75 | 3.00 | 89

NUMAN, GARY
See Radio Heart Featuring Gary Numan

NU SHOOZ
I CAN'T WAIT/Make Your Mind Up .... (Atlantic 7-89446) | .75 | 3.00 | 85
POINT OF NO RETURN/Goin' Thru The Motions .... (Atlantic 7-89392) | .75 | 3.00 | 86
DON'T LET ME BE THE ONE (EDIT)/Secret Message (LP Version) .... (Atlantic 7-89345) | .75 | 3.00 | 86
SHOULD I SAY YES?/Montecarlo Nite .... (Atlantic 7-89108) | .75 | 3.00 | 88
   (The promotional 45 issued with this sleeve has a different b-side, *Diciendo Sí*)
ARE YOU LOOKIN' FOR SOMEBODY NU/The Truth .... (Atlantic 7-89033) | .75 | 3.00 | 88
   (B-side featuring Maceo Parker)
DRIFTIN'/Doin' Alright .... (Atlantic 7-88978) | .75 | 3.00 | 88

NUTTY SQUIRRELS, THE
UH! OH! .... (Hanover 4540) | 5.00 | 20.00 | 59
PLEASE DON'T TAKE OUR TREE FOR CHRISTMAS/Nutty Noel .... (Columbia 4-41818) | 5.00 | 20.00 | 60

NYLONS, THE
SILHOUETTES/Princess Darkness .... (Open Air OA-0008) | .75 | 3.00 | 82
NA NA HEY HEY KISS HIM GOODBYE/It's What They Call Magic .... (Open Air OS-0022) | .75 | 3.00 | 87
HAPPY TOGETHER/Face In The Crowd .... (Open Air OS-0024) | .75 | 3.00 | 87

NYRO, LAURA
ELI'S COMIN/Sweet Blindness .... (Columbia 4-44531) | 3.75 | 15.00 | 68
   (Possibly a promotional issue only)

O

OAKEY, PHILIP
GOODBYE BAD TIMES/Goodbye Bad Times (Instrumental) .... (A&M 2755) | .75 | 3.00 | 85
   (Shown as by Philip Oakey and Giorgio Moroder)
   Also see Human League (Philip Oakey)

OAK RIDGE BOYS
TRYING TO LOVE TWO WOMEN .... (MCA 41217) | .75 | 3.00 | 80
EVERYDAY .... (MCA 52419) | 2.00 | 8.00 | 84
   (Promotional issue only, poster sleeve)
MAKE MY LIFE WITH YOU/Break My Mind .... (MCA 52488) | .75 | 3.00 | 84

		VG	NM	YR
LITTLE THINGS/The Secret Of Love .... (MCA 52556)		.75	3.00	85
COME ON IN (YOU DID THE BEST YOU COULD DO)/Roll Tennessee River .... (MCA 52722)		.75	3.00	85

O'BRIEN, RICHARD
(Songwriter/actor who played Riff Raff in *The Rocky Horror Picture Show*)

		VG	NM	YR
SHOCK TREATMENT/Overture .... (Warner Bros. 49799)		.75	3.00	81

(From the motion picture *Shock Treatment*)

O'BRYAN

		VG	NM	YR
LOVELITE .... (Capitol B-5329)		.75	3.00	84
BREAKIN' TOGETHER .... (Capitol B-5376)		.75	3.00	84

OCASEK, RIC

		VG	NM	YR
SOMETHING TO GRAB FOR/Connect Up To Me .... (Geffen 29784-7)		.75	3.00	82
EMOTION IN MOTION/P.F.J. .... (Geffen 28617-7)		.75	3.00	86
TRUE TO YOU/Hello Darkness .... (Geffen 28504-7)		.75	3.00	86

Also see the Cars

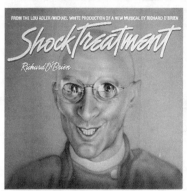

OCEAN, BILLY

		VG	NM	YR
LOVERBOY .... (Jive/Arista 9284)		.75	3.00	84
SUDDENLY/Lucky Man .... (Jive/Arista 9323)		.75	3.00	84
MYSTERY LADY/African Queen (No More Love On The Run) .... (Jive/Arista 9374)		.75	3.00	84
WHEN THE GOING GETS TOUGH, THE TOUGH GET GOING/ When The Going Gets Tough, The Tough Get Going (Instrumental) .... (Jive/Arista 9432)		.75	3.00	85
(From the motion picture *The Jewel Of The Nile*)				
THERE'LL BE SAD SONGS (TO MAKE YOU CRY)/If I Should Lose You .... (Jive/Arista 9465)		.75	3.00	86
LOVE ZONE/Love Zone (Instrumental) .... (Arista/Jive 9510)		.75	3.00	86
LOVE IS FOREVER/Dancefloor .... (Jive/Arista 9540)		.75	3.00	86
GET OUTTA MY DREAMS, GET INTO MY CAR/Showdown .... (Jive/Arista 9678)		.75	3.00	88
THE COLOUR OF LOVE/It's Never Too Late To Try .... (Arista/Jive 9707)		.75	3.00	88
TEAR DOWN THESE WALLS/Without You .... (Arista/Jive 9740)		.75	3.00	88
LICENCE TO CHILL/Pleasure .... (Jive/RCA 1283-7-J)		.75	3.00	89

Also see Ruby Turner (*If You're Ready*)

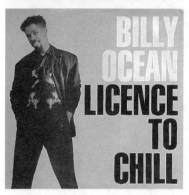

OCEANS, SONNY

		VG	NM	YR
PITY ME/ .... (Columbia 4-43422)		2.00	8.00	68

O'CONNOR, CARROLL
(Actor)

		VG	NM	YR
THOSE WERE THE DAYS .... (Atlantic 2847)		2.00	8.00	71

(Shown as by Carroll O'Connor & Jean Stapleton [as the Bunkers]. From the television series *All In The Family*. O'Connor, Stapleton, Rob Reiner, and Sally Struthers pictured.)

		VG	NM	YR
MOMENTS TO REMEMBER/Oh Babe What Would You Say/ They Can't Take That Away From Me .... (RCA 74-0962)		1.50	6.00	73

(Shown as by Carroll O'Connor & Jean Stapleton)

O'CONNOR, GLYNNIS
(Actress)
See Bobbie Gentry (*Ode To Billy Joe*)

O'CONNOR, HAZEL
See Ferry Aid

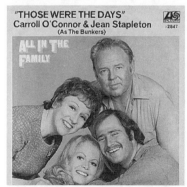

O'CONNOR, SINÉAD

		VG	NM	YR
MANDINKA/Drink Before The War .... (Chrysalis/Ensign VS4 43207)		1.25	5.00	87

OCTOBER, JOHNNY

		VG	NM	YR
GROWIN' PRETTIER/Young And In Love .... (Capitol 4267)		5.00	20.00	59

OCTOPUSSY
(Motion Picture)
See Rita Coolidge (*All Time High*)

ODE TO BILLY JOE
(Motion Picture)
See Bobbie Gentry (*Ode To Billy Joe*)

OFFICER AND A GENTLEMAN, AN
(Motion Picture)
See Joe Cocker (*Up Where We Belong*)

OFFSPRING, THE
EXTENDED PLAYS

		VG	NM	YR
GET IT RIGHT/HEY JOE/Baghdad/The Blurb .... (Nemesis 38)		.75	3.00	95

(Issued with a small-hole 33-1/3 RPM record)

OHIO PLAYERS
EXTENDED PLAYS

		VG	NM	YR
JIVE TURKEY/Heaven Must Be Like This/Skin Tight .... (Mercury SRM 1-705)		1.50	6.00	78

(Promotional issue only)

OINGO BOINGO

		VG	NM	YR
WEIRD SCIENCE .... (MCA 52633)		1.00	4.00	85
(From the motion picture *Weird Science*)				
JUST ANOTHER DAY .... (MCA 52726)		1.00	4.00	85
STAY .... (MCA 52789)		1.00	4.00	86
NOT MY SLAVE .... (MCA 53050)		1.00	4.00	87
WE CLOSE OUR EYES .... (MCA 53105)		1.00	4.00	87

Also see Danny Elfman

O'KANES, THE

		VG	NM	YR
CAN'T STOP MY HEART FROM LOVING YOU .... (Columbia 38-06606)		.75	3.00	87

O'KAYSIONS, THE

		VG	NM	YR
GIRL WATCHER .... (North State 1001)		12.50	50.00	68

O'KEEFE, DANNY

		VG	NM	YR
THE RUNAWAY/Just Jones .... (Warner Bros. 8489)		1.50	6.00	78

TITLE	LABEL AND NUMBER	VG	NM	YR
O'KEEFE, JOHNNY				
SHE'S MY BABY	(Liberty 55228)	3.75	15.00	60
OLAJUWON, AKEEM				
(Basketball Player)				
THE UNBEATABLE DREAM	(Macola 008)	6.25	25.00	87
(Promotional issue for Etonic Shoes, edition of 1,000)				
OLDFIELD, MIKE				
MAGIC TOUCH	(Virgin 7-99402)	.75	3.00	88
OLIVER				
JEAN/The Arrangement	(Crewe 334)	1.50	6.00	69
OLIVER, RICHARD				
TOGETHER, WE CAN MAKE IT HAPPEN/Tomorrow's Being Cancelled	(Rain 403)	.75	3.00	72
(A-side shown as by The Sound Of Rain Featuring Richard Oliver. Promotional issue for Cleveland Trust Bank.)				
OLMOS, EDWARD JAMES				
(Actor)				
See Mr. Mister (Stand And Deliver)				
OMD				
See Orchestral Manœuvres In The Dark				
ONCE BITTEN				
(Motion Picture)				
See 3 Speed (Once Bitten)				
O'NEAL, ALEXANDER				
FAKE	(Tabu ZS4-07100)	.75	3.00	87
CRITICIZE	(Tabu ZS4-07600)	.75	3.00	87
NEVER KNEW LOVE LIKE THIS	(Tabu ZS4-07646)	.75	3.00	88
(Shown as by Alexander O'Neal Featuring Cherrelle, both pictured)				
Also see Cherrelle (Saturday Love)				
O'NEAL, RYAN				
(Actor)				
See Frances Lai (Theme From Love Story)				
ONE AND ONLY, GENUINE, ORIGINAL FAMILY BAND, THE				
(Motion Picture)				
See Louis Armstrong (Ten Feet Off The Ground)				
ONE CRAZY SUMMER				
(Motion Picture)				
See Honeymoon Suite (What Does It Take)				
ONE EYED JACKS				
(Motion Picture)				
See Ferrante and Teicher (Love Theme From One Eyed Jacks)				
ONE FLEW OVER THE CUCKOO'S NEST				
(Motion Picture)				
See Jack Nitzsche (One Flew Over The Cuckoo's Nest)				
ONE LIFE TO LIVE				
(Television Soap Opera)				
Related see the Soaps and Hearts Ensemble				
ONE ON ONE				
(Motion Picture)				
See Seals & Crofts (My Fair Share)				
ONE 2 MANY				
DOWNTOWN/Welcome To My City	(A&M 1272)	.75	3.00	88
ONE TO ONE				
ANGEL IN MY POCKET	(Warner Bros. 28739-7)	.75	3.00	86
ONE WAY				
YOU BETTER QUIT	(MCA 53020)	.75	3.00	87
EXTENDED PLAYS				
SHOW ME	(MCA S-33-1754)	1.00	4.00	81
(Promotional issue only titled McDonald's Menu Music Chant, issued with a small-hole 33-1/3 RPM record. Also includes one song each, the titles are not listed on sleeve, by Donnie Iris, Terri Gibbs, and Rufus.)				
ONO, YOKO				
NOW OR NEVER	(Apple 1853)	2.50	10.00	72
(Shown as by Yoko Ono/The Plastic Ono Band)				
WALKING ON THIN ICE	(Geffen 49683)	1.00	4.00	81
(Originally issued with a lyric insert)				
NO, NO, NO/Will You Touch Me	(Geffen 49802)	1.00	4.00	81
MY MAN/Let The Tears Dry	(Polydor 2224)	.75	3.00	82
HELL IN PARADISE/Hell In Paradise (Instrumental)	(Polydor 883 455-7)	.75	3.00	85
Also see John Lennon				
ONTKEAN, MICHAEL				
(Actor)				
See Roberta Flack (Making Love)				
ORBISON, ROY				
I'M HURTIN'/I Can't Stop Lovin' You	(Monument 433)	6.25	25.00	60
RUNNING SCARED/Love Hurts	(Monument 438)	5.00	20.00	60
CRYING/Candy Man	(Monument 447)	5.00	20.00	61
DREAM BABY/The Actress	(Monument 456)	5.00	20.00	62
THE CROWD/Mama	(Monument 461)	5.00	20.00	62

		VG	NM	YR
LÉAH/Workin' For The Man	(Monument 467)	5.00	20.00	62
IN DREAMS/Shahdaroba	(Monument 806)	3.75	15.00	63
FALLING/Distant Drums	(Monument 815)	3.75	15.00	63
IT'S OVER/Indian Wedding	(Monument 837)	3.75	15.00	64
RIDE AWAY/Wondering	(MGM K-13386)	3.00	12.00	65
CRAWLING BACK/If You Can't Say Something Nice	(MGM K-13410)	3.00	12.00	65
BREAKIN' UP IS BREAKIN' MY HEART/Wait	(MGM K-13446)	3.00	12.00	65
TWINKLE TOES/Where Is Tomorrow?	(MGM K-13498)	3.00	12.00	66
TOO SOON TO KNOW/You'll Never Be Sixteen Again	(MGM K-13549)	3.00	12.00	66
CRY SOFTLY LONELY ONE/Pistolero	(MGM K-13764)	3.00	12.00	67
IN DREAMS/Leah	(Virgin 7-99434)	1.00	4.00	87
CRYING/Falling	(Virgin 7-99388)	1.00	4.00	87

(A-side shown as by Roy Orbison With k.d. lang. From the motion picture *Hiding Out*.)

		VG	NM	YR
YOU GOT IT/The Only One	(Virgin 7-99245)	1.00	4.00	89
SHE'S A MYSTERY TO ME/Dream Baby	(Virgin 7-99227)	.75	3.00	89

(A-side produced by Bono and written by David Evans, a.k.a. the Edge, and Paul Hewson, a.k.a. Bono)

		VG	NM	YR
CALIFORNIA BLUE/In Dreams	(Virgin 7 99202)	1.00	4.00	89
OH PRETTY WOMAN/Claudette	(Virgin 7 99189)	1.00	4.00	89

EXTENDED PLAYS

		VG	NM	YR
SWINGERS FOR COKE	(Coca-Cola no #)	12.50	50.00	66

(Promotional issue only with one "Coke" song each by the Drifters, Lesley Gore, Los Bravos, and Roy Orbison)

Also see Arlene Harden (*Crying*), Carl Perkins (*Birth Of Rock And Roll*), the Traveling Wilburys

ORBIT, WILLIAM
See Mickey Thomas (b-side of *Stand In The Fire*), Torch Song

ORCHESTRAL MANŒUVRES IN THE DARK

		VG	NM	YR
LOCOMOTION/Her Body In My Soul	(A&M/Virgin 2671)	1.00	4.00	84
SO IN LOVE/Concrete Hands	(A&M/Virgin 2746)	.1.00	4.00	85
SECRET/Firegun	(A&M/Virgin 2794)	1.00	4.00	85
IF YOU LEAVE/La Femme Accident	(A&M/Virgin 2811)	1.00	4.00	85

(A-side from the motion picture *Pretty In Pink*, Andrew McCarthy, Molly Ringwald, and Jon Cryer pictured on the front. Band members Andy McCluskey and Paul Humphreys pictured on the back.)

		VG	NM	YR
(FOREVER) LIVE AND DIE/This Town	(A&M/Virgin 2872)	.75	3.00	86
WE LOVE YOU/We Love You (Dub)	(A&M/Virgin 2897)	.75	3.00	86
DREAMING/Satellite	(A&M/Virgin 3002)	.75	3.00	88

ORIGINAL CASTE, THE

		VG	NM	YR
ONE TIN SOLDIER	(T-A 186)	1.50	6.00	69

ORIOLES, THE

		VG	NM	YR
WHAT ARE YOU DOING NEW YEAR'S EVE/Lonely Christmas	(Jubilee 5017)	125.00	500.00	54
OH HOLY NIGHT/The Lord's Prayer	(Jubilee 5017)	125.00	500.00	54

(Both Orioles sleeves were issued with second presssings of the record which had blue script Jubilee labels with a line under the logo)

ORION
See Jimy Ellis

ORLANDO, TONY

		VG	NM	YR
HALFWAY TO PARADISE/Lonely Tomorrows	(Epic 5-9441)	3.75	15.00	61
BLESS YOU/Am I The Guy	(Epic 5-9452)	3.75	15.00	61
HAPPY TIMES/Lonely Am I	(Epic 5-9476)	3.75	15.00	61
MY BABY'S A STRANGER/Talkin' About You	(Epic 5-9491)	3.75	15.00	62
AT THE EDGE OF TEARS/Chills	(Epic 5-9519)	3.75	15.00	62

ORLONS, THE

		VG	NM	YR
DON'T HANG UP/The Conservative	(Cameo 231)	3.00	12.00	62
SOUTH STREET/Them Terrible Boots	(Cameo 243)	3.00	12.00	63
NOT ME/My Best Friend	(Cameo 257)	3.00	12.00	63
CROSS FIRE!/It's No Big Thing	(Cameo 273)	3.00	12.00	63
BON-DOO-WAH/Don't Throw Your Love Away	(Cameo 287)	3.00	12.00	63
SHIMMY SHIMMY/Everything Nice	(Cameo 295)	3.00	12.00	64
RULES OF LOVE/Heartbreak Hotel	(Cameo 319)	3.00	12.00	64
KNOCK! KNOCK! (Who's There?)/Goin' Places	(Cameo 332)	3.00	12.00	64

ORPHAN'S CHORUS, THE

		VG	NM	YR
THIS OLD MAN	(20th Century 126)	1.50	6.00	58

ORPHEUS

		VG	NM	YR
BROWN ARMS IN HOUSTON	(MGM K-14022)	1.50	6.00	69

ORR, BENJAMIN

		VG	NM	YR
STAY THE NIGHT/That's The Way	(Elektra 7-69506)	.75	3.00	86
TOO HOT TO STOP/The Lace	(Elektra 7-69493)	.75	3.00	87

Also see the Cars

OSBORNE, JEFFREY

		VG	NM	YR
ON THE WINGS OF LOVE/I'm Beggin'	(A&M 2434)	1.00	4.00	82
WE'RE GOING ALL THE WAY/Two Wrongs Don't Make A Right	(A&M 2618)	.75	3.00	83
DON'T STOP/Forever Mine	(A&M 2687)	.75	3.00	84
YOU SHOULD BE MINE (THE WOO WOO SONG)/Who Would Have Guessed	(A&M 2814)	.75	3.00	86

(B-side with Portia Griffin)

		VG	NM	YR
ROOM WITH A VIEW/The Power	(A&M 2866)	.75	3.00	86
LOVE POWER/In A World Such As This	(Arista 9567)	.75	3.00	87

(A-side shown as by Dionne Warwick and Jeffrey Osborne, both pictured)

		VG	NM	YR
SHE'S ON THE LEFT/A Second Chance	(A&M 1227)	.75	3.00	88

Also see L.T.D., U.S.A. For Africa, Voices Of America

OSBOURNE, OZZY

		VG	NM	YR
FLYING HIGH AGAIN/I Don't Know (Live)	(Jet ZS5-02582)	1.00	4.00	81
SO TIRED/"B" Side	(CBS Associated ZS4-04383)	1.50	6.00	83
BARK AT THE MOON/Spiders	(CBS Associated ZS4-04318)	1.25	5.00	84
SHOT IN THE DARK/You Said It All	(CBS Associated ZS4-05810)	1.00	4.00	86

Also see Lita Ford (*Close My Eyes Forever*)

TITLE	LABEL AND NUMBER	VG	NM	YR

OSCAR
(Motion Picture)
See Tony Bennett (*Theme From Oscar*)

OSLIN, K.T.

WALL OF TEARS .... (RCA 5066-7-RAC)		1.25	5.00	84

(Promotional issue only, *For Promotional Use Only–Not For Sale* printed on sleeve)

80'S LADIES .... (RCA 5154-7-RAB)		1.00	4.00	87

(Promotional issue only, *Promotional Use Only–Not For Sale* printed on sleeve)

OSMOND, DONNY

SWEET AND INNOCENT .... (MGM K-14227)		1.25	5.00	71
THE TWELFTH OF NEVER / Life Is Just What You Make It .... (MGM K-14503)		1.25	5.00	73

(Four-color process used to print sleeve, good image detail. Top of sleeve is curve cut.)

THE TWELFTH OF NEVER / Life Is Just What You Make It .... (MGM K-14503)		1.25	5.00	73

(One-color brown used to print sleeve, image is soft and muddy-looking. Top of sleeve is straight cut.)

SOLDIER OF LOVE .... (Capitol B-44369)		1.00	4.00	89
SACRED EMOTION (EDIT) .... (Capitol 7PRO-79608)		1.50	6.00	89

(Promotional issue only, *Promotional Use Only Not For Sale* printed on sleeve)
Also see the Osmonds

OSMOND, LITTLE JIMMY

IF SANTA WERE MY DADDY / Silent Night .... (MGM K-14328)		1.50	6.00	72

OSMOND, MARIE

PAPER ROSES / Least Of All You .... (MGM K-14609)		1.50	6.00	73
THIS IS THE WAY THAT I FEEL / Play The Music Loud .... (Polydor/Kolob 14385)		1.00	4.00	77

(Thicker, soft-edged red lettering with a slight black accent used on front. Possibly a promotional issue.)

THIS IS THE WAY THAT I FEEL / Play The Music Loud .... (Polydor/Kolob 14385)		.75	3.00	77

(Thin, clean red lettering used on front. This may be a revised second printing.)

THERE'S NO STOPPING YOUR HEART .... (Capitol/Curb B-5521)		1.00	4.00	85
YOU'RE STILL NEW TO ME / New Love .... (Capitol/Curb B-5613)		.75	3.00	86

(Shown as by Marie Osmond with Paul Davis)

WITHOUT A TRACE .... (Capitol PB-44176)		.75	3.00	88

OSMONDS, THE

MR. SANDMAN / My Mom .... (MGM K-13281)		6.25	25.00	64

(Shown as by the Osmond Brothers)

LET ME IN .... (Polydor/Kolob K 14617)		1.50	6.00	73
I'M STILL GONNA NEED YOU / Thank You .... (MGM/Kolob M 14831)		1.50	6.00	75

Also see Donny Osmond

O'SULLIVAN, GILBERT

CLAIR .... (MAM/London 3626)		1.25	5.00	72

OTHER ONES, THE

WE ARE WHAT WE ARE / Islands .... (Virgin 99473-7)		.75	3.00	87
HOLIDAY / Dark Ages .... (Virgin 7-99428)		.75	3.00	87

O'TOOLE, PETER
(Actor)
See Tom Jones (*What's New Pussycat?*)

OUR DAUGHTER'S WEDDING

LAWNCHAIRS / Airline .... (Design 913)		2.00	8.00	80

Also see Keith Silva

OUTFIELD, THE

SAY IT ISN'T SO / Mystery Man .... (Columbia 38-05447)		.75	3.00	85
SAY IT ISN'T SO .... (Columbia 38-05447)		1.00	4.00	85

(Promotional issue, *Demonstration–Not For Sale* printed on sleeve)

YOUR LOVE / 61 Seconds .... (Columbia 38-05796)		.75	3.00	86
YOUR LOVE .... (Columbia 38-05796)		1.00	4.00	86

(Promotional issue, *Demonstration–Not For Sale* printed on sleeve)

ALL THE LOVE IN THE WORLD / Taking My Chances .... (Columbia 38-05894)		.75	3.00	86
ALL THE LOVE IN THE WORLD .... (Columbia 38-05894)		1.00	4.00	86

(Promotional issue, *Demonstration–Not For Sale* printed on sleeve)

EVERYTIME YOU CRY / Tiny Lights .... (Columbia 38-06295)		.75	3.00	86
EVERYTIME YOU CRY .... (Columbia 38-06295)		1.00	4.00	86

(Promotional issue, *Demonstration–Not For Sale* printed on sleeve)

SINCE YOU'VE BEEN GONE / Better Than Nothing .... (Columbia 38-07170)		.75	3.00	87
SINCE YOU'VE BEEN GONE .... (Columbia 38-07170)		1.00	4.00	87

(Promotional issue, *Demonstration–Not For Sale* printed on sleeve)

NO SURRENDER / Playground .... (Columbia 38-07384)		.75	3.00	87

OUTLOUD

IT'S LOVE THIS TIME .... (Warner Bros. 28264-7)		.75	3.00	87

OUT OF AFRICA
(Motion Picture)
See Melissa Manchester (*The Music Of Goodbye*), Al Jarreau (*The Music Of Goodbye*),

OUTSIDERS, THE

GIRL IN LOVE / What Makes You So Bad, You Weren't Brought Up That Way .... (Capitol 5646)		3.75	15.00	66
HELP ME GIRL / You Gotta Look .... (Capitol 5759)		3.75	15.00	66
I'LL GIVE YOU TIME (TO THINK IT OVER) / I Don't Want To Hurt You .... (Capitol 5843)		3.75	15.00	67
I'LL SEE YOU IN THE SUMMERTIME / And Now You Want My Sympathy .... (Capitol 5955)		3.75	15.00	67

OVER THE TOP
(Motion Picture)
See Sammy Hagar (*Winner Takes It All*), Kenny Loggins (*Meet Me Halfway*)

OWENS, BUCK

I'VE GOT A TIGER BY THE TAIL / Cryin' Time .... (Capitol 5336)		2.50	10.00	65
(I WANT) NO ONE BUT YOU / Before You Go .... (Capitol 5410)		2.50	10.00	65

TITLE	LABEL AND NUMBER	VG	NM	YR
GONNA HAVE LOVE/Only You (Can Break My Heart)	(Capitol 5465)	2.50	10.00	65
(Shown as by Buck Owens only but pictures Owens and the Buckaroos)				
SANTA LOOKED A LOT LIKE DADDY/All I Want For Christmas Dear Is You	(Capitol 5537)	2.50	10.00	65
THINK OF ME/Heart Of Glass	(Capitol 5647)	2.50	10.00	66
(Shown as by Buck Owens and the Buckaroos)				
OPEN UP YOUR HEART/No More Me And You	(Capitol 5705)	2.00	8.00	66
THE WAY THAT I LOVE YOU/Where Does The Good Times Go	(Capitol 5811)	2.00	8.00	67
(Shown as by Buck Owens and His Buckaroos)				
SAM'S PLACE/Don't Ever Tell Me Goodbye	(Capitol 5865)	2.00	8.00	67
(Shown as by Buck Owens and His Buckaroos)				
YOUR TENDER LOVING CARE/What A Liar I Am	(Capitol 5942)	2.00	8.00	67
(Shown as by Buck Owens and His Buckaroos)				
YOU LEFT HER TOO LONELY TOO LONG/It Takes People Like You	(Capitol 2001)	1.50	6.00	67
HOW LONG WILL MY BABY BE GONE/Everybody Needs Somebody	(Capitol 2080)	1.50	6.00	67
SWEET ROSIE JONES/Happy Times Are Here Again	(Capitol 2142)	1.50	6.00	67
(Shown as by Buck Owens and His Buckaroos)				
I CAN'T STOP/	(Capitol 2173)	1.50	6.00	68
I'VE GOT YOU ON MY MIND AGAIN/ That's All Right With Me (If It's All Right With You)	(Capitol 2300)	1.50	6.00	68
(Shown as by Buck Owens And The Buckaroos)				
CHRISTMAS SHOPPING/	(Capitol 2328)	1.50	6.00	68
WHO'S GONNA MOW YOUR GRASS/	(Capitol 2377)	1.50	6.00	68
JOHNNY B GOODE/Maybe If I Close My Eyes	(Capitol 2485)	1.50	6.00	69
TALL DARK STRANGER/Sing That Kind Of Song	(Capitol 2570)	1.50	6.00	69
BIG IN VEGAS	(Capitol 2646)	1.50	6.00	69
THE KANSAS CITY SONG/I'd Love To Be Your Man	(Capitol 2783)	1.50	6.00	70
I WOULDN'T LIVE IN NEW YORK CITY/	(Capitol 2947)	1.50	6.00	70
BRIDGE OVER TROUBLED WATER/(I'm Going) Home	(Capitol 3023)	1.25	5.00	71
ROLLIN' IN MY SWEET BABY'S ARMS/Corn Likker	(Capitol 3164)	1.25	5.00	71
HOT DOG/Second Fiddle	(Capitol B-44248)	1.00	4.00	88
STREETS OF BAKERSFIELD	(Reprise 27964-7)	.75	3.00	88
(Shown as by Dwight Yoakam and Buck Owens)				
Also see Buck Owens & Buddy Alan and the Buckaroos, Buck Owens and Susan Raye				

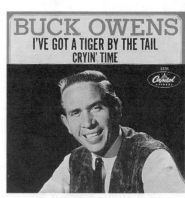

OWENS, BUCK, & BUDDY ALLAN AND THE BUCKAROOS

TITLE	LABEL AND NUMBER	VG	NM	YR
LET THE WORLD KEEP ON A TURNIN'/I'll Love You Forever And Ever	(Capitol 2237)	1.50	6.00	68
TOO OLD TO CUT THE MUSTARD/Wham Bam	(Capitol 3215)	1.50	6.00	71
Also see Buddy Alan, Buck Owens				

OWENS, BUCK, AND SUSAN RAYE

TITLE	LABEL AND NUMBER	VG	NM	YR
WE'RE GONNA GET TOGETHER/	(Capitol 2731)	1.50	6.00	70
TOGETHERNESS/	(Capitol 2791)	1.50	6.00	70
THE GREAT WHITE HORSE/Your Tender Loving Care	(Capitol 2871)	1.50	6.00	70
SANTA'S GONNA COME IN A STAGECOACH/One Of Everything You Got	(Capitol 3225)	1.50	6.00	71
LOOKING BACK/	(Capitol 3368)	1.50	6.00	70
Also see Buck Owens, Susan Raye				

OWENS, MARIE

TITLE	LABEL AND NUMBER	VG	NM	YR
LOVE'S GONNA COME TO YOU/Why Don't You Love Me Alone	(MCA 40018)	1.25	5.00	73
(Promotional issue only)				

OXO

TITLE	LABEL AND NUMBER	VG	NM	YR
WHIRLY GIRL/In The Stars	(Geffen 29765-7)	.75	3.00	83

OZARK MOUNTAIN DAREDEVILS, THE

TITLE	LABEL AND NUMBER	VG	NM	YR
JACKIE BLUE/Better Days	(A&M 1654)	1.50	6.00	75
YOU KNOW LIKE I KNOW/Arroyo	(A&M 1888)	1.25	5.00	76

P

PAAR, JACK

(Preceded Johnny Carson as the host of *The Tonight Show* from 1957-1962)

TITLE	LABEL AND NUMBER	VG	NM	YR
I-M-4-U (I AM FOR YOU)/Good Luck, Good Health, God Bless You	(Columbia 4-40628)	6.25	25.00	56
(Shown as by Jack Paar and Jack Haskell)				
FUNNY WHAT YOU LEARN FROM WOMEN/Blue Wiggle	(RCA Victor 47-7306)	6.25	25.00	58

PABLO CRUISE

TITLE	LABEL AND NUMBER	VG	NM	YR
WHATCHA GONNA DO?/Atlanta June	(A&M 1920)	1.25	5.00	77
LOVE WILL FIND A WAY/Always Be Together	(A&M 2048)	1.25	5.00	78
SLIP AWAY/That's When	(A&M 2373)	1.25	5.00	81

PACIFIC GAS AND ELECTRIC

EXTENDED PLAYS

TITLE	LABEL AND NUMBER	VG	NM	YR
MISS LUCY (Excerpt)	(Columbia AS 1)	1.25	5.00	70
(Promotional issue only titled *Dig This*, issued with a small-hole 33-1/3 RPM record. Also includes excerpts by Moondog, Nick Gravenites, Pete Seeger, Santana, Don Ellis, Raven, Firesign Theatre, and Tony Kosinec.)				

PACK, DAVID

TITLE	LABEL AND NUMBER	VG	NM	YR
THAT GIRL IS GONE	(Warner Bros. 28892-7)	.75	3.00	85

PAGE, BILL

TITLE	LABEL AND NUMBER	VG	NM	YR
SUNDAY WILL NEVER BE THE SAME	(Tower 349)	2.00	8.00	67

PAGE, JIMMY

TITLE	LABEL AND NUMBER	VG	NM	YR
WASTING MY TIME/Writes Of Winter	(Geffen 27821-7)	1.25	5.00	88
Also see the Firm, the Honeydrippers, Led Zeppelin, Willie and the Poor Boys, the Yardbirds				

PAGE, PATTI

TITLE	LABEL AND NUMBER	VG	NM	YR
CROSS OVER THE BRIDGE/	(Mercury 70302)	5.00	20.00	54
YOU WILL FIND YOUR LOVE (IN PARIS)/Fibbin'	(Mercury 71355)	3.00	12.00	58
(*Fibbin'* is listed as the b-side even though it was the song that made it to #39 on the Billboard Top 100)				
ONE OF US (WILL WEEP TONIGHT)/What Will My Future Be	(Mercury 71639)	2.00	8.00	60

TITLE	LABEL AND NUMBER	VG	NM	YR
I WISH I'D NEVER BEEN BORN/I Need You	(Mercury 71695)	2.00	8.00	60
DON'T READ THE LETTER/That's All I Need To Know	(Mercury 71745)	2.00	8.00	60
A CITY GIRL STOLE MY COUNTRY BOY/Dondi	(Mercury 71793)	2.00	8.00	61
YOU'LL ANSWER TO ME/Mom And Dad's Waltz	(Mercury 71823)	2.00	8.00	61
BROKEN HEART AND A PILLOW FILLED WITH TEARS/Dark Moon	(Mercury 71870)	2.00	8.00	61
GO ON HOME/Too Late To Cry	(Mercury 71906)	2.00	8.00	61
MOST PEOPLE GET MARRIED/You Don't Know Me	(Mercury 71950)	2.00	8.00	62
THE BOYS' NIGHT OUT/Three Fools	(Mercury 72013)	2.00	8.00	62
(A-side from the motion picture *The Boys' Night Out* co-starring Page)				
EVERYTIME I HEAR YOUR NAME/Let's Cry Together	(Mercury 72044)	2.00	8.00	62
HIGH ON A HILL OF HOPE/By A Long Shot	(Mercury 72078)	2.00	8.00	62
I'M WALKIN'/Invitation To The Blues	(Mercury 72123)	2.00	8.00	63
HAPPY BIRTHDAY JESUS/Christmas Bells	(Columbia 4-43447)	2.00	8.00	65

PAGE, TOMMY
A SHOULDER TO CRY ON	(Sire 27645-7)	.75	3.00	88

PAIGE, ELAINE
HEAVEN HELP MY HEART/Argument	(RCA PB-13958)	.75	3.00	84
(From the stage musical *Chess*. B-side shown as by Elaine Paige and Tommy Körberg. Benny Andersson, Tim Rice, and Björn Ulvaeus credited on front.)				

PAIGE, KEVIN
DON'T SHUT ME OUT	(Chrysalis 23389)	.75	3.00	89

PALEY BROTHERS, THE
ECSTASY/Hide N' Seek	(Sire 1001)	1.25	5.00	77
YOU'RE THE BEST/Magic Power	(Sire 1021)	1.00	4.00	78
TELL ME TONIGHT/Turn The Tide	(Sire 1033)	1.00	4.00	78
Also see the Beatles Costello (Andy Paley)				

PALMER, NICK
WORLDS OF TIME/If I Ever Love Again	(RCA Victor 47-9095)	2.00	8.00	66

PALMER, ROBERT
YOU ARE IN MY SYSTEM/Deadline	(Island 7-99866)	1.00	4.00	83
PRIDE	(Island 7-99835)	1.00	4.00	83
DISCIPLINE OF LOVE/Dance For Me	(Island 7-99597)	.75	3.00	85
ADDICTED TO LOVE/Let's Fall In Love Tonight	(Island 7-99570)	1.00	4.00	86
(First printing with photo of Palmer)				
ADDICTED TO LOVE/Let's Fall In Love Tonight	(Island 7-99570)	1.00	4.00	86
(Second printing with an image from the video featuring Palmer and four women)				
I DIDN'T MEAN TO TURN YOU ON/Get It Through Your Heart	(Island 7-99537)	.75	3.00	86
SWEET LIES/Want You More	(EMI Manhattan 7 99377)	.75	3.00	88
SIMPLY IRRESISTIBLE/Nova	(EMI Manhattan B-50133)	.75	3.00	88
EARLY IN THE MORNING/Disturbing Behavior	(EMI Manhattan B-50157)	.75	3.00	88
SHE MAKES MY DAY/Casting A Spell	(EMI B-50183)	.75	3.00	88
Also see Power Station				

PANDORAS
HOT GENERATION/You Don't Satisfy	(Voxx 45-1007)	1.50	6.00	84
IN AND OUT OF MY LIFE (IN A DAY)/The Hump	(Rhino 74402)	1.00	4.00	86

PANTER, GARY
ITALIAN SUNGLASS MOVIE/Tornader To The Tater	(Index 45-004)	2.50	10.00	81
(Limited edition of 2,500 poster sleeves. Production credited to the Residents.)				

PARACHUTE CLUB, THE
LOVE IS FIRE/Waves	(RCA 5056-7-R)	.75	3.00	86

PARENT TRAP, THE
(Motion Picture)

See Annette (*The Parent Trap*), Haley Mills (*Let's Get Together*)

PARIS, MICA
BREATHE LIFE INTO ME/Same Feeling	(Island 7-99178)	.75	3.00	89
MY ONE TEMPTATION/	(Island 7-99252)	.75	3.00	89

PARIS SISTERS, THE
DREAM LOVER/Lonely Girl	(MGM K-13236)	5.00	20.00	64
ONCE UPON A TIME/When I Fall In Love	(Mercury 72320)	3.00	12.00	64
ALWAYS WAITIN'/Why Do I Take It From You	(Mercury 72468)	3.00	12.00	65

PARKER, FESS
(Actor)
BALLAD OF DAVY CROCKETT/I Gave My Love (Riddle Song)	(Columbia J-252)	5.00	20.00	54
(This sleeve is for the 78 rpm, it is unknown if a sleeve exists for a 1954 45 RPM version)				
OLD BETSY	(Columbia 4-254)	7.50	30.00	55
(Shown as by Fess Parker and Buddy Ebsen)				
WRINGLE WRANGLE/The Ballad Of John Colter	(Disneyland F-43)	5.00	20.00	57
(From the motion picture *Westward Ho The Wagons*)				
THE BALLAD OF DAVY CROCKETT/Farewell	(Buena Vista F-426)	3.75	15.00	63
THE BALLAD OF DAVY CROCKETT/Daniel Boone	(RCA Victor 47-8429)	2.00	8.00	65

PARKER, GRAHAM
LOCAL GIRLS/I Want You Back	(Arista 0420)	1.25	5.00	79
(Shown as by Graham Parker and the Rumour)				
I WANT YOU BACK (ALIVE)/Mercury Poisoning	(Arista 0439)	1.50	6.00	79
(Shown as by Graham Parker and the Rumour. Front of sleeve states *A Special Blue Vinyl Collector's Edition*. Issued with a small-hole 33-1/3 RPM blue vinyl record.)				
STUPEFACTION/Women In Charge	(Arista 0523)	1.00	4.00	80
WAKE UP (NEXT TO YOU)/Bricks And Mortar	(Elektra 7-69654)	1.00	4.00	85
(Shown as by Graham Parker and the Shot)				
GET STARTED. START A FIRE/Ordinary Girl	(RCA 8639-7-R)	1.25	5.00	88

EXTENDED PLAYS
HOLD BACK THE NIGHT/(LET ME GET) SWEET ON YOU/
White Honey (Live)/Soul Shoes (Live) .... (Mercury 74000)   1.25   5.00   77
(Title on front of sleeve is *The Pink Parker*. Shown as by Graham Parker + The Rumour. Issued with either black or pink vinyl, black being harder to find.)

PARKER, LORI
GREEN WITH ENVY .... (Coral 62191)   2.00   8.00   60

PARKER, JAMESON
(Actor)
See Barry DeVorzon (*Theme From Simon & Simon*)

PARKER, MACEO
See Nu Shooz (featured on the b-side of *Are You Lookin' For Somebody Nu*)

PARKER, RAY, JR.
THAT OLD SONG .... (Arista 0616)   1.00   4.00   81
(Shown as by Ray Parker Jr. and Raydio)
CHRISTMAS TIME IS HERE .... (Arista 1035)   1.50   6.00   82
(Promotional issue only)
GIRLS ARE MORE FUN/I'm In Love .... (Arista 9352)   .75   3.00   85
ONE SUNNY DAY/DUELING BIKES FROM QUICKSILVER/How Long .... (Atlantic 7-89456)   .75   3.00   86
(A-side shown as by Ray Parker, Jr. and Helen Terry. B-side shown as by the Motor Band. From the motion picture *Quicksilver*. Parker and Terry pictured on front, actor Kevin Bacon on back.)
OVER YOU .... (Geffen 28152-7)   .75   3.00   87
(Shown as by Ray Parker Jr. With Natalie Cole, Parker pictured on front, Cole on back)
I DON'T THINK THAT MAN SHOULD SLEEP ALONE .... (Geffen 28417-7)   .75   3.00   87
Also see Raydio

PARLIAMENT
AQUA BOOGIE .... (Casablanca 950)   2.50   10.00   78
AQUA BOOGIE .... (Casablanca NB 950 D.J.)   3.75   15.00   78
(Promotional issue, *Loaned For Promotion Only, Not For Sale, Ownership & All Rights Reserved* printed on front)
Also see George Clinton, Bootsy Collins, Mudhoney (b-side of *Pump It Up*)

PARR, JOHN
MAGICAL/Treat Me Like An Animal .... (Atlantic 7-89568)   .75   3.00   85
ST. ELMO'S FIRE (MAN IN MOTION)/One Love .... (Atlantic 7-89541)   .75   3.00   85
(B-side shown as by David Foster. From the motion picture *St. Elmo's Fire*. Rob Lowe, Demi Moore, Emilio Estevez, Ally Sheedy, Judd Nelson, Mare Winningham, and Andrew McCarthy pictured on front.)
LOVE GRAMMAR/Treat Me Like An Animal .... (Atlantic 7-89484)   .75   3.00   85
TWO HEARTS (EXTENDED VERSION)/Two Hearts (Edit) .... (Atlantic 7-89403)   .75   3.00   86
(From the motion picture *American Anthem*, Mitch Gaylord pictured on back)
BLAME IT ON THE RADIO/Two Hearts .... (Atlantic 7-89333)   .75   3.00   86
DON'T WORRY 'BOUT ME/Two Hearts .... (Atlantic 7-89298)   .75   3.00   86
ROCK 'N' ROLL MERCENARIES/Execution Day .... (Atlantic 7-89303)   .75   3.00   87
(Shown as by Meat Loaf With John Parr, both pictured)

PARRISH
(Motion Picture)
See George Greeley (*Allison's Theme From Parrish*)

PARROTT, TOM
NEON PRINCESS/Groovy And Linda .... (Folkways 0201)   1.50   6.00   68

PARSONS, ALAN, PROJECT, THE
DON'T ANSWER ME .... (Arista 9160)   .75   3.00   84
LET'S TALK ABOUT ME/Hawkeye .... (Arista 9282)   .75   3.00   85
STANDING ON HIGHER GROUND/Inside Looking Out .... (Arista 9576)   .75   3.00   87
Also see the Hollies (Allan Clarke), Vitamin Z (Geoff Barradale), the Zombies (Colin Blunstone). All three individuals have provided vocals for the group.

PARSONS, GRAM, AND THE FALLEN ANGELS
EXTENDED PLAYS
MEDLEY (BONY MARONIE/40 DAYS/ALMOST GROWN)/
Conversations/Hot Burrito #1 .... (Sierra GP/EP 104)   1.50   6.00   82
(Promotional issue only, *Hot Burrito #1* shown as by Gene Parsons. Emmylou Harris credited on back with vocals and guitar. Issued with small-hole 33-1/3 RPM half speed master.)
Also see the International Submarine Band. Parsons was a member of, and recorded with, the Byrds for three months in 1968.

PARTLAND BROTHERS
SOUL CITY/Outside The City .... (Manhattan B 50065)   .75   3.00   86

PARTON, DOLLY
COAT OF MANY COLORS/Here I Am .... (RCA 74-0538)   2.50   10.00   69
BALLY PINBALL SLEEVE .... (Bally Pinball Division no #)   6.25   25.00   70s
(Promotional issue only. Generic hard cover sleeve pictures Parton next to the Dolly Parton Pinball Machine. Issued with a variety of Parton releases to jukebox vendors.)
9 TO 5/Odd Jobs .... (RCA PB-12133)   1.00   4.00   80
(From the motion picture *9 To 5*)
I WILL ALWAYS LOVE YOU .... (RCA PB 13260)   1.25   5.00   82
(From the motion picture *The Best Little Whorehouse In Texas*)
ISLANDS IN THE STREAM/I Will Always Love You .... (RCA PB-13615)   1.00   4.00   83
(First printing with a-side credited as *Duet With Dolly Parton* in a smaller type size than Rogers' name, both pictured)
ISLANDS IN THE STREAM/I Will Always Love You .... (RCA PB-13615)   .75   3.00   83
(Second printing with a-side credited as *Duet With Dolly Parton* in the same type size as Rogers' name, both pictured)
SWEET LOVIN' FRIENDS/God Won't Get You .... (RCA PB-13883)   1.00   4.00   84
(Shown as by Dolly Parton and Sylvester Stallone. From the motion picture *Rhinestone*.)
DOWNTOWN .... (RCA PB-13756)   1.00   4.00   84
REAL LOVE .... (RCA PB-14058)   1.00   4.00   85
(Credit on front reads *Duet With Kenny Rogers*, both pictured)
TO KNOW HIM IS TO LOVE HIM .... (Warner Bros. 28492-7)   1.00   4.00   87
(Shown as by Dolly Parton, Linda Ronstadt, Emmylou Harris)

TITLE	LABEL AND NUMBER	VG	NM	YR

THOSE MEMORIES OF YOU .... (Warner Bros. 28248-7) — 1.00 — 4.00 — 87
   (Shown as by Dolly Parton, Linda Ronstadt, Emmylou Harris)
THE RIVER UNBROKEN .... (Columbia 38-07665) — 1.25 — 5.00 — 87
I KNOW YOU BY HEART .... (Columbia 38-07727) — 1.25 — 5.00 — 88
   (Credit on front reads *Duet With Smokey Robinson*, only Parton pictured)
   Also see Emmylou Harris *(Light Of The Stable)*

PARTON, RANDY
(Brother of Dolly Parton)
OH, NO .... (RCA Victor 13087) — 1.50 — 6.00 — 82
   (Promotional issue only issued with clear gold vinyl)

PARTON, STELLA
(Sister of Dolly Parton)
I'LL MISS YOU .... (Townhouse B-1056) — 1.25 — 5.00 — 82

PARTRIDGE FAMILY, THE
I THINK I LOVE YOU/Somebody Wants To Love You Mind .... (Bell 910) — 1.50 — 6.00 — 70
DOESN'T SOMEBODY WANT TO BE WANTED/You Are Always On My Mind .... (Bell 963) — 1.50 — 6.00 — 71
   (Both sleeves picture the cast from the television series; Shirley Jones, David Cassidy, Susan Dey, Danny
   Bonaduce, Jeremy Gelbwaks, and Suzanne Crough. Only David Cassidy and Shirley Jones actually recorded.)
   Also see David Cassidy

PARTRIDGE FAMILY, THE
(Television Series)
   Related see Danny Bonaduce, David Cassidy, Ricky Segall (Bonaduce and Segal appeared on the series but did not record with the musical
   group)

PARTY PARTY
(Motion Picture)
   See Dave Edmunds *(Run Rudolph Run)*

PATIENCE & PRUDENCE
YOU TATTLETALE/Very Nice Is Bali Bali .... (Liberty 55084) — 7.50 — 30.00 — 57

PATRICK, BUTCH
(Child actor best known for the role of Eddie Munster in the television series *The Munsters* from 1964-1966)
WHATEVER HAPPENED TO EDDIE?/Little Monsters .... (Rocshire XR95041) — 2.50 — 10.00 — 83
   (Hard cover)

PATTI
I WANNA BE BOBBY'S GIRL .... (Metromedia 189) — 2.50 — 10.00 — 70
   (Bobby Sherman pictured)

PATTON, ROBBIE
DARLIN'/Never Comin' Down .... (Backstreet/MCA 41105) — 1.00 — 4.00 — 79

PAUL, LES, & MARY FORD
PUT A RING ON MY FINGER/Fantasy .... (Columbia 4-41222) — 2.50 — 10.00 — 58
JURA/It's Been A Long, Long Time .... (Columbia 4-41994) — 2.00 — 8.00 — 61
GOODNIGHT IRENE/ .... (Columbia 4-42291) — 2.00 — 8.00 — 61
YOUR CHEATIN' HEART/ .... (Columbia 4-42419) — 2.00 — 8.00 — 62
PLAYING MAKE BELIEVE/ .... (Columbia 4-42602) — 2.00 — 8.00 — 63
GENTLE IS YOUR LOVE/Move Along Baby .... (Columbia 4-42754) — 2.00 — 8.00 — 64

PAUL & PAULA
YOUNG LOVERS/Ba-Hey-Be .... (Philips 40096) — 3.75 — 15.00 — 63
FIRST QUARREL/School Is Thru .... (Philips 40114) — 3.75 — 15.00 — 63
NO OTHER BABY/Too Dark To See .... (Philips 40234) — 3.75 — 15.00 — 64

PAUPERS
MAGIC PEOPLE .... (Verve 5062) — 2.50 — 10.00 — 67

PAVAROTTI, LUCIANO
SCHUBERT: AVE MARIA/Bach-Gounod: Ave Maria .... (London 20102) — 1.25 — 5.00 — 80

PAVEMENT
MORE KINGS .... (Atlantic PR 6632-7) — 1.00 — 4.00 — 95
   (Promotional issue only)

PAVONE, RITA
REMEMBER ME/Just Once More .... (RCA Victor 47-8365) — 2.00 — 8.00 — 64
WAIT FOR ME/It's Not Easy .... (RCA Victor 47-8420) — 2.00 — 8.00 — 65

PAYNE, FREDA
CHERISH WHAT IS DEAR TO YOU/You Don't Owe Me A Thing .... (Invictus 9085) — 2.00 — 8.00 — 71

PAYOLAS
CHINA BOYS/TNT/Rose/Juke Box .... (I.R.S. 7701) — 1.00 — 4.00 — 80
   (Hard cover gatefold titled *Introducing Payolas*, issued with a small-hole 33-1/3 RPM record)
   Also see Paul Hyde and the Payolas, Rock and Hyde (Bob Rock, Paul Hyde)

PCU
(Motion Picture)
   See Mudhoney *(Pump It Up)*

PEACHES & HERB
CLOSE YOUR EYES .... (Date 2-1549) — 3.00 — 12.00 — 67
FOR YOUR LOVE .... (Date 2-1563) — 3.00 — 12.00 — 67
LOVE IS STRANGE .... (Date 2-1574) — 3.00 — 12.00 — 67
UNITED/Thank You .... (Date 2-1603) — 3.00 — 12.00 — 68
LET'S MAKE A PROMISE .... (Date 2-1623) — 3.00 — 12.00 — 68

PEANUT BUTTER CONSPIRACY, THE
IT'S A HAPPENING THING/Twice Is Life .... (Columbia 4-43985) — 5.00 — 20.00 — 67
   (Promotional issue only)
BACK IN L.A./Have A Little Faith .... (Challenge 500) — 3.00 — 12.00 — 69

TITLE	LABEL AND NUMBER	VG	NM	YR	203

PEARL HARBOR AND THE EXPLOSIONS
DRIVIN' / Release It .... (415 Records no #)   1.25   5.00   79

PEARL JAM
LET ME SLEEP (CHRISTMAS TIME) / Ramblings .... (Epic ZS7 4354)   6.25   25.00   91
  (Promotional issue only for fan club, *Demonstration Not For Sale* printed on sleeve, issued with a small-hole
  33-1/3 RPM record)
SONIC REDUCER / Ramblings Continued .... (Epic ZS7 4906)   5.00   20.00   92
  (Promotional issue only for fan club titled *Who Killed Rudolph. Demonstration Don't Pay Money For This* printed
  on sleeve. Issued with small-hole 45 RPM record.)
ANGEL / Ramblings .... (Epic ZS7 5610)   3.75   15.00   94
  (Promotional issue only for fan club, *Demonstration–Not For Sale* printed on sleeve.)
HISTORY NEVER REPEATS / Sonic Reducer (record 1) /
  SWALLOW MY PRIDE / My Way (record 2) .... (Sony EX 77628)   3.75   15.00   95
  (Promotional issue only gatefold issued with two 45s. All songs are live versions.)
SPIN THE BLACK CIRCLE / Tremor Christ .... (Epic 34 77771)   .75   3.00   95
NOT FOR YOU .... (Epic 34 77772)   .50   2.00   95
  (Red sleeve with black Epic logos, no artist or title credited)
IMMORTALITY .... (Epic 34 77873)   .50   2.00   95
  (Black half sleeve with blue Epic logos, no artist or title credited)
I GOT ID / Long Road .... (Epic 34 78199)   .50   2.00   95
WHO ARE YOU / Habit .... (Epic 34 78389)   .50   2.00   96
OFF HE GOES / Dead Man .... (Epic 34 78491)   .50   2.00   96
  Also see Green River (Jeff Ament, Stone Gossard), Mike Watt (Edward Vedder on *Big Train*)

PEASTON, DAVID
TWO WRONGS (DON'T MAKE IT RIGHT) .... (Geffen 27518-7)   .75   3.00   89

PEBBLES
GIRLFRIEND .... (MCA 53185)   .75   3.00   87
MERCEDES BOY .... (MCA 53279)   .75   3.00   88
TAKE YOUR TIME .... (MCA 53362)   .75   3.00   88
DO ME RIGHT .... (MCA 53406)   .75   3.00   88

PEBBLES AND BAMM BAMM
(Cartoon characters from the animated television series *The Flintstones*)
OPEN UP YOUR HEART / The Lord Is Counting On You .... (HBR 449)   7.50   30.00   65

PECK, GREGORY
(Actor)
  See Maurice Jarre (*Theme From Behold A Pale Horse*)

PECK, J. EDDIE
(Actor)
  See the Soaps and Hearts Ensemble

PEEL, DAVID
AMERIKA .... (Orange 8374)   1.25   5.00   90
  (Promotional issue included with book purchase)

PEEPLES, NIA
TROUBLE / Trouble (Instrumental) .... (Mercury 870 154-7)   .75   3.00   88
I KNOW HOW (TO MAKE YOU LOVE ME) /
  I Know How (To Make You Love Me) (Rap Version) ...... (Mercury 872 066-7)   .75   3.00   88

PELL, MEL
BRING ON THE CHINA / Smoke .... (SST 913)   .75   3.00   91
  (Issued with white vinyl)

PELUSO, LISA
(Actress)
  See the Soaps and Hearts Ensemble

PENDERGRASS, TEDDY
HOLD ME / Love .... (Asylum 7-69720)   .75   3.00   84
  (Duet with Whitney Houston although she is not credited on sleeve)
SOMEWHERE I BELONG / Hot Love .... (Asylum 7-69628)   .75   3.00   85
LOVE IS THE POWER / I'm Ready .... (Elektra 7-69422)   .75   3.00   88

PENFIELD, HOLLY
ONLY HIS NAME / Eyes Behind Your Eyes .... (Dreamland 102)   1.00   4.00   80

PEPSI & SHIRLIE
HEARTACHE / Surrender .... (Polydor 885 470-7)   .75   3.00   88
  Also see Ferry Aid

PENN, MICHAEL
NO MYTH / Big House .... (RCA 9111-7-R)   .75   3.00   90

PENNARIO, LEONARD
  See the Angel Listener (*Preview Highlights*)

PEPE
(Motion Picture)
  See Duane Eddy (*Pepe*)

PEPPERMINT RAINBOW, THE
DON'T WAKE ME IN THE MORNING, MICHAEL / Rosemary .... (Decca 732498)   2.00   8.00   69

PEPSI AND SHIRLIE
HEARTACHE / Surrender .... (Polydor 885 470-7)   .75   3.00   87
ALL RIGHT NOW / Feels Like The First Time .... (Polydor 887 277-7)   .75   3.00   88

PERE UBU
30 SECONDS OVER TOKYO / Heart Of Darkness .... (Hearthan 101)   12.50   50.00   75
  (Limited edition, the first 1,000 of 3,000 45s issued with sleeves)
FINAL SOLUTION / Cloud 149 .... (Hearthan 102)   18.75   75.00   76
  (Limited edition, the first 600 of 3,000 total issued with sleeves)

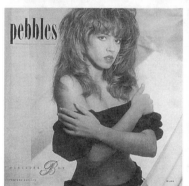

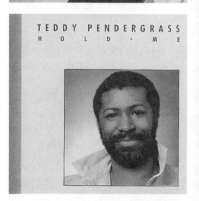

TITLE	LABEL AND NUMBER	VG	NM	YR

STREET WAVES/My Dark Ages .... (*Hearthan 103*) | 6.25 | 25.00 | 76
(Limited edition of 3,000)
THE MODERN DANCE/Heaven .... (*Hearthan 104*) | 7.50 | 30.00 | 77
(Limited edition of 1,000)
NOT HAPPY/Lonesome Cowboy Dave .... (*Rough Trade US 004*) | 2.50 | 10.00 | 81
30 SECONDS OVER TOKYO/Heart Of Darkness .... (*Hearthan 101*) | 1.00 | 4.00 | 97
(Originally included in the boxed set *The Hearpen Singles*, with "Notes" insert)
FINAL SOLUTION/Cloud 149 .... (*Hearthan 102*) | 1.00 | 4.00 | 97
(Originally included in the boxed set *The Hearpen Singles*)
STREET WAVES/My Dark Ages .... (*Hearthan 103*) | 1.00 | 4.00 | 97
(Originally included in the boxed set *The Hearpen Singles*)
THE MODERN DANCE/Heaven .... (*Hearthan 104*) | 1.00 | 4.00 | 97
(Originally included in the boxed set *The Hearpen Singles*, no artist name or song titles indicated)

BOXED SET

THE HEARPEN SINGLES .... (*Tim Kerr 957107*) | 10.00 | 40.00 | 96
(First edition. Complete set including four records in picture sleeves, explanatory insert, and cardboard box. Individually numbered edition of 2000 are identical reproductions of the original picture sleeves except they are reproduced on heavy, gloss coated paper.)
THE HEARPEN SINGLES .... (*Tim Kerr 957107*) | 7.50 | 30.00 | 97
(Second edition, identical to the first with the exception of the sticker on back indicating second edition. Complete set including four records in picture sleeves, explanatory insert, and cardboard box. Individually numbered edition of 2000 are identical reproductions of the original picture sleeves except they are reproduced on heavy, gloss coated paper.)
Also see Peter Laughner, They Might Be Giants (Tony Maimone). Anton Fier, of the Golden Palaminos, did not join Pere Ubu until 1982; after the sleeves were first issued.

PERFECT
(Motion Picture)
See Jermaine Jackson (*Perfect*)

PERKINS, AL
See Dwight Yoakam (b-side of *Santa Claus Is Back In Town*)

PERKINS, CARL
PINK PEDAL PUSHERS/Jive After Five .... (*Columbia 4-41131*) | 12.50 | 50.00 | 58
HOLLYWOOD CITY/The Fool I Used To Be .... (*Columbia 4-42405*) | 10.00 | 40.00 | 62
HAMBONE/Sister Twister .... (*Columbia 4-42514*) | 25.00 | 100.00 | 62
BIRTH OF ROCK AND ROLL/Rock And Roll (Fais Do Do) ...... (*America/Smash 884 760-7*) | 1.00 | 4.00 | 86
(B-side by Jerry Lee Lewis and Roy Orbison but not credited as such on sleeve)

PERKINS, TONY
(Actor best known for the role of Norman Bates in Alfred Hitchcock's classic *Psycho*)
INDIAN GIVER/Just Being Of Age .... (*RCA Victor 47-7155*) | 5.00 | 20.00 | 58

PERLMAN, ITZHAK
See the Angel Listener (*Preview Highlights*), Isaac Stern (*Happy Birthday, Isaac Stern*)

PERRI
I DON'T WANNA LOSE YOUR LOVE .... (*Zebra 53203*) | .75 | 3.00 | 88

PERRINE, VALERIE
(Actress)
See Village People (*Can't Stop The Music*)

PERRY, STEVE
OH SHERRIE .... (*Columbia 38-04391*) | .75 | 3.00 | 84
OH SHERRIE .... (*Columbia 38-04391*) | 1.00 | 4.00 | 84
(Promotional issue, *Demonstration Only Not For Sale* printed on sleeve)
SHE'S MINE .... (*Columbia 38-04496*) | .75 | 3.00 | 84
SHE'S MINE .... (*Columbia 38-04496*) | 1.00 | 4.00 | 84
(Promotional issue, *Demonstration Only Not For Sale* printed on sleeve)
Also see Journey, Kenny Loggins (*Don't Fight It*), U.S.A. For Africa, Voices Of America

PETER AND GORDON
NOBODY I KNOW/You Don't Have To Tell Me .... (*Capitol 5211*) | 3.00 | 12.00 | 64
I DON'T WANT TO SEE YOU AGAIN/I Would Buy You Presents .... (*Capitol 5272*) | 3.00 | 12.00 | 64
I GO TO PIECES/Love Me, Baby .... (*Capitol 5335*) | 3.00 | 12.00 | 65
TRUE LOVE WAYS/If You Wish .... (*Capitol 5406*) | 3.00 | 12.00 | 65
TO KNOW YOU IS TO LOVE YOU/I Told You So .... (*Capitol 5461*) | 3.00 | 12.00 | 65
THERE'S NO LIVING WITHOUT YOUR LOVING/Stranger With A Black Dove .... (*Capitol 5650*) | 3.00 | 12.00 | 66
TO SHOW I LOVE YOU/Start Trying Someone Else .... (*Capitol 5684*) | 3.00 | 12.00 | 66
KNIGHT IN RUSTY ARMOR/Flower Lady .... (*Capitol 5808*) | 3.00 | 12.00 | 66
SUNDAY FOR TEA/Hurtin' Is Lovin' .... (*Capitol 5864*) | 3.00 | 12.00 | 67

PETER, PAUL AND MARY
BIG BOAT/Tiny Sparrow .... (*Warner Bros. 5325*) | 3.75 | 15.00 | 62
A' SOALIN' .... (*Warner Bros. 5402*) | 3.75 | 15.00 | 64

PETERS, BERNADETTE
GEE WHIZ .... (*MCA 41210*) | 1.25 | 5.00 | 80
(Artwork by Alberto Vargas)
DEDICATED TO THE ONE I LOVE/Broadway Baby .... (*MCA 51152*) | 1.00 | 4.00 | 81
MAYBE MY BABY WILL .... (*MCA 51194*) | 1.00 | 4.00 | 81
(Artwork by Alberto Vargas)

PETERSEN, PAUL
(Juvenile actor on *The Donna Reed Show* and as a Mouseketeer on *The Mickey Mouse Club*)
SHE CAN'T FIND HER KEYS/Very Unlikely .... (*Colpix 620*) | 5.00 | 20.00 | 62
(B-side shown as by Paul Petersen & Shelley Fabares)
WHAT DID THEY DO BEFORE ROCK AND ROLL?/Very Unlikely .... (*Colpix 631*) | 15.00 | 60.00 | 62
(Shown as by Shelley Fabares With Paul Petersen)
KEEP YOUR LOVE LOCKED (DEEP IN YOUR HEART)/
Everything To Anyone You Love .... (*Colpix 632*) | 5.00 | 20.00 | 62
MY DAD/Little Boy Sad .... (*Colpix 663*) | 5.00 | 20.00 | 62

PETERSON, RAY
GOODNIGHT MY LOVE/Till Then .... (*RCA Victor 47-7635*) | 5.00 | 20.00 | 59

CORINNA, CORINNA/Be My Girl .... (Dunes 45-2002) 5.00 20.00 60
OH NO/If You Were Here .... (MGM 13269) 3.75 15.00 64
A HOUSE WITHOUT WINDOWS/Wish I Could Say No To You .... (MGM 13336) 3.75 15.00 64

PETE'S DRAGON
(Motion Picture)
    See Helen Reddy (Candle On The Water)

PET SEMATARY
(Motion Picture)
    See Ramones (Pet Sematary)

PET SHOP BOYS
WEST END GIRLS/A Man Could Get Arrested .... (EMI America B-8307) 1.25 5.00 85
OPPORTUNITIES (LET'S MAKE LOTS OF MONEY)/In The Night .... (EMI America B8321) 2.00 8.00 86
    (Withdrawn shortly after its release)
OPPORTUNITIES (LET'S MAKE LOTS OF MONEY)/Was That What It Was? (EMI America B8330) 1.00 4.00 86
    (Note the different b-side and catalog number from the previous entry)
LOVE COMES QUICKLY/That's My Impression .... (EMI America B-8338) 1.00 4.00 86
SUBURBIA/Jack The Lad .... (EMI America B8355) 1.00 4.00 86
IT'S A SIN/You Know Where You Went Wrong .... (EMI America B-43027) .75 3.00 87
WHAT HAVE I DONE TO DESERVE THIS?/A New Life .... (EMI Manhattan B-50107) .75 3.00 87
    (A-side shown as by Pet Shop Boys With Dusty Springfield, all three pictured on front)
DOMINO DANCING .... (EMI Manhattan B-50161) .75 3.00 88
LEFT TO MY OWN DEVICES/The Sound Of The Atom Splitting .... (EMI B-50171) .75 3.00 88

"What have I done to deserve this?"
Pet Shop Boys with Dusty Springfield.

PETTUS, GEORGE
MY NIGHT FOR LOVE .... (MCA 52894) .75 3.00 87
CAN YOU WAIT .... (MCA 53296) .75 3.00 88

PETTY, TOM, AND THE HEARTBREAKERS
LISTEN TO HER HEART/I Don't Know What To Say To You .... (Shelter 62011) 1.50 6.00 78
DON'T DO ME LIKE THAT/Casa Dega .... (Backstreet 41138) 1.00 4.00 79
REFUGEE/It's Rainin' Again .... (Backstreet 41169) 1.00 4.00 80
HERE COMES MY GIRL/Louisiana Rain .... (Backstreet 41227) 1.00 4.00 80
THE WAITING/Nightwatchman .... (Backstreet 51100) 1.00 4.00 81
A WOMAN IN LOVE (IT'S NOT ME)/Gator On The Lawn ...... (Backstreet 51136) 1.00 4.00 81
YOU GOT LUCKY/Between Two Worlds .... (Backstreet 52144) 1.00 4.00 82
CHANGE OF HEART/Heartbreakers Beach Party .... (Backstreet 52181) 1.00 4.00 83
    (Issued only with black vinyl. Red vinyl issued in a clear plastic sleeve with a title sticker.)
DON'T COME AROUND HERE NO MORE .... (MCA 5486) .75 3.00 84
MAKE IT BETTER (FORGET ABOUT ME)/Cracking Up ...... (MCA 52605) .75 3.00 85
REBELS .... (MCA 52658) .75 3.00 85
NEEDLES AND PINS (LIVE)/Spike (Live) .... (MCA 52772) .75 3.00 86
    (A-side shown as by Tom Petty and the Heartbreakers With Stevie Nicks)
JAMMIN' ME/Make That Connection .... (MCA 53065) .75 3.00 87
ALL MIXED UP .... (MCA 53153) .75 3.00 87
    Also see Bob Dylan (Band Of The Hand), Stevie Nicks (Stop Draggin' My Heart Around), Warren Zevon (Reconsider Me)

PEYTON PLACE
(Television Series)
    See Chris Connelly (Theme From Peyton Place)

PFEIFFER, MICHELLE
(Actress)
    See the Everly Brothers (Don't Worry Baby), the Beach Boys (Don't Worry Baby), Ann Wilson and Robin Zander (Surrender To Me)

PHAEDRA
(Motion Picture)
    See Gus Vali (Theme From Phaedra)

PHAIR, LIZ
CARNIVORE/Carnivore (Raw Version) .... (Minty Fresh 4) 2.50 10.00 93
    (Issued with either red or red/blue vinyl)
SUPERNOVA/Combo Platter .... (Matador/Atlantic OLE 103-7) 1.00 4.00 94
    (Hard cover issued with a small-hole 45 RPM blue vinyl record)

PHANTOM, THE
LOVE ME/Whisper Your Love .... (Dot 16056) 50.00 200.00 60

PHANTOM, ROCKER & SLICK
MEN WITHOUT SHAME .... (EMI America B-8292) 1.00 4.00 85
MY MISTAKE/Runnin' From The Hounds .... (EMI America B-8310) 1.00 4.00 86
    Also see Silver Condor (Earl Slick), the Stray Cats (Slim Jim Phantom, Lee Rocker)

PHILLIPS, LOU DIAMOND
(Actor)
    See Los Lobos (La Bamba), Mr. Mister (Stand And Deliver)

PHILLIPS, MICHELLE
NO LOVE TODAY/Aloha Louie .... (A&M 1824) 1.50 6.00 75
    Also see the Mamas and the Papas

PHILLIPS, PAUL
CHARLEY, MY BOY .... (Capitol CASF-4021) 2.00 8.00 58

PHILLIPS, SAM
(Also recorded earlier as Leslie Phillips but without any picture sleeves)
I DON'T KNOW HOW TO SAY GOODBYE TO YOU/Remorse ...... (Virgin 7-99301) 1.00 4.00 88

PHILLIPS, STU, AND ORCHESTRA
WILD PARTY/Intern Bash .... (Colpix 643) 1.50 6.00 63

PICKENS, SLIM
(Character Actor)
    See Wayne Newton (Stagecoach To Cheyenne)

TITLE	LABEL AND NUMBER	VG	NM	YR

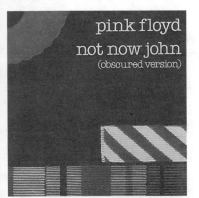

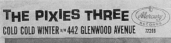

PICKETT, BOBBY (BORIS)

MONSTER MASH .... (Garpax 44167)		6.25	25.00	62
MONSTERS' HOLIDAY/Monster Motion .... (Garpax 44171)		6.25	25.00	62
(Shown as by Bobby [Boris] Pickett and the Crypt-Kickers)				
GRADUATION DAY/Humpty Dumpty .... (Garpax 44175)		6.25	25.00	63
(Shown as by Bobby Pickett)				

PICKETT, WILSON
See Elwood Blues Revue (Land Of A Thousand Dances)

PILLOW TALK
(Motion Picture)
See Doris Day (Pillow Talk)

PINK CADILLAC
(Motion Picture)
See Michael Martin Murphey (Never Givin' Up On Love), Southern Pacific (Any Way The Wind Blows)

PINK FLOYD

ARNOLD LAYNE .... (Tower 333)		200.00	800.00	67
(Promotional issue only)				
SEE EMILY PLAY .... (Tower 356)		150.00	600.00	67
(Promotional issue only, photo sleeve)				
SEE EMILY PLAY .... (Tower 356)		150.00	600.00	67
(Promotional issue only, title sleeve, no photo)				
ANOTHER BRICK IN THE WALL (Part II)/One Of My Turns .... (Columbia 1-11187)		1.25	5.00	79
WHEN THE TIGERS BROKE FREE/Bring The Boys Back Home .... (Columbia X18 03142)		1.50	6.00	82
(Fold open hard cover. Originally issued in shrink wrap with sticker stating *Limited edition collector's package with special photos from the movie*. A 50% premium would be added if the sleeve were still shrink-wrapped with sticker intact.)				
WHEN THE TIGERS BROKE FREE/Bring The Boys Back Home .... (Columbia X18 03142)		2.50	10.00	82
(Promotional issue, *Demonstration–Not For Sale* printed on sleeve. Fold open hard cover. Sleeve lists b-side even though the record has *When The Tigers Broke Free* on both sides)				
WHEN THE TIGERS BROKE FREE/Bring The Boys Back Home .... (Columbia X18 03176)		2.00	8.00	82
(Fold open hard cover. It is unknown if this sleeve is identical to *Columbia X18 03142* with the exception of the catalog number variation.)				
NOT NOW JOHN (OBSCURED VERSION)/The Hero's Return–Parts I and II . (Columbia 38-03905)		1.25	5.00	83
NOT NOW JOHN (OBSCURED VERSION) .... (Columbia AE7 1653)		2.00	8.00	83
(Promotional issue only, *Demonstration–Not For Sale* printed on sleeve. Issued with a small-hole 33-1/3 RPM record. Black and white artwork completely different from color stock sleeve.)				
LEARNING TO FLY/Terminal Frost .... (Columbia 38-07363)		1.00	4.00	87
ON THE TURNING AWAY/Run Like Hell (Live Version) .... (Columbia 38-07660)		1.00	4.00	87
Also see Syd Barrett, David Gilmour, Pete Townshend (Give Blood), Roger Waters				

PINK LADY

KISS IN THE DARK .... (Elektra/Curb 46040)		1.00	4.00	79

PINK PANTHER, THE
(Motion Picture)
See Henry Mancini (The Pink Panther Theme)

PINUPS, THE

SONG ON THE RADIO/It's Only Love .... (Columbia 18-02739)		1.00	4.00	82
SONG ON THE RADIO .... (Columbia 18-02739)		1.25	5.00	82
(Promotional issue, *Demonstration Only–Not For Sale* printed on sleeve)				

PIPES, THE

TEAMWORK .... (Carlton 575)		2.00	8.00	69

PIRATE MOVIE, THE
(Motion Picture)
See Christopher Atkins (How Can I Live Without Her)

PISCOPO, JOE

I LOVE ROCK 'N ROLL (Medley)/The First Rehearsal .... (Columbia 38-03253)		.75	3.00	82
I LOVE ROCK 'N ROLL (Medley) .... (Columbia 38-03253)		1.00	4.00	82
(Promotional issue, *Demonstration–Not For Sale* printed on sleeve)				
HONEYMOONMERS RAP/Fat Boy .... (Columbia 38-04939)		.75	3.00	85

PITNEY, GENE

I WANNA LOVE MY LIFE AWAY/I Laughed So Hard I Cried .... (Musicor 1002)		5.00	20.00	61
LOUISIANA MAMA/Take Me Tonight .... (Musicor 1006)		5.00	20.00	61
EVERY BREATH I TAKE/Mr. Moon, Mr. Cupid And I .... (Musicor 1011)		5.00	20.00	61
MECCA/Teardrop By Teardrop .... (Musicor 1028)		3.75	15.00	63
TWENTY FOUR HOURS FROM TULSA/Lonely Night Dreams Of Far Away Arms (Musicor 1034)		3.75	15.00	63
THAT GIRL BELONGS TO YESTERDAY/Who Needs It .... (Musicor 1036)		3.00	12.00	64
IT HURTS TO BE IN LOVE/Hawaii .... (Musicor 1040)		3.00	12.00	64
I'M GONNA BE STRONG/E Se Domani .... (Musicor 1045)		3.00	12.00	64
I MUST BE SEEING THINGS/Marianne .... (Musicor 1070)		2.50	10.00	65
I'M A FOOL TO CARE/Louisiana Man .... (Musicor 1097)		2.50	10.00	65
(Shown as by Gene Pitney and George Jones)				
YOUR OLD STANDBY/Big Job .... (Musicor 1115)		2.50	10.00	65
(Shown as by Gene Pitney and George Jones)				
BACKSTAGE .... (Musicor 1171)		2.50	10.00	66
COLD LIGHT OF DAY/The Boss' Daughter .... (Musicor 1200)		2.50	10.00	66
BILLY, YOU'RE MY FRIEND/Lonely Drifter .... (Musicor 1331)		2.00	8.00	68

PITTSBURGH STEELERS
See John Zov (One For The Thumb In 81)

PIXIES THREE, THE

BIRTHDAY PARTY .... (Mercury 72130)		5.00	20.00	63
COLD COLD WINTER/442 Glenwood Avenue .... (Mercury 72208)		5.00	20.00	63
IT'S SUMMERTIME U.S.A./The Hootch .... (Mercury 72288)		5.00	20.00	64

PLANES, TRAINS, AND AUTOMOBILES
(Motion Picture)
See Dave Edmunds *(Gonna Move)*

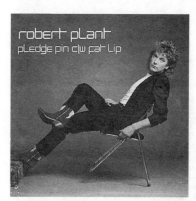

PLANET P
WHY ME?/Only You And Me .... (Geffen 29705-7) .75 3.00 83
Also see Tony Carey

PLANT, ROBERT
BURNING DOWN ONE SIDE/Moonlight In Samosa .... (Swan Song 7-99979) 1.50 6.00 82
PLEDGE PIN/Fat Lip .... (Swan Song 7-99952) 3.75 15.00 82
BIG LOG/Far Post .... (Es Paranza 7-99844) 1.00 4.00 83
IN THE MOOD/Horizontal Departure .... (Es Paranza 7-99820) 1.00 4.00 83
LITTLE BY LITTLE/Trouble Your Money .... (Es Paranza 7-99644) .75 3.00 85
TOO LOUD/Kallalou Kallalou .... (Es Paranza 7-99622) 1.50 6.00 85
HEAVEN KNOWS/Walking Towards Paradise .... (Es Paranza 7-99373) .75 3.00 88
TALL COOL ONE/White, Clean And Neat .... (Es Paranza 7-99348) 2.00 8.00 88
SHIP OF FOOLS/Billy's Revenge .... (Es Paranza 7-99333) .75 3.00 88
Also see the Honeydrippers, Led Zeppelin

PLATINUM BLONDE
CRYING OVER YOU/It Ain't Love Anyway .... (Epic 34-05593) .75 3.00 85
CRYING OVER YOU .... (Epic 34-05593) 1.00 4.00 85
(Promotional issue, *Demonstration–Not For Sale* printed on sleeve)
CONTACT/Tough Enough .... (Epic 34-07606) .75 3.00 87

PLATOON
(Motion Picture)
See the Miracles *(The Tracks Of My Tears)*, Percy Sledge *(When A Man Loves A Woman)*

PLATTERS, THE
HARBOR LIGHTS/Sleepy Lagoon .... (Mercury 71563) 5.00 20.00 60
RED SAILS IN THE SUNSET/Sad River .... (Mercury 71656) 5.00 20.00 60
TO EACH HIS OWN/Down The River Of Golden Dreams .... (Mercury 71697) 5.00 20.00 60
IF I DIDN'T CARE/True Lover .... (Mercury 71749) 3.75 15.00 61
TREES/Immortal Love .... (Mercury 71791) 3.75 15.00 61
I'LL NEVER SMILE AGAIN/You Don't Say .... (Mercury 71847) 3.75 15.00 61
SONG FOR THE LONELY/You'll Never Know .... (Mercury 71904) 3.75 15.00 62
IT'S MAGIC/Reaching For A Star .... (Mercury 71921) 3.75 15.00 62
MORE THAN YOU KNOW/Every Little Moment .... (Mercury 71986) 3.75 15.00 62
MEMORIES/Heartbreak .... (Mercury 72060) 3.75 15.00 63
ONCE IN A WHILE/I'll See You In My Dreams .... (Mercury 72107) 3.75 15.00 63
SINCERELY/P.S. I Love You .... (Mercury 72305) 3.75 15.00 63

PLAYING FOR KEEPS
(Motion Picture)
See Arcadia *(Say The Word)*

PLEASE DON'T EAT THE DAISIES
(Motion Picture)
See Doris Day *(Please Don't Eat The Daisies)*

PLIMSOULS, THE
A MILLION MILES AWAY/I'll Get Lucky .... (Shaky City 134) 2.00 8.00 82
A MILLION MILES AWAY/Play The Breaks .... (Geffen 29600-7) 1.25 5.00 83

PM
PIECE OF PARADISE .... (Warner Bros. 27779-7) .75 3.00 88

POCO
MY KIND OF LOVE/Hard Luck .... (Epic 10543) 1.50 6.00 70
UNDER THE GUN .... (MCA 41269) 1.00 4.00 80
GHOST TOWN/High Sierra (Instrumental) .... (Atlantic 7-89970) 1.00 4.00 82
CALL IT LOVE/Lovin' You Every Minute .... (RCA 9038-7-R) .75 3.00 89
NOTHIN' TO HIDE/If It Wasn't For You .... (RCA 9131-7-R) .75 3.00 89
Also see the Eagles (Timothy B. Schmit), the Illinois Speed Press (Paul Cotton), Randy Meisner, Loggins and Messina(Jim Messina), Timothy B. Schmit

POGUES, THE
See Shane MacGowan. Joe Strummer, of the Clash, was a member from 1991-1992.

POINDEXTER, BUSTER
(David Johansen)
HOT HOT HOT/Cannibal .... (RCA 5357-7) .75 3.00 87
(Shown as by Buster Poindexter And His Banshees Of Blue)
OH ME OH MY (I'M A FOOL FOR YOU BABY)/Cannibal .... (RCA 7638-7-R1) .75 3.00 88
(Shown as by Buster Poindexter And His Banshees Of Blue)
HIT THE ROAD JACK/Heart Of Gold .... (RCA 8914-7-R) .75 3.00 89
(Shown as by Buster Poindexter And His Banshees Of Blue. From the motion picture *The Dream Team*, Christopher Lloyd, Michael Keaton, Peter Boyle, and Christopher Furst pictured on back.)
ALL NIGHT PARTY/All Night Party (Power Mix) .... (RCA 9007-7-R) .75 3.00 89
Also see David Johansen, the New York Dolls

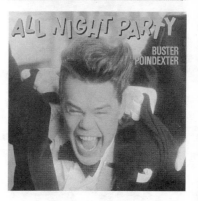

POINTER, BONNIE
FREE ME FROM MY FREEDOM/TIE ME TO A TREE (HANDCUFF ME) .... (Motown 1451F) 1.25 5.00 78
(Issued with either stock black or promotional red vinyl)
THE BEAST IN ME .... (Private I ZS4-04819) .75 3.00 85
(From the motion picture *Heavenly Bodies*, Cynthia Dale pictured on front)
THE BEAST IN ME .... (Private I ZS4-04819) 1.00 4.00 85
(Promotional issue, *Demonstration Only–Not For Sale* printed on sleeve. From the motion picture *Heavenly Bodies*, Cynthia Dale pictured on front.)
Bonnie Pointer left the Pointer Sisters in 1978, before any sleeves were released.

TITLE	LABEL AND NUMBER	VG	NM	YR

POINTER SISTERS
FIRE .... (Planet P-45901)		1.25	5.00	78
(Non-glossy uncoated paper)				
FIRE .... (Planet P-45901)		1.00	4.00	78
(Glossy coated paper)				
BABY COME AND GET IT/Operator .... (Planet YD-14042)		1.00	4.00	85
(Record bears the catalog number YB-14041)				
DARE ME .... (RCA PB-14126)		.75	3.00	85
TWIST MY ARM .... (RCA PB-14197)		.75	3.00	85
FREEDOM .... (RCA PB-14224)		.75	3.00	85
GOLDMINE/Sexual Power .... (RCA 5062-7-R)		.75	3.00	86
BE THERE .... (MCA 53120)		.75	3.00	87
(From the motion picture *Beverly Hills Cop II*, Eddie Murphy pictured)				
HE TURNED ME OUT/Translation .... (RCA 6865-7-R)		.75	3.00	88
(A-side from the motion picture *Action Jackson*, Carl Weathers and Vanity pictured on back.)				
POWER OF PERSUASION .... (Columbia 38-08015)		.75	3.00	88
Also see U.S.A. For Africa, Voices Of America				

POISON
TALK DIRTY TO ME .... (Capitol/Enigma B-5686)		1.00	4.00	86
I WANT ACTION .... (Capitol/Enigma B-44004)		1.25	5.00	86
(Poster sleeve)				
I WON'T FORGET YOU .... (Enigma/Capitol B-44038)		.75	3.00	87
NOTHIN' BUT A GOOD TIME .... (Enigma/Capitol B-44145)		.75	3.00	88
FALLEN ANGEL .... (Enigma/Capitol B-44191)		.75	3.00	88
EVERY ROSE HAS ITS THORN .... (Enigma/Capitol B-44203)		.75	3.00	88
YOUR MAMA DON'T DANCE .... (Enigma/Capitol B-44293)		.75	3.00	89

POLICE, THE
CAN'T STAND LOSING YOU/No Time This Time .... (A&M 2147)		2.50	10.00	79
MESSAGE IN A BOTTLE/Landlord (Live) .... (A&M 2190)		1.50	6.00	79
MESSAGE IN A BOTTLE/Landlord (Live) .... (A&M 2190)		2.50	10.00	79
(Poster sleeve)				
DE DO DO DO, DE DA DA DA/Friends .... (A&M 2275)		1.25	5.00	80
(Standard sleeve with group name and song titles)				
DE DO DO DO, DE DA DA DA/Friends .... (A&M 2275)		1.00	4.00	80
(Half sleeve with group name only. No song titles or catalog number indicated.)				
DON'T STAND SO CLOSE TO ME/A Sermon .... (A&M 2301)		1.00	4.00	81
EVERY LITTLE THING SHE DOES IS MAGIC/Shambelle .... (A&M 2371)		.75	3.00	81
SPIRITS IN THE MATERIAL WORLD/Flexible Strategies .... (A&M 2390)		.75	3.00	81
SECRET JOURNEY/Darkness .... (A&M 2408)		.75	3.00	82
EVERY BREATH YOU TAKE/Murder By Numbers .... (A&M 2542)		.75	3.00	83
KING OF PAIN/Someone To Talk To .... (A&M 2569)		.75	3.00	83
SYNCHRONICITY II/Once Upon A Daydream .... (A&M 2571)		.75	3.00	83
WRAPPED AROUND YOUR FINGER/Tea In The Sahara (Live) ..... (A&M 2614)		.75	3.00	83
DON'T STAND SO CLOSE TO ME '86/Don't Stand So Close To Me–Live ..... (A&M 2879)		.75	3.00	86
WALKING ON THE MOON/Message In A Bottle .... (A&M 2908)		1.25	5.00	86
Also see Stewart Copeland, Klark Kent (Stewart Copeland), Sting, Andy Summers				

POLYROCK
ROMANTIC ME/Your Dragging Feet .... (RCA PB-12141)		1.00	4.00	80

POMERANZ, DAVID, & SASHA MALININ
FAR AWAY LANDS .... (Cypress 661 126-7)		.75	3.00	85

PONCE, PONCIE
(Appeared in the television series *Hawaiian Eye* which aired from 1959-1963)
TEN CENT PERFUME/No Hu Hu (I Don't Care) .... (Warner Bros. 5244)		5.00	20.00	61

POOR COW
(Motion Picture)
    See Donovan (*Jennifer Juniper*)

POP, IGGY
CRY FOR LOVE/Winners And Losers .... (A&M 2874)		1.00	4.00	86
REAL WILD CHILD (WILD ONE)/Little Miss Emperor .... (A&M 2909)		1.00	4.00	86
PUSSY WALK/I Wanna Be Your Dog .... (Virgin 7PRO 11094)		2.00	8.00	96
(Promotional issue only, live at the Rock For Choice Benefit concert)				
Also see Iggy and the Stooges				

POP ART, THE
RUMPELSTILTSKIN .... (Epic # unknown)		1.25	5.00	

POPEYE
(Motion Picture)
    See Robin Williams (*I Yam What I Yam*)

POPP, ANDRE
THE WALTZ WITH A THOUSAND BEATS .... (Columbia 4-41570)		2.00	8.00	61

POPPEES
JEALOUSY/She's Got It .... (Bomp 106)		1.00	4.00	78

POPPIES, THE
HE'S READY .... (Epic 10019)		3.00	12.00	68

POPS AND 'TIMER
TELL ME SOMETHING SLICK .... (Warner Bros. 28725-7)		.75	3.00	86
(From the motion picture *Blue City*, Ally Sheedy and Judd Nelson pictured)				

PORKY'S REVENGE!
(Motion Picture)
    See Dave Edmunds (*High School Nights*)

PORTER, ROBIE
I HAVEN'T GOT ANYTHING BETTER TO DO .... (MGM K-13701)		2.00	8.00	67

PORTNOY, GARY
THEME FROM CHEERS (WHERE EVERYBODY KNOWS YOUR NAME) .... (Earthtone 7004)   2.00   8.00   82
     (From the television series *Cheers*)

POSEY, SANDY
SINGLE GIRL / Blue Is My Best Color .... (MGM K-13612)   2.00   8.00   66
I TAKE IT BACK / The Boy I Love .... (MGM K-13744)   2.00   8.00   67

POST, MIKE
THE THEME FROM HILL STREET BLUES / Aaron's Tune .... (Elektra 47186)   1.25   5.00   81
     (Shown as by Mike Post Featuring Larry Carlton. From the television series *Hill Street Blues*.)
THEME FROM MAGNUM P.I. / Gumbus Red .... (Elektra 47400)   2.00   8.00   82
     (From the television series *Magnum P.I.*, Tom Selleck and Mike Post pictured)
THEME FROM L.A. LAW / Jenny's Ayre .... (Polydor 887-145-7)   1.25   5.00   87
     (From the television series *L.A. Law*)

POSTER CHILDREN
POINTED STICK / Thinner-Stronger .... (Sub Pop 88)   1.25   5.00   90
     (Limited edition of 4,500 with the first 3,000 on bright pink vinyl and the remaining 1,500 on black)

POURCEL, FRANK
I ONLY WANT TO SAY (GETHSEMANE) .... (Paramount 0151)   1.50   6.00   69
     (From the Rock Opera *Jesus Christ Superstar*. Sleeve features a quote from Tim Rice and Andrew Lloyd Weber.)

POWELL, DOC
WHAT'S GOING ON / What I Like .... (Mercury 888 843-7)   .75   3.00   87

POWELL, JANE
(Actress/Entertainer)
THE WAY OF LIFE / Jamie .... (Ranwood 825)   1.50   6.00   76

POWERS, STEFANIE
(Actress)
See Wayne Newton (*Stagecoach To Cheyenne*)

POWERS, WILL
ADVENTURES IN SUCCESS .... (Island 7-99868)   .75   3.00   83
     (Song was co-written by Robert Palmer and Sting)

POWER STATION, THE
SOME LIKE IT HOT / The Heat Is On (Instrumental) .... (Capitol B-5444)   .75   3.00   85
GET IT ON .... (Capitol B-5479)   .75   3.00   85
COMMUNICATION .... (Capitol B-5511)   .75   3.00   85
     Also see Chic (Tony Thompson), Duran Duran (Andy and John Taylor), Robert Palmer, Andy Taylor, John Taylor

PRADO, PEREZ
MY ROBERTA / Tic Toc Polly Woc .... (RCA Victor 47-7540)   2.50   10.00   59
TERESITA LA CHUNGA / .... (RCA Victor 47-7873)   2.00   8.00   61
PRAIRIE CHIEFS, THE
BROKEN ARROW / Sweet Betsy From Pike .... (RCA Victor Bluebird WBY-69)   2.50   10.00   57
     (Children's series, from the television series *Broken Arrow*)

PRATT, ANDY
EXTENDED PLAYS
AVENGING ANNIE .... (Columbia AS 53)   1.50   6.00   73
     (Promotional issue only titled *New Comers As Featured In New Ingenue In August*, issued with a small-hole
     33-1/3 RPM record. Also includes one song each by Looking Glass, Johnny Nash, and Jimmie Spheeris.)
     Also see Bruce Springsteen (*Blinded By The Light-Playback*)

PREFAB SPROUT
WHEN LOVE BREAKS DOWN / The Yearning Loins .... (Epic 34-05464)   .75   3.00   85
WHEN LOVE BREAKS DOWN .... (Epic 34-05464)   1.00   4.00   85
     (Promotional issue, *Demonstration–Not For Sale* printed on sleeve)
APPETITE / When The Angels .... (Epic 34-05769)   .75   3.00   85
APPETITE .... (Epic 34-05769)   1.00   4.00   85
     (Promotional issue, *Demonstration Not For Sale* printed on sleeve)
CARS AND GIRLS / Vendetta .... (Epic 34-07922)   .75   3.00   88

PRENTISS, PAULA
(Actress)
See Connie Francis (*Where The Boys Are*)

PRESIDENTS OF THE UNITED STATES OF AMERICA, THE
PEACHES / Video Killed The Radio Star .... (Dry Hump 018)   .75   3.00   96
     (Hard cover with small-hole 45 RPM yellow vinyl)
     Also see Love Battery (Jason Finn)

PRESLEY, ELVIS
I WANT YOU, I NEED YOU, I LOVE YOU / My Baby Left Me .... (RCA Victor 47-6540)   300.00   1200.00   56
     (Promotional issue only "This Is His Life" cartoon strip style sleeve. No song titles or catalog number
     indicated.)
DON'T BE CRUEL / Hound Dog! .... (RCA Victor 47-6604)   25.00   100.00   56
     (*Don't Be Cruel* listed first)
HOUND DOG! / Don't Be Cruel .... (RCA Victor 47-6604)   18.75   75.00   56
     (*Hound Dog!* listed first)
LOVE ME TENDER / Any Way You Want Me (That's How I Will Be) .... (RCA Victor 47-6643)   37.50   150.00   56
     (Black and white)
LOVE ME TENDER / Any Way You Want Me (That's How I Will Be) .... (RCA Victor 47-6643)   18.75   75.00   56
     (Black and green)
LOVE ME TENDER / Any Way You Want Me (That's How I Will Be) .... (RCA Victor 47-6643)   10.00   40.00   56
     (Black and dark pink)
LOVE ME TENDER / Any Way You Want Me (That's How I Will Be) .... (RCA Victor 47-6643)   7.50   30.00   56
     (Black and light pink)
TOO MUCH / Playing For Keeps .... (RCA Victor 47-6800)   15.00   60.00   57
ALL SHOOK UP / That's When Your Heartache Begins .... (RCA Victor 47-6870)   15.00   60.00   57

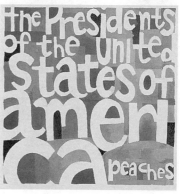

TITLE	LABEL AND NUMBER	VG	NM	YR

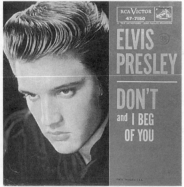

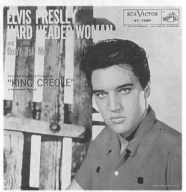

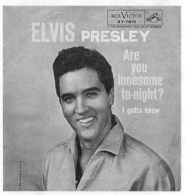

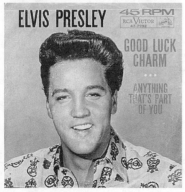

TREAT ME NICE/Nellie Was A Lady .... (Laurel 41 623) 1250.00 5000.00 57
(Black and white sheet affixed to a cardboard cover, no record exists. Made as a prop for the film Jailhouse Rock starring Presley. Shown as by Vince Everett but pictures Presley.)

JAILHOUSE ROCK/Baby I Don't Care .... (Laurel 41 624) 25.00 100.00 57
(Black and white sheet affixed to a cardboard cover, no record exists. Possibly made as a prop for the film Jailhouse Rock, but it's authenticity is in doubt. Shown as by Vince Everett but pictures Presley.)

YOUNG AND BEAUTIFUL/Don't Leave Me Now .... (Laurel 41 625) 25.00 100.00 57
(Black and white sheet affixed to a cardboard cover, no record exists. Possibly made as a prop for the film Jailhouse Rock, but it's authenticity is in doubt. Shown as by Vince Everett but pictures Presley.)

TEDDY BEAR/Loving You .... (RCA Victor 47-7000) 15.00 60.00 57

JAILHOUSE ROCK/Treat Me Nice .... (RCA Victor 47-7035) 15.00 60.00 57
(From the motion picture Jailhouse Rock starring Presley)

JAILHOUSE ROCK MEDIA PREVIEW .... (RCA Victor 47-7035) 375.00 1500.00 57
(Promotional issue only theatre ticket/sleeve created for the media preview of the film. Issued with the Jailhouse Rock sleeve and record. Deduct 50% if the ticket stub has been detached.)

DON'T/I Beg Of You .... (RCA Victor 47-7150) 12.50 50.00 58

WEAR MY RING AROUND YOUR NECK/Doncha' Think It's Time .... (RCA Victor 47-7240) 12.50 50.00 58

HARD HEADED WOMAN/Don't Ask Me Why .... (RCA Victor 47-7280) 12.50 50.00 58

ONE NIGHT/I Got Stung .... (RCA Victor 47-7410) 12.50 50.00 58

I NEED YOUR LOVE TONIGHT/A Fool Such As I .... (RCA Victor 47-7506) 200.00 800.00 58
(Back of sleeve advertises the Elvis Sails EP. Record shows the b-side title as [Now And Then There's] A Fool Such As I. The a-side made it to #4 on the Billboard charts while the b-side rose slightly higher to #2. Previously published values range from $500-$2000 and this averages those prices.)

I NEED YOUR LOVE TONIGHT/A Fool Such As I .... (RCA Victor 47-7506) 12.50 50.00 58
(Back of sleeve lists Presley EPs and Gold Standard singles. Record shows the b-side title as [Now And Then There's] A Fool Such As I. The a-side made it to #4 on the Billboard charts while the b-side rose slightly higher to #2.)

A BIG HUNK O' LOVE/My Wish Came True .... (RCA Victor 47-7600) 10.00 40.00 59

STUCK ON YOU/Fame And Fortune .... (RCA Victor 47-7740) 7.50 30.00 60
(Half sleeve with no song title listed. Sleeve reads Elvis' 1st New Recording For His 50,000,000 Fans All Over The World.)

IT'S NOW OR NEVER/A Mess Of Blues .... (RCA Victor 47-7777) 7.50 30.00 60

ARE YOU LONESOME TO-NIGHT?/I Gotta Know .... (RCA Victor 47-7810) 7.50 30.00 60

DON'T/Wear My Ring Around Your Neck .... (RCA Victor SP-45-76) 375.00 1500.00 60
(Promotional issue only)

SURRENDER/Lonely Man .... (RCA Victor 47-7850) 7.50 30.00 61
(B-side from the motion picture Wild In The Country starring Presley)

SURRENDER/Lonely Man .... (RCA Victor 37-7850) 250.00 1000.00 61
(Issued with Compact 33 Single. B-side from the motion picture Wild In The Country starring Presley.)

I FEEL SO BAD/Wild In The Country .... (RCA Victor 47-7880) 7.50 30.00 61
(B-side from the motion picture Wild In The Country starring Presley)

I FEEL SO BAD/Wild In The Country .... (RCA Victor 37-7880) 300.00 1200.00 61
(Issued with Compact 33 Single. B-side from the motion picture Wild In The Country starring Presley.)

HIS LATEST FLAME/Little Sister .... (RCA Victor 47-7908) 7.50 30.00 61
(Record shows a-side title as [Marie's The Name] His Latest Flame)

HIS LATEST FLAME/Little Sister .... (RCA Victor 37-7908) 500.00 2000.00 61
(Issued with Compact 33 Single. Record shows a-side title as [Marie's The Name] His Latest Flame. Sleeve correctly states "New-Orthophonic" in upper right.)

HIS LATEST FLAME/Little Sister .... (RCA Victor 37-7908) 550.00 2200.00 61
(Issued with Compact 33 Single. Record shows a-side title as [Marie's The Name] His Latest Flame. Sleeve erroneously states "Stereo-Orthophonic" in upper right.)

CAN'T HELP FALLING IN LOVE/Rock-a-Hula Baby .... (RCA Victor 47-7968) 6.25 25.00 61
(From the motion picture Blue Hawaii starring Presley)

CAN'T HELP FALLING IN LOVE/Rock-a-Hula Baby .... (RCA Victor 37-7968) 1000.00 4000.00 61
(Issued with Compact 33 Single. From the motion picture Blue Hawaii starring Presley.)

GOOD LUCK CHARM/Anything That's Part Of You .... (RCA Victor 47-7992) 6.25 25.00 62
(Song titles in blue and pink)

GOOD LUCK CHARM/Anything That's Part Of You .... (RCA Victor 47-7992) 6.25 25.00 62
(Song titles in rust and lavender)

GOOD LUCK CHARM/Anything That's Part Of You .... (RCA Victor 37-7992) 1250.00 5000.00 62
(Issued with Compact 33 Single)

SHE'S NOT YOU/Just Tell Her Jim Said Hello .... (RCA Victor 47-8041) 6.25 25.00 62

KING OF THE WHOLE WIDE WORLD/Home Is Where The Heart Is .... (RCA Victor SP-45-118) 50.00 200.00 62
(Promotional issue only with "Deejay Notes from RCA Victor" publicity sheet. A paragraph is devoted to each of the following: Elvis, Jimmy Elledge, and Sam Fletcher. This insert has minimal value because it is very difficult to distinguish photocopies from the originals.)

RETURN TO SENDER/Where Do You Come From .... (RCA Victor 47-8100) 6.25 25.00 62
(From the motion picture Girls! Girls! Girls! starring Presley)

ONE BROKEN HEART FOR SALE/They Remind Me Too Much Of You .... (RCA Victor 47-8134) 5.00 20.00 63
(From the motion picture It Happened At The World's Fair starring Presley)

(YOU'RE THE) DEVIL IN DISGUISE/Please Don't Drag That String Around (RCA Victor 47-8188) 5.00 20.00 63

BOSSA NOVA BABY/Witchcraft .... (RCA Victor 47-8243) 5.00 20.00 63
(Bottom of sleeve reads Coming Soon! "Fun In Acapulco" LP Album. A-side from the motion picture Fun In Acapulco starring Presley.)

BOSSA NOVA BABY/Witchcraft .... (RCA Victor 47-8243) 5.00 20.00 63
(Bottom of sleeve reads Ask For "Fun In Acapulco" LP Album. A-side from the motion picture Fun In Acapulco starring Presley.)

BOSSA NOVA BABY/Witchcraft .... (RCA Victor 47-8243) 5.00 20.00 63
(No mention of "Fun In Acapulco". A-side from the motion picture Fun In Acapulco starring Presley.)

KISSIN' COUSINS/It Hurts Me .... (RCA Victor 47-8307) 5.00 20.00 64
(A-side from the motion picture Kissin' Cousins starring Presley)

VIVA LAS VEGAS/What'd I Say .... (RCA Victor 47-8360) 5.00 20.00 64
(Coming Soon version at bottom. From the motion picture Viva Las Vegas starring Presley. The a-side made it to #29 on the Billboard charts while the b-side rose higher to #21.)

VIVA LAS VEGAS/What'd I Say .... (RCA Victor 47-8360) 10.00 40.00 64
(Ask For version at bottom. From the motion picture Viva Las Vegas starring Presley. The a-side made it to #29 on the Billboard charts while the b-side rose higher to #21.)

SUCH A NIGHT/Never Ending .... (RCA Victor 47-8400) 5.00 20.00 64

AIN'T THAT LOVING YOU BABY/Ask Me .... (RCA Victor 47-8440) 5.00 20.00 64
(Bottom of sleeve reads Coming Soon! 'Roustabout' LP Album. The a-side made it to #16 on the Billboard charts while the b-side rose higher to #12.)

AIN'T THAT LOVING YOU BABY/Ask Me .... (RCA Victor 47-8440) 5.00 20.00 64
(Bottom of sleeve reads Ask For 'Roustabout' LP Album. The a-side made it to #16 on the Billboard charts while the b-side rose higher to #12.)

DO THE CLAM/You'll Be Gone .... (RCA Victor 47-8500) 5.00 20.00 65

TITLE	LABEL AND NUMBER	VG	NM	YR
(SUCH AN) EASY QUESTION / It Feels So Right .... (RCA Victor 47-8585)		5.00	20.00	65

(Bottom of sleeve reads *Coming Soon! Special Tickle Me EP*. From the motion picture *Tickle Me* starring Presley.)

| (SUCH AN) EASY QUESTION / It Feels So Right .... (RCA Victor 47-8585) | | 5.00 | 20.00 | 65 |

(Bottom of sleeve reads *Ask For Special Tickle Me EP*. From the motion picture *Tickle Me* starring Presley.)

I'M YOURS / (It's A) Long Lonely Highway .... (RCA Victor 47-8657)		5.00	20.00	65
TELL ME WHY / Blue River .... (RCA Victor 47-8740)		5.00	20.00	65
FRANKIE AND JOHNNY / Please Don't Stop Loving Me .... (RCA Victor 47-8780)		5.00	20.00	66
SPECIAL EASTER PROGRAMMING KIT .... (RCA Victor no #)		250.00	1000.00	66

(Compete kit including the promotional singles *Joshua Fit The Battle* and *Milky White Way* in Gold Standard picture sleeves, mailer envelope, and an Easter greeting card from Presley. Approximately 80-90% is for the mailer itself.)

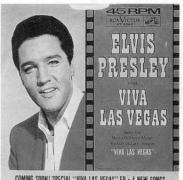

| LOVE LETTERS / Come What May .... (RCA Victor 47-8870) | | 5.00 | 20.00 | 66 |

(Bottom of sleeve reads *Coming Soon–Paradise Hawaiian Style*)

| LOVE LETTERS / Come What May .... (RCA Victor 47-8870) | | 5.00 | 20.00 | 66 |

(Bottom of sleeve reads *Ask For–Paradise Hawaiian Style*)

| COULD I FALL IN LOVE .... (Peca no #) | | 750.00 | 3000.00 | 66 |

(Color sleeve made as a prop for the film *Double Trouble*, no record exists. Shown as by Guy Lambert With George and His G-Men.)

| SPINOUT / All That I Am .... (RCA Victor 47-8941) | | 5.00 | 20.00 | 66 |

(Bottom of sleeve reads *Watch For Elvis' Spinout LP*. From the motion picture *Spinout* starring Presley.)

| SPINOUT / All That I Am .... (RCA Victor 47-8941) | | 5.00 | 20.00 | 66 |

(Bottom of sleeve reads *Ask For Elvis' Spinout LP*. From the motion picture *Spinout* starring Presley.)

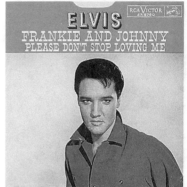

| IF EVERY DAY WAS LIKE CHRISTMAS / How Would You Like To Be .... (RCA Victor 47-8950) | | 7.50 | 30.00 | 66 |

(B-side from the motion picture *It Happened At The World's Fair* starring Presley)

| INDESCRIBABLY BLUE / Fools Fall In Love .... (RCA Victor 47-9056) | | 5.00 | 20.00 | 67 |
| HOW GREAT THOU ART / So High .... (RCA Victor SP-45-162) | | 50.00 | 200.00 | 67 |

(Promotional issue only, *Not For Sale* printed on front)

| LONG LEGGED GIRL (WITH THE SHORT DRESS ON) / That's Someone You Never Forget .... (RCA Victor 47-9115) | | 5.00 | 20.00 | 67 |

(Bottom of sleeve reads *Coming Soon–Double Trouble LP Album*. A-side from the motion picture *Double Trouble*.)

| LONG LEGGED GIRL (WITH THE SHORT DRESS ON) / That's Someone You Never Forget .... (RCA Victor 47-9115) | | 5.00 | 20.00 | 67 |

(Bottom of sleeve reads *Ask For–Double Trouble LP Album*. A-side from the motion picture *Double Trouble* starring Presley.)

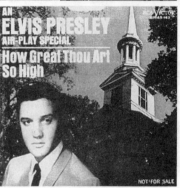

| THERE'S ALWAYS ME / Judy .... (RCA Victor 47-9287) | | 5.00 | 20.00 | 67 |

(The a-side made it to #78 on the Billboard charts while the b-side rose higher to #56)

| BIG BOSS MAN / You Don't Know Me .... (RCA Victor 47-9341) | | 5.00 | 20.00 | 67 |

(From the motion picture soundtrack *Clambake*, starring Presley, but not included in the film)

| GUITAR MAN / High Heel Sneakers .... (RCA Victor 47-9425) | | 5.00 | 20.00 | 67 |

(Bottom of sleeve reads *Coming Soon, Elvis' Gold Records, Volume 4*. A-side from the motion picture soundtrack *Clambake* but not included in the film.)

| GUITAR MAN / High Heel Sneakers .... (RCA Victor 47-9425) | | 5.00 | 20.00 | 67 |

(Bottom of sleeve reads *Ask For Elvis' Gold Records, Volume 4*. A-side from the motion picture soundtrack *Clambake* but not included in the film.)

| U. S. MALE / Stay Away .... (RCA Victor 47-9465) | | 5.00 | 20.00 | 68 |

(B-side from the motion picture *Stay Away, Joe* starring Presley)

| YOUR TIME HASN'T COME YET, BABY / Let Yourself Go .... (RCA Victor 47-9547) | | 5.00 | 20.00 | 68 |

(Bottom of sleeve reads *Coming Soon–Speedway LP*. From the motion picture *Speedway* starring Presley. The a-side made it to #72 on the Billboard charts while the b-side rose slightly higher to #71.)

| YOUR TIME HASN'T COME YET, BABY / Let Yourself Go .... (RCA Victor 47-9547) | | 5.00 | 20.00 | 68 |

(Bottom of sleeve reads *Ask For–Speedway LP*. From the motion picture *Speedway* starring Presley. The a-side made it to #72 on the Billboard charts while the b-side rose slightly higher to #71.)

| YOU'LL NEVER WALK ALONE / We Call On Him .... (RCA Victor 47-9600) | | 15.00 | 60.00 | 68 |
| ALMOST IN LOVE / A Little Less Conversation .... (RCA Victor 47-9610) | | 5.00 | 20.00 | 68 |

(From the motion picture *Live A Little, Love A Little* starring Presley. The a-side made it to #95 on the Billboard charts while the b-side rose higher to #69.)

| IF I CAN DREAM / Edge Of Reality .... (RCA Victor 47-9670) | | 3.75 | 15.00 | 68 |

(Sleeve reads *As Featured On His NBC-TV Special* although this version was not from the televised performance. The TV version was never officially released.)

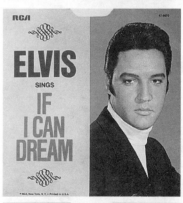

| IF I CAN DREAM / Edge Of Reality .... (RCA Victor 47-9670) | | 3.75 | 15.00 | 68 |

(No reference to Elvis' TV special)

| MEMORIES / Charro .... (RCA Victor 47-9731) | | 3.75 | 15.00 | 69 |

(A-side from the NBC-TV special *Elvis*)

| HOW GREAT THOU ART / His Hand In Mine .... (RCA Victor 74-0130) | | 37.50 | 150.00 | 69 |
| IN THE GHETTO / Any Day Now .... (RCA Victor 47-9741) | | 3.75 | 15.00 | 69 |

(Bottom of sleeve reads *Coming Soon "From Elvis In Memphis" LP Album*)

| IN THE GHETTO / Any Day Now .... (RCA Victor 47-9741) | | 3.75 | 15.00 | 69 |

(Bottom of sleeve reads *Ask For "From Elvis In Memphis" LP Album*)

| CLEAN UP YOUR OWN BACK YARD / The Fair Is Moving On .... (RCA Victor 47-9747) | | 3.75 | 15.00 | 69 |

(A-side from the motion picture *The Trouble With Girls* starring Presley)

| SUSPICIOUS MINDS / You'll Think Of Me .... (RCA Victor 47-9764) | | 3.57 | 15.00 | 69 |
| DON'T CRY DADDY / Rubberneckin' .... (RCA Victor 47-9768) | | 3.00 | 12.00 | 69 |

(From the motion picture *Change Of Habit* starring Presley)

KENTUCKY RAIN / My Little Friend .... (RCA Victor 47-9791)		3.00	12.00	70
WONDER OF YOU / Mama Liked The Roses .... (RCA Victor 47-9835)		3.00	12.00	70
I'VE LOST YOU / The Next Step Is Love .... (RCA Victor 47-9873)		3.00	12.00	70
YOU DON'T HAVE TO SAY YOU LOVE ME / Patch It Up .... (RCA Victor 47-9916)		3.00	12.00	70
I REALLY DON'T WANT TO KNOW / There Goes My Everything .... (RCA Victor 47-9960)		3.00	12.00	70

(Sleeve reads *Coming Soon–New Album*)

| I REALLY DON'T WANT TO KNOW / There Goes My Everything .... (RCA Victor 47-9960) | | 3.00 | 12.00 | 71 |

(Sleeve reads *Now Available–New Album*)

WHERE DID THEY GO, LORD / Rags To Riches .... (RCA Victor 47-9980)		3.75	15.00	71
LIFE / Only Believe .... (RCA Victor 47-9985)		7.50	30.00	71
I'M LEAVIN' / Heart Of Rome .... (RCA Victor 47-9998)		3.75	15.00	71
IT'S ONLY LOVE / The Sound Of Your Cry .... (RCA Victor 48-1017)		3.00	12.00	71
MERRY CHRISTMAS BABY / O Come, All Ye Faithful .... (RCA Victor 74-0572)		7.50	30.00	71
UNTIL IT'S TIME FOR YOU TO GO / We Can Make The Morning .... (RCA 74-0619)		3.00	12.00	72
HE TOUCHED ME / Bosom Of Abraham .... (RCA 74-0651)		30.00	120.00	72
AN AMERICAN TRILOGY / The First Time Ever I Saw Your Face .... (RCA 74-0672)		6.25	25.00	72
BURNING LOVE / It's A Matter Of Time .... (RCA 74-0769)		3.00	12.00	72
SEPARATE WAYS / Always On My Mind .... (RCA 74-0815)		3.00	12.00	72

(A-side from the motion picture *Elvis On Tour*)

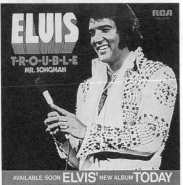

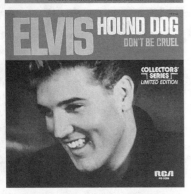

TITLE	LABEL AND NUMBER	VG	NM	YR
STEAMROLLER BLUES/Fool	(RCA 74-0910)	3.00	12.00	73
(A-side from the television special *Aloha From Hawaii Via Satellite*)				
RAISED ON ROCK/For Ol' Times Sake	(RCA APBO-0088)	3.00	12.00	73
I'VE GOT A THING ABOUT YOU BABY/Take Good Care Of Her	(RCA APBO-0196)	3.00	12.00	74
IF YOU TALK IN YOUR SLEEP/Help Me	(RCA APBO-0280)	3.00	12.00	74
PROMISED LAND/It's Midnight	(RCA PB-10074)	2.50	10.00	74
MY BOY	(RCA 2458EX)	37.50	150.00	74
(Green and black single sheet insert, printed on one side, meant to accompany *My Boy/Loving Arms* overseas. Not a picture sleeve but listed to distinguish it from *My Boy/Thinking About You*.)				
MY BOY/Thinking About You	(RCA PB-10191)	2.50	10.00	75
T-R-O-U-B-L-E/Mr. Songman	(RCA PB-10278)	2.50	10.00	75
BRINGING IT BACK/Pieces Of My Life	(RCA PB-10401)	2.50	10.00	75
HURT/For The Heart	(RCA PB-10601)	2.50	10.00	76
MOODY BLUE/She Thinks I Still Care	(RCA PB-10857)	2.50	10.00	76
WAY DOWN/Pledging My Love	(RCA PB-10998)	2.50	10.00	77
HOUND DOG/Don't Be Cruel	(RCA PB-11099)	1.00	4.00	77
(Originally included in the boxed sets *15 Golden Records–30 Golden Hits* and *20 Golden Hits In Full Color Sleeves*)				
IN THE GHETTO/Any Day Now	(RCA PB-11100)	1.00	4.00	77
(Originally included in the boxed sets *15 Golden Records–30 Golden Hits* and *20 Golden Hits In Full Color Sleeves*)				
JAILHOUSE ROCK/Treat Me Nice	(RCA PB-11101)	1.00	4.00	77
(Originally included in the boxed sets *15 Golden Records–30 Golden Hits*)				
CAN'T HELP FALLING IN LOVE/Rock-a-Hula Baby	(RCA PB-11102)	1.00	4.00	77
(Originally included in the boxed sets *15 Golden Records–30 Golden Hits* and *20 Golden Hits In Full Color Sleeves*)				
SUSPICIOUS MINDS/You'll Think Of Me	(RCA PB-11103)	1.00	4.00	77
(Originally included in the boxed sets *15 Golden Records–30 Golden Hits*)				
ARE YOU LONESOME TONIGHT/I Gotta Know	(RCA PB-11104)	1.00	4.00	77
(Originally included in the boxed sets *15 Golden Records–30 Golden Hits* and *20 Golden Hits In Full Color Sleeves*)				
HEARTBREAK HOTEL/I Was The One	(RCA PB-11105)	1.00	4.00	77
(Originally included in the boxed sets *15 Golden Records–30 Golden Hits* and *20 Golden Hits In Full Color Sleeves*)				
ALL SHOOK UP/That's When Your Heartaches Begin	(RCA PB-11106)	1.00	4.00	77
(Originally included in the boxed sets *15 Golden Records–30 Golden Hits* and *20 Golden Hits In Full Color Sleeves*)				
BLUE SUEDE SHOES/Tutti Frutti	(RCA PB-11107)	1.00	4.00	77
(Originally included in the boxed sets *15 Golden Records–30 Golden Hits* and *20 Golden Hits In Full Color Sleeves*)				
LOVE ME TENDER/Any Way You Want Me (That's How I Will Be)	(RCA PB-11108)	1.00	4.00	77
(Originally included in the boxed sets *15 Golden Records–30 Golden Hits* and *20 Golden Hits In Full Color Sleeves*)				
LOVING YOU/(Let Me Be Your) Tedddy Bear	(RCA PB-11109)	1.00	4.00	77
(Originally included in the boxed sets *15 Golden Records–30 Golden Hits* and *20 Golden Hits In Full Color Sleeves*)				
IT'S NOW OR NEVER/A Mess Of Blues	(RCA PB-11110)	1.00	4.00	77
(Originally included in the boxed sets *15 Golden Records–30 Golden Hits* and *20 Golden Hits In Full Color Sleeves*)				
RETURN TO SENDER/Where Do You Come From	(RCA PB-11111)	1.00	4.00	77
(Originally included in the boxed sets *15 Golden Records–30 Golden Hits* and *20 Golden Hits In Full Color Sleeves*)				
ONE NIGHT/I Got Stung	(RCA PB-11112)	1.00	4.00	77
(Originally included in the boxed sets *15 Golden Records–30 Golden Hits*)				
CRYING IN THE CHAPEL/I Believe In The Man In The Sky	(RCA PB-11113)	1.00	4.00	77
(Originally included in the boxed set *15 Golden Records–30 Golden Hits*)				
MY WAY/America	(RCA PB-11165)	2.50	10.00	77
MY WAY/America The Beautiful	(RCA PB-11165)	6.25	25.00	77
(Note the b-side title variation)				
UNCHAINED MELODY/Softly, As I Leave You	(RCA PB-11212)	2.50	10.00	78
(LET ME BE YOUR) TEDDY BEAR/Puppet On A String	(RCA PB-11320)	2.50	10.00	78
ARE YOU SINCERE/Solitaire	(RCA PB-11533)	2.50	10.00	79
I GOT A FEELIN' IN MY BODY/ There's A Honky Tonk Angel (Who Will Take Me Back In)	(RCA PB-11679)	2.50	10.00	79
GUITAR MAN/Faded Love	(RCA PB-12158)	2.50	10.00	81
THERE GOES MY EVERYTHING/You'll Never Walk Alone	(RCA PB-13058)	2.50	10.00	82
THE IMPOSSIBLE DREAM (THE QUEST)/An American Trilogy	(RCA JH-13302)	25.00	100.00	82
(Promotional issue only, souvenir given to visitors to Elvis' birthplace in Tupelo, Mississippi)				
THE ELVIS MEDLEY/Always On My Mind	(RCA PB-13351)	2.50	10.00	82
I WAS THE ONE/Wear My Ring Around Your Neck	(RCA PB-13500)	2.50	10.00	83
LITTLE SISTER/Paralyzed	(RCA PB-13547)	2.50	10.00	83
BABY, LET'S PLAY HOUSE/Hound Dog	(RCA PB-13875)	10.00	40.00	84
(Issued with gold vinyl)				
BLUE SUEDE SHOES/Tutti Frutti	(RCA PB-13885)	1.00	4.00	84
(Originally included in the boxed set *Elvis' Greatest Hits–Golden Singles, Vol. 1*. Issued with gold vinyl.)				
HOUND DOG/Don't Be Cruel	(RCA PB-13886)	1.00	4.00	84
(Originally included in the boxed set *Elvis' Greatest Hits–Golden Singles, Vol. 1*. Issued with gold vinyl.)				
I WANT YOU, I NEED YOU, I LOVE YOU/Love Me	(RCA PB-13887)	1.00	4.00	84
(Originally included in the boxed set *Elvis' Greatest Hits–Golden Singles, Vol. 1*. Issued with gold vinyl.)				
ALL SHOOK UP/(Let Me Be Your) Teddy Bear	(RCA PB-13888)	1.00	4.00	84
(Originally included in the boxed set *Elvis' Greatest Hits–Golden Singles, Vol. 1*. Issued with gold vinyl.)				
IT'S NOW OR NEVER/Surrender	(RCA PB-13889)	1.00	4.00	84
(Originally included in the boxed set *Elvis' Greatest Hits–Golden Singles, Vol. 1*. Issued with gold vinyl.)				
IN THE GHETTO/If I Can Dream	(RCA PB-13890)	1.00	4.00	84
(Originally included in the boxed set *Elvis' Greatest Hits–Golden Singles, Vol. 1*. Issued with gold vinyl.)				
THAT'S ALL RIGHT/Blue Moon Of Kentucky	(RCA PB-13891)	1.00	4.00	84
(Originally included in the boxed set *Elvis' Greatest Hits–Golden Singles, Vol. 2*. Issued with gold vinyl.)				
HEARTBREAK HOTEL/Jailhouse Rock	(RCA PB-13892)	1.00	4.00	84
(Originally included in the boxed set *Elvis' Greatest Hits–Golden Singles, Vol. 2*. Issued with gold vinyl.)				
LOVE ME TENDER/Loving You	(RCA PB-13893)	1.00	4.00	84
(Originally included in the boxed set *Elvis' Greatest Hits–Golden Singles, Vol. 2*. Issued with gold vinyl.)				
HIS LATEST FLAME/Little Sister	(RCA PB-13894)	1.00	4.00	84
(Originally included in the boxed set *Elvis' Greatest Hits–Golden Singles, Vol. 2*. Issued with gold vinyl.)				
ARE YOU LONESOME TONIGHT/Can't Help Falling In Love	(RCA PB-13895)	1.00	4.00	84
(Originally included in the boxed set *Elvis' Greatest Hits–Golden Singles, Vol. 2*. Issued with gold vinyl.)				
SUSPICIOUS MINDS/Burning Love	(RCA PB-13896)	1.00	4.00	84
(Originally included in the boxed set *Elvis' Greatest Hits–Golden Singles, Vol. 2*. Issued with gold vinyl.)				
BLUE SUEDE SHOES/Promised Land	(RCA PB-13929)	2.50	10.00	84
(Issued with blue vinyl)				
ALWAYS ON MY MIND/My Boy	(RCA PB-14090)	2.50	10.00	85
(Issued with purple vinyl)				

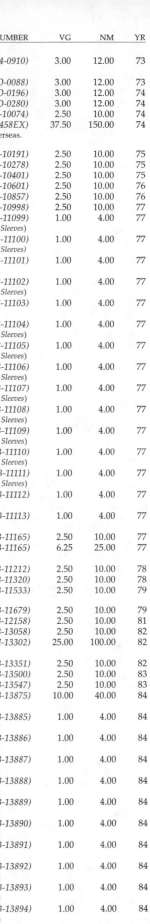

TITLE	LABEL AND NUMBER	VG	NM	YR
MERRY CHRISTMAS BABY/Santa Claus Is Back In Town .... (RCA PB-14237)		3.00	12.00	85
(Issued with either stock black or promotional green vinyl)				
HEARTBREAK HOTEL/Heartbreak Hotel .... (RCA 8760-7-R)		1.50	6.00	88
(Elvis and four others in a pink cadillac. B-side shown as by David Keith, from the motion picture *Heartbreak Hotel*.)				
HEARTBREAK HOTEL/Heartbreak Hotel .... (RCA 8760-7-R)		3.75	15.00	88
(Promotional issue, *Not For Sale–Demonstration* printed on back. Elvis and four others in a pink cadillac. B-side shown as by David Keith, from the motion picture *Heartbreak Hotel*.)				
HEARTBREAK HOTEL/Heartbreak Hotel .... (RCA 8760-7-R)		20.00	80.00	88
(Promotional issue only, man in an Elvis-style white jumpsuit pictured. B-side shown as by David Keith, from the motion picture *Heartbreak Hotel*.)				
DON'T BE CRUEL/Ain't That Lovin' You Baby (Fast Version) .... (RCA 64202)		1.25	5.00	92
(Generic white sleeve with "Elvis–The King Of Rock 'n' Roll" sticker affixed)				
BLUE CHRISTMAS/Love Me Tender .... (RCA 64203)		1.25	5.00	92
(Generic white sleeve with "Elvis–The King Of Rock 'n' Roll" sticker affixed)				
HEARTBREAK HOTEL/I WAS THE ONE/ Heartbreak Hotel (Alternate Take 5)/I Was The One (Alternate Take 2) ...... (RCA 07863 64476-7)		.75	3.00	96
GOLD STANDARD SERIES				
THAT'S ALL RIGHT/Blue Moon Of Kentucky .... (RCA Victor 447-0601)		50.00	200.00	64
GOOD ROCKIN' TONIGHT/I Don't Care If The Sun Don't Shine .... (RCA Victor 447-0602)		50.00	200.00	64
HEARTBREAK HOTEL/I Was The One .... (RCA Victor 447-0605)		50.00	200.00	64
HOUND DOG/Don't Be Cruel .... (RCA Victor 447-0608)		50.00	200.00	64
ALL SHOOK UP/That's When Your Heartache Begins .... (RCA Victor 447-0618)		50.00	200.00	64
KISS ME QUICK/Suspicion .... (RCA Victor 447-0639)		6.25	25.00	64
CRYING IN THE CHAPEL/I Believe In The Man In The Sky .... (RCA Victor 447-0643)		7.50	30.00	65
BLUE CHRISTMAS/Wooden Heart .... (RCA Victor 447-0720)		12.50	50.00	64
(Even though the catalog number indicates otherwise, this is the correct year of release)				
BLUE CHRISTMAS/Santa Claus Is Back In Town .... (RCA Victor 447-0647)		7.50	30.00	65
(Presley pictured on a Christmas card among wrapped gifts. *Gold Standard Series* in upper left corner-see 1977 release of the same songs.)				
PUPPET ON A STRING/Wooden Heart .... (RCA Victor 447-0650)		7.50	30.00	65
JOSHUA FIT THE BATTLE/Known Only To Him .... (RCA Victor 447-0651)		50.00	200.00	66
MILKY WHITE WAY/Swing Down Sweet Chariot .... (RCA Victor 447-0652)		50.00	200.00	66
BLUE CHRISTMAS/Santa Claus Is Back In Town .... (RCA Victor 447-0647)		2.50	10.00	77
(Presley pictured in a circle shape among ornaments. Does not indicate *Gold Standard Series* on sleeve although it is part of the series.)				
BOXED SETS				
15 GOLDEN RECORDS–30 GOLDEN HITS .... (RCA PP-11301)		15.00	60.00	77
(Complete set including fifteen records in picture sleeves, PB-11099 through PB-11113, and cardboard box)				
20 GOLDEN HITS IN FULL COLOR SLEEVES .... (RCA PP-11340)		20.00	80.00	77
(Complete set including ten records in picture sleeves, PB-11099, PB-11100, PB-11102, PB-11104 through PB-11109, PB-11111, and cardboard box.)				
ELVIS' GREATEST HITS–GOLDEN SINGLES, VOL. 1 .... (RCA PB-13897)		3.75	15.00	84
(Complete set including six gold vinyl records in picture sleeves, PB-13885 through PB-13890, and cardboard box.)				
ELVIS' GREATEST HITS–GOLDEN SINGLES, VOL. 2 .... (RCA PB-13898)		3.75	15.00	84
(Complete set including six gold vinyl records in picture sleeves, PB-13891 through PB-13896, and cardboard box.)				
Related see Daddy Bob (Elvis tribute), J.D. Sumner (Elvis tribute)				

PRESNELL, HARVE
(Actor/Entertainer)

TITLE	LABEL AND NUMBER	VG	NM	YR
IF YOU ARE BUT A DREAM/Charade .... (MGM K13189)		2.00	8.00	63

PRESTON, BILLY

TITLE	LABEL AND NUMBER	VG	NM	YR
THAT'S THE WAY GOD PLANNED IT/What About You .... (Apple 1808)		2.50	10.00	69
ALL THAT I'VE GOT (I'M GONNA GIVE IT TO YOU)/As I Get Older .... (Apple 1817)		2.50	10.00	70
SLAUGHTER/God Loves You .... (A&M 1380)		1.50	6.00	73
(From the motion picture *Slaughter*)				
SPACE RACE/We're Gonna Make It .... (A&M 1463)		1.50	6.00	73
NOTHING FROM NOTHING/My Soul Is A Witness .... (A&M 1544)		1.50	6.00	73
FANCY LADY/Song Of Joy .... (A&M 1735)		1.25	5.00	75
Also see Luther Vandross ('Til My Baby Comes Home)				

PRESTON, JOHNNY

TITLE	LABEL AND NUMBER	VG	NM	YR
CRADLE OF LOVE/City Of Tears .... (Mercury 71528)		5.00	20.00	60
FEEL SO FINE .... (Mercury 71651)		5.00	20.00	60
CHARMING BILLY/Up In The Air .... (Mercury 71691)		5.00	20.00	60
ROCK AND ROLL GUITAR/New Baby For Christmas .... (Mercury 71728)		5.00	20.00	60
LEAVE MY KITTEN ALONE/Token Of Love .... (Mercury 71761)		5.00	20.00	61
I FEEL GOOD/Willy Walk .... (Mercury 71803)		5.00	20.00	61
LET THEM TALK/She Once Belonged To Me .... (Mercury 71865)		5.00	20.00	61
FREE ME/Kissin' Tree .... (Mercury 71908)		5.00	20.00	61
BROKEN HEARTS ANONYMOUS/Let's Leave It That Way .... (Mercury 71951)		5.00	20.00	62
BIG BOSS MAN/The Day After Forever .... (Mercury 72049)		5.00	20.00	62

PRETENDERS, THE

TITLE	LABEL AND NUMBER	VG	NM	YR
STOP YOUR SOBBING/The Phone Call .... (Sire 49506)		1.00	4.00	79
LOUIE LOUIE/In The Sticks .... (Sire 49819)		1.00	4.00	81
BACK ON THE CHAIN GANG/My City Was Gone .... (Sire 29840-7)		.75	3.00	82
MIDDLE OF THE ROAD/2000 Miles .... (Sire 29444-7)		.75	3.00	83
SHOW ME/Fast Or Slow (The Law's The Law) .... (Sire 29317-7)		.75	3.00	83
THIN LINE BETWEEN LOVE AND HATE/Time The Avenger (Live Version) .... (Sire 29249-7)		.75	3.00	84
DON'T GET ME WRONG/Dance! .... (Sire 28630-7)		.75	3.00	86
HYMN TO HER (SHE WILL ALWAYS CARRY ON)/Tradition Of Love .... (Sire 28354-7)		.75	3.00	86
MY BABY/Room Full Of Mirrors .... (Sire 28496-7)		.75	3.00	87
IF THERE WAS A MAN .... (Warner Bros. 28259-7)		1.00	4.00	87
(From the motion picture *The Living Daylights*, Timothy Dalton and Maryam D'Abo pictured)				
WINDOWS OF THE WORLD/1969 .... (Polydor 887 816-7)		.75	3.00	88
(From the motion picture *1969*, Winona Ryder, Robert Downey, Jr., and Keifer Sutherland pictured)				
Also see UB40 (I Got You Babe)				

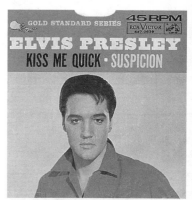

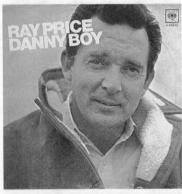

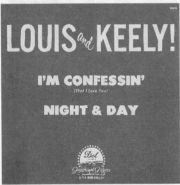

TITLE	LABEL AND NUMBER	VG	NM	YR

PRETTY IN PINK
(Motion Picture)
See Orchestral Manœuvres In The Dark (*If You Leave*), the Psychedelic Furs (*Pretty In Pink*)

PRETTY POISON
GIMME GIMME (YOUR AUTOGRAPH)/Kill You .... (*Poison Pops* no #) | | 1.50 | 6.00 | 81
  (Issued with small-hole 45 RPM record)
EXPIRATION/The Realm Of Existence .... (*Svengali 2913*) | | 1.25 | 5.00 | 81
  (Issued with 33-1/3 RPM record)
CATCH ME (I'M FALLING) (RADIO MIX)/Catch Me (I'm Falling) (Spanish Mix) (*Virgin 7-99416*) | | .75 | 3.00 | 87
  (Photo of lips on front and back)
CATCH ME (I'M FALLING) (RADIO MIX)/Catch Me (I'm Falling) (Spanish Mix) (*Virgin 7-99416*) | | .75 | 3.00 | 87
  (Photo of couple roller skating on front, from the motion picture *Hiding Out*.)
NIGHTIME/Nightime (Spanish Mix) .... (*Virgin 7-99350*) | | .75 | 3.00 | 88

PREVIN, ANDRE
See the Angel Listener (*Preview Highlights*)

PRICE, ALAN
I WANNA DANCE/Just For You .... (*Jet XW1119*) | | 1.25 | 5.00 | 77
  Also see the Animals

PRICE, LLOYD
BILLIE BABY/Try A Little Bit Of Tenderness .... (*Double-L 729*) | | 5.00 | 20.00 | 64

PRICE, RAY
MAKE THE WORLD GO AWAY .... (*Columbia 4-42827*) | | 3.75 | 15.00 | 63
  (Promotional issue only with red vinyl, insert, and letter)
DANNY BOY .... (*Columbia 4-44042*) | | 1.50 | 6.00 | 67

PRICK
COMMUNIQUE/Crack .... (*Nothing 5948*) | | 2.00 | 8.00 | 94
  (Promotional issue only split single, *Crack* shown as by Nine Inch Nails)

PRIDE, CHARLIE
IT'S GONNA TAKE A LITTLE BIT LONGER/
  You're Wanting Me To Stop Loving You .... (*RCA 74-0707*) | | 1.25 | 5.00 | 72

PRIEST, MAXI
WILD WORLD/On And On.. (*Virgin 7-99269*) | | .75 | 3.00 | 88
GOODBYE TO LOVE AGAIN/Problems .... (*Virgin 7-99235*) | | .75 | 3.00 | 89
  Also see Ferry Aid

PRIMA, LOUIS, & KEELY SMITH
THAT OLD BLACK MAGIC .... (*Capitol 4063*) | | 2.50 | 10.00 | 58
I'M CONFESSIN' (THAT I LOVE YOU)/Night & Day .... (*Dot 15978*) | | 2.50 | 10.00 | 59
  (Shown as by Louis and Keely!)
  Also see Keely Smith

PRINCE
MY LOVE IS FOREVER .... (*Warner Bros. 49050*) | | — | — | 79
  (There are unconfirmed reports of a withdrawn promotional only sleeve. If it does exist then a value of at least $75-$100 in near mint condition could be expected.)
WHY YOU WANNA TREAT ME SO BAD?/Baby .... (*Warner Bros. 49178*) | | 12.50 | 50.00 | 79
UPTOWN/Crazy You .... (*Warner Bros. 49559*) | | 5.00 | 20.00 | 80
1999/How Come U Don't Call Me Anymore .... (*Warner Bros. 29896-7*) | | 2.00 | 8.00 | 83
LET'S PRETEND WE'RE MARRIED/Irresistible Bitch .... (*Warner Bros. 29548-7*) | | 2.00 | 8.00 | 83
DELIRIOUS/Horny Toad .... (*Warner Bros. 29503-7*) | | 5.00 | 20.00 | 84
  (Poster sleeve)
WHEN DOVES CRY/17 Days .... (*Warner Bros. 29286-7*) | | 1.00 | 4.00 | 84
  (Originally issued with purple vinyl. From the motion picture *Purple Rain* starring Prince.)
LET'S GO CRAZY/Erotic City .... (*Warner Bros. 29216-7*) | | 1.50 | 6.00 | 84
  (Shown as by Prince and the Revolution. A-side background vocal credited to Sheila E. From the motion picture *Purple Rain* starring Prince.)
PURPLE RAIN .... (*Warner Bros. 29174-7*) | | 1.50 | 6.00 | 84
  (Plastic sleeve originally issued with purple vinyl. Shown as by Prince and the Revolution. From the motion picture *Purple Rain* starring Prince.)
I WOULD DIE 4 U/Another Lonely Christmas .... (*Warner Bros. 29121-7*) | | 1.00 | 4.00 | 84
  (Shown as by Prince and the Revolution. From the motion picture *Purple Rain* starring Prince.)
TAKE ME WITH U/Baby I'm A Star .... (*Warner Bros. 29079-7*) | | 1.00 | 4.00 | 85
  (Shown as by Prince and the Revolution. A-side credited on back as *Duet With Apollonia*. From the motion picture *Purple Rain* starring Prince.)
PAISLEY PARK/She's Always In My Hair .... (*Warner Bros. 29052-7*) | | — | — | 85
  (Another unconfirmed, withdrawn sleeve and record. If it does exist then a value of $300-$500 in near mint condition could be expected.)
AMERICA/Girl .... (*Paisley Park 28999-7*) | | .75 | 3.00 | 85
  (Shown as by Prince and the Revolution)
POP LIFE/Hello .... (*Paisley Park 28998-7*) | | .75 | 3.00 | 86
  (Shown as by Prince and the Revolution)
RASPBERRY BERET/She's Always In My Hair .... (*Paisley Park 28972-7*) | | .75 | 3.00 | 86
  (Shown as by Prince and the Revolution)
KISS/Love Or $ .... (*Paisley Park 28751-7*) | | .75 | 3.00 | 86
  (Shown as by Prince and the Revolution. Wendy Melvoin, of Wendy and Lisa, pictured on back.)
MOUNTAINS/Alexa De Paris .... (*Paisley Park 28711-7*) | | .75 | 3.00 | 86
  (Shown as by Prince and the Revolution. Lisa Coleman, of Wendy and Lisa, pictured on back.)
ANOTHERLOVERHOLENYOHEAD/Girls & Boys .... (*Paisley Park 28620-7*) | | .75 | 3.00 | 86
  (Shown as by Prince and the Revolution. Brown Marc pictured on back.)
SIGN "O" THE TIMES/La, La, La, He, He, Hee .... (*Paisley Park 28399-7*) | | .75 | 3.00 | 87
I WISH I WAS YOUR GIRLFRIEND/Shockadelic .... (*Paisley Park 28334-7*) | | .75 | 3.00 | 87
U GOT THE LOOK/Housequake .... (*Paisley Park 28289-7*) | | .75 | 3.00 | 87
  (Duet with Sheena Easton although she is not credited on the sleeve or record)
I COULD NEVER TAKE THE PLACE OF YOUR MAN/Hot Thing .... (*Paisley Park 28288-7*) | | .75 | 3.00 | 87
ALPHABET STREET .... (*Paisley Park 7-27900*) | | .75 | 3.00 | 88
  (Clear unprinted plastic sleeve with oval title sticker)
GLAM SLAM .... (*Paisley Park 7-27806*) | | .75 | 3.00 | 88
  (Clear unprinted plastic sleeve with arrow shaped title sticker)

		VG	NM	YR
I WISH U HEAVEN .... (Paisley Park 27745-7)		.75	3.00	88
BATDANCE/200 Balloons .... (Warner Bros. 22924-7)		.75	3.00	89
(From the motion picture *Batman*)				
SCANDALOUS/When 2 R In Love .... (Warner Bros. 22824-7)		.75	3.00	89
(From the motion picture *Batman*)				
PARTYMAN/Feel U Up .... (Warner Bros. 22814-7)		.75	3.00	89
(From the motion picture *Batman*)				
THE ARMS OF ORION .... (Warner Bros. 22757-7)		.75	3.00	89
(Shown as by Prince With Sheena Easton. From the motion picture *Batman*.)				
Also see Sheila E *(Koo Koo)*				

PRINCESS & STARBREEZE
		VG	NM	YR
IT'S GONNA BE LONELY .... (MCA 53150)		.75	3.00	87
BABY IT'S OVER .... (MCA 53302)		.75	3.00	88

PRINCESS BRIDE, THE
(Motion Picture)
See Mark Knofler *(Storybook Love)*, Willy DeVille *(Storybook Love)*

PRINE, JOHN
		VG	NM	YR
I SAW MOMMY KISSING SANTA CLAUS/Silver Bells .... (Oh Boy 1)		2.00	8.00	81
(Issued with red vinyl)				
EXTENDED PLAYS				
DEAR ABBY .... (Atlantic PR 195)		1.25	5.00	73
(Promotional issue only titled *Something For Nothing*. Also includes one song each, the titles are not listed on the sleeve, by Daryl Hall & John Oates, Barnaby Bye, and Delbert & Glen.)				

PRINCIPAL, VICTORIA
(Actress)
		VG	NM	YR
ALL I HAVE TO DO IS DREAM/Good Feeling .... (RSO 1065)		2.00	8.00	88
(Shown as by Andy Gibb and Victoria Principal, both pictured)				
Also see Floyd Cramer *(Theme From Dallas)*				

PRISM
		VG	NM	YR
DON'T LET HIM KNOW .... (Capitol B-5082)		1.00	4.00	82
(Illustration by Norman Rockwell)				
PRIVATE LIFE .... (Warner Bros. 27540-7)		.75	3.00	88

PRIVATE LIVES
		VG	NM	YR
LIVING IN A WORLD (TURNED UPSIDE DOWN)/Breakup .... (EMI America B-8210)		.75	3.00	84

PROBY, P.J.
		VG	NM	YR
MARIA/Good Things Are Coming My Way .... (Liberty 55850)		3.75	15.00	66
I CAN'T MAKE IT ALONE/If I Ruled The World .... (Liberty 55915)		3.75	15.00	67
WORK WITH ME ANNIE/You Can't Come Home Again .... (Liberty 55974)		3.75	15.00	67

PROCLAIMERS, THE
		VG	NM	YR
I'M GONNA BE (500 MILES)/Better Days .... (Chrysalis 43283)		1.25	5.00	88

PROCOL HARUM
		VG	NM	YR
SALTY DOG/Conquistador .... (A&M 1347)		1.50	6.00	72
A WHITER SHADE OF PALE/Lime Street Blues .... (A&M 1389)		1.25	5.00	72
GRAND HOTEL/Fire (Which Burnt Brightly) .... (Chrysalis 2013)		2.00	8.00	73

PROCTOR & BERGMAN
		VG	NM	YR
EXTENDED PLAYS				
GIVE US A BREAK .... (Mercury DJ 551)		2.00	8.00	78
(Promotional issue only, 11 tracks)				
Also see Firesign Theatre				

PROFESSOR LONGHAIR
		VG	NM	YR
MEET ME TOMORROW NIGHT/Doin' It .... (Dancing Cat 0013)		1.25	5.00	85
(Back of sleeve credits Clarence "Gatemouth" Brown on guitar)				
MARDI GRAS IN NEW ORLEANS/Jambalaya .... (Dancing Cat 0016)		1.25	5.00	85
(A-side credits Clarence 'Gatemouth' Brown on violin)				

PROGRAM 2
		VG	NM	YR
THE FEELING .... (Sire 41609)		.75	3.00	94

PROMISE CIRCLE
		VG	NM	YR
EASY TO TOUCH .... (Atlantic 7-89142)		.75	3.00	87

PROPER GROUNDS
		VG	NM	YR
MIND TEMPEST/Downtown Circus Gang .... (Maverick PRO-S-5788)		1.00	4.00	92
(Promotional issue only issued with small-hole 45 RPM yellow vinyl. An early release on Madonna's label.)				

PROPHET
		VG	NM	YR
SOUND OF A BREAKING HEART .... (Megaforce 7-89132)		.75	3.00	88

PROPHET, JEREMY
		VG	NM	YR
YOUR KINDA GUY/Rags To Riches .... (Philips 40450)		2.00	8.00	67

PSALMS, THE
		VG	NM	YR
A STORY I WAS TOLD/Christmas Island .... (Reilly PSA 431)		7.50	30.00	82

PSEUDO ECHO
		VG	NM	YR
A BEAT FOR YOU/Walkaway .... (EMI America B-8256)		.75	3.00	85

PSYCHEDELIC FURS, THE
		VG	NM	YR
THE GHOST IN YOU/Heartbeat (Remix) .... (Columbia 38 04416)		.75	3.00	84
THE GHOST IN YOU .... (Columbia 38 04416)		1.00	4.00	84
(Promotional issue, *Demonstration–Not For Sale* printed on sleeve)				
PRETTY IN PINK .... (A&M 2826)		.75	3.00	86
(From the motion picture *Pretty In Pink*)				
HEARTBREAK BEAT/New Dream .... (Columbia 38-06420)		.75	3.00	87
SHOCK/Presidential Gas (Live) .... (Columbia 38 07224)		.75	3.00	87
ALL THAT MONEY WANTS/Birdland .... (Columbia 38 07974)		.75	3.00	88

TITLE	LABEL AND NUMBER	VG	NM	YR

PUBLIC ENEMY

YOU'RE GONNA GET YOURS/Muzi Weighs A Ton	(Def Jam 38-07222)	1.00	4.00	87
NIGHT OF THE LIVING BASEHEADS/Cold Lampin' With Flavor	(Def Jam 38-08072)	1.00	4.00	88

Also see the Black Flames (b-side of *Are You My Woman?*)

PUCKETT, GARY, & THE UNION GAP

WOMAN, WOMAN/Don't Make Promises	(Columbia 4-44297)	2.50	10.00	67
(Shown as by The Union Gap Featuring Gary Puckett)				
YOUNG GIRL/I'm Losing You	(Columbia 4-44450)	2.50	10.00	68
(Shown as by The Union Gap Featuring Gary Puckett)				
LADY WILLPOWER/Daylight Stranger	(Columbia 4-44547)	2.50	10.00	68
OVER YOU/If The Day Would Come	(Columbia 4-44644)	2.50	10.00	68
LET'S GIVE ADAM AND EVE ANOTHER CHANCE/The Beggar	(Columbia 4-45097)	2.00	8.00	70

PUMPING IRON II

(Motion Picture)
See Skipworth & Turner (*Thinking About Your Love*)

PUNTS, THE

SHELLY'S BOYFRIEND/Rochambeau	(Bondage no #)	3.75	15.00	81

Also see Bonnie Hayes With The Wild Combo

PURE PRAIRIE LEAGUE

FADE AWAY/All The Way	(RCA PB-10880)	1.50	6.00	77

Also see Little Feat (Craig Fuller). Vince Gill was the lead singer from 1979-1983.

PURPLE RAIN

(Motion Picture)
See Prince (*Take Me With U, I Would Die 4 U, Purple Rain, Let's Go Crazy, When Doves Cry*)

PURSUIT OF HAPPINESS, THE

SHE'S SO YOUNG/Let My People Go	(Chrysalis VS4-43370)	.75	3.00	89

PYLON

COOL/Dub	(Caution no #)	2.00	8.00	79
CRAZY/M-Train	(DB 61)	1.50	6.00	81

PYRAMIDS, THE

PENETRATION/Here Comes Marsha	(Best 13002)	7.50	30.00	64
(Red version)				
PENETRATION/Here Comes Marsha	(Best 13002)	7.50	30.00	64
(Black version)				

Q

Q

SWEET SUMMERTIME/If It Ain't One Thing, It's Another	(Epic/Sweet City 8-50404)	1.00	4.00	77

Q-FEEL

DANCING IN HEAVEN (ORBITAL BE-BOP) LONG INTRO/ At The Top (All The Way To St. Tropez)	(Jive/RCA 1220-7-J)	.75	3.00	89

QUADROPHENIA

(Motion Picture)
See the Who (*5:15*)

QUAID, DENNIS

See Jerry Lee Lewis (*Great Balls Of Fire*)

QUARTERFLASH

FIND ANOTHER FOOL/Cruisin' With The Deuce	(Geffen 50006)	1.00	4.00	81
RIGHT KIND OF LOVE/You're Holding Me Back	(Geffen 29994-7)	1.00	4.00	82
TAKE ME TO HEART/Nowhere Left To Hide	(Geffen 29603-7)	.75	3.00	83
TAKE ANOTHER PICTURE/One More Round To Go	(Geffen 29523-7)	.75	3.00	83
TALK TO ME	(Geffen 28908-7)	.75	3.00	85
WALKING ON ICE	(Geffen 28894-7)	.75	3.00	85

Also see Seafood Mama

QUATEMAN, BILL

ONLY LOVE	(Columbia 4-45792)	1.50	6.00	73

EXTENDED PLAYS

SHOT IN THE DARK	(RCA JF-11225)	1.25	5.00	78

(Promotional issue only titled *The Music's On Us*, issued with a small-hole 33-1/3 RPM record. Also includes one song each by Aztec Two-Step, Scorpions, and Fandango.)

QUATRO, SUZI

ROCK HARD/State Of Mind	(Dreamland 104)	1.00	4.00	80

(From the motion picture *Times Square*)
Also see Ferry Aid

QUEEN

WE ARE THE CHAMPIONS/We Will Rock You	(Elektra 45441)	2.00	8.00	77
IT'S LATE/Sheer Heart Attack	(Elektra 45478)	2.00	8.00	77
BICYCLE RACE/Fat Bottomed Girls	(Elektra 45541)	1.50	6.00	78
PLAY THE GAME/A Human Body	(Elektra 46652)	1.25	5.00	80
FLASH'S THEME A/K/A FLASH/Football Fight	(Elektra 47092)	1.25	5.00	80
(From the motion picture *Flash Gordon*, Sam Jones pictured on back)				
UNDER PRESSURE/Soul Brother	(Elektra 47235)	1.25	5.00	81
(A-side shown as by Queen & David Bowie)				
BODY LANGUAGE	(Elektra 47452)	2.50	10.00	82
(First printing picturing a nude male and female, no b-side listed)				
BODY LANGUAGE/Life Is Real	(Elektra 47452)	1.50	6.00	82
(Second printing, white sleeve with red type)				
BACK CHAT/Staying Power	(Elektra 7-69941)	1.25	5.00	82
CALLING ALL GIRLS/Put Out The Fire	(Elektra 7-69981)	1.25	5.00	82

TITLE	LABEL AND NUMBER	VG	NM	YR
RADIO GA GA / I Go Crazy	(Capitol B-5317)	1.00	4.00	84
I WANT TO BREAK FREE / Machines (or 'Back To Humans')	(Capitol B-5350)	1.25	5.00	84
(John Deacon pictured on front)				
I WANT TO BREAK FREE / Machines (or 'Back To Humans')	(Capitol B-5350)	1.25	5.00	84
(Brian May pictured on front)				
I WANT TO BREAK FREE / Machines (or 'Back To Humans')	(Capitol B-5350)	1.25	5.00	84
(Freddie Mercury pictured on front)				
I WANT TO BREAK FREE / Machines (or 'Back To Humans')	(Capitol B-5350)	1.25	5.00	84
(Roger Taylor pictured on front)				
IT'S A HARD LIFE	(Capitol B-5372)	1.25	5.00	84
ONE VISION / Blurred Vision	(Capitol B-5530)	1.25	5.00	85
(From the motion picture *Iron Eagle*)				
PRINCES OF THE UNIVERSE	(Capitol B-5568)	1.25	5.00	86
(B-side of the 45 is *A Dozen Red Roses For My Darling* which was erroneously listed as the b-side for *A Kind Of Magic*. From the motion picture *Highlander*, Christopher Lambert pictured.)				
A KIND OF MAGIC / A Dozen Red Roses For My Darling	(Capitol B-5590)	1.00	4.00	86
(Sleeve lists the wrong b-side. The title on 45 b-side is *Gimme The Prize [Kurgan's Theme]*.)				
PAIN IS SO CLOSE TO PLEASURE	(Capitol B-5633)	1.00	4.00	86
I WANT IT ALL / Hang On In There	(Capitol B-44372)	1.25	5.00	89
Also see the Cross (Roger Taylor), Brian May and Friends, Freddie Mercury, Roger Taylor				

QUICKSAND
DIVORCE / Voice Killer	(Island 6896)	1.00	4.00	94
(Promotional issue only)				

QUICKSILVER
(Motion Picture)
See Roger Daltrey *(Quicksilver Lightning)*, Ray Parker, Jr. *(One Sunny Day/Dueling Bikes From Quicksilver)*.

QUIET RIOT
BANG YOUR HEAD (METAL HEALTH) / Bang Your Head (Metal Health) Live	(Pasha ZS4-04267)	.75	3.00	83
BANG YOUR HEAD (METAL HEALTH) / Bang Your Head (Metal Health) Live	(Pasha ZS4-04267)	1.00	4.00	83
(Promotional issue, *Demonstration Only–Not For Sale* printed on sleeve)				
MAMA WEER ALL CRAZEE NOW / Bad Boy	(Pasha ZS4-04505)	.75	3.00	84
MAMA WEER ALL CRAZEE NOW	(Pasha ZS4-04505)	1.00	4.00	84
(Promotional issue, *Demonstration Only Not For Sale* printed on sleeve)				
THE WILD AND THE YOUNG / Rise Or Fall	(Pasha ZS4-06174)	.75	3.00	86
THE WILD AND THE YOUNG / Rise Or Fall	(Pasha ZS4-06174)	1.00	4.00	86
(Promotional issue, *Demonstration Only–Not For Sale* printed on sleeve. Sleeve lists b-side although the 45 has *The Wild and the Young* on both sides.)				
Also see Hear 'N Aid				

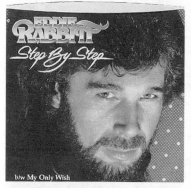

QUINN, AILEEN, AND THE ORPHANS
TOMORROW	(Columbia 18-02951)	1.00	4.00	82
(Promotional issue only, from the Broadway musical *Annie*)				

QUINN, ANTHONY
(Actor)
I LOVE YOU, YOU LOVE ME / Sometimes	(Capitol F5930)	3.00	12.00	67
Also see Maurice Jarre *(Theme From Behold A Pale Horse)*				

R

RABBITT, EDDIE
STEP BY STEP / My Only Wish	(Elektra 47174)	1.00	4.00	81
BOTH TO EACH OTHER (FRIENDS AND LOVERS)	(RCA PB-14377)	.75	3.00	86
(Shown as by Eddie Rabbitt With Juice Newton)				
BOTH TO EACH OTHER (FRIENDS AND LOVERS)	(RCA PB-14377)	1.00	4.00	86
(Promotional issue, shown as by Eddie Rabbitt With Juice Newton)				

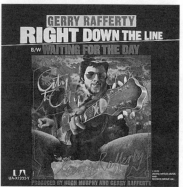

RADHA KRISHNA TEMPLE, THE
GOVINDA / Govinda Jai Jai	(Apple 1821)	2.00	8.00	70

RADIO HEART FEATURING GARY NUMAN
RADIO HEART / Mistasax Version #2 (Instrumental)	(Critique/Atco 7-99454)	.75	3.00	87

RADISH
DEAR AUNT ARCTICA / Bedtime	(Mercury 314 578 680-7)	.50	2.00	96

RAFFERTY, GERRY
RIGHT DOWN THE LINE / Waiting For The Day	(United Artists X1233-Y)	1.25	5.00	78
Also see Stealers Wheel				

RAGE AGAINST THE MACHINE
BULLET IN THE HEAD / Darkness	(Epic Associated 35 74927)	1.00	4.00	93

RAINBOW
STONE COLD / Rock Fever	(Mercury 76146)	.75	3.00	82
STREET OF DREAMS / Anybody There	(Mercury 815 660-7)	.75	3.00	83
Also see Deep Purple (Ritchie Blackmore). Tony Carey, Ronnie James Dio, and Cozy Powell left the group before these sleeves were released.				

RAINMAKERS, THE
LET MY PEOPLE GO-GO / Nobody Knows	(Mercury 884 907-7)	.75	3.00	86
SMALL CIRCLES /	(Mercury 888 943-7)	.75	3.00	87

RAINTREE COUNTY
(Motion Picture)
See Joni James *(Never Till Now)*.

RAITT, BONNIE
TOO LONG AT THE FAIR / Under The Falling Sky	(Warner Bros. 7645)	5.00	20.00	72
(Promotional issue only. Hard cover gatefold with 8-page booklet stitched inside used as a general promotional tool after the release of Raitt's second album *Give It Up*. No artist name, song titles, or catalog number listed on the outside of the sleeve.)				
YOU'RE GONNA GET WHAT'S COMING / The Glow	(Warner Bros. 49116)	1.25	5.00	79

TITLE	LABEL AND NUMBER	VG	NM	YR

DON'T IT MAKE YA WANNA DANCE/
Orange Blossom Special/Hoedown .... *(Full Moon/Asylum 47033)* | | 1.00 | 4.00 | 80
    (B-side shown as by Gilley's "Urban Cowboy" Band. From the motion picture *Urban Cowboy*, John Travolta pictured.)
BABY MINE/Mickey Mouse March .... *(A&M 1249)* | | .75 | 3.00 | 88
    (A-side shown as by Bonnie Raitt & Was [Not Was], b-side shown as by Aaron Neville)
THING CALLED LOVE .... *(Capitol B-44365)* | | .75 | 3.00 | 89
    Also see Artists United Against Apartheid

RAKIM
See Eric B. & Rakim

RALEIGH, KEVIN
MOONLIGHT ON WATER/The Art Of War .... *(Atlantic 7-88962)* | | .75 | 3.00 | 89
    Also see the Michael Stanley Band

RALSTON, ALFRED
JENNIE'S THEME/Entr'acte .... *(Angel SFO-36901)* | | 1.25 | 5.00 | 72
    (From the motion picture *Young Winston*)

RAMBO III
(Motion Picture)
    See Bill Medley (*He Ain't Heavy, He's My Brother*)

RAM JAM
EXTENDED PLAYS
BLACK BETTY .... *(CBS AE7-1128 AE7-1129)* | | 2.00 | 8.00 | 77
    (Promotional issue only titled *Music For Every Ear*, double single release issued with two small-hole 33-1/3 RPM records. Also includes one song each by Joan Baez, Cheap Trick, Crawler, Burton Cummings, and Dennis Wilson.)

RAMONES
I WANNA BE YOUR BOYFRIEND/
California Sun/I Don't Wanna Walk Around With You (Live) .... *(Sire 734)* | | 3.00 | 12.00 | 76
SWALLOW MY PRIDE/Pinhead .... *(Sire 738)* | | 3.00 | 12.00 | 77
SHEENA IS A PUNK ROCKER/I Don't Care .... *(Sire 746)* | | 3.00 | 12.00 | 77
    (First printing)
SHEENA IS A PUNK ROCKER/I Don't Care .... *(Sire 1006)* | | 2.50 | 10.00 | 77
    (Second printing identical to the first with the exception of the catalog number)
ROCKAWAY BEACH/Locket Love .... *(Sire 1008)* | | 2.50 | 10.00 | 77
DO YOU WANNA DANCE?/Baby Sitter .... *(Sire 1017)* | | 3.00 | 12.00 | 78
DON'T COME CLOSE/I Don't Want You .... *(Sire 1025)* | | 3.75 | 15.00 | 78
ROCK 'N' ROLL HIGH SCHOOL/Do You Wanna Dance? (Live Version) .... *(Sire 1051)* | | 2.00 | 8.00 | 79
    (A-side from the motion picture *Rock 'N' Roll High School*)
I WANNA BE SEDATED .... *(Sire 27663-7)* | | 1.50 | 6.00 | 88
PET SEMETARY/Sheena Is A Punk Rocker .... *(Sire 22911-7)* | | 1.50 | 6.00 | 89
    (From the motion picture *Pet Sematary*, Ramones pictured on back.)
    Also see Dust (Marky Ramone a.k.a. Marc Bell)

RANCID
TIME BOMB/The Wars End/Blast 'Em .... *(Epitaph 86455)* | | .75 | 3.00 | 95
RUBY SOHO/That's Entertainment/Disorder and Disarray .... *(Epitaph 86464-7)* | | .75 | 3.00 | 95
    (Hard cover with small-hole 45 RPM record)
EXTENDED PLAYS
I'M NOT THE ONLY ONE/BATTERING RAM/
The Sentence/Media Controller/Idle Hands .... *(Lookout 59)* | | .75 | 3.00 | 93

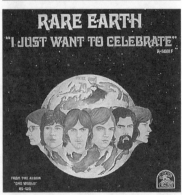

RAND, LEE
YOU KNOW/I Get So Lonely .... *(Destiny 507)* | | 2.50 | 10.00 |

RANDALL, TONY
(Comic Actor)
    See Doris Day (*Pillow Talk*)

RAN-DELLS, THE
MARTIAN HOP/Forgive Me Darling (I Have Lied) .... *(Chairman 45-4403)* | | 7.50 | 30.00 | 63

RANDOLPH, BOOTS
MICKEY'S TUNE .... *(Monument 852)* | | 2.50 | 10.00 | 64

RANJI
IT'S SO EASY TO BE BAD .... *(Anthem 51007)* | | 1.25 | 5.00 | 73

RANKIN, KENNY
PEACEFUL .... *(Mercury 72768)* | | 2.00 | 8.00 | 68

RARE EARTH
I JUST WANT TO CELEBRATE .... *(Rare Earth 5031)* | | 2.00 | 8.00 | 71
    (One of the few groups whose record label was named after them)

RASCALS, THE
YOU BETTER RUN/Love Is A Beautiful Thing .... *(Atlantic 2338)* | | 3.75 | 15.00 | 66
    (Shown as by the Young Rascals)
LONELY TOO LONG/If You Knew .... *(Atlantic 2377)* | | 3.75 | 15.00 | 67
    (Shown as by the Young Rascals)
GROOVIN'/Sueño .... *(Atlantic 2401)* | | 3.75 | 15.00 | 67
    (Shown as by the Young Rascals)
A GIRL LIKE YOU/It's Love .... *(Atlantic 2424)* | | 3.75 | 15.00 | 67
    (Shown as by the Young Rascals)
A BEAUTIFUL MORNING/Rainy Day .... *(Atlantic 2493)* | | 3.75 | 15.00 | 68
PEOPLE GOT TO BE FREE/My World .... *(Atlantic 2537)* | | 2.50 | 10.00 | 68
A RAY OF HOPE/Any Dance'll Do .... *(Atlantic 2584)* | | 2.00 | 8.00 | 68
SEE/Away, Away .... *(Atlantic 2634)* | | 2.00 | 8.00 | 69
CARRY ME BACK/Real Thing .... *(Atlantic 2664)* | | 2.00 | 8.00 | 69
I BELIEVE/Hold On .... *(Atlantic 2695)* | | 2.00 | 8.00 | 69
    (*I Believe* is shown as the a-side but failed to chart in the Billboard Hot 100, but *Hold On* managed to make it to #51)

GLORY GLORY .... (Atlantic 2743)   2.00   8.00   70
    (Back of sleeve credits backing vocals to the Sweet Inspirations)
    Also see Little Steven (Dino Danelli was a member of the Disciples of Soul)

RASPBERRIES
DON'T WANT TO SAY GOODBYE .... (Capitol 3280)   5.00   20.00   72
LET'S PRETEND .... (Capitol 3546)   2.50   10.00   73
    Also see Eric Carmen

RATT
ROUND AND ROUND/The Morning After .... (Atlantic 7-89693)   .75   3.00   84
WANTED MAN/She Wants Money .... (Atlantic 7-89618)   .75   3.00   84
LAY IT DOWN/Got Me On The Line .... (Atlantic 7-89546)   .75   3.00   85
DANCE/Take A Chance .... (Atlantic 7-89354)   .75   3.00   86
WAY COOL JR./Chain Reaction .... (Atlantic 7-88985)   .75   3.00   88
I WANT A WOMAN/What I'm After .... (Atlantic 7-88928)   .75   3.00   89

RAVEN
EXTENDED PLAYS
FRUMPY (Excerpt) .... (Columbia AS 1)   1.25   5.00   70
    (Promotional issue only titled *Dig This*, issued with a small-hole 33-1/3 RPM record. Also includes excerpts by
    Pacific Gas and Electric, Moondog, Nick Gravenites, Pete Seeger, Santana, Don Ellis, Firesign Theatre, and
    Tony Kosinec.)

RAVENS, THE
SIXTY MINUTE MAN .... (Media no #)   1.00   4.00   93

RAVERS, THE
IT'S GONNA BE A PUNK ROCK CHRISTMAS/Silent Night .... (Zombie/Ariola 7683)   1.25   5.00   77

RAVYNS
RAISED ON THE RADIO/Never Surrender .... (Full Moon/Asylum 7-69976)   .75   3.00   82
    (B-side shown as by Don Felder. From the motion picture *Fast Times At Ridgemont High*.)

RAWLS, LOU
TROUBLE DOWN HERE BELOW/The Life That I Lead .... (Capitol 5824)   2.00   8.00   67
THE STAR SPANGLED BANNER/Just A Closer Walk With Thee .... (MGM K-14527)   1.50   6.00   73
ARE YOU WITH ME .... (Epic 34-05831)   .75   3.00   86

RAY, DIANE
PLEASE DON'T TALK TO THE LIFEGUARD/That's All I Want From You .... (Mercury 72117)   5.00   20.00   63
WHERE IS THE BOY/My Summer Love Is Heading For An Early Fall .... (Mercury 72195)   5.00   20.00   63
SNOW MAN/Just So Bobby Can See .... (Mercury 72223)   3.75   15.00   63

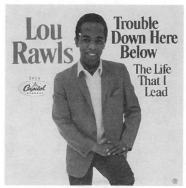

RAY, JOHNNIE
YOU DON'T OWE ME A THING/Look Homeward, Angel .... (Columbia 4-40803)   5.00   20.00   57

RAY, ROCKIN' RICHIE
HUMP A BABY/Baseball Card Lover .... (Rhino 004)   .75   3.00   77

RAYBURN, MARGIE
FREIGHT TRAIN .... (Liberty 55072)   3.75   15.00   57

RAYDIO
JACK AND JILL .... (Arista 0283)   1.00   4.00   77
    Also see Ray Parker Jr.

RAYE, SUSAN
MAYBE IF I CLOSE MY EYES/I Ain't Gonna Be Treated This Way .... (Capitol 2620)   1.25   5.00   69
HAPPY HEART/ .... (Capitol 3209)   1.25   5.00   71
    Also see Buck Owens and Susan Raye

REA, CHRIS
FOOL (IF YOU THINK IT'S OVER)/Midnight Love .... (United Artists/Magnet X1198-Y)   1.00   4.00   78
LET'S DANCE .... (Motown 1900 MF)   .75   3.00   87
LET'S DANCE .... (Motown 1900 MF)   1.00   4.00   87
    (Promotional issue, *Promotional Use Only/Not For Sale* printed on sleeve)
WORKING ON IT/Loving You Again (Live) .... (Geffen 27535-7)   .75   3.00   89
ON THE BEACH/Se Sequi .... (Geffen 22938-7)   .75   3.00   89

READY FOR THE WORLD
OH SHEILA .... (MCA 52636)   .75   3.00   85
SLIDE OVER .... (MCA 52713)   .75   3.00   85
DIGITAL DISPLAY/I'm The One Who Loves You .... (MCA 52734)   .75   3.00   85
LOVE YOU DOWN .... (MCA 52947)   .75   3.00   86
MY GIRLY .... (MCA 53337)   .75   3.00   88

REALITY BITES
(Motion Picture)
    See the Knack (*My Sharona*), Squeeze (*Tempted*)

REAL LIFE
CATCH ME I'M FALLING .... (MCA/Curb 52362)   .75   3.00   84
FACE TO FACE .... (MCA/Curb 52712)   .75   3.00   85

REASONS, THE
BABY BABY/My Kinda Guy .... (United Artists 50005)   2.00   8.00   66

REBEL HEELS
BREAK THE CHAIN/Robbing Me Blind .... (Atlantic 7-89016)   .75   3.00   88
EMPTY LOVE/Love Changes This .... (Atlantic 7-88982)   .75   3.00   88

RECKLESS SLEEPERS
IF WE NEVER MEET AGAIN/When You Get That Look .... (I.R.S. 53394)   .75   3.00   88
IF WE NEVER MEET AGAIN/When You Get That Look .... (I.R.S. S45-17630)   1.00   4.00   88
    (Promotional issue identical to stock copy except a sticker is placed on sleeve stating *S45-17630 For Promotion
    Only*. The record bears this catalog number.)
    Also see Jules and the Polar Bears, Jules Shear

RECORDS, THE
STARRY EYES / Paint Her Face .... (Virgin 67000) | 1.00 | 4.00 | 79
  (Hard cover)
TEENARAMA / Held Up High .... (Virgin 67002) | 1.00 | 4.00 | 79
  (Hard cover)
HEARTS IN HER EYES / So Sorry .... (Virgin 67008) | 1.25 | 5.00 | 80
  EXTENDED PLAYS
ABRACADABRA (HAVE YOU SEEN HER) / SEE MY FRIENDS / 1984 /
  Have You Seen Your Mother, Baby? (Standing In The Shadows) .... (Virgin PR 338) | 1.00 | 4.00 | 79
  (Sleeve states *Special limited edition available with the Records album VA 13130* which was their self-titled debut)

RED ARMY CHORUS, THE
  See David Foster (*Rendez-Vous*)

RED BOX
CHENKO (TENKA-IO) / Speeches .... (Sire 28206-7) | .75 | 3.00 | 87

REDD KROSS
YESTERDAY ONCE MORE .... (A&M 31458 0714 7) | .50 | 2.00 | 94
  (Side 9 of a 7 record box set titled *If I Were A Carpenter*. Each sleeve has a different face shot of Karen Carpenter on the front, Richard Carpenter on the back. No artist name or song titles indicated on sleeve. Complete set valued at $30.00 near mint.)

REDDY, HELEN
CANDLE ON THE WATER .... (Capitol 4521) | 1.25 | 5.00 | 77
  (From the motion picture *Pete's Dragon*)
DON'T TELL ME TONIGHT .... (MCA 52170) | 1.00 | 4.00 | 83

REDFORD, ROBERT
(Actor)
  See Melissa Manchester (*The Music Of Goodbye*), Al Jarreau (*The Music Of Goodbye*)

REDHEAD KINGPIN AND THE F.B.I.
DO THE RIGHT THING / A Shade Of Red .... (Virgin 7-99203) | .75 | 3.00 | 89

RED RIDER
WHITE HOT / Avenue "A" .... (Capitol 4845) | 1.00 | 4.00 | 80
HUMAN RACE / Sights On You .... (Capitol B-5211) | 1.00 | 4.00 | 83
YOUNG THING, WILD DREAMS (ROCK ME) .... (Capitol B-5335) | .75 | 3.00 | 84
BREAKING CURFEW .... (Capitol B-5383) | .75 | 3.00 | 84
BOY INSIDE THE MAN / Lasting Song .... (Capitol B-5591) | .75 | 3.00 | 86
  (Shown as by Tom Cochrane and Red Rider)
BIG LEAGUE / Vacation (In My Mind) .... (RCA 8750-7-R) | .75 | 3.00 | 88
  (Shown as by Tom Cochrane and Red Rider)

RED ROCKERS
BLOOD FROM A STONE / Burning Bridges .... (Columbia/415 38-04687) | .75 | 3.00 | 84
BLOOD FROM A STONE .... (Columbia/415 38-04687) | 1.00 | 4.00 | 84
  (Promotional issue, *Demonstration–Not For Sale* printed on sleeve)

REDS, THE
SELF REDUCTION / Victims .... (Eke 353) | 2.50 | 10.00 | 78
  (Early versions of songs to later appear on their A&M album and 10" releases)
(IT'S NOT THE) SAME THING / STRONGER SILENCE / Killing You .... (Ambition 45-104) | 2.00 | 8.00 | 81

RED 7
HEARTBEAT / Shades Of Grey .... (MCA 52531) | .75 | 3.00 | 85
WHEN THE SUN GOES DOWN .... (MCA 53012) | .75 | 3.00 | 87

REED, DAN, NETWORK, THE
GET TO YOU (LP Version) / Get To You (Spanish Version) .... (Mercury 870 421-7) | .75 | 3.00 | 88
RITUAL / Forgot To Make Her Mine .... (Mercury 870 183-7) | .75 | 3.00 | 88

REED, DONNA
(Actress)
  See Ray Bloch & Orchestra (*From Here To Eternity*)

REED, DONNA, SHOW
(Television Series)
  Related see Shelley Fabares, Paul Petersen, Donna Reed

REED, JERRY
HULLY GULLY GUITAR / Twist-A-Roo .... (Columbia 4-42533) | 2.50 | 10.00 | 62
ALABAMA WILD MAN / Take It Easy (In Your Mind) .... (RCA 74-0738) | 1.50 | 6.00 | 72
  Also see Chet Atkins (*Chet's Tune*)

REED, LOU
SEPTEMBER SONG / Oh Heavenly Salvation .... (A&M 2781) | 1.00 | 4.00 | 85
  (B-side shown as by Mark Bingham, Johnny Adams, and Aaron Neville. From the motion picture *Soul Man*.)
MY LOVE IS CHEMICAL / People Have Got To Move .... (Atlantic 7-89468) | 1.00 | 4.00 | 85
  (B-side shown as by Jenny Burton. From the motion picture *White Nights*, Mikhail Baryshnikov and Gregory Hines pictured.)
ROMEO HAD JULIETTE / Busload Of Faith .... (Sire 22875-7) | .75 | 3.00 | 89
  Also see Artists United Against Apartheid, the Smithereens (*Afternoon Tea/Long Way Back Again*), the Velvet Underground

REESE, DELLA
EVERYDAY / There's No Two Ways About It .... (RCA Victor 47-7750) | 2.50 | 10.00 | 60
AND NOW / There's Nothin' Like A Boy .... (RCA Victor 47-7784) | 2.50 | 10.00 | 60
I POSSESS / A Far Far Better Thing .... (RCA Victor 47-7884) | 2.50 | 10.00 | 61
I LOVE YOU SO MUCH IT HURTS / Blow Out The Sun .... (RCA Victor 47-8070) | 2.50 | 10.00 | 62
AS LONG AS HE NEEDS ME / .... (RCA Victor 47-8093) | 2.50 | 10.00 | 63
BE MY LOVE / I Behold You .... (RCA Victor 47-8145) | 2.50 | 10.00 | 63

REEVES, DEL
THE PRIVATE .... (United Artists 50157) | 1.50 | 6.00 | 67
WE'VE BEEN STRONG LONG ENOUGH .... (Koala 321) | 1.25 | 5.00 | 80
  (Shown as by Del Reeves & Liz Lyndell)

REEVES, JIM

I'M GETTIN' BETTER/I Know One .... (RCA Victor 47-7756)	2.50	10.00	60
AM I LOSING YOU/I Missed Me .... (RCA Victor 47-7800)	2.50	10.00	60
I'M GONNA CHANGE EVERYTHING/Pride Goes Before A Fall .... (RCA Victor 47-8080)	3.00	12.00	62
IS THIS ME?/Missing Angel .... (RCA Victor 47-8127)	2.50	10.00	62
GUILTY/Little Ole You .... (RCA Victor 47-8193)	2.50	10.00	63
SEÑOR SANTA CLAUS/ .... (RCA Victor 47-8252)	5.00	20.00	63
IS IT REALLY OVER?/ .... (RCA Victor 47-8625)	2.00	8.00	65

Also see Elvis Presley (Old Shep EP)

REEVES, SCOTT
(Actor)

See the Soaps and Hearts Ensemble

RE-FLEX

THE POLITICS OF DANCING/Flex It! .... (Capitol B-5301)	1.00	4.00	83
HURT .... (Capitol B-5348)	.75	3.00	84

REGAN, JOAN

I'M NO TOY .... (Columbia 4-43704)	2.00	8.00	66

REGINA

BABY LOVE/ .... (Atlantic 7-89417)	.75	3.00	86
BEAT OF LOVE/Beat Of Love (Edit) .... (Atlantic 7-89348)	.75	3.00	86
EXTRAORDINARY LOVE/ .... (Atlantic 7-89093)	.75	3.00	88

REID, MIKE

OLD FOLKS/Earthquake .... (RCA 6896)	.75	3.00	88

(Shown as by Ronnie Milsap and Mike Reid)

REINER, ROB
(Actor/Director)

See Carroll O'Connor & Jean Stapleton (Those Were The Days)

REIVERS

IN YOUR EYES .... (Capitol B-44091)	.75	3.00	87

(Sleeve states Formerly Known As Zeitgeist From Austin, Texas)
Also see Zeitgeist

RELATIONS, THE

BACK TO THE BEACH/Too Proud To Let You Know .... (Davy Jones 664)	5.00	20.00	60s

(It is presently unclear as to whether this sleeve is unique for this particular title or merely a generic Davy Jones half sleeve)

RELF, KEITH

SHAPES IN MY MIND .... (Epic 5-10110)	20.00	80.00	67
TOGETHER NOW/All The Falling Angels .... (MCCM 89-002)	1.50	6.00	89

Also see the Yardbirds

R.E.M.

RADIO FREE EUROPE/Sitting Still .... (Hib-Tone 0001)	18.75	75.00	81
RADIO FREE EUROPE/There She Goes Again .... (I.R.S. 9916)	3.75	15.00	83
S. CENTRAL RAIN (I'M SORRY)/King Of The Road .... (I.R.S. 9927)	2.00	8.00	84
(DON'T GO BACK TO) ROCKVILLE/Catapult (Live) .... (I.R.S. 9931)	2.00	8.00	84
CAN'T GET THERE FROM HERE/Bandwagon .... (I.R.S. 52642)	1.25	5.00	85
DRIVER 8/Crazy .... (I.R.S. 52678)	1.25	5.00	85
FEMME FATALE .... (The Bob 20)	10.00	40.00	86

(Available to subscribers of The Bob magazine. Sleeve to accompany a red or black, one-sided flexi-disc.)

FALL ON ME/Rotary Ten .... (I.R.S. 52883)	1.00	4.00	86
SUPERMAN/White Tornado .... (I.R.S. 52971)	1.00	4.00	86
THE ONE I LOVE/Maps And Legends .... (I.R.S. 53171)	1.00	4.00	87
ITS THE END OF THE WORLD AS WE KNOW IT (AND I FEEL FINE)/ Last Date .... (I.R.S. 53220)	1.00	4.00	87
STAND .... (Warner Bros. 27688-7)	.75	3.00	88

(Was also included in the boxed set Singleactiongreen)

GET UP/Funtime .... (Warner Bros. 22791-7)	.75	3.00	89

(Was also included in the boxed set Singleactiongreen)

POP SONG 89 .... (Warner Bros. 27640-7)	.75	3.00	89

(Was also included in the boxed set Singleactiongreen)

ORANGE CRUSH .... (Warner Bros. 927 652)	—	—	88

(This is an import that was included in the 4 record box set Singleactiongreen)

FAN CLUB/CHRISTMAS SLEEVES

PARADE OF THE WOODEN SOLDIERS/See No Evil .... (Fan Club U-23518M)	12.50	50.00	88

(Issued with green vinyl)

GOOD KING WENCESLAS/Academy Fight Song .... (Fan Club 122589)	10.00	40.00	89

(Poster sleeve)

GHOST REINDEER IN THE SKY/Summertime .... (Fan Club 122590)	7.50	30.00	90
BABY BABY/Christmas Griping .... (Fan Club 122591)	7.50	30.00	91
WHERE'S CAPTAIN KIRK/Toyland .... (Fan Club REM 92)	5.00	20.00	92

(There are reportedly 3 variations of this gray sleeve)

WHERE'S CAPTAIN KIRK/Toyland .... (Fan Club REM 92)	3.75	15.00	92

(White version)

SILVER BELLS/Christmas Time Is Here .... (Fan Club REM 1993)	3.75	15.00	93
SEX BOMB/Christmas In Tunisia .... (Fan Club REM 94)	3.75	15.00	94

(Originally issued with a magnet, stamps, and a sticker)

WICKED GAMES/Java .... (Fan Club REM 95)	2.50	10.00	95

BOXED SET

SINGLEACTIONGREEN .... (Warner Bros. 27688-7)	6.25	25.00	88

(Complete set including four records in picture sleeves, poster, and cardboard box)

Also see the Backbeat Band (Mike Mills), Golden Palaminos (Michael Stipe), Hindu Love Gods (Bill Berry, Peter Buck, Mike Mills), Robin Hitchcock & the Egyptians (Peter Buck)

REMAINS, THE

DIDDY WAH DIDDY .... (Epic 10001)	20.00	80.00	66

(Promotional issue only titled The Remains To Be Seen...And Heard!)

TITLE	LABEL AND NUMBER	VG	NM	YR

REMO–THE ADVENTURE BEGINS
(Motion Picture)
> See Tommy Shaw (*Remo's Theme*)

REMY ZERO
TEMENOS (HERE COME THE SHAKES)/Shadowcasting .... (Geffen PRO-S-0001-RZ) | 1.00 | 4.00 | 95
> (Promotional issue only with 4-3/4" x 4-3/4" insert)

REN AND STIMPY SHOW, THE
(Animated Television Series)
EXTENDED PLAYS
DOG POUND HOP/HAPPY, HAPPY, JOY, JOY/
> Kilted Yaksmen Theme/Big House Blues .... (Nickelodeon/Sony Wonder/Epic LS7 5402) | 2.50 | 10.00 | 93
> (Titled on front *Little Eediot!*, issued with a small-hole 33-1/3 RPM yellow vinyl record)

RENÉ, GOOGIE
THE SLIDE .... (Rendezvous 134) | 2.50 | 10.00 | 60

RENÉ AND ANGELA
I'LL BE GOOD/ .... (Mercury 884 009-7) | .75 | 3.00 | 85
YOU DON'T HAVE TO CRY/You Don't Have To Cry (Instrumental) .... (Mercury 884 587-7) | .75 | 3.00 | 86

RENE AND RENE
ANGELITO .... (Columbia 4-43045) | 3.00 | 12.00 | 64

RENO, MIKE
ALMOST PARADISE .... (Columbia 38-04418) | .75 | 3.00 | 84
> (Shown as by Mike Reno and Ann Wilson, both pictured. From the motion picture *Footloose*.)
> Also see Loverboy

REO SPEEDWAGON

DON'T LET HIM GO/I Wish You Were There .... (Epic 19-02127) | 1.25 | 5.00 | 80
SWEET TIME/Stillness Of The Night .... (Epic 14-03175) | 1.00 | 4.00 | 82
SWEET TIME .... (Epic 14-03175) | 1.25 | 5.00 | 82
> (Promotional issue, *Demonstration Not For Sale* printed on sleeve)
I DO' WANNA KNOW/Rock 'N Roll Star .... (Epic 34-04659) | .75 | 3.00 | 84
I DO' WANNA KNOW .... (Epic 34-04659) | 1.00 | 4.00 | 84
> (Promotional issue, *Demonstration Only Not For Sale* printed on sleeve)
CAN'T FIGHT THIS FEELING .... (Epic 34-04713) | .75 | 3.00 | 84
CAN'T FIGHT THIS FEELING .... (Epic 34-04713) | 1.00 | 4.00 | 84
> (Promotional issue, *Demonstration Only Not For Sale* printed on sleeve)
ONE LONELY NIGHT/Wheels Are Turnin' .... (Epic 34-04848) | .75 | 3.00 | 85
ONE LONELY NIGHT .... (Epic 34-04848) | 1.00 | 4.00 | 85
> (Promotional issue, *Demonstration Only Not For Sale* printed on sleeve)
THAT AIN'T LOVE/Accidents Can Happen .... (Epic 34-06656) | .75 | 3.00 | 87
THAT AIN'T LOVE .... (Epic 34-06656) | 1.00 | 4.00 | 87
> (Promotional issue, *Demonstration Only–Not For Sale* printed on sleeve)
VARIETY TONIGHT .... (Epic 34-07055) | .75 | 3.00 | 87
VARIETY TONIGHT .... (Epic 34-07055) | 1.00 | 4.00 | 87
> (Promotional issue, *Demonstration Only–Not For Sale* printed on sleeve)
IN MY DREAMS/Over The Edge .... (Epic 34-07255) | .75 | 3.00 | 87
IN MY DREAMS .... (Epic 34-07255) | 1.00 | 4.00 | 87
> (Promotional issue, *Demonstration Only–Not For Sale* printed on sleeve)
HERE WITH ME .... (Epic 34-07901) | .75 | 3.00 | 88
EXTENDED PLAYS
TIME FOR ME TO FLY .... (Columbia Special Products PV 16174) | 1.25 | 5.00 | 81
> (Promotional issue only used as an advertising tool for Nestle's $100,000 candy bar, issued with a small-hole
> 33-1/3 RPM record. Also includes one song each by Cheap Trick, Journey, and Molly Hatchet.)
> Also see Brian May & Friends (Alan Gratzer)

REPLACEMENTS, THE

I'M IN TROUBLE/If Only You Were Lonely .... (Twin/Tone 8120) | 3.00 | 12.00 | 81
CAN'T HARDLY WAIT/Cool Water .... (Sire 28151-7) | 1.00 | 4.00 | 87
I'LL BE YOU/Date To Church .... (Sire 22992-7) | 1.00 | 4.00 | 89

RESIDENTS, THE

FIRE/Aircraft Damage (Record 1)/LIGHTNING/Explosion (Record 2) .... (Ralph 1272) | 50.00 | 200.00 | 72
> (Double single release titled *Santa Dog*)
SATISFACTION/Loser=Weed .... (Ralph 0776) | 18.75 | 75.00 | 76
BEYOND THE VALLEY OF A DAY IN THE LIFE/Flying .... (Ralph 0577) | 18.75 | 75.00 | 77
SATISFACTION/Loser=Weed .... (Ralph 7803) | 1.00 | 4.00 | 78
> (Sleeve states *This record was previously released with a different cover.* Snakefinger credited on lead guitar.)
SANTA DOG '78/Fire .... (Ralph 7812) | 3.75 | 15.00 | 78
THIS IS A MAN'S MAN'S MAN'S WORLD/Safety Is A Cootie Wootie .... (Ralph 8422) | .75 | 3.00 | 84
> (Clear plastic sleeve with red "bloodshot" graphics silkscreened on one side. Issued with white vinyl.)
KAW-LIGA/Stars And Stripes Forever .... (Ralph 8622) | 1.00 | 4.00 | 86
> (Issued with either black or white vinyl)
HIT THE ROAD JACK/For Elsie (Excerpt) .... (Ralph 8722) | .75 | 3.00 | 87
> Also see Gary Panter, Snakefinger

RESTIVO, JOHNNY
THE SHAPE I'M IN/Ya Ya .... (RCA Victor 47-7559) | 5.00 | 20.00 | 59
I LIKE GIRLS/Dear Someone .... (RCA Victor 47-7601) | 5.00 | 20.00 | 59
THE MAGIC AGE IS SEVENTEEN/Doctor Love .... (20th Fox 279) | 5.00 | 20.00 | 61
> (Sleeve promotes *Seventeen* magazines's seventeenth birthday)

RESTLESS HEART

WHEELS/New York (Hold Her Tight) .... (RCA 5280-7-R) | .75 | 3.00 | 87

REVENGE OF THE NERDS II: NERDS IN PARADISE
(Motion Picture)
> See 38 Special (*Back To Paradise*)

REVENGE OF THE PINK PANTHER
(Motion Picture)
> See Inspector Clouseau (*Thank Heaven For Little Girls*)

REVERE, PAUL, AND THE RAIDERS, FEATURING MARK LINDSAY

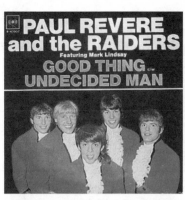

Title	Label and Number	VG	NM	YR
HUNGRY/There She Goes	(Columbia 4-43678)	3.75	15.00	66
THE GREAT AIRPLANE STRIKE/In My Community	(Columbia 4-43810)	3.75	15.00	66
GOOD THING/Undecided Man	(Columbia 4-43907)	3.75	15.00	66
SS 396/Camaro	(Columbia CSM-466)	7.50	30.00	67

(Promotional issue for Chevrolet. Flip side shown as by The Cyrkle.)

UPS AND DOWNS/Leslie	(Columbia 4-44018)	3.00	12.00	67
HIM OR ME–WHAT'S IT GONNA BE?/Legend Of Paul Revere	(Columbia 4-44094)	3.00	12.00	67
I HAD A DREAM/Upon Your Leaving	(Columbia 4-43678)	3.00	12.00	67
PEACE OF MIND/Do Unto Others	(Columbia 4-44335)	2.50	10.00	67
TOO MUCH TALK/Happening '68	(Columbia 4-44444)	2.50	10.00	68
DON'T TAKE IT SO HARD/Observation In Flight #285 In 3/4 Time	(Columbia 4-44553)	2.50	10.00	68
MR. SUN, MR. MOON/Without You	(Columbia 4-44744)	2.50	10.00	69
JINGLE BELLS/Jingle Bells	(Hitbound 102)	3.75	15.00	82

(Flip side shown as by Mike & Dean)
Also see Keith Allison, Brotherhood (Michael "Smitty" Smith, Drake Levin, Phil "Fang" Volk), the Cyrkle (Camaro), Jim "Harpo" Valley

REX
EXTENDED PLAYS

TROUBLE/TEN SECONDS OF LOVE/Feeling Better/Call Her "Easy"	(Columbia AE 71114)	1.25	5.00	76

(Promotional issue only, issued with a small-hole 33-1/3 RPM record)
Also see Rex Smith

REYNOLDS, BURT
(Actor)

LET'S DO SOMETHING CHEAP AND SUPERFICIAL	(MCA 51004)	1.25	5.00	80

(From the motion picture Smokey And The Bandit 2)

REYNOLDS, DEBBIE

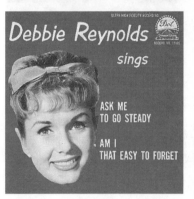

THE MATING GAME/Right Away	(MGM K-12761)	3.75	15.00	58
ASK ME TO GO STEADY/Am I That Easy To Forget	(Dot 15985)	2.50	10.00	60

(Ask Me To Go Steady is listed as the a-side but Am I That Easy To Forget was the song that reached #25 on the Billboard Top 40)

A TOUCH OF YOUR LOVE/City Lights	(Dot 16071)	2.50	10.00	60
HOME IN THE MEADOW/Raise A Ruckus	(MGM K-13140)	2.50	10.00	63

(From the motion picture How The West Was Won)

FOLLOW THE PIPER	(Piper 11-985)	2.50	10.00	60s

(Promotional sleeve for the Girl Scouts)

MOTHER EARTH AND FATHER TIME/Charlotte's Web	(Paramount 0220)	2.00	8.00	73

(From the motion picture Charlotte's Web)

REYNOLDS, JODY

ENDLESS SLEEP/Tight Capris	(Demon 1507)	6.25	25.00	58

RHINESTONE
(Motion Picture)
See Dolly Parton (Sweet Lovin' Friends), Sylvester Stallone (Sweet Lovin' Friends)

RHODES, EMITT

TAME THE LION/Golden Child Of God	(Dunhill 4315)	1.25	5.00	71

RHODES, LISA

HEAT IT UP/Born Rich	(Spindletop 113)	.75	3.00	85

RHYTHM CORPS

COMMON GROUND	(Pasha ZS4-07791)	.75	3.00	88

RHYTHM HERITAGE

THEME FROM "YOUNG FRANKENSTEIN"	(ABC Records 12063)	1.25	5.00	75

(From the motion picture Young Frankenstein)

RHYTHM ROCKERS, THE

WE BELONG TOGETHER/Oh, Boy!	(Satin 921)	25.00	100.00	60

RICH, BUDDY, BIG BAND, THE

MERCY, MERCY/Big Mama Cass	(World Pacific Jazz 88145)	2.00	8.00	67

RICH, CHARLIE

SHE LOVED EVERYBODY BUT ME/The Grass Is Always Greener	(Groove 58-0020)	6.25	25.00	63
FRANK JONES INTERVIEW WITH CHARLIE RICH	(Epic AE7-1065)	1.25	5.00	73

(Promotional issue only envelope sleeve with 3" flap. Sleeve reads An Exclusive Interview with Charlie Rich conducted by Frank Jones. Including musical excerpts from "Big Boss Man," "Nice 'N' Easy." "Life Has Its Little Ups And Downs." "Take It On Home." Issued with small-hole 33-1/3 RPM record.)

RICHARD, CLIFF

LUCKY LIPS/The Next Time	(Epic 5-9597)	5.00	20.00	63
IT'S ALL IN THE GAME/I'm Looking Out Of The Window	(Epic 5-9633)	5.00	20.00	63
I'M THE LONELY ONE/I Only Have Eyes For You	(Epic 5-9670)	5.00	20.00	64
I DON'T WANNA LOVE YOU/Look In My Eyes Maria	(Epic 5-9737)	5.00	20.00	64
BLUE TURNS TO GREY/I'll Walk Alone	(Epic 5-10018)	5.00	20.00	66
TIME DRAGS BY/La La La Song	(Epic 5-10101)	5.00	20.00	67
SUDDENLY	(MCA 51007)	1.00	4.00	80

(Shown as by Olivia Newton-John and Cliff Richard. From the motion picture Xanadu)

ALL I ASK OF YOU/The Phantom Of The Opera–Overture (Act II)	(Polydor 885 336-7)	1.00	4.00	86

(Shown as by Cliff Richard and Sarah Brightman, both pictured. B-side by The Royal Philharmonic Orchestra. From the musical The Phantom Of The Opera.)

GIVE A LITTLE BIT MORE/Keep On Looking	(EMI America 8076)	1.25	5.00	87
MY PRETTY ONE/Love Ya	(Striped Horse 7008)	1.00	4.00	87

(Hard cover)

SOME PEOPLE/Love Ya	(Striped Horse 7011)	1.00	4.00	88

(Hard cover)

RICHARD AND THE YOUNG LIONS

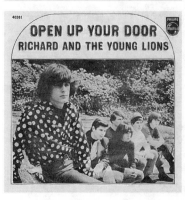

OPEN UP YOUR DOOR/Once Upon Your Smile	(Philips 40381)	5.00	20.00	66

RICHARDS, BARRY

BABY SITTIN' SANTA	(Epic 5-9564)	2.50	10.00	62

TITLE	LABEL AND NUMBER	VG	NM	YR

RICHARDS, KEITH

RUN RUDOLPH RUN .... (Rolling Stones 19311)		3.75	15.00	78
TAKE IT SO HARD/I Could Have Stood You Up .... (Virgin 7-99297)		.75	3.00	88
MAKE NO MISTAKE/It Means A Lot .... (Virgin 7-99240)		.75	3.00	89

Also see Aretha Franklin (Jumpin' Jack Flash), the Rolling Stones

RICHARDS, TURLEY

CRAZY ARMS .... (Columbia 4-43667)		2.00	8.00	66

RICHIE, LIONEL

YOU ARE/You Mean More To Me .... (Motown 1657MF)		1.00	4.00	82
MY LOVE/Round And Round .... (Motown 1677MF)		1.00	4.00	82
STUCK ON YOU .... (Motown 1746MF)		.75	3.00	84
PENNY LOVER .... (Motown 1762MF)		.75	3.00	84
SAY YOU, SAY ME .... (Motown 1819MF)		.75	3.00	85

(From the motion picture White Nights, although sleeve states the song is available exclusively on Richie's album. Gregory Hines and Mikhail Baryshnikov pictured on back.)

SAY YOU SAY ME .... (Motown 1819MF)		1.00	4.00	85

(Promotional issue half sleeve. White with black type that reads Radio-For All You Do...This Dub's For You. Finally Cleared By ASCAP and Brockman Music. No artist or title credited.)

DANCING ON THE CEILING .... (Motown 1843MF)		.75	3.00	86
DANCING ON THE CEILING .... (Motown 1843MF)		1.25	5.00	86

(Promotional issue, For Promotional Use Only Not For Sale printed on sleeve)

LOVE WILL CONQUER ALL .... (Motown 1866MF)		.75	3.00	86
LOVE WILL CONQUER ALL .... (Motown 1866MF)		1.25	5.00	86

(Promotional issue, For Promotional Use Only Not For Sale printed on sleeve)

DEEP RIVER WOMAN/Ballerina Girl .... (Motown 1873MF)		.75	3.00	86

(A-side credits background vocals to Alabama)

SE LA .... (Motown 1883MF)		.75	3.00	87

Also see Kenny Rogers (I Don't Need You), U.S.A. For Africa, Voices Of America

RICHMAN, JONATHAN, & THE MODERN LOVERS

NEW ENGLAND/Here Come The Martian Martians .... (Beserkley B-5743)		2.00	8.00	76

EXTENDED PLAYS

ICE CREAM MAN .... (Beserkley AE7-1120)		1.25	5.00	77

(Promotional issue only titled Great Ideas From Beserkley, issued with a small-hole 33-1/3 RPM record. Also includes 1 song each, the titles are not listed on sleeve, by the Rubinoos, Greg Kihn, and Earthquake.)

Also see the Cars (David Robinson), Earth Quake (b-side of Friday On My Mind), Talking Heads (Jerry Harrison)

RIDE

LEAVE THEM ALL BEHIND/She Calls .... (Sire/SBK number unknown)		1.25	5.00	92

(Promotional issue only, split single issued with blue vinyl. Flip side shown as by Slowdrive.)

RIDE THE WILD SURF

(Motion Picture)

See Jan & Dean (Ride The Wild Surf)

RIDDLE, NELSON, & HIS ORCHESTRA

THE MARKHAM THEME .... (Capitol 4244)		2.50	10.00	60
ORIGINAL MUSIC FROM THE TV SHOW THE UNTOUCHABLES .... (Capitol 4378)		2.50	10.00	60

(From the television series The Untouchables, Robert Stack pictured)

COME BLOW YOUR HORN/Connie's Theme .... (Reprise # unknown)		7.50	30	63

(From the motion picture Come Blow Your Horn, Frank Sinatra pictured)

Also see Linda Ronstadt (When You Wish Upon A Star)

RIDGWAY, STAN

DON'T BOX ME IN/Drama At Home .... (A&M 2604)		1.00	4.00	83

(A-side shown as by Stewart Copeland and Stanard Ridgway, b-side by Stewart Copeland, both pictured. From the motion picture Rumble Fish.)

CAMOUFLAGE/Stormy Side Of Town .... (I.R.S. 52875)		1.00	4.00	86

Also see Wall Of Voodoo

RIGHTEOUS BROTHERS, THE

JUST ONCE IN MY LIFE/The Blues .... (Philles 127)		3.75	15.00	65
EBB TIDE/(I Love You) For Sentimental Reasons .... (Philles 130)		3.75	15.00	65
THE WHITE CLIFFS OF DOVER/She's Mine, All Mine .... (Philles 132)		3.75	15.00	66
(YOU'RE MY) SOUL AND INSPIRATION/B Side Blues .... (Verve 10383)		2.50	10.00	66
HE/He Will Break Your Heart .... (Verve 10406)		2.50	10.00	66
GO AHEAD AND CRY/Things Didn't Go Your Way .... (Verve 10430)		2.50	10.00	66
STRANDED IN THE MIDDLE OF NO PLACE/Been So Nice .... (Verve 10551)		2.50	10.00	67

Also see Bill Medley

RILEY, JEANNIE C.

HARPER VALLEY P.T.A. .... (Plantation 173)		1.25	5.00	78

(From the motion picture Harper Valley P.T.A., caricature of Barbara Eden pictured. Issued with either black or green vinyl.)

RILEY, CHERYL PEPSII

THANKS FOR MY CHILD/Thanks For My Child (Confrontation Mix) .... (Columbia 38-07996)		.75	3.00	88
ME MYSELF & I/ .... (Columbia 38-08508)		.75	3.00	88

RINGWALD, MOLLY

(Actress)

See Orchestral Manœuvres In The Dark (If You Leave), Wang Chung (Fire In The Twilight)

RIOS, MIGUEL

A SONG OF JOY/El Rio .... (A&M 1193)		1.25	5.00	70

RIOT

OUTLAW/Rock City .... (Elektra 47218)		1.25	5.00	81

RIP CHORDS, THE

HERE I STAND .... (Columbia 4-42687)		12.50	50.00	63

(Promotional issue only issued with green vinyl)

GONE .... (Columbia 4-42812)		12.50	50.00	63

(Promotional issue only issued with blue vinyl)

Also see the Beach Boys (Bruce Johnston), Terry Day (a.k.a. Terry Melcher), Bruce Johnston

RIPPY, RODNEY ALLEN
(Child actor in commercials)
TAKE LIFE A LITTLE EASIER / World Of Love .... (Bell 45,403)   1.25   5.00   73

RISKY BUSINESS
(Motion Picture)
   See Bob Seger *(Old Time Rock & Roll)*

RITENOUR, LEE
MR. BRIEFCASE .... (Elektra 47185)   1.00   4.00   81

RITTER, TEX
THE PHANTON WHITE STALLION OF SKULL VALLEY / Froggy Went A-Courtin' (Record 1) /
   THE WRECK OF NUMBER NINE / Texas Rangers (Record 2) .... (Capitol CBSF-3010)   2.50   10.00   50
   (Hard cover gatefold for two 45s and is titled Children's Songs And Stories)
THE PONY EXPRESS / Billy The Kid (Record 1) /
   I LOVE MY ROOSTER / Night Herding Song (Record 2) .... (Capitol CBSF-3045)   2.50   10.00   50
   (Hard cover gatefold for two 45s and is titled Children's Songs And Stories)
BUMP TIDDIL DEE BUM BUM / I Just Can't Get Away (From These Old Memories) . (Capitol 2097)   2.00   8.00   68

RITTER, THELMA
(Actress)
   See Doris Day *(Pillow Talk)*

RIVERS, JOHNNY
MAYBELLINE / Walk Myself On Home .... (Imperial 66056)   3.00   12.00   64
SEVENTH SON / Unsquare Dance .... (Imperial 66112)   3.00   12.00   65
UNDER YOUR SPELL AGAIN / Long Time Man .... (Imperial 66144)   3.00   12.00   65
SECRET AGENT MAN .... (Imperial 66159)   3.00   12.00   66
   (From the television series Secret Agent)
POOR SIDE OF TOWN .... (Imperial 66205)   3.00   12.00   66
BABY I NEED YOUR LOVIN' .... (Imperial 66227)   3.00   12.00   67
THE TRACKS OF MY TEARS / Rewind Medley .... (Imperial 66244)   3.00   12.00   67
LOOK TO YOUR SOUL .... (Imperial 66286)   2.50   10.00   68
RIGHT RELATIONS / A Better Life .... (Imperial 66335)   2.50   10.00   68
MUDDY RIVER / Resurrection .... (Imperial 66386)   2.50   10.00   69
SEA CRUISE / Our Lady Of The Well .... (United Artists 50778)   2.50   10.00   71
HELP ME RHONDA / New Lovers And Old Friends .... (Epic 8-50121)   2.00   8.00   75

RIVINGTONS, THE
THE BIRD'S THE WORD .... (Liberty 55553)   6.25   25.00   63

R.J.'S LATEST ARRIVAL
OFF THE HOOK (RADIO EDIT) / Off The Hook (Midwest Version) .... (EMI Manhattan B-50132)   .75   3.00   88

ROARING BOYS
HOUSE OF STONE .... (Columbia 38-06114)   .75   3.00   86
HOUSE OF STONE .... (Columbia 38-06114)   1.00   4.00   86
   (Promotional issue, Demonstration–Not For Sale printed on sleeve)

ROB BASE & D.J. E-Z ROCK
JOY AND PAIN .... (Profile 5247)   .75   3.00   89

ROBBINS, MARTY
A WHITE SPORT COAT (AND A PINK CARNATION) / Grown-Up Tears .... (Columbia 4-40864)   7.50   30.00   57
THE STORY OF MY LIFE / Once-A-Week Date .... (Columbia 4-41013)   6.25   25.00   57
SHE WAS ONLY SEVENTEEN (HE WAS ONE YEAR MORE) /
   Sittin' In A Tree House .... (Columbia 4-41208)   6.25   25.00   58
THE HANGING TREE / The Blues Country Style .... (Columbia 4-41325)   5.00   20.00   59
   (A-side from the motion picture The Hanging Tree)
EL PASO / Running Gun .... (Columbia 4-41511)   3.75   15.00   60
BIG IRON / Saddle Tramp .... (Columbia 4-41589)   3.75   15.00   60
BALLAD OF THE ALAMO / A Time And A Place .... (Columbia 4-41809)   3.75   15.00   60
   (A-side from the motion picture The Alamo)
DON'T WORRY / Like All The Other Times .... (Columbia 4-41922)   3.75   15.00   61
JIMMY MARTINEZ / Ghost Train .... (Columbia 4-42008)   3.00   12.00   61
IT'S YOUR WORLD / You Told Me So .... (Columbia 4-42065)   3.00   12.00   61
   (Two versions with the same front but different imagery on the back)
I TOLD THE BROOK / Sometimes I'm Tempted .... (Columbia 4-42246)   3.00   12.00   61
LOVE CAN'T WAIT / Too Far Gone .... (Columbia 4-42375)   2.50   10.00   62
DEVIL WOMAN / April Fool's Day .... (Columbia 4-42486)   2.50   10.00   62
   (Green version)
DEVIL WOMAN / April Fool's Day .... (Columbia 4-42486)   2.50   10.00   62
   (Brown version)
RUBY ANN / Won't You Forgive? .... (Columbia 4-42614)   2.50   10.00   62
TEENAGER'S DAD / Cigarettes And Coffee Blues .... (Columbia 4-42701)   2.50   10.00   63
   (The b-side, Cigarettes And Coffee Blues, was the song to hit #93 on the Billboard Top 100)
NO SIGNS OF LONELINESS HERE / Not Ready Yet .... (Columbia 4-42781)   2.50   10.00   63
   (Uses the same photo of Robbins as Teenager's Dad sleeve with green background and Robbins looking directly at the camera)
NO SIGNS OF LONELINESS HERE / I'm Not Ready Yet .... (Columbia 4-42781)   2.50   10.00   63
   (Different photo of Robbins with brown background and looking to the upper left of sleeve)

ROBBINS, ROCKIE
YOU AND ME / Together .... (A&M 2231)   .75   3.00   80
WE BELONG TOGETHER .... (MCA 52516)   .75   3.00   85

ROBBS, THE
BITTERSWEET / End Of The Week .... (Mercury 72641)   3.00   12.00   66

ROBERTS, ERIC
(Actor)
   See Mike + the Mechanics *(Revolution)*

ROBERTSON, B.A.
HOLD ME / Spring Greens .... (Swan Song 72006)   .75   3.00   81
   (Shown as by B.A. Robertson & Maggie Bell)

TITLE	LABEL AND NUMBER	VG	NM	YR

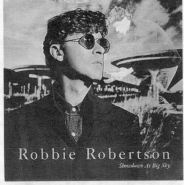

ROBERTSON, BAXTER
TIME AND AGAIN / Actions Speak Louder .... (Atco 7-99277) .75 3.00 88

ROBERTSON, DALE
(Actor in television and motion picture westerns)
TOO BUSY BEING ME / She's Still With Me .... (Liberty 56136) 2.00 8.00 69
FALLEN WOMAN / I Love Her World .... (Artco 502) 1.25 5.00 73

ROBERTSON, ROBBIE
SHOWDOWN AT BIG SKY .... (Geffen 28175-7) 1.00 4.00 87
SOMEWHERE DOWN THE CRAZY RIVER .... (Geffen 28111-7) 1.00 4.00 87
    Also see the Band

ROBINSON, BERT
HEART OF GOLD .... (Capitol B-44013) .75 3.00 87

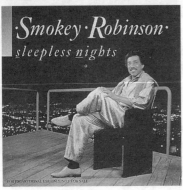

ROBINSON, HOLLY
(Actress)
21 JUMP STREET / Change With The Changing Times .... (I.R.S. 53468) 1.00 4.00 88
    (A-side from the television series 21 Jump Street, co-starring Robinson. B-side shown as by the dB's.)

ROBINSON, SMOKEY
HOLD ON TO YOUR LOVE .... (Tamla 1828MF) .75 3.00 85
HOLD ON TO YOUR LOVE .... (Tamla 1828MF) 1.00 4.00 85
    (Promotional issue, For Promotional Use Only/Not For Sale printed on back)
SLEEPLESS NIGHTS .... (Tamla 1839MF) .75 3.00 86
SLEEPLESS NIGHTS .... (Tamla 1839TF) 1.00 4.00 86
    (Promotional issue, For Promotional Use Only/Not For Sale printed on back)
JUST TO SEE HER .... (Motown 1877MF) .75 3.00 87
JUST TO SEE HER .... (Motown 1877MF) 1.00 4.00 87
    (Promotional issue, For Promotional Use Only/Not For Sale printed on back)
ONE HEARTBEAT / Love Will Set You Free (Theme From "Solarbabies") .... (Motown 1897MF) .75 3.00 87
    (Kenny G credited on back with saxophone solo)
WHAT'S TOO MUCH .... (Motown 1911MF) .75 3.00 87
WHAT'S TOO MUCH .... (Motown 1911MF) 1.00 4.00 87
    (Promotional issue, For Promotional Use Only/Not For Sale printed on back)
LOVE DON'T GIVE NO REASON .... (Motown 1925MF) .75 3.00 87
    Also see Kenny G (We've Saved The Best For Last), the Miracles, Dolly Parton (I Know You By Heart), U.S.A. For Africa, Voices Of America

ROBINSON, TOM
2-4-6-8 MOTORWAY / I Shall Be Released .... (Harvest 4533) 1.00 4.00 80
    (Shown as by Tom Robinson Band)
CAN'T KEEP AWAY / Mary Lynne / Dungannon .... (I.R.S. 9503) 1.00 4.00 80
    (Shown as by Tom Robinson Sector 27)

ROBINSON, VICKI SUE
GRAB THEM CAKES / Captain Lou's History Of Music .... (Epic 34-05688) .75 3.00 85
    (Shown as by Junkyard Dog With Vickie Sue Robinson. B-side shown as by Captain Lou Albano.)
GRAB THEM CAKES .... (Epic 34-05688) 1.00 4.00 85
    (Shown as by Junkyard Dog With Vickie Sue Robinson. Promotional issue, Demonstration–Not For Sale printed on back.)

ROCK, MONTI, III
FOR DAYS AND DAYS / Trouble .... (Mercury 72488) 3.00 12.00 65

ROCK AND HYDE
DIRTY WATER .... (Capitol B-5691) .75 3.00 87
I WILL .... (Capitol B-44020) .75 3.00 87
    Also see Paul Hyde and the Payolas

ROCKETS, THE
TURN UP THE RADIO .... (Capitol B-5262) 1.00 4.00 83
    Also see Mitch Ryder and the Detroit Wheels (James McCarty, Johnny Badenjek)

ROCKMELONS
NEW GROOVE / Dreams In The Empty City .... (Atlantic 7-88908) .75 3.00 88

ROCK 'N' ROLL HIGH SCHOOL
(Motion Picture)
    See Ramones (Rock 'N' Roll High School)

ROCKPILE
TEACHER TEACHER .... (Columbia 1-11388) 2.50 10.00 80
    (Promotional issue only, folding sleeve. No song title or catalog number indicated. Biographical history of the band printed inside.)
EXTENDED PLAYS
TAKE A MESSAGE TO MARY / CRYING IN THE RAIN /
Poor Jenny / When Will I Be Loved? .... (Columbia AE7 1219) 1.25 5.00 80
    (Included with the album Seconds Of Pleasure, titled Nick Lowe & Dave Edmunds Sing The Everly Brothers, issued with a small-hole 33-1/3 RPM record)

ROCKWELL, NORMAN
(Artist)
    See Wayne Newton (Stagecoach To Cheyenne), Prism (Don't Let Him Know)

ROCKY FELLERS, THE
LIKE THE BIG GUYS DO / Great Big World .... (Scepter 1254) 3.75 15.00 63

ROCKY HORROR SHOW, THE
(Stage Musical)
    See Tim Curry (Sweet Transvestite)

ROCKY IV
(Motion Picture)
    See John Cafferty and the Beaver Brown Band (Heart's On Fire), Survivor (Burning Heart), Robert Tepper (No Easy Way Out)

ROCKY III
(Motion Picture)
    See Survivor (*Eye Of The Tiger*)

RODGERS, EILEEN
WAIT TILL TOMORROW .... (Kapp 365)		2.00	8.00	61

RODGERS, JIMMIE
SECRETLY/Make Me A Miracle .... (Roulette 4070)		3.75	15.00	58
ARE YOU REALLY MINE/The Wizard .... (Roulette 4090)		3.75	15.00	58
RING-A-LING-A-LARIO/Wonderful You .... (Roulette 4158)		3.75	15.00	59
WOMAN FROM LIBERIA/Come Along Julie .... (Roulette 4293)		3.75	15.00	61
NO ONE WILL EVER KNOW/Because .... (Dot 16378)		2.50	10.00	62
I'LL NEVER STAND IN YOUR WAY/Afraid .... (Dot 16428)		2.50	10.00	63

RODGERS, PAUL
CUT LOOSE/Talking Guitar Blues .... (Atlantic 7-89749)		1.00	4.00	83
MORNING AFTER THE NIGHT BEFORE/Northwinds .... (Atlantic 7-89709)		1.00	4.00	84

    Also see Bad Company, the Firm, Free, Willie and the Poor Boys

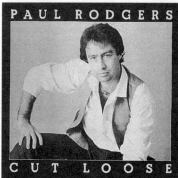

RODGERS, NILE
LET'S GO OUT TONIGHT .... (Warner Bros. 29049-7)		.75	3.00	85

    Also see Chic, John Hiatt (b-side of *Snake Charmer*), the Honeydrippers

RODGERS, RICHARD
(Composer)
    See Robert Russell Bennett (*Beneath The Southern Cross*)

RODNEY AND THE BRUNETTES
(Los Angeles disc jockey Rodney Bingenheimer, Diane Rovell, Diane Wilson, and Blondie)
LITTLE G.T.O./Holocaust On Sunset Boulevard .... (Bomp 127)		2.00	8.00	78

    Also see American Spring (Diane Rovell, Marilyn Rovell-Wilson), Blondie, the Honeys (Diane Rovell, Marilyn Rovell-Wilson)

RODRIGUEZ, JOHNNY
I COULDN'T BE ME WITHOUT YOU/Sometimes I Wish I Were You .... (Mercury 73769)		1.25	5.00	77

ROE, TOMMY
SUSIE DARLIN'/Piddle De Pat .... (ABC-Paramount 10362)		3.75	15.00	62
TOWN CRIER/Rainbow .... (ABC-Paramount 10379)		3.75	15.00	63
DOES ANYBODY KNOW MY NAME (TWO-TEN, SIX-EIGHTEEN)/				
Everytime A Bluebird Cries .... (ABC 10738)		3.00	12.00	65
IT'S NOW WINTERS DAY/Kick Me Charlie .... (ABC 45-10888)		2.00	8.00	66
JAM UP AND JELLY TIGHT/Moon Talk .... (ABC 45-11247)		2.00	8.00	69
WE CAN MAKE MUSIC/Gotta Keep Rolling Along .... (ABC 45-11273)		2.00	8.00	70

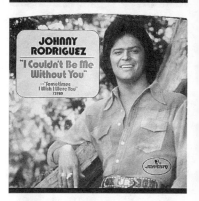

ROGER
(Roger "Zapp" Troutman)
I WANT TO BE YOUR MAN .... (Reprise 28229-7)		.75	3.00	87
THRILL SEEKERS .... (Reprise 27982-7)		.75	3.00	87
IF YOU'RE SERIOUS .... (Reprise 27897-7)		.75	3.00	87

    Also see Scitti Politti (*Boom! There She Was*)

ROGERS, DAVID
I'M IN LOVE WITH MY WIFE/Tessie's Bar Mystery .... (Columbia 4-44561)		1.50	6.00	68

ROGERS, EVAN
CALL MY HEART YOUR HOME .... (Capitol B-44327)		.75	3.00	89

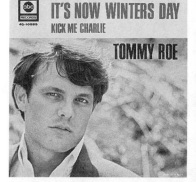

ROGERS, JULIE
LIKE A CHILD/The Love Of A Boy .... (Mercury 72380)		2.50	10.00	65

ROGERS, KENNY
SHE BELIEVES IN ME .... (United Artists X1273-Y)		1.00	4.00	79
YOU DECORATED MY LIFE/One Man's Woman .... (United Artists X1315-Y)		1.00	4.00	79
DON'T FALL IN LOVE WITH A DREAMER .... (United Artists X1345-Y)		1.00	4.00	80
(Shown as by Kenny Rogers with Kim Carnes)				
LADY/Sweet Music Man .... (United Artists X1380-Y)		1.00	4.00	80
I DON'T NEED YOU .... (Liberty 1415)		1.00	4.00	81
(Rogers and Lionel Richie pictured on back)				
SHARE YOUR LOVE WITH ME/Greybeard .... (Liberty A-1430)		1.00	4.00	81
KENTUCKY HOMEMADE CHRISTMAS .... (EMI P-A-1438)		1.00	4.00	81
LOVE WILL TURN YOU AROUND .... (Liberty B-1471)		1.00	4.00	82
(From the motion picture *Six Pack*)				
WE'VE GOT TONIGHT/You Are So Beautiful .... (Liberty B-1492)		.75	3.00	83
(A-side shown as by Kenny Rogers and Sheena Easton)				
ALL MY LIFE .... (Liberty B-1495)		.75	3.00	83
ISLANDS IN THE STREAM/I Will Always Love You .... (RCA PB-13615)		1.00	4.00	83
(First printing with a-side credited as *Duet With Dolly Parton* in a smaller type size than Rogers' name, both pictured)				
ISLANDS IN THE STREAM/I Will Always Love You .... (RCA PB-13615)		.75	3.00	83
(Second printing with a-side credited as *Duet With Dolly Parton* in the same type size as Rogers' name, both pictured)				
THIS WOMAN/Buried Treasure .... (RCA PB-13710)		.75	3.00	84
WHAT ABOUT ME? .... (RCA PB-13899)		.75	3.00	84
(Shown as by Kenny Rogers, Kim Carnes, and James Ingram, all three pictured. Top of sleeve is straight cut.)				
WHAT ABOUT ME? .... (RCA PB-13899)		.75	3.00	84
(Shown as by Kenny Rogers, Kim Carnes, and James Ingram, all three pictured. Top of sleeve is curve cut.)				
CRAZY/The Stranger .... (RCA PB-13975)		.75	3.00	84
MORNING DESIRE/People In Love .... (RCA PB-14194)		1.25	5.00	85
(Poster sleeve)				
CHRISTMAS WITHOUT YOU/A Christmas To Remember .... (RCA PB-14261)		.75	3.00	85
TOMB OF THE UNKNOWN LOVE/Our Perfect Song .... (RCA PB-14298)		.75	3.00	86
THE PRIDE IS BACK/Didn't We? .... (RCA PB-14384)		.75	3.00	86
(Shown as by Kenny Rogers With Nickie Ryder)				

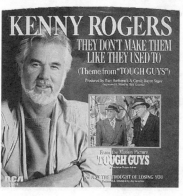

TITLE	LABEL AND NUMBER	VG	NM	YR

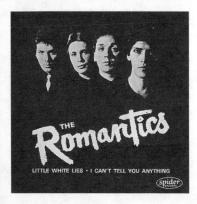

THEY DON'T MAKE THEM LIKE THEY USED TO (THEME FROM "TOUGH GUYS")/
Just The Thought Of Losing You? .... (RCA 5016-7-R) .75 3.00 86
(From the motion picture *Tough Guys*. Burt Lancaster and Kirk Douglas pictured front and back, Rogers on front.)

WHEN YOU PUT YOUR HEART IN IT .... (Reprise 27812-7) .75 3.00 88
(The Official Theme Song for the 1988 U.S. Gymnastics Team)

CHRISTMAS IN AMERICA/Joy To The World .... (Reprise 22750-7) .75 3.00 89
Also see the New Christy Minstrels, Dolly Parton (*Real Love*), U.S.A. For Africa, Voices Of America

ROGERS, ROY
See Rex Allen, Jr. (*Last Of The Silver Screen Cowboys*)

ROLIE, GREGG
THE HANDS OF TIME/I Will Get To You .... (Columbia 38-07351) .75 3.00 87
THE HANDS OF TIME .... (Columbia 38-07351) 1.00 4.00 87
(Promotional issue, *Demonstration Only–Not For Sale* printed on back)
Also see Journey, Santana

ROLLING STONES, THE
NOT FADE AWAY/I Wanna Be Your Man .... (London 45-9657) 37.50 150.00 64
TELL ME/I Just Wanna Make Love To You .... (London 45-9682) 20.00 80.00 64
IT'S ALL OVER NOW/Good Times, Bad Times .... (London 45-9687) 20.00 80.00 64
TIME IS ON MY SIDE/Congratulations .... (London 45-9708) 15.00 60.00 64
HEART OF STONE/What A Shame .... (London 45-9725) 75.00 300.00 64
THE LAST TIME/Play With Fire .... (London 45-9741) 15.00 60.00 64
I CAN'T GET NO SATISFACTION/The Under Assistant West Coast Promo Man (London 45-9766) 25.00 100.00 65
GET OFF OF MY CLOUD .... (London 45-9792) 7.50 30.00 64
AS TEARS GO BY .... (London 45-9808) 7.50 30.00 65
19TH NERVOUS BREAKDOWN .... (London 45-9823) 7.50 30.00 66
PAINT IT BLACK .... (London 45-901) 6.25 25.00 66
MOTHER'S LITTLE HELPER/Lady Jane .... (London 45-902) 6.25 25.00 66
HAVE YOU SEEN YOUR MOTHER, BABY, STANDING IN THE SHADOW? .... (London 45-903) 6.25 25.00 66
LET'S SPEND THE NIGHT TOGETHER/Ruby Tuesday .... (London 45-904) 6.25 25.00 67
(*Ruby Tuesday* made it to #1 on the Billboard charts while the a-side reached #55)
DANDELION/We Love You .... (London 45-905) 6.25 25.00 67
SHE'S A RAINBOW/2000 Light Years From Home .... (London 45-906) 6.25 25.00 67
JUMPIN' JACK FLASH/Child Of The Moon .... (London 45-908) 5.00 20.00 68
STREET FIGHTING MAN/No Expectations .... (London 45-909) 2000.00 8000.00 68
(Approximately 12 copies are known to exist)
HONKY TONK WOMEN/You Can't Always Get What You Want .... (London 45-910) 3.75 15.00 69
GENERIC ROLLING STONES HALF SLEEVE .... (Rolling Stones no #) .75 3.00 71
(Hard cover, with Rolling Stones tongue logo, used for a variety of releases from 1971-1986. No song titles listed.)
TIME WAITS FOR NO ONE .... (Rolling Stones PR 228) 7.50 30.00 76
(Promotional issue only)
BEFORE THEY MAKE ME RUN .... (Rolling Stones PR 316) 6.25 25.00 78
(Promotional issue only)
MISS YOU/Far Away Eyes .... (Rolling Stones 19307) 1.00 4.00 78
BEAST OF BURDEN/When The Whip Comes Down .... (Rolling Stones 19309) 150.00 600.00 78
SHATTERED/Everything's Turning To Gold .... (Rolling Stones 19310) 1.25 5.00 78
EMOTIONAL RESCUE/Down In The Hole .... (Rolling Stones 20001) 1.00 4.00 80
SHE'S SO COLD/Send It To Me .... (Rolling Stones 21001) 1.00 4.00 80
START ME UP/No Use In Crying .... (Rolling Stones 21003) 1.00 4.00 81
WAITING ON A FRIEND/Little T & A .... (Rolling Stones 21004) 1.00 4.00 81
GOING TO A GO GO (Live)/Beast Of Burden .... (Rolling Stones 21301) 1.00 4.00 82
TIME IS ON MY SIDE (Live)/Twenty Flight Rock (Live) .... (Rolling Stones 7-99978) 1.00 4.00 82
UNDERCOVER OF THE NIGHT/All The Way Down .... (Rolling Stones 7-99813) 1.00 4.00 83
SHE WAS HOT/Think I'm Going Mad .... (Rolling Stones 7-99788) 1.00 4.00 83
HARLEM SHUFFLE/Had It With You .... (Rolling Stones 38-05802) .75 3.00 86
HARLEM SHUFFLE .... (Rolling Stones 38-05802) 1.50 6.00 86
(Promotional issue, *Demonstration–Not For Sale* printed on sleeve)
ONE HIT (TO THE BODY)/Fight .... (Rolling Stones 38-05906) 1.00 4.00 86
ONE HIT (TO THE BODY) .... (Rolling Stones 38-05906) 1.50 6.00 86
(Promotional issue, *Demonstration–Not For Sale* printed on sleeve)
LOVE IS STRONG/The Storm/Love Is Strong (Ted Riley Extended Remix) .... (Virgin NR-38446) .75 3.00 94
OUT OF TEARS (DON WAS EDIT)/
Out Of Tears (Bob Clearmountain Remix Edit)/I'm Gonna Drive .... (Virgin NR-38459) .75 3.00 94
Also see Mick Jagger, Keith Richards, Peter Tosh (*Don't Look Back*), Willie and the Poor Boys (Charlie Watts, Bill Wyman), Bill Wyman

ROLLINS, HENRY
EARACHE MY EYE/You Know Me .... (Sub Pop 72) 3.75 15.00 90
(Shown as by the Rollins Band. Limited edition of 4,000 with the first 2,000 on pink vinyl and the remaining 2,000 on black.)
LET THERE BE ROCK/Carry Me Down .... (CZ 035) 2.50 10.00
(Shown as by Henry Rollins and the Hard Ons. Limited edition of 4,000.)
Also see Black Flag

ROMAN, LYN
THE TASTE OF LOVE/Unchained .... (Dot 45-17203) 1.50 6.00 69
(From the motion picture *The Brotherhood*)

ROMAN NUMERALS, THE
MATCHSTICK IN A WHIRLPOOL/The Come On .... (Columbia 4-44314) 2.00 8.00 67

ROMANTIC COMEDY
(Motion Picture)
See Peabo Bryson and Roberta Flack (*Maybe*)

ROMANTICS
LITTLE WHITE LIES/I Can't Tell You Anything .... (Spider 101) 1.50 6.00 77
TELL IT TO CARRIE/First In Line .... (Bomp 120) 1.50 6.00 78
(Issued with small-hole 45 RPM record)
WHAT I LIKE ABOUT YOU .... (Nemperor ZS9-7527) 2.00 8.00 79
ONE IN A MILLION/Do Me Anyway You Wanna .... (Nemperor ZS4-04373) .75 3.00 83

		VG	NM	YR
TEST OF TIME / Better Make A Move .... (Nemperor ZS4-05587)		.75	3.00	85
TEST OF TIME / Better Make A Move .... (Nemperor ZS4-05587)		1.00	4.00	85
(Promotional issue, *Demonstration–Not For Sale* printed on sleeve)				
MYSTIFIED / Make It Last .... (Nemperor ZS4-05684)		.75	3.00	85
MYSTIFIED .... (Nemperor ZS4-05684)		1.00	4.00	85
(Promotional issue, *Demonstration–Not For Sale* printed on sleeve)				

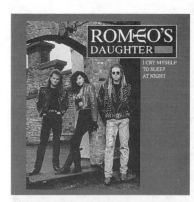

ROMEO, BOB
See James Dean (*Jungle Rhythm*)

ROMEO & JULIET
(Motion Picture)
See Nino Rota (*What Is Youth*)

ROMEO'S DAUGHTER
		VG	NM	YR
DON'T BREAK MY HEART / Wild Child .... (Jive/RCA 1140-7-J)		.75	3.00	88
I CRY MYSELF TO SLEEP AT NIGHT / Don't Look Back .... (RCA 1176-7-J)		.75	3.00	88

ROMEO VOID
		VG	NM	YR
WHITE SWEATER / Apache .... (415 Records 0012)		1.25	5.00	84
(Issued with small-hole 45 RPM record)				
SAY NO / Six Days And One .... (Columbia 38 04704)		1.00	4.00	84
SAY NO .... (Columbia 38 04704)		1.25	5.00	84
(Promotional issue, *Demonstration–Not For Sale* printed on sleeve)				

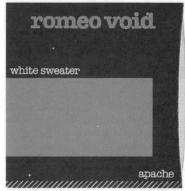

ROME SYMPHONY ORCHESTRA
		VG	NM	YR
THEME FROM BEN-HUR .... (MGM 12887)		1.25	5.00	60

ROME WILL NEVER LEAVE YOU
(Television Movie)
See Richard Chamberlain (*Rome Will Never Leave You*)

RONETTES, THE
		VG	NM	YR
WALKING IN THE RAIN / How Does It Feel .... (Philles 123)		12.50	50.00	64
BORN TO BE TOGETHER / Blues For Baby .... (Philles 126)		12.50	50.00	64
IS THIS WHAT I GET FOR LOVING YOU? / Oh, I Love You .... (Philles 128)		18.75	75.00	65
Also see Ronnie Spector				

RONNY AND THE DAYTONAS
		VG	NM	YR
DIANNE, DIANNE / All American Girl .... (RCA Victor 47-8896)		7.50	30.00	66

RONSON, MICK
		VG	NM	YR
SLAUGHTER ON 10TH AVENUE / GROWING UP AND I'M FINE / All Cut Up On You / Andy Warhol .... (RCA DJEO-0259)		6.25	25.00	74
(Promotional issue only. B-side shown as by Dana Gillespie.)				

RONSTADT, LINDA
		VG	NM	YR
UP TO MY NECK IN HIGH MUDDY WATER / Carnival Bear .... (Capitol 2110)		7.50	30.00	68
(Shown as by Linda Ronstadt & the Stone Poneys)				
BACK IN THE USA / White Rhythm And Blues .... (Asylum 45519)		1.25	5.00	78
HOW DO I MAKE YOU / Rambler Gambler .... (Asylum 46602)		1.00	4.00	80
GET CLOSER / Sometimes You Just Can't Win .... (Asylum 7-69948)		1.00	4.00	82
I KNEW YOU WHEN / Talk To Me Of Mendocino .... (Asylum 7-69853)		1.00	4.00	82
SOMEWHERE OUT THERE .... (MCA 52973A)		1.00	4.00	86
(Shown as by Linda Ronstadt and James Ingram. From the motion picture *An American Tail*.)				
WHEN YOU WISH UPON A STAR / Little Girl Blue .... (Asylum 7-69507)		1.00	4.00	86
(Shown as by Linda Ronstadt With Nelson Riddle & His Orchestra)				
TO KNOW HIM IS TO LOVE HIM .... (Warner Bros. 28492-7)		1.00	4.00	87
(Shown as by Dolly Parton, Linda Ronstadt, Emmylou Harris)				
THOSE MEMORIES OF YOU .... (Warner Bros. 28248-7)		1.00	4.00	87
(Shown as by Dolly Parton, Linda Ronstadt, Emmylou Harris)				
Also see Emmylou Harris (*Light Of The Stable*), Paul Simon (*Under African Skies*)				

ROOFTOPS
(Motion Picture)
See Etta James (*Avenue D*)

ROOFTOP SINGERS
		VG	NM	YR
TOM CAT / Shoes .... (Vanguard 35019)		2.00	8.00	63
MAMA DON'T ALLOW .... (Vanguard 35020)		2.00	8.00	63

ROOM, THE
(Motion Picture)
See Ken Jones (*Theme From Room 43*)

ROOMMATES, THE
		VG	NM	YR
GLORY OF LOVE .... (Valmor X 008)		5.00	20.00	61
(Possibly a promotional issue only)				
Also see Cathy Jean & the Roommates				

ROONEY, MICKEY
(Actor/Entertainer)
		VG	NM	YR
JIMMY McHUGH MELODY / Don't Blame Me .... (BER 842)		1.50	6.00	
(Shown as by Mickey Rooney and Ann Miller)				
LOVER OF THE SIMPLE THINGS / You Perfect Stranger .... (New Horizon # unknown)		1.50	6.00	

ROOTBOY SLIM & THE SEX CHANGE BAND WITH THE ROOTETTES
		VG	NM	YR
WORLD WAR III / Dare To Be Fat .... (Illegal 9007)		1.25	5.00	79

ROSE, THE
(Motion Picture)
See Bette Midler (*The Rose*)

ROSE, DAVID, AND HIS ORCHESTRA
		VG	NM	YR
FORBIDDEN PLANET / The Swan .... (MGM K-12243)		3.75	15.00	56
(A-side from the motion picture *Forbidden Planet*, b-side from the motion picture *Swan*. Each side of the sleeve pictures a scene from each film.)				

TITLE	LABEL AND NUMBER	VG	NM	YR

THE THEME FROM THE WONDERFUL WORLD OF THE BROTHERS GRIMM/
Black And Tan Fantasy .... (MGM K-13086) | 2.00 | 8.00 | 62
(A-side from the motion picture *The Wonderful World Of The Brothers Grimm*)

ROSE, TIM
MOTHER, FATHER WHERE ARE YOU/I'm Bringin' It Home .... (Columbia 4-43563) | 2.00 | 8.00 | 66
(Promotional issue only)
HEY JOE .... (Columbia 4-43648) | 3.00 | 12.00 | 66
(Promotional issue only)

ROSELLI, JIMMY
LAUGH IT OFF/Why Don't We Do This More Often .... (United Artists 866) | 1.25 | 5.00 | 65

ROSS, DIANA
REACH OUT & TOUCH (SOMEBODY'S HAND)/Dark Side Of The World .... (Motown 1165) | 2.00 | 8.00 | 70
AIN'T NO MOUNTAIN HIGH ENOUGH/Can't It Wait Until Tomorrow .... (Motown 1169) | 2.00 | 8.00 | 70
REMEMBER ME/How About You .... (Motown 1176) | 2.00 | 8.00 | 70
FIRST TV SPECIAL .... (Motown no #) | 2.50 | 10.00 | 71
(Half sleeve not issued with a specific 45. Front of sleeve states *Remember To Watch Diana Ross' First TV Special, Sun., April 18th, 10:00 p.m. EST on The ABC-TV Network*. Back of sleeve advertises the box set *The Motown Story*.)

GOOD MORNING HEARTACHE/God Bless The Child .... (Motown 1211F) | 2.00 | 8.00 | 73
(From the motion picture *Lady Sings The Blues*)
SORRY DOESN'T ALWAYS MAKE IT RIGHT .... (Motown 1335F) | 2.00 | 8.00 | 74
THEME FROM MAHOGANY (DO YOU KNOW WHERE YOU'RE GOING TO) (Motown M1377F) | 2.00 | 8.00 | 75
(Issued with either stock black or promotional yellow vinyl. From the motion picture *Mahogany*.)
I THOUGHT IT TOOK A LITTLE TIME .... (Motown 1387F) | 2.00 | 8.00 | 76
EASE ON DOWN THE ROAD .... (MCA/Motown/Epic 40947) | 1.50 | 6.00 | 78
(Shown as by Diana Ross/Michael Jackson. From the motion picture *The Wiz*.)
IT'S MY TURN .... (Motown 1496F) | 2.00 | 8.00 | 80
(From the motion picture *It's My Turn*. Michael Douglas and Jill Clayburgh pictured on back.)

MY OLD PIANO .... (Motown 1531) | 3.00 | 12.00 | 80
(Promotional issue only)
WE CAN NEVER LIGHT THAT OLD FLAME AGAIN .... (Motown 1626F) | 2.00 | 8.00 | 82
MUSCLES/I Am Me .... (RCA PB-13348) | 1.00 | 4.00 | 82
(Top of sleeve is curved and back of sleeve has a 1/2" white band at the top)
MUSCLES/I Am Me .... (RCA PB-13348) | 1.00 | 4.00 | 82
(Front of sleeve has a tab cut at the top and no white band on the back)
PIECES OF ICE/Still In Love .... (RCA PB-13549) | 1.00 | 4.00 | 83
ALL OF YOU/The Last Time .... (Columbia 38-04507) | .75 | 3.00 | 84
(A-side shown as by Julio Iglesias and Diana Ross)
ALL OF YOU/The Last Time .... (Columbia 38-04507) | 1.00 | 4.00 | 84
(Promotional issue, *Demonstration Only–Not For Sale* printed on sleeve. A-side shown as by Julio Iglesias and Diana Ross.)
SWEPT AWAY (Edited Version)/Fight For It .... (RCA PB-13864) | .75 | 3.00 | 84
(Photography by Francesco Scavullo)
MISSING YOU .... (RCA PB-13966) | .75 | 3.00 | 84
TELEPHONE/Fool For Your Love .... (RCA PB-14032) | .75 | 3.00 | 85
(Photography by Francesco Scavullo)
EATEN ALIVE .... (RCA PB-14181) | .75 | 3.00 | 85
CHAIN REACTION/More And More .... (RCA PB-14244) | .75 | 3.00 | 85
(A new mix was released in 1986 with the same catalog number. Whether or not a different sleeve was released is unknown.)
DIRTY LOOKS/So Close .... (RCA/Ross 5297-7-R) | .75 | 3.00 | 87
TELL ME AGAIN/I Am Me .... (RCA/Ross 5297-7-R) | .75 | 3.00 | 87
IF WE HOLD ON TOGETHER .... (MCA 53448) | .75 | 3.00 | 88
(From the motion picture *The Land Before Time*)
WORKIN' OVERTIME (WORK THAT 7" VERSION)/
Workin' Overtime (Work This Instrumental) .... (Motown 1964) | .75 | 3.00 | 89
(Three other catalog numbers are known of; 1924F, S45-17838, and S45-17886. It is unknown if there are actual sleeve variations for these releases.)

EXTENDED PLAYS
T'AINT NOBODY'S BIZNESS IF I DO/GOOD MARNING HEARTACHE/
My Man/You've Changed .... (Motown M-1531) | 2.50 | 10.00 | 72
(Promotional issue only, from the motion picture *Lady Sings The Blues*)
Also see the Supremes, U.S.A. For Africa, Voices Of America

ROSSELINI, ISABELLA
(Actress)
See Bobby Vinton *(Blue Velvet)*

ROSTAMO, DAVID
CULTURE VULTURE/Dead Poets .... (Sire 29019-7) | .75 | 3.00 | 84

ROTA, NINO
WHAT IS A YOUTH/Farewell Love Scene .... (Capitol 2502) | 1.50 | 6.00 | 69
(From the motion picture *Romeo & Juliet*, Leonard Whiting and Olivia Hussey pictured. Rota was the co-composer of the soundtrack. Glen Weston is the vocalist for the a-side and is credited on the record, not the sleeve. The b-side is dialogue highlights by Whiting and Hussey with original score.)
LOVE THEME FROM THE GODFATHER/The Godfather Waltz .... (Paramount 0152) | 1.50 | 6.00 | 72

ROTH, DAVID LEE
CALIFORNIA GIRLS .... (Warner Bros. 29102-7) | .75 | 3.00 | 85
JUST A GIGOLO/I AIN'T GOT NOBODY (MEDLEY) .... (Warner Bros. 29040-7) | .75 | 3.00 | 85
YANKEE ROSE .... (Warner Bros. 28656-7) | .75 | 3.00 | 86
GOIN' CRAZY!/¡Loco Del Calor! .... (Warner Bros. 28584-7) | .75 | 3.00 | 86
THAT'S LIFE/Bump And Grind .... (Warner Bros. 28511-7) | .75 | 3.00 | 86
JUST LIKE PARADISE/Bottom Line .... (Warner Bros. 28119-7) | .75 | 3.00 | 88
STAND UP .... (Warner Bros. 28108-7) | .75 | 3.00 | 88
DAMN GOOD .... (Warner Bros. 27825-7) | .75 | 3.00 | 88
Also see Van Halen

ROTTERS, THE
SIT ON MY FACE STEVIE NICKS/Amputee .... (Rotten 002) | 6.25 | 25.00 | 78

ROUSSOS, DEMIS
THAT'S ONCE IN A LIFETIME .... (Mercury 73992)   1.00   4.00   78

ROWAN & MARTIN'S LAUGH-IN
(Television Series)
    Related see Teresa Graves, Goldie Hawn, Lily Tomlin

ROWAN & MARTY
HANG ON THE BELL NELLIE .... (Epic 5-10042)   2.00   8.00   66

ROWELL, VICTORIA
(Actress)
    See the Soaps and Hearts Ensemble

ROWLAND, KEVIN
    See Dexy's Midnight Runners

ROWLAND, STEVE, AND THE RING LEADERS
OUT-RIDIN'/Here Kum The Karts .... (Cross Country 1-1818)   5.00   20.00   60s

ROWLES, JOHN
IN THE WORLD OF THE YOUNG .... (Kapp 2018)   2.00   8.00   71

ROXY MUSIC
JEALOUS GUY/To Turn You On .... (Atco 7329)   1.25   5.00   81
TAKE A CHANCE WITH ME/India .... (Warner Bros. 29978-7)   1.00   4.00   82
    Also see Bryan Ferry, Foreigner (Rick Wills). Founding member Brian Eno left the band in 1973.

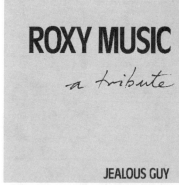

ROYAL, BILLY JOE
MAMA DIDN'T RAISE NO FOOLS/Get Behind Me Devil .... (Tollie 9011)   5.00   20.00   63
    (Promotional issue only)
I'LL PIN A NOTE ON YOUR PILLOW/A Place For A Heartache .... (Atlantic America 7-99404)   .75   3.00   87
OUT OF SIGHT AND ON MY MIND/She Don't Cry Like She Used To .. (Atlantic America 7-99364)   .75   3.00   87
IT KEEPS RIGHT ON HURTIN'/ .... (Atlantic America 7-99295)   .75   3.00   87
TELL IT LIKE IT IS/I Was Losing You .... (Atlantic America 7-99242)   .75   3.00   89
LOVE HAS NO RIGHT/ .... (Atlantic America 7-99217)   .75   3.00   89

ROYAL, ERNIE, AND THE MUTINEERS
BALLAD OF THE DEFIANT .... (Colpix 653)   2.50   10.00   62

ROYAL GUARDSMEN, THE
SNOOPY'S CHRISTMAS/It Kinda Looks Like Christmas .... (Laurie 3416)   3.75   15.00   68

ROYAL JACKS, THE
TAM-O-SHANTER/Anticipation .... (Amy 865)   3.75   15.00   62

ROYAL PHILHARMONIC ORCHESTRA, THE
    See Cliff Richard (B-side of All I Ask Of You)

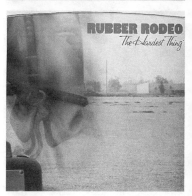

ROYALTY
WANNA MAKE IT UP TO YOU .... (Warner Bros. 27843-7)   .75   3.00   87
ANYONE IN LOVE .... (Warner Bros. 28345-7)   .75   3.00   87
BABY GONNA SHAKE .... (Sire 22988-7)   .75   3.00   89

RUBBER RODEO
JOLENE/Who's On Top .... (Rumble 02)   2.00   8.00   81
THE HARDEST THING/Woman Of Straw .... (Mercury 880 026-7)   .75   3.00   84

RUBIES, THE
SPANISH BOY/Deeper .... (Vee-Jay 596)   6.25   25.00   65
    (Promotional issue only, Promotion Copy Not For Sale printed on sleeve)

RUBINOOS, THE
I THINK WE'RE ALONE NOW/As Long As I'm With You .... (Beserkley 5741)   1.25   5.00   76
NOTHING A LITTLE LOVE WON'T CURE/Leave My Heart Alone .... (Beserkley 5810)   1.25   5.00   77
EXTENDED PLAYS
ROCK AND ROLL IS DEAD .... (Beserkley AE7-1120)   1.25   5.00   77
    (Promotional issue only titled Great Ideas From Beserkley, issued with a small-hole 33-1/3 RPM record. Also
    includes 1 song each, the titles are not listed on sleeve, by Greg Kihn, Earthquake, and Jonathan Richman &
    the Modern Lovers.)

RUBY AND THE ROMANTICS
HEY THERE LONELY BOY/Not A Moment Too Soon .... (Kapp 544)   3.75   15.00   63
YOUNG WINGS CAN FLY/Day Dreaming .... (Kapp 557)   3.75   15.00   63

RUCKER, SANDY
LAY ME DOWN/Lullabye .... (Monument ZS7 8560)   1.50   6.00   72

RUDE AWAKENING
(Motion Picture)
    See Mike + the Mechanics (Revolution)

RUFFIN, CALVIN (HOUN'DOG)
MY LITTLE HOME ON THE RANGE/Hurry-Hurry .... (Golden Crest 114)   3.75   15.00   50s

RUFFIN, DAVID
    See Daryl Hall & John Oates (The Way You Do The Things You Do), the Temptations

RUFUS
BRAND NEW DAY .... (Epic 5-10691)   2.50   10.00   71
EXTENDED PLAYS
LILAH .... (MCA S-33-1754)   1.00   4.00   81
    (Promotional issue only titled McDonald's Menu Music Chant, issued with a small-hole 33-1/3 RPM record. Also
    includes one song each, the titles are not listed on sleeve, by Donnie Iris, Terri Gibbs, and One Way.)
    Also see Chaka Khan

RULING CLASS
(Motion Picture)
    See Hugo & Luigi (Theme From The Ruling Class)

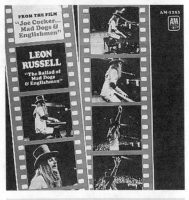

TITLE	LABEL AND NUMBER	VG	NM	YR

RUMBEL, NANCY
See Tingstad-Rumbel (*Fisherman's Dream*)

RUMBLE FISH
(Motion Picture)
    See Stewart Copeland and Stanard Ridgway (*Don't Box Me In*)

RUMBLES LTD.

| THE WILDEST CHRISTMAS/Santa Claus Is Coming To Town | (Dad's 103) | 3.75 | 15.00 | 66 |

RUNAWAYS, THE
See Lita Ford, Joan Jett, Cherie & Marie Currie. Micki (Michael) Steele left the group in 1978, before they recorded any material, and joined the Bangles in 1983.

RUNDGREN, TODD

| PARALLEL LINES | (Warner Bros. 22868-7) | 1.00 | 4.00 | 89 |

    Also see Nazz, Jim Steinman (*The Storm*), Utopia

RUN-D.M.C.

| MY ADIDAS/Peter Piper | (Profile 5102) | 1.00 | 4.00 | 86 |
| WALK THIS WAY/King Of Rock | (Profile 5112) | 1.00 | 4.00 | 86 |

    (Steve Tyler and Joe Perry of Aerosmith credited on back)

YOU BE ILLIN'/Hit It Run	(Profile 5119)	.75	3.00	86
IT'S TRICKY/Proud To Be Black	(Profile 5131)	.75	3.00	87
RUN'S HOUSE/Beats To The Rhyme	(Profile 5202)	.75	3.00	88
MARY MARY/Rock Box	(Profile 5211)	.75	3.00	88
I'M NOT GOING OUT LIKE THAT/How'd Ya Do It Dee	(Profile 5224)	.75	3.00	88

    Also see Artists United Against Apartheid

RUNNING SCARED
(Motion Picture)
    See Klymaxx (*Man Size Love*), Michael McDonald (*Sweet Freedom*), New Edition (*Once In A Lifetime Groove*), Kim Wilde (*Say You Really Want Me*)

RUSH

TOM SAWYER/Witch Hunt	(Mercury 76109)	2.00	8.00	81
NEW WORLD MAN/Vital Signs (Live)	(Mercury 76179)	1.50	6.00	82
THE BIG MONEY/Red Sector A (Live)	(Mercury 884 191-7)	1.25	5.00	85
TIME STAND STILL/High Water	(Mercury 888 891-7)	1.25	5.00	87

    Also see Bob & Doug McKenzie (Geddy Lee)

RUSH, JENNIFER

| FLAMES OF PARADISE/Call My Name | (Epic 34-07119) | .75 | 3.00 | 87 |

    (Sleeve states *Duet With Elton John*)

| FLAMES OF PARADISE | (Epic 34-07119) | .75 | 3.00 | 87 |

    (Promotional issue with a letter from the record company, *Demonstration–Not For Sale* printed on sleeve. Sleeve states *Duet With Elton John*)

RUSHEN, PATRICE

FORGET ME NOTS/Take You Down To Love	(Elektra 47427)	1.00	4.00	82
WATCH OUT/Over The Phone	(Arista 9562)	.75	3.00	87
COME BACK TO ME/Somewhere	(Arista 9644)	.75	3.00	87

RUSSELL, BRENDA

| PIANO IN THE DARK/This Time I Need You | (A&M 3003) | .75 | 3.00 | 88 |

    (A-side credits Joe Esposito on vocals)
    Also see Michael Franks (*When I Give My Love To You*)

RUSSELL, ELLIE

| I'LL NEVER STOP LOVING YOU/Hard To Get | (Bell 1103) | 1.25 | 5.00 | 60s |

    (Artist name not credited on sleeve)

RUSSELL, KURT
(Actor)
    See the Everly Brothers With the Beach Boys (*Don't Worry Baby*), Ann Wilson and Robin Zander (*Surrender To Me*)

RUSSELL, LEON

| THE BALLAD OF MAD DOGS & ENGLISHMEN/Let It Be | (A&M 1253) | 2.00 | 8.00 | 70 |

    (B-side shown as by Claudia Lennear who is pictured on the back)

IF I WERE A CARPENTER	(Shelter 40210)	1.25	5.00	74
ELVIS AND MARILYN/Anita Bryant	(Paradise 8667)	1.25	5.00	78
RESCUE MY HEART/Lost Love	(Paradise 631)	1.25	5.00	84

    Also see the Legendary Masked Surfers

RUSSO, TONY

| LOVE IS A MANY SPLENDORED THING/Autumn Leaves | (Bell 1106) | 1.00 | 4.00 | 60s |

    (Artist name not credited on sleeve)

RUTHERFORD, MIKE

| MOONSHINE/Working In Line | (Passport 7919) | 3.75 | 15.00 | 80 |

    (Promotional issue only)

| MAXINE/A Day To Remember | (Atlantic 7-89981) | 1.50 | 6.00 | 82 |

    Also see Peter Gabriel (*Walk Through The Fire*), Genesis, Mike + the Mechanics

RUTHLESS PEOPLE
(Motion Picture)
    See Dan Hartman (*Waiting To See You*) , Mick Jagger (*Ruthless People*), Billy Joel (*Modern Woman*)

RYAN, CHARLIE

| SIDE CAR CYCLE | (4 Star 1745) | 5.00 | 20.00 | 60 |

RYAN, IRENE
(Actress)

| GRANNY'S MINI-SKIRT/Bring On The Show | (Nashwood 100) | 7.50 | 30.00 | 68 |

    (Ryan pictured in character as Granny from *The Beverly Hillbillies*. Vocal backgrounds credited to the Marldeys.)

RYDELL, BOBBY

KISSIN' TIME/You'll Never Tame Me .... (Cameo 167)	5.00	20.00	59
WE GOT LOVE/I Dig Girls .... (Cameo 169)	5.00	20.00	59
WILD ONE/Itty Bitty Girl .... (Cameo 171)	5.00	20.00	60
SWINGIN' SCHOOL/Ding A Ling .... (Cameo 175)	5.00	20.00	60
(Red background, a-side from the motion picture *Because They're Young*)			
SWINGIN' SCHOOL/Ding A Ling .... (Cameo 175)	5.00	20.00	60
(Blue background, a-side from the motion picture *Because They're Young*)			
VOLARE/I'll Do It Again .... (Cameo 179)	3.75	15.00	60
SWAY/Groovy Tonight .... (Cameo 182)	3.75	15.00	61
GOOD TIME BABY/Cherie .... (Cameo 186)	3.75	15.00	61
THAT OLD BLACK MAGIC/Don't Be Afraid .... (Cameo 190)	3.75	15.00	61
THE FISH/The Third House .... (Cameo 192)	3.75	15.00	61
I WANNA THANK YOU/The Door To Paradise .... (Cameo 201)	3.75	15.00	61
JINGLE BELL ROCK/Jingle Bell Imitations .... (Cameo 205)	3.75	15.00	61
(Shown as by Bobby Rydell and Chubby Checker)			
I'VE GOT BONNIE/Lose Her .... (Cameo 209)	3.75	15.00	62
SWINGIN' TOGETHER/Teach Me To Twist .... (Cameo 214)	3.75	15.00	62
(Shown as by Bobby Rydell and Chubby Checker)			
I'LL NEVER DANCE AGAIN/Gee It's Wonderful .... (Cameo 217)	3.75	15.00	62
(The b-side originally on the sleeve, *Don't Ever Take Her For Granted*, has been overprinted with a dark green block of color. The new title, *Gee It's Wonderful*, is printed in silver on top of the dark green area.)			
THE CHA-CHA-CHA/The Best Man Cried .... (Cameo 228)	3.75	15.00	62
BUTTERFLY BABY/Love Is Blind .... (Cameo 242)	3.75	15.00	63
WILDWOOD DAYS/Will You Be My Baby .... (Cameo 252)	3.75	15.00	63
LITTLE QUEENIE/The Woodpecker Song .... (Cameo 265)	3.75	15.00	63
LET'S MAKE LOVE TONIGHT/Childhood Sweetheart .... (Cameo 272)	3.75	15.00	63
FORGET HIM/Love, Love Go Away .... (Cameo 280)	3.75	15.00	63
MAKE ME FORGET/Little Girl I've Had A Busy Day .... (Cameo 309)	3.75	15.00	64
A WORLD WITHOUT LOVE/Our Faded Love .... (Cameo 320)	3.75	15.00	64
I JUST CAN'T SAY GOODBYE/Two Is The Loneliest Number .... (Capitol 5305)	3.00	12.00	64

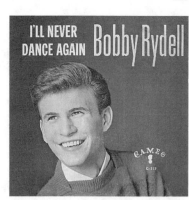

RYDER, MITCH, AND THE DETROIT WHEELS

SOCK IT TO ME-BABY!/I Never Had It Better .... (New Voice 820)	3.75	15.00	67
(1-1/4" band on top is black with type in color)			
SOCK IT TO ME-BABY!/I Never Had It Better .... (New Voice 820)	3.00	12.00	67
(1-1/4" band on top is white with type in black)			
TOO MANY FISH IN THE SEA & THREE LITTLE FISHIES/One Grain Of Sand .... (New Voice 822)	3.00	12.00	67
(Shown as by Mitch Ryder. Sleeve spells "Fishies", 45 spells "Fishes".)			
Also see Billy Lee & the Rivieras, the Rockets (James McCarty, Johnny Badenjek)			

RYDER, NICKIE
See Kenny Rogers (*The Pride Is Back*)

RYDER, WINONA
(Actress)
See the Pretenders (*Windows Of The World*)

S

SAAD, SUE, AND THE NEXT

WON'T GIVE IT UP/Kamonbaybeh .... (Planet 45912)	1.00	4.00	80

SADANE

ONE WAY LOVE AFFAIR .... (Warner Bros. 49663)	.75	3.00	81

SAD CAFÉ

LA-DI-DA/Love Today .... (Swan Song 72002)	1.00	4.00	80
Also see Paul Young, Mike + the Mechanics (Paul Young)			

SADE

HANG ON TO YOUR LOVE/Cherry Pie .... (Portrait 37-04664)	.75	3.00	84
HANG ON TO YOUR LOVE .... (Portrait 37-04664)	1.00	4.00	84
(Promotional issue, *Demonstration–Not For Sale* printed on sleeve)			
SMOOTH OPERATOR/Spirit .... (Portrait 37-04807)	.75	3.00	85
SMOOTH OPERATOR .... (Portrait 37-04807)	1.00	4.00	85
(Promotional issue, *Demonstration Not For Sale* printed on sleeve)			
YOUR LOVE IS KING/Love Affair With Life .... (Portrait 37-05408)	.75	3.00	85
YOUR LOVE IS KING/Love Affair With Life .... (Portrait 37-05437)	.75	3.00	85
(Sleeve is dated 1984 although it wasn't released until 1985. Note the catalog number variation from the previous title.)			
YOUR LOVE IS KING .... (Portrait 37-05437)	1.00	4.00	85
(Promotional issue, *Demonstration–Not For Sale* printed on sleeve)			
SWEETEST TABOO/You're Not The Man .... (Portrait 37-05713)	.75	3.00	85
SWEETEST TABOO (SHORT VERSION)/Sweetest Taboo (Long Version) .... (Portrait 37-05713)	1.00	4.00	85
(Promotional issue, *Demonstration–Not For Sale* printed on sleeve)			
NEVER AS GOOD AS THE FIRST TIME/Keep Hanging On (Live Instrumental) (Portrait 37-05846)	.75	3.00	85
NEVER AS GOOD AS THE FIRST TIME .... (Portrait 37-05846)	1.00	4.00	85
(Promotional issue, *Demonstration–Not For Sale* printed on sleeve)			
IS IT A CRIME?/Punch Drunk .... (Portrait 37-06121)	.75	3.00	86
(Photography by Helmut Newton)			
IS IT A CRIME? (SHORT VERSION)/Is It A Crime? (Long Version) .... (Portrait 37-06121)	1.00	4.00	86
(Promotional issue, *Demonstration–Not For Sale* printed on sleeve, photography by Helmut Newton)			
PARADISE/Super Bien Total .... (Portrait 37-07904)	.75	3.00	88
NOTHING CAN COME BETWEEN US/Make Some Room .... (Portrait 37-07977)	.75	3.00	88

SADLER, SSGT BARRY

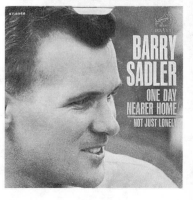

THE BALLAD OF THE GREEN BERETS/Letter From Vietnam .... (RCA Victor 47-8739)	2.00	8.00	66
THE "A" TEAM/An Empty Glass .... (RCA Victor 47-8804)	2.50	10.00	66
ONE DAY NEARER HOME/Not Just Lonely .... (RCA Victor 47-8966)	2.50	10.00	66
(Shown as by Barry Sadler)			

TITLE	LABEL AND NUMBER	VG	NM	YR

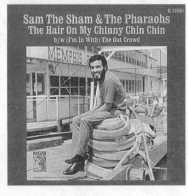

SA-FIRE
BOY, I'VE BEEN TOLD (CLUB EDIT)/Boy, I've Been Told ...... (Mercury/Cutting 870 514-7)	.75	3.00	88
THINKING OF YOU/Let Me Be The One ...... (Mercury/Cutting 872 502-7)	.75	3.00	89
GONNA MAKE IT (CLUB EDIT)/Gonna Make It ...... (Mercury/Cutting 874 278-7)	.75	3.00	89

SAGA
THE FLYER/The Sound Of Strangers ...... (Portrait 37-04178)	.75	3.00	83
THE FLYER ...... (Portrait 37-04178)	1.00	4.00	83
(Promotional issue, *Demonstration–Not For Sale* printed on sleeve)			
WHAT DO I KNOW?/Easy Way Out ...... (Portrait 37-05463)	.75	3.00	85
WHAT DO I KNOW? (LP VERSION)/What Do I Know? ...... (Portrait 37-05463)	1.00	4.00	85
(Promotional issue, *Demonstration–Not For Sale* printed on sleeve)			
ONLY TIME WILL TELL/The Way Of The World ...... (Atlantic 7-89195)	.75	3.00	88

SAGER, CAROLE BAYER
STRONGER THAN BEFORE/Somebody's Been Lying ...... (Boardwalk WS8-02054)	1.00	4.00	81
(Sager and her husband/producer Burt Bacharach pictured on back)			
Also see Dionne Warwick *(That's What Friends Are For)*			

SAHM, DOUG
I'M NOT A FOOL ANYMORE/Don't Fight It ...... (Teardrop 3482)	1.25	5.00	83
(Shown as by Doug Sahm & Augie Meyers, Sahm pictured)			
Also see the Sir Douglas Quintet (Doug Sahm)			

SAINT, EVA MARIE
(Actress)
See Joni James *(Never Till Now)*

ST. ELMO'S FIRE
(Motion Picture)
See John Parr *(St. Elmo's Fire)*

SAINTE-MARIE, BUFFY
SOULFUL SHADE OF BLUE ...... (Vanguard 35064)	5.00	20.00	83

ST. GEORGE AND TANA
SO TENDERLY ...... (Kapp 832)	2.00	8.00	67

ST. JOHN, KRISTOFF
(Actor)
See the Soaps and Hearts Ensemble

ST. PAUL
RICH MAN ...... (MCA 53110)	.75	3.00	87

SAINTS, THE
(I'M) STRANDED/No Time ...... (Sire 1005)	1.50	6.00	77

ST. THOMAS AQUINAS SCHOOL CHOIR
See Talking Heads *(Love For Sale)*

SALES, SOUPY
SOUPY SEZ/Pie In The Face ...... (Reprise 0368)	5.00	20.00	64
SPANISH FLEA/That Wasn't No Girl ...... (Capitol 5752)	5.00	20.00	66
USE YOUR NOGGIN/The Backwards Alphabet ...... (Capitol 5766)	5.00	20.00	66
SILLY SIDNEY ...... (Wonderland 187)	2.50	10.00	72
BINGITY BANGITY BUS ...... (Wonderland 342)	2.50	10.00	72

SALT-N-PEPA
SPINDERELLA'S NOT A FELLA (BUT A GIRL D.J.)/Shake Your Thang ...... (Next Plateau KF319)	.75	3.00	88
(B-side credit states *Featuring E.U.*)			
GET UP EVERYBODY (GET UP) (REMIX)/Twist And Shout ...... (Next Plateau KF321)	.75	3.00	88
(Front pictures Cheryl "Salt" James, Sandy "Pepa" Denton, and DJ "Spinderella" Roper side by side in a studio shot)			
GET UP EVERYBODY (GET UP) (REMIX)/Twist And Shout ...... (Next Plateau KF321)	.75	3.00	88
(Front pictures Cheryl "Salt" James, and Sandy "Pepa" Denton in a performance shot with DJ "Spinderella" Roper in the background)			

SALUGA, BILL
DANCIN' JOHNSON ...... (A&M 2140)	1.00	4.00	79

SAM THE SHAM AND THE PHARAOHS
JU JU HAND/Big City Lights ...... (MGM K-13364)	3.75	15.00	65
RING DANG DOO/Don't Try It ...... (MGM K-13397)	3.75	15.00	65
THE HAIR ON MY CHINNY CHIN CHIN/(I'm In With) The Out Crowd ...... (MGM K-13581)	3.75	15.00	66
HOW DO YOU CATCH A GIRL/The Love You Left Behind ...... (MGM K-13649)	3.75	15.00	66

SANBORN, DAVID
SLAM ...... (Reprise 27857-7)	.75	3.00	88
YOU ARE EVERYTHING ...... (Reprise 27623-7)	.75	3.00	88
Also see Randy Crawford *(Knockin' On Heaven's Door)*			

SAN DIEGO CHARGERS
(Football Team)
See Captain Q. B. & The Big Boys *(San Diego Super Chargers)*

SANDPIPERS, THE, AND MITCHELL MILLER AND ORCHESTRA
THE BALLAD OF DAVY CROCKETT ...... (Golden D197)	2.50	10.00	55
(Children's series issued with six-inch yellow vinyl)			
THE BALLAD OF DAVY CROCKETT/Green Grow The Lilacs ...... (Peter Pan Peanut Butter DF 100)	2.50	10.00	55
(Picture sleeve mailing envelope, premium item available by mail-order)			

SANDS, TOMMY
AFTER THE SENIOR PROM/Big Date ...... (Capitol 3985)	5.00	20.00	58
I'LL BE SEEING YOU/That's The Way I Am ...... (Capitol 4259)	5.00	20.00	59
THE PARENT TRAP/Let's Get Together ...... (Buena Vista 802)	10.00	40.00	61
(Shown as by Annette and Tommy Sands. From the motion picture *The Parent Trap*)			

SANTANA

BLACK MAGIC WOMAN/Hope You're Feeling Better .... (Columbia 4-45270)	3.00	12.00	70
OYE COMO VA/Samba Pa Ti .... (Columbia 4-45330)	2.00	8.00	71
NO ONE TO DEPEND ON .... (Columbia 4-45552)	2.00	8.00	72
THE SENSITIVE KIND/American Gypsy .... (Columbia 18-02178)	.75	3.00	81
THE SENSITIVE KIND/American Gypsy .... (Columbia 18-02178)	1.00	4.00	81

(Promotional issue, *Demonstration/Not For Sale* printed on sleeve. Sleeve lists b-side even though the 45 has *The Sensitive Kind* on both sides)

SAY IT AGAIN .... (Columbia 38-04758)	.75	3.00	85
SAY IT AGAIN .... (Columbia 38-04758)	1.00	4.00	85

(Promotional issue, *Demonstration Only/Not For Sale* printed on sleeve)

EXTENDED PLAYS

JINGO (Excerpt) .... (Columbia AS 1)	1.25	5.00	70

(Promotional issue only titled *Dig This*, issued with a small-hole 33-1/3 RPM record. Also includes excerpts by Pacific Gas and Electric, Moondog, Nick Gravenites, Pete Seeger, Don Ellis, Raven, Firesign Theatre, and Tony Kosinec.)

PERSUASION .... (Columbia Special Products CSS 1491)	1.50	6.00	70

(Promotional issue only titled *The Great American Sound*, issued with a small-hole 33-1/3 RPM record and a 6" x 6" insert for a mail-order Hershey Poster Offer. Also includes one song each by Blood Sweat and Tears, Chicago, and Aretha Franklin.)

Also see Dave Edmunds (Michael Schrieve on b-side of *High School Nights*), Hagar-Schon-Aaronson-Shrieve, Journey (Greg Rolie, Neal Schon), Gregg Rolie

SANTO & JOHNNY

LOVE LOST/Annie .... (Canadian American 118)	3.75	15.00	60
TWISTIN' BELLS/Bullseye .... (Canadian American 120)	3.75	15.00	60
I'LL REMEMBER (IN THE STILL OF THE NIGHT)/Song For Rosemary .. (Canadian American 164)	3.00	12.00	64
A THOUSAND MILES AWAY/Road Block .... (Canadian American 167)	3.00	12.00	60
GOLDFINGER/Sleep Walk .... (Canadian American 182)	3.00	12.00	64

SARAYA

LOVE HAS TAKEN ITS TOLL/ .... (Polydor 889 292-7)	.75	3.00	89

SARDO, FRANKIE

WHEN THE BELLS STOP RINGING/I Know Why And So Do You .... (20th Century Fox 208)	5.00	20.00	59

SARDUCCI, FATHER GUIDO

(Comedian Don Novello)

I WON'T BE TWISTING THIS CHRISTMAS/ Parco MacArthur (MacArthur Park) .... (Warner Bros. 49627)	1.00	4.00	80

SARIDIS, SAVERIO

LOVE IS THE SWEETEST THING/Here's Where I Belong .... (Warner Bros. 5243)	2.00	8.00	61

SARSTEDT, PETER

FROZEN ORANGE JUICE .... (World Pacific 77919)	2.00	8.00	69

SATURDAY NIGHT FEVER

(Motion Picture)

See KC and the Sunshine Band (*Boogie Shoes*), the Trammps (*Disco Inferno*)

SATURDAY NIGHT LIVE

(Television Series)

Related see Dan Aykroyd, John Belushi, the Blues Brothers (Dan Aykroyd, John Belushi), Billy Crystal, Eddie Murphy, Joe Piscopo

SAUCEDO, RICK, WITH THE JORDANAIRES

THE LEGEND LIVES ON/How Great Thou Art .... (Fraternity 3416)	2.50	10.00	78

SAUNDERS, RED

HAMBONE .... (Okeh 7166)	3.75	15.00	65

SAVAGE RESURRECTION

THING IN "E"/Fox Is Sick .... (Mercury 72778)	3.00	12.00	68

SAVAGE ROSE, THE

SUNDAY MORNING/Speak Softly .... (Gregar 71-0104)	5.00	20.00	60s

SAVAGE SEVEN, THE

(Motion Picture)

See Johnny Crawford (*Everyone Should Own A Dream*)

SAVOY BROWN

LAY BACK IN THE ARMS OF SOMEONE .... (Town House 1054)	1.00	4.00	81

SAWYER BROWN

BETTY'S BEIN' BAD .... (Capitol/Curb B-5517)	.75	3.00	85
HEART DON'T FALL NOW .... (Capitol/Curb B-5548)	.75	3.00	86
SOMEWHERE IN THE NIGHT .... (Capitol/Curb B-44054)	.75	3.00	87

SCAGGS, BOZ

LOWDOWN/What Can I Say/We're All Alone .... (Columbia AE 71100)	2.50	10.00	76

(Promotional issue only titled *The Feel Of "Silk Degrees"*, issued with a small-hole 33-1/3 RPM record)

HARD TIMES .... (Columbia 3-10606)	1.50	6.00	77
HEART OF MINE .... (Columbia 38-07780)	1.00	4.00	88

(Back of sleeve credits James Ingram on backing vocals)

COOL RUNNING .... (Columbia 38-07981)	1.00	4.00	88
WHAT'S NUMBER ONE? .... (Columbia 38-08068)	1.00	4.00	88

Also see Steve Miller (*Sitting In Circles*)

SCANDAL

OVER AND OVER/(You Were) Really Worth Waiting For .... (Pacific Rose no #)	2.00	8.00	78

(Hard cover)

LOVE'S GOT A LINE ON YOU/Another Bad Love .... (Columbia 38 03615)	.75	3.00	83
LOVE'S GOT A LINE ON YOU/Another Bad Love .... (Columbia 38 03615)	1.00	4.00	83

(Promotional issue, *Demonstration–Not For Sale* printed on sleeve)

WIN SOME LOSE SOME/Another Bad Love .... (Columbia 38 03987)	.75	3.00	83
WIN SOME LOSE SOME .... (Columbia 38 03987)	1.00	4.00	83

(Promotional issue, *Demonstration–Not For Sale* printed on sleeve)

TITLE	LABEL AND NUMBER	VG	NM	YR

THE WARRIOR/Less Than Half .... (Columbia 38-04424) .75 3.00 84
  (Shown as by Scandal Featuring Patty Smyth)
THE WARRIOR .... (Columbia 38-04424) 1.00 4.00 84
  (Promotional issue, *Demonstration–Not For Sale* printed on sleeve. Shown as by Scandal Featuring Patty Smyth.)
HANDS TIED/Maybe We Went Too Far .... (Columbia 38 04650) .75 3.00 84
  (Shown as by Scandal Featuring Patty Smyth)
HANDS TIED .... (Columbia 38 04650) 1.00 4.00 84
  (Promotional issue, *Demonstration–Not For Sale* printed on sleeve. Shown as by Scandal Featuring Patty Smyth.)
BEAT OF A HEART/Tonight .... (Columbia 38-04750) .75 3.00 84
  (Shown as by Scandal Featuring Patty Smyth)
BEAT OF A HEART .... (Columbia 38-04750) 1.00 4.00 84
  (Promotional issue, *Demonstration Not For Sale* printed on sleeve. Shown as by Scandal Featuring Patty Smyth.)
  Also see Patty Smyth

SCARBURY, JOEY
THE THEME FROM THE GREATEST AMERICAN HERO (BELIEVE IT OR NOT)/
  Little Bit Of Us .... (Elektra 47147) 1.25 5.00 81
  (From the television series *The Greatest American Hero*)

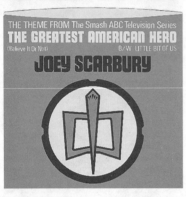

SCARFACE
(Motion Picture)
  See Debbie Harry (*Rush Rush*)

SCARLETT AND BLACK
YOU DON'T KNOW/Japan .... (Virgin 7-99405) .75 3.00 87
  Also see Doctor and the Medics (Sue West)

SCAVULLO, FRANCESCO
(Photographer)
  See Diana Ross (*Telephone, Swept Away*)

SCENT OF MYSTERY
(Motion Picture)
  See Eddie Fisher (*Scent Of Mystery*)

SCHAEFFER, LEONARD
LEONARD SCHAEFFER ENDORSEMENTS .... (Warner Bros.-Seven Arts PRO 301) 1.25 5.00 70s
  (Promotional issue only, issued with a small-hole 33-1/3 RPM record)

SCHATZ, WARREN, WITH THE UNIVERSAL CITY ORCHESTRA
STUCK ON T.V. .... (MCA 52137) .75 3.00 82

SCHIFRIN, LALO
THE ENTERTAINER–HELIOTROPE BOUQUET .... (MCA 52175) .75 3.00 82
  (From the motion picture *Sting II*)

SCHILLING, PETER
THE DIFFERENT STORY (WORLD OF LUST AND CRIME)/
  The Different Story (Instrumental) .... (Elektra 7-69307) .75 3.00 89

SCHMIT, TIMOTHY B.
SO MUCH IN LOVE/She's My Baby And She's Outta Control .... (Asylum 7-69939) 1.00 4.00 82
BOYS NIGHT OUT .... (MCA 53137) .75 3.00 87
  (Shown as by Timothy B)
  Also see Michael Dinner (*The Promised Land*), the Eagles, Poco

SCHNARRE, MONIKA
(Actress)
  See the Soaps and Hearts Ensemble

SCHNEIDER, HELEN
DARLIN' (FALLEN ANGEL) .... (Windsong JH-10991) 1.25 5.00 77
  (Promotional issue only)

SCHNEIDER, JOHN
(Actor-turned-country singer who played Bo Duke in the television series *The Dukes Of Hazzard*)
IT'S NOW OR NEVER/Stay .... (Scotti Brothers ZS6-02105) 1.00 4.00 81
STILL/ .... (Scotti Brothers ZS6-02489) 1.00 4.00 81
I'M GONNA LEAVE YOU TOMORROW/I Don't Feel Much Like A Cowboy Tonight (MCA 52648) .75 3.00 85
WHAT'S A MEMORY LIKE YOU (DOING IN A LOVE LIKE THIS)/
  The One Who Got Away .... (MCA 52723) .75 3.00 85

SCHON, NEAL
  See Hagar-Schon-Aaronson-Shrieve, Hear 'N Aid, Journey, Santana

SCORPIONS
ROCK YOU LIKE A HURRICANE/Coming Home .... (Mercury 818 440-7) 1.00 4.00 84
RHYTHM OF LOVE/We Let It Rock...You Let It Roll .... (Mercury 870-323-7) 1.00 4.00 88
EXTENDED PLAYS
STEAMROCK FEVER .... (RCA JF-11225) 1.25 5.00 78
  (Promotional issue only titled *The Music's On Us*, issued with a small-hole 33-1/3 RPM record. Also includes one song each by Bill Quateman, Aztec Two-Step, and Fandango.)

SCOTT, CLIFFORD
THE PLATINUM HORN .... (Omega # unknown) 2.50 10.00
  (Promotional issue only, no catalog number indicated on sleeve)

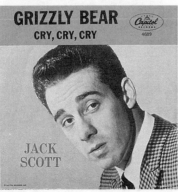

SCOTT, JACK
WITH YOUR LOVE/Geraldine .... (Carlton 483) 7.50 30.00 58
GOODBYE BABY/Save My Soul .... (Carlton 493) 7.50 30.00 58
BURNING BRIDGES/Oh, Little One .... (Top Rank 2041) 7.50 30.00 60
IS THERE SOMETHING ON YOUR MIND/Found A Woman .... (Top Rank 2093) 7.50 30.00 60
A LITTLE FEELING (CALLED LOVE)/Now That I .... (Capitol 4554) 7.50 30.00 61
MY DREAM COME TRUE/Strange Desire .... (Capitol 4597) 7.50 30.00 61
STEPS 1 AND 2/One Of These Days .... (Capitol 4637) 7.50 30.00 61

		VG	NM	YR
GRIZZLY BEAR/Cry, Cry, Cry .... (Capitol 4689)		7.50	30.00	62
THE PART WHERE I CRY/You Only See What You Want To See .... (Capitol 4738)		7.50	30.00	62

SCOTT, SHERREE

		VG	NM	YR
WHOLE LOT OF SHAKIN' GOIN' ON/Unhappy Birthday .... (Rocket 101)		25.00	100.00	58

SCOTT BROTHERS, THE

		VG	NM	YR
PART OF YOU/Kingdom Of Love .... (Skyline 502)		5.00	20.00	60

SCREAMING BLUE MESSIAHS, THE

		VG	NM	YR
I WANNA BE A FLINTSTONE/Little Baby Flintstone .... (Elektra 7-69433)		1.00	4.00	87

SCREAMING HEADLESS TORSOS

		VG	NM	YR
VINNIE/Kermes Macabre .... (Discovery 74506-7)		1.00	4.00	95
(Promotional issue only issued with pink vinyl)				

SCREAMING TREES

		VG	NM	YR
CHANGE HAS COME/Days (Record 1)/ FLASHES/Time Speaks Her Tongue (Record 2) .... (Sub Pop 48)		2.50	10.00	89
(Double single, poster sleeve titled *Change Has Come*. First pressing with one white vinyl and one black vinyl, second pressing with both on red vinyl.)				

SCRITTI POLITTI

		VG	NM	YR
PERFECT WAY .... (Warner Bros. 28949-7)		2.50	10.00	85
(Promotional issue only issued with a sheet of stamps. Cardboard, hand-letterpressed edition produced by Independent Project Press.)				
PERFECT WAY .... (Warner Bros. 28949-7)		.75	3.00	85
(Standard sleeve reproduction of Independent Project Press version)				
WOOD BEEZ (PRAY LIKE ARETHA FRANKLIN)/Wood Beez (Version) ...... (Warner Bros. 29152-7)		.75	3.00	84
BOOM! THERE SHE WAS/A World Come Back To Life .... (Warner Bros. 27976-7)		.75	3.00	88
(Shown as by Scritti Politti Featuring Roger)				
OH PATTI .... (Warner Bros. 27710-7)		.75	3.00	88

SCROOGED
(Motion Picture)

		VG	NM	YR
SCROOGED HALF SLEEVE .... (A&M no #)		.75	3.00	88
(Bill Murray pictured, no recording artist, song title, or catalog number listed. Used for singles from the soundtrack including *Put A Little Love In Your Heart* by Annie Lennox & Al Green and *Sweetest Thing* by New Voices Of Freedom)				

SCRUGGS, EARL
See Flatt & Scruggs, Nitty Gritty Dirt Band (*Honky Tonkin'*)

SEA, JOHNNY

		VG	NM	YR
GOING TO TULSA .... (Columbia 4-44423)		1.50	6.00	68

SEAFOOD MAMA

		VG	NM	YR
HARDEN MY HEART/City Of Roses .... (Whitefire no #)		6.25	25.00	80
Also see Quarterflash				

SEALS, DAN

		VG	NM	YR
EVERYTHING THAT GLITTERS (IS NOT GOLD)/So Easy To Need .... (EMI America B-8311)		.75	3.00	86
I WILL BE THERE (REMIX)/Gonna Be Easy Now .... (EMI America B-8377)		.75	3.00	87
ONE FRIEND .... (Capitol B-44077)		.75	3.00	87
Also see England Dan and John Ford Coley				

SEALS & CROFTS

		VG	NM	YR
MY FAIR SHARE .... (Warner Bros. 8405)		1.25	5.00	77
(From the motion picture *One On One*)				
Also see the Champs				

SEARCHERS, THE

		VG	NM	YR
NEEDLES AND PINS/ Ain't That Just Like Me .... (Kapp 577)		5.00	20.00	64
NEEDLES AND PINS/Ain't That Just Like Me .... (Kapp 577)		12.50	50.00	64
(Promotional issue which states *This is the Group and Record that knocked "The Beatles" out of first place in England*)				
AIN'T THAT JUST LIKE ME .... (Kapp 584)		12.50	50.00	64
(Promotional issue only)				
SOME DAY WE'RE GONNA LOVE AGAIN/No-One Else Could Love Me ...... (Kapp 609)		5.00	20.00	64

SEASE, MARVIN

		VG	NM	YR
CANDY LICKER/Candy Licker (Uncensored LP Edit) .... (London 888-798-7)		.75	3.00	87

SEBADOH

		VG	NM	YR
SOUL AND FIRE/Visibly Wasted .... (Sub Pop 211)		1.25	5.00	93
SKULL (REMIX) .... (Sub Pop 267)		1.25	5.00	94

EXTENDED PLAYS

		VG	NM	YR
SOULMATE .... (Sub Pop 171)		2.50	10.00	92
(Limited edition of 3,000 copies issued with green vinyl and insert. Promotional item given away to Sassy magazine readers on request. Also includes one song each by Velocity Girl, Codeine, and Sebadoh.)				
PRINCESS/1/2 UNDRESSED/Act Of Being Polite/Moisture/Suburban Bathers ...... (Sub Pop 367)		.50	2.00	96
(Limited edition of 2,000 issued with green vinyl)				
Also see Dinosaur Jr (Lou Barlow)				

SEBASTIAN, JOHN

		VG	NM	YR
SHE'S A LADY .... (Kama Sutra 254)		3.00	12.00	68
Also see the Lovin' Spoonful				

SECRET ADMIRER
(Motion Picture)
See Van Stephenson (*No Secrets*)

SECRET AGENT
(Television Series)
See Johnny Rivers (*Secret Agent Man*)

SECRET OF MY SUCCESS, THE
(Motion Picture)
See Night Ranger (*The Secret Of My Success*)

TITLE	LABEL AND NUMBER	VG	NM	YR

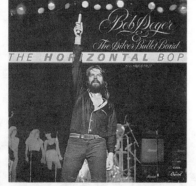

SECRETS, THE
TWIN EXHAUST / Hot Toddy .... (Swan 4097) | 10.00 | 40.00 | 62

SECRETS, THE
HEY, BIG BOY / The Other Side Of Town .... (Philips 40173) | 5.00 | 20.00 | 64

SECRETS, THE
ESCAPE / Ain't Life A Bitch .... (Motor City 1002) | 1.25 | 5.00 | 81
    (Folding sleeve)
    Also see MC5 (Dennis Thompson)

SEDAKA, DARA
(Daughter of Neil Sedaka)
MY GUY .... (RSO 892) | 1.00 | 4.00 | 78

SEDAKA, NEIL
YOU MEAN EVERYTHING TO ME / Run Samson Run .... (RCA Victor 47-7781) | 5.00 | 20.00 | 60
CALENDAR GIRL / The Same Old Fool .... (RCA Victor 47-7829) | 5.00 | 20.00 | 60
LITTLE DEVIL / I Must Be Dreaming .... (RCA Victor 47-7874) | 5.00 | 20.00 | 61
SWEET LITTLE YOU / I Found My World In You .... (RCA Victor 47-7922) | 5.00 | 20.00 | 61
KING OF CLOWNS / Walk With Me .... (RCA Victor 47-8007) | 5.00 | 20.00 | 62
BREAKING UP IS HARD TO DO / As Long As I Live .... (RCA Victor 47-8046) | 5.00 | 20.00 | 62
NEXT DOOR TO AN ANGEL / I Belong To You .... (RCA Victor 47-8086) | 5.00 | 20.00 | 62
ALICE IN WONDERLAND / Circulate .... (RCA Victor 47-8137) | 3.75 | 15.00 | 63
LET'S GO STEADY AGAIN / Waiting For Never (La Terza Luna) ... (RCA Victor 47-8169) | 3.75 | 15.00 | 63
THE DREAMER / Look Inside Your Heart .... (RCA Victor 47-8209) | 3.75 | 15.00 | 63
THE CLOSEST THING TO HEAVEN / Without A Song .... (RCA Victor 47-8341) | 3.75 | 15.00 | 64
LET THE PEOPLE TALK / In The Chapel With You .... (RCA Victor 47-8511) | 3.75 | 15.00 | 65
THE WORLD THROUGH A TEAR / High On A Mountain .... (RCA Victor 47-8637) | 3.75 | 15.00 | 65

SEEDS, THE
CAN'T SEEM TO MAKE YOU MINE / I Tell Myself .... (GNP Crescendo 354) | 5.00 | 20.00 | 67
MR. FARMER / Up In Her Room 4–14 .... (GNP Crescendo 383) | 7.50 | 30.00 | 67
A THOUSAND SHADOWS / The March Of The Flower Children ... (GNP Crescendo 394) | 5.00 | 20.00 | 67
SATISFY YOU / 900 Million People Daily .... (GNP Crescendo 408) | 10.00 | 40.00 | 68
    (Plastic sleeve)

SEEGER, PETE
EXTENDED PLAYS
BOTH SIDES NOW / MAYROWANA (Excerpts) .... (Columbia AS 1) | 1.25 | 5.00 | 70
    (Promotional issue only titled *Dig This*, issued with a small-hole 33-1/3 RPM record. Also includes excerpts by
    Pacific Gas and Electric, Moondog, Nick Gravenites, Santana, Don Ellis, Raven, Firesign Theatre, and Tony
    Kosinec.)

SEEKERS, THE
A WORLD OF OUR OWN / Sinner Man .... (Capitol 5430) | 2.50 | 10.00 | 65
    Also see the New Seekers

SEE NO EVIL
JUST WAITING / To Be Free / Is This Human? .... (CBS Associated ZS7-1908) | 1.00 | 4.00 | 89
    (Promotional issue only issued with small-hole 33-1/3 RPM record)

SEGALL, RICKY
(Child actor on the television series *The Partridge Family*)
SOONER OR LATER / Say Hey Willie .... (Bell 45-429) | 2.00 | 8.00 | 74

SEGER, BOB, & THE SILVER BULLET BAND
WE'VE GOT TONITE .... (Capitol 4653) | 1.25 | 5.00 | 78
OLD TIME ROCK & ROLL / Sunspot Baby .... (Capitol 4702) | 1.50 | 6.00 | 80
FIRE LAKE / Long Twin Silver Line .... (Capitol 4836) | 1.00 | 4.00 | 80
AGAINST THE WIND / No Man's Land .... (Capitol 4863) | 1.00 | 4.00 | 80
YOU'LL ACCOMP'NY ME .... (Capitol 4904) | 1.00 | 4.00 | 80
THE HORIZONTAL BOP / Her Strut .... (Capitol 4951) | 20.00 | 80.00 | 80
TRYIN' TO LIVE MY LIFE WITHOUT YOU .... (Capitol A-5042) | 1.00 | 4.00 | 81
FEEL LIKE A NUMBER .... (Capitol A-5077) | 1.25 | 5.00 | 81
SHAME ON THE MOON .... (Capitol B-5187) | 1.00 | 4.00 | 82
EVEN NOW .... (Capitol B-5213) | 1.00 | 4.00 | 83
ROLL ME AWAY .... (Capitol B-5235) | 1.00 | 4.00 | 83
OLD TIME ROCK & ROLL .... (Capitol B-5276) | 1.00 | 4.00 | 83
    (From the motion picture *Risky Business*, Tom Cruise pictured on back)
UNDERSTANDING .... (Capitol B-5413) | 1.00 | 4.00 | 84
    (From the motion picture *Teachers*)
AMERICAN STORM / Fortunate Son .... (Capitol B-5532) | .75 | 3.00 | 86
LIKE A ROCK / Livin' Inside My Heart .... (Capitol B-5592) | .75 | 3.00 | 86
IT'S YOU .... (Capitol B-5623) | .75 | 3.00 | 86
SHAKEDOWN .... (MCA 53094) | .75 | 3.00 | 87
    (Shown as by Bob Seger. From the motion picture *Beverly Hills Cop II*, Eddie Murphy pictured on back.)
    Also see Teegarden & Van Winkle (David Teegarden was a member of the Silver Bullet Band from 1978-81)

SELLECK, TOM
(Actor)
    See Mike Post (*Theme From Magnum P.I.*)

SELLERS, PETER
(Comic Actor)
    See Inspector Clouseau, Tom Jones (*What's New Pussycat?*)

SEMBELLO, MICHAEL
GREMLINS...MEGA MADNESS / Late For Work .... (Geffen 29255-7) | .75 | 3.00 | 85
    (B-side shown as by Jerry Goldsmith. From the motion picture *Gremlins*.)
GRAVITY / Mo' Gravity .... (A&M 2745) | .75 | 3.00 | 85
    (From the motion picture *Cocoon*)

SENSITIVE, PASSIONATE MAN, A
(Television Movie)
    See Melba Moore (*My Sensitive, Passionate Man*)

SEQUAL
TELL HIM I CALLED .... (Capitol B-44260)   .75   3.00   88

SERENADERS, THE
NIGHT OWL/I'm Gonna Love You .... (Starfire 115)   1.25   5.00   80
     (Issued with red vinyl)

SERENDIPITY SINGERS, THE
AUTUMN WIND/Same Old Reason .... (Philips 40236)   2.00   8.00   64
LITTLE BROWN JUG/High North Star .... (Philips 40246)   2.00   8.00   64
THE PHOENIX LOVE THEME/If You Come Back In Summer ..... (Philips 40356)   2.00   8.00   66

SETZER, BRIAN
THE KNIFE FEELS LIKE JUSTICE/Barb Wire Fence .... (EMI America B8301)   .75   3.00   86
     Also see the Stray Cats

SEVELLE, TAJA
LOVE IS CONTAGIOUS .... (Reprise/Paisley Park 28257-7)   .75   3.00   87
WOULDN'T YOU LOVE TO LOVE ME .... (Reprise/Paisley Park 28127-7)   .75   3.00   87

7A3, THE
GOES LIKE DIS/ .... (Geffen 22959-7)   .75   3.00   88
DRUMS OF STEEL/ .... (Geffen 27571-7)   .75   3.00   88
COOLIN' IN CALI/Groovin' .... (Geffen 27695-7)   .75   3.00   88

SEVENTY SEVENS, THE
A DIFFERENT KIND OF LIGHT/Closer To You .... (Exit/A&S EA-100EP)   .75   3.00   83
     (Promotional issue only, flip side shown as by Undercover, no song titles listed on sleeve. Issued with a small-
     hole 33-1/3 RPM.)

SEVERINSEN, DOC
COME TOGETHER .... (Command 4133)   1.25   5.00   70
SOMETIMES WHEN WE TOUCH .... (Frontline 9001-S)   1.25   5.00   80
     (Promotional issue only, hard cover)
THE TONIGHT SHOW THEME (JOHNNY'S THEME)/Skyliner .... (Amherst 310)   1.50   6.00   86
     (Shown as by the Tonight Show Band With Doc Severinsen)

SEVILLE, DAVID
GOTTA GET TO YOUR HOUSE/Camel Rock .... (Liberty 55079)   6.25   25.00   57
     Also see the Chipmunks

S-EXPRESS
THEME FROM S-EXPRESS .... (Capitol B-44181)   .75   3.00   88
SUPERFLY GUY/Funky Killer .... (Capitol B-44225)   .75   3.00   88

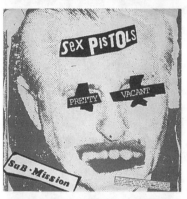

SEX PISTOLS
PRETTY VACANT/Sub-Mission .... (Warner Bros. 8516)   3.75   15.00   77

SEXTON, CHARLIE
BEAT'S SO LONELY .... (MCA 52715)   .75   3.00   85
IMPRESSED .... (MCA 52803)   .75   3.00   86
HOLD ME/Beat's So Lonely Extended Remix (Beat The Lonely Monster Mix) .... (MCA 52864)   .75   3.00   86
IN DEEP .... (MCA 53168)   .75   3.00   87
     (From the motion picture *Beverly Hills Cop II*, Eddie Murphy pictured on front, Sexton on back)

SEYMOUR, PHIL
PRECIOUS TO ME .... (Boardwalk WS8-5703)   1.25   5.00   87
     Also see the Textones, Dwight Twilley Band

SHADOWFAX
BROWN RICE/KARMAPA CHENNO/New Electric India .... (Windham Hill 0001)   .75   3.00   83
     (Promotional issue only, clear plastic sleeve with 5" x 3" sticker)

SHADOWS OF KNIGHT, THE
OH YEAH/Light Bulb Blues .... (Dunwich DX 122A)   5.00   20.00   66
BAD LITTLE WOMAN/Gospel Zone .... (Dunwich DX 128A)   7.50   30.00   66
I GOT MY MOJO WORKING/Interview/Potato Chip .... (Sundazed 123)   .50   2.00   96
     (Issued with blue vinyl)

SHADY DAZE, THE
EXTENDED PLAYS
I'LL MAKE YOU PAY/LOVE IS A BEAUTIFUL THING/
     Dennis Dupree From Danville/You Don't Know Like I Know .... (Sundazed 110)   .50   2.00   96
     (Hard cover issued with yellow vinyl)

SHAFER, HAL
MARCH OF THE VIKINGS .... (United Artists 130)   2.00   8.00   62

SHAGGY DOG, THE
(Motion Picture)
     See Roberta Shore (The Shaggy Dog)

SHAG, THE MOVIE
(Motion Picture)
     See Louise Goffin (Surrender)

SHAKESPEAR'S SISTER
     See Bananarama (Siobhan Fahey), Marcy Levy (Marcella Detroit)

SHALAMAR
DEAD GIVEAWAY/I Don't Wanna Be The Last To Know .... (Solar 69819)   .75   3.00   83
DANCING IN THE SHEETS/Dancing In The Sheets (Instrumental) .... (Columbia 38-04372)   .75   3.00   84
DON'T GET STOPPED IN BEVERLY HILLS .... (MCA 52594)   .75   3.00   85
     Also see Howard Hewett, Jody Watley

SHA NA NA
TOP FORTY OF THE LORD .... (Kama Sutra 528)   1.50   6.00   71
     (Record label shows title as *Top Forty*)

TITLE	LABEL AND NUMBER	VG	NM	YR

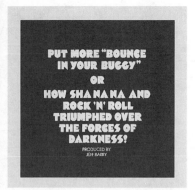

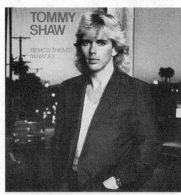

BOUNCE IN YOUR BUGGY .... (Kama Sutra 555)		2.00	8.00	72
(Promotional issue only)				
MAYBE I'M OLD FASHIONED .... (Kama Sutra 592)		1.25	5.00	74
Also see Tom Snow (Hurry Boy), John Travolta (Greased Lightnin')				

SHANICE
See Shanice Wilson

SHANKAR, RAVI

JOI BANGLA-OH BHAUGOWAN/Raga Mishra-Jhinjhoti .... (Apple 1838)		5.00	20.00	71

SHANNON
(Brenda Shannon Greene)

GIVE ME TONIGHT/Give Me Tonight (Dub Version) .... (Mirage 7-99775)		.75	3.00	84
DO YOU WANNA GET AWAY/Do You Wanna Get Away (Dub Mix) .... (Mirage 7-99655)		.75	3.00	85
CRIMINAL/Just That Type Of Girl .... (Atlantic 7-89164)		.75	3.00	87
(B-side shown as by Madame X. From the motion picture Fatal Beauty, Whoopi Goldberg pictured.)				

SHANNON
(Marty Wilde)

ABERGAVENNY .... (Heritage 814)		1.25	5.00	74

SHANNON, DEL

THINKIN' IT OVER/Runnin On Back .... (Liberty 56018)		5.00	20.00	68

SHAPE OF THINGS

YOU'VE GOT TO MAKE IT .... (Mega 16)		1.25	5.00	71

SHAPIRO, HELEN

KEEP AWAY FROM OTHER GIRLS .... (Epic 5-9549)		2.00	8.00	62

SHARIF, OMAR
(Actor)
See Maurice Jarre (Theme From Behold A Pale Horse)

SHARKEY, FEARGAL

A GOOD HEART/Anger Is Holy .... (A&M/Virgin 2804)		1.00	4.00	85
IF THIS IS LOVE/A Touch Of Blue .... (Virgin 7-99339)		.75	3.00	88

SHARP, DEE DEE

GRAVY/Baby Cakes .... (Cameo 219)		2.50	10.00	62
RIDE!/The Night .... (Cameo 230)		2.50	10.00	62
DO THE BIRD/Lover Boy .... (Cameo 244)		2.50	10.00	63
ROCK ME IN THE CRADLE OF LOVE/You'll Never Be Mine .... (Cameo 260)		2.50	10.00	63
WILD!/Why Doncha Ask Me .... (Cameo 274)		2.50	10.00	63
WHERE DID I GO WRONG/Willyam, Willyam .... (Cameo 296)		2.50	10.00	64
HE'S NO ORDINARY GUY/Never Pick A Pretty Boy .... (Cameo 329)		2.50	10.00	64
GOOD/Deep Dark Secret .... (Cameo 335)		2.50	10.00	65
I REALLY LOVE YOU/Standing In The Need Of Love .... (Cameo 375)		2.50	10.00	65
Also see Chubby Checker (Slow Twistin')				

SHAW, MARLENA

LOOK THROUGH THE EYES OF LOVE .... (Cadet 5618)		2.00	8.00	67

SHAW, RICKY

TEENAGE MARRIAGE .... (Golden Crest 109)		3.75	15.00	60s

SHAW, TOMMY

GIRLS WITH GUNS/Heads Up .... (A&M 2676)		1.00	4.00	84
FREE TO LOVE YOU/Come In And Explain .... (A&M 2715)		1.00	4.00	85
REMO'S THEME (WHAT IF)/Kiss Me Hello .... (A&M 2773)		.75	3.00	85
(A-side from the motion picture Remo Williams–The Adventure Begins)				
JEALOUSY/This Is Not A Test .... (A&M 2800)		.75	3.00	85
NO SUCH THING/The Outsider .... (Atlantic 7-89183)		.75	3.00	87
EVER SINCE THE WORLD BEGAN/The Outsider .... (Atlantic 7-89138)		.75	3.00	87
Also see Styx				

SHEAR, JULES

STEADY/Still I See You .... (EMI America B-8259)		1.00	4.00	85
Also see Jules and the Polar Bears, Reckless Sleepers				

SHEEDY, ALLY
(Actress)
See John Parr (St. Elmo's Fire), Pops and 'Timer (Tell Me Something Slick), Wang Chung (Fire In The Twilight)

SHEFFER, CRAIG
(Actor)
See Wild Blue (Fire With Fire)

SHEILA

LITTLE DARLIN' .... (Carrere ZS5 02564)		1.00	4.00	81
RUNNER .... (Carrere ZS5 02757)		1.00	4.00	81
RUNNER .... (Carrere ZS5 02757)		1.25	5.00	81
(Promotional issue)				

SHEILA E

THE GLAMOROUS LIFE/The Glamorous Life Part II .... (Warner Bros. 29285-7)		1.00	4.00	84
(Prince credited on back as The Starr)				
THE BELLE OF ST. MARK .... (Warner Bros. 29180-7)		1.00	4.00	84
(Prince credited on back as The Starr)				
A LOVE BIZARRE/A Love Bizarre, Part II .... (Paisley Park 28890-7)		.75	3.00	85
SISTER FATE/Sister Fate (Instrumental) .... (Paisley Park 28955-7)		.75	3.00	85
BEDTIME STORY/Dear Michaelangelo .... (Paisley Park 28786-7)		.75	3.00	86
HOLLY ROCK/Toy Box .... (Warner Bros./Paisley Park 28704-7)		.75	3.00	86
(A-side from the motion picture Krush Groove)				
HOLD ME/The World Is High .... (Paisley Park 28580-7)		.75	3.00	86

KOO KOO/Paradise Gardens .... (Paisley Park 28348-7)   .75   3.00   87
     (Photography by Prince)
     Also see Prince, U.S.A. For Africa, Voices Of America

SHELLEY, PETE
ON YOUR OWN/Please Forgive Me...But I Cannot Endure It Any Longer .... (Mercury 884 751-7)   1.00   4.00   86
     Also see the Buzzcocks

SHENANDOAH
(Motion Picture)
     See James Stewart (The Legend Of Shenandoah)

SHEPHERD, CYBILL
(Actress)
     See Al Jarreau (Since I Fell For You)

SHEPHERD, RED, AND THE FLOCK
SHE'S A GRABBER/I Can't Hold On .... (Philips 40398)   3.75   15.00   66

SHERIFF
WHEN I'M WITH YOU .... (Capitol B-5199)   1.25   5.00   82
     Also see Frozen Ghost (Wolf Hassel, Arnold Lanni)

SHERIFF, JAMIE
MY CAR/Sexy Thing .... (Polydor 2110)   1.25   5.00   80

SHERLEY, GLEN
LOOK FOR ME .... (Mega 41)   2.00   8.00   71

SHERMAN, ALLAN
HELLO MUDDUH, HELLO FADDUH! .... (Warner Bros. 5378)   2.50   10.00   63
HELLO MUDDUH, HELLO FADDUH! (NEW 1964 VERSION) .... (Warner Bros. 5449)   2.50   10.00   64

SHERMAN, BOBBY
IT HURTS ME .... (Decca 31741)   6.25   25.00   65
ANYTHING YOUR LITTLE HEART DESIRES/Goody Galum-Shus .... (Parkway 967)   5.00   20.00   65
COLD GIRL/Think Of Rain .... (Epic 5-10181)   3.75   15.00   67
LITTLE WOMAN .... (Metromedia 121)   1.25   5.00   69
LA LA LA (IF I HAD YOU) .... (Metromedia 150)   1.25   5.00   69
EASY COME, EASY GO .... (Metromedia 177)   1.25   5.00   70
HEY, MISTER SUN .... (Metromedia 188)   1.25   5.00   70
JULIE, DO YA LOVE ME .... (Metromedia 194)   1.25   5.00   70
GOIN' HOME .... (Metromedia 204)   1.25   5.00   70
CRIED LIKE A BABY .... (Metromedia 206)   1.25   5.00   70
THE DRUM .... (Metromedia 217)   1.25   5.00   71
WAITING AT THE BUS STOP .... (Metromedia 222)   1.25   5.00   71
JENNIFER .... (Metromedia 227)   1.25   5.00   71
TOGETHER AGAIN .... (Metromedia 240)   1.25   5.00   72
I DON'T BELIEVE IN MAGIC/Just A Little While Longer .... (Metromedia 249)   1.25   5.00   72
     Also see Patti (I Wanna Be Bobby's Girl)

SHERRICK
JUST CALL .... (Warner Bros. 28380-7)   .75   3.00   87
BABY I'M FOR REAL .... (Warner Bros. 28150-7)   .75   3.00   87

SHERRILL, JOYA
KATUSHA .... (Reprise 20,102)   1.50   6.00   62

SHE'S HAVING A BABY
(Motion Picture)
     See Dave Wakeling (She's Having A Baby)

SHINEHEAD
CHAIN GANG RAP .... (Elektra 7-69375)   .75   3.00   88

SHIRELLES, THE
FOOLISH LITTLE GIRL/Not For All The Money In The World .... (Scepter 1248)   6.25   25.00   63
DON'T SAY GOODNIGHT AND MEAN GOODBYE/I Didn't Mean To Hurt You ..... (Scepter 1255)   6.25   25.00   63

SHIRTS, THE
CAN'T CRY ANYMORE/I'm In Love Again .... (Capitol 4750)   1.25   5.00   79
     (Shown as by the Shirts Featuring Annie Golden)
DON'T YOU HESITATE/Ground Zero .... (Capitol 4783)   1.25   5.00   79
     Also see Darlene Love (b-side of River Deep, Mountain High)

SHIVA'S HEAD BAND
COUNTRY BOY/Such A Joy .... (Armadillo 811)   6.25   25.00   71

SHOCKED, MICHELLE
ANCHORAGE .... (Mercury 870 611-7)   1.00   4.00   88
WHEN I GROW UP/Fogtown .... (Mercury 872 590-7)   1.00   4.00   89

SHOCKING BLUE, THE
THE BUTTERFLY AND I/ACKA RAGH/Send Me A Postcard .... (Colossus PBCS-1000)   3.75   15.00   69
     (Promotional issue only titled Special Album Highlights, issued with a small-hole 33-1/3 RPM record. No song
     titles listed on sleeve.)
VENUS .... (Colossus 108)   2.50   10.00   69
MIGHTY JOE .... (Colossus 111)   2.00   8.00   70

SHOCK TREATMENT
(Motion Picture)
     See Richard O'Brien (Shock Treatment)

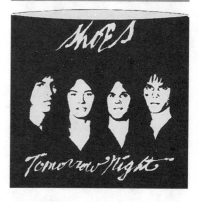

SHOES
TOMORROW NIGHT/Okay .... (Bomp 116)   2.50   10.00   78
TOO LATE/Now And Then .... (Elektra 46557)   1.50   6.00   79

TITLE	LABEL AND NUMBER	VG	NM	YR

Presidential Press Conference
the SICKniks   AMY · 824 · 45 rpm

WASHINGTON BAND STAND

Presidential
Press Conference
the SICKniks

SHONEN KNIFE
NEON ZEBRA/Bear Up Bison .... (Sub Pop 108)   1.50   6.00   91
   (Limited edition of 5,000 issued with gray vinyl. Produced in Germany and distributed in the U.S.)
SPACE CHRISTMAS/Christmas Message '91 .... (Rockville 6075)   1.50   6.00   91
TOP OF THE WORLD .... (A&M 31458 0706 7)   .50   2.00   94
   (Side 2 of a 7 record box set titled *If I Were A Carpenter*. Each sleeve has a different face shot of Karen Carpenter
   on the front, Richard Carpenter on the back. No artist name or song titles indicated on sleeve. Complete set
   valued at $30.00 near mint.)

SHOOTING STAR
YOU'VE GOT WHAT I NEED/Wild In The Streets .... (Virgin 67005)   1.25   5.00   79
WHERE YOU GONNA RUN/Do You Feel Alright .... (Virgin/Epic 14-03028)   1.00   4.00   82
SUMMER SUN .... (Geffen/Virgin 28994-7)   1.00   4.00   85

SHORE, DINAH
I'M YOUR GIRL .... (RCA Victor 47-5335)   3.00   12.00   53
EXTENDED PLAYS
YOU MEET THE NICEST PEOPLE/JINGLE BELLS/
  Silent Night/The Coventry Carol .... (Capitol Custom no #)   2.50   10.00   60
   (Promotional holiday issue sponsored by Chevrolet titled *Season's Best*. No song titles listed, back of sleeve
   promotes the album *Dinah Sings–Previn Plays*. Issued with a small-hole 33-1/3 RPM record.)
THE PUREX DINAH SHORE SPECIAL .... (Capitol Custom 3793)   2.50   10.00   61
   (Promotional issue only)

SHORE, ROBERTA
(Actress)
THE SHAGGY DOG/C'est Chiffon .... (Disneyland F-123)   3.75   15.00   59
   (From the motion picture *The Shaggy Dog*)

SHORROCK, GLENN
DON'T GIRLS GET LONELY .... (Capitol B-5267)   1.00   4.00   83
   Also see Little River Band

SHORT CIRCUIT
(Motion Picture)
   See El DeBarge (*Who's Johnny*)

SHORTER, RICK
CITY WOMAN .... (Columbia 4-43571)   2.00   8.00   66

SHRIEKBACK
GUNNING FOR THE BUDDHA/Bludgeoned (By The Chairleg Of The Truth)........ (Island 7-99480)   .75   3.00   87
GET DOWN TONIGHT/Big Fun .... (Island 7-99293)   .75   3.00   88
   Also see XTC (Barry Andrews)

SHY TALK
SHE WAS ALWAYS ON TIME (NOT ANYMORE)/I'm Only Human .... (Columbia 38 05799)   .75   3.00   86
SHE WAS ALWAYS ON TIME (NOT ANYMORE) .... (Columbia 38 05799)   1.00   4.00   86
   (Promotional issue, *Demonstration–Not For Sale* printed on sleeve)

SIBERRY, JANE
ONE MORE COLOUR/The Empty City .... (Open Air/Duke Street 0017)   1.00   4.00   85

SICKNICKS, THE
PRESIDENTIAL PRESS CONFERENCE .... (Amy 824)   3.75   15.00   61
   (Sleeve features a caricature of President John F. Kennedy)

SIEGEL, DAN
FRIDAY/Bad Habit .... (Inner City 46-45)   .75   3.00   80
   (B-side credits special guest John Klemmer)
FEELIN' HAPPY .... (CBS Associated ZS4-07667)   .75   3.00   87

SIFFRE, LABI
(SOMETHING INSIDE) SO STRONG/So Strong (Instrumental) .... (Chrysalis/China VS4 43102)   .75   3.00   87

SIGLER, BUNNY
LOVE TRAIN .... (Philadelphia International ZS7 3545)   1.50   6.00   74
LOVEY DOVEY/You're So Fine .... (Parkway 6000)   1.00   4.00   86

SIGUE SIGUE SPUTNIK
LOVE MISSILE F1-11/Hate Attack .... (Manhattan B-50035)   1.00   4.00   86

SILENCERS, THE
EXTENDED PLAYS
GIRL WAITING/LOVE IS BLIND/
  Romantic/Sidewalk Romeo (Angel Of Mercy) .... (Precision AE7-1233)   1.00   4.00   81
   (Promotional issue only, issued with a small-hole 33-1/3 RPM record)
   Also see Diamond REO (Frank Czuri)

SILENT MOVIE
(Motion Picture)
   See Lionel Newman (*The Silent Movie March*)

SILICONE TEENS
   See Dave Edmunds (b-side of *Gonna Move*)

SILK TYMES LEATHER
DO YOUR DANCE .... (Geffen 22958-7)   .75   3.00   89

SILLY KILLERS
EXTENDED PLAYS
NOT THAT TIME AGAIN/KNIFE MANUAL/Social Bitch/Sissy Faggots .... (No Threes 007)   3.75   15.00   82
   Also see the Fastbacks (Duff McKagan), Nirvana (Duff McKagan)

SILVA, KEITH
NIGHTLIFE/Raincoats and Silverware .... (Design 521)   1.00   4.00   80
   Also see Our Daughters Wedding

SILVERBIRD
GETTING TOGETHER/You .... (Columbia 4-45625) 1.50 6.00 72

SILVER CONDOR
YOU COULD TAKE MY HEART AWAY/Goin' For Broke .... (Columbia 18-02268) 1.00 4.00 81
    Also see Phantom, Rocker & Slick (Earl Slick)

SILVER CONVENTION
GET UP AND BOOGIE .... (Midland International 10571) 1.25 5.00 76

SILVERSTEIN, SHEL
SHOW IT AT THE BEACH/The Smoke-Off .... (Parachute/Casablanca RR518 DJ) 5.00 20.00 78
    (Infamous female nude sleeve, promotional issue only)
EXTENDED PLAYS
INVITATION/EIGHTEEN FLAVORS/SICK/JIMMY JET AND HIS TV SET/FOR SALE/
WARNING/THE YIPIYUK/Crocodile's Toothache/Stone Telling/Boa Constrictor/
Hug O' War/No Difference/My Hobby/Early Bird .... (Columbia AE7 1909) 1.50 6.00 84
    (Promotional issue only issued with small-hole 45 RPM record. Illustration by Silverstein.)

SILVESTRI, ALAN
NO MERCY MAIN TITLE .... (TVT Records no #) 1.25 5.00 87
    (Promotional issue only, Promotion Copy Not For Sale printed on sleeve. Issued with small-hole 45 RPM. From the motion picture No Mercy. Richard Gere and Kim Basinger pictured.)

SIMEONE, HARRY, CHORALE, THE
THE LITTLE DRUMMER BOY .... (20th Century-Fox 121) 2.00 8.00 58
THE LITTLE DRUMMER BOY .... (20th Century-Fox 121) 2.50 10.00 58
    (Promotional issue, sleeve states Prepare To Be Enchanted)
MARCH OF THE ANGELS .... (Mercury 72165) 1.50 6.00 62
THE LITTLE DRUMMER BOY ....(20th Fox 429) 1.50 6.00 63
THE LITTLE DRUMMER BOY ....(20th Fox 6429) 1.50 6.00 60s
    (Identical to 20th Century-Fox 429 except this sleeve states Distributed by ABC Records)

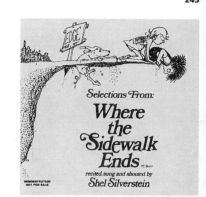

SIMON, CARLY
YOU BELONG TO ME/In A Small Moment .... (Elektra 45477) 1.25 5.00 78
VENGEANCE/Love You By Heart .... (Elektra 46051) 1.25 5.00 79
JESSE/Stardust .... (Warner Bros. 49518) 1.25 5.00 80
WHY/Why (Instrumental) .... (Mirage WTG 4051) 2.00 8.00 82
    (B-side shown as by Chic. From the motion picture Soup For One.)
YOU KNOW WHAT TO DO/Orpheus ....(Warner Bros. 29484-7) 1.25 5.00 83
TIRED OF BEING BLONDE/Black Honeymoon .... (Epic 34-05419) 1.00 4.00 85
TIRED OF BEING BLONDE .... (Epic 34-05419) 1.50 6.00 85
    (Promotional issue, Demonstration–Not For Sale printed on sleeve)
COMING AROUND AGAIN/Itsy Bitsy Spider .... (Arista 9525) 1.00 4.00 86
    (Color photo of Carly Simon on front. A-side from the motion picture Heartburn.)

COMING AROUND AGAIN/Itsy Bitsy Spider .... (Arista 9525) 1.00 4.00 86
    (Identical to color version with Carly Simon pictured except the entire sleeve is black and white. Some promotional copies were issued with this sleeve. A 7" x 14" insert folded to 7" x 7" was included, which may be mistaken for a separate sleeve. The insert would be of equal value to the sleeve. A-side from the motion picture Heartburn.)
COMING AROUND AGAIN/Itsy Bitsy Spider .... (Arista 9525) 1.25 5.00 86
    (Meryl Streep and Jack Nicholson pictured on front. A-side from the motion picture Heartburn.)
GIVE ME ALL NIGHT/Sleight Of Hand .... (Arista 9587) .75 3.00 87
    (Shown as by Carly)
THE STUFF THAT DREAMS ARE MADE OF/As Time Goes By .... (Arista 9619) .75 3.00 87
    (Shown as by Carly, b-side credits harmonica solo by Stevie Wonder)
ALL I WANT IS YOU/Two Hot Girls (On A Hot Summer Night) .... (Arista 9653) .75 3.00 87
    (Shown as by Carly)
YOU'RE SO VAIN (LIVE)/Do The Walls Come Down .... (Arista 9754) .75 3.00 88
LET THE RIVER RUN/The Turn Of The Tide .... (Arista 9793) .75 3.00 89
    (A-side from the motion picture Working Girl, Harrison Ford, Melanie Griffith, and Sigourney Weaver pictured on the back)
    Also see Jesse Colin Young (Fight For It)

SIMON, JOE
SAY .... (Gee Bee 077) 5.00 20.00 60s
TO LAY DOWN BESIDE YOU/Help Me Make It Through The Night .... (Spring 113) 1.50 6.00 71
THEME FROM CLEOPATRA JONES .... (Spring 138) 1.25 5.00 73
    (Shown as by Joe Simon Featuring The Mainstreeters. From the motion picture Cleopatra Jones, Tamara Dobson pictured.)

SIMON, LUCY
(Sister of Carly Simon)
MEET LUCY SIMON .... (RCA JF-10378) 1.50 6.00 75
    (Promotional issue only, interview and excerpts from the album Lucy Simon, issued with a small-hole 33-1/3 RPM record)

SIMON, PAUL
AMERICAN TUNE/One Man's Ceiling Is Another Man's Floor .... (Columbia 4-45900) 2.00 8.00 73
    (Paul Simon pictured on sleeve)
AMERICAN TUNE .... (Columbia AE7-1105) 3.00 12.00 76
    (Promotional issue only, American flag pictured on front. Note the date of release, this was probably reissued to coincide with the U.S. Bicentennial.)
LATE IN THE EVENING/How The Heart Approaches What It Yearns .... (Warner Bros. 49511) 1.25 5.00 80
THE BLUES/Same Girl .... (Warner Bros. 29803-7) 1.00 4.00 83
    (Shown as by Randy Newman and Paul Simon, only Newman pictured)
ALLERGIES .... (Warner Bros. 29453-7) 1.00 4.00 83
YOU CAN CALL ME AL .... (Warner Bros. 28667-7) .75 3.00 86
GRACELAND .... (Warner Bros. 28522-7) .75 3.00 86
THE BOY IN THE BUBBLE (REMIX) .... (Warner Bros. 28460-7) .75 3.00 86
DIAMONDS ON THE SOLES OF HER SHOES/
All Around The World Or The Myth Of Fingerprints .... (Warner Bros. 28389-7) .75 3.00 87
UNDER AFRICAN SKIES/I Know What I Know .... (Warner Bros. 28221-7) .75 3.00 87
    (A-side shown as by Paul Simon and Linda Ronstadt)
    Also see Simon and Garfunkel, U.S.A. For Africa, Voices Of America

TITLE	LABEL AND NUMBER	VG	NM	YR

SIMON AND GARFUNKEL

THE DANGLING CONVERSATION/The Big Bright Green Pleasure Machine ..(Columbia 4-43728)		5.00	20.00	66
AT THE ZOO ....(Columbia 4-44046)		10.00	40.00	67
THE BOXER/Baby Driver ....(Columbia 4-44785)		2.00	8.00	69
BRIDGE OVER TROUBLED WATER/Keep The Customer Satisfied ....(Columbia 4-45079)		2.00	8.00	70
CECILIA/The Only Living Boy In New York.......................................(Columbia 4-45133)		2.00	8.00	70
MY LITTLE TOWN/Rag Doll/You're Kind ....(Columbia 3-10230)		1.25	5.00	75

(*Rag Doll* shown as by Art Garfunkel, *You're Kind* shown as by Paul Simon)
Also see Art Garfunkel, Paul Simon, U.S.A. For Africa (Paul Simon), Voices Of America (Paul Simon)

SIMON & SIMON

(Television Series)
See Barry DeVorzon

SIMONE, NINA

MY SWEET LORD/Today Is A Killer/Poppies ....(RCA Victor 74-0871)		2.00	8.00	73

SIMON F

AMERICAN DREAM ....(Reprise 28237-7)		.75	3.00	87

SIMPLE MINDS

DON'T YOU (FORGET ABOUT ME)/A Brass Band In Africa ....(A&M 2703)		1.00	4.00	85
(A-side from the motion picture *The Breakfast Club*)				
ALIVE & KICKING/Up On The Catwalk (Live Version).............................(A&M 2783)		1.00	4.00	85
SANCTIFY YOURSELF/Sanctify Yourself (Dub Version).............................(A&M 2810)		.75	3.00	85
ALL THE THINGS SHE SAID/Don't You (Forget About Me) Live ....(A&M 2828)		.75	3.00	86
(Back of sleeve credits a-side additional lead vocals to Robin Clark)				
PROMISED YOU A MIRACLE/Book Of Brilliant Things ....(A&M 2954)		.75	3.00	87

SIMPLY RED

MONEY$ TOO TIGHT (TO MENTION)/Open Up The Red Box ....(Elektra 7-69607)		1.25	5.00	85
COME TO MY AID/Look At You Now ....(Elektra 7-69574)		1.00	4.00	85
MONEY$ TOO TIGHT (TO MENTION)/Picture Book (Dub) ....(Elektra 7-69528)		.75	3.00	86
(Sleeve design is identical to the 1985 release of the a-side with the exception of the b-side title and catalog number)				
THE RIGHT THING/There's A Light ....(Elektra 7-69487)		.75	3.00	87
INFIDELITY/Lady Godiva's Room ....(Elektra 7-69468)		.75	3.00	87
MAYBE SOMEDAY.../Broken Man ....(Elektra 7-69448)		.75	3.00	87
IT'S ONLY LOVE/Turn It Up ....(Elektra 7-69317)		.75	3.00	89
IF YOU DON'T KNOW ME BY NOW/Move On Out ....(Elektra 7-69297)		.75	3.00	89

SIMS, JOYCE

COME INTO MY LIFE (RADIO VERSION)/Come Into My Life (Dub Version) (Sleeping Bag LX-28)		.75	3.00	87

SINATRA, FRANK

ALL THE WAY ....(Capitol 596)		100.00	400.00	58
(Promotional issue only)				
TO LOVE AND BE LOVED ....(Capitol 4103)		100.00	400.00	58
(Promotional issue only)				
HIGH HOPES ....(Capitol 4214)		100.00	400.00	60
(Promotional issue only, shown as by Frank Sinatra and a Bunch of Kids. From the motion picture *A Hole In The Head*.)				
GRANADA/The Curse Of An Aching Heart ....(Reprise 20,010)		5.00	20.00	61
POCKETFUL OF MIRACLES/Name It And It's Yours ....(Reprise 20,040)		6.25	25.00	61
EVERYBODY'S TWISTIN'/Nothin' But The Best ....(Reprise 20,063)		6.25	25.00	62
ME & MY SHADOW/Sam's Song ....(Reprise 20,128)		6.25	25.00	62
(A-side shown as by Frank Sinatra and Sammy Davis, Jr., b-side by Dean Martin and Sammy Davis, Jr., all three pictured)				
RING-A-DING-DING ....(Reprise/Cal Nevada Lodge 101)		37.50	150.00	63
(Promotional souvenir available from the Cal Nevada Lodge)				
CALIFORNIA/America The Beautiful ....(Reprise 20,157)		125.00	500.00	63
(Promotional issue only, reportedly 1,000 made)				
COME BLOW YOUR HORN/I Have Dreamed ....(Reprise 20,184)		37.50	150.00	63
(Promotional issue only)				
LOVE ISN'T JUST FOR THE YOUNG/You Brought A New Kind Of Love To Me .... (Reprise 20,209)		7.50	30.00	63
THE OLDEST ESTABLISHED (PERMANENT FLOATING CRAP GAME IN NEW YORK)/ Fugue For Tinhorns ....(Reprise 20,217)		15.00	60.00	63
(Shown as by Frank Sinatra, Bing Crosby, and Dean Martin)				
MY KIND OF TOWN/I Like To Lead When I Dance ....(Reprise 0279)		37.50	150.00	64
(Promotional issue only)				
I HEARD THE BELLS ON CHRISTMAS DAY/The Little Drummer Boy ....(Reprise 0314)		7.50	30.00	64
WE WISH YOU THE MERRIEST/Go Tell It On The Mountain ....(Reprise 0317)		7.50	30.00	64
(Shown as by Frank Sinatra, Bing Crosby, and Fred Waring)				
IT WAS A VERY GOOD YEAR/Moment To Moment ....(Reprise 0429)		5.00	20.00	65
THAT'S LIFE ....(Reprise 0531)		5.00	20.00	66
(Sleeve reads *from the Frank Sinatra CBS Television Special "A Man And His Music" Part II. Dec 7, 1966*)				
FRANK AND SARAH AND NAT AND VIC SALUTE HAROLD ADAMSON ....(Harold Adamson Music Co. 100)		2.50	10.00	73
(Shown as by Frank Sinatra, Sarah Vaughan, Nat King Cole, and Vic Damone)				
I BELIEVE I'M GONNA LOVE YOU ....(Reprise 1335)		7.50	30.00	75
(Promotional issue only)				
A BABY JUST LIKE YOU/Christmas Mem'ries ....(Reprise 1342)		5.00	20.00	75
(Stock issue, red and black version)				
A BABY JUST LIKE YOU/Christmas Mem'ries ....(Reprise 1342)		7.50	30.00	75
(Promotional issue, blue version)				
STARGAZER/The Best I Ever Had ....(Reprise 1364)		3.75	15.00	76
(Promotional issue only, sleeve states *New Sinatra Single*)				
THEME FROM NEW YORK, NEW YORK/That's What God Looks Like To Me .... (Reprise 49233)		1.25	5.00	80
TO LOVE A CHILD/That's What God Looks Like To Me ....(Reprise 29903-7)		2.50	10.00	82
(Shown as by Frank Sinatra With the Reprise Children's Chorus Featuring Nikka Costa. Dedicated to Nancy Reagan.)				
L.A. IS MY LADY/Until The Real Thing Comes Along ....(Qwest 29223-7)		1.00	4.00	84
(Front of sleeve credits Quincy Jones and Orchestra)				

I'VE GOT YOU UNDER MY SKIN / Stay (Faraway, So Close!) .... (Island/Capitol 422-858 076-7) 1.00 4.00 93
(*Stay* shown as by U2. Both songs credited as the a-side.)
Also see Les Baxter (*Theme From The Manchurian Candidate*), Ray Bloch & Orchestra (*From Here To Eternity*), Nelson Riddle (*Come Blow Your Horn*)

SINATRA, NANCY
CUFF LINKS AND A TIE CLIP / Not Just Your Friend .... (Reprise 20,017) 5.00 20.00 62
LIGHTNING'S GIRL .... (Reprise 0620) 3.00 12.00 67
IS ANYBODY GOIN' TO SAN ANTONE .... (Reprise 0991) — — 71
(This sleeve has not been verified and may be an import sleeve only)

SINCEROS, THE
EXTENDED PLAYS
TAKE ME TO YOUR LEADER .... (Columbia AE7-1187) 1.00 4.00 79
(Promotional issue only titled *The Now Wave Sampler*, issued with small-hole 33-1/3 RPM record. Also includes one song each by the Beat, Hounds, and Jules and the Polar Bears.)

SINGING DOGS, THE
JINGLE BELLS / THREE BLIND MICE / Pat-A-Cake / Oh! Susanna .... (RCA Victor 47-6344) 2.50 10.00 55
HOT DOG ROCK & ROLL / Hot Dog Boogie .... (RCA Victor 47-6432) 2.50 10.00 56

SINGING NUN, THE
DOMINIQUE / Entre Les Etoiles (Among The Stars) .... (Philips 40152) 2.00 8.00 63
(Shown as by Soeur Sourire The Singing Nun)
TOUS LES CHEMINS (ALL THE ROADS) /
Frere Tout L'Monde (Brother Of All The World) .... (Philips 40165) 2.00 8.00 63
(Shown as by Soeur Sourire)

SINGLE BULLET THEORY
PEGGY GOT HER EYES FULL / There Is The Boy .... (Artifacts # unknown) 1.25 5.00 81
KEEP IT TIGHT / A Blink Of An Eye .... (Nemperor ZS4-03300) .75 3.00 82

SINGLETON, MARGIE
See Faron Young (*Keeping Up With The Jones*)

SINITTA
CROSS MY BROKEN HEART .... (Atlantic 7-89047) .75 3.00 88

SIOUXSIE AND THE BANSHEES
ISRAEL / Red Over White .... (PVC 1001) 1.25 5.00 80
DEAR PRUDENCE / Tattoo .... (Geffen/Wonderland 29358-7) 1.00 4.00 83
CITIES IN DUST .... (Geffen/Wonderland 28813-7) 1.00 4.00 85
PEEK-A-BOO / False Face .... (Geffen/Wonderland 27760-7) .75 3.00 88

SIR DOUGLAS QUINTET, THE
WHAT ABOUT TOMORROW / A Nice Song .... (Philips 40676) 3.00 12.00 70
Also see Doug Sahm

SIREN
ALL IS FORGIVEN / Master Of The Land .... (Mercury 872 448-7) .75 3.00 89

SIR MIX-A-LOT
POSSE' ON BROADWAY (THE GODZILLA REMIX EDIT) /
Posse' On Broadway (Video Edit) .... (Nastymix IGU 75555) .75 3.00 88
IRON MAN / I'll Roll You Up! .... (Nastymix IGU 76555-7) .75 3.00 89
(Craig Wells, Duke Erikson, Kirk Arrington, and Mike Howe, of Metal Church, credited on front)

SIRS, THE
OFF IN A DAYDREAM / Help Me .... (Amerco 103) 3.75 15.00 65

SISTER SLEDGE
FRANKIE / Peer Pressure .... (Atlantic 7-89547) 1.00 4.00 85

SISTERS OF MERCY, THE
THIS CORROSION / Torch .... (Elektra 7-69434) .75 3.00 87
LUCRETIA MY REFECTION / Long Train .... (Elektra 7-69378) .75 3.00 88
Tony James of Sigue Sigue Sputnik and Generation X did not join the group until 1990 and Wayne Hussey of Dead Or Alive left prior to 1987

SIX PACK
(Motion Picture)
See Kenny Rogers (*Love Will Turn You Around*)

SKAFISH
OBSESSIONS OF YOU / Sink Or Swim .... (I.R.S./Illegal 9011) 1.00 4.00 80
(Issued with small-hole 45 RPM record)

SKAGGS, RICKY
NEW STAR SHINING .... (Epic ES7 2569) .75 3.00 86
(Shown as by Ricky Skaggs & James Taylor. Promotional issue only, *Demonstration Not For Sale* printed on sleeve.)
EXTENDED PLAYS
YOU MAY SEE ME WALKIN' .... (CBS AE7 1429) 1.00 4.00 82
(Promotional issue only titled *Kickin Rock & Roll*, co-sponsored by Busch Beer and WBCN 104 FM and included in *The Phoenix* magazine. Also includes songs by George Jones, Merle Haggard, Larry Gatlin and the Gatlin Brothers Band, the Burrito Brothers, and Bobby Bare.)

SKELTON, RED
(Comedian)
THE CIRCUS / The Pledge Of Allegiance .... (Columbia 4-44798) 2.50 10.00 69

SKHY, A.B.
CAMEL BACK / Just What I Need .... (MGM K 14066) 2.00 8.00 69

SKID ROW
YOUTH GONE WILD / Sweet Little Sister .... (Atlantic 7-88935) .75 3.00 89
18 AND LIFE / Midnight / Tornado .... (Atlantic 7-88883) .75 3.00 89
I REMEMBER YOU / .... (Atlantic 7-88886) .75 3.00 89

TITLE	LABEL AND NUMBER	VG	NM	YR

SKIPWORTH & TURNER
THINKING ABOUT YOUR LOVE .... (4th and B'way 7414) | .75 | 3.00 | 85
  (From the motion picture *Pumping Iron II*)

SKYLARK
I'LL HAVE TO GO AWAY .... (Capitol P-3661) | 1.50 | 6.00 | 73

SKYLINERS, THE
THE LOVE BUG .... (Tortoise YB-11312) | 1.50 | 6.00 | 78

SLADES, THE
BABY/You Mean Everything To Me .... (Domino 100/200) | 18.75 | 75.00 | 58
  (Single sheet insert, not a true picture sleeve)
YOU CHEATED/The Waddle .... (Domino 500) | 18.75 | 75.00 | 58
  (Single sheet insert, not a true picture sleeve)
YOU GAMBLED/No Time .... (Domino 800) | 18.75 | 75.00 | 59
  (Single sheet insert, not a true picture sleeve)
JUST YOU/It's Better To Love .... (Domino 900) | 18.75 | 75.00 | 59
  (Single sheet insert, not a true picture sleeve, Also issued as Domino 901.)
IT'S YOUR TURN/Take My Turn .... (Domino 906) | 12.50 | 50.00 | 61
  (Single sheet insert, not a true picture sleeve)
SUMMERTIME/You Must Try .... (Domino 1000) | 12.50 | 50.00 | 61
  (Single sheet insert, not a true picture sleeve)

SLAUGHTER
(Motion Picture)
  See Billy Preston *(Slaughter)*

SLAYBACK, BILL
MOVE OVER BABE (HERE COMES HENRY) .... (Karen 714) | 12.50 | 50.00 | 73
  (Baseball legend Henry "Hank" Aaron pictured. Sleeve graphics and photo are identical to Richard "Popcorn" Wylie's release. Note that the catalog number of 714 was Babe Ruth's home run record that Aaron would eclipse on April 8, 1974.)

SLEDGE, PERCY
WHEN A MAN LOVES A WOMAN/Cover Me .... (Atlantic 7-89262) | .75 | 3.00 | 87
  (A-side from the motion picture *Platoon*)

SLEEPERS
MIRROR/Theory .... (Adolescent no #) | 1.00 | 4.00 | 80
MIRROR/Theory .... (Search & Destroy # unknown) | 3.75 | 15.00 | 80
MIRROR/Theory .... (Search & Destroy # unknown) | 1.25 | 5.00 | 80
  (Cardboard sleeve)
HOLDING BACK/B-Side .... (Mediumistic 200) | .75 | 3.00 | 94
  Also see Tuxedomoon

SLICK, GRACE
SUNFIGHTER/China .... (Grunt 65-0503) | 1.50 | 6.00 | 72
  (Shown as by Paul Kantner & Grace Slick)
SEASONS/Angel Of Night .... (RCA PB-11939) | 1.25 | 5.00 | 80
DREAMS .... (RCA PB-12041) | 1.25 | 5.00 | 80
  Also see Jefferson Airplane, Jefferson Starship, Starship

SLITS, THE
TYPICAL GIRLS/I Heard It Through The Grapevine .... (Antilles 102) | 2.50 | 10.00 | 79
  (Poster sleeve, identified as "Number 1 December 1979". Pictures the notorious photo of the nude, mud-covered band members when unfolded.)

SLOAN, P. F.
HALLOWEEN MARY .... (Dunhill 4016) | 5.00 | 20.00 | 65
SUNFLOWER, SUNFLOWER/The Man Behind The Red Balloons .... (Dunhill 4064) | 5.00 | 20.00 | 67

SLOWDIVE
SHE CALLS/Leave Them All Behind .... (Creation/SBK, Sire/Reprise PB 05468) | 1.00 | 4.00 | 92
  (Promotional issue only issued with blue vinyl. Sleeve reads *Limited Edition–Tour Collector's Item.* B-side side shown as by Ride.)

SLY AND THE FAMILY STONE
EVERYDAY PEOPLE/Sing A Simple Song .... (Epic 5-10407) | 2.50 | 10.00 | 68
STAND!/I Want To Take You Higher .... (Epic 5-10450) | 2.50 | 10.00 | 69
THANK YOU FALETTINME BE MICE ELF AGIN/Everybody Is A Star .... (Epic 5-10555) | 2.00 | 8.00 | 69
  Also see Larry Graham, Jesse Johnson *(Crazay)*

SLY FOX
STAY TRUE/If Push Comes To A Shove .... (Capitol B-5581) | .75 | 3.00 | 85

SMALL FACES
ALL OR NOTHING/Understanding .... (RCA Victor 47-8949) | 12.50 | 50.00 | 66
TIN SOLDIER/I Feel Much Better .... (Immediate ZS7-5003) | 5.00 | 20.00 | 68
  ("Tin Soldier" title in gold on front and not listed on back with b-side)
TIN SOLDIER/I Feel Much Better .... (Immediate ZS7-5003) | 5.00 | 20.00 | 68
  ("Tin Soldier" title in magenta on front and also listed on back with b-side)
REAL GOOD TIME .... (Warner Bros. 7442) | 5.00 | 20.00 | 70
  (Promotional issue only. Sleeve shows group name as Small Faces but record credits Faces.)
  Also see Humble Pie (Steve Marriot), Faces, Ronnie Lane, the Rolling Stones (Ronnie Wood), Rod Stewart, the Who (Kenney Jones). The original Small Faces consisted of Steve Marriott, Jimmy Winston (replaced by Ian McLagan in 1965), Ronnie Lane, and Kenney Jones. Rod Stewart and Ronnie Wood joined the group in 1969.

S*M*A*S*H
BARRABAS (PILOTED)/Turn On The Water .... (Sub Pop 276) | .75 | 3.00 | 95
  (Originally issued as part of a 4-record set titled *Helter Shelter*, which also included singles by Elastica, Supergrass, and Gene. Envelope sleeve issued with colored vinyl.)

SMASHING PUMPKINS, THE
I AM ONE .... (Limited Potential # unknown) | 5.00 | 20.00 | 90
TRISTESSA/La Dolly Vita .... (Sub Pop 90) | 2.50 | 10.00 | 91
  (Issued with either pink or black vinyl)
1979/Bullet With Butterfly Wings .... (Virgin 7243 8 38522 7 7) | .75 | 3.00 | 96

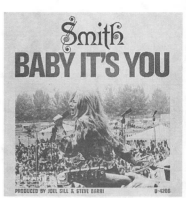

SMILER
LOVE TO LIVE .... (Ariola 7673) — 1.50 — 6.00 — 77

SMITH
BABY IT'S YOU .... (Dunhill 4206) — 1.50 — 6.00 — 69
WHAT AM I GONNA DO .... (Dunhill 4238) — 1.50 — 6.00 — 69

SMITH, BRO
BIGFOOT .... (Big Tree 16061) — 1.25 — 5.00 — 76

SMITH, CARL
TEN THOUSAND DRUMS/ .... (Columbia 4-41417) — 2.50 — 10.00 — 59

SMITH, COLUMBUS
WHERE SHALL I GO/ .... (Columbia 4-43838) — 2.00 — 8.00 — 66

SMITH, CONNIE
CINCINNATI, OHIO/Don't Feel Sorry For Me .... (RCA Victor 47-9214) — 1.50 — 6.00 — 67
    Also see Chet Atkins (*Chet's Tune*)

SMITH, JEAN
ASHES/Charcoal Ladder .... (Kill Rock Stars/Wordcore Volume Three) — .75 — 3.00 — 92
    (Folding sleeve with small-hole 45 RPM record)
    Also see Mecca Normal

SMITH, JENNIE
WE'LL BE TOGETHER/He's My Guy .... (RCA Victor PJ-340) — 7.50 — 30.00 — 57

SMITH, KATE
WHAT KIND OF FOOL AM I .... (RCA Victor 47-8279) — 2.00 — 8.00 — 63
GOD BLESS AMERICA .... (RCA Victor 47-8285) — 2.00 — 8.00 — 64

SMITH, KEELY
CLOSE .... (Dot 16089) — 2.00 — 8.00 — 60
    Also see Louis Prima & Keely Smith

SMITH, O. C.
DADDY'S LITTLE MAN/If I Leave You Now .... (Columbia 4-44948) — 2.00 — 8.00 — 69

SMITH, PATTI, GROUP
GLORIA/My Generation .... (Arista 171) — 2.50 — 10.00 — 76
HEY JOE (VERSION)/Piss Factory .... (Sire 1009) — 2.50 — 10.00 — 77
    (Back of sleeve credits, among others, Tom Verlaine on lead guitar)
BECAUSE THE NIGHT .... (Arista 0318) — 2.00 — 8.00 — 78
FREDERICK/Frederick (Live) .... (Arista 0427) — 2.00 — 8.00 — 79
(SO YOU WANT TO BE) A ROCK & ROLL STAR/
    54321 (Live)/A Fire Of Unknown Origin .... (Arista 0453) — 3.75 — 15.00 — 79

PEOPLE HAVE THE POWER/Wild Leaves .... (Arista 9689) — 1.00 — 4.00 — 88
    (Hard cover, shown as by Patti Smith. Photography by Robert Mapplethorpe. Back of sleeve credits, among
    others, Fred Sonic Smith on guitar.)
LOOKING FOR YOU (I WAS)/Up There Down There .... (Arista 9762) — 1.00 — 4.00 — 88
    (Shown as by Patti Smith. Back of sleeve credits, among others, Fred Sonic Smith on guitar and Kasim Sultan,
    of Utopia, on bass.)
    Also see Lenny Kaye, MC5 (Fred Sonic Smith)

SMITH, REX
YOU TAKE MY BREATH AWAY/You're Never Too Old To Rock & Roll .... (Columbia 3-10908) — 1.00 — 4.00 — 79
SOONER OR LATER/Never Gonna Give You Up .... (Columbia 1-11105) — 1.00 — 4.00 — 79
EVERLASTING LOVE/Still Thinking Of You/Billy And The Gun .... (Columbia 18-02169) — 1.00 — 4.00 — 81
    (A-side shown as by Rex Smith and Rachel Sweet. *Still Thinking Of You* shown as by Rex Smith and *Billy And
    The Gun* shown as by Rachel Sweet.)
EVERLASTING LOVE .... (Columbia 18-02169) — 1.25 — 5.00 — 81
    (Promotional issue, *Demonstration–Not For Sale* printed on sleeve. Shown as by Rex Smith and Rachel Sweet.)
    Also see Rex

SMITH, ROGER
(Actor and husband/manager of Ann Margret)
BEACH TIME/Cuddle Up A Little Closer .... (Warner Bros. 5068) — 3.75 — 15.00 — 59
LOVE OF TWO/Tick Tick Tick .... (Warner Bros. 5106) — 3.75 — 15.00 — 59

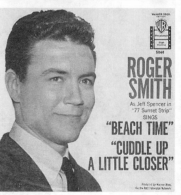

SMITH, SAMMI
HE'S EVERYWHERE .... (Mega 1) — 1.25 — 5.00 — 70

SMITH, SOMETHIN', AND THE REDHEADS
I DON'T WANT TO SET THE WORLD ON FIRE/You Made Me Love You .... (Epic 5-9280) — 3.00 — 12.00 — 58

SMITH, VERDELLE
JUANITA .... (Columbia 4-43296) — 2.00 — 8.00 — 65

SMITH, WILL
(Actor/Rapper)
    See D.J. Jazzy Jeff & The Fresh Prince

SMITH, WILLIAM
THE MEANING OF CHRISTMAS .... (Warner Bros. 5125) — 1.50 — 6.00 — 59

SMITHEREENS, THE
BEHIND THE WALL OF SLEEP/Blood And Roses .... (Enigma B-75002) — 1.25 — 5.00 — 86
IN A LONELY PLACE/Blood And Roses (Live) .... (Enigma B-75003) — 1.25 — 5.00 — 87
    (Back of sleeve credits Suzanne Vega with background vocal)
ONLY A MEMORY .... (Enigma/Capitol B-44150) — 1.00 — 4.00 — 88
HOUSE WE USED TO LIVE IN/Only A Memory .... (Enigma/Capitol B-44174) — 25.00 — 100.00 — 88
    (Unreleased promotional issue only that has been valued between $15 and $500 with no documented sales. It
    has been reported that the only copies of this sleeve are in the possession of the band.)
SICK OF SEATTLE/Keep Me Running (Demo)/Everything I Have Is Blue (Demo) .. (RCA 62803-7) — 2.50 — 10.00 — 94
    (Promotional issue only, *Not For Sale* printed on back.)
WAR FOR MY MIND/EVERYTHING I HAVE IS BLUE/
    Miles From Nowhere/Sleep The Night Away .... (RCA 62807-7 A/B) — 1.00 — 4.00 — 94
    (Originally included in the boxed set *A Date With the Smithereens*. Pat DiNizio pictured on front.)

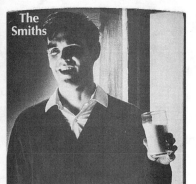

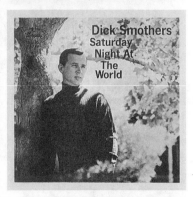

TITLE	LABEL AND NUMBER	VG	NM	YR
AFTERNOON TEA/LONG WAY BACK AGAIN/				
Love Is Gone/Point Of No Return ...... (RCA 62807-7 C/D)		1.00	4.00	94
(Originally included in the boxed set *A Date With the Smithereens*. Dennis Diken pictured on front. Lou Reed credited on back with lead guitar solos on *Point Of No Return* and *Long Way Back Again*.)				
GOTTI/SICK OF SEATTLE/Can't Go Home Anymore/Life Is So Beautiful .... (RCA 62807-7 E/F)		1.00	4.00	94
(Originally included in the boxed set *A Date With the Smithereens*. Jim Babjak pictured on front.)				
I'M SEXY/Keep Me Running (Demo)/				
Everything I Have Is Blue (4 Track Home Demo) ...... (RCA 62807-7 G/H)		1.00	4.00	94
(Originally included in the boxed set *A Date With the Smithereens*. Mike Mesaros pictured on front.)				
BOXED SET				
A DATE WITH THE SMITHEREENS ...... (RCA 62807-7)		7.50	30.00	94
(Complete set including four records in picture sleeves and cardboard box. See individual descriptions above.)				

SMITHS, THE
WHAT DIFFERENCE DOES IT MAKE? ...... (Sire/Rough Trade 29239-7)		3.00	12.00	84
HOW SOON IS NOW?/Shakespeare's Sister ...... (Sire/Rough Trade 29007-7)		2.00	8.00	85
STOP ME IF YOU THINK YOU'VE HEARD THIS ONE BEFORE ...... (Sire/Rough Trade 28136-7)		3.00	12.00	87
(Murray Head pictured on front.)				
Also see Morrissey, Aztec Camera (Craig Gannon)				

SMOKEY AND THE BANDIT 2
(Motion Picture)

See Burt Reynolds (*Let's Do Something Cheap And Superficial*)

SMOKING POPES
PURE IMAGINATION/O Holy Night ...... (Capitol 7PRO-11335/11336)		1.00	4.00	96
(Single sheet insert, not a true picture sleeve, edition of 1,500. Promotional issue only, *Promotional Use Only/Not For Sale* printed on insert. Issued with a small-hole 45 RPM.)				

SMOTHERS, DICK
SATURDAY NIGHT AT THE WORLD ...... (Mercury 72717)		6.25	25.00	67
Also see the Smothers Brothers, John Stewart (*Survivors*)				

SMOTHERS BROTHERS, THE
THE THREE SONG/The World I Used To Know ...... (Mercury 72483)		3.00	12.00	64
(B-side shown as by Dick Smothers)				
THE TOY SONG/Little Sacka Sugar ...... (Mercury 72519)		3.00	12.00	65
THE CHRISTMAS BUNNY (PARTS 1 & 2) ...... (Smothers Incorporated no #)		12.50	50.00	69
(Promotional issue only)				
Also see Dick Smothers, John Stewart (*Survivors*)				

SMYTH, PATTY
NEVER ENOUGH/Heartache Heard Round The World ...... (Columbia 38-06643)		.75	3.00	87
DOWNTOWN TRAIN/Tough Love ...... (Columbia 38-07112)		.75	3.00	87
Also see Scandal				

SNAKEFINGER
THE SPOT/Smelly Tongues ...... (Ralph 7805)		1.50	6.00	78
(Issued with blue vinyl)				
KILL THE GREAT RAVEN/What Wilbur? ...... (Ralph WIL7907)		1.25	5.00	79
(Back of sleeve states *Written and Produced by Snakefinger and the Residents*)				
THE MODEL/Talkin' In The Town ...... (Ralph 8005)		1.25	5.00	80
THE MAN IN THE DARK SEDAN/Womb To Worm ...... (Ralph 8051)		1.25	5.00	80
THERE'S NO JUSTICE IN LIFE/Move ...... (Ralph 8715)		1.00	4.00	87
I GAVE MYSELF TO YOU/(This Is Not A) Disco Song ...... (Undergrowth 1303)		2.00	8.00	80s
Also see the Residents (*Satisfaction*)				

SNAPPERS
MIRROR MAN ...... (Imperial 66422)		2.00	8.00	69

SNEAKER
MORE THAN JUST THE TWO OF US ...... (Handshake WS 9-02557)		.75	3.00	81

SNEEKERS, THE
SOUL SNEAKER/Sneaker Talk ...... (Columbia 4-43438)		2.00	8.00	65

SNIFF 'N' THE TEARS
See Loz Netto

SO
ARE YOU SURE/Don't Look Back ...... (EMI Manhattan B-50109)		.75	3.00	88

SNOW, HANK
THE MAN WHO ROBBED THE BANK AT SANTA FE/				
You're Losing Your Baby ...... (RCA Victor 47-8151)		2.00	8.00	63
Also see Chet Atkins (*Chet's Tune*), Elvis Presley (*Old Shep EP*)				

SNOW, PHOEBE
REELIN'/One-Eyed Jack ...... (A&M 2030)		1.00	4.00	78
(A-side shown as by Garland Jeffreys and Phoebe Snow)				
IF I CAN JUST GET THROUGH THE NIGHT/Soothin' ...... (Elektra 69305)		.75	3.00	89
Also see Dave Mason (*Dreams I Dream*)				

SNOW, TOM
HURRY BOY ...... (Capitol SPRO-8419)		1.50	6.00	76
(Promotional issue only, *For AOR Radio Only* printed on sleeve. Stevie Nicks, Elliot Randall of Sha Na Na, Jeff Porcaro and David Paich of Toto, Valerie Carter, and others are prominently credited.)				
ROCK & ROLL WIDOW ...... (Capitol PRO-8476)		1.50	6.00	76
(Promotional issue only)				

SNYDER, SUSAN MARIE
(Actress)

See the Soaps and Hearts Ensemble

SOAPS AND HEARTS ENSEMBLE, THE
MERRY CHRISTMAS WHEREVER YOU ARE/
  O Come All Ye Faithful/Joy To The World .... (RCA 07863-62979-7)   .75   3.00   94
    (The Soaps and Hearts Ensemble is a group of 29 actors and actresses representing 10 television soap operas.
    B-side shown as by Martha Byrne of *As The World Turns*.)

SOCIAL DISTORTION
MAINLINER/Playpen .... (Posh Boy 11)   3.00 12.00 81
1945/Under My Thumb/Playpen .... (Social Distortion # unknown)   5.00 20.00 82
MOMMY'S LITTLE MONSTER/Another State Of Mind .... (Social Distortion 4502)   3.75 15.00 83
ANOTHER STATE OF MIND/Mommy's Little Monster .... (Triple X 51023-7)   1.25   5.00 89
COLD FEELINGS/Bad Luck (Live) .... (Sony/Epic ES7-4568)   2.50 10.00 92
    (Promotional issue only with tour dates on back)

SOFT BOYS, THE
    See Katrina & the Waves (Kimberley Rew), Robyn Hitchcock and the Egyptians

SOFT CELL
TAINTED LOVE/Memorabilia .... (Sire 49855)   1.50   6.00 81
WHAT!/Memorabilia .... (Sire 29976-7)   1.25   5.00 82
LOVING YOU, HATING ME/It's A Mugs Game .... (Sire 29812-7)   1.25   5.00 82
    Also see Marc Almond

SOME, BELOUIS
IMAGINATION .... (Capitol B-5464)   .75   3.00 85
SOME PEOPLE .... (Capitol B-5492)   .75   3.00 85
LET IT BE WITH YOU .... (Capitol B-44021)   .75   3.00 87
ANIMAL MAGIC .... (Capitol B-44056)   .75   3.00 87

SOMEBODY UP THERE LIKES ME
(Motion Picture)
    See Perry Como (*Somebody Up There Likes Me*)

SOME KIND OF WONDERFUL
(Motion Picture)
    See Flesh For Lulu (*I Go Crazy*)

SOMETHING WILD
(Motion Picture)
    See Fine Young Cannibals (*Ever Fallen In Love*)

SOMMERS, JOANIE
I DON'T WANT TO WALK WITHOUT YOU/Seems Like So Long Ago .. (Warner Bros. # unknown)   6.25 25.00 67
    (Promotional issue only, half sleeve)
    Also see Edward Byrnes (*Kookie's Love Song*)

SONIC YOUTH
MAKING THE NATURE SCENE/
  I Killed Christgau With My Big Fuckin' Dick .... (Forced Exposure 001) 25.00 100.00 84
    (Color sleeve for test pressing, limited to only 25 copies)
MAKING THE NATURE SCENE/
  I Killed Christgau With My Big Fuckin' Dick .... (Forced Exposure 001)   7.50 30.00 84
    (Black and white sleeve)
DEATH VALLEY '69/Brave Men Run (In My Family) .... (Iridescence 12)   3.75 15.00 84
    (A-side shown as by Sonic Youth/Lydia Lunch)
DEATH VALLEY '69/Brave Men Run (In My Family) .... (My So Called Records 17)   2.50 10.00 84
    (A-side shown as by Sonic Youth/Lydia Lunch)
SILVER ROCKET/You Pose You Lose/Non-Metal Dude Wearing Metal Tee ... (Forced Exposure 012)   6.25 25.00 88
TOUCH ME I'M SICK/Halloween .... (Sub Pop 26)   3.75 15.00 88
    (Split single, *Halloween* shown as by Mudhoney. Limited to 3,000 copies with 500 on clear vinyl and 2,500 on
    black.)
IS IT MY BODY .... (Sub Pop 121)   2.50 10.00 91
    (Alice Cooper Tribute double single release limited to 5,500 copies with an unknown number on blue-gray
    vinyl. Also includes one song each by These Immortal Souls, Gumball, and Laughing Hyenas.)
SUPERSTAR .... (A&M 31458 0708 7)   .50   2.00 94
    (Side 3 of a 7 record box set titled *If I Were A Carpenter*. Each sleeve has a different face shot of Karen Carpenter
    on the front, Richard Carpenter on the back. No artist name or song titles indicated on sleeve. Complete set
    valued at $30.00 near mint.)
    Also see the Backbeat Band (Thurston Moore), Ciccone Youth, Thurston Moore

SONNIER, JO-EL
COME ON JOE .... (RCA 5282)   .75   3.00 87

SONNY AND CHER
LET THE GOOD TIMES ROLL/Love Is Strange .... (Reprise 0419) 10.00 40.00 65
    (Shown as by Salvatore Bono and Cher La Piere Also Known As Caesar & Cleo)
THE LETTER .... (Vault 45-916) 10.00 40.00 65
    Also see Cher

SON OF DRACULA
(Motion Picture)
    See Nilsson (*Daybreak*)

SON OF PETE
MANKIND .... (Beserkley 5739)   1.25   5.00 76
SILENT KNIGHT .... (Beserkley 5746)   1.25   5.00 76
BALLAD OF YUKON PETE .... (Organ 8669)   1.25   5.00

SONS OF CHAMPLIN, THE
JESUS IS COMING .... (Capitol 4668)   7.50 30.00 68
    (Issued with Compact 33 single originally available only by mail order)
    Also see Chicago (Bill Champlin)

SONS OF HEROES
LIVING OUTSIDE YOUR LOVE .... (MCA 52313)   1.00   4.00 83

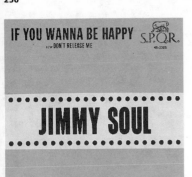

TITLE	LABEL AND NUMBER	VG	NM	YR
SONS OF THE PIONEERS				
SUGARFOOT	(Bluebird 105)	5.00	20.00	58
SOPWITH CAMEL				
POSTCARD FROM JAMAICA/Little Orphan Annie	(Kama Sutra 224)	2.50	10.00	67
SAGA OF THE LOWDOWN LET DOWN/The Great Morpheum	(Kama Sutra 236)	2.50	10.00	67
SOREL, LOUISE				
(Actress)				
See the Soaps and Hearts Ensemble				
S.O.S. BAND				
JUST THE WAY YOU LIKE IT (LONG VERSION)/Body Break	(Tabu ZS4-04523)	.75	3.00	84
THE FINEST /	(Tabu ZS4-05848)	.75	3.00	86
THE FINEST	(Tabu ZS4-05848)	1.00	4.00	86
(Promotional issue)				
SOUL, JIMMY				
WHEN MATILDA COMES BACK/Some Kinda Nut	(S.P.Q.R. 45-3302)	3.75	15.00	62
IF YOU WANNA BE HAPPY/Don't Release Me	(S.P.Q.R. 45-3305)	3.00	12.00	63
SOUL ASYLUM				
TIED TO THE TRACKS/Long Way Home	(Twin/Tone 8560)	3.75	15.00	85
SOMEBODY TO SHOVE	(Columbia 5024)	2.50	10.00	93
(Possibly a promotional issue only)				
MISERY/Hope	(Columbia 38 77959)	.50	2.00	95
PROMISES BROKEN/Can't Even Tell (Live)	(Columbia 38 78215)	.50	2.00	95
SOUL CLAN, THE				
(Solomon Burke, Arthur Conley, Don Covay, Ben E. King, and Joe Tex)				
SOUL MEETING/That's How It Feels	(Atlantic 2530)	3.75	15.00	68
Also see Ben E. King, Joe Tex				
SOUL MAN				
(Motion Picture)				
See Lou Reed (September Song)				
SOUL STING, THE				
See Linda Mackey				
SOUL SURVIVORS				
HAPPY BIRTHDAY, AMERICA (PARTS 1 & 2)	(Philadelphia International ZS8 3595)	1.25	5.00	76
(Promotional issue only, Demonstration–Not For Sale printed on sleeve)				
SOUL II SOUL				
KEEP ON MOVIN'	(Virgin 99205-7)	.75	3.00	89
SOUNDGARDEN				
ROOM A THOUSAND YEARS WIDE/H.I.V.Baby	(Sub Pop 83)	6.25	25.00	90
(Limited edition of 5,000 with the first 1,500 on purple vinyl and 3,500 on black)				
SOUND OF RAIN, THE				
See Richard Oliver				
SOUNDS UNLIMITED				
YOU DID IT BEFORE/OUR LOVE IS GONE/Gotta Get Away/She	(Tutman/Sundazed 104)	.50	2.00	95
(Issued with red vinyl)				
SOUP FOR ONE				
(Motion Picture)				
See Carly Simon (Why)				
SOURIRE, SOEUR				
(Popularly known as The Singing Nun)				
DOMINIQUE/Entre Les Etoiles (Among The Stars)	(Philips 40152)	2.00	8.00	63
TOUS LES CHEMINS (ALL THE ROADS)/				
Frere Tout L'Monde (Brother Of All The World)	(Philips 40165)	2.00	8.00	63
SOUTHER, J. D.				
GO AHEAD AND RAIN/All I Want	(Warner Bros. 29289-7)	1.00	4.00	84
SOUTHERN CULTURE ON THE SKIDS				
CLYDE'S LAMENT/CW James/Double-O Spy	(Moist # unknown)	.75	3.00	90
SOUTHERN PACIFIC				
MIDNIGHT HIGHWAY	(Warner Bros. 27952-7)	.75	3.00	88
HONEY I DARE YOU	(Warner Bros. 27691-7)	.75	3.00	88
ANY WAY THE WIND BLOWS	(Warner Bros. 22965-7)	.75	3.00	89
(From the motion picture Pink Cadillac)				
SOUTHSIDE JOHNNY & THE JUKES				
WALK AWAY RENEE/I Can't Wait	(Atlantic 7-89394)	1.00	4.00	86
Also see Jersey Artists For Mankind				
SPACEK, SISSY				
(Actress)				
COAL MINER'S DAUGHTER/I'm A Honky Tonk Girl	(MCA 41221)	1.00	4.00	80
(From the motion picture Coal Miner's Daughter)				
LONELY BUT ONLY FOR YOU/Old Home Town	(Atlantic America 7-99847)	.75	3.00	83
SPACE MONKEY				
COME WITH ME	(MCA 52623)	.75	3.00	85
(Originally issued with a biographical insert)				
SPANDAU BALLET				
TRUE/Gently	(Chrysalis VS4 42720)	1.00	4.00	83
GOLD/Gold (Live Version)	(Chrysalis VS4 42743)	.75	3.00	83

ONLY WHEN YOU LEAVE/Paint Me Down (recorded live) .... (Chrysalis VS4 42792) .75 3.00 84
HOW MANY LIES/Snakes And Lovers .... (Epic 34-06664) .75 3.00 86
HOW MANY LIES .... (Epic 34-06664) 1.25 5.00 86
    (Promotional issue, *Demonstration–Not For Sale* printed on sleeve)
    Also see Band Aid

SPANKY & OUR GANG
MAKING EVERY MINUTE COUNT .... (Mercury 72714) 2.00 8.00 67
LAZY DAY/(It Ain't Necessarily) Byrd Avenue .... (Mercury 72732) 2.00 8.00 67
SUNDAY MORNIN'/Echos Of My Mind .... (Mercury 72765) 2.00 8.00 68
    (Record shows b-side title as *Echoes*)
LIKE TO GET TO KNOW YOU .... (Mercury 72795) 2.00 8.00 68

SPARACINO, SPUTZY, AND DELILAH
THE WORLD INSIDE YOUR EYES/The Dead Walk .... (Saturn 2107-45) 1.50 6.00 85
    (Possibly a promotional issue only. 45 label shows a-side by Delilah & Sputzy. B-side shown as by Modern
    Man. From the motion picture *Day Of The Dead*.)

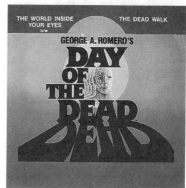

SPARKLEHORSE
HAMMERING THE CRAMPS/Too Late .... (Slow River no #) 1.00 4.00 95
    (Hard cover with small-hole 45 RPM record, no song titles on sleeve. Originally issued with insert listing song
    titles and credits.)
LONDON/Intermission .... (Capitol 11168) 2.00 8.00 95
    (Individually numbered, promotional issue only with white vinyl)

SPARKS
TALENT IS AN ASSET .... (Island 009) 1.50 6.00 74
ACHOO/Something For The Girl With Everything .... (Island 023) 1.50 6.00 74
I PREDICT/Moustache .... (Atlantic 4030) .75 3.00 82
COOL PLACES/Sports .... (Atlantic 7-89866) .75 3.00 83
    (A-side shown as by Sparks and Jane Wiedlin. Russell Mael and Wiedlin pictured on front.)
ALL YOU EVER THINK ABOUT IS SEX/
    I Wished I Looked A Little Better (Studio Version) .... (Atlantic 7-89797) .75 3.00 83
WITH ALL MY MIGHT/Sparks In The Dark .... (Atlantic 7-89645) .75 3.00 84
WHEN DO I GET TO SING "MY WAY" .... (Logic 59007) 1.50 6.00 95
    (Promotional issue only)

SPARKS, RANDY
JULIE KNOWS/At The End Of The Rainbow .... (Columbia 4-43138) 3.75 15.00 64
    Also see the Back Porch Majority, the New Christy Minstrels

SPARROW
TOMORROW'S SHIP/Isn't It Strange .... (Columbia 4-43755) 12.50 50.00 66
    (Promotional issue only)
    Also see Steppenwolf

SPECIAL AKA, THE
FREE NELSON MANDELA/Break Down The Door .... (Chrysalis VS 4-42794) 1.00 4.00 84
    (Nelson Mandela pictured on front. Back of sleeve credits backing vocals to and pictures, among others, Elvis
    Costello, Rankin Roger, and Dave Wakeling.)

SPECIALS, THE
GANGSTERS/The Selecter .... (Chrysalis/2 Tone 2374) 1.25 5.00 79
    (Generic Specials half sleeve probably used only for this release. No song title or catalog number indicated.)
    Also see Fine Young Cannibals (Andy Cox, David Steele), General Public (Dave Wakeling, Ranking Roger), the Special AKA (Dave Wakeling,
    Ranking Roger)

SPECTOR, PHIL
"A CHRISTMAS GIFT FOR YOU" SELECTIONS .... (Philles no #) 12.50 50.00 63
    (No artists or titles mentioned on sleeve, contents of this Christmas EP are unknown)
    Also see the Spectors Three

SPECTOR, RONNIE
TRY SOME, BUY SOME/Tandoori Chicken .... (Apple 1832) 2.50 10.00 71
SAY GOODBYE TO HOLLYWOOD/Baby Please Don't Go ..... (Epic/Cleveland International 8-50374) 3.75 15.00 77
    (Shown as by Ronnie Spector and the 'E' Street Band. Spector and Bruce Springsteen and the E Street Band
    pictured on front.)
SAY GOODBYE TO HOLLYWOOD .... (Epic/Cleveland International 8-50374) 5.00 20.00 77
    (Promotional issue, *Demonstration–Not For Sale* printed on sleeve. Shown as by Ronnie Spector and the 'E'
    Street Band. Spector with Bruce Springsteen and the E Street Band pictured on front.)
WHO CAN SLEEP/When We Danced .... (Columbia 38-07082) 1.00 4.00 87
WHO CAN SLEEP .... (Columbia 38-07082) 1.50 6.00 87
    (Promotional issue, *Demonstration–Not For Sale* printed on sleeve)
    Also see the Ronettes

SPECTORS THREE, THE
I REALLY DO/I Know Why .... (Trey 3001) 10.00 40.00 59
    Also see Phil Spector

SPEEDWAY
(Motion Picture)
    See Elvis Presley (*Let Yourself Go*)

SPENCE, BRIAN
COME BACK HOME .... (Polydor 887 718-7) .75 3.00 88

SPENCE, JUDSON
HOT & SWEATY .... (Atlantic 7-89010) .75 3.00 88
YEAH, YEAH, YEAH/Dance With Me .... (Atlantic 7-88999) .75 3.00 88

SPENCER, JON, BLUES EXPLOSION, THE
BIG YULE LOG BOOGIE/My Christmas Wish .... (Sub Pop 180) 2.50 10.00 92
    (Shown as by Jon Spencer. Limited edition of 2,218 issued with magenta vinyl.)
2 KINDSA LOVE/Lets Smerf .... (Matador/Capitol OLE 227-7) 1.00 4.00 96
    (Hard cover promotional issue only, *For Promotional Use Only - Not For Sale* printed on sleeve. Issued with
    small-hole 45 RPM record.)

TITLE	LABEL AND NUMBER	VG	NM	YR

SPENCER, TRACIE
SYMPTOMS OF TRUE LOVE .... (Capitol PB-44140) | .75 | 3.00 | 88
IMAGINE .... (Capitol PB-44268) | .75 | 3.00 | 89

SPHEERIS, JIMMIE
EXTENDED PLAYS
THE ORIGINAL TAP DANCING KID .... (Columbia AS 53) | 1.50 | 6.00 | 73
(Promotional issue only titled *New Comers As Featured In New Ingenue In August*, issued with a small-hole 33-1/3 RPM record. Also includes one song each by Johnny Nash, Looking Glass, and Andy Pratt.)

SPIDER
EVERYTHING IS ALRIGHT/Shady Lady .... (Dreamland 103) | 1.00 | 4.00 | 80
Also see Device (Holly Knight), Holly Knight

SPIDERS
NO NO BOY .... (Philips 40363) | 2.50 | 10.00 | 66

SPIES LIKE US
(Motion Picture)
See Paul McCartney (*Spies Like Us*)

SPINA, LITTLE BOBBY
LITTLE SIR ECHO .... (Soma 1415) | 3.75 | 15.00 | 65

SPINAL TAP
CHRISTMAS WITH THE DEVIL .... (Enigma 1143) | 1.50 | 6.00 | 84
Also see the Credibility Gap (Harry Shearer, Michael McKean), Hear 'N Aid

SPIN AND MARTY
THE TRIPLE-R SONG (YIPPI-I YIPPI-A YIPPI-O) .... (Am-Par DBR 58) | 2.00 | 8.00 |

SPINNERS
EXTENDED PLAYS
I'LL BE AROUND/ONE OF A KIND (LOVE AFFAIR) .... (Atlantic OP-7501) | 1.25 | 5.00 | 78
(Promotional issue only titled *Profiles In Gold Album 1*, issued with a small-hole 33-1/3 RPM record. Sold only at Burger King for 59¢ with the purchase of a Coke. Also includes two songs each by Abba, Firefall, and England Dan and John Ford Coley.)

SPINOSA, VICKY
DINKY LITTLE CABLE CAR/San Francisco Long Ago .... (Cavalier 804) | 1.00 | 4.00 | 84
(Shown as by Vicky Spinosa With Sal Carson and His Orchestra. 12-year old Spinosa pictured with San Francisco mayor Dianne Feinstein on front, Spinosa and Carson pictured on back.)

SPINOUT
(Motion Picture)
See Elvis Presley (*Spinout*)

SPIRIT
CADILLAC COWBOYS/Darkness .... (Epic 5-10849) | 2.00 | 8.00 | 72
NATURE'S WAY .... (Potato 1722) | 1.25 | 5.00 | 78
Also see Firefall (Mark Andes)

SPLIT ENZ
I GOT YOU/Double Happy .... (A&M 2252) | 1.50 | 6.00 | 80
I HOPE I NEVER/The Choral Sea .... (A&M 2285) | 1.50 | 6.00 | 80
ONE STEP AHEAD/In The Wars .... (A&M 2339) | 1.25 | 5.00 | 81
(Front of sleeve states *Laser Etched Single*)
ONE STEP AHEAD/In The Wars .... (A&M 2339) | 1.00 | 4.00 | 81
(Issued with black vinyl)
SIX MONTHS IN A LEAKY BOAT/Make Sense Of It .... (A&M 2411) | 1.00 | 4.00 | 82
Also see Crowded House, Tim Finn

SPOOKIE
DON'T WALK AWAY .... (Columbia 38-07782) | .75 | 3.00 | 88

SPOONER
MEAN OLD WORLD/Walking With An Angel .... (Boat SP 1018) | 1.00 | 4.00 | 86
(Folding sleeve)
EXTENDED PLAYS
DANCING DOLLS/WORKING GIRL/
Member Of The Family/From My Head To My Shoes .... (Boat SP 4001) | 1.00 | 4.00 | 79
(Hard cover, small-hole 33-1/3 record. Titled on front *Cruel School*.)

SPORTS, THE
HIT SINGLE/Who Listens To The Radio .... (Arista 0468) | 1.25 | 5.00 | 79

SPRING
See American Spring

SPRINGFIELD, DUSTY
STAY AWHILE/Something Special .... (Philips 40180) | 2.50 | 10.00 | 64
ALL CRIED OUT/I Wish I'd Never Loved You .... (Philips 40229) | 2.50 | 10.00 | 64
GUESS WHO/Live It Up .... (Philips 40245) | 2.50 | 10.00 | 64
LOSING YOU .... (Philips 40270) | 2.50 | 10.00 | 65
IN THE MIDDLE OF NOWHERE/Baby Don't You Know .... (Philips 40303) | 2.50 | 10.00 | 65
I JUST DON'T KNOW WHAT TO DO WITH MYSELF/Some Of Your Lovin' .... (Philips 40319) | 2.50 | 10.00 | 65
YOU DON'T HAVE TO SAY YOU LOVE ME/Little By Little .... (Philips 40371) | 2.50 | 10.00 | 66
(Green version)
YOU DON'T HAVE TO SAY YOU LOVE ME/Little By Little .... (Philips 40371) | 2.50 | 10.00 | 66
(Yellow version)
ALL I SEE IS YOU/I'm Gonna Leave You .... (Philips 40396) | 2.50 | 10.00 | 66
I'LL TRY ANYTHING/The Corrupt Ones .... (Philips 40439) | 2.50 | 10.00 | 67
GENERIC DUSTY SPRINGFIELD SLEEVE .... (Philips no #) | 2.50 | 10.00 | 67
(Front and back are identical to *I'll Try Anything* but without song titles on front.)
WHAT'S IT GONNA BE/Small Town Girl .... (Philips 40498) | 2.50 | 10.00 | 67
SON-OF-A PREACHER MAN/Just A Little Lovin' .... (Atlantic 2580) | 2.00 | 8.00 | 68
Also see Steve Dorff and Friends (*Theme From Growing Pains*), Pet Shop Boys (*What Have I Done To Deserve This?*)

SPRINGFIELD, RICK

Title	Label and Number	VG	NM	YR
SPEAK TO THE SKY / Why?	(Capitol 3340)	3.00	12.00	72
WHAT WOULD THE CHILDREN THINK	(Capitol 3466)	3.75	15.00	72
I'VE DONE EVERYTHING FOR YOU	(RCA PB-12166)	1.00	4.00	81
JESSIE'S GIRL / Carry Me Away	(RCA PB-12201)	1.25	5.00	80

(Sleeve refers to Springfield as Dr. Noah Drake from "General Hospital".)

Title	Label and Number	VG	NM	YR
LOVE IS ALRIGHT TONITE / Everybody's Girl	(RCA PB-13008)	1.00	4.00	81
DON'T TALK TO STRANGERS / Tonight	(RCA PB-13070)	1.00	4.00	82
I GET EXCITED / Kristina	(RCA PB-13303)	1.00	4.00	82
AFFAIR OF THE HEART / Like Father, Like Son	(RCA PB-13497)	1.00	4.00	83
SOULS (LIVE)	(RCA PB-13650)	.75	3.00	83
LOVE SOMEBODY / Great Lost Art Of Conversation	(RCA PB-13738)	.75	3.00	84

(From the motion picture *Hard To Hold*)

Title	Label and Number	VG	NM	YR
DON'T WALK AWAY / S.F.O. (Instrumental)	(RCA PB-13813)	.75	3.00	85

(From the motion picture *Hard To Hold*)

Title	Label and Number	VG	NM	YR
BOP 'TIL YOU DROP / Taxi Dancing	(RCA PB-13861)	.75	3.00	84

(B-side shown as by Rick Springfield and Randy Crawford. From the motion picture *Hard To Hold*.)

Title	Label and Number	VG	NM	YR
BRUCE / Guenevere	(Mercury 880 405-7)	1.25	5.00	84
CELEBRATE YOUTH / Stranger In The House	(RCA PB-14047)	.75	3.00	85
STATE OF THE HEART / The Power Of Love (The Tao Of Love)	(RCA PB-14120)	.75	3.00	85
ROCK OF LIFE / The Language Of Love	(RCA 6853-7-R)	.75	3.00	88
ENEMIES LIKE YOU AND ME / I Need You	(Epic 34 08115)	.75	3.00	88

SPRINGSTEEN, BRUCE

Title	Label and Number	VG	NM	YR
BLINDED BY THE LIGHT	(Columbia 4-45805)	50.00	200.00	73
HUNGRY HEART / Held Up Without A Gun	(Columbia 11-11391)	1.25	5.00	80
FADE AWAY / Be True	(Columbia 11-11431)	1.25	5.00	81

(First pressings of the 45 incorrectly show the b-side title as *To Be True* which is valued at $25 near mint)

Title	Label and Number	VG	NM	YR
SANTA CLAUS IS COMIN' TO TOWN	(Columbia AE7 1332)	5.00	20.00	81

(Promotional issue only, *Demonstration–Not For Sale* printed on sleeve)

Title	Label and Number	VG	NM	YR
DANCING IN THE DARK / Pink Cadillac	(Columbia 38-04463)	1.00	4.00	84
DANCING IN THE DARK	(Columbia 38-04463)	3.00	12.00	84

(Promotional issue, *Demonstration–Not For Sale* printed on sleeve)

Title	Label and Number	VG	NM	YR
COVER ME / Jersey Girl (Live)	(Columbia 38-04561)	1.00	4.00	84

(Springsteen and the E Street Band pictured on back)

Title	Label and Number	VG	NM	YR
COVER ME	(Columbia 38-04561)	3.00	12.00	84

(Promotional issue, *Demonstration–Not For Sale* printed on sleeve. Springsteen and the E Street Band pictured on back.)

Title	Label and Number	VG	NM	YR
BORN IN THE U.S.A. / Shut Out The Light	(Columbia 38-04680)	1.00	4.00	84

(Photography by Annie Leibovitz)

Title	Label and Number	VG	NM	YR
BORN IN THE U.S.A.	(Columbia 38-04680)	3.00	12.00	84

(Promotional issue, *Demonstration–Not For Sale* printed on sleeve. Photography by Annie Leibovitz)

Title	Label and Number	VG	NM	YR
I'M ON FIRE / Johnny Bye Bye	(Columbia 38-04772)	1.00	4.00	85

(Photography by Annie Leibovitz)

Title	Label and Number	VG	NM	YR
I'M ON FIRE	(Columbia 38-04772)	3.00	12.00	85

(Promotional issue, *Demonstration–Not For Sale* printed on sleeve. Photography by Annie Leibovitz)

Title	Label and Number	VG	NM	YR
GLORY DAYS / Stand On It	(Columbia 38-04924)	1.00	4.00	85

(Light beige background)

Title	Label and Number	VG	NM	YR
GLORY DAYS	(Columbia 38-04924)	3.00	12.00	85

(Promotional issue, *Demonstration–Not For Sale* printed on sleeve, medium tan background)

Title	Label and Number	VG	NM	YR
I'M GOIN' DOWN / Janey, Don't You Lose Heart	(Columbia 38-05603)	1.00	4.00	85
I'M GOIN' DOWN	(Columbia 38-05603)	3.00	12.00	85

(Promotional issue, *Demonstration–Not For Sale* printed on sleeve)

Title	Label and Number	VG	NM	YR
MY HOMETOWN / Santa Claus Is Comin' To Town	(Columbia 38-05728)	1.00	4.00	85

(Photography by Annie Leibovitz)

Title	Label and Number	VG	NM	YR
MY HOMETOWN	(Columbia 38-05728)	3.00	12.00	85

(Promotional issue, *Demonstration–Not For Sale* printed on sleeve. Photography by Annie Leibovitz)

Title	Label and Number	VG	NM	YR
WAR / Merry Christmas Baby	(Columbia 38-06432)	1.00	4.00	86

(Shown as by Bruce Springsteen & the E Street Band)

Title	Label and Number	VG	NM	YR
WAR	(Columbia 38-06432)	3.00	12.00	86

(Promotional issue, *Demonstration–Not For Sale* printed on sleeve. Shown as by Bruce Springsteen & the E Street Band)

Title	Label and Number	VG	NM	YR
FIRE / Incident On 57th Street (Live Version)	(Columbia 38-06657)	1.00	4.00	87

(Shown as by Bruce Springsteen & the E Street Band. No catalog number listed on sleeve. Photography by Annie Leibovitz)

Title	Label and Number	VG	NM	YR
FIRE	(Columbia 38-06657)	3.00	12.00	87

(Promotional issue, *Demonstration–Not For Sale* printed on sleeve. Shown as by Bruce Springsteen & the E Street Band. Photography by Annie Leibovitz)

Title	Label and Number	VG	NM	YR
BRILLIANT DISGUISE / Lucky Man	(Columbia 38-07595)	.75	3.00	87
TUNNEL OF LOVE / Two For The Road	(Columbia 38-07663)	.75	3.00	87

(Photography by Annie Leibovitz)

Title	Label and Number	VG	NM	YR
ONE STEP UP / Roulette	(Columbia 38-07726)	.75	3.00	88

(Photography by Annie Leibovitz)

Title	Label and Number	VG	NM	YR
SECRET GARDEN / Thunder Road (Live)	(Columbia 38 77847)	.50	2.00	95

EXTENDED PLAYS

Title	Label and Number	VG	NM	YR
BLINDED BY THE LIGHT	(Columbia AS 45)	12.50	50.00	72

(A series of promotional issues titled *Playback* issued with a small-hole 33-1/3 RPM record. Price includes generic *Playback* sleeve, individually valued at $5; and insert, individually valued at $45. Flip side by Andy Pratt. The record is valued at $100 near mint.)

Title	Label and Number	VG	NM	YR
THE CIRCUS SONG	(Columbia AS 52)	12.50	50.00	73

(A series of promotional issues titled *Playback* issued with a small-hole 33-1/3 RPM record. Price includes generic *Playback* sleeve, individually valued at $5; and insert, individually valued at $45. Also includes 1 song each by Loudon Wainright III, Taj Mahal, and Albert Hammond. The record is the most sought after of the *Playback* series and is valued at $200 near mint.)

Title	Label and Number	VG	NM	YR
ROSALITA	(Columbia AS 66)	12.50	50.00	73

(A series of promotional issues titled *Playback* issued with a small-hole 33-1/3 RPM record. Price includes generic *Playback* sleeve, individually valued at $5; and insert, individually valued at $45. Also includes songs by Johnny Winter and the Hollies. The record is valued at $150 near mint.)

Also see Artists United Against Apartheid, Jersey Artists For Mankind, Ronnie Spector (*Say Goodbye To Hollywood*), Bruce Springstone (parody), U.S.A. For Africa, Voices Of America

TITLE	LABEL AND NUMBER	VG	NM	YR

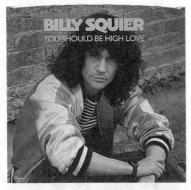

SPRINGSTONE, BRUCE
(MEET THE) FLINTSTONES / Take Me Out To The Ball Game .... (Clean Cuts 902) — 1.25 — 5.00 — 82
    (Tommy Keene on guitar credited on back of sleeve)
    Also see Tommy Keene

SPYRO GYRA
JUBILEE / Shaker Song .... (Infinity 50,041) — 1.00 — 4.00 — 79
MORNING DANCE / Song For Lorraine .... (Infinity 50,011) — 1.00 — 4.00 — 79

SQUALLS, THE
NA, NA, NA, NA / Crazy Hazy Kisses .... (I.R.S. 53049) — 1.00 — 4.00 — 87
    (B-side shown as by Flat Duo Jets. From the motion picture *Athens, GA–Inside/Out*. Issued with small-hole 45
    RPM record.)

SQUEEZE
COOL FOR CATS / Model .... (A&M 2146) — 1.25 — 5.00 — 80
IF I DIDN'T LOVE YOU / Pretty One .... (A&M 2229) — 1.25 — 5.00 — 80
PULLING MUSSELS (FROM THE SHELL) / Pretty One .... (A&M 2247) — 1.25 — 5.00 — 80
ANOTHER NAIL IN MY HEART / Going Crazy / What The Butler Saw .... (A&M 2263) — 1.25 — 5.00 — 80
IF I DIDN'T LOVE YOU / Another Nail In My Heart .... (A&M 1616) — 2.00 — 8.00 — 80
    ("Tiny Collector's Edition" sleeve issued with 5", small-hole 33-1/3 RPM record)
TEMPTED / Trust .... (A&M 2345) — 1.00 — 4.00 — 81
BLACK COFFEE IN BED / The Hunt .... (A&M 2424) — 1.50 — 6.00 — 82
HITS OF THE YEAR / Fortnight Saga .... (A&M 2776) — .75 — 3.00 — 85
HOURGLASS / Wedding Bells .... (A&M 2967) — .75 — 3.00 — 87
853 5937 / Take Me I'm Yours (Live) .... (A&M 2994) — 1.00 — 4.00 — 87
TEMPTED / My Sharona .... (A&M/RCA/Capitol 62800-7) — 1.00 — 4.00 — 94
    (Both songs listed as the a-side, *My Sharona* shown as by the Knack. From the motion picture *Reality Bites*.)
    Also see Paul Carrack, Difford and Tilbrook, Ferry Aid, Robyn Hitchcock, Jools Holland and His Millionaires

SQUIER, BILLY
YOU SHOULD BE HIGH LOVE .... (Capitol 4877) — 1.25 — 5.00 — 80
THE STROKE .... (Capitol 5005) — 1.00 — 4.00 — 81
MY KINDA LOVER .... (Capitol A-5037) — 1.00 — 4.00 — 81
IN THE DARK .... (Capitol A-5040) — 1.00 — 4.00 — 81
FAST TIMES / Interview .... (The Knight Club SPRO-9869) — 3.75 — 15.00 — 82
    (Originally available only to fan club members)
EMOTIONS IN MOTION .... (Capitol B-5135) — .75 — 3.00 — 82
EVERYBODY WANTS YOU .... (Capitol B-5163) — .75 — 3.00 — 82
SHE'S A RUNNER .... (Capitol B-5202) — .75 — 3.00 — 83
CHRISTMAS IS THE TIME TO SAY "I LOVE YOU" / White Christmas .... (Capitol B-5303) — 1.25 — 5.00 — 83
ROCK ME TONIGHT / Can't Get Next To You .... (Capitol B-5370) — .75 — 3.00 — 84
ROCK ME TONIGHT .... (Capitol B-5370) — 1.50 — 6.00 — 84
    (Promotional issue, *For Promotional Use Only. Not For Sale* printed on sleeve. No song titles listed on sleeve.)
ALL NIGHT LONG .... (Capitol B-5422) — .75 — 3.00 — 84
EYE ON YOU .... (Capitol B-5416) — .75 — 3.00 — 84
LOVE IS THE HERO .... (Capitol B-5619) — .75 — 3.00 — 86
SHOT O' LOVE .... (Capitol B-5657) — .75 — 3.00 — 86

SSQ
BIG ELECTRONIC BEAT / Fire .... (Enigma 16) — 2.50 — 10.00 — 83
SYNTHICIDE / Fire .... (EMI America B-8214) — 1.00 — 4.00 — 84
    Also see Stacey Q

STABILIZERS
ONE SIMPLE THING .... (Columbia 38-06700) — 1.00 — 4.00 — 87
ONE SIMPLE THING (EDITED VERSION) .... (Columbia 38-06700) — 1.25 — 5.00 — 87
    (Promotional issue, *Demonstration Only/Not For Sale* printed on sleeve)

STACEY Q
TWO OF HEARTS / Dancing Nowhere .... (Atlantic 7-89381) — .75 — 3.00 — 86
WE CONNECT / Don't Break My Heart .... (Atlantic 7-89331) — .75 — 3.00 — 86
DON'T MAKE A FOOL OF YOURSELF / Fly By Night .... (Atlantic 7-89135) — .75 — 3.00 — 88
I LOVE YOU / Dance The Night .... (Atlantic 7-89081) — .75 — 3.00 — 88
FAVORITE THINGS / Another Chance .... (Atlantic 7-88991) — .75 — 3.00 — 88
GIVE YOU ALL MY LOVE / .... (Atlantic 7-88893) — .75 — 3.00 — 89
    Also see SSQ

STACK, ROBERT
(Actor)
    See Nelson Riddle

STAGECOACH
(Motion Picture)
    See Wayne Newton (*Stagecoach To Cheyenne*)

STAIRSTEPS
FROM US TO YOU / Time .... (Dark Horse 10005) — 1.00 — 4.00 — 75

STALLONE, FRANK
(Brother of Sylvester Stallone)
DARLIN' / Album Medley .... (Polydor 821 382-7) — 1.00 — 4.00 — 84

STALLONE, SYLVESTER
(Actor)
SWEET LOVIN' FRIENDS / God Won't Get You .... (RCA 13883) — 1.00 — 4.00 — 84
    (Shown as by Dolly Parton and Sylvester Stallone. From the motion picture *Rhinestone*.)
    Also see John Cafferty and the Beaver Brown Band (*Voice Of America's Sons*), Survivor (*Burning Heart, Eye Of The Tiger*), Robert Tepper (*No Easy Way Out*)

STAMEY, CHRIS
THE SUMMER SUN / Where The Fun Is .... (Car/Ork 2/81982) — 3.75 — 15.00 — 78
    (Orange and black version)
THE SUMMER SUN / Where The Fun Is .... (Car/Ork 2/81982) — 1.50 — 6.00 — 78
    (Black and white version)

(I THOUGHT) YOU WANTED TO KNOW / If And When .... *(Car 7)*   3.75   15.00   78
    (Individually numbered, shown as by Chris Stamey and the dB's)
CHRISTMAS TIME / Occasional Shivers .... *(Coyote 8699)*   1.25   5.00   86
    (Plain white sleeve with gold sticker, issued with green vinyl)
    Also see the dB's, Golden Palaminos

STAMPLEY, JOE
SOUL SONG .... *(Dot 17442)*   1.50   6.00   72
    (Promotional issue only)

STAND AND DELIVER
(Motion Picture)
    See Mr. Mister *(Stand And Deliver)*

STANDELLS, THE
THE BOY NEXT DOOR / B. J. Quetzal .... *(Vee-Jay 643)*   10.00   40.00   65
POOR SHELL OF A MAN / Try It .... *(Tower 310)*   6.25   25.00   67
RIOT ON SUNSET STRIP / Black Hearted Woman .... *(Tower 314)*   6.25   25.00   67
CAN'T HELP BUT LOVE YOU / Ninety-Nine And One Half .... *(Tower 348)*   6.25   25.00   67
EXTENDED PLAYS
SOMETIMES GOOD GUYS DON'T WEAR WHITE / RIOT ON SUNSET STRIP /
  I Hate To Leave You / Why Pick On Me .... *(Sundazed 108)*   .50   2.00   95
    (Hard cover titled *Poor Boys Born In A Rubble,* issued with 45 RPM green vinyl)

STANG, ARNOLD
(Comic Actor)
LOT'SA LUCK CHARLIE .... *(MGM 12693)*   5.00   20.00   58

STANLEY, CHUCK, INTRODUCING ALYSON WILLIAMS
MAKE YOU MINE TONIGHT (REMIX) .... *(Def Jam 38-07425)*   .75   3.00   87
    (Both Stanley and Williams pictured)

STANLEY, MICHAEL, BAND, THE
SHOW ME SOMETHING / Somebody Else's Woman .... *(MSB Records 701)*   1.50   6.00   85
HARD DIE THE HEROES / Sound Track Medley: Journey-Dream-Quest-Fight   *(WEN Records R-54)*   2.50   10.00   86
    (Sleeve pictures Stanley with members of the Cleveland Browns football team in warrior costumes)
    Also see Kevin Raleigh

STANSFIELD, LISA
ALL AROUND THE WORLD / Affection .... *(Arista 9928)*   .75   3.00   89
    Also see Blue Zone UK, Coldcut

STANWYCK, BARBARA
(Actress)
    See Brook Benton *(Walk On The Wild Side)*

STAPLE SINGERS, THE
ARE YOU READY / Love Works In Strange Ways .... *(Private I ZS4-05565)*   1.00   4.00   85

STAPLES, MAVIS
20TH CENTURY EXPRESS / All The Discomforts Of Home .... *(Paisley Park 22968-7)*   .75   3.00   89

STAPLETON, JEAN
(Actress)
THOSE WERE THE DAYS .... *(Atlantic 2847)*   2.00   8.00   71
    (Shown as by Carroll O'Connor & Jean Stapleton [as the Bunkers]. From the television series *All In The Family.*
    O'Connor, Stapleton, Rob Reiner, and Sally Struthers pictured.)
MOMENTS TO REMEMBER /
  Oh Babe What Would You Say / They Can't Take That Away From Me .... *(RCA 74-0962)*   1.50   6.00   73
    (Shown as by Carroll O'Connor & Jean Stapleton)

STARFIRES, THE
SPACE NEEDLE / The Jordan Stomp .... *(Round 1016)*   12.50   50.00   62

STAR IS BORN, A
(Motion Picture)
    See Barbra Streisand *(Love Theme From A Star Is Born)*

STARLAND VOCAL BAND
LIBERATED WOMAN .... *(Windsong CB-10992)*   1.25   5.00   77

STARLETS, THE
    See the Blue Belles

STARPOINT
OBJECT OF MY DESIRE / Send Me A Letter .... *(Elektra 7-69621)*   .75   3.00   85
HE WANTS MY BODY / Satisfy Me Lover .... *(Elektra 7-69489)*   .75   3.00   87
SAY YOU WILL / .... *(Elektra 7-69373)*   .75   3.00   88

STARR, BRENDA K.
BREAKFAST IN BED .... *(MCA 53189)*   .75   3.00   87
I STILL BELIEVE .... *(MCA 53288)*   .75   3.00   88
WHAT YOU SEE IS WHAT YOU GET .... *(MCA 53367)*   .75   3.00   88

STARR, KAY
FOUR WALLS / Oh, Lonesome Me .... *(Capitol 4835)*   2.00   8.00   62

STARR, RINGO
BEAUCOUPS OF BLUES / Coochy-Coochy .... *(Apple 1826)*   10.00   40.00   70
    (Incorrect catalog number, Apple 1826, shown on sleeve)
BEAUCOUPS OF BLUES / Coochy-Coochy .... *(Apple 2969)*   6.25   25.00   70
    (Identical to previous sleeve but indicates correct catalog number of 2969)
IT DON'T COME EASY / Early 1970 .... *(Apple 1831)*   5.00   20.00   72
BACK OFF BOOGALOO / Blindman .... *(Apple 1849)*   5.00   20.00   72
    (Glossy coated paper, front of sleeve is black)
BACK OFF BOOGALOO / Blindman .... *(Apple 1849)*   5.00   20.00   72
    (Glossy coated paper, front of sleeve is gray)
BACK OFF BOOGALOO / Blindman .... *(Apple 1849)*   3.00   12.00   72
    (Non-glossy uncoated paper)

TITLE	LABEL AND NUMBER	VG	NM	YR

PHOTOGRAPH .... (Apple 1865) | 3.00 | 12.00 | 73
YOU'RE SIXTEEN .... (Apple 1870) | 3.75 | 15.00 | 73
ONLY YOU/Call Me .... (Apple 1876) | 3.00 | 12.00 | 74
IT'S ALL DOWN TO GOODNIGHT VIENNA/Oo-Wee .... (Apple 1882) | 3.00 | 12.00 | 75
WRACK MY BRAIN/Drumming Is My Madness .... (Boardwalk NB7-11-130) | 1.25 | 5.00 | 81

Also see Artists United Against Apartheid, the Beatles, Nilsson (Daybreak), John Stewart (Survivors)

STARSHIP
WE BUILT THIS CITY/Private Room (Instrumental) .... (Grunt FB-14170) | 1.00 | 4.00 | 85
SARA/Hearts Of The World (Will Understand) .... (Grunt FB-14253) | 1.00 | 4.00 | 86
   (Issued with either blue or black vinyl)
TOMORROW DOESN'T MATTER TONIGHT/Love Rusts .... (Grunt FB-14332) | 7.50 | 30.00 | 86
BEFORE I GO/Cut You Down To Size .... (Grunt FB-14393) | 1.00 | 4.00 | 86
NOTHING'S GONNA STOP US NOW/Layin' It On The Line (Live) .... (Grunt 5109-7-G) | .75 | 3.00 | 87
   (From the motion picture Mannequin, Andrew McCarthy pictured on front)
NOTHING'S GONNA STOP US NOW/Layin' It On The Line (Live) .... (Grunt 5109-7-G-1) | 1.50 | 6.00 | 87
   (Promotional issue only, Special Holiday Re-Service printed on sleeve, band pictured on front)
IT'S NOT OVER ('TIL IT'S OVER)/Babylon .... (RCA/Grunt 5225-7-G) | .75 | 3.00 | 87
BEAT PATROL/Girls Like You .... (Grunt 5308-7-G) | .75 | 3.00 | 87
WILD AGAIN/Layin' It On The Line .... (Elektra 7-69349) | .75 | 3.00 | 88
   (From the motion picture Cocktail)
IT'S NOT ENOUGH/Love Among The Cannibals .... (RCA 9032-7-R) | .75 | 3.00 | 89

Also see Jefferson Airplane, Jefferson Starship, Paul Kantner, Grace Slick, Mickey Thomas

STAR TREK
(Television Series)
THE TIME STEALER .... (Peter Pan 1514) | 1.00 | 4.00 | 79
   (8" tall hard cover, children's series)
   Related see Nichelle Nichols, Leonard Nimoy

STAR TREK–THE MOTION PICTURE
(Motion Picture)
   See Bob James (Main Theme From Star Trek–The Motion Picture)

STAR TREK III–THE SEARCH FOR SPOCK
(Motion Picture)
   See James Horner & Group 87 (The Search For Spock)

STAR WARS
(Motion Picture)
   See John Williams (Star Wars Main Title)

STAR WARS
(Television Special)
   See Jefferson Starship (Light The Sky On Fire)

STAR WARS INTERGALACTIC DROID CHOIR & CHORALE, THE
WHAT CAN YOU GET A WOOKIE FOR CHRISTMAS
   (WHEN HE ALREADY OWNS A COMB?)/R2-D2 We Wish You A Merry Christmas (RSO 1058) | 2.00 | 8.00 | 80
   (Star Wars character Chewbacca pictured on front. A-side actually performed by Meco, b-side by the Original
   Star Wars Cast: R2-D2/Anthony Daniels as C-3PO. No artist names credited on sleeve.)

STARZ
(SHE'S JUST A) FALLEN ANGEL/Monkey Business .... (Capitol 4343) | 1.50 | 6.00 | 76
CHERRY BABY/Rock Six Times .... (Capitol 4399) | 1.50 | 6.00 | 77
   (Originally issued with yellow vinyl)
SING IT, SHOUT IT/Subway Terror .... (Capitol 4434) | 1.50 | 6.00 | 77
   (Originally issued with yellow vinyl)
(ANY WAY THAT YOU WANT IT) I'LL BE THERE/Texas .... (Capitol 4546) | 1.50 | 6.00 | 78
SO YOUNG, SO BAD/Coliseum Rock .... (Capitol 4637) | 1.25 | 5.00 | 78

STATLERS, THE
ATLANTA BLUE .... (Mercury 818 700-7) | .75 | 3.00 | 84
EXTENDED PLAYS
A VERY MERRY CHRISTMAS .... (Mercury DJ 577) | 1.50 | 6.00 | 82
   (Promotional issue only, 4 tracks, shown as by the Statler Brothers)

STAY AWAY, JOE
(Motion Picture)
   See Elvis Presley (B-side, Stay Away)

STAYING ALIVE
(Motion Picture)
   See the Bee Gees (Someone Belonging To Someone, The Woman In You)

STEADMAN, RALPH
(Artist)
   See the Who (Happy Jack)

STEALERS WHEEL
STAR/What More Could You Want .... (A&M 1483) | 1.25 | 5.00 | 73
   Also see Gerry Rafferty

STEALS, JEAN
ARE YOU FOR ME .... (MCA 53342) | .75 | 3.00 | 88

STEAM
NA NA HEY HEY KISS HIM GOODBYE (WHITE SOX THEME) .... (Mercury C-30160) | 5.00 | 20.00 | 76
   (Chicago White Sox logo featured on sleeve)

STEARNS, JUNE
WHERE HE STOPS NOBODY KNOWS .... (Columbia 4-44575) | 1.50 | 6.00 | 68

STEELE, MAUREEN
SAVE THE NIGHT FOR ME .... (Motown 1787MF) | .75 | 3.00 | 85
SAVE THE NIGHT FOR ME .... (Motown 1787MF) | 1.00 | 4.00 | 85
   (Promotional issue, For Promotional Use Only/Not For Sale printed on sleeve)

STEELE, TOMMY
FORTUOSITY/I'm A Brass Band Today .... (Buena Vista F-457) | 2.50 | 10.00 | 66

STEELY DAN
EAST ST. LOUIS TOODLE-OO .... (ABC SPDJ-20) | 3.75 | 15.00 | 74
    (Promotional issue only, issued with a small-hole 33-1/3 RPM record)
    Also see Donald Fagen

STEGALL, KEITH
PRETTY LADY .... (Epic 34-04394) | .75 | 3.00 | 85
PRETTY LADY .... (Epic 34-04394) | 1.00 | 4.00 | 85
    (Promotional issue, *Demonstration Only–Not For Sale* printed on sleeve)

STEIN, FRANKIE, AND HIS GHOULS
WEERDO THE WOLF/Goon River .... (Power 338-45) | 5.00 | 20.00 | 64

STEINMAN, JIM
THE STORM/Rock And Roll Dreams Come Through .... (Epic/Cleveland International AE 7-1232) | 2.00 | 8.00 | 81
    (Promotional issue only, issued with a small-hole 33-1/3 RPM record. On back of sleeve the a-side credits the
    New York Philharmonic Orchestra. The b-side credits, among others, Todd Rundgren on electric guitar and
    background vocals, Max Weinberg of the E Street Band on drums, and Kasim Sultan on background vocals.)
LOST BOYS AND GOLDEN GIRLS .... (Epic/Cleveland International ZSS 169942) | 2.00 | 8.00 | 82
    (Promotional issue only released with half-speed mastered audiophile pressing)

STEPHENSON, VAN
MODERN DAY DELILAH .... (MCA 52376) | 1.00 | 4.00 | 84
WHAT THE BIG GIRLS DO .... (MCA 52437) | .75 | 3.00 | 84
NO SECRETS/Finale .... (MCA 52611) | .75 | 3.00 | 85
    (B-side shown as by Jan Hammer. From the motion picture *Secret Admirer*, C. Thomas Howell pictured.)
WE'RE DOING ALRIGHT .... (MCA 52755) | .75 | 3.00 | 86

STEPPENWOLF
RIDE WITH ME .... (ABC/Dunhill 4283) | 1.50 | 6.00 | 71
BORN TO BE WILD/The Pusher .... (ABC 11436) | 2.50 | 10.00 | 73
    (Featured in the motion picture *Easy Rider*)
STRAIGHT SHOOTIN' WOMAN/Justice Don't Be Slow .... (Mums ZS8 6031) | 1.50 | 6.00 | 74
    Also see Sparrow

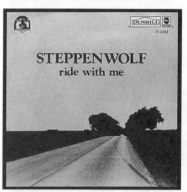

STERLING, JAN
(Actress)
    See Jerry Lee Lewis (*High School Confidential*)

STERN, ISAAC
EXTENDED PLAYS
HAPPY BIRTHDAY, ISAAC STERN/ISAAC STERN REMINISCES ABOUT
    THIS HISTORIC CONCERT/Album Highlights ....(Columbia AE71226) | 1.25 | 5.00 | 81
    (Promotional issue only, *Demonstration–Not For Sale* printed on sleeve, issued with a small-hole 33-1/3 RPM
    record. Stern, Pinchas Zukerman, Itzhak Perlman, and Zubin Mehta pictured on front.)

STETSON, GLENN
GIVE US THAT CHILD .... (Glenwood 45426) | 1.25 | 5.00 | 77

STEVENS, CAT
MOON SHADOW/I Think I See The Light .... (A&M 1265) | 1.50 | 6.00 | 71
PEACE TRAIN/Where Do The Children Play? .... (A&M 1291) | 1.25 | 5.00 | 71
MORNING HAS BROKEN/I Want To Live In A Wigwam .... (A&M 1335) | 1.25 | 5.00 | 72
SITTING/Crab Dance .... (A&M 1396) | 1.25 | 5.00 | 72
THE HURT/Silent Sunset .... (A&M 1418) | 1.25 | 5.00 | 73
OH VERY YOUNG/100 I Dream .... (A&M 1503) | 1.25 | 5.00 | 73
    (Illustration by Cat Stevens)
ANOTHER SATURDAY NIGHT/Home In The Sky .... (A&M 1602) | 1.25 | 5.00 | 74
GENERIC CAT STEVENS SLEEVE .... (A&M no #) | 1.25 | 5.00 | 74
    (Half sleeve used for miscellaneous Cat Stevens singles, no titles listed.)
BANAPPLE GAS .... (A&M 1785) | — | — | 76
    (Reports of this particular sleeve are most likely the generic Cat Stevens sleeve listed above)
(REMEMBER THE DAYS OF THE) OLD SCHOOLYARD/
    Land O'Freelove & Goodbye .... (A&M 1948) | 1.25 | 5.00 | 77

STEVENS, CONNIE
(Actress)
TOO YOUNG TO GO STEADY/A Little Kiss Is A Kiss .... (Warner Bros 5159) | 7.50 | 30.00 | 60
    Also see Edward Byrnes (*Kookie, Kookie*)

STEVENS, DODIE
PINK SHOE LACES/Coming Of Age .... (Crystalette 724) | 10.00 | 40.00 | 59

STEVENS, HUNT
JOHNNY ON THE SPOT/I Feel It For You .... (United Artists 107) | 6.25 | 25.00 | 58

STEVENS, JEFF
JOHNNY LUCKY AND SUZI 66 .... (Atlantic America 99259-7) | .75 | 3.00 | 88

STEVENS, RAY
JEREMIAH PEABODY'S POLY UNSATURATED QUICK DISSOLVING FAST
    ACTING PLEASANT TASTING GREEN AND PURPLE PILLS/Teen Years .... (Mercury 71843) | 6.25 | 25.00 | 61
SCRATCH MY BACK/When You Wish Upon A Star .... (Mercury 71888) | 5.00 | 20.00 | 61
AHAB, THE ARAB/It's Been So Long .... (Mercury 71966) | 6.25 | 25.00 | 62
SANTA CLAUS IS WATCHING YOU/Loved And Lost .... (Mercury 72058) | 5.00 | 20.00 | 62
HARRY, THE HAIRY APE .... (Mercury 72125) | 5.00 | 20.00 | 63
BUTCH BARBARIAN/Don't Say Anything .... (Mercury 72255) | 5.00 | 20.00 | 63
BUTCH BARBARIAN .... (Mercury DJ-66) | 7.50 | 30.00 | 63
    (Promotional issue only)
BUBBLE GUM THE BUBBLE DANCER/Laughing Over My Grave .... (Mercury 72307) | 5.00 | 20.00 | 64
BRIDGET THE MIDGET (THE QUEEN OF THE BLUES)/Night People .... (Barnaby ZS7 2024) | 2.00 | 8.00 | 70
    (2 sleeve variations exist, both of equal value)
I NEED YOUR HELP BARRY MANILOW/Daydream Romance .... (Warner Bros./Ahab 8785) | 1.00 | 4.00 | 79
SANTA CLAUS IS WATCHING YOU/Armchair Quarterback .... (MCA 52738) | 1.25 | 5.00 | 85
    (Issued with both the promotional red vinyl and stock black vinyl)

TITLE	LABEL AND NUMBER	VG	NM	YR

STEVENS, SHAKIN'
YOU DRIVE ME CRAZY/Baby You're A Child .... (Epic 14-02865) | 1.00 | 4.00 | 82
YOU DRIVE ME CRAZY/Baby You're A Child .... (Epic 14-02865) | 1.25 | 5.00 | 82
(Promotional issue, *Demonstration–Not For Sale* printed on sleeve. Sleeve lists b-side although the 45 has *You Drive Me Crazy* on both sides.)

STEVENS, STEVE
TOP GUN ANTHEM .... (Columbia 38-06282) | .75 | 3.00 | 86
(Shown as by Harold Faltermeyer and Steve Stevens. From the motion picture *Top Gun*.)
TOP GUN ANTHEM .... (Columbia 38-06282) | 1.00 | 4.00 | 86
(Shown as by Harold Faltermeyer and Steve Stevens. Promotional issue, *Demonstration Only–Not For Sale* printed on sleeve. From the motion picture *Top Gun*.)
Also see Michael Jackson (*Dirty Diana*)

STEWART, AL
NOSTRADAMUS/Terminal Eyes .... (Janus 243) | 1.50 | 6.00 | 74

STEWART, DAVE A.
IT'S MY PARTY .... (Platinum 4) | 1.50 | 6.00 | 81
(Shown as by Dave Stewart and Barbara Gaskin)
AVENUE D .... (Capitol B-44333) | .75 | 3.00 | 89
(Shown as by Etta James Featuring Dave A. Stewart, both pictured on back. From the motion picture *Rooftops*, James and Stewart.)
Also see Eurythmics

STEWART, GARY
PROMOTIONAL GARY STEWART SLEEVE .... (RCA JH-10351) | 1.50 | 6.00 | 75
(Promotional issue only, hard cover folding sleeve. No song titles listed. Stewart pictured on front and newspaper and magazine clippings are printed inside.)
BROTHERLY LOVE .... (RCA 13049) | 1.25 | 5.00 | 82
(Shown as by Gary Stewart and Dean Dillon)

STEWART, JAMES
(Actor)
THE LEGEND OF SHENANDOAH .... (Decca 31795) | 3.75 | 15.00 | 65
(Inspired by the motion picture *Shenandoah*)
THE CHEYENNE SOCIAL CLUB/Lonely Rolling Stone .... (National General 007) | 3.75 | 15.00 | 70
(Shown as by James Stewart and Henry Fonda)

STEWART, JERMAINE
WE DON'T HAVE TO TAKE OUR CLOTHES OFF/ Give Your Love To Me .... (Arista 9424) | .75 | 3.00 | 86
JODY/Dance Floor .... (Arista 9476) | .75 | 3.00 | 86
DON'T EVER LEAVE ME/Give Your Love To Me .... (Arista 9550) | .75 | 3.00 | 86
SAY IT AGAIN/You Promise .... (Arista 9636) | .75 | 3.00 | 87

STEWART, JOHN
SURVIVORS .... (RCA JB-10268) | 2.00 | 8.00 | 75
(Promotional issue only. Stewart shown with the cast of the Smothers Brothers TV show. Among those pictured are Steve Martin, Lily Tomlin, Tom and Dick Smothers, and Ringo Starr.)
Also see the Kingston Trio

STEWART, MARIO, AND HIS FOUR GUITARS
RIPTIDE/Surfer's Serenade .... (Souvenir 102) | 6.25 | 25.00 | 63

STEWART, MICHAEL
I WALK THE LINE/Garden Of Eden .... (Bell 17) | 1.25 | 5.00 |
(Flip-side by Artie Malvin, neither performer credited or pictured on sleeve)

STEWART, ROD
YOU WEAR IT WELL/True Blue .... (Mercury 73330) | 3.75 | 15.00 | 72
TWISTING THE NIGHT AWAY/True Blue/Lady Day .... (Mercury 73412) | 2.00 | 8.00 | 72
OH! NO NOT MY BABY .... (Mercury 73426) | 1.50 | 6.00 | 73
(Red plaid sleeve with no mention of artist name or song title, only record company logo and catalog number indicated)
MINE FOR ME/Farewell .... (Mercury 73426) | — | — | 74
(The existence of this sleeve has not been verified)
HOT LEGS .... (Warner Bros. 8535) | 1.50 | 6.00 | 77
I WAS ONLY JOKING .... (Warner Bros. 8568) | 1.25 | 5.00 | 77
DO YA THINK I'M SEXY?/Scarred and Scared .... (Warner Bros. 8724) | 1.00 | 4.00 | 78
(Rod Stewart donated all royalties from this single to UNICEF which totaled over $1,000,000)
AIN'T LOVE A BITCH .... (Warner Bros. 8810) | 1.00 | 4.00 | 78
I DON'T WANT TO TALK ABOUT IT .... (Warner Bros. 49138) | 1.00 | 4.00 | 79
PASSION/Better Off Dead .... (Warner Bros. 49617) | 1.00 | 4.00 | 80
YOUNG TURKS/Sonny .... (Warner Bros. 49843) | 1.00 | 4.00 | 81
TONIGHT I'M YOURS (DON'T HURT ME)/ Tora, Tora, Tora (Out With The Boys) .... (Warner Bros. 49886) | 1.00 | 4.00 | 81
HOW LONG/Jealous .... (Warner Bros. 50051) | 1.00 | 4.00 | 81
GUESS I'LL ALWAYS LOVE/Rock My Plimsoul .... (Warner Bros. 29874-7) | 1.00 | 4.00 | 82
BABY JANE/Ready Now .... (Warner Bros. 29608-7) | — | — | 83
(The existence of this sleeve is unconfirmed and is most likely an import only)
WHAT AM I GONNA DO .... (Warner Bros. 29564-7) | 1.00 | 4.00 | 83
INFATUATION/She Won't Dance With Me .... (Warner Bros. 29256-7) | .75 | 3.00 | 84
SOME GUYS HAVE ALL THE LUCK .... (Warner Bros. 29215-7) | .75 | 3.00 | 84
PEOPLE GET READY/Back On The Street .... (Epic 34-05416) | 1.00 | 4.00 | 85
(Shown as by Jeff Beck and Rod Stewart)
PEOPLE GET READY .... (Epic 34-05416) | 1.50 | 6.00 | 85
(Promotional issue, *Demonstration–Not For Sale* printed on sleeve. Shown as by Jeff Beck and Rod Stewart.)
LOVE TOUCH .... (Warner Bros. 28668-7) | .75 | 3.00 | 86
(From the motion picture *Legal Eagles*)
ANOTHER HEARTACHE .... (Warner Bros. 28631-7) | .75 | 3.00 | 86
EVERY BEAT OF MY HEART .... (Warner Bros. 28625-7) | .75 | 3.00 | 86
TWISTIN' THE NIGHT AWAY .... (Geffen 28303-7) | .75 | 3.00 | 87
(From the motion picture *Innerspace*)
LOST IN YOU .... (Warner Bros. 27927-7) | .75 | 3.00 | 88
FOREVER YOUNG/Days Of Rage .... (Warner Bros. 27796-7) | .75 | 3.00 | 88

		VG	NM	YR
MY HEART CAN'T TELL YOU NO .... (Warner Bros. 27729-7)		.75	3.00	88
DOWNTOWN TRAIN .... (Warner Bros. 22685-7)		.75	3.00	89

EXTENDED PLAYS

		VG	NM	YR
I'D RATHER GO BLIND/WHAT'S MADE MILWAUKEE FAMOUS (HAS MADE A LOSER OUT OF ME)/Italian Girls/Twistin' The Night Away .... (Mercury MEPL-28)		3.75	15.00	73

(Promotional issue only titled *A Rod Stewart Promotion Special*, issued with a small-hole 33-1/3 RPM record. No song titles listed.)

Also see Faces

STEWART, SANDY

		VG	NM	YR
MY COLORING BOOK .... (Colpix 669)		2.50	10.00	62

STEWART, SANDY

		VG	NM	YR
SADDEST VICTORY/Mind Over Matter .... (Modern 7-99774)		.75	3.00	84

Also see John Hiatt (*Snake Charmer*), Stevie Nicks (*Nightbird*)

STEWART, WYNN

		VG	NM	YR
HALF OF THIS, HALF OF THAT/The Happy Part Of Town .... (Capitol 5271)		2.00	8.00	64
'CAUSE I HAVE YOU/That's The Only Way To Cry .... (Capitol 5937)		2.00	8.00	67
WALTZ OF THE ANGELS/Love's Gonna Happen To Me .... (Capitol 2012)		2.00	8.00	67
SOMETHING PRETTY/ .... (Capitol 2137)		2.00	8.00	68
IN LOVE/ .... (Capitol 2240)		2.00	8.00	69

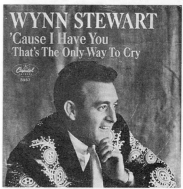

STICK

		VG	NM	YR
RESISTANCE/Drinking And Driving .... (Arista 07822-12612-7)		1.00	4.00	93

(Promotional issue only issued with small-hole, clear vinyl)

STICK

(Motion Picture)

See Anne Murray (*I Don't Think I'm Ready For You*)

STILLS, STEPHEN

		VG	NM	YR
CHANGE PARTNERS/Relaxing Town .... (Atlantic 2806)		1.50	6.00	71

(Glossy coated paper)

		VG	NM	YR
CHANGE PARTNERS/Relaxing Town .... (Atlantic 2806)		2.00	8.00	71

(Textured uncoated paper, this may be a promotional version)

		VG	NM	YR
STRANGER/No Hiding Place .... (Atlantic 7-89633)		.75	3.00	84

Also see Crosby/Stills/Nash, Crosby/Stills/Nash & Young

STING

		VG	NM	YR
IF YOU LOVE SOMEBODY SET THEM FREE/Another Day .... (A&M 2738)		.75	3.00	85

(First printing)

		VG	NM	YR
IF YOU LOVE SOMEBODY SET THEM FREE/Another Day .... (A&M 2765)		1.25	5.00	85

(Second printing with different catalog number)

		VG	NM	YR
FORTRESS AROUND YOUR HEART/Consider Me Gone (Live Version) .... (A&M 2767)		.75	3.00	85
LOVE IS THE SEVENTH WAVE/The Dream Of The Blue Turtles .... (A&M 2787)		.75	3.00	85
RUSSIANS/Gabriel's Message .... (A&M 2799)		.75	3.00	85
WE'LL BE TOGETHER/Conversation With A Dog .... (A&M 2983)		.75	3.00	87
BE STILL MY BEATING HEART/Ghost In The Strand .... (A&M 2992)		.75	3.00	87
ENGLISHMAN IN NEW YORK/If You There .... (A&M 1200)		.75	3.00	87
YOU STILL TOUCH ME/Let Your Soul Be Your Pilot .... (A&M 31458 1582 7)		.50	2.00	96

Also see Band Aid, the Police

STING II

(Motion Picture)

See Lalo Schifrin (*The Entertainer–Heliotrope Bouquet*)

STOKES, SIMON, AND THE NIGHTHAWKS

		VG	NM	YR
CAPTAIN HOWDY/I Fell For Her, She Fell For Him And He Fell For Me .... (Casablanca 0007)		1.25	5.00	74

STOLTZ, ERIC

(Actor)

See Flesh For Lulu (*I Go Crazy*)

STOMPBOX

		VG	NM	YR
NO WOODS (HAZARDOUS MIX)/Alcohol (Straight Edge Mix) .... (Columbia CS7 5639)		1.00	4.00	94

(Promotional issue only, *Demonstration–Not For Sale* printed on sleeve. Issued with small-hole 45 RPM.)

STONE COUNTRY

		VG	NM	YR
TIME ISN'T THERE (ANYMORE)/Life Stands Daring .... (RCA # unknown)		.5.00	20.00	68

STONE FURY

		VG	NM	YR
BREAK DOWN THE WALL .... (MCA 52464)		.75	3.00	84
LIFE IS TOO LONELY/Burns Like A Star .... (MCA 52523)		.75	3.00	85
LET THEM TALK .... (MCA 52942)		.75	3.00	86

Also see Kingdom Come (Lenny Wolf)

STONE PONEYS, THE

		VG	NM	YR
UP TO MY NECK IN HIGH MUDDY WATER/Carnival Bear .... (Capitol 2110)		7.50	30.00	68

(Shown as by Linda Ronstadt & the Stone Poneys)

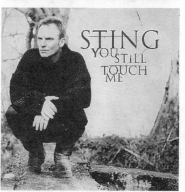

STOOGES, THE

See Iggy and the Stooges, Iggy Pop

STOP MAKING SENSE

(Motion Picture)

See Talking Heads (*Once In A Lifetime, Stop Making Sense*)

STORIES

		VG	NM	YR
I'M COMING HOME .... (Kama Sutra 545)		2.50	10.00	72

(Promotional issue only, hard cover)

Also see Dust, the Left Banke (Michael Brown). Kenny Aaronson (of Hagar-Schon-Aaronson-Shrieve) did not join Stories until 1973 and Rick Ranno (later in Starz) was a member in 1974.

STORM, BILLY

		VG	NM	YR
PLEASE DON'T MENTION HER NAME .... (HBR 474)		5.00	20.00	66

TITLE	LABEL AND NUMBER	VG	NM	YR

STORM, GALE
(Actress/Singer)

YOU/Angry .... (Dot 45-15734) | 6.25 | 25.00 | 58

STRAIT, GEORGE
THE CHAIR/In Too Deep .... (MCA 52667) | 1.25 | 5.00 | 85

STRANGE, BILLY, WITH THE TELSTARS
A LOTTA LIMBO .... (Coliseum 605) | 3.75 | 15.00 | 63

STRANGE ADVANCE
SHE CONTROLS ME .... (Capitol B-5214) | .75 | 3.00 | 83
WE RUN/Nor Crystal Tears .... (Capitol B-5470) | .75 | 3.00 | 85

STRANGLERS, THE
DUCHESS/The Raven .... (I.R.S. 9018) | 1.50 | 6.00 | 80

EXTENDED PLAYS

SOMETHING BETTER CHANGE/STRAIGHTEN OUT/
   (Get A) Grip (On Yourself)/Hanging Around .... (A&M 1973) | 1.25 | 5.00 | 77
   (Issued with a small-hole 33-1/3 RPM pink and white marbled vinyl record)

STRASSMAN, MARCIA
(Actress who co-starred in the television series *Welcome Back Kotter* and the motion picture *Honey I Shrunk The Kids*)

GROOVY WORLD OF JACK AND JILL/The Flower Shop .... (Uni 55023) | 3.00 | 12.00 | 67

STRAUSS, SHARON
DON'T KEEP OUR FRIENDS .... (ABC Paramount 10349) | 2.00 | 8.00 | 62

STRAY CATS, THE
STRAY CAT STRUT/You Don't Believe Me .... (EMI America B-8122) | 1.00 | 4.00 | 82
ROCK THIS TOWN/You Can't Hurry Love .... (EMI America B-8132) | .75 | 3.00 | 82
(SHE'S) SEXY +17/Lookin' Better Every Beer .... (EMI America B-8168) | .75 | 3.00 | 83
(SHE'S) SEXY +17/Lookin' Better Every Beer (Record 1)/
   CRUISIN'/Lucky Charm (Record 2) .... (EMI America BB-8169-1/2) | 1.25 | 5.00 | 83
   (Hard cover gatefold for two-record set)
LOOK AT THAT CADILLAC/Lucky Charm .... (EMI America B-8194) | .75 | 3.00 | 84
   Also see Phantom, Rocker & Slick (Slim Jim Phantom, Lee Rocker), Brian Setzer

STREEP, MERYL
(Actress)

   See Melissa Manchester (*The Music Of Goodbye*), Al Jarreau (*The Music Of Goodbye*), Carly Simon (*Coming Around Again*)

STREET, JANEY
SAY HELLO TO RONNIE .... (Arista 9265) | 1.00 | 4.00 | 84
   (Promotional issue only, *For Promotional Use Only Not For Sale* printed on sleeve)

STREETS OF FIRE
(Motion Picture)

   See Fire Inc. (*Tonight Is What It Means To Be Young*), Dan Hartman (*I Can Dream About You*)

STREISAND, BARBRA
SLEEP IN HEAVENLY PEACE/Gounod's Ave Maria .... (Columbia 4-43896) | 2.50 | 10.00 | 66
   (Promotional issue only)
JINGLE BELLS?/White Christmas .... (Columbia 4-44350) | 2.50 | 10.00 | 66
   (Promotional issue only)
HAVE YOURSELF A MERRY LITTLE CHRISTMAS/The Best Gift ...... (Columbia 4-44351) | 2.50 | 10.00 | 66
   (Promotional issue only)
THE CHRISTMAS SONG/My Favorite Things .... (Columbia 4-44352) | 2.50 | 10.00 | 66
   (Promotional issue only)
THE LORD'S PRAYER/I Wonder As I Wander .... (Columbia 4-44354) | 2.50 | 10.00 | 66
   (Promotional issue only)
   The above five sleeves all used the same photo and were released simultaneously to promote *Barbra Streisand– A Christmas Album*. A note from Harold Komisar, Columbia's National Album Promotion Manager, accompanied the releases.
SILENT NIGHT/Ave Maria .... (Columbia 4-43896) | 2.50 | 10.00 | 66
   (These are the same recordings as the promotional issue of the same catalog number listed above. The song titles have been changed for this release. This second sleeve variation is a title sleeve and has no photo.)
IF I CLOSE MY EYES (THEME FROM UP THE SANDBOX)/
   If I Close My Eyes (Theme From Up The Sandbox) Instrumental ..... (Columbia 4-45780) | 6.25 | 25.00 | 73
   (From the motion picture *Up The Sandbox* starring Streisand)
LOVE THEME FROM A STAR IS BORN (EVERGREEN) .... (Columbia 3-10450) | 1.25 | 5.00 | 76
   (From the motion picture *A Star Is Born* starring Streisand, Streisand and Kris Kristofferson pictured)
NO MORE TEARS (ENOUGH IS ENOUGH)/Wet .... (Columbia 1-11125) | 1.25 | 5.00 | 79
   (A-side shown as by Barbra Streisand/Donna Summer, both pictured)
THE WAY HE MAKES ME FEEL (Studio Version and Film Version) ...... (Columbia 38-04177) | 1.00 | 4.00 | 83
   (From the motion picture *Yentl* starring Streisand)
THE WAY HE MAKES ME FEEL (Studio Version) .... (Columbia 38-04177) | 1.25 | 5.00 | 83
   (Promotional issue, *Demonstration Only/Not For Sale* printed on sleeve. From the motion picture *Yentl* starring Streisand.)
PAPA, CAN YOU HEAR ME?/Will Someone Ever Look At Me That Way? .... (Columbia 38-04357) | 1.00 | 4.00 | 84
   (From the motion picture *Yentl* starring Streisand)
LEFT IN THE DARK .... (Columbia 38-04605) | 1.00 | 4.00 | 84
   (Among those credited on back of sleeve include the E Street Band's Roy Bittan and Max Weinberg, and Rick Derringer on lead guitar.)
LEFT IN THE DARK (WITH SPOKEN INTRO)/
   Left In The Dark (Without Spoken Intro) .... (Columbia 38-04605) | 1.25 | 5.00 | 84
   (Promotional issue, *Demonstration Only/Not For Sale* printed on back of sleeve. Among those credited on back of sleeve include the E Street Band's Roy Bittan and Max Weinberg, and Rick Derringer on lead guitar.)
MAKE NO MISTAKE, HE'S MINE .... (Columbia 38-04695) | 1.00 | 4.00 | 84
   (Credited as Duet with Kim Carnes, both are pictured on front)
MAKE NO MISTAKE, HE'S MINE .... (Columbia 38-04695) | 1.25 | 5.00 | 84
   (Promotional issue, *Demonstration Only/Not For Sale* printed on sleeve. Credited as a Duet With Kim Carnes, both are pictured on the front.)
EMOTION .... (Columbia 38-04707) | 1.00 | 4.00 | 85
EMOTION .... (Columbia 38-04707) | 1.25 | 5.00 | 85
   (Promotional issue, *Demonstration Only/Not For Sale* printed on sleeve)

Title	Label and Number	VG	NM	YR
SOMEWHERE	(Columbia 38-05680)	1.00	4.00	85
SOMEWHERE	(Columbia 38-05680)	1.25	5.00	85
(Promotional issue, *Demonstration Only/Not For Sale* printed on sleeve)				
SEND IN THE CLOWNS	(Columbia 38-05837)	1.00	4.00	86
SEND IN THE CLOWNS	(Columbia 38-05837)	1.25	5.00	86
(Promotional issue, *Demonstration Only/Not For Sale* printed on sleeve)				
ALL I ASK OF YOU	(Columbia 38-08026)	1.00	4.00	88
TILL I LOVED YOU	(Columbia 38-08062)	1.00	4.00	88
(Shown as by Barbra Streisand and Don Johnson, both are pictured front and back)				

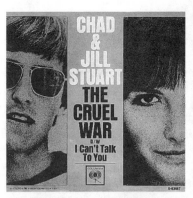

STRONG, BARRETT
STAND UP AND CHEER FOR THE PREACHER	(Epic 11011)	1.25	5.00	73

STRUTHERS, SALLY
(Actress)
See Carroll O'Connor & Jean Stapleton (*Those Were The Days*)

STRYPER
FREE/Calling On You	(Enigma B-75000)	1.00	4.00	87
HONESTLY/Sing-Along Song	(Enigma B-75009)	1.00	4.00	87
ALWAYS THERE FOR YOU/In God We Trust	(Enigma B-75019)	1.00	4.00	88
KEEP THE FIRE BURNING/The World Of You And I	(Enigma B-75032)	1.00	4.00	88

STUART, CHAD
GOOD MORNING SUNRISE/Paxton's Song	(Sidewalk 944)	3.00	12.00	68
Also see Chad and Jeremy, Chad & Jill Stewart				

STUART, CHAD & JILL
THE CRUEL WAR/I Can't Talk To You	(Columbia 4-43467)	3.00	12.00	65
Also see Chad and Jeremy, Chad Stuart				

STUART, MARTY
ARLENE	(Columbia 38-05724)	1.25	5.00	85

STUCKEY, NAT
SWEET THING	(Paula 243)	1.50	6.00	66

STYLE COUNCIL
MY EVER CHANGING MOODS/Mick's Company	(Geffen 29359-7)	1.00	4.00	84
YOU'RE THE BEST THING/The Big Boss Groove	(Geffen 29248-7)	.75	3.00	84
BOY WHO CRIED WOLF	(Geffen 28941-7)	.75	3.00	85
(WHEN YOU) CALL ME/Internationalists	(Geffen 28674-7)	.75	3.00	86
HOW SHE THREW IT ALL AWAY/Long Hot Summer	(Polydor 887 753-7)	.75	3.00	88
Also see Band Aid, the Jam (Paul Weller)				

STYLISTICS
YOU ARE BEAUTIFUL/Michael And Me	(Avco 4664)	1.50	6.00	76

STYX
COME SAIL AWAY/Put Me On	(A&M 1977)	1.50	6.00	80
FOOLING YOURSELF/The Grand Finale	(A&M 2007)	1.25	5.00	78
BLUE COLLAR MAN (LONG NIGHTS)/Superstars	(A&M 2087)	1.25	5.00	78
RENEGADE/Sing For The Day	(A&M 2110)	1.25	5.00	79
THE BEST OF TIMES/Lights	(A&M 2300)	1.00	4.00	80
MR. ROBOTO/Snowblind	(A&M 2525)	.75	3.00	83
DON'T LET IT END/Rockin' The Paradise	(A&M 2543)	.75	3.00	83
MUSIC TIME/Heavy Metal Poisoning	(A&M 2625)	.75	3.00	84
Also see Dennis De Young, Tommy Shaw				

SUAVÉ
MY GIRL (EDIT)/My Girl (Acappella)	(Capitol B-44124)	.75	3.00	88

SUBURBS, THE
WORLD WAR II/Change Agent	(Twin Tone 7909)	1.00	4.00	78

EXTENDED PLAYS
MEMORY/GO/STEREO/TEENAGE RUN-IN/CHEMISTRY SET/ Your Phone/Couldn't Care Less/You/Prehistoric Jaws	(Twin Tone 7801)	1.00	4.00	78

SUE ANN
ROCK STEADY	(MCA 53278)	.75	3.00	88
I'LL GIVE YOU LOVE	(MCA 53429)	.75	3.00	88

SUGAR BABES
I'LL EDUCATE YOU (ON MY LOVE)	(MCA 52930)	.75	3.00	86
THE PERFECT KIND OF LOVE	(MCA 53223)	.75	3.00	88

SUGARCUBES, THE
MOTORCRASH/Blue Eyed Pop	(Elektra 7-69355)	1.00	4.00	88
COLDSWEAT/Birthday	(Elektra 7-69377)	1.00	4.00	88

SUGARLOAF
TONGUE IN CHEEK/Woman	(Liberty 56218)	2.00	8.00	71
I GOT A SONG	(Brut 815)	1.50	6.00	73
(Shown as by Sugarloaf/Jerry Corbetta)				

SULLIVAN, ED, SINGERS AND ORCHESTRA
THE SULLI-GULLI (PARTS 1 AND 2)	(Columbia 4-44940)	2.00	8.00	69

SUMMER, DONNA
TRY ME… I KNOW… WE CAN MAKE IT	(Oasis 406)	2.00	8.00	76
HOT STUFF	(Casablanca 978)	—	—	79
(The existence of this sleeve has not been verified)				
NO MORE TEARS (ENOUGH IS ENOUGH)/Wet	(Columbia 1-11125)	1.00	4.00	79
(A-side shown as by Barbra Streisand/Donna Summer, both pictured. B-side shown as by Barbra Streisand.)				
THE WANDERER/Stop Me	(Warner Bros./Geffen 49563)	1.00	4.00	80

TITLE	LABEL AND NUMBER	VG	NM	YR
COLD LOVE/Grand Illusion	(Geffen 49634)	1.00	4.00	80
LOVE IS IN CONTROL (FINGER ON THE TRIGGER)/Sometimes Like Butterflies	(Geffen 29982-7)	1.00	4.00	82
STATE OF INDEPENDENCE/Love Is Just A Breath Away	(Geffen 29895-7)	1.00	4.00	82
THE WOMAN IN ME/Livin' In America	(Geffen 29805-7)	1.00	4.00	82
SHE WORKS HARD FOR THE MONEY/I Do Believe I Fell In Love	(Mercury 812 370-7)	.75	3.00	83
UNCONDITIONAL LOVE/Woman	(Mercury 814 088 7)	1.00	4.00	83
THERE GOES MY BABY/Maybe It's Over	(Geffen 29291-7)	.75	3.00	84
SUPERNATURAL LOVE	(Geffen 29142-7)	.75	3.00	84
DINNER WITH GERSHWIN	(Geffen 28418-7)	.75	3.00	87
ONLY THE FOOL SURVIVES	(Geffen 28165-7)	.75	3.00	87
(Shown as by Donna Summer With Mickey Thomas. Summer pictured on front, Thomas on back.)				
THIS TIME I KNOW IT'S FOR REAL/If It Makes You Feel Good	(Atlantic 7-88899)	1.00	4.00	89
MELODY OF LOVE (WANNA BE LOVED)/The Christmas Song	(Casablanca/Mercury 856 366-7)	.50	2.00	94

SUMMER, HENRY LEE
DARLIN' DANIELLE DON'T	(CBS Associated ZS4-07909)	.75	3.00	84

SUMMER AND SMOKE
(Motion Picture)
    See Peter Nero (Theme From Summer And Smoke)

SUMMER MAGIC
(Motion Picture)
    See Hayley Mills (Flitterin', Summer Magic)

SUMMER PLACE, A
(Motion Picture)
    See Percy Faith And His Orchestra (Theme From A Summer Place)

SUMMERS, ANDY
2010/To Hal And Back	(A&M 2704)	.75	3.00	84
(From the motion picture 2010)				
LOVE IS THE STRANGEST WAY	(MCA 53112)	.75	3.00	87
Also see the Police				

SUMNER, J. D.
ELVIS HAS LEFT THE BUILDING	(QCA 461)	2.50	10.00	77
(Sumner pictured with Elvis Presley)				

SUN
WANNA MAKE LOVE	(Capitol 4254)	1.25	5.00	76

SUNRAYS, THE
DON'T TAKE YOURSELF SO SERIOUSLY/I Look Baby, I Can't See	(Tower 256)	5.00	20.00	66
LOADED WITH LOVE/Time	(Tower 340)	6.25	25.00	66

SUNSET BOMBERS, THE
I CAN'T CONTROL MYSELF	(Zombie 7676)	1.25	5.00	78
Also see the Knack (Doug Feiger)				

SUNSHINE
(Television Movie)
    See Cliff De Young (My Sweet Lady)

SUPERGRASS
LOSE IT/Caught By The Fuzz	(Sub Pop 281)	.75	3.00	95
(Originally issued as part of a 4-record set titled Helter Shelter, which also included singles by Elastica, S*M*A*S*H, and Gene. Envelope sleeve issued with colored vinyl.)				

SUPERMAN THE MOVIE
(Motion Picture)
    See John Williams (Theme From Superman)

SUPERTRAMP
GIVE A LITTLE BIT/Downstream	(A&M 1938)	1.25	5.00	77
DREAMER/From Now On	(A&M 1981)	1.25	5.00	77
(Crime Of The Century album cover art)				
THE LOGICAL SONG/Just Another Nervous Wreck	(A&M 2128)	2.00	8.00	79
(Dark blue background with group name and song title in red)				
THE LOGICAL SONG/Just Another Nervous Wreck	(A&M 2128)	1.25	5.00	79
(Black background with group name and song title in orange)				
GOODBYE STRANGER/Even In The Quietest Moments	(A&M 2162)	1.00	4.00	79
TAKE THE LONG WAY HOME/Rudy	(A&M 2193)	1.00	4.00	79
(Yellow maze art)				
TAKE THE LONG WAY HOME/Rudy	(A&M 2193)	1.00	4.00	79
(Red maze art)				
TAKE THE LONG WAY HOME/Rudy	(A&M 2193)	1.00	4.00	79
(Green maze art)				
DREAMER/From Now On	(A&M 2269)	1.00	4.00	80
(Arc de Triomphe art)				
IT'S RAINING AGAIN/Bonnie	(A&M 2502)	.75	3.00	82
MY KIND OF LADY/Know Who You Are	(A&M 2517)	.75	3.00	82
CANNONBALL/Ever Open Door	(A&M 2731)	.75	3.00	85
FREE AS A BIRD/Thing For You	(A&M 2996)	.75	3.00	87
I'M BEGGIN' YOU/No Inbetween	(A&M 2985)	.75	3.00	87

SUPREMES, THE
YOUR HEART BELONGS TO ME/(He's) Seventeen	(Motown 1027)	25.00	100.00	62
WHERE DID OUR LOVE GO/He Means The World To Me	(Motown 1060)	6.25	25.00	64
BABY LOVE/Ask Any Girl	(Motown 1066)	6.25	25.00	64
STOP! IN THE NAME OF LOVE/I'm In Love Again	(Motown 1074)	6.25	25.00	65
BACK IN MY ARMS AGAIN/Whisper You Love Me Boy	(Motown 1075)	6.25	25.00	65
NOTHING BUT HEARTACHES/He Holds His Own	(Motown 1080)	6.25	25.00	65

THINGS ARE CHANGING .... (E.E.O.C. no #)   37.50   150.00   65
    (Promotional issue sponsored by the Equal Employment Opportunities Commission. Similar releases by the Blossoms and Jay & the Americans.)
CHILDREN'S CHRISTMAS SONG/Twinkle Twinkle Little Me .... (Motown 1085)   6.25   25.00   65
YOU CAN'T HURRY LOVE/Put Yourself In My Place .... (Motown 1097)   6.25   25.00   66
YOU KEEP ME HANGIN' ON/Remove This Doubt .... (Motown 1101)   6.25   25.00   66
I'M GONNA MAKE YOU LOVE ME/A Place In The Sun .... (Motown 1137)   5.00   20.00   68
    (Shown as by Diana Ross & The Supremes and The Temptations, all 8 are pictured. Back of sleeve promotes their television special on Monday, December 9th, 1968 NBC-TV.)
    Also see Florence Ballard, the Blue Belles (Cindy Birdsong), Diana Ross, U.S.A. For Africa (Diana Ross), Voices Of America (Diana Ross). Cindy Birdsong replaced Florence Ballard in 1967.

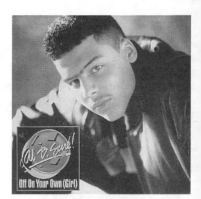

SURE, AL B.
NITE AND DAY .... (Warner Bros. 28192-7)   .75   3.00   88
OFF ON YOUR OWN (GIRL) .... (Warner Bros. 27870-7)   .75   3.00   88
KILLING ME SOFTLY .... (Warner Bros. 27772-7)   .75   3.00   88
RESCUE ME .... (Warner Bros. 27762-7)   .75   3.00   88
THE SECRET GARDEN .... (Qwest 19992)   .75   3.00   90
    (Shown as by Quincy Jones, Al B. Sure, James Ingram, El DeBarge, and Barry White)

SURFACE
LATELY .... (Columbia 38-07257)   .75   3.00   87
LATELY .... (Columbia 38-07257)   1.00   4.00   87
    (Promotional issue, *Demonstration Only Not For Sale* printed on sleeve)
I MISSED .... (Columbia 38-08018)   .75   3.00   88

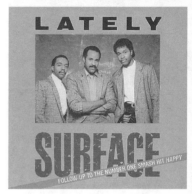

SURFARIS, THE
PUNK LINE/Scattershield .... (Koinkidink 101)   1.25   5.00   82

SURF MC'S
SURF OR DIE/Surf Or Die (Instrumental) .... (Profile 5150)   .75   3.00   87

SURVIVOR
EYE OF THE TIGER/Take You On A Saturday .... (Scotti Bros. ZS4-02912)   1.25   5.00   82
    (Featured in the motion picture *Rocky III*, Sylvester Stallone and Survivor pictured on sleeve)
EYE OF THE TIGER .... (Scotti Bros. ZS4-02912)   1.50   6.00   82
    (Promotional issue, *Demonstration–Not For Sale* printed on sleeve. Featured in the motion picture *Rocky III*, Sylvester Stallone and Survivor pictured on back)
AMERICAN HEARTBEAT/Silver Girl .... (Scotti Bros. ZS4-03213)   1.00   4.00   82
AMERICAN HEARTBEAT .... (Scotti Bros. ZS4-03213)   1.25   5.00   82
    (Promotional issue, *Demonstration Only–Not For Sale* printed on sleeve)
CAUGHT IN THE GAME/Slander .... (Scotti Bros. ZS4-04074)   1.00   4.00   83
CAUGHT IN THE GAME/Slander .... (Scotti Bros. ZS4-04074)   1.25   5.00   83
    (Promotional issue, *Demonstration Only Not For Sale* printed on sleeve. Sleeve lists b-side even though the 45 has *Caught In The Game* on both sides.)
I CAN'T HOLD BACK/I See You In Everyone .... (Scotti Bros. ZS4-04603)   .75   3.00   84
I CAN'T HOLD BACK .... (Scotti Bros. ZS4-04603)   1.00   4.00   84
    (Promotional issue, *Demonstration Only–Not For Sale* printed on sleeve)
HIGH ON YOU .... (Scotti Bros. ZS4-04871)   .75   3.00   84
HIGH ON YOU .... (Scotti Bros. ZS4-04871)   1.00   4.00   84
    (Promotional issue, *Demonstration Only Not For Sale* printed on sleeve)
THE SEARCH IS OVER/It's The Singer Not The Song ..... (Scotti Bros. ZS4-04871)   .75   3.00   85
THE SEARCH IS OVER .... (Scotti Bros. ZS4-04871)   1.00   4.00   85
    (Promotional issue, *Demonstration Only–Not For Sale* printed on sleeve)
FIRST NIGHT .... (Scotti Bros. ZS4-05579)   .75   3.00   85
FIRST NIGHT .... (Scotti Bros. ZS4-05579)   1.00   4.00   85
    (Promotional issue, *Demonstration Only/Not For Sale* printed on sleeve)
BURNING HEART .... (Scotti Bros. ZS4-05663)   .75   3.00   85
    (From the motion picture *Rocky IV*, Sylvester Stallone pictured)
BURNING HEART .... (Scotti Bros. ZS4-05663)   1.00   4.00   85
    (Promotional issue, *Demonstration Only–Not For Sale* printed on sleeve. From the motion picture *Rocky IV*, Sylvester Stallone pictured)
IS THIS LOVE .... (Scotti Bros. ZS4-06381)   .75   3.00   86
IS THIS LOVE .... (Scotti Bros. ZS4-06381)   1.00   4.00   86
    (Promotional issue, *Demonstration Only–Not For Sale* printed on sleeve)
MAN AGAINST THE WORLD .... (Scotti Bros. ZS4-07070)   .75   3.00   87

SUTHERLAND, KEIFER
(Actor)
    See the Pretenders *(Windows Of The World)*

SUTTONS, THE
LIVE IT UP (LOVE IT UP)/Kraazy .... (Rocshire XR95060)   .75   3.00   84
    (Hard cover)

SVT
NEW YEAR/Wanna See You Cry .... (SVT A)   1.00   4.00   79
    (Issued with small-hole, red vinyl)
HEART OF STONE/The Last Word .... (415 Records S0005)   1.00   4.00   79
    (Front of sleeve states *Jack Casady's [Hot Tuna] New Band*)
    Also see Hot Tuna, Jefferson Airplane

SWAGS, THE
ROCKIN' MATILDA/Blowing The Blues .... (West Wind 1003)   6.25   25.00   60

SWAN
(Motion Picture)
    See David Rose and His Orchestra

SWANN, BETTYE
DON'T TOUCH ME .... (Capitol 2382)   1.25   5.00   69

SWANSON, BERNICE
BABY I'M YOURS .... (Chess 1927)   2.00   8.00   65

TITLE	LABEL AND NUMBER	VG	NM	YR

SWANSONS, THE
ALL THESE THINGS WILL HAPPEN NOW/Shake/Marry Me .... *(Citizen X/Interscope PR 5843)* | .75 | 3.00 | 94
  (Hard cover issued with small-hole, blue vinyl)

SWATZELL, TOM
THE BALLAD OF JIMMIE RODGERS .... *(Showland 241973)* | 10.00 | 40.00 | 61
  (Shown as by Bernie Hess and Tom Swatzell)

SWAYZE, PATRICK
SHE'S LIKE THE WIND/Stay .... *(RCA 5363-7-R)* | 1.00 | 4.00 | 87
  (B-side shown as by Maurice Williams and the Zodiacs. From the motion picture *Dirty Dancing*.)
  Also see Bill Medley and Jennifer Warnes *(The Time Of My Life)*, Mickey Thomas *(Stand In The Fire)*

SWEAT, KEITH
I WANT HER/I Want Her, Part 2 .... *(Elektra 7-69431)* | .75 | 3.00 | 87

SWEET, MATTHEW
LET ME BE THE ONE .... *(A&M 31458 0716 7)* | .50 | 2.00 | 94
  (Side 12 of a 7 record box set titled *If I Were A Carpenter*. Each sleeve has a different face shot of Karen
  Carpenter on the front, Richard Carpenter on the back. No artist name or song titles indicated on sleeve.
  Complete set valued at $30.00 near mint.)
  EXTENDED PLAYS
WE'RE THE SAME/SPACE/SPEED RACER/You .... *(Zoo 42367)* | 1.25 | 5.00 | 95

SWEET, RACHEL
EVERLASTING LOVE/Still Thinking Of You/Billy And The Gun .... *(Columbia 18-02169)* | 1.00 | 4.00 | 81
  (A-side shown as by Rex Smith and Rachel Sweet. *Still Thinking Of You* shown as by Rex Smith and *Billy And
  The Gun* shown as by Rachel Sweet.)
EVERLASTING LOVE .... *(Columbia 18-02169)* | 1.25 | 5.00 | 81
  (Promotional issue, *Demonstration–Not For Sale* printed on sleeve. Shown as by Rex Smith and Rachel Sweet.)
HAIRSPRAY (THEME SONG) .... *(MCA 53303)* | 1.00 | 4.00 | 88
  (From the motion picture *Hairspray*, Ricki Lake and Jerry Stiller pictured)

SWEET CHARITY
(Motion Picture)
  See Sammy Davis, Jr. *(Rhythm Of Life)*

SWEETHEARTS OF THE RODEO
HEY DOLL BABY .... *(Columbia 38-05824)* | .75 | 3.00 | 86
HEY DOLL BABY .... *(Columbia 38-05824)* | 1.00 | 4.00 | 86
  (Promotional issue, *Demonstration–Not For Sale* printed on sleeve)

SWEET INSPIRATIONS, THE
  See the Rascals *(Glory Glory)*

SWEET SENSATION
TAKE IT WHILE IT'S HOT .... *(Atco 7-99352)* | .75 | 3.00 | 88
NEVER LET YOU GO .... *(Atco 7-99284)* | .75 | 3.00 | 88
SINCERELY YOURS .... *(Atco 7-99246)* | .75 | 3.00 | 89
  (Shown as by Sweet Sensation With Romeo J.D.)
HOOKED ON YOU .... *(Atco 7-99210)* | .75 | 3.00 | 89

SWIMMING POOL Q'S, THE
RAT BAIT/The A-Bomb Woke Me Up .... *(Chlorinated SPQR 079)* | 1.50 | 6.00 | 79
  (Orange version)
RAT BAIT/The A-Bomb Woke Me Up .... *(Chlorinated SPQR 079)* | 1.25 | 5.00 | 79
  (Gray version)
LITTLE MISFIT/Stingray .... *(DB 64)* | 1.25 | 5.00 | 82

SWINGERS, THE
LEAVING ON A JET PLANE .... *(Rumble 002)* | 1.25 | 5.00 | 81
COUNTING THE BEAT .... *(Backstreet 52080)* | 1.00 | 4.00 | 82

SWING OUT SISTER
BREAKOUT/Dirty Money .... *(Mercury 888 016-7)* | .75 | 3.00 | 86
SURRENDER/Who's To Blame .... *(Mercury 888 243-7)* | .75 | 3.00 | 87
TWILIGHT WORLD/Another Lost Weekend .... *(Mercury 888 484-7)* | .75 | 3.00 | 87
WAITING GAME/Coney Island Man .... *(Fontana 874 190-7)* | .75 | 3.00 | 89

SYLVAIN, SYLVAIN
EVERY BOY AND EVERY GIRL .... *(RCA PB-11937)* | 1.25 | 5.00 | 80
  (Issued with small-hole 45 RPM record)
  Also see David Johansen (pictured on the back of *Funky But Chic* sleeve as part of the David Johansen Group), the New York Dolls

SYLVERS, THE
STAY AWAY FROM ME .... *(Pride 1029)* | 1.50 | 6.00 | 73

SYLVESTER, TERRY
FOR THE PEACE OF ALL MANKIND .... *(Epic 8-20002)* | 2.00 | 8.00 | 74
  (Possibly a promotional issue only)
  Also see the Hollies

SYLVIA
DRIFTER .... *(RCA PB-12164)* | 1.00 | 4.00 | 81
THE MATADOR .... *(RCA PB-12214)* | 1.00 | 4.00 | 82

SYNDICATE OF SOUND
WHO'LL BE THE NEXT IN LINE? (LIVE)/The Spider & The Fly (Live) .... *(Sundazed 116)* | .50 | 2.00 | 96

SYREETA
(Syreeta Wright was married to Stevie Wonder)
HARMOUR LOVE .... *(Motown M1353F)* | 1.25 | 5.00 | 75

SYSTEM, THE
DON'T DISTURB THIS GROOVE/Modern Girl .... *(Atlantic 7-89320)* | .75 | 3.00 | 87
NIGHTTIME LOVER/Save Me .... *(Atlantic 7-89222)* | .75 | 3.00 | 87
COMING TO AMERICA .... *(Atco 7-99320)* | .75 | 3.00 | 88
  (From the motion picture *Coming To America*)
MIDNIGHT SPECIAL/Why You Wanna Hurt Me? .... *(Atlantic 7-88901)* | .75 | 3.00 | 89

T

TAKE 6
SPREAD LOVE .... (Reprise 27880-7) | .75 | 3.00 | 88

TALKING HEADS
LOVE GOES TO BUILDING ON FIRE/New Feeling .... (Sire 737)	2.50	10.00	77
UH-OH, LOVE COMES TO TOWN/I Wish You Wouldn't Say That .... (Sire 1002)	2.50	10.00	77
PSYCHO KILLER .... (Sire 1013)	2.50	10.00	78
TAKE ME TO THE RIVER/Thank You For Sending Me An Angel .... (Sire 1032)	1.50	6.00	78
BURNING DOWN THE HOUSE/I Get Wild/Wild Gravity .... (Sire 29565-7)	.75	3.00	83
THIS MUST BE THE PLACE (NAIVE MELODY)/Moon Rocks .... (Sire 29451-7)	.75	3.00	83
ONCE IN A LIFETIME/This Must Be The Place (Naive Melody) .... (Sire 29163-7)	.75	3.00	85

(A-side from the motion picture *Stop Making Sense*)

| STOP MAKING SENSE (GIRLFRIEND IS BETTER)/Heaven (Live) .... (Sire 29080-7) | .75 | 3.00 | 85 |

(A-side from the motion picture *Stop Making Sense*)

ROAD TO NOWHERE/Give Me Back My Name .... (Sire 28987-7)	.75	3.00	85
AND SHE WAS .... (Sire 28917-7)	.75	3.00	85
WILD WILD LIFE/People Like Us .... (Sire 28629-7)	.75	3.00	86

(B-side credit on back states *Featuring John Goodman: Lead Vocal*. From the motion picture *True Stories*.)

| LOVE FOR SALE/Hey Now .... (Sire 28497-7) | .75 | 3.00 | 86 |

(B-side shown as sung by the St. Thomas Aquinas School Choir. From the motion picture *True Stories*.)

| (NOTHING BUT) FLOWERS/Ruby Dear (Bush Mix) .... (Fly/Sire 27992-7) | .75 | 3.00 | 88 |
| BLIND/Bill .... (Fly/Sire 27948-7) | .75 | 3.00 | 88 |

Also see Jonathan Richman and the Modern Lovers (Jerry Harrison), Tom Tom Club (Tina Weymouth, Chris Frantz)

TALK TALK
| IT'S MY LIFE/Again, A Game...Again .... (EMI America B-81953) | 1.00 | 4.00 | 84 |
| LIFE'S WHAT YOU MAKE IT/It's Getting Late In The Evening .... (EMI America B8303) | 1.00 | 4.00 | 85 |

TALL, BARNY
| LITTLE LOVE LETTER/I'd Rather Be Wrong .... (Domino 907) | 12.50 | 50.00 | 61 |

(Single sheet insert, not a true picture sleeve)

| I'M ONLY HUMAN/Fleeting Love .... (Domino 909) | 12.50 | 50.00 | 61 |

(Single sheet insert, not a true picture sleeve)

TA MARA AND THE SEEN
| EVERYBODY DANCE/Lonely Heart .... (A&M 2768) | .75 | 3.00 | 85 |
| AFFECTTION/You Turn Me Up .... (A&M 2797) | .75 | 3.00 | 85 |

(Yes, this is the correct spelling for the a-side)

| THINKING ABOUT YOU/Long Cold Nights .... (A&M 2818) | .75 | 3.00 | 86 |

TAMBLYN, RUSS
(Actor)
| TOM THUMB'S TUNE/(It's Gotta Be) Now Or Never .... (M-G-M 58-XY-225) | 3.75 | 15.00 | 58 |

(A-side from the motion picture Tom Thumb. Back of sleeve tells the story behind *Tom Thumb* and also advertises the "delicious, nutritious Bosco Milk Amplifier".)
Also see Jerry Lee Lewis (*High School Confidential*)

T.A.M.I. SHOW, THE
(Motion Picture)
See Jan & Dean (*From All Over The World*)

TAMI SHOW
| SHE'S ONLY TWENTY/Don't Say No .... (Chrysalis VS4 43146) | .75 | 3.00 | 87 |
| CUPID'S SOLDIER/Stranger .... (Chrysalis VS4 43264) | .75 | 3.00 | 88 |

TANGIER
| ON THE LINE .... (Atco 7-99208) | .75 | 3.00 | 88 |

TANNER, MARC
See Cheryl Lynn (b-side of *At Last You're Mine*)

TANNO, MARC
| FIRST LOVE .... (20th Fox 185) | 2.50 | 10.00 | 60 |

TASHAN
| LOVE IS.../Got The Right Attitude .... (Columbia 38-07390) | .75 | 3.00 | 87 |

(Both songs credited on back as *Duet with Alyson Williams*)

TASTE OF HONEY, A
BOOGIE OOGIE OOGIE/World Spin .... (Capitol 4565)	1.25	5.00	78
SUKIYAKI .... (Capitol 4953)	1.00	4.00	81
I'LL TRY SOMETHING NEW .... (Capitol B-5099)	1.00	4.00	82

Also see Janice Marie Johnson

TAUPIN, BERNIE
(Elton John's lyricist partner)
| FRIEND OF THE FLAG/Backbone .... (RCA 5162-7-R) | 1.00 | 4.00 | 87 |
| CITIZEN JANE/White Boys In Chains .... (RCA 5216-7-R) | 1.00 | 4.00 | 87 |

TAXXI
THE HEART IS A LONELY HUNTER .... (Fantasy 928)	1.00	4.00	82
STILL IN LOVE .... (MCA 52612)	.75	3.00	85
THE REAL THING .... (MCA 52680)	.75	3.00	85

TAYLOR, ANDY
| TAKE IT EASY/Angel Eyes .... (Atlantic 7-89414) | .75 | 3.00 | 85 |

(From the motion picture *American Anthem*, Mitch Gaylord pictured on back. Among those credited on back are Terry Bozzio of Missing Persons on drums, Flo and Eddie on background vocals, and Steve Jones on sitar.)

| WHEN THE RAIN COMES DOWN .... (MCA 52946) | .75 | 3.00 | 86 |

(From the television series *Miami Vice*)

LIFE GOES ON .... (MCA 52999)	.75	3.00	87
I MIGHT LIE .... (MCA 53063)	.75	3.00	87
DON'T LET ME DIE YOUNG .... (MCA 53085)	.75	3.00	87

Also see Duran Duran, Power Station

TITLE	LABEL AND NUMBER	VG	NM	YR

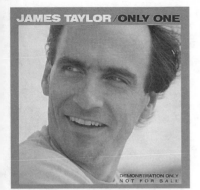

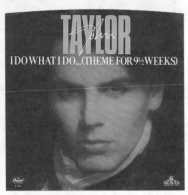

TAYLOR, B. E., GROUP
KAREN .... (Epic 34-05851) | .75 | 3.00 | 86
KAREN .... (Epic 34-05851) | 1.00 | 4.00 | 86
(Promotional issue, *Demonstration Only Not For Sale* printed on sleeve)
Also see Crack The Sky (Rick Withowski, Joe Macre, Joe D'Amico)

TAYLOR, BOBBY, AND THE VANCOUVERS
DOES YOUR MAMA KNOW ABOUT ME .... (Gordy 7069) | 7.50 | 30.00 | 68

TAYLOR, ELIZABETH
(Actress)
See Joni James (*Never Till Now*)

TAYLOR, JAMES
HARD TIMES/Summer's Here .... (Columbia 11-02093) | 1.00 | 4.00 | 81
EVERYDAY .... (Columbia 38-05681) | .75 | 3.00 | 85
EVERYDAY .... (Columbia 38-05681) | 1.00 | 4.00 | 85
(Promotional issue, *Demonstration Only–Not For Sale* printed on sleeve)
ONLY ONE/Mona .... (Columbia 38-05785) | .75 | 3.00 | 86
ONLY ONE .... (Columbia 38-05785) | 1.00 | 4.00 | 86
(Promotional issue, *Demonstration Only Not For Sale* printed on sleeve)
NEVER DIE YOUNG .... (Columbia 38-07616) | .75 | 3.00 | 87
BABY BOOM BABY .... (Columbia 38-07948) | .75 | 3.00 | 88
Also see Ricky Skaggs (*New Star Shining*)

TAYLOR, JOHN
I DO WHAT I DO...(THEME FOR 9 1/2 WEEKS)/Jazz ...... (Capitol B-5551) | 1.00 | 4.00 | 86
(Blue and black duotone on front. A-side from the motion picture *9 1/2 Weeks*.)
I DO WHAT I DO...(THEME FOR 9 1/2 WEEKS)/Jazz ...... (Capitol B-5551) | 1.00 | 4.00 | 86
(Blue halftone printed over solid silver on front. A-side from the motion picture *9 1/2 Weeks*.)
Also see Duran Duran, Power Station

TAYLOR, LIVINGSTON
(Brother of James Taylor)
CITY LIGHTS/Louie .... (Critique 7-99255) | .75 | 3.00 | 88
LOVING ARMS (COUNTRY VERSION)/Loving Arms (Pop Version) ... (Critique 7-99275) | .75 | 3.00 | 88

TAYLOR, R. DEAN
INDIANA WANTS ME .... (Rare Earth 5013) | 3.75 | 15.00 | 70
(Promotional issue only)
AIN'T IT A SAD THING .... (Rare Earth 5023) | 1.25 | 5.00 | 71

TAYLOR, ROGER
MAN ON FIRE/Killing Time .... (Capitol B-5364) | 1.00 | 4.00 | 84
Also see the Cross, Queen

TAYLOR, SUSANNE JEROME
WHY DID FOREVER HAVE TO END/Static .... (RCA PB-14211) | .75 | 3.00 | 85
Also see Drama

TEACHERS
(Motion Picture)
See Joe Cocker (*Edge Of A Dream*), Bob Seger (*Understanding*), 38 Special (*Teacher Teacher*)

TEARDROP EXPLODES, THE
See Julian Cope

TEARS FOR FEARS
MAD WORLD/Ideas As Opiates .... (Mercury 812 213-7) | 2.00 | 8.00 | 83
SHOUT/The Big Chair .... (Mercury 880 294-7) | 1.00 | 4.00 | 85
HEAD OVER HEELS/When In Love With A Blind Man ... (Mercury 880 899-7) | 1.00 | 4.00 | 85
MOTHERS TALK/Sea Song .... (Mercury 884 638-7) | 1.00 | 4.00 | 86
SOWING THE SEEDS OF LOVE/Tears Roll Down ... (Fontana 874 710-7) | .75 | 3.00 | 89
WOMAN IN CHAINS/Always In The Past ...... (Fontana 876 248-7) | .75 | 3.00 | 89
(A-side guest vocalist Oleta Adams pictured on back with Roland Orzabal and Curt Smith. Phil Collins credited on drums.)

TEASE
FIRESTARTER .... (Epic 34-05789) | .75 | 3.00 | 86
FIRESTARTER .... (Epic 34-05789) | 1.00 | 4.00 | 86
(Promotional issue, *Demonstration Only–Not For Sale* printed on sleeve)
I CAN'T STAND THE RAIN .... (Epic 34-07740) | .75 | 3.00 | 88

TECHNOTRONIC FEATURING FELLY
PUMP UP THE JAM .... (SBK 07311) | .75 | 3.00 | 89

TEEGARDEN & VAN WINKLE
GOD, LOVE AND ROCK & ROLL/Work Me Tomorrow ... (Westbound 170) | 1.25 | 5.00 | 70
Also see Bob Seger (David Teegarden was a member of the Silver Bullet Band from 1978-81)

TEELEY, TOM
SHE GOT AWAY/Heartland .... (A&M 2624) | .75 | 3.00 | 84

TEENAGE FANCLUB
FREE AGAIN/ .... (K 26) | 2.50 | 10.00 | 90
EVERYBODY'S FOOL/Primary Education/Speeder ... (Matador 007) | 2.50 | 10.00 | 90
GOD KNOWS IT'S TRUE/ .... (Matador 023) | 2.50 | 10.00 | 90

TEENA MARIE
FIX IT (PART 1)/Fix It (Part 2) .... (Epic 34-04124) | 1.25 | 5.00 | 83
LOVERGIRL/Lovergirl (Instrumental) .... (Epic 34-04619) | 1.00 | 4.00 | 84
LOVERGIRL/Lovergirl (Instrumental) .... (Epic 34-04619) | 1.25 | 5.00 | 84
(Promotional issue, *Demonstration Only/Not For Sale* printed on sleeve)
JAMMIN .... (Epic 34-04738) | .75 | 3.00 | 84
JAMMIN .... (Epic 34-04738) | 1.00 | 4.00 | 84
(Promotional issue, *Demonstration Only–Not For Sale* printed on sleeve)
OUT ON A LIMB/Starchild .... (Epic 34-04943) | .75 | 3.00 | 85

OUT ON A LIMB .... (Epic 34-04943) | 1.00 | 4.00 | 85
(Promotional issue, *Demonstration Only–Not For Sale* printed on sleeve)
14K .... (Epic 34-05599) | .75 | 3.00 | 85
(From the motion picture *The Goonies*)
14K .... (Epic 34-05599) | 1.00 | 4.00 | 85
(Promotional issue, *Demonstration Only–Not For Sale* printed on sleeve. From the motion picture *The Goonies*)
LIPS TO FIND YOU / Lips To Find You (Instrumental) .... (Epic 34-05872) | .75 | 3.00 | 86
LIPS TO FIND YOU / Lips To Find You (Instrumental) .... (Epic 34-05872) | 1.00 | 4.00 | 86
(Promotional issue, *Demonstration Only–Not For Sale* printed on sleeve. Sleeve lists b-side even though the 45 has *Lips To Find You* on both sides.)
LOVE ME DOWN EASY / Love Me Down Easy (Instrumental) .... (Epic 34-06292) | .75 | 3.00 | 86
LOVE ME DOWN EASY .... (Epic 34-06292) | 1.00 | 4.00 | 86
(Promotional issue, *Demonstration Only–Not For Sale* printed on sleeve)
LEAD ME ON .... (Columbia 38-06535) | .75 | 3.00 | 86
(From the motion picture *Top Gun*)
LEAD ME ON .... (Columbia 38-06535) | 1.00 | 4.00 | 86
(Promotional issue, *Demonstration Only–Not For Sale* printed on sleeve. From the motion picture *Top Gun*)
OOO LA LA LA / Sing One To Your Love (aka Instrumental Version of *Ooo La La La*)(Epic 34-07708) | .75 | 3.00 | 88
WORK IT / Work It (Instrumental) .... (Epic 34-07902) | .75 | 3.00 | 88

TEEN QUEENS, THE
DONNY (PARTS 1 & 2) .... (Antler 4016) | 10.00 | 40.00 | 60

TEE SET
MA BELLE AMIE .... (Colossus 107) | 1.50 | 6.00 | 69

TELEVISION
See Richard Hell and the Voidoids (Richard Hell), Richard Lloyd, Neon Boys (Richard Hell)

TELEX
PEANUTS / Basta (Dub) .... (Atlantic 7-89096) | .75 | 3.00 | 88

TELSTARS, THE
See Billy Strange and the Telstars

TEMPTATIONS, THE
MY GIRL / "Talking, 'Bout" Nobody But My Baby .... (Gordy 7038) | 20.00 | 80.00 | 65
BEAUTY IS ONLY SKIN DEEP / You're Not An Ordinary Girl .... (Gordy 7055) | 6.25 | 25.00 | 66
I'M GONNA MAKE YOU LOVE ME / A Place In The Sun .... (Motown 1137) | 5.00 | 20.00 | 68
(Shown as by Diana Ross & The Supremes and The Temptations, all eight are pictured. Back of sleeve promotes their television special on Monday, December 9th, 1968 NBC-TV.)
BALL OF CONFUSION (THAT'S WHAT THE WORLD IS TODAY) .... (Gordy 7099) | 3.75 | 15.00 | 70
TO BE CONTINUED / You're The One .... (Gordy 1871) | .75 | 3.00 | 86
TO BE CONTINUED .... (Gordy 1871) | .75 | 3.00 | 86
(Promotional issue, *For Promotion Only/Not For Sale* printed on sleeve)
A FINE MESS / Wishful Thinking .... (Motown 1837MF) | .75 | 3.00 | 86
(From the motion picture *A Fine Mess*)
I WONDER WHO SHE'S SEEING NOW / Girls (They Like It) .... (Motown 1908MF) | .75 | 3.00 | 87
I WONDER WHO SHE'S SEEING NOW / Girls (They Like It) .... (Motown 1908MF) | 1.00 | 4.00 | 87
(Promotional issue, *For Promotion Only/Not For Sale* printed on sleeve. Sleeve lists b-side even though the 45 has *I Wonder Who She's Seeing Now* on both sides.)
Also see Daryl Hall and John Oates (*The Way You Do The Things You Do*)

10
(Motion Picture)
See Henry Mancini (*Ravel's Bolero*)

10CC
I'M NOT IN LOVE .... (Mercury 73678) | 3.00 | 12.00 | 75
(Promotional issue only)
ART FOR ART'S SAKE / Get It While You Can .... (Mercury 73725) | 2.00 | 8.00 | 75
EXTENDED PLAYS
DONNA .... (UK 101) | 2.00 | 8.00 | 72
(Promotional issue only titled *What's So Great About UK Records*. Also includes tracks by other UK artists.)
Also see Godley & Creme, Wax (Graham Gouldman)

TEN CITY
THAT'S THE WAY LOVE IS .... (Atlantic 7-88963) | .75 | 3.00 | 89

TENDERLOIN
(Stage Musical)
See Bobby Darin (*Artificial Flowers*)

10,000 MANIACS
PEACE TRAIN / The Painted Desert .... (Elektra 7-69457) | 1.25 | 5.00 | 87
Peace Train was removed from later pressings of the album, *In My Tribe*, by request of the band after the song's writer, Cat Stevens, joined other Moslems in calling for the assassination of *Satanic Verses* author Salman Rushdie.
DON'T TALK / City Of Angels .... (Elektra 7-69439) | 1.00 | 4.00 | 87
LIKE THE WEATHER / A Campfire Song .... (Elektra 7-69418) | 1.00 | 4.00 | 88
WHAT'S THE MATTER HERE? / Cherry Tree .... (Elektra 7-69388) | 1.00 | 4.00 | 88
TROUBLE ME / The Lion's Share .... (Elektra 7-69298) | 1.00 | 4.00 | 89

TEPPER, ROBERT
NO EASY WAY OUT .... (Scotti Brothers ZS4-05750) | .75 | 3.00 | 85
(From the motion picture *Rocky IV*, Sylvester Stallone pictured on back)
NO EASY WAY OUT .... (Scotti Brothers ZS4-05750) | 1.00 | 4.00 | 85
(Promotional issue, *Demonstration Only Not For Sale* printed on sleeve. From the motion picture *Rocky IV*, Sylvester Stallone pictured on back.)
DON'T WALK AWAY .... (Scotti Brothers ZS4-05879) | .75 | 3.00 | 86
DON'T WALK AWAY .... (Scotti Brothers ZS4-05879) | 1.00 | 4.00 | 86
(Promotional issue, *Demonstration Only Not For Sale* printed on sleeve)

TERRY, HELEN
See Ray Parker, Jr. (*One Sunny Day/Dueling Bikes From Quicksilver*)

TERRY, SONNY
BLUE BOYS HOLLER / Blues Last Walk .... (Brut 804) | 1.50 | 6.00 | 73
(Shown as by Sonny Terry and Brownie McGhee)

TITLE	LABEL AND NUMBER	VG	NM	YR
TERRY, SUZANNE				
SOMEBODY TURNED MY WORLD	(Columbia 4-43523)	1.50	6.00	66
TERRY, TONY				
FOREVER YOURS	(Epic 34-07900)	.75	3.00	88
TESLA				
I JUST WANNA TESLAFY!	(Geffen PRO S-2692)	1.00	4.00	87
(Promotional issue only, hard cover issued with a small-hole 33-1/3 RPM record. Shown as by Al Coury with Marko Babineau. Spoken sales pitch for Tesla over the song *Modern Day Cowboy*.)				
LITTLE SUZI/Cumin' Atcha Live (Remix)	(Geffen 28353-7)	1.00	4.00	87
TEQUILA SUNRISE				
(Motion Picture)				
See the Everly Brothers With the Beach Boys (*Don't Worry Baby*), Ann Wilson and Robin Zander (*Surrender To Me*)				
TEX, JOE				
WOMAN STEALER/Cat's Got Her Tongue	(Dial 1020)	2.00	8.00	73
Also see the Soul Clan				
TEXTONES, THE				
SOME OTHER GIRL/Reason To Leave	(I.R.S./Faulty Products 01)	1.00	4.00	80
MIDNIGHT MISSION/Upset Me	(A&M GS-82016)	1.00	4.00	84
(Don Henley and Gene Clark credited with background vocals and Barry Goldberg on keyboards)				
Also see the Go-Go's (Kathy Valentine), Phil Seymour, Dwight Twilley Band (Phil Seymour)				
THANK GOD IT'S FRIDAY				
(Motion Picture)				
See Paul Jabara (*Trapped In A Stairway*)				
THEE MIDNIGHTERS				
THE MIDNIGHT FEELING/It'll Never Be Over For Me	(Whittier 501)	6.25	25.00	66
THEM				
WALKING IN THE QUEEN'S GARDEN	(Tower 384)	7.50	30.00	67
WE'VE ALL AGREED TO HELP	(Tower 461)	6.25	25.00	69
BABY PLEASE DON'T GO/Danger Heartbreak Dead Ahead	(A&M 1201)	.75	3.00	88
(B-side shown as by Marvelettes. From the motion picture *Good Morning, Vietnam*.)				
Also see Pete Bardens, Van Morrison				
THESE IMMORTAL SOULS				
LUNEY TUNE	(Sub Pop 121)	2.50	10.00	91
(Alice Cooper Tribute double single release limited to 5,500 copies with an unknown number on blue-gray vinyl. Also includes one song each by Sonic Youth, Gumball, and Laughing Hyenas.)				
THE THE				
HEARTLAND/Slow Train To Dawn	(Epic ES7-02718)	1.50	6.00	87
(Promotional issue only in conjunction with Tower Records. *Demonstration–Not For Sale* printed on sleeve.)				
THEY MIGHT BE GIANTS				
EVERYTHING RIGHT IS WRONG/You'll Miss Me	(Wiggle Diskette # unknown)	2.00	8.00	85
(Issued with a flexi-disc)				
WHY DOES THE SUN SHINE? (THE SUN IS A MASS OF INCANDESCENT GAS)/ Jessica	(Elektra 7-64602)	.75	3.00	93
O TANNENBAUM/Christmas Cards	(Elektra 7-64578)	.75	3.00	93
(Hard cover issued with green vinyl)				
Also see Pere Ubu (Tony Maimone)				
THICKE, ALAN				
(Comic actor and television talk-show host)				
THE WIZARD OF ODDS	(L.A. Records 10066)	1.50	6.00	
THICKE OF THE NIGHT/Grandma	(Atlantic 7-89701)	1.25	5.00	83
Also see Steve Dorff and Friends (*Theme From Growing Pains*)				
THIEF WHO CAME TO DINNER, THE				
(Motion Picture)				
See Henry Mancini (*Theme From The Thief Who Came To Dinner*)				
THIELEMANS, TOOTS				
See Billy Joel (*Leave A Tender Moment Alone*)				
THIEVES, THE				
EVERYTHING BUT MY HEART	(Bug P-B-44330)	.75	3.00	89
THIRD WORLD				
FORBIDDEN LOVE/Forbidden Love (Reprise)	(Mercury 874 054-7)	.75	3.00	89
13TH FLOOR ELEVATORS				
See Roky Erickson				
38 SPECIAL				
FANTASY GIRL/Honky Tonk Dancer	(A&M 2330)	1.00	4.00	81
CAUGHT UP IN YOU/Firestarter	(A&M 2412)	1.00	4.00	82
YOU KEEP RUNNIN' AWAY/Prisoners Of Rock 'N' Roll	(A&M 2431)	1.00	4.00	82
IF I'D BEEN THE ONE/Twentieth Century Fox	(A&M 2594)	.75	3.00	83
BACK WHERE YOU BELONG/Undercover Lover	(A&M 2615)	.75	3.00	83
TEACHER TEACHER	(Capitol B-5405)	.75	3.00	84
(From the motion picture *Teachers*)				
LIKE NO OTHER NIGHT/Heart's On Fire	(A&M 2831)	.75	3.00	86
SOMEBODY LIKE YOU/Against The Night	(A&M 2854)	.75	3.00	86
BACK TO PARADISE/Hold On Loosely	(A&M 2955)	.75	3.00	87
(From the motion picture *Revenge Of The Nerds II: Nerds In Paradise*)				
ROCK & ROLL STRATEGY/Love Strikes	(A&M 1246)	.75	3.00	88
THOMAS, B. J.				
GOD BLESS THE CHILDREN/On This Christmas Night	(MCA/Songbird 41134)	1.25	5.00	79
Also see Steve Dorff and Friends (*Theme From Growing Pains*)				

THOMAS, CARLA
LET ME BE GOOD TO YOU/Another Night Without My Man .... (Stax 188)   2.00   8.00   66

THOMAS, DANNY
(Actor/Comic)
THE FIRST CHRISTMAS/Christmas Story .... (RCA Victor 47-9342)   2.50   10.00   67

THOMAS, EVELYN
HIGH ENERGY .... (TSR 106)   .75   3.00   84

THOMAS, GUTHRIE
ARLO GUTHRIE ON GUTHRIE THOMAS .... (Capitol SPRO 8216/8217)   1.50   6.00   75
    (Promotional issue only, *Promotion Copy–Not For Sale* printed on sleeve. Guthrie Thomas pictured.)

THOMAS, JAMO, & HIS PARTY BROTHERS ORCHESTRA
I SPY (FOR THE FBI)/Snake Hip Mama .... (Thomas 303)   2.50   10.00   66

THOMAS, LILLO
I'M IN LOVE .... (Capitol B-5698)   .75   3.00   87

THOMAS, MICKEY
STAND IN THE FIRE/Opening Score .... (RCA PB-14273)   .75   3.00   85
    (B-side shown as by William Orbit. From the motion picture *Youngblood*, Cynthia Gibb, Rob Lowe, and Patrick
    Swayze pictured.)
    Also see Jefferson Starship, Starship, Donna Summer (*Only The Fool Survives*)

THOMAS, PAT
DESAFINADO/One Note Samba .... (MGM K-13102)   2.00   8.00   62

THOMAS, PHILIP-MICHAEL
(Actor who co-starred in the television series *Miami Vice*)
JUST THE WAY I PLANNED IT/All My Love .... (Atlantic 7-99581)   .75   3.00   85
FISH AND CHIPS/I'm In Love With The Love That You Give To Me .... (Atlantic 7-99560)   .75   3.00   85
DON'T MAKE PROMISES/Cosmic Free .... (Atlantic 7-99302)   .75   3.00   88
    Also see Chaka Khan (*Own The Night*) , Patti LaBelle (*The Last Unbroken Heart*)

THOMAS, VANEESE
(I WANNA GET) CLOSE TO YOU .... (Geffen 7-28216)   .75   3.00   87
LET'S TALK IT OVER .... (Geffen 7-28365)   .75   3.00   87

THOMPSON, CHRIS
LOVE AND LONELINESS/Empty House .... (Atlantic 7-89384)   .75   3.00   88
WHAT A WOMAN WANTS/She's Dangerous .... (Atlantic 7-89368)   .75   3.00   86
    Also see Manfred Mann's Earth Band, Night

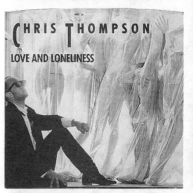

THOMPSON, HANK
LOST JOHN .... (Capitol 4649)   3.75   15.00   61
ROCKIN' IN THE CONGO .... (Churchill 7779)   1.25   5.00   81
COCAINE BLUES .... (Churchill 94003)   1.25   5.00   82

THOMPSON, KAY
ELOISE .... (Cadence 1286)   2.50   10.00   56

THOMPSON, LEA
(Actress)
    See Flesh For Lulu (*I Go Crazy*)

THOMPSON, MARC ANTHONY
SO FINE/Alot Of Girls (Would Turn) .... (Warner Bros. 29175-7)   .75   3.00   84

THOMPSON, SUE
WHAT'S WRONG BILL/I Need A Harbor .... (Hickory 1204)   3.75   15.00   63
TRUE CONFESSIONS/Suzie .... (Hickory 1217)   3.75   15.00   63

THOMPSON TWINS
LOVE ON YOUR SIDE/Love On Your Back .... (Arista 1056)   1.00   4.00   83
LOVE ON YOUR SIDE/Love On Your Back .... (Arista 9013)   1.00   4.00   83
    (A small sticker with the number AS1-9013 is placed over the original AS 1056 catalog number. Issued with the
    original 1056 number on the record. This appears to be an interim version until the revised 9013 number
    sleeves and 45 labels could be printed.)
LOVE ON YOUR SIDE/Love On Your Back .... (Arista 9013)   .75   3.00   83
    (It is assumed that this sleeve, with revised catalog number, was printed)
HOLD ME NOW/Let Loving Start .... (Arista 9164)   .75   3.00   84
DOCTOR! DOCTOR!/Nurse Shark .... (Arista 9209)   .75   3.00   84
YOU TAKE ME UP/Passion Planet .... (Arista 9244)   .75   3.00   84
LAY YOUR HANDS ON ME/The Lewis Carol (Adventures In Wonderland) .... (Arista 9396)   .75   3.00   85
KING FOR A DAY/Rollunder .... (Arista 9450)   .75   3.00   85
NOTHING IN COMMON/Nothing To Lose .... (Arista 9511)   1.00   4.00   86
    (From the motion picture *Nothing In Common*)
GET THAT LOVE/Perfect Day .... (Arista 9577)   .75   3.00   87
LONG GOODBYE/Dancing In Your Shoes .... (Arista 9609)   .75   3.00   87
SUGAR DADDY/Monkey Man .... (Warner Bros./Red Eye 22819-7)   .75   3.00   89
    Chris Bell, later of Gene Loves Jezebel, and Matthew Seligman, ex-Soft Boys bassist, were fired by the Thompson Twins manager prior to the
    release of these sleeves.

THOMSON, ALI
LIVE EVERY MINUTE .... (A&M 2260)   1.00   4.00   80

THORINSHIELD
LIFE IS A DREAM/The Best Of It .... (Philips 40492)   2.00   8.00   67

THORNALLEY, PHIL
LOVE ME LIKE A ROCK .... (MCA 53404)   .75   3.00   88

THORN BIRDS, THE
(Television Mini-Series)
    See Henry Mancini (*The Thorn Birds Theme*)

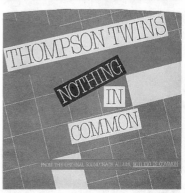

TITLE	LABEL AND NUMBER	VG	NM	YR

THOROGOOD, GEORGE, AND THE DESTROYERS
GENERIC GEORGE THOROGOOD SLEEVE .... (Rounder no #) | 1.25 | 5.00 | 80

(Sleeve reads *More George Thorogood and the Destroyers*, Thorogood pictured front and back. There is no specific mention of song titles or catalog number. This sleeve was used for the singles *I'm Wanted* and *Bottom Of The Sea*.)

I'M WANTED/Restless .... (Rounder 4540) | — | — | 80
(See *Generic George Thorogood Sleeve*)
BOTTOM OF THE SEA/Kids From Philly .... (Rounder 4536) | — | — | 80
(See *Generic George Thorogood Sleeve*)
NOBODY BUT ME .... (EMI America B-8123) | 1.00 | 4.00 | 82
BAD TO THE BONE/No Particular Place To Go (Live Version) .... (EMI America B-8140) | 1.00 | 4.00 | 82
ROCK AND ROLL CHRISTMAS/New Year's Eve Party .... (EMI America B-8187) | 1.00 | 4.00 | 83
TREAT HER RIGHT/You Can't Catch Me .... (EMI-Manhattan B-50121) | .75 | 3.00 | 88

THOROUGHLY MODERN MILLIE
(Broadway Musical)
See Julie Andrews (*Thoroughly Modern Millie*)

THOSE CALLOWAYS
(Motion Picture)
See Johnny Tillotson (*Angel*)

THREE DOG NIGHT
NOBODY .... (ABC/Dunhill 4168) | 7.50 | 30.00 | 68
(Promotional issue only, *Special Promotion Copy* printed on sleeve. Shown as by 3 Dog Night.)
MAMA TOLD ME (NOT TO COME) .... (ABC/Dunhill 4239) | 2.00 | 8.00 | 70
Also see Danny Hutton

3 MAN ISLAND
JACK THE LAD .... (Chrysalis VS4 43231) | .75 | 3.00 | 88
Also see Shriekback (Barry Andrews), XTC (Barry Andrews)

THREE O'CLOCK
NEON TELEPHONE .... (Paisley Park 27733-7) | .75 | 3.00 | 88

THREE RING CIRCUS
GROOVIN' ON THE SUNSHINE .... (RCA Victor 47-9537) | 2.00 | 8.00 | 68

3 SPEED
ONCE BITTEN/Just One Kiss .... (MCA/Curb 52717) | .75 | 3.00 | 85
(B-side shown as by Maria Vidal. From the motion picture *Once Bitten*.)

THREE STOOGES, THE
(Moe Howard, Larry Fine, and Joe de Rita)
SINKIN' THE ROBERT E. LEE/You Are My Girl .... (Epic 5-9402) | 7.50 | 30.00 | 60

THROCKMORTON, SONNY
ROSIE .... (Starcrest 73) | 1.25 | 5.00 | 76

THUDPUCKER, JIMMY
(Cartoon character from Garry Trudeau's comic strip *Doonesbury*)
GINNY'S SONG/Ginny's Song (Disco Version) .... (Warner Bros. 8245) | 1.50 | 6.00 | 76
(Shown as by Jimmy Thudpucker and the Walden West Rhythm Section. Among those credited on back as part of the Walden West Rhythm Section include Steve Cropper and Keith Moon.)
YOU CAN'T FIGHT IT/Take Your Life .... (Windsong CB-11230) | 1.25 | 5.00 | 78

THUNDER, JOHNNY
ROCK-A-BYE MY DARLING/The Rosy Dance .... (Diamond 132) | 5.00 | 20.00 | 63

THUNDERBALL
(Motion Picture)
See Tom Jones (*Thunderball*)

THURMAN, UMA
(Actress)
See Judas Priest (*Johnny B. Goode*)

TIA
BOY TOY/Boy Toy (Toy Breakdown) .... (RCA 5107-7-R) | .75 | 3.00 | 86

TICKLE ME
(Motion Picture)
See Elvis Presley (*Easy Question*)

TIFFANY
I THINK WE'RE ALONE NOW .... (MCA 53167) | .75 | 3.00 | 87
COULD'VE BEEN .... (MCA 53231) | .75 | 3.00 | 87
I SAW HIM STANDING THERE .... (MCA 53285) | .75 | 3.00 | 88
FEELINGS OF FOREVER/Out Of My Heart .... (MCA 53325) | .75 | 3.00 | 88
ALL THIS TIME/Can't Stop A Heartbeat .... (MCA 53371) | .75 | 3.00 | 88
RADIO ROMANCE/I'll Be The Girl .... (MCA 53623) | .75 | 3.00 | 89

TIGERS, THE
GEETO TIGER!/The Prowl .... (Colpix 773) | 37.50 | 150.00 | 65

TIKARAM, TANITA
TWIST IN MY SOBRIETY/I Love You .... (Reprise 7-22995) | .75 | 3.00 | 88

TILLIS, MEL
IF YOU'LL BE MY LOVE/ .... (Columbia 4-40944) | 7.50 | 30.00 | 57

TILLOTSON, JOHNNY
EARTH ANGEL/Pledging My Love .... (Cadence 1377) | 3.75 | 15.00 | 60
JIMMY'S GIRL .... (Cadence 1391) | 3.00 | 12.00 | 61
TALK BACK TREMBLING LIPS/Another You .... (MGM K-13181) | 2.50 | 10.00 | 63
WORRIED GUY/Please Don't Go Away .... (MGM K-13193) | 2.50 | 10.00 | 64
I RISE, I FALL/I'm Watching My Watch .... (MGM K 13232) | 2.50 | 10.00 | 64
WORRY/Sufferin' From A Heartache .... (MGM K-13255) | 2.50 | 10.00 | 64

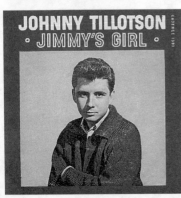

Title	Label and Number	VG	NM	YR
SHE UNDERSTANDS ME / Tomorrow	(MGM K-13284)	2.50	10.00	64
ANGEL / Little Boy	(MGM K-13316)	2.50	10.00	65
(A-side from the motion picture *Those Calloways*)				
THEN I'LL COUNT AGAIN / One's Yours, One's Mine	(MGM K-13344)	2.50	10.00	65
HEARTACHES BY THE NUMBERS / Your Mem'ry Comes Along	(MGM K-13376)	2.50	10.00	65
HELLO ENEMY / I Never Loved You Anyway	(MGM K-13445)	2.50	10.00	66

'TIL TUESDAY

Title	Label and Number	VG	NM	YR
VOICES CARRY / Are You Serious?	(Epic 34-04795)	1.00	4.00	85
VOICES CARRY	(Epic 34-04795)	1.25	5.00	85
(Promotional issue, *Demonstration–Not For Sale* printed on sleeve)				
LOOKING OVER MY SHOULDER / Don't Watch Me Bleed	(Epic 34-04935)	1.00	4.00	85
LOOKING OVER MY SHOULDER	(Epic 34-04935)	1.25	5.00	85
(Promotional issue, *Demonstration–Not For Sale* printed on sleeve)				
LOVE IN VACUUM / No More Crying	(Epic 34-05673)	1.00	4.00	85
LOVE IN VACUUM (SINGLE REMIX) / Love In A Vacuum (Long Version)	(Epic 34-05673)	1.25	5.00	85
(Promotional issue, *Demonstration–Not For Sale* printed on sleeve)				
WHAT ABOUT LOVE / Will She Just Fall Down	(Epic 34-06289)	.75	3.00	86
WHAT ABOUT LOVE	(Epic 34-06289)	1.00	4.00	86
(Promotional issue, *Demonstration–Not For Sale* printed on sleeve)				
COMING UP CLOSE / Angels Never Call	(Epic 34-06571)	.75	3.00	86
(BELIEVED YOU WERE) LUCKY / Limits To Love	(Epic 34-08059)	.75	3.00	88

TIMBUK 3

Title	Label and Number	VG	NM	YR
THE FUTURE'S SO BRIGHT, I GOTTA WEAR SHADES / I'll Do All Right	(I.R.S. 52940)	1.25	5.00	86
(Title in small type size)				
THE FUTURE'S SO BRIGHT, I GOTTA WEAR SHADES / I'll Do All Right	(I.R.S. 52940)	.75	3.00	86
(Title in larger type size)				
LIFE IS HARD / I Love You In The Strangest Way (Acoustic Version)	(I.R.S. 53017)	.75	3.00	87
ALL I WANT FOR CHRISTMAS / Medley: Blue Christmas-I Love You x 3	(I.R.S. 53221)	1.25	5.00	87
EASY / I Love You In The Strangest Way (Glass Eye Version)	(I.R.S. 53338)	.75	3.00	88

T.I.M.E.

Title	Label and Number	VG	NM	YR
TAKE ME ALONG / Make It Alright	(Liberty 56020)	3.00	12.00	68

TIME
(Stage Musical)
    See Julian Lennon (*Time Will Teach Us All*)

TIME GALLERY

Title	Label and Number	VG	NM	YR
VALERIE / The Letter	(Atlantic 7-89019)	.75	3.00	89
TAKING THE BEST /	(Atlantic 7-88926)	.75	3.00	89

TIMELORDS, THE

Title	Label and Number	VG	NM	YR
DOCTORIN' THE TARDIS	(TVT 4025)	.75	3.00	88
(Hard cover)				
BURN THE BEAT / Porpoise Song	(TVT 4045)	.75	3.00	88

TIMES SQUARE
(Motion Picture)
    See Marcy Levy and Robin Gibb (*Help Me!*), Suzi Quatro (*Rock Hard*)

TIMES TWO

Title	Label and Number	VG	NM	YR
CECILIA /	(Reprise 27871-7)	.75	3.00	88
STRANGE BUT TRUE / Come Over	(Reprise 27998-7)	.75	3.00	88
(Poster sleeve)				
CECILIA /	(Reprise 27871-7)	.75	3.00	88

TINGSTAD–RUMBEL
(Eric Tingstad and Nancy Rumbel)
EXTENDED PLAYS

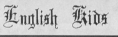

Title	Label and Number	VG	NM	YR
FISHERMAN'S DREAM	(Narada S33-17254)	1.00	4.00	86

(Promotional issue only titled *Narada Sampler–Excellence In New Acoustic Music*, issued with a small-hole 33-1/3 RPM record. Also includes one song each by Randy Mead, William Ellwood, Michael Jones, Matthew Montfort, Spencer Brewer, David Lanz, and Gabriel Lee.)

TIN HUEY

Title	Label and Number	VG	NM	YR
ROBERT TAKES THE ROAD TO LIEBER NAWASH / Squirm You Worm	(Clone 004)	1.00	4.00	78
(Front of sleeve titled *Breakfast With The Hueys*)				
ENGLISH KIDS / Sister Rose	(Clone 011)	1.00	4.00	80
(Hard cover)				

EXTENDED PLAYS

Title	Label and Number	VG	NM	YR
PUPPET WIPES / CUYAHOGA CREEPING BENT / Poor Alphonso (Live) / The Tin Huey Story	(Clone 002)	1.25	5.00	77

(Issued with a small-hole 33-1/3 RPM record)
Also see Chris Butler, the Waitresses (Chris Butler), Dennis Walsh and Friends (Harvey Gold, Stewart Justin)

TINT OF DARKNESS, A

Title	Label and Number	VG	NM	YR
SIXTY MINUTE MAN / Farewell My Love	(Starfire 113)	1.25	5.00	80
(Issued with "splash" vinyl)				
YOU SEND ME / Steal Away	(Starfire 109)	1.25	5.00	80
(Issued with "marble" vinyl)				

TINY TIM

Title	Label and Number	VG	NM	YR
COMIC STRIP MAN / Tell Me That You Love Me	(Solid Brass 101/103)	2.50	10.00	82
(Promotional issue only, *Special Promotion Copy* printed on sleeve)				

TKA

Title	Label and Number	VG	NM	YR
TEARS MAY FALL	(Tommy Boy 907-7)	.75	3.00	87
YOU ARE THE ONE	(Warner Bros. 22946-7)	.75	3.00	89

TLC

Title	Label and Number	VG	NM	YR
WATERFALLS / Waterfalls (Album Instrumental)	(LaFace/Arista 24107-7)	.50	2.00	95

TODD, DYLAN

Title	Label and Number	VG	NM	YR
THE BALLAD OF JAMES DEAN / More Precious Than Gold	(RCA Victor 47-6463)	12.50	50.00	56

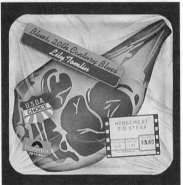

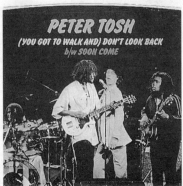

TITLE	LABEL AND NUMBER	VG	NM	YR

TODDY TEE
I NEED A ROLEX / You Haven't Heard Nothing .... (Warner Bros. 27542-7) | .75 | 3.00 | 89
  ("Double Artist Single", flip side shown as by Domination)

TOE FAT
JUST LIKE ME / Bad Side Of The Moon .... (Rare Earth 5019) | 3.00 | 12.00 | 70
  Also see Uriah Heep

TOKENS, THE
WHEN I GO TO SLEEP AT NIGHT / Dry Your Eyes .... (RCA Victor 47-7896) | 6.25 | 25.00 | 61
B'WA NINA / Weeping River .... (RCA Victor 47-7991) | 7.50 | 30.00 | 62
  (Sleeve does not refer to *The Lion Sleeps Tonight* album)
B'WA NINA / Weeping River .... (RCA Victor 47-7991) | 5.00 | 20.00 | 62
  (Sleeve refers to *The Lion Sleeps Tonight* album)
THE RIDDLE / Big Boat .... (RCA Victor 47-8018) | 6.25 | 25.00 | 62
LA BOMBA / A Token Of Love .... (RCA Victor 47-8052) | 5.00 | 20.00 | 62
I'LL DO MY CRYING TOMORROW / Dream Angel Goodnight .... (RCA Victor 47-8089) | 6.25 | 25.00 | 62
A BIRD FLIES OUT OF SIGHT / Wishing .... (RCA Victor 47-8114) | 6.25 | 25.00 | 63
TONIGHT I MET AN ANGEL / Hindi Lullabye .... (RCA Victor 47-8148) | 6.25 | 25.00 | 63
HEAR THE BELLS / ABC 1-2-3 .... (RCA Victor 47-8210) | 5.00 | 20.00 | 63
GREATEST MOMENTS IN A GIRL'S LIFE / Breezy .... (B.T. Puppy 591) | 5.00 | 20.00 | 66
PORTRAIT OF MY LOVE / She Comes And Goes .... (Warner Bros. 5900) | 3.75 | 15.00 | 67

TO LIVE AND DIE IN L.A.
(Motion Picture)
  See Wang Chung *(To Live And Die In L.A.)*

TOMITA
GOLLIWOG'S CAKEWALK / Clair De Lune .... (RCA DJBO-0308) | 1.00 | 4.00 | 74
  (Promotional issue only)
MARS / Venus .... (RCA JB-10819) | 1.00 | 4.00 | 76
  (Titled on front *The Tomita Planets*)
BOLERO / Pavan For A Dead Princess .... (RCA JB-11901) | 1.00 | 4.00 | 79

TOMLIN, LILY
(Actress / Comedienne)
BLUES, 20TH CENTURY BLUES .... (Polydor 14180) | 3.00 | 12.00 | 73
EDITH ANN / Detroit City .... (Polydor 14283) | 1.25 | 5.00 | 76
EXTENDED PLAYS
AND THAT'S THE TRUTH .... (Polydor ML 010) | 2.00 | 8.00 | 72
  (Promotional issue only including the tracks; A-side: Sister's Chocolate Milk, Babies, Chicken Delight, Dog
  Food, God, Mama's Tea Party; B-side: Super Markets, President's TV Show, Mama's Manicure Set, Bugs, If I
  Could Have A Baby, The Truth. No individual titles listed on sleeve.)
MODERN SCREAM .... (Polydor PRO-003) | 1.50 | 6.00 | 75
  (Promotional issue only with seven-track, 33-1/3 record; individual titles unknown)
LILY TOMLIN ON STAGE .... (Arista SP-10) | 1.50 | 6.00 | 77
  (Promotional issue only with four tracks, individual titles unknown)
  Also see Yvonne Elliman *(Moment By Moment)*, John Stewart *(Survivors)*

TOMMY
(Motion Picture)
  See the Who *(Listening To You/See Me Feel Me)*

TOM TOM CLUB
THE MAN WITH THE 4-WAY HIPS .... (Sire 29549-7) | .75 | 3.00 | 83
PLEASURE OF LOVE / Never Took A Penny .... (Sire 29437-7) | .75 | 3.00 | 83

TOM THUMB
(Motion Picture)
  See Russ Tamblyn *(Tom Thumb's Tune)*

TONE LOC
FUNKY COLD MEDINA .... (Delicious Vinyl 104) | .75 | 3.00 | 89

TONIGHT SHOW BAND WITH DOC SEVERINSEN, THE
THE TONIGHT SHOW THEME (JOHNNY'S THEME) / Skyliner .... (Amherst 310) | 1.50 | 6.00 | 86
  Also see Doc Severinsen

TONY! TONI! TONÉ!
BABY DOLL / Baby Doll (Edit of Album Version) .... (Wing 871 108-7) | .75 | 3.00 | 88
LITTLE WALTER / Little Walter (Instrumental) .... (Wing 887 385-7) | .75 | 3.00 | 88

TOP GUN
(Motion Picture)
  See Berlin *(Take My Breath Away)*, Cheap Trick *(Mighty Wings)*, Harold Faltermeyer & Steve Stevens *(Top Gun Anthem)*, Kenny Loggins *(Danger Zone)*, Teena Marie *(Lead Me On)*

TORCH SONG
PREPARE TO ENERGIZE .... (I.R.S. 9925) | .75 | 3.00 | 83
  Also see William Orbit

TOROK, MITCHELL
GUARDIAN ANGEL / I Want To Know Ev'rything .... (Guyden 2032) | 5.00 | 20.00 | 60
PINK CHIFFON / .... (Guyden 2034) | 5.00 | 20.00 | 60

TORRENCE, DEAN
  See Jan & Dean, Mike & Dean

TOSH, PETER
(YOU GOT TO WALK AND) DON'T LOOK BACK / Soon Come .... (Rolling Stones 19308) | 2.00 | 8.00 | 78
  (Tosh pictured with Mick Jagger)

TOTAL COELO
I EAT CANNIBALS / Mucho Macho .... (Chrysalis 42669) | 1.00 | 4.00 | 83

TOTAL CONTRAST
JODY/Jody (Instrumental) .... (London 886 179-7) .75 3.00 87
KISS/Sunshine .... (London 886-215-7) .75 3.00 87

TOTO
GOODBYE ELENORE/Live For Today .... (Columbia no #) 2.00 8.00 81
  (5.5" fold-out poster calendar issued with 5.25", small-hole, red vinyl 33-1/3 RPM. Promotional issue only, no song titles listed on sleeve.)
MAKE BELIEVE/We Made It .... (Columbia 38-03143) 1.00 4.00 82
MAKE BELIEVE .... (Columbia 38-03143) 1.25 5.00 82
  (Promotional issue, *Demonstration Not For Sale* printed on sleeve)
I WON'T HOLD YOU BACK/Afraid Of Love .... (Columbia 38-03597) 1.00 4.00 82
I WON'T HOLD YOU BACK .... (Columbia 38-03597) 1.25 5.00 82
  (Promotional issue, *Demonstration–Not For Sale* printed on sleeve)
STRANGER IN TOWN .... (Columbia 38-04672) .75 3.00 84
STRANGER IN TOWN .... (Columbia 38-04672) 1.00 4.00 84
  (Promotional issue, *Demonstration Only/Not For Sale* printed on sleeve)
HOLYANNA .... (Columbia 38-04752) .75 3.00 85
HOLYANNA .... (Columbia 38-04752) 1.00 4.00 85
  (Promotional issue, *Demonstration Only/Not For Sale* printed on sleeve)
I'LL BE OVER YOU .... (Columbia 38-06280) .75 3.00 86
I'LL BE OVER YOU .... (Columbia 38-06280) 1.00 4.00 86
  (Promotional issue, *Demonstration Only/Not For Sale* printed on sleeve)
WITHOUT YOUR LOVE .... (Columbia 38-06570) .75 3.00 86
WITHOUT YOUR LOVE .... (Columbia 38-06570) 1.00 4.00 86
  (Promotional issue, *Demonstration Only/Not For Sale* printed on sleeve)
PAMELA .... (Columbia 38-07715) .75 3.00 88
STRAIGHT FOR THE HEART .... (Columbia 38-07945) .75 3.00 88
  Also see Far Corporation (Dave Paich), Night (Steve Porcaro), Tom Snow (*Hurry Boy*), Voices Of America

TOUGH GUYS
(Motion Picture)
  See Kenny Rogers (*They Don't Make Them Like They Used To*)

TOWNSHEND, PETE
FACE DANCES PART TWO/Man Watching .... (Atco 7-99884) 1.25 5.00 83
BARGAIN/Dirty Water .... (Atco 7-99884) 1.25 5.00 83
FACE THE FACE/Hiding Out .... (Atco 7-99590) 1.00 4.00 85
GIVE BLOOD/Magic Bus (Live) .... (Atco 7-99577) 1.00 4.00 85
  (B-side shown as by Pete Townshend with David Gilmour and Deep End. Gilmour pictured on back with Townshend.)
BAREFOOTIN'/Behind Blue Eyes .... (Atco 7-99499) 1.00 4.00 86
A FRIEND IS A FRIEND/Man Machines .... (Atlantic 7-88875) .75 3.00 89
  (B-side shown as by Pete Townshend with Simon Townshend)
  Also see Artists United Against Apartheid, the Who

TOWNSHEND, SIMON
(Brother of Pete Townshend)
I'M THE ANSWER/Into The Memory .... (Polydor/21 Records 815 992-7) 1.00 4.00 83
BARRIERS/House On Fire .... (Polydor/21 Records 883 138-7) .75 3.00 85
  (Shown as by Simon Townshend's Moving Target)
  Also see Pete Townshend (*A Friend Is A Friend*)

TOYS IN THE ATTIC
(Motion Picture)
  See Jack Jones (*Toys In The Attic*)

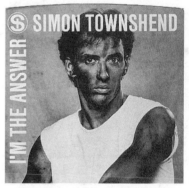

T'PAU
HEART AND SOUL/On The Wing .... (Virgin 7-99466) .75 3.00 87
BRIDGE OF SPIES/No Sense Of Pride .... (Virgin 7-99417) .75 3.00 87
CHINA IN YOUR HAND/ .... (Virgin 7-99369) .75 3.00 87

TRAFFIC
HOLE IN MY SHOE .... (United Artists 50218) 5.00 20.00 67
  Also see the Jim Capaldi, Spencer Davis Group (Steve Winwood), Dave Mason, Steve Winwood

TRAMAINE
IN THE MORNING TIME/With All My Heart .... (A&M 2805) .75 3.00 85

TRAMMPS
DISCO INFERNO .... (Atlantic 3389) 1.50 6.00 77
  (Featured in the motion picture *Saturday Night Fever*)

TRANSLATOR
COME WITH ME .... (Columbia 38-04911) .75 3.00 85
COME WITH ME .... (Columbia 38-04911) .75 3.00 85
  (Promotional issue, *Demonstration–Not For Sale* printed on sleeve)

TRANSVISION VAMP
TELL THAT GIRL TO SHUT UP/God Save The Royalties .... (Uni 50001) 1.25 5.00 88

TRASHMEN, THE
WHOA DAD/Walkin' My Baby .... (Garrett 4012) 25.00 100.00 64
DANCING WITH SANTA/Real Live Doll .... (Garrett 4013) 37.50 150.00 66
HENRIETTA (Live)/Rumble (Live) .... (Sundazed 102) .75 3.00 90
LUCILLE/Green Onions .... (Sundazed 103) .75 3.00 90
ROLL OVER BEETHOVEN/Betty Jean (Instrumental) .... (Sundazed 105) .75 3.00 92
  (Issued with blue marbled vinyl)
DANCIN' WITH SANTA/Real Live Doll .... (Sundazed 112) .50 2.00 96
  (Issued with red vinyl)

TRAVALENA, FRED
(Impressionist)
LA'S MY SPOT .... (Travlo 8061) 1.25 5.00 83
  (Originally included an insert)

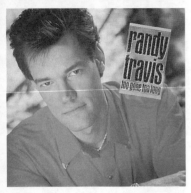

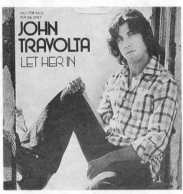

TRAVELING WILBURYS

TITLE	LABEL AND NUMBER	VG	NM	YR
HANDLE WITH CARE/Margarita	(Wilbury 27732-7)	1.00	4.00	88
END OF THE LINE/Congratulations	(Wilbury 27637-7)	1.00	4.00	88

Also see the Beatles (George Harrison), Bob Dylan, Electric Light Orchestra (Jeff Lynne), George Harrison, Roy Orbison, Tom Petty

TRAVERS, PAT, BAND

SNORTIN' WHISKEY/Statesboro Blues (Live)	(Polydor 2107)	1.25	5.00	80

TRAVIS, MERLE

See Nitty Gritty Dirt Band (Honky Tonkin')

TRAVIS, RANDY

TOO GONE TOO LONG	(Warner Bros. 28286-7)	1.00	4.00	87
I TOLD YOU SO	(Warner Bros. 27969-7)	1.00	4.00	87
HONKY TONK MOON/Young Guns	(Warner Bros. 27833-7)	.75	3.00	88
AN OLD TIME CHRISTMAS/How Do I Wrap My Heart Up For Christmas	(Warner Bros. 27707-7)	1.00	4.00	88
DEEPER THAN THE HOLLER	(Warner Bros. 27689-7)	.75	3.00	88
IT'S JUST A MATTER OF TIME/Rock, Rhythm & Blues	(Warner Bros. 22841-7)	.75	3.00	89

TRAVOLTA, JOEY
(Brother of John Travolta)

I DON'T WANNA GO/Where Do We Go From Here	(Millenium 615)	1.25	5.00	78

TRAVOLTA, JOHN
(Actor)

LET HER IN/Big Trouble	(Midland International MB-10623)	1.25	5.00	76
LET HER IN	(Midland International JH-10623)	2.00	8.00	76
(Promotional issue only, Not For Sale For DJs Only printed on sleeve)				
WHENEVER I'M AWAY FROM YOU/Razzamatazz	(Midland International MB-10780)	1.25	5.00	76
ALL STRUNG OUT ON YOU/Easy Evil	(Midland International MB-10907)	1.25	5.00	77
SLOW DANCING/Moonlight Lady	(Midsong International MB-10977)	1.25	5.00	77
RAZZAMATAZZ/What Would They Say	(Midsong International MB-11206)	1.25	5.00	78
(B-side from the motion picture The Boy In The Plastic Bubble)				
BIG TROUBLE	(Midsong International MI-1000)	1.25	5.00	78
YOU'RE THE ONE THAT I WANT/Alone At A Drive-In Movie (Instrumental)	(RSO 891)	1.25	5.00	78
(Shown as by John Travolta and Olivia Newton-John, both pictured. From the motion picture Grease.)				
GREASED LIGHTNIN'/Rock "N Roll Is Here To Stay	(RSO 909)	1.25	5.00	78
(B-side shown as by Sha Na Na. From the motion picture Grease.)				

Also see Jimmy Buffett (Hello Texas), Yvonne Elliman (Moment By Moment), Jermaine Jackson (Perfect), Olivia Newton-John (Livin' In Desperate Times), Bonnie Raitt (Don't It Make Ya Wanna Dance)

TREMELOES, THE

SILENCE IS GOLDEN/Carrie Anne	(Epic 5-10184/80)	12.50	50.00	67
(Promotional issue only issued with red vinyl. Flip side shown as by the Hollies.)				
SILENCE IS GOLDEN	(Epic 5-10184)	3.00	12.00	67
EVEN THE BAD TIMES ARE GOOD	(Epic 5-10233)	3.00	12.00	67

TREMULIS, NICHOLAS

MORE THAN THE TRUTH/Hold On Tight	(Island 7-99432)	.75	3.00	87

TREVOR, VAN

YOU'VE BEEN SO GOOD TO ME/Sunday Morning	(Date 1565)	2.50	10.00	67

T. REX

THE GROOVER/Born To Boogie	(Reprise 1161)	6.25	25.00	73

TRILLION

HOLD OUT	(Epic 8-50670)	1.25	5.00	78
(Promotional issue only, Demonstration/Not For Sale printed on sleeve)				

TRIO

BOOM BOOM/Out In The Streets	(Mercury 814 501-7)	1.50	6.00	83

TRIPLETS, THE
(Fran Warren, Eileen Barton, and Kay Brown)

LOYALTY/Together (We Were Meant To Be Together)	(MGM K12751)	3.75	15.00	58
(From the motion picture Mardi-Gras)				

TRIUMPH

HOLD ON/Just A Game	(RCA PB-11569)	1.50	6.00	79
SPELLBOUND/Cool Down	(MCA 52520)	1.00	4.00	85
FOLLOW YOUR HEART/Stranger In A Strange Land	(MCA 52540)	1.00	4.00	85
(Issued with red vinyl)				
SOMEBODY'S OUT THERE	(MCA 52898)	.75	3.00	87
JUST ONE NIGHT	(MCA 53014)	.75	3.00	87

TROGGS, THE
EXTENDED PLAYS

IF YOU'VE GOT THE TIME	(Miller Beer 621)	3.75	15.00	66
(Promotional issue only radio spots for Miller Beer; three by the Troggs, two by Brook Benton, and one by Johnny Mack)				

TROLLS, THE

STUPID GIRL/I Don't Recall	(Warrior 173)	5.00	20.00	66

TROOP

MAMACITA/Mamacita (Instrumental)	(Atlantic 7-89078)	.75	3.00	88
MY HEART/My Heart (Single Edit-East Coast Remix)	(Atlantic 7-89023)	.75	3.00	88
STILL IN LOVE/	(Atlantic 7-88974)	.75	3.00	88

TROOPER

SANTA MARIA/Whatcha Gonna Do About Me	(MCA 40685)	1.50	6.00	76

TROUBLE FUNK

GOOD TO GO	(Island 7-99538)	.75	3.00	86

TROUBLE WITH GIRLS (AND HOW TO GET INTO IT), THE
(Motion Picture)
See Elvis Presley (*Clean Up Your Own Backyard*)

TROY, BOB
I NEVER WORRY .... (Columbia 4-43734) — 1.50 — 6.00 — 66

TRUE, ANDREA, CONNECTION
MORE MORE MORE ....(Buddah 515) — 2.00 — 8.00 — 76

TRUE LOVE
(Motion Picture)
See A'me Lorain (*Whole Wide World*)

TRUE STORIES
(Motion Picture)
See Talking Heads (*Love For Sale, Wild Wild Life*)

TRUTH, THE
EXCEPTION OF LOVE/I'm A Man .... (I.R.S. 52600) — .75 — 3.00 — 85
WEAPONS OF LOVE/This Way Forever .... (I.R.S. 53084) — .75 — 3.00 — 87

TSUNAMI
LEFT BEHIND/Warm/Crawl .... (Sub Pop 137) — 1.50 — 6.00 — 92
(Split single, limited edition of 4,000 issued with red vinyl. *Warm* and *Crawl* shown as by Velocity Girl.)
COULD HAVE BEEN CHRISTMAS/Merry Christmas, I Love You .... (Simple Machines 14) — 1.50 — 6.00 — 93
(Front of sleeve reads *Seasons Greetings from Tsunami and Velocity Girl*. Both songs listed as the a-side, *Merry Christmas, I Love You* shown as by Velocity Girl.)

TUBB, JUSTIN
TAKE A LETTER MISS GRAY .... (Groove 0017) — 5.00 — 20.00 — 58

TUBES, THE
WHITE PUNKS ON DOPE .... (A&M 1733) — 2.50 — 10.00 — 75
DON'T WANT TO WAIT ANYMORE .... (Capitol B-5007) — 1.00 — 4.00 — 81
SHE'S A BEAUTY .... (Capitol B-5217) — 1.25 — 5.00 — 83
THE MONKEY TIME .... (Capitol B-5254) — 1.00 — 4.00 — 83
PIECE BY PIECE .... (Capitol B-5443) — 1.00 — 4.00 — 85
Also see Fee Waybill

TUCKER, MARSHALL, BAND
See Marshall Tucker Band

TUCKER, MAUREEN
AROUND AND AROUND/Will You Love Me Tomorrow? .... (Trash 82644) — 2.50 — 10.00 — 81
(*Will You Love Me Tomorrow?* listed first on front of sleeve but *Around And Around* is clearly labeled as the a-side on the back of sleeve and 45 label)
Also see the Velvet Underground

TUCKER, SOPHIE
SOME OF THESE DAYS/Life Begins At Forty .... (Decca 1-703) — 2.50 — 10.00 — 51
(Decca "Curtain Call" series of reissues)

TUCKER, TANYA
DELTA DAWN .... (Columbia 4-45588) — 1.50 — 6.00 — 77
SAVE ME .... (MCA 40902) — 1.00 — 4.00 — 78
NOT FADE AWAY/Texas (When I Die) .... (MCA 40976) — 1.00 — 4.00 — 78
ONE LOVE AT A TIME .... (Capitol B-5533) — .75 — 3.00 — 86
JUST ANOTHER LOVE/You Could Change My Mind .... (Capitol B-5604) — .75 — 3.00 — 86
LOVE ME LIKE YOU USED TO .... (Capitol B-44036) — .75 — 3.00 — 87

TUFF DARTS
(I WANNA KNOW) WHO'S BEEN SLEEPING HERE?/Rats .... (Sire 1015) — 1.00 — 4.00 — 78
Also see Robert Gordon

TUNES OF GLORY
(Motion Picture)
See Mitch Miller (*Tunes Of Glory*)

TUNIE, TAMARA
(Actress)
See the Soaps and Hearts Ensemble

TURNER, BAKE
(Football player for the New York Jets)
IS ANYONE GOING TO SAN ANTONE?/Love Is Not For Me .... (Kapp 2075) — 1.25 — 5.00 — 69

TURNER, IKE AND TINA
NO TEARS TO CRY/A Fool For A Fool .... (Warner Bros. 5433) — 6.25 — 25.00 — 64
I WANNA JUMP/Treating Us (Women Funky) .... (Minit 32077) — 3.75 — 15.00 — 69
Also see Tina Turner

TURNER, JESSE LEE
TEEN-AGE MISERY/That's My Girl .... (Fraternity 855) — 10.00 — 40.00 — 59
BABY PLEASE DON'T TEASE/Thinkin' .... (Carlton 509) — 5.00 — 20.00 — 59

TURNER, RUBY
IF YOU'RE READY (COME GO WITH ME) .... (Jive 1027-7-J) — .75 — 3.00 — 85
(Shown as by Ruby Turner With Jonathan Butler, Turner Butler, and producer Billy Ocean pictured on back)

TURNER, TINA
LET'S STAY TOGETHER .... (Capitol B-5322) — 1.25 — 5.00 — 84
WHAT'S LOVE GOT TO DO WITH IT .... (Capitol B-5354) — 1.00 — 4.00 — 84
BETTER BE GOOD TO ME/When I Was Young .... (Capitol B-5387) — 1.00 — 4.00 — 84
PRIVATE DANCER/Nutbush City Limits .... (Capitol B-5433) — 1.00 — 4.00 — 84
SHOW SOME RESPECT/Let's Pretend We're Married .... (Capitol B-5461) — 1.00 — 4.00 — 85
WE DON'T NEED ANOTHER HERO (THUNDERDOME)/
We Don't Need Another Hero (Thunderdome) .... (Capitol B-5491) — 1.00 — 4.00 — 85
(From the motion picture *Mad Max–Beyond Thunderdome*, Turner and Mel Gibson pictured)

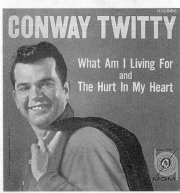

TITLE	LABEL AND NUMBER	VG	NM	YR
ONE OF THE LIVING	(Capitol B-5518)	1.00	4.00	85
(From the motion picture *Mad Max–Beyond Thunderdome*)				
IT'S ONLY LOVE/The Only One	(A&M 2791)	.75	3.00	85
(A-side shown as by Bryan Adams/Tina Turner, b-side by Bryan Adams, both pictured)				
TYPICAL MALE/Don't Turn Around	(Capitol B-5615)	.75	3.00	86
TWO PEOPLE	(Capitol B-5644)	.75	3.00	86
WHAT YOU GET IS WHAT YOU SEE	(Capitol B-5668)	.75	3.00	86
BREAK EVERY RULE/Take Me To The River	(Capitol B-44003)	.75	3.00	87
THE BEST	(Capitol B-44442)	.75	3.00	89
STEAMY WINDOWS	(Capitol B-44473)	.75	3.00	89
Also see Ike and Tina Turner, U.S.A. For Africa, Voices Of America				

TURN OF THE CENTURY

TITLE	LABEL AND NUMBER	VG	NM	YR
LOVE MEANS (YOU NEVER HAVE TO SAY YOU'RE SORRY)/ One Teardrop (Una Lágrima)	(Ranwood 909)	1.25	5.00	70s

TURRENTINE, STANLEY

TITLE	LABEL AND NUMBER	VG	NM	YR
I TOLD JESUS/Storm	(CTI Records OJ-8)	2.00	8.00	72

TURTLES, THE

TITLE	LABEL AND NUMBER	VG	NM	YR
HAPPY TOGETHER/Like The Seasons	(White Whale 244)	5.00	20.00	67
SHE'D RATHER BE WITH ME	(White Whale 249)	6.25	25.00	67
YOU KNOW WHAT I MEAN	(White Whale 254)	3.00	12.00	67
SHE'S MY GIRL	(White Whale 260)	3.00	12.00	67
SOUND ASLEEP	(White Whale 264)	3.00	12.00	68
THE STORY OF ROCK & ROLL	(White Whale 273)	7.50	30.00	68
ELENORE	(White Whale 276)	2.50	10.00	68
YOU SHOWED ME/Buzz Saw	(White Whale 292)	2.50	10.00	69
YOU DON'T HAVE TO WALK IN THE RAIN	(White Whale/Blimp 308)	2.50	10.00	69
LOVE IN THE CITY	(White Whale/Blimp 326)	2.50	10.00	69
HAPPY TOGETHER	(Rhino 74406)	1.25	5.00	87
(Hard cover. From the motion picture *Making Mr. Right*. Ann Magnuson and John Malkovich pictured on the front, an ad for the album *The Best of The Turtles* on the back.)				
Also see Flo & Eddie (Howard Kaylan, Mark Volman), Jefferson Airplane (John Barbata), Jefferson Starship (John Barbata)				

TUXEDOMOON

TITLE	LABEL AND NUMBER	VG	NM	YR
JOE BOY (THE ELECTRONIC GHOST)/Pinheads On The Move	(Tidal Wave 101)	3.75	15.00	78
JOE BOY (THE ELECTRONIC GHOST)/Pinheads On The Move	(Time Release 1018)	2.50	10.00	78
STRANGER/Love/No Hope	(Time Release 102)	2.00	8.00	79
(Shown as by Tuxedomoon With Winston Tong)				
WHAT USE?/Crash	(Ralph 8003)	1.25	5.00	80
DARK COMPANION/59 To 1 Remix	(Ralph 8054)	1.25	5.00	80
Also see Sleepers				

TWEETS, THE

TITLE	LABEL AND NUMBER	VG	NM	YR
DANCE LITTLE BIRD (THE BIRDIE SONG)	(Satril 1006)	1.00	4.00	82

TWENNYNINE WITH LENNY WHITE

TITLE	LABEL AND NUMBER	VG	NM	YR
KID STUFF/Slip Away	(Elektra 47043)	1.00	4.00	80

TWICE AS MUCH

TITLE	LABEL AND NUMBER	VG	NM	YR
SITTIN' ON A FENCE/Baby I Want You	(MGM 13530)	5.00	20.00	68

21 JUMP STREET
(Television Series)
See Holly Robinson (*21 Jump Street*)

TWIGGY
(Model/Actress)

TITLE	LABEL AND NUMBER	VG	NM	YR
OVER AND OVER/When I Think Of You	(Capitol 5903)	3.75	15.00	67

TWILLEY, DWIGHT

TITLE	LABEL AND NUMBER	VG	NM	YR
GIRLS/To Get To You	(EMI America B-8196)	1.00	4.00	84
LITTLE BIT OF LOVE/Max Dog Theme	(EMI America B-8206)	1.00	4.00	84
WHY YOU WANNA BREAK MY HEART/Chilli D's Theme (Instrumental)	(EMI America B-8235)	1.25	5.00	84
(From the motion picture *Body Rock*)				
SEXUAL/Wild Dogs	(CBS Associated ZS4-06050)	.75	3.00	86
Also see Dwight Twilley Band				

TWILLEY, DWIGHT, BAND

TITLE	LABEL AND NUMBER	VG	NM	YR
I'M ON FIRE	(Shelter 40380)	2.00	8.00	75
YOU WERE SO WARM	(Shelter 40450)	2.00	8.00	75
COULD BE LOVE	(Shelter 62003)	1.50	6.00	76
TWILLEY DON'T MIND	(Arista 0278)	1.50	6.00	77
Also see Phil Seymour, the Textones (Phil Seymour), Dwight Twilley				

TWINKLE

TITLE	LABEL AND NUMBER	VG	NM	YR
TERRY	(Tollie 9040)	10.00	40.00	65
(Promotional issue only)				

TWINS, THE

TITLE	LABEL AND NUMBER	VG	NM	YR
JO-ANN'S SISTER/Who Knows The Secret	(RCA Victor 47-7235)	5.00	20.00	58

TWISTED SISTER

TITLE	LABEL AND NUMBER	VG	NM	YR
WE'RE NOT GONNA TAKE IT/You Can't Stop Rock 'N' Roll	(Atlantic 7-89641)	.75	3.00	84
I WANNA ROCK/The Kids Are Back	(Atlantic 7-89617)	.75	3.00	84
LEADER OF THE PACK/I Wanna Rock	(Atlantic 7-89478)	.75	3.00	85
YOU WANT WHAT WE GOT/Shoot 'Em Down	(Atlantic 7-89445)	.75	3.00	86
HOT LOVE/Tonight	(Atlantic 7-89215)	.75	3.00	87
Also see Hear 'N Aid				

TWITTY, CONWAY

TITLE	LABEL AND NUMBER	VG	NM	YR
WHAT AM I LIVING FOR/The Hurt In My Heart	(MGM K12886)	6.25	25.00	60
IS A BLUE BIRD BLUE/She's Mine	(MGM K12911)	6.25	25.00	60
C'EST SI BON (IT'S SO GOOD)/Don't You Dare Let Me Down	(MGM K12969)	6.25	25.00	60

		VG	NM	YR
THE NEXT KISS (IS THE LAST GOODBYE)/Man Alone .... (MGM K12998)		6.25	25.00	61
IT'S DRIVIN' ME WILD/Sweet Sorrow .... (MGM K13034)		5.00	20.00	61
THE CLOWN/The Boy Next Door .... (Elektra 47302)		1.25	5.00	82
THE ROSE/It's Only Make Believe .... (Elektra 7-69854)		1.25	5.00	82
WHITE CHRISTMAS .... (Warner Bros. 29129-7)		1.00	4.00	86

2 MEN AND A DRUM MACHINE
See the Wee Papa Girl Rappers

TWO OF A KIND
(Motion Picture)
See Olivia Newton-John (Livin' In Desperate Times, Twist Of Fate)

2010
(Motion Picture)
See Andy Summers (2010)

TYLER, BONNIE

		VG	NM	YR
IF I SING YOU A LOVE SONG/Heaven .... (RCA PB-11349)		1.50	6.00	78
TAKE ME BACK/Getting So Excited .... (Columbia 38-04246)		1.00	4.00	83
TAKE ME BACK/Take Me Back (Edit) .... (Columbia 38-04246)		1.25	5.00	83
(Promotional issue, *Demonstration Not For Sale* printed on sleeve)				
HOLDING OUT FOR A HERO .... (Columbia 38-04370)		1.00	4.00	84
(From the motion picture *Footloose*)				
HOLDING OUT FOR A HERO .... (Columbia 38-04370)		1.25	5.00	84
(Promotional issue, *Demonstration Only–Not For Sale* printed on sleeve. From the motion picture *Footloose*)				
HERE SHE COMES .... (Columbia 38-04548)		1.00	4.00	84
(From the motion picture *Metropolis*)				
HERE SHE COMES .... (Columbia 38-04548)		1.25	5.00	84
(Promotional issue, *Demonstration Only Not For Sale* printed on sleeve. From the motion picture *Metropolis*)				
IF YOU WERE A WOMAN (AND I WAS A MAN)/Under Suspicion .... (Columbia 38-05839)		1.00	4.00	86
IF YOU WERE A WOMAN (AND I WAS A MAN) .... (Columbia 38-05839)		1.25	5.00	86
(Promotional issue, *Demonstration Not For Sale* printed on sleeve)				

TYMES, THE

		VG	NM	YR
SO MUCH IN LOVE/Roscoe James McCain .... (Parkway 871)		3.75	15.00	63
WONDERFUL! WONDERFUL!/Come With Me To The Sea .... (Parkway 884)		3.75	15.00	63
SOMEWHERE/View From My Window .... (Parkway 891)		3.75	15.00	63
TO EACH HIS OWN/Wonderland Of Love .... (Parkway 908)		3.75	15.00	64
THE MAGIC OF OUR SUMMER LOVE/With All My Heart .... (Parkway 919)		3.75	15.00	64
HERE SHE COMES/Malibu .... (Parkway 924)		3.75	15.00	64

TYRONE A'SAURUS AND HIS CRO-MAGNONS

		VG	NM	YR
THE MONSTER TWIST .... (Warner Bros. 5305)		3.75	15.00	62

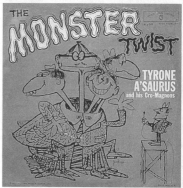

U

UB40

		VG	NM	YR
PLEASE DON'T MAKE ME CRY/Food For Thought (Live Version) .... (A&M 2630)		.75	3.00	84
I GOT YOU BABE/Nkomo A Go Go .... (A&M 2758)		.75	3.00	84
(Brown background, shown as by UB40 With Chrissie Hynde)				
I GOT YOU BABE/Nkomo A Go Go .... (A&M 2758)		.75	3.00	84
(Green background, shown as by UB40 With Chrissie Hynde)				
DON'T BREAK MY HEART (Specially Remixed Version)/Mek Ya Rok .... (A&M 2792)		.75	3.00	85
RAT IN MI KITCHEN/Rat In Mi Kitchen (Dub Version) .... (A&M 2898)		.75	3.00	86
SING OUR OWN SONG/Sing Our Own Song (Dub Version) .... (A&M 2858)		.75	3.00	86
(Back credits guest vocal to Mo Birch)				
Also see Afrika Bambaataa and Family (Reckless)				

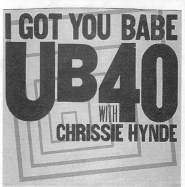

UFO

		VG	NM	YR
TOO HOT TO HANDLE .... (Chrysalis 2157)		1.50	6.00	77
(Originally issued with red vinyl)				
CHERRY .... (Chrysalis 2239)		1.50	6.00	78

ULLMAN, TRACEY
(Actress/Comedienne)

		VG	NM	YR
THEY DON'T KNOW .... (MCA 52347)		1.00	4.00	83
BREAK-A-WAY .... (MCA 52385)		1.00	4.00	83

ULMER, JAMES BLOOD

		VG	NM	YR
WHERE DID ALL THE GIRLS COME FROM/Night Lover .... (Columbia 7-1358)		1.00	4.00	81
(Promotional issue only)				

ULTRAVOX

		VG	NM	YR
DANCING WITH TEARS IN MY EYES/Building .... (Chrysalis VS4 42781)		1.25	5.00	84
Also see Band Aid, Midge Ure				

UNDERCOVER

		VG	NM	YR
CLOSER TO YOU/A Different Kind Of Light .... (Exit/A&S EA-100EP)		.75	3.00	83
(Promotional issue only, flip side shown as by the Seventy Sevens, no song titles listed on sleeve. Issued with a small-hole 33-1/3 RPM.)				

UNDERGROUND LOVERS

		VG	NM	YR
SUPERSTAR/Eastside Stories .... (Polydor 42285 1710 7)		1.00	4.00	95
(Hard cover, promotional issue only, *For promotional use only—not for sale* printed on sleeve)				

UNDERWORLD

		VG	NM	YR
UNDERNEATH THE RADAR .... (Sire 27968-7)		.75	3.00	88
SHOW SOME EMOTION .... (Sire 27788-7)		.75	3.00	88
STAND UP .... (Sire 22852-7)		.75	3.00	89

UNFORGIVEN, THE

		VG	NM	YR
I HEAR THE CALL/The Ghost Dance .... (Elektra 7-69540)		.75	3.00	86

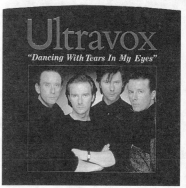

TITLE	LABEL AND NUMBER	VG	NM	YR

UNIFICS
THE BEGINNING OF MY END/Sentimental Man .... (Kapp 957) — 2.00 — 8.00 — 68
IT'S A GROOVY WORLD .... (Kapp 985) — 2.00 — 8.00 — 69

UNION
MAINSTREET U.S.A./Invitation .... (Portrait 12-02149) — 1.00 — 4.00 — 81
(Randy Bachman credited on back as writer and producer)
MAINSTREET U.S.A. .... (Portrait 12-02149) — 1.50 — 6.00 — 81
(Promotional issue, *Demonstration/Not For Sale* printed on back of sleeve. Randy Bachman credited as writer and producer.)

UNIQUES, THE
MERRY CHRISTMAS DARLING/Rockin' Rudolph .... (Demand 2936) — 20.00 — 80.00 — 63

UNIT GLORIA
THE LAST SEVEN DAYS/The Merry Dance .... (Elektra 45678) — 1.50 — 6.00 — 69

UNTOUCHABLES, THE
WHAT'S GONE WRONG/The Lonely Bull .... (Stiff/MCA 52775) — 1.00 — 4.00 — 85
I SPY (FOR THE F.B.I.) .... (Stiff/MCA 52725) — 1.00 — 4.00 — 85
FREAK IN THE STREET .... (Stiff/MCA 52988) — 1.00 — 4.00 — 87

UNTOUCHABLES, THE
(Television Series)
See Nelson Riddle

UP THE SANDBOX
(Motion Picture)
See Barbra Streisand (If I Close My Eyes)

URBAN COWBOY
(Motion Picture)
See Jimmy Buffett (Hello Texas), Bonnie Raitt (Don't It Make Ya Wanna Dance), Joe Walsh (All Night Long)

URE, MIDGE
IF I WAS/Piano .... (Chrysalis VS4 42905) — .75 — 3.00 — 85
DEAR GOD/Music #1 .... (Chrysalis VS4 43319) — .75 — 3.00 — 88
Also see Ultravox

URGENT
RUNNING BACK/Dedicated To Love .... (Manhattan B-50005) — .75 — 3.00 — 85

URGE OVERKILL
WICHITA LINEMAN/Head On .... (Touch N Go 27) — 3.00 — 12.00 — 87
TICKET TO L.A./(I'm On A) Drunk .... (Touch N Go 55) — 1.25 — 5.00 — 90
(Some copies were stamped with a signature on the back which would double or possibly triple the value)
NOW THAT'S THE BARCLORDS/What's This Generation Coming To? .... (Sub Pop 109) — 2.00 — 8.00 — 91
(Limited edition of 5,000 with yellow vinyl. Produced in Germany and distributed in the U.S.)

URIAH HEEP
THAT'S THE WAY THAT IT IS/Son Of A Bitch .... (Mercury 76177) — 1.25 — 5.00 — 82
Also see Toe Fat

U.S.A. FOR AFRICA
WE ARE THE WORLD .... (Columbia US7-04839) — 1.00 — 4.00 — 85
WE ARE THE WORLD .... (Columbia US7-04839) — 1.50 — 6.00 — 85
(Promotional issue, *Demonstration Only–Not For Sale* printed on sleeve)
Also see Dan Aykroyd, Harry Belafonte, Lindsey Buckingham, Kim Carnes, Ray Charles, Bob Dylan, Bob Geldof, Daryl Hall & John Oates, James Ingram, the Jacksons (Jackie Jackson, Marlon Jackson, Michael Jackson, Randy Jackson, Tito Jackson), La Toya Jackson, Michael Jackson, Al Jarreau, Waylon Jennings, Billy Joel, Quincy Jones, Cyndi Lauper, Huey Lewis & the News, Kenny Loggins, Bette Midler, Willie Nelson, Jeffrey Osborne, Steve Perry, Pointer Sisters, Lionel Richie, Smokey Robinson, Kenny Rogers, Diana Ross, Sheila E., Paul Simon, Bruce Springsteen, Tina Turner, Voices Of America, Dionne Warwick, Stevie Wonder

UTOPIA
SALLY BAD .... (Fortune 568) — 2.50 — 10.00 — 63

UTOPIA
CRYBABY/Winston Smith Takes It On The Jaw .... (Passport/Utopia 7923) — 1.00 — 4.00 — 84
Also see Nazz (Todd Rundgren), Todd Rundgren, Patti Smith (Kasim Sultan), Jim Steinman (The Storm)

U2
I WILL FOLLOW/Out Of Control (Live) .... (Island 49716) — 3.75 — 15.00 — 81
(Top of sleeve is straight cut)
I WILL FOLLOW/Out Of Control (Live) .... (Island 49716) — 3.75 — 15.00 — 81
(Top of sleeve is curved)
I WILL FOLLOW/Out Of Control (Live) .... (Island 49716) — 7.50 — 30.00 — 81
(Promotional only poster sleeve)
I WILL FOLLOW/Boy-Girl .... (Island 49716) — — — — — 81
(This has not been confirmed as a U.S. sleeve, it may be an import only)
TWO HEARTS BEAT AS ONE/Endless Sleep .... (Island 7-99861) — 2.50 — 10.00 — 83
PRIDE (IN THE NAME OF LOVE)/Boomerang 11 .... (Island 7-99704) — 1.25 — 5.00 — 84
(Martin Luther King, Jr. pictured on back)
WITH OR WITHOUT YOU/
Luminous Times (Hold On To Love)/Walk To The Water .... (Island 7-99469) — .75 — 3.00 — 87
WITH OR WITHOUT YOU/
Luminous Times (Hold On To Love)/Walk To The Water .... (Island 7-99469) — 1.00 — 4.00 — 87
(Hard cover)
I STILL HAVEN'T FOUND WHAT I'M LOOKING FOR/
Spanish Eyes/Deep In The Heart .... (Island 7-99430) — .75 — 3.00 — 87
I STILL HAVEN'T FOUND WHAT I'M LOOKING FOR/
Spanish Eyes/Deep In The Heart .... (Island 7-99430) — 1.00 — 4.00 — 87
(Hard cover)
WHERE THE STREETS HAVE NO NAME/Silver And Gold/Sweetest Thing .... (Island 7-99408) — .75 — 3.00 — 87
WHERE THE STREETS HAVE NO NAME/Silver And Gold/Sweetest Thing .... (Island 7-99408) — 1.00 — 4.00 — 87
(Hard cover)
IN GOD'S COUNTRY/Bullet The Blue Sky/Running To Stand Still .... (Island 7-99385) — .75 — 3.00 — 87
IN GOD'S COUNTRY/Bullet The Blue Sky/Running To Stand Still .... (Island 7-99385) — 1.00 — 4.00 — 87
(Hard cover)

ANGEL OF HARLEM/A Room At The Heartbreak Hotel .... (Island 7-99254) .75 3.00 88
  (Billie Holiday pictured on back.)
ANGEL OF HARLEM/A Room At The Heartbreak Hotel .... (Island 7-99254) 1.00 4.00 88
  (Hard cover; Billie Holiday pictured on back.)
DESIRE/Hallelujah Here She Comes .... (Island 7-99250) .75 3.00 88
DESIRE/Hallelujah Here She Comes .... (Island 7-99250) 1.25 5.00 88
  (Hard cover gatefold)
WHEN LOVE COMES TO TOWN/Dancing Barefoot .... (Island 7-99225) .75 3.00 89
  (Shown as by U2 With BB King)
WHEN LOVE COMES TO TOWN/Dancing Barefoot .... (Island 7-99225) 1.00 4.00 89
  (Hard cover, shown as by U2 With BB King)
ALL I WANT IS YOU/Unchained Melody .... (Island 7-99199) .75 3.00 89
ALL I WANT IS YOU/Unchained Melody .... (Island 7-99199) 1.00 4.00 89
  (Hard cover)
STAY (FARAWAY, SO CLOSE!)/I've Got You Under My Skin .... (Island/Capitol 422-858 076-7) 1.00 4.00 93
  (I've Got You Under My Skin shown as by Frank Sinatra with Bono. Both songs listed as the a-side.)
  Also see Band Aid, Roy Orbison (She's A Mystery To Me)

VAGRANTS, THE
I CAN'T MAKE A FRIEND/Young Blues .... (Vanguard 35038) 15.00 60.00 66

VALE, JERRY
THE LIGHTS OF ROME .... (Columbia 4-42994) 2.00 8.00 64
HAVE YOU LOOKED INTO YOUR HEART .... (Columbia 4-43181) 2.00 8.00 64
  (Promotional issue only issued with red vinyl)
SANTA MOUSE/Silent Night, Holy Night .... (Columbia 4-44280) 2.00 8.00 67

VALENS, RITCHIE
THAT'S MY LITTLE SUZIE/In A Turkish Town .... (Del-Fi 4114) 18.75 75.00 59
LITTLE GIRL/We Belong Together .... (Del-Fi 4117) 18.75 75.00 59
  (Add $15 if the Concerning This Record insert is included, Limited Valens Memorial Series label)
STAY BESIDE ME/Big Baby Blues .... (Del-Fi 4128) 12.50 50.00 60
(THE ORIGINAL) DONNA/La Bamba .... (Kasey 7040) 5.00 20.00 60s

VALENTINE, GARY
THE FIRST ONE/Tomorrow Belongs To You .... (Beat 001) 1.50 6.00 78

VALENTINE, SCOTT
(Actor)
  See Intimate Strangers (Let Go)

VALERY, DANA
I'D LOVE YOU TO LOVE ME/I Never Had It So Good .... (Phantom 10316) 1.25 5.00 75

VALI, GUS
THEME FROM PHAEDRA .... (United Artists 522) 1.50 6.00 62
  (From the motion picture Phaedra)

VALINO, JOE
LEGEND OF THE LOST/Declaration Of Love .... (United Artists 101) 7.50 30.00 57

VALJEAN
THEME FROM BEN CASEY/Theme From Dr. Kildare .... (Carlton 573) 2.50 10.00 62
  (A-side from the television series Ben Casey, b-side from the television series Dr. Kildare)
TILL THERE WAS YOU/The Eighteenth Variation .... (Carlton 576) 2.50 10.00 62

VALLEY, JIM "HARPO"
TRY, TRY, TRY/Invitation .... (Dunhill 4096) 3.00 12.00 67
  Also see Paul Revere and the Raiders

VALLI, FRANKIE
THE PROUD ONE .... (Philips 40407) 3.00 12.00 66
CAN'T TAKE MY EYES OFF YOU .... (Philips 40446) 3.00 12.00 67
I MAKE A FOOL OF MYSELF .... (Philips 40484) 3.00 12.00 67
TO GIVE (THE REASON I LIVE) .... (Philips 40510) 3.00 12.00 67
THE GIRL I'LL NEVER KNOW .... (Philips 40622) 3.00 12.00 69
CAN'T SAY NO TO YOU .... (Capitol B-5115) 1.25 5.00 82
  (Shown as by Frankie Valli and Cheryl Ladd)
  Also see the 4 Seasons

VALLI, JUNE
GUESS THINGS HAPPEN THAT WAY/Tell Him For Me .... (Mercury 71750) 2.00 8.00 61

VANDALS, THE
IT'S LIKE NOW BABY/Wet And Wild .... (Golden Gate 0011) 3.75 15.00 66

VANDENBERG
FRIDAY NIGHT/I'm On Fire .... (Atco 7-99792) .75 3.00 84

VAN DOREN, MAMIE
(Actress)
  See Louis Armstrong (The Beat Generation), Jerry Lee Lewis (High School Confidential)

VANDROSS, LUTHER
I'LL LET YOU SLIDE/I'll Let You Slide (Instrumental) .... (Epic 34-04231) .75 3.00 83
'TIL MY BABY COMES HOME/'Til My Baby Comes Home (Instrumental Version) (Epic 34-04760) .75 3.00 83
  (Organ solo by Billy Preston credited on back)
IT'S OVER NOW .... (Epic 34-04944) .75 3.00 85
GIVE ME THE REASON .... (Epic 34-06129) .75 3.00 86
  (From the motion picture Ruthless People)
GIVE ME THE REASON .... (Epic 34-06129) 1.00 4.00 86
  (Promotional issue, Demonstration Only–Not For Sale printed on sleeve. From the motion picture Ruthless People.)

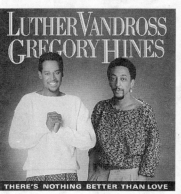

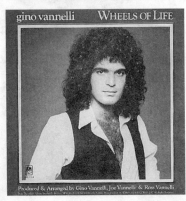

TITLE	LABEL AND NUMBER	VG	NM	YR
STOP TO LOVE/Stop To Love (Instrumental)	(Epic 34-06523)	.75	3.00	86
STOP TO LOVE	(Epic 34-06523)	1.00	4.00	86
(Promotional issue, *Demonstration Not For Sale* printed on sleeve)				
THERE'S NOTHING BETTER THAN LOVE/				
There's Nothing Better Than Love (Instrumental)	(Epic 34-06978)	.75	3.00	87
(Shown as by Luther Vandross and Gregory Hines)				
THERE'S NOTHING BETTER THAN LOVE	(Epic 34-06978)	1.00	4.00	86
(Promotional issue, *Demonstration Not For Sale* printed on sleeve. Shown as by Luther Vandross and Gregory Hines.)				

VAN DYKE, DICK
(Comic Actor)

TITLE	LABEL AND NUMBER	VG	NM	YR
THREE WHEELS ON MY WAGON/Underwater Wonderland	(Jamie 1256)	6.25	25.00	61
SUPER-CALI-FRAGIL-ISTIC-EXPI-ALI-DOCIOUS/A Spoonful Of Sugar	(Buena Vista F-434)	3.00	12.00	65
(A-side shown as by Julie Andrews, Dick Van Dyke, and the Pearlies. From the motion picture *Mary Poppins*.)				
CHIM CHIM CHEREE/Step In Time	(Buena Vista F-441)	3.00	12.00	65
(From the motion picture *Mary Poppins*)				

VAN DYKE, LEROY

TITLE	LABEL AND NUMBER	VG	NM	YR
NIGHT PEOPLE	(Mercury 72232)	2.00	8.00	64

VAN EATON, LON & DERREK

TITLE	LABEL AND NUMBER	VG	NM	YR
SWEET MUSIC/Song Of Songs	(Apple 1845)	2.50	10.00	72
WHO DO YOU OUT DO	(A&M 1662)	1.25	5.00	75
(Record shown as by Lon & Derrek)				

VANGELIS

TITLE	LABEL AND NUMBER	VG	NM	YR
MAIN THEME/Eric's Theme	(Polydor 2189)	1.00	4.00	81
(From the motion picture *Chariots Of Fire*)				

VAN HALEN

TITLE	LABEL AND NUMBER	VG	NM	YR
RUNNIN' WITH THE DEVIL	(Warner Bros. 8556)	6.25	25.00	78
DANCE THE NIGHT AWAY	(Warner Bros. 8823)	3.00	12.00	79
SO THIS IS LOVE?/Hear About It Later	(Warner Bros. 49751)	2.00	8.00	81
PRETTY WOMAN/Happy Trails	(Warner Bros. 50003)	1.50	6.00	82
(First printing)				
(OH) PRETTY WOMAN/Happy Trails	(Warner Bros. 50003)	1.00	4.00	82
(Second printing with revised a-side title)				
JUMP/House Of Pain	(Warner Bros. 29384-7)	.75	3.00	83
I'LL WAIT	(Warner Bros. 29307-7)	.75	3.00	84
PANAMA	(Warner Bros. 29250-7)	1.00	4.00	84
HOT FOR TEACHER	(Warner Bros. 29199-7)	1.00	4.00	84
HOT FOR TEACHER	(Warner Bros. 29199-7)	1.50	6.00	84
(Clear plastic double pocket gatefold sleeve with folded insert)				
WHY CAN'T THIS BE LOVE	(Warner Bros. 28740-7)	.75	3.00	86
LOVE WALKS IN	(Warner Bros. 28626-7)	.75	3.00	86
BEST OF BOTH WORLDS/Best Of Both Worlds (Live)	(Warner Bros. 28505-7)	.75	3.00	86
BLACK AND BLUE/A Apolitical Blues	(Warner Bros. 27891-7)	.75	3.00	88
WHEN IT'S LOVE	(Warner Bros. 27827-7)	.75	3.00	88
FINISH WHAT YA STARTED	(Warner Bros. 27746-7)	.75	3.00	88
Also see Sammy Hagar, Brian May & Friends (Edward Van Halen), David Lee Roth				

VANILLA FUDGE

TITLE	LABEL AND NUMBER	VG	NM	YR
THAT'S WHAT MAKES A MAN/The Spell That Comes After	(Atco EP 4527)	5.00	20.00	68
(Promotional issue only)				
Also see King Kobra (Carmen Appice)				

VANITY

TITLE	LABEL AND NUMBER	VG	NM	YR
PRETTY MESS	(Motown 1752MF)	1.00	4.00	84
MECHANICAL EMOTION	(Motown 1767MF)	.75	3.00	84
(Credit on front reads *Background: Morris Day*)				
MECHANICAL EMOTION	(Motown 1767MF)	1.00	4.00	84
(Promotional issue, *For Promotional Use Only/Not For Sale* printed on sleeve. Credit on front reads *Background: Morris Day*.)				
UNDER THE INFLUENCE/Wild Animal	(Motown 1833MF)	.75	3.00	86
UNDER THE INFLUENCE	(Motown 1833MF)	1.00	4.00	86
(Promotional issue, *For Promotional Use Only/Not For Sale* printed on sleeve)				
ANIMALS/Gun Shy	(Motown 1848MF)	.75	3.00	86
ANIMALS	(Motown 1848MF)	1.00	4.00	86
(Promotional issue, *For Promotional Use Only/Not For Sale* printed on sleeve)				
Also see Pointer Sisters (*He Turned Me Out*), Vanity 6				

VANITY 6

TITLE	LABEL AND NUMBER	VG	NM	YR
HE'S SO DULL/Make-Up	(Warner Bros. 29955-7)	1.25	5.00	82
Also see Apollonia 6 (Brenda Bennett, Susan Moonsie), Vanity				

VANNELLI, GINO

TITLE	LABEL AND NUMBER	VG	NM	YR
HOLLYWOOD HOLIDAY/	(A&M 1449)	1.50	6.00	73
POWERFUL PEOPLE/Lady	(A&M 1652)	1.50	6.00	74
LOVE OF MY LIFE/Omens Of Love	(A&M 1861)	1.25	5.00	76
I JUST WANNA STOP/The Surest Things Can Change	(A&M 2072)	1.25	5.00	78
WHEELS OF LIFE/Mardi Gras	(A&M 2114)	1.25	5.00	78
(Poster sleeve)				
LIVING INSIDE MYSELF/Stay With Me	(Arista 0588)	1.25	5.00	81
(Top of sleeve curved)				
LIVING INSIDE MYSELF/Stay With Me	(Arista 0588)	1.25	5.00	81
(Top of sleeve straight cut)				
NIGHTWALKER/	(Arista 0613)	1.25	5.00	81
THE LONGER YOU WAIT/Bandito	(Arista 0664)	1.25	5.00	82
BLACK CARS/Imagination	(HME/PRA WS4-04889)	1.00	4.00	84
HURTS TO BE IN LOVE/Here She Comes	(HME/CBS Associated ZS4-05586)	.75	3.00	85
HURTS TO BE IN LOVE	(HME/CBS Associated ZS4-05586)	1.00	4.00	85
(Promotional issue, *Demonstration Only–Not For Sale* printed on sleeve)				

	VG	NM	YR
IN THE NAME OF MONEY/ .... (CBS Associated ZS4-06663)	.75	3.00	87
IN THE NAME OF MONEY .... (CBS Associated ZS4-06663)	1.00	4.00	87

(Promotional issue, *Demonstration Only–Not For Sale* printed on sleeve)

	VG	NM	YR
WILD HORSES/ .... (CBS Associated ZS4-06699)	.75	3.00	87
WILD HORSES .... (CBS Associated ZS4-06699)	1.00	4.00	87

(Promotional issue, *Demonstration Only–Not For Sale* printed on sleeve)

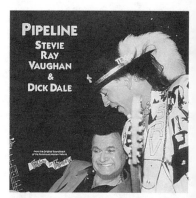

VAN-ZANT

	VG	NM	YR
YOU'VE GOT TO BELIEVE IN LOVE .... (Geffen/Network 29037-7)	1.00	4.00	85

(Group led by Johnny Van Zant, the younger brother of Ronnie Van Zant of Lynyrd Skynyrd and Donnie Van Zant of 38 Special

VARDAS, PETER

	VG	NM	YR
HE THREW A STONE/Checkerboard Love .... (Phase 867)	2.00	8.00	60s

VARGAS, ALBERTO
(Pinup Artist)

See the Cars (*It's All I Can Do*), Bernadette Peters (*Maybe My Baby Will, Gee Whiz*)

VAUGHAN, SARAH

	VG	NM	YR
SOLE, SOLE, SOLE .... (Mercury 72300)	2.00	8.00	65
FRANK AND SARAH AND NAT AND VIC SALUTE HAROLD ADAMSON .... (Harold Adamson Music Co. 100)	2.50	10.00	73

(Shown as by Frank Sinatra, Sarah Vaughan, Nat King Cole, and Vic Damone)

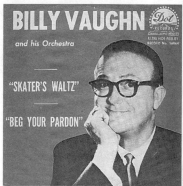

VAUGHAN, STEVIE RAY

	VG	NM	YR
PIPELINE .... (Columbia 38-07340)	1.50	6.00	87

(Shown as by Stevie Ray Vaughan & Dick Dale, both pictured. From the motion picture *Back To The Beach*.)

	VG	NM	YR
PIPELINE .... (Columbia 38-07340)	2.00	8.00	87

(Promotional issue, *Demonstration Only–Not For Sale* printed on sleeve. Shown as by Stevie Ray Vaughan & Dick Dale, both pictured. From the motion picture *Back To The Beach*.)

VAUGHN, BILLY

	VG	NM	YR
CIMARRON/You're My Baby Doll .... (Dot 15836)	1.50	6.00	58

(Back of sleeve lists discography of single records, extended play albums, and long play albums)

	VG	NM	YR
HAWAIIAN WAR CHANT/ .... (Dot 15900)	1.50	6.00	59
TRADE WINDS/ .... (Dot 15906)	1.50	6.00	59
CARNIVAL IN PARIS/Wabash Blues .... (Dot 15976)	1.50	6.00	59
SKATER'S WALTZ/Beg Your Pardon .... (Dot 16064)	1.50	6.00	60

(Shown as by Billy Vaughan and his Orchestra)

	VG	NM	YR
THE LAST SAFARI/ .... (Dot 17045)	1.50	6.00	67

Also see Walter Brennan (*Dutchman's Gold*)

VEE, BOBBY

	VG	NM	YR
DEVIL OR ANGEL/Since I Met You Baby .... (Liberty 55270)	3.75	15.00	60
RUBBER BALL/Everyday .... (Liberty 55287)	3.75	15.00	60
STAYIN' IN/More Than I Can Say .... (Liberty 55296)	3.75	15.00	61
HOW MANY TEARS/Baby Face .... (Liberty 55325)	3.75	15.00	61
PLEASE DON'T ASK ABOUT BARBARA/I Can't Say Goodbye .... (Liberty 55419)	3.75	15.00	62
PUNISH HER/Someday .... (Liberty 55479)	5.00	20.00	62

(B-side shown as by Bobby Vee with the Crickets)

	VG	NM	YR
CHARMS/Bobby Tomorrow .... (Liberty 55530)	3.00	12.00	63
BE TRUE TO YOURSELF/A Letter From Betty .... (Liberty 55581)	3.00	12.00	63
STRANGER IN YOUR ARMS/1963 .... (Liberty 55654)	3.00	12.00	64
MAYBE JUST TODAY/You're A Big Girl Now .... (Liberty 56014)	2.50	10.00	68

(Shown as by Bobby Vee and the Strangers)

VEGA, SUZANNE

	VG	NM	YR
LUKA/Night Vision .... (A&M 2937)	1.00	4.00	87
LUKA (VERSION EN ESPAÑOL)/Luka (English Version) .... (A&M 35084)	1.50	6.00	87
SOLITUDE STANDING/Tom's Diner .... (A&M 2960)	1.00	4.00	87
GYPSY/Left Of Center .... (A&M 2988)	7.50	30.00	87

(Promotional issue only)
Also see the Smithereens (*In A Lonely Place*)

VEGA, TATA

	VG	NM	YR
MISS CELIE'S BLUES (SISTER) .... (Qwest 28754-7)	.75	3.00	86

(From the motion picture *The Color Purple*)

VELA, ROSIE

	VG	NM	YR
MAGIC SMILE/2nd Emotion .... (A&M 2856)	.75	3.00	86
INTERLUDE/Taxi .... (A&M 2886)	.75	3.00	86

VELOCITY GIRL

	VG	NM	YR
I DON'T CARE IF YOU GO/Always .... (Slumberland 004)	3.75	15.00	90
MY FORGOTTEN FAVORITE/Why Should I Be Nice To You .... (Slumberland 010)	2.50	10.00	91
WARM/CRAWL/Left Behind .... (Sub Pop 137)	2.00	8.00	92

(Split single, limited edition of 4,000 issued with red vinyl. *Left Behind* shown as by Tsunami.)

	VG	NM	YR
CRAZY TOWN/Creepy .... (Sub Pop 137)	1.25	5.00	92

(The first 2,000 issued with green vinyl)

	VG	NM	YR
MERRY CHRISTMAS, I LOVE YOU/Could Have Been Christmas .... (Simple Machines 14)	1.25	5.00	93

(Front of sleeve reads *Seasons Greetings from Tsunami and Velocity Girl*. Both songs listed as the a-side, *Could Have Been Christmas* shown as by Tsunami.)

	VG	NM	YR
SORRY AGAIN/Marzipan .... (Sub Pop 257)	.75	3.00	94

(Hard cover)

	VG	NM	YR
NOTHING/Anatomy Of A Gutless Wonder .... (Sub Pop 341)	.50	2.00	96

EXTENDED PLAYS

	VG	NM	YR
CRAWL .... (Sub Pop 171)	2.50	10.00	92

(Limited edition of 3,000 copies issued with green vinyl and insert. Promotional item given away to *Sassy* magazine readers on request. Also includes one song each by Beat Happening, Codeine, and Sebadoh.)

VELORE & DOUBLE-O

	VG	NM	YR
YOUR UGLY .... (Virgin 7-99421)	.75	3.00	87

VELVETEENS

	VG	NM	YR
I FEEL SORRY FOR YOU BABY/Ching Bam Bah .... (Golden Artists 614)	3.00	12.00	67

TITLE	LABEL AND NUMBER	VG	NM	YR

VELVET MONKEYS
COLORS PART 1/Colors Part 2 .... (Bona Fide 7002)		1.50	6.00	85
ROCK THE NATION/Why Don't We Do It In The Road? .... (Sub Pop 102)		1.25	5.00	91

(Limited edition of 7,000 with the first 4,000 on clear vinyl and the remaining 3,000 on black)

Also see Backbeat Band (Thurston Moore), Dinosaur Jr (J Mascis), Gumball (Don Fleming, Jay Spiegel), Thurston Moore, Sonic Youth (Thurston Moore), Ciccone Youth (Thurston Moore), Mike Watt (J Mascis on *Big Train* and *E-Ticket Ride*)

VELVET UNDERGROUND, THE
ALL TOMORROW'S PARTIES/I'll Be Your Mirror .... (Verve 10427)		1000.00	4000.00	66

(Promotional issue only, shown as by Nico and the Velvet Underground. There has been only one reported sale, of $4,000 in near mint condition, in 1992. It is difficult to estimate what a similar copy would sell for, if one ever surfaces again, but $5,000-6,000 would not be surprising.)

EXTENDED PLAYS
VELVET UNDERGROUND RADIO SPOTS .... (MGM VU-1)		250.00	1000.00	66

(Promotional issue only)

Also see John Cale, Lou Reed, Maureen Tucker

VENETIANS, THE
SO MUCH FOR LOVE .... (Chrysalis VS4 43056)		.75	3.00	87
BITTER TEARS/Heartbeat .... (Chrysalis VS4 43242)		.75	3.00	88

VENTURES, THE
PERFIDIA/No Trespassing .... (Dolton 28)		7.50	30.00	60
WALK—DON'T RUN '64/The Cruel Sea .... (Dolton 96)		5.00	20.00	64
SLAUGHTER ON 10TH AVENUE/Rap City .... (Dolton 300)		5.00	20.00	64
BLUE STAR/Comin' Home Baby .... (Dolton 320)		3.75	15.00	66
GREEN HORNET THEME/Fuzzy And Wild .... (Dolton 323)		3.75	15.00	66
PENETRATION/Wild Thing .... (Dolton 325)		3.75	15.00	66
INDIAN SUN/Squaw Man .... (United Artists 50800)		2.50	10.00	70
THE YOUNG AND THE RESTLESS/Eloise .... (United Artists 369)		2.00	8.00	74
THE YOUNG AND THE RESTLESS/Fur Elise .... (United Artists 369)		2.00	8.00	74
SURFIN' AND SPYIN'/Showdown At Newport .... (Tridex 501)		1.25	5.00	81

(A-side shown as by the Ventures with Charlotte Caffey and Jane Wiedlin)

VERA, BILLY, & THE BEATERS
THE BIBLE SALESMAN/Are You Coming To My Party? .... (Atlantic 45-2628)		2.50	10.00	69

(Shown as by Billy Vera)
I CAN TAKE CARE OF MYSELF .... (Alfa 7002)		2.00	8.00	81

(Poster sleeve, promotional issue only. Shown as by Billy & The Beaters.)
AT THIS MOMENT/Someone Will School You, Someone Will Cool You .... (Alfa 7005)		1.50	6.00	81

(Shown as by Billy & The Beaters)
I CAN TAKE CARE OF MYSELF/Millie, Make Some Chili .... (Rhino 74404)		1.00	4.00	87
LET YOU GET AWAY/Anybody Seen Her? .... (Rhino 74405)		1.00	4.00	87

(From the motion picture *Blind Date*. Bruce Willis and Kim Basinger pictured on the front, Billy Vera & the Beaters on the back.)
LET YOU GET AWAY/Anybody Seen Her? .... (Rhino 74405)		1.00	4.00	87

(Hard cover, from the motion picture *Blind Date*. Bruce Willis and Kim Basinger pictured on the front, Billy Vera & the Beaters on the back.)
BETWEEN LIKE AND LOVE .... (Capitol B-44149)		.75	3.00	88

VERLAINE, TOM
See Neon Boys, Patti Smith (*Hey Joe*). Television released no U.S. sleeves.

VERNE, LARRY
MISTER LIVINGSTON/Roller Coaster .... (Era 3034)		5.00	20.00	60

VESTA
See Vesta Williams

VIBES
(Motion Picture)

See Cyndi Lauper (*Hole In My Heart*)

VIBES, THE
BEAT OF MY HEART/Oh Darlin .... (Starfire 108)		1.25	5.00	80
TELL ME I'M YOUR LOVE/Up On The Mountain .... (Starfire 106)		1.25	5.00	80

(Issued with blue vinyl)

VICTORY AT SEA
(Television Special)

See Robert Russell Bennett (*Beneath The Southern Cross*)

VIDAL, MARIA
BODY ROCK/Do You Know Who I Am .... (EMI America B-8233)		.75	3.00	84

(B-side shown as by Ashford & Simpson. From the motion picture *Body Rock*.)

Also see 3 Speed (b-side of *Once Bitten*)

VIDÉO, MONTE, AND THE CASSETTES
SHOOP-SHOOP, DIDDY-WOP, CUMMA-CUMMA, WANG-DANG/				
Don't Mention My Name .... (Geffen 29494-7)		.75	3.00	83

VIERRA, CHRISTINA
YOU CAN FLOAT IN MY BOAT .... (Warner Bros. 27879-7)		.75	3.00	88

VIEW FROM THE HILL
NO CONVERSATION .... (EMI/Capitol B-44095)		.75	3.00	87

VIEW TO A KILL, A
(Motion Picture)

See Duran Duran (*A View To A Kill*)

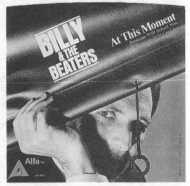

VIGNON, JEAN-PAUL
GOODBYE GOODBYE COQUETTE .... (Philips 40502)		1.50	6.00	69
YOU (TOÍ) (SI)/Let Me Get To Know You .... (Nelson Barry/TK 7900)		1.50	6.00	77

(Farrah Fawcett Majors pictured on the front and Jean-Paul Vignon on the back, titles not listed on sleeve. Record shows a-side by Farrah Fawcett and Jean-Paul Vignon, b-side by Jean-Paul Vignon.)

VILLAGE PEOPLE

IN THE NAVY .... (Casablanca NB 973)	2.00	8.00	79
(Promotional issue only)			
CAN'T STOP THE MUSIC/Milkshake .... (Casablanca NB 2261)	1.50	6.00	80
(From the motion picture Can't Stop The Music, Bruce Jenner, Valerie Perrine, Steve Guttenberg, and Village People pictured)			
5 O'CLOCK IN THE MORNING/Food Fight .... (RCA PB 12258)	1.50	6.00	81

VILLAGE STOMPERS, THE

WASHINGTON SQUARE .... (Epic 5-9617)	2.00	8.00	63
BLUE GRASS .... (Epic 5-9655)	2.00	8.00	64
BROTHER CAN YOU SPARE A DIME .... (Epic 5-9785)	2.00	8.00	65

VILLECHAIZE, HERVÉ

(French actor best known for his role of Tattoo on the television series *Fantasy Island* from 1978-83)

WHY/When A Child Is Born .... (Epic/Cleveland International 19-50947)	1.25	5.00	80
WHY/When A Child Is Born .... (Epic/Cleveland International 19-50947)	1.50	6.00	80
(Promotional issue, *Demonstration: Not For Sale* printed on sleeve. Sleeve lists b-side even though the 45 has *Why* on both sides.)			

VINCENT, GENE

RIGHT NOW/The Night Is So Lonely .... (Capitol F4237)	375.00	1500.00	59

VINCENT, JAN-MICHAEL

(Actor)

See Marvin Hamlisch (*Love Theme*)

VINCENT, VINNIE, INVASION

ANIMAL/Boyz Are Gonna Rock .... (Chrysalis VS7 42447)	1.25	5.00	86
(Promotional issue only titled *Are You Ready To Rock?*, *Promotional* printed on back of sleeve. No song titles listed on sleeve, issued with pink vinyl.)			
ALL SYSTEMS GO SNEAK PEEK MEDLEY .... (Chrysalis VS4 43253)	1.25	5.00	88
(Promotional issue only issued with one-side record)			
Also see Kiss (Vinnie Vincent)			

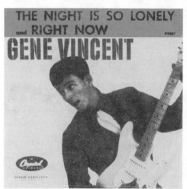

VINE, MARTY

CHERYL .... (Epic 5-9382)	2.00	8.00	60

VINTON, BOBBY

ROSES ARE RED/You And I .... (Epic 5-9509)	2.50	10.00	62
(Vinton looking to the lower right)			
ROSES ARE RED/You And I .... (Epic 5-9509)	2.50	10.00	62
(Vinton looking straight ahead with his chin in his hand)			
RAIN RAIN GO AWAY/Over And Over .... (Epic 5-9532)	2.50	10.00	62
TROUBLE IS MY MIDDLE NAME/Let's Kiss And Make Up .... (Epic 5-9791)	2.50	10.00	62
OVER THE MOUNTAIN/Faded Pictures .... (Epic 5-9577)	2.50	10.00	63
BLUE ON BLUE/These Little Things .... (Epic 5-9593)	2.00	8.00	63
BLUE VELVET/Is There A Place (Where I Can Go) .... (Epic 5-9614)	2.00	8.00	63
THERE! I'VE SAID IT AGAIN/The Girl With The Bow In Her Hair .... (Epic 5-9638)	2.00	8.00	63
MY HEART BELONGS TO ONLY YOU .... (Epic 5-9662)	2.00	8.00	64
TELL ME WHY .... (Epic 5-9687)	2.00	8.00	64
CLINGING VINE .... (Epic 5-9705)	2.00	8.00	64
MR. LONELY .... (Epic 5-9730)	2.00	8.00	64
DEAREST SANTA .... (Epic 5-9741)	2.00	8.00	64
LONG LONELY NIGHTS/Satin .... (Epic 5-9768)	2.00	8.00	65
L-O-N-E-L-Y/Graduation Tears .... (Epic 5-9791)	2.00	8.00	65
THEME FROM HARLOW (LONELY GIRL) .... (Epic 5-9814)	2.00	8.00	65
(From the motion picture *Harlow*, Carroll Baker and Vinton pictured individually)			
CARELESS/Satin Pillows .... (Epic 5-9869)	2.00	8.00	65
DUM-DE-DA .... (Epic 5-10014)	2.00	8.00	66
PETTICOAT WHITE (SUMMER SKY BLUE) .... (Epic 5-10048)	2.00	8.00	66
COMING HOME SOLDIER .... (Epic 5-10090)	2.00	8.00	66
FOR HE'S A JOLLY GOOD FELLOW .... (Epic 5-10136)	2.00	8.00	67
RED ROSES FOR MOM .... (Epic 5-10168)	2.00	8.00	67
PLEASE LOVE ME FOREVER/Miss America .... (Epic 5-10228)	2.00	8.00	67
JUST AS MUCH AS EVER .... (Epic 5-10266)	2.00	8.00	67
TAKE GOOD CARE OF MY BABY .... (Epic 5-10305)	2.00	8.00	68
HALFWAY TO PARADISE .... (Epic 5-10350)	2.00	8.00	68
(Photo of Vinton from 1968)			
HALFWAY TO PARADISE .... (Epic 5-10350)	2.50	10.00	68
(Younger image of Vinton used)			
I LOVE HOW YOU LOVE ME .... (Epic 5-10397)	2.00	8.00	68
TO KNOW YOU IS TO LOVE YOU .... (Epic 5-10461)	2.00	8.00	69
THE DAYS OF SAND AND SHOVELS .... (Epic 5-10485)	2.00	8.00	69
MY ELUSIVE DREAMS .... (Epic 5-10576)	2.00	8.00	70
NO ARMS CAN EVER HOLD YOU .... (Epic 5-10629)	1.50	6.00	70
WHY DON'T THEY UNDERSTAND .... (Epic 5-10651)	1.50	6.00	70
EVERY DAY OF MY LIFE .... (Epic 5-10822)	1.50	6.00	72
SEALED WITH A KISS/All My Life .... (Epic 5-10861)	1.50	6.00	72
BUT I DO .... (Epic 5-10936)	1.50	6.00	72
HE/My First And Only Love .... (Tapestry 003)	1.25	5.00	80
SANTA MUST BE POLISH/Santa Claus Is Coming To Town .... (Tapestry 100)	1.00	4.00	87
BLUE VELVET .... (Epic 34-06537)	2.50	10.00	87
(Hard cover promotional issue only, *Special Souvenir Single For Instore Play* printed on sleeve. From the motion picture *Blue Velvet*, Kyle MacLachlan and Isabella Rossellini pictured.)			

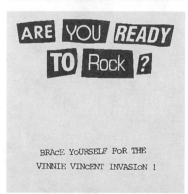

VIRGINIA WOLF

WAITING FOR YOUR LOVE/Take A Chance .... (Atlantic 7-89459)	.75	3.00	86

VISION QUEST

(Motion Picture)

See Journey (*Only The Young*), John Waite (*Change*)

TITLE	LABEL AND NUMBER	VG	NM	YR

VITAMIN Z
BURNING FLAME .... (Geffen 29039-7) | .75 | 3.00 | 85
   Also see Alan Parsons Project (Geoff Barradale)

VIVA LAS VEGAS
(Motion Picture)
   See Elvis Presley (Viva Las Vegas)

VIXEN
EDGE OF A BROKEN HEART/Cruisin' .... (EMI Manhattan B-50141) | 1.00 | 4.00 | 88
EDGE OF A BROKEN HEART/Cruisin' .... (EMI Manhattan B-50141) | 1.25 | 5.00 | 88
   (Poster sleeve)
CRYIN'/Desperate .... (EMI B-50167) | 1.00 | 4.00 | 88
LOVE MADE ME/Hellraisers .... (EMI B-50195) | 1.00 | 4.00 | 89

VOICE OF THE BEEHIVE
I SAY NOTHING/Things You See When you Don't Have Your Gun (Live) .... (London 886 334-7) | 1.25 | 5.00 | 87
DON'T CALL ME BABY/There's A Barbarian In The Back Of My Car .... (London 886 500-7) | 1.25 | 5.00 | 88

VOICES OF AMERICA
HANDS ACROSS AMERICA/We Are The World .... (EMI America B-8319) | 1.00 | 4.00 | 86
   (Basic track credited to members of Toto. Originally issued with a registration slip for the Sunday, May 25, 1986 event.)
   Also see Toto, U.S.A. For Africa

VOICES OF EAST HARLEM
ANGRY/(We Are) New York Lightning .... (Elektra 45775) | 1.25 | 5.00 | 71

VOLLENWEIDER, ANDREAS
FLIGHT FEET/Behind The Gardens, Behind The Wall, Under The Tree... .... (CBS 38-04755) | 1.00 | 4.00 | 84
FLIGHT FEET .... (CBS 38-04755) | 1.25 | 5.00 | 84
   (Promotional issue, For Promotion Only printed on sleeve)
NIGHT FIRE DANCE/The Play Of The Five Balls/The Five Planets .... (CBS 38-06155) | 1.00 | 4.00 | 86

VOODOOIST CORPORATION, THE
   See Deborah Harry (Liar, Liar)

VOX HUMANA
LUNAR TUNES/The Fountain Of Youth .... (Rhino 005) | 1.25 | 5.00 | 77

VOYAGE OF THE ROCK ALIENS
(Motion Picture)
   See Jermaine Jackson (When The Rain Begins To Fall), Pia Zadora (When The Rain Begins To Fall)

VOYAGE TO THE BOTTOM OF THE SEA
(Motion Picture)
   See Frankie Avalon (Voyage To The Bottom Of The Sea)

VOYEUR
KEEP ON LOVIN' YOU/Midnight Dancer .... (MCA 52532) | .75 | 3.00 | 85
PARADISE/Midnight Dancer .... (MCA 52563) | .75 | 3.00 | 85

W

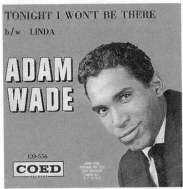

WADE, ADAM
SPEAKING OF HER/Blackout Of The Moon .... (Coed 536) | 2.50 | 10.00 | 60
FOR THE WANT OF YOUR LOVE/Pursuit Of Happiness .... (Coed 539) | 2.50 | 10.00 | 60
GLORIA'S THEME/ .... (Coed 541) | 2.50 | 10.00 | 60
THE WRITING ON THE WALL/Point Of No Return .... (Coed 550) | 2.50 | 10.00 | 61
AS IF I DIDN'T KNOW/Playin' Around .... (Coed 553) | 2.50 | 10.00 | 61
TONIGHT I WON'T BE THERE/Linda .... (Coed 556) | 2.50 | 10.00 | 61
I'M CLIMBIN' (THE WALL)/They Didn't Believe Me .... (Epic 5-9521) | 2.50 | 10.00 | 62
THERE'LL BE NO TEARDROPS TONIGHT/Here Comes The Pain .... (Epic 5-9557) | 2.50 | 10.00 | 62
THEME FROM IRMA LA DOUCE (LOOK AGAIN) .... (Epic 5-9609) | 2.50 | 10.00 | 63

WADE, BRANDON
LETTER FROM A TEENAGE SON .... (Philips 40503) | 1.50 | 6.00 | 68

WAGNER, JACK
ALL I NEED/Tell Him (That You Won't Go) .... (Qwest 29238-7) | .75 | 3.00 | 84
PREMONITION/Lady Of My Heart .... (Qwest 29085-7) | .75 | 3.00 | 84
   (The a-side made it to #101 on the Billboard charts while the b-side rose higher to #76)
TOO YOUNG .... (Qwest 28931-7) | .75 | 3.00 | 85
LOVE CAN TAKE US ALL THE WAY .... (Qwest 28790-7) | .75 | 3.00 | 85
   (Credited on front as Duet With Valerie Carter)
WEATHERMAN SAYS .... (Qwest 28387-7) | .75 | 3.00 | 87
ISLAND FEVER .... (Qwest 28267-7) | .75 | 3.00 | 87

WAGNER, ROBERT
(Actor, married to Natalie Wood, who starred in the television series It Takes A Thief, Switch, and Hart To Hart)
SO YOUNG/Almost Eighteen .... (Liberty 55069) | 7.50 | 30.00 | 57

WAGONEERS
EVERY STEP OF THE WAY .... (A&M 1230) | 1.50 | 6.00 | 88
   (Half sleeve)

WAGONER, PORTER
   See Chet Atkins (Chet's Tune)

WAINRIGHT III, LOUDON
   See Bruce Springsteen (The Circus Song)

WAITE, JOHN
MISSING YOU/For Your Love .... (EMI America B-8212) | .75 | 3.00 | 84
TEARS/Dreamtime/Shake It Up .... (EMI America B-8238) | .75 | 3.00 | 84

		VG	NM	YR
RESTLESS HEART / Euroshima	(EMI America B-8252)	.75	3.00	84
CHANGE / White Heat	(Chrysalis VS4-42606)	.75	3.00	85

(A-side from the motion picture *Vision Quest*, Matthew Modine and Linda Fiorentino pictured on back)

		VG	NM	YR
EVERY STEP OF THE WAY	(EMI America B-8282)	.75	3.00	85
WELCOME TO PARADISE	(EMI America B-8278)	.75	3.00	85
IF ANYBODY HAD A HEART	(EMI America B-8315)	.75	3.00	86

(From the motion picture *"About Last Night..."*)

		VG	NM	YR
THESE TIMES ARE HARD FOR LOVERS / Wild One	(EMI America B-43018)	.75	3.00	87
DON'T LOSE ANY SLEEP (Single Version) / Wild One	(EMI Manhattan B43040)	.75	3.00	87

Also see the Babys

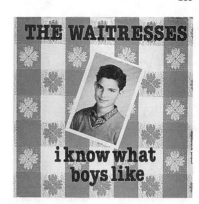

WAITRESSES, THE
		VG	NM	YR
CLONES / Slide	(Clone 006)	2.00	8.00	77

(Front of sleeve reads *Waitresses in "Short Stack"*. *Slide* shown as the a-side on the record label.)

		VG	NM	YR
I KNOW WHAT BOYS LIKE / No Guilt	(Antilles 105)	1.25	5.00	80

(Hard cover. A-side released later the same year on Polydor without a picture sleeve.)
Also see Chris Butler, Tin Huey (Chris Butler)

WAKELING, DAVE
		VG	NM	YR
SHE'S HAVING A BABY / Drummin' Man	(I.R.S. 53238)	.75	3.00	88

(B-side shown as by Topper Headon. A-side from the motion picture *She's Having A Baby*, Kevin Bacon and Elizabeth McGovern pictured on back.)
Also see General Public, the Special AKA, the Specials

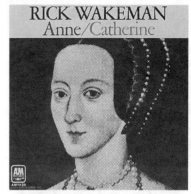

WAKELY, JIMMY
		VG	NM	YR
SLIPPING AROUND	(Shasta 107)	3.75	15.00	58

WAKEMAN, RICK
		VG	NM	YR
ANNE / Catherine	(A&M 1430)	2.50	10.00	73

WALDORF SALAD
		VG	NM	YR
LOOK AT THE CHILDREN	(A&M 1436)	1.50	6.00	73

WALKER, BILLY
		VG	NM	YR
HEART BE CAREFUL	(Columbia 4-42792)	2.00	8.00	63
CROSS THE BRAZOS AT WACO	(Columbia 4-43120)	2.50	10.00	65

(Promotional issue only issued with red vinyl)

		VG	NM	YR
THE OLD FRENCH QUARTER / How Do You Ask	(Monument 45-932)	2.00	8.00	66
CHARLIE'S SHOES	(Columbia 4-44287)	2.00	8.00	67

WALKER, DUB
		VG	NM	YR
FREEDOM MARCH / Battle Hymn Of The Republic	(Domino 908)	12.50	50.00	61

(Single sheet insert, not a true picture sleeve)

WALKER, JIMMY
(Comedian)
		VG	NM	YR
ABBADABBA HONEYMOON	(Buddah 529)	2.00	8.00	76

WALKER, JR., AND THE ALL-STARS
		VG	NM	YR
SHOTGUN / Hot Cha	(Soul 35008)	5.00	20.00	65
HOW SWEET IT IS (TO BE LOVED BY YOU) / Nothing But Soul	(Soul 35024)	3.75	15.00	66

(Shown as by Jr. Walker)

WALKER, TONJA
(Actress)
See the Soaps and Hearts Ensemble

WALKER BROTHERS, THE
		VG	NM	YR
MAKE IT EASY ON YOURSELF / Doin' The Jerk	(Smash 5-2009)	3.00	12.00	65
MY SHIP IS COMIN' IN / You're All Around Me	(Smash 5-2016)	3.00	12.00	65
THE SUN AIN'T GONNA SHINE (ANYMORE) / After The Lights Go Down	(Smash 5-2032)	3.75	15.00	65

Also see Scott Engel

WALK ON THE WILD SIDE
(Motion Picture)
See Brook Benton (*Walk On The Wild Side*)

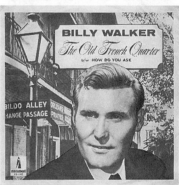

WALK THE MOON
		VG	NM	YR
DADDY'S COMING HOME	(MCA 53173)	.75	3.00	87
SHE FLIES	(MCA 53267)	.75	3.00	87

WALK THIS WAY
		VG	NM	YR
IN MY ROOM	(Mercury 870 249-7)	.75	3.00	88

WALLACE, JERRY
		VG	NM	YR
DIAMOND RING / All My Love Belongs To You	(Challenge 59027)	3.00	12.00	58
LITTLE COCO PALM / Mission Bell Blues	(Challenge 59060)	2.50	10.00	60

WALLEY, DEBORAH
(Actress)
EXTENDED PLAYS
		VG	NM	YR
SUMMER MAGIC / FLITTERIN' / BEAUTIFUL BEULAH / UGLY BUG BALL / On The Front Porch / Pink Of Perfection / Femininity	(Buena Vista 4023)	3.75	15.00	63

(Promotional issue sponsored by Alcoa Wrap. Shown as by Burl Ives, Hayley Mills, Eddie Hodges, and Deborah Walley. From the motion picture *Summer Magic*, Burl Ives and Hayley Mills pictured on front.)

WALL OF VOODOO
		VG	NM	YR
MEXICAN RADIO / Call Of The West	(I.R.S. 9912)	1.00	4.00	82
MEXICAN RADIO	(I.R.S. 70693)	1.25	5.00	82

(Promotional issue only, the specific differences between the stock and promo sleeves are unknown)

		VG	NM	YR
DO IT AGAIN / Back In The Laundromat	(I.R.S. 53136)	1.00	4.00	87

Also see Stan Ridgway

WALSH, DENNIS, AND FRIENDS
		VG	NM	YR
IN THE MORNING / Friends	(Celestial no #)	1.00	4.00	79

(Harvey Gold and Stewart Justin, members of Tin Huey, are among "Friends" credited on sleeve)

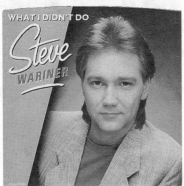

TITLE	LABEL AND NUMBER	VG	NM	YR

WALSH, JOE
ALL NIGHT LONG/Orange Blossom Special .... *(Full Moon/Asylum 46639)* | 1.00 | 4.00 | 80
    (B-side shown as by Gilley's "Urban Cowboy" Band. From the motion picture *Urban Cowboy*.)
WAFFLE STOMP/Things .... *(Full Moon/Asylum 7-69951)* | 1.25 | 5.00 | 82
    (A-side from the motion picture *Fast Times At Ridgemont High*)
SPACE AGE WHIZ KIDS/Theme From Island Weirdos .... *(Full Moon/Warner Bros. 29611-7)* | 1.25 | 5.00 | 83
THE RADIO SONG .... *(Full Moon/Warner Bros. 28304-7)* | 1.00 | 4.00 | 87
    Also see Michael Dinner *(The Promised Land)*, the Eagles (Walsh joined the Eagles in 1976)

WANG CHUNG
DON'T LET GO/There Is A Nation .... *(Geffen 29377-7)* | .75 | 3.00 | 83
DANCE HALL DAYS/Ornamental Elephant .... *(Geffen 29310-7)* | .75 | 3.00 | 83
FIRE IN THE TWILIGHT/The Reggae (Instrumental) .... *(A&M 2728)* | 1.00 | 4.00 | 85
    (B-side shown as by Keith Forsey. From the motion picture *The Breakfast Club*, Emilio Estevez, Molly Ringwald, Judd Nelson, Anthony Michael Hall, and Ally Sheedy pictured.)
TO LIVE AND DIE IN L.A. .... *(Geffen 28891-7)* | .75 | 3.00 | 85
    (From the motion picture *To Live And Die In L.A.*)
EVERYBODY HAVE FUN TONIGHT .... *(Geffen 28562-7)* | .75 | 3.00 | 86
LET'S GO/The World In Which We Live .... *(Geffen 28531-7)* | .75 | 3.00 | 86
HYPNOTIZE ME .... *(Geffen 28359-7)* | .75 | 3.00 | 87
PRAYING TO A NEW GOD .... *(Geffen 22969-7)* | .75 | 3.00 | 89

WAR
SPILL THE WINE/Magic Mountain .... *(MGM 70L 1277)* | 2.50 | 10.00 | 70
    (Shown as by Eric Burdon & War)
SUN OH SON/Lonely Feelin' .... *(United Artists 50746)* | 2.00 | 8.00 | 71
WHY CAN'T WE BE FRIENDS? .... *(United Artists XW-629X)* | 1.50 | 6.00 | 75
LOW RIDER .... *(United Artists XW706-Y)* | 1.50 | 6.00 | 75
GALAXY/Galaxy Part II .... *(MCA 40820)* | 1.25 | 5.00 | 77
HEY SENORITA/Sweet Fighting Lady .... *(MCA 40883)* | 1.25 | 5.00 | 78
    (Half sleeve)

WARD, BILLY, AND HIS DOMINOES
LUCINDA/Stardust .... *(Liberty 55071)* | 10.00 | 40.00 | 57
    Clyde McPhatter left the group in 1953 to form the Drifters and Jackie Wilson left for a solo career in 1956, both before this single was recorded. The vocalist on this release is Eugene Mumford previously of the Serenaders and the Larks.

WARD, DALE
BIG DALE TWIST/Here's Your Hat .... *(Boyd 118)* | 5.00 | 20.00 | 62
    Also see the Crescendos

WARD, RACHEL
(Actress)
    See Phil Collins *(Against All Odds)*, Henry Mancini *(The Thorn Birds Theme)*

WARD, ROBIN
LOSER'S LULLABYE/Lolly Too Dum .... *(Songs Unlimited 37)* | 3.75 | 15.00 | 63

WARD BROTHERS, THE
CROSS THAT BRIDGE (NY Mix)/Cross That Bridge (Kitchen Sink Edit) .... *(A&M/Virgin 2911)* | .75 | 3.00 | 86
WHY DO YOU RUN?/Madness Of It All (Instrumental) .... *(A&M/Virgin 2928)* | .75 | 3.00 | 86

WARINER, STEVE
WHAT I DIDN'T DO/Your Love Has Got A Hold On Me .... *(MCA 52506)* | .75 | 3.00 | 84
YOU CAN DREAM OF ME/I Let A Keeper Get Away .... *(MCA 52721)* | .75 | 3.00 | 85

WARING, FRED
WE WISH YOU THE MERRIEST/Go Tell It On The Mountain .... *(RCA Victor 0317)* | 7.50 | 30.00 | 64
    (Shown as by Frank Sinatra, Bing Crosby, and Fred Waring)

WAR LOVER
(Motion Picture)
    See Bernie Leighton

WARNER, FLORENCE
ONLY LOVE .... *(Mercury 76154)* | .75 | 3.00 | 82

WARNES, JENNIFER
UP WHERE WE BELONG .... *(Island 7-99996)* | 1.00 | 4.00 | 82
    (Shown as by Joe Cocker and Jennifer Warnes. From the motion picture *An Officer and a Gentleman*, Richard Gere and Debra Winger pictured front and back.)
FIRST WE TAKE MANHATTAN .... *(Cypress 661-115)* | 1.25 | 5.00 | 86
SIMPLY MEANT TO BE .... *(Warner Bros. 28388-7)* | .75 | 3.00 | 87
    (Shown as by Gary Morris and Jennifer Warnes. From the motion picture *Blind Date*, Kim Basinger and Bruce Willis pictured.)
(I'VE HAD) THE TIME OF MY LIFE/Love Is Strange .... *(RCA 5224-7-R)* | 1.00 | 4.00 | 87
    (A-side shown as by Bill Medley and Jennifer Warnes, b-side by Mickey and Sylvia. From the motion picture *Dirty Dancing*, Patrick Swayze and Jennifer Gray pictured.)

WARREN, FRAN
    See the Triplets *(Loyalty)*

WARREN, RUSTY
EXTENDED PLAYS
KNOCKERS UP/BASIN STREET/
    Bounce Your Boobies/I Wish I Could Shimmy Like My Sister Kate .... *(Jubilee EP-45-2039)* | 3.00 | 12.00 | 62

WARWICK, DIONNE
EMPTY PLACE/Wishin' And Hopin' .... *(Scepter 1247)* | 2.00 | 8.00 | 63
THAT'S WHAT FRIENDS ARE FOR/Two Ships Passing In The Night .... *(Arista 9422)* | .75 | 3.00 | 85
    (Shown as by Dionne & Friends Featuring Elton John, Gladys Knight and Stevie Wonder. Warwick, John, Knight, and Wonder pictured on front. Warwick, John, Knight, Wonder, and the song's authors, Burt Bacharach and Carole Bayer Sager, pictured on back.)
WHISPER IN THE DARK/Extravagant Gestures .... *(Arista 9460)* | .75 | 3.00 | 85
    (Shown as by Dionne)
LOVE POWER/In A World Such As This .... *(Arista 9567)* | .75 | 3.00 | 87
    (A-side shown as by Dionne Warwick and Jeffrey Osborne. Warwick and Osborne pictured on front.)

RESERVATIONS FOR TWO/For Everything You Are .... (Arista 9638)   .75   3.00   87
    (A-side shown as by Dionne Warwick and Kashif. Warwick pictured on front and Kashif on back.)
ANOTHER CHANCE TO LOVE/Cry On Me .... (Arista 9656)   .75   3.00   87
    (A-side shown as by Dionne Warwick and Howard Hewett)
I DON'T NEED ANOTHER LOVE/Heartbreaker .... (Arista 9940)   .75   3.00   90
    Also see U.S.A. For Africa, Voices Of America

WASHINGTON, DINAH
A ROCKIN' GOOD WAY .... (Mercury 71629)   3.75   15.00   60
    (Shown as by Brook Benton and Dinah Washington)
WE HAVE LOVE/Looking Back .... (Mercury 71744)   2.50   10.00   61
DO YOU WANT IT THAT WAY/Early Every Morning .... (Mercury 71778)   2.50   10.00   61
OUR LOVE IS HERE TO STAY/Congratulations To Someone .... (Mercury 71812)   2.50   10.00   61
    (Uses the same photo of Washington as *Do You Want It That Way* and has the same back)
SEPTEMBER IN THE RAIN/Wake The Town And Tell The People .... (Mercury 71876)   2.50   10.00   61
TEARS AND LAUGHTER/If I Should Lose You .... (Mercury 71922)   2.50   10.00   62
SUCH A NIGHT/Dream .... (Mercury 71958)   2.50   10.00   62
    (*Dream* listed second as the b-side although it was the song that charted at # 92 on Billboard)
COLD COLD HEART/ .... (Mercury 72040)   2.50   10.00   62

WASHINGTON, GROVER, JR.
JUST THE TWO OF US/Make Me A Memory (Sad Samba) .... (Elektra 47103)   1.00   4.00   80
    (Bill Withers provides vocals but was not credited on sleeve)
BE MINE (TONIGHT)/ .... (Elektra 47246)   1.00   4.00   82

WAS (NOT WAS)
BABY MINE/Mickey Mouse March .... (A&M 1249)   .75   3.00   88
    (A-side shown as by Bonnie Raitt & Was [Not Was]. B-side shown as by Aaron Neville.)
SPY IN THE HOUSE OF LOVE/Dad I'm In Jail .... (Chrysalis VS4 43266)   .75   3.00   88
WALK THE DINOSAUR/Wedding Vows In Vegas .... (Chrysalis VS4 43331)   .75   3.00   88
ANYTHING CAN HAPPEN (POP)/Anything Can Happen (R&B) .... (Chrysalis VS4 43365)   .75   3.00   89

W.A.S.P.
SCREAM UNTIL YOU LIKE IT .... (Capitol B-44063)   1.00   4.00   87
    (From the motion picture *Ghoulies II*)

WATERFRONT
CRY/Saved .... (Polydor 871 110-7)   .75   3.00   89

WATERS, ROGER
RADIO WAVES/Going To Live In LA .... (Columbia 38-07180)   1.00   4.00   87
RADIO WAVES .... (Columbia 38-07180)   1.25   5.00   87
    (Promotional issue, *Demonstration–Not For Sale* printed on sleeve)
SUNSET STRIP/Money (Live) .... (Columbia 38-07364)   1.00   4.00   87
    (B-side shown as by Roger Waters with the Bleeding Heart Band which features Paul Carrack as guest
    vocalist.)
    Also see Pink Floyd

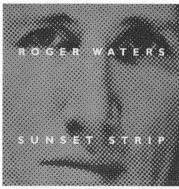

WATKINS, GREG
(Actor)
    See the Soaps and Hearts Ensemble

WATLEY, JODY
LOOKING FOR A NEW LOVE .... (MCA 52956)   .75   3.00   86
LOOKING FOR A NEW LOVE .... (MCA S45-17291)   1.25   5.00   87
    (Poster sleeve)
STILL A THRILL .... (MCA 53081)   .75   3.00   87
DON'T YOU WANT ME .... (MCA 53162)   .75   3.00   87
SOME KIND OF LOVER .... (MCA 53235)   .75   3.00   87
MOST OF ALL .... (MCA 53484)   .75   3.00   88
REAL LOVE/Real Love (Instrumental) .... (MCA 53484)   .75   3.00   89
    Also see Shalamar

WATSON, DOC
    See Nitty Gritty Dirt Band (*Honky Tonkin'*)

WATT, MIKE
BIG TRAIN/Amnesty Report .... (Columbia 38 77898)   .75   3.00   95
    (Artists credited on back include Dave Grohl from Nirvana, Edward Vedder from Pearl Jam, J Mascis from
    Dinosaur Jr, Cris and Curt Kirkwood from Meat Puppets, Perry Ferrell and Stephen Perkins from Jane's
    Addiction)
E-TICKET RIDE/The Big Bang Theory/Dominance And Submission .... (Columbia CS7 7400)   1.00   4.00   95
    (Promotional issue only, *Demonstration Only–Not For Sale* printed on sleeve. Back of sleeve credits a slew of
    guest artists including Mike D. from Beastie Boys, Stephen Perkins from Jane's Addiction, and J Mascis from
    Dinosaur Jr.)
    Also see Minutemen

WA WA NEE
SUGAR FREE/When The World Is A Home .... (Epic 34-07283)   .75   3.00   87

WAX
SHADOWS OF LOVE/Magnetic Heaven .... (RCA PB-14403)   .75   3.00   86
    Also see Andrew Gold, 10cc (Graham Gouldman)

WAYBILL, FEE
YOU'RE STILL LAUGHING .... (Capitol B-5399)   .75   3.00   84
    Also see the Tubes

WAYNE, PAULA
NEVER LESS THAN YESTERDAY/In The Name Of Love .... (Columbia 4-43727)   2.00   8.00   66

WAYSTED
HEAVEN TONIGHT .... (Capitol B-5685)   .75   3.00   87

WEATHERLY, JIM
THE NEED TO BE/Like Old Times Again .... (Buddah 420)   1.25   5.00   74

TITLE	LABEL AND NUMBER	VG	NM	YR

WEATHERS, CARL
(Actor)
    See Pointer Sisters (*He Turned Me Out*)

WEAVER, DENNIS
(Actor)
HUBBARDVILLE STORE/Prairie Dog Blues .... (*Ovation 1056*) | 1.25 | 5.00 | 75

WEAVER, PATTY
(Actress, appeared in the soap opera *The Young And The Restless*)
ONE LOVE TOO LATE/Part Time Man .... (*Warner Bros. 50023*) | 1.00 | 4.00 | 82

WEAVER, SIGOURNEY
(Actress)
    See Carly Simon (*Let The River Run*)

WEBB, JOYCE
RIGHT HERE/I'll Cry After You've Gone .... (*Domino 300/400*) | 12.50 | 50.00 | 58
    (Single sheet insert, not a true picture sleeve)
AIN'T THAT JUST LIKE A MAN/I Don't Care .... (*Domino 600*) | 12.50 | 50.00 | 58
    (Single sheet insert, not a true picture sleeve)

WEBBER, ANDREW LLOYD
(Composer)
    See Sara Brightman (*Pie Jesu*)

WEEDS, THE
NO GOOD NEWS/Stop .... (*N.W.I. 2745*) | 6.25 | 25.00 | 69

WEEMS, TED
HEARTACHES/Out Of The Night .... (*Decca 1-718*) | 3.00 | 12.00 | 53
    (Decca "Curtain Call" series of reissues)

WEE PAPA GIRL RAPPERS, THE
HEAT IT UP/Heat It Up (Instrumental) .... (*Jive/RCA 1158-7-J*) | .75 | 34.00 | 88
    (Shown as by the Wee Papa Girl Rappers Featuring 2 Men And A Drum Machine)

WEIRDOS, THE
DESTROY ALL MUSIC/Why Do You Exist/A Life Of Crime .... (*Bomp 112*) | 1.50 | 6.00 | 77
WE GOT THE NEUTRON BOMB/Solitary Confinement .... (*Dangerhouse 1063*) | 2.50 | 10.00 | 78
SKATEBOARDS TO HELL/Adult Hood .... (no label or #) | 3.00 | 12.00 | 79

WEIRD SCIENCE
(Motion Picture)
    See Oingo Boingo (*Weird Science*)

WEISSBURG, TIM
STREAK-OUT .... (*a&m 1520*) | 1.25 | 5.00 | 73

WELCH, BOB
HOT LOVE, COLD WORLD .... (*Capitol 4588*) | 1.25 | 5.00 | 77
CHURCH .... (*Capitol 4719*) | 1.00 | 4.00 | 79
    Welch was a member of Fleetwood Mac until 1975, two years before their first sleeve was issued, and was replaced by Lindsey Buckingham.

WELCH, TINA
SHOW AND TELL .... (*Belmont 626*) | 1.25 | 5.00 | 81

WELCOME BACK KOTTER
(Television Series)
    Related see Gabriel Kaplan, Marcia Strassman, John Travolta

WELK, LAWRENCE
WEARY BLUES/In The Alps .... (*Coral 61670*) | 3.75 | 15.00 | 56
    (Shown as by the McGuire Sisters and Lawrence Welk, all four pictured)

WELKER, FRANK
(Comedian and voice for many television and film cartoon characters)
A TOTALLY RIDICULOUS 12 DAYS OF CHRISTMAS/
    Floppy The Christmas Bunny .... (*Down The Hall* # unknown) | 1.25 | 5.00 | 86

WELLER, PAUL
    See Band Aid, the Jam

WELLES, ORSON
(Actor/Writer/Director best known for his film classic *Citizen Kane*)
I KNOW WHAT IT IS TO BE YOUNG/Love Is A Lovely Word .... (*Max no #*) | 1.50 | 6.00 | 84

WELL RED
GET LUCKY/Get Lucky (Dub) .... (*Virgin 7-99398*) | .75 | 3.00 | 87
    (George Clinton credited on front with vocal and dub mix)

WELLS, KITTY
GUILTY STREET/Shape Up Or Get Out .... (*Decca 32455*) | 2.00 | 8.00 | 69

WELLS, MARY
BYE BYE BABY/Please Forgive Me .... (*Motown 1003*) | 18.75 | 75.00 | 61
I DON'T WANT TO TAKE A CHANCE/I'm So Sorry .... (*Motown 1011*) | 12.50 | 50.00 | 61
STRANGE LOVE/Come To Me .... (*Motown 1016*) | 12.50 | 50.00 | 61
THE ONE WHO REALLY LOVES YOU/I'm Gonna Stay .... (*Motown 1024*) | 10.00 | 40.00 | 62
YOU BEAT ME TO THE PUNCH/Old Love (Let's Try It Again) ...... (*Motown 1032*) | 10.00 | 40.00 | 62
WHAT'S THE MATTER WITH YOU BABY/Once Upon A Time .... (*Motown 1057*) | 10.00 | 40.00 | 64
    (Shown as by Marvin Gaye and Mary Wells)
HE'S A LOVER/I'm Learnin' .... (*20th Century-Fox 590*) | 6.25 | 25.00 | 65

WENCES, SEÑOR
(Ventriloquist)
S'ALL RIGHT? S'ALL RIGHT/Deefeecult For You .... (*Joy 228*) | 2.50 | 10.00 | 60s

WENDY AND LISA
WATERFALL .... (Columbia 38-07243)   .75   3.00   87
WATERFALL .... (Columbia 38-07243)   1.00   4.00   87
     (Promotional issue, *Demonstration–Not For Sale* printed on sleeve)
HONEYMOON EXPRESS .... (Columbia 38-07661)   .75   3.00   87
     Also see Prince (*Mountains, Kiss*)

WEREWOLVES, THE
HOLLYWOOD MILLIONAIRE/City By The Sea .... (RCA PB-11283)   1.25   5.00   78
BABY EYES/Summer Weekends/No More Blues .... (RCA JE-11459)   1.25   5.00   78
     (Promotional issue only titled *Ship Of Fools* on front, song titles listed on back.)

WERNER, DAVID
WHIZZ KID .... (RCA APBO-0253)   1.50   6.00   75
EXTENDED PLAYS
WHAT'S RIGHT .... (Epic AE71185)   2.50   10.00   79
     (Promotional issue only released in conjunction with Washington DC radio station DC 101 to benefit the
     Special Olympics. Includes one song each by Cheap Trick and Molly Hatchett. Issued with a yellow vinyl,
     small-hole 33-1/3 RPM record.)

WESLEY, KASSIE
(Actress)
     See the Soaps and Hearts Ensemble

WEST, DOTTIE
ARE YOU HAPPY BABY?/Right Or Wrong .... (Liberty 1392)   1.25   5.00   80
     Also see Chet Atkins (*Chet's Tune*)

WEST, LESLIE
     See the Vagrants. West also recorded with Mountain but the group released no U.S. sleeves.

WEST, MAE
(Actress, Hollywood's first sex symbol)
DAY TRIPPER/Treat Him Right .... (Tower 260)   3.75   15.00   67
SHAKIN' ALL OVER/If You Gotta Go .... (Tower 261)   3.75   15.00   67
HARD TO HANDLE/You Gotta Taste All The Fruit .... (20th Century-Fox 6718)   7.50   30.00   67
     (From the motion picture *Myra Breckinridge*)

WESTON, KIM
I GOT WHAT YOU NEED/Someone Like You .... (MGM 13720)   2.50   10.00   67

WESTWARD HO THE WAGONS
(Motion Picture)
     See Bill Hayes (*Wringle Wrangle*), Vaughn Monroe (*Wringle Wrangle*), Fess Parker (*Wringle Wrangle*)

WESTWORLD
SONIC BOOM BOY .... (RCA 7613-7)   .75   3.00   87

WET WET WET
WISHING I WAS LUCKY/Words Of Wisdom .... (Uni 50000)   .75   3.00   88
SWEET LITTLE MYSTERY/Don't Let Me Be Lonely Tonight .... (Uni 50002)   .75   3.00   88
ANGEL EYES/We Can Love .... (Uni 50006)   .75   3.00   88

WET WILLIE
COUNTRY SIDE OF LIFE .... (Capricorn 0031)   1.50   6.00   73
     (Promotional issue only)

WHAM!
YOUNG GUNS (GO FOR IT)/Going For It .... (Columbia 38 036112)   1.50   6.00   83
     (Shown as by Wham! U.K.)
YOUNG GUNS (GO FOR IT) .... (Columbia 38 036112)   2.00   8.00   83
     (Promotional issue, *Demonstration–Not For Sale* printed on sleeve. Shown as by Wham! U.K.)
WAKE ME UP BEFORE YOU GO-GO/
     Wake Me Up Before You Go-Go (Instrumental) .... (Columbia 38-04552)   1.25   5.00   84
WAKE ME UP BEFORE YOU GO-GO .... (Columbia 38-04552)   1.50   6.00   84
     (Promotional issue, *Demonstration–Not For Sale* printed on sleeve)
CARELESS WHISPER/Careless Whisper (Instrumental) .... (Columbia 38-04691)   1.25   5.00   84
     (Full color first printing. Shown as by Wham! Featuring George Michael.)
CARELESS WHISPER .... (Columbia 38-04691)   1.50   6.00   84
     (Promotional issue, *Demonstration Not For Sale* printed on sleeve. Full color first printing. Shown as by Wham!
     Featuring George Michael.)
CARELESS WHISPER/Careless Whisper (Instrumental) .... (Columbia 38-04691)   1.00   4.00   84
     (Black and white second printing with completely different design. Shown as by Wham! Featuring George
     Michael.)
EVERYTHING SHE WANTS/Like A Baby .... (Columbia 38-04840)   .75   3.00   85
EVERYTHING SHE WANTS .... (Columbia 38-04840)   1.25   5.00   85
     (Promotional issue, *Demonstration–Not For Sale* printed on sleeve)
FREEDOM/Heartbeat .... (Columbia 38-05409)   .75   3.00   85
FREEDOM .... (Columbia 38-05409)   1.25   5.00   85
     (Promotional issue, *Demonstration–Not For Sale* printed on sleeve)
I'M YOUR MAN/Do It Right (Instrumental) .... (Columbia 38-05721)   .75   3.00   85
I'M YOUR MAN .... (Columbia 38-05721)   1.25   5.00   85
     (Promotional issue, *Demonstration Not For Sale* printed on sleeve)
THE EDGE OF HEAVEN/Blue (Live In China) .... (Columbia 38-06182)   .75   3.00   86
THE EDGE OF HEAVEN .... (Columbia 38-06182)   1.25   5.00   86
     (Promotional issue, *Demonstration–Not For Sale* printed on sleeve)
WHERE DID YOUR HEART GO?/Wham! Rap '86 .... (Columbia 38-06294)   .75   3.00   86
WHERE DID YOUR HEART GO? .... (Columbia 38-06294)   1.25   5.00   86
     (Promotional issue, *Demonstration–Not For Sale* printed on sleeve)
     Also see Band Aid, George Michael

WHAT IF
WHAT IF/Love Is A Fire .... (RCA 5218-7-R)   .75   3.00   87

WHAT'S NEW PUSSYCAT?
(Motion Picture)
     See Tom Jones (*What's New Pussycat?*)

TITLE	LABEL AND NUMBER	VG	NM	YR

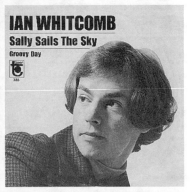

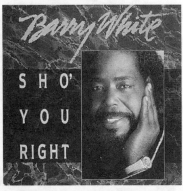

WHEELER, BILLY EDD
HALF A MAN .... (Kapp 842)   1.50   6.00   67

WHEELER, ONIE
SUNNYLAND FARMER .... (Epic 5-9540)   2.00   8.00   62

WHELCHEL, LISA
(Juvenile actress who appeared on The New Mickey Mouse Club in 1977 and played Blair Warner in the television series *The Facts Of Life* from 1979-1989)
HOW HIGH, HOW DEEP, HOW WIDE .... (Nissi SGL 4606)   1.50   6.00   84
     (Promotional issue only, *For Promotional Use Only Not For Resale* printed on sleeve. Song title is printed on a sticker placed on the front of the sleeve.)

WHEN IN ROME
HEAVEN KNOWS / Whatever The Weather .... (Virgin 7-99253)   .75   3.00   88

WHERE LOVE HAS GONE
(Motion Picture)
     See Jack Jones *(Where Love Has Gone)*

WHERE THE BOYS ARE
(Motion Picture)
     See Connie Francis *(Where The Boys Are)*

WHISPERS, THE
A SONG FOR DONNY / A Song For Donny (Instrumental) .... (Solar YB-11739)   1.25   5.00   79
EMERGENCY / Only You .... (Solar 48008)   1.25   5.00   82

WHITAKER, JOHNNY
(Child actor who played Jody on the television series *Family Affair* from 1966-1971)
FRIENDS / You You .... (Chelsea 0056)   2.00   8.00   72

WHITCOMB, IAN
POOR LITTLE BIRD / Where Did Robinson Crusoe Go With Friday On Saturday Night (Tower 274)   2.50   10.00   66
SALLY SAILS THE SKY / Groovy Day .... (Tower 385)   3.00   12.00   68

WHITE, BARRY
ANYTHING YOU WANT ME TO / I'll Do For You Anything You Want Me To ... (20th Century 2208)   1.50   6.00   75
SHO' YOU RIGHT / You're What's On My Mind .... (A&M 2943)   .75   3.00   87
FOR YOUR LOVE / I'm Ready For Love .... (A&M 3000)   .75   3.00   87
THE SECRET GARDEN .... (Qwest 19992)   .75   3.00   90
     (Shown as by Quincy Jones, Al B. Sure, James Ingram, El DeBarge, and Barry White)

WHITE, JOHN
CAN'T GET YOU OUT OF MY SYSTEM .... (Geffen 28332-7)   .75   3.00   87
VICTIM .... (Geffen 7-28170)   .75   3.00   87

WHITE, KARYN
FACTS OF LOVE .... (Warner Bros. 28588-7)   .75   3.00   86
     (Shown as by Jeff Lorber Featuring Karyn White)
SUPERWOMAN / Language Of Love .... (Warner Bros. 27783-7)   .75   3.00   88
THE WAY YOU LOVE ME .... (Warner Bros. 27773-7)   .75   3.00   88

WHITE, LENNY
     See Twennynine With Lenny White

WHITE, MAURICE
STAND BY ME .... (Columbia 38-05571)   .75   3.00   85
STAND BY ME .... (Columbia 38-05571)   1.00   4.00   85
     (Promotional issue, *Demonstration Only Not For Sale* printed on sleeve)
I NEED YOU .... (Columbia 38-05726)   .75   3.00   86
     Also see Earth Wind & Fire

WHITE LION
WAIT / Don't Give Up .... (Atlantic 7-89126)   .75   3.00   88
TELL ME / .... (Atlantic 7-89051)   .75   3.00   88
WHEN THE CHILDREN CRY / Lady Of The Valley .... (Atlantic 7-89015)   .75   3.00   88
LITTLE FIGHTER / Let's Get Crazy .... (Atlantic 7-88874)   .75   3.00   89

WHITE NIGHTS
(Motion Picture)
     See Phil Collins and Marilyn Martin *(Separate Lives)*, John Hiatt *(Snake Charmer)*, Lou Reed *(My Love Is Chemical)*, Lionel Richie *(Say You, Say Me)*

WHITESNAKE
FOOL FOR YOUR LOVING / Black And Blue .... (Mirage 3672)   1.50   6.00   80
LOVE AIN'T NO STRANGER / Guilty Of Love .... (Geffen 29171-7)   1.00   4.00   84
HERE I GO AGAIN .... (Geffen 28339-7)   .75   3.00   87
IS THIS LOVE .... (Geffen 28233-7)   .75   3.00   87
GIVE ME ALL YOUR LOVE .... (Geffen 28103-7)   .75   3.00   88
     Also see Deep Purple (Jon Lord, Ian Paice). David Coverdale was with Deep Purple from 1973-1976.

WHITE ZOMBIE
SUPER-CHARGER HEAVEN (PSYCHOHOLIC) .... (label and # unknown)   2.00   8.00   95
     (Promotional issue only issued with green vinyl)
     Also see Wickerman (Jay Yuenger)

WHITFIELD, BARRENCE, AND THE SAVAGES
     See A'me Lorain *(Whole Wide World)*

WHITING, LEONARD
(Actor)
     See Nino Rota *(What Is Youth)*

WHITLOCK, BOBBY
PUT ANGELS AROUND YOU / Here, There and Everywhere .... (Swan Song 7-99907)   .75   3.00   83
     (Shown as by Maggie Bell & Bobby Whitlock, both pictured on back)

TITLE	LABEL AND NUMBER	VG	NM	YR

WHO, THE
HAPPY JACK .... (Decca 32114) — 6.25 — 25.00 — 67
   (Illustration by artist Ralph Steadman)
PINBALL WIZARD/Dogs Part II .... (Decca 732465) — 3.75 — 15.00 — 69
SEE ME, FEEL ME/Overture From Tommy .... (Decca 732729) — 3.75 — 15.00 — 70
SUBSTITUTE/Young Man's Blues .... (Decca 32737) — 50.00 — 200.00 — 70
   (Promotional issue only; was also intended for use with stock copies but the records were never pressed)
LISTENING TO YOU/SEE ME FEEL ME/Overture From Tommy .... (Polydor 15098) — 2.00 — 8.00 — 75
   (From the motion picture *Tommy*)
SQUEEZE BOX .... (MCA 40475) — 6.25 — 25.00 — 75
   (Promotional issue only, *Promotion Copy Not For Sale* printed on sleeve. Connect-the-dot drawing by John Entwistle.)
5:15/I'm One .... (Polydor 2022) — 1.50 — 6.00 — 79
   (From the motion picture *Quadrophenia*)
I'M THE FACE/Zoot Suit .... (Mercury DJ 570) — 1.50 — 6.00 — 80
   (Shown as by the High Numbers)
YOU BETTER YOU BET/The Quiet One .... (Warner Bros. 49698) — 1.00 — 4.00 — 81
ATHENA/It's Your Turn .... (Warner Bros. 29905-7) — 1.00 — 4.00 — 82
   Also see Roger Daltrey, Small Faces (Kenney Jones), Jimmy Thudpucker (Keith Moon), Pete Townshend

WHODINI
FUNKY BEAT/Funky Beat (Instrumental) .... (Jive/Arista 9461) — .75 — 3.00 — 86
ROCK YOU AGAIN (AGAIN & AGAIN)/Now That Whodini's Inside The Joint . (Jive/Arista 9607) — .75 — 3.00 — 87

WHO'S THAT GIRL
(Motion Picture)
   See Michael Davidson (*Turn It Up*), Madonna (*Causing A Commotion, Who's That Girl*)

WICKERMAN
SHITKICKER/Slack .... (Imago 72787-25088-1) — .75 — 3.00 — 94
   (J, a.k.a. guitarist Jay Yuenger, from White Zombie credited on *Shitkicker*)

WIEDLIN, JANE
BLUE KISS/Somebody's Going To Get Into This House .... (I.R.S. 52674) — .75 — 3.00 — 85
RUSH HOUR/The End Of Love .... (EMI-Manhattan B-50118) — .75 — 3.00 — 88
INSIDE A DREAM/Song Of The Factory .... (EMI-Manhattan B-50145) — .75 — 3.00 — 88
   Also see Frosted, the Go-Go's, Sparks (*Cool Places*), the Ventures (*Surfin' and Spyin'*)

WILCOX, HARLOW, AND THE OAKIES
GROOVY GRUBWORM .... (Plantation 28) — 1.50 — 6.00 — 69
   (Originally issued with green vinyl)

WILD
HURRICANE .... (Columbia 38-07936) — .75 — 3.00 — 88

WILD, JACK
SOME BEAUTIFUL .... (Capitol 2742) — 1.25 — 5.00 — 70

WILD BLUE
FIRE WITH FIRE/Taboo .... (Chrysalis VS4 42985) — .75 — 3.00 — 86
   (From the motion picture *Fire With Fire*, Craig Sheffer and Virginia Madsen pictured)

WILDE, DANNY
TIME RUNS WILD .... (Geffen 27987-7) — .75 — 3.00 — 88
   Also see Great Buildings

WILDE, EUGENE
DON'T SAY NO TONIGHT/Gotta Get You Home Tonight .... (Philly World 7-99608) — .75 — 3.00 — 85

WILDE, KIM
KIDS IN AMERICA/You'll Never Be So Wrong .... (EMI America B-8110) — 1.00 — 4.00 — 86
GO FOR IT/Lovers On A Beach .... (MCA 52513) — 1.50 — 6.00 — 84
   (Poster sleeve)
SAY YOU REALLY WANT ME .... (MCA 52952) — .75 — 3.00 — 86
YOU KEEP ME HANGIN' ON .... (MCA 53024) — .75 — 3.00 — 86
SAY YOU REALLY WANT ME .... (MCA 53130) — .75 — 3.00 — 87
   (Second release for this title, this time featured in the motion picture *Running Scared*)
ANOTHER STEP (CLOSER TO YOU) .... (MCA 53192) — .75 — 3.00 — 87
   (Credit on back reads *Features Guest Appearance By Junior*. Wilde and Junior pictured on back.)
YOU CAME .... (MCA 53370) — .75 — 3.00 — 88
   Also see Ferry Aid

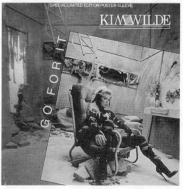

WILDER, GENE
(Comic actor married to Gilda Radner)
PURE IMAGINATION/Cheer Up Charlie .... (Paramount 0106) — 2.50 — 10.00 — 70
   (From the motion picture *Willie Wonka And The Chocolate Factory*)

WILDER, MATTHEW
BOUNCIN' OFF THE WALLS/Love Of An Amazon .... (Private I ZS4-04617) — .75 — 3.00 — 84
BOUNCIN' OFF THE WALLS/Love Of An Amazon .... (Private I ZS4-04617) — 1.00 — 4.00 — 84
   (Promotional issue, *Demonstration Only–Not For Sale* printed on sleeve. Sleeve lists b-side even though the 45 has *Bouncin' Off The Walls* on both sides.)

WILD IN THE COUNTRY
(Motion Picture)
   See Elvis Presley (b-side of *Surrender*, b-side of *I Feel So Bad*)

WILDLIFE
SOMEWHERE IN THE NIGHT/Sun Don't Shine .... (Swan Song 7-99842) — .75 — 3.00 — 83

WILD LIFE, THE
(Motion Picture)
   See Bananarama (*The Wild Life*)

WILD ONES, THE
MY LOVE/Lord Love A Duck .... (United Artists 971) — 3.00 — 12.00 — 66
COME ON BACK .... (Sears 6-6576) — 7.50 — 30.00 — 66
   (Cardboard cover, photography by Richard Avedon)

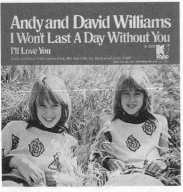

TITLE	LABEL AND NUMBER	VG	NM	YR
WILD PAIR, THE				
See Paula Abdul (*Opposites Attract*)				
WILL AND THE KILL				
HEART OF STEEL	(MCA 53318)	.75	3.00	88
WILLIAMS, ALYSON				
See Chuck Stanley Introducing Alyson Williams, Tashan				
WILLIAMS, ANDY				
THE VILLAGE OF ST. BERNADETTE	(Cadence 1374)	2.50	10.00	59
DANNY BOY/Fly By Night	(Columbia 4-42199)	1.25	5.00	61
THE WONDERFUL WORLD OF THE YOUNG/	(Columbia 4-42265)	1.25	5.00	62
STRANGER ON THE SHORE/I Want To Be Wanted	(Columbia 4-42451)	1.25	5.00	62
DON'T YOU BELIEVE IT/Summertime	(Columbia 4-42523)	1.25	5.00	62
CAN'T GET USED TO LOSING YOU/Days Of Wine And Roses	(Columbia 4-42674)	1.25	5.00	63
AND ROSES AND ROSES/	(Columbia 4-43257)	2.00	8.00	68
BATTLE HYMN OF THE REPUBLIC/Ave Maria	(Columbia 4-44650)	2.00	8.00	68
(Robert Francis Kennedy pictured front and back)				
REMEMBER/	(Columbia 4-45985)	1.25	5.00	73
CHRISTMAS PRESENT/	(Columbia 1-10054)	1.25	5.00	74
IT'S THE MOST WONDERFUL TIME OF THE YEAR/				
Kay Thompson's Jingle Bells	(Columbia AE7-1108)	1.50	6.00	76
(Promotional issue only)				
WILLIAMS, ANDY AND DAVID				
(Sons of Andy Williams)				
I WON'T LAST A DAY WITHOUT YOU/I'll Love You	(Kapp 2179)	1.25	5.00	72
ONE MORE TIME/Stay With Me Awhile	(MCA 40085)	1.25	5.00	73
Also see Williams Bros				
WILLIAMS, ANSON				
(Actor, played Potsie on the television series *Happy Days*)				
DEEPLY/I Want To Believe In This One	(Chelsea 3061)	1.25	5.00	77
WILLIAMS, BARRY				
(Actor, played Greg Brady on the television series *The Brady Bunch*)				
SUNNY/Sweet Sweetheart	(Paramount 0122)	5.00	20.00	70
WILLIAMS, CHRISTOPHER				
TALK TO MYSELF/Sweet Memories	(Geffen 22936-7)	.75	3.00	89
WILLIAMS, CINDY				
(Comic actress)				
See Laverne & Shirley				
WILLIAMS, DARNELL				
PURE SATISFACTION	(My Disc ZS4-04085)	.75	3.00	83
(Promotional issue only)				
WILLIAMS, DENIECE				
DO WHAT YOU FEEL	(Columbia 38-03807)	.75	3.00	83
DO WHAT YOU FEEL	(Columbia 38-03807)	1.00	4.00	83
(Promotional issue, *Demonstration Only–Not For Sale* printed on sleeve)				
LET'S HEAR IT FOR THE BOY	(Columbia 38-04417)	.75	3.00	84
LET'S HEAR IT FOR THE BOY	(Columbia 38-04417)	1.00	4.00	84
(Promotional issue, *Demonstration Only–Not For Sale* printed on sleeve)				
NEXT LOVE	(Columbia 38-04537)	.75	3.00	84
NEXT LOVE	(Columbia 38-04537)	1.00	4.00	84
(Promotional issue, *Demonstration Only–Not For Sale* printed on sleeve)				
WISER AND WEAKER/Wiser And Weaker (Instrumental)	(Columbia 38-06157)	.75	3.00	86
WISER AND WEAKER/Wiser And Weaker (Instrumental)	(Columbia 38-06157)	1.00	4.00	86
(Promotional issue, *Demonstration Only Not For Sale* printed on sleeve)				
I SURRENDER ALL	(Sparrow 1121)	1.25	5.00	86
I CAN'T WAIT	(Columbia 38-08014)	.75	3.00	88
WILLIAMS, DON				
WE'VE GOT A GOOD FIRE GOIN'	(Capitol B-5526)	.75	3.00	85
I WOULDN'T BE A MAN	(Capitol PB-44066)	.75	3.00	87
WILLIAMS, GEOFFREY				
CINDERELLA	(Atlantic 7-89060)	.75	3.00	88
THERE'S A NEED IN ME	(Atlantic 7-89122)	.75	3.00	88
WILLIAMS, HANK				
YOUR CHEATIN' HEART	(MGM 13305)	2.50	10.00	65
WILLIAMS, HANK, JR.				
LONG GONE LONESOME BLUES/Doesn't Anybody Know My Name?	(MGM K-13208)	2.50	10.00	64
LOVESICK BLUES/	(MGM K-13305)	2.50	10.00	65
I'M SO LONESOME I COULD CRY/Is It That Much Fun To Hurt Someone	(MGM K-13318)	2.50	10.00	65
YOU'RE RUININ' MY LIFE/	(MGM K-13392)	2.50	10.00	64
HEAVEN CAN'T BE FOUND	(Warner Bros./Curb 28227-7)	1.00	4.00	87
YOUNG COUNTRY	(Warner Bros./Curb 28120-7)	1.00	4.00	88
EARLY IN THE MORNING AND LATE AT NIGHT	(Warner Bros./Curb 27722-7)	1.00	4.00	88
WILLIAMS, JOHN				
THEME FROM CLOSE ENCOUNTERS OF THE THIRD KIND	(Arista 300)	1.00	4.00	77
(From the motion picture *Close Encounters Of The Third Kind*)				
STAR WARS MAIN TITLE/Cantina Band	(20th Century-Fox 2345)	1.50	6.00	78
(From the motion picture *Star Wars*. Front and back feature artwork of the film's main characters.)				
THEME FROM SUPERMAN (MAIN TITLE)/Love Theme From Superman	(Warner Bros. 8729)	1.00	4.00	78
(From the motion picture *Superman The Movie*)				
THEME FROM E.T. (THE EXTRA-TERRESTRIAL)	(MCA 52072)	1.00	4.00	82
(From the motion picture *E.T. The Extra Terrestrial*)				
RAIDERS MARCH	(Warner Bros. 22931-7)	1.00	4.00	89
(From the motion picture *Indiana Jones And The Last Crusade*. Front of sleeve features artwork of the film's main characters.)				

WILLIAMS, JOHNNY, ORCHESTRA
MONTREAL .... (Columbia 4-42516) | 1.50 | 6.00 | 62

WILLIAMS, LARRY
SLOW DOWN/Dizzy, Miss Lizzy .... (Specialty 626) | 18.75 | 75.00 | 58
(*Slow Down* is listed first as the a-side and did not appear in Billboard's Top 100, but *Dizzy, Miss Lizzy* did make it to #69)

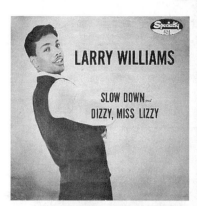

WILLIAMS, LENNY
See Kenny G (*Don't Make Me Wait For Love*)

WILLIAMS, MASON
SATURDAY NIGHT AT THE WORLD .... (Warner 7248) | 1.50 | 6.00 | 69
(Promotional issue only)

WILLIAMS, MAURICE, AND THE ZODIACS
See Patrick Swayze (*She's Like The Wind*)

WILLIAMS, PAT
A WHITER SHADE OF PALE .... (Verve 5075) | 2.00 | 8.00

WILLIAMS, PAUL
LOOK WHAT I FOUND/The Lady Is Waiting .... (A&M 1429) | 1.25 | 5.00 | 73

WILLIAMS, ROBIN
I YAM WHAT I YAM/He Needs Me .... (Boardwalk WS8-5701) | 1.50 | 6.00 | 80
(B-side shown as by Shelley Duvall. From the motion picture *Popeye*, Williams and Duvall pictured.)
EXTENDED PLAYS
ELMER FUDD SINGS BRUCE SPRINGSTEEN (FIRE)/NICHOLSON/THROBBING PYTHON
OF LOVE/The Falklands/Richard Simmons .... (Casablanca 2367 DJ-7) | 1.50 | 6.00 | 83
(Promotional issue only titled *Throbbing Sampler, For DJ Use Only* printed on sleeve)
ONE LINERS/Excerpts .... (Columbia CS7-2526) | 1.50 | 6.00 | 86
(Promotional issue only titled *A Night At The Met, Demonstration–Not For Sale* printed on sleeve. A-side is 24 one liners which are individually listed on the back of the sleeve.)
Also see Louis Armstrong (*What A Wonderful World*)

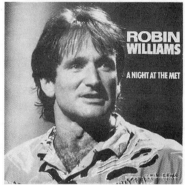

WILLIAMS, ROGER
AUTUMN LEAVES .... (Kapp 116-x) | 2.50 | 10.00 | 55
SUNRISE SERENADE .... (Kapp 301) | 2.00 | 8.00 | 60
I GET A KICK OUT OF YOU .... (Kapp 364) | 2.00 | 8.00 | 60
MARIA .... (Kapp 437) | 2.00 | 8.00 | 61

WILLIAMS, VANESSA
THE RIGHT STUFF/The Right Stuff (Edited Version) .... (Wing/PolyGram 887 386-7) | .75 | 3.00 | 88
(HE'S GOT) THE LOOK/The Right Stuff (Rex's Mix) .... (Wing/PolyGram 887 7816-7) | .75 | 3.00 | 88
DREAMIN'/The Right Stuff (Instrumental) .... (Wing/PolyGram 871 078-7) | .75 | 3.00 | 88
DARLIN' I/The Right Stuff (The Rex Groove) .... (Wing/PolyGram 871 936-7) | .75 | 3.00 | 89

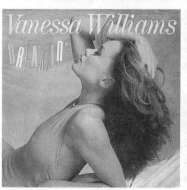

WILLIAMS, VESTA
DON'T BLOW A GOOD THING/I'm Coming Back .... (A&M 2926) | .75 | 3.00 | 86
(Sleeve shown as by Vesta, the record indicates her full name)

WILLIAMS BROS.
(Two sons of Andy Williams)
SOME BECOME STRANGERS .... (Warner Bros. 28403-7) | .75 | 3.00 | 87
HOW LONG .... (Warner Bros. 28275-7) | .75 | 3.00 | 87
Also see Andy and David Williams

WILLIE AND THE POOR BOYS
BABY PLEASE DON'T GO/Poor Boy Boogie .... (Passport 7928) | 1.00 | 4.00 | 85
THESE ARMS OF MINE/Let's Talk It Over .... (Passport 7929) | 1.00 | 4.00 | 85
Also see Bad Company (Paul Rodgers), Free (Paul Rodgers), Led Zeppelin (Jimmy Page), Jimmy Page, Paul Rodgers, the Rolling Stones (Bill Wyman, Charlie Watts), Bill Wyman, the Yardbirds (Jimmy Page). Kenny Jones of the Who and Chris Rea also participated but were not credited on the sleeve.

WILLIE WONKA AND THE CHOCOLATE FACTORY
(Motion Picture)
See Gene Wilder (*Pure Imagination*)

WILLIO & PHILLIO
ALL WINTER LONG .... (Wizard S102) | 1.50 | 6.00 | 78
GOIN' QUACKERS/Vacuum Cleaner Hoses .... (Disneyland 505) | 2.00 | 8.00 | 80
(Promotional issue only. Shown as by Willio & Phillio and Donald Duck.)

WILLIS, BRUCE
(Actor)
RESPECT YOURSELF/Fun Time .... (Motown 1876MF) | .75 | 3.00 | 87
RESPECT YOURSELF .... (Motown 1876MF) | 1.00 | 4.00 | 87
(Promotional issue, *For Promotional Use Only Not For Sale* printed on sleeve)
YOUNG BLOOD/Flirting With Disaster .... (Motown 1886MF) | .75 | 3.00 | 87
YOUNG BLOOD .... (Motown 1886MF) | 1.00 | 4.00 | 87
(Promotional issue, *For Promotional Use Only/Not For Sale* printed on sleeve)
UNDER THE BOARDWALK/Jackpot (Bruno's Bop) .... (Motown 1896MF) | .75 | 3.00 | 87
UNDER THE BOARDWALK .... (Motown 1896MF) | 1.00 | 4.00 | 87
(Promotional issue, *For Promotional Use Only/Not For Sale* printed on sleeve)
Also see Al Jarreau (*Since I Fell For You*), Gary Morris and Jennifer Warnes (*Simply Meant To Be*), Billy Vera & the Beaters (*Let You Get Away*)

WILSON, AL
BABY, I WANT YOUR BODY .... (Playboy 6076) | 1.50 | 6.00 | 76

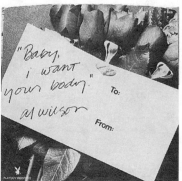

WILSON, ANN
ALMOST PARADISE .... (Columbia 38-04418) | .75 | 3.00 | 84
(Shown as by Mike Reno and Ann Wilson, both pictured. From the motion picture *Footloose*.)
THE BEST MAN IN THE WORLD .... (Capitol B-5654) | .75 | 3.00 | 86
(From the motion picture *The Golden Child*)
SURRENDER TO ME .... (Capitol B44288) | .75 | 3.00 | 88
(Shown as by Ann Wilson and Robin Zander. From the motion picture *Tequila Sunrise*. Wilson and Zander pictured on the front, Mel Gibson, Michelle Pfeiffer, and Kurt Russell pictured on the back.)
Also see Heart

TITLE	LABEL AND NUMBER	VG	NM	YR

WILSON, BRIAN

LET'S GO TO HEAVEN IN MY CAR/Too Much Sugar	(Sire/Reprise 28350-7)	1.25	5.00	88
LOVE AND MERCY/He Couldn't Get His Poor Old Body To Move	(Sire/Reprise 27814-7)	1.25	5.00	88
NIGHT TIME	(Sire/Reprise 27787-7)	12.50	50.00	88

(Promotional issue only, no stock records released)
Also see the Beach Boys, the Legendary Masked Surfers

WILSON, DENNIS
EXTENDED PLAYS

RIVER SONG	(CBS AE7-1128 AE7-1129)	2.00	8.00	77

(Promotional issue only titled *Music For Every Ear*, double single release issued with two small-hole 33-1/3 RPM records. Also includes one song each by Joan Baez, Cheap Trick, Crawler, Burton Cummings, and Ram Jam)
Also see the Beach Boys

WILSON, DOOLEY
(Vaudeville entertainer, played the piano player "Sam" in the motion picture *Casablanca*)

AS TIME GOES BY/Dialogue from "Casablanca"	(Warner Bros. 7741)	2.50	10.00	73

(Promotional issue only, from the motion picture *Casablanca*)

WILSON, JACKIE

THAT'S WHY (I LOVE YOU SO)/Love Is All	(Brunswick 55121)	6.25	25.00	59
TALK THAT TALK/Only You, Only You	(Brunswick 55165)	6.25	25.00	59
NIGHT/Doggin' Around	(Brunswick 9-55166)	6.25	25.00	60
ALONE AT LAST/Am I The Man?	(Brunswick 55170)	5.00	20.00	60
THE TEAR OF THE YEAR/My Empty Arms	(Brunswick 55201)	5.00	20.00	60
THE WAY I AM/My Heart Belongs To Only You	(Brunswick 55220)	3.75	15.00	61
THE GREATEST HURT/There'll Be No Next Time	(Brunswick 55221)	3.75	15.00	61
A GIRL NAMED TOMIKO/What Good Am I Without You?	(Brunswick 55236)	3.75	15.00	62
(A-side from the motion picture *A Girl Named Tomiko*)				
LET THIS BE A LETTER (TO MY BABY)/Didn't I?	(Brunswick 55435)	2.50	10.00	70
REET PETITE/You Better Know It	(Columbia 38-07329)	1.00	4.00	87
REET PETITE	(Columbia 38-07329)	1.25	5.00	87

(Promotional issue, *Demonstration–Not For Sale* printed on back of sleeve)

WILSON, NANCY

DON'T COME RUNNING BACK TO ME	(Capitol 5340)	1.50	6.00	65

WILSON, SHANICE

(BABY TELL ME) CAN YOU DANCE/Summer Love	(A&M 2939)	.75	3.00	87
NO 1/2 STEPPIN'/Summer Love	(A&M 2990)	.75	3.00	87
THIS TIME/Wait So Long	(Arista 9772)	.75	3.00	89

(Shown as by Kiara & Shanice Wilson)

WILSON PHILLIPS
(Trio featuring Carnie and Wendy Wilson, daughters of Brian Wilson, and Chynna Phillips, daughter of John and Michelle Phillips of the Mamas & the Papas)

HOLD ON/Over And Over	(SBK Records B-07322)	.75	3.00	90

WINANS, THE

AIN'T NO NEED TO WORRY	(Qwest 29274-7)	.75	3.00	85
(Shown as by the Winans and Anita Baker)				
LET MY PEOPLE GO (PART I)/Let My People Go (Part II)	(Qwest 28874-7)	.75	3.00	85
LOVE HAS NO COLOR	(Qwest 28147-7)	.75	3.00	87
(Shown as by the Winans Featuring Michael McDonald)				
GIVE ME YOU	(Qwest 27929-7)	.75	3.00	87
LEAN ON ME	(Warner Bros. 27533-7)	.75	3.00	89

(Shown as by Thelma Houston and the Winans)
Also see Be Be & Ce Ce Winans

WINANS, BE BE & CE CE

I.O.U. ME	(Capitol P-B-44009)	.75	3.00	87
CALL ME	(Capitol P-B-44041)	.75	3.00	87

Also see the Winans

WINBUSH, ANGELA

ANGEL	(Mercury 888 831-7)	.75	3.00	87

WINDING, KAI

MONDO CANE NO. 2/Portrait Of My Love	(Verve 10313)	2.50	10.00	64

(From the motion picture *Mondo Cane No. 2*)

WINGER

MADALAINE/Higher And Higher	(Atlantic 7-89041)	.75	3.00	88
SEVENTEEN/Poison Angel	(Atlantic 7-88958)	.75	3.00	88
HEADED FOR A HEARTBREAK/State Of Emergency	(Atlantic 7-88922)	.75	3.00	89
HUNGRY/Time To Surrender	(Atlantic 7-88859)	.75	3.00	89

Also see Fiona (Kip Winger duet on *Everything You Do*)

WINGER, DEBRA
(Actress)
See Joe Cocker (*Up Where We Belong*)

WINGS
See Paul McCartney

WINNINGHAM, MARE
(Actress)
See John Parr (*St. Elmo's Fire*)

WINTER, EDGAR, GROUP, THE

ROUND & ROUND/Catchin' Up	(Epic 5-10922)	1.25	5.00	72

Also see Dan Hartman, the Legends (Dan Hartman). Rick Derringer joined the group in 1973.

WINTER, JOHNNY

TITLE	LABEL AND NUMBER	VG	NM	YR
ROLLIN' & TUMBLIN'	(Sonobeat 107)	18.75	75.00	68
(Sleeve pictures the Vulcan Gas Co., an Austin nightclub)				
ROLLIN' & TUMBLIN'	(Sonobeat 107)	12.50	50.00	68
(Sleeve does not picture the Vulcan Gas Co.)				
(It is unclear as to whether this is the correct title that was released with these particular sleeves)				
Also see Bruce Springsteen (Rosalita)				

WINTERHALTER, HUGO, AND HIS ORCHESTRA

TITLE	LABEL AND NUMBER	VG	NM	YR
THE PEANUT VENDOR/Delicado	(RCA Victor 61-8516)	1.50	6.00	65
(Hard cover)				

WINWOOD, STEVE

TITLE	LABEL AND NUMBER	VG	NM	YR
WHILE YOU SEE A CHANCE/Vacant Chair	(Island 49656)	1.25	5.00	80
ARC OF A DIVER/Dust	(Island 49726)	1.25	5.00	80
HIGHER LOVE	(Island 28710-7)	.75	3.00	86
FREEDOM OVERSPILL	(Island 28595-7)	.75	3.00	86
THE FINER THINGS	(Island 28498-7)	.75	3.00	86
BACK IN THE HIGH LIFE AGAIN	(Island 28472-7)	.75	3.00	86
VALERIE/Talking Back To The Night (Instrumental Version)	(Island 28231-7)	1.00	4.00	88
TALKING BACK TO THE NIGHT	(Island 28122-7)	1.00	4.00	88
ROLL WITH IT/The Morning Side	(Virgin 7-99326)	.75	3.00	88
DON'T YOU KNOW WHAT THE NIGHT CAN DO?/ Don't You Know What The Night Can Do? (Instrumental)	(Virgin 7-99290)	.75	3.00	88
HOLDING ON/Holding On (Instrumental)	(Virgin 7-99261)	.75	3.00	88
HEARTS ON FIRE/Hearts On Fire (Instrumental)	(Virgin 7-99234)	.75	3.00	89
Also see the Spencer Davis Group, Traffic				

WIRE TRAIN

TITLE	LABEL AND NUMBER	VG	NM	YR
I'LL DO YOU/It's Only Dark	(Columbia 38-04386)	.75	3.00	84
I'LL DO YOU	(Columbia 38-04386)	1.00	4.00	84
(Promotional issue, Demonstration–Not For Sale printed on sleeve)				
LAST PERFECT THING/L'Adresse De L'Ete	(Columbia 38-05691)	.75	3.00	85

WITHERS, BILL

TITLE	LABEL AND NUMBER	VG	NM	YR
THE GIFT OF GIVING/Let Us Love	(Sussex 247)	1.50	6.00	72
USA/Paint Your Pretty Picture	(Columbia 18-02651)	1.25	5.00	81
SOMETHING THAT TURNS YOU ON/You Tried To Find A Love	(Columbia 38-05424)	1.25	5.00	85
Also see Grover Washington, Jr. (Just The Two Of Us)				

WITNESS FOR THE PROSECUTION

(Motion Picture)

See Bob Carroll (Song From Witness For The Prosecution)

WIZ, THE

(Motion Picture)

See Michael Jackson (Ease On Down The Road), Diana Ross (Ease On Down The Road)

WOLF

TITLE	LABEL AND NUMBER	VG	NM	YR
PAPA WAS A ROLLIN' STONE/Window On A Dream	(Constellation 7-69849)	.75	3.00	82

WOLF, PETER

TITLE	LABEL AND NUMBER	VG	NM	YR
LIGHTS OUT/Poor Girl's Heart	(EMI America B-8208)	.75	3.00	84
I NEED YOU TONIGHT/Billy Bigtime	(EMI America B-8241)	.75	3.00	84
OO-EE-DIDDLEY-BOP!/Crazy	(EMI America B-8254)	.75	3.00	85
COME AS YOU ARE/Thick As Thieves	(EMI America B-8350)	.75	3.00	87
CAN'T GET STARTED/Mamma Said	(EMI America B-43012)	.75	3.00	87
Also see Artists United Against Apartheid, the J. Geils Band				

WOLF & WOLF

TITLE	LABEL AND NUMBER	VG	NM	YR
DON'T TAKE THE CANDY	(Morocco 1729CF)	.75	3.00	84
(Promotional issue only, For Promotional Use Only Not For Sale printed on sleeve. Issued with yellow vinyl.)				

WOMACK, BOBBY

TITLE	LABEL AND NUMBER	VG	NM	YR
I'LL STILL BE LOOKING UP TO YOU	(MCA 52467)	.75	3.00	85
(Shown as by Bobby Womack and Wilton Felder)				
I WISH HE DIDN'T TRUST ME SO MUCH	(MCA 52624)	.75	3.00	85
GYPSY WOMAN	(MCA 52793)	.75	3.00	85
(I WANNA) MAKE LOVE TO YOU	(MCA 52955)	.75	3.00	86
LIVING IN A BOX	(MCA 53190)	.75	3.00	87

WOMACK AND WOMACK

(Cecil and Linda Womack, Cecil is Bobby Womack's brother and Linda is Sam Cooke's daughter. Bobby Womack's first wife was Sam Cooke's widow, Barbara.)

TITLE	LABEL AND NUMBER	VG	NM	YR
TEARDROPS/Conscious Of My Conscience	(Island 7-99337)	.75	3.00	88

WOMAN IN RED, THE

(Motion Picture)

See Stevie Wonder (I Just Called To Say I Love You, Love In Flight)

WONDER, STEVIE

TITLE	LABEL AND NUMBER	VG	NM	YR
PART 1–2 (I CALL IT PRETTY MUSIC, BUT...) THE OLD PEOPLE CALL IT THE BLUES	(Tamla 54061)	12.50	50.00	62
(Shown as by Little Stevie Wonder)				
FINGERTIPS-PART 1 & 2	(Tamla 54080)	7.50	30.00	63
(Shown as by Little Stevie Wonder)				
HEY HARMONICA MAN/This Little Girl	(Tamla 54096)	7.50	30.00	64
BLOWIN' IN THE WIND/Ain't That Asking For Trouble	(Tamla 54136)	6.25	25.00	66
A PLACE IN THE SUN/Sylvia	(Tamla 54139)	6.25	25.00	66
SIR DUKE	(Tamla 54281F)	2.00	8.00	77
SEND ONE YOUR LOVE	(Tamla 54303F)	1.25	5.00	79
OUTSIDE MY WINDOW	(Tamla 54308F)	1.25	5.00	80
MASTER BLASTER (JAMMIN')	(Tamla 54317 F)	1.25	5.00	80

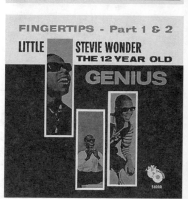

TITLE	LABEL AND NUMBER	VG	NM	YR
EBONY AND IVORY/Rainclouds	(Columbia 18-02860)	1.00	4.00	82
(Shown as by Paul McCartney Additional Vocals By Stevie Wonder)				
EBONY AND IVORY	(Columbia 18-02860)	2.00	8.00	82
(Promotional issue, *Demonstration–Not For Sale* printed on sleeve. Shown as by Paul McCartney Additional Vocals By Stevie Wonder.)				
RIBBON IN THE SKY/Black Orchid	(Tamla 1639TF)	.75	3.00	82
USED TO BE/I Want To Come Back As A Song	(Motown 1650MF)	.75	3.00	82
(A-side shown as by Charlene & Stevie Wonder, b-side shown as by Charlene)				
I JUST CALLED TO SAY I LOVE YOU/ I Just Called To Say I Love You (Instrumental)	(Motown 1745MF)	.75	3.00	84
(From the motion picture *The Woman In Red*)				
LOVE IN FLIGHT/It's More Than You	(Motown 1769MF)	.75	3.00	84
(From the motion picture *The Woman In Red*)				
PART-TIME LOVER/Part-Time Lover (Instrumental)	(Tamla 1808TF)	.75	3.00	85
PART-TIME LOVER	(Tamla 1808TF)	1.00	4.00	85
(Promotional issue, *For Promotional Use Only/Not For Sale* printed on sleeve)				
THAT'S WHAT FRIENDS ARE FOR/Two Ships Passing In The Night	(Arista 9422)	.75	3.00	85
(Shown as by Dionne & Friends Featuring Elton John, Gladys Knight and Stevie Wonder. Warwick, John, Knight, and Wonder pictured on front. Warwick, John, Knight, Wonder, and the song's authors, Burt Bacharach and Carole Bayer Sager, pictured on back.)				
GO HOME/Go Home (Instrumental)	(Tamla 1817TF)	.75	3.00	85
GO HOME/Go Home	(Tamla 1817TF)	1.00	4.00	85
(Promotional issue, *For Promotional Use Only Not For Sale* printed on sleeve)				
OVERJOYED/Overjoyed (Instrumental)	(Tamla 1832TF)	.75	3.00	85
OVERJOYED	(Tamla 1832TF)	1.00	4.00	85
(Promotional issue, *For Promotional Use Only Not For Sale* printed on sleeve)				
LAND OF LA LA	(Tamla 1846TF)	.75	3.00	85
LAND OF LA LA	(Tamla 1846TF)	1.00	4.00	85
(Promotional issue, *For Promotional Use Only Not For Sale* printed on sleeve)				
SKELETONS	(Motown 1907MF)	.75	3.00	87
SKELETONS	(Motown 1907MF)	1.00	4.00	87
(Promotional issue, *For Promotional Use Only Not For Sale* printed on sleeve)				
YOU WILL KNOW	(Motown 1919MF)	.75	3.00	87
YOU WILL KNOW/You Will Know (With Interview)	(Motown 1919MF)	1.00	4.00	87
(Promotional issue, *For Promotional Use Only Not For Sale* printed on sleeve)				
GET IT	(Motown 1930MF)	.75	3.00	88
(Shown as by Stevie Wonder and Michael Jackson)				
GET IT	(Motown 1930MF)	1.25	5.00	88
(Promotional issue, *For Promotional Use Only Not For Sale* printed on sleeve. Shown as by Stevie Wonder and Michael Jackson.)				
MY EYES DON'T CRY	(Motown 1946)	.75	3.00	88
MY LOVE	(Columbia 38-07781)	.75	3.00	88
(Shown as by Julio Iglesias Featuring Stevie Wonder)				
Also see Julian Lennon (*Time Will Teach Us All*), Carly Simon (*The Stuff That Dreams Are Made Of*), U.S.A. For Africa, Voices Of America				

WONDERFUL WORLD OF THE BROTHERS GRIMM, THE
(Motion Picture)
    See David Rose (*The Theme From The Wonderful World Of The Brothers Grimm*)

WONDER WHO?, THE
DON'T THINK TWICE/Sassy	(Philips 40324)	3.75	15.00	65
(Song titles not listed on sleeve, connect-the-dots graphics spell out "We are your favorites")				
ON THE GOOD SHIP LOLLIPOP/You're Nobody 'Til Somebody Loves You	(Philips 40380)	3.75	15.00	66
LONESOME ROAD	(Philips 40471)	3.75	15.00	66
Also see the 4 Seasons				

WONDER WOMAN
(Television Series)
    See New World Symphony (*Wonder Woman*)

WOO, GERRY
HOW LONG/Get It Tonight	(Polydor 887 126-7)	.75	3.00	87

WOOD, LAUREN
PLEASE DON'T LEAVE	(Warner Bros. 49043)	1.00	4.00	79
HALF AS MUCH/Dark December Night	(Warner Bros. 49713)	1.00	4.00	81
Also see Sam Harris (*I'd Do It All Again*)				

WOODELL, PAT
(Actress, played the role of Bobbie Jo Bradley on the television series *Petticoat Junction*)
WHAT GOOD WOULD IT DO/Somehow It Got To Be Tomorrow Today	(Colpix 772)	3.00	12.00	65

WOODS, DEBBY
JUST ONE MORE CHANCE/About A Quarter To Nine	(Epic 5-9489)	1.50	6.00	62

WOOL
MEDICATION/Marky St. James	(London 162 117 001)	1.00	4.00	92
(Promotional issue only issued with red vinyl)				

WOOLEY, BRUCE, & THE CAMERA CLUB
EXTENDED PLAYS
VIDEO KILLED THE RADIO STAR/CLEAN CLEAN/ Trouble Is/Only Babies Can Fly	(Columbia 1-11264)	1.25	5.00	80
(Promotional issue only, *Demonstration: Not For Sale* printed on back of sleeve)				
Also see Thomas Dolby				

WOOLEY, SHEB
SANTA AND THE PURPLE PEOPLE EATER	(MGM K12733)	2.50	10.00	58
SKIN TIGHT, PIN STRIPED, PURPLE PEDAL PUSHERS/ Till The End Of The World	(MGM K13013)	2.50	10.00	61
OLD RAG JOE/Hootenanny Hoot	(MGM K13166)	2.50	10.00	62

WORKING GIRL
(Motion Picture)
    See Carly Simon (*Let The River Run*)

WORLD PARTY
SHIP OF FOOLS/Holy Water .... (Ensign/Chrysalis VS4 43052)   .75   3.00   87
ALL COME TRUE/World Groove (Do The Mind Guerrilla) .... (Ensign/Chrysalis VS4 43132)   .75   3.00   87

WORLD'S GREATEST ATHLETE, THE
(Motion Picture)
    See Marvin Hamlisch (Love Theme)

WORTH, MARION
I THINK I KNOW/ .... (Columbia 4-41799)   2.50   10.00   61
SHAKE ME I RATTLE (SQUEEZE ME I CRY)/Tennessee Teardrops .... (Columbia 4-42640)   2.50   10.00   62

WRAY, LINK
SLINKY/Rendezvous .... (Epic 5-9343)   12.50   50.00   59
RUMBLE MAMBO/Ham Bone .... (Okeh 7166)   10.00   40.00   63
VENDETTA/Facing All The Same Tomorrows .... (Norton 003)   .75   3.00   89
    (A-side shown as by Link Wray and His Raymen)
FRIDAY NIGHT DANCE PARTY/The Girl Can't Dance .... (Norton 046)   .50   2.00   96
    (A-side shown as by Link Wray and the Raymen with Bunker Hill. B-side shown as by Bunker Hill with Link
    Wray and the Raymen.)
GENERIC LINK WRAY & THE RAYMEN SLEEVE .... (Norton 801-810)   .50   2.00   95
    (Half sleeve for Norton's reissue juke box series of ten 45s)
    Also see Robert Gordon (Fire)

WRESTLERS, THE
LAND OF 1,000 DANCES?!!?/Captain Lou's History Of Music/Captain Lou .... (Epic 34-05709)   .75   3.00   85
    (B-side shown as by Captain Lou Albano)

WRIGHT, BERNARD
WHO DO YOU LOVE/Who Do You Love (Instrumental) .... (Manhattan B-50011)   .75   3.00   85

WRIGHT, ROBIN
(Actress)
    See Willy DeVille (Storybook Love), Mark Knopfler (Storybook Love)

WYATT, SHARON
(Actress)
    See the Soaps and Hearts Ensemble

WYCOFF, MICHAEL
THE CHRISTMAS SONG/Love Is So Easy .... (RCA PB-13366)   .75   3.00   82

WYLDE HEARD, THE
STOP IT GIRL/Take It On Home .... (Philips 40454)   3.75   15.00   66

WYLIE, RICHARD "POPCORN"
COME TO ME/Weddin' Bells .... (Epic 5-9543)   3.00   12.00   62
MOVE OVER BABE (HERE COMES HENRY) .... (Carla 715)   7.50   30.00   74
    (Baseball legend Henry "Hank" Aaron pictured. Sleeve graphics and photo are identical to Bill Slayback's
    release. Note that the catalog number of 715 was the number of home runs Aaron needed to break Babe Ruth's
    record, which Aaron would accomplish on April 8, 1974.)

WYMAN, BILL
IN ANOTHER LAND/The Lantern .... (London 45-907)   7.50   30.00   67
    (A-side credited to Bill Wyman and appeared on the Rolling Stones album Their Satanic Majesties Request. B-
    side shown as by the Rolling Stones.)
(SI SI) JE SUIS UN ROCK STAR/Rio De Janeiro .... (A&M/Ripple 2367)   2.00   8.00   81
    Also see the Rolling Stones, Willie and the Poor Boys

WYNETTE, TAMMY
SINGING MY SONG .... (Epic 5-10462)   1.50   6.00   69
WHITE CHRISTMAS .... (Epic AS 60)   1.50   6.00   73
    (Promotional issue only)
EXTENDED PLAYS
BEDTIME STORY .... (Epic AS7-1040)   1.50   6.00   72
    (Promotional issue only envelope sleeve with 3" flap. Sleeve reads ...an Exclusive Interview with Tammy
    Wynette...including musical excerpts from "Stand By Your Man," "We Sure Can Love Each Other," "Good Lovin'",
    "Run, Woman, Run," "Take Me," and "He Loves Me All The Way." Issued with a small-hole 33-1/3 RPM record.)
INTERVIEW AND EXCERPTS .... (Epic AS 44)   1.50   6.00   73
    (Promotional issue only, shown as by George Jones and Tammy Wynette)

WYNN, KEENAN
(Actor)
    See Wayne Newton (Stagecoach To Cheyenne)

X

X
ADULT BOOKS/We're Desperate .... (Dangerhouse 88)   5.00   20.00   78
    (Folding sleeve)
WHITE GIRL/Your Phone's Off The Hook (But You're Not) .... (Slash 106)   2.50   10.00   80
    (Blue version)
WHITE GIRL/Your Phone's Off The Hook (But You're Not) .... (Slash 106)   2.50   10.00   80
    (Green version)
BLUE SPARK/Dancing With Tears In My Eyes .... (Elektra 7-69885)   3.00   12.00   82
BREATHLESS/Riding With Mary .... (Elektra 7-69825)   1.00   4.00   83
    (From the motion picture Breathless, Richard Gere and Valerie Kaprisky pictured on the front, X on the back)
BURNING HOUSE OF LOVE/Love Shack .... (Elektra 7-69626)   1.00   4.00   85
    (Front and back artwork co-created by Exene Cervenka)
4TH OF JULY/Positively 4th Street .... (Elektra 7-69462)   1.00   4.00   87
COUNTRY AT WAR/You Wouldn't Tell Me .... (Big Life/Mercury PRO 1036-7)   2.00   8.00   93
    (Promotional issue only issued with small-hole red vinyl)
    Also see Exene Cervenka

TITLE	LABEL AND NUMBER	VG	NM	YR

by XTC

XANADU
(Motion Picture)
See Electric Light Orchestra (*All Over The World, I'm Alive*), Olivia Newton-John (*Suddenly, Magic*)

XTC
TEN FEET TALL/Helicopter/The Somnambulist .... (Virgin 67004)		1.00	4.00	79
MAKING PLANS FOR NIGEL/This Is Pop/Meccanik Dancing (Oh We Go) .... (Virgin 67009)		1.00	4.00	79
THE MAYOR OF SIMPLETON/One Of The Millions .... (Geffen/Virgin 27552-7)		.75	3.00	89
KING FOR A DAY/Toys .... (Geffen/Virgin 22953-7)		.75	3.00	89

Also see Shriekback (Barry Andrews), 3 Man Island (Barry Andrews)

Y&T
DON'T STOP RUNNIN'/Forever .... (A&M 2669)		.75	3.00	84
ALL AMERICAN BOY/Go For The Throat .... (A&M 2789)		.75	3.00	85

Also see Hear 'N Aid

YANKOVIC, "WEIRD AL"
RICKY/Buckingham Blues .... (Rock 'N' Roll ZS4-03849)		1.25	5.00	83
(Rick Derringer credited on guitars)				
EAT IT .... (Rock 'N' Roll ZS4-04374)		.75	3.00	84
EAT IT .... (Rock 'N' Roll ZS4-04374)		1.00	4.00	84
(Promotional issue, *Demonstration Only–Not For Sale* printed on sleeve)				
KING OF SUEDE .... (Rock 'N' Roll ZS4-04451)		.75	3.00	84
KING OF SUEDE .... (Rock 'N' Roll ZS4-04451)		1.00	4.00	84
(Promotional issue, *Demonstration Only–Not For Sale* printed on sleeve)				
I LOST ON JEOPARDY/I'll Be Mellow When I'm Dead .... (Rock 'N' Roll ZS4-04469)		.75	3.00	84
I LOST ON JEOPARDY .... (Rock 'N' Roll ZS4-04469)		1.00	4.00	84
(Promotional issue, *Demonstration Only–Not For Sale* printed on sleeve)				
THIS IS THE LIFE .... (Rock 'N' Roll ZS4-04708)		.75	3.00	84
(From the motion picture *Johnny Dangerously*)				
THIS IS THE LIFE .... (Rock 'N' Roll ZS4-04708)		1.00	4.00	84
(Promotional issue, *Demonstration Only–Not For Sale* printed on sleeve. From the motion picture *Johnny Dangerously*.)				
LIKE A SURGEON/Slime Creatures From Outer Space .... (Rock 'N' Roll ZS4-04937)		.75	3.00	85
LIKE A SURGEON .... (Rock 'N' Roll ZS4-04937)		1.00	4.00	85
(Promotional issue, *Demonstration Only–Not For Sale* printed on sleeve)				
I WANT A NEW DUCK .... (Rock 'N' Roll ZS4-05578)		.75	3.00	85
I WANT A NEW DUCK .... (Rock 'N' Roll ZS4-05578)		1.00	4.00	85
(Promotional issue, *Demonstration Only–Not For Sale* printed on sleeve)				
ONE MORE MINUTE .... (Rock 'N' Roll ZS4-05606)		.75	3.00	85
ONE MORE MINUTE .... (Rock 'N' Roll ZS4-05606)		1.00	4.00	85
(Promotional issue, *Demonstration Only–Not For Sale* printed on sleeve)				
LIVING WITH A HERNIA/Don't Wear Those Shoes .... (Rock 'N' Roll ZS4-06400)		.75	3.00	86
LIVING WITH A HERNIA .... (Rock 'N' Roll ZS4-06400)		1.00	4.00	86
(Promotional issue, *Demonstration Only–Not For Sale* printed on sleeve)				
CHRISTMAS AT GROUND ZERO .... (Rock 'N' Roll ZS4-06588)		1.25	5.00	86
FAT .... (Rock 'N' Roll ZS4-07769)		.75	3.00	88
LASAGNA .... (Rock 'N' Roll ZS4-07961)		.75	3.00	88

EXTENDED PLAYS
ANOTHER ONE RIDES THE BUS (LIVE)/HAPPY BIRTHDAY/				
Gotta Boogie/Mr. Frump In The Iron Lung .... (Placebo 3626)		2.50	10.00	80

YANOVSKY, ZALMAN
AS LONG AS YOU'RE HERE .... (Buddah 12)		2.00	8.00	67

Also see the Lovin' Spoonful

YARBROUGH, GLENN
BABY THE RAIN MUST FALL/I've Been To Town .... (RCA Victor 47-8498)		2.00	8.00	65

Also see the Limeliters

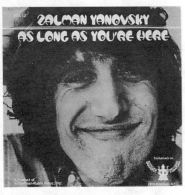

YARDBIRDS, THE
I WISH YOU COULD/A Certain Girl .... (Epic 5-9709)		150.00	600.00	64
(On the back of the sleeve is an ad for Denim Tones socks. It seems even the Yardbirds were not beyond commercial exploitation. It's ironic that the sleeve Epic decides to use for advertising an unrelated product didn't make it into the Billboard Top 100.)				
HEART FULL OF SOUL .... (Epic 5-9823)		7.50	30.00	65
OVER UNDER SIDEWAYS DOWN .... (Epic 5-10035)		6.25	25.00	66
HAPPENINGS TEN YEARS TIME AGO .... (Epic 5-10094)		6.25	25.00	66

Also see Jeff Beck, the Bunburys (Eric Clapton), Eric Clapton, Randy Crawford (Eric Clapton), Donovan (Jeff Beck), the Honeydrippers (Jeff Beck, Jimmy Page), Led Zeppelin (Jimmy Page), Jimmy Page, Keith Relf, Willie and the Poorboys (Jimmy Page)

YATES, LORI
SCENE OF THE CRIME .... (Columbia 38-08055)		.75	3.00	88

YA YA
CAUGHT IN A LIE/Fear Of Flying .... (Atco 7-99298)		.75	3.00	88

YAZ
SITUATION/Situation (Dub Version) .... (Sire 29953-7)		2.00	8.00	82
(Shown as by Yazoo)				
SITUATION/Situation (Dub Version) .... (Sire 29953-7)		1.50	6.00	82

Also see Erasure (Vince Clarke), Alison Moyet

YAZOO
See Yaz

YAZZ AND THE PLASTIC POPULATION
STAND UP FOR YOUR LOVE RIGHTS/Stand Up For Your Love Rights (R & B 7" Remix)(Elektra 7-69311)		.75	3.00	88
(Shown as by Yazz)				
THE ONLY WAY IS UP .... (Elektra 7-69365)		.75	3.00	88

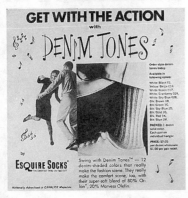

YELLO
BIMBO/I.T. Splash .... (Ralph YL-8058-S) — 1.25 — 5.00 — 80
I LOVE YOU/Rubber West .... (Elektra 7-69824) — 1.25 — 5.00 — 83
OH YEAH/Oh Yeah (Indian Summer Music) .... (Mercury 884 930-7) — 1.25 — 5.00 — 86
  (Multi-color sleeve)
OH YEAH/Oh Yeah (Indian Summer Music) .... (Mercury 884 930-7) — 1.00 — 4.00 — 87
  (Yellow sleeve, featured in the motion picture *Ferris Bueller's Day Off*)
CALL IT LOVE/l'Hôtel .... (Mercury 888 311-7) — 1.00 — 4.00 — 87

YELLOW MAGIC ORCHESTRA
COMPUTER GAME "THEME FROM THE CIRCUS"/
  Yellow Magic (Tong Poo) .... (Horizon/A&M 127) — 1.00 — 4.00 — 80
A MESSAGE FROM YMO/edited songs from X Multiplies ...... (A&M/YMO # unknown) — 1.50 — 6.00 — 80
  (Promotional issue only poster sleeve)
MICRO SAMPLER .... (A&M/YMO5) — 1.50 — 6.00 — 80
  ("Mini" 5 inch sleeve issued with yellow vinyl)
BEHIND THE MASK/ .... (A&M 2261) — 1.00 — 4.00 — 80

YELLOW SUBMARINE
(Motion Picture)
  See the Beatles (*Yellow Submarine*)

YENTL
(Motion Picture)
  See Barbra Streisand (*The Way He Makes Me Feel*)

YES
OWNER OF A LONELY HEART/Our Song .... (Atco 7-99817) — .75 — 3.00 — 83
LEAVE IT/Leave It (Acappella) .... (Atco 7-99787) — .75 — 3.00 — 84
IT CAN HAPPEN/It Can Happen (Live Version) .... (Atco 7-99745) — .75 — 3.00 — 84
LOVE WILL FIND A WAY/Holy Lamb (Song For Harmonic Convergence) ... (Atco 7-99449) — .75 — 3.00 — 87
RHYTHM OF LOVE/City Of Love (Live) .... (Atco 7-99419) — .75 — 3.00 — 87
  Also see Jon Anderson, Anderson, Bruford, Wakeman, Howe, GTR (Steve Howe), Rick Wakeman

YESTER, JERRY
I CAN LIVE WITHOUT YOU/Garden Of Imagining .... (Dunhill 4061) — 2.50 — 10.00 — 66
  Also see the Lovin' Spoonful

Y KANT TORI READ
COOL ON YOUR ISLAND/Heart Attack At 23 .... (Atlantic 7-89021) — 12.50 — 50.00 — 88
  Also see Guns N' Roses (Matt Sorum)

YOAKAM, DWIGHT
GUITARS, CADILLACS .... (Reprise 28688-7) — 1.25 — 5.00 — 86
LITTLE SISTER .... (Reprise 28432-7) — 1.00 — 4.00 — 87
LITTLE WAYS .... (Reprise 28310-7) — 1.00 — 4.00 — 87
SANTA CLAUS IS BACK IN TOWN/
  Christmas Eve With The Babylonian Cowboys/"Jingle Bells" ...... (Reprise 28156-7) — 1.25 — 5.00 — 87
  (B-side shown as With Dwight Yoakam and Al Perkins)
ALWAYS LATE WITH YOUR KISSES .... (Reprise 27994-7) — .75 — 3.00 — 88
STREETS OF BAKERSFIELD .... (Reprise 27964-7) — .75 — 3.00 — 88
  (Shown as by Dwight Yoakam and Buck Owens)
I SANG DIXIE .... (Reprise 27715-7) — .75 — 3.00 — 88

"YOU KNOW WHO" GROUP, THE
THIS DAY LOVE/Hey You And The Wind And The Rain .... (International Allied 823) — 3.75 — 15.00 — 65

YOU NEVER GAVE ME ROSES
(Motion Picture)
  See Megan McDonough (*If I Could Only Reach You*)

YOUNG, BARRY
A HEART WITHOUT A NAME .... (Columbia 4-43594) — 1.50 — 6.00 — 66
A YEAR, A MONTH, A DAY .... (Mercury 72769) — 1.50 — 6.00 — 68

YOUNG, FARON
BACKTRACK/I Can't Find The Time .... (Capitol 4616) — 2.00 — 8.00 — 61
THREE DAYS/ .... (Capitol 4696) — 2.00 — 8.00 — 61
KEEPING UP WITH THE JONES/ .... (Mercury 72237) — 1.50 — 6.00 — 64
  (Shown as by Faron Young and Margie Singleton. Two versions exist for this sleeve, their differences are unknown.)
SHE WENT A LITTLE BIT FARTHER/ .... (Mercury 72774) — 1.50 — 6.00 — 68

YOUNG, JESSE COLIN
FIGHT FOR IT/Hidin' Away .... (Elektra 7-69953) — .75 — 3.00 — 82
  (A-side shown as by Jesse Colin Young and Carly Simon)
  Also see the Youngbloods

YOUNG, KATHY
A THOUSAND STARS/Eddie My Darling .... (Indigo 108) — 12.50 — 50.00 — 60
HAPPY BIRTHDAY BLUES/Someone To Love .... (Indigo 115) — 7.50 — 30.00 — 61
MAGIC IS THE NIGHT/Du Du'nt Du .... (Indigo 125) — 7.50 — 30.00 — 61
  Also see Chris & Kathy

YOUNG, NEIL
COMES A TIME/Motorcycle Mama .... (Reprise 1395) — 1.25 — 5.00 — 78
HEY HEY, MY MY (INTO THE BLACK) RUST NEVER SLEEPS/
  My My, Hey Hey (Out Of The Blue) Rust Never Sleeps ...... (Reprise 49031) — 2.00 — 8.00 — 79
  (Shown as by Neil Young & Crazy Horse)
HAWKS & DOVES/Union Man .... (Reprise 49555) — 1.00 — 4.00 — 80
LITTLE THING CALLED LOVE/We R In Control .... (Geffen 29887-7) — 1.00 — 4.00 — 82
WONDERIN'/Payola Blues .... (Geffen 7-29574) — 1.00 — 4.00 — 83
WEIGHT OF THE WORLD .... (Geffen 28623-7) — .75 — 3.00 — 86
TEN MEN WORKIN' .... (Reprise 27908-7) — 1.50 — 6.00 — 88
  (Shown as by Neil Young & the Bluenotes)

TITLE	LABEL AND NUMBER	VG	NM	YR
THIS NOTE'S FOR YOU	(Reprise 27848-7)	1.00	4.00	88
(Shown as by Neil Young & the Bluenotes)				
ROCKIN' IN THE FREE WORLD	(Reprise 22776-7)	1.00	4.00	89
Also see Crosby/Stills/Nash/Young, Emmylou Harris (*Light Of The Stable*)				

YOUNG, PAUL

TITLE	LABEL AND NUMBER	VG	NM	YR
WHEREVER I LAY MY HAT/Tender Trap	(Columbia 38 04071)	.75	3.00	83
WHEREVER I LAY MY HAT/Tender Trap	(Columbia 38 04071)	1.00	4.00	83
(Promotional issue, *Demonstration–Not For Sale* printed on sleeve)				
COME BACK AND STAY/Yours	(Columbia 38 04313)	.75	3.00	84
COME BACK AND STAY	(Columbia 38 04313)	1.00	4.00	84
(Promotional issue, *Demonstration–Not For Sale* printed on sleeve)				
LOVE OF THE COMMON PEOPLE/Behind Your Smile	(Columbia 38-04453)	.75	3.00	84
LOVE OF THE COMMON PEOPLE	(Columbia 38-04453)	1.00	4.00	84
(Promotional issue, *Demonstration–Not For Sale* printed on sleeve)				
EVERYTIME YOU GO AWAY/This Means Anything	(Columbia 38-04867)	.75	3.00	85
EVERYTIME YOU GO AWAY	(Columbia 38-04867)	1.00	4.00	85
(Promotional issue, *Demonstration–Not For Sale* printed on sleeve)				
I'M GONNA TEAR YOUR PLAYHOUSE DOWN/Broken Man	(Columbia 38-05577)	.75	3.00	85
I'M GONNA TEAR YOUR PLAYHOUSE DOWN	(Columbia 38-05577)	1.00	4.00	85
(Promotional issue, *Demonstration–Not For Sale* printed on sleeve)				
EVERYTHING MUST CHANGE/Give Me My Freedom	(Columbia 38-05712)	.75	3.00	85
EVERYTHING MUST CHANGE	(Columbia 38-05712)	1.00	4.00	85
(Promotional issue, *Demonstration–Not For Sale* printed on sleeve)				
SOME PEOPLE/Steps To Go	(Columbia 38-06423)	.75	3.00	86
SOME PEOPLE	(Columbia 38-06423)	1.00	4.00	86
(Promotional issue, *Demonstration–Not For Sale* printed on sleeve)				
WHY DOES A MAN HAVE TO BE STRONG/A Matter Of Fact	(Columbia 38-06630)	.75	3.00	87
WHY DOES A MAN HAVE TO BE STRONG	(Columbia 38-06630)	1.00	4.00	87
(Promotional issue, *Demonstration–Not For Sale* printed on sleeve)				
Also see Band Aid, Mike + the Mechanics, Sad Café				

YOUNG, VAL

TITLE	LABEL AND NUMBER	VG	NM	YR
PRIVATE CONVERSATIONS (RADIO VERSION)/				
Private Conversations (Instrumental Version)	(Amherst 312)	.75	3.00	87

YOUNG AND THE RESTLESS, THE
(Television Soap Opera)
   Related see Michael Damian, David Hasselhoff, the Soaps and Hearts Ensemble, Patty Weaver

YOUNGBLOOD
(Motion Picture)
   See Mickey Thomas (*Stand In The Fire*)

YOUNGBLOODS, THE

TITLE	LABEL AND NUMBER	VG	NM	YR
GRIZZLY BEAR/Tears Are Falling	(RCA Victor 47-9015)	2.50	10.00	66
Also see Jesse Colin Young				

YOUNG FRANKENSTEIN
(Motion Picture)
   See Rhythm Heritage (*Theme From Young Frankenstein*)

YOUNG MC

TITLE	LABEL AND NUMBER	VG	NM	YR
BUST A MOVE/Got More Rhymes	(Delicious Vinyl 105)	.75	3.00	89
PRINCIPAL'S OFFICE/Principal's Office (Instrumental)	(Delicious Vinyl 7-99137)	.75	3.00	89
I COME OFF (7" REMIX)/I Come Off (L.P. Version)	(Delicious Vinyl 7-98993)	.75	3.00	90

YOUNG RASCALS, THE
   See the Rascals

YOUNG WINSTON
(Motion Picture)
   See Alfred Ralston (*Jennie's Theme*)

YUTAKA

TITLE	LABEL AND NUMBER	VG	NM	YR
LOVE LIGHT	(Alfa 7004)	1.00	4.00	81

Z

ZADORA, PIA

TITLE	LABEL AND NUMBER	VG	NM	YR
ROCK IT OUT/Give Me Back My Heart	(MCA/Curb 52294)	1.00	4.00	83
WHEN THE RAIN BEGINS TO FALL/Substitute	(MCA/Curb 52521)	.75	3.00	84
(A-side shown as by Jermaine Jackson and Pia Zadora, both pictured. B-side shown as by Pia Zadora. A-side from the motion picture *Voyage Of The Rock Aliens*.)				
I AM WHAT I AM/For Once In My Life	(CBS Associated ZS4-06322)	.75	3.00	86
(On back credited as *Pia Zadora Singing with the London Philharmonic Orchestra*)				
I AM WHAT I AM	(CBS Associated ZS4-06322)	1.00	4.00	86
(Promotional issue, *Demonstration Only–Not For Sale* printed on sleeve. On back credited as *Pia Zadora Singing with the London Philharmonic Orchestra*.)				

ZAGER & EVANS

TITLE	LABEL AND NUMBER	VG	NM	YR
HYDRA 15,000/I Am	(Vanguard 35125)	2.50	10.00	71

ZANDER, ROBIN

TITLE	LABEL AND NUMBER	VG	NM	YR
SURRENDER TO ME	(Capitol B44288)	.75	3.00	88
(Shown as by Ann Wilson and Robin Zander. From the motion picture *Tequila Sunrise*. Wilson and Zander pictured on the front, Mel Gibson, Michelle Pfeiffer, and Kurt Russell pictured on the back.)				
Also see Cheap Trick				

ZAPP
   See Roger

TITLE	LABEL AND NUMBER	VG	NM	YR

301

ZAPPA, DWEEZIL
(Son of Frank Zappa)
MY MOTHER IS A SPACE CADET / Crunchy Water .... (Barking Pumpkin WS4 03366) — 1.25 — 5.00 — 82
    (Shown as by Dweezil, pictured with his pubescent bandmates and his sister Moon Zappa)
LET'S TALK ABOUT IT / Electric Hoedown .... (Barking Pumpkin B-74204) — 3.75 — 15.00 — 86

ZAPPA, FRANK
I DON'T WANNA GET DRAFTED! .... (Zappa ZR 1001) — 2.00 — 8.00 — 80
    (First printing)
I DON'T WANNA GET DRAFTED! .... (Zappa WS7-73000) — 2.50 — 10.00 — 80
    (Second printing identical to the first printing except for the Barking Pumpkin catalog number. Uncertain as
    to whether a record exists with this catalog number.)
VALLEY GIRL .... (Barking Pumpkin WS9-02972) — 1.25 — 5.00 — 82
    (Shown as by Frank & Moon Zappa, both pictured. Record shown as by Frank Zappa.)

ZAPPA, MOON
(Daughter of Frank Zappa)
    See Dweezil Zappa (My Mother Is A Space Cadet), Frank Zappa (Valley Girl)

ZASLOW, MICHAEL
(Actor)
    See the Soaps and Hearts Ensemble

ZEBRA
BEARS / One More Chance .... (Atlantic 7-89605) — .75 — 3.00 — 84

ZEITGEIST
WHEREHAUS JAM / Freight Train Rain / Electra .... (DB 76) — 1.50 — 6.00 — 84
    Also see the Reivers

ZENTNER, SI, AND HIS ORCHESTRA WITH THE JOHNNY MANN SINGERS
MISSISSIPPI MUD .... (Liberty 55437) — 1.50 — 6.00 — 62

ZEROS, THE
WILD WEEK-END / Beat Your Heart Out .... (Bomp 118) — 1.50 — 6.00 — 78
BOTTOMS UP / Sneakin' Up .... (Rockville 6091) — 1.25 — 5.00 — 92

ZEVON, WARREN
LEAVE MY MONKEY ALONE / Leave My Monkey Alone (Latin Rascals Dub) .... (Virgin 99440-7) — .75 — 3.00 — 87
RECONSIDER ME / Factory .... (Virgin 7-99370) — .75 — 3.00 — 87
    (Don Henley, Roy Bittan of the E Street Band, and Mike Campbell and Benmont Tench of the Heartbreakers
    credited on back)
    Also see Hindu Love Gods

ZIGGY STARDUST/THE MOTION PICTURE
(Motion Picture)
    See David Bowie (White Light/White Heat)

ZIMBALIST, EFREM, JR.
(Actor)
ADESTE FIDELIS (OH, COME ALL YE FAITHFUL) /
    Deck The Halls With Boughs Of Holly / Caroling, Caroling .... (Warner Bros. 5126) — 3.75 — 15.00 — 60
    (B-side shown as by the Guitars Inc.)

ZOMBIES, THE
TELL HER NO / Leave Me Be .... (Parrot 45-9723) — 6.25 — 25.00 — 65
SHE'S COMING HOME .... (Parrot 45-9747) — 6.25 — 25.00 — 65
BUTCHERS TALE / This Will Be Our Year .... (Date 2-1612) — 7.50 — 30.00 — 68
    (Possibly a promotional issue only)
    Also see the Alan Parsons Project (Colin Blunstone)

ZORN, JOHN
    See Golden Palaminos

ZOV, JOHN
ONE FOR THE THUMB IN 81 .... (Thumbs Up Enterprises Inc. 1000) — 1.25 — 5.00 — 80

ZUCKERMAN, PINCHAS
    See Isaac Stern (Happy Birthday, Isaac Stern)

ZWOL
(Walter Zwol)
NEW YORK CITY (SHORT VERSION & LONG VERSION) .... (EMI America 8005) — 1.50 — 6.00 — 78
    (Promotional issue only issued with square, small-hole, white vinyl)

ZZ TOP
TUSH .... (London 220) — 2.00 — 8.00 — 75
IT'S ONLY LOVE .... (London 241) — 1.50 — 6.00 — 76
GIMME ALL YOUR LOVIN / If I Could Only Flag Her Down .... (Warner Bros. 29693-7) — 1.00 — 4.00 — 83
LEGS / Bad Girl .... (Warner Bros. 29272-7) — 1.00 — 4.00 — 84
SLEEPING BAG .... (Warner Bros. 28884-7) — .75 — 3.00 — 85
STAGES .... (Warner Bros. 28810-7) — .75 — 3.00 — 85
ROUGH BOY .... (Warner Bros. 28733-7-7) — .75 — 3.00 — 86
DOUBLEBACK .... (Warner Bros. 19812-7) — .75 — 3.00 — 90
    (From the motion picture Back To The Future Part III)

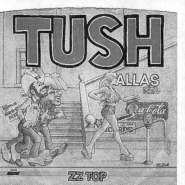

Bibliography

Barack, Burt, and George Denham, *Thirty Years of Forty-Five RPM Picture Sleeves*. Avon: Lorell Press, 1983.

Cates, Jim, *The Official Picture Sleeve Price Guide*. Topeka: Educational Concepts Corporation, 1986.

DelBuono, Robert and Cindy, *The Beatles: A Collection*. Philadelphia: The George H. Buchanan Company, 1982.

Heggeness, Fred, *Goldmine's Country Western Record & CD Price Guide*. Iola: Krause Publications, 1996.

Heggeness, Fred, *Goldmine's Promo Record & CD Price Guide*. Iola: Krause Publications, 1995.

Lofman, Ron, *Goldmine's Celebrity Vocals*. Iola: Krause Publications, 1994.

McNeil, Alex, *Total Television: A Comprehensive Guide To Programming from 1948 to the Present*. New York: Penguin Group, 1996.

Neely, Tim, *Goldmine Price Guide to Alternative Records*. Iola: Krause Publications, 1996.

Neely, Tim, ed., *Goldmine's Price Guide to 45 RPM Records*. Iola: Krause Publications, 1996.

Osborne, Jerry, *The Official Price Guide to Elvis Presley Records and Memorabilia*, First Edition. New York: House of Collectibles, 1994.

Osborne, Jerry, *The Official Price Guide to Movie/TV Soundtracks and Original Cast Albums*, Second Edition. New York: House of Collectibles, 1997.

Osborne, Jerry, *The Official Price Guide to Records*, Eleventh Edition. New York: House of Collectibles, 1994.

Osborne, Jerry, and Bruce Hamilton, *Osbourne & Hamilton's Original Record Collector's Price Guide*, Fourth Edition. Phoenix: O'Sullivan, Woodside & Co., 1983.

Osborne, Jerry, and Bruce Hamilton, *Popular & Rock Price Guide for 45's*, Third Edition. Chicago: Follett Publishing Company, 1981.

Philip Lief Group, *Blockbuster Entertainment Guide to Movies and Videos 1998*. New York: Dell Publishing, 1997.

Romanowski, Patricia, and Holly George-Warren, ed., *The New Rolling Stone Encyclopedia of Rock & Roll*. New York: Rolling Stone Press, 1995.

Robbins, Ira A., ed., *The Trouser Press Guide to 90's Rock: The All-New Fifth Edition of The Trouser Press Record Guide*. New York: Simon & Schuster, 1997.

Umphred, Neal, *Goldmine's Rock 'N Roll 45 RPM Record Price Guide*. Iola: Krause Publications, 1994.

Whitburn, Joel, *Top Pop Singles 1955–1993*. Menomonee Falls: Record Research Inc., 1994.

Notes

Notes